CURRENT TRENDS IN LINGUISTICS

VOLUME IV

CURRENT TRENDS IN LINGUISTICS

Edited by

THOMAS A. SEBEOK

IV: Ibero-American and Caribbean Linguistics

Associate Editors:

ROBERT LADO

NORMAN A. MCQUOWN

SOL SAPORTA

Assistant Editor: YOLANDA LASTRA

1968

MOUTON

THE HAGUE · PARIS

LIBRARY CONGRESS CATALOG CARD NUMBER 64-3663

Printed in the Netherlands by Mouton & Co., Printers, The Hague.

EDITOR'S INTRODUCTION

The twin clichés, "population explosion" and "information explosion", succinctly point up complaints shared by the linguistic profession with other scientific disciplines as well as, increasingly, with the humanities. It is not always appreciated, however, that the two "explosions" are coupled in a dialectic relationship: the more linguists are trained, the more research is produced and therefore the more of its results will be published; on the other hand, the more information is available, the more specialists will be required to process pertinent portions of the total output. Given the limitations of time — his scarcest resource — every linguist must reach a compromise between two alternatives: he can, in varying degree, yield to the pressure to spend more and more time reading and thus have less and less time left over for creative work; or, by lowering his standards of "keeping up", he can narrow the scope of his activities and thus risk being inadequately informed.

The most frequently suggested solution to this dilemma calls for the establishment of some sort of abstracting service. The arguments for such a service (cf. T. J. Condon, "Abstracting scholarly literature: a view from the sixties", *ACLS Newsletter* 18.1-14 [1967]) are usually based on the mirage that unwanted information can be rejected with confidence by reading about it in some abstract form. Reading abstracts is, in fact, not only unreliable but also extremely boring, and there is good evidence to indicate that it actually takes less time to skim a paper than to read an abstract of it and, if the paper is judged relevant, to then get to the original without delay.

By striking a workable balance between relevance and coverage, the *Current Trends in Linguistics* series attempts to provide linguists with quite another solution to the problem: dependence on a human network, the most essential ingredient of which is good judgment. Our series is meant to function as a kind of "invisible college", in which the readers are invited to participate in a manner depicted in an insightful editorial by P.H. Abelson: "Outside their own specialties they rely on colleagues they can trust to lead them to experts who can be trusted, who in turn either directly provide the needed information or guide them to the most reliable relevant literature. ... Reliance on this human network provides more than raw information. It provides judgment, and suggestions of more feasible approaches to the problem being considered. In view of the many strengths of this information network, computer technology has far to go to match it in effectiveness and especially in cost" (*Science* 159:3815 [1968]).

The articles in this series are assigned to the best available scholar for any given subject, as determined by the Editorial Board for that volume. Trustworthiness of treatment is thus assured. Each paper is a highly individualistic contribution, hopefully interesting in itself. Guided by the table of contents, the indexes, and the extensive bibliographic controls, the reader is invited to maximize for himself the product of relevance and coverage, which is quality. Naturally, the quality inherent in the various volumes and, within them, the various articles, will inevitably reflect the state of linguistic sophistication in each region and in each subdiscipline as represented in the part of the world under scrutiny. The purpose is not to improve on reality but to represent this as it exists in a given place at a given time, and — to repeat — to do so as reliably and interestingly as possible under very differing circumstances.

The first volume in this series appeared in 1963. Shifts in editorial policy were stated and the reasons for them discussed in my Introduction to Vol. II; they apply, *mutatis mutandis*, to this fourth volume as well. There has also been, in the meantime, a change in the source of financial support: whereas Vols. I-III were sponsored, with three successive grants, by the National Science Foundation, the preparation of this volume and of Vols. V and VI was made possible by three successive contracts between the United States Office of Education and the Indiana University Foundation. The contract for Vol. IV bore the identification USOE OEC 5-14-017. I hereby gratefully acknowledge this indispensable aid.

The outline for the master plan for *Current Trends in Linguistics*, most recently published in my Introduction to Vol. II, now stands as follows:

Vol. I, *Soviet and East European Linguistics*, which had been sold out by 1967, was reprinted in 1968 and is once again available.

Vol. II, *Linguistics in East Asia and South East Asia*, has been off press for some months.

Vol. III, *Theoretical Foundations*, first published in 1966, is still available as a whole, and the chapters by Chomsky, Greenberg, and Hockett in separate booklets as well (*Janua Linguarum*, Series Minor 56, 59, and 60, respectively).

Vol. V, *Linguistics in South Asia*, is completely composed and the authors and editors are currently reading their first proofs; the book should, therefore, appear late in 1968.

Vol. VI, *Linguistics in South West Asia and North Africa*, is being prepared in collaboration with Associate Editors Charles A. Ferguson (Stanford University, Carleton T. Hodge (Indiana University), and Herbert H. Paper (University of Michigan), and Assistant Editors John R. Krueger (Indiana University) and Gene M. Schramm (University of Michigan). The book is in press, scheduled to appear sometime in 1969.

Vol. VII, *Linguistics in Sub-Saharan Africa*, is being prepared in collaboration with

Associate Editors Jack Berry (Northwestern University) and Joseph H. Greenberg (Stanford University), and Assistant Editors David Crabb (Princeton University) and Paul Schachter (University of California, Los Angeles). This book is likewise in press, and is also scheduled to appear in 1969.

Vol. VIII, *Oceanic Linguistics*, is being prepared in collaboration with Associate Editors J. Donald Bowen (University of California, Los Angeles), Isidore Dyen (Yale University), George W. Grace (University of Hawaii), and Stephen A. Wurm (Australian National University), and Assistant Editor Geoffrey O'Grady (University of Victoria). Many articles have been received and the book is expected to go to press in the Winter of 1968 and, accordingly, appear late in 1969.

Vol. IX, *Linguistics in Western Eurpe*, is being prepared in collaboration with Associate Editors Werner Winter (University of Kiel) and Einar Haugen (Harvard University), and Assistant Editor Curtis Blaylock (University of Illinois). The deadline for manuscripts has been set for the end of 1968, and they are expected to go to press in the Spring of 1969, envisaging a publication date early in 1970.

Vol. X, *Linguistics in North America*, is being prepared in collaboration with Associate Editors William Bright (University of California, Los Angeles), Dell Hymes (University of Pennsylvania), John Lotz (Center for Applied Linguistics), Albert H. Marckwardt (Princeton University), Jean-Paul Vinay (University of Victoria). The table of contents has been designed. The Editor expects to issue invitations shortly, setting a deadline for late 1969; the book is scheduled, therefore, to appear late in 1970 or early the following year.

At least two more volumes, as previously announced, are under consideration to round this cycle out sometime in the early 1970's. Their thematic focus is slowly crystallizing. One of these volumes is certain to deal with linguistics in its relationships with adjacent arts and sciences; and the other with the three cardinal methods of language classification, the genetic, the areal, and the typological, with special reference to the scholarly literature concerning those extinct languages not treated in previous volumes. Editorial Boards are currently being assembled for both. Correspondents and reviewers have also made some suggestions, and the Editor would welcome further constructive opinions as to the manner in which the series could be made as useful as possible.

This work — like Vol. III — was conceived amidst the excitement of the 1964 Linguistic Institute of the Linguistic Society of America, held in Bloomington, and the added turmoil of the partially overlapping Inter-American Symposium on Linguistics and Language Teaching (August 3-8; cf. LSA *Bulletin* 38.32-33 [1965]). This book is thus at least the sixth to appear as a direct consequence of that Linguistic Institute; one other, which should certainly be singled out here, is the Instituto Caro y Cuervo's *El Simposio de Bloomington, agosto de 1964*; *Actas, Informes y Comunicaciones*, published in Bogota, in 1967.

At my request, during the Summer of 1964, the Program's Executive Committee appointed a special committee to work with the Editor on the development of this book; the members of this committee then became *de facto* the Editorial Board for Vol. IV. Most of the contributors were initially invited while the Symposium was in session.

As the perceptive reader will suspect, more chapters were conceived in our original design than now appear within these covers: in Part One, missing are chapters on Grammar, as well as on Comparative and Historical Linguistics; in Part Two, we had hoped to include a discussion on the Linguistics of 19th and 20th Century Immigration; and in Part Three, there was to have been a study of the National Languages of the Caribbean. Alas, the respective authors invited to write on these subjects withdrew too late for us to find a suitable substitute.

The deadline for completion of the manuscripts was set for the end of 1965 — and most of the authors scrupulously met their obligation; but due to unforeseen delays some of the currency of the articles was inevitably lost. This unfortunate circumstance — although partially remedied in proof — must be kept in mind when judging the timeliness of certain contributions.

Seven chapters — those by Barthel, Cisneros, Coseriu, Escobar, Guitarte and Torres, Lope, and Martinez — appear here in English translation. Credits are as follows: Barthel's and Coseriu's were rendered from the German, the former by Clifton Butcher, the latter under Professor Coseriu's own supervision. The other five came to us in Spanish; Claire Stevens translated Guitarte-Torres, and Cesar Bandera translated the remaining four.

It is cheerful to be able to report here that linguistics in Latin America has come a long way since this undertaking got under way, at least if organizational activities give an accurate indication of academic achievement. The First Inter-American Linguistic Institute was held in Montevideo, in January-February, 1966, sponsored by the Inter-American Program and by ALFAL (acronym for the Asociación de Lingüística y Filología de América Latina). The Second Inter-American Linguistic Institute was held in Mexico City, from November 1967 to February 1968, at the Escuela Nacional de Antropología e Historia, under the joint auspices of the Program and ALFAL and with the collaboration of several Mexican cultural institutions. Over 120 students registered, coming from every part of the Hemisphere (excepting only Paraguay and some of the Central American countries). The IV. Symposium of the Inter-American Program was also held in Mexico City, in January 1968, with 65 delegates and 42 observers in attendance. The third Institute and the fifth Symposium are going to be held in São Paulo; the fourth Institute and sixth Symposium are already being planned for Puerto Rico, and the succeeding one will probably take place in Canada.

Mention should be made of certain developments which are not elsewhere reported in this book.

(1) A new acronym, which is increasingly coming to be used for the Program referred to above, is PILEI, for Programa Interamericano de Linguistica y Enseñanza de Idiomas.

(2) ALILEME, which is discussed on p. 608 of the book, has, in the meantime, ceased to function as a separate organization, since a new Departamento de Lingüística Computacional has been organized within ALFAL.

(3) Because of the current political situation in Argentina, some linguists (such as L. J. Prieto) have left that country; others have changed their institutional affiliation.

(4) A new journal, *Estudos Linguisticos*, was started in São Paulo.

(5) In Bolivia, a notable event was the founding of an Instituto de Estudios Lingüísticos (INEL), by Martha Hardman-de-Bautista.

Professor Manrique has requested the following addendum: "Since the time this paper was written, many changes have occurred in the institutional affiliations of people referred to [in his article]; some tasks have been completed and others have faced unexpected problems. [His] survey is outdated in some of its details, but the general picture is still valid as of 1968."

The Master List of Abbreviations, Index of Languages, and Index of Names were compiled by Yolanda Lastra. The Editor wishes to express his appreciation to her for attending to these chores and many others; her help in seeing this book through press has been invaluable. Thanks are also due to the other three editorial associates — Robert Lado, Norman A. McQuown, and Sol Saporta — for giving of their time and wisdom; Albert S. Storm and Julia A. Petrov, of the U.S. Office of Education, for their benevolent patience; and the staff of Mouton & Co. for their splendid cooperation.

Bloomington, March 15, 1968 THOMAS A. SEBEOK

CONTENTS

PART IV: SOURCES AND RESOURCES

LIST OF ABBREVIATIONS

AA	American Antiquity. Menasha, Wisconsin.
AAA	American Anthropological Association.
AAWL	Abhandlungen der Akademie der Wissenschaften und der Literatur in Mainz, Geistes- und sozialwissenschaftliche Klasse. Wiesbaden.
ACALE	Actas del III Congreso de Academias de la Lengua Española. Bogotá, 1960.
ACIA	Actas y Memorias del Congreso Internacional de Americanistas.
ACLR	Actes du Colloque International de Civilisations, Littératures et Langues Romanes. Bucarest, 1959.
ACP	Acción Cultural Popular. Colombia.
Acta Salm	Acta Salamanticensia. Universidad de Salamanca. Facultad de Filosofía y Letras.
ACU	Argentina, Chile, Uruguay.
AdL	Anuario de Letras. México.
AEA	Anuario de Estudios Atlánticos. Madrid.
AEAM	Anuario de Estudios Americanos. Sevilla.
AEH	Acta Ethnographica Academiae Scientiarum Hungaricae.
AFCl	Anales de Filología Clásica. Lima.
Afr S	African Studies. Johannesburg.
AGI	Archivio Glottologico Italiano. Firenze.
AIAK XXXIV	Akten des 34. Internationalen Amerikanistenkongresses. Wien, 1960.
AID	Agency for International Development. United States.
AIL	Anales del Instituto de Lingüística de la Universidad Nacional de Cuyo. Mendoza, Argentina.
AION-L	Annali, Istituto Universitario Orientale, Sezione linguistica. Napoli.
AION-SR	Annali, Istituto Universitario Orientale, Sezione romanza. Napoli.
AJF	American Journal of Folklore.
AJPh	American Journal of Philology. Baltimore.
ALEC	Atlas Lingüístico-Etnográfico de Colombia.
ALet	Anuario de Letras. México.
ALFAL	Asociación de Lingüística y Filología de América Latina.
ALILEME	Asociación Latinoamericana para la Investigacion Lingüística mediante Equipos Mecánico-Electrónicos.
AmA	American Anthropologist. Menasha, Wisconsin.
Anales de la Soc. Argent. de Est. Geogr.	Anales de la Sociedad Argentina de Estudios Geográficos.
AnINA	Anales del Instituto Nacional de Antropología e Historia. México.
Anl	Anthropological Linguistics. Bloomington, Indiana.
AnnLat	Annali Lateranensi. Pubblicazione del Pontificio Museo Missionario Etnologico. Città del Vaticano.
AO	Archivum. Oviedo.
APIL	Asociación de Profesores e Investigadores de Lenguas, Lingüística y Literatura. Chile.
Arch V	Archiv für Völkerkunde. Wien.
ArL	Archivum Linguisticum. Glasgow.
AS	American Speech. A Quarterly of Linguistic Usage. New York.
ASal	Acta Salmanticensia. Salamanca.
AVF	Archivos Venezolanos de Folklore. Caracas.

AV Ph	Archiv für vergleichende Phonetik. Berlin.
BAAL	Boletín de la Academia Argentina de Letras. Buenos Aires.
BAC	Boletín de la Academia Colombiana. Bogotá.
BACL	Boletín de la Academia Cubana de la Lengua. La Habana.
BAE	Boletín de la Real Academia Española. Madrid.
BAH	Boletín de la Academia Hondureña de la Lengua. Tegucigalpa.
BBMP	Boletím de la Biblioteca Menendez Pelayo. Santander.
BDE	Breve Diccionario Etimológico.
BDH	Biblioteca de Dialectología Hispanoamericana.
BF	Boletim de Filología. Lisboa.
BFL	Boletim de Filologia. Lisboa.
BFM	Boletín de Filología. Montevideo.
BFR	Boletim de Filologia. Rio de Janeiro.
BFS	Boletín de Filología. Santiago de Chile.
BFS	Bulletin de la Faculté des Lettres de Strasbourg. Strasbourg.
BFUCh	Boletín de Filología, Instituto de Filología de la Universidad de Chile. Santiago de Chile.
BHi	Bulletin Hispanique. Annales de la Faculté des Lettres de Bordeaux. Bordeaux.
BICC	Thesaurus. Boletín del Instituto Caro y Cuervo. Bogotá.
Bijdr TLV	Bijdragen tot de Taal-, Land- en Volkenkunde, uitgegeven door het Koninklijk Instituut voor Taal-, Land- en Volkenkunde, 's-Gravenhage.
BIV	Boletín Indigenista Venezolano. Caracas.
BNC	BiNational Center.
BSL	Bulletin de la Société de Linguistique de Paris. Paris.
BSVasc	Boletín de la Real Sociedad Vascongada de Amigos del País. San Sebastían.
BT	The Bible Translator. Periodical for the Assistance of Bible Translators. London.
CA	Cuadernos Americanos. México.
CAnthr	Current Anthropology. A world journal of the sciences of man. Chicago.
CARE	Cooperative for American Relief Everywhere.
CCE	Centro de Cálculo Electrónico. México.
CDC	Control Data Corporation.
CdM	Colegio de México.
CEEM	Comisión para el Estudio de la Escritura Maya.
CEPAL	Comisión Económica para America Latina.
CETA	Centre d'Etudes pour la Traduction Automatique du Centre National de la Recherche Scientifique. Grenoble.
CHA	Cuadernos Hispanoamericanos. Madrid.
CREFAL	Centro Regional de Educación Fundamental para el Desarrollo de la Comunidad en América Latina.
CTL	Current Trends in Linguistics.
CU	Cultura Universitaria. Caracas.
DCEC	Diccionario Crítico Etimológico de la Lengua Castellana.
DCELC	Diccionario Crítico Etimológico de la Lengua Castellana.
DFL	Departamento de Filología. Universidad de San Marcos.
DLLCl	Departamento de Lingüística y Literaturas Clásicas. Bueros Aires.
DLM	Departamento de Lingüistica de la Universidad de la República, Montevideo.
EA	Estudios Americanos. Sevilla.
ED	Etudes dahoméennes. Port-Novo, Dahomey.
ELT	English Language Teaching. London.
ELTG	Etnographia e Lingua Tupi Guaraní.
ELTH	Amado Alonso, Estudios lingüísticos: Temas hispanoamericanos.
EMP	Estudios dedicados a Menéndez Pidal. Madrid.
ER	Estudio Romanischs.
Fi	Filología. Buenos Aires.
Fil	Filología. Buenos Aires.
FL	Foreign language.

FLES	Foreign Language Elementary Schools.
FLT	Foreign language teaching.
GL	General Linguistics. Lexington, Kentucky.
GP	Gross product.
Homenaje Krüger	Homenaje a Fritz Krüger. Mendoza, 1952, 2 vols.
Homenaje Martinet	Miscelanea Homenaje a André Martinet. Universidad de la Laguna, Canarias, 3 vols.
Homenaje Millás	Homenaje a Millás-Vallicrosa. Barcelona, 1954.
HR	Hispanic Review. Philadelphia.
HSAI	Handbook of South American Indians. Bulletin 143, Bureau of American Ethnology. Washington.
IAA	Instituto de Filología y Letras Hispánicas, 'Dr. Amado Alonso'. Buenos Aires.
IAm	Ibero-American.
IBM	International Business Machines.
ICC	Instituto Caro y Cuervo. Bogotá.
IEDES	Institut d'études de développement économique et social. University of Paris.
IFAB	Instituto de Filología 'Andrés Bello'. Universidad Central, Caracas.
IFUCh	Instituto de Filología. Universidad de Chile, Santiago.
IJAL	International Journal of American Linguistics. Baltimore.
ILC	Instituto de Lingüística. Universidad de Cuyo, Mendoza, Argentina.
ILCA	Instituto Lingüístico Colombo-Americano. Bogotá.
ILV	Institute Lingüístico de Verano.
INI	Instituto Nacional Indigenista. Mexico.
IRAL	International Review of Applied Linguistics in Language Teaching. Heidelberg.
JPS	The Journal of the Polynesian Society. Wellington, N.Z.
JSAm	Journal de la Société des Americanistes. Nouvelle série. Paris.
LAE	Ecuadorian Literacy League.
Lg	Language. Journal of the Linguistic Society of America. Baltimore.
Ling. Bibl.	Linguistic Bibliography.
LL	Language Learning. Ann Arbor.
LN	Lingua Nostra. Firenze.
LSA	Linguistic Society of America.
LWC	Languages of wider communication.
MLJ	Modern Language Journal. Ann Arbor, Michigan.
MLN	Modern Language Notes. Baltimore.
MLR	The Modern Language Review. Cambridge.
MSCALE	Memorias del Segundo Congreso de Academias de la Lengua Española. Madrid, 1956.
MSLL	Monograph Series on Languages and Linguistics. Georgetown University, Washington, D.C.
NAL	North American descriptive linguistics.
NCTE	National Council of teachers of English.
NF	neue Folge.
NRFH	Nueva Revista de Filología Hispánica. México.
NWIG	Nieuwe West-Indische Gids. 's-Gravenhage.
OAS	Organization of American States.
OFINES	Oficina Internacional de Información y Observación del Español.
ONEC	Office Nationale d'Education Communautaire. Haiti.
PFLE	Presente y Futuro de la Lengua Espanola (Actas de la Asamblea de Filología del Primer Congreso de Instituciones Hispánicas). Madrid, 1964, 2 vols.
Ph	Phonetica. Basel.
PICAm	Proceedings of the International Congress of Americanists.
PMLA	Publications of the Modern Language Association of America. New York.
PSA	Papeles de Son Armadans. Palma de Mallorca, España.

PyH	La Palabra y el Hombre. Jalapa, México.
QIA	Quaderni Ibero-Americani. Torino.
RBF	Revista Brasileira de Filologia. Rio de Janeiro.
RCA	Revista Colombiana de Antropología. Bogotá.
RCF	Revista Colombiana de Folclor. Bogotá.
RdL	Revista de Letras. Assis. São Paulo.
RDyTP	Revista de Dialectología y Tradiciones Populares. Madrid.
REMQ	Revue des études maya - quichés. Paris.
Rev. de la Fac. de Human. y Ciencias	Revista de la Facultad de Humanidades y Ciencias. Montevideo.
Rev de la Univ. de Buenos Aires	Revista de la Universidad de Buenos Aires.
Rev. de Phil. e Hist.	Revista de Philologia e História. Rio de Janeiro.
Rev Ib	Revista Iberoamericana. México.
RF	Romanische Forschungen. Vierteljahrsschrift für romanische Sprachen und Literaturen. Frankfurt a. M.
RFE	Revista de Filología Española. Madrid.
RFH	Revista de Filología Hispanica. Buenos Aires.
RI	Revista Iberoamericana. México.
RIB	Revista Interamericana de Bibliografía. Washington, D.C.
RJb	Romanistisches Jahrbuch. Hamburg.
RL	Ricerche Linguistiche. Bollettino dell-Istituto di Glottologia dell'Università di Roma. Rome.
RLA	Revista de Lingüistica Aplicada. Concepción, Chile.
RLiR	Revue de linguistique romane. Lyon.
RLR	Revue de Linguistique Romane. Lyon & Paris.
RMEA	Revista Mexicana de Estudios Antropológicos. México.
RMNac	Revista del Museo Nacional. Lima.
RMPaul	Revista do Museu Paulista. São Paulo.
RNC	Revista Nacional de Cultura. Caracas.
Rom Helv	Romanica Helvetica. Zurich.
RomPh	Romance Philology. Berkeley and Los Angeles.
RPF	Revista Portuguesa de Filologia. Coimbra.
RPh	Romance Philology. Berkeley and Los Angeles.
RR	The Romanic Review. New York.
SAm	Spanish America.
SCIDE	Servicio Cooperativo Interamericano de Educación.
SEP	Secretaría de Educación Pública. México.
Sil	Studies in Linguistics. Buffalo, New York.
SIL	Studies in Linguistics. Buffalo, New York.
SIL	Summer Institute of Linguistics.
SJA	Southwestern Journal of Anthropology. Albuquerque, New Mexico.
SL	Studia Linguistica, Revue de Linguistigue générale at comparée. Lund.
SNPh	Studia Neophilologica. A Journal of Germanic and Romanic Philology. Uppsala.
SovEtn	Sovtskaja ètnografija. Moskva.
SPh	Studia Philologica (Homenaje a Dámaso Alonso). Madrid, 3 vols.
TAT	Thematic Apperception Test.
Te	Estudios Lingüísticos. Temas españoles.
Th	Estudios Linguisticos. Temas hispanoamericanos.
Thesaurus	Thesaurus, Boletín del Instituto Caro y Cuervo. Bogotá.
TIL	Travaux de l'Institut de Linguistique. Faculté des Lettres de l'Université de Paris. Paris.
TILAS	Travaux de l'Institut d'Etudes Latino-Americains de l'Université de Strasbourg.
Tl	Tlalocán. Atzcapotzalco, México.

TT	Taal en tongval. Antwerpen.
UCLA	University of California, Los Angeles.
UCPL	University of California Publications in Linguistics. Berkeley and Los Angeles.
UCWI	University College of the West Indies.
UNAM	Universidad Nacional Autónoma de México.
UNESCO	United Nations Educational, Social, and Cultural Organization.
UNESCO-IBE	United Nations Educational, Social, and Cultural Organization and International Bureau of Education.
UNP	Unión Nacional de Periodistas. Quito.
USAID	United States Agency for International Development.
USIA	United States Information Agency.
USIS	United States Information Service.
VKNA	Verhandelingen van de Koninklijke Nederlandse Akademie van Wetenschappen, afdeling Letterkunde. Nieuwe Reeks. Amsterdam.
VKR	Voprosy kul'tury reči. Moskva.
VR	Vox Romanica. Annales Helvetici explorandis linguis Romanicis destinati. Bern.
YMLS	The Year's Work in Modern Language Studies. London.
ZEthn	Zeitschrieft für Ethnologie. Organ der Deutschen Gesellschaft für Völkerkunde. Braunschweig.
ZFSL	Zeitschrift für französische Sprache und Literatur. Wiesbaden.
ZPhon	Zeitschrift für Phonetik und allgemeine Sprachwissenschaft. Berlin.
ZRPh	Zeitschrift für romanische Philologie. Tübingen.

PART I

GENERAL AND IBERO-AMERICAN LINGUISTICS

INTRODUCTION

SOL SAPORTA

A careful reading of the six chapters which make up the section on general linguistics in Latin America, particularly the two contributions on General Perspectives and Hispanic Philology, yields an over-all assessment which one cannot consider particularly gratifying. In spite of occasional brilliant moments to the contrary, the long-range contribution of Latin America to general linguistic theory and methodology has been 'modest', to use Malkiel's carefully chosen term. One sees repeated references in the following chapters to an area of research which is 'in its infancy' or to an area where 'no activity is recorded'.

The tradition for linguistic studies in Latin America has focused almost exclusively on studies of the Spanish and Portuguese languages. The emphasis has generally been local, specific, and nontheoretical. The result has been that serious study has been restricted to essentially three areas: (1) the history and philology of the languages involved, with occasional attempts at descriptive works; (2) dialect and lexical differences in Latin America; (3) concern with the influences of native languages on Spanish and Portuguese, primarily in the area of lexicon. This emphasis has, for the most part, not been conducive to creative work of a philosophical nature on the nature and function of language, or epistemological questions on the nature of linguistic science. In addition, perhaps due to the absence of a classical or Indo-European tradition in Latin America, questions of general theoretical importance in historical linguistics have similarly been neglected.

The result has been an intellectual atmosphere with relatively little original scholarship in linguistic method and theory, but rather with emphasis on the accumulation and elaboration of detailed examples, sometimes of some of the more superficial aspects of the languages involved, aspects which have not failed to attract the often misguided enthusiasm of amateurs and dilettantes. In questions of general linguistic import, Latin America has consistently functioned as audience rather than as participator in the international dialogue.

Mattoso Câmara's introductory text written in Portuguese is virtually the only recent book by a Latin-American scholar which attempts to present an over-all view of linguistic research. Heles Contreras' forthcoming *Elementos de lingüística descriptiva* is a partial attempt to fill the need which till now has been met mostly by translations.

Furthermore, the fact that the humanistic tradition which prevails in Latin America does not make clear distinctions between linguistics, philology, stylistics, and more traditional literary analysis, has perhaps contributed to the lack of a coherent, well-formulated position emerging in Latin-American linguistics. There are great names in Latin-American linguistics: Alonso, Bello, Hanssen, Lenz; but no Sapir or Trubetskoy. There have been important centers of linguistic research: Buenos Aires, Santiago, Bogotá, but no Prague or Copenhagen.

It is perhaps not atypical that there have been recent, not always profound efforts at the application to the languages of Latin America of neo-Bloomfieldian linguistics, precisely at the time when this position is being most severely criticized in the United States; it is painful to have to report that the linguistic revolution that has permeated scholarship in this country and abroad for the last decade has not only had no apparent effect in Latin America, but is virtually unknown. One cannot avoid the conclusion that in the field of linguistic scholarship, Latin America has become insulated to the rest of the academic community.

Contributions to the data for lexicographic and dialect study have been prolific and of varied interest. However, the limitations of such data in the absence of any significant theoretical considerations soon become apparent. And conversely, in the few cases where there is an awareness of the vacuum in linguistic theory, it tends to lead to an almost indiscriminate eclecticism, whereby 'everything which appears to be scientific is in principle equally good and worth adopting (Coseriu).' Similarly, in the area of languages in contact, the typical efforts are catalogues of forms in lieu of explanations.

It must be a matter of genuine concern to all scholars interested in Latin America to read that 'the foremost problem of I(bero) A(merican) linguistics is to overcome its backwardness in the general field of scientific linguistics as such' (Coseriu). It is probably this one area, more than any other, which has enabled linguistics to emerge as an exciting discipline with an increasingly significant impact on neighboring fields. To the extent that the above evaluation is an accurate reflection of the present climate, it is extremely disheartening to those who have been optimistic about the potential and the future of the study of language in Latin America.

There are indications that some sensitivity to the situation is developing, and that efforts to remedy it are being made. Indicative of a possible reversal of this trend is the recent Latin-American Linguistic Institute, held in Montevideo, where scholars with a variety of training and interests met to deal with current issues. A second such institute is being discussed. Hopefully, the sustained interaction of colleagues beyond national boundaries will result in the elimination of a certain degree of parochialism which has been manifested in the past, and which has resulted in such fruitless debates as those patriotic discussions about the relative worth of 'native sons', or the polemics on 'purism'. One can then look forward to an increased maturity in the scholarly position of general linguistics in Latin America.

GENERAL PERSPECTIVES

EUGENIO COSERIU

O. PRELIMINARIES

0.1. In these 'Perspectives' I intend to lay out the main lines of the recent development in Ibero-American [IAm] linguistics as well as its present situation, a general account of its results, and its possibilities for further development. Consequently, I shall consider the following points:

(1) The external conditions — historico-cultural and others — which have determined and still determine the development of linguistics in Ibero-America [IAm];

(2) The centers of linguistic research in IAm, and the amount and character of their work;

(3) The principal IAm journals of linguistics and their characteristic features;

(4) The information which is available for linguistic work in IAm, the influences which have shaped this work, and the theoretical and methodological trends which it displays;

(5) The prevailing attitudes of IAm linguistics and two experiences which I interpret as attempts to overcome them;

(6) The specific fields in which IAm linguists have worked and the positive results they have so far obtained;

(7) The repercussion of IAm linguistics in the scientific world;

(8) Perspectives for the future.

0.2. It would not be possible to avoid, in a survey such as this, overlappings with other sections in this volume devoted to single disciplines. I have tried, however, to limit overlappings to the indispensable minimum, restricting specific references to what seemed to be important from a theoretical or methodological point of view or, at any rate, what appeared to be symptomatic of linguistics in IAm. I have made more detailed references only with regard to linguistic theory and general linguistics and to those disciplines which are not considered in special chapters (stylistics, philosophy of language, history of linguistics).

0.3. A general survey of IAm linguistics would be incomplete and distorted, if Brazil were excluded. Thus I could not avoid referring to Brazil, although Brazilian linguistics is treated in a separate chapter. In this case too I have reduced references to what was apparently necessary for a coherent outline, particularly where the basic similarities and differences between Brazil and the rest of IAm were in question.

0.4. With a few exceptions, dictated by the nature of the subject, I shall exclusively consider the development of IAm linguistics during the last twenty-five years (1940-65). As to the material to be discussed, it seemed to be impossible to confine this survey to the newer trends (structural or functional linguistics). This would have seriously distorted the outline, since those newer trends are scarcely represented in IAm. I have consequently adopted a different delimitation by confining it to scientific or 'academic' linguistics, i.e. to linguistics commonly treated in university courses and academic publications with scientific aims and with a minimum of acceptable methodological and technical background, excluding only non-specialized and methodologically non-scientific linguistics. This delimitation implies a value judgement in a general sense, but not in each particular case. It does not necessarily mean that everything which has been produced with scientific aims and methods is valuable as such nor that non-specialized linguistics has only obtained results of no interest. Above all, it does not imply denying the usefulness of many non-specialist achievements. Indeed, the scientific linguists of IAm must very frequently turn to the material and the results obtained by non-specialist investigators, empirical grammarians, or amateur linguists. Non-specialized linguistics, however, continues a line of activity which is not at all in accordance with any present trend in our science. In addition, non-scientific linguistics is not characteristic of IAm, except perhaps from a quantitative point of view, since it is more or less the same everywhere.

0.5. Because of the situation stated in 7.1., it is likely that, in spite of my efforts, certain facts may have escaped me, for which I apologize in advance. The first hand data at my disposal concerning the southern part of the South American continent by far exceed my information about the northern part of South America and about Central America, which in addition is mostly second hand. I hope however that eventual involuntary omissions have not seriously affected the basic lines of the survey. For the same reason I had to refer to my personal experience in Montevideo, with a frequency that may possibly appear overstressed. For this too I apologize beforehand.

0.6. The information published so far about recent IAm linguistics is scarce and fragmentary. Homero Serís' *Bibliografía* — referred to in fn. 25 —, which could have supplied substantial information, cannot be trusted in this respect. The critical notices contained in the *Handbook of Latin American Studies* (Cambridge, Mass., 1937ff.; later, 1951ff., Gainesville, Fla.) are excellent but they concern the research on IAm languages (aboriginal and non-aboriginal), not properly linguistics in IAm. Other useful sources are the following: Ana María Barrenechea and Narciso Bruzzi Costas, 'Bibliografía lingüística argentina (1939-47)'; Serafim Silva Neto, 'A filologia portuguesa no Brasil (1939-48)'; Max Leopold Wagner, 'Crónica bibliográfica hispanoamericana', all three included in *Os estudos de linguística românica na Europa e na América desde 1939 a 1948: Suplemento bibliográfico da 'Revista Portuguesa de Filologia'*, I, Manuel de Paiva Boléo, Ed., pp. 147-74, 340-68 and 369-98, respectively (Coimbra, 1951); Rafael Heliodoro Valle, 'Bibliografía hispanoamericana del español',

Hispania 37.274-84 (1954); Hersley C. Woodbridge, 'Central American Spanish: a bibliography. 1940-53', *RIB*, 6, 2.104-15 (1956). Concerning Chile, we have the ample and well-balanced report by Ambrosio Rabanales, 'Pasado y presente de la investigación lingüística y filológica en Chile', *BFUCh*, 16.121-43 (1964). Concerning Brazilian linguistics: Zdeněk Hampejs, 'Filólogos brasileiros', *BFUCh*, 13.165-234 (1961, published 1962) and Sílvio Elia, 'Os estudos filológicos no Brasil', in *Ensaios de filologia*, 157-232 (Rio de Janeiro, 1963). On the particularly important activity of Amado Alonso in Buenos Aires: Ángel Rosenblat, 'Amado Alonso', *CU*, 31.61-71 (1952); Eugenio Coseriu, *Amado Alonso* (Montevideo, 1953); Guillermo Guitarte, 'Amado Alonso', *Fi*, 4.3-7 (1952-53). As for Serafim Silva Neto: Manuel de Paiva Boléo, 'In Memoriam Serafim da Silva Neto', *RPF*, 10.409-18 (1960) and Sílvo Elia, *RBF*, 5.9-13 (1959-60). Concerning the work done in Montevideo: Josef Dubský, 'Z jiho-americké lingvistiky', *Sbornik prací Filosofické Fakulty Brněnské University*, A 8, 9.140-41 (1960) and the reviews referred to below in section 7, fn. 171.

0.7. The term 'North American' will be conventionally employed here as an adjective referring to the United States; the terms 'Ibero-America' and 'Ibero-American' [IAm] refer to the Spanish and Portuguese speaking countries of America. 'Spanish America' [SAm] and 'Hispano-American' refer to the Spanish speaking countries. The expression 'modern linguistics' will be applied to all linguistic trends which have appeared and/or spread in the twentieth century (including dialect geography, Vosslerian idealism, etc.); the term 'traditional' refers to all pre-structural linguistics.

0.8. I may finally point out that I shall consider in this survey the linguistics done in IAm, not the linguistics which has IAm as its object.

1. EXTERNAL CONDITIONS

1.0. Elsewhere, particularly in Europe, the situation in linguistics, as in other sciences at a given historical moment, normally depends, above all, on the personalities of certain scholars and on the trends of ideas which they determine. Contrary to this, the present state of IAm linguistics, which is not ideologically and methodologically autonomous, rather depends on the environmental conditions under which it has developed. This fact radically distinguishes IAm linguistics from linguistics elsewhere, particularly from that of Western Europe. The problem of the DIRECTION in the development of IAm linguistics is not so relevant as the problem of the DEGREE of its development. A minimum knowledge of these conditions, which are historico-cultural as well as material, is therefore necessary for a well-founded appreciation of the achievements, deficiencies and possibilities of IAm linguistics.

1.1. The first condition to be named is the short tradition of IAm linguistics. The scientific tradition of Hispano-American linguistics revolves around four great names: the genial Venezuelan grammarian Andrés Bello (d. 1865), whose philological activity developed chiefly in Chile; the remarkable Hispanic philologist Rufino José Cuervo

(d. 1911), a Colombian; the Hispanist Federico [Friedrich] Hanssen (d. 1919) and the linguist and grammarian Rodolfo [Rudolf] Lenz (d. 1938), both Germans who were active in Chile (the former from 1889, the latter from 1890). Furthermore, this tradition has either been discontinuous or indirect, or both, in the Spanish-American countries, with the sole exception of Chile, where there has been a practically uninterrupted tradition beginning with Hanssen and Lenz, followed by R. Oroz and continued by younger linguists. The properly scientific tradition of Brazil, except for a few forerunners, is of an even more recent date; it was however steadier and more compact. While the generation of the initiators (Said Ali, Sousa da Silveira, Antenor Nascentes, Augusto Magne) was still active, a second generation successfully engaged in the battle for scientific linguistics (Ernesto Faria, Mattoso Câmara, Silva Neto, Sílvio Elia, Maurer Jr., Celso Cunha, etc.) and a third and fourth generation of younger linguists came into existence, without a breach of continuity. Apart from this feeble or late scientific tradition, almost the entire realm of older IAm linguistics is limited to pre-scientific linguistics: Spanish and Portuguese empirical grammar, essays on regional dialects (particularly from the lexical point of view and mainly with normative aims), and study of aboriginal languages on a non-specialized level.[1]

1.2. As a second condition we can consider the relative newness and instability of academic linguistics. The oldest Institute of philology among those which have had a certain amount of continuity is that of Buenos Aires, which was founded in 1923. The others are all of a more recent date. The majority of the existing Institutes furthermore are Institutes of 'philology'. Departments or Institutes of linguistics only exist in Montevideo and in a number of universities in Argentina. In addition, the Institutes are not as numerous as one might suppose. As a matter of fact, there are fewer Institutes in the vast area of IAm than in a relatively small European country such as Italy for example.[2] The majority of IAm universities too are of recent origin, and most of the Faculties of Arts are even newer (e.g., in Brazil and Uruguay) and this is particularly true in the case of the professorships for linguistics. In many cases the latter do not exist at all, at least not on a specialized scientific level. And where they do exist, they are insufficient and often unstable, since they depend on local possibilities for finding qualified persons to fill these positions, as well as on the university

[1] I am leaving aside, of course, certain etymological and comparative enterprises (as e.g. attempts to relate the Quechua language to Sanskrit or Hebrew or to derive Spanish from Greek and the like) — by the way common everywhere among a certain type of amateurs — which do not even belong to the modest prescientific linguistics, but rather to pseudo-linguistics and to fanciful invention.

[2] It must also be pointed out that an institute does not necessarily imply the existence of a team of investigators. The team of Mendoza at the time of Corominas consisted of the director and two assistants. The Departamento de Lingüística of Montevideo was founded with a chief and a secretary and had no other staff members until 1962 (what was called in publications in Europe and America the 'school of Montevideo' actually was a group of enthusiasts and unselfish, voluntary collaborators). Similar was the situation of the Instituto de Filología Hispánica of Buenos Aires in 1960. In other cases the collaborators were and still are few in number, at least as far as linguistics is concerned (thus in Santiago and in Caracas). The Instituto Caro y Cuervo of Bogotá with its complex organization is in this respect unique in Spanish America.

curricula, which are frequently subject to reform in many countries.[3] As far as I know, no university has the four professorships for General Linguistics, Romance Linguistics, Spanish and Hispano-American (or Portuguese and Brazilian) Linguistics and Amerindian Linguistics, which one would expect for an adequate linguistic curriculum in IAm, not to speak of Indoeuropean Linguistics or General Phonetics, the teaching of which is exceptional in IAm.[4] Even in those countries where linguistics is most advanced the four professorships are not found. Thus the linguistic subjects commonly taught in Argentine universities — leaving aside the courses on foreign and classical languages and literatures — are General Linguistics, Grammar (General and Spanish) and History of the Spanish Language (the teaching of Romance Philology has been eliminated). The situation is similar in Chile (Santiago), where as a consequence of a recent reform Romance Linguistics is no longer taught. In Brazil there are chairs for Romance and Portuguese Philology, but no chairs for General Linguistics. The situation in Montevideo is probably the most favorable: the University there has chairs for General and Indo-European Linguistics and Romance Linguistics, besides a special chair for 'Ciencias del Lenguaje' devoted to the study of Spanish, and the curriculum of the Instituto de Profesores includes Introduction to Linguistics, History of the Spanish Language, Theory of Grammar (i.e. General and Spanish Grammar) and Philosophy of Language.

1.3 Owing to the newness of linguistics taught on a university level, there is an inevitably acute and lasting shortage of specialized teachers and particularly of research workers with a strictly scientific training.[5] In many cases the first IAm professors of necessity were, and still are, either specialists in other subjects (for ex., in the Classical Arts), high school professors transferred to the university, self-trained persons with scientific interests,[6] or young men with hasty or incomplete education — all these appointed to fulfill immediate needs of teaching rather than to promote research. Thus the number of centers of linguistic activity by no means corresponds to the number of universities (which in certain parts of IAm has increased rapidly during the last years), nor does it correspond to the number of those universities where linguistic subjects are taught. As a matter of fact, linguistics understood as research is either altogether lacking or scarcely represented in vast areas of IAm. Only in a few

[3] Moreover the number of chairs does not correspond to the actual number of professors for linguistic subjects, since one person mostly occupies two or three — and here and there even four or five — different chairs, in the same or in different institutions (and sometimes even in two different countries).

[4] Also because a specialization in linguistics as such does not exist. Commonly, the courses on linguistic subjects for the greater part belong to the curricula of Spanish Language and Literature (or Romance Languages and Literatures).

[5] Such exceptions as Rodolfo Oroz, with his philological training received in Germany, or Ángel Rosenblat, who studied under Amado Alonso in Buenos Aires, then in Paris and Berlin, and collaborated in the Centro de Estudios Históricos of Madrid, before he came to occupy a university chair, are very rare and possible unique in IAm, in the older generation.

[6] Some self-taught linguists have certainly proved to be excellent investigators and masters, particularly in Brazil, where the existence of good linguists partly preceded the creation of Faculties of Arts; but in this survey I am not concerned with individual cases and exceptions, but rather with a general IAm situation.

countries has noticeable progress been made, but there too scientific linguistics is concentrated in the capitals and only occasionally, as in Argentina and Brazil, in some other university towns.

For the same reason, many of the initiators and promoters of linguistic studies in America, following Hanssen and Lenz, were foreigners trained abroad (mainly Europeans). Among those who directed or created research centers and were particularly influential as to the development of linguistics in IAm, are the Spaniard Amado Alonso, in Buenos Aires, whose direct or indirect influence has been most conspicuous and partly continues to be effective today; the Spaniard Juan Corominas and the German Fritz Krüger, in Mendoza; the Italian trained Rumanian Eugenio Coseriu, in Montevideo. Others, whose temporary activity, independent of its intrinsic value, had a less directly noticeable influence were the Italian Terracini, the Dane Uldall, the Spaniard Tovar, all three in Tucumán; the Spaniard Zamora Vicente in Buenos Aires; the Rumanian Gazdaru (La Plata and Buenos Aires), the Spaniard Hernando Balmori (Tucumán and La Plata), the North American Swadesh (Mexico City), the Italian Ferrario (Montevideo) — although Terracini and Tovar have certainly been influential through their works published in Argentina, and Swadesh's activity has unquestionably had repercussion among students of native languages.[7]

The lack of teachers and specialized research workers is slowly being overcome in some countries. The number of linguists locally trained by national or foreign masters has increased to some extent (thus, particularly, disciples of Amado Alonso either occupied or are now occupying chairs in several universities), and younger linguists have specialized or have been educated in Europe or in the United States.[8] But in many countries the situation has changed very little. As a rule, the number of specialists is still very limited in comparison with the number of universities and with the actual tasks of IAm linguistics.

1.4. The newness and instability of organized academic linguistics also determine the nature and size of the facilities, chiefly of specialized libraries. There are few linguistic libraries in IAm and they are for the most part very incomplete, particularly for certain types of research (thus e.g. for historical and comparative linguistics). This is partly due to the fact that the libraries were founded only recently and with very limited funds, partly to the conditions under which they developed.[9] Either because

[7] Among other IAm linguists and philologists of foreign origin — excepting the Spanish and Portuguese — I mention the Italian Bucca in Argentina; the Germans Bunse (Pôrto Alegre, Brazil), Moldenhauer (Rosario, Argentina), and Schulte-Herbrüggen (Santiago de Chile); the Jugoslav Marcovich (Mérida, Venezuela); the Poland trained Russian Altuchow (Montevideo); and the Italian Meo Zilio, who was active for several years in Montevideo. From 1938 to 1945 the German Ulrich Leo, a Romance Philologist, was active in Venezuela. I do not know what repercussions the temporary activity of the North American Norman McQuown in Mexico had or that of the German Gerold Ungeheuer in Colombia (Popayán).

[8] Thus, e.g. in Germany, the Brazilian Dall'Igna Rodrigues and the Peruvian Escobar; in Spain, the Ecuadorian Toscano Mateus and the Argentinean Guitarte; in the United States, the Peruvian Martha Hildebrandt, the Argentinean Suárez and the Chilean Heles Contreras.

[9] The library of the Mendoza Institute, for instance, about which concrete information was published, possessed 700 volumes in 1941 and 1010 volumes in 1944. The Departamento of Montevideo

of the lack or insufficiency of initial funds or because of the material difficulty in obtaining out of print books and journals, to which must be added the instability of the currency in several countries, it was generally impossible to build up organically designed libraries. These rather grew at random by means of donations, exchanges, and what could be found on the local market. An important exception is the library of the Instituto de Filología Hispánica of Buenos Aires, which was methodically enlarged at the time of Amado Alonso and later completed and partly kept up to date thanks to the untiring efforts of Guillermo Guitarte, secretary of the Institute for several years, in its most critical period. But normally the libraries grew haphazardly, judging from those which I personally visited.[10] This situation affects especially expensive works, such as linguistic atlases and collections of journals. In spite of the interest in dialect geography in IAm, there is not one public library, as far as I know, which possesses *all* Romance linguistic atlases.[11] As for the journals, it is very common that in an Institute some collections are to be found, while others, equally important and relating to the same field, are lacking, simply because there are no exchange arrangements with them.[12] It should also be mentioned that normally an IAm Institute can only rely upon its own bibliographical sources, which is another basic difference between IAm and many European countries or the United States concerning research possibilities. In most cases the specialized libraries are scattered about different countries, hundreds or thousands of miles apart from each other, and exchange arrangements either do not exist at all or are very limited.[13]

---

began with no library at all and with a minimum annual fund for acquisitions; and this situation can be repeatedly encountered in IAm.

[10] More organical sometimes are certain private libraries. Thus, that of Serafim Silva Neto in Rio de Janeiro, with the help of which several Brazilian linguists have worked. The work of Montevideo too was done mostly with the aid of the present writer's private library. A rather organical library with basic works of general and English linguistics was built up by Max Bertens in the Instituto Pedagógico of Concepción (Department of English).

[11] In 1959, the richest library in this regard was the private library of Silva Neto, followed by that of the Instituto de Filología Hispánica of Buenos Aires.

[12] Particularly such journals as *Language*, *IJAL*, *Voprosy Jazykoznanija* are (or not long ago were) bibliographical rarities in IAm.

[13] Although my information about the libraries is incomplete and partly indirect, I give it here, as it could serve as a first hint to foreign scholars who want to work in IAm. The richest library for linguistic works and also for specialized journals (General and Indo-European Linguistics, Classical Linguistics and Philology, Romance Linguistics and Philology) still is that of the two Buenos Aires institutes, although several journal collections stayed incomplete since the transfer of Amado Alonso to the U.S.A. and of the *RFH* to Mexico. It is followed, although with specialization in more limited fields, by those of the Instituto Caro y Cuervo in Bogotá, the Colegio de México, the Instituto of Mendoza (presently possessing an important stock of journals of Romance linguistics) and the Instituto 'Andrés Bello' of Caracas (with a good Hispanic fund for Spanish and American Spanish studies). More limited are the stocks of the Instituto of Santiago de Chile and of the already mentioned Department of English of Concepción, and even more limited are those of the institutes of La Plata and Rosario, in Argentina, and of the Departamento de Lingüística of Montevideo, Uruguay. In Rio de Janeiro the National Library has a good supply in linguistics. Elsewhere too one can find linguistic stocks in the National Libraries (or in the general libraries of the universities or Faculties). Extraordinarily wealthy and complete as to Romance and Portuguese linguistics (including all major journals in these fields) was Silva Neto's private library. I do not know what happened to it.

1.5. The character of the basic information at the disposal of IAm linguists largely depends on the situation which has just been sketched, particularly in the case of general linguistics and linguistic theories. As for its quantity, this information is not scarce, but, in so far as it depends on local possibilities, it is unsystematic and fragmentary. If an IAm linguist quotes concepts of Brøndal or Jakobson, Frei or Hockett, this does not necessarily mean that he either adheres to one or another doctrine or that he has deliberately made a choice among several possibilities — it might simply result from a casual contact with some writing of the author quoted. Furthermore, the information as a whole is not homogeneous, i.e. it is not the same in the different research and teaching centers. The foreign teachers too contribute to this situation: they certainly open new horizons, but, at the same time, they determine the basic information of their pupils in accordance with their origin, their education, and their personal preferences, which can lead to unevennesses, especially if ONE linguistic theory is identified with linguistic theory as such, as is often the case. The heterogeneous character of the basic information is another feature which clearly distinguishes IAm linguistics from that of North America, at least from the descriptive linguistics which as a whole can be called 'Bloomfieldian'. Whereas two different North American descriptive linguists, independent of their specialization and their personal positions, possess to a certain extent the same basic information and therefore a common stock of concepts and terms, two IAm linguists trained in different centers may dispose of equally great (or even greater) but at the same time radically different bulks of information. This can certainly be the case also with two European linguists belonging to different schools or countries. In IAm, however, the difference often depends rather on the material conditions of information (e.g. whether or not the respective libraries contain certain books and journals), than on a coherent system of linguistic thought. So what elsewhere normally is a matter of orientation or of conception, can be a matter of information in IAm.

1.6. In another sense the intimate connection between Hispano-American and Spanish (and between Brazilian and Portuguese) linguistics must be taken into account. This connection is, in effect, the determining condition for what is homogeneous in the activity of the IAm research centers as to the basic information and the methodological orientation, in a positive as well as in a negative sense. That is to say, if the average Hispano-American linguist is acquainted with the essentials of the history of linguistics, this is due to the fact that a translation of the well-known short treatise by Thomsen appeared in Spain (*Historia de la lingüística*, Barcelona, 1945), as well as to Antonio Tovar's book, *Lingüística y filología clásica. Su situación actual* (Madrid, 1944). The fact that Stenzel and Bühler are almost universally known names among the Hispano-American linguists and are referred to by them with a frequency that is unusual in most European countries and inconceivable in the United States, is also due to Spanish translations (resp., *Filosofía del lenguaje*, Madrid, 1935, and *Teoría del lenguaje*, Madrid, 1950).[14] If, on the other hand, structuralism reached Spanish America only

[14] It is strange that these names are much more often quoted in IAm than in the German speaking

lately, one of the reasons for this fact is that it was also only lately introduced in Spain.[15] And if North American descriptive linguistics is relatively unknown in Spanish-America, this is surely related to the very feeble response which this trend called forth among the Spanish linguists.[16]

1.7. Another condition which is effective in the same sense is the limited knowledge of languages among the average IAm linguists. In most parts of IAm (particularly in South America) French still is the best known foreign language. Thus the works of French linguists (or those published in the French language) are more widely spread than works in German or English. This explains the utmost importance of translations for the works written in the latter languages. If Vossler has been more influential in IAm than any other German scholar (e.g. Paul is still widely unknown there), this is due to the fact that his works were translated. And if stylistics has spread far in IAm, this is not only due to the orientation of many IAm linguists nor only to the writings of Amado Alonso, but also to translations and to the contributions of Vossler and Spitzer to IAm periodicals. In the same way, Jespersen's *Mankind*, which was translated into Spanish, is much better known and quoted more often than his *Language*; and Sapir is now becoming a generally known name, thanks to his being translated into Spanish and Portuguese.[17]

1.8. Finally, mention must be made of the influence of political situations on cultural life, which in some instances has been of serious consequence for teaching and research; e.g. the changes which the Buenos Aires Instituto de Filología has undergone and the lack of continuity in its work have been mainly for political reasons.

2. RESEARCH CENTERS

2.0. As has been indicated above (1.2.) most of the centers of linguistic work in IAm (and to some extent, all of them) are 'philological' centers. Linguistics prevails in

---

countries, where Bühler was influential to some extent, whereas the response to Stenzel was very limited among linguists. This is because they are just TWO among other theorists of language in the German speaking countries, while they are THE German theorists par excellence for most IAm linguists. The same also occurs in other fields of culture with translated authors.

[15] It must be said that certain topics, such as the problems of the distinction between morphology and syntax or Hjelmslev's general grammar, have come to be known to the average Hispano-American linguist through Spanish books of a very low scientific quality, as are the two by Antonio Llorente Maldonado de Guevara, *Los 'Principios de gramática general' de Hjelmslev y la lingüística* (Granada, 1953) and *Morfología y sintaxis. El problema de la división de la gramática* (Granada, 1955). Generally, the Spanish publications enjoy a great prestige in Spanish America; from this follows that certain Spanish works on 'modern' linguistics were widely accepted, which, however, would rather deserve to be forgotten: cf. Coseriu, *Reseñas* 2.11-13 (Montevideo, 1954).

[16] In this connection one can rather expect a spreading in the reverse direction — from Spanish America to Spain — as it was the case with other modern trends at the time of Amado Alonso.

[17] It must further be stated that in teaching it does not matter which languages the teacher knows or uses, since the bibliography which can be given to the students, primarily (and sometimes exclusively) is that in the national languages (in Brazil, also the bibliography in Spanish).

some cases, but it is never exclusive. This is due to the old unity between linguistics and philology, which has been preserved up to the present day in particular fields, to the needs of teaching, and, above all, to a very deep-rooted Spanish and Portuguese tradition. Most of the IAm linguists are therefore philologists at the same time, i.e. besides linguistics they also cultivate cultural history in a broader sense, literary studies, or textual criticism. As for work in linguistics, the officially organized centers (those of Spanish America), as they do not have any specific delimitations except for a few cases, could actually cultivate any glottological discipline or language. In fact, they devote themselves especially to the study of Spanish and particularly to the study of local Spanish. In addition, they depend for their activity chiefly on the personalities and the specific interests of their directors.

2.1. Leaving aside the Language Academies, which have different aims, there are nine centers in Spanish America, where scientific linguistics is cultivated with certain diligence, as shown by more or less numerous publications. They are the following:

In ARGENTINA: the Instituto de Filología y Letras Hispánicas 'Dr. Amado Alonso' [IAA] and the Departamento de Lingüística y Literaturas Clásicas [DLLCl] of Buenos Aires, and the Instituto de Lingüística of the University of Cuyo [ILC], in Mendoza;

In CHILE: the Instituto de Filología of the University of Chile [IFUCh], in Santiago;

In COLOMBIA: the Instituto Caro y Cuervo [ICC], in Bogotá;

In MEXICO: the Centro de Estudios Lingüísticos y Literarios of the Colegio de México [CdM], in Mexico City;

In PERU: the Departamento (formerly Instituto) de Filología of the University of San Marcos [DFL], in Lima;

In URUGUAY: the Departamento de Lingüística of the Universidad de la República (Facultad de Humanidades y Ciencias), in Montevideo [DLM];

In VENEZUELA: the Instituto de Filología 'Andrés Bello' [IFAB], of the Universidad Central, in Caracas.

2.1.1. The IAA is a continuation of the former Instituto de Filología of the University of Buenos Aires. It was founded in 1923 — with the assistance of the Centro de Estudios Históricos of Madrid — under the honorary direction of Ramón Menéndez Pidal and with Américo Castro as acting director. This Institute was at first the only center of importance and later (until 1946) the most important of all the philological and linguistic research centers in Ibero-America. During the first years of its existence — a period in which it changed direction several times — this Institute already did excellent work and published a number of valuable contributions. But especially from 1927 to 1946, under the direction of Amado Alonso, it displayed an intensive and manifold activity, becoming one of the most important centers of the Hispanic world and even the foremost at the time when philological and linguistic activity decreased in Spain. Between the years 1930 and 1946 it published the deservedly famous *Biblioteca de Dialectología Hispanoamericana* [*BDH*] (6 volumes and three supplements);[18] in 1931 it initiated a *Colección de estudios indigenistas*; between

[18] Volume 7, already prepared at the time of Amado Alonso, was not published until 1949.

1932 and 1942 it published a *Colección de estudios estilísticos* (three volumes and one supplement),[19] and between 1939 and 1946 the *RFH* (and two supplements of it, with a literary character), along with other works issued outside of these collections or outside of the University. About 1941, during the most splendid period of the Institute, Amado Alonso gathered around it a large number of collaborators: Pedro Henríquez Ureña (d. 1946), Eleuterio Tiscornia (d. 1945), Ángel Battistessa, Ángel Rosenblat, Marcos Morínigo, Raimundo Lida, María Rosa Lida, Berta Elena Vidal de Battini, Ana María Barrenechea, and others, a number of whom had been his own pupils. In 1946, however, Amado Alonso was compelled to move to the United States. Many of his team dispersed[20] and the Institute entered a critical phase of its existence, which it has not yet completely overcome. Associated at first with the Instituto de Literaturas Clásicas, as the Sección Románica of a new Instituto de Filología directed by Enrique François, it practically ceased to operate. The Sección Románica was changed to Instituto de Filología Románica in 1950, then in 1953 to Instituto de Filología Hispánica, which assumed its present form in 1962. In these successive forms the Institute had another period of rather intensive activity, although very short-lived (1949-51), under the direction of Alonso Zamora Vicente; then another period of inactivity or limited activity (from 1954 to 1958 it was completely unproductive). Since 1959 it has been in a process of recovering, but because of the difficulties it passed through, it does not today have a team of collaborators comparable to that of its former times. In Amado Alonso's days, the Instituto de Filología was a center open to various modern linguistic trends; under the direction of Zamora Vicente, it was a good center for Hispanic studies in the Spanish tradition; in its last form, under the guidance of Ana María Barrenechea, it seems to have turned its attention toward structural grammar, although without abandoning other interests. Journal: *Fi.*

2.1.2. The DLLCl is a continuation of the former Instituto de Literaturas Clásicas. The DLLCl also underwent several transformations, before it reached its present state: Sección Clásica of the Instituto de Filología, Instituto de Filología Clásica (with a Section for Linguistics), Departamento de Filología Clásica y Lingüística. It was directed for many years in its various phases and up to its penultimate phase by the Latinist Enrique François (d. 1956?). At present it is directed by Salvador Bucca. Under the direction of François the DLLCl had a period of somewhat assiduous activity — although of a rather informative character — particularly between 1944 and 1949. During this period the DLLCl published, in addition to a number of Latin texts and works on literary history, a linguistic series including translations of Pernot, Vendryes, Lejeune, and Marouzeau and Antonio Tovar's important book *Estudios sobre las primitivas lenguas hispánicas* (1949). From 1950 to 1955 the DLLCl displayed a more limited activity[21] and later, until 1959, was altogether silent. This Institute was

[19] Another supplement and a further volume were issued in 1948 and in 1951, respectively.

[20] María Rosa Lida (d.1962) and Morínigo went to the United States, Rosenblat to Venezuela, and Raimundo Lida to Mexico.

[21] In 1955 it published: Giacomo Devoto, *Los fundamentos de la historia lingüística*, translated by Carlos Alberto Ronchi March, and Romualdo Ardissone, *Aspectos de la glotogeografía argentina.*

for many years a center for classical philology, also interested in historical and comparative (Indo-European) linguistics. In its new form, it seems to turn towards general and Amerindian linguistics and has shown interest for structuralism.[22] Journal: *AFCl.*

2.1.3. The ILC was founded in 1940 and had a first period of activity until 1945, under the direction of the Hispanist Juan Corominas. After an interruption of several years, it again took up activity in 1949, under the direction of the well-known Romance philologist Fritz Krüger.[23] In its first phase the ILC above all engaged in the study of (Hispanic) etymology. Under the direction of Krüger it turned towards linguistic-ethnographical Romance and Argentine studies. Journal: *AIL.*

2.1.4. The IFUCh was founded in 1943 (as a continuation of the Sección de Filología of the Instituto Pedagógico, which has been in existence since 1935) and has been directed from the beginning by Rodolfo Oroz. It is a research institute exclusive of teaching. In 1949 it became a section of a larger Instituto de Investigaciones Histórico-Culturales. The IFUCh has devoted itself particularly to the study of Spanish in Chile. Its collaborators are: Luis Cifuentes (d. 1956), Ambrosio Rabanales, Lidia Contreras — all of them Hispanists — and Anselmo Raguileo, a student of native languages. The general orientation of this Institute is traditional, but among its collaborators a certain interest for structuralism has been shown. Journal: *BFUCh.*

2.1.5. The ICC, officially founded in 1942 (but actually organized only in 1944), has continually developed and enlarged, particularly in the last years. From 1944 to 1948 it was directed by Félix Restrepo (1887-1965; honorary president from 1948-1965); since 1948 it has been directed by José Rivas Sacconi, with Rafael Torres Quintero as associate director. It is now, in structure, the most powerful organism devoted to linguistics in IAm. Although it does not exclusively dedicate itself to linguistic research, it has among its five departments two linguistic departments: a department of lexicography and another of dialectology (directed by Fernando Antonio Martínez and Luis Flórez, respectively), besides a department of classical philology (directed by Jorge Páramo Pomareda) and a large team of industrious collaborators. Among these, besides those already named, José Joaquín Montes deserves special mention.[24] The Seminario 'Andrés Bello', a teaching section of the Institute, created in 1958, organizes postgraduate courses, partly with the collaboration of foreign teachers and lecturers, in which scholarship holders from different countries participate. Since the old group of Buenos Aires dispersed, the ICC has become the leading center of America for Spanish American studies, although it lacks the continental orientation of the Instituto de Filología (in fact, it has concentrated its attention almost exclusively on the

[22] During recent years it published some informative pamphlets (cf. fn. 48) and began a series of *Cuadernos de lingüística indígena* (2 numbers in 1964).

[23] Concerning his activity in Germany and in Argentina see: Gerardo Moldenhauer, *Fritz Krüger. Notice biographique et bibliographique* (Louvain, 1959). The University of Cuyo published two huge volumes of an *Homenaje a Fritz Krüger* (Mendoza, 1952 and 1954), with important foreign (mainly European) contributions.

[24] From 1940 to 1949 the Spaniard Pedro Urbano González de la Calle was also active in Colombia and collaborated with the ICC since its foundation. Later he went to Mexico.

Spanish of Colombia) and has not reached in certain aspects the rigor and technical perfection of the work done in Argentina. Besides two bibliographical series, it is publishing: *Publicaciones del ICC*, *Publicaciones del ICC. Series Minor*, *Filólogos colombianos*, *Clásicos colombianos* (19, 9, 3, and 4 volumes, respectively, until 1964).[25] The ICC has also taken care of a facsimile reprint of the published part of Cuervo's *Diccionario de construcción y régimen de la lengua castellana* (2 vols., Freiburg im Breisgau, 1953-54) and is now publishing its continuation (under the direction of Fernando Antonio Martínez and with Corominas acting as an adviser). It is also preparing the *Atlas Lingüístico-Etnográfico de Colombia* [*ALEC*] (under the direction of Luis Flórez). The general orientation of the linguistic work done by the ICC is traditional, as is usual in the fields of lexicology and dialectology. However, through foreign participation in the Seminario 'Andrés Bello', the ICC has helped to spread structural ideas and methods. Some of its collaborators have also manifested some interest in structuralism. Journal: *BICC*.

2.1.6. The principal interests of the CdM — an institute for post-University studies, founded in 1943 — are more of a literary and historico-cultural nature. Among its collaborators in the field of linguistics Juan M. Lope Blanch (also at the Universidad Nacional Autónoma de México) deserves special mention.[26] In the comprehensive and philologically important series of its publications only occasionally does a work appear related to linguistics.[27] The linguistic interests of the CdM are more readily expressed in its journal: *NRFH*.

2.1.7. The DFL, partly in conjunction with the Riva-Agüero Institute of the Universidad Católica, is displaying a rather manifold activity, although it is primarily philological in nature and not on a strictly academic level. The following belong to the Lima group of philologists: Fernando Tola Mendoza (Classical Philology, Sanskrit), José Jiménez Borja and Luis Jaime Cisneros (General and Spanish Linguistics), Teodoro Meneses (native languages), Martha Hildebrandt (Phonetics and native languages; after several years of activity in Venezuela she again joined the DFL in 1962), Alberto Escobar (Romance languages). The DFL published a comprehensive

[25] In this series there appeared in the domain of linguistics works of exceptional interest, as the published and unpublished writings of Cuervo: very useful handbooks, as Rohlfs' *Manual de Filología hispánica* (1957); valuable studies, as Delos Lincoln Canfield's *La pronunciación del español en América* (1962) and the dialectological works of Flórez; useful popularizing books (also by Flórez); but unfortunately also a few works which are close to amateur linguistics, as Homero Serís' *Bibliografía de la lingüística española* (1964) — very rich to be sure, but unsystematic, careless and arbitrary in the selection and arrangement of the material and full of naive affirmations and of serious inaccuracies — as well as some works far beneath the level of scientific acceptability, as Celia Hernández de Mendoza's *Introducción a la Estilística* (1962).

[26] The linguistic contributions of Raimundo Lida — who was active in the Colegio between 1946 and 1952 and since 1953 has been a teacher at Harvard — mostly belong to his activity in Buenos Aires, prior to 1946.

[27] The same can be said about the series *Publicaciones de la NRFH*, also edited by the Colegio, into which linguistics enters only partially, in the form of stylistics. Some linguistic works were in turn published by the Universidad Nacional Autónoma de México in the series *Publicaciones del Centro de Estudios literarios*.

series of pamphlets mainly designed to be used in teaching. Journal: *Sphinx*.

2.1.8. The DLM, founded in 1951, was directed by the present writer from its beginning until March, 1963. Following my transfer to Germany, it remained in charge of my former pupil José Pedro Rona, who, after some attempts in the Indo-European field, has been specializing in Hispano-American dialectology. The DLM — in addition to those materials designed for its own use — is publishing two series of *Publicaciones*, one printed and one mimeographed, and a series of *Cuadernos de Filosofía del Lenguaje* (17, 14, and 2 items, respectively, until 1964). The DLM has also published 2 volumes of the series *Filología y Lingüística* of the Facultad de Humanidades. From 1952 to 1962 the DLM was the most active linguistic center in IAm and the most modern in its orientation, being at the same time the only IAm center for research in general linguistics. Concerning its aims and collaborators see 5.1.2. No journal.

2.1.9. The IFAB, founded in 1947, has been directed from its beginning by the Argentine Ángel Rosenblat (in Venezuela since 1946; cf. fn. 20), the first and the most famous of Amado Alonso's disciples.[28] Unfortunately, because of external circumstances, the IFAB does not have a large group of collaborators. In spite of this it has accomplished important work. Spanish, American Spanish, and especially Venezuelan Spanish are its subjects of research. The IFAB has so far published two volumes of a major series of publications as well as a series of excellent *Cuadernos* — partly of a popularizing character, but nevertheless with a serious scientific foundation and on a high level — almost all written by its director.[29] In his personal activity Dr. Rosenblat has remained true to his traditional linguistic education; but among the collaborators of the Institute structural orientation is also found.[30] No journal (but cf. fn. 37).

2.2. It may be said that about four-fifths (or more) of scientific Hispano-American linguistics during the last twenty-five years — i.e. with a few exceptions (cf. 1.1., 2.1.1., and 2.1.4.), of ALL scientific linguistics in Spanish America — has been accomplished in or by the Institutes just enumerated. Outside of these Institutes and independent of several other less active or recently founded Institutes, there only remains to be mentioned the individual and more or less isolated activity of a limited number of linguists. In certain cases, the activity of these linguists coincides with that of the centers they represent and, to a certain extent — apart from such countries as Argen-

[28] Professor Rosenblat presently is the leading figure in Hispano-American linguistics. Among other things, he is the best connoisseur of American Spanish and at the same time the best IAm connoisseur of the history of Spanish. About his activity in Venezuela, see María Rosa Alonso, 'Ángel Rosenblat y el español de Venezuela', *CU* 64.74-78 (1958).

[29] The most extensive work, a *Diccionario de venezolanismos*, still is in preparation. Specimens of this dictionary are found in Rosenblat's two volumes *Buenas y malas palabras en el castellano de Venezuela. Primera Serie*[2] and *Segunda Serie* (Caracas, 1960; the first edition of the first series appeared in 1956).

[30] From 1953 to 1961 the Peruvian structuralist Martha Hildebrandt was a collaborator of the Instituto (cf. 2.1.7. and fn. 8) and was moreover dealing with native languages in the Comisión Indigenista Nacional. One can further mention the young Hungarian Esteban Emilio Mosonyi, who has also devoted himself to the study of native languages applying structural methods.

tina, Chile and Mexico — with THE scientific linguistics of their respective countries.

Thus, in ARGENTINA, the activity of the well-known structuralist Luis Jorge Prieto (Córdoba); of Gerardo [Gerhard] Moldenhauer and Germán Fernández Guizzetti (Rosario); and of Clemente Hernando Balmori (La Plata) (d. 1965) should be mentioned. In Tucumán the successive presence of several linguists (cf. 1.3.) has not led to the establishment of a permanent research center; nevertheless, Terracini published two important works there[31] and initiated a collection of students' pamphlets, of which two items were issued. In Buenos Aires, where he established himself after World War II, the Romance philologist Gazdaru has displayed a significant activity while collaborating intermittently with the two Institutes of the University.[32]

For CHILE we still have to mention: in Santiago, the activity of the grammarian Claudio Rosales (d. 1951) and that of the linguist Heinz Schulte-Herbrüggen; in Concepción, the activity of the Anglicist Max Bertens Charnley (who has also done some work in the field of American Spanish) and the very recent and somewhat hurried but nevertheless promising activity of Heles Contreras. It is possible that Concepción will in time become a second important center of linguistic research in Chile: there are encouraging signs for it.

In MEXICO the activity of Morris Swadesh and of the Spanish archeologist and Indoeuropean scholar P. Bosch-Gimpera in the Instituto de Historia of the Universidad Nacional Autónoma (Mexico City) and the activity of Juan A. Hasler (Veracruz) ought to be mentioned; in ECUADOR, that of Humberto Toscano Mateus (Quito, d. 1966); in COSTA RICA, that of Arturo Agüero Chaves (San José). In PUERTO RICO besides the vast lexicographical work done by Augusto Malaret, the activity of Manuel Álvarez Nazario in the same field should also be remembered.

In other centers and countries there has been some sporadic work worth mentioning, but no extensive or continuous linguistic activity. The above can thus give an idea of the vast empty areas shown by the map of scientific linguistics in Spanish America.

2.3.0. In Brazil linguistic work has not usually been concentrated in research Institutes. It rather centered around professorships and university courses and generally has a strictly individual character. Consequently, 'center of linguistic activity' will mean in this case concentration of individual activity in a single town.

2.3.1. Rio de Janeiro has been and still is the major center of linguistics in Brazil. As far as the first generation of Brazilian linguists is concerned (cf. 1.1.), the activity of Manuel Said Ali (1861-1953) and of Álvaro Fernando Sousa da Silveira (born 1883) belongs for the most part to the period preceding that considered in this survey; but Antenor Nascentes (born 1886) and Augusto Magne (born 1887) continue to be productive in the present period. The activity of most of those linguists whom I called the second Brazilian generation — Joaquim Mattoso Câmara Jr., Ernesto Faria (1906-62), Serafim da Silva Neto (1917-60), Sílvio Elia, Celso Ferreira da Cunha —

[31] *¿Qué es la lingüística?* (1942) and *Perfiles de lingüistas. Contribución a la historia de la lingüística comparada* (1946).

[32] See Nydia G. B. de Fernández Pereiro, 'Dimitrie Gazdaru', *Orbis* 11.393-404 (1962).

is also concentrated in Rio. Ismael de Lima Coutinho (d. 1965), Gladstone Chaves de Melo, Antônio Houaiss too, and perhaps some others, can be included in this group. Mattoso Câmara (born 1904), the oldest of this generation, has also been the most modern in his orientation, since he introduced structuralism in Brazil (and indirectly even in Portugal). In turn Silva Neto, an indefatigable promoter of all kinds of linguistic studies, who was recognized as a master by the linguists of his own generation and also by older ones, has been the main representative of historical linguistics in his country and is so far the most outstanding figure in Brazilian linguistics in more than one sense. The main subjects of research for this and the preceding generation have been Portuguese and Brazilian Portuguese (history, phonetics, grammar, lexicology, dialectology, stylistics, critical text editions). Other topics, however, were not ignored; thus, general linguistics (Mattoso Câmara), Romance linguistics (Silva Neto), Latin studies (Faria), history of linguistics (Silva Neto, Sílvio Elia) and Amerindian linguistics (Mattoso Câmara).

In other Brazilian centers too there has been a notable or at least promising development in linguistics. For São Paulo, we can mention the activity of Francisco da Silveira Bueno, a student of Portuguese, and particularly that of the Latinist and Romance philologist Theodoro Henrique Maurer Jr. Elsewhere, the following names, among others, have to be remembered: Rosário F. Mansur Guérios (Curitiba), Heinrich Bunse and Albino de Bem Veiga (Pôrto Alegre), Florival Seraine and R. Valnir C. Chagas (Fortaleza), Ángela Vaz Leão (Belo Horizonte). A promising new center was until recently that of Brasília, including Aryon Dall'Igna Rodrigues (Native languages), Adriano Da Gama Kury (Portuguese) and Nelson Rossi (Romance languages); this center dispersed however in 1965. Some linguistic activity has also been recorded in Recife, Salvador and Florianópolis.

2.3.2. While most linguistic publications in Spanish America are issued by the universities and research institutes, the situation is different in Brazil in this respect too, which seems to indicate a greater public interest in linguistics. Although a number of works were published by institutions (such as the Instituto Nacional do Livro, Casa de Rui Barbosa, Rio de Janeiro Faculty of Arts, São Paulo University), most of them are issued by commercial publishing houses, as in Western Europe and the United States.[33]

2.4.1. In order to complete this survey, we must also remind the reader of those centers primarily devoted to the study of native languages. Important centers for this field exist in Mexico City, Guatemala, Caracas, Asunción, São Paulo and Brasília. These centers are radically different from the linguistic-philological centers considered above — from which, by the way, they are totally separate — and represent, so to say, 'another' linguistics in IAm. In these centers linguistics is not associated with philology, but rather with anthropology and ethnology (by the way, they are not exclusively

[33] In this connection there must be mentioned above all the *Biblioteca Brasileira de Filologia* of the Livraria Acadêmica, the publications of the Livros de Portugal Press as well as the meritorious, although very variable *Coleção 'Rex'* of the Organização Simões (all three in Rio de Janeiro).

linguistic centers, but indeed anthropological and ethnological centers). Strangely enough, these centers are sometimes more advanced than are the philological-linguistic centers. The students of native languages generally have less philological training than other IAm linguists and know much less about traditional historical linguistics, but they are in certain cases better acquainted with modern descriptive techniques, and the influence of North American descriptivism has in several instances proved to be decisive among them.[34] At any rate, independent of its occasional intrinsic value, the activity in the field of native languages is marginal in the whole of IAm linguistics and has so far scarcely affected its general development. The leading centers of IAm linguistics are the philological-linguistic centers, not only because they are much more numerous and have more resources, but also because the linguistics which they represent is that which predominates (or is exclusive) in teaching and has infinitely greater possibilities for both national and continental diffusion, whereas the native language work, owing to its very subject, can only call forth a local and limited response. A description of the Guajiro language awakens very little interest in Chile or Argentina and, vice versa, a description of Araucanian is not likely to arouse interest in Colombia or Venezuela. This is particularly true if one considers the present situation in IAm linguistics, in which the facts investigated are of more interest than the methods which are used. Even in those countries where the studies of indigenous languages are carried out, they mostly remain confined to the circles of native lore students.[35]

2.4.2. In the same connection we must remember the intensive and indefatigable activity displayed by the Summer Institutes of Linguistics, i.e. by Pike and his collaborators, an activity at first limited to Mexico, but later extended to Peru, Guatemala, Colombia, Ecuador, Bolivia, and, recently, to Brazil (Rio, Brasília, Belém). Unfortunately this activity has not had repercussion in IAm linguistics either (except in some centers for native language studies). This is due partly to its character, partly to what has been said in 2.4.1. and to the fact that it was displayed above all in Central America and in the northern countries of South America, whereas IAm linguistics, from Rio to Santiago de Chile, is concentrated mainly in the southern part of the Continent.

2.5. In another sense, the activity of several linguistic associations should be mentioned, which are however not oriented towards research but rather towards information and discussion. In Uruguay a 'Centro Lingüístico de Montevideo' was founded in 1951; in Chile a 'Círculo Lingüístico de Santiago' arose in 1957, and similar circles were set up in Valparaíso and in Concepción in 1959. I have also had notice of such a circle in Buenos Aires, and it is possible that there are other similar associations elsewhere. Finally in 1962 an 'Asociación de Lingüística y Filología de América Latina' was organized on an Inter-American level. This association held its first congress in

[34] The union between linguistics, anthropology, and ethnology is also typical in this sense.

[35] Certain ties — mostly fragile and of a local character — between the non-native and the native language studies were established with the help of those linguists who worked in both fields, such as Mattoso Câmara, Mansur Guérios, Hernando Balmori, Ferrario or Cisneros, who were ALSO concerned with native languages, or Martha Hildebrandt, Dall'Igna Rodrigues, Fernández Guizzetti, who were PRIMARILY concerned with native languages.

Viña del Mar (Chile) in January 1964. Several people have placed much hope in it, but its possibilities to stimulate effectively the progress of linguistics in IAm, once the first moments of enthusiasm are passed, seem to be doubtful.

3. JOURNALS

3.0. Two general facts have to be taken into account concerning the IAm linguistic journals. The first is that all journals like the Institutes are journals of 'philology', i.e. alongside with linguistics they also publish historical and literary articles, which often prevail over the linguistic part (the same is true of course of the book reviews).[36] The second is that articles published in the IAm journals exceed the limits of what has actually been worked out in IAm. Indeed, whereas the contributions of IAm linguists to journals other than IAm are relatively few, foreign contributions are abundant in the principal IAm journals, and in some of them (*NRFH*, *AIL*, *Ibérida*) they even prevail. Except for the general characterization of the journals, only their linguistic part and only the IAm contribution thereof will be considered here.

3.1.0. There are seven outstanding journals of linguistics (and philology) among those published in IAm. These will be examined here in the chronological order of their foundation.

3.1.1. The *Boletín de Filología* [*BFUCh*] published under this name since volume 5, 1947-49 (volume 4, 1944-46 appeared as *Boletín del Instituto de Filología de la Universidad de Chile*), 16 volumes until 1964, directed since its foundation by Rodolfo Oroz, can be considered the oldest of the seven journals as it continues, even in the enumeration of its volumes, a former *Sección de Filología* in the University of Chile *Anales de la Facultad de Filosofía y Educación*, of which 3 volumes were issued between 1936 and 1943. Since volume 10, 1958, the *Boletín* appears regularly at the rate of one volume annually. It included for many years abundant foreign (European) contribution, but during recent years IAm and particularly Chilean contributions have increased. The book reviews, of an informative character especially during the last years, vary greatly from one volume to another — numerous in some of them, they are lacking completely in others. The linguistic studies published by the *BFUCh* mainly deal with Chilean dialectology and lexicology and Spanish grammar. The general outlook of this journal is traditional. Nevertheless, it was the first to publish studies which employ North American descriptive methods (cf. 4.2.1.) and a review by Heles Contreras of Chomsky's *Syntactic Structures* (14.251-7, 1962). Particularly important is volume 8, *Homenaje a Rodolfo Oroz* (1954-55).

3.1.2. The *Revista de Filología Hispánica* [*RFH*], 8 volumes published, Buenos

[36] The only exclusively or almost exclusively linguistic journal, *Investigaciones Lingüísticas* (5 vols., Mexico City, 1933-8), belongs to a period prior to that considered here. From a journal *Folia Linguistica Americana* offprints of contributions to no. 1 (announced for 1952) were distributed, but the journal itself, as far as I know, was not issued.

Aires, 1939-46, continued as *Nueva Revista de Filología Hispánica* [*NRFH*], Mexico City, 1947ff. (16 vols. until 1962), is the most important among IAm philological journals and the principal Hispanic organ in America, owing to its wealth and variety of content as well as to its scientific and technical level. Founded by Amado Alonso in its two forms, it was directed by him until his death (1952), then by Alfonso Reyes (d. 1959) and since 1962 by Antonio Alatorre and Ángel Rosenblat.[37] Since its foundation it included important foreign contribution which has considerably increased in the *NRFH*. The *RFH* was mainly an organ of the Buenos Aires Instituto de Filología and of Hispanists or Romance philologists, either Argentine or resident in Argentina. The *NRFH* has become an organ of continental Hispanic studies (including North America). Under the direction of Amado Alonso it kept, in its two forms, a certain balance between linguistics and philology. In the following period the interest for literature prevailed. Only during recent years does it seem to have regained a balance between philology and linguistics, particularly in the book review section, thanks to Lope Blanch. The articles it publishes deal mainly with Spanish (European and American), but general linguistics, Romance linguistics, and philosophy of language are also represented, above all in the book reviews. It has always been an organ open to the various trends of modern linguistics, including structuralism to a certain extent (but cf. 4.2.1.). Most useful is its *Bibliografía* elaborated in systematic connection with that of the *Revista Hispánica Moderna*. Particularly important are the volumes in honor of Amado Alonso (7, 1953) and of Alfonso Reyes (15, 1961).

3.1.3. The *Anales del Instituto de Lingüística* of the University of Cuyo [*AIL*], Mendoza, 1942ff. (with an interruption from 1946 to 1949), first directed by Juan Corominas (vols. 1-3, 1941-43, issued 1942-45) and then by Fritz Krüger (1950ff.), 8 volumes until 1962, represent in a certain sense two different journals as to favorite topics and to the origin of the contributions. In the first phase the *Anales* were almost a single accomplishment of Corominas and Spitzer, with interests chiefly for etymology. In their second phase they became an international journal devoted to the study of Romance languages and folklore (particularly Hispanic, as well as Hispano-American and Argentine), with predominantly European collaboration. As to its orientation it practically is a continuation of the journal *Volkstum und Kultur der Romanen* formerly edited by Krüger in Hamburg. Local contribution was relatively limited in both phases (if one excludes that of its directors). The book reviews, mostly due to Krüger himself, are numerous in the second period.

3.1.4. The *Boletín del Instituto Caro y Cuervo* [*BICC*], Bogotá, 1945ff. (since volume 7, 1951 called: *Thesaurus. Boletín del Instituto Caro y Cuervo*), very regularly published (19 volumes until 1964), and directed by José Rivas Sacconi, includes an almost equal

[37] The *RFH* was edited by the Instituto de Filología of Buenos Aires and the Instituto de las Españas (Hispanic Institute) of the Columbia University, New York; the *NRFH*, by the CdM (1947-57) and later by the CdM and the University of Texas, Austin, Texas (1958-61); since 1962 it is edited by the Centro de Estudios Lingüísticos y Literarios of the CdM and the IFAB. In the periods, when the direction was interrupted, the appearance of the *NRFH* was secured by its secretaries (at first, Raimundo Lida; later, Antonio Alatorre).

amount of philological and linguistic articles, considered on the whole, although philology is prevalent in certain volumes. European and North American collaboration is abundant, but IAm and, in particular, Colombian contribution have gradually increased. The topics of its local contributions are Colombian dialectology and lexicology (practically lacking is historical linguistics). Other linguistic topics are found almost exclusively in the book reviews. The latter have recently become numerous and varied owing above all to José Joaquín Montes. The general outlook of the journal is traditional, sometimes open to structuralism through the foreign collaboration and a few reviews. Special mention should be given to volume 5 (1949, issued 1950), *Homenaje a Félix Restrepo.*

3.1.5. *Filología* [*Fi*], Buenos Aires, 1949ff. (with an interruption between 1954 and 1958), directed successively by Alonso Zamora Vicente (1-3, 1949-51), Arturo Berenguer (4, 1952-53), Marcos Morínigo (5-6, 1959-60), and finally by Ana María Barrenechea (1961ff.), 8 volumes until 1962, reflects the ups and downs of the Instituto de Filología of Buenos Aires after what happened in 1946 (cf. 2.1.1.). Under the direction of Zamora Vicente this journal had a good period and presented a clearcut physiognomy. The following period was rather one of decay and disorientation. Since the last volumes the *Fi* has been recovering to some extent and is at the same time gaining a definite character. Its contributions are mostly Hispano-American and Argentine (a good number of the collaborators remain those trained in the school of Amado Alonso and who belonged to the *RFH* group). Its content was more linguistic than philological during the first years; later, the reverse. In the latest volumes it seems to aim at a balance between linguistics and historico-literary erudition. The linguistic articles mostly deal with European and American (Argentine) Spanish, and to some extent with Romance linguistics (Gazdaru). Linguistic book reviews are numerous in the three first volumes, much less however in the following. The general outlook of *Fi* is traditional, approaching structuralism in the recent years. Volume 8 (1962), *Homenaje a María Rosa Lida de Malkiel*, deserves particular mention.

3.1.6. The *Revista Brasileira de Filologia* [*RBF*], Rio de Janeiro, 1955ff., founded by Serafim Silva Neto and directed by him until volume 4 (1958), since volume 6 by a committee (Nascentes, Lima Coutinho, Mattoso Câmara, Sílvio Elia), 6 volumes until 1961, is the leading philological-linguistic journal of Brazil. It appeared regularly under the direction of Silva Neto and less regularly after his death. In some volumes there is an abundancy of foreign contribution; generally however, Brazilian contributors (linguists belonging to the Rio, Pôrto Alegre and, to a smaller extent, to the São Paulo groups) prevail. Its content is to a much greater extent linguistic than philological. The topics of the *RBF* are European and Brazilian Portuguese, but it also publishes articles and book reviews concerning general and Romance linguistics. Together with the *RFH-NRFH* it is the IAm journal which devotes most interest to historical linguistics. Its book reviews are numerous and generally extensive. Although its orientation is fundamentally traditional (historical), it is the IAm journal which grants most space to structuralism, in its articles as well as in its review section (the *Crônica lingüística* by Mattoso Câmara ought to be mentioned in this respect). Vol. 4, dedicated to the 100th anniversary of José Leite de Vasconcelos, is of particular importance.

3.1.7. *Ibérida*, Rio de Janeiro, 1959ff., directed by Celso Cunha, Antônio Houaiss, and Israël Salvador Révah (in the beginning only by the former two), is a properly 'IAm' journal, in the sense that it grants almost equal space to the Portuguese and the Spanish languages in its philological parts (which prevail) as well as in the linguistic parts (concerned mainly with historical linguistics). Its foreign collaboration, particularly Spanish, is very abundant. Local contribution is however scarce. Its review section is almost exclusively of a philological character. Volume 1 of *Ibérida* was dedicated to Menéndez Pidal; Volume 3, to Sousa da Silveira; Volumes 5-6, to Marcel Bataillon.

3.2. Among the remaining philological journals in IAm worth mentioning are above all the Buenos Aires *Anales de Filología Clásica* [*AFCl*] (under this name since volume 4, 1947-49; the first volumes, 1939-46 appeared as: *Anales del Instituto de Literaturas Clásicas*), directed at first by Enrique François and since 1960 by Salvador Bucca, 7 volumes until 1960 — a journal for Greek and Latin philology, which, however, between 1949 and 1954 (vols. 4-6) published a number of valuable linguistic articles by foreign contributors (Chantraine, Marouzeau, Pisani, Tovar), numerous linguistic reviews (mainly on historical and comparative linguistics) and important contributions by Gazdaru on the history of linguistics in the nineteenth century (cf. 6.3.7.).

Other journals are either of less interest from the point of view of scientific linguistics or of a very recent date. *Sphinx* (Lima), a yearbook of the DFL, which reached vol. 15 in 1962, in its second phase, is a philological journal of a very general nature, publishing articles on classical and oriental philology, translations, literary studies, etc., and occasionally articles on Spanish, Romance, or Amerindian linguistics. The *Jornal de Filologia*, São Paulo, 1953ff., directed by Francisco da Silveira Bueno, publishes articles on philology and linguistics (in particular on Brazilian Portuguese) at rather different scientific levels; its review section seems to be above all a personal mouthpiece of its director. The *Boletín de Filología* [*BFM*], Montevideo, 1936ff., issued by the Sección de Filología of the Instituto de Estudios Superiores, under the direction of Adolfo Berro García, is a review of quite irregular appearance (it reached vol. 9, nos. 58-60, in 1962); although very erratic as to its quality (for the most part prescientific), it deserves to be mentioned for the materials it has published (lexical and others); in the last volume it initiated a good review section. Of very irregular appearance and of limited interest is the *Boletim da Sociedade de Estudos Filológicos* of São Paulo (3 issues published form 1943 to 1959). I do not know the *Anuario de Filología* of Maracaibo (Venezuela). *Indianoromania*, published by the Seminario de Filología of the Riva-Agüero Institute (Catholic University of Peru, Lima) under the direction of Luis Jaime Cisneros (one issue in 1962, with mainly foreign contributions), is too new to have a definite character. In Concepción, Chile, a *Revista de Lingüística aplicada* began to appear in 1963, which I have not yet been able to see.[38]

Among the journals of the Academies mention should be made of the *Boletín de la Academia Argentina de Letras*, Buenos Aires, 1933ff., which often publishes linguistic articles (mainly of a lexicological nature), as well as linguistic book reviews; also of the *Revista Filológica*, published by the Academia Brasileira de Filologia.

Among those journals which are no longer published the *Boletim de Filologia* [*BFR*], Rio de Janeiro, 1946-49 (10 issues) particularly deserves to be remembered. It was edited by Nascentes, Mattoso Câmara, Silva Neto and Sílvio Elia, including articles mostly by the same, especially on Portuguese. The first reviews of structural works (Swadesh, Jakobson, Trubetzkoy) which appeared in Brazil were published in this journal by Mattoso Câmara. It also published the first articles on Portuguese phonemics by the same author.

3.3. The journals so far enumerated can be considered as specialized organs. Linguistic studies are in addition published by non-specialized journals, above all by periodicals of the Faculties of Arts such as: *Humanidades* (La Plata), *Humanitas* (Tucumán), *Letras* (Curitiba), *Letras* (Lima), *Revista de la Facultad de Humanidades y Ciencias* (Montevideo); and more recently: *Revista de Letras* (Assis, Brazil), *Revista de la Facultad de Humanidades* (San Luis Potosí, Mexico), *Anuario de Letras* (Mexico City). The general journals of several universities also publish linguistic articles — e.g. *Atenea* (Concepción, Chile), *Anales de la Universidad de Chile* (Santiago), *Cultura Universitaria* [*CU*] (Caracas) and the journals of several Argentine universities — and so do several broader cultural journals, as the *Mercurio Peruano* (Lima), *Revista Nacional* (Montevideo), *Revista Nacional de Cultura* [*RNC*] (Caracas)[39] and the modest yet meritorious *Revista de Cultura* of Tomás Fontes (Rio de Janeiro), as well as journals devoted to other disciplines, e.g. the excellent *Revista de Antropologia* of Egon Schaden (São Paulo), and of course the bulletins and journals for native studies.

4. INFORMATION, INFLUENCES, AND TRENDS

4.0. As has been pointed out above in 1.5., speaking about IAm linguistic trends does not mean dealing with conceptions and methods which arose in IAm, but rather with conceptions which spread and methods which were adopted in IAm, i.e. with the ideological and methodological bases of IAm linguistics. If we would confine ourselves, as has been done before in the *Current Trends in Linguistics*, to the new and specific views of IAm linguistics (i.e. to views different from those known in Europe and the

[38] The periodical series *Cuadernos del Sur* published by the Instituto de Humanidades of the Universidad Nacional del Sur (Bahía Blanca, Argentina), in which among others a few contributions relating to linguistics appeared, is not properly a journal. I do not know the series *Lenguaje y ciencias* of Trujillo, Peru (which reached no. 12 in 1964).

[39] Numbers 112-113 of this journal (1955) constituted an *Homenaje a Andrés Bello*.

United States) or to the original IAm contribution to linguistic theory and methodology, this survey would have no reason to be written or it would have been a very limited one. As to its trends, the outlook of IAm linguistics is determined by what it received, not by what it could offer. For this very reason the problem of orientations for IAm coincides to a high degree with the problem of information and will be considered here from this point of view.

4.1.0. In what follows I shall consider primarily what has been produced in the field of information in IAm and then the general results so far obtained in this field.

4.1.1.1. The first vein of general linguistic information in IAm undoubtedly is translations.

A true program of linguistic translations expertly prefaced and annotated, was developed by Amado Alonso in Buenos Aires, with the assistance of Raimundo Lida. This program was carried out partly by the Instituto de Filología and partly through the series *Filosofía y Teoría del Lenguaje* directed by Alonso himself and issued by Losada Publishers. In the Instituto series two selections of articles appeared: K. Vossler, L. Spitzer, and H. Hatzfeld, *Introducción a la estilística romance*, translation and notes by A. Alonso and R. Lida (1932), and Charles Bally, Elise Richter, A. Alonso, R. Lida, *El impresionismo en el lenguaje* (1936). To the Losada series belong: Ch. Bally, *El lenguaje y la vida* [Le Langage et la vie], transl. by A. Alonso (1941); K. Vossler, *Filosofía del lenguaje* [Gesammelte Aufsätze zur Sprachphilosophie], translation and notes by A. Alonso and R. Lida (1943); F. de Saussure, *Curso de lingüística general* [Cours de linguistique générale], transl. by A. Alonso (1945).[40] These translations, several of which were printed more than once,[41] have enjoyed a wide diffusion and have been highly influential, not only in Spanish America but also in Brazil, Spain and Portugal.

Except for this enterprise, there has not been a regular or rational translation program in IAm. Yet University and above all commercial presses published several important works, such as: *Psicología del lenguaje* [Psychologie du langage = *Journal de psychologie*, 30. 1933; an incomplete translation] (Buenos Aires, 1952); Jespersen, *Humanidad, nación, individuo desde el punto de vista lingüístico* [Mankind, Nation and Individual from a Linguistic Point of View] (Buenos Aires, 1947); Sapir, *El lenguaje* [Language] (Mexico City, 1954); Bertil Malmberg, *La fonética* [La Phonétique] (Buenos Aires, 1964). In Brazil Mattoso Câmara excellently translated Sapir, *A linguagem. Introdução ao estudo da fala* [Language] (Rio de Janeiro, 1954) and *Lingüística como ciência* (a selection of 9 articles; Rio de Janeiro, 1961). Works of

[40] After the death of Alonso, a further volume appeared in this collection: K. Vossler, *Cultura y lengua de Francia* [Frankreichs Kultur und Sprache], transl. by Elsa Tabernig and Raimundo Lida (1955). At the time of Alonso the following were moreover announced as being in preparation: Jespersen, *Philosophy of Grammar*, and Meillet, *Linguistique historique et linguistique générale*; from what I heard, a translation of Trubetzkoy's *Grundzüge* had also been planned.

[41] The translation of de Saussure reached its 4th impression in 1961.

good[42] or less good[43] philosophy of language also circulated as translations and were influential among linguists.[44] Translations of works by Bertrand Russell were not so readily received by linguists and there are not yet any signs of an influence of logical semanticists.[45]

Unfortunately, those translations neither done nor directed by specialists, are inconvenient in two ways: on the one hand they often are deficient, particularly as to their linguistic terminology (thus, among others, the translation of Jespersen's *Mankind*), and on the other hand they are not selected with sound criteria.[46] The latter implies a rather serious danger, as a book having been translated is often interpreted by non-specialists as a guarantee of excellence.[47]

4.1.1.2. Another vein of information is represented by the book reviews and chronicles published in journals and particularly by a number of works with historical-informative aims. Among these last the following have a general character: the two works by Terracini cited in fn. 31 (especially the former); *Panorama de la lingüística moderna* by the Spaniards Antonio M. Badía Margarit and José Roca Pons — published as introduction to the second Spanish edition of Vendryes' *El lenguaje* (Mexico City, 1958) —, unfortunately a fragmentary and hardly trustworthy or critical survey, particularly concerning more recent trends (glossematics, North American descriptive linguistics), and hardly more than an enumeration of names and titles as far as the latest developments of linguistics in Italy, Germany, England, etc. are concerned; Sílvio Elia's *Orientações da lingüística moderna* (Rio de Janeiro, 1955) — particularly on Vossler, dialect geography, Hjelmslev, Trubetzkoy and European phonemics; and Silva Neto's excellent *Manual de filologia portuguesa* (Rio de Janeiro, 1952; 2nd ed., 1957), which supplies ample information concerning the methods of historical linguistics and the dialectology. Especially on dialectology: Silva Neto, *Guia para estudos dialectológicos* (Florianópolis, 1955; 2nd ed., Belém, 1957), and Coseriu, *La geografía lingüística* (Montevideo, 1956). Very detailed information on a particular problem of

[42] Thus: Cassirer, *Mito y lenguaje* [Sprache und Mythos] (Buenos Aires, 1954) — and among those works not exclusively on philosophy of language: *Antropología filosófica* [Essay on Man] (Mexico, 1945) and *Las ciencias de la cultura* [Zur Logik der Kulturwissenschaften] (Mexico, 1951); Wilbur Marshall Urban, *Lenguaje y realidad* [Language and Reality] (Mexico, 1952).

[43] Such as Ogden & Richards, *El significado del significado* [The Meaning of Meaning] (Buenos Aires, 1954).

[44] In this field even a Russian work was translated: D. P. Gorskij, Ed., *Pensamiento y Lenguaje* [Myšlenie i jazyk] (Montevideo, 1958), which certainly is not the most adequate to represent the thinking of the best Soviet theorists of language.

[45] They are nevertheless represented by a good *Antología semántica*, compiled by Mario Bunge (Buenos Aires, 1960).

[46] In fact, besides important or at least useful works, also other works of doubtful utility were translated, such as the superficial booklets on semantics, stylistics, and grammar by Guiraud or works which from the point of view of present day linguistics are not useful at all, such as *La Vie du langage* and *La Philosophie du langage* by Albert Dauzat. And a Buenos Aires publisher reissued Max Müller, *La ciencia del lenguaje* [The Science of Language] in 1944, without indicating to which epoch this work belongs.

[47] Thus, Max Müller and Dauzat are listed in some IAm bibliographies next to Saussure and Bloomfield, and Dauzat even figures as a philosopher of language (!).

historical linguistics (Vulgar Latin) is given in Silva Neto's *História do latim vulgar* (Rio de Janeiro, 1957).[48]

4.1.1.3. Thirdly, the introductory handbooks of linguistics can be considered as informative compendia. The first of them, Mauricio [sic] Swadesh, *La nueva filología* (Mexico City, 1941), also the first work to introduce the principles and methods of North American descriptive linguistics to IAm, was not very influential, partly on account of what is said in 7.1., but especially because it is a book unfortunate in many ways (primarily, because it is written in a manner inappropriate to be accepted by IAm linguists and because it contains expressions of political passion altogether out of place).[49] Almost simultaneously with this unsuccessful attempt appeared Mattoso Câmara's book *Princípios de lingüística geral* (Rio de Janeiro, 1941), which since its second edition (Rio, 1954) has become the best handbook for the introduction to linguistics so far published in a Latin country.[50] These two handbooks are now joined by Heles Contreras' modest and imperfect course *Elementos de lingüística descriptiva* (Concepción, 1963), which is not more than a summary of some aspects of North American descriptive linguistics, but which can claim the merit of being the first IAm handbook to contain a section on transformational techniques.

4.1.2. The preceding refers to the properly informative work achieved in IAm. There must be added, of course, information spread by popularizing publications (relatively numerous) or by research and critical publications, and by the teaching activity of IAm linguists, as well as what was derived from the two countries traditionally influential in IAm: Spain and France (and also Portugal, as far as Brazil is concerned).[51]

4.1.3. Owing to the facts just stated, the general level of linguistic information considerably increased in IAm, particularly in such countries as Argentina and Brazil and above all among young linguists, who usually are better informed than the old.

[48] During recent years the DLLCl of Buenos Aires too (cf. 2.1.2.) began to contribute to the diffusion of information by a series of either translated or original pamphlets. I have seen two of them: Robert A. Hall, Jr., *Lingüística norteamericana*, 1925-1950 [American Linguistics, 1925-1950, *ArchL* 3.101-25, 1951, and 4.1-16, 1952] (1960), and Ivonne Bordelois, *Perspectivas de la estilística* (1962), in which, curiously enough, just the very recent trends are lacking, particularly all the North American efforts in stylistics, glossematic stylistics and Antonio Pagliaro's most important 'critical semantics'; I do not know the second pamphlet, *Cuatro artículos de lingüística estructural* (1962). Among other significant translations I mention: Kurt Baldinger, *La semasiología* [Die Semasiologie] (Rosario, 1964). I am leaving aside, of course, the translated articles published in journals. Among the articles, the following is not specified as, but probably is, a translation: John van Horne, En torno a la gramática descriptiva, *BFUCh* 8.101-26 (1954-5); it presents a rather superficial and partially distorted view of North American descriptivism.

[49] Bloomfield, *Lg*. 19.168-70 (1943), perhaps praised too much the positive aspects of this work, although he did not fail to allude to its negative aspects.

[50] Based on sound, well selected, and well elaborated information, this book keeps an intelligent balance between traditional and structural linguistics and, within the latter, between European and North American structuralism, which seems to be very reasonable for an introductory handbook.

[51] Among the bibliography originated in Spain the *Biblioteca Románica Hispánica* (Editorial Gredos, Madrid) has been very important and spread all over the IAm countries (including Brazil, where it spread even more than in some of the Spanish speaking countries).

The first results are partly tangible: such names as Vendryes, de Saussure, Vossler, Spitzer, Bally, Bühler are well known to IAm linguists and are usually included in the lists of readings in those universities where linguistics is taught, alongside with the leading Spanish linguists (and Portuguese linguists in Brazil). These are followed by names such as: Humboldt,[52] Meillet, Sapir, Trubetzkoy,[53] Wartburg,[54] and some others.

4.1.4. Less directly known are other linguists and so are entire trends of present-day linguistics.

North American descriptive linguistics (Bloomfieldian and post-Bloomfieldian) [NAL] still is the great unknown, in spite of Swadesh's book and of some recent efforts.[55] Indeed, if one excludes some native language students, it is known only in a few centers (such as Rio de Janeiro, Montevideo, Buenos Aires, Córdoba, Concepción) and there rather to isolated persons, and not to all those working in the field of scientific linguistics. There are several reasons for this situation: The external conditions pointed out in 1.6. and 1.7., the limited possibilities to apply the new North American methods to the traditional and specific domains of IAm linguistics (lexicology, lexical dialectology, philology),[56] the general resistance to antimentalism and to its consequences for linguistics (e.g. the scarce or very recent attention devoted by NAL to semantics and stylistics), the fact that most of the foreign teachers in IAm have been Europeans (possibly representatives of very different views), the fact that many IAm linguists were trained in Europe, and last but not least, the fact that NAL mostly ignores the European tradition[57] or is opposed to it. IAm linguistics was and still is

[52] Who, however, is known almost exclusively through the very imperfect and questionable selection included in the booklet of José María Valverde, *Guillermo de Humboldt y la filosofía del lenguaje* (Madrid, 1955).

[53] Known above all through the French translation by Cantineau and through Alarcos Llorach's *Fonología española.*

[54] Known for his *Einführung in Problematik und Methodik der Sprachwissenschaft*, a book which circulated in IAm in its French translation (*Problèmes et méthodes de la linguistique*, Paris, 1946), as well as in the Spanish translation (*Problemas y métodos de la lingüística*, Madrid, 1951). I point out that, when I speak of a more or less ample knowledge, I refer to the works of a general character by the listed authors, not to their investigations in particular fields (I do not refer e.g. to Vendryes as a Celtist or to Trubetzkoy as a Slavist or as a Caucasiologist).

[55] NAL is ignored in Terracini's *¿Qué es la lingüística?* (where Sapir, *Totality* is incidentally quoted). Thirteen years later NAL is not treated either in Sílvio Elia's *Orientações* (in which, however, some North American works are quoted).

[56] Symptomatic in this connection is the case of Martha Hildebrandt, who, a structuralist in her native language studies, employs, however, traditional philological methods in *La lengua de Bolívar, I. Léxico* (Caracas, 1961).

[57] Thus, e.g. an identification of Wilhelm von Humboldt with Alexander von Humboldt, as can be found in Harry Hoijer, Ed., *Language in Culture* 93 and 286, is simply inconceivable among the well informed IAm linguists. Equally — independent of the practical justification it may have in the United States — the well informed IAm linguist is vexed by the fact that the North American handbooks so often ignore the great European linguists whom he knows and esteems, e.g. that neither Gilliéron nor Bartoli are quoted in connection with dialect geography, as is the case in Hockett, *A Course in Modern Linguistics* 484 (where, instead of Bartoli's well known norm of the lateral areas, only an unpublished formulation by Isidore Dyen is quoted about this same norm) or that the name of de Saussure simply does not appear in this same book.

basically an extension of European linguistics; consequently, to the extent NAL deviated from European linguistics, it also remained distant from IAm linguistics as a whole.[58]

English linguistics and untranslated German linguistics are also little known; Soviet linguistics is almost completely unknown,[59] and so is linguistics exclusively published in less widespread European languages, due to what is said in 1.7.

Strangely enough and contrary to what one might suppose, even Italian linguistics does not enjoy a wide acquaintance. Undoubtedly, the activity of Terracini in Argentina, the reviews of Bucca (*AIL*), Ronchi March (*AFCl*), Montes (*BICC*) and others, and the translation of Devoto's book quoted in fn. 21 must have contributed to its diffusion; however, judging from the publications, it does not seem that specific ideas of Italian linguistics have penetrated into IAm linguistics, excepting Montevideo (where Bartoli, Pagliaro, Terracini, Pisani, Devoto are frequently used) and, to some extent — particularly as far as historical linguistics is concerned — Rio de Janeiro. Croce has certainly been remarkably influential in many cases, but mostly through Vossler.[60] Finally, glossematics did not spread far either.[61] Some information in this field was provided by the following: Salvador Bucca, 'Consideraciones sobre la glosemática', *AIL* 5.17-21 (1952), based on a few articles by Hjelmslev and Uldall and on Martinet's review, *BSL* 52.19-42; Martha Hildebrandt, 'La glosemática', *RNC* 104.119-29 (1954), based on lectures held by Hjelmslev and Eli Fischer-Jørgensen in the United States; Sílvio Elia, *Orientações* 145-66 (where glossematics is treated under the name of 'structuralism'). The first and so far only attempt at a critical and ample discussion of glossematics published in IAm is found in Coseriu, *Forma y sustancia en los sonidos del lenguaje* (Montevideo, 1954).

4.1.5. The varying familiarity with the latter fields implies perceivable differences as to information levels in the various IAm centers, in spite of what can be considered as more or less uniform. Relatively high levels of information are recorded above all in Rio de Janeiro, Montevideo, Buenos Aires and Santiago, still judging from the

[58] Certainly, this situation is gradually changing with the growing knowledge of the English language and the specialization of a number of young people in the United States, and there already are a few signs of a change in attitude. Thus the subscriptions to *Language*, few until 1959, rapidly increased in recent years (doubling between 1960 and 1963), although chiefly among the native language students and teachers of English. This change of attitude, however, has not yet led to a general trend of interest for NAL. In addition, several North American centers have started a policy of approach to IAm linguistics. This policy, although welcome as such, in my opinion will not be successful, however, if it only is an attempt to transplant NAL and if the own traditions and peculiarities of IAm linguistics are ignored.

[59] In this respect one can only mention a few reviews by Montes (*BICC*). Some Russian bibliography was used by Schulte-Herbrüggen in his book cited in 4.2.2.

[60] In one South American bibliography, which can be regarded as well informed, I find: 74 French titles (and 10 translations from the French), 24 English (and 11 translations) [12 North American titles in both categories], 4 German (and 16 translations), 3 Italian titles (and 2 translations), and 124 Spanish titles, 78 of them Hispano-American (45 among these by local authors). Except for the English titles, which normally are less numerous, these proportions seem to be typical for linguistics in Spanish America.

[61] A little better known is the preglossematic Hjelmslev, although mostly indirectly; cf. fn. 15.

publications. An optimum of information, including all those fields referred to as less known in 4.1.4. and such disciplines as history of linguistics and philosophy of language, was achieved in Montevideo between 1952 and 1962.[62]

4.2.0. In connection with the diffusion of information, I spoke of 'influences' exerted on IAm linguistics. But this calls for an explanation. It is certainly possible in some cases to speak properly of influences, implying the critical incorporation of borrowed elements to new or at least organic and definable conceptions. In this sense one can trace direct influence of Vossler and Husserl in Amado Alonso, of Jakobson and Sapir in Mattoso Câmara, of Martinet and glossematics in Luis Jorge Prieto, of Italian linguistics, a number of language philosophers and several forms of European structuralism in the theoretical works of Montevideo. In most cases, however, one cannot speak of influences in this sense, but rather of a total or partial adherence to a certain doctrine or even of an occasional application or use of views and methods for particular or circumscribed aims. In the following I shall not, however, insist on this distinction, which, strictly speaking, can only be made for each particular linguist and sometimes only for single works. I shall rather refer to those views, methods, and techniques of modern linguistics which were either accepted or applied and used in IAm, without implying in each case a total adherence on the part of the cited linguists. Indeed, the most general feature of IAm linguistics in this connection is its eclecticism: the simultaneous presence of different views and methods in the activity of the same linguists and sometimes in the same work.

4.2.1. Chronologically linguistic idealism in its Vosslerian form was the first of modern linguistic trends to spread in IAm, and it has been widely accepted by IAm linguists as a theory as well as in the first of its applied forms, i.e. stylistics. Amado Alonso basically was an idealist in his general view of language, and some of his idealism was passed on to all of his disciples. Jiménez Borja[63] and Escobar in Peru, and Sílvio Elia in Brazil also profess to be idealists. Idealistic principles, even if they are eventually not identified as such, can further be found in most IAm linguistics and have also penetrated into the teaching of language and grammar in schools. A peculiar form of idealism, closer to Hegel and Humboldt than to Vossler and stylistics, is found in the theoretical works of Montevideo.[64]

Idealism was followed by dialect geography, which was widely adopted during recent years, particularly in the form of onomasiology, a field in which the geographical method coincides and combines with the Wörter und Sachen method and with ethnographical linguistics. Dialect geography continues to spread and presently seems to constitute the most vital trend of IAm linguistics; see 6.2.1.

As a third trend, although noticeably distant from the two first trends — chronologically separate from the former and quantitatively from the latter — structuralism

[62] In part, and especially since 1957, the DLM has been active in different ways also as a center for the diffusion of linguistic information to several other IAm centers.

[63] Cf. his booklet *El idealismo en la lingüística y su derivación metodológica* (Lima, 1931).

[64] Concerning the stylistic application of idealism, see 6.2.3.

can be mentioned. European structuralism of the Prague School came to be known in IAm only after 1940 and began to spread with certain continuity, although very slowly, only since 1950. North American structuralism, if one excludes Swadesh's book cited in 4.1.1.3., began to be known even later and did not show signs of diffusion until about 1960, except for a few isolated cases. Silva Neto pointed to Trubetzkoy's *Grundzüge* in 1941 and Terracini reviewed it in the *RFH* in 1942. In 1944 and 1945 Amado Alonso published articles on phonemics: 'La identidad del fonema', *RFH* 6.280-3, and 'Una ley fonológica del español', *HR* 13.91-101; he also successively employed phonemic concepts in his works on historical phonemics. This did not provoke, however, a structuralistic trend in Spanish America, and even in Buenos Aires this line of activity was interrupted. The *BFUCh* published the first review on a structuralistic work along with the first structuralistic article in 1953, but this did not change the orientation of the Institute either, nor caused broader repercussions. The first reviews on structuralistic works were published by the *NRFH* only in 1955 and 1957; these reviews were by the way written by North American linguists, and up to the present day this same journal has not published any structuralistic article by a Hispano-American linguist. The first research center to have a structuralistic orientation and to be continually active in this field in Spanish America was the Departamento de Lingüística of Montevideo, where structuralist works have been published since 1952. A structuralist since the beginning of his activity (1952) Luis Jorge Prieto, however, has published most of his contributions in Europe. The first structuralistic work about American Spanish published by a Hispano-American was Washington Vásquez' *El fonema /s/ en el español del Uruguay* (Montevideo, 1953), followed in the same year by Ismael Silva Fuenzalida's 'Estudio fonológico del español de Chile', *BFUCh* 7.153-76 (1952-53). The first critical discussion of the foundation of Bloomfieldian linguistics in comparison with other forms of structuralism is found in Coseriu, *Forma y sustancia* 13-21 (1954). In Buenos Aires the structuralistic line was again taken up by Guillermo Guitarte, although with a single article: 'El ensordecimiento del žeísmo porteño', *RFE* 39.261-83 (1955, issued 1956). Somewhat different is the situation in Brazil, where since 1946 we observe Mattoso Câmara's activity in the field of structuralism,[65] whose orientation was transmitted to some of his pupils and partly penetrated as far as school grammars.[66] All in all, between 1950 and 1960, if one excludes a few native language students, there was no other continuous structuralistic activity in IAm than that displayed by Mattoso Câmara, by Coseriu and some of his disciples and collaborators, and by Luis Jorge Prieto and Silva Fuenzalida (the latter by the way residing in the United States and thus removed from IAm

[65] In 1946, Mattoso Câmara published reviews of structural works in the *BFR*, an activity which he continued in the following years; in 1949 he began to publish in the same journal his first studies on Portuguese phonemics (the first phonemic contributions in the Luso-Brazilian world), which culminated in his book: *Para o estudo da fonêmica portuguêsa* (Rio de Janeiro, 1953).

[66] See Adriano Da Gama Kury, *Pequena gramática para a explicação da nova nomenclatura gramatical* (Rio de Janeiro, 1959).

linguistics). This situation has somewhat changed during the last years, although not much. The following have since then directed their attention towards structuralism: Ana María Barrenechea, Mabel Manacorda de Rosetti, Fernández Guizzetti and Jorge Suárez in Argentina; Rabanales and Heles Contreras in Chile; and a certain interest for structuralism also appeared in Colombia (Patiño Rosselli, Montes). European structuralism (including Jakobson) generally met with broader acceptance and sometimes also penetrated into non-structuralistic works, especially in the form of phonemics. North American methods were applied by: Silva-Fuenzalida, Martha Hildebrandt, Fernández Guizzetti, Jorge Suárez and Heles Contreras. But North American structuralism was by no means assimilated and incorporated into IAm linguistics, so that the contributions of these latter linguists are for the time being rather foreign bodies in it: they are pieces of North American linguistics casually produced in IAm.

4.2.2. Certain trends as well as certain methods and techniques of very recent linguistics have not been recorded so far in IAm or they are found only sporadically. Thus there has not been any adherence to glossematics (although glossematical concepts were used here and there) nor to Guillaumism, which is strange, when one considers its recent diffusion in France. The only representative of Weisgerber's Neo-Humboldtism — and thus also of what is called in the U.S.A. the 'Sapir-Whorf hypothesis' — is Schulte-Herbrüggen, with his book *El lenguaje y la visión del mundo* (Santiago de Chile, 1963).[67] Heles Contreras is the only one who has been dealing with generative grammar.[68] No activity is recorded in the field of mathematical linguistics or machine translation.[69] Swadesh's glottochronology has not been widely received either, and this time one may say fortunately. This technique certainly aroused interest and some naive expectations among native language students and ethnologists and was applied in Mexico, and here and there in Brazil, where it was received with uncritical enthusiasm in one case,[70] and with sympathy, although not without reservations, in another.[71] But beyond this it was either explicitly opposed as lacking rational foundation,[72] or considered with welcome scepticism[73] or, as in most cases, simply ignored.

[67] Juan Corominas' 'Rasgos semánticos nacionales', *AIL* 1.1-29 (1941, publ. 1942) is rather connected with Vossler's linguistic characterology.

[68] Cf. 4.1.1.3. and see Heles Contreras and Sol Saporta, 'The Validation of a Phonological Grammar', *Lingua* 9.1-15 (1960) and Sol Saporta and Heles Contreras, *A Phonological Grammar of Spanish* (Seattle, Wash., 1962).

[69] In this field I only know a small book translated from the Russian: S. A. Lebedev and D. I. Panov, *La máquina electrónica de calcular y la traductora automática* (Buenos Aires, 1957).

[70] Aryon Dall'Igna Rodrigues, 'Eine neue Datierungsmethode der vergleichenden Sprachwissenschaft', *Kratylos* 2.1-13 (1957).

[71] Joaquim Mattoso Câmara, Jr., 'Glotocronologia e estatística léxica', *RBF* 5.209-15 (1959-60). In its moderated and less unreasonable form represented by Sarah Gudschinsky, glottochronology has been applied by Professor Mattoso Câmara to native languages of Brazil, in collaboration with Sarah Gudschinsky herself.

[72] Eugenio Coseriu, 'Critique de la glottochronologie appliquée aux langues romanes', *Actes du Xe Congrès International de Linguistique et Philologie Romanes. Strasbourg 1962* 87-96 (Paris, 1965).

[73] Olaf Blixen, *La glotocronología. Examen crítico de su validez* (Montevideo, 1964) (= *Cuadernos de Antropología*, 2).

5. TYPICAL ATTITUDES AND NEW EXPERIENCES

5.0. IAm linguistics as a whole can be characterized by two basic attitudes which constitute, so to speak, its typical style: the attitude it assumes concerning linguistic theories and methodology and the attitude it reveals in the delimitation of its objective field of activity.[74] These attitudes have been implicitly or explicitly opposed, particularly by the Instituto de Filología of Buenos Aires and the Departamento de Lingüística of Montevideo, which can therefore be considered as representatives of a different style.

5.1.0. As far as the former attitude is concerned, IAm linguistics is characterized by its RECEPTIVITY. In this respect it resembles, to a certain point, Soviet linguistics during the years immediately following Marrism: it is inclined to absorb information and to adopt and apply methods which have already been tried elsewhere, however without the intention to participate in the international dialogue of linguistics, but rather for immediate and local purposes. By the way, the adopted methods are not necessarily selected because of their newness or intrinsic quality. The foremost problem of IAm linguistics is to overcome its backwardness in the general field of scientific linguistics as such. Thus, everything which appears to be scientific is in principle equally good and worth adopting. One often hears or reads the phrase: 'In IAm we have not yet this or that type of study'; a typical aspiration of most IAm linguists is therefore to accomplish such investigations as are lacking in IAm, conforming to European and recently also to United States models.[75] All this can undoubtedly be justified by the actual objective situation, as was seen above, but at the same time it implies a previous renunciation to carry imported theories and methods further. IAm linguists certainly want to contribute to the qualitative progress of LINGUISTICS IN IAM and to elevate it to the level of European or North American linguistics, but they are usually not inclined to contribute to qualitative progress — theoretically and methodologically — of LINGUISTICS AS A WHOLE. In this respect they rather aim at a quantitative progress, i.e. to extend already existing scientific linguistics to fields either unexplored or barely explored. Thus, IAm linguistics is a linguistics which generally does not strive for originality and which has no theoretical or methodological ambitions.[76] Its motto is absorbing and applying, rather than creating and renovating. During the last years a methodological advance has been perceivable, but, strictly speaking, through the importation of new methods, rather than through an internal methodological renovation or development of original methods. For the same reason

[74] Strictly speaking these two attitudes could be reduced to just one, since in both cases we have to do with what is regarded by IAm linguistics as its specific task. It is, however, proper to examine them separately.

[75] In certain cases this leads to the explicit adaptation of particular models, e.g. of a certain European book.

[76] Sometimes this lack of interest is presented as a virtue and eventual theoretical and methodological speculations are considered as inopportune or as not corresponding to the proper task of IAm linguistics.

theoretical and critical discussions are relatively rare in IAm: facts and opinions are discussed on the basis of theories already there, but usually not theories as such and their epistemological foundations. In this sense the book reviews published in the journals, which are primarily informative, as was shown above, are symptomatic. Their critical part, if it exists at all, is usually limited to information and facts (possibly to IAm facts ignored by the author being reviewed), and when dealing with a theoretical or methodological work of some importance (particularly with a European or North American work), the review tends to be a mere summary.[77]

5.1.1. A remarkable exception within the general picture of IAm linguistics in this respect too was the activity of the Buenos Aires Instituto de Filología at the time of Amado Alonso. Although this Institute did not renounce the task of informing and spreading information — on the contrary (cf. 4.1.1.1.) —, it strove to elevate the level of linguistics in IAm, setting an example of original and critical work. Thus the *RFH* was a journal with an international tenor, which did not accept European linguistics in a passive manner but rather established the dialogue with it on its own level. And more generally the entire activity of Buenos Aires did not consist in adopting and adapting; it rather was an autonomous activity often showing theoretical and methodological initiative. This is explicitly revealed in a few theoretical works,[78] but is above all implicitly expressed in the entire work of the Institute, in its attitude and its way of facing problems. Thus, the activity of the Instituto de Filología was a factual and — given the early period in which it developed — an almost ante litteram overcoming of the receptive attitude still prevailing in IAm linguistics today.

5.1.2. Another effort in the same sense — and this time always explicit and more systematical and more deliberately ideological than that of Buenos Aires — was made by the present writer in the DLM, which in fact is characterized especially by its critical, methodological, and theoretical activity. Since this effort was an attempt unique in its kind in IAm, I shall consider it in some detail.

The DLM did not disdain the task of informing and training either but treated it almost exclusively as an ancillary task in view of its own research activity.[79] As regards to this activity, the DLM strove first of all to embrace as many linguistic fields as possible. Thus it dealt with the following disciplines: linguistic theory (Coseriu), theory of grammar (Coseriu, Luis Juan Piccardo), phonemics (Coseriu, Washington Vásquez), stylistics (Coseriu, Carlos M. Rey), philosophy of language (Coseriu, Arnaldo Gomensoro, Mercedes Rein), historical linguistics (Coseriu, José

[77] In this connection one can even observe a regress parallel to the rapid methodological advances of linguistics in Europe and in the United States: the linguistic book reviews in the *RFH* were on the whole much more critical than those in the *NRFH*, and the reviews by Oroz in the first volumes of the *BFUCh* were more critical than the reviews published by his collaborators in the last volumes of the same journal. Also in linguistic polemics — frequent especially in Brazil — the information complex is prevailing: one does not discuss what the adversary thinks, but rather what he knows concerning facts as well as conceptions and methods.

[78] Cf. above all Amado Alonso's preface to his translation of de Saussure's *Cours*.

[79] With this aim in view a great number of texts by European and American linguists were translated and/ or multiplied for the internal use of the Departamento.

Pedro Rona), dialectology (Coseriu, Rona), besides several particular problems such as translation (Olaf Blixen), interlinguistic contacts (Rona, Juan Meo Zilio), extra-linguistic expressive activities (Meo Zilio), and the teaching of grammar (Piccardo). As to languages the following were included: Romance languages (Coseriu), Spanish of Uruguay and America (Rona, Vásquez, Meo Zilio), Italian (Meo Zilio), native languages (Benigno Ferrario [d. 1959], Blixen, Vásquez), Sanskrit (Nicolás Altuchow).[80] Secondly the DLM undertook to discuss critically the main trends of modern linguistics and the respective methods, examining their value in each case. The formula characterizing the critical activity of Montevideo is: 'scope and limits', since it tried in each case to determine the validity and at the same time the limitations of the various views and methods under discussion. Thus Coseriu examined the distinction between language and speech and the validity of Saussureanism in this connection (*Sistema norma y habla*, 1952); the relation between form and substance in the sounds of language, the interrelation between phonetics and phonemics and the scope and limits of the various phonemic theories and of glossematics (*Forma y sustancia en los sonidos del lenguaje*, 1954); the range and limits of dialect geography (*La geografía lingüística*, 1956); the foundations of grammar and the scope and limits of grammatical logicism, psychologicism and formalism (*Logicismo y antilogicismo en la gramática*, 1957); the relation between functioning and change in language and between description and history in linguistics, the rational sense of phonetic laws and the foundations and possibilities of diachronical structuralism (*Sincronía, diacronía e historia*, 1958). Coseriu and Vásquez outlined a scheme for the unification of the phonic sciences, fixing their application levels (*Para la unificación de las ciencias fónicas*, 1953). Piccardo critically examined two basic points of grammatical theory: the problem of word categories (*El concepto de 'partes de la oración'*, 1952) and the problem of sentence (*El concepto de 'oración'*, 1954); Rona, partly developing ideas of Coseriu, examined the specific problems of Hispano-American dialectology and established a number of new methodological principles for this discipline (*Aspectos metodológicos de la dialectología hispanoamericana*, 1958). Thirdly the DLM undertook to elaborate a linguistic theory in accordance with the reality of language, in its functioning as well as in its historical development, a task undertaken by Coseriu, who performed it simultaneously with his critical activity.[81] The basic principles of this theory are that the first condition of any linguistic theory is its adequacy to its object and that its basis must necessarily be the 'original knowledge', i.e. the knowledge which man possesses about himself as a speaker. It follows from the latter that the different lin-

[80] Among the collaborators of the Departamento the following deserve special mention: Luis Juan Piccardo, Washington Vásquez — who, unfortunately, abandoned linguistics — Nicolás Altuchow, Juan [Giovanni] Meo Zilio and José Pedro Rona. I should like to underline particularly the excellent work done by Professor Piccardo, whose *Concepto de oración*, as a synthesis as well as an original contribution, ranks among the best written on this topic, and not only in IAm.

[81] Especially in *Sistema, norma y habla; Forma y sustancia; Sincronía, diacronía e historia*. The two former were reprinted in Eugenio Coseriu, *Teoría del lenguaje y lingüística general* (Madrid, 1962).

guistic theories are necessarily based on valid intuitions, although they will eventually become partialized, distorted, and dogmatized in the course of further elaboration. In the construction of his theory, Coseriu therefore starts by noticing the essential exactness of two traditional intuitions: the intuition referring to the dynamic, i.e. creative character of language, affirmed since Humboldt by linguistic idealism, and the intuition concerning the systematic character of language, also already expressed by Humboldt, but developed above all by linguistics of positivistic origin (Saussure, Bloomfield and their followers).[82] Consequently, he tries to reconcile these two equally correct intuitions and to justify rationally their unity, and thus he comes to a conception in which language is regarded as a creative activity implying at the same time a systematic technique, and in which any essential difference between the functioning and the change of language is denied. This leads him furthermore to distinguish between external and internal structures of historical languages and between several structure levels of the linguistic technique (norm — system — linguistic type), as well as to a theory of contexts and of the use of non-linguistic instruments on behalf of linguistic technique.[83] The theory developed by Coseriu as a whole is structuralistic and functionalistic, but not formalistic. It is equally removed from those formalizations which ignore the substance in the two sides of language as also from those which exclude the meaning as uninvestigable or try to reduce it to different phenomena (situation, distribution, etc.).[84]

5.1.3. Besides these two main efforts, which by the way were rather different, the anti-receptive attitude, i.e. the aspiration to contribute originally to linguistic theory and methodology is only to be seen in a few individual cases. Thus in the first place in the isolated but important activity of Luis Jorge Prieto, whose distinction between opposition and contrast and whose contributions designed to establish a functional discipline of the content plane (noology) parallel to what phonemics is for the expression plane (cf. 6.3.4.) are well known and have been favorably received in international circles. In the same connection mention should be made of Félix Martínez Bonati (Chile) concerning linguistic theory of literature (cf. 6.2.3.). Some signs to overcome the purely receptive attitude are also to be found in the activity of Ana María Barrenechea, Rabanales, and some Brazilian linguists (Mattoso Câmara).[85]

5.2.0. As to the latter attitude, IAm — or rather Hispano-American — linguistics

[82] Basically it is the same assumption which transformational theory — starting from other premises and with different aims in view — would maintain years later.

[83] The latter in 'Determinación y entorno. Dos problemas de una lingüística del hablar', *RJb* 7.29-54 (1955-6).

[84] Particularly the thesis that 'linguistics without meaning is meaningless' — which today is beginning to gain ground even in the North American linguistics of the strictest antimentalist tradition (cf. Roman Jakobson, in *Proceedings of the Ninth International Congress of Linguists* 1141) — has always been a basic norm of the work of Montevideo, not only as a mere preferential option, but as a theoretically founded principle; cf. *Forma y sustancia* 17-8; *Logicismo y antilogicismo* 14-6.

[85] I am excepting, of course, those European or North American linguists who worked more or less in isolation in IAm.

(cf. 5.4.) is characterized by its LOCALISM. This means that it tends to limit itself to the study of local material and to be IAm or even regional IAm (Chilean, Colombian, etc.) also in its research subjects. This limitation too can be partly justified by external circumstances;[86] it is, however, at the same time a matter of attitude, even of a deliberate attitude.[87] Indeed, the studies of a local character are often presented in Hispano-American writings as the immediate aim and as the leading or even exclusive task of linguistics in IAm. This would be strange if said elsewhere: Nobody would maintain indeed that the leading or exclusive task of German linguistics should be the study of German and its dialects or that North American linguistics should confine itself to English spoken in the United States. The factual and even deliberate localism is however normal among most Hispano-American linguists, and it is also characteristic of the activity of some of the research institutes.

Localism is often joined by what could be called DIFFERENTIALISM or PECULIARISM, i.e. the tendency to record among local facts only those which are differential or peculiar for the respective region.[88] This radically distinguishes the native language studies from the studies on the regional varieties of Spanish. Whereas the native language studies aim at a total description of the languages dealt with or at least at a description of partial systems of these languages, the studies on Spanish are mostly limited to recording and discussion of single facts which differ from general Spanish or from standard Spanish of Spain. Such a procedure, if useful for certain ends, nevertheless implies a serious limitation from the point of view of descriptive linguistics, since the recorded facts usually are not examined within that system in which they function, but rather in relation to another more or less ideal system.[89] In addition, the localistic limitation even affects the validity of the statements about the peculiarity of these facts: as the comparison is normally made only with one level of Spanish spoken

86 In fact, certain investigations are difficult to carry out in Spanish America (cf. 1.4). The fields, which offer less material difficulties, are general linguistics, American Spanish and native languages, and of course American Spanish is the field of easiest access.

87 One could assert that other types of studies would not arouse interest in local environments. But this would be a vicious circle, since, if there is not any interest, it is because it was not created. Cf. e.g. the different situation found in Brazil concerning historical studies (5.4.).

88 Thus at least three of the six items in the program of the Instituto de Filología of Santiago have a localistic character: 'b) the study of the peculiarities of Chilean Spanish (pronunciation, grammatical forms, vocabulary, anthroponymy, toponymy); c) the elaboration of a linguistic atlas for Chile and a complete dictionary of Chileanisms; d) the elaboration of a Chilean linguistic bibliography' (*BFUCh* 4.5, 1944-6); two of these items show at the same time a peculiaristic orientation ('peculiarities', 'Chileanisms'). The history and description of non-American Spanish are not included in this program.

89 For this reason most investigations on American Spanish are rather collections of material complementary to the Gramática of the Spanish Academy and particularly to its dictionary, than studies properly speaking. Even the general contributions about the Spanish of this or that country do not present the whole Spanish language of the respective country (or at least systematic examples of it), but in fact single aspects considered as differential. In reality one can say that there are many comparative examinations of American Spanish (as far as it differs from General Spanish and from the Spanish of the Real Academia), but that genuine descriptions of the varieties of American Spanish are lacking.

in Spain, the possible diffusion of these same facts in other levels of the same Spanish or in other regions of America is left out of consideration.[90]

5.2.1. The exceptions, at least the deliberate exceptions, are not very numerous in this case either. Peculiarism seems to be slowly overcome by dialect geography and by a few systematic local studies. The reactions to localism are, however, fewer. European students as Corominas, Terracini, Krüger, Gazdaru, Ferrario and others were not localists, of course: they simply continued in IAm an earlier activity, already directed towards other interests; and due to the very nature of their object, the grammarians usually are not localists either, as they are concerned with Spanish grammar as such rather than with Hispano-American grammar. A clearly non-localistic attitude has been characteristic for the DLM, as is shown by the languages it has dealt with (cf. 5.1.2.) and by other signs.[91] Nor would it have been possible for the old Instituto de Filología Clásica of Buenos Aires to be localistic, given its specialization (cf. 2.1.2. and 3.2.). Non-locally limited interests are also shown by the DFL (cf. 2.1.7.) and by some isolated scholars.

5.2.2. The great exception in this respect was, however, the Instituto de Filología of Buenos Aires, which since its beginning was a center for Hispanic, not simply Argentine studies. Amado Alonso kept up and stressed this orientation, always working on a general Hispanic level, even when dealing with American and local problems, which permitted him to correct a number of errors committed because of the narrow localistic outlook.[92] This same attitude to overcome localism by viewing local Hispano-American facts in a broader Hispanic perspective,[93] is revealed moreover in all the publications of the Instituto, especially in the *BDH* and the *RFH*. Amado Alonso's attitude was transmitted to his disciples, first of all to Ángel Rosenblat, who even in his studies on local facts, proceeds as a Hispano-Americanist and a Hispanist (not

[90] The differentialistic attitude seemingly continues the tradition begun by Cuervo, who, in fact, often examined local peculiarities. It must be observed, however, that Cuervo usually regarded the peculiarities from a general Hispanic point of view, and that local facts were for him mainly starting points for true Hispanic monographies. It is indeed possible to investigate peculiarities without adopting a peculiaristic attitude.

[91] In dialectology, Rona, *Aspectos metodológicos* 18-22, stressed the necessity of overcoming localism by studying single phenomena characteristic for the entire Spanish of America; cf. 6.2.1.

[92] Cf. e.g. his famous article 'Examen de la teoría indigenista de Rodolfo Lenz', *RFH* 1.313-50 (1939).

[93] This does not imply, of course, any concession to peculiarism. On the contrary, Amado Alonso expressed his opposition to such an attitude in terms which deserve to be fully quoted: 'I suppose that a word such as *yapa* is as common in Peru as *padre* or *mano*. But the compilers of vocabularies include *yapa* and not *padre* nor *mano*. Why is this so? Because *yapa* is a curiosity in Madrid. In other words, the guiding principle for the inclusion of a word is a fact which is external to the system being studied; it is included because it is unusual in another area. All the pieces that make up the machine and how they work do not matter, only those individual pieces which seem surprising somewhere else.' (*RFH*, 3. 162, 1941). Further on Alonso observes that such a proceeding is legitimate only, if one wishes to establish a supplement to the Dictionary of the Academy, but not, if one has to describe a modality of American Spanish. Many Hispano-American dialectologists consider Amado Alonso as their ideal master, but his teachings in this respect were not faithfully followed indeed.

simply as an Argentineanist or a Venezuelanist). This attitude has partly been kept up also as a proper tradition of the IAA (cf. 2.1.1. and 3.1.5.).

5.3. In the development of IAm linguistics the parallelism between the Instituto de Filología of Buenos Aires and the DLM, the two centers which had the ambition to open new ways for language studies in IAm, is symptomatic, particularly if one considers that there never existed a direct relationship between them.[94] Undoubtedly, there are also perceptible differences between these two centers. In Buenos Aires philology was maintained along with linguistics, whereas the DLM has been almost exclusively linguistic; in Buenos Aires much attention was directed towards stylistics, whereas the DLM paid more attention to the methodology of descriptive linguistics, grammatical theory, and philosophy of language; the Instituto de Filología has been a center for Hispanic linguistics, whereas the DLM has been orientated towards general and Romance linguistics. Yet this does not make the similarities between the two centers less conspicuous. Both centers have displayed an intensive critical activity, striving to overcome both the receptive attitude and localism, although the work in Montevideo has above all been directed towards the former aim, in Buenos Aires more towards the latter (the amount of descriptive and historical publications of Montevideo cannot of course be compared to what was achieved in Buenos Aires in these fields). And, above all, the activity displayed in both cases reveals coherent linguistic conceptions. The leading conception in Buenos Aires is implicit in the practice of research and has been manifested only in part or in connection with particular problems;[95] in Montevideo, on the contrary, there has been an effort to develop properly a linguistic theory, i.e. an explicit and critically founded conception.

5.4. In Brazil, the situation concerning the two basic attitudes just considered is different. Whereas the receptive attitude in methods and conceptions is also prevailing among Brazilian linguists, this is not the case with localism. Certainly, local and differential studies were published in Brazil too, although much less than in Spanish America, but Brazilian scientific linguistics considered as a whole never was localistic. On the contrary, Brazilian linguists have always considered the whole tradition of the Portuguese language as their own and thus have dealt with Medieval Portuguese and Portuguese etymology, have written historical grammars and histories of the language, so that their activity is a section of Portuguese linguistics in general, only separating from the common Luso-Brazilian body in the dialectological studies and in the studies on contemporary Brazilian Portuguese. This is also the reason why Brazilian linguistics presents itself above all as historical linguistics, while Hispano-American linguistics presents itself more as dialectology.

[94] None of the members of the Montevideo group was a pupil of Amado Alonso. Moreover, the activity of Montevideo began when that of Buenos Aires had ceased.

[95] It would be interesting to single out in a synthesis all of Amado Alonso's general ideas on language. Such a synthesis in my opinion would comprise much more than what is contained in Diego Catalán Menéndez-Pidal, *La escuela lingüística española y su concepción del lenguaje* (Madrid, 1955).

6. WORK FIELDS: RESULTS SO FAR OBTAINED

6.0. In this section I shall enumerate and examine shortly the topics on which IAm linguists have concentrated. I do not intend to give a complete list of all the works published or to dwell on their analysis. I shall only mention their general features and their amount in the different fields, in order to stress the focuses of interest of IAm linguistics and to outline a balance of its results. I shall only refer to the theoretical and methodological aspects and to the general results of those linguistic disciplines treated in separate chapters of this book. Consequently, the account sketched in this section must be completed by what is contained in these other chapters. For the same reason I shall not deal with the studies on native languages, except for a reference to general works. The enumeration of the topics will not strictly follow a systematic classification of the linguistic disciplines but will be adapted to a compromise between such a classification and the work fields characteristic of IAm linguistics.

6.1.0. In the pre-scientific as well as in the scientific tradition of IAm linguistics the two favorite and almost exclusive work fields are: that of national languages (subdivided into a) lexicology; b) dialectology; c) problem of the standard language; d) school grammar), and that of native languages. During the period we are dealing with a number of works of synthesis have appeared for these fields, which constitute at the same time starting points for further studies.

6.1.1. The first Hispano-American synthesis in lexicology (i.e. the collecting of lexical Americanisms), Augusto Malaret's *Diccionario de americanismos* (Mayagüez, P. R., 1925), belongs to a prior period; but the third revised and enlarged edition of this work was published in the period dealt with here (Buenos Aires, 1946). Another very rich synthesis, however in various aspects inferior to that of Malaret, is Francisco Javier Santamaría's *Diccionario general de americanismos*, 3 vols. (Mexico City, 1942-43).[96] There is no synthesis comparable to these two in Brazil.

6.1.2. In Hispano-American dialectology a fundamental stage is represented by the *BDH* (cf. 2.1.1.) which, however, is not really a synthesis but rather a corpus of dialectological studies. For Brazil there is nothing comparable to this corpus (also because dialect studies are not very numerous there anyway); on the other hand there is available for Brazil an important historical-descriptive synthesis: Serafim Silva Neto's *Introdução ao estudo da língua portuguêsa no Brasil*[2] (Rio de Janeiro, 1963), the like of which is lacking in Spanish America.[97]

6.1.3. Concerning the problem of the standard language Amado Alonso's *El problema de la lengua en América* (Madrid, 1935) still preserves its entire value. Also

[96] The first syntheses on semantic aspects are those by the North American Charles E. Kany: *American-Spanish Semantics* and *American-Spanish Euphemisms* (both: Berkeley and Los Angeles, 1960).

[97] The only general synthesis for American Spanish — on an elemental and popular level — is due to a German student: Max Leopold Wagner, *Lingua e dialetti dell'America spagnola* (Florence, 1949). About syntax and pronunciation we have two works due to North American students: Kany, *American-Spanish Syntax* (Chicago, 1945; 2nd ed., 1951), and Canfield's work referred to in fn. 25.

excellent is Ángel Rosenblat's initiation, *La lengua y la cultura de Hispanoamérica. Tendencias actuales* (Berlin, 1933), several times republished (last edition: Caracas, 1962).[98] In Brazil, a work similar to that of Alonso as far as the basic attitude is concerned is Sílvio Elia's *O problema da língua brasileira*[2] (Rio de Janeiro, 1961).[99]

6.1.4. In the field of school grammar an important stage was reached by the renovating work of Amado Alonso and Pedro Henríquez Ureña, *Gramática castellana* (2 vols.; Buenos Aires, 1938), several times republished. There is nothing equal in Brazil, although there exist a number of school grammars written by linguists (Nascentes, Rocha Lima, Silveira Bueno, Celso Cunha).

6.1.5. For the native languages a general synthesis is Antonio Tovar's *Catálogo de las lenguas de América del Sur* (Buenos Aires, 1961), an outcome of his activity in Tucumán, which contains short characterizations of these languages and their classification, as well as 168 pages of bibliography.[100]

6.2.0. In the period with which we are concerned here, three disciplines are prevailing in IAm linguistics: dialectology, lexicology and stylistics (which in the opinion of most IAm linguists belongs to linguistics),[101] all three applied to the national languages. For Brazil historical linguistics must be added, which even prevails there over the others (c.f. 6.4.2.).

6.2.1. Dialectology — although in an absolute sense it still is in an initial stage (e.g. concerning the determination of dialect borders) — is presently the most vital section of IAm linguistics from the point of view of the amount of work and of collected materials, and has perceptibly advanced in the recent years, at least in some countries (Argentina, Chile, Colombia, Puerto Rico, Uruguay). Here I shall only point out in which sense progress has been made.

The contributions on principles and methods of dialectology are not numerous indeed. Besides the introductions by Silva Neto and Coseriu cited in 4.1.1.2. and the information contained in more general works, one should mention Rona's booklet,

[98] Cf. by the same author, *El castellano de España y el castellano de América. Unidad y diferenciación* (Caracas, 1962). The work of the Spaniard Américo Castro, *La peculiaridad lingüística rioplatense y su sentido histórico* (Buenos Aires, 1941; new ed. 1960) is impressionistic and very questionable; it has provoked many controversies. The same problem is dealt with in Rodolfo A. Borello, 'Actitud del argentino medio frente a la lengua' and Ángel J. Battistessa, 'El argentino y sus principales interrogantes frente a los problemas de la unidad de la lengua', both in *Presente y futuro de la lengua española. Actas de la Asamblea de Filología del I Congreso de Instituciones hispánicas* 1. 193-8, and 199-208, respectively (Madrid, 1964); and in Rosenblat's important historical study, 'Las generaciones argentinas del siglo XIX ante el problema de la lengua', *Revista de la Universidad de Buenos Aires*, 5th period, 5.539-84 (1960), also published separately (Buenos Aires, 1961).

[99] [Alexandre] Barbosa Lima Sobrinho adopts a point of view rather socio-cultural than linguistic in his *A língua portuguêsa e a unidade do Brasil* (Rio de Janeiro, 1958). An interesting discussion of the same subject is found in Antônio Houaiss' *Sugestões para uma política da língua* 74-129 (Rio de Janeiro, 1960).

[100] An initiation including also the North American languages is Dick E. Ibarra Grasso's *Lenguas indígenas americanas* (Buenos Aires, 1958). I have not yet seen Mattoso Câmara, *Introdução às línguas indígenas brasileiras*[2] (Rio de Janeiro, 1965).

[101] Heles Contreras, 'Stylistics and Linguistics', in: Sol Saporta et alii, *Stylistics, Linguistics, and Literary Criticism* 23-31 (New York, 1961), represents a North American point of view.

Aspectos metodológicos pointed out above (cf. 5.1.2. and fn. 91), in which the necessity to distinguish in dialectology the different levels of language and to fix the dialect zones on an IAm scale[102] beyond national borders is maintained. Ambrosio Rabanales' *Introducción al estudio del español de Chile. Determinación del concepto de chilenismo* (Santiago, 1953) can also be named.[103] The descriptive studies are in turn numerous, and some of them contain methodological observations too.

Concerning the methods of investigation, a first immediate progress was made through research trips and inquiries, either direct or by correspondence, for which Tomás Navarro's *Cuestionario lingüístico hispanoamericano* (Buenos Aires, 1943; 2nd ed., 1945) was an important instrument. More decisive progress, going far beyond simple inquiries, was represented by the introduction of dialect geography. So far the only linguistic atlas for an American Spanish region is found, preceded by an ample study, in Tomás Navarro's *El español en Puerto Rico. Contribución a la geografía lingüística hispanoamericana* (Río Piedras, P.R., 1948). Since this work, however, dialect geography has advanced in Argentina (Vidal de Battini), in Uruguay (Rona), and above all in Colombia, where the ICC has become the foremost center for dialect geography in Spanish America, and where the preparation of the *ALEC* (cf. 2.1.5.) has fairly advanced.[104] Linguistic atlases are either in preparation or at least being planned for other IAm countries too.[105] About the onomasiological studies related to dialect geography, see 6.2.2. Besides these methodological improvements and partly independent of them, general studies, usually of a differential nature, on Spanish spoken in different Hispano-American countries[106] or smaller regions[107] have continued to be published.

[102] Rona himself applied these principles in '«Vulgarización» o adaptación diastrática de neologismos o cultismos', *Revista Nacional* 205.385-409 (also published separately: Montevideo, 1962), and in 'El uso del futuro en el voseo americano', *Fi* 7.121-44 (1961).

[103] Cf. the discussions by Rona, *BFM* 7 and by Juan M. Lope Blanch, *NRFH* 12.410-2.

[104] See: Tomás Buesa Oliver and Luis Flórez, *El Atlas lingüístico-etnográfico de Colombia (ALEC). Cuestionario preliminar* (Bogotá, 1954 [publ. 1956]) and *Cuestionario para el Atlas lingüístico-etnográfico de Colombia. Segunda edición, en experimentación* (Bogotá, 1960; a third edition without the names of the authors was published in 1961); also several articles by Flórez: 'El español hablado en Colombia y su atlas lingüístico', *Presente y futuro de la lengua española* 1.5-77 (with 50 maps); 'El Atlas lingüístico-etnográfico de Colombia (ALEC). Nota informativa', *BICC* 16. 77-125 (with 23 maps); 'Principios y métodos del Atlas lingüístico-etnográfico de Colombia (ALEC)', *BICC* 19.201-9.

[105] In Uruguay Adolfo Berro García has been preparing a linguistic atlas; in Chile the Instituto de Filología of Santiago has planned a similar work; another atlas has been planned for Costa Rica: cf. Arturo Agüero, 'El español de Costa Rica y su atlas lingüístico', *Presente y futuro de la lengua española* 1.135-52. For Brazil a linguistic atlas has been planned by the Casa de Rui Barbosa (Rio de Janeiro).

[106] The outstanding among these studies are the following: Humberto Toscano Mateus, *El español en el Ecuador* (Madrid, 1953); Berta Elena Vidal de Battini, *El español en la Argentina* (Buenos Aires, 1964; a first and shorter version was published in 1954); and, for his manner of posing problems, the pamphlet by Ángel Rosenblat, *Lengua y cultura de Venezuela* (Caracas, no date). *Presente y futuro de la lengua española* 1. includes articles on the Spanish of Mexico, Chile, Ecuador, Paraguay, Puerto Rico, by Lope Blanch, Oroz, Toscano Mateus, Luis De Gásperi, Rubén del Rosario; and on Argentinean Spanish, by Luis Alfonso and Vidal de Battini.

[107] Such as the remarkable study by Vidal de Battini, *El habla rural de San Luis*, I (= *BDH* 7; Buenos

Generally, IAm dialectology is mostly phonetical and lexical. Studies on grammatical dialectology were published by: Rosenblat, Lope Blanch, Flórez, José Joaquín Montes, Rona, Alfredo F. Padrón (Cuba) and some others.[108] There have also been some studies on stylistic aspects.[109]

The most important general result of Hispano-American dialectology was a revision — or for the time being rather a rejection — of the dialect division traditionally accepted since Pedro Henríquez Ureña's article 'Observaciones sobre el español en América', *RFE* 7.357-90 (1921). Along with several European and North American students a number of IAm linguists have also contributed to this.[110]

6.2.2. The almost exclusively differentialistic IAm lexicology generally has not introduced new methods and there are hardly any theoretical and methodological contributions in this field.[111] In fact, it is almost always a particular form of dialectology, different from the latter only because it is limited to words and does not intend to establish dialect borders (but IAm dialectology usually does not establish them either). Therefore the properly new contributions in the field of lexicology are rather the onomasiological studies, partly related to dialect geography and partly to the Wörter und Sachen method. Such studies were published in Spanish America by Oroz, María E. Zappacosta, Oreste Plath and especially by Vidal de Battini, Flórez and Montes; in Brazil, by Heinrich Bunse and Florival Seraine.[112] A work which can be placed in between onomasiology, semantics, and stylistics is Lope Blanch's *Vocabulario mexi-*

Aires, 1949). In Brazil an important analogous study on a regional variety of Portuguese is: Antenor Nascentes, *O linguajar carioca*² (Rio de Janeiro, 1953). About the phonic aspects of a local variety of American Spanish the most comprehensive contribution is Luis Flórez, *La pronunciación del español en Bogotá* (Bogotá, 1951).

108 Among these studies the following particularly deserve to be mentioned: Rosenblat, 'Notas de morfología dialectal', *BDH* 2. 103-316 (Buenos Aires, 1946), and Lope Blanch, *Observaciones sobre la sintaxis del español hablado en México* (México, 1953).

109 Thus: Ambrosio Rabanales, 'Uso tropológico, en el lenguaje chileno, de nombres del reino vegetal', *BFUCh* 5.137-243 and 'Recursos lingüísticos, en el español de Chile, de expresión de la afectividad', *BFUCh* 10.205-302; and Cecilia Enet, '1200 comparaciones populares argentinas', *AIL* 6.325-73. Elements of a study on the styles of language are contained in Ismael Silva-Fuenzalida, 'El uso de los morfemas 'formales' y 'familiares' en el español de Chile', *BFUCh* 8.439-55. Stylistic aspects are also treated by Frida Weber, 'Fórmulas de tratamiento en la lengua de Buenos Aires', *RFH* 3.105-139, and María Beatriz Fontanella, 'Algunas observaciones sobre el diminutivo en Bogotá', *BICC* 17. 556-73.

110 Concerning the present state of the problem, cf. José Pedro Rona, 'El problema de la división del español americano en zonas dialectales', *Presente y futuro de la lengua española* 1.215-26, where also new criteria for a dialect classification are proposed.

111 An exception is Fernando A. Martínez, 'Contribución a una teoría de la lexicografía española', *BICC* 3.61-116.

112 Flórez even contributed to onomasiology with two books: *Habla y cultura popular en Antioquia. Materiales para un estudio* [the onomasiological part: 175-339] (Bogotá, 1957) and *Léxico de la casa popular urbana en Bolívar, Colombia* (Bogotá, 1962). The contributions by Zappacosta and Plath appeared in *AIL*; those by Vidal de Battini mostly in *Fi*; those by Montes in *BICC* (in which also other onomasiological studies were published). The contributions by Krüger in the same field belong rather to Romance linguistics.

cano relativo a la muerte (Mexico City, 1963). A methodologically interesting contribution, whose subject is a native language, is Anselmo Raguileo's 'Los nombres de parentesco en la familia mapuche', *BFUCh* 7.343-59.[113]

6.2.3. Many IAm linguists have dealt with stylistics, either with 'stylistics of the langue' (Bally stylistics) or with 'stylistics of speech', i.e. literary texts stylistics (Vossler-Spitzer stylistics). I shall here mention the main theoretical works in this field and some of the most important applications.

The leading promoter of stylistics in Hispano-America was Amado Alonso, who devoted a great part of his activity to it. Among his theoretical and methodological contributions the following must be remembered: 'Carta a Alfonso Reyes sobre la estilística', published in the newspaper *La Nación* of Buenos Aires (February, 9, 1941) and 'The Stylistic Interpretation of Literary Texts', *MLN* 57.489-96 (1942).[114] In Brazil Mattoso Câmara drew a theoretical sketch of stylistics together with a short stylistic characterization of the Portuguese language, *Contribuição para uma estilística da língua portuguêsa* (Rio de Janeiro, 1952; 2nd edition, 1953: *Contribuição à estilística portuguêsa*). Coseriu wrote about several theoretical problems of stylistics; thus, about the position of stylistics in relation with other linguistic disciplines, in *Sistema, norma y habla*, particularly 63, and 'Determinación y entorno' (cf. 5.2.1.); about the different possible stylistics, in *Reseñas* 7-8 (Montevideo, 1953); about the conditions and modalities of metaphorical creation, in *La creación metafórica en el lenguaje* (Montevideo, 1956). An important and philosophically well-founded theoretical work on the relation between language and literature and on the work of verbal art is Félix Martínez Bonati's *La estructura de la obra literaria* (Santiago de Chile, 1960). An excellent introduction to stylistics (even the best initiation to prestructural stylistics of all I know) is Roberto Fernández Retamar's *Idea de la estilística* (Universidad Central de Las Villas [Santa Clara, Cuba], 1958).[115] A criticism of Spitzer's stylistics was tried by Ángela Vaz Leão in *Sôbre a estilística de Spitzer* (Belo Horizonte, 1960); a criticism of Devoto's stylistics is found in Coseriu's *Reseñas* cited above.

As to the application of stylistics, Amado Alonso's most important achievement is *Poesía y estilo de Pablo Neruda* (Buenos Aires, 1940; 2nd ed., 1951).[116] Mattoso

[113] The work of Rosenblat referred to in fn. 29 contains genuine historico-critical monographs on lexical problems, although written in a popular style. The lexicographical contributions on slang, which remain to be mentioned in this domain, are usually due to non-specialists. An important exception is Antenor Nascentes, *A gíria brasileira* (Rio de Janeiro, 1953). To Nascentes we also owe a *Dicionário de sinónimos* (Rio de Janeiro, 1957).

[114] Both reprinted in: Amado Alonso, *Materia y forma en poesía* 95-106 and 107-32, respectively (Madrid, 1955).

[115] Cf. also the more succinct and modest initiation by Luis Jaime Cisneros, *El estilo y sus límites* (Lima, 1958), and the informative pamphlet referred to in fn. 48.

[116] Less accomplished (and less stylistic) is his work *Ensayo sobre la novela histórica. El modernismo en La Gloria de Don Ramiro* (Buenos Aires, 1942). Cf. also the other essays included in *Materia y forma en poesía.* Alonso's contributions to stylistics of the Spanish language belong to a period prior to that here considered.

Câmara applied his ideas on stylistics in some of his essays collected in *Ensaios Machadianos. Língua e estilo* (Rio de Janeiro, 1962).[117]

6.3.0. The IAm contributions to general linguistics, beyond those mentioned in 6.2., are not very numerous, if the purely informative contributions are left aside. Besides, almost all of them are concerned with particular disciplines or problems.

6.3.1. The main contributions to linguistic theory and the general foundations of linguistics are those by Coseriu cited and commented on in 5.1.2. (cf. also 7.2.). To these the book by Schulte-Herbrüggen cited in 4.2.3. can be added. On a seemingly particular problem, which, however, is connected with the basic function of language, Amado Alonso and Raimundo Lida, 'El concepto lingüístico de impresionismo', *El impresionismo en el lenguaje* (cf. 4.1.1.) 121-251, and Amado Alonso, 'Por qué el lenguaje en sí mismo no puede ser impresionista', *RFH* 2.379-86, should be remembered. A genuine theory of standard language is displayed in Alonso's *El problema de la lengua en América*. General ideas on language are found in several descriptive and historical studies by this same author; cf., e.g. his interpretation of the notion of 'interior form' in 'Sobre métodos: Construcciones con verbos de movimiento en español', *RFH* 1.105-38, and in 'Preferencias mentales en el habla del gaucho', *El problema de la lengua en América* 143-79.[118] The complementarity between different views of language was affirmed by Coseriu, *La creación metafórica* 5-15.

6.3.2. The following have contributed to the theory of phonemics: Amado Alonso, 'La identidad del fonema' (containing a psychologistic notion of the phoneme, much closer to Baudouin de Courtenay and Sapir than to the latter views of Trubetzkoy); Coseriu, *Sistema, norma y habla* (on the distinction between system and norm in the phonic plane of language); Coseriu and Vásquez, *Para la unificación de las cienicas fónicas* (cf. 5.1.2.); Coseriu, *Forma y sustancia* (on the problems of identification and delimitation of phonemes); Coseriu, *Sincronía, diacronía e historia* (on the scope and limits of diachronical phonemics); Luis Jorge Prieto, 'Remarques sur la nature des oppositions distinctives basées sur l'accentuation monotonique libre', *Revista de la Facultad de Filosofía y Humanidades* 4, numbers 1-3 (Córdoba, Argentina, 1952), and 'Traits oppositionnels et traits contrastifs', *Word* 10.43-59 (on the distinction between opposition and contrast, also applicable outside of phonemics). Cf., furthermore, the work by Contreras and Saporta referred to in fn. 68 (a reinterpretation of phonic facts, particularly of facts of distribution, in transformational terms). A summary of

[117] Among other studies, at least partially relating to stylistics, the following can be remembered: Enrique Anderson Imbert, *El arte de la prosa en Juan Montalvo* (Mexico, 1948); Ángel Rosenblat, 'La lengua de Cervantes', in the collective volume *Cervantes* 47-129 (Caracas, 1949); Ana María Barrenechea, 'Borges y el lenguaje', *RFH* 7.551-69, and *La expresión de la irrealidad en la obra de Jorge Luis Borges* (Mexico, 1957); Ulrich Leo, *Interpretaciones hispanoamericanas. Ensayos de teoría y práctica estilísticas. 1939-1958* (Santiago de Cuba, 1960); on a French text: Carlos M. Rey, *Una fábula de La Fontaine. Análisis métrico-estilístico* (Montevideo, 1956). Cf. moreover, the contributions on stylistics of the langue referred to in fn. 109.

[118] Reprinted — the latter with many modifications and under the title of 'Americanismo en la forma interior del lenguaje' — in Amado Alonso, *Estudios lingüísticos. Temas españoles* 230-87 (Madrid, 1951) and *Estudios lingüísticos. Temas hispanoamericanos* 73-101 (Madrid, 1953), respectively.

the phonemic theory is found in Mattoso Câmara's *Para o estudo da fonêmica portuguêsa* 7-52.[119]

6.3.3. There are many more contributions to the theory of grammar and to the discussion of grammatical notions. The main studies on the foundations of grammar are: Coseriu, *Logicismo y antilogicismo* and 'Determinación y entorno';[120] on basic grammatical notions, the two studies by Piccardo cited in 5.1.2.[121] Important and modern are further Ana María Barrenechea's 'El pronombre y su inclusión en un sistema de categorías semánticas', *Fi* 8.241-72 and 'Las clases de palabras en español, como clases funcionales', *RomPh* 17.301-9. Concerning the distinction between coordination and subordination Eduardo J. Prieto's small pamphlet *Parataxis e hipotaxis* (Rosario, 1959) can be remembered; on the neutralization in grammar: Mattoso Câmara, 'Sur la neutralisation morphologique', *TIL* 2.76-77. About several other grammatical notions and problems: Coseriu, 'El plural en los nombres propios', *RBF* 1.1-15; 'Sobre el futuro romance', *RBF* 3.1-18; and *Sobre las llamadas 'construcciones con verbos de movimiento': un problema hispánico* (Montevideo, 1962). Among other contributions the following can be mentioned: Luis Cifuentes García, 'Acerca del aspecto', *BFUCh* 8.57-63; Gastón Carrillo Herrera, 'Las oraciones subordinadas', *BFUCh* 15.165-21; José Joaquín Montes, 'Sobre la división de la gramática en morfología y sintaxis', *BICC* 18.679-85. An attempt to adapt Tesnière's structural syntax to some aspects of Spanish is Jorge Páramo Pomareda, 'Elementos de sintaxis estructural', *BICC* 16.185-207. A number of grammatical distinctions drawn with modern criteria, although not further developed, are found in the program of Rabanales recorded in 6.3.5. Grammatical notions are moreover exposed and discussed in Mattoso Câmara's *Introdução* and also in Luis Jaime Cisneros, *Lengua y estilo, I* (Lima, 1959).[122]

119 Among the applications — besides Mattoso Câmara's *Fonêmica*, the studies by Alonso, Vásquez, Silva-Fuenzalida and Guitarte pointed out in 4.2.2., and the pamphlet by Saporta and Contreras referred to in fn. 68 — there must be mentioned: Silva-Fuenzalida, 'La entonación en el español y su morfología', *BFUCh* 9.177-87, and Antônio Houaiss, *Tentativa de descrição do sistema vocálico do português culto na área dita carioca* (Rio de Janeiro, 1959). An interesting study, which raises new problems with regard to the phonemic distribution in Spanish is Ambrosio Rabanales, 'Las siglas: un problema de fonología española', *BFUCh* 15.327-42. In general, studies of experimental phonetics are lacking in IAm, although there are a number of laboratories for phonetics. The only general study which can be mentioned in this field is Mercedes V. Álvarez Puebla de Chaves, *Problemas de fonética experimental* (La Plata, 1948). Among the applications: Alonso Zamora Vicente, 'Rehilamiento porteño', *Fi* 1.5-22, and the study by the Portuguese Armando de Lacerda and the Brazilian Nelson Rossi, 'Particularidades fonéticas do comportamento elocucional do falar do Rio de Janeiro', *Revista do Laboratório de Fonética Experimental* 4.5-102 (Coimbra, 1958).

120 These studies were also reprinted in *Teoría del lenguaje y lingüística general*, together with those pointed out in fn. 81 and with 'El plural en los nombres propios'.

121 Both reprinted, togehter with others, in Luis Juan Piccardo, *Estudios gramaticales* (Montevideo, 1962).

122 The following published important grammatical studies on the national languages — in Spanish America: Rosenblat, Rosales, Lidia Contreras, Lope Blanch, Cisneros, Mabel Manacorda de Rosetti; in Brazil: Nascentes, Mattoso Câmara, Maurer Jr., Carlos Henrique da Rocha Lima, Vaz Leão, Evanildo Bechara and others. In Brazil most of these grammatical studies are descriptive and historical at the same time; in Spanish America they are mainly descriptive and interpretative.

6.3.4. Semantics is represented in IAm by just a few contributions and generally continues to be understood as a discipline which studies the changes in the meaning of words. The best known work in this respect, Félix Restrepo's *Diseño de semántica general. El alma de las palabras*, which reached its 5th edition (Bogotá, 1958), does not belong to the period considered here. Francisco da Silveira Bueno, *Tratado de semântica geral aplicada à língua portuguêsa do Brasil* (São Paulo, 1947; third edition, 1960: *Tratado de semântica brasileira*), is an adaptation and application to Portuguese of the classifications proposed by Albert Carnoy, *La science du mot. Traité de sémantique* (Louvain, 1927).[123] More recent trends in semantics have not yet entered IAm investigation, if one excepts the neo-Humboldtian trend — present in some of Amado Alonso's contributions (particularly in 'Preferencias mentales en el habla del gaucho', cited in 6.3.1.) and in the already mentioned book by Schulte-Herbrüggen — and the stimulus coming from anthropology, to which Raguileo's article cited in 6.2.2. is indebted. From IAm in turn came an important novelty in semantics, which at the same time is one of the most important IAm contributions to linguistic theory. That is the functional analysis of content — an analysis which, of course, embraces both grammar and the lexical level — undertaken by Luis Jorge Prieto in a number of contributions[124] published since 1954 and which culminated in his *Principes de noologie* (The Hague, 1964). In these *Principes* an attempt is made to establish minimal unities of simultaneous realization for content (noemes), analogous to the phonemes on the expression plane of language.[125]

6.3.5. A number of IAm contributions of theoretical or methodological interest concern particular problems of general linguistics or applied linguistics.

Thus linguistic taboo is treated in Coseriu, *La creación metafórica* 23-7, and Mansur Guérios, *Tabus lingüísticos* (Rio de Janeiro, 1956). Women's language is dealt with in: Hernando Balmori, 'Habla mujeril', *Fi* 8.123-38. About the extra-linguistic expressive activities, Rabanales, 'La somatolalia', *BFUCh* 8.355-78; and Meo Zilio, 'Consideraciones generales sobre el lenguaje de los gestos', *BFUCh* 12.225-48, and 'El lenguaje de los gestos en el Uruguay', *BFUCh* 13.75-163,[126] should be mentioned, the latter being the first contribution in which a large number of gestures are interpreted in terms of functional oppositions and distinctive features.

[123] Roberto Vilches Acuña, *Semántica española* (Buenos Aires, 1954; 2nd ed., 1959) and *Elementos de semántica* (Santiago de Chile, 1959) have a popular character.

[124] 'Signe articulé et signe proportionnel', *BSL* 50.134-43; 'Contributions à l'étude fonctionnelle du contenu', *TIL* 1.23-41; 'Figuras de la expresión y figuras del contenido', *Miscelánea homenaje a André Martinet. 'Estructuralismo e historia'* 1.243-9 (La Laguna, 1957); 'D'une asymétrie entre le plan de l'expression et le plan du contenu de la langue', *BSL* 53.86-95; 'Rapport paradigmatique et rapport syntagmatique sur le plan du contenu', *Omagiu lui Iorgu Iordan* 705-13 (Bucarest, 1958).

[125] The contributions to structural semantics by Coseriu initiated in Montevideo did not begin to be published until his transfer to Europe. The first of them is 'Pour une sémantique diachronique structurale', *Travaux de linguistique et de littérature* 2.1.139-86 (Strasbourg, 1964).

[126] Both were also published in one volume *El lenguaje de los gestos en el Río de La Plata* (Montevideo, 1961). Cf., moreover, by the same author 'Los sonidos avulsivos en el Río de La Plata' and 'Sonidos extralingüísticos en el habla ríoplatense', *AION-L* 2.113-20 and 221-33.

The most important theoretical contribution to the problem of translation published in IAm is Benvenuto Terracini's 'El problema de la traducción' in *Conflictos de lenguas y de cultura* 43-103 (Buenos Aires, 1951). Furthermore, there should be remembered: Alfonso Reyes, 'De la traducción' in *La experiencia literaria* 116-28 (Buenos Aires, 1952); Paulo Rónai, *Escola de tradutores*² (Rio de Janeiro, 1956); Olaf Blixen, *La traducción literaria y sus problemas* (Montevideo, 1954).[127] On linguistic terminology, there is nothing to be mentioned in Spanish America; in Brazil in turn, several works appeared in this field: Nascentes, *Léxico de nomenclatura gramatical brasileira* (Rio de Janeiro, 1946); Mattoso Câmara, *Dicionário de fatos gramaticais* (Rio de Janeiro, 1956; 2nd ed., São Paulo, 1964: *Dicionário de filologia e gramática referente à língua portuguêsa*); Sílvio Elia et alii, *Dicionário gramatical*³ (Pôrto Alegre 1962; 1st ed., 1953). The most sensible essay on the teaching of grammar in secondary schools is Piccardo's *Gramática y enseñanza* (Montevideo, 1956),[128] partly based on ideas of Pagliaro and Fries.[129] A detailed program for the teaching of general and Spanish grammar in university courses was published by Rabanales: *Gramática española. Programas. Cuestionarios. Bibliografías.* (Santiago, 1959). A remarkable work concerned with the teaching of modern foreign languages was published in Brazil: R. Valnir C. Chagas, *Didática especial de línguas modernas* (São Paulo, 1957). Two important works on the teaching of Latin are also due to Brazilian linguists: Ernesto Faria, *O latim e a cultura contemporânea* (Rio de Janeiro, 1941), in the second considerably enlarged edition: *Introdução à didática do latim* (Rio de Janeiro, 1959); and Sílvio Elia, *O ensino do latim. Doutrina e métodos* (Rio de Janeiro, 1957).

6.3.6. Problems of philosophy of language are treated in several of Coseriu's works, particularly in *Forma y sustancia*, in *Logicismo y antilogicismo*, in 'Determinación y entorno' and in *Sincronía, diacronía e historia*, and also in Martínez Bonati's book cited in 6.2.3. Philosophical problems are moreoever discussed in the contributions on impressionism by Alonso and Lida pointed out in 6.3.1. More than by original works, philosophy of language is however represented in IAm by critical and informative contributions.[130] In this connection the activity of Raimundo Lida should be named first of all, although it belongs almost entirely to a period prior to that considered here.[131] In the series *Cuadernos de filosofía del lenguaje* of the Departamento

[127] I do not know Ernesto Zierer, *Teoría y práctica de la traducción. Ensayo de lingüística aplicada* [= *Lenguaje y ciencias*, 10] (Trujillo, Peru, 1963).

[128] Reprinted in *Estudios gramaticales*, 87-109.

[129] Further, one can remember the important notice by Amado Alonso, 'Los nuevos programas de lengua y literatura', *RFH* 2. 55-57, and María Delia Paladini, *Fundamentos para la enseñanza de la lengua en la escuela secundaria* (Tucumán, 1947). I only heard indirectly about a booklet by Manacorda de Rosetti on structural grammar in high school teaching, published in Buenos Aires.

[130] I deliberately leave out some strange enterprises which have little to do with philosophy and nothing at all with linguistics.

[131] His main contributions in this field are: 'Croce y Gentile, filósofos del lenguaje', *Cursos y Conferencias* 7.572-87 (Buenos Aires, 1935), and 'Bergson, filósofo del lenguaje', *Nosotros* 80.5-49 (Buenos Aires, 1933), the latter reprinted in his book *Letras hispánicas* 45-99 (Mexico, 1958). Later, too, Lida continued to deal occasionally with philosophy of language; cf. his indications in *Letras hispánicas* 10.

de Lingüística of Montevideo the following were published: Arnaldo Gomensoro, *John Dewey y la filosofía del lenguaje* (1956), and Mercedes Rein, *Ernst Cassirer* (1959).[132] In Chile, Martínez Bonati published an important study: *La concepción del lenguaje en la filosofía de Husserl* (Santiago, 1960). Moreover there can be mentioned: Víctor Li Carrillo, *Platón, Hermógenes y el lenguaje* (Lima, 1959), and about Spanish speaking thinkers: Juan David García Bacca, 'Filosofía de la gramática y gramática universal según Andrés Bello', *RNC* 9:65.7-23 (1947), Carlos Blanco Aguinaga, *Unamuno, teórico del lenguaje* (Mexico, 1954); Ángel Rosenblat, *Ortega y Gasset: Lengua y estilo* (Caracas, 1958).

6.3.7. Comparatively many contributions are found in IAm, and particularly in Spanish America, on the history of linguistics. They refer to European linguistics (and sometimes to North American) as well as, and above all, to IAm linguistics.

To the history of linguistics belong Terracini's two books cited in footnote 31.[133] The former is a general outline, in which, according to the conviction of the author, recent linguistics is practically identified with Croce-Vossler idealism (to which only Saussureanism is opposed). The latter contains several keen essays interpreting Bopp, Ascoli, Meyer-Lübke and Meillet, Gilliéron, Schuchardt, Claudio Giacomino.[134] Very important are the studies by Gazdaru on various aspects of linguistics in the nineteenth century based on hitherto unpublished documents (from the Ascoli archive in Rome), which are issued together with these studies. The most important among them are the following: 'La controversia sobre las leyes fonéticas en el epistolario de los principales lingüistas del siglo XIX', *AFCl* 4.211-328; 'A propósito de Stammbaumtheorie y Wellentheorie', *AFCl* 5.99-116; 'Cartas inéditas de Adolfo Mussafia. La 'ley sintáctica Tobler-Mussafia' y otros problemas filológicos', *Fi* 4.8-48.[135]

Concerning the history of Spanish linguistics some studies on Nebrija should be particularly mentioned.[136] As for IAm linguistics, the main studies are concerned with

[132] In 1959 further pamphlets (on Aristotle, St. Augustine, Locke, Hegel, Humboldt and Richard Hönigswald) were in preparation.

[133] Both were reprinted in one volume in Italian *Guida allo studio della linguistica storica. I. Profilo storico-critico* (Rome, 1949).

[134] Two of these studies, those on Bopp and Schuchardt, were published for the first time in this book; the others had been published in European journals. Furthermore, Terracini published in Argentina: 'W.D. Whitney y la lingüística general', *RFH* 5.105-47. This study was also included in the Italian edition referred to in the preceding footnote.

[135] Other studies belonging to this series are: 'Cuatro cartas de Friedrich Diez a G. I. Ascoli', *Fi* 3.105-10; 'Epistolario inédito de 1878 sobre una nueva edición de la Gramática de Friedrich Diez', *Homenaje a Fritz Krüger* 2.659-83 (Mendoza, 1954); 'Un conflicto 'dialectológico' del siglo pasado. Contribución a la historia de la filología retorrománica', *Orbis* 11.61-74. Gazdaru further published 'Influjos de Benedetto Croce sobre la lingüística contemporánea' in *Benedetto Croce. Conmemoración. Ensayos. Testimonios. Bibliografía* 118-45 (Buenos Aires, 1954), as well as several brief articles on the history of Rumanian linguistics, in his stenciled journal *Cuget romînesc* (Buenos Aires, 1951 ff.).

[136] Pedro U. González de la Calle, *Elio Antonio de Nebrija (Aelius Antonius Nebrissensis). Notas para un bosquejo histórico* (Bogotá, 1945); Piccardo, 'Dos momentos en la historia de la gramática española. Nebrija y Bello', *Revista de la Facultad de Humanidades y Ciencias* 4.87-112 (Montevideo, 1949), reprinted in his *Estudios gramaticales* 7-34. Of great importance is Amado Alonso's interpretative study 'Examen de las noticias de Nebrija sobre antigua pronunciación española', *NRFH* 3.1-82.

the four important linguists who constitute its older tradition: Bello, Cuervo, Hanssen and Lenz. The essential studies on Bello are: Amado Alonso, 'Introducción a los estudios gramaticales de Andrés Bello', and Ángel Rosenblat, 'Las ideas ortográficas de Bello', both in *Obras completas de Andrés Bello*, respectively, 4. *Gramática* IX-LXXXVI and 5. *Estudios gramaticales* IX-CXXXVIII.[137] The most ample contribution concerning Cuervo is: Fernando Antonio Martínez, 'Estudio preliminar', in Rufino José Cuervo, *Obras* 1. XI-CXLVI (Bogotá, 1954).[138] About Lenz there must be mentioned, in the first place, the study of the Chilean Alfonso M. Escudero, 'Rodolfo Lenz', *BICC* 18.445-84, which takes into account almost all earlier contributions.[139] On Hanssen: Eladio García, 'La obra científica de Federico Hanssen', and Julio Saavedra Molina, 'Bibliografía de Don Federico Hanssen' in Hanssen, *Estudios. Métrica-Gramática-Historia literaria* 1.9-26 and 3.245-55, respectively (Santiago, 1958). Much more than the title promises is offered in the important historico-critical study by Guillermo Guitarte, 'Cuervo, Henríquez Ureña y la polémica sobre el andalucismo de América', *VR* 17.363-416, reproduced and amplified in *BICC* 15.3-64.[140]

6.4.0. With respect to historical linguistics concerning the national languages I shall proceed in the same manner as I did in the case of dialectology and lexicology, confining myself to aspects of a general or theoretical character and to those which seem to be symptomatic for a comparison between Spanish America and Brazil.

[137] The second of these studies is a genuine history of the ideas on Spanish orthography. Cf. also the study by Piccardo referred to in the preceding footnote; that of García Bacca cited in 6.3.6.; Ángel Rosenblat, *El pensamiento gramatical de Bello* (Caracas, 1961); and the study by the Spaniard Samuel Gili Gaya, 'Introducción a los estudios ortológicos y métricos de Bello', in *Obras completas de Andrés Bello. 6. Estudios filológicos* 1. XI-CIII (Caracas, 1954). Furthermore (among others): Claudio Rosales, 'Cien años de señorío de la gramática de Andrés Bello', *BFUCh* 4.247-59; Juan B. Selva, *Trascendencia de la Gramática de Bello y el estado actual de los estudios gramaticales* (Buenos Aires, 1950); Baltasar Isaza Calderón, *La doctrina gramatical de Bello* (Panama, 1960). In view of such abundant bibliography, it must be said that few linguists in the world have been so minutely studied and interpreted as Bello.

[138] Together with a bibliography of Cuervo by Rafael Torres Quintero also in F. A. Martínez and R. Torres Quintero, *Rufino José Cuervo. Estudio y bibliografía* (Bogotá, 1954). In addition: González de la Calle, 'Formación general lingüística del Maestro Rufino José Cuervo. Apuntes para un ensayo', *BICC* 1.212-41.

[139] Particularly important among these are two critical studies by Amado Alonso: 'Rodolfo Lenz y la dialectología hispanoamericana', *BDH* 6.269-78, and that referred to in fn. 92.

[140] Other historical contributions are: Piccardo, *Acotaciones al Diálogo de la lengua* [Valdés] (Montevideo, 1941); Sílvio Elia, *O romantismo em face da filologia* (Pôrto Alegre, 1956), reprinted under the title of 'Origens românticas da filologia moderna' in the already mentioned *Ensaios de filologia* 11-37; Moldenhauer, 'Notas sobre el origen y la propagación de la palabra 'linguistique' (>lingüística) y términos equivalentes', *AIL* 6.430-44; Lope Blanch, 'La *Gramática española* de Jerónimo de Texeda', *NRFH* 13.1-16; Emmanuel Pereira Filho, 'As 'Regras de Orthographia' de Pero de Magalhães Gândavo', *RBF* 6.3-31; and the two editions: Mateo Alemán, *Ortografía castellana*, published by José Rojas Garcidueñas, with a preliminary study (pp. XIII-XXXIX) by Tomás Navarro, 'La Ortografía de Mateo Alemán' (Mexico, 1950), and Olmar Guterres da Silveira, *A 'Grammatica' de Fernão d'Oliveyra* (Rio de Janeiro, 1954). Contributions to the history of linguistics are also found in Silva Neto, *Ensaios de filologia portuguêsa* (São Paulo, 1956), and *Lingua, cultura e civilização* (Rio de Janeiro, 1960). Cf. also the informative works pointed out in 4.1.1.2. and the studies referred to in 0.6.

6.4.1. The only theoretical study of a general nature on linguistic change and the foundations of linguistic history published in IAm is Coseriu, *Sincronía, diacronía e historia*. With single theoretical aspects of linguistic history are concerned: Amado Alonso's 'Substratum y superstratum', *RFH* 3.209-18; and Terracini's 'Cómo muere una lengua' and 'Lengua y cultura' in *Conflictos de lenguas y de cultura* 11-42 and 104-96, respectively. General problems relating to linguistic change are moreover treated in works of Alonso and Silva Neto, and in Mattoso Câmara's *Introdução*.

6.4.2. Historical linguistics as such is scarcely represented in Spanish America. The only continuous activity concerning the general history of the Spanish language is that of Amado Alonso (articles published in the *RFH*, *NRFH*, *BICC* and elsewhere). Coseriu and Guitarte have also dealt with problems of the history of Spanish. But since Hanssen[141] no historical grammar or history of the language has so far been written in Spanish America, and studies on ancient Spanish are also lacking.[142] The situation in Brazil is very different. There, besides a number of historical studies, a good historical grammar[143] and two histories of the Portuguese language appeared, which are the most extensive so far published in the Portuguese-Brazilian world;[144] several students (Augusto Magne, Silva Neto, Celso Cunha, Bem Veiga) published important critical editions of ancient Portuguese texts.

Somewhat more encouraging is the picture of the history of American Spanish, a field in which however Ángel Rosenblat has been the only great specialist since the death of Henríquez Ureña and Alonso.[145] During the last years two essentially important events were recorded in this field. On the one hand Rosenblat's fundamental work *La población indígena y el mestizaje en América* (2 volumes, Buenos Aires, 1954),[146] about the history of the hispanization of America and the external relations between Spanish and the native languages, was published. On the other hand, concerning the problem of the historical basis of American Spanish, the anti-Andalusian

[141] His *Gramática histórica de la lengua castellana* was published in Halle in 1913 and was reprinted in Buenos Aires in 1945.

[142] Coseriu, *La Hispania romana y el latín hispánico. Breve introducción al estudio histórico del español* (Montevideo, 1953) is a concise summary of problems and facts designed for beginners. As far as ancient text editions are concerned, I can only name Rodolfo A. Borello, *Jaryas andalusíes* (Bahía Blanca, Argentina, 1959).

[143] Ismael de Lima Coutinho, *Pontos de gramática histórica*[4] (Rio de Janeiro, 1958 [since then a 5th edition was published, which I have not seen]). This work is the best, by the way, but it is not the only one of its kind in Brazil.

[144] Silveira Bueno, *A formação histórica da língua portuguêsa*[2] (Rio de Janeiro, 1958); Silva Neto, *História da língua portuguêsa* (Rio de Janeiro, 1952-7).

[145] Along with him one can only mention Guillermo Guitarte, the best historian among the younger linguists (many of whom simply ignore historical linguistics).

[146] Cf., by the same author 'La hispanización de América. El castellano y las lenguas indígenas desde 1492', *Presente y futuro de la lengua española* 2.189-216 (Madrid, 1964). Among other contributions to this topic there are: Marcos A. Morínigo, 'Difusión del español en el Noroeste argentino', in his *Programa de filología hispánica* 71-100 (Buenos Aires, 1959), and the book by Ardissone referred to in fn. 21. A general history of the Romanization of America, however not comparable to Rosenblat's work, was published in Brazil: Joaquim Ribeiro, *História da romanização da América* (Rio de Janeiro, 1959).

thesis, which had been universally admitted since the contributions of Henríquez Ureña[147] on this problem and the acceptance of his results by Amado Alonso, was thrown into the discussion and basically rejected. Guillermo Guitarte, with his article cited in 6.3.7., decisively contributed to this revision, along with some Spanish and North American students.[148]

6.4.3. Scarcely cultivated in Spanish America are also certain disciplines of a historical character as etymology and historical toponymy, although there are abundant extemporaneous etymologists among the pre-scientific and non-scientific linguists, and although there exist studies on descriptive toponymy and collections of such place names as are immediately etymologizeable (at least in a generic sense). The principal etymological investigations are due to Corominas (articles published in the *AIL*, *RFH* and elsewhere). Others who also dealt with etymology are: Amado Alonso, Henríquez Ureña, Krüger, Rosenblat, Hernando Balmori, Gazdaru, Coseriu, Rona, Cisneros and a few others. An exemplary etymological investigation is Rosenblat's 'Origen e historia del *che* argentino', *Fi* 8.325-401.[149] The works on historical toponymy worth mentioning first of all, also belong to Rosenblat: *Argentina. Historia de un nombre* (Buenos Aires, 1949), 2nd edition: *El nombre de la Argentina* (Buenos Aires, 1964), and *El nombre de Venezuela* (Caracas, 1956).[150] In Brazil Nascentes, Augusto Magne, Silva Neto and A. G. Cunha have contributed to etymology.

6.4.4. A number of contributions concerning interlinguistic contacts are found in Spanish America as well as in Brazil. Many Hispano-American linguists have been concerned with the contacts with native languages (among them: Morínigo, Oroz, Rosenblat).[151] Nevertheless, the general problem of the influence of these languages on American Spanish has remained in the same stage in which Amado Alonso left it (in the study cited in fn. 92) and which needs to be revised. Meo Zilio above all devoted himself to the Hispano-Italian contacts (local influences in both directions).[152] The first contributions on Hispano-Portuguese contacts from a dialectological point of view are due to Rona.[153] The main contribution on the cultural influence of

[147] In particular *Sobre el problema del andalucismo dialectal de América* (Buenos Aires, 1932).

[148] Partial doubts concerning anti-Andalusianism were also expressed by Coseriu, *Amado Alonso* 11 (Montevideo, 1953).

[149] About some theoretical and methodological aspects of etymology, cf. Coseriu, '¿Arabismos o romanismos?', *NRFH* 15.4-22 (particularly 17-18).

[150] An interesting methodological problem was raised by Rona, '*Uruguay*. (The Problem of Etymology of Place Names of Guarani Origin)', *Names* 8.1-5.

[151] Especially the Paraguayan Morínigo paid much attention to these contacts, primarily to the influence of Spanish on Guarani. His most important work, *Hispanismos en el guaraní* (Buenos Aires, 1931) elaborated under the direction of Amado Alonso, is prior to the period considered here. Among his ulterior contributions there are: 'Influencia del español en la estructura lingüística del guaraní', *Fi* 5.237-47 and 'La penetración de los indigenismos americanos en el español', *Presente y futuro de la lengua española* 2. 217-26.

[152] In numerous articles published above all in *LN* since 1955 and in 'Italianismos generales en el español rioplatense', *BICC* 20.68-119.

[153] *La frontera lingüística entre el portugués y el español en el Norte de Uruguay* (Pôrto Alegre, 1963), and, among the preprinted contributions of the DLM, *El dialecto 'fronterizo' del Norte de Uruguay* and *El 'caingusino': un dialecto mixto hispano-portugués* (both 1959).

English is Ricardo J. Alfaro's *Diccionario de anglicismos* (Panama, 1950; new ed., Madrid, 1964).[154]

6.5.0. Little attention has been given to languages other than national languages in IAm, in Spanish America even less than in Brazil.

6.5.1. Romance linguistics has been cultivated in Spanish America almost exclusively by linguists of foreign origin: Terracini, Coseriu and especially Krüger and Gazdaru. In Brazil, in turn, an interesting activity has been displayed in this field by several Brazilian linguists, and four important works on Vulgar Latin were published,[155] besides some other works of a general character,[156] to which Spanish America has either little or nothing to oppose.[157] Researches on single Romance languages other than national are altogether lacking, however, in Spanish America as well as in Brazil.[158] Not even investigations on Portuguese are found in Spanish America,[159] whereas there were some contributions concerning Spanish in Brazil (Nascentes, Hélcio Martins [d. 1966]).

6.5.2. Even less is found outside of the Romance field. Concerning the English language I do not know contributions worth mentioning other than those by Bertens Charnley, published in European or North American journals. Nothing has come to my knowledge concerning other modern non-Romance languages: if such contributions do exist, they did not spread and were not influential in IAm linguistics as a whole. As far as the classical languages are concerned, I only know some contributions of a rather philological character and some grammars designed for use in teaching. Among these, Rodolfo Oroz' *Gramática latina* (Santiago, 1932; 3rd ed., 1953; Portuguese translation, Rio de Janeiro, 1938) deserves to be mentioned. In Brazil two works of a good scientific level are recorded in this field: Ernest Faria's *Fonética histórica do latim*

154 Lidia Contreras, 'Los anglicismos en el lenguaje deportivo chileno', *BFUCh* 7.177-341, can furthermore be remembered.

155 Silva Neto, *Fontes do latim vulgar. O Appendix Probi* (Rio de Janeiro, 1938;3rd ed., 1956) and *História do latim vulgar* (Rio de Janeiro, 1957); Maurer Jr., *Gramática do latim vulgar* (Rio de Janeiro, 1959) and *O Problema do latim vulgar* (Rio de Janeiro, 1962).

156 Such as Maurer Jr., *A unidade da România ocidental* (São Paulo, 1951), interesting for its main thesis, although modest and questionable in its realization. There can also be mentioned an introduction to Romance linguistics: Nascentes, *Elementos de filologia romanica* (Rio de Janeiro, 1954).

157 Coseriu, *El llamado 'latín vulgar' y las primeras diferenciaciones romances. Breve introducción a la lingüística románica* (Montevideo, 1954) is an initiation for students based on well known facts, whose originality is limited to the manner in which several problems are posed (among these, the problem of Vulgar Latin itself). More than modest is Cisneros' *Appendix Probi* (Lima, 1952). An effort of a certain interest is Heles Contreras' 'Una clasificación morfo-sintáctica de las lenguas románicas', *RomPh* 16.261-8. I do not know A. Luco's handbook *Lingüística románica* (Santiago de Chile, 1955).

158 About Catalan one must remember *Miscel.lània Fabra. Recull de treballs de lingüística catalana i romànica dedicats a Pompeu Fabra* (Buenos Aires, 1943), in which Amado Alonso published his important study 'Partición de las lenguas románicas de Occidente' (pp. 81-101), and Corominas a contribution on toponymy, 'Noms de lloc catalans d'origen germànic' (pp. 108-132). Corominas also dedicated a few other contributions to Catalan. Gazdaru dedicated several contributions to the Rumanian language.

159 Coseriu, '*Fiz* y *tenho feito*. Contribución al estudio del sistema de tiempos y aspectos del verbo portugués', a contribution submitted to the fourth Colóquio Internacional de Estudos Luso-Brasileiros (Salvador, Brazil, 1959), has not yet been published.

(Rio de Janeiro, 1955) and *Gramática superior da língua latina* (Rio de Janeiro, 1958). Strangely enough, a language which found a certain number of cultivators in IAm, although almost exclusively from a philological point of view, has been Sanskrit, with which Fernando Tola, González de la Calle, Miroslav Marcovich (Venezuela), Bucca, Altuchow, Jorge Bertolaso Stella (Brazil) have dealt. As far as I know the only linguistic work in this field is Nicolás Altuchow's *Gramática sánscrita elemental* (Montevideo, 1962).[160] In the field of Indo-European linguistics I do not know anything worth mentioning beyond Tovar's work cited in 2.1.2. and P. Bosch-Gimpera's important work on prehistory, *El problema indoeuropeo* (Mexico, 1960).[161] Outside of the Indo-European domain there are practically no scientific contributions to be mentioned, if one excludes the studies on native languages.[162]

6.6. Summarizing: in Spanish America linguistics is mostly concentrated on Spanish, particularly on American Spanish and even more on present American Spanish. In Brazil, Portuguese is the main subject of linguistics, but historical interests are prevailing at the scientific level: from this follows the 'unitarian' attitude in contrast to the 'differentialistic' attitude of Spanish America, and the greater attention devoted to Romance and Latin linguistics.

6.7. A few words remain to be said about the technical level of IAm publications, as far as the authors are concerned (exactness of quotations, correctness and completeness of bibliographical data, systematic arrangement of material, etc.), as well as to editorial aspects (print, mistakes, etc.). An elevated technical level was achieved in Buenos Aires in former times, where the *RFH* constituted an example in this connection. Technically excellent are the publications of the CdM in Mexico. A high technical level is also presented, with a few exceptions, by the printed publications of the DLM, as well as by the recent publications of Santiago and Bogotá, where considerable progress has been made in the last years. Elsewhere the technical level is lower. Leaving aside those countries where scientific linguistics virtually does not exist, the publications show a low technical level in Peru and in many instances also in Brazil, although some Brazilian printings have perceptibly improved during recent years in this respect.

7. REPERCUSSIONS

7.0. Generally speaking, the repercussions of IAm linguistics in the scientific world do not correspond to its value: on the one hand, they are less than this value; on the

[160] Of linguistic interest is also his excellent annotated translation *El Tarkasamgraha de Annambhaṭṭa. Texto sánscrito con introducción, traducción y notas* (Montevideo, 1959).

[161] The contributions of O. F. A. Menghin 'Veneto-Illyrica I' and 'Veneto-Illyrica II', *AFCl* 4.151-81 and 5.61-69, and some others are also concerned with prehistory and archeology.

[162] The Africanistic activity displayed by Benigno Ferrario in Montevideo has had no repercussions; see his 'La protohistoria a la luz de la glotología (Área etiópico-egipcio-bérbera)', *Revista del Instituto de Antropología de la Universidad Nacional de Tucumán* 2.3.37-63 (1941). In Brazil, too, a number of Africanistic contributions have been recorded, whose value I do not know. I have not seen Ernesto Zierer's booklet *Introducción a la lengua japonesa hablada* (Trujillo, Peru, 1964).

other hand, they are varying and haphazard, and show no sound selection criteria, so that unrepresentative works often are better known than representative ones. This is to some extent due to language difficulties (deficient knowledge of Spanish and Portuguese in international spheres). But primarily it is due to a wide lack of acquaintance with IAm culture, which is considered more as an object for research than as a possible contribution to research, and which usually arouses interest only among specialists of IAm studies. Thus IAm linguistics too is almost exclusively known among Ibero-Americanists, and even among these mostly as Ibero-Americanistics (not e.g. as a contribution to general linguistics), and particularly for the material it gathered. This ignorance in the linguistic as well as in other cultural fields, by the way, begins with the IAm countries themselves. Indeed, there exists a profound mutual ignorance between the Hispano-American countries. Therefore the unity of language, traditions, and conditions implies an ANALOGOUS but not a UNITARIAN development of linguistics as well as of other forms of culture in these countries. Culturally Lima, Quito, or Bogotá are much further apart from Buenos Aires or Santiago de Chile than are Paris, Rome, or New York.[163] There is an even more marked lack of acquaintance, although unilateral, between Spanish and Portuguese America. Further on IAm linguistics is, of course, widely ignored by European linguistics and even more so by North American linguistics.

7.1. The scarce acceptance of IAm linguistics in Spanish America is due to its mainly local and localistic character, as well as to a great critical insecurity and to a certain timidity in evaluating directly what originates in other IAm countries, which constitutes a kind of inferiority complex of this linguistics, i.e. all that comes from Europe or the United States must be good in itself, but what comes from other IAm countries is probably bad. This explains why certain IAm works reach other IAm countries only by way of Europe. Actually only the works of Amado Alonso and his group had repercussions practically all over Spanish America. A work such as Fernández Retamar's *Idea de la estilística* has remained widely unknown (otherwise it cannot be explained why other inferior introductions to stylistics were published), and the same can be said of Martínez Bonati's *La estructura de la obra literaria*. The important works of Piccardo too are still ignored by most Hispano-American grammarians.[164] Concerning the knowledge of Brazilian linguistics the situation is even worse. The vast activity of Silva Neto and such excellent works as Mattoso Câmara's *Introdução* (which could have been adopted as a handbook all over Latin America) and his *Fonêmica*, or such useful works as Valnir Chagas' *Didática*, Sílvio Elia's

[163] Thus, in Argentina or in Uruguay it is much easier to obtain books published in Europe or in the United States than books from other Hispano-American countries (except for Mexico). In fact, only from two centers (Buenos Aires and Mexico) the diffusion of publications in Spanish America is constant and goes on under more or less acceptable conditions.

[164] Most of the publications of Montevideo are not listed in Serís' *Bibliografía*; there even are lacking a good number of those registered in the bibliographical repertories or reviewed (and even published) in journals, which the compiler of the bibliography apparently consulted.

Orientações and the works of Faria on Latin, have had either no or few repercussions in Spanish America.[165] The old Instituto de Filología of Buenos Aires tried to overcome this mutual ignorance and distrust and was at the time of Amado Alonso a center interested in the development of linguistics in the Hispano-American countries and in Brazil. But since 1946 the situation has become worse instead of becoming better.[166]

Very different is the attitude of the Brazilian linguists, who generally follow with enough attention what is being published in Spanish America,[167] and review and use Hispano-American works.[168]

7.2. In Spain it was above all Amado Alonso who met with wide acceptance as he is considered there — not without reason — as a representative of Spanish linguistics. But beyond Alonso the repercussions of IAm linguistics are not so far-reaching as one might suppose, and, what is worse, scientific and pre-scientific linguistics are sometimes badly confused, owing to a strange lack of insight.[169] IAm activity concerning linguistic theory, grammatical theory, and general linguistics after Alonso is known to the more advanced Spanish linguists, but is still ignored by most of the others.[170] Elsewhere in Europe only Amado Alonso, Coseriu and Luis Jorge Prieto are relatively known names, and even Alonso is mainly known to students of Romance and Hispanic languages. Nevertheless, judging from reviews and quotations, European

[165] The *Introdução* by Mattoso Câmara has not yet been reviewed, from what I know, by any of the great Hispano-American journals.

[166] Thus, e.g. the first and very sporadic reviews of publications of the DLM — which are found reviewed in European journals since 1952 — appeared in the *BICC* in 1957 and not until 1958 in the *BFUCh* and in the *NRFH*, and no reviews of these publications have hitherto appeared in Buenos Aires. In the 8 volumes of the *RFH* one can find 11 reviews of Portuguese works (almost all of them Brazilian), 6 of them on linguistics; in turn, the 16 volumes of the *NRFH* only contain 5 reviews of works in Portuguese and only one of them on linguistics (by the way, a work by the German linguist Piel). In the *BFUCh* there are only four reviews of Brazilian linguistic works; in *Fi* none at all. Reviews of Portuguese and Brazilian publications are relatively numerous only in the *AIL* (from volume 4 on), but they almost exclusively concern contributions about ethnography or ethnographical linguistics.

[167] With exceptions, of course. Thus F. Gomes de Matos, *Lg* 40.631 (1964) believes that IAm linguistics has awakened from its lethargy only in the last three years, which evidently is far from being true.

[168] The Hispano-American bibliography mentioned in fn. 60 does not include any Portuguese titles; in turn, a similar — and more limited — Brazilian bibliography lists 26 Spanish titles, 14 of them Hispano-American. The *RBF*, too, regularly publishes reviews of Spanish and Hispano-American works. In this same connection, I can point out that the DLM has had much closer and earlier relations with Rio de Janeiro than, e.g. with Buenos Aires.

[169] Works of very low scientific value, which do not enjoy any prestige in the Hispano-American countries themselves, are quoted and praised in Spanish publications. And more than one amateur linguist received excellence attestations from famous Spanish scholars. Cf. Coseriu, *Reseñas* 13 (Montevideo, 1953).

[170] Thus Fernando Lázaro Carreter, *Diccionario de términos filológicos*² (Madrid, 1962), which even includes terms proposed by some obscure European linguists and never employed by anybody, does not include any of the terms proposed and regularly employed by IAm linguists and generally ignores (deliberately?) all the theoretical IAm contributions. In this respect the attitude of Portuguese linguists towards Brazilian linguistics is very different: the best Brazilian linguists are well known in Portugal and their works figure regularly in the lists of lectures recommended to students of linguistics.

linguistics seems to pay more attention to the development of IAm linguistics than does North American linguistics. In fact, in the United States IAm linguistics is almost exclusively known and made use of by Hispanists and Ibero-Americanists (although in this case probably more than in Europe). Thus the publications of the DLM, which have had ample repercussions in Western[171] as well as in Eastern Europe,[172] are practically ignored in the United States and have not been reviewed so far either in *Lg*, *Word*, or *IJAL*. Except for some occasional reviews by Romance philologists and a few sporadic indications, the North American reader has available only the completely distorted, malevolent, and curiously anachronistic presentation by Robert A. Hall, Jr.: *Idealism in Romance Linguistics* 85-8 (Ithaca, N.Y., 1963). Strangely enough, the theory developed in Montevideo has remained unknown even to the promoters of generative grammar, although they assert a number of principles which have been maintained in Montevideo since 1952, e.g. a) the conception of languages as 'rule-governed creativity';[173] b) the dynamic interpretation of language as a technique to express and understand also what is new and what was never said before; c) the criticism of antimentalism and the stressing of the importance of the speakers' intuition, which is considered as the very subject and foundation of linguistic theory; d) the necessity for re-interpreting and re-evaluating traditional grammar in so far as it corresponds to the actual functioning of language; e) the necessity for describing languages as systems for linguistic creation.[174] In the transformationalists' writings one can sometimes find textual coincidences with former writings of Montevideo, coincidences which are evidently due to an analogous point of view. It is regrettable that the transformationalists should have ignored this, since generative grammar would have found in the Montevideo writings a clear distinction of levels of grammaticality, the determination of the actual nature of the speaker's intuition, and its relation to scientific analysis as well as its theoretical basis,[175] and, more generally, those philosophical foundations which it lacks and is still searching, not always in adequate places. In addition, the theory developed in Montevideo has gone much further than transformational grammar, which explicitly limits itself to

[171] Cf., e.g. the reviews by Martinet, *BSL* 52.19-23 and 263 (1956); by Pisani, *AGI* 61.58-68 (1956) and *Paideia* 17.82-92 (1962); and by René Gsell, *RLR* 23.165-6 (1959); and N. C. W. Spence, 'Towards a New Synthesis in Linguistics: the Work of Eugenio Coseriu', *ArchL* 12.1-34 (1960).

[172] Coseriu, *Sincronía, diacronía e historia* was translated into Russian in V. A. Zvegincev, Ed., *Novoe v lingvistike* 3.123-343 (Moscow, 1963).

[173] Cf. *Sincronía, diacronía e historia* 53, fn. 47.

[174] Cf. the latest formulation of such exigency in *Sincronía* 155: 'In fact, for the speakers themselves the present-day language is not only a collection of forms which have already been realized and can be used as models (*norm*), but also a technique to go beyond what has been realized, a system of possibilities (*system*). The description, therefore, has to account for the possibilities of all that which is a productive pattern, a schema which is applicable to the realization of that which does not yet exist as a norm. This is true not only in morphology but also in syntax, lexicon (derivation and composition of words) and even in the phonological system where the possibilities of realization are not identical for each functional unit'.

[175] Cf. *Sincronía* 32-3.

synchrony,[176] as it has shown that linguistic technique not only works synchronically, but also diachronically, i.e. that 'linguistic change' is the historical realization of this system of possibilities, which each language is.[177]

8. FUTURE PERSPECTIVES

8.0. The survey just outlined may seem to be pessimistic. Indeed, apart from a few exceptions, there is not really an IAm linguistics which might be characterized by a specific conceptual and methodological content, as there is a North American, or even an English or Italian linguistics. What really exists rather is a SITUATION of linguistics in IAm; consequently the characterization I tried to give had to refer to this situation, to the typical attitudes of IAm linguistics and to its style, rather than to its contribution to the internal progress of linguistics. Nevertheless, it seems to me that the achievements of IAm linguistics are remarkable, if one considers the conditions mentioned in 1., besides others which I could not enumerate, and I believe that there are good perspectives for future development, not only for an external progress — extension and application of linguistics existing today — but also for internal progress, i.e. for overcoming linguistics imported from Europe and the United States.

8.1. As to the external progress, a great development can be expected first of all in Brazil. It is true that Brazil has not yet had organized centers for progressive linguistic work such as those of Buenos Aires and Montevideo. But these latter were shortlived efforts and under the present circumstances it cannot be said how far the weakened IAA will be able to renew and continue the tradition of Amado Alonso in all its dimensions, nor does it seem probable that the DLM can uphold and continue the universalistic orientation it had between 1951 and 1962. Moreover, the achievements in scientific linguistics so far made in Brazil, in proportion surpass the achievements of Spanish America. One must further add that, whereas there does not exist one uniform Hispano-American linguistics, in Brazil there already exists an uninterrupted Brazilian linguistic tradition, which is beginning to acquire its own definite features. And what is more, in Brazil the universities are much more interested in linguistics, and the remarkable circulation of certain linguistic works[178] allows the hope that a young generation with a good and homogeneous preparation will soon exist there.

[176] Cf. Noam Chomsky, *Current Issues in Linguistic Theory* 22 (The Hague, 1964).

[177] The coincidences in views and intentions do not imply, however, that I agree with transformational technique. On the contrary I consider this technique as inadequate and as a further form of an arbitrary partialization of the concrete linguistic experience. 'Inadequate', as in the case of other abstract and dogmatized models, of course, means 'only partially adequate'.

[178] It was seen that Mattoso Câmara's *Introdução* already had four editions and Lima Coutinho's *Gramática histórica* five, and that even books implying a stricter especialization had several editions; thus, Silva Neto, *Fontes do latim vulgar* had three, and Faria's *Fonética histórica do latim* had two editions.

In Spanish America a future development can be expected above all in Argentina, where several linguistic centers are already existing and where a new generation of well-prepared linguists with a modern outlook is rising: Ana María Barrenechea, L. J. Prieto, Guitarte (presently at the Boston College), Suárez, Fernández Guizzetti. A future development can also be expected in Chile (Santiago and Concepción), and, of course, in Colombia, especially provided that the ICC can overcome localism in its research (as it is doing now in teaching), that its publications are subjected to a more rigorous selection, and if it can keep up the orientation towards broader information as is observed e.g. in the case of Montes.

8.2. It is more difficult to predict how far IAm will be able to contribute to the theoretical and methodological progress of linguistics. IAm linguistics presently is, as was seen, in a receptive phase, and there are no indications that this phase will be overcome in the near future and on a sufficiently large scale. But precisely in receptivity lies the possibility for a qualitative progress of linguistics as of other fields of culture. What seems to be — and even is — at a certain time eclecticism, is also, in a broader historical perspective, ideological openness and anti-dogmatism, non-limitation to a single tradition. One only needs to have a look at the bibliographical background of some of the books published in IAm. While most North American linguistic books and also many Western European books are primarily based on local and national traditions, while neglecting all other traditions and what happens elsewhere, in IAm the information tends towards a balance between the local, the European and the North American traditions. A writing or bibliography in which such names as Humboldt, de Saussure, Bloomfield, Trubetzkoy, Jakobson, Harris, Terracini, Pagliaro, Frei, Martinet appear together, is exceptional elsewhere, whereas it is not so in some IAm centers. Such contributions as Rulon S. Wells' 'De Saussure's System of Linguistics', *Word* 3.1-31 (1947) or Einar Haugen's 'Directions in Modern Linguistics', *Lg* 27.211-22 (1951) are classical in North American linguistics, not only because of their unquestionable intrinsic value, but also because they were exceptional in their environment and at the time when they appeared. In IAm, however, a good knowledge of de Saussure and the co-existence of European and North American linguistics are by no means exceptional among the better informed linguists. If aspects of pre-scientific linguistics, which persevere in many countries of IAm, including on the academic level, are eliminated, and if IAm linguistics matures, acquires self-confidence, and thus passes from a receptive to a critical and creative phase, this linguistics, which is today indefinite, will be able to attain an impartial and anti-dogmatic synthesis of all traditions combined in it and to contribute to the advance and unity of international linguistics in a way which cannot now be foreseen. In this sense I can conclude this survey with convinced optimism.

8.3. But general progress will of course depend on various circumstances, such as: the intensification of contacts and interchanges between the IAm centers of activity, the intensification of interchanges with European and North American centers, the creation of a greater number of regular linguistic courses, the creation of linguistic institutes and specialized libraries with sufficient endowment, the training of young linguists in foreign countries, and the translation of a number of classical linguistic works, be it in the theoretical or didactic field (as e.g. Humboldt, Paul, Bloomfield, Trubetzkoy, Hjelmslev, Pagliaro, Harris, Gleason).[179]

[179] A recent Peruvian translation of Bloomfield's *Language* (*Lenguaje* [sic], Lima 1964) should be disregarded altogether: it is full of errors of every sort and kind and, in its present form, cannot reasonably be recommended to anybody.

HISPANIC PHONOLOGY

ERICA GARCIA

1. Latin American research on Hispanic Phonology can be said to fall into three stages: the normative, the historical, and the structural — divisions largely associated with a difference in views concerning the basic relation between American Spanish and the language of Spain.

During the first stage, which runs approximately from 1870 to the 1920's, the main emphasis rested on the study of local forms. The language spoken in Latin America was generally regarded as a corrupt version of Spanish, and its peculiarities were recorded with the normative purpose of improving speech in the new republics. The amount of work done in phonology during that first period is negligible. Some information as to early pronunciation in the several Latin American countries can be gleaned from lexicons of local terms, as well as from works denouncing defective speech forms, but since the material is generally very sketchy and naturally leaves many crucial questions unanswered, discussion of the work of this period is not likely to be very productive.

The second stage has given us most of the material now available on the phonology of Spanish in Latin America. Its chief aim was to relate historically the language of Latin America to the Spanish of Spain. Scholars such as Cuervo, and especially Lenz, can be regarded as bridging the gap between the interests of the first and the second stages. The historical orientation of this period becomes particularly clear in the long controversy over the Andalusian origin of many features of Latin American Spanish, and primarily in the large literature devoted to the history of *seseo*.[1]

The second, or historical stage, was followed by a third, or structuralist period, which began roughly in the fifties. In this last stage the emphasis rests on the structural description of the phonology of the Latin American dialects, although an occasional paper with historical orientation may appear as an exception to the norm.

2. Quite naturally, work on Hispanic Phonology has been mainly concerned with Latin American dialects. Some studies deal, however, with what could be called questions of 'general phonology', but they are very few and bear little relation to the

[1] By *seseo* is generally meant the merger of /s/ and /θ/ into /s/, characteristic of Southern Spain and all of Latin America. Much valuable work on these questions was done by Henríquez Ureña. For a penetrating evaluation of his position, cf. Guillermo L. Guitarte, 'Cuervo, Henríquez Ureña y la polémica sobre el andalucismo de América', *Thesaurus* 14.20-81 (1959).

specific problems of Hispanic Phonology. A striking feature of most of the work done in phonology in Spanish America is precisely the degree to which theory and facts have managed to preserve their independence.

The number of those writing on theoretical questions appears restricted to Alonso, Coseriu and Prieto. Of these, the general writings of Alonso are closely related to his historical and dialectological interests, leaving only Coseriu and Prieto, who have done serious original thinking on some basic phonological issues.

Coseriu has devoted much attention to the problems posed by the relation between phonetics and phonology (as related to the *langue-parole* opposition), on the one hand, and the planes of expression and content, on the other. His theoretical roots are in de Saussure, with some influence of the Italian school. Among his papers, those dealing with the concepts of system, norm and speech ('Sistema, norma y habla') and with the opposition of form and substance in speech sounds ('Forma y sustancia en los sonidos del lenguaje') are worthy of mention for their perceptive remarks on the essentially non-physical nature of phonic realization. But they appear to have had little influence on the practice of other Latin American linguists, perhaps because it is not too clear in just what way his conclusions may be relevant to the task of actual linguistic analysis.

Prieto's theoretical writings on phonology are essentially a development of certain ideas implied in the works of the Prague school, especially in connection with syntagmatic phenomena. He has repeatedly shown that differences in order or succession are not to be equated with those involving an exclusion of terms, since they do not involve the sound system in the same way. He has therefore proposed that these two kinds of difference be kept distinct by the terms 'contrast' and 'opposition'.[2] However, as in the case of Coseriu, we do not find that Prieto's ideas have had any noticeable influence on the analysis of Spanish dialects.

One might finally raise the question of the degree to which phonological studies in Spanish have had the benefit of experimental phonetic techniques. Occasional use of kimograms and of palatograms has been made (especially by Zamora Vicente and by Alonso); Mercedes A. Puebla de Chaves began in Argentina a program of research on regional intonation patterns, using amplified oscillograms, but this was never carried to completion.

3. It was pointed out above that the first purely normative stage was followed by a period of predominantly historical orientation. The break between the two, however, was not a complete one, since the purist's interest in correct ways of speaking was enriched rather than replaced by the philologist's curiosity in the differences between the speech of Latin America and Spain.

The ideal to which the scholars of this second period aspired appears to have been to find the distinctive features of the various Spanish dialects and to describe their

[2] These same notions appear in the neo-Firthian distinction between 'structure' and 'system'.

spatial extent fully, both as a goal in itself, and because geographic distribution might shed some light on the historical origin of the various divergences. In other words, they wished to describe geographically and to explain historically the major isoglosses cutting across the Hispanic world. Even more briefly, what they strove for was a philologically annotated linguistic atlas.

This is clearly the goal that inspired the work of Amado Alonso, whose studies are by far the best of this period. For instance, his papers on the evolution of *ll* and *y*, the merger of implosive *-l* and *-r*, and the history of *seseo*, integrate a number of geographical, phonetic and philological facts, all of which contribute equally to a balanced appraisal of the particular dialectal feature studied. There is no doubt that the goal of this period was an eminently reasonable one. As it happened, however, a series of factors — some inherent in the very approach adopted by the scholars of this period, some merely fortuitous — combined to doom the whole enterprise to failure.

The first problem faced by this generation of scholars was the paucity of data on Latin American dialects. The different dialects of Spain were not very well described either, to be sure, but at least there was, on the continent, a tradition of monograph writing, based on the work of Menéndez Pidal, which could be expected to yield the necessary facts.

The need to cope with this lack of information on Latin American speech inspired what are probably the most influential works of the second period: the *Biblioteca de Dialectología Hispanoamericana* (usually abbreviated *BDH*), put out under the direction of Alonso by the Instituto de Filología of Buenos Aires, and Navarro Tomás' *Cuestionario lingüístico hispanoamericano*.

The *Biblioteca de Dialectología Hispanoamericana* was intended to be a storehouse of information on Hispanic dialectology and is, to this day, the only general collection of material on this subject. It contains original studies on specific Latin American dialects, such as Henríquez Ureña's description of the Spanish of Santo Domingo, or Battini's work on the rural speech of San Luis in Argentina, as well as older works, many of which were no longer available in their original editions (e.g. Espinosa's description of New Mexican Spanish, which makes up volumes 1 and 2 of the *BDH*, a collection of brief studies and old glossaries dealing with Mexican Spanish and Central American dialects in vol. 4, Lenz's famous essay on the Araucanian substratum of Chilean in vol. 6, etc.) The editions of early works were enriched with careful notes by Alonso and Angel Rosenblat on parallel developments in other regions of the Spanish speaking world.

It should be pointed out that phonology was not the primary concern of the *BDH*, since the philological orientation of its founder and, indeed, of this entire period, led quite naturally to a concentration on the study of morphological and lexical variations. However, it is in the *BDH* that we find most clearly expressed the theoretical principles, or rather perhaps the linguistic goals, that underlay the historical period. In his Introduction to the *BDH*,[3] Alonso states that the purpose of this collection is to relate

[3] *BDH*, 1. 6. 'Queremos, pues, ser colaboradores, anudando cada problema con el estado actual de

geographically each dialectal form to its counterpart in other Hispanic regions. A more insightful remark on the nature of dialectological studies is buried in a footnote to his paper on 'acoustic equivalence', where Alonso pointed out[4] that in sifting through the dialectal material available he had observed that practically all variants found in one dialect also appeared in a number of others. Linguistic geography would consequently have to be aimed, not at the collection of facts, but at the characterization of dialects in terms of their peculiar features.

The idiosyncratic features of each dialect, however, could only be determined by elimination of all the ones common to the remainder. For such a task, the studies contained in the *BDH* provided no more than the groundwork. Fresh material had to be obtained, and to make this possible was the goal of Navarro Tomás' *Cuestionario*.

Since the political splintering of Latin America into a score of independent nations made it extremely unlikely that a general linguistic atlas of American Spanish would ever become a reality, it was highly desirable that such studies as were undertaken should prove as homogeneous as possible. In this way a series of partial monographs might substitute for a general atlas. To ensure the comparability of future studies on American Spanish dialects was the purpose of Navarro Tomás' *Cuestionario*, which drew the attention of the prospective collector to a number of points that had been found of interest in dialects already more or less well investigated.

It appears, then, that the scholars of the second period had not only a clear program of action, defined by Alonso and exemplified in his work, but also a practical tool with which to gather the necessary data. That the enterprise did not yield the anticipated results was probably chiefly due to three factors which will be discussed below.

In the first place, both Alonso and Navarro Tomás can be characterized as philologists rather than linguists. In the second place, Navarro Tomás, besides being a philologist, was also an excellent phonetician. This left clear traces in his questionnaire, thereby influencing the many works that were based on it. Finally, it must be borne in mind that most, if not all the scholars of the second period, studied the language from a double point of view. On the one hand they were pure descriptivists, interested in the dialectal evolution of Spanish and in the parallel it offered to the

---

la Filología ... Nuestra labor más dura consiste en relacionar geográficamente cada forma dialectal con la correspondiente de todas las regiones hispánicas ... También en América es posible intentar estudios de geografía lingüística ... es suficiente la consignación de variantes por grandes regiones — casi siempre por naciones — para levantar una bandada de cuestiones científicas nuevas: permanente separación de convergencias y divergencias (Meillet) en el desarrollo lingüístico hispanoamericano....'

[4] 'Equivalencia acústica', in *BDH* I, 440-69, esp. p. 442, footnote 3. 'Esta sorprendente comprobación de que la mayoría de las variantes fonéticas denunciadas en un dialecto castellano ... se repiten en los demás ya premia suficientemente nuestra afanosa rebusca de documentaciones dialectales ... ellas nos han impuesto, con este descubrimiento, la necesidad de orientar los estudios de dialectología castellana de modo muy diferente del hasta hoy seguido. Si queremos caracterizar un habla regional, tendremos que separar cuidadosamente los desarrollos convergentes en todos los dialectos (que por ser los de más bulto se citan como peculiares de cada uno) de los verdaderamente divergentes.'

splintering of the Romance speech-community.[5] But on the other, they were vitally concerned, as men of letters and educators, in preserving the unity of the Spanish language. This essentially normative goal could not help colouring their approach to the data, since it naturally led them to concentrate on dialectal differences for their standard or sub-standard value, rather than because of the role they played within the regional sound systems.

The confluence of these factors, in combination, of course, with the particular interests, ability, and degree of thoroughness of the various investigators, accounts for the contents of most of the available descriptions of American Spanish. As representative examples one may mention Flórez's work on the Spanish of Colombia, Battini's description of San Luis, Navarro Tomás' book on Puerto Rico, and Boyd-Bowman's study of the speech of Guanajuato in Mexico. All these works are characterized by what, from a system-oriented point of view, can best be described as an atomistic approach. This approach appears to result from the factors mentioned above, which made themselves felt in various ways.

In the first place, the sections on 'phonetics' of these studies, and of the many others like them, are not analyses of phonological systems. They are descriptions of the different ways in which 'things are pronounced' in America. The things pronounced turn out to be the letters of ordinary Spanish orthography, a clear instance of the philological tradition affecting dialectology. One particularly neat example of the letter-bound orientation of this period is the ambiguous value of the terms *yeísmo* and *seseo* in Spanish linguistics. These words refer primarily to the pronunciation of *ll* (a palatal lateral in Castilian) as [j], and of *c* and *z* ([θ] in Castilian) as [s], respectively. Since in both cases these phonetic changes have resulted in mergers, *yeísmo* and *seseo* have acquired the secondary value of 'no distinction is made between *ll* and *y* (or *c*, *z* and *s*)'. It is precisely because some dialects retain a distinction that others have lost, that the phenomena of *yeísmo* and *seseo* are so important in Spanish dialectology. However, some dialects in which a distinction *is* made between *ll* and *y* still qualify technically as having *yeísmo* because in them *ll* is pronounced with the phonetic substance that corresponds to the outcome of the merger in some other dialects. This situation was labelled by Alonso 'distinguishing *yeísmo*'. Though the phrase at first blush appears self-contradictory, it makes sense within a tradition that dealt primarily with the pronunciation of letters.

It follows quite naturally from this view of phonology, that as long as the letters preserved their form-distinguishing power, no essential change had taken place: the Spanish system remained intact. This is the conclusion arrived at repeatedly by Flórez in describing Colombian dialects, and by Navarro Tomás in his work on Puerto Rican Spanish.

The concern with grammatical and lexical forms rather than speech sounds charac-

[5] This parallel is clearly drawn in Bertil Malmberg's 'L'espagnol dans le nouveau monde', *SL* 1.79-216 (1947) and 2.1-36 (1948), which is an excellent synthesis of the interests and findings of this period.

teristic of this period is also reflected in the presentation of the material: for each letter, the various divergences from Standard Spanish are listed. In most works no attempt is made at drawing a line between clearly phonological phenomena, statable as general rules, and individual shifts affecting particular lexical items. Cases of metathesis, isolated archaisms, and, say, perfectly regular hardening or weakening of certain consonants are presented as equally significant instances of the realization of this particular letter in this dialect.

Such an approach to the data had a fatal consequence. The type of enlightened philological study so brilliantly exemplified in Alonso's work could only be pursued further while there were fresh questions to investigate. Now the problems studied by Alonso were the obvious ones, the differences of which Spanish speakers had long been aware. For this tradition to persist, it would have required new problems to study. Such new questions could hardly be raised, however, by an approach lacking in theoretical interests and aimed at what in practice often turn out to be incoherent accumulations of facts.

That the descriptive works so often happen to be masses of raw data, is largely due to the phonetic orientation of Navarro Tomás' questionnaire, which chiefly stresses accuracy in description, rather than points of theoretical interest. The questions deal, in most cases, either with details of phonetic realization (e.g. Is *a* predominantly velar or palatal? How is *s* pronounced? Is the diphthong *ei* lowered so that it almost sounds like *ai*? etc.) or with the distribution of phonemes in certain lexical items (e.g., What words retain an 'aspirated h'?) The notion that is least stressed in this work is that of opposition between phonemes. Reference is occasionally made to the possibility of merger, or of new phonemes arising as a consequence of the loss of final consonants,[6] but the general principles of phonological opposition which explain such phenomena are not mentioned in the introduction, nor made the basis of the questions.

The works based on this questionnaire might still be expected to yield a wealth of detailed phonetic data on various dialects, waiting only to be adequately analyzed. Unfortunately, this expectation is not realized owing, in this case, to a fortuitous outside factor: economic reasons made it impossible to use phonetic type in most of these works (though some contain passages in phonetic transcription in an appendix). We are consequently left with a mass of largely unanalyzed field notes presented in ordinary Spanish orthography.

The consequences of adopting an atomistic, purely descriptive approach to the data, with the concomitant failure to seek for general principles that will explain more than one phenomenon, appear to be clearly illustrated by the treatment in the literature of hiatus and accent shift in such words as *país*, *caído*, etc. All the descriptions of Spanish dialects deal with these questions in more or less lengthy sections. An attempt to relate these phenomena has recently been made by Rabanales, who points out that diphthongization and loss of hiatus are essentially one and the same phenomenon.

[6] Cf. T. Navarro Tomás, 'Desdoblamiento de fonemas vocálicos', *Revista de Filología Hispánica* 1.165-67 (1939).

But he goes no further than a neat classification of the various circumstances under which the changes take place, and a comparison of these shifts to similar ones in Vulgar Latin. As a general explanation he invokes a tendency to simplify the distributional pattern of Spanish, but his claim remains unsubstantiated.

There is, however, another very common phenomenon in Spanish dialects which Rabanales leaves unmentioned. This is the apparent neutralization, in sub-standard speech, of the opposition between high and mid vowels in unstressed syllables. All descriptions of Spanish dialects carefully record the alternations of *i* and *e*, *u* and *o* when unstressed, and it seems clear from the data that what confronts us here is a three-vowel system occurring under weak stress. This will automatically explain the diphthongization in words such as *peor*, *toalla*, since these words are really /pIor/, /tUała/, in sub-standard as well as in rapid speech. Automatic diphthongization in these words, however, greatly reduces the number of instances of hiatus. It is not surprising, then, that items like *país*, *caído*, etc. should give up their hiatus too and follow the by now almost general rule whereby stress falls on the segment with greater sonority. Once the class of *país* is adapted to this rule (the adaptation being manifested by a shift in stress), the only aberrant items left are words like *amoníaco*, *océano*, etc., with both hiatus and stress on the less sonorous segment (which is, however, a member of a five vowel system). These too finally yield to the prevalent pattern and turn up as [amonjáko] and [osjáno].

It appears that these various shifts of pattern in substandard speech can easily be accounted for if one assumes a three-vowel system in unstressed syllables. It is, however, connections and assumptions of this type that regularly fail to be made in the works of the second period.

Reference should be made, finally, to the normative interest that was shared by most of these scholars. The attitude is well illustrated in Battini's work *El español de la Argentina*. The purpose of the book (which, incidentally, contains most valuable maps on the geographic distribution of a number of dialectal features, carefully based on many years of field work) is to describe and to evaluate socially the various differences in pronunciation, etc., found in Argentina, so that grade-school teachers, for whom the work is written, may know what features in their students' speech are totally unacceptable and should therefore be corrected.

The puristic orientation of many scholars also accounts for the relative importance attached to the phenomena described. If we are reasonably well informed, for instance, on the extent of the areas retaining the *ll*/*y* opposition, this is not because this particular distinction was viewed as somehow crucial to the phonological system, but simply because finding a new area that kept it provided fresh ammunition in the long-drawn battle for its preservation or re-acquisition.

As we attempt to summarize the achievements of the historical period, we find that the better works[7] give us a collection of useful field notes; in the case of the less

For instance, the work of Navarro Tomás, Battini and Robe.

thorough or conscientious workers, we have an atomistic hodge-podge of examples.[8] The original goal of geographic description turns up in practice as a mention of the *general* spread of each phenomenon, rather than as detailed information on its geographic or social diffusion within a particular country. As a consequence, the same information is repeated in work after work. As for the further aim of historical explanation, it generally materializes as a listing of archaisms, and in careful study of what particular lexical items retain an aspirated *h* from Latin *f*.

It is not surprising that the approach to Hispanic Phonology discussed so far should have failed to yield new isoglosses, since every feature found in some dialect was also discovered to occur elsewhere. The moral drawn from this situation — one no doubt highly comforting to prescriptivists bent on preserving the unity of the language — was that there really were no isoglosses, and that essentially the same system was current over the whole Spanish world. In their role of descriptivists, however, they felt that something had been missed, since the reality of dialects, as entities, could hardly be ignored and is, indeed, sensed by every Spanish speaker. Recourse was thus had to the old stand-by 'accent', which could safely be invoked to explain the differences between Chilean and Mexican, but was never described any further.

The identity of the dialects could probably have been explained much better than by invoking accent if the scholars of this period had concentrated on the various patterns of co-occurrence of dialectal features. It may well be that a truly peculiar and individual trait (such as the strong assibilation of *y* in the River Plate region) is the exception rather than the rule among American Spanish dialects. Still, what makes for the individuality of a dialect is the particular way and the degree in which it combines certain of the features found in most, but not necessarily all, Spanish-speaking areas. The historicists, it turns out, should have been on the look-out not for striking differences like *yeísmo* and *seseo*, but rather for the subtle balance in which dialectal features co-exist in each variety of Spanish.

Such a finding, however, was almost sure to elude them, since patterns of this type would be perceived by scholars interested in systems, rather than in particular items. It seems, then, that the philological tradition that inspired such very reasonable goals, also made their achievement practically impossible. One of the consequences of the failure of this period was that students of Spanish largely gave up historical questions and turned instead to the structural description of synchronic systems.

4. The third stage, which manifests itself primarily in a proliferation of structural descriptions of the Spanish of different countries, is characterized by two features: in the first place, American Spanish is no longer studied within the framework of general Spanish dialectal developments; second, Latin American scholars began to be influenced by foreign, i.e. non Hispanic, schools of linguistics.[9]

[8] In this category falls much of the work of Flórez, Lacayo, Toscano Mateus, and Boyd Bowman.

[9] On the other hand, some foreign scholars are still working in essentially the Navarro Tomás tradition in the sixties, e.g. D. Lincoln Canfield, *La pronunciación del español en América* (Bogotá, 1962). This book is to be recommended for its excellent bibliography.

For instance, Trager's description of Castilian is clearly the model followed by Chavarría-Aguilar and Silva-Fuenzalida in their studies of Costa Rican and Chilean Spanish. These papers, as also King's on Mexican, concentrate primarily on matters of allophonic and phonemic distribution, and on the problem raised by junctures, but generally give very little information on the actual phonetic realization of the phonemes.

Both Chavarría-Aguilar and Silva-Fuenzalida depart from the traditional analysis of Spanish by adding one phoneme to the inventory. Costa Rican in said to have an /ŋ/ because of intervocalic contrasts between [ŋ] and [n], e.g. *con eso* 'with that' [koŋeso] vs. *conejo* 'rabbit' [konexo]. This contrast has usually been handled (implicitly or explicitly) in terms of open juncture, even in cases where an [ŋ]/[n] contrast arises in word final position, owing to vowel elision.[10] Such a situation appears to exist in Nicaragua, according to Lacayo, where the difference between Standard Spanish *un imbécil* and *una imbécil* is rendered by [uŋimbésil] vs. [unimbésil]. Unfortunately, Chavarría-Aguilar does not discuss at all the advantages and disadvantages of his analysis, with an extra phoneme, over one involving juncture.

Silva-Fuenzalida's addition to the usual inventory is an /h/, found as the realization of pre-pausal *s*, as in *los amigos* 'the friends' [lohamiγoh]. His reluctance to ascribe this phone to /s/ is not based on considerations of substance, i.e. the difficulty one encounters in finding some phonetic feature common to [s] and [h] that is not shared by any other phoneme. Silva-Fuenzalida is more concerned with the contradictions such a solution would introduce in his definition of allophones in terms of distribution with respect to various kinds of juncture. His argument for /h/ consequently appears rather circular, since it is never made quite clear why it is preferable to postulate an extra phoneme, rather than to change the juncture system.

The Prague school of phonology does not appear to have affected Spanish American linguists, save in the River Plate region. The application of Prague phonology to the study of language change by Martinet has influenced Guitarte's very interesting paper on Buenos Aires *yeísmo*, to which reference will be made below. On the other hand, synchronic concepts like neutralization, and the emphasis on substance rather than distribution that one usually associates with Prague, are well represented in the controversy over the phonemic assignment of 'aspirated *s*.'[11]

The aspiration of post-vocalic pre-consonantal *s* is not an exclusive trait of River Plate Spanish; it is found in varying degrees in many other dialects, both in Latin America and in Spain, where it has even led (as in Puerto Rico) to a change in the

[10] Cf. Ruth L. Hyman, '[ŋ] as an Allophone denoting Open Juncture in Several Spanish-American-Dialects', *Hispania* 39.293-99 (1956). Juncture is postulated by Stockwell, Bowen and Silva-Fuenzalida to cover not only the [ŋ]/[n] problem, but also the contrasts between [w] and [gw], [s] and [h] [j] and [y̌] in some Caribbean and Central American dialects, in their paper on 'Spanish Juncture and Intonation', *Lg*. 32.641-65 (1956)

[11] It is interesting to compare the problem-oriented discussion of this question by Ricci and Rona with the simple listing of allophones which makes up Richard Beym's 'Porteño /s/ and [h] [hᵘ] [s] [x] [Ø] as Variants' in *Lingua* 12.199-204 (1963).

vowel system, by phonemicization of the more open, pre-*s* allophones, when the aspirated /s/ drops entirely.

The essential phonetic facts for the River Plate dialect were given by Malmberg, who describes the weakening of /s/ in implosive position as ranging all the way from [s] through [h] to zero, the actual degree of weakening depending on social factors, as well as on the phonetic context. A similar study of Uruguayan speech was made by Vásquez, who, like Malmberg, refrains from tackling the analytical problem of how this range of sounds is to be phonemicized. In allowing /s/ to cover such widely divergent allophones as [s], [h] and [x], he agrees no doubt with Coseriu's views, who allows for the possibility that certain phonemes in a system be defined not only in terms of positive (i.e. invariant) features, but also of negative ones, i.e. it will suffice that these phonemes be merely different from the ones to which they are related by their positive features.[12]

On the same question Ricci took a different position.[13] After discussing how the sound corresponding to the letter *s* in such a work as *mosca* 'fly'[14] would be phonemicized within different theoretical approaches, he concludes that it should be assigned to /x/ on grounds of phonetic similarity. Rona takes issue with this solution in his review of Ricci, and claims that he hears [h][15] and not [x] in *mosca.* He also claims that the aspiration perceived before /k/ is really a normal implosive allophone of /s/, since in syllable final position there is a neutralization of the grave/acute opposition, which keeps /s/ and /x/ apart when syllable initial. Rona relates this to two other phenomena of Spanish:

(1) the grave/acute neutralization of ŋ and n, also in syllable final position, i.e. the syllable initial acute [n] is matched in many dialects by a syllable final grave [ŋ], and

(2) the neutralization of the compact/diffuse opposition in syllable initial position, as evidenced by such variants as *fuego/juego* 'fire', *bueno/güeno* 'good', even *puchara/ cuchara* 'spoon'.

He therefore concludes that Ricci is mistaken in viewing the problem of [h] as one of simple phonemicization, since the aspiration is merely an instance of a very general rule of Spanish.

What Rona is in effect operating with here is the notion of neutralization without the archiphoneme. Only so (i.e. by ignoring the fact that the [h] before /k/ is really an archiphoneme) can he feel free to assign it to /s/, even when one of the features of /s/

[12] Cf. E. Coseriu, *Sincronía, diacronía e historia*, p. 103, fn. 8.

[13] Ricci's work is known to me only through Rona's review in *B.F.M.*

[14] Phonetically this sound ranges from [h] to [x], but is apparently perceived by native speakers as just as good an /s/ as the one in *sí* 'yes.' However, in other Spanish-speaking areas, for instance in Colombia, speakers who aspirate their *s*'s are said to *jotear*, i.e., to use the *jota*, name of the letter that corresponds to /x/.

[15] His reason for disagreeing with Ricci is not entirely clear, since by [h] Rona means a velar voiceless fricative.

is no longer distinctive. The theoretical implications of this position are unfortunately explored no further.

Upon closer analysis it appears, however, that Rona is not aware of the full consequences of adopting Jakobsonian features. If the oppositions of place of articulation are split up by means of the features compact/diffuse and grave/acute, then /s/ and /x/ are opposed, at best, as diffuse to compact, or as diffuse acute to compact (grave). In other words, gravity can never be the only feature distinguishing these two phonemes, since there is always an /f/ to keep apart, unless it is claimed that /s/ is really a palatal (i.e., a compact) fricative.[16] Similarly in the case of [n- -ŋ], the neutralization of the grave/acute opposition would presumably link /n/ and /m/, and by no means explain the appearance of [ŋ] in the position of neutralization. It would seem then that what we have in the syllable final aspiration, as well as in the syllable final nasal, are the fricative and the nasal archi-phonemes respectively.

The more recent developments in phonological theory associated with the 'generative transformational' approach to language have as yet had very little impact on Latin American phonology. The new theory has however inspired a description of (general) Spanish where most dialectal features are ignored, i.e. Saporta and Contreras' *A Phonological Grammar of Spanish.*

The work is essentially a restatement, in terms of phrase structure and transformational rules, of Spanish phonotactics. It sheds no new light on our knowledge of Spanish phonology, and the more or less original deviations from traditional analysis (such as phonemicizing the intervocalic flap in *pero* 'but' as /r/ plus a syllable boundary, a possibility already pointed out by Bello) are not the happiest features of the work.[17] This little grammar may be useful, however, as an original introduction to the techniques of generative grammar.

Some promising connections have been pointed out by Saporta on the relation between dialectal divergences and the ordered rules of a generative grammar. It seems likely, indeed, that though the same rules may occur in various dialects, they may yield very different outputs owing to the different order in which they have been incorporated into the grammar. Saporta's paper, which is chiefly programmatic, is based mainly on material from Chilean Spanish.

Whatever their shortcomings, the structural studies have had the great virtue of introducing into the analysis of Spanish dialects the concept of system which, as was pointed out above, had been conspicuously lacking. At the same time, however, most of the structural descriptions are somehow lacking in interest. One seems to detect a lack of fit between the theoretical framework in which most of these studies have been conceived and the real problems on which the study of American Spanish can be expected to shed light. After all, as was correctly perceived during the historical

[16] Such a claim is possible for Castilian Spanish, but hardly justified for Latin America. The structural implications of a dental articulation of /s/ are discussed below in section 5.c. (1).

[17] Not surprisingly, many of the facts and problems of phonemic distribution were already known, and discussed in essentially modern terms, in works of a normative bent. Cf. Alfredo F. Padrón, *Sobre -TL- como grupo medial. Estudio fonético ortológico* (La Habana, 1938).

period, the true challenge facing the linguist is to describe the development of the various dialects and to account for the diverging solutions given in them to the initial 'problem', i.e. the phonological system inherited from Spain at the end of the Middle Ages.

5. One would hope that more satisfying results could be obtained from Spanish-American phonology than it has yielded so far if the phonetic phenomena observed could somehow be related to an adequate theoretical framework; this framework could serve at once to explain the observations and to raise new questions for further investigation. In this section we shall attempt to sketch a number of problems where a system and theory oriented approach seems to promise interesting results.

a) Of the many problems that require investigation in Hispanic Phonology, one that immediately comes to mind is that of contact between Spanish and various African and American Indian languages. Most descriptions of Caribbean Spanish, for instance, mention the existence of forms with /ñ/ for a /y/ in Standard Spanish, e.g. *ñamar*, St. Spanish *llamar* (usually /yamar/) 'to call', and attribute them to a Negro substratum. A suggestion that is hardly acceptable when based on racial and anatomical considerations becomes worth entertaining when one considers that in Yoruba, for instance, [ñ] is the allophone of /y/ before nasal vowels.

The influence of Quechuan on the Spanish vowels of Ecuador and Perú has long been recognized, and it seems fairly clear that the confusion of /e/ and /i/, /u/ and /o/ in, say, Ecuadorian Spanish, can be ascribed to the three vowel system of Quechuan. However, a work written in the fifties still blames the 'careless' pronunciation of the Spanish vowels by bilinguals on the fact that Quechua is not a written language.

An opposition between /ł/ and /y/ in many Indian languages has occasionally been invoked as the reason for the retention of this contrast in the few Latin American Spanish dialects that do not have *yeismo*. It would be interesting to know whether the Spanish opposition is, as it were, merely parasitic on its presence in other languages, or whether it survives in cases where the Indian language is no longer spoken or has lost the opposition.

Quite clearly, far more information is necessary than is now available both on the indigenous languages and on the phonetic peculiarities of the co-territorial varieties of Spanish. Caudmont claims, for instance, that the contact between Spanish and Ingan in Colombia has resulted not only in the preservation of /ł/ in the Spanish of the region, but also in the phonologization of [w] as /w/ vs. /u/ in the Spanish of the bilinguals, owing to pressure of the Ingan system. It would be desirable to know whether this alleged phonemicization of [w] has had any overt effect on either its realization or its distribution, or whether the change is inferred merely from the study of the two systems in contact.

The influence of an Indian substratum has most often been invoked in connection with intonation features; it goes almost without saying in Spanish

American phonological studies that the very striking differences between the various dialects, with regard to prosodic features, are due to the intonation patterns inherited from the different Indian languages, but these claims remain unsupported by factual evidence. Since in many cases the Indian languages which may have contributed a 'tonada' are no longer spoken, it would appear highly desirable to make the most of those that still are, in order to substantiate the validity of these assertions.

This problem is not only of great interest to Spanish phonology and to the study of language contact but may bear indirectly on such theoretical questions as the place of intonation in the phonological component of a generative grammar.[18] One would like to find out whether a feature as intimately associated with syntactic structure as intonation is claimed to be can readily be adopted from a totally unrelated language in dialect after dialect. It would be even more interesting to know whether, in view of the differences in intonation, an analyst might not perhaps be forced to posit different grammatical structures for, say, Bolivian and Mexican Spanish.

b) The distributional patterns of Spanish are so well known that they have been mentioned only in connection with deviations from the standard, and in lieu of general statements one usually finds long lists of examples. It might be preferable to face the question from the following point of view: What differences are there, both in the stock of phonemes, and in the distributional pattern, as one moves from standard to sub-standard speech, and from careful to colloquial pronunciation? The influence of spelling is no doubt to blame for the marginal, but nonetheless very real, existence of phonemes like /v/, /θ/, and /ł/ in many American dialects, the distinction between /y/ and /ž/ in River Plate Spanish, and the pronunciation of the letter *x* as [ks]. The interpretation of these phenomena in terms of co-existing phonological systems would seem to be a promising possibility. A beginning in this direction is made in Honsa's interesting paper on geographical and social differentiation of the phonological system of Spanish in Argentina. Though he occasionally lapses into inaccuracies (e.g. with respect to the Standard Buenos Aires system) and makes some daring claims, for instance on the social motivations of the devoicing of *porteño* /ž/, one can only hope that more studies like his will be made on the Spanish of other Latin American countries.

c) Finally, there seem to be even greater opportunities in the study of the phonetic facts themselves, within a theoretical framework firmly grounded in the Saussurean notion of opposition: Since the function of phonemes is, after all, to remain safely aloof from each other, in order to preserve their distinguishing power, a change in the realization of one phoneme will very seldom fail to affect the remainder of the system.

The introduction of these principles into diachronic phonology has chiefly been the

18 The discussion of prosodic features in connection with syntax appears limited so far to brief studies by Kahane and Beym, and by Silva-Fuenzalida, on syntactic juncture in Mexican and Chilean Spanish respectively.

work of Martinet, and it seems that his concepts of functional load, phonological space, and structural pressures might be fruitfully applied to the study of Hispanic Phonology. An excellent example of such an application is Guitarte's analysis of the devoicing of *porteño yeísmo*. Starting with the questions discussed by Guitarte, a number of problems will be raised where a systemic approach proves illuminating.

(1) One of the areas where the usefulness of a systemic approach seems obvious is that of the phonetic realization of /s/. It is known that in practically all of Spanish America /s/ is a pre-dorsal convex denti-alveolar sibilant, while it is apico-alveolar and concave in Spain. In his paper on *yeísmo*, Guitarte has suggested that both the shift in articulation and the concomitant change in acoustic quality can be interpreted as reflecting a change in the internal organization of the phonological system: In those varieties of Spanish which retain the /θ/-/s/ distinction, the 'phonological space' available is most efficiently utilized if /s/ is closer to a palatal than to a dental sibilant, and indeed, /s/ is often regarded as the fricative counterpart of the palatal stop /č/.[19] On the other hand, the dialects characterized by *seseo*, i.e. the loss of the /θ/-/s/ opposition, almost uniformly exhibit a clearly dental articulation of /s/; in other words, /s/ can be said to have become in these dialects the fricative counterpart of /t/.[20]

There are remarkably few exceptions to the situation we have sketched. It would seem that the few cases where it does not hold (some regions in Perú and Colombia) can be explained either by contact with Indian languages, or on the basis of extra-linguistic factors (a strong puristic, Spain-oriented tradition). Guitarte's suggestion, which is extremely plausible, could be checked by detailed information on the nature of /s/ in all Latin American dialects, as well as in the co-territorial Indian languages.

(2) In connection with the aspiration of /s/, and the consequent phonemicization of vowel allophones in certain dialects, one is reminded of Vásquez' remark that /s/ is the most frequent phoneme in Spanish. A study on the relative frequency of syllables ending in vowel, in vowel plus /s/, vowel plus liquid and vowel plus nasal would probably be of interest in accounting for the effect the loss of post-vocalic /s/ might be expected to have, besides shedding light on the widespread neutralization of implosive /l/ and /r/.

(3) Malmberg has pointed out a very interesting contrast between [h] and [x] in the speech of Buenos Aires, as in *testo* 'I make a will' vs. *texto* 'text', the pronunciation in careful speech being [testo] vs. [teksto], but in colloquial form, [tehto] vs. [texto]. He does not say how consistently the difference is made, but this certainly seems a point worth investigating. One would expect the learned cluster /ks/ to reduce to /s/ in colloquial pronunciation, but if a difference is beginning to be made between the two, this could have two consequences: First, there would be no possibility of regarding [h] as representing the /s/-/x/ archiphoneme, and second, it might even lead to the establishment of /h/ as an independent phoneme.

[19] Cf. E. Alarcos Llorach, *Fonologia española*, p. 118 (Madrid, 1950).

[20] Of course the /s/ in these dialects is, from the phonetic point of view, the reflex of Old Spanish *ç* and *z*; the point has therefore been made that most of Spanish is characterized by historical *ceceo*.

(4) The possibility of an independent /h/ should also be investigated in connection with the historical problem of 'aspirated h' from Latin *f*. According to most of the available literature (as well as to the spelling, i.e. *j* is usually employed to indicate aspiration of *h*) words like *huir*, when pronounced with 'aspirated h', are to be phonemicized as having /x/). However, many descriptions fail to make this statement explicitly. Should there be a contrast between *jugar* and aspirated *huir*, the historical question would have important synchronic consequences.

(5) In this connection one might mention the fact that in a large area of Central America /x/ has shifted to /h/. It might be argued that the new [h] so conspicuous in Caribbean Spanish is merely a matter of realization, and does not entail any systemic change, so that words like *jugar* and *general* still begin with the fricative counterpart of /k/. It seems far more likely, however, that the shift of /s/ to /h/ is not a mere phonetic one, but a change affecting the entire phonemic system, where it leaves a hole in the pattern: The velar order no longer resembles the labial and dental ones in their symmetrical make-up of voiceless stop-voiceless fricative-voiced obstruent.

That this is so seems to be shown by a further change that has taken place in some of the dialects where /x/ has become /h/, and apparently nowhere else: there the hole left by /x/ has been filled from what seems at first blush a most unlikely source, i.e. /r̄/. As a matter of fact, the route is actually a very simple one. /r̄/ is opposed in Spanish only to /r/, the opposition being of a quite different nature from all others in the system. It can then legitimately be regarded as an unintegrated phoneme, whose precise realization in terms of place of articulation may be irrelevant, since it must differ from /r/ only in having greater length. And indeed, in all Spanish-speaking areas uvular trills and fricatives are found as realization of /r̄/, as idiosyncratic departures from the norm.

However, in some social dialects of some areas in the Caribbean, especially in Puerto Rico, /r̄/, i.e. the long partner of /r/, has regularly become a uvular trill, and sometimes even a uvular fricative. /r̄/, or rather /R/, thus approaches, phonetically, the hole in the pattern left by the shift of /x/. The elimination, by devoicing, of the remaining difference between /R/ and the hole, is almost to be expected. The change has indeed taken place both in Puerto Rico and in parts of Colombia, probably as a result of two pressures: one, the need to avoid merger with the fricative allophone of /g/, and second, the fact that the combination of features implied by the 'hole' [x] was, as it were, available to realize a phoneme of the language. The development of /r̄/ into /x/ can almost certainly be regarded as due to structural pressures, since it is found both in Puerto Rico and in Colombia, the only common feature between the two dialects apparently being the weakening of (original) /x/ to /h/.

When one reads Matluck's statement (1961) that the names of the letters *j* and *rr* are in Puerto Rico [la hota i la exe] one can hardly agree with Navarro Tomás' assertion that Puerto Rico has the same phonemic system as 'general Spanish'.

(6) Similar pressures appear to be at work in many Latin American dialects, refashioning the palatal order. Guitarte has suggested, very plausibly, that the devoicing

of Buenos Aires /ž/[21] into /š/ can be understood in terms of an optimum realization of the palatal stop/fricative opposition, especially in view of the absence of any /š/.

Guitarte also points out that the more or less pronounced *rehilamiento* (approximately stridency)[22] of /y/ may well be related to the phenomenon of *yeísmo*. The original phonemic system, still preserved in Castilian, has the following oppositions among the resonants:

n —— ñ
l —— ł
y

Now both /ł/ and /ñ/ appear to be weak points in the system. /ñ/ is in many dialects in process of merging with /ni/; /ł/ has gone further along the road to extinction, since almost everywhere in Latin America (as well as in large areas in Spain) it has fallen together, as it also did in French, with /y/, not with /li/.[23]

In systems with only a (threatened) /ñ/, the palatal glide /y/ is practically an unintegrated phoneme. It is consequently free to develop more fricative allophones, and sometimes it even becomes /ž/, the voiced counterpart of /č/.

It seems reasonable to assume, as Guitarte points out, that this development of /y/ into /ž/ will take place only where there is *yeísmo*, i.e. where /ł/ and /y/ have merged. Otherwise, /y/ can be expected to remain in the non-obstruent part of the system, where it will be supported as a palatal glide by its opposition to /ł/ and /ñ/. And indeed, this seems to be largely the case. The only confirmed exceptions to this rule appear to be the dialects of Santiago del Estero, in Argentina, and parts of the Sierra in Ecuador (in both of which there may be Quechuan influence at work), as well as Northwestern Salmantino, in Spain, where dialect mixture is probably involved.[24]

21 This is a very strong palatal fricative that corresponds etymologically to other dialects' /y/, and is represented by *y* or *ll* in the orthography.

22 On the rather elusive concept of *rehilamiento* in Spanish phonetics there is now an interesting study by Bès, who points out that *rehilamiento* requires a tense articulation at the point of stricture, plus high pressure of the breath stream, thus allowing for local vibration, as in [v], [ẓ], [z], [ž], and [ẓ̌].

23 The difference in the paths taken by /ł/ and /ñ/ and the coincidence between the Spanish and French developments suggests that an explanation in terms of functional load may be the most promising, besides showing that the palatal order was not very stable to begin with.

24 In the American dialects, /ł/ has shifted to /ž/, while /y/ remains as a palatal glide. In Spain, on the other hand, Northwestern Salmantino preserves /ł/, but pronounces /ž/ for words with etymological /y/. The preservation of the opposition with different phonetic realizations points to very different causes in Spain and in America; moreover, Northwestern Salmantino appears to have undergone a period of *yeísmo* (in the sense of merger) realized as /ł/. Cf. Antonio Llorente Maldonado de Guevara, 'Importancia para la historia del español de la aspiración y otros rasgos fonéticos del salmantino noroccidental', *RFE* 42.151-65 (1958-59) Another exception to this rule appears to exist in the Province of Corrientes (Argentina), on which there is contradictory information. Gandolfo points out that Correntino has a [ǰ] in words spelled with *y*, i.e. where other Spanish dialects have a palatal glide /y/. This overstridency of /y/ is quite unexpected in a dialect that retains the opposition with /ł/, and may be due to Guaranitic substratum, as suggested by Battini, who, however, describes the sound as a *voiceless* palatal affricate which she represents as [ŷ]. Cf. *El español de la Argentina*, p. 72. Finally, Honsa sets up the Correntino phonemic system with a [j], not a [ǰ]. More information on this point, as well as on the phonetics of Guarani, would be desirable.

Unfortunately, the descriptions of these crucial American dialects, as well as of the varieties of Quechuan spoken there, are far from adequate.

Though one may then fairly safely assume that *rehilamiento* of /y/ implies *yeísmo*, the converse does not hold. There are vast areas in Latin America where there is *yeísmo*, but where /y/ is still pronounced as a pure palatal glide,[25] e.g. in San Luis, Argentina. This leaves the system with an unintegrated /č/, lacking /š/ and /ž/ counterparts to match the organization /p-f-b/ or /t-s-d/.

However, in many dialects /č/ seems to be adopting as fricative partner another 'unintegrated' phoneme, i.e. /r̄/. The assibilation of /r̄/ is a well-known phenomenon in Latin American dialectology, where it has usually been discussed in connection with the assibilation of /tr/ (especially prominent in Chilean and Costa Rican). But it would seem that the two developments may well be structurally independent, since in San Luis (Argentina), /r̄/ has developed into a retroflex [ẓ̌], while /tr/, formerly also assibilated, as in Chilean Spanish, now has the same pronunciation as in, say, Buenos Aires, where /r̄/ is a strong apical trill.

We then expect /r̄/ to assibilate, i.e. to develop into /ž/, either in the regions where there is no *yeísmo* (the areas which retain an /ł/-/y/ opposition)[26] or in those where /y/ is still a palatal glide. This hypothesis appears to be confirmed by the available information, with the exception of a few small areas, the largest being the Province of Entre Ríos, in Argentina, where there is both a /ž/ (from old /y/) and a retroflex /ẓ̌/ from /r̄/.[27] Since Entre Ríos lies between Corrientes, with a strongly assibilated *rr*, and the River Plate region, with strong *rehilamiento* of *y*, dialect mixture seems a plausible explanation.

(7) The assibilation of /tr/ is usually discussed from a purely phonetic point of view, and in total independence of the rest of the system. One would, however, expect that any shift of /tr/ in the direction of [č] would have some effect on /č/ itself. And indeed the literature points out that in many areas, /č/ appears to be losing its fricative element, thus developing into a palatal stop.[28] One would expect this shift to be connected with the assibilation of /tr/.

The shift of /tr/ into an affricate may have not only systemic consequences but even be due, in part, to systemic pressures, since such a shift would have the effect of regularizing the distributional pattern. /tr/ is, in fact, a weak point in the system of Spanish clusters, since on the one hand it lacks a partner in /tl/, while on the other its voiced counterpart /dr/ seems to be falling together with /gr/ in many areas.[29]

[25] The pronunciation of /y/ as a palatal glide in areas of *yeísmo* is probably linked to the vitality of the /ñ/-/ni/ opposition.

[26] This is strikingly confirmed by the tests carried out by Gandolfo in Corrientes: her *porteño* /ž/, corresponding etymologically to *ll* and *y*, was understood (and written) by Correntino informants as *rr*.

[27] Cf. Battini, 'Extensión de la *rr* múltiple'.

[28] For instance in Colombia (cf. Flórez, Thesaurus 16.17-125 (1961)), in Puerto Rico and the Dominican Republic (cf. Navarro Tomás 1956), and in Bolivia (cf. D. Lincoln Canfield, *op. cit.* p. 92). In Cuba, on the other hand, /č/ appears to be moving to [š]. (Cf. Henríquez Ureña, *BDH* V, p. 139).

[29] For instance, in Colombia (cf. Flórez, Thesaurus 5.124-62 (1949)) and in Panama (cf. Stanley L. Robe, *The Spanish of Rural Panama*, p. 43.).

Unfortunately, the available studies on Latin American Spanish, both of the historical and the structuralist persuasion, uniformly fail to establish these connections. One would, for instance, like to know whether the merger of /dr/ and /gr/ is more than a chance occurrence in the dialects where /tr/ is highly assibilated. It would also be desirable to know what the phonetic realization of /č/ is in, say, Costa Rica, where Gagini already pointed out that *tronco* sounded like *chonco*. But most of these questions have been left unanswered, because unasked, by analysts with access to the data.

One can only hope that future work in Hispanic Phonology will profit from the insights of theory in the framing of the questions it sets itself, as well as using the rich material of American Spanish to teach us more about the nature of language.

BIBLIOGRAPHY

Biblioteca de Dialectología Hispanoamericana (Buenos Aires, 1930-49).

Néstor Almendros, 'Estudio fonético del español en Cuba', *Boletín de la Academia Cubana de la Lengua* 7.138-76 (1958).

Amado Alonso, *Estudios lingüísticos. Temas españoles* and *Temas hispanoamericanos* (Madrid, 1961) (abbreviated *Te* and *Th* respectively).

——, 'La identidad del fonema', *Revista de Filología Hispánica* 6.280-83 (1944); reprinted in *Estudios lingüísticos*; *Te* 253-58.

——, 'Una ley fonológica del español', *HR* 13.91-101 (1945); reprinted in *Estudios lingüísticos*; *Te* 237-49.

——, 'Examen de las noticias de Nebrija sobre antigua pronunciación española', *NRFH* 3.1-82 (1949).

——, 'Formación del timbre ciceante en la "ç", "z" española', *NRFH* 5.121-72 and 263-312 (1951).

——, 'Historia del ceceo y del seseo españoles', *Thesaurus* 7.111-200 (1951).

——, 'La pronunciación de "rr" y de "tr" en España y América', *Estudios lingüísticos*; *Th* 123-58.

——, 'Orígenes del seseo americano', *Estudios lingüísticos*; *Th* 84-122.

——, 'La "ll" y sus alteraciones en España y América', *Estudios lingüísticos*; *Th* 159-212.

——, '"-r" y "-l" en España y América', *Estudios lingüísticos*; *Th* 213-60.

Berta E. Vidal de Battini, *El habla rural de San Luis* Parte I. Fonética, morfología, sintaxis. *BDH* VII (1949).

——, 'Extensión de la *rr* múltiple en la Argentina', *Filología* 3.181-85 (1951).

——, *El español de la Argentina* (Buenos Aires, 1954).

Gabriel G. Bès, 'Examen del concepto de rehilamiento', *Thesaurus* 19.18-42 (1964).

Richard Beym, 'Porteño /s/ and [h] [hˇ] [s] [x] [Ø] as Variants', *Lingua* 12.199-204 (1963).

J. Donald Bowen, see Ismael Silva-Fuenzalida.

Peter Boyd-Bowman, 'La pérdida de vocales átonas en la altiplanicie mexicana', *NRFH* 6.138-40 (1952).

——, *El habla de Guanajuato* (México, 1960).

María Josefa Canellada y Alonso Zamora Vicente, 'Vocales caducas en el español mexicano', *NRFH* 14.221-41 (1960).

D. Lincoln Canfield, *La pronunciación del español en America* (Bogotá, 1962).

Jean Caudmont, 'La influencia del bilingüismo como factor de transformación de un sistema fonológico', *RCA* 2.207-18 (1954).

Heles Contreras, *see* Sol Saporta.

Eugenio Coseriu (with Washington Vásquez), 'Para la unificación de las ciencias fónicas. (Esquema provisional)', *Revista de la Facultad de Humanidades y Ciencias* 10.183-91 (Montevideo, 1953).

——, *Sincronía, diacronía e historia* (Montevideo, 1958).

——, 'Sistema, norma y habla'', and 'Forma y sustancia en los sonidos del lenguaje', *Teoría del lenguaje y lingüística general* (Madrid, 1962).

O. L. Chavarría-Aguilar, 'The Phonemes of Costa Rican Spanish', *Lg.* 27.248-53 (1951).

Mercedes V. Alvarez Puebla de Chaves, 'Algunas consideraciones relativas al timbre en fonética', *Humanidades* 31.593-626 (1948).

Luis Flórez, 'Cuestiones del español hablado en Montería y Sincelejo', *Thesaurus* 5.124-62 (1949).

——, 'El habla del Chocó', *Thesaurus* 6.110-16 (1950).

——, *La pronunciación del español en Bogotá* (Bogotá, 1951).

——, *Habla y cultura popular en Antioquia* (Bogotá, 1957).

——, 'Pronunciacipon del español en Bolívar (Colombia)', *Thesaurus* 15.174-79 (1960).

——, 'Del habla popular en Santander (Colombia)', *Revista Colombiana de Folclor* 2.9-14 (1960).

——, 'Observaciones generales sobre la pronunciación del español an el Departamento de Bolívar (Colombia)', *ibid.* 155-60.

——, 'El Atlas Lingüístico-Etnográfico de Colombia, (ALEC), Nota informativa', *Thesaurus* 16.77-125 (1961).

Adriana Gandolfo, 'Spanish *ll*, *y* and *rr* in Buenos Aires and Corrientes', *Proceedings of the Ninth International Congress of Linguists* 212-15 (The Hague, 1964).

Guillermo L. Guitarte, 'El ensordecimiento del žeísmo porteño. Fonética y fonología', *RFE* 39.261-83 (1955).

——, 'Cuervo, Henríquez Ureña y la polémica sobre el andalucismo de América', *Thesaurus* 14.20-81 (1959).

Pedro Henríquez Ureña, *El español en Santo Domingo BDH V* (1940).

Vladimir Honsa, 'The Phonemic System of Argentinian Spanish', *Hispania* 48.275-83 (1965).

Ruth L. Hyman, '[ŋ] as an Allophone denoting Open Juncture in Several Spanish-American Dialects', *Hispania* 39.293-99 (1956).

Henry R. Kahane and Richard Beym, 'Syntactical Juncture in Colloquial Mexican Spanish', *Lg.* 24.387-96 (1948).

Harold V. King, 'Outline of Mexican Spanish Phonology', *SIL* 10.51-62 (1952).

Heberto Lacayo, 'Apuntes sobre la pronunciación del español de Nicaragua', *Hispania* 37.267-68 (1954)..

——, *Cómo pronuncian el español en Nicaragua* (México, 1962).

Bertil Malmberg, 'L'espagnol dans le nouveau monde', *SL* 1.79-116 (1947) and 2.1-36 (1948).

——, *Etudes sur la phonétique de l'espagnol parlé en Argentine*, (= Lunds Universitets Årsskrift 45) (Lund, 1950).

——, 'Note sur la structure syllabique de l'espagnol mexicain', *Z Phon* 17.251-55 (1964).

Humberto Mateus Toscano, *El español en el Ecuador*. Anejo 61, *RFE* (Madrid, 1953).

Joseph Matluck, *La pronunciación en el español del Valle de México* (México, 1951).

——, 'La pronunciación del español en el valle de México', *NRFH* 6.109-20 (1952).

——, 'Fonemas finales en el consonantismo puertorriqueño', *NRFH* 15.332-42 (1961).

Tomás Navarro Tomás, 'Desdoblamiento de fonemas vocálicos', *Revista de Filología Hispánica* 1.165-67 (1939).

——, *Cuestionario lingüístico hispanoamericano* (Buenos Aires, 1943).

——, *El español en Puerto Rico* (Universidad de Puerto Rico) (Río Piedras, 1948).

——, 'Apuntes sobre el español dominicano', *Revista Iberoamericana* 21.417-29 (1936).

Alfredo F. Padrón, *Sobre -TL- como grupo medial. Estudio fonético ortológico* (La Habana, 1938).

Luis Prieto, 'Remarques sur la nature des oppositions distinctives basées sur l'accentuation monotonique libre', *Revista de la Factultad de Filosofía y Humanides* (Universidad de Córdoba), 4.407-11 (1952).

——, 'Traits oppositionels et traits contrastifs'', *Word* 10.43-59 (1954).

Ambrosio Rabanales, 'Diptongación y monoptongación en el español vulgar de Chile', *RJb* 11.319-27 (1960).

——, 'Hiato y antihiato en el español vulgar de Chile', *BFUCh* 12.197-223 (1960).

Julio Ricci, *Un Problema de interpretatión fonológica en el español del Uruguay* (Montevideo, 1963).

Stanley L. Robe, *The Spanish of Rural Panama. Major dialectal features* (University of California Press, 1960).

José Pedro Rona, Review of Ricci, *BFM* 9.199-204 (1962).

Ismael Silva-Fuenzalida, 'Syntactical Juncture in Colloquial Chilean Spanish', *Lg.* 27.34-7 (1951).

——, 'Estudio fonológico del español de Chile', *BFUCh* 7.153-76 (1952-53).

Ismael Silva-Fuenzalida, Robert P. Stockwell and J. Donald Bowen, 'Spanish Juncture and Intonation', *Lg.* 32.641-65 (1956).

Sol Saporta, 'Ordered rules, dialect differences, and historical processes', *Lg.* 41.218-24 (1965).

Sol Saporta and Heles Contreras, *A Phonological Grammar of Spanish* (Seattle, University of Washington Press, 1962).

Robert Stockwell, *see* Ismael Silva-Fuenzalida.

George L. Trager, 'The Phonemes of Castilian Spanish', *Travaux du Cercle Linguistique de Prague* VIII. 217-22.

Washington Vásquez, 'El fonema /s/ en el español del Uruguay', *Revista de la Facultad de Humanidades y Ciencias* 10.87-94 (Montevideo, 1953).

——, *see* also E. Coseriu.

Alonso Zamora Vicente, 'Rehilamiento porteño', *Filología* 1.5-22 (1949).

——, *see* also María Josefa Canellada.

LEXICOGRAPHY

FERNANDO ANTONIO MARTÍNEZ

1.1. Lexicography, in Spanish America more than anywhere else, has been intimately connected with the historical evolution of the language. In general, it can be said that the problems of language change have had a direct influence on the development of lexicography.[1]

1.2. The Spaniards arrived on the American Continent and encountered a diversity of languages, which was to leave an imprint on their own. From this fact, simple in itself, important consequences follow: (1) the establishment and gradual expansion of Spanish throughout the different regions of the New World; (2) the contribution of the indigenous languages to the language of the first immigrants and their descendents; (3) the diverse nature of such contributions which, in a way, reflected the existing differences among indigenous languages; (4) the geographic area of each of these languages, which had formerly been fairly unified, but which was already changing upon the arrival of the Spaniards, and which created the beginning of a distribution later altered and diversified until it came to be the present configuration of Spanish-American nations.

1.3. To these facts, another should be added, of no less importance for lexicography and, in general, for the linguistic development of Spanish America. The language of the conquerors, fifteenth century Spanish,[2] was not uniform; on the other hand, it

[1] What follows is no more than a simple outline of Spanish-American lexicography. Certainly, it is not a history or even an account of all the main works in the field, not even those of recent works. It is more important, in our opinion, to underline the main tendencies, general problems, and crucial developments in the field. These are problems which originate the particular situation of Spanish in America and which arise within lexicography itself. What is important is the existence of a Spanish-American lexicography relatively independent from the Spanish one, with problems that should examined here before they can be integrated into Spanish lexicography at large, or into the more general problem of the situation of Spanish in America. We make no attempt to deal with specific problems or with lexicographic techniques. Only in order to illustrate some of these points (without losing sight of the most recent developments in methods and orientations in European tradition), we refer to the volume of *IJAL*, Part IV, 28:2 *Problems in Lexicography* edited by Fred W. Householder and Sol Saporta (Bloomington, 1962). As for bibliography, both with regard to Spanish in general and Spanish-America in particular, we refer to the undoubtedly most complete *Bibliografía de la lingüística española* by Homero Serís, Publicaciones del Instituto Cary y Cuervo 19 (Bogotá, 1964), which should be kept in mind for all the works mentioned here, as well as those which have remained unmentioned.

[2] Rufino José Cuervo, *El español en Costa Rica* in *Obras*, ed. Instituto Caro y Cuervo 2.627 (1954); Rodolfo Lenz, *El español en Chile*, *BDH* 6.217; M. L. Wagner, *Lingua e dialetti dell' America Spagnola*,

had a definite popular character.[3] These two features, of undeniable importance in the creation of a Spanish-American regional vocabulary, are clearly apparent in the basis of the formation of the different lexicons and especially in the criteria for evaluation of so-called Americanisms.[4]

1.4. Coming now to the lexicon proper, the following observations can be made: immediately after the conquest, America provided the bases for the study of the Spanish vocabulary which had just been propagated and consolidated, and for a preliminary differentiation of the various lexicographic repertoires. These bases are of two kinds: (1) the terms which slipped into, or were intentionally used in the writings of the first chroniclers; (2) the various dictionaries which were compiled, particularly by the clergy, to meet the pressing need for communication with the native population. It is true, though, as Cuervo[5] indicated, that once these tongues disappeared, the data furnished by the dictionaries could not be accurately checked or verified; but the research scholar must take them into account, collect them, and try to solve the problems they present, particularly in determining the degree of credibility that should be granted to the chroniclers.

1.5. Be that as it may, there is a contrast between Spain and America in what concerns the making of the first dictionaries. Those known by the names of Palencia and Nebrija date from the end of the fifteenth century, the moment at which the process of the general unification of the language was reaching full maturity, while its expansion was being promoted and accelerated by the prospects offered by a New World. Both Palencia and Nebrija stand on a border-like situation: they close one period and open another. For example, in Nebrija's lexicon of 1493 is found the word *canoa*, the first-born of American terms, as Cuervo calls it. In America, on the other hand, the writing of dictionaries begins at the very moment when the establishment of the language in remote, vast, and diverse lands, has barely begun; here Spanish has no past. Numerous dictionaries are made to meet the needs of communication; they stand at the doorstep of the conquest and colonization and are, consequently, the most important documents in the process of extinction of a whole group of languages and the triumph of a new one.

1.6. This difference is significant in at least one way: in Spanish America study of the lexical inventory precedes the consideration of language from a grammatical point of view, a result which is also due in part to the absence of a tradition of classical languages. Since the languages is expanding throughout new territories, the main

p. 11 (Firenze, 1949); see also the important work by Angel Rosenblat, 'Base del español de América', *BFUCh* 16.171 (1964).

[3] Rufino José Cuervo, *El castellano en América* 2. 535-536.

[4] By Americanisms is generally understood: (1) terms of native origin in a particular country or region coming from an indigenous language, (2) all the modifications undergone by Spanish in each of the different countries of Spanish-America. Neither of these definitions necessarily implies a Panamerican frame of reference, which, however, is generally understood when talking about Americanisms.

[5] Rufino José Cuervo, *Apuntaciones críticas sobre el lenguaje bogotano*, no. 979, p. 657 (1914).

concern is, first, vocabulary, then grammar; and this is true not only during the period of conquest and colonization but also later. As in the Spain of Nebrija there are a few cases of more or less simultaneous elaboration of grammars (*artes*) and dictionaries here. From 1560 we have the *Lexicon o vocabulario de la lengua general del Perú* of Fr. Domingo de Santo Tomás, who said that 'It is not enough to have the grammar of a language, even if it is thoroughly done, if one does not have a large number of words which is what the grammar shows how to order.'[6]

The *Arte de la lengua mexicana* and the *Vocabulario en lengua castellana y mexicana* of Alonso de Molina, date from 1571. Alonso de Molina says, however, that the vocabulary was printed a few years ago.[7] Grammar and vocabulary go together in the *Gramática y vocabulario mexicanos* of Antonio del Rincón. It is to be noticed that in these works the grammatical part deals primarily with the grammar of the aboriginal language and secondly, with that of Spanish, which is used as a language of reference to illustrate or explain the new language, whether it was known or was to be known. For our purposes, we may disregard the lexicons of the native languages, and take instead as the starting point of Spanish American systematic lexicography the date 1786, when Alcedo gathers the first group of America provincialisms. One has to travel a long way — to 1846 — to arrive at Andrés Bello's *Gramática*, written with the purpose of teaching Spanish-American speakers, and a work in which the Spanish of these regions is something to be acknowledged on its own grounds. Between these two dates, though, there is an absolute predominance of lexicon over grammar. These dictionaries reflect an interest in regional vocabularies (regional with regard to Spain); grammar is ignored almost completely. The mother tongue, peninsular Spanish, is kept on a secondary level.

1.7. Our foregoing remarks confronts us with a new important fact in the field of Spanish-American lexicography. With Bello's *Gramática* comes a desire to consider the language of Spanish America as an expression of national unity, a unity which has a linguistic counterpart. This expression is at the same time American and Spanish, that is to say, Spanish-American. Bello writes for his Spanish-American brothers, and after a few paragraphs the language appears to him as a group of words, and dictions, i.e. vocabulary. Ten years before the *Gramática*, in the *Observaciones* of 1836, lexicon and grmmar appear together with the purpose of fostering national, or rather Spanish-American, unity. Bello did not recommend purism; but a consequence of his *Gramática* and the acceptance and diffusion with which it met and still meets in South American countries has been that of stressing the criterion of correctness, much more effective with regard to vocabulary than with regard to grammar. This fact (non-existent in Peninsular Spanish) gives rise, from a practical point of view, to the composition of American regional vocabularies. The language of the mother country, which before had only a secondary place, comes, as an unexpected but logical conse-

[6] Fray Domingo de Santo Tomás, *Lexicon o vocabulario de la lengua general del Perú*, p. 6 (Lima, 1951).

[7] Alonso de Molina, Ed. facs., *Epist. nuncup* (Madrid, 1944).

quence, to assume first place, and becomes, both in grammar and lexicon, the norm, the archetype, the correct one, the pure one. Regional dictionaries will reflect this tendency.

1.8. As is widely recognized, only since Rufino J. Cuervo has American Spanish been the subject of scientifically valid consideration. But rather more important was the type of linguistic corpus subjected to this approach. In his *Apuntaciones críticas sobre el lenguaje bogotano* the language studied was that of a region, of a city; it anticipated the study of that of the other cities or capitals, which in turn represented different nationalities or different linguistic conditions. Thus, Cuervo provides Spanish-American dialectology with serious foundations for the first time. In some cases the criteria for solving linguistic problems have repercussions on the lexicography of several countries.

1.9. When Rodolfo Lenz arrived in Chile in 1890, the situation was as follows: modern linguistic methods were being used mainly in phonetics, in the rigorous description of a given regional speech. Following Cuervo's inspiration, these methods tried to describe, objectively and systematically, the linguistic physiognomy of a country, which in the case of Chile brought about the problem of the substratum.

Both in the case of Cuervo and that of Lenz, lexical problems are taken up for the first time in a scientific way and begin to be considered and to be studied as a separate set of problems following rigorous techniques. Prescriptivism yields to scientific norms.

1.10. The work of these two scholars created two well-defined fields in Spanish-American linguistics: that of the language system (the description and analysis of its grammatical structure), and that of the lexicon (the independent study of the vocabularies of different areas, their historical connections, origins, etc.), including the folkloristic usage, which Lenz considered.

From then on the dictionary could profit from the results obtained in the field of grammar and thus become a discipline in itself, without precluding the possibility of paying special attention to specific language sectors, for example, the vocabulary of individual authors, works, periods.

1.11. But in the century of Cuervo and Lenz, Spanish-American education opens itself widely and intensively to European trends. The literary contacts, together with commercial exchanges, immigration, and other factors, bring the influence of French culture, which leaves a permanent imprint on the language. This influence does not come exclusively and directly from France; it comes, in many cases, through Peninsular Spanish, which since 1800 had thus renovated its lexicon. In Spanish America, however, this influence has a particular character: it brings about an extensive and profound reaction, i.e., antigallicism. A substantial puristic trend sets in which later results in an attempt on the part of Spanish-American lexicography to combat gallicisms in the vocabulary. Times change and with them cultural forms and their center of gravity, which is transferred from one place to another. The cultural development, particularly technological, carried out by the United States (whose sphere of influence is stronger every day in Spanish-American countries), presents today, as the French influence did before, the problem of a constant inflow of anglicisms in American Spanish. Dictionaries are beginning to take notice of this and to gather and explore this new field.

1.12. In other words, provincial and regional Spanish-American vocabularies, as well as other lexicographic endeavours, reflect this new trend in a twofold way: — with regard to the items included and the treatment they are accorded.

2.1. The discovery and conquest of the territories which today make up all the Spanish-American countries were carried out in little more than fifty years. It is not without interest to notice that lexicography begins precisely in those years of discovery and conquest. The *Relaciones* of Columbus already contain words such as *canoa, cacique, maiz* which become permanently incorporated, as native American terms, into the general Hispanic vocabulary. With the publication in Alcalá (1516) of the first three *Décadas* of Pedro Mártir Anglería, there appears what can be considered the first glossary of American terms.[8]

From what has been said above (1.4), it can be seen that from the very beginning there are two areas in the study of vocabulary: the collection of native terms which are gradually incorporated into Spanish, and the study of those other native terms which survive in the first lexicons, as more or less distorted relics of the basic vocabulary of preconquest languages.[9] The cultivator of one or the other field did in time

[8] Cuervo, *Apuntaciones*, no. 980, p. 657.; Marcos A. Morínigo, *La penetración de los indigenismos americanos en el español, OFINES, PFLE* 218 (Madrid, 1964).

[9] In fact, Spanish American lexicography was to distinguish between those words, which from the very beginning, by being profoundly assimilated, become widespread or tend to be so, and those other words which, being less susceptible to the process of assimilation, remain circumscribed in their use to certain regions. From the start, the former assert their presence in the language at large, while the latter still today keep a very restricted character. It is precisely these words which offer in their linguistic affiliations a close relationship with the vocabularies of certain other languages, and can, therefore, be considered as true relics. Words such as *ají, guayaba, guanábana, iguana, yuca, mamei*, etc. or those like *canoa, caimán, papa*, etc., represent objects, products, or animals belonging to the aboriginal life and culture, and which the Spaniards adopted in their original forms (sometimes, however, as in the case of the last three mentioned, Spanish terms were used which were later abandoned: cfr. Cuervo, *Apuntaciones*, 979). These words entered into Spanish once and for all, their use being generalized for the reasons indicated, and also because this use originated in the first — and therefore the most influential — centers of expansion of colonial establishments. But this is not the case with words like *chajuán, chisa, chusque, guapucha, guascas, quincha*, etc., which although they belong to the same type of objects, remain till today rooted in certain areas, possibly as a result of their aboriginal languages having become localized. As Cuervo demonstrated (*Apuntaciones*, 986), they are words of *Chibcha* origin. They can be considered as relics or remnants known to us because they are documented in some lexicons (in this particular case the *Vocabulario de la lengua mosca o chibcha*). In the case of words of widespread general use, what interests us, in the first place, is their assimilation from the very beginning by the standard language, although later on it has at times been possible to determine their specific origin.

Furthermore, the difference between the two types of words is occasionally reflected both in the repertories of Spanish language or in more specialized works. Thus, of those quoted, none is included in the otherwise most complete *Semántica* by Kany or in the *Buenas y malas palabras* of Rosenblat; *guayaba*, on the other hand, is included and studied in the *DCEC* of Corominas; *guayuco*, however, is

result in the compilation of regional lexicons, and in the creation and composition of dictionaries of pre-Colombian languages.

2.2. It is only logical that lexicographic work would have started here, in spite of royal ordinances (like that of 1550 in the *Leyes de Indias*) restricting the use of native languages in favor of the growing expansion and use of Spanish.[10] The teaching of such languages, in Mexico and in Lima, encourage the writing of grammars (*Artes*) and catechisms and consequently also of glossaries (this we have to assume even where no written records have been preserved). At any rate, this period, never surpassed in the extension and depth of its work, extends to the end of the eighteenth century. Its main characteristic consists in collecting and illustrating the vocabulary of primitive tongues, and also in reflecting some principles of geographic distribution which at times may reflect an ethnic background: Caribbean, Tainan, Quechua, or Chibchan.

2.3. It is fortunate that for each of the first three centers of discovery, conquest, and colonization, that is, the Antilles and Central America, Mexico, and Peru and other South American countries, there are one or more dictionaries: the *Diccionario caribe-francès* of Breton (1665), the *Vocabulario en lengua mexicana* of Alonso de Molina (1571), and the *Lexicon o Vocabulario de la lengua general del Perú* of Fray Domingo de Santo Tomás (1586). Of the three centers mentioned, the first, which includes the area of Arawak and Carib, is less important than the other two. The most important is the third where there are some truly notable works, such as the anonymous *Arte y vocabulario de la lengua general del Perú* (1586),[11] the *Vocabulario de Diego González Holguín* (1608). Besides, there are those concerning the speech of a particular region or group, such as the *Vocabulario guaraní* of Fr. Ruiz Montoya (1640), the *Vocabulario aimará* of Fr. Bertonio (1612) or the *Arte y vocabulario* of Fr. Tahuste for Cumanagoto (1680); and finally, the *Arte y gramática general* of Valdivia, also with vocabulary, for Chile (1606).

2.4. From the standpoint of the orientation of these dictionaries, this period of Spanish-American lexicography ends towards the last years of the eighteenth century, when it gives rise to what can be called the linguistics of indigenous languages. The appearance of this field of study as an independent discipline is intimately connected with that first period. It should not be forgotten, though, that the preparation of vocabularies and dictionaries for almost three centuries had the purpose of providing a lexical inventory of the unknown languages, illustrating them with references to the known language. These repertories are basically connected with the European tradition, and specifically, with the Spanish tradition. Thus, for example, Fray

---

not. The difference becomes even more obvious when we consider words like *ambil* or *ambir*, which are strictly local and whose affiliation has not yet been determined. Something similar could be said of *carate*, with its variant *carare* according to Rosenblat.

10 Antonio Tovar, *Catálogo de las lenguas de América del Sur*, p. 186 (Buenos Aires, 1961). See, also, Angel Rosenblat, *La Hispanización de América, OFINES*, 2-189-216.

11 Antonio Tovar, *Catálogo*, pp. 209-10.

Domingo de Santo Tomás explains that: this vocabulary follows the same order as Nebrija's with the alphabet divided in two sections.[12]

2.5. Mayans, in his *Orígenes*, pointed out that from the terms introduced into Spanish through commerce with the Indies a useful and interesting dictionary could be made. He quoted some himself.[13] However, it is with Alcedo that Spanish-American lexicography of provincial terms begins, and with it a new stage in the development of lexicography. Two basic lexicographic aspects are already present in his *Vocabulario* (1789): (1) words originated in Spain and modified through contact with indigenous languages (2) words from these languages introduced into Spanish and modified by the Spanish-American speaker.[14] To this we should add the broad

[12] Fray Domingo of Santo Tomás, *op. cit., prólogo*, p. 12.

[13] Cf. La Viñaza, *Biblioteca histórica de la filología castellana* (Madrid, 1893) col. 1816.

[14] It is a generally established fact that Spanish vocabulary undoubtedly began to undergo modifications (particularly semantic) from the very time of the Conquest. But perhaps it is not entirely accurate to say that these modifications came about through contact with the indigenous languages ('the contact with native languages had a vital influence on the development of Spanish-American speech', says Charles E. Kany, *Semántica hispanoamericana*, introd.). It was rather through contact with the new American environement. Nonetheless, within the whole of such modifications, it would seen appropriate to distinguish between those brought about under the normal and general processes of evolution in Spanish, and those which are properly due to the adaptation of Spanish vocabulary to the new milieu. If, for instance, the word *cuchilla* as 'the crest of a mountain range or of a mountain' is simply a special application of *cuchilla* as 'a kind of wide-blade knife' (Cuervo finds this meaning documented in Valbuena), this, it seems, would have to be distinguished from a word like *botalón* 'a post to tie up to or hold cows' (Bogotá), a meaning which the nautical term *botalón* 'pole reaching towards the outer part of a boat' (Corominas, DCEC, verb *botar*), acquires in the new American environment. Something similar could be said of *estantillo*, meaning 'estacón' (Cuervo, *Apuntaciones*, 530) and of other terms which, in the opinion of Kany (*Semántica hispanoamericana, introd.*) show an evolution which 'was not in accordance with Peninsular usage'. A detailed investigation in this regard would, of course, lead to a chronology of semantic changes in Spanish-American vocabulary. Thus, for example, the difference between *pozos* (Amer. 'any stagnant water') and *pozas* (Sp. 'a hollow place with still water in it') probably dates back to a state of vacillation which, according to Cuervo (*Apunt.* 528), is already documented in the records of some chroniclers (Cieza de León, el Inca Garcilaso) and originates at that time. Of *quebrada* as 'brook' Cuervo himself thinks it is a meaning undoubtedly developed in America at the time of the Conquest (*Apunt.* 603).
It this is what happened with the vocabulary of Spanish, regarding the meaning of words, something similar happened with the vocabulary of aboriginal languages incorporated into Spanish, particularly from the point of view of word forms. Corominas (*Indianorománica*, RFH, VI, p. 7) quotes the testimony of the Inca Garcilaso with regard to the substitution of *g* for *k* (or *q*) in the Quechua of Peru, and adds that this kind of substitution becomes almost a phonetic law: *minga, porongo, chingana, guarango*, all replacing voiceless stops, likewise: *condor, tambo* (from *kuntur, tampu*). There are, besides, other cases in which the influence of Spanish on the vocabulary of indigenous origin seems clear. Thus, we know (from Las Casas) that the pronunciation of the *i* in *areíto* was long, but Castellanos already pronounced *aréito* (as if it were Sp. *pleito*). We also know (from Las Casas) that the *i* in *ceíba* was long, but in the pronounciation of Castellanos it became *céiba* (as Sp. *reina*): cf. Pedro Henríquez Ureña, *Palabras antillanas* in *Para la historia de los indigenismos*, p. 111. It is likewise known that *nagua* and *enagua* are Castilianized modifications of *naguas* which 'is the primitive form, whose Taino origin is unquestionable' (Henríquez Ureña, ibid. p. 119). Cuervo thinks, on the basis of Castellanos, that *guádua* is a modification from *guáduba* (*Apunt.* 922, note). And not only in pronounciation, but also in the gender of certain nouns: for example, in *guanábana, guanábano* (the first one from Las Casas, the second from Oviedo) the distinction was taken from the pattern *manzana -no, ciruela -lo* (Henríquez Ureña, *ibid.* p. 113). It is possible that this would happen with other words, for example *guácima* and *guácimo*, etc.

concept which is the basis of his *Vocabulario*.[15] Its purpose is to provide a contemporary lexical view of the American world: plants, birds, animals, their features and characteristics. It is a concept similar to the one that inspires the *Diccionario de voces cubanas* of Pichardo, which opens nineteenth century lexicography, and which springs from living experience with the language and with different neighboring countries (Cuba, Santo Domingo, and Puerto Rico). It offers a direct testimony of lexical varieties, of their sources (terms from other languages), and their most marked changes in meaning.[16]

This second period, which extends until 1900 — even though Cuervo's *Apuntaciones* appear in 1867 — is the most fertile in Spanish-American lexicography, and, undoubtedly, the most important one. And this for two reasons: because of the number of works published, and, above all, because in it the basic problems confronting the study of Spanish American vocabulary are stated, although not always, of course, with the necessary methodological rigor. Before we point out these problems, let us quickly glance at the development which Spanish-American lexicography takes in two further stages.

A third period includes the years between 1900 and 1930. Cuervo's *Diccionario de construcción y régimen* points out, in the domain of lexicon, the general direction of the language, much as Bello had previously indicated with regard to grammar. Cuervo died in 1911 but, fortunately for America, a new man, Rodolfo Lenz, arrived in Chile in the last decade of the century and continued his activity until 1938. Chile is a good point of reference to characterize this period; Echeverría y Reyes's *Voces usadas en Chile* dates from 1900, 'the best and best ordered dictionary of provincialisms on any country of the Americas', according to Lenz. The *Diccionario de chilenismos* of M. A. Román, dates from 1901-1918 and the *Diccionario etimolójico de las voces chilenas derivadas de lenguas indíjenas americanas*[17] of R. Lenz from dates 1904-1910. Elsewhere, the *Diccionario de argentinismos* of Garzón dates from 1910, and the *Vocabulario de Mexicanismos* of García Icazbalceta from 1899-1905 (incomplete). These and others are representative works of this period.

A new stage begins in 1930 which can be characterized by the influence of Amado Alonso's *Biblioteca de Dialectología Hispanoamericana* in different fields, but especially in dialectology. Alonso's wise orientation is also present in the *Revista de Filología*

[15] 'Since he did not intend a historical review of the process, but rather a register of what was going on in his time and place, many of the items documented in older works are missing. Its documental interest for the study of American life and language is unequalled because its vocabulary is a reflexion of its epoch, the fundamental change in life which had taken place in the preceding century which was that of consolidation of regional life and therefore of differentiation among regions' (Morínigo, *La penetración*, 222).

[16] 'A book which merits loud praise, whose technique, more than a century after its publication, has been unsurpassed. Pichardo's *Diccionario* pointed the way for the compilation and publication of many similar works throughout Spanish America. Unfortunately, not all were as meritorious, but they are useful as documents for our history of language in America and for our study of the lexical sources of American Spanish' (Morínigo, *La penetración*, 223-4).

[17] cf. Ambrosio Rabanales, *La investigación lingüística y filológica en Chile*, *BFUCh* 16.132 (1964).

Hispánica. His influence has been manifold and long in its reach; not only are the volumes of his *Biblioteca* an indispensable tool for the dialectologist but also for the lexicographer, who through them can establish a methodological criterion for the selection and analysis of Spanish-American regional vocabulary, while it offers in itself carefully selected materials. Also in the *Revista* we find valuable observations by Alonso and his collaborators on lexicographic and dialectal works. This serious and deep influence has been felt in linguistic studies in general, but particularly (one would think of Henriquez Ureña, Rosenblat, and Morínigo's contributions to native language studies) in what concerns provincial or local lexicography in Spanish America.

3.1. The first basic problem of Spanish-American lexicography is that of Americanisms. As indicated before, it is with Alcedo and Pichardo that the idea of a Spanish-American common bond is established, although not explicitly. It is with reference to this idea that we can view the effort of A. de los Ríos, in 1855, to gather from the work of one of the most important chroniclers, Fernández de Oviedo, the totality of specifically American terms used in it. In a more systematic way, this is the guiding principle of the Spanish lexicographer Salvá, who introduces this problem in the general domain of Hispanic lexicography with his *Diccionario* (1846). To this effect, we could mention some later works, for example the *Vokabular* of Blumentritt (1882-85), Toro y Guisbert's *Americanismos* (1912), the *Tesoro* of Lentzner, and others. Although with some defects (nothing uncommon in this type of work, undertaken by a single individual), Malaret's *Diccionario de americanismos* (1925 2nd ed. 1931) is the most complete effort in this regard, together with the *Amerikanistisches Woerterbuch* of G. Friedrici (1947), a fundamental book, even though modestly presented as an aid to historians, ethnographers, geographers, and naturalists interested in the sources of Spanish-American cultural history. Its purpose is not the study of a Pan-american lexicon, but, so to speak, of that which panindigenous. However, while investigating the latter it greatly contributes to the general study of Americanisms.[18] On the other hand, this Panamericanist idea lies at the basis of criticisms of the *Diccionario de la Academia* or of the Academia itself, for example, J. T. Medina's *Los americanismos del Diccionario de la Academia Española* (1927), or D. Rubio's *Los llamados mexicanismos de la Academia Española* (1917).

3.2. The second problem is that of provincialisms.[19] Each Spanish-American country (at times even each lexicographer) looks for and finds a vocabulary geographically differentiated from that of the other countries. This problem is a basic one in

[18] Cf. Fritz Krueger, *NRFH* 2.381 (1948).

[19] In Spanish-American lexicography, provincialisms and regionalisms are usually confused with each other (fortunately, without any serious consequences). What should be understood by regionalisms hardly needs explanation. However, the term provincialisms has been used to describe the totality of the vocabulary of a country. Thus, for example, Santamaría, *Diccionario de mexicanismos*, p. 12. 'The only thing that would fit the narrow framework of a provincial or national vocabulary, in any case limited to one of the Spanish speaking countries, is the word whose structure and meaning are pure'. (Mexico, 1959).

more than one sense. In the already existing dictionaries no matter how lacking in rigor they are, a provincialism means a vocabulary item used in a limited geographical area which coincides with present-day national frontiers. This definition is, in general, correct, even though in many instances elements are included in it which do not pertain to the lexicographic study of provincialisms; such, for instance, as the inclusion of phonetic peculiarities considered to be errors or of archaisms taken as inadmissible for present-day use due to the more or less important phonetic alterations or changes in meaning, or the treatment of neologisms as a corrupting influence with regard to the unity of the language. In spite of all this, there is an attempt to record the vocabulary features of a country as something peculiar to it. This is the guiding idea in one of the most important collections of provincialisms of the last century, the *Diccionario de barbarismos y provincialismos de Costa Rica* of C. Gagini (1892). It was revised and expanded by the author and published with a prologue by Cuervo who had pointed out that what had appeared to be entirely peculiar to Costa Rica could also be found in other countries. In this second edition of 1919 Gagini abandons the idea of barbarisms. Along the same lines, although not with as vast a vision as Gagini, we can mention the *Peruanismos* of Arona (1883) the *Provincialismos de Guatemala* of Batres Jáuregui (1892), the *Hondureñismos* of Membreño (1895), and, very especially, the *Vocabulario de mexicanismos* of García Icazbalceta (1899),[20] whose publication was encouraged by Cuervo, which is unfortunately incomplete. To be sure, this is the field in which lexico-grammatical purism has left deepest imprint, damaging the objective recording of the lexicon in each country. There has also been a confusion in this field with the type of more restricted vocabularies, which we will now discuss.

3.3. The problem of vast dialectal areas or zones necessarily leads, from Henriquez Ureña to M. L. Wagner, to the exploration, study, and recording of a regional lexicon. Henriquez Ureña himself anticipated the existence, within his five areas, of further subdivisions. Other scholars have determined them for different countries.[21] It has been, above all, Morínigo who has lately insisted on the problem of the formation of a regional lexicon, pointing out, among other things, the importance of recording the vocabulary of mechanics and technology.[22] It seems evident now that a special lexicographic study has a place in the study of regional linguistic areas. To this effect, we have, for instance, the testimony of Pichardo who noticed with reference to Cuba that in its Eastern half native terms were especially numerous as well as those from neighbouring Haiti, while in its Western half those of Mexico prevailed. Something similar must occur in other countries, particularly those where the influence of native languages existed, or still exists.

In this regard, we must mention an important nineteenth century work, the *Tesoro*

[20] In the still unpublished letter. F. J. Santamaría's *Diccionario de mejicanismos* is intended to continue and complete that of García Icazbalceta; cf. Serís. *Bibliografía*, no. 1565a. p. 767.

[21] cf. Homero Serís, *Bibliografía*, pp. 706-8; for Ecuador, P. Boyd-Bowman, *NRFH* 7.222-3 (1953).

[22] Marcos Morínigo, *La formación léxica regional hispanoamericana*, *NRFH* 7.234-41 (1953).

de catamarqueñismos of Lafone Quevedo (1895, second ed. 1898), with reference to an Argentinian region; another, of no less importance with regard to Mexico is *El provincialismo tabasqueño* of Santamaría (1921). These two works, which in a way mark the two basic aspects of regional lexicons, began a type of study which has continued and increased today — thanks not only to dialectological studies but also to the various projects for linguistic atlases in Spanish America. Also recent lexicographic research of the type of 'words and things', of crafts, industries, activities, etc., is carried on with reference to the two mentioned aspects of regional vocabularies: influence of native languages in a more or less restricted area, and typical Spanish regionalisms of a certain locality. The vocabularies of special activities or occupations will show how much more detailed Spanish-American lexicography can become. Let us remember in this connection the two studies of B. E. Vidal de Battini, *Voces marinas en el habla rural de San Luis* (1949) and *El léxico de los yerbateros* (1953).

3.4. Aboriginal languages have been studied either as separate and complete totalities or in their surviving elements. These surviving elements are those which, more or less distorted, have been introduced from the time of the conquest, into documents, literary sources, chronicles, or have been preserved in the oral tradition of regional speech. Both those items in the complete repertories of aboriginal languages and those preserved in written sources or the oral tradition (sometimes of a purely local nature), have become an essential part of the total corpus of Americanisms. Spanish-American lexicography has been interested in recording out of the total speech of a region those items originating in the native language, even though they have not always been incorporated into general Spanish use, because a large proportion of them are used in places still remote and insufficienctly explored.[23] The study of this portion of regional vocabularies which can be properly called indigenous vocabulary, has a model in Henriquez Ureña's *Para la historia de los indigenismos* (1935-38), a series of studies which in his own opinion are, preliminary efforts for the historical dictionary ïndigenous vocabulary of America, a project cherished by the Instituto de Filología de Buenos Aires, and which, as far as we know, has not been continued. To be sure, the nineteenth century also looked on this field as one of the most attractive and rewarding and devoted to it the contributions of such authors as A. Rojas, *Glosario de voces indígenas de Venezuela* (1881); Fernández Ferraz, *Nahuatlismos de Costa Rica* (1892); Robelo, *Diccionario de aztequismos* (1904); and others. In this respect, the most extensive and well documented work is R. Lentz's *Diccionario etimolójico de voces chilenas derivadas le lenguas indíjenas* (1904-1910) a book which for many year has been the great dictionary of indigenous vocabulary used by linguistics, not yet surpassed in its richness in lexical items.[24]

[23] Morínigo, *La penetracion*... p. 218: 'Besides the fact that in many cases the diffusion of these words was restricted to the area of the extension of the source language because they referred to local customs.'

[24] Guillermo L. Guitarte, 'Bosquejo histórico de la filología hispanoamericana', *El Simposio de Cartagena* 230-44 (Bogotá 1965).

Efforts have continued in this field with progressively more solid contributions, some of them excellent. Let it suffice to remember, among others, the *Estudios de voces tucumanas* of Lizondo (1927), for Quechua; *Las voces guaranies del Diccionario académico* of Morínigo (1935); the lexicon of *Quechuismos usados en Colombia*, L. Tascón (1934, second ed. 1961); and more recently, A. Pazos' *Glosario de Quechuismos colombianos* (1961); and O. D'Costa's essay *Mestizaje del castellano en Colombia* (1950), in which besides Quechua words, Taino terms are also included. In Lemos Ramírez's important *Semántica o ensayo de lexicografía ecuatoriana* Quechua elements in national names are recorded. Also important are the following works: Davila Garibi's *Del nahuatl al español* (1939) for Mexico; Vivanco Diaz's *Diccionario americanista* (1957) for Cuba; and A. Rosenblat's *El castellano de Venezuela* (1958) for Venezuela. Two works deserve special mention: *Palabras indígenas de la isla de Santo Domingo* (1935) of Emiliano and Emilio Tejera, a book, in the opinion of A. Alonso, 'of inestimable linguistic worth, exceptional in our vocabularies'[25] and the above-mentioned *Amerikanistisches Woerterbuch* of Friederici, where the scholar finds, in the words of M. L. Wagner, 'a rich and well-documented source of information on all subjects touching on the cultural and linguistic history of America'.[26]

3.5. It is not surprising that in Spanish-American lexicography, names of plants, fruits, and animals form a rather homogeneous chapter. The spectacle of nature was the first obstacle that the conquistador found in his understanding of the American world, and, at the same time, it was the first stage for linguistic assimilation through the exercise of the colonists' creativity to coin new words or propagate the native ones. Not always, of course, was this new vocabulary extended to the Hispanic world at large; in fact, it has been restricted to areas almost exclusively American. Its richness, on the other hand, is enormous, and the attention it has received since the last century by lexicography is well justified. Thus, Colmeiro, already in 1871, can be said to have opened this field of investigation in a systematic way, with his *Diccionario de los diversos nombres vulgares de muchas plantas usuales o notables del Antiguo y Nuevo Mundo*, and his *Primeras noticias acerca de la vegetación americana* (1892) — a field which is now explored with ever growing attention in every one of the Spanish-American countries. There exists, of course, the serious problem of separating what is peculiar to one country from what is common to several or many of them. However, José T. Medina could offer a good account of *Voces chilenas de los reinos animal y vegetal* in 1917, and also dating from the same year is Toro y Guisbert's *Ensayo de una sinopsis de nombres científicos y vulgares de la fauna americana*. Not is it surprising that the possibility of errors of documentation or interpretation is greater here than in other domains. Unless one has the qualifications of a naturalist (this is why the work of Pichardo is still so admirable), it is difficult to determine which is present-day popular terminology, or inherited from native languages, or the

[25] RFH, II, p. 70 (1940).
[26] RFE, XXXIV, p. 317 (1950).

more or less universal scientific terminology. But more important than establishing the similarities or coincidences of a regional speech with that of other regions, is recording, exploring, determining the areas from which the preserved items expand — items which in many cases provide the basis for present use, even though this may seem at times capricious and arbitrary. Without going into a thorough review of the many monographs done in every country (Bondenbender's for Argentina; S. E. Ortiz, A. María and J. J. Montes' for Colombia; Poey, Gundlach, and Roig y Mesa's for Cuba; Armengol, Oroz, and Rabanales' for Chile, etc.) it is important to make special mention of A. Malaret's essay *Lexicon de fauna y flora* (1961), the first effort towards a global view of this large sphere of lexicography, where the use of metaphor offers interesting possibilities of expression, as R. Oroz and later A. Rabanales have shown.

3.6. The study of place-names is another of the basic fields of Spanish-American lexicography — a field which was also explored by nineteenth century scholars and whose importance should be underlined. It is a sector which may be threatened by extra-linguistic factors. 'Toponymy', writes M. Pidal, 'is not only the history of the proper names most common in a language; it is interesting as a record of primitive languages, often the only one remaining. Place-names are the living voices, transmitted from generation to generation, of those people who have disappeared.'[27] Unfortunately (in Colombia, for example) place-names have been abandoned arbitrarily in order to be replaced by new ones, and as a consequence their tradition and its development, be it Hispanic or indigenous, have been interrupted. This is a tendency which can lead to the eradication of essential features in Spanish-American speech — features that could throw light on indigenous languages, and could contribute in more than one case to emphasize the present-day nature of different linguistic problems.

Two types of contributions exist in this lexicographic field: first, there are the geographic dictionaries (Paz Soldán's, 1877, for Perú; Peñafiel's, 1885, for Mexico), in which accounts of a rather practical nature are given of place-names — always useful and sometimes indispensable for the scholar. Secondly, there are more specific works dealing with concrete problems of toponymy (those dealing with the name America, or the names of the different countries, the main capital cities, regions, etc.), works that begun in the second half of the nineteenth century. Thus, we have the work of Buschman about Aztec toponymy (1853), or that of A. de la Rosa (1895, with an English translation the same year), and R. Hill's in 1896.

Of these two types of contributions some take a more traditional Hispanic attitude, like that of Groussac who sees the Spanish origin of place-names along the Patagonian coast, and others which deal almost exclusively with the indigenous aspect of the problem, for example P. Groeber with regard to Araucanian toponymy. In general, however, the indigenous aspects of toponymy have prevailed in the studies of every country, although there does not seem to be a real justification for this, since the

[27] Ramon Menendes Pidal, *Toponimia prerrománica hispana*, *ed.* Gredos, p. 5. See also H. Krahe, *Ortsnamen als Geschichtsquelle*, (Heidelberg, 1949).

toponymy of Hispanic origins is in fact vastly extended throughout America. So far the works published in this field are not exactly lexical repertories (the date for a general dictionary of American place-names is still remote). However, one should mention in this respect the work of Paz y Niño, *Las lenguas indígenas del Ecuador*, which is a toponymic dictionary (1946-52), and the *Diccionario de etimologías mayas* of S. Pacheco Cruz (1953).

3.7. A complex network of interrelations at different levels can be established when we consider the number of indigenous elements in American Spanish in their relations first with Spanish in general, and with other languages. There is first the lexical flow of indigenous vocabulary which became assimilated into the general stock of Spanish vocabulary both among the different Spanish-American countries and in Peninsular Spanish. There is also the incorporation of certain Americanisms, which reflect the living conditions of our countries, into other European countries (let us remember the *rastacuero* and *butaca* of which Rosenblat speaks).[28] Furthermore, one would have to consider the relations between Spanish and other European languages through the contacts between Spanish Americans and successive waves of immigrants, and in some cases the status of Spanish as a minority language with relation to the indigenous languages (for example, in some areas of Peru).

A general view of the significance of this complex situation, with reference in particular to the influence of other European languages on American Spanish, can be seen in *Das ausländische Sprachgut im Spanischen des Rio de la Plata* of R. Grossman (1926); with specific reference to Italian, in R. Donghi's *Contribución al estudio del italianismo en la Argentina* (1925); and on the influence of English, Barabino's *English influence on the common speech of the River Plate* (1950), which shows how strong this influence is, much as it was in the last century in the case of French, although for different reasons. In this respect, Baralt's book, *Diccionario de galicismos* (1855),[29] is already a classic, still valuable and useful today, in spite of the fact that French influence has greatly decreased in Spanish America (see J. Guasch Leguizamón's *Galicismos aceptados, aceptables y vitandos*, 1951). Of course, also pertaining to this lexical domain are the influences of Spanish-American speech on other languages, although this influence is rather limited to that of the vocabulary of native languages. Thus, see for instance Ph. Motley Palmer's *Der Einfluss der neuen Welt auf dem deutschen Wortschatz* (1933) and Lokotsch's *Etymologisches Woerterbuch der amerikanischen (indianischen) Woerter in Deutschen* (1926).

The influence of Spanish on indigenous languages is a most important one, as shown, in the case of Guaraní, in the excellent book of Morínigo, *Hispanismos en el guaraní* (1931), and the study of W. Giese, *Hispanismos en el mapuche* (1947). Illuminating and full of insights and suggestions is A. Tovar's book, *Español y lenguas indígenas* (1964).

[28] *Buenas y malas palabras*, Serie I, pp. 115-8 and 412-8.

[29] For Colombia, R. Uribe, *Diccionario abreviado de galicismos, provincialismos y correcciones de lenguaje* (Medellín, 1887).

3.8. Finally, we find in Spanish-American lexicography the domain of the lexicon of individual authors, both from the colonial period and from modern times. It is a domain of considerable importance due to have an ever increasing development. Its results will undoubtedly be important for the examination of the vocabulary of American Spanish in general. Not much has been done yet, when one thinks of the vastness of this field, but there are already some contributions which can be considered definitive: such is the case with E. F. Tiscornia's *La lengua de Martín Fierro* (I, 1925), and the solidly documented *La lengua de Bolivar* (I, 1961) of M. Hildebrandt; of a more general character, but devoting some attention to vocabulary, is I. J. Pardo's *Juan de Castellanos* (1961). On the other hand, not infrequently one finds works like M. Ferragu's *Colombianismos de vocabulario y de sintaxis en José Eustausio Rivera* (1954), which points to the consideration of those elements considered national in the speech of an author. We shall have to wait for greater attention to be given to works or authors from the colonial period in each country. In them, Americanisms and indigenous elements will find valuable documentation.

3.9. Nowhere better than in the lexicon of an individual can we find supporting evidence for semantic innovations, which are always interesting, and not as dangerous to the unity of the language as Lenz believed. Unfortunately, semantic studies as an independent discipline have received so little attention that work in this field is almost non-existent. As an applied discipline, applied above all to dictionary-making, it is worth noticing Lenz's *Die indianischen Elemente im chilenischen Spanish*, which in the words of Corominas, is valuable because it groups words in semantic fields.[30] But without embracing the whole of a vocabulary, semantic studies can be restricted to more specific areas of it, or concentrate on its special uses. Be that as it may, the question is, is there such a thing as Spanish-American semantics? The answer is yes, both in principle and in fact.

Since a great many Americanisms are caused by new semantic developments in the general vocabulary of Spanish, it is clear that Spanish American lexicon, seen from this particular perspective, offers a wide field for lexico-semantic investigations. On the other hand, also in the practice of observing the semantic development of words from indigenous sources, one can find certain features which, once recorded an systematically analyzed, could perhaps show some processes peculiar to America. Furthermore, it is also possible in this connection to study the problems of what is or is not peculiar to one country (perhaps this is the sense of some of J. B. Selva's works for Argentina), or what is common to two or more of them (thus, for example, P. Benvenuto Murrieta's work regarding Peru and Puerto Rico).[31] However, before such tasks can be successfully undertaken it is necessary first to determine what is, semantically, Spanish-American. This is what, in a praiseworthy effort, A. Malaret has done in his small book *Semántica americana* (1943). Finally, with Ch. E. Kany's *American-Spanish Semantics* (1960), a full systematization has seen attempted. This

[30] Joan Corominas, *DCEC*, *Ind. bibl.*, p. 47.
[31] *BFM*, 1937, nos. 4-5, pp. 53-9.

is a book bound to exercise a profound influence in this particular domain, as well as in the general field of study of American Spanish.

3.10. For the present time, there do not seem to be any plans in Spanish American lexicography for a general inventory of the language. This, in spite of the fact that Baralt, author of the *Diccionario de galicismos*, had plans in 1850 for a *Diccionario matriz de la lengua castellana*, of which P. Grases[32] said he only published 'a prospectus with the outline of the undertaking and some samples belonging to the letter A', enough, however, to show how capable this illustrious lexicographer was. Cuervo's initiative (and that of his colleague V. G. Manrique) to plan a Spanish dictionary dates from 1863 ('similar to Webster's and Bescherlle's'). Although the project was completely abandoned, there remained the *Muestra* which, apart from its intrinsic value, is a representative document in this field. But the author of the *Apuntaciones*, who aspired — especially in its last edition — to reflect the status of Spanish both as a literary and a popular language, started, in 1871, his monumental *Diccionario de construcción y régimen de la lengua castellana* (A-B, 1886; C-D, 1893), a unique contribution, in its class, to Spanish American lexicography. Of course, there is no question in this *Diccionario* of taking up the totality of the Spanish vocabulary, but, as its title indicates, only of those items which offer a variety of constructions in their syntactic functions as well as a variety of meanings according to whether the construction is modified by the presence of a certain preposition, adverb, etc. It is, thus, a syntactic dictionary, and its originality, apart from its wise and rigorous execution, comes from having applied the most demanding concepts of nineteenth century lexicography to Spanish syntax. Only two volumes were published, and reprinted in 1953 by the Instituto Caro y Cuervo which has undertaken to continue the work.[33]

4. Thus far, we have dealt with the work of specific individuals in the field of Spanish American lexicography. Let us now turn to the work and influence of institutions. We have already made reference in passing to how the Instituto de Filología of the Universidad de Buenos Aires once sponsored, probably through the initiative of Henriquez Ureña, the project for a *Diccionario histórico de indigenismos americanos*. The final disappearence of that model institute — for reasons quite foreign to scholarship — definitively put an end to the project. Meanwhile, other institutions have been created, such as the Instituto Caro y Cuervo (1942) under the direction of J. M. Rivas Sacconi, now in charge of continuing Cuervo's *Diccionario de construcción y régimen*; the Instituto Andrés Bello in Caracas, where materials are being gathered for the *Diccionario de venezolanismos* under the direction of A. Rosenblat; and finally, though it is chronologically the first, the Instituto de Filología de la Universidad de Chile, founded and directed since 1935 by Rodolfo Oroz, where

[32] P. Grases *Don Rufino José Cuervo, conjunción de tres filólogos venezolanos*, p. 8 (Caracas, 1945).
[33] Fascicles 1, *ea-empeorar* (1959) and 2, *emperezar-émulo* (1962) of vol III have been published.

Ambrosio Rabanales and a small group of collaborators are preparing the *Diccionario del léxico común del español de Chile*, which aspires to be the most complete of its kind. The Academias de la Lengua are also engaged in lexicographic projects: That of Colombia has a Comisión de Vocabulario Técnico, carefully studying this particular field of contemporary life; and the Academia Argentina de Letras constantly publishes in its *Boletín* studies directly related to the problems of Spanish American lexicography.

5. To summarize, Spanish-American lexicography, through its different stages mentioned above has been essentially concerned with two basic problems: (1) Spanish vocabulary, the vocabulary of general Spanish, which is the heritage of all Spanish speaking people, is modified on American soil in many different ways: nationally, regionally, locally. This is the aspect that links, through its various implications, Spanish American lexicography to Hispanic lexicography in general. (2) That general Spanish vocabulary is enriched with and at times also modified by the contribution of typically American Terms, remnants of the basic vocabularies of the aboriginal languages which, more or less changed, are incorporated into the common language. This is the specifically Spanish-American aspect of general Spanish lexicography. In the first case, we have the dictionaries carried out under different criteria, such as respect for the academic norms, grammatical propriety, purism, or objective and rigorous observation of facts, and which can hardly be properly called repertoires of Americanisms. In the second case, we have the lexicons which do not necessarily exclude indigenist elements and that can be called collections of Americanisms. It would seem that this is an arbitrary simplification of many facets which reduces the field of Spanish American lexicography, but it seems nonetheless to be a realistic view.

In 1944, J. Corominas published a most provocative study (provocative in name and content) called *Indianorrománica.*[34] According to Corominas, that which is specifically American consists, not in the aboriginal terms that have been adopted into Spanish, but in the development that Castilian words have undergone in the new continental atmosphere. In other words, what is reflected from this new life in the terms called Americanisms is the proper subject matter for vocabularies of Americanisms — a complex and rich subject matter which fully justifies the creation of such vocabularies. But perhaps one should insist on the abundance of indigenous terms, and the complexity of their history. There exists in this regard a rather biased idea that the influx of indigenous elements is small because interest has usually been limited to the vocabulary which has gone beyond the frontiers of Spanish America to be incorporated into the general vocabulary of Spanish, and occasionally also into other languages. One of the future tasks of Spanish American lexicography, however, should be the study and systematic collecting of the indigenous vocabulary, without, of course, any disregard for the other aspect of Spanish American speech.

It is important in this respect to point out that A. Rosenblat, the foremost scholar

[34] Joan Corominas, 'Indianorománica: Estudios de lexicología hispanoamericana', *RFH* 6.1-35, 209-248 (1944).

today in Spanish American philology and the best qualified to understand the Spanish of the different countries, has noticed (after he reduced the figures of indigenous terms given by Alvarado for Venezuela and by Lenz for Chile) that some three thousand indigenous terms can be recognized in the Spanish of Venezuela. This does not mean that all of them are present in the common language, but they represent nonetheless a considerable number.[35] What happens, as Rosenblat writes, is that in each town, in each hamlet a rich terminology, largely of indigenous origin, is used in naming plants, animals, and household goods. Some of the terms are used in large regions, but most are limited to small areas and their fate is to give way gradually to more general or more prestigious terms.[36]

All this terminology, this vocabulary, is still far from having been recorded lexicographically. The task, then, is urgent, and more so, because of what Antonio Tovar has recently said, something which deserves careful consideration: The survival of our language is also linked to that of the great Indian languages. These, or at least some of them, will determine the evolution of local Spanish, and if, as we hope, the unity of the language is maintained and it continues to be mutually intelligible on both sides of the Atlantic, those indigenous contributions will continue to give a certain hue to general Spanish, in a different way, but just as they already influence it with the imported words which have been general use for a long time.[37]

6.1. Now that we are at the end of this survey, we should ask ourselves on what theoretical grounds the results of lexicography can be based, as well as, what the solution is to the different problems taken up by dictionaries in Spanish-America. However, the answer is not easy, since, on the one hand, it would depend on what answer Hispanic lexicography in general could provide in this respect. On the other hand, a thorough review of the concepts involved in the composition of each dictionary and in the formulation of partial solutions would be necessary. Given the nature of this survey, it is not possible here to undertake such a review. It may them seem more adequate, since we are dealing with lexicography, to ask to what extent a lexicographic theory is implied in the composition of the different vocabularies. In this case, we should talk of methodology rather than theory although lexicographers themselves attach little importance to an explicit formulation of their methodology.[38] A brief sketch can, however, be attempted by examining the various types of dictionaries, their different levels, and the different periods in which they were composed.

Of course, such methodology leads back to the very objectives of lexicography — objectives which are characterized by the fact that the compilation of dictionaries pursues primarily practical, not theoretical ends, unless, of course, the conscious scientific attitude of the compiler becomes explicit. From this point of view the

[35] *Buenas y malas palabras*, Serie II, pp. 393-5.

[36] Ibid p. 395.

[37] Antonio Tovar, 'Español y lenguas indígenas. Algunos ejemplos', *PFLE* II, *OFINES* 245-57, 251 (Madrid, 1964).

[38] 'The indifference which lexicography displays towards its own methodology is astonishing'. Uriel Weinreich, *Lexicographic Definition in Descriptive Semantics*, *IJAL* 28:2, 26.

object of lexicography coincides with the ways in which the lexical body of a language can be recorded. Thus, the two main lines along which the composition of repertories is effected become immediately clear: alphabetical recording, on the one hand, and methodical and systematic recording on the other.[39] In Spanish lexicographic methodology three basic criteria are usually taken into account in the compilation of a general dictionary: quantitative, functional, and material, with more specific criteria in each case. With regard to quantity, a more selective criterion would try to cover most of the lexicon (including or excluding scientific or technical terms, terms from the arts and occupations, dialectal words, slang, borrowings, archaisms, neologisms) or the totality of it. With regard to the second criterion, a more specific one would be grammatical, trying to classify vocabulary by the grammatical category of the words, their semantic nucleus, and their definition (descriptive, logical, technical) or exemplification (documented with literary or dialectal texts), which in turn leads to various forms of presentation (empirical, scientific, historical). Thirdly, a criterion of orthographic recording of the word according to its usual pronunciation (confirmed or explained by etymology) or, more infrequently, by means of a phonetic transcription, may be used. These criteria are subject to the particular attitude of the lexicographer, an attitude which can be determined by one of the following tendencies: adherence to grammatical norms (correctness), to usage (objective recording without evaluation), or to a scientific consideration (total predominance of the linguistic or philological education of the lexicographer). From the point of view of the formulation of a lexicographic methodology it is in this last tendency that the elaboration of lexical material offers a wider theoretical foundation.[40]

The methodology of systematic dictionaries (by which we mean dictionaries ordered not alphabetically, but by semantic groups) seems less well developed. Julio Casares has reviewed the subject for Spanish.[41] It is, however, to be noticed that the ideological dictionary, in spite of its systematic elaboration, is subject to compliance with practical needs.[42] More important than the presentation or summary of the methodological principles by which this type of dictionary can be made,[43] is the fact that the arrangement of vocabulary items by meaning groups or word families opens up a new perspective on lexicology.[44]

[39] cf. Bruno Migliorini, *Che cos'è un vocabolaro*, p. 4 (Firenze, 1951).

[40] In this sense, Spanish-American lexicography offers two cases of special importance, those of R. J. Cuervo and of R. Lenz in the introductory pages of their respective works.

[41] Julio Casares, *Nuevo concepto del diccionario de la lengua y otros problemas de lexicografía* 21-125, Madrid, 1941).

[42] cf. J. Casares *op. cit.*, p. 111 and Rudolf Hallig und Walter von Wartburg, *Begriffssystem als Grundlage für die Lexikographie* p, 6, (Berlin, 1952).

[43] See, for example, the fundamental presentation of that bv Hallig-Wartburg, *op. cit.* 9-22, compared with that of Dornseiff, *Der deutsche Wortschatz nach Sachgruppen* (Berlin-Leipzig, 1934); besides, Kurt Baldinger, *Die Gestaltung des wissenschaftlichen Wörterbuchs*, in *Romanistisches Jahrbuch* 5.65-94 (1952).

[44] In relation, of course, to the existence of these groups or families and their special investigation, but not in their relationship with methodological outlines, since these are based 'a priori, extralin-

6.2. Ideological dictionaries (and somehow also those of synonyms) establish an organic distribution of lexicon by groups or by families of words, thus acknowledging the fact that lexicon has an internal coherence with sections within the general vocabulary, which requires a criterion other than the purely external alphabetical one for their presentation and elaboration. The ideological dictionary assumes that, beyond the apparent chaos of a vocabulary, there is a certain order of ideas, of related notions, of semantic fields held together by an ideal nexus; in other words, the basis for these dictionaries is the feeling of the existence of a lexical system within the language.[45]

The existence of this lexical system is confirmed from the point of view of semantic fields which postulates together with a conceptual field a lexical field.[46] This lexical field, although bounded, forms, with others, larger fields, until the totality of the vocabulary is encompassed.[47] Accordingly, lexicon — to use an expression of H. A. Gleason — is something more than a miscellaneous remnant;[48] it can be considered part of the structure of the language. Within the lexical system of the language, the existence of organic fields provides each word with a meaning by contrasting it with others in that field.

Gleason, asking whether lexicon should be properly considered a part of the structure of the language, notes that this would not be so if in fact the lexicon were not internally organized *in some form*,[49] in some way specific to itself. But today we know that it is indeed so organized, at least in some sections.[50] What is the significance — Gleason wonders — of the fact, for example, that not in every language are there fully structured segments of vocabulary, such as colors?[51] Perhaps as in phonology or grammar, the structure would be more clearly visible against the background of the entire system than it would be if isolated parts were examined separately. Furthermore, it may be that what we have called lexicon is merely a residue of unanalyzed material, but out of which a system or number of systems of different types could still be selected. This could be 'the most likely situation'.[52]

6.3. To be sure, neither the view of lexicon offered by ideological dictionaries, nor the one offered by the theory of semantic fields can be equated in the lexicology as an autonomous discipline. Lexicology indeed shares with them consideration of the meaning or semantic nucleus of a word, but its field is delimited in a different way.

---

guistic considerations and do not arise from the semantic material itself'. Stephen Ullman, 'Descriptive Semantics', in *Word* 9:3. 227.

45 Cf. Hallig-Wartburg, *op. cit.*, p. 5.

46 Suzanne Öhman, 'Theories of the Linguistic Fields', in *Word* 9:2. 126.

47 *Ibid.*, p. 127.

48 H. A. Gleason, 'The Relation of Lexicon and Grammar', in *IJAL* 28:2. 96.

49 Ibid., p. 97. Italics are mine.

50 Suzanne Öhman, *Wortinhalt und Weltbild*. 76-83 (Stockholm, 1951).

51 Cf. S. Ullman, 'Descriptive Semantics', op. cit., p. 227, and S. Öhman, *Theories*, op. cit., p. 130.

52 *Op. cit.*, p. 97.

Unfortunately lexicology is, in general, a domain insufficiently explored.[53] We are witnessing, however, a moment of theoretical formulation of lexicology as the science of words.[54] The object of lexicology is the study of words as units of vocabulary, each an invariable relationship between a sound complex and a meaning.[55] But since the manifestations of a word are variable both phonologically and grammatically, the task of lexicology is the study of these variations in what they have of invariance. Consequently, lexicology tries to isolate the lexical meaning of a word and make it recognizable within its phonological, grammatical and semantic variations. It is precisely here that lexicology attempts to determine what the 'lexical meaning' is, 'distinct' — as Weinreich observes — 'from that simple relation between a sign-vehicle and a class of phenomena which is studied by a generalized semantics.'[56] A simple naming relationship is characterized by the monosemy of the linguistic sign (and by its stable content in the context where it occurs), while the typically linguistic sign in itself is polysemous, and, furthermore, the secondary meanings (submeanings) of a word are subject to successive specialization according to the grammatical context in which they appear. If, then, a meaning can, even partially, be specified through the participation of a sign in a series of synonyms, it is clear that a polysemous word which has acquired other specialized contextual meanings will participate in different series of synonyms depending on which secondary meaning is involved. Hence, while for general semantics polysemy and contextual specialization are but special deviations of a pure naming relationship, for lexicology they are its main object of study. From the point of view of lexicology the grammatically free word (unrestricted), monosemous and susceptible of literal application, is an irregular case (degenerate) and linguistically atypical.

Weinreich, who achieves these determinations of the object of lexicology by studying its progress in Soviet linguistics, proposes, in accordance with such determinations, an organic program of lexicology based on the following: the *monosemous* or *polysemous* character of words extended over the vocabulary as a whole; a stage of their development (systematizing the results of the first two criteria in a descriptive way: *descriptive lexicology*) or studying them through their history (comparing the results of descriptive lexicology and applying them to the different historical stages of a language: *historical lexicology*), and this with reference to a group of related languages (*comparative lexicology*) or to language in general (*general lexicology*). This is, of course, the skeleton, of the program, but Weinreich points out how, for each subdivision,

[53] 'Lexicology is largely an unexplored field'. I. J. Gelb, *Lexicography, Lexicology, and the Akkadian Dictionary*, in *Miscelánea Homenaje a André Martinet* 2.65 (Canarias, 1958).

[54] S. Ullman, 'Language and Meaning', in *Word* 2:2. 118, and also, *The Principles of Semantics*, 2nd enlarged edition, 24-42 (1957).

[55] Uriel Weinrich, 'Lexicology', in *Current Trends in Linguistics*, I (1963), p. 66. What follows in the text is based on this excellent study of fundamental importance in many aspects.

[56] Ibid., p. 67.

sections can be established to approximate the lexicological field, which would eventually provide the exact contours of this discipline and make it valid, through its subsequent application, for any language.[57]

[57] 'To qualify as a 'discipline' at all, lexicology must comprise a system of related and researchable questions which can be answered for every language in a repeatable way' (p. 63).

HISPANIC DIALECTOLOGY

JUAN M. LOPE BLANCH

A. SPANISH-AMERICAN STUDIES

1. *The unity of Spanish*

Since the end of World War II, the future of the Spanish language across the widespread territories where it is spoken has been a matter of great concern to scholars in the field of Spanish letters. Towards the end of the nineteenth century, Rufino José Cuervo took a very pessimistic view of the problem, considering the fragmentation of Spanish into different American languages as inevitable. Contrary to this pessimism, however, twentieth-century linguists have thought for the most part that the unity of Spanish was firmly established. Max Leopold Wagner echoed this optimistic opinion when he stated, in *Lingua e dialetti dell'America Spagnola* (Firenze, 1949), that 'le forze centripete sono più forti di quelle centrifughe' (p. 147), considering that the relative lexical and phraseological diversity characterizing each of the different varieties of conversational language in the Spanish speaking countries was restrained and counterbalanced by the leveling impact of the learned and written language, while also being amply compensated by a basic phonetic and grammatical unity. In his opinion, the situation of American Spanish could be described by the formula 'varietà nell'unità e unità nella differenziazione'. In 1949, Avelino Herrero Mayor (*Tradición y unidad del idioma. El diccionario y otros ensayos*, Buenos Aires, 1949), who for several years had been devoting himself to the same question, argued — taking as a basis an address by R. M. Pidal read in 1944[1] — that the fundamental unity of the language was guaranteed for years to come, although he warned of the dangers posed by barbarism and negligence, a reason for his proposal to wage a decisive battle against all corrupting factors, under the strategic direction of the Real Academia Española de la Lengua.

Again in 1956, the problem was restated in clearer and more rigorous terms. Now it was Ramón Menéndez Pidal who, on the occasion of the Second Congress of the Academias de la Lengua in Madrid, reaffirmed his confidence in the future uniformity of the language.[2] He pointed out that modern channels of communication (books,

[1] 'La unidad del idioma', included in the book *Castilla, la tradición, el idioma*, *Colección Austral* 501.171-218 (Buenos Aires, 1945).

[2] Menéndez Pidal, 'Nuevo valor de la palabra hablada y la unidad del idioma', *Memorias del*

radio, newspapers, transoceanic travel, etc.) are entirely different from those which existed at the time of the Roman Empire. Thus the phenomenon of linguistic fragmentation in the case of Latin need not be repeated in the case of Spanish. However, Dámaso Alonso again warned of the dangers besetting the life of the language, fearing that Cuervo's prophecy of 1899 about dialectal fragmentation would, in the long run, come true.[3] Taking as a basis some concrete examples, he reached the following conclusions: 'Everywhere within the Hispanic linguistic body, a disintegrating process is underway; a process which affects phonetics, syntax, morphology, and lexicon. All these aspects of the process foreshadow serious trouble in the future... The edifice of our linguistic community is already breaking apart' (p. 43). With regard to the lexicon, he pointed out a split into two large American zones: a Northern zone (Mexico, Central America, and the Northern part of South America) under the influence of English, and the Southern zone (Central and South America) under the influence of French.

Nonetheless, the majority of linguists did not share this pessimism. Also in 1956, Vicente García de Diego published 'El sentimiento americano del castellano', *Homenaje a Bello, Caro y Cuervo* 431-38 (Madrid, Real Academia Española, 1956), a brief study expressing his confidence in the unity of the language and showing how the linguistic nationalism that flared up in some American countries in the last century had already disappeared. He also indicated how the language remained uniform in the basic field of grammar, as much in morphology as in syntax, as opposed to its relative diversity in lexicon. Angel Rosenblat, in turn, while updating his old study *Lengua y cultura de Hispanoamérica. Tendencias actuales* (Caracas, 1962),[4] stated several reasons for not admitting the possibility of fragmentation, i.e. linguistic nationalism has already been abandoned; unifying influence of the learned language; the spreading of the literary language; an awareness of belonging to a common language; the weak influence of substratum forces, steadily receding; and the stability of Hispanic cultural roots. All together, these reasons lead him to the conclusion that 'American Spanish, far from tending towards linguistic independence, shows an increasing orientation towards unity'.

Shortly afterwards, A. Rosenblat restated his optimism in *El castellano de España y el castellano de América. Unidad y diferenciación* (Caracas, 1962). Together with the regional differentiation, which may puzzle the tourist so much, he explained, there is a certain tendency towards a Spanish-American linguistic unity — a unity that lies in what the speech of Spanish America has in common with the overall pattern of Castil-

---

Segundo Congreso de Academias de la Lengua Española 487-95 (Madrid, 1956). This speech was also published in *BAAL* 21.429-43 (1956); and in *CHA* 7:78/79.253-62 (1956).

[3] Dámaso Alonso, 'Unidad y defensa del idioma', *MSCALE* 33-48 (Madrid, 1956). It can be seen also in *CHA* 7:78/79.277-88 (1956); and in his book *Del Siglo de Oro a este siglo de siglas* 237-60 (Madrid, 1962).

[4] A lecture delivered for the first time in Jena, 1933, and later published in Caracas, *Anales del Instituto Pedagógico*, 1949; in Paris, Librairie des Éditions Espagnoles, 1951; and in Lima, Universidad Nacional de San Marcos, 1960 (offprint of *Sphinx* 13.68-88).

ian, rather than in the features which are peculiar to American Spanish compared with Peninsular Spanish. In other words it is unity which rests on the common Hispanic root (phonological, as well as grammatical and even lexical) of American Spanish. 'The destiny of the language reflects the cultural ideal of its speakers'. Rosenblat was of the opinion that the ideal tended towards universality on the basis of a common language which, in turn, is the result of a common Hispanic culture.

When this disturbing problem was presented in the Asamblea de Filología of the First Congress of Hispanic Institutions in Madrid, in June of 1963, all the linguists present declared their confidence in the future of the language.[5] G. Carrillo Herrera, in 'Tendencias a la unificación idiomática hispanoamericana e hispana. Factores externos', *PFLE* 2. 17-34,[6] placed a special emphasis on the differences which exist between contemporary cultural conditions and those present at the time of the downfall of the Roman Empire. A unifying element today, he indicated, lies in the process of urbanization of rural speech, which is a consequence of the migration to big urban centers of provincial people, a fact that brings with it the elimination of dialectal varieties under the leveling impact of the standard language instead of promoting their further propagation.

V. García de Diego, in 'Los malos y buenos conceptos de la unidad del castellano', *PFLE* 2.5-16, based his optimism on the assured predominance of language (*lengua*) speech organized into a system and discipline, over speech (*habla*), which is free and thus carries a diversifying tendency. He pointed out that the differences which exist in American Spanish are perhaps smaller than those existing among the different regions of the Peninsula. A similar confidence was revealed by A. Herrero Mayor in 'Presente y futuro de la lengua española en América', *PFLE* 2.109-26,[7] and by Luis Alfonso in 'Tendencias actuales del español en la Argentina', *PFLE* 1.161-82 (1964), although Alfonso showed the dangers to which the language is exposed and considered that it was necessary to keep a vigilant and active attitude. Dámaso Alonso, in 'Para evitar la diversificación de nuestra lengua', *PFLE* 2.259-68 (1964),[8] proposed several measures to offset those dangers, such as to create an institution for overseeing and protecting Castilian. This institution would operate in collaboration with the Asociación de Academias de la Lengua and would be entrusted to expand education — especially linguistic education — in the schools and universities, also to unify the lexicon, a mainly technical task; its motto should be 'unification rather than purism'. A concrete result from this congress was the creation of the Oficina Internacional de Información y Observación del Español, seated in Madrid and made up of linguists from all Spanish-speaking countries. Its primary mission will be to take care of the unity of the language, trying to eliminate differences and channeling its harmonious evolution.

[5] The text of these addresses has been published in two volumes (Madrid, Oficina Internacional de Información y Observación del Español, 1964).

[6] Published also in *Arbor* 55:211/212.21-42 (1963).

[7] Published in *BAAL* 38.55-87 (1963), basically following the ideas of his book of the same title published in Buenos Aires by the Institución Cultural Española in 1943.

[8] Also published in *Arbor* 55:211/212.7-20 (1963).

2. *General Studies*

There are not enough studies available for an overall understanding of American Spanish in its basic characteristics. A general work of synthesis[9] is almost impossible for lack of reliable national monographs. The only manual which presents such global vision is the little book by Max L. Wagner mentioned above, *Lingua e dialetti dell'America Spagnola* (Firenze, 1949). It is a work for the general public, summing up the data which were available at that moment, and offering a rather complete bibliography. Basically using lexical material, it shows the strong archaism typical of American Spanish and highlights its surprising homogeneity as a consequence of the short time in which the colonization of Spanish America took place, carried out mostly by men of the low social classes. He lists the main evolutionary facets of the process — which coincide with those that took place in the Peninsula — and then points out the lexical and semantic differences (nautical terms, indigenous terms, neologisms, derivative suffixes). Likewise, he takes up the problem of the influence of substratum languages, a question to which we will refer later. Finally, he lists the main peculiarities of each of the large zones into which he considers American Spanish to be divided: Mexico and Central America; the Antilles; the Andes zone; Chile; and the Plate River area. Later studies have forced us to modify some of Wagner's statements.

In a chapter devoted to the 'Español de América', Alonso Zamora Vicente quickly goes over, in *Dialectología española*, 306-61 (Madrid, 1960), the main peculiarities of American Spanish and makes a rapid survey of the most important problems, such as indigenous influence, andalucianism, and *voseo*. He also presents a list of the typical features (phonetic, grammatical, lexical) of the different Spanish-American areas, although he occasionally makes some imprecise generalizations.

Joaquim Ribeiro, in *História da romanização da América* (Rio de Janeiro, 1959), has tried to sum up the data presently available on the development of Portuguese, Spanish, and French in the New World, although he concentrates almost entirely on Portuguese and ignores many important studies about American Spanish. The best analyzed aspect is the lexical one.

Arturo Agüero Chaves offers a modest but well organized survey of the linguistic history of Spanish America in his books about *El español en América* (San José de Costa Rica, 1960), and *El español de América y Costa Rica* (San José, 1962). Less valuable is the study by M. Sanchís Guarner, 'Sobre los problemas de la lengua castellana en América', *PSA* 19.138-68 (1960), because his résumé is based on relatively antiquated studies already surpassed by later investigations. Thus, for example, Sanchís Guarner denies the Andalucian influence, considering — like Henríquez

9 Aurelio M. Espinosa Jr. spoke of this sad situation of Spanish American dialectology in 'Unsolved problems in Spanish and Spanish American linguistics', *Hispania* 34.233-39 (1951), showing the big lacunae in our knowledge of American speech. Some of the errors of the dialectological investigation done in Mexico were shown in my address to the first meeting of *ALFAL*, entitled 'Dolencias de la dialectología mexicana' (Viña del Mar, 1964).

Ureña — that the American *seseo* is an independent development from Andalusian. He seemingly ignores the studies of Lapesa, Menéndez Pidal, Catalán, and others which I will mention later and which were published before 1960. It seems evident that in order to make an overall, and at the same time, detailed study of American Spanish, it is necessary to rely on the availability of a whole series of specific studies dealing with the different dialectal zones of each of the Spanish-American countries.[10]

An idea of how much is still needed can be found in the inventory by Gerardo Moldenhauer, *Filología y lingüística. Esencia, problemas actuales y tareas en la Argentina* (Santa Fe, 1952). This study reveals that, in spite of all the work already accomplished in one of the countries with a strong philological tradition, it is still necessary, 1) to organize complete bibliographical catalogues of an analytical nature; 2) to carry out an urgently needed study of indigenous languages, viewed in themselves as well as substratum tongues; 3) to calibrate the influence of adstratum tongues (that of immigrants); 4) to do thorough lexicographical studies (particularly studies of archaisms, neologisms, and regionalisms), as well as studies of folklore, family names, and place names.

3. *Methodology and Linguistic Geography*

There are also insufficient methodological studies. These studies could guide and facilitate a rigorous investigation of American Spanish. One of the most instructive in this respect is Eugenio Coseriu's *La geografía lingüística* (Montevideo, 1956), a clear and concise explanation of methods, problems, aims, and results of linguistic geography. He describes the different types of linguistic maps and analyzes the criteria and procedures followed in the main atlases then available, i.e. Gilliéron's for French, Jaberg and Jud's for Italian and Southern Swiss, Bottiglioni's for Sardinian, Pușcariu's for Rumanian, Griera's for Catalan, etc.

T. Navarro Tomás' *Cuestionario lingüístico hispanoamericano* (Universidad de Buenos Aires, 1943; 2ª edición, 1945) was the first one to be published in Spanish America, and has served as a basis for later questionnaires — the Colombian one, for instance — and also as a guide for many studies of local speech to which I will refer later. Although this work is a general guide to be adapted to the specific requirements of each zone, it is undoubtedly a most useful one, for it gives ample consideration to grammatical problems, especially morphology, an aspect of language very often neglected by other questionnaires.

José Pedro Rona studies certain basic principles of dialectal investigation in his *Algunos aspectos metodológicos de la dialectología hispanoamericana* (Montevideo, 1958). It is indispensable, he says, to define dialectal levels exactly, as well as the

[10] Unfortunately, this situation is not likely to materialize soon, since Angel Rosenblat, some years ago, decided to write a general manual of American Spanish with the means then available and his own knowledge of Spanish-American speech, an enterprise so vast that he has not yet been able to complete it.

different cultural strata (which are not the same in America as in Spain), and to determine the number and real extension of the different Spanish-American dialects, using only linguistic tools. He also considers it necessary to study the causes of dialectal fragmentation, both those which are not within the system (indigenous substrata, adstratum languages, etc.) and those which are systematic (implicit tendencies in the Spanish linguistic system, the influence of the dialects spoken by Spanish colonists). Stanley Robe has also made some 'Sugerencias para una metodología de la dialectología hispanoamericana' in his address to the 1st Meeting of the Asociación de Lingüística y Filología de América Latina (Viña del Mar, 1964; still unpublished). Ambrosio Rabanales, in his *Introducción al estudio del español de Chile* (Santiago de Chile, 1953), presented a very important question: the definition of the linguistic concept of *americanismo* and, consequently, those of *chilenismo*, *mexicanismo*, *argentinismo*, etc. After showing the disadvantages and limitations of the different criteria thus far used, he reaches the limited conclusion that only the origin of the different forms can help define and characterize them. Thus, he only considers a true chilenism 'every expression, be it oral, written or somatological, originated in Chile regardless of its grammatical nature'.

The relative homogeneity of the Spanish spoken in America (higher, even, than that of Peninsular Spanish) is something noticed by many specialists. However, José Pedro Rona, in 'El problema de la división del español americano en zonas dialectales', *PFLE* 1.215-26, considers this homogeneity only apparent and wrongly based on the simplistic dialectal division of Spanish America into five large zones, as was done by Henríquez Ureña almost half a century ago, using extrasystematic criteria (cf. *RFE* 7.357-90 [1921]). Taking into account the phenomena of *yeísmo* (/ļ/ and /y/ equated), of *žeísmo* (*rehilamiento* of /y/) and the *voseo* (in its four different morphological manifestations) Rona thinks it is possible to distinguish among twenty-three different zones in American Spanish. Naturally, the phenomena used to establish these dialectal partitions should only be considered useful to exemplify a particular case. They would not be valid to establish a dialectal division in countries or regions where the *voseo* does not occur or where there is overall *yeísmo*. However, these phenomena reveal how necessary it is to rely on linguistic facts, rather than on extrasystematic data, in order to establish dialect regions.

The work of linguistic geography is still embryonic in Spanish America. So far, the only complete study already published is that of Tomás Navarro, *El español en Puerto Rico. Contribución a la geografía lingüística hispanoamericana* (Río Piedras, 1948), which is not only a careful description of the present state of Spanish in this Caribbean island but is also an excellent methodological approach to how the main questions of dialect geography should be treated — an approach applicable to other Ibero-American countries. Because of the small size of Puerto Rico, the forty-three localities chosen by Tomás Navarro to make his survey — with a questionnaire of 445 questions, including those phonetic, grammatical, and lexical — form a really tight network. The results of his investigation are reflected in seventy-five maps in which the author has tried to summarize each phonetic or grammatical phenomenon, allowing for manifestations of certain lexical items carefully selected, instead of making an accumulation of maps referring to all and each one of these items, many of which would have no illustrative value. It is surprising, with regard to the lexicon, the variety of designations gathered in such a small territory, although it is not possible to establish a clear demarcation of dialect zones, since the isoglosses of the different phenomena do not always coincide. Navarro seeks out carefully the explanation for the different linguistic facts, be it in the tradition of Peninsular rural Spanish, the independent development of the system in Puerto Rico, in the native substratum or African influence or, finally, in the regional (western) ancestry of colonists of the island.

With the exception of Puerto Rico, no other country in America has been mapped. For several years now, the Instituto Caro y Cuervo in Bogotá has been preparing the complete linguistic atlas of Colombia, and the field surveys, directed by Luis Flórez, are already well advanced. Tomás Buesa Oliver and Luis Flórez, in *El atlas lingüístico-etnográfico de Colombia. Cuestionario preliminar* (Bogotá, 1954),[11] have carefully explained the procedure followed in the realization of what will be the first atlas of one of the large Spanish-American countries. In the preparation of the preliminary questionnaire, they took into consideration the questionnaires used in the main European atlases (basically that of Navarro Tomás for the *Atlas lingüístico de la Península Ibérica*). They also expanded the questions relative to the lexicon in order to cover the realities proper to the Colombian way of life. They selected some 250 localities, not symmetrically distributed, but according to the prospective linguistic interest in each zone. Approximately 46,000 speakers belong to each of those areas of investigation. They decided to use informants of both sexes and of the same generation — between forty and sixty years of age — and always taperecord all interviews, in order to start building an archive of Colombian speech. In that first publication, the authors of the project provided the phonetic transcription which was to be used — an extremely detailed system, perhaps excessively complicated, since it is difficult to admit that any human ear could distinguish more than fifty allophones of vowel /e/ and as many of /o/, all of which have specific symbols in their phonetic transcription. The first surveys revealed the impossibility of using that preliminary questionnaire, which included over 8,000 questions — an excessive number for any atlas, and more particularly so for an atlas of nationwide scope. Tomás Buesa and Luis Flórez admitted that themselves in *Cuestionario para el atlas lingüístico-etnográfico de Colombia. Segunda redacción, en experimentación* (Bogotá, 1960). They had to simplify and modify significantly the preliminary questionnaire, reducing the number of questions to 1,348, and completely eliminating the vocabulary of certain particular industries established only in a few places. Thus, they produced a very practical questionnaire, perfectly adequate to the realities of a tropical environment, although the authors stated that

[11] It is an offprint of the article published in *BICC* 10.147-315 (1954). Luis Flórez gave a brief notice of the project in *Orbis* 5.391-92 (1956).

possibly they would have to introduce some changes in this simplified questionnaire when they made the surveys of the mountainous regions of Colombia.

A few years later, this colossal enterprise began to yield its first results. Luis Flórez, in 'El atlas lingüístico-etnográfico de Colombia. Nota informativa', *BICC* 16.77-125 (1961), explained the stage at which the investigations were at the moment, and the modifications (dictated by experience) made to the original plan. Finally, he offered a sample of the phonetic, lexical, and grammatical material already gathered in the districts of Bolívar and Santander, together with some linguistic maps showing the existing differences between the two provinces.[12] Again, Luis Flórez gave an account of the progress made in the project in his address to the Philological Assembly of the 1st Congress of Hispanic Institutions, 'El español hablado en Colombia y su atlas lingüístico', *PFLE* 1.5-78,[13] when he presented fifty-three maps — mostly on lexical questions — in which he included the results obtained in the seventy-three localities visited up to 1962.

This is all that has been done for the moment. There are other projects for linguistic mapping in Spanish America, but it does not seem likely that they will materialize. Arturo Agüero, in 'El español en Costa Rica y su atlas lingüístico', *PFLE* 1.151-2, has voiced his pessimism with regard to the immediate possibility of doing the atlas of Costa Rica, an enterprise much desired and pondered upon, but paralyzed for different reasons before it could be set in motion. Given the small territorial extension of Costa Rica, visits had been planned to only forty localities, which would have allowed the project to be carried through rather briefly.

Other projects exist, such as the linguistic atlas of Chile, but its realization does not seem probable in the near future. Due to the enormous territorial extension of most Spanish-American countries, it is evident that linguistic mapping in America should be done by regions, not entire nations. This is suggested by the experience of the Colombian project. After ten years of work, the Atlas Lingüístico-Etnográfico de Colombia, in spite of the enthusiasm shown by its sponsors, is only half finished. For this reason Luis Flórez has already mentioned the advisability of doing only regional atlases, which would gradually be covering the different geographic zones of Colombia (*BICC* 16.96, 1961).[14] This is precisely what is being done in the countries of Europe — territorially smaller than those of America — since Albert Dauzat made the suggestion. [15] It is true, though, that this fragmentation of territories will make it

[12] Later on (p. 144) I refer to other monographic studies of a descriptive nature — not linguistic geography — which are also the results of field research for the *ALEC*.

[13] Also published in *BICC* 18.269-356 (1963).

[14] This is what is being done in Brazil, where the *Atlas Prévio dos Falares Baianos* of Nelson Rossi has appeared this year (1964).

[15] Cf. A. Dauzat, *Le nouvel atlas linguistique de la France par régions* (Luçon, 1942) also in *Le Français moderne* 10.1-10 (1942). In the Iberian Peninsula only there are now in preparation or in full progress the following regional atlases: Andalusia, by Manuel Alvar, already finished and about to be published; Aragón, the Canary Islands, Rioja, Ayerbe, Navarra, Cataluña, and the Gallician-Portuguese area.

necessary to prepare different questionnaires — at least in part — for each zone. But it is also true that this would allow a deeper understanding of the realities and peculiarities proper to each region, a fact that would amply compensate for the plurality the relative heterogeneity of the questionnaires, and hence, of the results. To be sure, in order to produce these future regional atlases, it will be necessary to determine beforehand — even if it is only provisionally — which are the different dialectal regions of each country or of each zone of the American continent. Hence, the importance of preliminary studies on 'El problema de la división del español americano en zonas dialectales', to which J. P. Rona referred in the above mentioned paper; this problem has received the rigorous and detailed attention it deserves in very few countries.[16]

4. *The substratum languages of American Spanish*

Another question of great importance for Spanish-American dialectology concerns the substratum languages. Since R. Lenz said that the Castilian of Chile was a type of Spanish with Araucanian sounds, that is, a variety of Spanish profoundly modified by the Mapuche substratum, there have been many linguists who have taken up the question to refute or set limitations to Lenz's statement, or to support his theory of the deep influence of substrata on American Spanish. During the last year, several important works about this problem have been published. The books of Angel Rosenblat about Amerindians, *La población indígena de América desde 1492 hasta la actualidad* (Buenos Aires, 1945), and *La población indígena y el mestizaje en América*, 2nd. ed. (Buenos Aires, 1954; 2 volumes), are important as a starting point for this kind of investigation. In his works, the author studies in detail the distribution of population (Indian, White, Negro, and Mestizo) in the different regions of America, using the last demographic data available, and carrying his study in a regressive chronological progression up to the moment of arrival of the Spaniards in the New World. Rosenblat's calculation is that the indigenous population of America at that time was slightly over thirteen million inhabitants, distributed in the following way: approximately one million Indians north of the Río Grande; some 5,600,000 in the Antilles, Mexico, and Central America, out of which four and a half millions lived in the territories that make up today's Mexico; some 6,785,000 Indians lived in South America. Rosenblat also makes a careful analysis of the intermarriage and acculturation processes in each of the American regions and a study of the different castes that were being formed.

[16] Later on, when we deal with studies of a regional or nationwide scope, I will summarize what has been said about the dialectal areas into which Ecuador, Argentina, Chile, and other countries, can be divided. But, of course, whenever those regional lines are established, extreme care should be exercised, paying attention to significant linguistic factors minutely investigated. The research scholar must avoid any impressionistic classification, similar to what P. Henríquez Ureña anticipated with regard to Mexico, without a basis on preliminary field research (see *RFE* 8.359-61 [1921]); or what P. Boyd-Bowman 'suspected' with regard to the so-called 'central area' of this country.

The Araucanian thesis of Lenz was already disputed by Max Leopoldo Wagner in 1920 and by Amado Alonso in 1939.[17] Wagner noticed that many of the phonetic features in the Spanish of Chile that Lenz thought were of Araucanian origin were, in fact, Hispanic, although he admitted some of Lenz's assumptions: for instance, the sibilant pronunciation of /r̄/, the prepalatal articulation of the cluster /tř, the alveolar pronunciation of /d, t, n, s/ when in contact with /r/. Amado Alonso later demonstrated that all these peculiarities of Chilean Spanish could be easily explained within the linguistic system of Castilian. With these developments, the theories about the importance of the substrata in determining the peculiarities of American Spanish were greatly undermined. It was then that the idea of turning to the substratum languages to explain those peculiarities was seriously questioned. Nonetheless, the substratum influence was still acknowledged in many particular cases. The outlook of the question towards the end of World War II was well reflected in the second chapter of M. L. Wagner's book, already mentioned, *Lingua e dialetti dell'America Spagnola*: there is an obvious influence of the native languages in the lexicon, especially from Caribbean languages, which were the first to come in contact with Spanish (*maíz*, *batata*, *sabana*, etc.); there follow in numerical importance items taken from *Náhuatl* (*jícara*, *cacahuate*, *petaca*, etc.), and then — in smaller proportion — words of *Quechua* origin (*cóndor*, *guano*, etc.), from the *Guaraní* (*tapir*, *ñandú*), and from *Araucanian* (*gaucho*). The substratum influence is also evident on intonation, and not lacking either — although in a much smaller scale — on the phonetic system, a fact particularly recognizable on the articulation of glottalized /k', p', t', s'/ through Mayan influence, a characteristic of Yucatan Spanish; or in the consistent use of stress on the syllable before last, which is characteristic of some regions of the Andes (*hácer*), due perhaps to *Quechua* substratum. It is even possible to recognize certain native influences in the morphology and syntax of Spanish in American regions (suffix *-eco*, from Náhuatl *écatl*, for example).[18]

Such was the situation when Bertil Malmberg published a brief but most important article, 'L'espagnol dans le Nouveau Monde', *Studia Linguistica* 1.79-116 (1947) and 2.1-36 (1948),[19] in which he presented the problem of the substrata in American Spanish as a case of interest to general linguistics; i.e. it is possible to analyze in Spanish America, in a living reality, the conflicts originating from the encounter of two different languages. Malmberg is of the opinion that lexical borrowings should not be considered cases of substratum influence, but only those cases showing the effects upon

[17] M. L. Wagner, 'Amerikanisch-Spanisch und Vulgarlätein', *ZRPh* 40.286-312 and 385-404 (1920). Spanish translation, 'El español de América y el latín vulgar', *Cuadernos del Instituto de Filología de la Universidad de Buenos Aires* 1.45-110 (Buenos Aires, 1924). A. Alonso, 'Examen de la teoría indigenista de Rodolfo Lenz', *RFH* 1.313-350 (1939). Also included in his book *ELTH* 2.332-98 (Madrid, 1953).

[18] Some of the Mexican constructions to which Wagner refers are highly disputable: *vuestras personitas de ustedes*, *vosotrititos*, etc., with the use of second person plural pronouns. Nor are the cases of false agreement observed in 'indios que recién chapurrean castellano' (Indians who are just beginning to jabber in Castilian) very illustrative.

[19] It has been published separately in book form (Lund, 1948; 74 pp.)

the grammatical and phonetic system of the invading languages by the substratum language. The analysis of the peculiarities of present Peruvian Spanish (an extremely conservative and 'castiza' variety: apicoalveolar *s*, unaspirated final *-s*, absence of *voseo*, velar *x*), in Chile (a rural variety: aspiration of *-s*, palatalization of *x*, the existence of *voseo*, the abundance of diminutive forms, etc.), in Paraguay (a hybrid variety: traditionally 'castiza' in the preservation of *ḷ*, the hiatuses and the regularly unaspirated final *-s*; in turn influenced by the *Guaraní* in the existence of an initial fricative *ƀ*-, an intervocalic affricate *-ŷ-*, and alveolar *t* and *d*), and in Argentina (an anarchic and rural variety: *voseo*, *y* 'rehilada' > *ž*, aspiration of final *-s*, frequent nasalizations) leads him to the conclusion that 'l'action du substrat est due au *niveau cultural* des vaincues. Elle n'est pas une conséquence immédiate de leur nombre'. Malmberg thinks that, in fact, the traditional and conservative Spanish of Peru can be explained by the cultural history of this zone, where the first American University was founded, and where the *criollos*, numerically inferior to the Indians and *mestizos*, became purists, as always happens with minority groups. That is why neither the phonetics of Quechua nor the Aymará could influence the phonetic system of Peru and Bolivia. On the contrary, the Spanish of Chile, a territory colonized by farmers, has a rural character, without presenting any Araucanian influence in its peculiarities. The cultural situation of Paraguay is, however, very different. There, Guaraní continues to be the mother tongue, the family tongue of all the people, and indeed it enjoys the highest prestige; consequently it may influence the realization of the Castilian phonetic system, which in its capacity of being the official and learned language preserved the Castillian system intact. The cultural situation of Argentina (an isolated region at first, linguistically independent, and later subjected to a strong current of inmigration) also explains the peculiarities of the Castilian spoken there: its popularism and its anarchy. Thus, except in Paraguay — where the cultural conditions of the indigenous substratum are very special — no substantial substratum influence can be detected in the Spanish spoken in America. None of the phonetic or morphological features of American Spanish (*seseo*, *yeísmo*, reduction of the opposition /f/ — /ḥ/, aspiration of *-s*, palatalization of *x*, velarization of final *-n*, diphthongization of hiatuses, *loísmo*, *voseo*, disappearance of morpheme *-se* in the imperfect subjunctive, etc.) need to be explained through influences extraneous to the linguistic system of Spanish.

In spite of the criticisms and objections raised against Malmberg's study,[20] his fundamental theory of the historical and cultural conditions necessary for the effective influence of the substratum seems to have convinced many scholars. Malmberg restated his thesis in the Colloque International des Civilizations, Littératures et Langues Romanes, which took place in Bucarest in 1959, in his 'L'extension du castillan et le problème des substrats', *ACLR* 249-60 (1959). He reached the following conclusions: 1) A general explanation of any linguistic fact is always preferable to a special one; 2) An internal explanation is preferable to any external one (i.e. the substratum

[20] Cf., for instance, those by A. Rosenblat in *NRFH* 4.404-8 (1950); and by Marcos A. Morínigo, *RPh* 4.318-26 (1950-51), included in his book *Programa de filología hispánica* 130-49.

influence); 3) If a linguistic change implies the loss of functional distinctions or functional units, it is better to explain it as a case of reduction on the periphery of the language rather than as a case of substratum influence; 4) Interference (substratum influence) can only be assumed when the change brings about an increase in the number of functional contrasts or a reinterpretation of their interrelations; 5) Substratum influence should only be invoked when the *social* (cultural) situation of a community is such that the cases of interference can be accepted and adopted by the ruling classes.

Again in 1963, B. Malmberg insisted on his point of view with the publication of 'Tradición hispánica e influencia indígena en la fonética hispanoamericana', *PFLE* 2.227-44. In this article he has demonstrated how the phonetic peculiarities of American Spanish generally correspond to the structure or 'genius' of the Castilian phonological system, which is characterized 'by an overwhelming number of open syllables, by the weak pronunciation of implosive consonants which, however, exist, and by a very small number of implosive phonemic contrasts as compared with the overall number of contrasts in syllable initial position' (p. 230). Thus, with the exception of Paraguayan Spanish, evidently influenced by Guaraní, none of the peculiarities of American Spanish 'contradicts the general tendencies of phonetic evolution in Ibero-romance, and, furthermore, none of them has an exclusively American character'. That is why these peculiarities 'should not be explained by the influence of any native tongue' (p. 239). The *seseo*, i.e. the neutralization of the opposition /s/ — /θ/ is nothing but a case of *reducción en la periferia* (peripheral reduction), just like the *yeísmo* and other Spanish-American phonic peculiarities.

In the opinion of Marcos Morínigo, 'La penetración de los indigenismos americanos en el español', *PFLE* 2.217-66, the lexical influence of native American tongues upon Castilian is, undoubtedly, the most important one. He explains how the slow borrowing process into Castillian was effected. But he very accurately points out that 'present day dictionaries of Americanisms compete in adding to their lexicon the greatest number of indigenisms, whether they are used or not in American Spanish, thus distorting the real situation of the indigenous languages and confusing scholars'.

Most studies about substratum influence made in Spanish America continue to be of an exclusively lexical nature. Such is the work of E. Otero D'Costa, 'Mestizajes del castellano en Colombia', *BICC* 2.166-75 (1946) and 6.15-80 (1950), which only with lexical samples — some of them very well documented — reveals the influence of the different native tongues upon Colombian Spanish; particularly by the Taino group and Quechua, and — in a lesser degree — by other Carib languages and Chibcha. Also of an exclusively lexical character is the old study (1935) of Emiliano Tejera, *Palabras indígenas de la isla de Santo Domingo*, reprinted in Ciudad Trujillo in 1951. It is a fairly useful work, in spite of its serious philological limitations, because it offers an interesting documentation of each old word, with quotations from chroniclers, geographers, and historical documents.

In 'Argentinismos de origen indígena', *BAAL* 20.37-95 (1951), Juan B. Selva has gathered a fairly large number of Quechua, Araucanian, and Guaraní words, alphabetically listed. Very seldom does he give the etymology of words, or the geographic extension of the area in which they are used, and even more rarely does he offer the cultural environment to which they belong. And what is worse, he includes doubtful terms or even words that obviously are not of American origin. The dictionary assembled by Walterio Meyer Rusca, *Voces indígenas del lenguaje popular sureño. 550 chilenismos* (Osorno, 1952) is not very valuable either, because it is based on rather old studies (especially the *Diccionario etimológico* of R. Lenz), stripping them of all their erudite apparatus — his being a work addressed to the general public — and making few and not very fortunate additions.

Also a work for the general public is the study of L. Flórez, 'Algunas voces indígenas en el español de Colombia', *RCA* 4.285-310 (1955), in which he has some commentaries about different words from Arahuaco, Carib, Náhuatl, Quechua, and Chibcha. I. Bar-Lewaw's article 'Traces of the Nahuatl language in Mexican Castilian', *AION-SR* 5.183-99 (1963), collects some words from Aztec used today in Mexican Spanish — especially plant names, domestic implements and meals, place names, and some other Nahuatl words which have spread down to Costa Rica. Undoubtedly more rigorous and scientific is the lexicon gathered by Hugo Gunckel, 'Nombres indígenas relacionados con la flora chilena', *BFS* 11.191-327 (1959), which is part of a *Diccionario de nombres de plantas chilenas*, in preparation. In his article he includes more than 1,500 terms and variations with their phonetic transcriptions, corresponding to almost 600 plants.[21]

Other aspects of the possible influence of substratum have occupied the attention of Angel Rosenblat in *El castellano de Venezuela: la influencia indígena* (Caracas, 1958),[22] who thinks that such influence is unquestionable in the different intonations of the different regions in the country. Perhaps some examples would be the strength of consonantism in the Andes, the strongly sibilant character of its /s/, also the pronunciation *-ún* instead of *-ón* typical of the Palmar region and, perhaps also the suffixes *-oco* (*zaperoco* 'alboroto') and *-eco*. On the other hand, he reports no case of syntactic influence, and points to the scarcity of native terms in the Spanish of Venezuela. Antonio Mediz Bolio, in *Interinfluencia del maya con el español de Yucatán* (Mérida, 1951),[23] believes it is possible to find enough Maya features in Yucatan Spanish to

[21] Lexical studies of this nature abound in Spanish America. About the lexical influence of Quechua, I understand that during the past few years the following studies, among others, have been published: Manuel M. Muñoz Cueva, *La pesca de José Mendes o correcciones al lenguaje usual* (Cuenca, Ecuador, 1959); Arturo Pazos, *Glosario de quechuismos colombianos* (Bogota, 1961); María Delia Millán de Palavecino, 'Lexicografía de la vestimenta en el area de influencia del quechua', *Folia Lingüística Americana* 1:1.37-69 (1952); J. M. B. Farfán, 'Quechuismos. Su ubicación y reconstrucción etimológica', *RMNac* 26.52-64 (Lima, 1957); 27.40-58 (1958); 28.19-39 (1959); O. Corvalán, 'El substratum quechua en Santiago del Estero', *Humanitas* 3.85-94 (Tucumán, 1956), who thinks that certain phonetic, grammatical, and lexical features are of Quechua origin, although they can well be explained without recourse to this native language, as David Lagmonovich demonstrated in 'Sobre el español de Santiago del Estero', *Humanitas* 3:8.55-70 (1957), in reply to Corvalán's article.

[22] An offprint of the article published in the *BIV* 3-5:1-4.89-107 (1955-57).

[23] Also published in *Yikal Maya Than* 12.153-54, 156-61, 167-68, 171-74 (Mérida, 1951); and in *Memorias de la Academia Mexicana de la Lengua* 14.29-41 (1956).

consider that variety of Spanish as a hybrid language. He thinks the characteristic intonation of Yucatan is of Mayan origin, as well as certain syntactic units which are common in that region (impersonal active construction in passive form: *Este vestido me lo regalaron por mi hermana*) and some other examples which may very well have a Hispanic root. In a rather impressionistic way, J. I. Dávila Garibi feels that there is a 'possible Náhuatl influence in the use and abuse of the diminutive in Mexican Spanish' (*Estudios de Cultura Náhuatl* 1.91-4, 1959), but there are no reasons to believe that such a phenomenon is not a strictly Spanish development. J. I. Dávila Garibi himself, in his *Algunas analogías fonéticas entre el romanceamiento castellano de voces latinas y la castellanización de vocablos nahuas* (México, 1954), has attempted to describe the general rules followed by Nahua terms when brought into Castilian: loss of unstressed vowels or of the vowel in the Aztec suffix (*huacalli* > *huacal*); palatalization of *tz-* (*tzictli* > *chicle*); sonorization of intervocalic *-p-* (*Tlacopan* > *Tacuba*); opening of final *-i* (*molli* > *mole*). But since 'the formation of Nahuatlisms was not uniform throughout the country', these general rules have a very limited value.

It can be seen, consequently, from all I have said, that the study of the influence of native tongues upon Castilian has barely begun. It would be necessary for those engaged in the investigation of American Spanish to have a relatively profound knowledge of the substratum languages, or that the specialists in these native tongues would be more interested in analyzing the peculiarities of American Spanish. There is, unfortunately, a serious lack of communication between the Indianists and the Hispanicists. This is a situation which causes, in many cases, the mutual influences between Spanish and the substratum languages, of which scholars speak, to be nothing but sheer impressions, more or less justified intuitions. It so happens that sometimes facts which are taken to originate in a specific substratum influence are also found in other parts of America with different substratum tongues, or even in parts of the Iberian Peninsula. There seems to be some unanimity in considering the particular intonation of each American zone as a phenomenon due to indigenous influence. However, there are no serious comparative studies of the indigenous intonations held responsible for these Spanish-American peculiarities, nor has there been enough consideration of the fact that sometimes very different Castilian intonations exist in a region subjected to the influence of only one substratum, differences which perhaps depend on the different cultural levels of the speakers. On lexical grounds, where the substratum influences are more easily perceived, there has been much exageration, as M. A. Morínigo has very well pointed out in the above mentioned work. It has even happened that native etymologies have been given of words which are well documented in fifteenth-century Spanish. It would be necessary to indicate the vitality of each of the indigenisms gathered in the different countries of Spanish America, because in many dictionaries prepared without regard for geographic or cultural facts, many words are gathered which are unknown by the majority, or even the totality, of speakers in the country. Obviously, not the same interest is offered by a native term of general use in the standard language of the country, as a specialized one, such as words referring to the flora or the toponymy peculiar to a certain region, which, strictly speaking, are not even part of the lexical system of the language. Furthermore, on the whole, the immense majority of words gathered in the vocabularies of indigenisms are words of fauna or flora or local toponymies while common terms which designate everyday realities hardly add up to a hundred. As long as thorough and careful research is not carried out in this domain, B. Malmberg's theory about the absolute weakness of the substratum influence would have to be accepted almost without reservations.

5. *The problem of the Andalusian influence*

Henríquez Ureña reacted strongly in 1921 against the general opinion believing in the Andalusian character of American Spanish, an opinion which had been formulated in a rather impressionistic and imprecise form at the end of the seventeenth century, and which had been echoed by Menéndez Pidal, Wagner, and other linguists. In the ensuing polemic with Wagner,[24] he completely denied any Andalusian character in American Spanish, considering that American *seseo* and *yeísmo* are independent from Andalusian *seseo* and *yeísmo*, and even chronologically prior to the latter. Besides, he believed that the number of Andalusian colonists was no greater than that of Castilians or of other people from other regions of Spain. So ardently did Henríquez Ureña maintain his anti-Andalusian position[25] that he carried along many other linguists,[26] including M. L. Wagner. Wagner, in fact, upon the publication in 1949 of his *Lingua e dialetti dell'America Spagnola*, renounces the Andalusian theory (80-1) and admits that the conquerors of America came 'da tutte le province della Spagna' (p. 18). Amado Alonso, a friend and collaborator of Henríquez Ureña, dedicated himself to the task of proving how unfounded the Andalusian theory was. In order

[24] Cf. *RFE* 8.357-90 (1921); 14.20-32 (1927); 17.277-84 (1930); 18.120-48 (1931); and *Cuadernos del Instituto de Filología de Buenos Aires* 1:2.114-22 (Buenos Aires, 1925).

[25] Guillermo L. Guitarte has published an excellent study titled 'Cuervo, Henríquez Ureña y la polémica sobre el andalucismo de América', *VR* 17.363-416 (1958), reprinted in *BICC* 14.20-81 (1959), in which he shows how Henríquez Ureña had approached this linguistic question with an inflamed patriotic fervor, according with the 'Americanist nationalism' prevailing in his time. Besides, he offers very pertinent evaluations about what had been written at the time about that problem.

[26] Thus, A. Rosenblat wrote in 1933: 'El pretendido andalucismo de América es un mito que desecha la moderna investigación histórica y filológica' (The pretended Andalusianism of American Spanish is a myth rejected by modern historical and philological research). It is true, though, that not all were carried by Henríquez Ureña's opinion, perhaps because they did not know about it, or perhaps because they did not consider it convincing. This is what happens, for instance, in the case of W. J. Entwistle, in *The Spanish Language* (London, 1936), who maintained his conviction about the general Andalusian character of American Spanish, a particularly intense character in the lowlands. A long time afterwards, D. Molina y Vedia (*BICC* 1.367-74 (1945)) insisted on defending the Andalusian theory, indicating a new way to prove it by comparing Andalusian with the Spanish-American lexicon; his observations, however, were insufficient.

to do that, he attempted to demonstrate rigorously that the American *seseo* and *yeísmo* are independent from the parallel phenomena of the Andalusian dialect[27] and that American *yeísmo* in particular could not have an Andalusian origin since it was a hundred years older than Andalusian *yeísmo*[28] (252-3). 'Andalusia has probably been the first place where *yeísmo* has been developed within Spain, but *yeísmo* has not had the same extension elsewhere as in Andalusia. ... The phenomenon is unquestionably autochthonous in America, in the various American regions' (252-3). And this is so, because the oldest documentation of this phenomenon is American (in Lima, towards 1680), while the first documented proof of Andalusian *yeísmo* dates from the last decades of the eighteenth century. Of the same opinion is Tomás Navarro in 'Nuevos datos sobre el yeísmo en España', *BICC* 19.1-17 (1964), when he comments on some data included in the first volume of the *Atlas lingüístico de la Península Ibérica*: 'Literary attestations on Andalusian *yeísmo* begin in the second half of the eighteenth century, a century after those of Spanish-American *yeísmo*. One would suppose that each arose independently because of analogous tendencies and that they existed in speech for a longer or shorter period before being reflected in literature' (p. 14). Amado Alonso's assumption that each of the focal points of *yeísmo* should have sprung up spontaneously and independently seems to find confirmation in the fact that, during the last centuries of the Middle Ages, examples of *yeísmo* developed in Aragonese regions, as revealed by Juan Corominas in 'Para la fecha del yeísmo y del lleísmo', *NRFH* 7.81-7 (1953). Alvaro Galmés de Fuente in 'Le—yeísmo y otras cuestiones lingüísticas en un relato morisco del siglo XVII', *EMP* 7.273-307 (1957), on the other hand, thinks that it is possible to date Peninsular *yeísmo*, specifically Andalusian, back to the first decade of the seventeenth century, in accordance with a Moorish manuscript reflecting the state of the language in 1609. According to this, he believes that Andalusian *yeísmo* should be related to the *yeísmo* of the Andalusianized regions of America, i.e. coastal regions. But still, A. Alonso, in his study 'La base lingüística del español americano',[29] denied the Andalusian basis of American Spanish for the same reasons and because he considered that Andalusian colonists were not more numerous than Castilians (p. 15). However, during the last years of his life, A. Alonso softened substantially his anti-Andalusian position. Already in his revision of the article mentioned in note 27, which he published under the title 'Orígenes del seseo americano', *ELTH* 102-50, he acknowledges that Andalusian *seseo* existed prior to the time he had thought it did (the confusion of *-z* and *-s* in final position is already documented for the fourteenth century), and he also admits that the great number of Andalusians who migrated to America could create a favorable ground for this confusion, although he in no way admits that they were the cause of it, since the two

[27] Cf., for instance, 'La pronunciación americana de la *z* y la *ç* en el siglo XVI', *Universidad de La Habana* 4:23.62-83 (1939), where he states that the process of Spanish American *seseo* (equating *z* = /ẑ̦/, *ç* = /ș̂/ and *s*) is independent from Andalusian.

[28] Cf. A. Alonso's 'La *ll* y sus alteraciones en España y América', *EMP* 2.41-90 (1951). Also in his book *ELTH* 2.196-262 (Madrid, 1962).

[29] Included also in this book *ELTH* 2.7-72.

developments are somewhat different: 'This Andalusian linguistic process and that of American *seseo* are heterogeneous, and it is therefore linguistically impossible that one be the continuation of the other' (p. 141).[30] A similar opinion is also maintained in his article 'Historia del ceceo y del seseo españoles', *BICC* 7.111-200 (1951), where he states that the phenomenon of the *ceceo-seseo* developed 'preferably in the area of imported Castilian (Andalusia and the areas abroad) and more particularly in those where it was taken by regionally heterogeneous settlers', because there is usually in this type of community a tendency towards linguistic simplification. Given the fact that 'the change did not have one, but many focal areas', he still believes that American *seseo* is an independent development which fit the general state of the language in the sixteenth century. He admits, nonetheless, that in this process of linguistic leveling directed towards the creation of a common and homogeneous linguistic vehicle 'Andalusians did not ferment but did foment the change' (p. 200). Only in one particular instance did A. Alonso admit the Andalusianism of an American feature: that of the confusion between implosive *-r* and *-l* the results of which coincide both in Andalusia and the Caribbean and show an indubitable Caribbean Andalusianism, understood 'in its origins as a style as the dominance of the Andalusian modality', which later 'Negro populations carried to extremes' (A. Alonso y R. Lida 'Geografía fonética: *-r* y *-l* en España y América', *RFH* 7.313-45 [1945]; and in A. Alonso's book *Temas hispanoamericanos*, 263-331; cf. p. 327 and 331).

Later investigations by several linguists have modified substantially the anti-Andalusianist theory of Henríquez Ureña and even of A. Alonso.[31] First, Peter Boyd-Bowman's studies about the regional origins of American colonists[32] revealed that the small amount of data used by Henríquez Ureña was totally insufficient and distorted the real situation. Boyd-Bowman's statistics show that all throughout the

[30] A. Tortoló's 'La legitimidad gramatical del seseo hispanoamericano', *CHA* 27.311-19 (1956) simply echoes this opinion. He makes of it a question of Spanish-American honor when he requests from the Academia de la Lengua the orthoëpic recognition of the *seseo*. Again A. Tortoló, in 'La legitimidad gramatical de la pronunciación hispanoamericana', *BACL* 5.50-124 (1956), made a passionate apologia for the American *yeísmo* and *seseo*, using previous studies somewhat superficially, particularly studies by A. Alonso, in order to end agitation for the Academia to sanction Spanish-American orthoëpic pattern with its authority, recognizing that this pattern is different, but as honorable as Castilian.

[31] I think it is pertinent to recall that the authoritative studies by A. Alonso were not enough to convince some linguists, who maintained their support of the Andalusian theory. Such was the case, for instance, with D. Lincoln Canfield, who in 'Andalucismos en la pronunciación salvadoreña', *Hispania* 36.32-3 (1953), considered many of the peculiarities of Salvadoran Spanish of Andalusian roots, such as: its articulatory weakening (nasalization of vowels, which weakens or eliminates nasals, diphthongization of hiatuses, unvoicing of final vowels, velarization of final *-n*, aspiration of *-s*, etc.); its archaism (occlusive pronunciation of *-b-*, *-d-*, and *-g-*, aspiration of *h-*, etc.) and cases of over correction. Cf. also his 'Andalucismos en la pronunciación hispanoamericana', *Kentucky Foreign Language Quarterly* 8.177-81 (1961).

[32] Boyd-Bowman has now in press a very extensive study, called *Indice geobiográfico de* 40.000 *pobladores españoles de América en el siglo XVI*, which will be published by the Instituto Caro y Cuervo of Bogota in several volumes. As preview of his investigation he has published some articles: 'Regional origins of the earliest Spanish colonists of America', *PMLA* 71.1152-72 (1956), and 'La emigración peninsular a América: 1520-1539', *Historia Mexicana* 13.165-92 (1963).

sixteenth century the proportion of Andalusian colonists was far superior to those from other Spanish regions. Especially during the first period of the conquest (Caribbean period: 1493-1519), a period of formation of the Spanish transplanted to the New World, the Andalusians accounted for forty percent of the Spanish immigrants. They came for the most part from the provinces of Sevilla and Huelva. Beginning in 1520, the number of Andalusians somewhat diminishes, but they still outnumber Castilians. From 1580 the percentage of Andalusians again rises substantially, particularly those from Sevilla. It is also interesting to notice that the number of women going to the New World were for the most part Andalusians, making up sixty-seven per cent during the Caribbean period, while the number of women from Old Castile was only eight per cent. Boyd-Bowman also takes into account the destination of these immigrants, pointing out that the Andalusian population in Santo Domingo was as large as that made up by all the other Spanish regions together; the proportion was not so favorable to the Andalusians in the case of Peru.

Another significant fact is brought out by J. Pérez Vidal's observations in 'Aportación de Canarias a la población de América', *AEA* 1.91-197 (1955), to the effect that the majority of immigrants sailing from the Canary Islands during the first half of the sixteenth century were Andalusians — particularly from the Atlantic provinces of Andalusia — Cádiz, Sevilla, Huelva — and from Extremadura. Pérez Vidal thinks that a true linguistic community existed between Andalusia and America, with the Canary Islands acting as a link. This linguistic community is evidenced by the type of *s* which is more of the Andalusian type than Castilian, an end result from the old sibilants *s*, *ss*, *ç*, and *z*; by the aspiration of syllable final *-s* (*dehpuéh*); by the assimilation of *s* to the following consonant (*mimmo*); by the resulting *j* from the group *-sg-* (*dijusto*); by the aspiration of *h-* from *f-*; by the reduction of /x/ to a weak voiceless aspiration; by the disuse of *vosotros* replaced by *ustedes*; by the frequent use of the diminutive in its *-ito* form; by the widespread use of the periphrasis *ir* + gerund (*voy a ir cavando*); by the preservation of certain archaisms (*candela*, *demorar*); and by the abundance of certain maritime terms (*balde*, *bandazo*, *jalar*, *fletar*).

Furthermore, Rafael Lapesa has demonstrated in 'Sobre el ceceo y el seseo en Hispanoamérica', *RI* 21.409-16 (1946), (an advance and résumé of the more extensive work titled 'Sobre el ceceo y seseo andaluces', *Homenaje a Martinet*, 1.67-94, 1957), that Spanish-American *seseo* indeed has — contrary to what A. Alonso thought — an Andalusian origin. In fact, Andalusian *seseo* was already in progress when the first trips of Columbus took place; new testimonies gathered by Lapesa prove that the confusion is very old in Andalusia (documented in the *Cancionero de Baena*, collected before 1445: *çatan*, *çedal*) and that this phenomenon enjoyed a great vitality towards the end of the fifteenth century, even though it did not succeed in higher cultural levels until 1560 or 1570. On the other hand, what today is called *seseo* — and what was called *ceceo, zezeo* during the sixteenth century — was historically *çeçeo* or *zezeo*, since it meant the substitution of coronal or predorsal convex /s/ for the apicoalveolar concave /s/, resulting from old *ç* or *z*; that is to say, it meant that the alveolar sibilants were articulated as dental or interdental: the two dental affricates *ç* or *c* [= ŝ] and *z* [= ẑ] came to be articulated as dental *fricatives* and later were assimilated with the two apicoalveolar fricatives *s*- or *ss* [= ṡ] and -*s*- [= ż], forcing the latter into a dental pronunciation. The Andalusian confusion of *ss, s, ç, z* was pronounced either with the hissing *siseo* of coronal or predorsal [s] or with the soft muffled *ciceo* of [θ̣] or [θ]; both were varieties of the so-called *ceceo* — *zezeo*, since both originate from the old *ç* or *z*, and not from the apicoalveolar *s*. In America, the variety was the hissing *siseo* — as it was first in Seville and later in Cordoba and other Andalusian regions; the American regions presently using *ceceo* could be the remnants of a fluctuating period, which perhaps existed during the first years of the colonization, or perhaps the result of an independent and modern evolution of convex dental [s]. All this — together with the geobiographical data provided by Boyd-Bowman — leads Lapesa to the conviction that indeed there was Andalusianism in the Spanish brought to America by the colonists, especially in the linguistic leveling that occurred during the Caribbean period.

Diego Catalán, in 'El çeçeo-zezeo al comenzar la expansión atlántica de Castilla', *BF* 16.306-34 (1957), has reached conclusions similar to those of Lapesa: the *ceceo* (pronunciation of apicoalveolar /ss/ and /s/ as dorso-dental /ç/ and /z/) came gradually into being during the fifteenth century, so that during the first quarter of the sixteenth century it was already a common phenomenon in Seville, and, for that matter, not a vulgar one or belonging to the speech of the underworld (*habla germanesca*), a fact which 'decidedly leads one to discard the idea, so generally accepted nowadays, that the origin of American *çeçeo* is completely independent of Andalusian *çeçeo*' (p. 332). Shortly afterwards, Diego Catalán reiterated, in *Génesis del español atlántico. Ondas varias a través del océano* (La Laguna de Tenerife, 1958),[33] his theory not only of the Andalusian character of American Spanish, but even of its 'sevillano' character as implicit in the data furnished by Boyd-Bowman, which clearly show 'that during the Antilles period of colonization the Andalusians from Seville clearly dominate in number, unity and prestige' (p. 236). The Caribbean process of leveling — with its typical *çezeo* — is very similar to that in the Spanish of the Canary Islands where this phenomenon had already taken root most definitely towards 1500. This fact allows the supposition that the Canary Islands acted as a link between Andalusian and American Spanish.[34]

Ramón Menéndez Pidal, in 'Sevilla frente a Madrid. Algunas precisiones sobre el

[33] An address delivered at the *Simposio de Filologia Românica*, 233-42 (Rio de Janeiro, 1959).

[34] Confirming the data presented by J. Pérez Vidal in 'Aportación de Canarias a la población de América', (cf. supra), in which he points to the obvious influence of the Canary Islands in the speech of St. Bernard, Louisiana (cf. R. R. MacCurdy mentioned on page 141), there is also a parallel case in Brazilian Portuguese, especially that of Rio Grande do Sul and Santa Catarina, where a notable influence of the speech of the Azores can be perceived. It was from the Azores that a strong migration took place at the beginning of the seventeeth century (cf. M. de Paiva Boléo, *Filologia e História: A emigração açoriana para o Brasil* (Coimbra, 1945).

español de América', *Homenaje Martinet* 3.99-165 (1962), and Diego Catalán in 'El español canario. Entre Europa y América', *BF* 19.317-37 (1960), have come even further concerning the Andalusian character of American Spanish. Menéndez Pidal notices how many other phenomena of an Andalusian nuance are repeated in American Spanish — and, according to D. Catalán, in the Spanish of the Canary Islands as well: aspiration of final *-s*; neutralization of implosive *-r* and *-l*; assimilation and aspiration of *-r* followed by *n-* or *l-*; dephonemicization of /x/ — /ḥ/; weakening of intervocalic *-d-*; velarization of word final *-n*; and, of course, the phenomenon of *yeísmo*. Menéndez Pidal is of the opinion that the Andalusian character of American Spanish occurs especially in coastal areas — as Wagner had already suggested — but he does not believe it is due to climatic but to historical reasons; i.e. the fleets departing from Andalusia periodically reached the ports of those coastal regions, thus producing there a constant process of linguistic Andalusianism. These fleets 'were yearly loaded with Andalusianism and scattered it on the shores where they docked' (p. 143). This is why he proposes that instead of talking of 'lowlands' and 'highlands' the distinction be between maritime lands or lands 'of the fleet' and inlands. Such a distinction seems evident in the case of Mexican Spanish, which has an Andalusian character along the coast, while the inlander of the plateau speaks a Spanish closer to Castillian. But of course, viceroys, governors, law agents, ecclesiastics and other learned men, whose destinations were the capitals of the viceroyalties, also traveled in these fleets. These people of higher learning brought to Mexico, Lima, and other big cities the courtly innovations of the metropolis (the *tuteo* and the learned *yeísmo*). Chronologically speaking, American Spanish could very well have been Castilian at the beginning (with *-ḷ-* and *-d-* preserved) with a certain Andalusian not very pervasive tonality (*çeçeo*). Soon a gradual differentiation would be effected between the coastal speech (strongly Andalusianized and, in particular, with features typical of Seville) and the speech of the inlands, closer to that of Madrid, to the Castilian court. Of these three types of speech there remain representative zones in America: areas of conservative speech, archaic (with *ḷ*, *-d-*), areas of a popular Andalusian type of speech (maritime zones), and areas of learned speech, less Andalusian (the central points of the viceroyalties, with courtly *tuteo* and *yeísmo*). D. Catalán shows how those peculiarities of Andalusianized coastal speech in America are also found in the Spanish of the Canary Islands.

A synthesis of the present state of the problem has been made by Rafael Lapesa in 'El andaluz y el español de América', *PFLE* 2.173-82, in the following terms: 'There can be no longer any doubt as to the Andalusian origin of some of the most peculiar features of American pronunciation: *seseo*, which is the most general one; very probably, *yeísmo*; certainly, even though not found throughout America, the confusion of final *r* and *l*, the aspiration of final *s* and the substitution of *j* by *h*. All of these features are found in Spain, not only in Andalusia but in other southern regions, particularly Extremadura. It goes without saying that American Spanish is not only a variety of Andalusian. Whatever is Andalusian or from southern Spain is one of the elements which entered into its make up... The Andalucianism thesis... leads one to leave aside the opposition between Spanish from Spain and American Spanish; at least as far as phonetics is concerned, it would be more proper to refer to Castilian and Atlantic Spanish. The latter term would reflect the common features which are shared by the Andalusian variety and that of the Spanish-American countries (p. 182).[35]

6. *Studies of continental scope*

Very few phonetic studies have yet been made of a general Spanish-American scope. Besides those already mentioned with regard to the question of Andalusianism, the most important is D. L. Canfield's *La pronunciación del español en América. Ensayo histórico descriptivo* (Bogotá, 1962), a valuable summary of the present state of our knowledge in this field, with two objectives: geographically first, to determine the allophonic variations of the most characteristic phonemes in Spanish-American pronunciation (all of which are duly mapped); and, secondly, to show the origin and chronology of the first manifestations and subsequent spreading of those variations. Canfield distinguishes between two periods in the history of Spanish-American phonology: the initial one — sixteenth century — with a predominance of Andalusian over Castilian, and the subsequent one — seventeenth century — with the *criollo* variety prevailing over the peninsular one, although this second period is also in its origin and tonality Andalusian (characterized by certain innovations — for instance, *yeísmo* — which did not reach the mountainous regions). This basic Andalusianism of Spanish America can be detected both in the early stages of its evolution (*çeçeo-seseo*, aspiration or palatal articulation of *x*, etc.), as well as in its later development (aspiration of *-s*, confusion of *-l* and *-r* implosive, velarization of *n* in open transition, leveling of *ḷ-y*). He distinguishes two large American zones in the territorial distribution of these phenomena, a distinction unrelated to either the historical distribution of the indigenous languages or the present political demarcations, but depending on the degree to which those regions were exposed to Andalusian phonological influence. In other words, coastal areas, with strong Andalusian influence, as against highland areas, were removed from this influence. Thus he concurs for the most part with the above mentioned theory of Menéndez Pidal. The indigenous influence is, according to Canfield, very small, although it is quite apparent in some particular cases: confusion of *e-i* and *o-u* in the areas with a Quechua substratum; the Yucatan articulation of *č* with the typical Mayan glottalization; affricate pronunciation of *-ŷ-* in Paraguay, characteristic of Guaraní.

Amado Alonso and Raimundo Lida, in 'Geografía fonética: *-r* y *-l* en España y

[35] J. Pérez Vidal's 'Las Canarias, vía de introducción de portuguesismos en América', *Actas do Colóquio de Estudos etnográficos «Dr. Leite de Vasconcelos»* 3.359-67 (Porto, 1959-60), deals with the occidental character of Spanish-American lexicon, a question of which Juan Corominas had already spoken in 'Indianorománica: II, Occidentalismos americanos', *RFE* 6.139-75 and 209-54 (1944).

América', *RFH* 7.313-45 (1945),[36] have studied in detail the leveling process of *-r* and *-l*, noticing that the different forms of articulatory alteration in both phonemes coalesce in their vocalization and their loss or dephonemicization, 'are all realizations of the same fact: "the weakening of syllable final consonants"'. They draw attention to the tremendous geographic extension of the phenomenon and to the fact that neither in Spain nor in America does it occur with geographic continuity, but in scattered places, which suggests that it is a case of parallel and independent development. 'Nevertheless, among the regions that change the character of *r* and *l*, there are two, one in Spain and one in America, which do it with common forms which are at the same time typical of them only: Andalusia and the Caribbean, with their vocalization (*poique*), aspiration (*buhla*), loss (*animá, comé*), and even occasional nasalization (*vingen*)... so that the idea of their being related obviously occurs to one' (p. 343 = p. 326 of the book).

Daniel N. Cárdenas, in 'The geographic distribution of the assibilated *r*, *rr* in Spanish America', *Orbis* 7.407-14 (1958), has arranged and summarized the existing data regarding the assibilation of *r̄*, and has attempted to provide a phonological explanation of its displacement, which he considers to be the result of the attraction exerted by the two palatals of the Spanish phonemic system, ɲ and λ [= l̹], in order to establish a geometric correlation.

Ruth L. Hyman, in '[ŋ] as an allophone denoting open juncture in several Spanish-American dialects', *Hispania* 39.293-9 (1956), notices that in the Spanish of Cuba, Costa Rica, Honduras, Mexico, Nicaragua, Panama, Venezuela, and Peru, velar *-n* in word final position before pause is just an allophone of /n/, but if followed by a word beginning with a vowel it is a sign of open juncture and is in complementary distribution with [n], which appears in word initial or middle position.

Dwight L. Bolinger's 'Evidence on X', *Hispania* 35.49-63 (1952), is a series of very detailed statistics — based on questionnaires sent by mail to several cultural centers in different Spanish-American countries — in which he reached the conclusion that the pronunciation [ks] is more frequent in Spanish America than the articulation [*s*], both in intervocalic and preconsonantal position; besides, there exists among Spanish speakers — even among those who say they pronounce [s] — the awareness that the refined articulation [ks] is to be preferred, that it is 'the correct one'. Tomás Navarro, in 'La pronunciación de la *x* y la investigación fonética', *Hispania* 35.330-1 (1952), criticizes Bolinger's work as totally unsuitable and not scientific[37] by pointing out the method he used — mailing and addressing the question to the very same person whose pronunciation he was to determine.

The detailed annotations made by Angel Rosenblat, in 'Notas de morfología dialectal', *BDH* 2.105-316, to the work of Aurelio M. Espinosa about the Spanish of New Mexico, are — for their richness and large scope, covering practically all Spanish-

[36] Published with a brief but important addition in A. Alonso's book *ELTH*, 263-331.

[37] Bolinger replied to Navarro in the same volume of *Hispania*: 'The pronunciation of *x* and puristic anti-purism', 442-4.

speaking territories — the best available work for the understanding of the grammatical features in American Spanish and their close relationship with their corresponding Peninsular features, as well as of their historical origins. Many phonetic phenomena and even some of a syntactic character are also explained in that work, which offers an ample bibliography of each of the facts under consideration. In the domain of syntax, the book by Charles E. Kany, *American Spanish Syntax* (Chicago, 1945), is of great importance, even if it does not study in detail all the compiled phenomena. This book offers a large number of American constructions and of morphological as well as lexical peculiarities, systematically classified and amply documented with literary examples — particularly from works that try to reflect the living language, since Kany does not fail to notice the existing separation in Spanish America between the written and the spoken language. Naturally, not all the peculiarities in the syntax of American Spanish find a place in this book, but one has to take into consideration that such an enterprise will be absolutely impossible as long as there is a lack of monographic investigations of the speech of each of the different regions and zones in Spanish America. Rosenblat and Kany have used almost all the bibliography that could be used at the moment and have carried out a most worthy effort of investigation. Their works continue to be an indispensable reference for those who may try to do any grammatical study of American Spanish.

There are not many specific studies of continental scope either. Juan B. Selva, in 'Sufijos americanos', *BICC* 5.192-213 (1949), has paid some attention to the study of suffixes *-ango* (a very productive one), *-ingo*, *-ongo*, *-ungo*, which he considers to be American, because they have either originated in America or predominate among indigenous terms — especially names of tribes — although they are also frequent among words of African origin. All of them usually have a derogatory meaning, both in native terms and in those of Castilian in which they appear. Max L. Wagner's 'El sufijo hispanoamericano *-eco* para denotar defectos físicos y morales', *NRFH* 4.105-14 (1950), finds the suffix *-eco* almost exclusively in the area of Nahuatl influence (Mexico and Central America), a reason he thinks it is a derivative from the Nahuatl adjectival ending *-ic* or *-tic*; the *e* of the suffix could be due either to the analogical influence of Spanish suffix *-eto*, also derogatory, or to the cross with the suffix *-eco* from Nahuatl; he also studies suffixes *-enco* and *-engo*, and their mutual interferences.

From a purist standpoint, J. Mallo, in 'El empleo de las formas del subjuntivo en *-ra* con significación de tiempos del indicativo', *Hispania* 30.484-7 (1947), fears that the use of the imperfect subjunctive in substitution for the imperfect as well as the simple and compound preterites of the indicative — of frequent use in old speech — may eventually weaken spoken American Spanish deeply, although he recognizes that those uses belong to a stilted literary language 'of low quality'. He believes that such a phenomenon has a Gallician ancestry. In the face of criticisms by Wright (*Hispania* 30.488-95, 1947) and Bolinger (*Hispania* 31.341-2, 1948), he holds to his opinion on the basis of a statistical count of the functions of the form *-ra* (twelfth to twentieth century). He demonstrates that the use of the imperfect in *-ra* with an indicative value is typical of Medieval language and, in modern times, of Gallician writers, granting, however, that the phenomenon does not really exist in the language of Spanish America, but only in the literature of second-rate writers.

Although limiting his investigation to the written language of Colombia, Charles N. Staubach, in 'Current variations in the past indicative use of the *-ra* form', *Hispania* 29.355-62 (1946), reached the conclusion, on the basis of another statistical count, that the form in *-ra* with indicative meanings is still fairly common among the novelists and journalists of Colombia, but with a difference: its value as pluperfect is more frequent among careful and well known writers, while the other uses (as imperfect, absolute preterite, and present perfect [*antepresente*]) are most current among journalists and little known writers.

José Pedro Rona, in 'Sobre sintaxis de los verbos impersonales en el español americano', *Romania, Homenaje a F. Piccolo*, 391-400 (Napoli, 1962), considers that the use of the subject pronoun — instead of the dative — to designate the 'logical subject' of impersonal verbs of the type *me parece* is a normal and generalized phenomenon in America, which he tries to explain by stating that the construction *yo me parece* is the nonemphatic form of American Spanish (the corresponding Castilian form being, according to Rona, *me parece*), as opposed to the emphatic Spanish Spanish-American form *a mí me parece*. This is in accordance with his opinion that all Spanish America uses the subject pronoun almost necessarily for the non-emphatic form. Again, J. P. Rona, in 'El uso del futuro en el voseo americano', *Fi* 7.123-44 (1961), thinks that the multiplicity of future forms in the regions of *voseo* should be explained by analyzing separately the singular forms (of the type *andarás*) from the plural ones (*andarés, andarís, andaréis*), which are normal derivations from the Spanish archetype *-e(d)es*, while the former are obviously forms from the singular. To the analysis of diatopic and diastratic distribution, one should add considerations of frequency; in this case, the forms *andarés, andarís, andaréis* belong to the language that has been 'passed on', while the form *andarás* belongs to the language learned in school and thus appears as an imposed form, above all in the areas and in the levels in which the periphrastic future is normally used.

It is evident that, with the exception of the general studies by Kany and Rosenblat, very little has been written about the numerous grammatical problems of American Spanish. This is also the case — although in a lesser degree — with Peninsular Castilian. The grammatical aspect of the language is the least studied of all. Such fundamental questions as the simplification of the verbal paradigm in the spoken language, for instance, have not yet received the attention they deserve. There are, as we will see further on, some praiseworthy grammatical studies of a local, regional or even national scope, but they are not enough for the moment to warrant the realization of an overall American study. Hence, there is the urgent need for research in the different dialect regions of each of the Spanish-American countries. Without such investigations it will not be possible to arrive at a full understanding of the dialectal complex of American Spanish.

For many years, the most widely studied field in Spanish-American linguistics has been the lexical one. Besides the numerous vocabularies of indigenous terms, there are numberless works which in a more or less systematic way account for the lexical peculiarities of American Spanish. It is true, however, that there are not many dictionaries of a continental scope, but on the other hand, national and regional lexicons do abound. During the last twenty years some general studies of unquestionable importance have been published. In this respect is Marcos A. Morínigo's 'La formación léxica regional hispanoamericana', *NRFH* 7.234-41 (1953). Also his book *Programa de filología hispánica* (pp. 56-70) is of particular interest. In this book, he enumerates the different general procedures to which the Spanish language has had recourse to give a name to those American realities unknown to the European man. At the beginning, the conquerors tended to give Arabic names to those new realities, since they thought that the lands of America were those regions already visited by the Arabs (*las Indias*); thus, canoes were called *almadías*, the Indians were *gandules*, and their arms *azagayas*. Later, the vocabulary took on an 'American' character, through the incorporation of indigenism (*ají*, *caimán*, *iguana*, etc.), or by means of analogical derivations (*gallinazo*, *aguilucho*), or by some other descriptive (*armadillo*) or metaphorical processes (*predicador* 'tucán'). The scarcity of Spanish-American technical vocabulary can be explained by the fact that Spanish artisans left their manual work in the hands of the natives, who did not know any specialized vocabulary and used the general terms of Castilian.

We owe to Augusto Malaret the most complete lexical counts of American Spanish. The third edition of his *Diccionario de americanismos* (Buenos Aires, 1946) is the result of more than twenty years of constant work,[38] an accomplishment not yet surpassed and an indispensable reference work, in spite of some deficiencies, the questionable accuracy of some etymologies, and the limitations imposed by considerations of space. Malaret avoids the use of references and all the textual documentation that would have made his work of an unmanageable size. He prefers to offer the end results, already synthesized, of his work, a work which undoubtedly implies a tremendous number of consultations and confrontations. He also accounts for the idiomatic expressions of American Spanish and determines, in so far as this is possible, the geographic extension where the terms registered are used. The appreciable imprecision of some of these geographic demarcations could be due to the inaccuracy of his sources. The *Lexicón de fauna y flora*, published by A. Malaret in Bogotá, 1961,[39] is a necessary complement to his *Diccionario de americanismos* (3rd ed., Buenos Aires, 1946), of which it could be considered a part intentionally separated by the author, so that the *Diccionario* would not become excessively big. Some other studies of his about the same topic — *Los americanismos en la copla popular y en el lenguaje culto* (New York,

[38] The first edition was published in Mayagüez (1925). The second one in San Juan de Puerto Rico (1931).

[39] It had been published previously in *BICC* 1-15 (1945-59).

1947)[40] and 'Los americanismos en el lenguaje literario', *BFUCh* 7.1-113 (1952-3) — are good proof of the untiring endeavors of A. Malaret. In these two works, he has collected several hundred American words that enrich the Spanish language, determining their geographic extension and documenting them with folklore and literary quotations.

Also of great value is the work of Georg Friederici, *Amerikanistisches Wörterbuch und Hilfswörterbuch für den Amerikanisten*, 2nd edition (Hamburg, 1960),[41] a historical study, amply documented, of all the exotic terms used by the historians of the Conquest, of interest not only for linguistics but also for ethnography and natural history. Not only American terms are documented there, but also many which are Spanish, Portuguese, and from other sources, used by the chroniclers of America (historians, travelers, botanists, geographers, etc.) who in some way applied them to American realities.

Charles E. Kany has simultaneously published two very interesting works: *American-Spanish Semantics*, and *American-Spanish Euphemisms* (Berkeley-Los Angeles, 1960).[42] In them he analyzes in detail — on the basis of a surprisingly vast amount of material, covering all the geography of Spanish speaking territories — the processes and motivations of lexical creation. He notices that the awareness of belonging to a common language restrains and counterbalances the tendency towards lexical fragmentation proper to popular speech, a tendency due to many different reasons: the influence of the different indigenous tongues; the variety of realities proper to each of the geographic areas of Spanish America; the inevitable evolution of the language in each territory; and the different waves of immigrants into each American country.

Armando Levy Cardoso's book, *Amerigenismos* 1. (Rio de Janeiro, 1961), is a modest although useful résumé of previous works about American terms incorporated into Spanish and Portuguese. There are some errors in it, especially concerning etymological questions, which can be blamed on the sources he uses.

Some particular topics have already been studied on a continental scope: Horacio Jorge Becco's *Lexicografía religiosa de los afroamericanismos* (Buenos Aires, 1952)[43] contains an alphabetical catalogue of African or Castilian terms designating deities, beliefs or superstitions, ceremonies, and rites of the Negro population in America, generally indicating the countries where each of those terms is used. Another aspect of popular vocabulary — that indicating drunkenness — has been studied, somewhat superficially and without the use of all necessary documentation, by Raúl R. Madueño, in several leaflets: *Léxico de la borrachera* (Buenos Aires, 1953), *Más voces para un léxico* (Buenos Aires, 1955), and *Ampliación y corrección de un léxico* (Buenos Aires,

[40] A complement to this book is his article 'Cancionero de americanismos', *BFM* 7.272-99 (1951) where he only exemplifies a couple of hundred words already included in the third edition of his *Diccionario de americanismos*, using some popular songs.

[41] The first edition of *Amerikanistisches Wörterbuch* was done in Hamburg (1947); that of the *Hilfswörterbuch* in 1926.

[42] Of the first one there is a Spanish translation titled *Semántica hispanoamericana* (Madrid, 1963).

[43] An offprint from *BAAL* 20.305-38 (1951).

1958). On the other hand, the historical-semantic study of Pedro Grases, 'La idea de 'alboroto' en castellano. Notas sobre dos vocablos: *bululú* y *mitote*', *BICC* 6.384-430 (1950), is excellent. In it he shows how those terms have followed an ideological evolution, pertaining specially to a certain area of the American continent, until they finally ended in the concept of *tumulto, alboroto*. He also studies a series of words which, although originally meaning very different things, have come to be used as synonyms of *alboroto, pendencia*, in Peninsular Castilian, as well as Venezuela and other American countries. Kurt Baldinger also, in his 'Designaciones de la 'cabeza' en Hispanoamérica', *ALet* 4.25-56 (1964), has analyzed the process of metaphoric creation — generally with a humorous intent — proper to the spoken language, on the basis of the different denominations of a very concrete concept, allowing, however, a free expansion of popular fantasy.

A very interesting aspect of Spanish-American lexicon consists of terms of a maritime origin, firmly rooted in American Spanish. Julio Guillén Tato, in 'Algunos americanismos de origen marinero', *AEAm* 5.615-34 (1948), Berta Elena Vidal de Battini, in 'Voces marineras en el habla rural de San Luis', *Fi* 1.105-50 (1949), and Delfín L. Garasa, in 'Origen náutico de algunas voces de América', *Tradición* [Cuzco], year I, 2.21-9 (1950), and in 'Voces náuticas en Tierra Firme', *Fi* 4.169-209 (1952-3), have demonstrated, following the path of Cuervo, Gagini, and other philologists, how the long sea travels and the contacts which they created between travelers and sailors gave to the speech of the colonizers a strong nautical flavor.

The sailors' vocabulary — veterans as they were in the adventure of the New World — would enjoy a high prestige among the colonists, who could find in it a means to designate realities or activities previously unknown. In addition, one must not forget that direct participation by sailors in the conquest of America must have been more important, numerically, than historical data (such as lists of passengers and other official documents) would allow one to suppose. Hence, there is the fact that in American Spanish words such as *botar, fletar, rumbo, rancho, chicote, chicotear, abarrote, balde, abordar*, and many others[44] are of common and widespread use.

In the domain of lexicon, it has also been noticed that American Spanish, as a peripheric and colonization language, keeps many old words and grammatical forms which have become archaic in the Peninsula. Cuervo, Eusebio R. Castex, and other linguists many years ago discussed this problem. In recent years, C. Martínez Vigil (*BFM*, I-IV), J. Cornejo and A. F. Padrón (Montevideo, 1942), E. D. Tovar y Ramírez (*BAAL* 13.493-659 [1944]), J. D. Díaz-Caneja (*Escorial* 5-8 [1941-2]) and J. B. Selva (Buenos Aires, 1944 and *Revista de Educación* 3:1.156-64 [La Plata, 1958]) have dealt with this question and have gathered many words, as well as phonetic variations and popular alterations, and idiomatic expressions, which, being of normal use in Spanish America, have gone out of use or are only used in rural areas in the

[44] In this regard, H. Ch. Woodbridge's thesis *Spanish nautical terms of the Age of Discovery* (Urbana, Ill., 1950) is very useful. Woodbridge offers historical documentation for many of those maritime terms which were later rooted in American Spanish.

Peninsula. This archaic tendency exists side by side with the neologistic trend of the ever active forces of lexical creativity. Rodolfo M. Ragucci in his *Neologismos de mis lecturas* (Buenos Aires, 1947-51),[45] J. B. Selva, in 'Verbos nuevos', *BAAL* 15.179-9 (1946), and F. Restrepo, in *El castellano naciente* (Bogotá, 1956), have gathered a great number of words, which although of general use in Spanish America or in some other Spanish-speaking countries, are not found in the *Diccionario* of the Real Academia. Of course, most of these neologisms, because of their general use, do not have any dialectal significance. It would be necessary to determine the formative processes and areas of use in all those cases in which the neologisms could reveal some kind of dialectal differentiation.

Finally, the question of Anglicisms and Gallicisms has also occupied the attention of Spanish-American philologists, although they have not always given their investigations an adequate and useful direction. On the whole, lexicographers, while tackling this problem, have adopted a purist attitude, one of *casticismo*, of correction and repression — drawing the attention of Spanish speakers to the dangers of 'corruption' entailed in the adoption of foreign terms.

Other times they devote themselves to the task of unrestrictedly accumulating foreign terms — even though some of them are only found once in some Spanish publication — without stopping to consider whether such words are really part of the living language, or only occasional products. Thus, in the most voluminous work of this type published lately, Ricardo J. Alfaro in *Diccionario de anglicismos* (Panamá, 1950),[46] gathers, together with the most used English terms in present Spanish, a great number which are just simple errors of translation found in books, magazines, and newspapers of very uneven quality, as if they were deeply rooted Anglicisms in Spanish. Since no mention is made in that work of geographic factors or of the sources of those Anglicisms, the *Diccionario* is of little interest for dialectal studies in American Spanish. It has, though, a great deal of practical and pedagogical value, particularly for translators. Naturally, it would be necessary to analyze the real extent of penetration and diffusion of those foreign terms in Spanish, not limiting this kind of investigation to the purely lexical or semantic aspect, but particularly paying attention to the possible syntactic influence, a subject of a more difficult nature, but, undoubtedly, of deeper significance.

A simple catalogue of English or French terms more or less extensively used in Spanish lacks any real dialectological interest. It is true, however, that these catalogues[47] — purist or not, critical or just descriptive — would be of some help for the proposed analytical job.

[45] Cf. also the series of articles published in the *BAAL* 16/26 (1947 and 1961) respectively.

[46] Second edition, Madrid (1964). The prologue to this dictionary, a theoretical justification, had previously appeared with the title 'El anglicismo en el español contemporáneo', *BICC* 4.102-28 (1948).

[47] Some titles: R. Restrepo, *Apuntaciones idiomáticas y correcciones de lenguaje* (Bogota, 1943; 2nd ed. Bogota, 1955); Ch. N. Staubach 'English terms in Bogota', *Hispania* 29.56-66 (1946); J. Guasch Leguizamón, *Galicismos aceptados, aceptables y vitandos* (Buenos Aires, 1951); L. Flórez. 'Galicismos y anglicismos del español de Colombia' in his book *Lengua española* 189-214 (Bogota, 1953); J. Mallo,

B. NATIONWIDE STUDIES

Within the more reduced limits of national areas, there have been many studies published in the last two decades. Not all of them, of course, have the same value, nor have they been done following similar methods or goals. The speech of some countries is presently being studied in a systematic way, while our knowledge of some other areas depends on the sporadic endeavors of some isolated scholars.

1. *The Antilles*

Puerto Rico. — Rubén del Rosario has on some occasions made a quick description of the phonetic, grammatical, and lexical peculiarities of Puerto Rican Spanish.[48] He notices that its phonetic system shows some peculiarities which make it different from Peninsular Spanish (velar *r*; the frequency of the phoneme *ñ*; a seven vowel vocalic system, with /ę/ and /ǫ/ as plural morphemes). Some of these features may be due to the substratum influence or the Negro influence; but he notices that those features relate Puerto Rican Spanish to the speech of other American areas. Also the morphological-syntactical system of Castilian remains unchanged in the island. He believes that English influence on Puerto Rican Spanish, either phonetic or lexical, is not as strong as some linguists would tend to think.

M. Alvarez Nazario has studied, in fairly good detail, two aspects of Puerto Rican Spanish: archaism and the African influence, in *El arcaísmo vulgar en el español de Puerto Rico* (Mayagüez, 1957), and *El elemento afronegroide en el español de Puerto Rico* (San Juan, 1961). The conservative character of Puerto Rican speech, reflected not only in its vocabulary but also in its phonetics, morphology, and syntax, could be explained by the early establishment of Castilian on the island, by its later cultural immobility, and by the lack of communications between the colony and the metropoli and even among the different regions of the island. The influence of African tongues, only appreciable in phonetics and lexicon, is due to the great number of slaves, particularly Sudanese and Bantu, transported in successive waves to Puerto Rico. Those Bantu and Sudanese tongues must have acted as either determinants of certain Puerto Rican features or helped in the development of some Spanish tendencies; this, in particular, must have been the case with the weakening and elimination of consonantal sounds in word final position.

Thomás Navarro, author of the best work on Puerto Rican Spanish (cf. p. 111), in

---

'La plaga de los anglicismos', *Hispania* 37.135-40 (1954) and 'La invasión del anglicismo en la lengua española de América', *CA* 28:4.115-23 (1959); J. J. Salcedo Figueroa, *Filtros del lenguaje: acribología* (Caracas, 1961); O. Echeverri Mejía, 'Anglicismos, galicismos y barbarismos de frecuente uso en Colombia', *PFLE* 2.91-102.

[48] Cf. 'La lengua de Puerto Rico', *Asomante* 2.95-103 (1946); *La lengua de Puerto Rico. Ensayos* (San Juan, 1956); *Consideraciones sobre la lengua en Puerto Rico* (San Juan, 1958); 'Estado actual del español en Puerto Rico', *PFLE* 1.153-60.

his brief article 'The old aspirated *H* in Spain and the Spanish of America', *Word* 5.166-9 (1949), has compared the results of the Spanish evolution of *ḥ* with those gathered by himself in his study of Puerto Rican Spanish. He shows how words with aspirated *h* are more scattered on the island than in Spain. There are articulatory differences not only among different communities but also among persons of different social and cultural levels, and even in the speech of a single person. All this could be explained by the particular history of Puerto Rican colonization. Joseph H. Matluck, in 'Fonemas finales en el consonantismo puertorriqueño', *NRFH* 15.332-42 (1961), talks of the great reduction operated in the phonetic system of the island: as against the seven possibilities in standard Castilian, only two can occur in word final position in Puerto Rico (/l/ and /ŋ/), and only three in middle syllable final position: /s/ (and its allophone [h], /l/, and /n/ (with its variant consisting in the nasalization of the preceding vowel), as compared with the seven Castilian phonemes with their fifteen allophones. He points out the strong Anglicism of Puerto Rican Spanish, noticing that even words of English origin can be adapted to the simplified phonetic system of the island.[49]

Cuba. — Very useful for the understanding of Cuban Spanish are the commentaries and additions that Alfredo F. Padrón made, page by page and point by point, to the first edition of *American Spanish syntax* by Kany, as well as the answers that he gathered to many of the questions included in the *Cuestionario lingüístico* of T. Navarro,[50] although they do not seem to be the result of direct field research but based on his vast personal knowledge of Cuban speech. N. Almendros, in 'Estudio fonético del español en Cuba', *BACL* 7.138-76 (1958), made a quick exposé of the more common phonetic features in the speech of the western region of the island. He added some brief observations concerning the problem of the Andalusian character of *criollo* Spanish and the influence of prehispanic and African tongues, particularly in regard to pronunciation. The works of Esteban Rodríguez Herrera are of interest in the lexical field, especially his *Léxico mayor de Cuba* (2 volumes, La Habana, 1958-9), a useful work, since it covers satisfactorily vocabulary aspects which had not been studied by Pichardo, Dihigo and other previous lexicographers, although sometimes his explanations about the origin and evolution of Cuban terms are controversial and not well founded.[51] It is evident that there is still much to do in the study of Cuban

[49] With a puristic criterion, Washington Lloréns, in 'El español de Puerto Rico', *BAH* 3:447-57 (1956), also deplores the contaminating influence of English in Puerto Rican Spanish.

[50] Cf. A. F. Padrón, 'Giros sintácticos corrientes en el habla popular, culta y semiculta cubanas', *BFM* 5.467-95 (1948); 'Giros sintácticos usados en Cuba', *BICC* 5.163-75 (1949); 'Comentarios acerca de sintaxis cubana', *Revista Bimestre Cubana* 64.195-210 (1949); 'Giros sintácticos en las hablas cubanas', *Revista Bimestre Cubana* 6.634-48 (1951).

[51] Cf. some other of his previous work, such as, 'El plebeyismo en Cuba', *BFUCh* 8.407-37 (1954-55), and 'La gramática, el lenguaje y los periódicos', *BACL* 1.387-463 (1952). Also, Mary Coult's additions, in *Dictionary of the Cuban Tobacco industry* (Washington, 152), to José E. Perdomo's lexicon on tobacco.

Spanish, which is of great interest due to the importance the island had in the first period of the American conquest, during the so-called Caribbean period.

Santo Domingo. — Still less has been done with regard to the Spanish of Santo Domingo, in spite of the importance that a detailed knowledge of this island's speech can have for Spanish-American dialectology, for the same reason as that of Puerto Rican Spanish. We are in debt to T. Navarro 'Apuntes sobre el español dominicano', *RI* 21.417-29 (1956), an interesting though brief phonetic study, written with data collected more than thirty years ago. He studies the differences in vowel and consonant articulation observed in the speech of nine peasants representative of the three areas of the country. He notices that compared with the consistency of vowel articulation, many variants can be distinguished in the consonants in closed syllable final — something that can be also observed in other parts of America. These variants coincide with those observed in other Caribbean countries and in southern Spain.

A very special situation is that of the Spanish spoken in Trinidad, as R. W. Thompson has demonstrated in 'A preliminary survey of the Spanish dialect of Trinidad', *Orbis* 6.353-72 (1957), and 'Préstamos lingüísticos en tres idiomas trinitarios', *EAt* 12.249-54 (1956). In spite of the fact that it survives as a family language only, under the pressure of English and French, this variety of Spanish — similar to that of the Venezuelan Guiana, (with neutralization of *x-h*, aspiration of *f-*, mixed *r̄*, velar *n*, with archaic morphology) — is not a creolized language, but is in a state of rapid decadence; young people of Hispanic origin prefer the use of English.

2. *North and Central America*

Mexico. — Substantially more has been written in the last two decades about the spoken language of Mexico, although much more needs to be done. The large territory of the country poses a difficulty to investigations of a nationwide scope, for only a few regions have been studied in detail. Hence, Mexican Spanish is still largely considered one unitary whole, even though differences among different regions can be very easily perceived. Recently, J. M. Lope Blanch wrote a very brief exposition of the peculiarities of the Spanish spoken in Mexico City — as an ideal norm of learned speech practiced in many other regions — 'Estado actual del español en México', *PFLE* 1.79-91, mentioning the weakness of the substratum — except in vocabulary — as well as the archaic character of certain features of Mexican Spanish, some developments of tendencies proper to Spanish, and some other cases of morphological simplification of the system. Daniel Huacuja, in 'En defensa del idioma', *ACALE* 287-99, (1960), spoke, as a purist, of the most common mispronunciations and errors of construction and lexicon, especially in the language of journalists and radio speakers, which he considers seriously influenced by English.

Although Alfred B. Gaarder's doctoral thesis, *El habla popular y la conciencia colectiva* (Mexico, 1954), is of a sociological or psychological nature, it has some linguistic interest for the rich materials of spoken language that he gathers: vocabulary, expressions, peculiarities of women's language, the use of diminutive suffixes, jargon, etc.

More research has been done with regard to phonetics. Joseph H. Matluck, *La pronunciación en el español del valle de México* (Mexico, 1951),[52] carefully studies the phonetic system of the rural speech of the valley, comparing its features with those of other Hispanic areas. He notices as the most relevant features the strong consonantism of the region (preservation of final consonants, and of voiced intervocalics, the tense pronunciation of /s/ and /š/, a resistance against the reduction of 'learned' sound groups, etc.) a tendency towards equating open and closed vowels in an intermediate timbre, a weakening and loss of unstressed vowels, and the special intonation 'with its curious circumflex final cadence'.

Harold V. King, 'Outline of Mexican Spanish phonology', *SiL* 10.51-62 (1952), made a brief description of the vocalic and consonantal phonemes, their allophones, junctures, types of intonation, pauses, etc., observed in two speakers from Mexico City. The question of the weakening and loss of unstressed vowels, which had already been noticed with regard to the Mexican high plateau by Henríquez Ureña in 1921, has lately again occupied the attention of some scholars: P. Boyd-Bowman, in 'La pérdida de vocales átonas en la altiplanicie mexicana', *NRFH* 6.138-40 (1952), observed that this phenomenon occurs almost exclusively when in contact with *s*, and he pointed out that the particular sharp timbre of Mexican *s*, of a long duration, could be related to the sibilants proper to the substratum language.

A. Zamora Vicente and María J. Canellada, in 'Vocales caducas en el español mexicano', *NRFH* 14.221-41 (1960), discovered that this phenomenon occurred not only with unstressed vowels, but even with stressed vowels, thus producing several syllabic consonants. Also, they discovered that it occurs equally at all cultural levels in Mexico City, a reason they considered it 'the most curious and astonishing phenomenon' of Mexican Spanish.

Finally, J. M. Lope Blanch, in 'En torno a las vocales caedizas del español mexicano', *NRFH* 17.1-19 (1963), has studied this phenomenon statistically, observing that it occurs not in a small number of speakers — almost always occasionally and concurring with cases of devoicing — and that it appears conditioned by the consonant in contact with the vowel, almost always a sibilant, /s/ or /š/. Besides, he notices that the phenomenon extends beyond the limits of the plateau, since it occurs — under the same conditions — in the speech of Colombia, El Salvador, Perú, Bolivia, Ecuador, and Argentina, a reason it should not perhaps be explained as a phenomenon determined by the influence of the substratum language. Joseph H. Matluck, in 'La *é* trabada en la ciudad de México: estudio experimental', *ALet* 3.5-34 (1963), has made a detailed spectrographic analysis of stressed /e/. It shows the notable differences

[52] Cf. also the summary of this work in *NRFH* 6. 109-20 (1952).

existing between its Mexican varieties and those compiled by T. Navarro in the learned speech of Madrid, as well as the unsystematic nature of those varieties in different individuals, and even with a single one on different occasions. Another detailed spectrographic analysis of vocalic sounds in two speakers (one of them the author himself) from two different countries, Mexico and Colombia, has been carried out by Daniel N. Cárdenas in 'Acoustic vowel loops of two Spanish idiolects', *Phonetica* 5.9-34 (1960), in order to show the enormous variety of allophones, the distribution of which does not correspond to present theoretical principles. In 'Nasal variants after final *s* in the Spanish of Jalisco', *PMLA* 60.556-61 (1955), again D. N. Cárdenas discovers that the nasal resonance of *-s* is not so widespread in Jalisco as it was thought, and that it is also found in other regions, which makes it difficult to explain it either through the influence of the substratum or as a simple physiological phenomenon.

In grammar there has not been much progress. J. M. Lope Blanch, in *Observaciones sobre la sintaxis del español hablado en México* (Mexico, 1953), has simply catalogued the more common syntactic peculiarities in Mexico City, with some superficial and not too systematic morphological annotations. With greater precision, Lope Blanch, in 'Sobre el uso del pretérito en el español de México', *StPh* 2.373-85 (1961), has shown the different aspect values that distinguish the simple preterite (perfective and punctual) from the compound preterite (imperfective or reiterative), stating that this distinction is not a consequence of a confusion in the Spanish pattern rule, but a result of an independent evolution from the state of Castilian in the sixteenth century. Henry R. Kahane, in 'The position of the actor expression in colloquial Mexican-Spanish', *Lg* 26.236-63 (1950), has made a rigorous descriptive study of the position in the phrase of the subject-actor, noticing a notable flexibility in the construction, since the place of the actor depends on very different factors, such as the number of elements appearing in the phrase, the perfective or imperfective nature of the action, its transitive or intransitive character, the formal category (substantive, pronoun, etc.) of the actor, and others.[53] In fairly good detail, María E. Miquel i Vergés, in 'Fórmulas de tratamiento en la ciudad de México', *ALet* 3.35-86 (1963), has compiled a catalogue of the usual forms of address in the different situations and social relations of urban speech, according to age, social position, degree of acquaintance or family relationship among the speakers.[54]

In the domain of lexicography, one should mention the work of Francisco J.

[53] Henry R. Kahane and Richard Beym's study, 'Syntactical juncture in colloquial Mexican Spanish', *Lg* 24.388-96 (1948), is a valuable one, in which the authors study the relative distribution of closed and open junctures, with results which do not always coincide with T. Navarro's conclusions in *Manual de entonación española* 51-2 (New York, 1944); thus, for example, in the subjective clause the subject may not always be in close juncture with the predicate.

[54] In this respect, other similar studies have already been made in different American countries. In the last few years, the most complete are: Javier Sologuren, 'Fórmulas de tratamiento en el Perú', *NRFH* 8.241-67 (1954); L. Flórez, 'Algunas fórmulas de tratamiento en el español del departamento de Antioquia', *BICC* 10.78-88 (1954); J. A. Pérez, 'Fórmulas de tratamiento en Colombia', *Filosofía, Letras y Educación* 28.47-62 (Quito, 1959-60); and Luisa Eguiluz, 'Fórmulas de tratamiento en el español de Chile', *BFUCh* 15.169-233 (1962).

Santamaría, whose *Diccionario de mejicanismos* (Mexico, 1959) is a fundamental work for the understanding of Mexican speech and even that of other American countries, because of its numerous references to lexical studies published all over Spanish America. However, this work is somewhat bulky, since many words and expressions are included which are not peculiar to Mexico, but are from standard Spanish, and also because the author echoes occasionally unjustified or erroneous etymological suppositions, particularly in dealing with words of a possible American origin. In any case, this is one of the few fundamental works now existing on Mexican Spanish. Also useful is the work of Marcos E. Becerra, *Rectificaciones y adiciones al Diccionario de la Real Academia Española* (Mexico, 1954), especially for its high number of indigenisms — names of animals and plants in particular — included, with indication of their particular geographic distribution and their corresponding etymologies, even though the latter are doubtful or disputable at times. Of less value is the *Diccionario rural mexicano* (Mexico, 1961) by Leovigildo Islas Escárcega,[55] because, in spite of some new materials like peasant words, sayings, and proverbs, many definitions are vague, geographic demarcations imprecise, and the etymologies of some words of Nahuatl origin doubtful. Juan M. Lope Blanch has done a monographic study of three special concepts, 'muerte, morir y matar', in *Vocabulario mexicano relativo a la muerte* (Mexico, 1963), where he classifies ideologically several hundred words and expressions, which are usually built around expressive patterns of regular Spanish, but which are capable of innumerable specific forms.

Even though they are not the work of linguists, the books by Francisco Padrón, *El médico y el folklore* (San Luis Potosí, 1957), by M. Velasco Valdés, *Vocabulario popular mexicano* (Mexico, 1957), and by A. Jiménez, *Picardía mexicana* (Mexico, 1960), have some interest for the rich linguistic material gathered directly from the living language.

With regard to dialectological investigations of regional or local character, it should be noticed that the only monographs of real value done in Mexico have been published during the last decades. The first one chronologically was that of Víctor M. Suárez, *El español que se habla en Yucatán* (Merida, 1945), a rather complete work, in spite of its errors and limitations. The main phonetic, morphological, and syntactic features of the Spanish of the Yucatan peninsula are included in this work, which also gathers some expressions peculiar to that region. The author devotes special attention to the Maya influence in Yucatan Spanish, a rather strong influence in phonetics as well as in lexicon, owing to the vitality of the indigenous language, which survives as a family language in almost all the territory. However, some of the facts considered of Mayan origin are not well justified.

Much more rigorous and to the point is the work of P. Boyd-Bowman, *El habla de Guanajuato* (Mexico, 1960), done with a basis on the *Cuestionario lingüístico* of T. Navarro. It is now the most complete description of a Mexican local speech, especially in what concerns morphology and phonetics. Basically using the seven volumes of the

[55] It is a very enlarged second edition of his *Vocabulario campesino nacional* (Mexico, 1945).

BDH, all the accounted phenomena are placed in relation to their corresponding forms in other Spanish-American regions. Another serious description of a local speech is that of Estrella Cortichs de Mora, *El habla de Tepotzotlán* (Mexico, 1951), although linguistic facts are here analyzed with less detail and rigor than in Boyd-Bowman's book.[56] Unfortunately, it has not yet been possible to publish Daniel N. Cárdenas' work, *El español de Jalisco*.[57] However, Cárdenas published an article with the same title, in *Orbis* 3.62-7 (1954), in which he advances the conclusions of his work done in thirty-nine localities of the state, also using the *Cuestionario* of T. Navarro. On the other hand, the study of Susana Francis Soriano, *Habla y literatura popular en la antigua capital chiapaneca* (Mexico, 1960) has no other merit than that of drawing attention to a dialectal variety very different from those of the rest of the country — a very archaic and rural variety, with *voseo* and perhaps fairly influenced by substratum languages. Juan A. Hasler's brief study, 'Situación de las tareas de la investigación lingüística en Veracruz', *PyH* 2:5.43-9 (1958), is interesting because it reveals that Nahuatl is being rapidly replaced by Spanish in the state of Veracruz. Hasler distinguishes three varieties of Spanish: Huastecan, highland, and coastal. Finally, Max A. Luria's 'Judeo-Spanish dialects and Mexican popular speech', *Homenaje Millás* 1.789-810 (1954) is a worthwhile and systematic analysis of the existing points of contact between popular Mexican speech and the two varieties of Judeo-Spanish dialects, eastern and western.

United States. — The Spanish spoken in the different regions of the United States has been the subject of several studies, brief for the most part and basically on the lexicon. There are no comprehensive studies or complete descriptions of each of its dialectal varieties, similar to that done by Aurelio M. Espinosa on the Spanish of New Mexico so many years ago. In several North American universities some doctoral dissertations have been written on this subject, but for the most part they have not been published. This is regrettable, given the receding character and state of inferiority in which the Spanish of those regions finds itself, a situation which forebodes its rapid disappearance. John H. Burma has written on the general distribution of the Spanish-speaking population of the United States, in *Spanish-Speaking groups in the United States* (Durham, 1954), with an emphasis on the special — marginal — living conditions of Mexican groups (about three million people living mostly in the South), of Puerto Ricans (some 300,000 in New York), and of the Philippinos (approximately 40,000 on the West Coast), all of which are in a deficient economic situation and ill-integrated in the country by reason of their language, race, and temperament. R. M. Duncan, in 'Algunas observaciones sobre la fonología de la *s* palatal en el español de Nuevo Méjico', *ASal* 10:2.223-8 (1956), observes a clear tendency towards weakening

[56] The chapter dealing with 'Palabras y cosas' was also published independently in *NRFH* 8.137-55 (1954).

[57] Presented as a thesis to Columbia University in 1953. The linguistic peculiarities of the area are: firm consonantism, vowels of a medium timbre (unvoiced in word final position), *rehilamiento* of *r̄*, an abundance of verbal periphrasis, use of the adverb *recién* before simple preterite.

in the articulation of *ĉ* (> *š*) in northern Mexico and occasionally in New Mexico. He thinks that the few cases preserved of etymological *š* in Nahuatl words prove that Spanish *š* must have disappeared (> *x*) before the colonization of that territory.

Jacob Ornstein, in 'The archaic and the modern in the Spanish of New Mexico', *Hispania* 34.137-42 (1951), briefly mentions certain lexical and grammatical peculiarities (archaic or rustic) in the area south of the city of Socorro; he also mentions, in passing, some expressions proper to *pachuco*. R. S. Boggs, in 'Phonetics of words borrowed from English by New Mexican Spanish', *Homenaje Krüger* 2.305-32 (1952), briefly studies the process of phonetic adaptation of English words used in two counties of New Mexico and shows how those words have been adapted to the phonetic system of Spanish, especially in their endings and final sounds. With regard to lexicon, Lawrence B. Kiddle's '*Turkey* in New Mexican Spanish', *RomPh* 5.190-7 (1951-2) again examines a subject which had previously occupied the author's attention, *Hispania* 24.213-6 (1941), showing in a linguistic map the areas where eight different denominations of the word *pavo* are used. In his 'Problemas lexicográficos del español del Sudoeste', *Hispania* 40.139-43 (1957), Aurelio M. Espinosa Jr. has made some brief observations about certain peculiarities in words of Hispanic origin (archaisms, regionalisms, lexical weakening, derivations) in indigenous words and in terms taken from English, many of which have been completely Hispanicized in their form. We owe to Gilberto Cerda, Berta Cabaza, and Julieta Farías one of the most important lexicographic works done till now, their *Vocabulario español de Texas* (University of Texas Hispanic Studies, 1953). One should point out, however, that it has not been done with a very rigorous criterion, and there are some deficiencies in it. At any rate, it is a very complete and useful codification, which shows that the most powerful lexical tendencies in the area are — as could be expected — those of English and Mexican Spanish. Many forms are also documented which are simply phonetic variations of Spanish words (*máistro, ajuera, usté*).

Interesting, though relatively brief, is the article by Anthony G. Lozano, 'Intercambio de español e inglés en San Antonio, Texas', *AO* 11.111-38 (1961), in which he shows, through the study of the speech of four bilingual persons, the interferences existing in the phonetic systems of Spanish and English in this type of speaker. He notes that such interaction is not as intense as could be imagined, and it seems that the two phonetic systems are kept well separated from each other, while lexical interferences are more frequent.[58]

Although not as detailed as could be desired, the work of Raymond R. MacCurdy, *The Spanish dialect in St. Bernard Parish, Louisiana* (Albuquerque, 1950), is of great interest and value. It is one of the few studies done lately on the Spanish of the United States which try to cover all the fundamental aspects of language: phonetics, morphology, and vocabulary (in which he also includes simple phonetic variations).

[58] On the other hand, Lester Beberfall's brief study, 'Some linguistic problems of the Spanish-speaking people of Texas', *MLJ* 42.87-90 (1958), deals with the use of Hispanic constructions and phonemes by Spanish-speaking Texans when they express themselves in English.

This variety of Spanish coincides basically with the speech of the Canary Islands, since it was taken into Louisiana in the eighteenth century by immigrants from those islands. For this reason, it is very similar to Dominican Spanish, since in the eighteenth century many colonists from the Canary Islands also arrived in Santo Domingo.

Finally, Francis C. Hayes' 'Anglo-Spanish speech in Tampa, Florida', *Hispania* 32.48-52 (1949) and Carmelita L. Ortiz' 'English influence on the Spanish of Tampa', *Ibidem* 300-4, have demonstrated how strong the influence of English is in the lexicon, semantics, and even syntax of the Spanish spoken in Tampa by Cuban, Spanish and Italian immigrants.

Central America. — Central America continues to be one of the least studied regions, even though much has been done lately in some countries, and we expect that several projects will be carried out in some others. Until now, one of the least known varieties of Spanish is that of Guatemala, and there are no indications that this situation is going to change in the immediate future. During the last twenty years only some isolated and unimportant studies have been published. D. Lincoln Canfield, in 'Guatemalan *rr* and *s*: A recapitulation of old Spanish sibilant gradation', *Florida University Studies* 3.49-51 (1951), finds traces of the old Castilian distribution of dental and alveolar sibilants, which is proof of historical continuity and tenacity in pronunciation as a basic indication of cultural tradition.

Richard L. Predmore's 'El sufijo *-al* en el español de Guatemala', *NRFH* 6.140-4 (1952) draws attention to the extraordinary vitality of that suffix. He thinks that the influence of indigenous tongues is to be reckoned with in this phenomenon, although his reasoning is not very convincing. In *Pequeño diccionario etimológico de voces guatemaltecas* (2nd ed., Guatemala, 1954),[59] Jorge Luis Arreola collected a series of native terms (Quiché, Cakchiquel, Nahuatl, Mayan, etc.), place-names for the most part, with etymologies that do not always seem accurate. K. Kunath's 'La casa rural en el este de Guatemala', *AIL* 4.140-56 (1950) offers a systematic study of 'words and things' about lodging, in an area with an entirely Castillian basis, in which, naturally, some native terms have been incorporated. In Gustavo Correa's interesting book *El espíritu del mal en Guatemala* (New Orleans, 1955), although of an extralinguistic scope, numerous names of the devil and its personifications are gathered, which are of interest to the philologist.

The phonetics of the Spanish of El Salvador is relatively well known to us, thanks to the works of D. Lincoln Canfield, *La pronunciación del español en El Salvador* (San Salvador, 1953) and, above all, 'Observaciones sobre el español salvadoreño', *Filología* 6.29-76 (1960). Following point by point the linguistic *Cuestionario* of T. Navarro, he has studied the vocalic and consonantal systems of Salvadoran speech, adding some very brief grammatical and lexicographic annotations. The pages of phonetic transcription annexed to the study are very useful. The lexical contribution of Enrique D. Tovar y R., 'Contribución al estudio del lenguaje salvadoreño. Algo sobre

[59] First edition (Guatemala, 1941).

el léxico de flora', *BICC* 2.421-59 (1946), is well conceived and includes a fairly good number of Nahuatl, Carib or Hispanic terms with different meanings from the ones they have in the Iberian Peninsula.

Still less progress has been achieved in the study of Honduran and Nicaraguan Spanish. There are only a few lexicographic studies of varied extension and interest worth mentioning. C. Izaguirre's 'Hondureñismos', *BAH* 1.55-124 (1955) greatly expands the old work of A. Membreño of the same title. F. Fuguerva's 'Hondureñismos', *BAHo* 1.131-38 has some brief annotations to the lexicon of Olonchano. Alfonso Valle's *Diccionario del habla nicaragüense* (Managua, 1948) is more ambitious and complete. He includes and studies — at times with an excessively purist mind — some eight thousand words, many of which are of native origin, although there are no indications of how current each one of them is.[60]

We owe to Arturo Agüero Chaves two valuable contributions to the study of Costa Rican speech. In one of them, 'El español en Costa Rica y su atlas lingüístico', *PFLE* 1.135-52, after a brief historical summary of the Spanish colonization, he enumerates the main phonetic and grammatical characteristics of the Spanish — particularly popular Spanish — spoken in the Central Valley, comparing it briefly with the speech of the province of Guanacaste. Agüero himself had already studied this region (which is very similar to Nicaragua, culturally and linguistically) — together with regular Costa Rican speech — in his other work, *El español en Costa Rica* (San José, 1960). It would be most interesting if Agüero Chaves could soon carry out his project for a linguistic atlas of Costa Rica, which I have mentioned before (cf. p. 113). Also of interest is the brief but well organized study of O. L. Chavarría-Aguilar, 'The phonemes of Costa Rica Spanish', *Lg* 27.248-53 (1951), a phonemic description of the Costa Rican phonological system with its main allophones.

Slightly larger, and with better results, is the work done lately on the speech of Panama. Stanley L. Robe's *The Spanish of Rural Panama* (Berkeley-Los Angeles, 1960) is of particular interest. It is a very detailed descriptive study, done with modern criteria, of the peasant speech in four central provinces of the country; it is a rigorous synchronic description, objectively done, of the phonemic and morphological system, without establishing comparisons with the corresponding phenomena observed in other areas of Spanish America. What is most original in this work is the observation of the phonological system of Panamanian speech together with purely phonetic facts, something which is barely beginning to be done in the specific studies of other regions. However, there is no mention in the book of syntactic facts and hardly any of lexical peculiarities; there is only mention, in passing, of some examples of words originating in the aboriginal languages or from other sources. The study is fundamentally synchronic, although in chapter two, Robe makes an historical exposé of the

[60] Also lexical is the brief article by Douglas Taylor, 'Loanwords in Central America Carib', *Word* 4.187-95 (1948), in which he studies the speech of the descendants of Negroes deported from Santo Domingo to Central America, a speech whose lexicon has been enriched by successive waves of words of French, English, and Spanish origin.

origin of the Panamanian colonists and their particular living conditions. The author had previously taken up the subject in his article 'Algunos aspectos históricos del habla panameña', *NRFH* 7.209-20 (1953), in which he explained how most of the territory of Panama remained apart from communication routes, thus being isolated and culturally backward, even though Panama was a center of communications and a bridging link during the conquest of America. This diachronic aspect had been followed previously by Miguel Amado in 'El lenguaje de Panamá', *BAAL* 14.641-66 (1945) and 18.339-88 (1949), in which a study was made of the process of historical formation of Panamanian Spanish within the cultural framework of the area, on the basis of documents from that period.

In the strictly lexical domain, Luisa Aguilera Patiño has worked with fair success in *El panameño visto a través de su lenguaje* (Panama, 1947) and 'Diccionario de panameñismos', *BAAL* 20.405-506 (1951). She has collected alphabetically a rich lexical material commonly used in Panama — and, in many cases, in other American countries or in standard Spanish — simply indicating the meaning of each term in Panama, and only occasionally providing possible etymologies, some of which are purely fanciful.

3. *South America*

The study of the different regions of this area has also been very uneven. Unfortunately, there is very little concerning some countries, but, on the other hand, with regard to some others, there have been done or are now in progress the best and most systematic investigations in Spanish-American dialectology. Most praiseworthy is the work being done at the Instituto Caro y Cuervo of Bogota, an institution which for more than a decade has been sustaining the compilation tasks of the first linguistic atlas of a large American country. Also in Argentina, Chile, and Uruguay the progress continues in a serious and profitable way, although in these countries most of the progress is due to the enthusiasm and effort of some individual scholars who have tried to continue the work initiated by Amado Alonso in the Instituto de Filología of Buenos Aires almost forty years ago.

Colombia. — We owe to Luis Flórez much of the merit of this encouraging situation. Besides directing the work for the atlas of Colombia and personally contributing a great deal in it, he has been publishing a series of studies about Colombian Spanish which are of real interest. We have him and his associates to thank for the fact that Colombian Spanish is now the most widely studied and perhaps the best known of the New World.

Lately, Luis Flórez has provided us with what can be termed a general glance at Colombian Spanish, a useful one as a start, in 'El español en Colombia', *PFLE* 1. 5-78.[61] Here he mentions the most common phonetic, grammatical, and lexical

[61] Also published in *BICC* 8.268-356 (1963).

features of Colombian Spanish (and also some of a regional character), which seem to show a tendency towards linguistic unification, mainly as a consequence of the expansion of the speech of the big cities. He has studied in detail the phonetic system of urban speech, in *La pronunciación del español en Bogotá* (Bogotá, 1951), comparing it with the speech of other areas of the country, particularly those on the coast and Antioquia region. It is a very detailed descriptive work in which he shows the basic unity of the phonological system of Bogotá Spanish and of Peninsular Spanish, in spite of certain phonetic differences (aspiration of *x*, assibilation of *r̄* and *tr*, a weak articulatory tension, flat predorso-alveolar *s*, etc.). He also tries to discover the possible Negro influence in some articulations (neutralization of /l/ and /r/, strong nasalization of vowels and even consonants, velar articulation of *r̄* in the Cauca, and some others).

In the grammatical domain even though it is, as in the other countries, the least investigated, some interesting contributions have been published. José Joaquín Montes' 'Sobre la categoría de futuro en el español de Colombia', *BICC* 17.527-55 (1962) studies the different forms and values of the etymological form in *-re* — not in use today — the periphrastic forms (*haber de* + infinitive, *ir a* + infinitive, *pensar* + infinitive) and some other substitutes for the future (present indicative), using the materials used by certain works of *costumbrista* literature, newspapers, and also examples taken from the living language. With such materials concerning especially the speech of Antioquia and Calda, J. J. Montes has also studied, in 'Perífrasis con *ir* en Colombia', *BICC* 18.384-43 (1963), the gerund and infinitive constructions, systematically classifying their different aspect values (durative, incoative, iterative, intensive, etc.). María Beatriz Fontanella has written 'Algunas observaciones sobre el diminutivo en Bogotá', *BICC* 18.556-73 (1962), analyzing the distribution of the *-ito*, *-ico* suffixes and their different values (affective, superlative, emphatic, etc.). Luis Flórez has written a brief article, called '*Vos* y la segunda persona verbal en Antioquia', *BICC* 9.380-6 (1953), about the different forms of tenses in relation to the *voseo* used in the department of Antioquia.

With regard to lexicon, a fairly large number of works have been published lately in which many usual Colombian terms are included which are not in the *Diccionario de la Academia* or are given different meanings from those which they have in Colombian Spanish. Of all these works, perhaps the most comprehensive one is that by Julio Tobón Betancourt, *Colombianismos y otras voces de uso general* (Medellín, 1947; 2nd ed. Bogotá, 1953), using a large amount of materials, although terms of a general Hispanic character are included as well as simple phonetic variations found in popular speech.[62]

[62] Other lexicographic contributions of interest: Wenceslao Montoya, 'Colombianismos', *Universidad de Antioquia* 21.395-410 (1947) and 22.115-30 and 287-98 (1948) — these are additions, particularly from the speech of Antioquia, to Tobón's book; L. A. Acuña, *Diccionario de bogotanismos* (Bogotá, 1951), with many examples illustrating popular use; Abilio Lozano Caballero, 'Vocabulario de lenguaje popular colombiano', *BAC* 9.367-94 (1959), an advance work regarding letter *A*; Félix

The works done about certain aspects of regional speech in the interior of the country have more dialectological interest. Most of these works are the results of the research done during the compilation of materials for the Atlas Lingüístico-etnográfico de Colombia. Luis Flórez, in *Habla y cultura popular en Antioquia* (Bogotá, 1957), has studied the most important syntactic, morphological, and phonetic features of Antioquia speech, using the *Cuestionario* by T. Navarro, and finishing his research with a rigorous and detailed study of an ethnographic-linguistic nature, according to the 'words and things' method. Also to L. Flórez we owe the following descriptive works of regional speech: 'El español hablado en Segovia y Remedios', *BICC* 7.18-110 (1951), and 'Cuestiones del español hablado en Montería y Sincelejo', *BICC* 5.124-62 (1949). In both works he lists the most important grammatical and phonetic features and prepares ideological vocabularies of the popular speech of the departments of Antioquia and Bolivar respectively. On other occasions Flórez has devoted himself exclusively to the phonetic aspects of regional speech: 'El español hablado en Santander' *ALet* 4 (1964), 'La pronunciación del español en Bolívar', *BICC* 15.174-9 (1960), and 'Observaciones generales sobre la pronunciación del español en el departamento de Bolívar', *RCF* 5.155-68 (1960). A complement to the last two articles is the study by J. J. Montes 'Del español hablado en Bolívar', *BICC* 45.82-112 (1959), in which he organizes several morphological and syntactical data obtained in sixteen localities of the department: changes of gender, observations on number, use of some pronominal forms, morphology of the verb, and above all, the processes of nominal formation (derivation, composition, and parasynthesis). Emilio Robledo's 'Orígenes castizos del habla popular de Antioquia y Caldas', *BICC* 5.176-91 (1949), and *Universidad de Antioquia*, 32.413-26 (1956), explains the archaic character, phonetic and lexical, typical of these mountainous regions as a result of their isolation for several centuries. He tries to demonstrate this archaism by comparing certain linguistic facts in Antioquia with the language of Golden Age writers. Finally, J. J. Montes, in 'Algunos aspectos del habla popular en tres escritores caldenses', *BICC* 15.180-213 (1960), offers a brief literary documentation of some phonetic and grammatical phenomena in the speech of Caldas, as well as a more detailed vocabulary — neologisms or semantic changes — used in that region. The research carried out by Flórez and his associates as part of these studies of regional speech, following the 'words and things' method, is of considerable interest. All these works which have an ethnolinguistic and sociological interest are done with rigour, although with a documentation of uneven value. Some of them are accompanied by brief, though useful, annotations of a phonetic and grammatical nature.[63]

Restrepo, 'Correcciones al diccionario manual de la lengua española', *BAC* 10.7-25 (1960); Pedro Lira, 'Voces usadas en Colombia y en Chile', *ACALE* 353-69; Julio César García, 'Colombianismos históricos', *Universidad de Antioquia* 25.643-52 (1950), 26.99-108, 317-33, 547-72 (1951); José Joaquín Montes, 'Algunas fitonimias colombianas', *BICC* 18.163-86 (1963); José Antonio León Rey, 'Riñas de gallos y vocabulario de gallística', *RCF* 1:2.79-96 (1953).

[63] The most important are: L. Flórez, *Léxico de la casa popular urbana en Bolívar* (Bogota, 1962); María L. Rodríguez de Montes, 'Cunas, andadores y canciones de cuna en Bolívar, Santander,

Strictly lexical are some published works of varied extension and value, although always interesting because they offer materials gathered directly from the living language in the different dialectal areas of Colombia. In this respect, we should mention the work of Gonzalo Cadavid Uribe, *Oyendo conversar al pueblo* (Bogotá, 1953), as well as 'El saber popular', *Universidad Pontificia Bolivariana* 23:84.360-94 (1958). He has included a large number of words, sayings, idioms, and proverbs used in the department of Antioquia.[64]

Venezuela. — With regard to Venezuelan Spanish, one should mention the fairly useful study by H. L. A. Van Wijk, *Contribución al estudio del habla popular de Venezuela* (Amsterdam, 1946), with a well documented account of many syntactic, morphological and phonetic facts intimately related to other Hispanic speech areas and to old Castilian. However, this work is handicapped because it has not been done on the basis of field research, but on the data provided by *costumbrista* literature; for this reason it is not very reliable, especially in what concerns phonetics. It is well known that *costumbrista* writers *create* a popular language which does not always reflect the living one. Besides, since most of his literary sources are Rómulo Gallegos' novels, what his study reflects is basically the speech of the *llanos*. Finally, some of the features which Van Wijk considers to be typically Venezuelan (conservation of the future subjunctive, certain periphrasis with gerunds) are also found in other Spanish-American areas.

Angel Rosenblat's *Lengua y cultura de Venezuela* (Caracas, 1955) is a general description of Venezuelan speech with morphological and lexical examples in order to show how Venezuelan Spanish is, on the one hand, very conservative, but on the other hand has been adding different innovations to the classical foundation, be it by means

---

Antioquia y Nariño', *BICC* 17.313-48 (1962), which is essentially a folklore study because of the large number of cradle songs included; Jennie Figueroa Lorza, 'Léxico de la caña de azúcar en Palmira y La Cumbre, Valle del Cauca', *BICC* 18.553-621 (1963); María L. Rodríguez de Montes, 'Léxico de la alimentación popular en algunas regiones de Colombia', *BICC* 19.43-98 (1964); L. Flórez, 'Alimentación en Coyaima, Tolima', *Revista de Folklore* 3.173-292 (1948); J. J. Montes 'Apuntes sobre el vocabulario del tabaco en Bolívar y Santander', *BICC* 17.30-50 (1962); Luis R. Simbaqueba, 'Apuntes lexicográficos sobre la industria del ladrillo en Bogotá', *BICC* 13.57-82 (1958); Jennie Figueroa and Eduardo Camacho, 'Léxico de la carpintería en Bogotá', *BICC* 14.258-70 (1959); Eduardo Amaya and L. Flórez, 'Transporte y elaboración de la sal en Zipaquirá', *BICC* 3.171-227 (1947); J. J. Montes, 'Del castellano hablado en Manzanares', *BICC* 12.154-73 (1957), a vocabulary about coffee and its cultivation; and also by J. J. Montes, 'Del habla y el folclor en Manzanares', *BICC* 13.175-87 (1958), a vocabulary about sugar cane and the preparation of sugar loaf ('panela'); finally, C. E. López, 'Terminología de la embriaguez en las regiones caldenses de Calarcá y otras del mismo departamento', *Studium* 3:7-8.193-224 (Bogotá, 1959).

[64] Some other recent lexicographic studies about the speech of some Colombian regions: J. Sánchez Camacho, *Diccionario de voces y dichos del habla santandereana* (Bucaramanga, 1958); Leonardo Tascón, *Diccionario de provincialismos y barbarismos del Valle del Cauca y quechuismos usados en Colombia* (Cali, 1961); L. Flórez, 'Medicina, magia y animismo en Segovia de Antioquia', *Revista de Folklore* 6.185-236 (1951); F. Sánchez Arévalo, 'Notas sobre el lenguaje de Río de Oro', *BICC* 6.214-52 (1950), a vocabulary preceded by a very brief phonetic description of this dialectal speech.

of semantic extensions, or highly productive derivations, or simply by lexical creation within the atmosphere of popular speech. Also by A. Rosenblat is the best lexical study of Venezuelan speech published in the last decades: *Buenas y malas palabras en el castellano de Venezuela*² (Caracas-Madrid, 1960, 2 Vols.).[65] Although the book is presented in a form accessible to the non-linguist, there is in it an enormous amount of philological erudition; in each case, the origin, history, evolution, and geographic distribution of the term or expression are offered. This work is a preview of the dictionary of Venezuelan which Rosenblat has been preparing at the Institute Andrés Bello of the University of Caracas.[66]

Also lexical are the ethnolinguistic studies of S. Rodulfo Cortés, 'La curiara del Orinoco', *AVF* 4-5.195-206 (1957-8), 'Folklore del café en la región de El Haltillo', *AVF* 6.7-34 (1959-60), and of J. Marcano Rosas, 'Los usos del taparo en la isla de Margarita', *AVF* 4-5.231-53 (1957-58), and of J. A. de Armas Chitty, 'Vocabulario del hato', *AVF* 10-11.21-151 (1961-62).

Ecuador. — Although there have not been very many studies on Ecuadorian Spanish lately, this variety of Spanish has been the subject of one of the largest and most detailed general descriptions done recently about Spanish. This has been the work of Humberto Toscano Mateus, *El español en el Ecuador* (Madrid, 1956).[67] In a rather minute way he describes Ecuadorian Spanish in its phonetic, morphological, lexical, and syntactic aspects. Mainly he uses as a basis the speech of Quito, although he constantly refers to the dialectal areas in the interior of the country in order to show existing differences, particularly between the speech of the Sierra (archaisms with *leísmo*, strong consonantism, and vacillating vowels, with an appreciable native influence) and that of the Coast, whose phonetics is very similar to that of other maritime areas of America (with laxness of consonant system, strong vocalism, *loísmo* and *yeísmo*). Toscano pays considerable attention to the influence of the Quechua substratum which he thinks important, not only in the lexicon but also in phonetics and syntactic constructions.

The phonetic aspect of Ecuadorian Spanish has also been the subject of a brief study by P. Boyd-Bowman, 'Sobre la pronunciación del español en el Ecuador', *NRFH* 7.221-33 (1953), who, on the basis of the speech of three informants only, coincides with Toscano's distinction between the Andes zone (strong consonantism, Quechua influence in the vowels, in stress and the pronunciation of ř) and the coastal one, whose phonetics is not a continuation of that peculiar to the coasts of Colombia and Peru (with *yeísmo* and lax consonants). With regard to lexicon, Alfonso Cordero

[65] The first edition, in one volume, was made in Caracas - Madrid (1956).

[66] Compared with it, there is little interest in what other lexicographic studies contributed during those years, such as Inés de Müller's *Venezolanismos y otras palabras muy usadas* (Caracas, 1961), and Pedro Lira Urquieta, 'Venezolanismos y chilenismos y barbarismos que dejaron de serlo', *Boletín de la Academia Chilena* 14:45 (1954) and *Boletín de la Academia Venezolana* 23.68-73 (1955).

[67] H. Toscano himself made a summary description of Ecuadorian speech, based on this work, in his address 'El español hablado en Ecuador', *PFLE* 1.111-26.

Palacios' *Léxico de vulgarismos azuayos* (Cuenca, 1957) is very useful, in spite of a certain stylistic overflowering in his definitions and the doubtful nature of some etymologies. It is rich in materials from the provinces of Azogues and Cuenca. Lately, Julio Tobar Donoso has written a study on *El lenguaje rural en la región interandina del Ecuador* (Quito, 1961).

Central Areas. — Extremely little has been the progress made lately with regard to the Spanish of Peru, Bolivia, and Paraguay. The works published in Peru are of a lexical nature, and all of them are of very limited scope. Rubén Vargas Ugarte's *Glosario de peruanismos* (Lima, 1953)[68] includes some terms and proverbs used in Peru, alphabetically arranged (many of them are of common use in other Spanish-American countries, or in general standard Spanish). He exemplifies the meaning of these items with historical or literary quotations,[69] sometimes from the seventeenth century (names of coins, for instance). Essentially lexical also is the study of Martha Hildebrandt,[70] 'El español en Piura. Ensayo de dialectología peruana', *Letras* 43.256-72 (Lima, 1949), a valuable work because it offers several archaisms used in Piura — although they have been forgotten in Lima — and other interesting lexical examples (neologisms, words of doubtful origin, semantic changes, etc.). A. Tam Fox has studied another vocabulary aspect recently, in 'Notas lexicográficas en torno a la cocina limeña', *Sphinx* 14.185-201 (1961).

The Spanish of Bolivia remains almost forgotten. H. L. Van Wijk has shown an interest in its phonetics, 'Bolivianismos fonéticos en la obra costumbrista de Alfredo Guillén Pinto', *BFUCh* 13.49-73 (1961). He finds an existing phonetic continuity among the Andean zones of Argentina, Bolivia, and Peru (opposition *ll-y*, preservation of final *-s*, assibilation of *rr* and *tr*, etc.) and certain influences from the phonetics of Aymará on the speech of the northcentral region of the Bolivian high plateau; but since the study has been done on the basis of literary texts, one could question the real significance and value of the data recorded by the novelist and used by Van Wijk. Some grammatical peculiarities of Bolivian Spanish have been studied by Charles E. Kany in 'Some aspects of Bolivian popular speech', *Hispania* 15.193-205 (1947), where he expands what he had already mentioned in *American Syntax* about *voseo*, the use of the article and the unstressed personal pronoun, some functions of verbal tenses, and other grammatical points which could reveal a certain indigenous influence from Quechua and Aymará. Bertil Malmberg's 'Notas sobre la fonética del español en el Paraguay', *Yearbook of the New Society of Letters* (Lund, 1947), 18 pp., are of particular interest because the phonetic peculiarities that he mentions (alveolar arti-

[68] Published again in Lima (1956) and a third time in Lima [no date].

[69] Another case of dialectological research done on the written language is C. A. Angeles Caballero's *Los peruanismos en la literatura peruana* I (Lima, 1956), an unquestionably useful work, given the lack of rigorous studies about Peruvian Spanish.

[70] She is also the author of a detailed and well documented study on *La lengua de Bolívar* (I, *Léxico*; Caracas, 1961), in which Spanish-American scholars can find interesting data about indigenisms, archaisms, and provincialisms in Peru and Venezuela, as well as foreign terms used by Bolívar.

culation of *t*, affricate *ŷ*, assibilation of *r̄* and *tr*, preservation of ḷ and also of hiatuses) help him to present his theory about the special situation of Paraguayan Spanish as a learned official language, to which we referred while talking about the problem of substratum (see pp. 115-16).

Argentina. — Argentinian is at present one of the best studied varieties of Spanish. The Institute of Philology of the University of Buenos Aires perpetuated dialectological investigation, which already has a tradition in the country. Of particular interest is the work of Berta Elena Vidal de Battini during several years of research. She started with a valuable and detailed geographical and linguistic study about certain phonetic phenomena peculiar to Argentinian Spanish (intonation, articulation of *s*, *r̄* and *ll-y*), providing excellent linguistic maps for all of them.[71] Later she expanded her phonetic and morphological investigations (*voseo*) in 'El español de la Argentina', *PFLE* 1.183-90, with considerable grammatical and phonetic annotations.

Recently she has published *El español de la Argentina* (Buenos Aires, 1964) which is an expanded edition of all those previous works and a valuable general description of Argentinian Spanish, including detailed analyses of the most characteristic phenomena, all of them illustrated in fourteen magnificent maps.

Bertil Malmberg's *Etudes sur la phonétique de l'espagnol parlé en Argentine* (Lund, 1950), in spite of certain errors of interpretation, is of great interest, a most detailed study of Argentinian Spanish using modern structural methods by a scholar who is an excellent phonetician. His analysis of Argentinian peculiarities of pronunciation (lengthening of stressed vowels, *rehilamiento* and unvoicing of *ž* coming from *ll-y*, aspiration of final *-s*, etc.) leads him to the same conclusion he presented in 'L'espagnol dans le nouveau Monde' (see p. 115) i.e. linguistic changes should be explained by trying first to find the reason within the system in the light of the specific historical, social, and cultural conditions of the area, with recourse to the influence of substrata only when these conditions would warrant such an explanation. Malmberg notices that Argentinian Spanish follows the general characteristics of Spanish. The problem of the unvoicing of *ž* resulting from *y-ll* was the subject of a study by A. Zamora Vicente, 'Rehilamiento porteño', *Fi* 1.5-22 (1949), who considered that *š*, its unvoiced manifestation, is of a popular basis and the most frequent in Buenos Aires. Guillermo L. Guitarte replied to this — after a polemic in which A. Alonso, Boyd-Bowman, Malmberg and Ana María Barrenechea took part — in 'El ensordecimiento del žeismo porteño. Fonética y fonología', *RFE* 39.261-83 (1955), a statistical study showing that the unvoicing, a phenomenon peculiar to the middle class rather than to the lower classes, occurred only in 16% of the speakers. Guitarte tried to find a structural explanation for it: the *rehilamiento* was due, he said, to the tendency to make a clearer correlation between /ĉ/ and /y/, giving to the /y/ a (*chicheante*) timbre similar to

[71] Cf. *El español de la Argentina* (Buenos Aires, 1954). Her article about the 'Extensión de la *rr* múltiple en la Argentina', *Filología* 3.181-84 (1951) is a preview of one of the chapters in this little book.

that of /č/; but with *rehilamiento* the laryngeal vibrations are weakened, thus the /ž/ tends progressively to be unvoiced and the pair of sounds goes from a relation based on voicing, /ĉ/-/ž/, to one of plosion versus friction, /ĉ/-/š/. The grammatical aspect of Argentinian Spanish has been less studied. We owe to Giovanni Meo Zilio a series of brief studies about the influence of Italian on the Spanish of the Rio de la Plata, both Argentinian and Uruguayan.[72] He refers to the means of propagation of Italian influence in that region and to certain obvious cases of lexical and morphological influence (some suffixes occasionally used).[73]

Berta Elena Vidal de Battini's *El habla rural de San Luis* (Buenos Aires, 1949; and *BDH* VII [1948]) is fundamental for the understanding of the language of the interior provinces. It is one of the most complete and rigorous descriptions of a regional Spanish-American speech. This volume covers only phonetics, with a particular emphasis on intonation problems and grammar, but so many examples of derivation and composition are provided that the lexical aspect is also fairly well covered. This a region of particular interest because in a certain way it is part of two linguistic orbits: during the colonial period it was part of Chile, but later, in the seventeenth century, it became linguistically related to the speech of the Argentinian coast of Buenos Aires, from which it differs in some phonetic and morphological respects.

Some suggestive ideas are expressed by Federico E. País in *Algunos rasgos estilísticos de la lengua popular catamarqueña* (Tucumán, 1954). While studying the main phonological, grammatical, and lexical features in the speech of Catamarca, he maintains that it is not possible to confine oneself to quoting isolated lexicographic facts, but that it is necessary to analyze them in their living function, within the total system of the language. Thus he speaks of the reorganization of the morphological system in the speech of that region, while observing that two tendencies can be appreciated which have merged in the *criollo* speech: the learned tendency, conservative and archaic, and the innovating forces, with popular rooting, within which one could place the indigenous influence. Also very useful are the studies of 'words and things' done by Vidal de Battini with the utmost care: 'El léxico de los buscadores de oro de La Carolina, San Luis', *Homenaje Krüger* 1.303-333; with an abundance of terms of maritime origin, as well as archaic and Quechua terms; 'El léxico de los yerbateros', *NRFH* 7.190-208 (1953), with a Guaraní basis; and 'El léxico ganadero de la Argen-

[72] Cf. 'Alcune tendenze sintattiche e stilistiche nello spagnolo medio rioplatense', *QIA* 3:22.417-27 (1958); 'Un morfema italiano con funzione stilistica nello spagnolo rioplatense', *LN* 19.58-64 (1958); 'Una serie di morfemi italiani con funzione stilistica nello spagnolo nell'Uruguay', *LN* 20.49-54 (1959); 'Sull' elemento italiano nello spagnolo rioplatense', *LN* 21.97-103 (1960); and 'Canali e veicoli dell'italianismo in Uruguay', *LN* 23.117-21 (1962).

[73] The magnificent study *El argentinismo 'Es de lindo'* (Madrid, 1960) by Fritz Krüger, goes completely beyond the limits of Argentinian dialectology and is really a masterful work of comparative Romanic syntax, done on the basis of Hispanic construction also usual in Argentina. The debated book *La peculiaridad lingüística rioplatense* by A. Castro, of which a second revised edition has been made in Madrid, 1960 (the first one was in Buenos Aires, 1941), approaches linguistic facts a more from historical-cultural standpoint than a strictly dialectological one. Nonetheless, it clarifies some aspects of philological problems with observations which should not be disregarded by a dialectologist.

tina. La oveja en la Patagonia y en Tierra del Fuego', *Fi* 5.135-189 (1959). There has been a notable increase in these ethnolinguistic studies in Argentina. Several of them are masterfully done by A. Dornheim: 'La alfarería criolla en Los Algarrobos', *Homenaje Krüger* 1.335-64; 'Algunos aspectos arcaicos de la cultura popular cuyana', *AIL* 5.303-36 (1952), which is a complete vocabulary of agricultural tasks and tools; 'Posición ergológica de los telares cordobeses en Sudamérica', *Revista del Instituto Nacional de la Tradición*, I (Buenos Aires, 1949); 'La vivienda rural en el valle de Nono', *Anales de Arqueología y Etnología*, X (Mendoza, 1948). Also according to the 'words and things' method, different aspects of popular culture have been studied by Víctor Barrionuevo Imposti, *El uso de la madera en el valle de San Javier* (Córdoba, 1949); María E. Zappacosta, 'La vitivinicultura de Mendoza', *AIL* 6.375-459 (1957), with a short appendix of words relative to drunkenness;[74] A. Anastasi, 'El riego rural en Mendoza', *Homenaje Krüger* 2.519-34; and J. F. Calderón, 'El barrilete. Notas para el léxico de la artesanía argentina', *Fi* 2.65-71 (1950).

As in the rest of America, lexical studies, not all of the same value, are the most numerous. One of the richest and most valuable is the one by Tito Saubidet, *Vocabulario y refranero criollo* (Buenos Aires, 1943),[75] with an abundance of linguistic and folklore materials, particularly those relative to horses and other manifestations of rural life in the southern part of the Buenos Aires province, although this is not the work of a linguist and no philological study is made in it. Also very rich and useful is the work of José Vicente Solá, *Diccionario de regionalismos de Salta* (Buenos Aires, 1947; also 1950 and 1957) ,where he gathers a large number of words from pre-Hispanic origin, especially Quechua, relative to both toponymy and fauna and flora, and even some other lexical aspects.[76]

Uruguay. — With regard to phonetics, Washington Vázquez has done a rigorous phonological study about 'El fonema *s* en el español del Uruguay', *Revista de la*

[74] Cf. also by María E. Zappacosta, 'Designaciones argentinas de la embriaguez', *AIL* 6.426-9 (1957), without any reference to the similar studies by R. R. Madueño mentioned on page 00.

[75] And successive editions, also in Buenos Aires, 1945, 1949, and 1952.

[76] In order not to make this account too long, I will just list other lexicographical studies: Guillermo A. Terrera, 'Voces y refranero del caballo criollo', *BAAL* 17.409-70 (1948), a detailed study, though not very precise in its etymological comments; Pedro Inchauspe, *Más voces y costumbres del campo argentino* (Buenos Aires, 1954); Carlos Villafuerte, *Voces y costumbres de Catamarca* (Buenos Aires, 1954; *BAAL*, 24.133-64, 305-92 [1959]); F. E. Mendilaharzu, 'Experiencias del campo. Algunas aportaciones lingüísticas tucumanas', *BAAL* 25.543-89 (1960); Luis A. Flores, 'Vocabulario de regionalismos correntinos', *BAAL* 23.399-450 (1958) and 'Contribución al conocimiento de los regionalismos de Córdoba', *BAAL* 25.365-98 (1960); Julio Viggiano Essain, *Vocabulario tradicional cordobés* (Córdoba, 1956; with an indication of its geographic distribution); Julián Cáceres Freyre, *Diccionario de regionalismos de la provincia de La Rioja* (Buenos Aires, 1961); Miguel A. Esteva Sáenz, 'Voces entrerrianas', *BAAL* 28.303-70 (1963); O. di Lullo, *Contribución al estudio de voces santiagueñas* (Buenos Aires, 1946; toponymy, fauna, and flora); Teófilo Sánchez de Bustamante, 'Regionalismos jujeños', *BAAL* 20.195-247 (1951). The vocabulary of *Martín Fierro* has been studied lately by M. Manso (Tucuman, 1945), Francisco I. Castro (Buenos Aires, 1950; words and expressions), and by Pedro Inchauspe (Buenos Aires, 1955); that of *Don Segundo Sombra*, by Horacio J. Becco, *BAAL* 19.49-80 (1950; there is also the enlarged edition of Buenos Aires, 1952).

Facultad de Humanidades y Ciencias 10.87-94 (1953). One of the allophones of this phoneme in word final position [s] points to a possible change in the immediate future of the Uruguayan vocalic system, with phonemes *a:*, *ɛ*, *ɔ* as number morphemes. José Pedro Rona, in 'Vulgarización o adaptación diastrática de neologismos o cultismos' (offprint from *Revista Nacional*), speaks of a 'normalizing' force operating on anomalous forms within the popular system, and concerning both phonetics and morphology.

The conflict arising from two languages in contact with each other has been exemplified by J. P. Rona in two books: *El dialecto fronterizo del norte del Uruguay* (Montevideo, 1959) and *La frontera lingüística entre el portugués y el español en el norte del Uruguay* (Pôrto Alegre, 1963). By means of an analysis of the two phonological systems and of some grammatical facts, he sees several zones of transition and notices that the distribution of these zones is not due to historical, ethnic, oı cultural reasons. He assumes that also on the Brassilian side Portuguese must offer some Hispanic features, at least in its lexicon. In 'La lengua española en el Río Grande del Sur', *PFLE* 1.361-6 Dionisio Fuertes Alvarez confirms Rona's supposition indicating that Spanish influence can be observed not only in its lexicon but also in its morphology.

With regard to the lexicon, and besides some Argentinian studies about the Rio de la Plata speech which are also applicable to Uruguay, one should mention J. C. Guarnieri's useful *Nuevo vocabulario campesino rioplatense, con las locuciones más usadas en el Uruguay* (Montevideo, 1957), based on firsthand data and also materials from literary works.

Chile. — Rodolfo Oroz' 'El español de Chile', *PFLE* 1.93-110, is a very detailed though very condensed enumeration of the peculiarities of Chilean popular speech, both phonetic and grammatical. He also speaks of the dialectal division of the country into four zones: northern, central, southern, and that of Chiloé. I. Silva-Fuenzalida's 'Estudio fonológico del español de Chile', *BFUCh* 7.153-76 (1952-3) is a rigorous application of phonemic principles and methods (especially those of Trager) in order to minutely describe the phonetic system of standard Chilean speech. Ambrosio Rabanales, in 'Hiato y antihiato en el español vulgar de Chile', *BFUCh* 12.197-223 (1960), makes a detailed study of the different solutions used by popular speech with regard to hiatuses, in order to maintain the unstable equilibrium of the vocalic system. He points out that the tendency towards monophthongization and the creation of hiatuses through consonantal syncopation are Latin and Hispanic habits of articulation. In another article, 'Diptongación y monoptongación en el español vulgar de Chile', *RJb* 11.319-27 (1960), A. Rabanales has analyzed the diphthongs originating from the vocalization of grouped consonants (*b*, *d*, *g*), and the cases of popular monophthongization due to a dissimilation or elimination of infrequent occurrences within the system.

The grammatical aspects of Chilean Spanish have been the subject of some noteworthy studies. Rodolfo Oroz's 'Prefijos y pseudoprefijos en el español actual de

Chile', *BFUCh* 7.115-32 (1952-3) deals with the uses and vitality of certain prefixes (*super-*, *ultra-*, *sub-*, etc.), common both in the written or technical language and in colloquial speech. Rabanales, in 'Recursos lingüísticos, en el español de Chile, de expresión de la afectividad', *BFUCh* 10.205-302 (1958), studies in detail the main phonetic, morphological, syntactic, and lexical methods used in familiar or popular speech to reveal affections or emotions, most of which are also those of general standard Spanish. 'El uso de los morfemas formales y familiares en el español de Chile', *BFUCh* 8.439-55 (1954-5) by I. Silva-Fuenzalida, has a sociolinguistic orientation, in which the author evaluates the respectful and familiar forms of Chilean Spanish according to the social condition of the speakers, their emotional states of mind, their individual characteristics, etc.

In Chile several ethnolinguistic investigations have also been done lately following the 'words and things' method, such as Rodolfo Oroz's 'La carreta sureña', *Homenaje Krüger* 1.365-88, which is very detailed and well documented; Bernardo Valenzuela Rojas' 'El horno campesino y su función panificadora', *BFUCh* 13.235-82 (1961); Oreste Plath's 'Alimentación y lenguaje popular', *Revista Médico-asistencial* (Santiago, 1949), 18 pp.; Stella Moder Pérez de Valenzuela's 'Chilenismo de Maintecillo. El lenguaje pesquero', *BFUCh* 5.379-422 (1947-9); and Elba Koller's 'El cultivo del arroz en la provincia de Ñuble y su terminología', *BFUCh* 9.87-103 (1956-57). Another contribution to the lexical study of Chilean speech is A. Rabanales and L. García Cifuentes' 'Primer viaje de investigación', *BFUCh* 4.157-220 (1944-46), an alphabetical compilation of Chilenisms used in the province of Coquimbo, preceded by some methodological considerations. Also by Rabanales 'Uso tropológico, en el lenguaje chileno, de nombres del reino vegetal', *BFUCh* 5.137-263 (1947-9) is a rich catalogue of words, always with their phonetic transcriptions, classified ideologically. R. Oroz's 'Metáforas relativas a las partes del cuerpo humano en la lengua popular chilena', *BICC* 5.85-100 (1949) refers mainly to the similarity of form between the object and the image it suggests. The strong influence of English in a particular aspect of Spanish vocabulary can be observed in the studies of Lidia Contreras, 'Los anglicismos en el lenguaje deportivo chileno', *BFUCh* 7.177-341 (1952-3) and *Diccionario histórico del deporte* (Santiago de Chile, 1962). Useful materials are also offered by Oreste Plath's article, 'Aportaciones populares sobre el vino y la chicha', *AIL* 8.361-413 (1962), and Elisa Carrasco's 'Terminología pesquera de la provincia de Valparaíso', *BFUCh* 9.15-33 (1956-7).

From this quick survey of Spanish-American dialectology, one can infer that we have come a long way in the last two decades, especially in some areas. But, taking a closer look, it is apparent that a much longer and difficult road still appears ahead of us. With regard to some American regions we ignore almost completely how their spoken Spanish really is. With regard to other zones, we possess only scattered data which are not always trustworthy; some erroneous or inaccurate facts, owing to a lack of rigorous investigation, are passed on from book to book. Immense and urgent tasks await

Spanish-American dialectology; these will require the team effort of many investigators.

Perhaps one would need to start by knowing in full detail the true situation of spoken Spanish in the big urban centers of America at present. These are the main centers for linguistic expansion; it is there that the fundamental peculiarities in the speech of each country arise, and from there that the pattern-norms of the language extend into regional speeches, stifling them or leveling them into national uniformity. Buenos Aires, Bogota, Santiago, Mexico, La Habana, Montevideo, Caracas, Lima, and other capitals are focuses of linguistic effervescence, whose evolutionary tendencies may not be similar to one another, or to the general pattern of the language. These capitals usually provide expressive norms to the rest of the country, and in them the principal varieties of American Spanish are represented. All of these basic varieties of the cultural-linguistic totality, which Spanish America is, must be studied urgently, systematically described in their phonetic, grammatical and lexical aspects, as a starting point for studies of a regional character within each country, and as fundamental ingredients of the Spanish-American linguistic picture.

Another urgent task would be the exact demarcation of the different dialectal areas of each of the American countries. Naturally, this should be done not on the basis of impressionistic arguments, as has been the case sometimes, but by means of a direct exploration of each national territory. Before determining dialectal lines, it would be necessary to study the fundamental phonetic, lexical, and grammatical realities of each region. With the help of carefully planned basic questionnaires, this would not be a difficult task, nor would the territorial extension of some countries prove an insurmountable obstacle. The demarcation of dialectal lines within each country would permit us to start the job of drawing regional linguistic atlases, an enterprise which is practically impossible for the moment in most parts of America.

It seems evident that Spanish-American dialectology would progress rapidly if there could be some kind of coordination of the different individual efforts. It would be extremely beneficial for each investigator to orient his efforts, regardless of how minimal and specific they might be, towards a common goal, as an integral part of a higher *totum*. In order to do that it would be necessary to use a uniform methodology and to determine concrete goals of general interest. It is absolutely necessary to 'modernize' linguistic studies in Spanish America, using working procedures whose effectiveness has been amply proven in Europe. It will also be necessary to give a structural orientation to these studies, without confining oneself to providing isolated observations concerning this or that particular problem. Phonetic analyses, fundamental as they are in any dialectological study, must be supplemented with the phonemic interpretation of the elements in the system. It should become equally important that works of a lexical nature be more than simple alphabetical compilations of words and expressions; and that there be an effort to establish the value of each term within its own semantic field and to define geographic, historical, and cultural factors. In other words, it is necessary to arrive at the internal form of each Spanish-American linguistic variety.

Of course, it would also be desirable to devote greater attention to grammatical phenomena. In many of the works published lately, there is a concern only for phonetic and lexical facts, while grammatical structure, the backbone of the language, remains ignored. For centuries, grammar has only been concerned with the written language. The changing reality of spoken language seemed impossible to grasp. It is true that the compilation and study of grammatical phenomena, especially speech phenomena, require a greater effort, due to the higher complexity of certain constructions; but today we have at our disposal adequate means to fix spoken language and reproduce it in all its complex reality. One single syntactic feature can be more significant than a whole series of lexical peculiarities.

We must avoid simplifying generalizations because they can distort the reality of a language. In an area such as Spanish America, with an intense linguistic effervescence, where a multifaceted linguistic situation is evident in all its aspects, any scholarly preconceived judgment may become disastrous for the exactitude and rigor of investigation, and any simplification of this complex instability can basically deform reality. This is why detailed and minute monographs on the speech of small regions or localities are necessary, together with general studies of a continental scope. Without this type of monograph any global synthesis will never be more than a more or less accurate intuition, a more or less dangerous adventure.

Another one of the great common tasks of Spanish-American dialectology should consist, I believe, in a dispassionate analysis of the problem of substratum languages. The changes undergone by American Spanish, as well as its peculiarities, should be explained in terms of the internal system of the language, whenever this is possible. Blaming any peculiarity of American Spanish on the influence of substratum languages is a comfortable and easy solution, but entirely gratuitous unless it is perfectly justified — particularly when the structure of the substratum languages is generally unknown. In this respect, Malmberg's attitude, an extreme one according to some scholars, seems to be very reasonable. Even in the lexical domain one has to act carefully. A simple catalogue of prehispanic terms, most of them toponymy or terms of the fauna and flora peculiar to a particular region, is not very useful. It is necessary to evaluate the vitality of these indigenous terms, to weigh their importance within the internal structure of the language. It would likewise be important to obtain the collaboration of specialists in these native languages in order to elucidate the true influence of the substratum and therefore to work on the basis of accurate knowledge and thus avoid gratuitous statements one way or the other.

It would be advisable to make clear to what extent the simplification of at least some aspects of the Spanish-American linguistic system is caused by the fact that American Spanish is a peripheric or colonization language. This simplification or morphological reduction is, on the other hand, offset by an increase in periphrastic, analytical forms. The readjustments operatant in the morphosyntactic system could be compared with those operatant within the lexical system in the different regions; that is to say, they could be compared with national semantic changes. Perhaps the archaic character of some Spanish American speech areas could have a basis in this particular condition of American Spanish as a peripheral language, a condition which could also explain, perhaps, the impetus with which some evolutional tendencies peculiar to the Spanish system have developed.

Another task of common interest should be the historically documented and linguistic investigation of the possible areas of Spanish dialectal influence due to the different regional origin of the colonists. The Andalusian character of the Caribbean area seems to be a proven fact; the relationship of certain other areas to the speech of the Canary Islands is no less probable; the occidental features of American Spanish have also been revealed by Corominas. It would be worth pursuing on these problems in a systematic way. A historical and documental study might throw new light upon many other questions of American Spanish, as Angel Rosenblat has profitably shown on some occasions;[77] it would be advisable to go further and further in this direction. Spanish-American historical philology has not yet materialized.

[77] Lately, for instance, in 'Las generaciones argentinas del siglo XIX ante el problema de la lengua', *Revista de la Universidad de Buenos Aires* 5:4.539-84 (1960).

HISPANIC PHILOLOGY*

YAKOV MALKIEL

I. INTRODUCTION

In assessing Latin America's, all told, modest share in current inquiries into Hispanic philology, it is essential to remember, from the outset, the characteristic scope of the Spanish keywords *filología* and *filólogo*. Whereas present-day American English usage tends to accept philology in a fairly narrow sense ('critical study of ancient texts, within the matrix of cultural history — frequently as a preliminary step toward literary or linguistic analysis'), the more conservative Spanish usage, consecrated by the German-inspired preferences of R. Menéndez Pidal and his Madrid School, influential on both sides of the Atlantic, uses *filología* almost as an equivalent of 'Humanities' and makes *filólogo* a counterpart of 'humanist'. As a result, bulletins, journals, monograph series, book ventures, research institutes, and academic curricula emblazoning *filología* in their names may be expected to include in the range of their scholarly concern and curiosity not only the hard core of philology proper, esp. paleographic and critical editions of texts, glossaries, and bibliographic inventories, but also motley bits of folklore, *Wörter-und-Sachen* studies, dialectology, metrics, historical grammar, etymology, descriptive sketches, esthetic, social, or philosophic ('existentialist') interpretations of literature as well as its historical background, and the like.

On the Spanish American scene this semantic discrepancy marks not only a point of fluctuating terminology; it has far deeper and more important connotations. With rare, if very notable, exceptions, the relatively few native Hispano-American intellectuals at all addicted to 'philology' have been concerned with those ingredients of the Spanish heritage which have lingered on, from colonial times, in their own local cultures. This is particularly true of folklore and dialectology, whose most sophisticated spokesmen, steeped in the mythological, literary, and linguistic cross-currents of three millennia of European culture, have specialized in seeking out noteworthy archaisms in their country's (or their continent's) native traditions. As a consequence, much of the soundest folkloristic and dialectological research on the local scene is not strictly synchronic, but adorned with introductory sketches of the Old World background or studded with vivid 'flashbacks'.[1] The separation of antiquarian 'philology'

* It is a pleasure to record here my gratitude to Marilyn May Vihman for her perceptive critical reading of this chapter in manuscript and, later, in galley-proof.

[1] The inclusion of a very generous slice of European antecedents can be closely observed in the case of the trail-blazing booklet by María Rosa Lida, *El cuento popular hispano-americano y la literatura*

from these other disciplines with which it happens to be organically interwoven in actual practice is, within the fabric of Spanish American culture, somewhat constrained, not to say artificial.

As a collateral heir to the metropolitan Spanish tradition of scholarship, South and Central America's school of philology suffers from one very severe handicap: Until fairly recently there did not develop on Spanish soil any organized body of or apparatus for research geared to classical studies;[2] serious Oriental studies (with the exception of investigations into classical Arabic and, on a minor scale, Biblical Hebrew and related languages) are to this day virtually non-existent;[3] and, most surprising of all, 'modern philology', whether viewed as an essentially medievalistic discipline or as one principally focusing on the last five centuries of 'Western culture', represents in Spain a very recent innovation, postdating the Civil War.[4] Given the strong dependence of Spanish American academic standards on those favored in Spain — a dependence far more pronounced in the 20th than in the 19th century, it is small wonder that no sustained work in, say, comparative Romance, Germanic, Slavic, Indic, or Chinese philology could evolve anywhere on an impressive scale in the Spanish-speaking section of the New World.

It is exceedingly difficult to delimit territorially the cis-Atlantic realm of native Hispanic philology, to set off the temporal limits of its 'modern' period, and to vindicate one's assertions with references to the biographies of the unfolding drama's chief protagonists. By standards normally applied elsewhere, Andrés Bello (1781-1865) could at best qualify for the role of a precursor; but the pride his native Venezuela — if not his adopted country Chile — takes in him has of late been translated

(Buenos Aires, 1941), which was to start the future Mrs. Malkiel on a meteoric career of philological scholarship at its least adulterated. Cf. Stanley L. Robe's perceptive review, in *RomPh* 19.99-103 (1965-66), esp. 102, of Susana Chertudi, *Cuentos folklóricos de la Argentina*, Vol. 1 (Buenos Aires, 1960).

[2] On the timid re-awakening of classical scholarship south of the Pyrenees see Arnold G. Reichenberger, 'Herodotus in Spain; comments on a neglected essay (1949) by María Rosa Lida de Malkiel', *RomPh* 19.235-249 (1965-66), esp. 246ff.

[3] The string, not to say dynasty, of influential Spanish Arabists, spanning a century of sustained research principally in the realm of Hispano-Arabic philology, includes Francisco Codera, Julián Ribera y Tarragó, the many-sided and highly productive Miguel Asín Palacios, and Emilio García Gómez; at the present juncture, etymology and toponymy in this domain are most assiduously cultivated by Jaime Oliver Asín. Two meritorious late-19th-century scholars stood off from the main stream of events: the lexicographer L. Eguílaz y Yanguas and that penetrating student and unsurpassed connoisseur of Mozarabic antiquities F. J. Simonet. The Hebraists form no comparable corps, and have appeared on the scene only quite sporadically. Their number includes the rigorous paleographer and archivist Pe Fidel Fita; the cataloguer of rabbinical manuscripts and collector of Old Judeo-Spanish lexical gems M. Gaspar Remiro; the Catalan experts J. M. Millás Vallicrosa and I. González Llubera (d. 1962), the latter a long-time resident of Belfast and Cambridge (England) and the author of numerous publications in English; and the current representative in Madrid of paleo-Semitic and Sephardic studies, F. Pérez Castro.

[4] To the best of my knowledge, the periodical *Filología moderna*, founded in 1960, is the first Spanish-language journal of its kind, trailing decades behind its counterparts in France, Great Britain, and the United States, and a century behind Herrig's *Archiv für das Studium der neueren Sprachen*.

into a monumental edition of his scattered writings, each volume preceded by a major critical sketch from the pen of a living expert;[5] and since the ranks of these contemporary analysts include A. Alonso, Á. Rosenblat and S. Gili Gaya, Bello's work continues to be a modern focus of discussion, much as W. von Humboldt's in Germany and, on balance, more so than W. D. Whitney's in the States. Bello's contact with British philologists during the years of his diplomatic mission to London was, despite its fruitfulness, episodic; in contrast, the Parisian stay of his intellectual successor R. J. Cuervo (b. 1844) was so prolonged as to make one wonder to what extent his work should be credited to his Colombian background rather than to the broadly European if not narrowly French tradition of late 19th-century linguistics. Cuervo's claim to a place of distinction on the contemporary scene, despite his death over half a century ago (1911), could be staked out with a reference to the belated posthumous publication (1944) of two of his most meritorious treatises and to the continued appearance — under the aegis of a Bogotá institute honoring his name — of studies he left unfinished.[6] The concluding decades of the 19th century were marked by the transfer to Santiago de Chile of two young German scholars, R. Lenz and F. Hanssen, who jointly transformed that city's Instituto Pedagógico into a citadel of Spanish

[5] In this impressive series of *Obras completas*, Vol. 4 (1951), containing the classic *Gramática de la lengua castellana destinada al uso de los americanos*, includes A. Alonso's prefatory essay (ix-lxxxvi): 'Introducción a los estudios gramaticales de Andrés Bello'; similarly, Vol. 5 (1951), a miscellany of *Estudios gramaticales*, is ushered in by Á. Rosenblat's remarks (ix-cxxxviii) on 'Las ideas ortográficas de Bello', while S. Gili Gaya's 'Introducción a los estudios ortológicos y métricos de Bello: arte y ciencia de la poesía' (xii-ciii) paves the reader's way to Vol. 6 (1955): *Estudios filológicos*, Part 1.

[6] Bogotá's state-sponsored and well-endowed Instituto Caro y Cuervo, which issues a weighty *Boletín* (= *Thesaurus*; Vol. 1: 1945), has published a useful, meticulously documented pamphlet: *Bibliografía de Rufino José Cuervo* (1951), from the pen of Rafael Torres Quintero. This guide contains — aside from an informative Introduction (9-31) and an annotated list of Cuervo's not too recklessly scattered writings (37-61) — a most helpful record of critical reactions to the chosen author's publications (65-104). Other symptoms of a 'Cuervo Renaissance': not only have the two volumes of the torso of his unique 'syntactic dictionary' been reissued by the Institute, but at least two fascicles of the previously unavailable Vol. 3 (EA-EM, including the book-length entry on the definite articles *el*, *la*, etc.), totalling 200 large-format, two-column pages, have been successfully salvaged under the scrupulous editorial leadership of Fernando Antonio Martínez (1959, 1961). There is further available at present a two-volume edition of Cuervo's works (*Obras*, 1954), again sponsored by the Institute and jointly packing well over three thousand pages tidily printed on extra-thin but solid paper. Of these, Vol. 1, containing by way of Forematter a substantial essay by F. A. Martínez (vii-cxlvi), includes all of Cuervo's major writings short of the dictionary, notably a reproduction of the 6th, posthumous edition of the 'Bible' of American Spanish philology: the *Apuntaciones críticas sobre el lenguaje bogotano*; the author's notes to Bello's standard grammar of Spanish (see above, fn. 5); and the long-hidden treatise 'Castellano popular y castellano literario', which became available for the first time in the *Obras inéditas de Rufino J. Cuervo* (1944). Vol. 2, supervised by the same Rafael Torres Quintero who had previously assembled and rigorously edited Cuervo's shorter writings — a few of them forgotten, inaccessible, or unknown (*Disquisiciones sobre filología castellanas* [1950]) — contains, in addition to these less elaborate pieces, a selection of fragments, drafts, significant epistolary statements, non-technical ventures, and other items of heightened concern to the student of Colombian *Gelehrtengeschichte*. An intimate glimpse of Cuervo cast in the less formal role of a letter writer is provided by J. Ignacio Tellechea Idígoras in *Thesaurus* 16.577-613 (1961). For the latest information consult J. J. Montes, 'Bibliografía del español de Colombia', *Thesaurus* 20.425-465 (1965), an inventory comprising 342 items.

philology; again, it is difficult to apportion the credits, though one may state that both European-trained scholars brilliantly measured up to the challenge of the New World: Lenz rose to the occasion by adding to his original pioneering competence in phonetics a new skill in anthropological linguistics (Araucanian, Papiamento), in syntax (psychologically tinged, in the Wundtian tradition), and in the theory of language teaching; Hanssen, a run-of-the-mill Latinist at the start of his career, became, through a sharp reorientation, a trail-blazing explorer of Old Spanish conjugation, syntax, dialectology, metrics, and textual criticism.[7] Both founding fathers of Chilean philology have left direct students — not a few of them still alive and even actively engaged in research, but their particular lines of inquiry were not pursued with any degree of energy after their demise.

Throughout the next act of the play, which takes us to the mid-'twenties, Buenos

[7] The intellectual legacy of Lenz and Hanssen has been badly neglected, perhaps because, being foreigners by birth, education, and training as well as by range, slant, and style of creative activity, they have not qualified for belated recognition as national 'heroes' — very much unlike Bello, Cuervo, and even such men of lesser stature as the Chilean J. T. Medina and the Venezuelan L. Alvarado.

The accessibility and potential impact of Hanssen's writings have been gravely impaired by the original publication of most of them in such out-of-the-way series as the *Anales de la Universidad de Chile* and, worse, the *Verhandlungen des deutschen wissenschaftlichen Vereins in Santiago*; by the failure of his direct students to collect them into two or three manageable volumes, carefully cross-referenced and indexed; by the unwillingness or inability of the Argentine publisher who in 1943 reprinted Hanssen's *Gramática histórica de la lengua castellana* (orig. Halle, 1913) to have this important book brought up to date and annotated; and by the unavailability of any dependable bibliographic guide to Hanssen's writings except for the sketchy — and avowedly partial — bibliography compiled, upon his death, by E. C. Hills, with stray addenda suggested by C. Carroll Marden and K. Pietsch, see *MLN* 35.183-184, 505 (1920). Yet Hanssen's monographs contain the seeds of promising studies not yet undertaken to this day; I fell back on some of them in preparing my articles 'Toward a reconsideration of the Old Spanish imperfect in *-ía* ~ *-ié*', *HR* 27.435-81 (1959; *Joseph E. Gillet Memorial*) and 'Diphthongization, monophthongization, metaphony: Studies in their interaction in the paradigm of the Old Spanish *-ir* verbs', *Lg* 42.430-72 (1966).

Lenz, whose active teaching at Santiago spanned a period of forty years (1890-1930), has, on balance, aroused greater interest as the stronger personality and keener mind of the two. The earliest bibliography of his writings, hidden away in the obscure *Revista de bibliografía chilena y extranjera* (May, 1914), was expanded by R. Vilches to include a total of 91 items and appeared in the Lenz Memorial — originally planned as a testimonial on the occasion of the master's 75th birthday — which occupies Vol. 2:1.1-169 (1938) of the University of Chile's *Anales de la Facultad de Filosofía y Educación*, Secc. de Filología (= *Boletín del Instituto de Filología*); see pp. 160-169. This miscellany also contains an introductory vignette by C. Vicuña (7-10) and, more important, A. Alonso's note, 'Rodolfo Lenz y la fonética del castellano', in which Alonso's own — and T. Navarro's — phonetic term 'rehilamiento' is equated with the 'Schleimhautvibration' as observed by Lenz. It was of all contributors A. Alonso who, in collaboration with Raimundo Lida, reserved Vol. 6 (1940) of his prestigious 'Biblioteca de dialectología hispanoamericana' almost in its entirety for an annotated translation from the German of three epoch-making articles (1891-94) which Lenz had published in European journals immediately upon his transfer to Santiago (*El español en Chile*). It was Alonso, too, who, despite his sharp disagreements with Lenz, kept alive the reverberations of the latter's work in polemic articles such as the celebrated and exciting 'Examen de la teoría indigenista de Rodolfo Lenz', *Revista de filología hispánica* 1.313-50 (1939). At present, further criticism is brought to bear on Lenz's approach by Jorge A. Suárez, a young Argentine scholar imbued with the doctrine and practice of modern structuralism as ministered in this country; see his two stimulating articles 'Problemas de lexicografía hispanoindia' (*RomPh* 17.155-69 [1963-64]) and 'Indigenismos e hispanismos vistos desde la Argentina' (*ibid.* 20.68-90 [1966-67]).

Aires, a typical latecomer among the continent's urban centers, rose to great prominence, though again the specifically Argentine share in the success of that community of scholars is difficult to determine. The decline of German prestige after the First World War and the emergence of a new Madrid School of philology, championed by Menéndez Pidal, were reflected in the invitations issued by the Argentine government to such students of his as A. Castro and, after a brief interlude, a young A. Alonso to head the newly founded Instituto de Filología. Alonso's almost twenty years of forceful and imaginative directorship of that Institute (1927-46), prior to his transfer to Harvard, represent beyond dispute the all-time peak of Hispanic philology in this hemisphere, possibly through his unique personal magnetism and managerial skill even more than through the sheer weight of his scholarship. A close friend of leading poets, a literary critic and historian in his own right, the offspring — excitingly enough — of a Basque-speaking Navarrese family, a scholar professionally trained in instrumental phonetics at Hamburg, and a deft all-around student of historical grammar and dialectology, A. Alonso typified, to the Argentine intelligentsia, the progressive, versatile, elastic new-style philologist, where the straight classicist and medievalist Hanssen had been a mouthpiece for cumbersome old-style philology and Lenz had represented the stringent line of unadulterated linguistic inquiry (slightly reminiscent in his unyielding austerity of L. Bloomfield). But his *œuvre* falls into a Spanish, an Argentine, and an American period; should it be discussed in these different geographic contexts? The best-known of his associates, P. Henríquez Ureña, a Dominican by birth, had studied and taught at Minnesota and had risen to fame in Mexico before joining the faculty of La Plata and entrenching himself in Buenos Aires. Among A. Alonso's closest students a few remain in Argentina, a sprinkling have drifted to other Hispanic centers such as Caracas (Á. Rosenblat) and Mexico City (E. S. Speratti Piñero). Some — like M. A. Morínigo, R. Lida, the late M. R. Lida de Malkiel, and J. B. Avalle Arce — struck root in this country, at least one carries on the tradition in France (D. Devoto); and of two European scholars who — not without some encouragement from Alonso — found a temporary asylum in Argentine universities in the critical lustrum of the early 'forties' one at present shuttles between Chicago and Barcelona and the other has settled down in Turin.[8]

A more general appraisal in retrospect has been contributed by Alfonso M. Escudero in *Thesaurus* 18.445-84 (1963).

[8] The importance attributed to A. Alonso's activities and the grief felt at his untimely death (1952) can be inferred from the publication of three memorials, by the journals *NRFH* 6 (1953: Mexico City), *Archivum* 4 (1954: Oviedo, Spain), and *Fil.* 5 (1959: Buenos Aires). The first of these ventures contains the definitive bibliography, replacing the tentative list of his writings which figured in the plaquette issued by a grateful inner circle of students on the occasion of the revered teacher's fiftieth birthday, with a tasteful Preface by María Rosa Lida (Buenos Aires, 1946). For a retrospective appraisal of A. Alonso's stand as a linguist see my review, in *RomPh.* 9.237-52, of his magnum opus left unfinished, *De la pronunciación medieval a la moderna en español* (1954). The galvanizing effect of Alonso's teaching as well as certain flaws inherent in his doctrine were carefully assayed by E. Coşeriu in his 9-page critical necrology, *Rev. de la Fac. de Human. y Ciencias* (Montevideo) 7:10 (1953).

Among the handful of students whom Alonso, a victim of the Perón revolution, left behind in

These examples of cultural mobility and osmosis could be multiplied, with occasional side-glances at Montevideo's Instituto de Lingüística, at Bogotá's Instituto Caro y Cuervo, and at Mexico City's Colegio de México. Thus, it was, characteristically, a Spaniard, A. Salazar, who opened the Mexicans' eyes to hidden connections between one ingredient of musicology and one facet of lexicology (Golden Age names of instruments); another Spaniard, A. Millares Carlo, has for years expounded paleography and coördinated bibliography at the Colegio; a Spanish classicist, P. U. González de la Calle, identified the sources tapped by Cuervo in his long-entombed monographs; and a seasoned Spanish dialectologist, T. Navarro, quite apart from his own spade-work in Puerto Rico, made it possible through his *Cuestionario* for aficionados like the Yucateco V. M. Suárez to plan and work out their dialect monographs. Other names of short-term appointees, seasonal visitors, transient scholars (E. Coşeriu, A. Tovar, A. Zamora Vicente), and aged newcomers to the local scene (F. Krüger) come readily to mind, a state of flux in academic staffing quite faithfully mirroring the Latin republics' pathetic instability in matters political, social, and economic. This situation must be pointed out, because it has been a crucial, if not always beneficial, co-determinant of current trends and because it accounts for a probably unavoidable residue of arbitrariness in the doling-out of credit for scholarly achievements. The philological traditions of stable countries like, say, Sweden and Italy, almost hermetically closed at the level of academic personnel, hardly lend themselves to meaningful comparison with such an earthquake area as one discerns all over South and Central America.

Given the general haziness of the term 'philology' — doubly so, I repeat, on Spanish-American soil — plus the critical lack of any organic growth of the discipline in its range from northern Mexico to Patagonia, no analyst of Spanish American humanities can presume to erect a neatly architectured edifice of recent, current, and prospective research in this particular province of knowledge. But one can with due modesty attempt to provide a few loosely integrated surveys or cross-sections of inquiries into such domains as (a) linguistically flavored history of colonial (and more recent) immigration and settlement; (b) lexicography and etymology as geared to local needs; (c) older stages of Peninsular Spanish, with equal attention to the periods of the *Reconquista* and of the *Conquista*; (d) historical ingredients of dialectology; (e) social implications of regional speech; (f) stylistically isolable elements of the literary language; (g) the realm of proper names (toponyms and anthroponyms). Conversely, inquiries into such areas as descriptive dialectology have been assigned to separate chapters in this volume and will therefore be deliberately omitted here except for intermittent side-glances. The above-mentioned sequence of narrower analyses will be preceded by a brief appraisal of the few attempts at a global grasp of American Spanish, a bundle of dialects sometimes calibrated in conjunction with local manifestations of fine literature or against a broadly cultural background. The

---

Buenos Aires upon his enforced transfer to Harvard (1946), the two most strongly, if not exclusively, addicted to linguistic research have been Ana María Barrenechea and Frida Weber de Kurlat.

conclusion will necessarily be confined not to a prognosis of actual expectations (since in Latin America conceivably more than elsewhere the course of scholarship all too often depends on extraneous factors), but rather to a sober assessment of latent possibilities of undisturbed intellectual progress. An effort will be made to encompass in this purview, at least peripherally, significant and influential probings by and large carried out on other continents but inextricably interwoven, through personal ties and academic vicissitudes, with the main fabric of South and Central America's researches in Hispanic philology.

II. ATTEMPTS AT A GLOBAL VIEW OF AMERICAN SPANISH

Interestingly enough, even those New World pioneers of Hispanic philology who evinced active concern with general linguistics timidly favored concentration on a single major variety of American Spanish; thus, even though Cuervo's total grasp of Hispanic culture and of linguistic scholarship steadily grew in firmness and finesse from one edition of his *Apuntaciones críticas* to the next (1867-72, 1876, 1881, 1885, 1907, 1914), it was at no time his intention to cross the precinct of a single city dialect in monographic researches (his Preface to C. Gagini's Costa Rican vocabulary must rank as an exception). Similarly, the three sensational articles which, it will be recalled, Lenz published in quick succession at the outset of his Chilean career ('Zur spanisch-amerikanischen Formenlehre'; 'Chilenische Studien'; 'Beiträge zur Kenntnis des Amerikanospanisch') were — despite the deceptive breadth of two of their titles — quite sharply focused on the lower-class speech of his adopted country. It took a relative outsider, the aspiring German comparativist Max Leopold Wagner (who was only for a brief spell exposed to the realities of Mexican life), to envision the ramification of New World Spanish dialects as a tempting object of linguistic curiosity, with special emphasis on the issues of structural differentiation and territorial fragmentation. Wagner's monograph also added an entirely new dimension to the problem — as a versatile Romance scholar in the full and rich sense of the label he formally raised the question: To what extent is it permissible to liken the split of Latin, in late Antiquity, into the family of Romance languages to the allegedly threatening fission of a more or less unified Spanish, as originally imported, into semi-autonomous overseas varieties?[9] The problem is more intricate than Wagner surmised, inasmuch

[9] 'Amerikanisch-Spanisch und Vulgärlatein', *ZRPh.* 40.286-312, 385-404 (1920); cf. F. Krüger, *RFE* 8.193-4 (1921); translated, with A. Castro's encouragement no doubt, by Carlos M. Grünberg and published, under the title 'El español de América y el latín vulgar', in the ephemeral *Cuadernos del Instituto de Filología* 1:1.43-110 (1924). The original was reprinted in Vol. 2 of *Meisterwerke der romanischen Sprachwissenschaft* (ed. L. Spitzer) 208-63 (München, 1930); cf. the editor's comment (344-5). For the most thorough of the three presently available partial bibliographies of Wagner's hopelessly scattered writings see G. Manuppella, *BF* 15.39-124 (1954-55); as a substitute for the missing tail sections one may use H. Serís, *Bibliografía de la lingüística española* (Bogotá, 1964), a reference book whose usefulness can be enhanced through joint consultation of Hensley C. Woodbridge's microscopic appraisal in *RomPh* 20.107-12 (1966-67). My own necrology of Wagner (1963) was channeled through the same quarterly (16.281-9) and has been reprinted in *Portraits of*

as the dynamics of the essentially subliminal 'drift' can be accelerated, slowed down, scotched, or even reversed by a volitional attitude on the part of the élites of South and Central America's speech communities, whose leaders are at liberty to foster, on the educational level, a form of language-centered pan-Hispanism, inclusive or exclusive of metropolitan Spain.[10] Also, the underlying image of a gradually dilapidating monolith is assuredly misleading: The spoken Spanish brought to the shores of the New World was most certainly not homogeneous, and the processes which ensued were not all slanted in the direction of divergence and endlessly repeated splitting.[11]

Through a historical accident, the year 1492 marked not only the establishment of the westward prong of Spanish speech beyond the Canary Islands, but also the severance of Judeo-Spanish from the main stock, as a result of the banishment and dispersal of the Sephardim at the behest of the Catholic Sovereigns. Through a further coincidence, M. L. Wagner's extended residence in Constantinople, a traditional center of the Judeo-Spanish diaspora, sharpened his awareness of the implications of Judeo-Spanish for the general Hispanist;[12] while he was not the first student of that language, no linguist before him had combined expertise in American-Spanish and familiarity with Judeo-Spanish, plus the ability to trace these two bifurcating branches to the common trunk — Old Spanish — and, even beyond, to the ultimate

linguists (ed. T. A. Sebeok) 2.463-74 (Bloomington and London, 1966).

While Wagner published many more articles, notes, and reviews on Spanish American themes, his one relatively late attempt at a semipopular synthesis: *Lingua e dialetti dell'America spagnola* (Florence, 1949) is, all told, a weak and unoriginal booklet, as was, a quarter-century before, his superfluous foray into straight literary history (*Die spanisch-amerikanische Literatur in ihren Hauptströmungen*). In the concluding decade of Wagner's life his once scintillating etymological studies also began to show regrettable cracks: for details see *RomPh* 9.50-68 (1954-55).

10 The cultured Latin-American's preoccupation with his own language was the life-long concern of A. Alonso ever after his transfer to Buenos Aires. Some fruits of his thinking will be found in the miscellany *El problema de la lengua en América* (Madrid, 1935), esp. in the chapter 'Hispanoamérica, unidad cultural'; in the more sharply focused, provocative book *Castellano, español, idioma nacional: historia espiritual de tres nombres* (Buenos Aires, 1938; 2d ed. [enlarged and revised], 1943); and in the treatise *La Argentina y la nivelación del idioma* (Buenos Aires, 1943), for which the pamphlet *Argentina: a new proving ground for the Spanish language*, tr. Margaret S. de Lavenás (Buenos Aires, 1941), may have served as the trial balloon. The socio-cultural side of American-Spanish has likewise fascinated Á. Rosenblat, another immigrant; his brochure-sized publications bearing on this issue extend from *La lengua y la cultura de Hispanoamérica; tendencias lingüístico-culturales* (Jena and Leipzig, 1933) to *El castellano de España y el castellano de América; unidad y diferenciación* and *Lengua y cultura de Hispanoamérica: tendencias actuales* (both pamphlets issued in Caracas in 1962; of the former there also exists a 1965 ed.). For a general appraisal, predominantly in a severe key, of Rosenblat as a linguist, see Carlos P. Otero, 'Gramaticalidad y normativismo', *RomPh* 20.53-68 (1966-67).

11 The need for stressing the ever-present possibility of convergence of dialects as heavily as has been, by generations of scholars, their divergence, was dramatized by A. Martinet, in his note 'Dialect', *RomPh* 8.1-11 (1954-55) and in Chap. 5 of his book *Éléments de linguistique générale* (Paris, 1960-61).

12 Wagner's weightiest contribution along this line, *Beiträge zur Kenntnis des Judenspanischen von Konstantinopel* (Vienna, 1914), immediately made him the leading expert by eclipsing J. Subak's earlier probings. In the *Caracteres generales del judeo-español* (*RFE*, Suppl. 12; Madrid, 1930) he addressed himself to the general reader in an attempt at 'haute vulgarisation' and, less successfully, at generalization. The weakest link in the chain of his researches, on the scales of novelty, tidy workmanship, and wealth of implications, is 'Espigueo judeo-español', *RFE* 34.9-106 (1950).

'Vulgar Latin' roots. On the side of folklore, meanwhile, Menéndez Pidal began to cultivate a similar perspective in his masterly joint inquiries into Peninsular, Sephardic, and New World balladry.[13] There is a certain irony in the fact that numerous Sephardic families, as a result of latter-day turmoils, upheavals, and persecutions, have reëstablished themselves in Latin American urban centers, notably in Buenos Aires, thus becoming reabsorbed by a Spanish-speaking environment. When Paul Bénichou, equally rooted in the traditions of Paris and of Tetuán-Oran, found himself temporarily stranded in Argentina, a victim of the turbulent 'forties, the contact with a — to him — new and bubbling variety of Spanish provided a powerful stimulus for reëxamining North African specimens of traditional Spanish balladry and folk speech familiar from childhood and adolescence.[14]

Again, it is probably more than sheer coincidence that Pedro Henríquez Ureña, a scion of an old and distinguished family from Santo Domingo, should have neatly recognized the cultural contours of Spanish America (in their linguistic and literary projections) at a painfully long distance from his Caribbean homestead, on the cold premises of the University of Minnesota where he earned his doctorate and temporarily held down a teaching position.[15] To Henríquez Ureña we owe the first tentative classification of Spanish American dialects,[16] an unpretentious schema a revision of

[13] All earlier monographs by the author and by his predecessors alike were overshadowed by the two monumental volumes *Romancero hispánico* (*hispano-portugués, americano y sefardí*); *teoría e historia* (*Obras* 9 and 10; Madrid, 1953). For a digest and a perceptive appreciation see S. Griswold Morley's review in *RomPh* 11.311-17 (1957-58).

[14] Bénichou's parallel studies in balladry and dialectology appeared first in installments (*Revista de filología hispánica* 6.36-76, 105-38, 255-79, 313-81 [1944]: 'Romances judeo-españoles de Marruecos'; ibid. 7.209-58 [1945]: 'Observaciones sobre el judeo-español de Marruecos'), later as a book-length reprint which did not hit the market but elicited several substantial (and preëminently favorable) reactions from critics; cf. S. Griswold Morley, 'A new Jewish-Spanish *romancero*', *RomPh* 1.1-9 (1947-48). Despite his growing preoccupation with modern literature Bénichou has since returned at intervals to these earlier themes, with preponderant emphasis on the folkloristic component; cf. 'Variantes modernas en el romancero tradicional: *Sobre la muerte del Príncipe Don Juan*', *RomPh* 17.235-52 (1963-64).

[15] For a necrology, by Á[ngel] J. B[attistessa], and a preliminary bibliography of Henríquez Ureña's writings (1900-46), compiled by [J]ulio C[aillet]-B[ois], see *Revista de filología hispánica* 8.194-210 (1946); small wonder that, now that his many-pronged activities have become something of a legend, the continued fascination exerted by his *œuvre* should be powerful enough to justify the posthumous reprinting of many classic essays and monographs, sometimes with addenda and corrigenda culled from his notes, cf. the *Estudios de versificación española*, ed. M. A. Morínigo (Buenos Aires, 1961), and the appreciation of this omnibus volume by Oliver T. Myers in *RomPh* 17.519-20 (1962-63). Much of the influence that Henríquez Ureña exerted on the younger generation was due to his skill as enticing lecturer and captivating causeur and raconteur; on these — to most of us elusive — features of his personality see María Rosa Lida de Malkiel's cameo, 'Una conversación con Pedro Henríquez Ureña', *Gaceta* 3:21 (México, May 1956), cols. 1*ab* and 4*a-c*. A much-delayed collection of papers dedicated to his memory — some evoking his activities, others embodying fruits of independent research — appeared in the *Revista iberoamericana* 21 (1956). His own essays — the genre in which he really excelled — were carefully collected and edited by E. S. Speratti Piñero under the title *Obra crítica* (México, 1960), with a Preface by Jorge Luis Borges and a definitive bibliography by the compiler (751-93); cf. also *RevIb* 21.195-242 for an earlier version of that chrono-bibliography.

[16] 'Observaciones sobre el español en América (1-3)', *RFE* 8.357-90 (1921), 17.277-84 (1930), 18.120-48 (1931). In later linguistic writings the author gravitated more and more toward insular

which, in the light of countless new findings, is critically overdue; but, though conversant with the less abstract approaches to linguistics, he remained to the last a thoroughly sophisticated, cosmopolitan philologist at heart, steeped in knowledge of history and literature acquired at first hand[17] and able to mediate brilliantly between these disciplines wherever an alliance of skills and flairs is *de rigueur*, as in his string of inquiries into versification, colonial settlement, and culturally saturated etymology (see the relevant sections below). His prolonged stay in Mexico, on top of his links to Santo Domingo and to the United States, and his stylistic prowess and plain command of the literary *métier* made him the logical person to survey and systematize our synchronic and diachronic understanding of American Spanish as spoken, sung, and written in North America as well as in continental and insular Central America — a far-flung territory indeed which must have acquired a certain sharpness of contour when viewed by an experienced eye from the extreme 'southern' vantage points of Buenos Aires and La Plata (two university centers between which Don Pedro divided his time in the concluding years of his life). Unfortunately Henríquez Ureña's linguistic ventures remain a fragment, and there is nobody to whom he could have bequeathed his contagious zest, pleasing broad-mindedness, unrivalled propensity for synthesizing, and special knack for viewing Greater Mexico, the Carribean, and continental South America from northern and southern observation posts.

Amado Alonso must unquestionably have toyed with the possibility of providing a global view of New World Spanish (and even of its implications for general linguistics); his competent and readable supplements to Vol. 1 (1930) of the revised and translated version of A. M. Espinosa-padre's monograph on New Mexican Spanish point in this direction, as do his — to the taste of many readers — excessively circumstantial papers on the prehistory of the *seseo*.[18] Regrettably, Alonso delayed action on any

---

Caribbean Spanish and toward circumjacent continental varieties of his native language; cf. 'Palabras antillanas en el Diccionario de la Academia', *RFE* 22.175-86 (1938); the hundreds upon hundreds of pages of running commentary in the important miscellany *El español en Méjico, los Estados Unidos y la América Central* (Buenos Aires, 1938); also the appended 'Datos sobre el habla popular de Méjico' (277-324; the sources range from García Icazbalceta's and Ramos y Duarte's dictionaries via A. M. Carreña's Open Letter to J. M. Dihigo [1916] to four then recent contributions to the periodical *Investigaciones lingüísticas*) and the more original 'Mutaciones articulatorias en el habla popular' (329-79), with reference to Greater Mexico, cf. the Introduction (ix-xxii); plus his crowning achievement, *El español en Santo Domingo* (Buenos Aires, 1940) — the last two books constituting Vols. 4 and 5, respectively, of A. Alonso's Biblioteca de dialectología hispanoamericana. For one sample of the latest thinking on American Spanish in dialectal projection see J. P. Rona, 'El problema de la división del español americano en zonas dialectales' (with 2 maps), *Presente y futuro de la lengua española* 1.215-26 (Madrid, 1964).

[17] His three major ventures comprise: (a) *La versificación irregular en la poesía castellana* (Madrid, 1920; rev. 2d ed., 1933; 3d ed. as part of the *Estudios* [1961] identified in fn. 15); (b) *La cultura y las letras coloniales en Santo Domingo* (Buenos Aires, 1936); (c) *Literary currents in Hispanic America*; The Charles Eliot Norton Lectures, 1940-41 (Cambridge, Mass., 1945), also available in Spanish: *Las corrientes literarias en la América Hispánica*, tr. J. Díez-Canedo (Mexico, 1949; 3d ed., 1964) and, comparable in scope, *Historia de la cultura en la América Hispánica* (Mexico, 1947).

[18] Unfortunately, Alonso came perilously close to miring in the swampy ground of the prehistory of *ceceo* and *seseo*, i.e., *stricto sensu*, of the lisping vs. the non-lisping pronunciation of the sound represented by *z* and $c^{e,i}$ in standard Spanish. Some of the bulky material that he accumulated since

such project until, in 1946, a sudden change in circumstances veered his curiosity in a different direction; what has actually come to fruition is, on balance, a series of sparklingly phrased essays and a few heavily documented research papers on uncoördinated points of phonology.[19] Alonso's direct students, to the extent that they could at all be recruited for linguistics, have not inherited their teacher's enthusiasm about general problems of methodology, which animated even his minutely technical investigations and gave point to his austere collections of data. Rosenblat's consecutive exposures to the social and intellectual climates of Buenos Aires, Quito, and Caracas lends, it is true, a triple focus to his current researches, and in his 'Notas de morfología dialectal' as well as in several articles extracted from a doctoral thesis devoted to the category of gender he has scrupulously assembled a profusion of filtered data from every available scrap of information on American Spanish[20] — a laudable show of

---

the earliest awakening of his curiosity to this web of problems (cf. *RFE* 20.68-75 [1933]) was released in such papers as 'Orígenes del ceceo y del seseo españoles', *Thesaurus* 7.111-200 (1951), 'La pronunciación francesa de la *c* y de la *z* españolas', *NRFH* 5.1-37 (1951), and 'Formación del timbre ciceante en la *c, z* española', ibid. 121-73, 263-312, 'Cronología de la igualación *c-z* en español', *HR* 19.37-58, 143-64 (1951), beside the relevant chapter, overburdened with documentation, in *De la pronunciación medieval a la moderna en español*; cf. the summary in *RomPh* 9.243-6 (1955-56). A fatally stricken Alonso's final summation of his views is found in the 1952 postscript (132-50) to Part 3 ('Orígenes del seseo americano' [101-32], apparently drafted in 1938) of his essay 'Algunas cuestiones fundamentales' (7-150) incorporated into his *Estudios lingüísticos: temas hispano-americanos* (Madrid, 1953; reprinted in 1961), an essay which in turn represents a kind of emergency distillate of an all-important book never completed but tentatively entitled *Caracteres generales del español de América.* On these unfulfilled promises see *Estudios* 16. After Alonso's death several leading Spanish scholars voiced their opinions, invariably nuanced and sometimes divergent from Alonso's, of this complex of problems; cf. Diego Catalán, 'The end of the phoneme /z/ in Spanish', *Word* 13.283-322 (1957); Rafael Lapesa, 'Sobre el *ceceo* y *seseo* andaluces', *Estructuralismo e historia*: *Miscelánea-homenaje a André Martinet* 1.67-94 (La Laguna, 1957) beside 'Sobre el *ceceo* y el *seseo* en Hispanoamérica', *RI* 21.409-16 (1956); Menéndez Pidal, 'Sevilla frente a Madrid; algunas precisiones sobre el español de América', *Estructuralismo e historia* 3.99-165 (1962), see below. It was, incidentally, Catalán who, by dedicating to Alonso's memory one of his own juvenilia (*La escuela lingüística española y su concepción del lenguaje* [Madrid, 1955]) and by sympathetically scrutinizing in that booklet the general linguistic concepts underlying Alonso's analyses, vindicated for Spain many inquiries falling into Alonso's fruitful Argentine period.

19 'El grupo *tr* en España y América', *Homenaje a Menéndez Pidal* 2.167-91 (Madrid, 1925), included under the more accurately descriptive title 'La pronunciación de *rr* y de *tr* en España y América' in the author's posthumous *Estudios lingüísticos* 150-95; 'La *ll* y sus alteraciones en España y América', *Estudios dedicados a Menéndez Pidal* 2.41-89 (1951), reprinted in the *Estudios lingüísticos* 196-262; (in collaboration with R. Lida), 'Geografía fonética: *-l* y *-r* implosivas en español', *Revista de filología hispánica* 7.313-45 (1945), included, under the title '*-r* y *-l* en España y América' and, unceremoniously enough, without reference to Lida's co-authorship, in the *Estudios lingüísticos* 263-331. Regrettably, this latter volume has received not the slightest editorial attention and leaves the reader completely unforewarned as to where the pieces selected originally appeared (if they were at all published) and, more important, as to whether the author's vanishing strength had allowed him to introduce last-minute improvements.

20 The 'Notas' form part of the concluding volume of the translation and revision, by A. Alonso and Á. Rosenblat, of A. M. Espinosa-padre's *Estudios sobre el español de Nuevo Méjico* (Buenos Aires, 1930-46), thus furnishing a pendant, without equaling them in value, to Alonso's imaginative 'Problemas de dialectología hispanoamericana', appended to the opening volume and also issued separately. For one encomiastic appraisal see H. Meier, *RF* 63.424-7 (1951). Espinosa's Chicago dis-

disciplined *détaillisme* which, even on the positive side, falls short of providing the much-needed synthesis and, on the negative side, testifies to the author's total divorce from any hue of modern thinking about language.

Characteristically, it was again an uninhibited foreign observer — this time a Swede, Bertil Malmberg — who made the next significant attempt to encompass, within a single study, if not the total landscape of Spanish-speaking America, at least the most conspicuous summits of that landscape.[21] Though a Romance philologist of conservative persuasions by early training, Malmberg at the critical juncture was trying hard to slough off that first academic hide and to address himself preëminently to readers manning the front-line of advanced linguistics. Selected problems of New World Spanish come up briskly for discussion to the extent that they exemplify thought-provoking situations, provide fine-grained answers, or seduce the author into raising questions of special pertinence to a thoroughly revamped brand of general linguistics.

While organized vehicles of research recognize on an increasing scale the wisdom of dealing with New World Spanish as a single, if many-faceted, phenomenon — witness the symptomatic record and configuration of latter-day congresses, symposia, yearbooks, bibliographies, and the like,[22] actual progress along this unifying line is

---

sertation ('Studies in New Mexican Spanish') appeared initially in Vol. 1 (1909) of the short-lived *Revue de dialectologie romane*; in retrospect, Alonso and Rosenblat's decision to pour such copious and useful information of their own into the annotated translation of a monograph quite obsolete by the standards of 1930 and 1946 must be viewed as a grave strategic error (though it was doubtless meant as a tribute and a friendly gesture).

Among the published fragments of Rosenblat's erudite dissertation on the morphology of gender in Spanish the most noteworthy are: (a) 'Género de los sustantivos en *-e* y en consonante: vacilaciones y tendencias', *Estudios dedicados a Menéndez Pidal* 3.159-202 (1952) and (b) 'Comportamiento de las terminaciones *-o, -a*', *NRFH* 16.31-80 (1962). One shorter extract or companion piece, 'Vacilaciones de género en los monosílabos' (Caracas 1951), provoked sharp and richly deserved criticism from Joseph H. Silverman, *RomPh* 7.205-9 (1953-54).

[21] B. Malmberg, 'L'espagnol dans le Nouveau Monde; problème de linguistique générale', *SL* 1.79-116 (1947), 2.1-36 (1948), a paper aiming, above all, at a careful qualification of the frequently exaggerated agency of substrata and superstrata. For a fundamentally friendly appraisal, with just a few barbs on the side of methodology and with numerous corrections of factual details, see the balanced review by M. A. Morínigo in *RomPh* 4.318-26 (1950-51). Malmberg's broadening concern with Hispano-Romance in all its ramifications broke through in his ambitious and provocative article 'Linguistique ibérique et ibéroromane: problèmes et méthodes', *SL* 15.57-113 (1961).

[22] While most bibliographies lump together metropolitan and overseas Spanish (and Portuguese) — witness the annual *Linguistic bibliography* published by Spectrum (Utrecht-Antwerp) — a separate section whimsically entitled 'Latin American language', originally from the pen of Charles E. Kany but authored by Daniel S. Wogan starting with Vol. 18 (1952), appears in the *Handbook of Latin American studies*, a reference tool launched in 1936 by Harvard University Press under the stewardship of Lewis Hanke and issued at present by Florida University Press. Characteristic of the current overlaps and incongruities pervading all channels of information is the fact that this traditionally slender chapter adjoins the section on literature, while the chapter on the same territory's indigenous languages, expertly surveyed by Norman A. McQuown, forms part of each volume's anthropological section, with little or no mutual coördination. Symptomatic of the modern trend is the establishment of a separate section 'Latin American studies' in *YWMLS*, for the first time in Vol. 26 (1964); the subsection on American Spanish, qua language, has been entrusted to P. Russell-Gebbett.

hampered by the fact that most native workers available for this kind of research are motivated by some quaint provincialism, not to say sentimentally tinged parochialism, while the very few foreigners available, for all their broad horizons, rarely acquire more than a nodding acquaintance with the crucially important raw facts. There has thus developed a disquieting chasm between the broad-gauged curiosity and analytical felicity of outsiders, who know how properly to tilt the research (had they only the leisure to do so), and the narrow-gauged competence and dogged devotion of the insiders, tragically cut off from the main avenues of advanced contemporary thinking.

Whereas in theory it is perfectly well known that, in a future division of labor and responsibilities, one ideally suitable 'slice' of material would include a package of certain present-day Peninsular dialects (especially Andalusian), plus the aggregate of Judeo-Spanish, plus the tell-tale speech of the mid-Atlantic Canary Islands[23] and of

---

Among recent conferences, the First International Congress of Hispanists (held in Oxford, September 1962, entirely in Spanish; the Transactions [*Actas*], published by Dolphin [Oxford], appeared two years later) gave limited prominence to philology and linguistics and placed lighter emphasis on Ultramarine than on Peninsular research, reflecting in this pattern the composition of its participants. Any appraisal of the Second Meeting (Nimwegen, 1965) must, to command respect, be based on the published summaries of papers offered rather than on the announced program. Latin America's share in such periodic events as International Congresses of Linguists (e.g. the Ninth, held in Cambridge, Mass., August 1962) and Meetings of the Société de Linguistique Romane (the latest convened in Madrid in 1965) has traditionally been modest, though the former sparked the organization of an autonomous 'Asociación de Lingüística y Filología de América Latina' (= ALFAL), which has weathered all storms of apathy and inertia and, in fact, held its own assembly in Montevideo early in 1965; the activities of this group must be distinguished from mixed gatherings of North and Latin American experts ('Inter-American Program in Linguistics and Language Teaching') at Cartagena (1963) and Bloomington, Ind. (1964), co-sponsored by the Instituto Caro y Cuervo and the U.S. Center for Applied Linguistics and slanted in the direction of pedagogy, data-gathering, and the like. Worthy of note are also the recently institutionalized joint meetings, at intervals, of the Academies of all Spanish-speaking countries (1951, 1956, 1960).

Far and away the most promising venture of this kind, on account of its sharp programmatic focus (*Presente y futuro de la lengua española*) and of its appeal to speakers of Spanish on both sides of the Atlantic, has been the inaugural Congress of 'Instituciones hispánicas', whose proceedings are now open to inspection (Madrid: OFINES, 1964); see the wittily phrased, if less than incisive, digest in *YWMLS* 26.274-6 of individual contributions by L. Alfonso (Argentina), D. Alonso (Spain), G. Carrillo Herrera (Chile), L. Flórez (Colombia), R. Lapesa (Spain), J. Lope Blanch (Mexico), B. Malmberg (Sweden), M. Muñoz Cortés (Spain), R. Oroz (Chile), Á. Rosenblat (Venezuela, previously Argentina and Ecuador), and A. Zamora Vicente. Characteristically, the key note, struck by Carrillo Herrera (who had been the driving force behind ALFAL), was the prospect of unification from above, rather than any further dismemberment at the lower social level, of American Spanish, despite the acknowledged presence of powerful centrifugal forces. The papers displaying the strongest technical scaffolding were offered by Lapesa (ties between Andalusian and American Spanish, see below) and Malmberg (abiding phonetic tendencies of Spanish); Flórez's contribution was the most searchingly detailed, and has since become separately available in revised form: 'El español hablado en Colombia', with 53 dialect maps (*Thesaurus* 18.268-356 [1963]).

23 M. L. Wagner's substantial review in *RFE* 12.78-86 (1925) of a less than distinguished dialect glossary (L. y A. Millares, *Léxico de Gran Canaria* [Las Palmas, 1924]) undoubtedly served as a first eye-opener; nevertheless until the mid-'forties research in Canary Islands Spanish, through a concatenation of circumstances, failed to get off the ground, if one disregards J. Álvarez Delgado's concern with the Guanche substratum. By that time, with the Universidad de La Laguna acting as a magnet, José Pérez Vidal started publishing a number of shorter investigations in quick succession; he also reissued (1946), embedded in a heavy critical apparatus, Sebastián de Lugo's pioneering

the entire New World all the way west to the Philippine Islands, the whole spiced by a generous dosage of 15th- and 16th-century texts of varying social level, regional provenience, and artistic intent (if any), there exist as of today neither research institutes geared to this type of investigation, nor, worse, powerful personalities able to face a challenge of such magnitude.

One obstacle into which Latin American philologists are bound to run in aiming at a total picture of the linguistic facet of their culture is that even the most industrious among them start out, as a rule, with a project involving a narrowly confined territory, then try to expand it by annexing adjacent areas, as it were, without bothering to change the lens of critical inspection. Take the matter of lexicography, for example: Of the two authors of general dictionaries of New World Spanish A. Malaret began as a modest collector of Puerto Rican lexical idiosyncrasies, while Francisco J. Santa-

---

'Colección de voces y frases provinciales de Canarias', compiled a century before that date and for the first time published in 1920, without any philological elaboration. Simultaneously a new dimension was added to Canarian studies through the arrival on the scene, as a permanent resident, of an authentic Romance linguist trained by Karl Jaberg, namely Max Steffen, who before long engaged in etymological studies (*Lexicología canaria*, 2 fascicles, 1945-49). Next, Manuel Alvar, a Spanish dialectologist well-versed in Aragonese and, especially, in Andalusian, and endowed with an enviable knack for field work, issued a sizable monograph based on notes taken in a few weeks of feverishly concentrated interviewing (March 1954): *El español hablado en Tenerife* (*RFE* Suppl. 69; Madrid, 1959). Though the first impression left by this book was one of copiousness of field data, accuracy of transcription, skillful harnessing of cartography and *Wörter und Sachen* approach, and, above all, deft coördination with descriptive and historical inquiries into Peninsular and American Spanish — an impression favorable enough to have earned the author an 'Antonio de Nebrija' Prize (1955), Alvar's tactical workmanship was later seriously questioned on this side of the Ocean; see Emanuel S. Georges' objections, geared to minutiae, in *RomPh* 16.467-74 (1962-63), beside M. Steffen's lexical elaborations in *VR* 20.81-93 (1961). A far more penetrating critique, from the pen of Diego Catalán — a Spaniard who, unlike Alvar, spent several dreary years at La Laguna and thus ranks as a first-rate observer of local conditions, in addition to being a top-notch analyst — is to appear soon in the *ZRPh*. In this exemplary 'Auseinandersetzung' Catalán's chief methodological criticism bears on the indefensible, if widespread, equation of techniques used in preparing linguistic atlases (esp. the use of a questionnaire) and those underlying dialect monographs, an equation taken for granted by Alvar. Concomitantly, Catalán points out in no uncertain terms the need for stressing, in studies of the speech behavior of newly colonized territories ('Español atlántico', 'Neo-español meridional y marítimo'), the socio-cultural stratification, rather than the strictly geographical configuration, characteristic of European settlements influenced by age-old political divisions. Though Catalán's bold vista encompasses the inflection of the verb, pronominal as well as verbal syntax, and even the lexicon, it is the phonetic chapter — in particular the authoritative, unequivocal comments on the free alternation of [ş] and [θ̧], on the recent diffusion of *yeísmo*, on the restoration of intervocalic *-d-*, on the secondary limitation of /*h*/ to contexts where it matches Cast. /x/ rather than zero, and on the 'general crisis of implosive consonants' (especially of *s*)—that marks a genuine break-through which, if his advice is heeded, bids fair to revolutionize future research in New World Spanish. For a parallel, non-polemic preview of Catalán's image of Canarian Spanish see his paper 'El español en Canarias', *Presente y futuro de la lengua española* 1.238-80.

Note that the dialects of the Madeira, Cabo Verde, and Azores Archipelagos are increasingly viewed as possible bridges between South Portuguese (esp. Algarve) and Brazilian dialects; cf. Francis M. Rogers' articles in *HR* 14.235-53 (1946), 16.1-32 (1948), and 17.47-70 (1949), all three embodying the results of a phonetically tilted Harvard dissertation (1940); also his papers in *BF* 7.17-29 (1940) and in *MLN* 62.361-70 (1947), as well as the perspectives opened in Rogers' inspired review of Göran Hammarström, *Étude de phonétique auditive sur les parlers de l'Algarve* (1953); finally J. G. C. Herculano de Carvalho's monograph *Coisas e palavras* (Coimbra, 1953; reprinted from *Biblos*) and

maría first specialized, on a comparable scale, in his native Tabasqueño, a variety of Southern Mexican.[24] In reality, the compilation of an ambitious dictionary ranging over roughly one third of a hemisphere presupposes a training, an approach, a technique, and a degree of refinement completely at variance with those required for strictly local recording made on familiar ground. It takes no special competence in *Gestaltpsychologie* to realize that a mere sum of details is no true equivalent of a whole.

On the other hand, the relatively few foreigners — North Americans and a sprinkling of Dutchmen, Germans, Swiss — who have of late shown active interest in, say, American Spanish dialectology have, with the exception of Malmberg, set themselves far more narrowly circumscribed goals than Lenz or Wagner.[25]

III. LINGUISTIC ASPECTS OF IMMIGRATION AND SETTLEMENT

Whereas in this country, despite the strenuous efforts of H. Kurath, the strands of dialectologically oriented linguistics and of demography (history of settlements and migrations) have not, or not yet, become intimately interwoven, Latin American

---

my critique of it in *Lg.* 33.54-76 (1957), which is to be included in the volume *Essays on linguistic themes* (Oxford, 1968).

[24] Malaret's trajectory led from such modest beginnings as his Puerto Rican *Diccionario de provincialismos* (San Juan, 1917) to the ambitious *Diccionario de americanismos* (Mayagüez, 1925; 2d ed., San Juan, 1931, with two supplements in the early 'forties; 3d ed., Buenos Aires, 1946). Santamaría, a lawyer by profession, started out with ventures of strictly local appeal, e.g. *El provincialismo tabasqueño; ensayo de un vocabulario* (*A-C*) and *Americanismo y barbarismo; entretenimientos lexicográficos y filológicos* (both books published in Mexico City in 1921), then almost overreached himself in a premature attempt at a synthesis: *Diccionario general de americanismos* (3 vols., Mexico, 1942), finally recovered his equilibrium in his best-balanced compilation by far: *Diccionario de mejicanismos* (Mexico, 1959), see E. M. Hernández's scrupulously fair assessment in *RomPh* 18. 479-85 (1964-65). Malaret's research library, which fed his dictionary projects, has been sold to the New York Public Library; Santamaría's holdings now form part of the University of California's Berkeley Library; the two sets of source books are worthy of inspection, on account of numerous handwritten marginal and interlinear notes, by the individual authors and by the two original owners of the copies involved.

On the general landscape of Latin American lexicography see my typologically and bibliographically slanted paper in *RomPh* 12.366-99 (1958-59) and 13.111-55 (1959-60) beside its more abstractly worded epitome in *IJAL* 28:2:4. 1-24 (1962; *Problems in lexicography*, eds. F. W. Householder and S. Saporta), which is to enter, in slightly retouched form, into the miscellany *Essays on linguistic themes*.

[25] Let me briefly mention, on the North American side, Peter M. Boyd-Bowman (Canadian, but Harvard-trained), D. Lincoln Canfield, Roger L. Hadlich, Henry R. Kahane (and his closer students), Charles E. Kany, Lawrence B. Kiddle, J. H. Matluck, Juan B. Rael, Stanley L. Robe, William F. Shipley. Of these, most have traveled and many have resided in Latin America for the purposes of teaching or field work; a few have to their credit publications in Spanish. It is, consequently, hazardous to disentangle the tightly interwoven strands of North as against Latin American contributions to this domain. My own share is exceedingly modest, being confined to the twin reviews of V. M. Suárez, *El español que se habla en Yucatán; apuntamientos filológicos* (see *HR* 16.175-83 [1948]; cf. *IJAL* 14.74-6 [1948]), and of Berta Elena Vidal de Battini, *El habla rural de San Luis* (see *RomPh* 3.191-201 [1949-50]), though I have made it a point in most of my studies to utilize collaterally American-Spanish material, wherever it is relevant.

In Europe a disappointingly meager number of Hispanists have concerned themselves, typically in a small way, with overseas Spanish: Giuseppe Bellini in Italy; W. Giese in Germany; H. L. A. van Wijk in the Netherlands; Konrad Huber in Switzerland.

philologists, responding to the challenge of European-style *Siedlungsgeschichte*, have teamed up with local historians and joined forces with a few foreigners to elucidate some of these — to them burning — interdisciplinary questions. The standard treatise has of late been Á. Rosenblat, *La población indígena de América desde 1492 hasta la actualidad* (Buenos Aires, 1945); but the key problem, that of the *andalucismo* of American Spanish, has been attacked by several experts in a number of short stabs (brilliantly executed in part) rather than in any large-scale encircling movement.

The slogan *andalucismo* is not free from ambiguity, which may be at the root of the long-drawn-out dispute and of the impasse reached. The term can mean either 'Andalusian PROVENIENCE of some salient common features of New World Spanish dialects' or, with a smaller measure of commitment, the mere 'RESEMBLANCE (open to various interpretations) of southern Peninsular Spanish to the most characteristic branches of Overseas Spanish'. Silhouetted against the half-century-old debate is the vivid remembrance of the monopoly that Seville for centuries enjoyed as Spain's gateway to the New World.

The pioneers — Lenz (1893-94), Hanssen (1913), Navarro (1918), Menéndez Pidal — were vaguely aware of the strong mutual affinity of Andalusian and American Spanish, but came up with only incidental and impressionistic statements, except for Cuervo who, at the peak of his activity (1901), categorically stated his belief in the fairly equal representation of all sections of ancient Spain in the exploration of the Western hemisphere.[26] The next important step was taken by Wagner, who, in the aforementioned monograph on American Spanish vs. Vulgar Latin (1920), advanced a 'refined' Andalucist hypothesis: Instead of Andalusia proper all of southern Spain was to be viewed as the purveyor of the speech forms at issue, and only selected portions of Spanish America were to figure at the receiving end of the line. These views, for the defense of which Wagner took up the cudgels seven years later,[27] were assailed

[26] Cuervo's tone-setting paper 'El castellano en América' appeared in *BHi* 3.35-62 (1901); see esp. 41-2. Henríquez Ureña identified some hints made by pioneers at the turn of the century in footnotes to his monograph *Sobre el problema del andalucismo* ... 122-3 and to the earlier article underlying that particular chapter; cf. here fn. 28, below. For a while Navarro remained aloof from any historical commitment, while admitting surface resemblance between Andalusian and American Spanish; see such syntheses of his as the *Manual de pronunciación española* and the *Compendio de ortología española* (Madrid, 1927), cf. *RFE* 17.282. He limited himself to the rigorous delimitation of zones for *seseo* and *ceceo* and established tentative backward links with Hispano-Arabic in his classic study, supported by A. M. Espinosa-hijo and L. Rodríguez-Castellano, 'La frontera del andaluz', *RFE* 20. 225-77 (1933), with an unprecedented wealth of accurate cartographic illustrations. However, in the 'Notas preliminares' (22-3) to his book, based on much earlier field notes, *El español en Puerto Rico; contribución a la geografía lingüística hispanoamericana* (Río Piedras, 1948), Navarro resolutely joined Henríquez Ureña and A. Alonso in averring that Castilians, Basques, and Galicians had a discernibly heavier share in the colonization of the Caribbean island than had the Andalusians.

[27] 'El supuesto andalucismo de América y la teoría climatológica', *RFE* 14.20-32 (1927). The 'climatological theory' of recent vintage does not, needless to say, operate with any direct influence of climate on human speech. The point at issue is that immigrants have, demonstrably, been often influenced in their choice of a new homestead by climatic preferences acquired at earlier stages of their lives. Wagner limits the South Spanish influence to such lowlands as the Antilles, the most accessible sections of Chile, and the Atlantic coastlands of Mexico, Venezuela, and Colombia beside the Río de la Plata zone.

on three occasions (1921, 1925, 1932) by Henríquez Ureña, who painstakingly assembled every scrap of information that could be extracted from the *historiadores de Indias* to prove Cuervo right in affirming that no one province of the mother country was favored over any other throughout the *Conquista* period. In the last and most forceful of his inquiries Henríquez Ureña pointedly remarked that mere similarity of two dialects does not of necessity imply the descent of one from the other; this atom of theory was indeed the crux of the entire controversy.[28]

A. Alonso's intervention at this dramatic juncture was to be expected, but he considerably delayed entering the fray, siding in the end with Henríquez Ureña, except that he allowed for a very special exposure of Antillean Spanish to Andalusian.[29] In this intellectual climate permeating Argentine university centers a quarter-century ago one must also appreciate J. Corominas' string of lexical studies purporting to demonstrate extra-close ties between the vocabularies of Western Peninsular and American Spanish.[30] Aside from their exceptional value, the notes, inexplicitly,

[28] Henríquez Ureña's growing concern with this genetic relation falls into four discernible phases. In Part 1 of his 'Observaciones ...' the problem was a mere side issue, see (a) 8.357-90 (1921), esp. 359 Four years later it became the focus of a discussion kindled by certain passages in Wagner's provocative 1920 monograph, cf. (b) 'El supuesto andalucismo de América', *Cuadernos del Instituto de Filología* 1:2 (1925). Wagner's polite rebuttal of the year 1927 led to an exquisitely courteous (c) counter-rebuttal in Part 2 of the 'Observaciones', see *RFE* 17.277-84 (1930). The notes listed under (b) and (c) were conjoined, provided with some prefatory remarks, and transformed, awkwardly enough, again under the title 'El supuesto andalucismo de América', into Part 2 (119-36) of (d) a book-length publication, *Sobre el problema del andalucismo dialectal de América* (see fn. 26, above), which forms Supplement 2 (1938) to A. Alonso's Biblioteca de dialectología; the opening 118 pages of the book, subtitled 'Comienzos del español en América', involve an expansion of Part 3 of the author's 'Observaciones', *RFE* 18.120-48 (1931), and have appeared in abridged form in *Cursos y Conferencias*, a journal sponsored by the Colegio Libre de Estudios Superiores (Buenos Aires, 1936). For one last summation of the author's views see Chap. 11 ('Semejanzas con la fonética andaluza' 164-7) of his monograph *El español en Santo Domingo* (1940). After Henríquez Ureña's death in 1946 the linguistic residue of his personal archive was channeled, upon A. Alonso's initiative, to P. Boyd-Bowman.

[29] Alonso's book project *Nivelación, diferenciación y renivelación en el español de América*, announced as forthcoming in 1932 (see Henríquez Ureña, *Sobre el problema* 122), has never materialized; one is left wondering whether the torso was absorbed into another venture which for a while captured the author's imagination in the late 'thirties', *Caracteres generales del español de América* (see fn. 18, above). Alonso's unequivocal rejection of the Andalucist thesis is found in 'Algunas cuestiones fundamentales' (*Estudios*: *temas hispanoamericanos* 13-16), but one finds hints scattered over earlier papers, e.g. 'El grupo *tr* en España y América' (1925) and 'Cambios acentuales' (1930), attached to Vol. 1 of the expanded Espinosa monograph. For this unbending attitude E. Coşeriu took him to task in his necrology (1953).

[30] Corominas' cluster of etymological notes ('Occidentalismos americanos', *Rev. de Fil. Hisp.* 6. 139-75, 209-54 [1944]; cf. fn. 143, below) forms part of an ambitious series, 'Indianoromanica', which along with his 'Problemas del diccionario etimológico' (*RomPh.* 1.23-36, 79-104 [1947-48]) — likewise written during his Argentine period — blazed the trail for his monumental four-volume venture *Diccionario crítico etimológico* (1954-57); see below. In the opening article of his own journal ('Rasgos semánticos nacionales', *AIL* 1.1-29 [1941-42]), esp. 9-13, 25-29, Corominas pointed out the recurrent semantic shift which helped transform countless nautical terms into terra firma equivalents (*ensenada, estero, farellón, placer* 'reef, sandbank', *rancho*, and others), a theme on which B. E. Vidal de Battini was later to embroider with her usual thoroughness ('Voces marinas en el habla rural de San Luis', *Fil.* 1.105-49 [1949]), and which, still later, stimulated D. L. Garasa; cf. fn. 139, below. In all likeli-

mediated between Wagner's and Henríquez Ureña's views, showing that certain metropolitan dialects were in fact far more strongly represented than others in the compositional formula for American Spanish, but at the same time deflecting the readers' attention from Andalusian in the direction of the untapped resources of Asturo-Leonese.

Significant progress in the discussion of this problem can be achieved through two reciprocally complementary avenues of approach: increasingly solid historical underpinning and the instrumentality of a less rigid linguistic analysis. On the historical side, A. Alonso was fortunate enough, in 1950, to persuade the one linguistically inclined student he had at Harvard, Peter M. Boyd-Bowman, to take over the researches Henríquez Ureña had left unfinished and to expand that scholar's collections of data, especially as regards the regional backgrounds of the early generations of newcomers to the 'Indies', a topic that had independently claimed the attention of straight historians, such as L. Rubio y Moreno, J. Rodríguez Arzúa, V. A. Neasham, and J. Friede. The result is an impressive *Índice geobiográfico de cuarenta mil pobladores españoles de América en el siglo XVI*, of which Vol. 1, concerned with the period 1493-1519, has recently made its appearance (Bogotá, 1964).[31] Most of the book contains meticulously classified and indexed raw data on an estimated 20% of the total immigration from Spain until 1600, with special emphasis on periodization, but part of the Introduction (vii-xxxiv) includes a preliminary digest of the results obtained, and these results, ironically, tend to foil the expectations of the very same scholars with whom the author no doubt hoped to be in a position to agree. In the first quarter-century of Spanish settlement (the 'Antillean' Period), we learn, one in every group of three colonists was an Andalusian, also, conceivably more important, one in five hailed from the Province of Seville, and one in six was either a denizen or at least a native of the city of that name (xii). Even if, as seems likely, the preëminence of the Andalusian ingredient was to fade in subsequent decades, the strong South

hood this vocabulary reflects, in part, the colonists' unique experiences during their long transoceanic journey, in part their earlier familiarity with the sea (and to this extent casts oblique light on their widespread original links with Spain's coastlands).

[31] Much of the Forematter in Boyd-Bowman's book (esp. the 'Prólogo', vii-xxv) embodies the adaptation of an earlier article from his pen, 'The regional origin of the earliest Spanish colonists of America', *PMLA* 71.1152-72 (1956); pp. 1164-72 include a diagram, a map, and tables. The bulk of the book contains a roster of 'emigrants' (xxvii; one would have preferred the tag 'immigrants'), listed by their full names, with adequate attention to their birthplace, the year of their entry, and their principal movements across the New World, the whole subdivided on the basis of (modern) province and locality (1-166); further details are supplied only where they can be smoothly extracted from the primary source of information (on all philological and statistic criteria see xxvii-xxxiv). The book further contains Addenda, subdivided according to large sections of the mother country (Catalonia, Old Castile, etc.), with special attention to foreigners and Basques (167-78); and three major indexes: one of family-names, a boon to future students of anthroponymy (181-224); one of trades and ranks (225-38), of concern to students of social history and to linguists (the latter will discover in it a valuable companion piece to Paul M. Lloyd's unpublished Berkeley dissertation [1960] *A linguistic analysis of Old Spanish occupational terms*); the last, a composite list — which will benefit the toponymist — of colonial regions and cities toward which the newcomers were heading (239-54). The Bibliography (xliii-lviii) records sources on the growth of the colonies as late as 1650.

Spanish flavor of the primitive layer of American Spanish could not have been demonstrated more incisively and must henceforth be unquestioningly accepted.

Midway between historical and linguistic insights is the growing realization that the role of 'remigrants' (*Rückwanderer*), i.e. of persons reared in the European mother country, then exposed for years or decades to the New World environment, and finally reabsorbed by their country of birth, has been grossly neglected in the study of coincidences between certain varieties of Peninsular and of American Spanish. The content of the 'melting pot', in other words, is wont to spill over, and not a few drops will hit Andalusia (and other maritime sections of Spain) without being immediately recognized for what they are. A systematic study of this process, in socio-economic and linguistic terms, remains to be carried out.

Far more exciting for the theorist and practitioner of general linguistics is yet another explanation of striking convergences between Southern Peninsular and American Spanish, a hypothesis still *in statu nascendi* whose contours are dimly recognizable in some of the latest writings by Lapesa, Malmberg, and Catalán. The link assumed is typological rather than genetic, but a concrete socio-historical setting is part of the ensemble of circumstances held responsible for the phenomenon observed.[32] If one may reduce their pronouncements to a common denominator, representatives of this school of thought argue persuasively that the Spanish language, taken as an abstraction, as a system, is moving in a certain direction, especially as regards the ideal configuration of the syllable (Cons. + Vowel) and the specific sound changes stemming therefrom. It would seem that in areas of flux and insecurity, particularly in territories where Spanish, as a result of conquests and violent upheavals, has overlaid some other language (Granadino Arabic in 13th-16th century-Andalusia, Guanche in the Canary Islands, a profusion of indigenous Indian languages in the New World), the built-in resistances to these impending tendential changes have been broken down far more effectively than, say, in Castile proper, virtually monolingual for a distinctly greater length of time. This analysis, let me add on my own, parallels a new style of thinking in other branches of comparative linguistics: Whereas half a century ago a common innovation (e.g. the reflexive construction) in most or, better still, in all Romance languages would have prompted scholars to affirm that the innovation had already won out in the parent-tongue at the stage of the split, the modern, kinetically phrased alternative is to assert that the feature at issue was merely on its way to winning out, but that the counterpart originally preferred (e.g.

[32] See the separate contributions of Lapesa and Malmberg to the *Presente y futuro* ... miscellany (cf. fn. 22, above). The concept of an 'Atlantic expansion' of Castilian, which ties together Western Andalusia, the Canary Islands, and the New World, was launched by D. Catalán in an important paper ('El *çeçeo-zezeo* al comenzar la expansión atlántica de Castilla', *BF* 16.306-34 [1956-57; published in 1958]), an article which, on the one hand, testified to the author's fruitfully close collaboration with Lapesa, L. F. Cintra, and A. Galmés de Fuentes (309) and, on the other, disclosed a pleasant rapport (333-4) with Boyd-Bowman's statistically oriented opening study of the year 1956. The piece also marked an unequivocal withdrawal (332) from A. Alonso's polygenetic thesis according to which Latin America's *seseo* had arisen quite independently from Andalusia's.

the medio-passive voice of classical Latin) may perfectly well have still been in wide use, if heading at varying speeds for retreat and ultimate extinction.

To sum up: The prospects of overcoming a painful deadlock are bright. The latest historical analysis has not, to be sure, demonstrated any majority of Andalusians over Spaniards from all other sections of the Peninsula combined, but it has identified a hard shell of early colonists from two southern provinces, Seville and Huelva, and has individuated the preëminent role played by Seville-City. That strong homogeneous nucleus was confronted with a numerically superior, but not nearly so unified, assemblage of heterogeneous dialects, which it could easily have outweighed. For the assumed *andalucismo* we must substitute the more solidly buttressed hypothesis of *sevillanismo*.[33] Add to this sharper focus the fresh insight into the leveling part played by 'remigrants' from the New World. Over against these newly defined external factors it seems perfectly legitimate to place internal factors, such as the uninhibited or even accelerated phonetic development in areas of new settlement (Southern Spain and the New World alike) characterized by weakening resistance to change. All that is needed to reconcile these mutually complementary agencies is the willingness, on the part of the analyst, to operate with the assumption of multiple or complex, rather than simple, causation.[34]

The problem of *andalucismo* (or *sevillanismo*) owes its triple appeal to the size of the

[33] With refreshing vigor, Menéndez Pidal, enlisting the aid of D. Catalán, lately brought to completion a project which he let lie fallow in 1941, giving it a structuralistic twist and an explicitly Sevillian, rather than hazily Andalusian, cultural focus: 'Sevilla frente a Madrid; algunas precisiones sobre el español de América', *Estructuralismo e historia* 3.99-165 (1962). Not least important is the section 'Continuada renovación del español colonial' (135-65), in which the future Spanish American dialects are surveyed in their embryonic shapes. In his masterly conclusion, the author distinguishes between (a) an early variety of American Spanish, superficially exposed to Andalusian ('castellano con un sello andaluz poco profundo'), which struck root in territories of relative socio-economic stagnancy, chiefly the interior of Colombia, Ecuador, and Peru, plus a bloc comprising Bolivia, Tucumán, and the adjoining Northwest of Argentina; and (b) a later, more advanced variety, heavily exposed to the impact of the Sevillian brand of Andalusian ('andalucismo más recargado y dialectal'); this variety is characteristic of territories open to all manner of traffic, commerce, and communication and lacking any barriers of cultural conservatism: the Antilles, the outlying sections of Mexico, the Atlantic coastland of Colombia and Venezuela, almost the entire length of the Pacific Coast, the Río de la Plata.

This daring thesis, which at first glance opens up unlimited vistas, runs afoul of one difficulty: While it assumes an ASCENDING intensity of Andalusian infiltration (with special reference to syllable-final *-s*, *-l*, and *-r*, to intervocalic *-d-*, to the neatness of *j* /x/ and *ll* /λ/), the statistical data show a gradual DECREASE in the representation of Andalusians among settlers. Menéndez Pidal's answer to any objection of this kind would be that such phonetic fashions are not necessarily controlled by sturdy colonists, but rather by those agile 'traficantes' who, in the wake of the Spanish merchant marine, imposed on the impressionable, perhaps gullible, settlers the cultural standards of Seville as the greatly admired maritime capital of the 'old country'.

One additional consideration: Must we not reckon with major developments WITHIN (Sevillian) Andalusian from 1500 to 1800 and with the stronger receptiveness to innovations from those New World dialects which, as a consequence of the general flux of local societies, were still malleable?

[34] On this point of theory see my contribution to Mouton's latest venture, *To Honor Roman Jakobson* 2.1228-47 ('Multiple versus simple causation in linguistic change') and my 1965 Presidential Address, LSA ('Linguistics as a genetic science'), to appear in an issue of *Lg* corresponding to the year 1967.

territory affected by the issue, to the prestige of the disputants, and to a chain of dramatic reversals in the fortunes of 'vogues' and 'fashions'. Debates around other problems bearing on the linguistic effects of colonization have exuded less glamour, but their cumulative weight has been by no means negligible. It is the merit of Sra. Vidal de Battini to have demonstrated beyond the shadow of a doubt that her native Central Argentine province of San Luis initially gravitated toward Santiago de Chile rather than toward Buenos Aires, as did of course also the adjacent territory to the West, e.g. Cuyo.[35] This discovery makes the very use of labels such as 'Argentine Spanish' problematic; it also shows that contrasts between Indian substratum languages, such as Aztec vs. Maya in Mexico, need not be principally responsible for any major discrepancies between national frontiers and dialect boundaries in Latin America. Finally, the author's spade work confirms the findings of W. D. Elcock and other explorers of Pyrenean dialects to the effect that the opposing slopes of high mountain chains frequently attract settlers of similar background,[36] with the result that such ranges, for all their seeming impassability, do not, as a rule, constitute sharp language boundaries.

Any classification of language material on the basis of these writers' and speakers' nationality or citizenship is consequently untenable, in the context of linguistic analysis. The practically unlimited reliance on this criterion is one of the two serious flaws marring C. E. Kany's *Spanish American syntax* (an inventory otherwise tidily compiled),[37] the other blemish being the historically meaningless confrontation of an

[35] See the judicious booklet *El español de la Argentina* (Buenos Aires, 1954), with 11 maps, briefly digested in *RomPh* 9.401-2 (1955-56), and Part 1 — the only one published — of the aforementioned monograph *El habla rural de San Luis*, which has elicited a spate of reviews.

[36] Cf. Elcock's dissertation *De quelques affinités phonétiques entre l'aragonais et le béarnais* (Paris, 1938), especially the entertaining Introduction.

[37] On account of its wide range, topical novelty, wealth of factual information, and consistently high standard of typographic neatness Kany's *Syntax* has elicited a number of more than casual reactions; cf. the reviews by F. Alegría, *Hispania* 30.140-2 (1947); W. J. Entwistle, *MLJ* 41.336-7 (1946); L. Flórez, *Thesaurus* 2.372-85 (1946); F. Krüger, *AIL* 4.301-14 (1950); A. Malaret, *RR* 38.282-4 (1947); H. Meier, *BF* 8.368-70 (1945-47); J. B. Rael, *HR*, XIV (1946), 357-361; Á. Rosenblat, *NRFH* 4.57-67 (1950). The 2d ed (1951), though only superficially revised on the tactical and not at all on the strategic level, provoked further discussions, this time by A. M. Badía i Margarit, *ER* 3.263-5 (1951-52 [1954]); Luis Cifuentes G., *BFUCh* 7.391-410 (1952-53); L. Flórez, *Thesaurus* 8.215-7 (1952); and L. B. Kiddle, *RomPh* 7. 366-72 (1953-54).

These two cycles of discussions of Kany's *Syntax* amount, at least in the bulk of data freshly unearthed or newly adduced, to a book-length publication in their own right. Cifuentes contributes a rich platter of *chilenismos*, with numerous excursuses set off in small print. Entwistle praises the predominance of (verifiable) written sources and singles out for favorable mention the chapter on *voseo*. Flórez, in his first critical venture, spreads out a string of 81 remarks, for the most part addenda carved from living Bogotá usage, which the reviewer is careful not to pass off as exclusive Colombianisms; the second venture embodies a sober and precise comparison of the two editions. Kiddle, far and away the most perceptive and incisive among Kany's critics, pays tribute to the author's learning and acknowledges the usefulness of the book, but firmly states his serious reservations about the preceptive slant, finds the underlying concept of 'Standard Spanish' highly debatable, and questions the wisdom of using literary records as prime evidence in dialect studies. Krüger, applauding the copiousness of the documentation and seemingly unaware of any methodological issues directly or obliquely involved, piles up supplementary data and parallels, not a few from Peninsular usage

academic, artificial standard of Peninsular Spanish with a spectrum of samples of uninhibited, untutored speech culled from all over the New World. Those in search of an authentic European foil to New World colloquial usage will be rewarded by the use of W. Beinhauer's specimens of racy Peninsular Spanish, extracted, not unlike Kany's, from appropriately light-weight sources even more than from unobtrusive direct observation.[38]

IV. LEXICOGRAPHY AND ETYMOLOGY GEARED TO LOCAL NEEDS

It has been asserted that linguistics — a notoriously fluid discipline — lends itself all too easily to either GRAMMATICALIZATION or LEXICALIZATION. If the mid-20th-century panorama of linguistic research in the United States suggests almost exclusive orientation toward grammatical analysis (with, increasingly, logico-mathematical overtones), the landscape of Hispanic philology to the south of the Mexican border is dominated by lexicological and lexicographic preoccupations (if one may by these two labels distinguish between genuine researches in the lexicon and mere compilations of reference tools in the realm of words). For this slant any close observer of the scene might adduce several explanations, of which a particularly cogent — if less than complimentary — one is the circumstance that much philological research throughout Latin America has traditionally been carried on by aficionados. Now it is a widely acknowledged fact that intelligent amateurs can do far more competent work in the collection and definition of conspicuous lexical units than in, say, phonetic or syntactic dissections, which demand thorough formal specialization and a deliberate weaning-away of the trainee from popular and scholastic misconceptions. This pattern of ranking does not apply to etymology, however, because the tracing of words to their ultimate origins requires a constant interplay of analytical rigor, philological conscientiousness, and historical 'flair' bordering on artistic insight. As a result of these stiff requirements, considerable harm has, unfortunately, been done in Latin America by undertrained would-be etymologists.

(including Portuguese and, surprisingly enough, Catalan). Malaret's review is a bouquet of compliments, but appended to it are a few stray lexical addenda. Meier, likening Kany's book to Keniston's earlier *Syntax of Castilian prose* (which has remained a torso), views it as an accurate catalogue of facts, divorced from any explicative commitment, and stresses the lexical (i.e. atomistic) rather than functional, truly syntactic slant of the whole. Rael's objections (in contrast to those of Kiddle) bear on minute details, mostly in the area of object pronouns, provoking by their acerbity Alegría's rebuttal. Rosenblat makes allowances for the didactic bias of the book, recognizes its link not only to lexicology but also to inflection (esp. in the 40-page section on the *voseo*), and offers a profusion of elaborative remarks, tapping his reservoir of personal recollections of Argentinian, Ecuadorian, and Venezuelan usage.

A short companion piece by Kany is 'Some aspects of Bolivian popular speech', *HR* 15.193-205 (1947); for a list of preparatory studies from his pen — usually limited to a single idiomatic phrase (incl. its variants) or to a single construction — see *Ling. Bibl.* 2.357 (1950).

[38] Beinhauer's *Spanische Umgangssprache* (Berlin and Bonn, 1930; 2d ed., rev. and enl., Bonn [1958]) is avowedly patterned, in its tone, technique, and underlying assumptions, on Leo Spitzer's once fashionable *Italienische Umgangssprache* (Bonn and Leipzig, 1922).

Whether we insist on using logical classificatory criteria or remain content with distinguishing between certain 'styles' of research (or else 'plateaux of analytical sophistication'), the lexical studies carried on in Latin America and bearing on the native varieties of Spanish fall into certain easily recognizable categories.[39]

There is, first, the recurrent collection of picturesque local expressions (*argentinismos, chilenismos*, etc.), typically believed by the compiler to be restricted to his own province, state, or country, provided he is one of the overwhelmingly numerous avocational philologists. Few of these well-intentioned workers have bothered to reflect on the accurate definition of, say, *chilenismo*.[40]

Second, the lexical vehicle of a province of human endeavor or curiosity may be at the center of a monograph. Suitable topics include the straight and the metaphoric uses of names of plants and animals; terms used in certain trades, crafts, and arts, also in games and sports, etc. The standard of style in this domain has been set the world over by the *Wörter-und-Sachen* approach and by a series of elaborate linguistic atlases and dialect studies which in Europe reached their peak thirty years ago. The techniques that have stood the test of two or three inquisitive generations — the inclusion of plates with drawings and photographs, the use of questionnaires, the (optional) phonetic transcription of forms elicited, the organization of lexical data in terms of the corresponding patterns and processes of material civilization, and so forth — have been successfully imitated by local field-workers. Middle-sized monographs so oriented have long been known as ideal 'chunks' of investigation for all manner of theses and dissertations.

Third, as a bow in the direction of the *Languages-in-contact* approach, one encounters studies of certain foreign lexical strains in local varieties of Spanish (e.g. Gallicisms or Anglicisms; or, for that matter, elements borrowed from Indian languages such as Mapuche = Araucanian, Quechua, and Guaraní). Inverting the perspective, the linguist may focus his attention on clusters of Spanish words or whole streaks of the lexicon that have, for once, penetrated into these very same donor languages or into tongues that are found only at the receiving end.

A fourth type of inquiry allocates the center of the discussion to the biography of a

[39] See, in addition to my two papers identified toward the close of fn. 24, above, the following articles displaying the same proclivity: 'The uniqueness and complexity of etymological solutions', *Lingua* 5.225-52 (1956), and 'A tentative typology of etymological studies', *IJAL* 23.1-17 (1957). Both are to be included, in slightly revised form, in the miscellany *Essays on linguistic themes*.

[40] We owe the best-known theoretical investigation to Ambrosio Rabanales O[rtiz]: *Introducción al estudio del español en Chile; determinación del concepto del chilenismo* (Suppl. 1 [1953] to *BFUCh*). The author's non-puristic definition at the outset of Part 2: 'The Chileanism is any oral, written or kinesic [= mimetic, gesture-like] expression created in Chile by Chileans who speak Spanish as their native language or by foreigners residing in Chile who have assimilated that language' clashes with J. T. Medina's, who confined his selective curiosity to the parlance of upper-class residents of the national capital, and implies disagreement, *mutatis mutandis*, with the notions underlying the sampling techniques of Batres Jáuregui, Calcaño, Membreño, and Rivodó. For one strong objection to the insistence on origin as the sole determinant of such a regionalism see L. B. Kiddle's otherwise laudatory review in *RomPh* 12.310-4 (1958-59), notable also for the critic's ability to pit many self-observed Peruvianisms against Rabanales' Chileanisms.

word — preferably one less than transparent in its ultimate descent and rich in linguistic vicissitudes and cultural implications (say, *gaucho* or *peón*). Some etymologists will favor very elaborate reconstructions of a single tangled trajectory; others tend to group together several word biographies more sketchily drawn, through thinner documentation or sparser indulgence in excursuses. Instead of a lexeme (i.e., a root morpheme), the thread holding together a number of speech forms may be a sementeme (i.e., a gloss), as when the analyst, rather than asking himself: What have been the shades of meaning and the derivational offshoots of Word *X* in the course of its diffusion over the New World?, elects the alternative phrasing: What has been the distribution of all American Spanish regionalisms sharing Meaning *Y* ('bean' or 'turkey', for instance)? Among Romance scholars these two mutually complementary slants of word studies have been known as 'semasiological' and 'onomasiological'.[41]

Between these four approaches there exist, needless to say, overlaps, as when a scholar's curiosity ranges over Chilean athletic terms of English provenience, urging him to press into simultaneous service the exploratory devices of the second and the third approach.[42] Also, it is undeniable that in matters lexicographic one cannot always hermetically shut off Latin America from the remainder of the world, and that the intellectually ambitious and well-trained expert will be tempted, again and again, to transcend any such parochialism. In fact, how could one possibly gauge the specifically 'exotic' admixture of American Spanish without constant eliminative reference to Peninsular Spanish, pan-Romanic, and even circum-Mediterranean antecedents?[43]

The four principal categories of lexical research isolated here now deserve some closer inspection. The collection of regionalisms, with a country rather than a province (state) or a city (village) serving as the yardstick of delimitation, boasts a venerable tradition in Latin America, going back to E. Pichardo's Cuban dictionary published as early as 1836 (and reissued, incidentally, in 1953, newly revised and expanded by E. Rodríguez Herrera — an unusual lifespan indeed for a book venture of this kind). This lexicographic genre reached its summit at the turn of the century,

[41] For the best survey turn to Bruno Quadri, *Aufgaben und Methoden der onomasiologischen Forschung*; *eine entwicklungsgeschichtliche Darstellung* (Rom. Helv. 37; Bern, 1952). Fine specimens of these two closely interwoven threads of investigative technique are offered by K. Jaberg, *Aspects géographiques du langage* (Paris, 1936), and by B. Hasselrot, 'L'abricot; essai de monographie onomasiologique et sémantique', *SNPh.* 13.45-79, 226-52 (1940-41).

[42] Cf. Lidia Contreras F., 'Los anglicismos en el lenguaje deportivo chileno', *BFUCh* 7.177-341 (1952-53): a list of 404 items, preceded by a grammatical sketch (181-97), with drawings and an alphabetic index.

[43] Characteristically, a single middle-sized *Festschrift* venture (*Homenaje a Rodolfo Oroz* = *BFUCh* 8 [1954-55]) elicited three such responses from European scholars (familiar at first hand with Latin America) as included American Spanish in their scope, but exceeded it by a wide margin: J. Corominas, 'Falsos occidentalismos americanos' (65-70), a bit of autocriticism brought to bear on an earlier article (*RFH* 6.139-75, 209-54); F. Krüger, 'Preludio de un estudio sobre el mueble popular en los países románicos' (127-204, with plates), an article which, true to its title, has acted as a wedge for bulky book-length monographs of later vintage (cf. fn. 56 below); and M. L. Wagner, 'Anthropomorphe Bilder für Geländebezeichnungen vornehmlich in den iberoromanischen Sprachen' (465-74).

witness the dates of A. Membreño's celebrated *Hondureñismos* (1895; 2d ed., 1897; 3d ed., 1912), but many compilations of this sort continued to appear until the mid-century point. Recently, the production along this once promising line has shown symptoms of progressive slackening,[44] whether on account of the appearance of general dictionaries of American Spanish such as those by Malaret and Santamaría,[45] or as a consequence of the gradual absorption of *americanismos* by Madrid's tone-setting Academy Dictionary, a reversal of policy which obviates the manufacture of of separate supplements. The change in the rate of output, however, is due not only to the reassessment of actual needs, but also to the fact that a certain lexicographic fad has at length run its course.

It may be argued, at first blush, that such vocabularies, now in their declining stage, are in any event the concern of dialectologists rather than of philologists and that their inclusion under this rubric is indefensible. This objection can easily be parried on two grounds. First, in the matter of selection of noteworthy forms, constructions (syntactic and phraseological), and shades of meanings, most authors of such dictionaries to this day aspire to little more than the filling of small gaps in the Academy Dictionary with lexical florilegia of their own choosing (occasionally — but far more seldom at present than, say, fifty years ago — to the tune of puristic condemnation); in other words, the frame of reference is textual. Second, and more important, many of these glossaries contain optional or obligatory illustrations of local usage with passages extracted from *costumbista* writers.[46] At this point contact has been established between lists of regionalisms adorned with literary endorsements and — a separate, but related genre — collections of lexical oddities excerpted from prestigious writers on the suspicion that they may have served to evoke a certain local atmosphere.[47]

[44] Nevertheless, one runs across new titles such as *Chilenismos*, by J. M. Yrrarázaval Larrain (Santiago de Chile, 1945), and *Glosario de peruanismos*, by R. Vargas Ugarte (Lima, 1953), to say nothing of accretions to older ventures like the *Suplemento al Diccionario de peruanismos* (ed. Estuardo Núñez; Lima 1957) by P. Paz Soldán y Unanue (= 'Juan de Arona', 1839-95), salvaged from dust-covered issues (1891-93) of the periodical *El Chispazo*.

[45] Under the directorship of A. Alonso (1927-46), the librarian of the Instituto de Filología at Buenos Aires, aside from acquiring one copy of each purchasable dialect vocabulary for the reference shelf, was instructed to buy two additional copies, from which each entry could be conveniently cut out, pasted onto a standard-sized slip or sheet, and kept in a master-file. These valuable clippings formed a kind of steadily renewable stream of lexical information with — unlike any concrete dictionary project — no foreseeable cut-off point. I wonder whether that University's remodeled Instituto de Filología y Literaturas Hispánicas has kept up this excellent practice.

[46] One finds, in fact, two kinds of literary quotations in such dictionaries, sometimes picturesquely intermingled: passages extracted from local fiction, with — understandably enough — special attention to descriptions and to dialogue; and passages from Peninsular classics purporting to illustrate the earlier currency of such words, constructions, and phrases in the prestigious metropolitan tradition of *belles-lettres*.

[47] One fairly recent specimen is the indefatigable A. Malaret's book-length paper 'Los americanismos en el lenguaje literario', *BFUCh* 7.1-113 (1952-53). The more common approach is to have a relative tyro (as part of his basic training) distill 'Americanisms' — for the most part of the lexical order — from a single full-sized novel, or from characteristic writings of a single author (or closely connected group of authors); cf. J. J. Monte, 'Algunos aspectos del habla popular en tres escritores caldenses',

While the wide-meshed dictionary encompassing the lexical idiosyncrasies of a major country is a genre now past its crest (Santamaría's aforementioned *Diccionario de mejicanismos* may mark its rear guard), smaller geographic units — be they exiguous independent countries, or mere provinces or states subsumable under the larger entities — are more and more recognized as appropriately delimited objects of a home-grown lexicographer's labor of love. Take L. Sandoval's monumental *Diccionario de guatemaltequismos*,[48] an undertaking in which the compiler's ear was so finely attuned to the narrowly circumscribed material that he could, with authority, record not only formations actually overheard but, I strongly suspect, also items (in particular, derivatives) only latently present. On the Argentine scene, the older large-scale ventures attempting to do justice to the entire far-flung country are yielding the right of way, before our eyes, to sharply pinpointed repertories of the usage of a single province, e.g. Salta or Catamarca.[49] The systematic exploration of varying speech forms in urban and rural communities, along valleys, and in provinces (states, departments) has of late been most effectively pushed in Colombia,[50] where some of

Thesaurus 15.180-213 (1960), and Hugo Rivera, 'Glosario de la novela chilena *Chicago Chico* de Armando Méndez Carrasco y otros autores', *BFUCh* 17.281-361 (1965). The antecedents of this category of research are traceable to such early exploratory lists of regionalisms as M. de Toro y Gisbert — an Argentinian longtime resident of Paris, 'El idioma de un argentino: *La guerra gaucha* de Leopoldo Lugones', *BAE* 9.526-48, 705-28 (1922), and J. Alemany [Bolufer] — interestingly, a Spaniard, 'El castellano en la Argentina, según la novela de Don Carlos Quiroga, titulada *La raza sufrida*', ibid. 17.303-52 (1930), almost in its entirety an annotated word-list (306-52). Based exclusively on readings is H. L. A. van Wijk's Amsterdam thesis (1946) *Contribución al estudio del habla popular de Venezuela*, which of course represents a European's approach to American Spanish.

Radically distinct from the documentation, based on written sources, of racy and predominantly rustic localisms is the study of written Spanish, as favored by the educated and even the highly cultured, in the various New World countries. [illegible]tep in this direction is R. Oroz's article 'Prefijos y seudoprefijos en el español actual de Chil[illegible]Ch 7.115-32 (1952-53); here the author, visibly influenced by B. Migliorini's probings into contemporary written Italian, focuses attention on neologisms exhibiting such 'international' morphemes as *pre-*, *ante-*, *post-*, *anti-*, *sub-*, *inter-*, *trans-*, *super-/sobre-*, *extra-*, *ultra-*, *archi-*, *hiper-*, i.e. essentially on Latinisms and Hellenisms; the titles of some similarly inspired writings by that author can be culled from Lidia Contreras' analytical Bibliography (ibid. 8.481-516). Since studies of this kind bear fundamentally on the scripta ('Schriftsprache'), it seems more apposite and, above all, more economic to plan them on a pan-Hispanic rather than on a strictly regional scale.

48 The alternative title of this book, *Semántica guatemalense* (Guatemala [City], 1941-42), visibly chosen in imitation of G. Lemos R[amírez]'s *Semántica, o ensayo de lexicografía ecuatoriana* (Guayaquil, 1920), is misleading, insofar as the book is not restricted to recording noteworthy shades of meaning.

49 Cf. J. V. Solá, *Diccionario de regionalismos de Salta* (*República Argentina*) (Buenos Aires, 1947; 2d ed., 1950); and Carlos Villafuerte, *Voces y costumbres de Catamarca*, 2 vols. (Buenos Aires: Academia Argentina de Letras, 1961). Similarly, even in a country the size of Ecuador: A. Cordero Palacios, *Léxico de vulgarismos azuayos* (Cuenca del Ecuador, 1957). This is not tantamount to affirming that small-scale lexical surveys were heretofore unavailable: Distinctly earlier specimens can indeed be adduced for the island of Chiloé in Chile, for the state of Tabasco and the Yucatan Peninsula in Mexico, etc. But they were previously the exception rather than the rule.

50 Much of the work currently done in Colombia comprises by-products or companion pieces of the ambitious project of a national 'Sprach- und Sachatlas' (in the tradition of K. Jaberg and J. Jud's celebrated Italian and Southern Swiss model), namely the *Atlas Lingüístico-Etnográfico de Colombia*

the field-work and subsequent publication of finished monographs has been coördinated and supervised by Bogotá's dialectologically slanted Instituto Caro y Cuervo, during a wholesome respite from political upheavals. In this particular pursuit the 'data-oriented' Bogotá institute has shown greater skill and initiative than have its otherwise no less active counterparts in Caracas, Montevideo, Buenos Aires, Mendoza, and Santiago de Chile.

As regards major city dialects, there exists, to be sure, an old native tradition for grappling with their lexical problems — witness Ricardo Palma's artistically suffused concern with the speech of Lima — and for coming to grips with local grammar and lexicon alike, as attested by Cuervo's life-long preoccupation with Bogotá. The sound system of an urban dialect can be a worth-while problem in its own right, and the record of research along this by-path extends from a North American pioneer's spadework in the Mexican capital seventy years ago (C. C. Marden, *The phonology of the Spanish dialect of Mexico City*) to a now fifteen-year old monograph by a younger Colombian trained by the ranking European expert (T. Navarro) at New York's Columbia University (L. Flórez, *La pronunciación del español en Bogotá*); but nothing has yet become available that could be pitted, with respect to a blend of austerely linguistic and sociological sophistication, against, say, David DeCamp's

= *ALEC*. From the pen of the senior investigator L. Flórez we now have a programmatic 'Nota informativa', *Thesaurus* 16.77-125 (1961), and, in collaboration with the cartographer Jennie Figueroa, the aforementioned key-article, accompanied by 53 maps: 'El español hablado en Colombia y su Atlas Lingüístico' (1963); the preliminary questionnaire used for field work was prepared in advance by Flórez in collaboration with Tomás Buesa Oliver and is available in print (Bogotá, 1957). It is in this broad context of rigorous data-gathering, under controlled conditions, that one can best appreciate the collection of riddles, from the lips of native speakers, made by Gisela Beutler in Nariño, Antioquia, and Northern Santander (*Thesaurus* 16.367-451 [1961], 18.98-140, 404-27 [1963]), as well as the parallel transcription of cradle songs carried out by María Luisa Rodríguez de Montes, 'Cunas, andadores y canciones de cuna en Bolívar, Santander, Antioquia y Nariño (Colombia)', ibid. 17.313-48 (1962). These glotto-ethnographic researches are, *grosso modo*, on the same level of rigor and sophistication as those carried out by the North American counterparts of the Colombian investigators; cf. Peter Boyd-Bowman's conservatively planned inquiry into the speech of a Mexican mining town and its environs, *El habla de Guanajuato* (Mexico, 1960), and the hard core of Stanley Robe's more progressively styled studies in Panamanian: *The Spanish of rural Panama; major dialectal features* (UCPL 20; Berkeley and Los Angeles, 1960). In Boyd-Bowman's and Robe's books the lexicon plays, of course, a subordinate role.

In its ultimate roots, the fruitful activity of the Instituto Caro y Cuervo is based on a far-reaching and deeply rooted alertness of Colombian intellectuals to problems of linguistic propriety and regional nuancing. The peculiar status of the country's northern coast, opening up on the Caribbean, was already the particular concern of devoted lexicographers such as Adolfo Sundheim (1922); cf. also P. M. Revollo, *Costeñismos colombianos* (Barranquilla, 1942). Leonardo Tascón's posthumous *Diccionario de provincialismos y barbarismos del Valle del Cauca*, salvaged by his sons, has recently been reissued (Cali, 1961), along with the author's *Quechuismos usados en Colombia*, in a joint volume which includes an appreciation (7-22) of the devoted puristic zealot (1858-1921) from the pen of A. Romero Lozano; cf. fn. 78, below. Add such items, of marginal scholarly value, as Gonzalo Cadavil Uribe, *Oyendo conversar al pueblo, acotaciones al lenguaje popular antioqueño* (Bogotá, 1953); Jorge Sánchez Camacho, *Diccionario de voces y dichos del habla santandereana* (Bucaramanga, 1958); and P[e] Julio Tobón Betancourt, *Colombianismos y otras voces de uso general* (Medellín, 1947; 2d ed., Bogotá, 1953).

sparkling Berkeley dissertation (1953) *The pronunciation of English in San Francisco.*[51] The lexicographic side of urbanistic research is, at this stage, perhaps the least developed. There exists on the market a fringe of usually slender books or pamphlets containing annotated lists of, to cite concrete examples, *arequipeñismos* (in Peru) or *bogotanismos* (in Colombia), but even by local standards they occupy one of the lowest rungs on the ladder of organized linguistic scholarship.[52] The relatively most imaginative type of lexically oriented inquiry that has been made into city parlances has set itself the goal to isolate a certain social argot or some transitional ('mixed') language used in immigrants' quarters.[53] We are still far removed from the prospect of having, at our fingers' tips, reliable many-tiered monographs on the socially and culturally stratified lexicon of a modern megalopolis such as Lima, Mexico City, or Buenos Aires.

In accord with the scheme established here, the second 'subgenre' of lexicographic research comprises the study of the lexical reflexes of a province of human endeavor or curiosity. Here an amalgam of (α) linguistics and (β) research in material civilization (= *Sachforschung*) and ethnography (= *Volkskunde*) may and in fact should be achieved; this combination, clearly traceable to the somewhat stale Central European tradition of field-work (*Aufnahmen an Ort und Stelle*) and subsequent cultural interpretation, must not be confused with ultra-fashionable American-style 'ethnolinguistics', which has independently left stray vestiges to the south of the Mexican border.[54]

If we choose, in the wake of Meringer and Schuchardt, *Wörter-und-Sachen* as a common denominator for lexical studies geared to interviews, accompanied by drawings and photographs of tools, containers, dwellings, etc., underpinned by a

[51] Serialized in *Orbis*; the first installment appeared in 7.372-91 (1958); the second in 8.54-77 (1959).

[52] Cf. M. A. Ugarte, *Arequipeñismos* (Arequipe, 1942), and L. A. Acuña, *Diccionario de bogotanismos* (Bogotá [n.d.]).

[53] This applies to the *cocoliche* spoken by certain nuclei of Italian immigrants in Buenos Aires and to comparable parlances observed in the capitals of Argentina and of Uruguay; the first synthesis was supplied by R. Grossmann, *Das ausländische Sprachgut im Spanischen des Río de la Plata* (Hamburg, 1926), and several shorter pieces have of late been furnished by Giovanni Meo-Zilio, himself a resident of Montevideo over a period of ten years; cf. his latest article, just off the press: 'Italianismos meridionales en el español rioplatense', *BFUCh* 17.225-35 (1965), and three contributions in the mid-'fifties to Vols. 16 and 17 of *LN*; for details see fn. 68 below. This systematic distillation of (dialectal) Italianisms overlaps with the general study of low-class speech in the Buenos Aires area, a social dialect colored by its close ties both to ethnic minority groups and to a criminal argot (*lunfardo*); cf. T. Gobello, *Lunfardía; introducción al estudio del lenguaje porteño* (Buenos Aires, 1953). There exist comparable lexical probings, at the corresponding educational and economic level, into the speech of Mexico City; these studies range from M. L. Wagner's half-century old 'Mexikanisches Rotwelsch' (*ZRPh* 39.513-50) to R. S. Boggs' 'Términos del lenguaje popular y caló de la capital de Méjico', *BFUCh* 8.35-43 (1954-55); cf. fn. 141, below. But while these probings, with their inevitable emphasis on piquant tidbits, may be the etymologist's delight, they do not compensate for the lack of balanced and objective descriptions of multilayered urban dialects.

[54] Thus, Ismael Silva-Fuenzalida — characteristically, addicted to the phonemic approach ('Estudio fonológico del español de Chile', *BFUCh* 7.152-76 [1952-53]), has, in the wake of F. G. Lounsbury, spearheaded inquiries straddling the contiguous domains of socio- and ethno-linguistics, cf. 'El uso de los morfemas 'formales' y 'familiares' en el español de Chile', ibid. 8.439-55 (1954-55).

firm grasp of the relevant technology, and coördinated with cartographic projections, then it is probably correct to trace the early stages of Spanish American research so slanted to the 'thirties and early 'forties.[55] It was in particular a seasoned European champion of this approach, Fritz Krüger, who, after practicing it for a quarter-century at Hamburg's Hansische Universität and after successfully imparting to many German disciples and an occasional foreigner his knowledge of underlying theory and pertinent rules-of-thumb, implanted this type of investigation in West Argentinian soil (after accepting the directorship of an Institute at Mendoza, Prov. of Cuyo), from where the technique spread over several centers of Spanish-speaking America.[56] At this juncture Colombia, through the special facilities and opportunities

[55] The initiative lay, at the preliminary stage, in the hands of non-professionals. Thus José E. Perdomo, the author of the *Léxico tabacalero cubano* (Havana, 1940), held down, of all positions, the job of 'Director-Jefe de Propaganda y Defensa del Tabaco Habano'. Small wonder that of the 920 technical terms and expressions of the tobacco industry he collected, no less than four hundred were brand names! Still less surprising is the fact that a book meant to serve as an authoritative guide in drawing up and judicially interpreting contracts and all manner of transactions was normative in tone, to the detriment of purely linguistic concerns; cf. the slightly Quixotic appraisal by A. Alonso in *RFH* 4.390-2 (1942). On the North American side one may adduce, as pioneering examples of the *Wörter-und-Sachen* approach brought to bear on American Spanish, such papers by L. B. Kiddle (Univ. of Michigan) as his well-known *jícara* monograph (New Orleans, 1944) and the note '"Turkey" in New Mexican Spanish', *RomPh* 5.190-7, with two maps (1951-52; *Antonio G. Solalinde Memorial*).

[56] In Hamburg Krüger's influence was all-pervasive in the 16 volumes (1928-44) of his quarterly *Volkstum und Kultur der Romanen* and in the monograph series (chiefly embodying doctoral theses written under his direction) *Hamburger Studien zu Volkstum und Kultur der Romanen.* Characteristic of the *Wörter-und-Sachen* investigative technique was, among the writings of his students, the monograph by W. Bierhenke, *Ländliche Gewerbe der Sierra de Gata*; *eine wort- und sachkundliche Untersuchung* (Hamburg, 1932); also H. Messerschmidt, 'Haus und Wirtschaft in der Serra da Estrêla (Portugal)', *VKR* 4.72-163, 246-305 (1931), and W. Ebeling, 'Die landwirtschaftlichen Geräte im Osten der Provinz Lugo (Spanien)', ibid. 5.50-151 (1932). Krüger's own crowning achievement was the multipronged monograph *Die Hochpyrenäen*, published, through different channels, in four parts, totaling six massive volumes, from the mid-'thirties to the early 'forties.

After the Second World War the tide of academic taste and intellectual preference changed radically in and around Hamburg, witness that research center's new outlet, the *RJb*, founded in 1947. Simultaneously, Krüger's approach conquered new strongholds (a) in a spate of dialectologically oriented Madrid dissertations, e.g. those written by M. J. Canellada (1944) and M. C. Casado Lobato (1948) — see my reviews in *Lg* 23.60-6 (1947) and 25.291-307, 437-46 (1949); (b) in the temporarily influential, at present side-tracked Coimbra journal *RPF* (founded in 1947), directed by M. Paiva Boléo, a former associate of Krüger's at Hamburg and at present his most ardent follower in Europe; (c) in the West Argentine periodical *AIL* — launched by Corominas, but taken over, after a five-year break, by Krüger, as a result of his transfer, in 1948, to the Universidad de Cuyo (Mendoza); cf. the Preface to Vol. 4 (1950; readied for the printer in 1949).

Krüger's most ambitious undertaking in the last quarter-century and one aptly illustrating his hunger for factual information, his bibliographic prowess, and his total aloofness from any topic even remotely redolent of 'arts and letters' has been his bulky monograph on the Romance rustic nomenclature of pieces of furniture (*El mobiliario popular en los países románicos*), of which Part A appeared as a supplement to the *RPF*, Part B, on 'seats', fills two hundred-odd pages of Vol. 7 (1959) of the *AIL*, while Part C, on the 'cradle', is to be channeled through Madrid's *RDyTP*; cf. fn. 43, above.

In the years 1952 and 1954 the University of Cuyo issued, in two volumes packing over one thousand pages, the *Homenaje a Fritz Krüger*, a unique miscellany of learned papers which became a meeting-ground for European and Spanish American scholars, with an occasional North American participant admitted for good measure; see Stanley L. Robe's admirably balanced assessment in

for research vested in its nationally supported Instituto Caro y Cuervo, is in all likelihood more hospitable to this current than any other Hispanic country on this side of the Atlantic.[57]

Certain isolable ingredients of this — culturally rewarding — style of research can be extracted from the compound known as *Wörter-und-Sachen* and presented alternatively in some other context. A. Salazar's masterly inquiry into the music, musical instruments, and dances described or evoked by Cervantes is a case in point:[58] While the material is not arranged in a way to be most serviceable to the lexicographer, the synoptic tables (132f.), the alphabetic index (172-3), the folding table containing the 'family trees' of instruments, plus the 74 appended excursuses (133-72), as distinct from footnotes, jointly make it possible to use the monograph as a handy and extremely precise reference tool. In as much as Daniel Devoto's early parallel training — in large part, self-training — in musicology, folklore, and classical literature goes back to his Buenos Aires period, it is proper to credit Argentina with some of the researches that he has been conducting during the subsequent Parisian segment of his career, after falling under the spell of Marcel Bataillon; the article on difficult lexical items in the poetry of Gonzalo de Berceo (an author no living expert knows more intimately than Devoto) thus deserves mention at this point because it shows the author in command of skills that make him the logical continuator of Salazar.[59] Of course, one

RomPh 9.68-72 (1955-56) and 10.270-3 (1956-57). In more than one respect the venture represents a bridge between the Old and the New World, with special reference to the glotto-ethnographic analysis here at issue. Some papers deal with slices of material civilization transferred to Europe across the Atlantic, cf. M. Menéndez García, 'El maíz y su terminología en Asturias' (2.369-402). Krüger's old companions-in-arms from Hamburg here reappear at a 'convocation' held at the foot of the Andes, contributing papers keyed to the *Wörter-und-Sachen* approach or, at least, to the study of *realia* and attuned to Peninsular topics, as is true of the articles by W. Bierhenke (1.207-30: 'Agavefasern und ihre Verarbeitung in Algarve') and by R. Wilmes (2.157-92: 'Contribución a la terminología de la fauna y de la flora pirenaica: Valle de Vió [Aragón]'). More important, native Argentinians and immigrants from Germany close ranks in bringing newly furbished, if not novel, tools to bear on local problems, cf. B. E. Vidal de Battini, 'El léxico de los buscadores de oro de La Carolina, San Luis' (1.303-33) and A. Dornheim, 'La alfarería criolla en Los Algarrobos [Prov. de Córdoba]' (1.335-64).

[57] Two examples selected at random: J. J. Montes, 'Apuntes sobre el vocabulario del tabaco en Bolívar y Santander', *Thesaurus* 17.30-50 (1962); and Jennie Figueroa L., 'Léxico de la caña de azúcar en Palmira y La Cumbre (Valle del Cauca, Colombia)', ibid. 18.553-621 (1963). Similar research papers have of late been prepared in Chile: Elba Koller, 'El cultivo del arroz en la provincia de Ñuble y su terminología', *BFUCh* 9.87-103 (1956-57; word-list: 98-103), and Elisa Carrasco, 'Terminología pesquera de la provincia de Valparaíso' [158 expressions arrayed in semantic groups and alphabetically cross-indexed], ibid. 9.15-33. Some of these papers are little more than neat and conscientious seminar reports on the predoctoral level, hence, typically, pieces authored by unknowns. In South America, as in Portugal, this kind of research project, perhaps on account of the 'home economics' element, increasingly seems to attract young women.

[58] 'Música, instrumentos y danzas en las obras de Cervantes', *NRFH* 2.21-56, 118-73. The author, though a long-term resident of Mexico City and a staff member of its élite institution Colegio de México, was a displaced Spanish intellectual.

[59] See his 'Notas al texto de los *Milagros de Nuestra Señora* de Berceo', *BHi* 59.5-25 (1957); Devoto's related medievalistic studies come up for mention infra, cf. fnn. 121 and 125. He is also the author of a major article on balladry known for its peculiar methodological twist, 'Sobre el estudio folklórico del Romancero español', ibid. 57.233-91 (1955), with emphasis on erotic rather than heroic

can resolutely veer away from the semantic zone of tangible objects without straying too far from this path, as when P. Grases, upon settling in Venezuela, selected the finely graded Spanish expressions for 'uproar' to test his aptitude for lexicographic probings[60] — strictly speaking, a venture into the realm of synonymy.

As regards the third 'subgenre', namely the lexical contacts of American Spanish with other languages — if one may, for once, lump together borrowings due to (a) readings, (b) the showing of motion pictures, (c) translations by hack writers and hasty journalists, (d) bidirectional travels by tourists, businessmen, and diplomats, (e) exposure to educational institutions, (f) infiltration or large-scale settlement of immigrants of widely varying stocks and social categories —, it seems proper to consider jointly current studies in Gallicisms, Anglicisms (of British and American provenience), Italianisms, and Lusisms[61] and to oppose this clearly delimited domain

themes and with special attention to the use of rationally unjustified variants, a bent of curiosity which helped him establish a precarious rapport with some phonologists. Devoto's early roots in Argentine philology and musicology appear in numerous minor contributions to A. Alonso's *RFH*, particularly middle-sized book reviews, as well as in a major article bespeaking the range of his bibliographic information: 'La canción tradicional y la música culta', *Rev. de la Univ. de Buenos Aires* 3:2:1.73-91 (1944), a dormant journal at that very moment revived and given editorial sparkle by R. Lida. Least familiar to linguists and philologists are such studies by Devoto as are entombed in musicological miscellanies, e.g. 'La enumeración de instrumentos musicales en la poesía medieval castellana', in Vol. 1 of *Miscelánea en homenaje a Mons. Higinio Anglès* (Barcelona, 1958-9).

60 'La idea de "alboroto" en castellano. Notas sobre dos vocablos: *bululú* y *mitote*', *Thesaurus* 6.384-430 (1950). In this model study Grases traces Am.-Sp. *bululú* 'riot, uproar, excitement' to its Peninsular antecedents: 'one-man theatrical troupe' (386-92), identifies Aztec *mitotl* as the etymon of *mitote* (393-4), then reviews 26 Spanish American near-synonyms, e.g. *bochinche*, *brollo*, *bronca*, *bullaranga*, *cómica* (395-413), and a generous sampling of noteworthy Peninsular counterparts: *bulla*, *chirinola*, *fandango*, *galimatías*, *guirigay*, etc. (415-23), concluding with a critical retrospect and some generalizations. One could also record here miscellaneous inventories of vernacular phytonyms and zoönyms, such as J. J. Montes, 'Algunas fitonimias colombianas', ibid. 18.167-86 (1963), and 'Algunas voces relacionadas con los animales domésticos', ibid. 20.1-47 (1965), with a profusion of maps, phonetic transcription, references to Peninsular Spanish and other Romance dialects and a handy word-index, as well as studies in figurative uses — some of them highly entertaining — of plant and animal names, e.g. A. Rabanales Ortiz, 'Uso tropológico, en el lenguaje chileno, de nombres del reino vegetal' (*BFUCh* 5.137-262 [1947-49; separatum dated 1950]), the latter a pendant to W. Beinhauer's European-flavored study of all manner of animal metaphors in Peninsular Spanish: *Das Tier in der spanischen Bildsprache* (Hamburg, 1949). On the border-line of folklore (superstitions, ritual) one may place J. M. Lope Blanch's *Vocabulario mejicano relativo a la muerte* (Mexico, 1963); the author, I understand, is a Spaniard now firmly established in Mexico.

61 No systematic inquiry seems to have been made into the gradual dissolution of Yiddish speech into such surrounding city dialects as that of Buenos Aires. Judging from parallel situations observed at close range elsewhere (Berlin, Vienna, New York City), such a process is bound to leave certain sediments, at least of the lexical order, in the parlance of the majority group.

I have as yet made no attempt to unearth the few and scattered — if at all available — scraps of information on contacts, past and present, between Hispano-Romance and German (Chile, Brazil), Dutch (Surinam), Japanese (Southern Brazil), Indic (Guiana, West Indies), and Central African (Caribbean, Brazil) — except that there exists a sizable literature on the Afro-Cuban strain. Upon occasion Latin American periodicals have acted as vehicles for studies on Gypsy-Spanish, but only those from the pens of European contributors; cf. M. L. Wagner, 'A propósito de algunas palabras gitano-españolas', *Fil* 3.161-80 (1951), and several notes by C. Clavería tied together by the unifying thread of the title 'Miscelánea gitano-española' (on *mangante* and *pirandón*: *NRFH* 2.373-6 [1948]; on *pagüe* and its synonyms: ibid. 4.43-9 [1950], etc.).

en bloc to the equally important and in some respects far more exciting field of research in Hispano-Indian symbiosis.

The hazard of Gallicisms has been very real in Spanish culture at three separate segments of its historical trajectory, of which the last and longest includes the periods of the Enlightenment and of France's 19th- and early 20th-century supremacy in fine literature and certain branches of science. This risk was, for a while, exacerbated in Spanish America, as a result of the eagerness of many locally tone-setting intellectuals to spend their formative years in, of all places, Paris — in marked (not to say militant) preference to Madrid. Small wonder that the jeopardy was most vigorously diagnosed by a Venezuelan, Rafael María Baralt (1810-60), to whom, as to Cuervo, unassailably pure usage meant the immobilized standard of the Golden Age; Baralt apparently did not suspect that the allegedly 'castizo' lexicon of Cervantes and Lope was also shot through with Gallicisms of earlier date, in heavy disguise. Because of a change in winds, this 'danger' has at present subsided and elicits little additional comment.[62]

It is the Anglicism (or rather the [North] Americanism), then, that represents the order of the day, on a small scale in Spain proper[63] and, in much bolder projection, all over Latin America, where the danger of 'contagion' is at its most acute in Mexico City, in the Isthmus (particularly the Panama Canal zone), in Puerto Rico, and in crowded urban centers of the Río de la Plata area. Characteristically, it is Panamanians like Luisa Aguilera Patiño and, especially, Ricardo J. Alfaro who, aroused by this situation in their closest environment, have become articulate about the 'Anglo-Hispanic' problem, so rich in controversial cultural and political implications.[64]

[62] Baralt's *Diccionario de galicismos*, with a Preface by the influential writer and archivist-librarian J. E. Hartzenbusch (Madrid, 1855), has gone through several posthumous printings (1874, 1918, etc.). The author, born in Maracaibo, was, fundamentally, a historian of his native country, whose flair for flawless style and puristically conceived propriety of usage alerted him to the menace of adulteration. A smaller lexicographic venture of his, the *Diccionario matriz de la lengua castellana* (Madrid, 1850), was reproduced in facsimile on the occasion of the tenth anniversary (1957) of the Universidad del Zulia founded in his native city.

[63] On Lapesa's position one may profitably consult his paper 'La lengua desde hace cuarenta años', *Revista de Occidente* (New Ser.), Nos. 8-9 (Nov.-Dec. 1963), pp. 193-208, esp. 196-8 (note the shrewd remark on the continued trickle of Gallicisms, not a few of which reach Spanish via an English detour) as well as several passages — identifiable through the Index, s.v. *inglés* — in the consecutive editions of his book *Historia de la lengua española*. Lapesa's influence in Spanish America has in recent years been reinforced through several highly successful visits to such hubs of intellectual activity as the Universidad de La Plata (Argentina) and the Colegio de México. Because he and his Italian counterpart, Bruno Migliorini (Florence), conspicuously share a dual commitment to language history and to enlightened normativism and because two languages of such mutual affinity as Spanish and Italian happen at present to be similarly exposed to the pressure of English, it would be worthwhile to compare, point by point, Lapesa's reaction to this challenge to Migliorini's sharply profiled attitude, as expressed in 'Cento anni di lessico italiano' (forming part of the miscellany *Cento anni di lingua italiana [1861-1961]* (Milano, 1962) — where his essay flanks G. Devoto's stimulating piece, 'Cento anni in cinque ventenni', in which the phonemic implications of such Anglicisms as *tram* and *sport* are explicated. See G. Costa's review in *RomPh* 18.337-40 (1964-65) and the same critic's perceptive appraisal of Migliorini's *Lingua contemporanea*, ibid. 19.618-21.

[64] Alfaro, a scholar-politician who reached the pinnacle of his career as President of the Republic of Panama, started his lexicographic probings with an exploratory article ('El anglicismo en el español contemporáneo' [a speech given before the local Academy], *Thesaurus* 4.102-28 [1948]), from there

Important research has independently been carried on elsewhere, as far south as Chile, and there has been no dearth of competent if small-sized contributions by North American observers, which need not be surveyed here.[65] It should be stressed, however, that Anglo-Spanish lexical relations have been 'acted out in real life' and kept under close surveillance by three generations of analysts in another part of the New World, namely the southwestern belt of the United States, or the south if one were to include Tampa and Miami. Here, A. M. Espinosa-padre and E. C. Hills, both concerned with New Mexico, spearheaded a movement aimed at a steadily expanding territory which was to include California, Arizona, Colorado, Texas, Florida, and — not least — New York City, reeling under the sudden influx of Puerto Ricans.[66] Some of the studies have been conducted under almost ideal laboratory conditions and have been paralleled or preceded by all manner of sociological probings into the patterns of adjustment of native speakers of Spanish to several dimensions of North American culture. A vast synthesis of these scattered researches, to the extent that they touch upon language, has become a prime desideratum, and systematic comparison with the findings of Spanish American investigators made on their native soil seems to be the next logical step. A third ingredient in the future over-all study of the confrontation of Spanish and English throughout the post-colonial New World might well be the scrutiny of the changing lexical relations in the Philippine Islands between

---

proceeded to the writing of a book-length dictionary: *Diccionario de anglicismos; enumeración, análisis y equivalencias castizas de los barbarismos, extranjerismos, neologismos y solecismos de origen inglés* (Panamá [City], 1950). Pruned of its flamboyant subtitle but not shorn of its belligerently puristic bias, the book appeared in a revised ed. (Madrid, 1964) under the imprint of the Biblioteca Románica Hispánica (Series V, Vol. 4); the 1948 article now transformed into the Introduction (7-25) is substantial, but bristles with partisan views in the classic tradition of *Fremdwörterhass.*

Another center of research in Anglicisms has been Chile. I have not consulted and therefore cannot calibrate *Anglicismos*, by Elizabeth V. Peyton and Guillermo Rojas Carrasco (Valparaíso, 1944) — reputedly a word-list of 500 items, one third of them already sanctioned by the Academy —, but I must commend Lidia Contreras' monograph on Anglicisms in the jargon of sports (see fn. 42, above) for its exemplary rigor and detachment. Split, characteristically enough, between loyalties to Panama and to Chile has been the checkered career of Luisita V. Aguilera Patiño, a student, above all, of narrative folk traditions (1949, 1952, 1956) and of local paroemiology (*Refranero panameño* ..., a monumental Univ. of Chile thesis, 1955); her lexicographic inventory, *El panameño visto a través de su lenguaje* (Panamá [City], ca. 1955), includes 115 Anglicisms.

65 Many of the shorter and less pretentious pieces have appeared in *Hispania.* For a bird's-eye view and level-headed appraisal of these (and related) activities see Einar Haugen, *Bilingualism in the Americas: a bibliography and research guide*, Publ. of the American Dialect Society, No. 26 (1956); cf. W. F. Shipley's warm appreciation in *RomPh* 13.84-86 (1959-60).

66 Most of the earlier studies (by Kercheville, Post, Rael, and others) can easily be located through the bibliographies appended to A. Alonso's Bibl. de Dial. hisp.-am., Vols. 2, 4, and 7. The student work assembled and issued by M. Romera Navarro stands apart, in that linguistic analysis is reduced to a minimum; see Stanley M. Sapon's rev. in *RomPh* 8.163 (1954-55) of Gilberto Cerda, Berta Cabazo, and Julieta Farias, *Vocabulario español de Texas* (Austin, 1953). On border argots in this territory see M. L. Wagner, 'Ein mexikanisch-amerikanischer Argot: das *Pachuco*', *RJb* 6.237-66 (1953-54), with a handy word-list (246-66), and Lurline Coltharp's sociologically slanted monograph: *The tongue of the 'tirilones'; a linguistic study of a criminal argot* (Univ. of Alabama Press, 1965); cf. W. Sinclair's review in *RomPh* 21.110-3 (1967-68).

Important material on the assimilation of Spanish words to American English is hidden away in

the two great contenders and between each of them on the one hand, and Tagalog as the leading indigenous language on the other.

Despite some progress, the current analyses of Anglicisms are not as fine-grained as one has a right to expect on the strength of advances achieved elsewhere. Two lacunae in particular come to mind. Insufficient emphasis has been placed on the different impact of (a) such irreducibly 'Anglo-Saxon' words as *bloomers*, *bluff*, *boycott* (Sp. *blúmers*, *blóf*, *boicot-eo*) and (b) English words of Graeco-Latin or French-Italian ancestry: *circulate*, *citizenry*, *scientist*. Both categories are thought-provoking to the detached observer and constitute latent 'threats' to the watchful zealot, but their agencies are different in kind and degree of intensity. Group (a) adds entirely new word families to the local Spanish stock, activates the mechanism of certain synchronic sound correspondences (as when the peculiar /ə/ [ʌ] of E. *bluff* becomes /o/), and sets in motion the existing derivational machinery (*blof-ear*, *boicot-eo*). Group (b), ordinarily not 'borrowed' but absorbed into the existing stock through assimilation to transparent cognates, blurs the traditional semantic and syntactic contours of those congeners, as when *circular* begins to develop an unprecedented transitive use; *ciudadanía*, originally abstract, is pressed into service as a mass-noun; and *científico*, in emulation of E. *scientist*, is substituted for authentically Spanish *hombre de ciencia*.

The second point that some purists habitually miss is the dubious advantage, in terms of 'casticismo', of a concealed loan translation over a candid borrowing. Three different situations can be set off. Since the terminology of motor vehicles is traceable, in its ultimate roots, to the jargon of wheelwrights, one is not too hard put to replace *bearings* by *cojinetes*, *fender* by *guardafango*, *clutch* by *embrague*, etc. But surely Alfaro's regret at the obsolescence of such old-style card games (not all of them, he forgets to add, of strictly Spanish background) as *bacará*, *báciga*, *berlanga*, *briscán*, *monte*, *mus*, *pechigonga*, *quínolas*, *rentoy* (< Fr. *rends-toi!*), *rocambor*, *sacanete*, *tresillo*, *truque*, and *tute* is not tantamount to an invitation to attach these labels to the new currently fashionable games imported from the English-speaking countries? And can he and patriots of like persuasion seriously believe that loan translations as typical alternatives to loan-words (say, *balompié* for *football*) 'defile' Spanish less than do easily recognizable straight lexical transfers, when in reality they merely represent cases of subtler, hence often ineradicable, penetration?

The problem of Italianisms is altogether different. If one disregards the Italo-Luso-

---

collections of place-names, cf. those by E. G. Gudde for California and by W. C. Barnes and B. H. Granger for Arizona; in critical reactions to them (cf. W. Bright's and W. F. Shipley's mutually complementary critiques of the latter); and in notes and articles flowing from them, cf. Madison S. Beeler, 'The Californian oronym and toponym *Montara*', *RomPh* 20.35-39 (1966-67). On residual Hispanisms in Colorado English one finds a few slivers of helpful information in Clyde T. Hankey, *A Colorado word geography*, Publ. of the Amer. Dial. Soc., No. 34 (1960); see my digest in *RomPh* 18.524 (1964-65). The standard guide remains H. W. Bentley, *A dictionary of Spanish terms in English, with special reference to the American Southwest* (New York, 1932).

A splinter of Canary Islands Spanish has been wedged into the French-speech area of the bayous; see Raymond R. MacCurdy, *The Spanish dialect in St. Bernard parish, Louisiana* (Albuquerque, 1950), and the reviews by W. A. Read, *RomPh* 5.231-2 (1951-52) and by myself, *Lg* 27.405-11 (1951).

Castilian 'Mischsprache' or *lingua franca* favored by crews and commanders — including Columbus — of early expeditions (this cant must surely have left a few lexical deposits in New World Spanish),[67] we are essentially faced with the 20th-century speech of the *barrio italiano* in a metropolis like Montevideo and Buenos Aires; comparable problems must have crystallized in southern Brazil, especially in São Paulo. One distinguishes two socio-educational levels in this process of Italo-Spanish amalgam. The low-class speech absorbs a large number of Italian dialect words, which further sifting, such as underlies Meo Zilio's latter-day research, may assign to its European sources: Genoese, Neapolitan, Sicilian, etc. Far more elusive is the influence of the second-generation immigrant, especially if he embarks on the career of a journalist or editor: While he has sufficiently mastered the essentials of Spanish to avoid the pitfall of gross 'grammatical' errors, his style — as regards propriety of word order, precise delimitation of lexical meaning, and other delicate features — may continue to show traces of childhood exposure to a Romance language other than Spanish. As a result, unless he watches himself, his manner of writing will be, at best, colorless and, at worst, thoroughly unenjoyable. Close observers of the Italianate side of the Buenos Aires scene have been Renata Donghi, Américo Castro, and Amado Alonso.[68]

67 The classic analysis of Columbus' lexicon is found in Menéndez Pidal's article 'La lengua de Cristóbal Colón', now readily accessible in a collection of essays so entitled (Colección Austral 280; Mexico and Buenos Aires, 1942), pp. 9-49; orig. *BHi* 45.5-28 (1940) with a companion note in *Correo erudito* 98-101 (Madrid, 1940).

68 After an early feeler ('Contribución al estudio del italianismo en la República Argentina', 1925; cf. M. L. Wagner, *RFE* 15.191-5 [1928]) by Renata Donghi [de Halperín], who was stimulated to engage in this project by A. Castro's first stint as Director of the newly founded Instituto de Filología, the leading Spanish philologist, on his second visit to Buenos Aires in the very late 'thirties, made a number of observations on the Argentine capital's bundle of dialects. Some of these thoughts and retrospective second thoughts, after Castro's eventual transfer to this country, were presented at the 1940 Conference of Teachers of Spanish American Literature which convened at UCLA, and were still later expanded into a highly controversial book: *La peculiaridad lingüística rioplatense y su sentido histórico* (Buenos Aires, 1941), which unleashed a furious debate among the country's leading intellectuals. Though far more restrained in his judgments, A. Alonso also commented repeatedly on the diluted character of middle-class Porteño, not least as used among intellectuals. As regards idiosyncrasies of the low-class parlance of Italian immigrants as well as of native speakers of Spanish exposed to that parlance, see the above-mentioned writings by Gobello, Grossmann, and G. Meo Zilio, esp. the latter's notes: 'Influenze dello spagnolo sull'italiano parlato nel Rio de la Plata', *LN* 16.16-22 (1955); 'Fenomeni lessicali ...', ibid. 16.53-5; 'Fenomeni di contaminazione morfologica nel cocoliche rioplatense', ibid. 16.112-7; 'Un morfema italiano con funzione stilistica nello spagnolo rioplatense', ibid. 19.58-64 (1958); 'Una serie di morfemi italiani con funzione stilistica nello spagnolo nell'Uruguay', ibid. 20.49-54 (1959); 'Sull'elemento italiano nello spagnolo rioplatense', ibid. 21.97-103 (1960); 'Canali e veicoli dell'italianismo in Uruguay', *ibid.* 23.116-21 (1962); 'Settanta italianismi gastronomici nello spagnolo d'America', *ibid.* 26.48-54 (1965); also: 'Italiano e spagnolo in Uruguay', in *La Navicella* 20ff. (Montevideo, 1957) and, with reference to phonology (applied to pedagogy), syntax, and semantics, 'Alcune tendenze sintattiche e stilistiche dello spagnolo medio rioplatense', *QIA* 22.417-27 (1958); 'Interferenze sintattiche nel cocoliche rioplatense', *LN* 17.54-9 (1956); 'Fenomeni stilistici del cocoliche rioplatense', ibid. 17.88-91; 'Notas de fono- y auto-fonodidáctica italo-hispánica', *Anales del Instituto de Profesores Artigas* (Montevideo, 1957), No. 2, pp. 28. The well-informed and sophisticated author, a student of C. Tagliavini's whose thinking has to some extent been moulded by his next-door neighbor in Montevideo, E. Coşeriu, and by A. Menarini, has

Lusisms in American Spanish, particularly in the La Plata zone, are due either to the very strong immigration from Galicia at the turn of the century, or to the open cultural frontier, especially in the period 1700-1900, between the estuary of La Plata and southern Brazil. A systematic inquiry, beyond the few available probings,[69] into the *galleguismos*, as against the *brasileñismos*, of both Uruguayan and Porteño low-class speech, and, conversely, into the *castellanismos* lingering on all over southern Brazil, remains a prime desideratum.

Given such an ensemble of auspicious circumstances as the infinite variety of autochthonous Indian languages all over Latin America, the superb preservation of numerous indigenous cultures, and the frequent occurrence of all manner of glotto-hybridism (including the continued rise of 'Creole' languages[70]), the study of linguistic, especially lexical, contacts between American Spanish and the diverse Amerindian substrata and adstrata holds out the promise of truly unlimited possibilities. Measured by these tempting prospects, the research is still in its infancy at present, a remark which would not hold of Indianistic inquiries in North America. There are other, equally sharp differences between Anglo-Indian and Hispano-Indian RELATIONS and STUDIES alike — contrasts, either ineradicable or apt to be gradually smoothed away, which will forthwhith command our attention.

Meanwhile it is helpful to remember that, despite these incompatibilities, the ties between North American and Latin American investigations so directed are rapidly becoming indissoluble. Whereas, unlike the times of Lenz and Wagner, such European Indianists as can also pass muster as experts in Hispano-Romance are at present distressingly few and may run into the teeth of severe New World criticism,[71] the

finally distilled ca. 700 Platense words of Italian parentage, which are to be jointly presented in a book-length synthesis provisionally entitled *El elemento italiano en el español rioplatense*; see *LN* 21.99, fn. 9. Meanwhile we have from Meo Zilio's pen an article affording a panoramic view: 'Italianismos generales en el español rioplatense', *Thesaurus* 20.58-119 (1965), with a conveniently arrayed alphabetic word-list. From lexicocentric studies he has lately struck out in the direction of extrasystemic sounds, significant gestures, and related phenomena, again and again in reference to his favorite hunting ground hugging the Rio de la Plata. At proof I learn that his latest output includes: 'Algunos septentrionalismos italianos en el español rioplatense', *RJb* 15.297-301 (1964).

[69] For the evocation of the social milieu — an assortment of ranch hands, itinerant workers, cattle thieves, contrabandists — in which many Brazilianisms, from the outpost of Portuguese in Rio Grande do Sul, could ooze through into Platense Spanish (and vice versa), I refer the reader to the suggestive short story 'El muerto' by Jorge Luis Borges, modern Argentina's outstanding literary figure. Not fortuitously, perhaps, Borges, as a theorist and a polemist, has also been passionately interested in the problem of Argentinian Spanish, facing that problem, in his role of insider, not at all from the same angle as the most qualified observers from Spain, A. Castro and A. Alonso. See his pamphlet *El idioma de los argentinos* (Buenos Aires, 1928), bound, in the 1953 reprint, with José Edmundo Clemente's essay *El idioma de Buenos Aires*.

[70] Through a lucky coincidence, Robert A. Hall's latest book *Pidgin and Creole languages* (Ithaca, N.Y., 1966) has just come off the press. Unfortunately, its tidy Selected Bibliography (163-77), while possibly doing justice to the full range of the author's own writings (no less than 59 items are listed), is sparing in its inventory of Douglas M. Taylor's papers and critically deëmphasizes some of William A. Read's latter-day contributions.

[71] Thus, if W. Giese's 'Hispanismos en el mapuche' (*BFUCh* 5.115-32 [1948-49]) provoked only elaborations on the part of A. Rabanales O[rtiz]: 'Observaciones a "Hispanismos en el mapuche"' (*ibid.*

rapprochement between Latin American scholars and the separate teams of North American Romanists and Indianists is likely to advance by leaps and bounds.[72] There has been of late growing understanding in this country for the exceptional worthwhileness of lexically slanted studies bearing on such areas as the Caribbean or the Southwest of the United States and involving equal expertise in American English, American Spanish, and at least one local Indian language.[73] William Shipley's brilliant study of Hispanisms in the entire linguistic subsoil of California's culturally

---

7.133-51 [1952-53]: 64 comments on sound features and 146 lexical vignettes), a straight Indianistic classificatory monograph by a Spanish Indo-Europeanist proved not immune to a fatally damaging verdict meted out by an Argentine critic: see J. A. Suárez's assessment in *IJAL* 28.286-93 (1962) of Antonio Tovar's *Catálogo de las lenguas de América del Sur* (Buenos Aires, 1961).

[72] Early experiments have yielded papers such as G. L. Trager, 'Spanish and English loanwords in Taos', *IJAL* 10.144-58 (1944), and Robert F. Spencer, 'Spanish loanwords in Keresan', *SJA* 3.130-46 (1947). Semitechnical notes coming from Romance quarters have been contributed by L. B. Kiddle, arising at the point of convergence of that scholar's separate concerns with general dialectology, Romance philology, and American Spanish lexicography; see in particular 'Spanish loanwords in American Indian languages', *Hispania* 35.179-84 (1952), and 'The Spanish language as a medium of cultural diffusion in the Age of Discovery', *AS* 27.241-56 (1952). Interestingly, A. Marshall Elliott (d. 1910), often regarded — at least in Johns Hopkins circles — as the founder of Romance philology in the United States, wrote a pioneering study (1884) on one Creole language functioning as 'lingua franca', a paper not so difficult of access as to have escaped the attention of P. Henríquez Ureña (see his 1938 omnibus volume, p. 325-6): 'El hispano-náhuatl del *Güegüence*', lit. 'Dancer'. Elliott's comments followed quickly upon the publication of the text — half-comedy, half-ballet — by D. G. Brinton (1883). *Güegüence* reflects Azt. *huehuentzin*, i.e. /howen¢in/, etym. 'old man', a traditional comic role in Middle American folk dance (information supplied by W. Bright).

[73] Read's *Louisiana-French* (Baton Rouge, 1931; 2d ed. [posthumous], with Addenda, 1963) is far more meritorious on the lexico-etymological than on the phonic side; cf. the two mutually complementary statements by W. Bright in *RomPh* 18.350-2 (1964-65) and 19.490-5 (1965-66). Read's concluding Indiano-Romanic papers, written at the end of an exceptionally long career, were 'Some words from French Louisiana', *RomPh* 7.180-6 (1953-54), and 'Four Indiano-Brazilian lexical notes', *ibid.* 9.370-1 (1955-56). The same journal published two important papers from the pen of D. R. Taylor (several others have appeared in *Lg*, *Word*, and *IJAL*): 'Lexical borrowing in Island-Carib' and, with a running commentary by Hans Erich Keller, 'Remarks on the lexicon of Dominican [i.e., involving the island of Dominica] French Creole', 16.143-52 and 402-15 (1962-63); cf. fn. 94, below.

Active concern in the Western United States with past stages of Spanish-Indian symbiosis overlaid by a present-day stratum of American-English culture is currently at its all-time peak. Fine specimens of small-scale researches — frequently mere by-products of straight Indianistic projects — include W. and E. Bright, 'Spanish words in Patwin', *RomPh* 13.161-4 (1959-60); W. Bright, 'Animals of acculturation in the California Indian languages', *UCPL* 4:4.215-46 (1960), with four maps (for a Hispanic distillate of this monograph see *RomPh* 14.360-1); Alan R. Taylor, 'Spanish *manteca* in Alaskan Eskimo', *RomPh* 16.30-2 (1962-63); and Jesse O. Sawyer, 'The implications of /r/ and /rr/ in Wappo history', *ibid.* 18.165-77 (1964-65). A number of parallel inquiries have appeared in *IJAL*; notably Wick R. Miller, 'Spanish loanwords in Acoma' [an Indian pueblo situated between Albuquerque and Gallup, N. Mex.; but the actual interviewing was done in the San Francisco Area], 25.147-53 (1959), 26.41-9 (1960). Though the generation of Miller's informant no longer spoke Spanish, he surmised that the variety of Spanish underlying the borrowings was grosso modo identical with the dialect analysed by G. L. Trager and G. Valdez, 'English loans in Colorado Spanish', *AS* 12.34-44 (1937). Among immediately forthcoming contributions let me mention Sally McLendon, 'Spanish words in Eastern Pomo', to appear in *RomPh*.

At this point, the separate North American and Spanish American researches are moving closer and closer to interpenetration and ultimate merger, as North Americans, some of them missionaries, in the course of their field work acquire a feeling for the ever-present Hispano-Indian osmosis, while

variegated Central Valley is a gem of historically saturated comparativistic research.[74]

Nowhere in Spanish America,[75] not even in a country as passionately responsive to the challenge of cultural anthropology and pre-Columbian archeology as Mexico has been for decades,[76] has there crystallized any vigorous tradition of progressive high-level research in indigenous languages, even remotely comparable in sheer dynamism to the activities sparked in this country by Boas, Sapir, and L. Bloomfield. On the positive side of the ledger, this otherwise sad situation has had two redeeming consequences. First, in the absence of any well-organized cadre of professional Indianists, not a few versatile intellectuals have developed a range of interests conducive to bridging the gap between Amerindian linguistics and Spanish philology. Second, consistently strong emphasis has been placed on lexical problems, to the detriment, one is forced to admit, of phonology and grammatical structure, in part because lexicology bristles with fewer technical difficulties, in part because the link to other facets of 'cultural interaction' is far more obvious if one starts out from the lexicon.

---

intuitively perceptive Spanish Americans, to study the subsoil of their own culture with the requisite rigor, flock to the graduate schools and research institutes of their neighbors to the north. Witnesses to this rapprochement are the papers by Jacob A. Loewen, 'Spanish loanwords in Waunana' [Noanamá village on the San Juan River of the Colombian Chocó], *IJAL* 26.330-44 (1960; field work carried out in 1951-53), with a word-list containing 173 items; Donald Olson, 'Spanish loanwords in Pame' [an Otomanguean language spoken in the SE corner of the Mexican State of San Luis Potosí], ibid. 29.219-21 (1963); and William Bright and Robert A. Thiel, 'Hispanisms in a modern Aztec dialect', *RomPh* 18.444-52 (1964-65). On the other hand, the writings of not a few younger Latin American analysts bespeak thorough familiarity with the North American *modus operandi*; note in particular Martha Hildebrandt, *Sistema fonémico del macoíta* (Caracas, 1958) and Yolanda Lastra, 'Fonemas segmentales del quechua de Cochabamba' [Bolivia], *Thesaurus* 20.48-67 (1965), esp. p. 58 (borrowings from Spanish) — quite apart from I. Silva-Fuenzalida's debt to ethnolinguistics. Conversely, L. J. Prieto (Santiago de Chile) has been toeing the line of Parisian structuralism (André Martinet).

74 'Spanish elements in the indigenous languages of Central California', *RomPh* 16.1-21 (1962-63), with a map, several tables, and a carefully drawn-up comparative word-list (17-21). In as much as the paper dwells on predominantly unpublished material collected and sifted by Catherine Callaghan, Jesse O. Sawyer, William and Elizabeth Bright, Harvey Pitkin, Sylvia Broadbent (engaged in teaching and research at Bogotá before her recent return to California), and Sydney M. Lamb, it affords a preview of intensified concentration on such topics.

75 Current Indianistic research — most of it digested in the Abstracts Section of *IJAL* — is channeled through such media as *América Indígena* (Mexico), *Antropológica* and *Boletín Indigenista Venezolano* (Caracas), *Tradición* (Cuzco) and *Perú Indígena* (Lima), *Revista de Antropologia* (São Paulo). In dramatic anticlimax to the situation on the North American scene, diligent data-gathering seems not to have given rise to any theoretical reappraisal or methodological reorientation, except of course where it has been carried on by outsiders such as M. Swadesh and members of the Kenneth L. Pike family.

76 Rather characteristically, the five volumes (1933-38) of *Investigaciones lingüísticas* — a venture piloted by Mariano Silva y Aceves and discontinued after his death — contained a motley assortment of papers, some of them more pedagogical than scholarly. Among those strictly investigative in tone and content, some deal with local varieties of Spanish (e.g. Clotilde Evelia Quirarte, 'El español usado en Nochistlán', 1.68-102, 164-200), some with standard Spanish without any conspicuous reference to Mexico (e.g. Hugo Leicht, 'Arabismos presentes en el español registrados por temas ideológicos' [i.e., Arabisms semantically grouped], 1.200-51), a great many with Zapotec and other indigenous languages viewed in isolation, but surprisingly few with problems of Hispano-Indian symbiosis; among these exceptions note J. Ignacio Dávila Garibi, 'Ortografía de nombres geográficos de origen

Here are some illustrations of joint active curiosity, on the part of many-sided Latin Americans, about Indian languages and the Hispanic tradition (also, in some privileged instances, about their actual osmosis), a curiosity recurrently moving in the lexicologic groove. By way of prelude, one recalls such zigzagging lines of intellectual commitments as those traced by A. Membreño (1859-1921), who at first compiled a straight list of *Hondureñismos* (Tegucigalpa, 1895), i.e., of local Spanish regionalisms; who two years later expanded his slender book into a venture more than twice its original size through the inclusion of supplements containing lists of Carib, Zambo, Sumo, Paya, Jicaque, Lenca, and Chorti words (the last-mentioned being an extinct language); who by 1901 published a list of indigenous toponyms from Honduras (and seven years later produced a parallel list for El Salvador), and in 1907 issued a pamphlet with a roster of Aztec words recorded in Honduras.[77] This straddling of interests is by no means exceptional; witness, in Colombia, Leopoldo Tascón, whose puristically inspired abhorrence of 'provincialisms and barbarisms' sullying the speech of the Cauca Valley did not deter him from collecting unobjectionable Quechua words.[78] (After all, the Indian, being a 'noble savage', cannot defile the Spanish language by injecting into it a dose of exoticism; the picturesque inlayings of Quechua words are consequently not on a par with ugly and avoidable Gallicisms.) In neighboring Venezuela, Lisandro Alvarado (1858-1929), currently the object of a rising cult,[79] is not only the author of an exemplary bifocal study of Venezuelan-Spanish

nahuatl' (1.104-15) and the section 'Mayismos usados en Tabasco' (303-5) in Rosario M. Gutiérrez Eskildsen, 'Cómo hablamos en Tabasco' (1.265-312).

Similarly, the other major Mexican venture, *NRFH* — founded and directed from Harvard (1947-52) by Amado Alonso, but actually managed at its embryonic stage by R. Lida, later nominally headed by the critic and polygraph Alfonso Reyes, still later supervised de facto by A. Alatorre, who is currently installed as official editor in collaboration with Á. Rosenblat — has paid disappointingly limited attention to Hispano-Indian contacts. Exceptions include short papers by M. L. Wagner, 'El sufijo hispanoamericano *-eco* para denotar defectos físicos y morales', 4.105-14 (1950), and Richard L. Predmore, 'El sufijo *-al* en el español de Guatemala', 6.141-4 (1952), both of which I discuss below, and an occasional piece by Marcos A. Morínigo. M. Sandmann's note 'Un problema de geografía lingüística antillana' (9.383-5 [1955]), provoked by R. W. Thompson's earlier remarks on 'The mushroom in the Greater Antilles', actually serves to show that Jam. *junjo* is a distortion of Fr. *champignon.* (Both Thompson and Sandmann temporarily taught at the University of the West Indies.)

[77] The 3d and final ed. (Mexico, 1912) of Membreño's *Hondureñismos* marked, it is true, a sharp reduction in size. An aftermath of Addenda, Henríquez Ureña reported (1938), appeared in the *Revista de la Universidad de Honduras* (Tegucigalpa, 1922-23). The titles of the author's other writings here alluded to are: *Nombres geográficos indígenas de la República de Honduras* (Tegucigalpa, 1901); *Aztequismos de Honduras* (Mexico, 1907); *Nombres geográficos de la República del Salvador, estudio etimológico* (Mexico, 1908).

[78] After the author's death his two lexicographic life-time ventures appeared, first separately (Bogotá, c. 1934), then jointly (1961); cf. fn. 50, above.

[79] The nationally supported project of Alvarado's *Obras completas* (5 vols.) was launched in 1953 and concluded three years later by Santiago Key-Ayala, a local expert in the history of scholarship; cf. *RomPh* 14.187 (1960-61) for a summary of his companion booklet *Obra inducida de L. S.; piezas de su archivo* (Buenos Aires, 1958). The *Datos etnográficos de Venezuela* appeared twice posthumously: initially in 1945, then again (with a Preface by M. Acosta Saignes) in 1956, as the second-to-last link in the chain of *Obras.* The *Glosarios del bajo español* (orig. 1929), a uniquely arranged ref-

low-class speech (first focus: semantic idiosyncrasies; second focus: archaisms and innovations), but also of a *realia*-oriented *Glosario de voces indígenas de Venezuela.* In this compilation the 'voces chainas y cumanagotas' from the East, the Caracas area included, are kaleidoscopically intermingled with specimens of Carib and Taíno, all of them conventionally, i.e. inadequately, transliterated but, on the other hand, tidily defined, circumstantially described, and copiously documented from miscellaneous written sources — works of scholarship and belles-lettres alike. Add to this enviable record Alvarado's minor works: his observations on the Carib spoken in the lowlands of Barcelona, the posthumously published guide to indigenous Venezuelan toponyms, a collection of ethnographic materials, alongside strings of phonological and grammatical remarks bearing on local varieties of colloquial Spanish. On the Chilean scene, one might be equally justified to characterize, in similar terms, the bi- or rather multi-furcation of the encyclopedic interests of José Toribio Medina.[80] In the Caribbean area, we once again cross the path of that talented scholar Pedro Henríquez Ureña (d. 1946), whose elastic mind reconciled significant work in all phases and projections of Hispanic verbal culture with the patient mosaic-like reconstruction of exciting lexical trajectories: *ají* 'chili', *boniato* 'sweet potato', *papa* and *patata* 'potato', *caribe* in its relation to *caníbal*, and with probings into the Antillean lexicon.[81] Marcos A. Morínigo's Paraguayan-Argentine background has made him,

---

erence work, now occupies Vols. 2 and 3 (1954-55) of the *Obras*, where it is prefaced by P. Grases (cf. fn. 60, above) and is flanked by several minor writings, including 'Sufijos en el lenguaje criollo' and 'Anacronismo lingüístico'. The *Glosario de voces indígenas* (orig. 1921), enriched by a previously unavailable excursus 'Voces geográficas' (367-422), forms Vol. 1 of the set. The slim pamphlet *Observaciones sobre el caribe hablado en los llanos de Barcelona* (Caracas, 1919) thus turns out to have functioned as the author's pilot study.

80 The interplay of restrictive purism as regards the Hispanic lexical stock and of tolerance in reference to the autochthonous strain characterizes such writings of Medina's as his *Chilenismos; apuntes lexicográficos* (Santiago, 1928) in contrast to *Voces chilenas de los reinos animal y vegetal ...* (Santiago, 1927). But the author's total scholarly personality was, of course, far too many-faceted to be compressed into any such rigid dichotomy. Were it not for my self-imposed confinement at this juncture to native Spanish American 'eruditos', I could have commented profusely on the ability of one naturalized Chilean, R. Lenz, to straddle the two domains; witness, alongside that author's aforementioned controversial researches in American-Spanish, his strictly Indianistic *Estudios araucanos* (Santiago, 1895-97; reprinted from the *Anales* of his University), a book which still feeds current research, cf. J. A. Suárez, 'The phonemes of an Araucanian dialect' [the Perquenco dialect near Púa, Prov. of Malleco], *IJAL* 25.177-81 (1959). Even more noteworthy in this respect are Lenz's two magna opera, the *Diccionario etimológico de voces chilenas derivadas de lenguas indígenas americanas* (Santiago, 1905-10), the lengthy Introduction to which contains the fullest and most reliable analysis of relevant 19th-century research, far in excess of Chile proper; and its syntactic counterpart, *La oración y sus partes* (Madrid, 1920; 3d ed., 1935), in which Araucanian, contrasted with the European languages, serves the same end as do Tagalog and Central Algonquian in L. Bloomfield's writings on general linguistics.

81 The full flavor of Henríquez Ureña's *Para la historia de los indigenismos* (Buenos Aires, 1938) — a monograph which, incidentally, has absorbed an earlier string of notes on Antillean words — cannot be enjoyed without due attention to two circumstances. First, here a spokesman for Spanish America was offering a collection of elegantly worded articles interweaving historico-archival and dialectal evidence, in an effort to piece together trade routes, sea lanes, trends of cultural fashion, with the same expertise and sophistication as was being displayed by the most authoritative European spokesmen

with some encouragement from A. Alonso, the logical choice for the exploration of a bidirectional process: the filtering-through of Hispanisms into his native Guaraní and, conversely, of Guaraní exoticisms into local varieties and thence even into the standard form of Spanish.[82] It has also alerted him to the régime of bilingualism which — not unlike the present state of affairs in and around Asunción — prevailed, at the turn of the century, in Santiago del Estero, except that there the language vying with Spanish for supremacy was Quechua.[83] But since Morínigo has also evinced a strong side-interest in Golden Age literature, especially in the theater and in the 'historiadores de Indias', he has naturally attempted to combine the lexicologic bent pushing him in the direction of 'Indianoromanica' with his legitimate literary proclivity. The result was the study of reflections, in Lope de Vega's inexhaustibly rich verbal cosmos, of Spain's new colonial empire, including the infiltration of certain 'indigenismos' into his vocabulary, as well as the parallel painstaking inquiry, which has not yet reached full maturation, into the ancestry and spread of the earliest Indian words, real or supposed, that oozed into the flow of the Spanish lexicon — this time with the assistance of historiographic sources.[84]

(K. Jaberg, V. Bertoldi, B. Hasselrot, P. Aebischer, say) for this kind and style of research, which was at that very moment riding the crest of success. Second, the pre-publication of some of these studies, in slightly less elaborate form, in a Porteño newspaper of such prestige and circulation as *La Nación* aroused tremendous lay interest in these inquiries, producing a response comparable to the impact left by certain paper-back editions in this country (cf. the powerful topical influence of Ruth Benedict's *Patterns of culture*).

Henríquez Ureña's mastery in this domain appeared also in an occasional book review; cf. his generous appraisal, in *RFH* 7.288-90 (1945), of Kiddle's meritorious paper on *jícara* < Azt. *xicalli*. He exerted a palpable and wholesome influence not only on M. A. Morínigo (see below) but also, more subtly, on M. R. Lida de Malkiel; witness her note on *Patagonia* (*HR* 20.321-3 [1952]), which has provoked much lively discussion, and her tasteful article on the cultural and literary history of chocolate, 'Elixir de América', *Libro jubilar de Alfonso Reyes* 191-201 (Mexico, 1955).

[82] Alonso placed Morínigo's principal monograph, *Hispanismos en el guaraní*; *estudio sobre la penetración de la cultura española en la guaraní, según se refleja en la lengua* (Buenos Aires, 1931), at the head of his planned series Colección de estudios indigenistas, a project which later fizzled out. For critical reactions to that monograph see G. Cirot, *BHi* 36.116-8 (1935); C. Monteiro, *Rev. de Phil. e Hist.* (Rio), 2.490-3 (1934); and especially M. L. Wagner, *ZRPh* 54.119-22 (1934), who examined the book in conjunction with F. Boas' note 'Spanish elements in Modern Nahuatl', *Todd Memorial Volumes* 1.85-9 (New York, 1930) and with his own paper 'Algunas apuntaciones sobre el folklore mexicano', *AJF* 40.105-43 (1927). The companion piece to *Hispanismos* was Morínigo's article 'Las voces guaraníes del Diccionario Académico', *BAAL* 3.5-71 (1935). Characteristically, Morínigo has shrunk back from the task of describing the sound system and the grammatical structure of Guaraní, even after settling in this country; this became, in the early 'sixties, the dual target of two Cornell-trained Argentinians, Jorge A. Suárez and Emma Gregores de Suárez. Aside from fostering research in Spanish-Guaraní contacts, Argentine scholarship a quarter-century ago unearthed Patagonian-Spanish word-lists (Tsonik, Yamana) traceable to the end of the colonial period. See M. A. Vignati, *BAAL* 8.160-202, 637-63 (1940).

[83] See his non-technical communication 'Difusión del español en el noroeste argentino', *Hispania* 35.86-95 (1952), with comments on the present-day confinement of Quechua to the territory between the Río Salado and the Río Dulce in the province of Santiago and to the preservation of Atacameño in the 'puna' (i.e. Andine tableland) of Atacama — two dwindling speech islets.

[84] To the mention of his well-known book *América en el teatro de Lope de Vega* (Buenos Aires, 1946; *RFH*, Suppl. 2) one may add the titles of several complementary or supplementary articles: 'Indigenismos americanos en el léxico de Lope de Vega', *RNC* 12(84).72-95 (1951); 'La

The relevance of Indianistic research to Spanish philology is clearest where some kind of interpenetration of form or meaning between the imported and the locally autochthonous language is amenable to observation. The social setting of rural Spanish America, with its widespread bilingualism, leaves ample room for all manner of blends and overlaps; these contacts have been observed by native and foreign analysts alike and have been discussed preponderantly in Spanish American learned journals. Thus, commenting on the Mexican and Central American suffix *-eco* (var. *-eque*) in local Spanish designations of physical and moral defects, as in *patuleco* 'crooked-legged' for *pernituerto*, fam. *zanquituerto*, Wagner judiciously separates it from the age-old Peninsular cluster *-aco*, *-eco*, *-oco*/*-ueco*, of pre-Latin parentage, as are many other Romance derivational morphemes displaying a vocalic gamut. He then links it to Azt. *-ik*, wondering whether the semantic affinity to Hispanic *-eto* might have cast the borrowed morpheme in this erratic mold as regards the stressed front-vowel, since the expected reflex would have been **-ico*, var. **-ique*.[85] Perhaps, as J. A. Suárez muses (*RomPh* 20:1), it might have been wiser to trace to Aztec only the *-eco* that appears in names of inhabitants ('gentilicios'), such as *guatemalteco*, *yucateco* (from *-ecatl*). Similarly, in focusing attention on Guatem. *-al* in designations

formación léxica regional hispanoamericana', *NRFH* 7.234-41 (1953): exoticisms vs. adjusted Spanish words used in the New World nomenclature of flora, fauna, and various trades and crafts; 'Para la etimología de *poncho*', ibid. 9.32-4 (1955): retreat from the traditional indigenous etymon (Arauc. *pontho*) in favor of an unidentified Peninsular base, on the strength of the usage of the chronicler and cosmographer Alonso de Santa Cruz. Several of Morínigo's articles were collected in a miscellany, *Programa de filología hispánica* (Buenos Aires, 1959), unfortunately without any corrections — an oversight lamented by J. M. Lope Blanch, *NRFH* 14.145 (1966). A new collection of the latest crop of his scattered papers has, I understand, very recently become available.

[85] 'El sufijo hispanoamericano *-eco* para denotar defectos físicos y morales', *NRFH* 4.105-14 (1950). In some respects this article represents an offshoot of Part 3 (*ZRPh* 64.321-37 [1944]) of Wagner's 'Iberoromanische Suffixstudien'. It also reverberates some ideas voiced in Wagner's book *Lingua e dialetti dell'America spagnola* and can be fruitfully consulted in conjunction with several critical reactions to that book, esp. K. Huber's richly informative review in *VR* 10.313-21 (1948-49), studded with data personally collected in Peru. Other filters for Wagner's slightly muddy flow of information have been provided by Á. Rosenblat, *NRFH* 4.404-6 (1950) — with equal attention to the Hispano-Latin and Indian ingredients; by A. Tovar, *AIL* 4.298-301 (1950) — who, surprisingly, deëmphasized the Indian elements; by A. Zamora Vicente, *RPF* 3.348-53 (1949-50), whose strength lay in the combined knowledge, at first hand, of one branch of South Spanish (Extremeño) and of Platense; and, from the vantage point of a comparative Romanist, by K. Baldinger, *ZRPh* 66.227-32 (1950). Wagner's final onslaught on American Spanish as a whole, in his 'Crónica bibliográfica hispano-americana' (*Os estudos de linguística românica na Europa e na América desde 1939 a 1948*, ed. M. de Paiva Boléo, Supl. bibl. 1 a *RPF* [Coimbra, 1951], pp. 369-98) shows a general slackening of his power. The country-by-country survey contains, to be sure, useful summaries of certain well-known books, such as the monographs by V. M. Suárez (1945), T. Navarro (1948), and B. E. Vidal de Battini (1949), and occasionally guides the reader (375) to neglected items, e.g. to Ignacio Alcocer, *El español que se habla en México; influencia que en él tuvo el idioma mexicano o náhuatl* (Tacubaya, D.F., 1936). But one finds nothing beyond a few non-committal generalities (397) in reference to G. Friederici's *Amerikanistisches Wörterbuch* (Hamburg, 1947), a pathetic retreat from the vigor and incisiveness with which Wagner himself once dissected (*RFE* 15.294-7 [1928]) that same author's far less arresting *Hilfswörterbuch für den Amerikanisten* (Halle, 1926).

Independent information on *-eco*, *-enco*, *-engo*, etc. can be gleaned from my monograph *The Hispanic suffix '-(i)ego': a morphological and lexical study based on historical and dialectal sources*, UCPL 4:3.111-213 (1951), and from the twenty-odd reviews which it has elicited.

of groves, patches of planted terrain, etc., Richard L. Predmore asks himself whether Azt. *-tla(n)* 'abundance' and *-tlalli* 'earth', also, independently, Maya *pakal* 'plant(ing)' (segmented *pak-al* by speakers of Spanish) could not have locally reinforced one traditional semantic nuance of Sp. *-al*, var. *-ar* < Lat. -ĀLE, as used in mass-nouns.[86]

The intertwining of the Hispanic and the indigenous lexical strands may show an entirely different pattern, and the resulting skein may be even more difficult to unravel. Instead of the convergence of derivational suffixes we may be facing the contamination of root morphemes qua actual sound sequences or merely qua semantic schemes, a hypothetical situation whose plausibility, from case to case, may be tested by the application of rule-of-thumb analysis. Take an area like the Yucatan Peninsula, marked by the coexistence and increasing reciprocal influence of Maya and (Mexican) Spanish. Sp. *acechar* (from OSp. *assechar* 'to pursue' < Lat. ASSECTĀRĪ) means everywhere 'to pry, espy, stalk', but in Yucatan it has evolved the additional meaning 'to make a short visit, drop in'. The fact that in Maya *c̓eneb* designates both 'prying, stalking' and 'dropping in' supplies the obvious explanation (emulated polysemy). On the other hand, the circumstance that Sp. *apesgar* 'to press, weigh' has sharpened its connotation to the point where it suggests 'to exert pressure on', 'to weigh on' (with the bare hands or with an appropriate tool) does not necessarily militate in favor of any conflation with Maya *petś'ah* 'to press, lay hand on'. Whether OSp. *a-*, *em-pesgar* directly reflects a type *PĒNS-ICĀRE (from PĒNSUM 'weight') or goes back, via **-pezgar*, to IMPEDICĀRE 'to ensnare, catch, trap' and thus presupposes only secondary attraction by *peso* 'weight' is a matter of bitter controversy among Romance etymologists, but the involvement of the Latin-Romance word for 'weight' at some point of *apesgar*'s trajectory has never been questioned. If there ensued a local contact in Yucatan with the Maya word implicated, it must have been minimal, amounting in all likelihood to an additional lease on life for the Spanish word elsewhere slightly obsolescent.[87] — In certain particularly intricate situations both root morphemes and derivational suffixes, in their physical shapes and in their semantic ambits alike, may lend themselves to widely ranging interpretations as regards the classic dilemma Hispano-Romance vs. Amerindian. For incisiveness of argument and sheer drama of identification I commend Jorge A. Suárez's vignettes on Sp. *avechucho* 'ugly night bird of prey', coll. 'bum, scalawag', Per. Chil. *lacho* = *chulo* (i.e., 'flashy, snappy, foxy, sporty [fellow]'), Arg. Ec. *rabincho* 'knife without handle, tailless animal', and

[86] 'El sufijo *-al* en el español de Guatemala', *NRFH* 6.141-4 (1952). The writer, currently engaged in historical and literary inquiries, is the author of an unpublished Columbia dissertation in Central American dialectology, directed by T. Navarro. His earlier interest comes to the fore, perhaps for the last time, in his imaginative review (*RomPh* 7.216-9 [1953-54]) of J. Matluck, *La pronunciación en el español del valle de México*. The latest thinking on the Peninsular use of *-al* in dendronyms and names of plantations is embodied in the note by W. E. Geiger: 'Fruit, fruit-tree, and grove in Spanish: a study in derivational patterning', *RomPh* 20.176-86 (1966-67).

[87] For criticism of these two conjectures of hybridism posited by A. Barrera Vásquez (1943) and V. M. Suárez (1945) see my note 'On analyzing Hispano-Maya blends', *IJAL* 14.74-6 (1948). My article on *assechar* and its variants appeared the following year in *HR* 17.183-232. A radically revised analysis is embodied in my paper 'Latin *pedica*, *pēnsum*, and *pertica* in Hispano-Romance', reserved for the *Mélanges Alf Lombard.*

chulengo 'ostrich, guanaco [= cameloid ruminant], small donkey'. Suárez, though a practicing Indianist, has trained himself to view with wholesome skepticism indigenous etyma, for all their picturesque suggestiveness, and, after weighing every circumstance, favors in all four instances the assumption of Peninsular extraction (as did before him, independently, Morínigo in the case of *poncho*).[88] — Yet another possibility, already alluded to apropos of P. Grases' inquiry into the Hispanic words for 'uproar' (fn. 60, above), is to place a lexical item of, say, unassailably identified Aztec ancestry in the organic context of its near-synonyms of different filiation. — Finally, as regards the configuration of lexical itineraries, there emerge before our eyes several previously unsuspected possibilities. One of the most felicitous discoveries that have been credited to Henríquez Ureña (*Para la historia de los indigenismos*, 1938) is the ever-present alternative to lexical diffusion along land routes within the former Spanish colonial empire: A word may, at first, have been imported into the metropolis (from the Antilles, say), only to have bounded back from Seville to the more outlying stretches of the New World possessions (e.g., the La Plata estuary). Knotty problems of stratification may also arise — to the exclusion of any 'feed-back' from the mother country — where several indigenous languages abut on each other. Thus, Porteño investigators endowed with the finesse of Ricardo L. J. Nardi and Jorge A. Suárez have been asking themselves, with regard to NW Argentina, whether one Indian language may have influenced another through the instrumentality of Spanish (i.e., at a relatively late date) or whether, in a given territory, a pre-Columbian language was first overlaid by Quechua, which then transmitted to Spanish some of the words it may have absorbed, with the European language acting as the uppermost layer.[89]

As regards the astonishing variations in actual standards of performance, one is tempted to set up some kind of pyramid, marked by an extra-broad base and a very modest elevation; in fact, throughout the interval separating the vintage years of Lenz's activity and the recent crystallization of a new, for the most part foreign-trained, avant-garde, we are confronted with a truncated pyramid. To the foundation of this geometric figure we would have to assign the rather numerous writings in Hispano-Indian lexicology which, despite a certain display of erudition, do not attain the level of professionally acceptable workmanship. Examples can be adduced from many quarters. Thus, though E. W. de Moesbach has the advantage of actually speaking Araucanian and though his fellow-missionary W. Meyer Rusca has a knack (which he has exploited to the hilt) for extracting linguistically pertinent information

[88] The four etymological incrustations are found toward the end of J. A. Suárez's studiedly austere review article 'Indigenismos e hispanismos, vistos desde la Argentina', *RomPh* 20.68-90 (1966-67). The opposite hypothesis of autochthonous provenience was espoused by two Argentinian scholars (Carlos Albarracín Sarmiento and María Estela de Souza), who contributed miscellaneous notes and elaborations to Berta Koessler-Ing's folkloristic monograph *Tradiciones araucanas* (Suppl. 1 to *Rhesis*; Buenos Aires, 1962), prefaced by C. Hernando Balmori.

[89] Cf. Suárez's critique, included in 'Indigenismos e hispanismos ...', of Nardi's perceptive monograph 'El quichua de Catamarca y la Rioja' [two sub-Andine provinces], reprinted from the *Cuadernos del Instituto Nacional de Investigación Folklórica* (Buenos Aires, 1962), pp. 189-285.

from archival material, the three monographs on hybridisms in Southern Chile which these two enthusiasts have written either jointly or separately are vitiated by such shortcomings as laxity in sound correspondences and inability to generalize, as well as the unwarranted assumption that, just because present-day Araucanians live in a given territory, every exotic-sounding word or toponym observed in the area at issue must necessarily be traced to that language.[90] A recent ambitious attempt, made on the Argentine side of the Andes, to replace F. J. de Augusta's old (1916) bidirectional Araucanian-Spanish dictionary by something more attractive must be written off as a failure, in the light of Suárez's and Nardi's strictures. Aside from serious flaws of transcription, lacunae in the bibliography, etc., the book in question lacks consistency in the inclusion of Hispanisms in Araucanian, is imprecise in defining those included, shows such gaucherie in the handling of 17th-, 18th-, and 19th-century sources (Luis de Valdivia, Bernardo Havestadt, Andrés Febrés, E. W. Middendorf, etc.) as to awaken little confidence in the reader concerned with Araucanianisms in American Spanish, and, as if this were not enough, falls short of expectations in winnowing out Quechua ingredients from the lexical patrimony of Araucanian (orig. North Araucanian?).[91] Similar lack of critical discernment in the selection of material detracts from the value of very recent writings by such Argentine aficionados — not necessarily concerned with their country's southern provinces — as F. H. Casullo and G. A. Terrera. A romantic predisposition in favor of 'indigenismos' prompted the former so to analyze *garúa* 'drizzle', *piola* 'houseline', and *poncho*, while the latter, using earlier glossaries and steering clear of the onerous chores of field work, threw in for good measure *chancho* 'pig', *guapo* 'bold, gallant, handsome', and *guaso* 'coarse, uncouth'.[92]

[90] Cf. Moesbach, *Voz de Arauco. Explicación de los nombres indígenas de Chile* (Padre Las Casas [Chile], 1946); Meyer Rusca, *Voces indígenas del lenguaje popular sureño; 550 chilenismos* (Osorno, 1952), reviewed by J. A. Suárez, *RomPh* 15.390-1 (1961-62); Meyer Rusca and Moesbach, *Diccionario geográfico-etimológico indígena de las provincias Valdivia, Osorno y Llanquihue* (Osorno, 1955), reviewed by Suárez, *RomPh* 14.351-2 (1960-61). The complex inner stratification of Araucanian has, of course, long been known to specialists; cf. P. Englert, *Los elementos derivados del aymará y quichua en el idioma araucano* (Santiago de Chile, 1934).

[91] Esteban Erize, *Diccionario comentado mapuche-español; araucano, pehuenche, pampa, picunche, rancülche, huilliche* (Buenos Aires, 1960); a 550-page book, with maps and drawings, published for the Instituto de Humanidades of the Univ. Nac. del Sur. See the review by Nardi in *Cuadernos del Instituto Nacional de Investigaciones Folklóricas* 2.269-72 (1961) and the devastating critique by Suárez, 'Problemas de lexicografía hispanoindia', *RomPh* 17.155-69 (1963-64; *María Rosa Lida de Malkiel Memorial*, Part 1). Significantly, Buenos Aires played host to the 17th International Congress of Americanists as early as 1910, an occasion on which Lenz, then at the zenith of his power, offered the paper 'Los elementos indios del castellano de Chile' (published in the transactions two years later).

[92] Casullo's *Voces indígenas en el idioma español* (Buenos Aires, 1964; Preface by D. L. Garasa) and Terrera's *Antiguo vocabulario iberoindígena y su vigencia actual* (Buenos Aires, 1964), along with Berta Koessler-Ing's *Tradiciones araucanas*, are reviewed with uncompromising honesty in Suárez's oft-quoted paper 'Indigenismos e hispanismos ...', *RomPh* 20:1. The locus of Corominas' original article on *garúa* and of reactions to it can now be identified through the entry to his dictionary; see also the Supplement (4.1014). On *piola*, a cognate of *pihuela* 'jess' (i.e., 'short strap round the leg of a hawk') see my own study 'Hispano-Latin *PEDIA and *MANIA: History and prehistory of *pihuela* ...', *Studies in the reconstruction of Hispano-Latin word families*, UCPL 11. 22-39, 96-154 (1954).

— At mid-elevation one might set off monographs showing, be it only in tone, their authors' limited exposure to advanced scholarship and partial familiarity with the existing literature — qualities which have restrained any amateurish indulgence in freewheeling conjectures and have elicited helpful collections of data without allowing any real break-through.[93] At the very top one is free to place specimens of research showing the craftsmen in full command of philological evidence and linguistic sophistication; at present Nardi and Suárez come closest to deserving this rating and may thus be viewed as the legitimate successors of Lenz.[94]

If one disregards the extinct native languages of the Caribbean, it is fair to state that, from the angle of Hispanic philology as practiced of late in Central and South America (to the exclusion of Brazil), the contact with current research in the major Indian languages, especially the 'lenguas generales', has been most fruitful. This

[93] At this altitude one may conceivably find a niche for the Mayisms highlighted by V. M. Suárez, *El español que se habla en Yucatán* (Mérida, 1945). Taking his cue from T. Navarro's propaedeutically slanted *Cuestionario lingüístico hispanoamericano*: 1. *Fonética, morfología, sintaxis* (Buenos Aires, 1943), Suárez, in no way a professional, nevertheless turned in a better performance than his predecessor P. Patrón Peniche, who had no crutch to lean on; cf. the latter's *Léxico yucateco: barbarismos* [9-118], *provincialismos* [119-56] *y mayismos* [157-75] (México, 1932), originally published in the 'Sociedad científica Antonio Alzate's' *Mem. y revista* 52.73-178 (1932). I cannot determine whether it is apposite to place at this level such studies as E. Otero D'Costa's 'Mestizajes del castellano en Colombia', *Thesaurus* 6.15-80 (1950), which encompasses *tainismos* (15-18: 'De cómo penetraron al corazón del país') and *quechuismos* (19-80) — the latter, I repeat, the object of L. Tascón's separate attention (1934). See also D'Costa's pilot study, under the same title, ibid. 2.166-75 (1946). Nor can I appraise with any degree of competence reference works like M. Lizondo Borda's *Voces tucumanas derivadas del quichua* (Tucumán, 1927), still less the implications for Hispanic philology of P. A. Guasch's *Diccionario guaraní precedido de una síntesis gramatical y de la fauna y flora guaraníticas*[3] (Buenos Aires, 1948). I record, without having seen them, two very recent publications: T. Buesa Oliver, *Indoamericanismos léxicos en español* (Madrid, 1965), and H. Toscano Mateus, 'Interjecciones quichuas en el español de América', *RJb* 15.288-96 (1964); for a digest see *Thesaurus* 21.199-200 and 225 (1966).

[94] With Suárez and Nardi, who are abreast of structural analysis, imbued with philological fervor, interested in American Spanish — cf. the latter's note 'Paul Groussac y el español de la Argentina', *Fil* 6.114-21 (1960) — and au courant of the latest thinking on Indian dialectology (to the extent of being in a position to formulate the assumed kinship between varieties of Quechua spoken in Cuzco, Catamarca [until ca. 1900], and Santiago del Estero), native Spanish American investigators have reached a plateau of respectability inviting a dialogue with their best-qualified European and North American counterparts. Nardi in his Quechua studies could afford to parry weighty arguments by J. H. Rowe (*IJAL* 16.137-48 [1948]); Suárez, a student of C. H. Hockett's and the translator for EUDEBA of *A course in modern linguistics*, produced a Quechua parallel to the infiltration of /š/ into Mexican Spanish, as observed by H. V. King, *SIL* 10.51-62 (1952), etc. In regard to hybridism one is here reminded of Douglas R. Taylor's stimulating papers 'Lexical borrowing in Island-Carib', *RomPh* 16.143-52 (1962-63) — a study of an Arawakan language carried from the Lesser Antilles to the Bay of Honduras and overlaid by Karina (=True Carib), Spanish, English, and French; and 'Remarks on the lexicon of Dominican French Creole', ibid. 16.402-15 — comments on a pidginized congeries of Western French patois, with a sprinkling of Spanish, Portuguese, African, and native Amerindian elements; cf. fn. 73, above. Taylor's widely-scattered papers — some of them channeled through *Lg* and *IJAL* — are, in turn, admittedly based on spade work carried out by the Dutchman C. H. de Goeje (b. 1879), notably in 'Nouvel examen des langues des Antilles', *JSAm* (N.S.) 31.1-120 (1939) and *Études linguistiques caraïbes*, 2 vols. (Amsterdam, 1909-46).

The impact being left by the two young Argentine scholars is the stronger as their respective spouses have lent their activities added support. Emma Gregores de Suárez, originally a classicist engrossed

statement applies to Aztec, Maya, Arawak, Quechua, Aymará, Guaraní, and Araucanian (Mapuche).[95]

Only a few fleeting remarks are needed at this point on the fourth 'sub-genre' here isolated, namely etymology proper, in as much as it seems well-nigh impossible, in practice, to extricate it completely from the other contexts of lexical research on which we have already trained our lens. Witness our earlier comments on such analyses of lexical problems rich in etymological implications as Henríquez Ureña's many-splendored studies in 'indigenismos' and J. A. Suárez's inquiries into genetically controversial items like *lacho* and *rabincho* — mosaic-like reconstructions matched on the North American side by L. B. Kiddle's probings into *jícara* and Mex. *guajalote* 'turkey' (and its synonyms).[96] True, not all New World practitioners of Hispano-Romance philology have shown any pronounced finesse in this particular direction: A scholar as versatile and in many respects elastic as A. Alonso trespassed rarely on this slippery terrain, and his relatively best-known foray, the article on Am.-Sp. *zonzo* 'tasteless, inane; boob, simpleton', unfortunately borders on a failure.[97]

Though the relative brevity of J. Corominas' stint at the University of Cuyo (Mendoza, Arg.) in the early 'forties may have prevented him from becoming the

---

by the Graeco-Latin background of Spanish Golden Age writers (see *Anales de Filología Clásica* 6.91-105 [1953-54]), later became a convert to descriptive linguistics (see 'Las formaciones adverbiales en *-mente*', *Fil* 6.77-102 [1960]), and earned her doctorate at Cornell on the strength of an Indianistic thesis. Susana Chertudi de Nardi is a leading folklorist and has collaborated with Ricardo Nardi on certain projects straddling their two specialties (cf. S. L. Robe's reviews in *RomPh* 16.232-3 [1962-63] and 19.99-103 [1965-66]).

[95] Quiché seems to have lost its appeal to students of linguistic diffusion; things were different in the concluding years of the 19th century, when S. I. Barberena published his *Quicheísmos, contribución al estudio del folklore americano* (San Salvador, 1894) as an implied answer to Z. Fernández Ferraz's *Nahuatlismos de Costa Rica* (San Juan, 1892). It is the Aztec words which continue to arouse interest in the Isthmus republics; Edward M. Hernández draws my attention to V. Arroyo, 'Nahuatismos y nahuatlismos en Costa Rica', *Tlatoani* 2:7.13-7 (1953), and to P. Geoffroy Rivas, *Toponimia náhuatl de Cuscatlán* (San Salvador, 1961).

[96] I have published a number of etymological articles — three or four of monograph length — in South and Central American journals. Despite the Spanish garb in which they appeared, these studies — be it on account of the themes selected or as a consequence of the techniques favored — have produced few reverberations to the south of the Mexican border; thus even the most elaborate among them deserve no more than bare mention here: 'La historia lingüística de *peón*', *Thesaurus* 7.3-46 (1951); 'La familia *lazerar, laz(d)rar, lazeria:* estudios de paleontología lingüística', *NRFH* 6.209-76 (1952); '*Apretar, pr(i)eto, perto*: historia de un cruce hispanolatino', *Thesaurus* 9.1-139 (1953); '*Cundir*: historia de una palabra y de un problema etimológico', *BFUCh* 8.247-64 (1954-55); 'En torno a la etimología y evolución de *cansar, canso, cansa(n)cio*', *NRFH* 9.225-76 (1955); 'Antiguo español y gallegoportugués *trocir* "pasar"', ibid. 10.385-95 (1956); 'Etimología y cambio fonético débil; trayectoria iberorrománica de *medicus, medicāmen, medicina*', *Homenagem a Marcel Bataillon: Ibérida* 6.127-71 (Dec. 1961 [June 1963]); 'Sobre el núcleo etimológico de esp. ant. *desman(d)ar, desman(o)*: lat. DĒ-, DĪ-MĀNĀRE', *Fil* 8.185-211 (1962 [1964]) — with numerous passages badly garbled by a careless typesetter. In several of these studies American Spanish receives a lion's share of authorial attention.

[97] 'Las prevaricaciones idiomáticas de Sancho, 1: *çonço*', *NRFH* 2.1-9 (1948); included in the miscellany *Estudios lingüísticos: temas hispanoamericanos* under the revised title '*Çonço* y su origen' (399-414). For criticism see Part 2 of my paper 'Fuentes indígenas y exóticas de los sustantivos y adjetivos verbales en *-e*', *RLiR* 24.201-53 (1960), esp. 225-6.

ranking etymologist of his generation on the Spanish American scene, the thoroughness and originality of many of his pilot articles plus the sweep and monumental size of his four-volume dictionary, on the one hand, and, on the other, his continued links to Central and South American research centers, after his transfer to Chicago twenty years ago,[98] jointly militate in favor of placing his *œuvre* in the present context.

The first stage of Corominas' meteoric career as etymologist coincides with his years of apprenticeship and early mastership in his native Barcelona. From there he lost no time in branching out to Madrid, to work under R. Menéndez Pidal, and to Zurich, to associate with J. Jud and A. Steiger. The German-Swiss training and Central Europe's intellectual environment in the mid-'thirties left an especially deep imprint on him, converting him (as they did J. Hubschmid and, for a while, P. Aebischer; also many lesser luminaries) into a 'pure' etymologist, i.e., one for whom linguistics outside the lexico-onomastic domain either seems to have a narrowly ancillary function (phonology) or almost dwindles into nothingness (morphosyntax). But as a Romance etymologist, with balanced emphasis on Spanish and on Catalan, Corominas has no peers within his generation. During his Argentine period, he was the lone, by no means idle, New World representative of Catalan philology,[99] which has now become virtually extinct in Central and South America.

[98] A model of a middle-sized etymological study, by the standards of a quarter-century ago, is the article 'Los nombres de la lagartija y del lagarto en los Pireneos', *RFH* 5.1-20 (1943), in constructive criticism of W. D. Elcock, 'The enigma of the lizard in the Aragonese dialect', *MLR* 35.483-93 (1940); for a parallel reaction see L. Spitzer in *AIL* 1.182-4 (1941-42). Worthy of mention and commendation, in addition to several titles already cited, are: 'Nuevas etimologías españolas', *AIL* 1.119-53 (1941-42): *allende* 'beyond', *aquende* 'this side of', *caracol* 'snail', *hueco* 'hollow', *joroba* 'hump', *vera* (=Ptg. *beira*) 'edge', *tatara-* 'great-grand-' (in kinship terms), *tropezar* 'to stumble' (cf. my elaboration in *UCPL* 11.30-3, 120-39 [1954]); 'Problemas para resolver', *ibid.* 1.166-81: *alondra* 'lark' beside *golondrina* 'swallow', *orín* 'rust', and *lindo* 'beautiful', orig. 'well-mannered' (the author justifiably supports LĒGITIMUS against Menéndez Pidal's LĪMPIDUS); 'Espigueo de latín vulgar', ibid. 2.128-54 (1942-44): *desear* 'to desire' (from DĒSIDIA 'indolence', not from DĒSĪDERĀRE), Pyr. *esplu-ca, -ga* 'small cavity underneath a rock', *esquilmar* 'to harvest, drain' beside dial. *quima* 'branch', *golpe* 'blow' alongside *dolobre* 'stone hammer', *morcuero* = *majano* 'stone heap' beside *miércoles* 'Wednesday', *porfía* 'stubbornness' (lit. 'perfidiousness'), *sanguijela* 'leech' (=Cat. *samaruga*), *sarta* 'string, file', and *tosco* 'uncouth' (from UICUS TUSCUS). Also traceable to the transitional period in Corominas' career is the article, published in this country but drafted, if not written, in Argentina: 'Problemas del diccionario etimológico', *RomPh* 1.23-38, 79-104 (1947-48). Among the word-origins subjected to scrutiny there figure those of *alrededor* 'around' (OSp. *redor* < RETRŌ 'backward'), *bellaco* 'cunning, knavish', *bostezar* 'to yawn' beside *acezar* 'to pant', *escarmiento* 'punishment' > 'caution' (explained as syncopated *escarnimiento* 'cruel mockery'), *garra* 'claw', *guisante* 'pea' [plant and seed], *mojiganga* 'mummery', *se-, je-ta* 'mushroom', *tez* 'complexion', *zalagarda* 'ambush' beside (coll.) *zaragata* 'row, scuffle'. Of the solutions advocated, the first-mentioned was impugned by F. Lecoy, *RomPh* 7.35-43 (1953-54); cf. Corominas' bitter rebuttal, ibid. 7.330-2.

While a resident of the United States Corominas has served as etymological and lexicographic consultant to Bogotá's Instituto Caro y Cuervo and has contributed a few important articles and reviews to Mexico City's *NRFH*, on whose editorial masthead his name appears.

[99] Witness his critical edition, with glossary and full-blown grammatical commentary, of 'Las vidas de santos rosellonesas del manuscrito 44 de París', *AIL* 3.126-211 (1943-45), as well as his stewardship of an important and unique *Festschrift* in honor of a trailblazing Catalanist, *Miscel·lània* [*Pompeu*] *Fabra* (Buenos Aires, 1944), a volume which contains, in addition to several expertly edited studies on

Because Corominas spent the mid-'forties in Argentina, working at intervals in A. Alonso's Instituto de Filología at Buenos Aires and simultaneously building up his own research center in far-off Mendoza while laying the foundations for his future dictionary project (*Diccionario crítico etimológico de la lengua castellana*, Vols. 1-4 [Bern, 1955-57]), that dictionary — the author's life work — contains inordinately numerous nuggets of information on American Spanish usage, culled from newspapers, casually overheard conversations, glossaries of regionalisms, and other heterogeneous sources. In fact, these particular slivers of motley material have been collected in such random fashion as to sometimes give the impression of flotsam. Even so, the data on both the local semantic hues of standard words and on genuine regionalisms — not a few within their ranks are of indigenous parentage — constitute one of the most attractive features of an exceptionally ambitious venture, unevenly (not to say capriciously) executed, hence meritorious in some respects while irremediably controversial in others.[100] One is all the more chagrined to observe that the Spanish-American reaction to the *DCELC*, as against the gratifyingly vigorous European and North American response, has been singularly weak.[101]

If it is true that, once the readers discount Corominas' innumerable quirks and whims, that scholar, on the strength of his *DCELC's* originality and range of information, has carved out a niche for himself in the pantheon of leading etymologists, it is equally certain that Á. Rosenblat's record of accomplishments in lexicology is distressingly modest by comparison. To begin with, the very title of the book in which

Catalan themes, A. Alonso's broad-gauged article 'Partición de las lenguas románicas de Occidente' (81-101). Corominas' own lexical research later achieved a perfect meshing of the Catalan and the Castilian strains, e.g. in his substantial, if unnecessarily harsh, review of J. Terlingen's dissertation on Italianisms in classical Spanish.

100 The two severest pronouncements on the *DCELC* were made by W. von Wartburg, *RLiR* 23.207-60 (1959), from the angle of Gallo-Romance, and by the author of these lines, in *Word* 12.35-50 (1956), against the backdrop of general linguistics. Most of the other fuller appraisals concern themselves with individual problems and are predominantly or even overwhelmingly favorable; cf. J. E. Gillet, *HR* 26.261-95 (1958); L. Spitzer, *MLN* 71.71-83, 373-86 (1956); 72. 579-91 (1951); and 74.127-49 (1959); G. Rohlfs, *RLiR* 21.294-319 (1957); M. L. Wagner, *RF* 69.236-72 (1959); also, on a more modest scale, K. Baldinger, V. Cocco (*RPF* 8.358-68 [1957-59]), J. M. Piel, and others. On the Basque side add L. Michelena, *BSVasc.* 10.373-84 (1954), 11.283-97 (1955), 12.366-73 (1960), and 13.494-500 (1961). Ten years after the completion of the project there still exists no exhaustive, reliable guide to the literature it has provoked; ironically, Corominas' own rosters of critical reviews, the first preceding the Supplement (*DCELC* 4.897*b*-898*a*), the second ushering in the epitome (*Breve diccionario etimológico ...* =*BDE* 10 [Madrid, 1961]), bristle with minor inaccuracies (e.g., under Pottier) and suffer from unaccountable gaps (thus, even the eulogistic judgment of I. González Llubera remains unmentioned). To compound the trouble, such otherwise dependable reference works as Spectrum's annual *Bibliographie linguistique* are, for once, of small avail, because cross-references to those review articles which have appeared under separate titles have not been consistently furnished. It is difficult to ferret out oblique assessments; for one clue to A. Steiger's thinking see *VR* 15.115 (1956). Of course, Corominas' writings have long been the bibliographer's despair, inasmuch as the author has elected to spell his own name in an intriguing number of ways (Joan, Juan, John; Corominas, -es). For a helpfully balanced appraisal of *BDE* turn to Paul M. Lloyd, *HR* 31.256-9 (1963).

101 The 'Adiciones y rectificaciones' by R. Martínez-López, *BFUCh* 11.5-26 (1959 [1960]) contain an unexciting string of lexical minutiae, of limited bearing on the kernels of the problems at issue. Other depressing reviews of this kind, which seem to evade the main questions and issues and to

he has assembled his lexical feuilletons, *Buenas y malas palabras*, is predestined to be a source of severe irritation to fellow linguists, who must bristle at the implied extra-linguistic scale of values.[102] In fact, the inauspicious title turns the clock back, taking us behind Julio Calcaño (1840-1919), *El castellano en Venezuela; estudio crítico* (Caracas, 1897; 2d ed., 1950), not to speak of Lisandro Alvarado's sequel (1929). The book itself, let me hasten to add, is distinctly better than its title and shows, rather consistently, a level of performance that calls to mind, on the North American scene, C. E. Kany's three major writings: the aforementioned *Syntax* as well as the subsequent twin ventures into the contiguous domains of semantics and of euphemisms,[103] all three in the twilight zone between analytical and applied linguistics.

What detracts from the scholarly merit of Rosenblat's book — despite its fundamental judiciousness, the writer's remarkable control over many sources diligently excerpted, and well-nigh flawless typographic tidiness, which must not be taken for granted in Spanish America — is the obnoxious interplay of three pervasive weaknesses: first, the author's willingness to compromise at every step between straight historico-philological learning and his public's demand for pedagogical guidance and quickly assimilable normative decisions, quite apart from its craving for genteel entertainment; second, the disproportion between the writer's formidable expertise in the surface manifestations of American Spanish and his relative helplessness in the general Romance substructure of Spanish philology; and, third, his pervasive lack of curiosity — explicit or, at least, implied — about linguistic methodology.[104] Let a

serve as outlets for long-dormant *fichiers*, include C. C. Smith, 'Los cultismos literarios del Renacimiento ...', *BHi* 61.236-72 (1959); B. Pottier, 'Recherches sur le vocabulaire hispanique', *BHi* 57.442-53 (1955), 58.84-91 and 355-64 (1956), 59.209-18 (1957); O. Macri, 'Alcune aggiunte ... (*A-J*)', *RFE* 40.127-70 (1956) and, as if this display of pedantry were not enough, 'Nuevas adiciones ..., con apéndice sobre neologismos en Juan Ramón [Jiménez]' (*A-Y*), *BBMP* 38.231-384 (1962). — I have not inspected the lone Brazilian reaction by A. G. Cunha in *RBF* 2:1.114-23 (1956).

102 The first, one-volume edition of the book — whose full title, emblazoned on the inner title page, is *Buenas y malas palabras en el castellano de Venezuela* — appeared in 1956 (Caracas: EDIME), with a Preface by Mariano Picón-Salas — a writer whose style Rosenblat later eulogized in a commemorative essay (*Thesaurus* 20.201-12 [1965]). The revised and expanded edition, whose two volumes, each embodying a 'series', jointly pack almost one thousand pages, reached the book market four years later. Each volume boasts a separate word index, and the first includes a workmanlike Venezuelan bibliography (467-84). Of Rosenblat's few lexical notes post-dating this semi-erudite anthology and channeled through learned journals let me single out for mention the meticulously documented monograph 'Origen e historia del *che* argentino', *Fil* 8.325-401 (1962 [-64]): Here the author retraces, step by step, the transformation of an age-old deictic particle ('llamada interjectiva') into an introductory or modulating element ('partícula matizadora del diálogo'). Has the use of *che* as a nickname applied to Argentinians residing in other parts of the hemisphere (say, in Cuba: witness *Ernesto* '*Che*' *Guevara*) eluded the author's vigilance? For rather trenchant criticism of this article see J. J. Montes, *Thesaurus* 20.650 (1965). B. Malmberg tries to mediate between Rosenblat's Romance and J. P. Rona's Guaraní derivation of *che*, viewing the problem as panchronic (*SL* 18.47-54 [1964]).

103 See Stanley L. Robe's review (*RomPh* 17.179-84 [1963-64]) of Kany's *American-Spanish semantics* and *American-Spanish euphemisms*, two parallel offshoots (Berkeley and Los Angeles, 1960) of a single research project. For a European reaction to the book on semantics (of which there exists a Spanish translation by L. E. Bareño [Madrid, 1962]) see B. Malmberg, *SL* 17.54-9 (1963).

104 The desire to entertain a large circle of newspaper readers may have prompted Rosenblat to inject an innocuous dosage of anecdotal 'cuteness' into an otherwise serious article, well-reasoned

single example suffice: One of the most elaborate pieces, '¿Incorrección o creación?' (1.453-61), bears on local post-verbals in *-a*, *-o*, *-e* and, specifically, on such competing doublets as *desbarro* and *desbarre* 'slip, blunder, folly'. While the author's display of seasoned knowledge regarding untold details of usage is most impressive throughout, he happens to miss the main point: Only the *-o* and the *-a* series of arrhizotonic abstracts are traditionally peculiar to Spanish and Portuguese (as they are, barring minor discrepancies, to Italian). The *-e* series developed as late as the 15th century, sprouting from such pairs of Gallicisms (including Provençalisms and Catalanisms) in late Old Spanish as *afeit-ar* 'to embellish' ~ *afeit-e* 'embellishment'.[105] Since we are here confronted with a striking innovation in pre-classical rather than medieval Spanish, the discrepancies between Peninsular and overseas Spanish might have lent themselves to a particularly exciting discussion had the author, unfortunately more attracted by the trees than the forest, properly heeded the nuclear problem.

V. PHILOLOGICAL APPROACH TO OLDER STAGES OF PENINSULAR SPANISH

If one disregards the pioneering efforts of Andrés Bello, text-centered philology (including, as its adjuncts, critical editions, paleography, the study of medieval *realia*, and a thick slice of historical grammar and etymology) has hardly struck any deep roots in Spanish American academic tradition. F. Hanssen, a man long stationed in Santiago de Chile, hence particularly well-informed on all available resources of New World scholarship, listed in the Bibliography (pp. ix-xiv) of his *Gramática histórica* (1913) a single Old Spanish text published in South or Central America, namely G. Euzaguirre Rouse's ed. of the *Crónica general de España* by Fray García de Eugui,

and abundantly documented, cf. his remarks on Ven. P.-Ric. *pollina* beside Mex. *burrito* or *cerquillo* 'bangs' = Sp. *flequillo* ('mechón de pelo que cae habitualmente sobre la frente del asno o borrico' > 'peinado infantil': 1.116-8). It is less comforting to watch a downright confusion of levels of discourse, as when a flawlessly argued note (1.113-6) on Venez. *ostinao* 'bored, annoyed' (*obstinado* × *hostigado*) is marred at the end by gratuitous meditations on the 'carácter nacional' of Venezuelans. Of course, there exists an old tradition in Spanish America of appreciating philology as a pastime or entertainment (see *RomPh* 13.123-4 [1959-60]); it was this facetious approach that A. Alonso, one gathers, sought to eradicate.

The palpable unevenness of Rosenblat's scholarship emerges also from his note on '*Andes, andenes y andinos*' (2.312-8). The discussion of *Ande(s)* < Quechua *anti* 'East' is brief and to the point, and the subsequent transfer of the Pacific Coast oronym to the Venezuelan mountain range, originally called *Sierras Nevadas*, is studied in almost excessively lavish detail; yet the etymology of *andén*, which may be less superficially picturesque for the layman but which in fact involves real linguistic problems concerning Spanish, is taken care of via a nonchalant, uncritical reference to a dictionary entry; for a multi-faceted discussion of *andén* 'sidewalk, sidepath, platform' and *andana* 'row, line, tier' see my note 'The Romance word family of Latin AMBĀGŌ', *Word* 3.59-72 (1947).

105 Only prolonged immersion in the early history of Gallicisms can serve as an eye-opener in such matters; cf. Anita Katz Levy, 'Contrastive development in Hispano-Romance of borrowed Gallo-Romance suffixes' (I) in *Rom Ph*, 18.399-429 (1964-65; to continue) as well as my own papers, 'Préstamos y cultismos', *RLiR* 21.1-61 (1957); 'Fuentes indígenas y exóticas de los sustantivos y adjetivos verbales en *-e*', ibid. 23.80-111 (1959), 24.201-53 (1960; Part 3 to follow), and 'Genetic analysis of word-formation', *CTL* 3.305-64 (1966).

bishop of Bayonne.[106] Hanssen personally did of course busy himself, even more than many of his European peers, with details of the manuscript tradition, dialectal coloring, metric structure, and comparable 'technical' features of numerous key-texts of medieval literature, including Berceo's *Vida de Santo Domingo de Silos*;[107] but the corpus of his researches, for all their intrinsic merit, remained something alien and highly atypical — a kind of inlaying of solid German philology within the fabric of Hispanic culture, an incrustation quite unlikely to kindle local enthusiasm or to spark emulation. Characteristically, Argentina's initial answer to the feverish activity of the Teuto-Chileans was provided by French immigrants such as Paul Groussac; and just as Hanssen's weightiest books appeared, of all places, in Halle, so Groussac (and his counterpart Luciano Abeille on the side of dialectology) saw to it that their most ambitious writings were channeled through Parisian publishing houses and journals.[108]

The period stretching from the mid-'twenties to the late 'thirties may properly be described as the time of the growing hegemony of Argentina, which kept its leadership unimpaired until the mid-'forties, when the entire edifice collapsed under the weight of Perón's dictatorship. The motley group that vigorously forged ahead in and around Buenos Aires throughout these two decades was composed of (a) intellectuals imported from a temporarily progressive and cosmopolitan Spain and (b) immigrants and their immediate descendants, two nuclei at the last stage supplemented by (c) a heterogeneous group of refugees from totalitarian or war-torn parts of Europe. Two additional ingredients of this unique compound were (d) a few Argentinians of

[106] Hanssen lists only the reprint, which, as if to compound the difficulty, he fails to date. The text originally appeared in several installments spread over Vols. 121-2 (1908) of the National University's *Anales*; see esp. 122.1-66 and 387-515. There is no dearth of differently colored Chilean sources feeding Hanssen's grammar: models of parliamentary rhetoric (M. L. Amunátegui), historiography (D. Barros Arana), and folk-speech (A. Orrego).

[107] Significantly, the 'Notas' devoted to this Berceo text (*Anales* 120.715-63 [1907]) were based on John D. Fitzgerald's Paris thesis (1904), while Hanssen's nearly contemporary review article 'Sobre un compendio de gramática castellana anteclásica' (ibid. 122.671-95 [1908]) contains a promptly delivered critique of A. Zauner's *Altspanisches Elementarbuch*.

[108] To European medievalists Groussac (1848-1929) has been chiefly known from his two major contributions to the *Revue hispanique*: 'Le commentateur du *Laberinto*' (11.164-219 [1904], with a postscript added upon receipt of a missive from M. de Unamuno: elaborate corroboration of R. Foulché-Delbosc's assertion that the 'Comendador griego' [1499] was Hernán Pérez de Toledo) and 'Le livre des *Castigos e Documentos* attribué au roi D. Sanche IV' (15.212-339 [1906], followed by a lengthy editorial comment from the pen of Foulché-Delbosc). Groussac here pays tribute to the austere tradition of 'analyse des sources et discussion des documents'. On his homeground the Toulouse-born Frenchman, acclimatized in Argentina as early as 1866 (college professor in Tucumán and Buenos Aires; from 1885 director of the National Library), became more of a versatile *polígrafo*, writing historical plays (*La divisa punzó*, set in the Rosas period), assembling his essays and feuilletons — which contain such gems as 'Philologie amusante' (1903) —, annotating collections of documents, specializing in provincial history, observing the mores of his adopted country (*Fruto vedado: costumbres argentinas*, 1884), and polemizing with the British Crown on either country's titles to the Malvinas Archipelago. The far less prominent Abeille published two books in Paris: *Idioma nacional de los argentinos* (1900), an unmentionable treatise, and *L'esprit démocratique de l'enseignement secondaire argentin* (1910), a centennial retrospect.

old stock, not all of them Porteños, and (e) a mere handful of other Latin Americans.[109] The prelude to the amalgam was the founding (1923) of the Instituto de Filología at the University of Buenos Aires (a research center which was soon to eclipse Santiago's Instituto Pedagógico) and the appearance on the scene of such a colorful figure as Américo Castro for a short-term directorship.[110] The Instituto's rapid climb to international prestige, accentuated by the temporary débacle and continued weakness of Madrid, is associated with the name of Amado Alonso. Since 1946 the Instituto has passed through several reorganizations, none of which has restored it to its earlier status of leadership.

The growth of the Instituto is marked by several research efforts. To Castro's initiative one must credit the seven fascicles of its short-lived *Cuadernos*, oriented toward such problems as were being raised and discussed in Spain's and Germany's *inter-bella* philological centers; the combination of historical linguistics with a medievalistic focus in literary inquiries was the hallmark of that approach.[111] The next break-through was the foundation of the Argentine Academy of Letters (1933), endowed with funds for editing its own *Boletín* (= *BAAL*), which has hereafter been chiefly piloted by Arturo Marasso. Straight philology, Argentine dialectology,

[109] The five components which A. Alonso succeeded in deftly balancing against each other may be briefly exemplified with the following names: (a) A. Castro, A. Alonso; (b) Á. Rosenblat, R. and M. R. Lida, A. M. Barrenechea, F. Weber de Kurlat; (c) B. A. Terracini, J. and H. Corominas, P. Bénichou; (d) E. F. Tiscornia, B. E. Vidal de Battini; (e) P. Henríquez Ureña, M. A. Morínigo. The publications of the Instituto (its *Revista* in particular) received added glitter from contributions by scholars residing in other countries; these formed a sixth group, as it were, a group also represented, and by no means sparingly, on the editorial board of the journal, with a certain preference given, for once, to North Americans over Europeans. Thus, one finds side by side the names of J. Casalduero and Á. del Río; H. A. Hatzfeld and L. Spitzer; W. J. Entwistle; D. C. Clarke, S. Gilman, H. L. Johnson, H. Keniston, and J. Ornstein; etc.

[110] At the height of the Civil War A. Castro briefly reappeared in Buenos Aires. From there he went to the University of Texas, to Princeton University, and to the University of California, at Los Angeles and eventually at San Diego (La Jolla). It was to Castro that A. Cortina (b. 1902) dedicated his edition of the 'Diálogo entr' el Amor y un Viejo', *BAAL* 1.319-71 (1933), a venture which in a way, parallels that writer and scholar-critic's book-length edition of the *Cancionero de Jorge Manrique* (Madrid, 1929). On the other hand, M. Schneider inscribed A. Alonso's name on his experiment with historical grammar: 'El colectivo en latín y las formas en *-a*', *BAAL* 2.25-92 (1934). These facts are worth pondering because Cortina and Schneider later drifted away from Alonso's inner circle. On the crystallization of that circle see Á. Rosenblat's commemorative essay 'Amado Alonso', originally published in Caracas' *Cultura Universitaria* 31.61-71 (1952), now available in the miscellany *La primera visión de América* ... 273-85. Stray data on the incubative period of the Instituto can likewise be culled from a piece unsigned, but clearly inspired and anthorized by its Director, in *BAAL* 1.87-90 (1933). A buoyantly optimistic Alonso, one observes, here tragically overestimated his own and his group's actual chances, announcing as forthcoming such items as Vol. 2 of the *Biblia medieval romanceada*, M. A. Morínigo's *Historia del español en el Río de la Plata*, his own *Caracterización del español de América* (none of which ever came to fruition, cf. fnn. 18 and 29 above), just as he was later (1939) ill-advised in announcing the project, to be carried out by himself and by María Rosa Lida, *Primitivos estudios dialectales sobre el castellano en la Argentina* — a project which never got off the ground.

[111] The *Cuadernos* contained such medievalistic items as Á. J. Battistessa, *La biblioteca de un jurisconsulto toledano del siglo XV* (No. 3), and Ana Julia Darnet, *Un diálogo de Luciano romanceado en el siglo XV* (No. 4), beside grammatical and lexical monographs.

literature viewed as art, and normative linguistics cut to daily needs have all four ever since been within the purview of that bulletin, on whose early issues Alonso's dynamism, personal taste, and range of friends and disciples left an indelible imprint; witness his inaugural article 'Intereses filológicos e intereses académicos en el estudio de la lengua' 1.7-14 (1933). The final step in the upward surge was the launching six years later, with Alonso in sole command, of the *Revista de Filología Hispánica*, which for eight critical years — bracketing the War — shared with Zurich's *Vox Romanica* the distinction of being the world's best-edited and most skillfully managed mouthpiece of organized Romance scholarship.

Combined attention to language and literature — especially through joint study of their older stages — was an ideal, preached by Castro and Alonso, which could be translated into action in different manners. One relatively modest means of implementing a program so conceived was to furnish neatly edited texts, which could later be put to use by independent teams of experts. Two ventures of this kind, separated by eighteen years, actually mark off the rise and the decline of the Instituto: the edition of the Old Spanish Pentateuch (1927), by A. Castro in collaboration with the Spanish paleographer A. Millares Carlo and with a local scholar, Ángel J. Battistessa, signaled an auspicious start,[112] while the publication of the Alfonsine *Setenario* by Kenneth H. Vanderford (1945)[113] preceded by the thinnest of margins the irremediable diaspora of Alonso's original staff.

A second, equally effective technique of cross-fertilization between history of language and history of literature consists in first establishing certain hard facts, at once pertaining to chrono-biography and to regional localization, then in simultaneously filling, with these newly clarified facts, characteristic gaps in the two rival

112 This is a composite text, containing excerpts from three Escorial MSS: I-j-3, I-j-8, and I-j-6. A few years after his return to Madrid A. Castro succeeded in persuading a talented young refugee from the Nazified University of Berlin, Georg (= George E.) Sachs, to resume the study of the Old Spanish Bible, a project which Sachs, upon his expulsion from Falangist Spain, continued in New York until his untimely death (1939) at the age of thirty; cf. the posthumous 'Fragmento de un estudio sobre la *Biblia medieval romanceada*', *RomPh* 2.217-28 (1948-49) and, in its wake, the comments by O. H. Hauptmann, Max Berenblut, and R. Levy, ibid. 3.157-9, 258-61, and 261-2, as well as R. D. Abraham's supplementary note, ibid. 14.237-44 (1960-61). Taking up where his teacher Castro had left off, A. G. Solalinde assigned to one of his own favorite students at Wisconsin, Oliver H. Hauptmann, the edition of the parallel Escorial MS I-j-4, a project whose first fruits, in the guise of a slim selective glossary, appeared by 1942 (*HR* 10.34-46), while the scrupulous edition of the entire Pentateuch had to wait for another eleven years; see I. González-Llubera's delayed, if substantial, review in *RomPh* 12.94-100 (1958-59). The unpublished portion of Hauptmann's material is now in the hands of Margherita Morreale. While the Buenos Aires project, all promises notwithstanding, failed to develop under Alonso, a Chilean scholar, R. Oroz, later prepared a superficially annotated glossary to that portion of the text which reflects the language of MS Esc. I-j-8; see *BFUCh* 4.261-434 (1944-46).

113 The handsomely printed book-length edition followed upon an impressive article, '*El Setenario* y su relación con las *Siete Partidas*', *RFH* 3.233-301 (1941); the research project was carried out in Chicago, and the lion's share of initiative and guidance must be credited to H. Keniston. The lexical material entombed in this text has, in part, been lifted to the surface in Corominas' etymological dictionary and in Glen D. Willbern's Chicago thesis, as distilled in his book *Elementos del vocabulario castellano del siglo XIII* (Mexico, 1953).

disciplines. This unusual feat A. Alonso and his followers have accomplished in coming to grips with the obscure figure and *œuvre* of a Mexican-Spanish poet of the colonial era, Fernán González de Eslava (active between 1567 and 1600), long believed to have been born in the New World, but now known to have immigrated in 1558; he was possibly a native Navarrese, and, like his contemporaries Juan de Castellanos and Ortiz de Vergara, he exemplifies the perfectly smooth adjustment of some youthful, mentally elastic newcomers to their new environment. A. Alonso himself and, in his wake, a former student of his and now a prolific scholar in her own right, Frida Weber de Kurlat, have inserted the data scrupulously gathered and verified in the separate slots of historical grammar and of the history of colonial *belles-lettres*.[114]

The third reconciliation of the divergent interests of linguistic and literary savants can be engineered through critical, annotated editions of ancient texts. If the given text happens, for esthetic reasons, to carry an inherently powerful appeal, and if its accessibility has been blocked by lexical and grammatical difficulties alone, then the deft removal of these obstacles can produce a real outburst of euphoria among a sizable group of long-frustrated lay readers. Some such response of unparalleled intensity seems to have greeted, a quarter-century ago, the appearance of a slender volume of tastefully edited 'selections' from Juan Ruiz's *Libro de buen amor* (ca. 1330-45), one of the pearls of world literature that had been whetting the appetites of thousands of famished readers. The editor of the extracts, María Rosa Lida, whom A. Alonso had lured from a blind-alley apprenticeship in Hellenistic studies to

[114] González de Eslava's posthumously published book, *Coloquios espirituales y sacramentales y Canciones divinas*, appeared in 1610 and was re-issued in 1877, through the efforts of J. García Icazbalceta. Alonso's initial onslaught on the problems surrounding the fortunes of that poet took the form of an extended biographic essay ('Biografía de Fernán González de Eslava', *RFH* 2.213-321 [1940]), but significant implications of his life story were later presented in an austerely linguistic context, e.g. under the heading 'Orígenes del seseo americano', see *Estudios lingüísticos: temas hispanoamericanos* 116-22. For the latest and fullest treatment of the author's plays see F. Weber de Kurlat, *Lo cómico en el teatro de Fernán González de Eslava* (Buenos Aires [1963]); a book carefully and sympathetically analyzed by Oliver T. Myers in *RomPh* 18.243-8. As the critic — himself a superb connoisseur of the artistically stylized rustic *Sayagués* dialect — remarks, the book offers far more than the title suggests, presupposes familiarity with historically skewed dialectology and with intricacies of 16th-century literature (picaresque novel, early theater) alike, and may serve as an opening wedge for a much-needed critical edition of the chosen writer.

Though Frida Weber de Kurlat owes the topical and methodological inspiration for this book to A. Alonso, she has never disavowed her equal indebtedness to an American teacher of European background, Joseph E. Gillet, under whose guidance she worked, as a beginner, at Bryn Mawr during the tenure of a fellowship. It was Gillet who aroused her curiosity about the primitive theater, who initiated her into Sayagués, and who strengthened her determination to bridge the — currently fashionable — gap between literary and linguistic research; it is also the common link with Gillet that accounts for the striking affinity of her work to the painstaking researches conducted by Charlotte Stern, cf. the latter scholar's article 'Fray Íñigo de Mendoza and medieval dramatic ritual', *HR* 33.197-245 (1965). Other studies from Sra. de Kurlat's pen testifying to this unabashedly philological slant include 'Sobre el negro como tipo cómico en el teatro español del siglo XVI', *RomPh* 17.380-91 (1963-64) and 'El tipo cómico del negro en el teatro prelopesco; Fonética', *Fil* 8.139-68 (1962 [-64]). Her latest piece, 'Gil Vicente y Diego Sánchez de Badajoz ...', ibid. 9.119-62 (1963[-65]), more strictly literary in its approach, attests the growing influence on her of María Rosa Lida de Malkiel.

mastery and real break-throughs in the medieval and Renaissance domains, had just started to establish her reputation as a refined critic and historian of literature.[115] The new dimension that the 'selections' added to her earlier equipment was the ability, rare in a literary expert and unprecedented in Argentina, to cut a swath through the heavy underbrush of linguistic and philological exegesis.[116] This ability, which remained ancillary within the ensemble of her scholarly endowments, María Rosa Lida de Malkiel demonstrated in a long succession of books, monographic studies, notes, and searching book reviews, with special reference to nuances and intricacies of lexicon, syntax, and style; the majority of these researches, and those most admirably balanced, fall into her California period (1948-1962).[117] Her excellent self-imposed training in the classics and her self-acquired knowledge of the medieval Romance vernaculars — both Peninsular and extra-Hispanic, plus her ever-present discipline and repudiation of amateurism, made her a particularly competent judge of the artful literary language, especially of the hermetic style heavily larded with Greek and Latin reminiscences, with Oriental arabesques, and with subtly disguised slivers of Oïl, Oc, and Italian ingredients. Much as her prowess as an applied linguist manifested itself

[115] As general bio-bibliographic guides to that author one may elect to use my Necrology (*RomPh* 17.9-32 [1963-64]) and preliminary analytical bibliography (ibid. 33-52) as well as the recent provisional supplement to the bibliography (ibid., 20.44-52); one prime purpose of these commemorative writings has been to assemble as conveniently as possible the hopelessly scattered reactions to her well-nigh two hundred books, articles, and reviews, so as to place in a sharply silhouetting perspective the diversified activities which María Rosa Lida de Malkiel compressed into her tragically short lifespan (1910-62), terminated ten years after A. Alonso's no less untimely death.

It is customary to regard her article 'Transmisión y recreación de temas grecolatinos en la poesía lírica española', *RFH* 1.20-63 (1939) as the starting-point of a meteoric rise. Actually, that article was preceded by a half-dozen shorter pieces, of which one bore on a linguistic subject ('Los grecismos del español según Juan de Valdés'). Her unpublished juvenilia include drafts of studies on the grammatical category of gender, especially its history (1934), and on the Greek elements in Spanish, with particular emphasis on patterns of stress and configuration, and on the uniqueness of some lexical trajectories (1936).

[116] The more technical issues that arose in the process of elaboration of the light-winged booklet (inspired by F. Lecoy's 1938 monograph) were attacked in the erudite companion piece 'Notas para la interpretación, influencia, fuentes y texto del *Libro de buen amor*', *RFH* 2.105-50 (1940), harbingered by the brief comment, '*Tumbal* "retumbante"', ibid. 1.65-7 (1939). The author's final views on the poem were embodied in *Two Spanish masterpieces* (1961), after the settling of all scores on controversial matters in the heavily polemic 'Nuevas notas ...', *NRFH* 13.17-82 (1959).

[117] The titles do not invariably reveal the full import of the linguistic ingredient of certain studies from her pen. Thus, 'La *General estoria*: notas literarias y filológicas', *RomPh* 12.111-42 (1958-59), 13.1-30 (1959-60), contains a singularly competent, if unobtrusive, dissection of the Alfonsine vocabulary (esp. 27-9), to say nothing of the masterly inquiry into the medieval art of translation (passim). Priceless bits of information on 15th-century Spanish at its most opaque are found in the author's book on Juan de Mena (1950), an expanded doctoral dissertation, and in the seldom consulted companion article 'La prosa de Juan de Mena', *BAAL* 18.393-432 (1949), noted for its neat discrimination between the Cordovan writer's didactic, narrative, and ornamental style. The long-hidden stylistic connection between Spain's late-medieval and early-16th-century writers has never been more vigorously exposed than in the article 'Fray Antonio de Guevara; Edad Media y Siglo de Oro español', *RFH* 7.346-88 (1945), which derives added point and poignancy from the author's firm stand in her courteous polemic with Menéndez Pidal. The topic later attracted the attention of Juan Marichal: 'Sobre la originalidad renacentista en el estilo de Guevara', *NRFH* 9.113-28 (1955).

in an astonishingly wide range of first-rate translations into her native Spanish, so her keenness as an analytical linguist, if only on a modest scale, served to support her monumental inquiries into the artistry of Juan de Mena and of *La Celestina*, bolstered her one short experiment in straight textual criticism (a skill brought to bear on Berceo's *Vida de Santa Oria*), and shone forth on those regrettably few occasions on which she strayed into the lexico-etymological field.[118]

A. Alonso's circle and its derivatives (created through the dispersal of his students, chiefly in the late 'forties[119]) gave rise to but few linguistically slanted critical editions; of these not all involved medieval texts, witness Dorothy McMahon's recent edition of Book V of Agustín de Zárate's *Historia del Perú*, a project sponsored and prefaced by M. A. Morínigo.[120] In the closest vicinity of such severely academic editions one may place scrupulously accurate modernizations of ancient texts, one of the most delicate tasks a philologist or near-philologist can set himself, involving as it does a modicum of exposure to analytical linguistics and a maximum of flair for artistic verbalization, especially where verse is involved. In this context Francisca Chica Salas' and Daniel Devoto's independent adaptations of Berceo deserve high

[118] From among the author's thoroughly documented, artistically or intellectually piquant articles tracing the history of semantic hues, metaphors, and set phrases, provided these were rich in memorable literary implications, let me cite these: '*Civil* "cruel"', *RFH* 1.80-85 (1939); '*Estar en (un) baño, estar en un lecho de rosas*', ibid. 3.263-270 (1941); '*Saber* "soler" en las lenguas romances y sus antecedentes grecolatinos', *RPh* 2.269-83 (1948-49); 'Arpadas lenguas', *Estudios dedicados a Menéndez Pidal* 2.227-52 (Madrid, 1951). On top of these ambitious items she wrote a number of competent book reviews on linguistic themes. To these must be added, in turn, mosaic-like reconstructions of 'topoi' (which are always bound to cast off fringe-benefits for the leisurely lexicographer); cf. 'El amanecer mitológico en la poesía narrativa española', *RFH* 8.77-110 (1946) — an almost overelaborate inventory — and the two comments on the 'bee' motif (1944, 1954-63). At no forbidding distance from the center of linguistics are such paroemiological studies as 'Los refranes en las obras de don Juan Manuel', *RomPh* 4.163-8, 187-9 (1950-51), echoing the author's early side-interest in folklore. A firm grasp of all facets of the linguistic situation serves as a tool of exquisite textual criticism in 'Notas para el texto de la *Vida de Santa Oria*', *RomPh* 10.19-33 (1956-57). For an attempt to appreciate the author's unflagging concern with self-improvement see my note 'Cómo trabajaba M. R. L. de M.', in *Homenaje a Antonio Rodríguez-Moñino* 1.337-44 (Madrid, 1966). In one baffling instance, a brief incidental remark by the author (anent the fixed binomial *flor y rosa*) sparked a debate in which L. Spitzer, E. Jareño, P. Groult, and K.-D. Uitti emerged as the chief participants or referees (for details see *RPh* 17.35).

[119] Raimundo Lida went to Mexico City (Colegio de México), from there to Ohio State and to Harvard; María Rosa Lida went to Harvard, thence to Berkeley, and (after her marriage) held visiting professorships at various American universities, returning—fatally stricken—to the Facultad de Filosofía y Letras of her native city in the Fall of 1961; Ángel Rosenblat went to a teaching and research position at Caracas via a short stint in Ecuador; E. Anderson Imbert has reached Harvard via Michigan; J. B. Avalle Arce teaches at Smith; Daniel Devoto has settled in Paris; M. A. Morínigo went to Southern California and Florida, then briefly returned to Buenos Aires as a dean, and is now at Illinois; Emma Susana Speratti Piñero has moved to the Colegio de México. The members of the group who have remained in Argentina and maintained their active interest in research are mostly women: Ana María Barrenechea (Ph. D. Pennsylvania), Frida Weber de Kurlat, Berta Elena Vidal de Battini, Celina S. de Cortázar. (Julio Caillet-Bois has not, to my knowledge, trespassed on the territory of philological linguistics.)

[120] Published, under the title *Historia del descubrimiento y conquista del Perú* (Buenos Aires: Facultad de Filosofía y Letras [1965]), with two university institutes acting as joint sponsors. Note in the back the bulging section of historical and linguistic comments.

praise;[121] on the less exciting side of prose, one may cite Á. Rosenblat's edition of a modernized *Amadís de Gaula* (1940).

The fourth bridge between literary and linguistic commitments has been, traditionally, metrics (*stricto sensu* or, broadly viewed, as an inalienable part of poetics). In the Spanish-speaking world the bonds between metrics and linguistics have been dramatized by the dual range of T. Navarro's researches, an affinity which became especially pronounced after his transfer to this hemisphere; note, in particular, his concern with versification in the miscellany *Estudios de fonología española* (Syracuse, N.Y., 1946) and the general tenor of the vastly more important and influential *Métrica española: reseña histórica y descriptiva* (Syracuse, 1956).[122] On the Spanish-American scene, the penchant for metric studies of a person of such magnetic appeal as P. Henríquez Ureña could not fail to become contagious.[123] Among the most talented of his followers, María Rosa Lida de Malkiel combined this flair for metrics with her solid grasp of two millennia of intellectual and artistic history,[124] while Daniel Devoto added a more than

[121] Francisca Chica Salas, though a graduate of the capital's Facultad de Filosofía y Letras, does not rank as a trained philologist; an inspired poet following an independent path of creative writing (see her three 'recueils' *Romancero porteño* [1939], *El límite* [1941], and *Fragilidad de la tierra* [1963]), she relied for technical guidance in preparing her translations from Berceo (*Milagros* and fragments of other poems; Buenos Aires, 1943) on the expertise of her closest friend, María Rosa Lida, who later dedicated to her that posthumous 'magnum opus' of her own, *La originalidad artística de* '*La Celestina*' (Buenos Aires, 1962) and who became, in turn, the beneficiary of several evocative essays from Da. Francisca's pen, notably the piece 'Permanencia de M. R. L. de M.', *Fil* 8.1-5 (1962 [-64]). Daniel Devoto's modernization of Berceo's *Milagros de Nuestra Señora* (Valencia, 1957; rev. 2d ed., 1965) derives its scholarly value from the appended Glossary and Notes (pp. 168-266) and has, as its strictly academic pendants, a string of textual comments (*BHi* 59.5-23 [1957]), a scintillating analysis (ibid. 65.206-37 [1963]) of the canticle *¡ Eya velar !* inserted in Berceo's *Duelo de la Virgen*, plus an unpublished monumental Sorbonne thesis bearing on the Riojano poet. Through an amusing coincidence, the best earlier interpretation of the canticle at issue, rivaling Spitzer's and Trend's, must be credited to an Argentine scholar of the same generation (see Germán Orduna, 'La estructura ...', *Humanitas* [Tucumán], 4:10.75-104 [1958]; Orduna has likewise done original research in Juan Ruiz). A less distinguished exercise in modernization, coming from a different quarter, is Clemente Canales Toro's version of Berceo's *Signos de juicio final* ([Santiago de Chile] 1955). — At proof let me record the recent publication of a long awaited book by Francisca Chica Salas: *Elegía a María Rosa Lida y once poemas de piedad* (Buenos Aires, 1966).

[122] For a summary and brief appraisal of the *Estudios* see my critique in *HR* 17.174-9 (1949); a few reactions to the book were more severely qualified or downright negative. The *Métrica* elicited a major review article: P. Le Gentil, 'Discussions sur la versification espagnole médiévale — à propos d'un livre récent', *RomPh* 12.1-32 (1958-59); the sharply opposing views of Madrid (even where its ranking spokesman was displaced to Manhattan) and of Paris were expounded anew in this latest fencing match.

[123] The discussion of the 'versificación irregular' in Old Spanish — a problem neatly isolated by Henríquez Ureña in 1920 — has continued unabated over the last half-century. For a useful digest of the 'état présent des études' and the valiant championship of a minority view see Robert A. Hall, Jr., 'Old Spanish verse and Germanic superstratum', *RomPh* 19.227-34 (1965-66). Henríquez Ureña's personal involvement with metric problems transcended the writing and consecutive revisions of his sensationally successful book; characteristically, his last contribution to his favorite Porteño journal was 'Sobre la historia del alejandrino', *RFH* 8.1-11 (1946).

[124] Her article 'La métrica de la Biblia: un motivo de Josefo y San Jerónimo en la literatura española', *Estudios hispánicos: Homenaje a Archer M. Huntington* 335-59 (Wellesley, Mass., 1952), ties in with other studies carved out from an unfinished monograph on Josephus. The inquiries into Spanish

welcome personal touch of erudite amenity through his unique musicological sophistication.[125]

The fifth and last bridge here visualized as leading from linguistics to literature is the systematic scanning of ancient grammars and philological treatises, an approach conducive not only to new partial insights into remote stages of the language, but also to fresh attacks on the history of ideas. Thus, A. Alonso's microscopic inspection of the post-medieval sibilants forced him to concern himself at length with the biographies and academic backgrounds (if any) of his chief Renaissance authorities; aside from clearing this ground from a heavy overgrowth, he made it a point to examine the basic frame of Nebrixa's theoretical thinking as a prelude to the reconstruction of the actual sound system posited or implied in that pioneer's writings.[126]

Apart from these five special communication lanes every exposure to ancient texts is apt to serve as an occasional pretext and point of departure for 'fichiers' organized around selected dubious or controversial issues of etymology, lexical semantics, syntax, and style. With a measure of diligence, *savoir faire*, and sheer luck an experienced worker will succeed in extracting a few middle-sized articles or at least notes from such collections of raw data, after previous sifting and categorizing. Nobody in Spanish America mastered this *métier* better than P. Henríquez Ureña, to whose unflagging industriousness we owe — to cite one example among many — a lexico-syntactic piece on *ello* 'it' closely fitting this description.[127]

---

versification were woven into the book *Juan de Mena, poeta del prerrenacimiento español* (Mexico, 1950) and numerous shorter writings, including the sharply polemic review, in *Speculum* 26.174-9 (1951) and 28.905-8 (1953), of P. Le Gentil, *La poésie lyrique espagnole et portugaise à la fin du moyen âge* (Rennes, 1949 and 1952-53). These investigations were paralleled by studies of metaphors; cf. 'La hipérbola sagrada en la poesía castellana del siglo XV', *RFH* 8.121-30 (1946).

125 See his aforementioned inquiry into Berceo's canticle *¡ Eya velar !* (*BHi* 65.206-37 [1963]), a paper that benefited greatly, so the author avers, from the sympathetic attention of Mlle Solange Corbin, a noted student of older Spanish and Portuguese liturgy. In his conclusion, the author departs from earlier critics in adjudging the canticle not to folk lyric, but to imitations of liturgic songs; in this context he pays heightened attention to the hybrid Latin-Spanish refrain. Though in the rigor of its bibliographic elaboration this paper clearly pertains to the author's Parisian period, it perpetuates, in a way, a line of competence and curiosity traceable to his years of apprenticeship in Buenos Aires; cf. 'Sobre la música tradicional española', *RFH* 5.344-66 (1943).

126 A. Alonso's lifelong preoccupation with *seseo* and *ceceo* cast off such interim reports as 'Trueques de sibilantes en antiguo español' (*NRFH* 1.1-12 [1947]; this item invites comparison with my own rather overdocumented piece 'Spanish *cosecha* and its congeners', *Lg* 23.389-98 [1947]). The same bent seduced Alonso into entering the labyrinth of Hispano-Arabic symbiosis and osmosis; cf. his mutually complementary papers, marking his transfer to Harvard, 'Las correspondencias arábigo-españolas en los sistemas de sibilantes', *RFH* 8.12-76 (1946) and 'Árabe *st* > esp. *ç*; esp. *st* > árabe *ch*', *PMLA* 63.325-38 (1947), the latter reprinted in *Estudios lingüísticos: temas españoles* (Madrid, 1951). Of rather incidental and anecdotal value in this context is the note 'Identificación de gramáticos españoles clásicos', *RFE* 35.221-36 (1951), aiming as it does to elucidate the vicissitudes in the lives and publications of 'El Anónimo de Lovaina', Cristóbal de Villalón, and Antonio de Corro. On the other hand, Alonso's massive 'Examen de las noticias de Nebrija sobre la antigua pronunciación española', *NRFH* 3.1-82 (1949), includes in its initial section ('Principios y supuestos': 3-20) a genuine and stimulating contribution to the history of ideas, while the remainder of the monograph is cut to the technical needs of phonemic analysis.

127 See *RFH* 1.209-29 (1939); also *El español en Santo Domingo* 226-31 (Buenos Aires, 1940).

It is small wonder that problems of medieval Peninsular usage acted as a strong stimulant preponderantly among Hispanists of loose ties (or no direct ties) to the Spanish American scene. The bitter twenty-year old controversy between A. Castro and L. Spitzer regarding the alternative assignment of certain phrases, constructions, extensions of meaning in Old Spanish to the Latin or to the Arabic tradition provoked considerable restlessness in Europe and in the United States,[128] but produced few ripples on the surface of Latin American intellectual life; the one truly important exception to this trend, namely the belated participation of E. Coşeriu in this dispute,[129] involves, characteristically enough, a Roumanian linguist trained in Italy who, to the regret of many New World observers, had to wend his way back to a European university (Tübingen).[130] There are, of course, on record in South and Central America some recent or fairly recent instances of medievalistic research linked by no direct or indirect threads to pre-Peronian Buenos Aires, but these inquiries, as a rule, lack any linguistic dimension.[131] Conversely, such studies contributed to Mexico's prestigious *NRFH* as do have a bearing on Old Spanish (qua language) have seldom, if ever, emanated from Latin American quarters.[132]

[128] The discussion was sparked by A. Castro's interpretative book: *España en su historia; cristianos, moros y judíos* (Buenos Aires, 1948) and spilled over onto the pages of the *NRFH* (3.141-58 [1949]). Among those who sided with Castro was, understandably, R. Lapesa, both in his extremely benevolent review (*NRFH* 3.294-307 [1949]) and in the relevant chapter of his *Historia de la lengua española*, starting with the 2d ed. (Madrid, 1950); J. R. Andrews and J. H. Silverman bore down on Spitzer, as critic of Castro and of Castro's student S. Gilman, in a long-winded, bizarrely philosophical, review article which passed almost unnoticed ('On destructive criticism ...', *Modern Language Forum* [Los Angeles], 42.3-24[1957]).

[129] '¿Arabismos o romanismos?', *NRFH* 15.4-22 (1961: *Homenaje a Alfonso Reyes*). For the most part Coşeriu's views coincide with Spitzer's rather than with Castro's.

[130] Coşeriu's weightiest monograph, published at the height of his Uruguayan period, was *Sincronía, diacronía e historia. el problema del cambio lingüístico* (Montevideo, 1958). Earlier writings from his pen, frequently mere brochures reprinted from obscure periodicals, include *Sistema, norma y habla* (1952); (with W. Vásquez) *Para la unificación de las ciencias fónicas* (1953); *Forma y sustancia en los sonidos de la lengua* (1954); and *La creación metafórica en el lenguaje* (1958). Attempts to bring the author's philosophical training to bear on specific problems of Romance linguistics include studies on the plural of proper names (1955) and on the Romance future (1957), both published in Spanish by the *Revista Brasileira de Filologia*. For one — conceivably premature — attempt to appraise this scholar's *œuvre* as a whole see N. C. W. Spence, 'Towards a new synthesis in linguistics: the work of Eugenio Coşeriu', *ArL* 12.1-34 (1960). My chief reason for so thinking is that, after his transfer to Tübingen the author has turned to new problems and developed a novel style, veering away from precedents; for one sample see his latest article, '*Tomo y me voy*; ein Problem vergleichender europäischer Syntax', *VR* 25.13-55 (1966).

[131] Examples in point are Irma Césped, 'Los *fabliaux* y dos cuentos de Juan Ruiz', *BFUCh* 9.35-65 (1956-57), and Luciana de Stefano (Caracas), 'La sociedad estamental en las obras de Don Juan Manuel', *NRFH* 16.329-54 (1962 [-64]); cf. the same social historian's more fully developed book *La sociedad estamental de la baja Edad Media española a la luz de la literatura de la época* (Caracas, [1966]; with a Preface by Á. Rosenblat). Articles of this type usually contain, as a by-product, a few crumbs of useful and easily assimilable information for the lexicographer and the stylistician. The survival of medieval themes in rural Spanish American transmission has never failed to fascinate local workers; cf. Y. Pino Saavedra, 'Santa María Egipciaca en la tradición oral chilena', *BFUCh* 8.333-45 (1954-55).

[132] This is true of such studies in Old Southeast Spanish as Álvaro Galmés de Fuentes, 'El mozárabe levantino en los *Libros de los repartimientos de Mallorca y Valencia*' (4.313-46 [1950]), and of J. Corominas' composite review article 'Notas de lingüística italo-hispánica, con ocasión de dos libros

VI. HISTORICAL INGREDIENTS OF DIALECTOLOGY

Most present-day dialectologists — in Spanish America as elsewhere — have resolutely veered away from the philological moorings of their discipline. Whether the investigator is concerned with a set of phonetic problems[133] or leans toward lexicology (with its almost inevitable *Wörter-und-Sachen* paraphernalia[134]), the stringently synchronic perspective is bound to prevail to the point of exclusiveness. However, the conservative rather than innovating character of most varieties of rural speech carries with it the perennial temptation for the analyst to point out correspondences between older stages of the written language and current regional folk-usage. As a result, not a few dialect studies of varying degrees of sophistication and progressiveness contain useful pellets of philological information through strings of references to historical grammars, ancient texts, or both.[135]

VII. SOCIAL IMPLICATIONS OF REGIONAL SPEECH

Under this heading it may be admissible to array two clearly heterogeneous classes of linguistic studies. On the one hand, the surveyor may set off probings into special milieux and neatly silhouetted subsocieties, to the extent that these conspicuous environments and the unique linguistic climates prevailing in them cannot be satis-

nuevos' (10.144-86 [1956]), bearing on Angelico Prati's etymological dictionary (1951) and on Gerhard Rohlfs' dialectologically tinted historical grammar (1949-54). While Fritz Krüger's 'Cosas y palabras del Noroeste ibérico' (4.231-53 [1950]) moves in a groove familiar to the reader of that scholar's earlier investigations, he has lately encroached on the slippery grounds of onomatopoeia, expressivism, and substratum: 'Acerca de las raíces onomatopéyicas *casc-*, *cosc-*, *coc-* y *croc-*' (6.1-32 [1952]), a type of study that one inclines to associate with H. Schuchardt's tradition. Cf., in topical and methodological proximity to that article, the book-length inquiry: *Problemas etimológicos: las raíces CAR-, CARR- y CORR-* (Madrid, 1956), involving an assault on J. Hubschmid's preserve which the latter, as one would expect, has tried to parry, through full use of Basque and Celtic material (*RomPh* 13.31-49 [1959-60]).

133 Cf. Joseph Matluck, 'La pronunciación del español en el Valle de México', *NRFH* 6.109-20 (1952), an article based on the slightly earlier book *La pronunciación en el español del Valle de México*.

134 By way of supplement to my earlier references to Argentina and Colombia (fnn. 56 and 57) let me cite, as an average rather than superior achievement, Estrella Cortichs de Mora, 'El habla de Tepotzotlán', *NRFH* 8.137-55 (1954). The chosen area occupies the extreme east of the border-zone between the States of Mexico and Hidalgo. The topics discussed include, in routine sequence, the daily toils, housing, the construction and manipulation of the water pump (*bambilete*), the yoke, the plough, and the culture of maize and maguey. The author uses, albeit sparingly, parallel findings in other parts of the hemisphere (B. E. Vidal de Battini) and of Spain (Krüger, Canellada).

135 One extreme example (in Peninsular research) is provided by the dissertation of María Josefa Canellada, *El bable de Cabranes* (Madrid, 1946). Of course, any study of a dialect viewed through the prism of a single writer's usage — a hybrid genre of research of dubious merit; for one example see A. Zamora Vicente, 'El dialectalismo de José María Gabriel y Galán', *Fil* 2.113-75 (1950) — is of necessity philologically flavored. (Zamora Vicente, a Spaniard trained in his own country, served as a temporary replacement for Amado Alonso in Argentina at the height of the Perón regime.) The keenest theorist among the continent's numerous devotees of dialectology is undoubtedly J. P. Rona; see his *Aspectos metodológicos de la dialectología hispanoamericana* (Montevideo, 1958) — reviewed by R. A. Hall, Jr. in *RomPh* 16.378-9 [1962-63] — and his aforementioned contribution to *Presente y futuro*.

factorily described in terms of ethnic nuclei alone, as examined above. On the other hand, one recognizes in the standard discourse, and may attempt to individuate, certain characteristic strains far more strongly conditioned by social pressures than are others.[136]

Perhaps no social group has of late haunted the imagination of South American intellectuals quite so strongly as the nearly extinct loose pampa confederacy of the *gauchos* (= Braz. *gaúchos*). One can speak of a Gauchesque streak in Argentine literature and, stretching the facts a little, even of its dimly discernible counterpart in philology. For twenty long years the towering figure in this latter domain was Eleuterio F. Tiscornia (1879-1945), a native Argentine educator who, at the ripe age of forty-odd years, was mentally still elastic enough and sufficiently free from invidiousness to join forces with a distinctly younger, more magnetic, and — as if to make things more difficult — newly imported A. Alonso.[137] Tiscornia's main effort was directed at annotating, with fastidious rigor, José Hernández's classics *El gaucho Martín Fierro* (1872) and *La vuelta de Martín Fierro* (1879), with special attention to the elusive lexicon; he also gave sporadic attention to B. Hidalgo's trail-blazing *Diálogos*, to H. Ascasubi's *Santos Vega* (1851, 1872), and to E. del Campo's mock-epic *Fausto* (1870).[138] The enthusiasm which presided over this output (and which, through a freak of fortune, was channeled into serious, objective research) cannot be fully appreciated without some reference to the general mood that gripped Argentinian intellectuals in the mid-'twenties. Their country, it was widely felt, was at long last coming into its own, in fact, was reaching out for continental leadership; *gaucho* living, a colorful kaleidoscope of the hinterland's romantic past, was now being recaptured for posterity by front-line novelists,[139] and the few qualified linguists

[136] One could of course argue in favor of transfering to this section such discussions of the general problem of colonial settlement as have been sociologically shored up, notably Á. Rosenblat's latest 'mise au point': 'Base del español de América: nivel social y cultural de los conquistadores y pobladores', *BFUCh* 16.171-230 (1964); see the detailed summary by Jennie Figueroa Lorza in *Thesaurus* 20.399-403 (1965).

[137] Born in Gualeguaychú (Entre Ríos) into a provincial surrounding, Tiscornia made his career in Buenos Aires, becoming the principal of the Colegio Manuel Belgrano and a professor at the influential and intellectually discriminating Teachers' College (Instituto Nacional del Profesorado Secundario); in the end he was elected to membership in the exclusive Argentine Academy of Letters. A. Alonso not only absorbed his best publications into two series over which he exercised control ('Colección de estudios literarios' and 'Biblioteca de dialectología hispanoamericana'), but himself prepared an edition of E. del Campo's *Fausto* (Buenos Aires, 1943; reissued in 1947 and in 1951), contributing to it an important study: 'El manuscrito del *Fausto* en la Colección Martiniano Leguizamón' (pp. xxxix-lxi). See also the chapter 'Americanismos en la forma interior del lenguaje', in *Estudios lingüísticos: temas americanos* 73-101.

[138] The hard core of Tiscornia's philological and linguistic exegesis is embodied in the two respective volumes '*Martín Fierro*' *comentado y anotado* (1925; new ed., substantially enlarged, 1941) and *La lengua de* '*Martín Fierro*' (1930). Other ventures include the reader *Poetas gauchescos: Hidalgo, Ascasubi, del Campo* (1940; 2d ed., 1945); the pamphlet *La vida de Hernández y la elaboración del* '*Martín Fierro*' (1937); and the edition of R. L. Dillon, *Advertencias del gaucho Martín Fierro a los marineros de la armada nacional* (1942, 1943). All of these books appeared in Buenos Aires.

[139] Not for nothing were those years marked by the appearance of Ricardo Güiraldes' masterpiece, *Don Segundo Sombra* (1926), which, critics affirm, represents the apogee of the genre of *gaucho* novel.

available could hardly expect to find a more suitable and more rewarding outlet for their energies and talents than the scrupulous piecing-together of a shattered way of life — doomed to oblivion, yet somehow symbolic of an imperishable Argentina. Artistic evocation and scholarly reconstruction for once went hand in hand; their felicitous blend, so seldom attainable, came to fruition in Tito Saubidet's delightful *Vocabulario y refranero criollo*, a publication[140] — half-book, half-album — whose diagrams, sharp-edged drawings, and pleasing color plates — so richly suggestive of all phases of unhampered life in the pampa — were contributed by the same aficionado artist who, turning an amateur linguist, compiled a dictionary noted for its sober, precise, and polished definitions, and for its pointed exemplifications as well.

Another social dialect, characterized by a special humor, matched to a peculiar technique of 'encoding' information so as to make it unintelligible except to those initiated, and spiced by borrowings from certain favored languages, is the cant of the criminal world, Sp. *caló*. This argot has its known antecedents in early-17th-century Spanish (*germanía*), boasts strong cross-connections to other national varieties of an essentially international 'Gaunersprache', and is marked by an astonishingly rapid rate of attrition in the lexical domain, a speed of decay that steadily produces new vacua crying out for immediate replacements, either through bold metaphoric extensions of the conventional semantic ranges or through some formal device. The study of such material is beset by particular difficulties (including the safe collection of dependable raw data) and has appealed, in Spanish America as elsewhere, to a few daredevils and seekers after the unusual and pungent.[141]

Such was the atmospheric pressure in this direction that the Argentine writer, Enrique Rodríguez Larreta, acclaimed as the master of the historical novel — for all its 'modernism' *La gloria de Don Ramiro* (1908) is acted out in the Spain of Philip II, cf. A. Alonso's searching critical monograph (1942) — as a mature man (b. 1875) succumbed to the temptation of writing an undistinguished gauchesque novel, *Zogoibi* (1926). Gauchesque motifs abound in the finely chiseled short stories of Jorge Luis Borges. On the side of folklore studies, J. A. Carrizo at that very moment issued his *Antiguos cantos populares argentinos* (Buenos Aires, 1926), followed in rapid succession by provincial *Cancioneros populares* for Salta (1933), Jujuy (1934), Tucumán (1937), and La Rioja (1943), and by the synthesis *Antecedentes hispano-medievales de la poesía tradicional argentina* (1945). Small wonder that a scholar of the stature of Tiscornia was swept onto the crest of this powerful vogue, rather than continuing such unexciting, if meritorious, chores as the edition (1926) of *El discurso sobre la poesía castellana* by G. Argote de Molina (1549-90). Even a literary historian as austerely addicted to research in the Middle Ages and the Renaissance and as stubbornly independent in her tastes and attitudes as was María Rosa Lida de Malkiel for one fleeting moment allowed herself to be swayed ('Carta a Andrés Ramón Vázquez sobre [la cinta] *Way of a Gaucho*', *Buenos Aires Literaria* 5.27-30 [Febr. 1953]). Note the fact that the gauchesque theater of Florencio Sánchez (1875-1910; an Uruguayan acclimatized in Buenos Aires) chronologically mediates between the peaks of the gaucho epic (ca. 1870) and the gaucho novel (ca. 1925).

[140] The original edition, magnificently printed by an aggressive Porteño publisher (G. Kraft Ltda.), appeared in 1943; the 4th edition, or rather printing, is traceable to 1952; the 5th, to 1957-58. In the early 'fifties Bartolomé J. Ronco, a seasoned student of the La Plata area's colonial past, was at work on a copiously documented *Glosario gauchesco de voces ganaderas*, on whose wealth he allowed A. Alonso to draw.

[141] The classic treatise, at least for Argentina, is A. Dellepiane, *El idioma del delito* (Buenos Aires, 1894), whose Peninsular pendant, of almost equally old vintage, has been R. Salillas, *El delincuente*

The alternative type of social implications of dialect speech would, I repeat, involve such chosen elements of the standard language as convey enhanced 'social messages' in comparison to the, in this respect, relatively neutral context. This whole area of socially extra-relevant ingredients of speech still awaits its major investigators in Spanish America, where some of the preparatory groundwork has been laid by foreigners,[142] and is thus not subject to minute inspection here. Forms of address are definitely pertinent and have been studied in some detail for Platense and Peruvian Spanish. One also thinks of hypocoristics, especially those used in a milieu of pronounced intimacy; of nicknames and the like; of colorful phraseology permeated with recollections of a remote seafaring way of life or shot through with allusions to dance and music, not only among 'swingers' and 'hipsters'. For all these tempting lines of curiosity a few model studies can now be cited.[143]

VIII. STYLISTICALLY ISOLABLE ELEMENTS OF THE LITERARY LANGUAGE

Inasmuch as stylistics, as practiced in Spanish America, bears not on 'style in language' (to quote T. A. Sebeok's felicitous formula),[144] but on the peculiarities of individual

---

español: el lenguaje (Madrid, 1896). On the old *germanía* there are available to the researcher two important books by J. M. Hill, *Poesías germanescas* (1945) and *Voces germanescas* (1949). The leading 20th-century authority on all nooks and crannies of this field has been M. L. Wagner (cf. his article 'Apuntaciones sobre el caló bogotano', *Thesaurus* 6.181-213 [1950]), while C. Clavería has achieved a certain expertise in the connections of Gypsy-Spanish to cant. In close vicinity to this domain one may place inquiries into regional low-class speech (cf. E. Rodríguez Herrera, 'El plebeyismo en Cuba', *BFUCh* 8.407-37 [1954-55], with a 12-page word-list) as well as those concerned with the lexical idiosyncrasies of certain close-knit socio-ethnic minorities, e.g. the group of underprivileged Italian immigrants in the Río de la Plata area (*lunfardía*); cf. fn. 53, above.

142 The most comprehensive guide to the slippery terrain of euphemisms is C. E. Kany's book *American-Spanish euphemisms*, a companion volume to his *American-Spanish semantics*; see the joint review by D. L. Canfield in *Thesaurus* 15.302-5 (1960) and cf. fn. 103, above. Kany's oft-quoted treatment of *voceo* in his earlier book on syntax may now be supplemented by A. Nascentes' note, 'O tratamento de *você* no Brasil', *BFUCh* 8.307-14 (1954-55).

143 The latest research in Romance diminutives has been ably summarized and shrewdly assessed in Jerry R. Craddock's far-reaching review article (oriented, it is true, toward Europe), 'A critique of recent studies in Romance diminutives', *RomPh* 19.286-325 (1965-66); add to his bibliography Delmira Maçãs, 'O sufixo *-inho* junto a adjectivos na linguagem familiar portuguesa', *BFUCh* 8.219-32 (1954-55). As regards regionally favored forms of address, a straight path leads from Frida Weber's 'Fórmulas de tratamiento en la lengua de Buenos Aires', *RFH* 3.105-39 (1941) to Javier Sologuren's 'Fórmulas del tratamiento en el Perú', *NRFH* 8.241-67 (1954). On hypocoristics see P. M. Boyd-Bowman, 'Cómo obra la fonética infantil en la formación de los hipocorísticos', *NRFH* 9.337-66 (1955). The transfer of maritime terms and phrases to a landlocked environment — a problem first tackled, I repeat, by J. Corominas and by B. E. Vidal de Battini — comes again to the fore in D. L. Garasa's piece 'Voces náuticas en tierra firme', *Fil* 4.169-209 (1952-53). The musical orchestration and terpsichorean enrichment of Porteño lexicon and phraseology receives almost disproportionate attention at the hands of D. Devoto, bent, as always, on maximum accuracy and wealth of critically sifted information ('Sobre paremiología musical porteña'. *Fil* 3.6-83, 206 [1951]).

144 Bally's *Traité de stylistique française* (Heidelberg, 1909; 3d ed., 1951), which has served in many quarters as a model for the 'style in language' approach, was neither translated nor adapted to Spanish

writers and schools of verbal artistry, i.e., on a zone of overlap between language and literature, it hardly invites any searching discussion in the framework of this survey. Perhaps the one fact deserving mention, and even a certain emphasis, is the spread of active curiosity, among Spanish American theorists and practitioners of philology, over a spectrum of disciplines including major chunks of both the literary and the linguistic landscape. Indisputably, this liberal spread of intellectual commitment is praiseworthy and greatly benefits research in stylistics; regrettably, it produces an occasional diffraction of attention and, even more serious, entails one-sided concentration on Spanish material, almost to the exclusion of first-rate inquiries into languages and literatures other than the vehicle of the national heritage.

Joint concern with language and literature need not result in any partiality to the stylistic approach, nor must one expect any other type of cross-fertilization to ensue at once. One may be hard put to characterize P. Henríquez Ureña's parallel studies of *La cultura y las letras coloniales en Santo Domingo* (Buenos Aires, 1936) and *El español en Santo Domingo* (1940) in other terms than as two separate lines of investigation, with obvious topical rather than hidden disciplinary cross-connections. Also, a gap seems, at first glance, to be interposed between Raimundo Lida's dialectological researches, undertaken in the company of his teacher and mentor A. Alonso, and his numerous literary essays and monographs. But the exemplary rigor with which R. Lida examines such an elusive issue as the matter of periodization in literature (*RFH* 3.166-80 [1941]) may involve a dual debt to his formal training in philosophy, with special stress on esthetics, and to his ten years or so of active concern with linguistics; and if it is true that his excellent articles on Quevedo — the first fruits of an eagerly awaited book-length project? — do not overtly display any linguistic predilection, some of his shorter pieces (e.g. an elegant paper on the derivational devices used by Juan Ramón Jiménez) betray, without pedantry, the critic's long exposure to technical work in a linguistic laboratory.[145] Similarly, Ana María Barrenechea's austerely analytical work, some of it revolving around functional linguistics,[146] is subtly and unobtrusively connected with her writings on literary themes, such as

---

conditions along the lines of Reto Roedel's Italianization (*Lingua e elocuzione, esercizi di stilistica italiana* [San Gallo, 1940]; cf. the review by E. Werder in *VR* 6.324-8 [1941-42]) or of Cesare Segre's more recent adaptation (1963) of Bally's *Linguistique générale et linguistique française* (1932; rev. ed., 1944); see Fred M. Jenkins's exhaustive analysis in *RomPh* 19.58-68 (1965-66). However, Bally's *Le langage et la vie* (1926; rev. ed. 1935, 1952) contained a section 'Stylistique et linguistique générale', which was included in A. Alonso's translation (1941) of the 2d ed., published under the title *El lenguaje y la vida*. The miscellany *El impresionismo en el lenguaje*, eds. A. Alonso and R. Lida (Buenos Aires, 1936), encompasses annotated writings by Bally paired off with others by Elise Richter.

[145] A good sampler of R. Lida's scattered essays is *Letras hispánicas, estudios, esquemas* (Mexico, 1958). His craftsmanship as a polished Quevedo scholar is best exemplified with these two pieces: 'Quevedo y su España antigua', *RomPh* 17.253-71 (1963-64), and 'Sobre Quevedo y su voluntad de leyenda', *Fil* 8.273-306 (1962 [-64]). The analysis of suffixation used as a stylistic device — a topic dear to L. Spitzer (1910) — pervades R. Lida's contribution to the Alfonso Reyes Memorial, 'Palabras de Juan Ramón', *NRFH* 15.617-24 (1961 [-63]).

[146] 'Las clases de palabras en español, como clases funcionales', *RomPh* 17.301-9 (1963-64); 'El pronombre y su inclusión en un sistema de categorías semánticas', *Fil* 8.241-72 (1962 [-64]).

La expresión de la irrealidad en la obra de Jorge Luis Borges.[147] In the researches of her protégée and fellow-worker Emma Susana Speratti Piñero, an expert on Valle-Inclán, microscopically precise lexicology (with special attention to the distillation of 'americanismos') and literary anatomy go hand in hand.[148]

The academic tradition calling for one scholar to embrace, through a vigorous grip on a single culture (preferably his own), both its linguistic and its literary strains goes back to early-20th-century Spain and is readily associated with such prestigious names as Menéndez Pidal and A. Castro;[149] the obvious link to Spanish America would then be Amado Alonso, [150] who, aside from leaning on a pattern firmly established at Madrid's venerable Centro de Estudios Históricos (the prototype of Argentina's incipient Instituto de Filología), could and did fall back on the range of activities of such much-admired versatile Central European 'Romanists' as K. Vossler and L. Spitzer. The fact that, on both sides of the Atlantic, this peculiar tradition, with its patent advantages and no less obvious drawbacks, should have survived undiminished

[147] An English version of this book (Mexico, 1957) has appeared, entitled *Borges, the Labyrinth Maker*; tr. R. Lina (New York, 1965). A. M. Barrenechea is also the joint author, with E. S. Speratti Piñero, of the five-pronged book *La literatura fantástica en Argentina* (Mexico, 1957): L. Lugones, H. Quiroga, M. Fernández, J. L. Borges, and J. Cortázar.

[148] A designedly technical paper such as 'Los americanismos en *Tirano Banderas*', *Fil* 2.225-91 (1950), was one of the stepping stones to her synthesis, *La elaboración artística en 'Tirano Banderas'* (Mexico, 1957); cf. C. Blanco Aguinaga's appraisal in *NRFH* 11.410-3 (1957). Through an amusing coincidence, one writer far less celebrated than Valle-Inclán, namely Ciro Bayo, who provided a model for the novel at issue, also straddled the domains of fine letters and (dilettantish) dialectology; see J. H. Silverman, 'Valle-Inclán y Ciro Bayo: sobre una fuente desconocida de *Tirano Banderas*', *NRFH* 14.73-88 (1966). The model, in matters lexical and phraseological, was Bayo's novel *Los marañones.*

[149] The compatibility and interlocking of concerns with language and literature was intensified by the fact that in early- and mid-20th-century Spain there arose whole generations of scholar-writers. M. de Unamuno's many-faceted *œuvre* is an example in point; one of the less well-known facets is his early indebtedness to W. D. Whitney and his later occasional returns to linguistic themes, in articles and scattered comments. Pedro Salinas, a younger poet-professor, steered clear of any formal commitments vis-à-vis linguistics (and is reported to have railed at etymologists), but at least espoused the cause of medieval studies, not only through his tasteful modernization of that venerable epic *Cantar de Mio Cid*, but also through erudite essays such as *Jorge Manrique; tradición y originalidad* (Buenos Aires, 1947). At this juncture one is reminded of pre-revolutionary Russia, which had its share of poets steeped in erudition (Vjačeslav Ivanov, Valerij Brjusov), attending university courses in philology (Aleksandr Blok), and — in the end — attaining remarkable expertise in chosen fields (Osip Mandelštam in Old Italian literature, Anna Axmatova in Puškin studies).

This situation has been reënacted on the Spanish American scene, where Alfonso Reyes, the acknowledged coryphaeus of Mexican littérateurs, evinced signal interest in classical Greek as well as in Spanish medieval literature (*Cid, Libro de buen amor*). On the Argentine side, the undisputed artistic and intellectual pace-setter of an entire generation, Jorge Luis Borges, has taken time off to plunge into such unorthodox ventures as the writing of the pamphlet *El idioma de los argentinos* (Buenos Aires, 1928; reissued in 1953 and bound with J. E. Clemente, *El idioma de Buenos Aires*) or the private study of Old Germanic metrics; cf. fn. 69, above.

[150] Easily the single most ambitious gambit in this direction was A. Alonso's book — launched at the zenith of his career — *Poesía y estilo de Pablo Neruda* [a Chilean poet eight years his junior]; *interpretación de una poesía hermética* (Buenos Aires, 1940; rev. 2d ed., 1951). The most pertinent of his studies were posthumously collected — and, in part, salvaged — through the efforts of a devoted disciple, Raimundo Lida: *Materia y forma en poesía* (Madrid, 1955; 3d ed., 1965).

until the late 'sixties, long after its eclipse in most other western countries,[151] will perhaps be acidly interpreted by some unfriendly observers as just another manifestation of the general slowness and resultant backwardness of Hispanic culture; or at least be equated with the propensity toward 'tradicionalidad y misoneísmo' and with the delight taken in 'late fruits' — to abide by R. Menéndez Pidal's famous characterization (*Los españoles en su historia* [1947], ed. 1951, pp. 26-30).

Such a pessimistic appraisal, however, would be one-sided and unfair. With the pendulum in linguistics currently swinging everywhere in the direction of semantics, syntax, stylistics, and poetics, the discrepancy between world opinion and Spanish America's private taste in these philological matters is bound to dwindle, possibly to the point of gradual disappearance. Not implausibly, all that will soon be needed to invigorate the ailing discipline is an enlightened, resourceful, and imaginative leader.[152]

IX. ONOMATOLOGY

For a variety of reasons the study of proper names must be relegated to the periphery of philology. For one thing, it is not always feasible to draw a sharp line of demarcation between lexicology (as bearing on common nouns) and toponymy, inasmuch as place names, at least in their pristine shape, ordinarily involve a heavy dosage of

[151] In metropolitan Spain this tradition has been upheld in the sensationally successful output of D. Alonso. In a less flashy manner, Rafael Lapesa has divided his time between commitments to such topics as, on the one hand, *Asturiano y provenzal en el Fuero de Avilés* (Acta Salm. 2:4; Salamanca, 1948) and, on the other, *La trayectoria poética de Garcilaso* (Madrid, 1948) and *La obra literaria del Marqués de Santillana* (Madrid, 1957). Both D. Alonso and R. Lapesa have, through lectures and teaching, strengthened their hold on Spanish American intellectuals: the former at the University of Buenos Aires, the latter at La Plata and the Colegio de México. The old splendid tradition has survived into the current activities of Diego Catalán Menéndez-Pidal. It has its share of hazards, easily seducing a less than iron-willed worker into superficiality. Thus, Carlos Clavería has won M. L. Wagner's acclaim (*RomPh* 7.360-6 [1953-54]) as a student of Gypsy-Spanish, while incurring C. Blanco Aguinaga's wrath (*NRFH* 8.430-2 [1954]) for his unexciting performance in *Temas de Unamuno* (Madrid, 1953). Worse, A. Zamora Vicente — imported from Spain, I repeat, to serve as A. Alonso's temporary successor in Buenos Aires, then, upon his return to the Peninsula, a professor at Salamanca and, later, a senior staff member of the Madrid Academy's Lexicographic Seminary — has spread himself perilously thin through his ill-advised decision to include within his purview, without the necessary safeguards, Peninsular and overseas dialectology, medieval epic and Golden Age drama, to say nothing of a fling he had at modernist literature (Valle-Inclán), with the foreseeable result that all dimensions of his scholarship have suffered irremediable damage. The first reviewer who correctly diagnosed his vulnerability to serious criticism was María Rosa Lida de Malkiel; see her abrasive remarks, in *NRFH* 3.182-5 (1949), on Zamora Vicente's hastily executed edition (1946) of the *Poema de Fernán González*.

[152] One paradox of the present-day situation is that a worker may adopt, from different teachers, several techniques without bothering about their ultimate reconcilability. For one eloquent example of the resultant gap compare Martha Hildebrandt's 'humanistic' monograph *La lengua de Bolívar*, 1: *Léxico* (Caracas, 1961; cf. the review by Leonie F. Sachs in *RomPh* 17.476-8 [1963-64]) with the same scholar's aforementioned 'behavioristic' *Sistema fonémico del macoíta*. It will be particularly interesting to watch M. Hildebrandt's attitude in Vol. 2 of her Bolívar study, which is to bear on morphology, syntax, and style.

common nouns. This is particularly true of the autochthonous (Indian) constituents of Spanish American toponymy.[153] Aside from this hazy delimitation within linguistics, the discipline suffers from its constant encroachments on other realms of knowledge (archeology, history, etc.). In Spanish America its lineaments are further blurred by a certain parochialism of outlook: Not only are references to the European mother-country conspicuously scarce,[154] but even isolated attempts at a global view of New World conditions have not yet reached the blueprint stage. What we do possess at present is a small collection of local onomastic word-lists underpinned by scrupulous archival research, a genre of which Benjamín Núñez's roster of topographic terms culled from colonial Argentine sources (A.D. 1516-1810)[155] is a fair example. There also exist a few monographs on privileged toponyms and names of countries which lend themselves to a lively historical account by virtue of the exciting cultural context in which they happen to be embedded; witness Á. Rosenblat's reports on the crystallization of *Argentina* and *Venezuela*,[156] reminiscent — in tone, bias, and documentation — of A. Alonso's full-blown essay on the three competing labels 'Spanish', 'Castilian', and 'National Language'. A few timid efforts have been made to examine, mostly on a local scale, derivatives from family-names and from place-names (the latter group, called 'gentilicios', encompasses adjectives and names of inhabitants alike; in some instances also names of indigenous languages pinpointed on a map; cf. Calif. Diegueño, Luiseño).[157] In this direction, a somewhat bolder cross-country perspective would be most desirable. Thus, with the new information on the genesis of the suffixes *-í/ -in(o)* and *-eño* readily available,[158] it should be rewarding to prepare an

[153] Aside from Membreño's older monographs (see fn. 77, above, and cf. fn. 76) and the ill-fated experiments of Teuto-Chilean missionaries (see fn. 90, above), note the Supplement (273-80) to Koessler-Ilg's more recent repository of Argentine-Araucanian folklore; cf. P. Groeber, *Toponimia araucana* (Buenos Aires, 1926; reprinted from *Anales de la Soc. Argent. de Est. Geogr.*).

[154] Not surprisingly, they stem, as a rule, from European contributors to Spanish-American journals; cf. R. Menéndez Pidal, '*Murcia* y *Mortera*: dos topónimos hidrográficos', *Fil* 3.1-5 (1951). (For further information on the Hispanic descendants of *murcidus* see the opening section of my article 'Multiple versus simple causation in linguistic change', in the new testimonial volume *To Honor Roman Jakobson*, 2.1228-47.)

[155] The monograph, entitled *Términos topográficos en la Argentina colonial (1516-1810): un análisis lingüístico cultural* (Instituto Pan-Americano de Geografia e História; Coleção 'Têrmos geográficos', No. 2; Rio de Janeiro, 1965), was originally suggested by T. Navarro during the author's training period at Columbia University. It includes a conscientiously documented glossary of 472 items, of which as many as 381 are either entirely absent from the Academy Dictionary or, at least, have not been identified with the appropriate meaning. The glossary is ushered in by an introductory essay (11-54; with 8 full-page maps, some of which illustrate the diffusion of key-words); at its end the major findings are summarized in a handy conclusion, from which one learns, e.g., that the indigenous toponyms comprise 6.6% of the total.

[156] *Argentina, historia de un nombre* (Buenos Aires, 1949) — a narrative epitomized by W. L. Stover, Jr. in *RomPh* 5.75-6 (1951-52) — and, clad in a new garb, *El nombre de la Argentina* (Buenos Aires, 1964); also, *El nombre de Venezuela* (Caracas, 1952).

[157] A. Berro García, 'Los gentilicios uruguayos', *BFUCh* 8.15-34 (1954-55); R. Oroz, 'Sobre los adjetivos derivados de apellidos en la lengua española', ibid. 9.105-20 (1956-57).

[158] For a mere prospectus of the monograph actually needed see G. Sachs, 'La formación de los gentilicios en español', *RFE* 21.393-9 (1934). On *-í/ -in(o)*, nourished by Latin and Arabic sources, see my review in *HR* 16.262-8 (1946) of F. Mateu y Llopis, *Glosario hispánico de numismática*, esp.

exhaustive inventory of the highly productive *-eño* — as in *diegu-eño*, *luis-eño* (California), *tabasqu-eño* (Mexico), *panam-eño* (Isthmus), *lim-eño* (Peru), *santiagu-eño* (Argentina; but *-ino* in Chile and *-és* in Galicia), *port-eño* (from *puerto* 'harbor', used in reference to Buenos Aires City) — in hemispheric projection and to interweave such a geographic account with the temporally slanted annals of conquest and colonization.

X. CONCLUSION

Despite the diversity and sporadic intensity of philological activities observed, it would be an exaggeration to claim that Hispanic philology is currently passing through a period of flowering or even that the outlook for the immediate future is particularly bright. From the Río Grande to Tierra del Fuego one finds at present a greater number of active research centers, of journals and bulletins, of trained field workers and competent analysts than at any earlier stage of organized scholarship. But leadership in a grand style, as regards both originality of thinking and bold initiative in planning and implementing, is sorely lacking everywhere; and this critical weakness is fraught with heightened hazards in a culture accustomed to looking up for directions to talented, colorful individuals endowed with charismatic power.

Not all Spanish-speaking countries have so far been represented in philological experiments and accomplishments in correct proportion to the general vitality (or potentialities) of their intellectual fermentation. While Chile and Argentina have had their moments of pride, a country as original in its cultural configuration and as influential in numerous respects as Mexico has scored very modestly in matters philological — to the severe disappointment of its many friends.[159] Though the *Diccionario de peruanismos* by Pedro Paz Soldán y Unanue (pseud. Juan de Arjona) started publication in 1861,[160] i.e., ten years before Zorobabel Rodríguez's pioneering *Diccionario de chilenismos*, the subsequent record of Peruvian philology has remained disillusioningly meager. There have been some stirrings in Ecuador and in Uruguay — even in the Caribbean, which most of the time has been writhing in political agony —, but none worth mentioning, to my knowledge, either in Paraguay or in Bolivia, and the Isthmus republics have, all told, been dormant. Perhaps the two countries marked by the steadiest output, relatively speaking, from the threshold of this century to the

264-6. Counter to Meyer-Lübke's conjecture, Sp. *-eño* and It. *-igno* perpetuate Lat. *-ĭneu*, not *-ignu*; see my note 'The Latin base of the Spanish suffix *-eño*', *AJPh* 65.372-81 (1944), and G. Bonfante's embroidery ('Babbo di legno, mamma di legno') in *RomPh* 5.157-8 (1951-52).

[159] Through one of its institutions — the Colegio de México — and certain publishing houses (esp. the Fondo de Cultura Económica) — Mexico, needless to say, has obligated many foreign literary historians, philologists, and linguists, and favorable mention has already been made of some of its all too few native researchers in the domain under study, such as A. Alatorre, V. M. Suárez, and F. J. Santamaría. In this context Juan M. Lope Blanch's syntactic investigations, notably the book-length monograph *Observaciones sobre la sintaxis del español hablado en México*, deserve listing.

[160] The finished book appeared in Lima as late as 1883.

present juncture (with two thirds of the century behind us) have been Colombia and Venezuela. In fact, at this point Bogotá and Caracas show a level of alertness and productivity which puts them in a class with Mexico City, Santiago de Chile, and Buenos Aires.

If this geographic bird's-eye view reveals a damaging unevenness in the distribution of responsibilities and achievements, the acephalous character of the available contingent of workers will emerge from the comparison of a few temporally spaced cross-sections. In 1905 very few real experts were at work, but the publications of Lenz and Hanssen in Santiago and of Cuervo in distant Paris set off this parsimoniousness of staffing by the highest standard of inspired workmanship. Twenty years later, of these three trail-blazers only Lenz remained alive, and he was at that point discernibly past his crest; but by then Venezuela had found in L. Alvarado a worthy successor to Calcaño, P. Henríquez Ureña's star was just beginning to rise, and A. Castro's first ephemeral visit to Buenos Aires kindled considerable philological interest oriented toward German-style *Romanistik*. European scholars of other than Spanish background, notably M. L. Wagner, responded to the challenge. By 1940 A. Alonso's personal magnetism and a set of favorable circumstances transformed Argentina (and, in particular, Buenos Aires) into a first-rate focus of Spanish philology. Carriers of native talent, hard-working immigrants from Europe, harassed political refugees from Spain and Italy, and visitors from other South and Central American countries were welded into an excellent, universally admired team, into which, for the first time, sufficient self-confidence was instilled. Ten years later, the Alonso group — weakened on its homeground by the untimely disappearance (1946) of Henríquez Ureña — was dispersed and its founder dead (1952), but a few of the original members remained not only startlingly active, but, more important, capable of further, self-propelled growth. This was notably true of D. Devoto in Paris and of R. Lida at Harvard (with strong links to Mexico), while in the classic writings of María Rosa Lida de Malkiel's Berkeley period, until six years ago, the entire movement reached its highest summit, so far as the literary ingredient of philology is concerned. Simultaneously, the development of its linguistic ingredient, which actually was closer to A. Alonso's heart, rapidly began to lose momentum.

By 1965 all older traditions of philological linguistics had almost completely evaporated, in part as a result of the dynamic regrouping of forces and skills and commitments in Europe and in North America, in part as a consequence of Spain's erosive cultural decay. Many Latin Americans in positions of influence have meanwhile become thoroughly aware of the resultant gap, and some haphazard attempts have been made to remedy the situation. By dint of reading, traveling, and studying abroad, several younger Spanish American philologists and linguists have of late familiarized themselves with the tenets of structuralism and related 'modernistic' currents of thought and corresponding techniques.

In so doing, they have upon occasion overreacted, allowing themselves to be dazzled by a new standard of abstract elegance and a novel style of terminology. As a result, some have been tempted to jettison their heritage completely, instead of critically selecting the truly useful features of 'modernism', salvaging that part of their own heirloom which merits preservation, and harmoniously blending the new theoretical insights with the facts distillable by the traditional historico-philological methods.[161] In their current soul-searching Spanish America's younger philological linguists will before long discover that they stand no chance of scoring any revolutionary break-through without embedding their researches in the fertile matrix of Romance linguistics, a decision which may also entail the rendering of a major service to the general study of language.

ADDENDA at page-proof (Jan. 1968). — *Ad* fn. 9: J. L. Butler's addenda and corrigenda to Manuppella's bibliography are to appear in *RPh.* — *Ad* fn. 18: A refreshingly original counterpart to Menéndez Pidal's article is supplied by W. G. Boltz, 'Canton, the Seville of China', *RPh* 21.171-4 (1967-68). — *Ad* fn. 23: Catalán's review article has now appeared in *ZRPh* 82.467-506 (1966), followed immediately by M. Alvar's harshly phrased rejoinder. — *Ad* fn. 35: Of *El español de la Argentina* there exists at present a new ed., aiming in particular at grade-school teachers (Buenos Aires, 1964; pp. 226 and 14 color maps, with a Preface by Á. Rosenblat). — *Ad* fn. 44: Though not primarily a lexicographic venture, the *magnum opus* of R. Oroz, *La lengua castellana en Chile* (Santiago, 1966; dedicated to the memory of Lenz) boasts a fully developed section on vocabulary and phraseology (pp. 403-481) and may be easily put to use for lexical research thanks to a handy word index (pp. 499-535), — *Ad* fn. 50: The latest published progress report on *ALEC*, from the pen of J. J. Montes Giraldo, can be read in *Thesaurus* 22.94-100 (1967). — *Ad* fn. 53: OFINES now sponsors a bi-hemispheric study group 'Estudio coordinado del habla culta en las principales ciudades del mundo hispano'; the first colloquium (1966) took place in Madrid; the second (1967), in Bogotá. — *Ad* fn. 68: Meo Zilio's latest contribution to his favorite domain is "Genovesismos en el español rioplatense", *NRFH* 17.245-63 (1963-64 [1967]). *Ad* fnn. 82 and 95: The Cornell dissertations of Emma Gregores and Jorge A. Suárez have now been consolidated into a single book: *A description of colloquial Guaraní* (The Hague and Paris: Mouton & Co., 1967) — an unprecedented 'inquadramento' for a Spanish-American research project. — *Ad* fn. 105: The concluding installment of Anita Katz Levy's article has now appeared (*RPh* 20.296-320). — *Ad* fn. 116: For the latest retrospective appreciation of Lida de Malkiel's Ruiz studies see J. Corominas' critical ed. of the *Libro de Buen Amor* (Madrid, 1967), Introduction (pp. 7-68, passim).

[161] The need to test, balance, and reciprocally qualify rough-hewn structural analysis (or any latter-day substitute for it) and the more delicately shaded historical findings has been stated quite explicitly by Diego Catalán Menéndez-Pidal, especially in his perceptive article 'Nuevos enfoques de la fonología española', *RomPh.* 18.178-91 (1964-65), which embodies a penetrating dissection of the rev. 3d ed. (1961) of E. Alarcos Llorach's *Fonología española.* Such interweaving of old and new strains is not necessarily facilitated by the kind of hero-worship of pioneers as 'native sons' of certain countries, a cult which, for better or worse, remains eminently characteristic of the intellectual climate all over Spanish America.

BRAZILIAN LINGUISTICS

J. MATTOSO CÂMARA Jr.

I. BACKGROUND

Linguistic studies in Brazil have always centered upon the Portuguese language. Neither Classical, or Indo-European philology, on the one hand, nor any philosophical discussion on the origin, scope and functions of language, on the other, have found any interest in Brazilian scholarship. Focusing on Portuguese, Brazilian scholars have had three main fields of interest: history and philology of Portuguese, the establishment of a standard language for Brazil, and Brazilian dialectology.

The historical study of the language was stimulated by the example of the historical linguistics school in Portugal, which started in the latter part of the nineteenth century with Adolfo Coelho and José Leite de Vasconcelos, a thorough neogrammarian scholar. Brazil for a long time reechoed what was said in Portugal without any mark of original investigation. We can only cite João Ribeiro, who dissented in many points from Leite de Vasconcelos and counteracted the neogrammarian bias of the Portuguese scholar. Ribeiro had been strongly influenced by the neogrammarians' opponents when he studied philology in Germany and stressed idealistic viewpoints of Vossler in dealing with problems of Portuguese historical grammar.

Notwithstanding, in the thirties of our century Brazil made a substantial great contribution to the historical studies of Portuguese with the publication of an etymological dictionary by Antenor Nascentes.[1] It is the first overall work on the subject, both for Portugal and Brazil. Until now no other has satisfactorily replaced it. Nascentes does not give the meaning of the words listed. On moot points he registers all the etymologies that have been proposed but avoids to proposing new etymologies. His aim has been evidently to state what had been discussed and/or established until then.

Dialectological inquiry centered upon the collection of regional vocabularies. This activity was marred by technical defects, the main ones being a very vague delimitation of regional usage and the omission of any kind of phonetic transcription. Words are represented in the standard orthography and no clue is given of their truly phonetic shape in regional usage. Moreover, well chosen contexts are lacking in defining clearly the semantic area of each word. We find a more ambitious in-

[1] Antenor Nascentes, *Dicionário Etimológico da Língua Portuguesa* (Rio de Janeiro, 1932).

vestigation by Amadeu Amaral on the dialect called 'Caipira'.[2] The main part is also a vocabulary, but some attention is paid to phonetics and grammar. It was a regional dialect of the hinterland of the state of São Paulo which was already obsolescent at the time of the research. Amadeu holds the hypothesis that 'o fundo do dialecto representa um estado atrasado do português ... sôbre êsse fundo se vieram sucessivamente entretecendo os produtos de uma evolução divergente'[3]. It is the concept of an isolated area that is thus postulated instead of the more usual explanation for dialectal features in Brazil: Indian or African substrata.

The problem of a standard language focused first on phonetics. At the beginning of the twentieth century Felipe Franco de Sá tried to establish a received pronunciation for Brazil.[4] He compared the Brazilian usage with the findings of Gonçalves Viana for Portugal. Franco de Sá was not a well-trained phonetician, but his work is commendable as a statement of the chief phonetic traits in Brazil. He was followed in this kind of research by Antenor Nascentes and José Oiticica, who disagreed strongly with one another on many concrete points and on phonetic theory.[5] Oiticica, for instance, considers /l̦, n̦, š, ž/ as modifications of /l, n, s, z/ respectively and, like these last four, dental consonants, while Nascentes insists on their palatal articulation in the face of dental /l, n, s, z/. Oiticica denies also the velar articulation of postvocalic /l/, which is undeniable, and even has shifted to /w/ in the colloquial speech; he also rejects the presence of a nasal consonant closure for nasal vowels before a stop, which has been accurately posited by Viana for Portugal and by Nascentes for Brazil. He is right, however, when he dissents from Nascentes in reference to an affricate nature of the intervocalic voiced stops.

Nascentes, who remained more in accordance with Franco de Sá, was the more accepted orthoëpist in school teaching. His conclusions were approved by the Primeiro Congresso de Lingua Cantada, in 1936 in São Paulo, which dealt with the orthoëpy of the chant in Portuguese. It was stated that the standard pronunciation of Brazilian Portuguese ought to follow the 'Carioca' features (city of Rio de Janeiro) and not those of the north of the country or of São Paulo.

Lexicography had its first important work at the beginning of the nineteenth century with Antonio de Morais Silva.[6] From the fourth edition onwards the book has received so many additions and modifications from anonymous editors that it became quite a new work. Much later we have to cite a great dictionary by Laudelino

[2] Amadeu Amaral, *O Dialecto Caipira* (São Paulo, 1920).
[3] Amadeu Amaral, *O Dialecto Caipira* 55 (São Paulo, 1920).
[4] Felipe Franco de Sá, *A Lingua Portuguesa, dificuldades e dúvidas* (Maranhão, 1915).
[5] They exchanged letters on the subject after the Congresso da Língua Cantada. The letter by Oiticica, who insisted on his old ideas (José Oiticica, *Estudos de Fonologia* (Rio de Janeiro, 1916), was included with commentary by his student Almir Matos Peixoto, in José Oiticica, *Roteiros em Fonética Fisiológica, Técnica do Verso e Dição* 159-211 (Rio de Janeiro. 1955). The answer by Nascentes is to be found in Antenor Nascentes, *Estudos Filológicos* 119-43 (Rio de Janeiro, 1938).
[6] Antonio de Morais Silva, *Dicionário da Língua Portuguesa*[4] (Lisboa, 1831).

Freire and L. Campos.[7] With respect to grammatical theory and standard grammar there were many divergencies. One trend was towards a strict acceptance of the standards of the literary language of Portugal. Others, on the contrary, defended the autonomy and even the independence of the literary language of Brazil. The discussion became rather confusing because many different problems were brought into it. The basic question was the urgency of abandoning the stylistic classical patterns of the sixteenth and seventeenth centuries; but there was also the plea for the acceptance of colloquial peculiarities of Brazilian Portuguese and even for adopting in the literary style popular traits not received in the standard speech and more or less dialectal.

Writers, politicians, and journalists participated in the discussion in a passionate way. The philologists were little heard and moreover did not, in the main, have neat and coherent ideas on the subject. João Ribeiro advocated the adoption of the designation 'língua nacional' instead of Portuguese and later justified his opinion: 'Sinto ainda a necessidade de novamente escrever acerca do que podiamos chamar a 'língua nacional' dos brasileiros. Não era a defêsa nem a apologia intencional de solecismos, de barbaridades e de defeitos indesculpáveis. Era muito mais erguido e alevantado o meu propósito. Tratava-se da independência do nosso pensamento e da sua imediata expressão'.[8]

II. GENERAL LINGUISTICS

What we may call the current trends of linguistic studies in Brazil begins in the forties. It is simultaneous with the development of Faculdades de Letras, Ciências e Filosofia, also referred to more concisely as Faculdades de Filosofia, in the Brazilian universities. These include the study of the biological and physical sciences alongside with the humanities and the social sciences.

The first thorough teaching of linguistics was started in the Universidade do Distrito Federal (Rio de Janeiro), created in 1935. Linguistics was envisaged as a background for language teachers and students aiming at literary criticism. It was therefore considered as a part of the humanities and under that aspect was taught for two years until 1939, when the University was closed by the City Administration. Joaquim Mattoso Câmara Jr. was in charge of the linguistic courses. Later, in 1950, he was called again to teach linguistics in the Faculdade Nacional de Filosofia of the Universidade do Brasil (Rio de Janeiro). In the meanwhile he had published a book on the subject (1941), which is now in its fourth edition.[9] It is a handbook, the only one extant in Portuguese for some time. The author was influenced at first by the French school of linguistics, through George Millardet, visiting professor at the

[7] Laudelino Freire e J. L. Campos, *Grande e Novíssimo Dicionário da Língua Portuguesa*[3] (Rio de Janeiro, 1957).

[8] João Ribeiro, *A Lingua Nacional, notas aproveitáveis*[3] (São Paulo, 1933), 16.

[9] J. Mattoso Camara Jr., *Principios de Linguística Geral, como introdução aos estudos superiores da lingua portuguesa*[4] (Rio de Janeiro, 1964).

Universidade do Distrito Federal. Afterwards he studied in the United States of America under the guidance of Roman Jakobson and Louis Gray. The reader may form an idea of the book by the rather divergent reviews of Sol Saporta and Emilio Alarcos Llorach on the third edition.[10]

The author also tried to disseminate the linguistic idea of Edward Sapir in Brazil. He translated Sapir's *Language* and edited a selection of papers by Sapir under the title of *Linguística como Ciência* (1961) using the title of the first paper in the anthology ('The state of linguistics as a science').

Those publications mark a new interest for linguistics in Brazil. Two other scholars have also turned to linguistics: Aryón Dall'Igna Rodrigues and Sílvio Edmundo Elia. Rodrigues is a specialist in Tupi, and his chief interest is the study of Brazilian Indian languages. But he has also devoted himself primarily to anthropological linguistics as the head of the Department of Linguistics at the Universidade de Brasilia. Unlike Mattoso Câmara, whose connections are chiefly with the Prague Circle, the Saussurian orientation, and the linguistic philosophy of Sapir, Rodrigues tends toward the Bloomfieldian mechanicism. Silvio Elia, on the other hands, keeps himself aloof from any kind of structuralism, either European or American. He is mainly a disciple of Vossler and envisages linguistics as philosophical thinking rather than as an empirical science. Like Vossler he sees in linguistics the basis for the study of literature and literary style. His first book was a discussion of the concept of the Brazilians' language as a continuance of the language of Portugal and a criticism of the opposite viewpoint.[11] He takes the opportunity to expound his theoretical linguistic views and to emphazise the approach of Vossler towards language. He subsequently wrote a more ambitious book on the contemporary linguistic ideas,[12] taking issue with structuralists, especially Hjelmslev; his criticism of glossematics relies heavily on the well-known essay by Siertsema.

III. DESCRIPTIVE PORTUGUESE LINGUISTICS

The interest in general linguistics favored a more systematic, and therefore better study of Brazilian standard Portuguese. Phonetic investigation was replaced by a thorough phonemic approach in a little book published in 1953;[13] it envisaged the standard pronunciation of Rio de Janeiro in its formal style. In spite of the term *phonemics* in the title, the book is linked to the doctrine of the Prague school, especially through Jakobson. It abandons the old classification of consonants strictly

[10] Sol. Saporta, *Lg*, 36:1.89-96 (1960). E. Alarcos Llorach, *Rom Ph*, 15:3.335-8 (1962).

[11] Silvio E. Elia, *O Problema du Lingua Brasileira*[2] (Rio de Janeiro, 1961).

[12] Silvio E. Elia, *Orientações da Linguística Moderna* (Rio de Janeiro, 1955).

[13] J. Mattoso Câmara Jr., *Para o Estudo da Fonêmica Portuguesa* (Rio de Janeiro, 1953). The work was written some years before. Its pivotal chapter 'Os Fonemas em Português' was published in 1949 in a linguistic journal; J. Mattoso Câmara Jr., 'Para o estudo da fonemica portuguesa. Os fonemas em portuguêsa, *BFR*, 1 (Rio de Janeiro, 1949). It was commented on by Paul Garvin in *SIL*, 8:4.93-6 (1950).

based on the place of articulation to accept, instead of it, the triadic classification of Jakobson — labial, front and back consonants — in which the position of the narrowest stricture is emphasized. The 'chiantes' /š/ and /ž/ are considered back consonants, in opposition to /f/ and /s/ and /v/ and /z/ respectively. Among the nasals /ŋ/ is opposed to /m/ and /n/ in the same way. The triadic arrangement was maintained for the liquids by means of an interpretation of the two kinds of trills in Portuguese as positional allophones of a phoneme /r/: The phoneme /r/ is assumed to correspond to fortis [r̃], the lenis [r] being interpreted as an allophone in intervocalic position. At the same time there is posited a gemination /rr/ in this position to account for the fortis [r̃] in distinctive opposition to lenis [r], the first /r/ — postvocalic — actualized as zero and the second — prevocalic — actualized as [r̃]; in this way [r̃] is not considered intervocalic and instead of an opposition /r̃/ and /r/ between vowels there is /rr/ versus /r/.

By now the author has given up this interpretation, which indeed sacrificed too much the phonetic reality to the symmetry of the system; he admits an opposition of two phonemes, which is neutralized in any position but the intervocalic one.

Profound innovations are found in the book respecting the Brazilian Portuguese vowels. Since Franco de Sá the unstressed vowels have been considered per se in their rich and complex variety of timbre. European and Brazilian Portuguese diverge widely in timbre. Franco de Sá posited a class of 'vogais reduzidas' in unstressed position, from a hint of Gonçalves Viana for the European Portuguese in quite another sense.[14] Franco de Sá considered the 'vogais reduzidas' with an intermediary timbre between /e/ and /i/ and /o/ and /u/ respectively; but they are allophones of /i/ and /u/ in some environments. The absence of stress brings neutralization to the oppositions of the seven Portuguese vowel phonemes and gives rise to allophones. The nasal vowels were interpreted in the book as a sequence of vowel plus nasal, since there are vowel plus sibilant and vowel plus liquid in Portuguese syllables. The nasalization of the vowel was considered as an automatic consequence of the presence of a postvocalic nasal, which is phonetically eliminated before pause. The nasalization of the vowel in contact with a nasal in the following syllable, a normal occurrence in Brazilian Portuguese, is not phonemic. What is relevant is the nasal closure of the vowel (an archiphoneme /N/ in post-vocalic position); hence the neat opposition between *sem mana* /seNmana/ 'without sister' and *semana* /semana/ 'week', in spite of a nasal [ẽ] in both sequences.

The phonemic approach has not been adopted, however, in a clear and decided way. Nascentes included some phonemic interpretations in the second edition (1953) of his essay on *O Linguajar Carioca em 1922*, and some concessions were made to phonemics in descriptive studies of Brazilian Portuguese. There was a polemic between Elia and Oiticica, because Oiticica criticized the inclusion of some

[14] This was made very clear in a doctoral dissertation at the Universidade da Guanabara: Leodegário A. de Azevedo Filho, *A Fonêmica Descritiva e a Nomenclatura Gramatical Brasileira* 19 (Rio de Janeiro, 1961).

viewpoints of the Prague school in a school grammar of Elia; but the polemic only touched marginal points and was far from revealing.[15]

Traditional phonetics held its ground and the purport and the implications of the phonemic approach are not yet well understood among Brazilian scholars. In a recent statement of grammatical terminology, sponsored by the Ministério de Educação for high school teaching, the ideas of Franco de Sá were maintained, in the main, and phonemics was discarded as a questionable approach.[16] We can say with Brian Head of the best phonetic study in recent times — a statement of Brazilian vowels in the speech of Rio de Janeiro, by Antonio Houaiss,[17] that 'the distinction between phonetic data and phonemic structure is not explicit'.[18] This study was read as a paper in the Congresso Brasileiro de Língua Falada no Teatro (Bahia, 1956), and in this conference on the orthoëpy of speech in Brazilian drama the discussions were conducted on purely phonetic lines.

Moreover, the phonetic approach has not made great advances since the work of Franco de Sá, Nascentes and Oiticica. It is based on impressionistic techniques and the ear training of the researchers is not of a high level. Nascentes has advocated the installation of laboratories of experimental phonetics, but there is only one so far in the Universidade da Bahia. It was planned by the Portuguese phonetician Armando de Lacerda on the model of his own laboratory at the Universidade de Coimbra. The Bahia laboratory was left to Nelson Rossi, who, however, afterwards left Bahia for a chair of Portuguese at the Universidade de Brasilia. Lacerda and Rossi did experimental research on the speech of Rio de Janeiro, which was published in Coimbra.[19]

Grammatical description was kept in the background. Mattoso Câmara, at the Faculdade Nacional de Filosofia and the Museu Nacional (Rio de Janeiro), and Aryón Rodrigues at the Universidade de Brasilia have tried to stimulate descriptive grammatical studies of standard Brasilian Portuguese and the spoken language, but those efforts have been confined to the university milieu of their own students, although in a grammatical dictionary, now in its second edition,[20] Mattoso Câmara has emphasized the importance of descriptive linguistics. In descriptive grammar no valuable improvement has been made since the works of Manuel Said Ali in the twen-

[15] For the articles by Elia: Silvio E. Elia (Apêndice), *Orientações da Linguística Moderna*, 203-39 (Rio de Janeiro, 1955).

[16] Ministério da Educação e Cultura, *Nomenclatura Gramatical Brasileira* (Rio de Janeiro, 1958). Ministério da Educação e Cultura, *Nomenclatura Gramatical Brasileira e sua Elaboração, organização de Antonio José Chediak* (Rio de Janeiro, 1960).

[17] Antonio Houaiss, *Tentativa de Descrição do Sistema Vocálico do Português Culto na Área Dita Carioca* (Rio de Janeiro, 1958).

[18] Brian F. Head, 'A Survey of the Study of Dialectology and Phonetics in Portugal and Brazil', *A Comparison of the Segmental Phonology of Lisbon and Rio de Janeiro* 300 (Austin, 1964).

[19] Armando de Lacerda e Nelson Rossi, 'Particularidades Fonéticas do Comportamento Elocucional do Falar do Rio de Janeiro, em confronto com o português normal de Portugal', *Revista do Laboratório de Fonética Experimental de Coimbra* 4.5-102 (1958).

[20] J. Mattoso Câmara Jr., *Dicionário de Filologia e Gramática*[2] (Rio de Janeiro, 1964).

ties. Said Ali was a keen grammarian but still addicted to traditional grammar. Said Ali's approach for instance, to the study of the root vowel alternations in Portuguese verbs is still mantained in spite of the fact that through phonemics and some phonological rules much more systematic and economical results would be obtained. We can cite, notwithstanding, a commendable unpublished study of Joselice Andrade Macedo, of the Universidade da Bahia, who has made a computer study of the morphemes of Portuguese, using a corpus of 111, 000 words taken from recorded conversations.

IV. ROMANCE LINGUISTICS

In the historical outlook of Portuguese, on the contrary, a deeper and broader view has been attained.

One very important aspect was the introduction into historical studies of a romanic dimension through the attention paid to Vulgar Latin. In Brazil the chief Romance languages are not studied in a thorough manner. The only exception is French, which for a long time was the best known foreign language and only now is beginning to be superseded by English. French philology and literature have always been met with much interest by Brazilian scholars. It was, however, a very narrow basis on which to develop Romance linguistics and on which to give a good perspective of Portuguese in its relation to the other offshoots of Latin. This situation has not changed, but contemporary historical Romance linguistics developed in a vertical way, so to say, by turning to Vulgar Latin and the direct Latin sources of Portuguese.

The great step was taken by Serafim Silva Neto, a brilliant scholar who died too soon and to whom we shall refer more than once, for he was a researcher of many interests Silva Neto had been strongly influenced by Leite de Vasconcelos and the historicist school of Portugal.[21] But he was also an enthusiast of the methodology of Hugo Schuchardt whose example awoke his interest in detailed research in connection with ethnography and the history of culture.

He paid special attention to the prehistory of Portuguese. It was in this sense that he focused on the debatable problems of Vulgar Latin. He wrote many papers on it and finally proposed the new denomination of 'Latim Corrente', a free translation of the term *Lateinische Umgangssprache*, adopted for instance by J. B. Hofmann. He was less than twenty years old when he published a book on Vulgar Latin.[22] It was a critical text of the *Appendix Probi* with detailed and rich commentaries stressing the points of interest for Portuguese. It was subsequently revised and enlarged.

[21] He devoted his attention to a critical and historical survey of the development of linguistics and philology in Portugal. Serafim Silva Neto, *Manual de Filologia Portuguesa, história, problemas e métodos*[2] (Rio de Janeiro, 1957).

[22] Serafim Silva Neto, *Fontes do Latim Vulgar, o Appendix Probi* [3] (Rio de Janeiro, 1956). The first draft of the book was written in 1935.

Vulgar Latin was also the focus of Teodoro Maurer Jr., of the Universidade de São Paulo. He is the author of two books on the subject.[23] In one he discusses the concept of Vulgar Latin. In the other he sketches a theoretical structure of late Latin before the emergence of the Romance languages.

Joaquim Ribeiro, a son of João Ribeiro, had another view in his study of the romanization of America.[24] In a review of the book, Nascentes made the following evaluation: 'Na romanística estava faltando un trabalho que se ocupasse com a romanizaçáo dos continentes fora do europeu. O professor Joaquim Ribeiro acaba de resolver o problema quanto à America. A história da romanização da América, diz êle, veio abrir novos horizontes no campo da România ... Novos problemas apresentam-se aos romanistas'. Nascentes stresses, however, 'um êrro capital' in Ribeiro's book: to include Italian on the same level as Portuguese and Spanish as a language of romanization, since Italian came much later with European immigration in the same manner as German or Polish.[25]

V. HISTORICAL STUDY OF PORTUGUESE

Brazil has now a thorough historical grammar of Portuguese to offer alongside those of J. J. Nunes in Portugal, and Edwin Williams in the United States of America, namely, the one by Ismael da Lima Coutinho, of the Universidade do Estado do Rio de Janeiro.[26] It is a more rigorous and reliable book than that of Francisco da Silveira Bueno, of the Universidade de São Paulo.[27]

A new approach to diachronic Portuguese linguistics was launched by Serafim Silva Neto in a lengthy work first published in fascicles.[28] He places the history of the language in the framework of political and cultural history. The first chapters, dealing with Iberian Latin and the evolution of Portuguese from the ninth century onwards, are specially commendable. He traces a rough but neat outline of the Iberian Atlantic territory and its ethnic and cultural conditions 'before the Romans' and at the time of 'the Romans', commenting on the linguistic conditions and the evolution of a 'Hispanic Latin'. The survey of the phonetic, morphological, and syntactical historical features, which are at the basis of Portuguese, is rather schematic and lacks of a truly structural approach. The study of the basic vocabulary, on the other hand, is detailed and rich with keen observations related to ethnographic data. He also gives a good cultural sketch of the Germanic and the Arabic periods. A sound

[23] Teodoro Maurer Jr., *Gramática do Latim Vulgar* (Rio de Janeiro, 1959). Teodoro Maurer Jr., *O Problema do Latim Vulgar* (Rio de Janeiro, 1962).

[24] Joaquim Ribeiro, *Histório da Romanização da América* (Rio de Janeiro, 1959).

[25] Antenor Nascentes, *Revista Brasileira de Filologia* 6:1.135-7 (Rio de Janeiro, 1961).

[26] Ismael da Lima Coutinho, *Gramática Histórica*[4] (Rio de Janeiro, 1958).

[27] Francisco da Silveira Bueno, *A Formação Histórica da Lingua Portuguesa*[2] (Rio de Janeiro, 1958).

[28] Serafim Silva Neto, *História da Lingua Portuguesa* (Rio de Janeiro, 1952).

idea basic to the book is the ethnic, cultural, and linguistic opposition between North and South since pre-Roman times. The romanization, which was much stronger in the South, and the much longer Arabic domination in the South have contributed to a sharp linguistic division. He stresses at the same time the importance of the so-called Christian Latin owing to the expansion of Christianity, that 'à semelhança da cultura romana, partiu do sul para o Norte'.[29] The divergent evolution of the Latin clusters *cl-* and *pl-* (*plāga* > *Chaga*, *praga*), a moot point in Portuguese historical grammar, is explained by Silva Neto as an instance of the linguistic northern and southern opposition. According to this theory, *cr-* and *pr-* are southern features, while *ch-* is ascribed to a pre-Roman substratum. Silva Neto's theory of linguistic evolution, on which he comments in the 'Introdução' of the book, is a mixture of substratum ideas and a rather loose concept of 'drift', picked up from Sapir; he also emphasizes the influence of school teaching and of the literary writers. In a chapter on 'A Língua' he expounds his ideas on what should be understood by Vulgar Latin: he rejects the concept of 'Proto-Romance' as a theoretical reconstructed language and sticks to concrete data, like Schuchardt; but he correctly stresses the overall character of Vulgar Latin as the colloquial language of the Roman Empire. 'Êsse é fato fundamental; ao contrário, é acessório e até extra linguístico, o fato de que, com a decadência politico-social do Império, o nível da lingua padrão tenha ido progressivamente decrescendo'.[30] The chapters of the book dealing with Old, Classical, and Modern Portuguese are unfortunately too poor and even insufficient within the implicit scope of the book. Silva Neto centered upon the literary language, or better said, made a sketchy evaluation of the style of some authors that he considered representative and important in the establishment of the standards of the literary language in the past and in the present. A very serious ailment is, no doubt, responsible for this defect of the book.[31]

Silva Neto also envisaged the history of Portuguese in Brazil. In his *História da Lingua Portuguesa,* cited above, he had already considered the theme in a study of Portuguese expansion in Asia, Africa and America.

It is the subject of a small book of his published in 1950.[32] According to his method he associates the history of the language and its expansion in the new territory and its differentiation into dialects with the political and cultural events of Portuguese colonization. He compiles a rich body of facts from many historical sources, but somewhat at random, and does not organize them in a comprehensive framework. His essential thesis, a very debatable one indeed, is the evolution of a 'dialeto crioulo' through the contact of the Portuguese colonists with the Indians and the African

[29] Serafim Silva Neto, *História da Língua Portuguesa* 146 (Rio de Janeiro, 1952). The influence of the southern Romance population under the Arabs' dominion was also studied by Rosário F. Mansur Guérios, 'O Romanço Moçarábico Lusitano', *Letras* 5/6.123-53 (Curitiba, 1956).

[30] Serafim Silva Neto, *História da Língua Portuguesa* 108 (Rio de Janeiro, 1952).

[31] He died at last in 1960 when only 43 years old. The last fascicle is of 1957.

[32] Serafim Silva Neto, *Introdução ao Estudo da Língua Portuguesa no Brasil* (Rio de Janeiro, 1950).

slaves. Later, as he assumes, the intensification of the Portuguese immigration, the establishment of urban centers, the diffusion of schools (chiefly confieded to the Jesuits), and the strengthening of the colonial administration were to change the situation completely. Hence he divides the history of Portuguese in Brazil into three stages: from 1532 to 1654, when 'é escassíssimo o elemento branco, que se vê afogado na maré dos índios e dos africanos';[33] from 1654 to 1808, which is the year of the establishment of the royal Portuguese family in Brazil fleeing from Napoleon's invasion of Portugal; from 1808 onwards. He ascribes a great role to this last stage through a process of urbanization in contrast with the importance of rural life in the colonial times. Urbanization brought with it the emergence of a standard language based on urban usage and literary patterns. In this way, Silva Neto is inclined to see in rural Brazilian dialects the result of 'isolated areas' of the kind posited by Amadeu Amaral for the 'dialecto Caipira'.[34] Unlike Amaral, however, Silva Neto assigns great importance to Indian and African influences in those dialects; in a rather biased view of linguistic structure he considers Brazilian dialectal features as a 'cicatriz do primitivo aprendizado tosco da língua portuguêsa'.[35] He makes a schematic and rather atomistic survey of Brazilian dialectical traits.

Another book on the historical background of Brazilian Portuguese is by Gladstone Chaves de Melo, who at the time was assistant professor in the Universidade do Brasil.[36] He discusses the Indian and African influence on Brazilian Portuguese, arguing against those who emphasize them, and offers us a critical bibliography on the subject. In the chapter 'A Língua Popular' he outlines the more discussed traits of Brazilian Portuguese, but, like Silva Neto, in an atomistic way. He considers at last 'A Língua Literária', evaluating its divergence from standard European Portuguese as a stylistic one under the formula 'língua comum e estilos diversos'. This viewpoint, an erroneous one indeed, had been advanced earlier by Silvio Elia in *O Problema da Língua Brasileira*, who, however, rejected it in the second edition of his book.

In all these historical investigations of Brazilian Portuguese the philological biases of the researchers have somewhat distorted the true nature of the problem. There is the implicit idea that the literary language, or, what is worse, the stylistic mannerism of writers represents the standard language; on the opposite side is placed the vulgar language and its 'spurious' traits. Moreover, there is the hope of linking any Brazilian Portuguese feature to Classical Portuguese, or, on the contrary, to assert it as a quite new feature associated with an original Brazilian culture and the excellencies of ethnic mixture. In fact in the divergence between standard European Portuguese and standard Brazilian Portuguese we have to take into account a diver-

[33] Serafim Silva Neto, *Introdução ao Estudo da Língua Portuguesa no Brasil* 88 (Rio de Janeiro, 1950).
[34] See note 3.
[35] Serafim Silva Neto, *Introdução ao Estudo da Língua Portuguesa no Brasil* 177 (Rio de Janeiro, 1950).
[36] Gladstone Chaves de Melo, *A Língua do Brasil* (Rio de Janeiro, 1946).

gent structural evolution owing to geographical separation and different social milieus. Silvio Elia, for instance, overestimated the role of written literature in language in his essays on 'A Contribuição Linguística do Romantismo' and 'A Contribuição Linguistica do Modernismo' to Brazilian Portuguese.[37]

VI. DIALECTOLOGY

Brazilian dialectology has made some progress in the face of what we have inherited from the past. Brazilian scholars are now aware of the false approaches that have been taken. There is a keen perception of the urgency of accurate phonetic research and a better understanding of the techniques of field work. In the curricula of Brazilian universities, however, no place has been given until now to phonetic training and practice with informants.

Nascentes and Silva Neto have advocated the application of the techniques of linguistic geography in dialectology. The Casa de Rui Barbosa, a research department of the Ministério de Educação, sponsored these efforts. Nascentes published an outline guide for a linguistic atlas of Brazil[38] and Silva Neto planned a center of dialectology in the Museu Nacional (Centro de Estudos de Dialectologia Brasileira) that was not brought to life. He also delivered lectures on Brazilian dialectology at the Universidade de Minas Gerais (Belo Horizonte) and at the Universidade do Rio Grande do Sul (Porto Alegre). He also published a manual on linguistic geography.[39] In 1954, the Casa de Rui Barbosa invited the European dialectologist Sever Pop to conduct a course on linguistic geography in Rio de Janeiro. Pop envisaged the methods and theoretical implications of linguistic geography from the viewpoint of European Romance linguistics. In it, linguistic geography, since Gilliéron, is chiefly a diachronic discipline for Romance historical linguistics. The problem in Brazil and in America at large is, of course, different. It must be essentially a synchronic investigation. What matters is the distribution and typological classification of dialectal divergences.

Until recently things remained on theoretical ground. Now, however, we have a first concrete achievement: the Instituto Nacional do Livro, a research department of the Ministério de Educação, was the publisher of a preliminary atlas of Bahia by Nelson Rossi with the aid of a staff of researchers.[40] The research was sponsored by the Universidade da Bahia when Rossi was a member of its faculty. It includes two kinds of charts: 154 charts of basic words and phrases investigated in fifty rural localities and forty-four supplementary 'cartas-resumo' to exhibit for some special

[37] Silvio E. Elia, 'A Contribuição Linguística do Romantismo', 'A Contribuição Linguística do Modernismo', *Ensaios de Filologia*, 39-146, Rio de Janeiro, 1963.

[38] Antenor Nascentes, *Bases para a Elaboração do Atlas Linguístico do Brasil* (Rio de Janeiro, 1958).

[39] Serafim Silva Neto, *Guia para estudos dialectológicos* (Florianópolis, 1955).

[40] Nelson Rossi, *Atlas Prévio dos Falares Baianos* (Rio de Janeiro, 1963).

items the different designations in a succinct way. In the set of 154 charts, which constitutes the bulk of the atlas, the distribution of forms according to the fifty localities visited is given in phonetic transcription. This phonetic transcription, a narrow one, was adopted from the system of Armando de Lacerda, described in his journal of the phonetic laboratory in Coimbra, with the additions of Göran Hammarström in his phonetic research in Algarve,[41] but Rossi added some symbols that 'a aplicação do sistema ao português do Brasil revelou necessários' and changed the manner of marking the stress.[42] For each locality two informants are questioned, but both answers are registered only when there is a descrepancy between them. The itemization is divided under four headings: H = *Homem biológico* 'man and his life', P = *Pecuária* 'cattle-breeding', T = *Terra* 'Earth', V = *Vegetais* 'vegetation'. There are, moreover, eleven preliminary charts: a map of the state of Bahia, Brazilian linguistic areas according to the division of Antenor Nascentes, the delimitation of the 'falar baiano' according to Nascentes, the physiography of the state of Bahia, the official names of the localities visited,[43] their names according to the local usage, their old names that have been substituted in the course of time, demography and administrative status of the localities, the 'freguesias' where they are included, chief economical activities, and data about the informants.

The plan of the work thus followed the linguistic-ethnographic method of Jaberg and Jud, which Silva Neto had advocated for a linguistic atlas of Brazil. It is also on purely synchronic lines. The number of localities visited are scarce, owing to the enormous difficulties of transportation in the hinterland of Brazil, but they were very well chosen both as to their geographical distribution in the state and as to their ethnographic aspects. We can therefore consider this first tentative work of Rossi as a very commendable and auspicious achievement.

Of course, linguistic geography in Brazil cannot aim at an overall atlas of the country. We have to content ourselves with a series of local atlases conducted step by step according to available material possibilities.

It ought also to expand its aims, envisaging the statement of local phonemic patterns and the patterns of grammatical morphemes. For this the items must be chosen with a view to phonemic and morphemic description, broadening the purely ethnographic interests.

VII. PHILOLOGY

Notwithstanding the progress made in general linguistics, Portuguese linguistics, and dialectology, philology in its narrow sense continues to assert its claims to the main

[41] Armando de Lacerda e Göram Hammarström, *Transcrição Fonética do Português Normal* (Coimbra, 1953); Göran Hammarström, *Etude de Phonétique Auditive sur les parlers de l'Algarve* (Uppsala, 1953).

[42] Nelson Rossi, 'Tıanscrição Fonética', *Atlas Prévio dos Falares Baianos* (Rio de Janeiro, 1963).

[43] It is usual in Brazil to ascribe official new names to localities with old traditional names, which are stubbornly mantained in usage.

attention of Brazilian scholarship. The teaching of Portuguese in Brazilian universities is chiefly of a philological character and merges often with literary studies. The overwhelming importance of philology in Brazil is well illustrated in a book by Gladstone Chaves de Melo.[44] He advocates the study of linguistics as a precious aid to philological research and no more. It is true that in a second edition he somewhat modified this minimizing view of linguistics.

Of late Brazilian philology has given great attention to critical editions of literary works of Old and Modern Portuguese. In the past there were neither clear ideas nor sound methods in this field. The ancient editions of Brazilian writers are on the whole inaccurate and the old and classical Portuguese authors were often quoted from unreliable editions.

Silva Neto fought against that situation. He was an enthusiastic bibliophile and had his own rich collection of old Portuguese books and microfilms of old manuscripts. He envisaged, for instance, a comparative study of biblical Portuguese texts of the Middle Ages under the title of *A Biblia Medieval Portuguesa;* he published some preliminary essays on the subject. His chief philological work is, however, a critical edition of a sixteenth century book 'de devoção' by the humanist André de Rezende,[45] according to a copy extant in the Biblioteca Nacional of Rio de Janeiro. His notes and commentaries to the text constitute an impressive critical apparatus.

Much earlier, however, two scholars of a former generation had turned their attention to the philology of literary texts: the Jesuit Augusto Magne, who later became a professor of Romance philology at the Faculdade Nacional de Filosofia of the Universidade do Brasil, and Alvaro Ferdinando Sousa da Silveira.

Magne, a versatile philological researcher, faced two ambitious works, at the same time both of which he left incomplete: a dictionary of Old Portuguese[46] and a Latin Etymological dictionary.[47] He has also begun some critical editions of Old Portuguese texts. He has completed an old Portuguese text (fourteenth century) of a novel of the Round Table cycle.[48] The manuscript is in Vienna (Hofbibliotek zu Wien), and only some fragments had been published till then. Magne made a detailed study of the manuscript and added a rich glossary to the text. The text, however, is not quite reliable, because the editor indulged in some arbitrary amendments. Later, he edited a facsimile of the manuscript, with a close transcription at its side in Roman type.[49]

Sousa da Silveira, in the twenties, edited two classical texts of the sixteenth century: the eclogue *Crisfal* and the elegy of Luis de Camões *Sobolos rios*, with an impressive critical apparatus. From 1940 onwards, in charge of the Portuguese chair at the

44 Gladstone Chaves de Melo, *Iniciação á Filologia Portuguesa*[2] (Rio de Janeiro, 1957).

45 André de Rezende, *A Santa Vida e Religiosa Conversação de Frei Pedro* (Rio de Janeiro, 1947).

46 There are only two volumes, both still under the letter *A*.

47 There are four volumes from *A* to *CR*.

48 Augusto Magne, *A Demanda do Santo Graal*, 3 vols. (Rio de Janeiro, 1944).

49 It is the 1st volume of a planned new edition.

Faculdade Nacional de Filosofia of the Universidade do Brasil, until his retirement in 1954, Sousa da Silveira gave a philological emphasis to his teaching. As an indirect result he edited the critical texts of two 'autos' of Gil Vicente (beginnings of the sixteenth century)[50] and the classical tragedy *Castro* of Antonio Ferreira, of the same century.[51] He also wrote a treatise of what he called 'syntactic phonetics': a methodical survey of the external sandhi in Old and Classical Portuguese; he extracts from that survey some conclusions for a reliable critical edition of old texts[52]. The more valuable work of Sousa da Silveira is a critical edition of the writings of Casimiro de Abreu, a Brazilian romantic poet who lived in the middle of the nineteenth century.[53] His poetry is spontaneous; its meters are rather irregular; and the language borders on colloquial usage. For those reasons he is often frowned upon by literary critics. Since he died very young and the Brazilian reading public is very fond of him, his poems fell in the hands of unscrupulous publishers and there is much controversy about 'errors' of language and versification for which the poet is really responsible. Sousa da Silveira prepared a careful and thorough, revised text and in copious notes discussed Casimiro's language and meters. Those notes go beyond their overt purpose: they present an excellent evaluation of Brazilian literary language, compared to the patterns of Portugal, and they outline a general study of Portuguese versification.

This work of Sousa da Silveira focused attention on the urgent need for critical editions of the chief Brazilian writers as a prior step to the philological study of their writings. Gladstone Chaves de Melo prepared a critical edition, of the novel *Iracema* by José de Alencar.[54] The special philological importance of this text is the fact that the novel is the love story of an Indian girl, and Alencar included in it borrowing from Tupi. He intended in this way to enrich the literary language of Brazil and to give to it an indigenous flavor; moreover, he departed from the classical literary patterns and accepted many things from Brazilian colloquial usage. Chaves de Melo discussed the grammatical ideas of Alencar, who had been somewhat inconstant in his opinions, and tried to evaluate his role in the development of the Brazilian literary language.

The Instituto Nacional do Livro enthusiastically sponsored critical editions of Brazilian and Portuguese writers. There is an ambitious plan to prepare critical editions of the works of Machado de Assis, Brazil's best novelist, and Antonio Houaiss has outlined a method for doing it.[55]

[50] A. F. Sousa da Silveira, *Dois Autos de Gil Vicente* (Rio de Janeiro, 1951).

[51] *Castro* was included in a volume also including the *Auto da Alma* of Gil Vicente, *Crisfal* and *Sobolos rios:* A. F. Sousa da Silveira, *Textos Quinhentistas* (Rio de Janeiro,, 1945).

[52] A. F. Sousa da Silveira, *Fonética Sintática* (Rio de Janeiro, 1952).

[53] A. F. Sousa da Silveira, *Obras de Casimiro de Abreu*, 2 vols. (Rio de Janeiro, 1955).

[54] Gladstone Chaves de Melo, 'Introdução Notas e Apêndice: Alencar e a Língua Brasileira', *Iracema, lenda do Ceará* (Rio de Janeiro, 1948).

[55] Antonio Houaiss, 'Introdução ao texto crítico das *Memórias Póstumas de Brás Cubas* de Machado de Assis'. It is a paper read at the IV Colóquio Internacional de Estudos Luso-Brasileiros (Bahia, 1959).

The successor to Sousa da Silveira in the Portuguese chair at the Faculdade Nacional de Filosofia of the Universidade do Brasil, Celso Ferreira da Cunha, is also a philologist. He devoted his attention to the old Portuguese poets of the thirteenth and fourteenth centuries, such as Joan Zorro and Martin Codax.[56] He also dealt with the problems of medieval Portuguese meter.[57] In the same tradition Albino de Bem Veiga, of the Universidade do Rio Grande do Sul, prepared a critical edition of the *Virgeu da Consolação*, according to an old Portuguese manuscript, debated the authorship of the religious treatise, and sketched the grammar of the text.[58]

VIII. STYLISTICS

It is necessary to stress that these philological achievements did not lead Brazilian scholars to stylistics in the modern sense of the word. Machado de Assis, for instance, has been the object of an enormous mass of studies. They have been focused on his life, his personality, the covert philosophy of his writings, the plots of his novels, their characters, but very little has been said of his stylistic resources, which are subtle and varied.[59]

Linguistic stylistics is almost ignored in Brazilian scholarship. The only exception is perhaps a theoretical essay by Mattoso Câmara, who tried to place stylistics in the area of the concepts of *Kundgabe* and *Appell* of Karl Bühler.[60] Among Brazilian scholars there is the dangereous tendency to confuse style with Saussure's concept of *parole;* hence the way is barred to the development of stylistics along structural lines.

In Brazil stylistics is falsely understood, either as a counteraction to prescriptive school grammar or as the sum of psychological individual idiosyncrasies. In the first sense it was the subject of a book by Manuel Rodrigues Lapa, a Portuguese philologist who lived for some time in Brazil.[61]

IX. VERSE TECHNIQUE

The study of verse technique, on the other hand, made good progress. We have already cited the investigation by Sousa da Silveira in the critical apparatus of the *Obras de Casimiro de Abreu*. Also Manuel Bandeira, a most important contemporary Brazilian poet, has turned his attention to metrical problems in Brazilian poetry, especially in a critical edition of the works of the romantic poet Gonçalves Dias.[62]

[56] Celso Ferreira da Cunha, *O Cancioneiro de Joan Zorro* (Rio de Janeiro, 1949); Celso Ferreira da Cunha, *O Cancioneiro de Martin Codax* (Rio de Janeiro, 1956).

[57] Celso Ferreira da Cunha, *À Margem da Poética Trovadoresca* (Rio de Janeiro, 1950).

[58] Albino de Bem Veiga, *Virgeu da Consolação* (Porto Alegre, 1958).

[59] *See:* Benjamin M. Woodbridge Jr., *RomPh*, 17:2.522-3 (1963).

[60] J. Mattoso Câmara Jr., *Contribuição à Estilistica Portuguesa*², (Rio de Janeiro, 1953).

[61] Manuel Rodrigues Lapa, *Estilística da Língua Portuguesa*⁴, (Rio de Janeiro, 1965).

[62] A. Gonçalves Dias, *Obras Poéticas, organização e notas de Manuel Bandeira* (São Paulo, 1944).

We have seen that Ferreira da Cunha is a specialist in medieval Portuguese versification.

There is a very valuable essay on Portuguese verse technique by M. Cavalcanti Proença.[63] Instead of the metrical foot, Proença prefers to speak of the metrical cell.[64] He perceived very neatly the necessary link extant between rules of meter and the prosodic features of Portuguese and counteracted the tendency to see in meter a mechanical sequence of unstressed and stressed syllables apart from normal elocution and the semantic contents of the message.

It is true that he insists on the importance of a secondary accent, assuming it to be in apparently unstressed syllables in order to have in Portuguese words of more than three syllables, a series of iambs, trochees and so on; he even goes so far as to assume, like Said Ali,[65] a secondary stress in the last syllable of Portuguese proparoxytones (for instance: *balsâmicas* constituting two iambs, *balsá/micás*). But at the same time he admits: 'é possível fugir ao acento secundário'.

Like other critics of verse technique, he minimizes the role of word boundaried, stress groups, and pause; but he correctly disagrees with those who see the basis of Portuguese verse in a constant number of syllables, and he does not see any essential difference between traditional verse with a regular number of syllables and free verse. In the 'Prefácio',[66] he insists that one should not give 'preferência pela pianola em detrimento do pianista', and, asserting 'a existência de acentos secundários' as 'real e inegável' he observes, however, that the long quantity of stressed syllables before pause, which varies according to the importance of the pause, introduces in meter a very complex rhythm instead of the 'noção de tonicidade mecânica'.[67]

X. CLASSICAL PHILOLOGY

A new aspect of contemporary Brazilian linguistic studies was for a time an effort to create a classical philology based on Classical Latin. Those efforts came from Ernesto Faria, who held the chair of Latin and Roman literature in the Faculdade Nacional de Filosofia. It could be a first step toward establishing a philological study of Latin in the frame of Indo-European comparative philology. But Faria relied on the French school of latinists in the first decades of our century and did not keep pace with the more recent theories in the field of Indo-European. Moreover he had little Greek and less Sanskrit and he was, therefore, unable to fill the gap in thorough Classical philological studies in Brazilian scholarship. His best work is a treatise on Latin historical phonetics.[68]

63 M. Cavalcanti Proença, *Ritmo e Poesia* (Rio de Janeiro, 1955).
64 M. Cavalcanti Proença, *Ritmo e Poesia*, 21 (Rio de Janeiro, 1955).
65 Manuel Said Ali, *Tratado de Versificação* (Rio de Janeiro, s/d).
66 M. Cavalcanti Proença, *Ritmo e Poesia*, 6-7 (Rio de Janeiro, 1955).
67 M. Cavalcanti Proença, *Ritmo e Poesia*, 7 (Rio de Janeiro, 1955).
68 Ernesto Faria, *Fonética Histórica do Latim*[3] (Rio de Janeiro, 1957).

XI. LEXICOGRAPHY

We have seen how lexicography was fostered in Brazil from the beginnings of the nineteenth century. At present the Instituto Nacional do Livro has considered lexicography one of its more important aims. The Instituto accepted the task of publishing the continuation of an old Portuguese dictionary by Antonio Joaquim de Macedo Soares. This work[69] of the seventies and eighties of the nineteenth century was intended to be an assertion of the colloquial language of Brazil, under the slogan: 'Já é tempo dos brasileiros escreverem como se fala no Brasil, e não como se escreve em Portugal'.[70] Macedo Soares, however, had only published a 147 page volume ending with the word *candeieiro* in its rural meaning in Brazil.[71] A son of the author, the judge Julião Rangel de Macedo Soares, delivered his father's manuscript material, to the Instituto, but he failed to organize and select that material and even made obstrusive additions.[72] The Instituto also planned for some time a Brazilian encyclopedia, this project was later abandoned. Now the Instituto is favoring the edition of glossaries and partial vocabularies as a preliminary step for a more ambitious work.

A small but very commendable dictionary was edited under the responsibility of Hildebrando Lima and Gustavo Barroso, but the real editor since the second edition was the philologist Aurelio Buarque de Holanda, who worked on it as a very skilled lexicographer.[73] Recently the Academia Brasileira de Letras began at last to fulfill one of its old desiderata: the publication of a large standard dictionary of Portuguese on the lines of the Spanish dictionary of the Real Academia Española. The task was assigned to Antenor Nascentes, and the two first volumes of the work are now published.[74]

XII. FINAL REMARKS

From this exposition we can see that the current trends of linguistic studies in Brazil are somewhat outdated in the face of current linguistic trends in the United States of America and Europe. There has been technical progress in areas of study that are now of a much lesser interest than they enjoyed in the past, such as philology and lexicography. Diachronic linguistics has not expanded according to the views that

[69] Antonio Joaquim de Macedo Soares, *Dicionário Brasileiro da Língua Portuguesa, elucidário etimológico-crítico* (Rio de Janeiro, 1875).

[70] Antonio Joaquim de Macedo Soares, *Dicionário Brasileiro da Língua Portuguesa, elucidário etimológico-crítico*, 3 (Rio de Janeiro, 1875).

[71] A kind of cowboy or a kind of rural dance. In standard Portuguese the meaning is 'lamp', a derivation of *candeia* also 'lamp'. The standard phonological form is *candieiro* (/e/ changes to /i/ in hiatus before a stressed /e/); but Macedo Soares prefers a Brazilian variant with a diphthongization, though he also registers *candieiro* at its side.

[72] The work consists of three volumes (1954, 1955) ending in the word *zura*, slang for *usurario* 'miser'.

[73] *Pequeno Dicionário Brasileiro da Lingua Portuguesa*[11] (Rio de Janeiro, 1964). Now Holanda appears as the author.

[74] Academia Brasileira de Letras, *Dicionário da Língua Portuguesa, elaborado por Antenor Nascentes*, Vol. 1, A-C (Rio de Janeiro, 1961), Vol. 2, D-I (Rio de Janeiro, 1964).

structuralism has opened to it, though the approach of Silva Neto keeps pace with important contemporary European currents. Linguistic geography, in its beginnings in Brazil, is yet to be placed in the larger framework of structural dialectology.

The crucial point is the development of general linguistics, which is to change many things in a fundamental way. Linguistics is by now a basic course in the curricula of Brazilian Faculdades de Filosofia. But there are two drawbacks to its full blooming. Brazilian universities are still lacking well-trained personnel to cope with the needs of linguistic teaching and research. On the other hand, linguistics is only placed in the 'cursos de letras' as a part of the humanities. Only the Universidade de Brasilia has an independent department of linguistics. The general situation assigns a subordinate place in the curriculum to linguistics, reduces the scope of its teaching, and is bound to emphazise the old and erroneous idea of considering linguistics a handmaid of philology and literary criticism. Moreover, within that general framework, there is very little possibility of developing the new paths that have given to modern descriptive linguistics its truly scientific and rigorous character.

The study of Brazilian Portuguese, which has been and ought to be the pivotal problem of Brazilian scholarship, is strictly dependent on the solving of those crucial points.

SUPPLEMENTARY BIBLIOGRAPHY

For detailed and not necessarily selective information of the linguistic studies in Brazil since the beginnings of the nineteenth century, the following works can be consulted supplementarily:

Bechara, Evanildo, 'Manuel Said Ali Ida', *Letras*, 167-82 (Curitiba, 1956).

Mattoso Câmara Jr., J., 'Os Estudos Linguísticos Regionais', *BFR* 5.3-17 (Rio de Janeiro, 1947).

——, 'Filologia, bibliografia', *Manual de Estudos Brasileiros sob a direção de Rubens Borba de Morais e William Berrien*, 257-84 (Rio de Janeiro, 1949).

——, 'As Idéias Gramaticais de João Ribeiro', *Letras*, 22-35 (Curitiba, 1961).

——, 'Said Ali e a Língua Portuguesa', *Vozes*, 55:6.415-9 (Petrópolis, 1961).

Elia, Silvio E. 'Os estudos Filológicos no Brasil', *Ensaios de Filologia*, 157-232 (Rio de Janeiro, 1963).

Head, Brian F., 'A Survey of the Study of Dialectology and Phonetics in Portugual and Brazil', *A Comparison of the Segmental Phonology of Lisbon and Rio de Janeiro*, 269-305 (Austin, 1964).

Nascentes, Antenor, 'A Filologia no Brasil, esbôço histórico', *Estudos Filológicas*, 21-45 (Rio de Janeiro, 1939).

——, 'Instituto de Filologia', *Estudos Filológicos*, 61-9 (Rio de Janeiro, 1939).

——, 'O Colégio Pedro II e a Filologia Portuguesa', *Estudos Filológicos*, 89-96 (Rio de Janeiro, 1939).

——, 'Panorama Atual dos Estudos Filológicos no Brasil', *Estudos Filológicos*, 145-55 (Rio de Janeiro, 1939).

Silva Neto, Serafim, *Manual de Filologia Portuguesa, história, problemas e métodos*², (Rio de Janeiro, 1957).[75]

[75] Silva Neto pays little attention to Brazil, focusing essentially on the history of linguistic studies in Portugal.

PART II

LINGUISTICS OF NON-IBERO-AMERICAN LANGUAGES

INTRODUCTION

NORMAN A. McQUOWN

It is appropriate that at the moment when the First Inter-American Linguistic Institute has just been concluded at the University of Uruguay in Montevideo (January and February, 1966), thus extending to Ibero-America the tradition established in the United States of (North) America in 1928, that a survey of work in Ibero-American and Caribbean linguistics be undertaken. It is especially appropriate that current work in the areas of indigenous linguistics, and of creole linguistics, be outlined at a time when there has been a resurgence of activity in indigenous linguistics in Mexico, Central and South America, and in the study of the pidginized or creolized outcomes of language-contact situations in the Caribbean.

To establish a base-point for these studies in Ibero-America and the Caribbean, it seemed desirable to consider the indigenous languages found there by European discoverers, conquerors, and missionaries, both in their pre-Discovery period as evidenced in indigenous writing systems (Barthel) and in their post-Discovery state as found in manuscript and printed materials in Latin-based alphabetic writing introduced by Catholic missionaries (Suárez). Materials in both writing systems still constitute a challenge to present-day scholars, both linguists and non-linguists. The Maya writing system, for example, still undeciphered, is becoming the focus of increasing interest on the part of a variety of scholars, whose efforts are outlined by Barthel, and in whose activities Barthel himself has played an important part. It is to be hoped that within the next decade, a team of appropriately chosen specialists (linguist, archeologist, and culture historian, cryptologist, and computer programmer) will find it possible to work together long enough and effectively enough to yield a definitive solution to the problem and thus make available to linguist and culture historian alike the contents of the only extensive pre-Discovery written records available. Possibly even more arduous and more consuming of time and effort is the task of making maximally available in a form to permit maximal exploitation, both toward the goals of linguistics and toward those of culture history, the records in indigenous languages of the nature of indigenous culture and of its contact with the culture of the Discoverers. A critical survey of the quality of work done toward the accomplishment of this task, as well as suggestions for its improvement, are presented by Suárez. From his presentation it is amply clear that only the first steps have thus far been taken toward the full exploitation of the legacy left us by the early missionaries and their indigenous emanuenses, and that not one but a dozen teams will be required to carry out the task.

With this indirect knowledge of pre-and immediate post-Discovery indigenous languages and cultures, it will become possible to situate in historical context the results of recent work in direct contact with speakers of indigenous languages. This work is of two kinds, descriptive contemporary, and reconstructive historical. Grimes outlines for us descriptive work in recent times, Longacre summarizes the work of linguistic comparison and reconstruction, and Mayers bridges the gap between these two orientations with his programmatic discussion of current work in indigenous dialectology.

Grimes prefers to orient his discussion from the point of view of the contributions of descriptive work on Ibero-American indigenous languages toward the development of descriptive theory and techniques. Indeed, the quantity of this work in recent times, particularly during the last decade, is such that Ibero-American Indian languages have constituted a major proving ground for a developing theory and technique of linguistic description. Most of this testing has been carried out by associates of the Wycliffe Bible Translators, and the principal theories and techniques tested have been those of certain of its more active theoreticians, most notably of Kenneth L. Pike. The quantity and variety of this American Indian linguistic material, whatever its mode of presentation, constitute a major source of contrastive data for general linguistics. The chief impediment to its full exploitation is the tremendous current lag in publication. For every brief article which has appeared in a linguistics journal, there are at least a full descriptive grammar, an ample collection of spontaneously proferred indigenous text materials, and a full dictionary, all still in the files. It is urgent that the elaboration of these materials be completed and that they be made more generally available.

Longacre reviews in considerable detail a very considerable quantity of work in indigenous linguistic comparison and reconstruction which has been carried out in the past decade. In time perspective, if not in bulk nor in detail, this work now exceeds that accomplished in some established Old World linguistic families, such as Indo-European, and begins to approach the scope of as yet hypothetical constructs such as Afro-Asiatic (Hamito-Semitic). Both areally restricted families such as Macro-Otomanguean in Middle America, and geographically widespread families such as Uto-Aztecan in the Great Basin and in the Southwest in the United States, and in Mexico, have received increasing attention in recent times. The work of reconstruction has progressed from Proto-languages ancestor to small groups of relatively closely related languages (Pamean or Manguean) to ever more remote proto-languages reconstructed from these. On the basis of the reconstructed proto-lexicon, organized in semantic domains, inferences as to the cultural content referenced by such lexicon have been derived, and some glimpses of the culture of the speakers of the proto-languages have been presented (Proto-Mixtecan and Proto-Amuzgo-Mixtecan).

Comparison and reconstruction have begun to flesh out what was heretofore only a skeleton or only an unsubstantiated hypothesis of probable close relationship. It seems not unlikely that the reconstruction of linguistic history and of culture history traced with its aid may be able to forego the long period of infancy through which it has progressed in the Old World and may, in the New World, spring into full maturity in a relatively brief span. Here, as in contrastive linguistics, the principal impediment is the unavailability of most of the descriptive material collected over the last thirty years in Ibero-America and the Caribbean.

Mayers presents a program for dialect study, both in survey and in depth, not only of the linguistic varieties spoken by groups of individuals in the communities of an area, but also of the features of cultural heritage and of social organization evidenced by such individuals in such groups in such communities. His placing of studies of linguistic variation firmly in their sociocultural context poses a data-gathering task of considerable complexity for what is inevitably a team of linguist and sociocultural anthropologist and a data-processing task of such difficulty that only with computer aid will it be possible to synthesize the results of such studies and correlate the linguistic with the sociocultural findings. Needless to say, the model which he sets up is at present almost entirely programmatic, although some beginnings have been made in separate studies in Chiapas (Tzeltal-Tzotzil) in Mexico and in Guatemala (Pokomchi).

Hall's survey of recent studies of contact languages in the Caribbean completes the current picture of New World non-Ibero-American linguistics south of the Rio Grande.

It is to be hoped that the Inter-American Program in Linguistics and Language Teaching, the on-going Interamerican Linguistic Institutes (Mexico City, 1967-68, São Paulo, 1969) which it sponsors, and the effort encouraged by its Symposia (Cartagena, 1963, Bloomington, 1964, Montevideo, 1966, Mexico City, 1968, São Paulo, 1969), and by its standing committees (Theoretical and Applied Linguistics, Indigenous and Creole Languages, Ibero-American Linguistics and Dialectology, Language Teaching, Ethnolinguistics and Sociolinguistics, and Computational Linguistics) may constitute a new force which will collaborate effectively with those already functioning in the area to stimulate still greater activity in linguistic studies in Ibero-America and the Caribbean.

CLASSICAL LANGUAGES

JORGE A. SUAREZ

0.1. The absence of a clearly defined group of Indian languages to which the term 'classical' unquestionably applies is the first lacuna we meet in the literature on classical Indian languages. Nor has it been explicitly stated what characteristics, of time or others, some old period of an Indian language should have in order to qualify as classical. The term is firmly established for Nahuatl texts of chiefly the sixteenth century, but it is not universally applied to other languages. A few examples will suffice.

In the general introduction to Amerindian languages of *Les langues du monde*[1] we find only the expression 'langues de civilisation', applied to Quechua, Nahuatl, and Tupi-Guarani. But in the pertinent sections, apart from 'Aztec classique' (1058), the adjective is added only to Yucatec (1071) — somewhat hesitantly, to judge by the quotation marks enclosing it. McQuown[2] gives the name of Classical Yucatec to the language of the fifteenth century down to the middle of the seventeenth century. The cautious use of the term reappears for the Quechua of Cuzco: Trimborn[3] resorts also to including 'classical' between quotation marks, whereas Rowe[4] refers to sixteenth-century Cuzco Quechua, 'for convenience', as Classical Inca (but most of his sources belong, in fact, to the seventeenth century). On the other hand, no mention of Classical Quechua is to be found in the introduction of Rivet and de Créqui-Montfort's bibliography,[5] and when the designation appears, only once, in the complete alphabetic index, it is with reference to the paper by Rowe already mentioned. Cadogan speaks in various places[6] of Classical Guarani, meaning the Guarani of the seventeenth century, as attested by Ruiz de Montoya. For other languages in a

[1] A. Meillet and M. Cohen (ed.), *Les langues du monde*[2] 602 (Paris, 1952).

[2] Norman A. McQuown, *An Outline of (Classical) Yucatec*. To appear in the *Handbook of Middle-American Indians* (in press).

[3] Francisco de Ávila, *Dämonen und Zauber im Inkareich*, aus dem Khetschua übersetzt und eingeleitet von Dr. Hermann Trimborn. *(Quellen und Forschungen. Geschichte der Geographie und Völkerkunde*, vol. 4) 15 (Leipzig, 1938).

[4] John H. Rowe, 'Sound patterns in three Inca dialects', *IJAL* 16. 137-48 (1950).

[5] P. Rivet and G. de Créqui-Montfort, *Bibliographie des langues aymará et kičua*, 4 vols. (Paris, 1951-6).

[6] E.g. in León Cadogan, 'En torno al bilingüismo en el Paraguay', *Revista de Antropologia* 6.24 (São Paulo, 1958).

similar situation, the term 'old' is used instead of 'classical': Old Quiche[7] or Old Tupi,[8] for example.

Apparently, neither the type of available texts nor the period in which they were written are determinants, as especially a comparison between Nahuatl and Guarani may illustrate. In the case of the former, a great amount of texts, which reflect the indigenous culture, were written by, or collected from, native speakers in the sixteenth century. In the case of Guarani, most of the texts were written by Spanish missionaries and, even when they were not, all have the same Catholic content; of those texts, grammars and vocabularies are from the seventeenth century, while all the extensive texts belong to the following century.

The criteria for setting the limits, within each language, of the period to be considered classical are not always explicitly stated and, in any case, appear to vary widely. For Nahuatl and Yucatec, the designation is restricted in such a way as to cover only those texts that are freer from the influence of European culture. But in the case of Quechua the same criterion would yield only a handful of short texts of pre-Hispanic origin and perhaps an isolated work by Francisco de Ávila, belonging in the seventeenth century.[9] The extension of the term to all the literature of the seventeenth century and part of the following century appears, therefore, to depend exclusively on the use of the language as a literary medium. For Guarani, in turn, the classical period corresponds to the years of Jesuit missionary work, and comes to an end together with the end of the missions.

Notwithstanding so many dissimilarities, it is possible to discover certain common traits which some indigenous languages share, at least partially, and which show that the common designation of 'classical' may be applied to them in not as arbitrary a way as our remarks above may lead to infer. Those traits are the following: a large body of texts; the use of the language as a literary medium; the development of a literary style; a special form of the language, characteristic of the higher strata of native culture (e.g. Nahuatl); local identification (e.g. Cuzco Quechua), and freedom from heavy Spanish or Portuguese borrowing (e.g. the Guarani of the missions, contrasted for its 'purity' to that spoken elsewhere).

0.2. For want of a standard accepted list, our selection of the languages to be considered classical for the purpose of the present survey has obeyed exclusively a practical consideration: that of including only those on which some significant or systematic work has been published during the period we intend to cover; namely, Nahuatl, Yucatec, Quiche, Quechua, Tupi, and Guarani. The addition of Cakchiquel to this list is intended as an example of an undoubtedly classical language for which investigation has been so far virtually nonexistent.

[7] E.g. Johannes Friedrich, *Kurze Grammatik der alten Quiché-Sprache im Popol Vuh*. *AAWL* No. 4 (1955).

[8] E.g. A. Lemos Barbosa, *Curso de Tupi antigo*² (Rio de Janeiro, 1956).

[9] Cf. fn. 3: *Dämonen* 3 and 13.

As the point of departure for this survey we have chosen 1940, a date somewhat removed, mainly because of the relatively slow rate of production in this field; but also because around that date some important collections of texts began to appear. In addition, we have found it convenient to include as well a few significant works that were published in the late thirties.

In a field such as this, in which amateurish work is so abundant, a great part of the total production had perforce to be left out. But the line was not easy to draw consistently, because it is difficult in some cases, due precisely to the relative scarcity of contributions, to consider any one of them as completely worthless.

1.0. *Editions and textual criticism.* It is obvious that one prerequisite of linguistic study in this field is the availability of the relevant sources — not only texts, but also old grammars and vocabularies. The editorial activity so far carried out for making them accessible has not been meager, and it is precisely in the edition of texts where the total output has been greater. Though, on the whole, the rate of publication is only moderate, nevertheless it is significant that a number of collections which are or have recently been under way show both system and continuity.[10] These collections, together with other less systematic efforts, have increased considerably in recent years the number of available texts. Of course, 'availability' in this connection does not only mean that previously unpublished documents have been published, but also that texts known so far only in rare or poor versions have been re-edited in a reasonably accurate way.

As it is to be expected, not all the languages have been equally favored. Thus the number of Nahuatl texts that have been published and translated in recent years is larger than that of any other classical language, and some of them have had more than one edition. Owing to its importance, Sahagún's work has been the most favored. We may especially mention the edition by Dibble and Anderson[11] of the manuscript known as *Florentine Codex*; the partial editions of the other manuscript (the *Matritensis*) made by Schultze Jena;[12] an edition based on both manuscripts, in course of publication under the direction of Garibay;[13] and another text by Sahagún edited by Lehmann and Kutscher.[14] Some of the most important historical documents in

[10] *Corpus* (1942-); *Quellenwerke* (1938-); *Fuentes* (1958-); *ELTG* (1939-56).

[11] Bernardino de Sahagún, *Florentine Codex. General History of the Things of New Spain.* Translated from the Aztec into English, with notes and illustrations, by A. J. O. Anderson and C. E. Dibble. 9 vols. (Santa Fe, New Mexico, 1950-63).

[12] *Wahrsagerei, Himmelskunde und Kalender der alten Azteken*, aus dem aztekischen Urtext Bernardino de Sahagún's übersetzt und erläutert von Dr. Leonhard Schultze Jena. *Quellenwerke* No. 4 (1950). *Gliederung des alt-aztekischen Volks in Familie, Stand und Beruf*, aus dem aztekischen Urtext Bernardino de Sahagún's übersetzt und erläutert von Dr. Leonhard Schultze Jena. *Quellenwerke* No. 5 (1952).

[13] Miguel León-Portilla, *Ritos, sacerdotes y atavíos de los dioses. Fuentes (Informantes de Sahagún* No. 1, 1958). Ángel María Garibay K., *Veinte himnos sacros de los nahuas. Fuentes (Informantes de Sahagún* No. 2, 1958). Ángel María Garibay K., *Vida económica de Tenochtitlán I. Pochtecayotl ('Arte de traficar'). Fuentes (Informantes de Sahagún* No. 3, 1961).

[14] *Sterbende Götter und christliche Heilbotschaft.* Wechselreden indianischer Vornehmer und

Nahuatl, such as the *Historia tolteca-chichimeca*,[15] the *Códice Chimalpopoca*,[16] the *Anales de Tlatelolco*,[17] and the historical works of Chimalpahin[18] and Tezozomoc,[19] have been published in facsimile and/or paleographic versions. Other texts of significance, like the *Cantares mexicanos*, were partially edited by Schultze Jena.[20] This incomplete list[21] represents only the works of widest compass, but there have also been numerous publications of shorter documents, many of them due to the untiring activity of Garibay.[22] It is apparent, therefore, that even if there still are many unpublished texts, the Nahuatl corpus available is quite considerable.

For the Mayan languages the picture is somewhat different. The additions have

---

spanischer Glaubensapostel, 'Colloquios y doctrina christiana' des Fray Bernardino de Sahagún aus dem Jahre 1564. Spanischer und mexikanischer Text mit deutscher Übersetzung von Walter Lehmann. Aus dem Nachlass herausgegeben von Gerdt Kutscher. *Quellenwerke* No. 3 (1949).

15 *Historia Tolteca-Chichimeca.* Die mexikanische Bilderhandschrift Historia Tolteca-Chichimeca. Die Manuskripte 46-58bis der Nationalbibliothek in Paris. Übersetzt und erläutert von Konrad Theodor Preuss und Ernst Mengin. Teil I: Die Bilderschrift nebst Übersetzung, *Baessler Archiv*, Beiheft 9 (1937); Teil II: Der Kommentar, *Baessler Archiv* 21.1-66 (1938). *Historia Tolteca-Chichimeca.* Liber in lingua nahuatl manuscriptus picturisque ornatus, ut est conservatus in Bibliotheca Nationis Gallicae Parisiensi sub numeris XLVI-LVIIIbis, edidit Ernst Mengin. *Corpus* vol. 1 (1942).

16 *Die Geschichte der Königreiche von Colhuacan und Mexico.* Text mit Übersetzung von Walter Lehmann. *Quellenwerke* No. 1 (1938). *Códice Chimalpopoca. Anales de Cuauhtitlán. Leyenda de los Soles*, edición fototípica y traducción de Primo Feliciano Velázquez. Instituto de Historia, Universidad Nacional (México, 1945).

17 *Unos Anales históricos de la Nación Mexicana.* Die manuscrits mexicains Nr. 22 und 22bis der Bibliothèque Nationale de Paris übersetzt und erläutert von Ernst Mengin. Teil I: Die Handschrift nebst Übersetzung; Teil II: Der Kommentar. *Baessler Archiv* 22.67-168 (1939); 23.115-39 (1940). *Unos Annales históricos de la Nación Mexicana.* Liber in lingua nahuatl manuscriptus paucisque picturis linearibus ornatus, ut est conservatus in Bibliotheca Nationis Gallicae Parisiensi sub numero XXII. Archetypum. Ejusdem operis exemplum aetate posterius nonnullisque picturis linearibus ornatum, ut est conservatum in Bibliotheca Nationis Gallicae Parisiensi sub numero XXIIbis, edidit Ernst Mengin. *Corpus* vol. 2 (1945).

18 *'Diferentes historias originales de los reynos de Colhuacan, y México, y de otras provincias'. El autor de ellas dicho Don Domingo Chimalpahin.* Liber in lingua mexicana manuscriptus, ut est conservatus in Bibliotheca Nationis Gallicae Parisiensi sub numero LXXIV, edidit Ernst Mengin. *Corpus* 3:1-3 (1949, 1950, 1952).

Das Memorial Breve acerca de la Fundación de la Ciudad de Colhuacan, und weitere ausgewählte Teile aus den 'Diferentes Historias Originales' von Domingo de San Antón Muñon Chimalpahin Quauhtlehuanitzin. Aztekischer Text mit deutscher Übersetzung von Walter Lehmann und Gerdt Kutscher. *Quellenwerke* No. 7 (1958).

Günter Zimmermann (ed.), *Die Relationen Chimalpahin's zur Geschichte México's. Teil I: Die Zeit bis zur Conquista* 1521. *Teil II: Das Jahrhundert nach der Conquista (*1522-1615*)*. Universität Hamburg, *Abhandlungen aus dem Gebiet der Auslandskunde*, vols. 68, 69, series B: *Völkerkunde, Kulturgeschichte und Sprachen* vol. 38, 39 (Hamburg, 1963, 1965).

19 Fernando de Alvarado Tezozomoc, *Crónica Mexicayotl.* Paleografía y traducción directa del náhuatl por Adrián León. Publicación del Instituto de Historia, Primera Serie No. 10, Universidad Nacional Autónoma de México (México, 1949).

20 *Alt-Aztekische Gesänge.* Nach einer in der Biblioteca Nacional von Mexico aufbewahrten Handschrift übersetzt und erläutert von Dr. Leonhard Schultze Jena. Nach seinem Tode herausgegeben von Gerdt Kutscher. *Quellenwerke* No. 6 (1957).

21 Cf. Concepción Basilio, 'Bibliografía sobre cultura náhuatl 1950-58', *Estudios de Cultura Náhuatl* 1.125-66 (1959); 'Bibliografía sobre cultura náhuatl 1959', *ibid.* 2.209-17 (1960).

22 Cf. the bibliography in *Estudios de Cultura Náhuatl* 4.20-6 (1963).

been significant but few: the *Popol Vuh*[23] and indigenous chronicles,[24] for Quiche; the *Memorial de Tecpán Atitlán,*[25] for Cakchiquel. As it has been recently pointed out by E. Mengin,[26] the key elements for analyzing these sources, i.e. grammars and dictionaries, are for the most part still in manuscript or in unreliable editions. The gap is very great for some of the languages: as against the publication of a short *Confesionario,*[27] and of the *Memorial* already mentioned, a recent survey by Sáenz de Santa María[28] lists for Cakchiquel twelve vocabularies, five grammars, and six collections of sermons.

For Classical Quechua we have had editions of Jurado Palomino,[29] of Francisco de Ávila[30] (although some parts of his work are still unpublished[31]), of the dramas *Usca paucar,*[32] *El pobre más rico,*[33] and *Ollantay.*[34] There have also been various attempts at establishing the original text of the hymns collected by Cristóbal de Molina.[35]

[23] *Popol Vuh. Das Heilige Buch der Quiché-Indianer von Guatemala.* Nach einer wiedergefundenen alten Handschrift neu übersetzt und erläutert von Dr. Leonhard Schultze Jena. *Quellenwerke* No. 2 (1944).

[24] Adrián Recinos, *Crónicas indígenas de Guatemala* (Guatemala, 1957).

[25] *Memorial de Tecpán-Atitlán (Sololá). Historia del antiguo reino del Cakchiquel dicho de Guatemala.* Liber in lingua cakchiquel manuscriptus, ut est conservatus in Bibliotheca Musei Universitatis Pennsylvaniensis Philadelphiae sub Br. 498.21/CAr15, edidit Ernst Mengin. *Corpus* vol. 4 (1952).

[26] 'Die wichtigste Ergebnisse und Aufgaben der Maya-Sprachforschung', *AIAK XXXIV* 743-62 (1962).

[27] Ernesto Chinchilla Aguilar, 'Un confesionario del siglo XVII, escrito por Fray Antonio del Saz, O.F.M.', *Antropología e Historia de Guatemala* 11.32-9 (1959).

[28] C. Sáenz de Santa María, 'Una ojeada a la bibliografía lingüística guatemalteca', *Revista de Indias* 19:76.255-71 (1959).

[29] Bartholomaei Juradi Palomini, *Catechismus Quichuensis.* Ad fidem editionis limensis anni MDCXLVI. Edidit, latine uertit, analysi morphologica synopsi grammatica, indicibus auxit Prof. Dr. Hippolytus Galante. Hispanice e latino reddedit Eliseus B. Viejo Olero. Consejo Superior de Investigaciones Científicas, Instituto Gonzalo Fernández de Oviedo (Madrid, 1943).

[30] Francisci de Ávila, *De priscorum huaruchiriensium origine et institutis.* Ad fidem MSPTI 3169 Bibliothecae nationalis Matritensis edidit Prof. Dr. Hippolytus Galante. Consejo Superior de Investigaciones Científicas, Instituto Gonzalo Fernández de Oviedo (Madrid, 1942). See also fn. 3.

[31] Hermann Trimborn, 'Ante una nueva edición del manuscrito quechua de Francisco de Ávila', *Letras* 49.233-9 (Lima, 1953).

[32] Teodoro L. Meneses, 'El "Usca Paucar", un drama religioso en quechua del siglo XVIII', *Documenta* 2.1-178 (Lima, 1949-50).

[33] Gabriel Centeno de Osma, *El pobre más rico, comedia quechua del siglo XVI* (Texto quechua y traducción castellana con reproducción facsimilar del manuscrito. Transcripción y traducción española de J. M. B. Farfán y Humberto Suárez Álvarez). Instituto Superior de Lingüística y Filología de la Universidad Nacional Mayor de San Marcos (Lima, 1938).

[34] J. M. B. Farfán, *El drama Quechua Apu Ollantay* (Lima, 1952). Hipólito Galante, *Ollantay.* Ad fidem codicis Pastor-Justinianiensis Archiuii Nationalis Limensis recensuit latine uertit integra codicis Sahuaraurensis lectione analysi morphologica grammatica indicibus dissertationibus scholiis auxit (Lima, 1938).

[35] John H. Rowe, 'Eleven Inca prayers from the Zithuwa ritual', *The Kroeber Anthropological Society Papers* (The Walter B. Cline Memorial Volume) 8-9.82-99 (Berkeley, 1953). Lucas Guerra, 'Traducción y comentario de una de las oraciones incaicas de Cristóbal de Molina', *Revista de la Sección Arqueología de la Universidad Nacional* 3.148-67 (Cuzco, 1946). J. M. B. Farfán, 'Textos y glosario quechua, anexo a "Las curaciones por las fuerzas del espíritu en la medicina aborigen" de Juan B. Lastres', *Revista del Museo Nacional* 14.72-6, (Lima, 1945).

A facsimile reimpression of a text by Nicolás Yapuguay[36] and six volumes of the collection *Etnografia e Língua Tupi-Guaraní* containing several 'Doctrinas' and 'Catecismos'[37] are the chief contributions, in this respect, to Classical Guarani, whose most important sources are, at least, not in manuscript. More has been done in Tupi: the most extensive text, Araujo's *Catecismo* whose first edition had become rare, has been re-edited in facsimile,[38] and important vocabularies have been published[39] as well as some studies on their relations to one another.[40] Other six volumes of *Etnografia e Língua Tupi-Guaraní* are devoted to Tupi texts; the publication of those by Anchieta, here and elsewhere, has been especially in charge of M. de Paula Martins.[41]

1.1. If we consider all this work from the point of view of philological technique, its degree of achievement appears disparate. We shall comment on some of these editions only, taking each of them as representative of a group. Although we will not consider

[36] *Sermones y exemplos en lengua guaraní por Nicolás Yapuguay con direction de vn religioso de la Compañia de Iesús.* Edición facsimilar de la edición príncipe del año 1727 (Buenos Aires, 1953).

[37] *El Tesoro de la Doctrina Christiana en lengua Guaraní (Catecismos varios* I). Prólogo de Plinio Ayrosa. *ELTG* No. 24 (1952). *Doctrina Christiana por el P. Gaspar Astete, traducida en lengua guaraní por otro Padre de la misma Compañia (Catecismos varios* II*).* Prefacio de Plinio Ayrosa. *ELTG* No. 27 (1953). *Catecismo por el P. M. Gerónimo de Ripalda, traducido en Guaraní por Francisco Martínez, con cuatro tratados muy devotos (Catecismos varios* III). *ELTG* No. 29 (1954). *Catecismo mayor o Doctrina Christiana clarissima y brevissimamente explicada... por un Padre de la Compañía de Jesús (Catecismos varios* IV*). ELTG* No. 30 (1955). *Varias doctrinas en lengua guaraní, por el P. Simón Bandini, de la Compañía de Jesús (Catecismos varios* V*). ELTG* No. 31 (1956). *Compendio de la Doctrina Christiana para niños, compuesto en lengua francesa por el R. P. Francisco Pomeij. Traducido en lengua guaraní por el P. Christoval Altamirano (Catecismos varios* VI*). ELTG* No. 32 (1956).

[38] Antonio de Araujo, *Catecismo na lingua brasilica.* Reprodução fac-similar da 1ª edição (1618) com apresentação por A. Lemos Barbosa. *Biblioteca da Língua Tupi* vol. 1 (Río de Janeiro, 1952).

[39] Carlos Drumond, *Vocabulário na lingua brasilica*, 2ª edição revista e confrontada com o Ms. fg. 3144 da Biblioteca Nacional de Lisboa. *ELTG* Nos. 23, 26 (1952, 1953). Plinio Ayrosa, *Vocabulário Português-Brasilico. ELTG* No. 21 (1951).

[40] Maria de Lourdes de Paula Martins, *Notas sôbre relações verificadas entre o Diccionário Brasiliano e o Vocabulário na língua Brasilica, ELTG* No. 7 (1945); 'O Diccionário Brasileiro Português e o Ms. 11481 da Biblioteca Nacional', *Boletim bibliográfico da Biblioteca Pública Municipal de São Paulo* 6.69-83 (1946); 'Notas referentes ao Diccionário Portugês-Brasiliano e Brasiliano-Português', *ibid.* 12.121-47 (1949); 'Vocabulários Tupis. O problema do Vocabulário na Língua Brasilica', *ibid.* 13.59-93 (1949).

[41] Plinio Ayrosa, *Poemas Brasílicos do Pe Cristóvão Valente S. J. ELTG* No. 2 (1941); *Orações e dialogos da Doutrina Cristã na lingua Brasilica. Mss. do século XVIII transcritos e anotados por ... ELTG* No. 17 (1950); *Nomes dos membros do corpo humano e outros designativos na lingua Brasilica. Mss. do século XVIII transcritos e anotados* por ... *ELTG* No. 19 (1950). Maria de Lourdes de Paula Martins, 'A "Cantiga por o sem ventura" do Pe. José de Anchieta', *Revista do Arquivo Municipal de São Paulo* 72.201-14 (1940); 'Literatura Tupi do Padre Anchieta', *ibid.* 79. 281-85 (1941); *Contribuição para o estudo do teatro Tupi de Anchieta: Diálogo e Trilogia (segundo manuscritos originais do século XVI), ELTG* No. 3 (1941); *Poesias Tupis (Século XVI), ELTG* No. 6 (1945); 'Teatro Tupi. Restituição de uma peça de Anchieta', *Revista do Arquivo Municipal de São Paulo* 114.223-51 (1947); *Auto representado na festa de São Lourenço (de José de Anchieta). Peça trilingue do sec. XVI.* Museu Paulista (São Paulo, 1948); *José de Anchieta, S.J.: Poesias, ms. do sec. XVI em Português, Latim e Tupi.* Transcrição, traduções e notas da ... Museu Paulista (São Paulo, 1954).

mere reproductions of earlier editions or of manuscripts, we want at least to make special mention of the excellent ones in facsimile made by E. Mengin.[42]

In the paleographic edition of Chimalpahin, carefully prepared by Lehmann and Kutscher,[43] we find a technical description of the manuscript, detailed information on the difficulties of various readings, together with indication of interpolations, of improper linking of words, etc., and some quotations from old grammars or dictionaries, seemingly for justifying the (German) translation. As far as formal philological technique is concerned, this — as all the rest of the *Quellenwerke* — is on the whole the most satisfactory. Also of a high standard is T. Meneses's edition of *Usca paucar*,[44] based on a recently discovered manuscript. Both the original Quechua text and the established one are given, together with variants from the only manuscript formerly known, the translation into Spanish, and abundant critical notes.

In numbers 2 and 19 of *Etnografia e Lingua Tupi-Guaraní*,[45] Plinio Ayrosa does not give the text in facsimile, but only in the transcription adopted throughout the whole collection (a transcription based on an unexplained phonetic interpretation of the old texts). Number 3 of the same collection[46] is representative of the editorial practice of Paula Martins (also that of Ayrosa in number 17[47]) to offer either the facsimile or the paleographic version, followed by the transcription with corrections — the reasons for those emendations are given in notes, together with numerous, rather unsophisticated, linguistic remarks. In the two volumes edited by C. Drumond[48] it is impossible to know with certainty what parts come from one or other of the manuscripts utilized (unless we check on a previous edition by Ayrosa[49]), nor what are the 'minor' corrections introduced by the editor. Notwithstanding their many apparent shortcomings, a very positive aspect in the editions made by Ayrosa and Paula Martins is that they pay predominant attention to linguistic problems in the notes, and that they frequently bring in their support evidence from old grammars, vocabularies, and other texts.

In his edition of Francisco de Ávila[50] H. Galante gives the facsimile reproduction of the manuscript, the emended text, and the critical apparatus; but that the latter is insufficient appears clearly from a comparison of the facsimile with the emended text, in which many of the changes have been introduced without any indication at all. The editor's decision of transcribing the text in González Holguín's 'classical' orthography is a rather bold step for which no reasons are adduced: the three stop series of Classical Quechua are not distinguished in Ávila's manuscript, and this might be due to dialectal differences of which Galante seems to be entirely unaware. Even less

[42] *Cf.* fn. 10: *Corpus.*
[43] *Cf.* fn. 18: *Das Memorial Breve.*
[44] *Cf.* fn. 32.
[45] *Cf.* fn. 41: *Poemas Brasílicos* and *Nomes dos membros.*
[46] *Cf.* fn. 41: *Contribuição.*
[47] *Cf.* fn. 41: *Orações.*
[48] *Cf.* fn. 39.
[49] *Vocabulário na língua Brasílica.* Manuscrito português-tupi do século XVII coordenado e prefaciado por Plinio Ayrosa. *Coleção do Departamento de Cultura*, vol. 20 (São Paulo, 1938).
[50] *Cf.* fn. 30.

satisfactory is his edition of Jurado Palomino.[51] It reproduces the original edition of 1649 and also includes the emended text, but this time with no critical apparatus. It is necessary to compare both texts word by word in order to become aware of the changes made by the editor. In the two editions the original is translated directly into Latin, and the Spanish version made after it. It is difficult to see the reason for this; certainly not because of Latin being less removed — at least lexically — from Quechua than Spanish is.

In his edition of Sahagún[52] Garibay utilizes mainly the Madrid manuscript, with mention of the variants found in the *Florentine Codex*; but not of all of them, 'o por ser vulgares, o por ser sin importancia' (10). However the relation between both manuscripts is not agreed upon (18-9), and their respective evaluation appears not to depend on internal comparison as much as on chronological arguments. Garibay's edition of another text collected by Sahagún[53] contains detailed information on the manuscript; the notes include an account of the emendations, of the reasons that led the editor to disagree in many points with Seler's translation, and a detailed justification of the translation here presented; but the numerous corrections made upon the manuscript of its crossings-out, repetitions, wrong separation of words, and so on are only partially accounted for (14).

In his edition of *Ollantay*[54] Farfán explicitly disclaims its being a work of textual criticism, but nevertheless several variants are mentioned, and the text is a mixture of different manuscripts with emendations introduced by the editor; on the other hand, the orthography is that of modern Cuzco Quechua. T. Meneses,[55] in his fitting criticism of this edition, has pointed out that the author does not even follow, as regards the manuscripts he in fact utilizes, what he claims in the introduction. Meneses's critique concerning the exuberance of historical-literary studies, as well as translations, of the *Ollantay* at a time in which 'la etapa filológica no ha sido debidamente cumplida' (145), applies also to most Quechua sources, especially those of pre-Hispanic origin. And, to a great extent, it may serve to characterize as well the situation for other classical languages.[56]

As for the mentioned attempts at reconstructing the original text of the Quechua hymns,[57] Rowe has justly pointed out the principal weakness of his predecessors — which also applies to L. Guerra, unmentioned by him: the treatment of the language as if it had not undergone any changes, which leads to establishing the text in modern Cuzco dialect. Rowe's attempt, on the other hand, is sound in its conservative assumptions concerning the origin of the copyist's errors, the reliability of Molina's

[51] *Cf.* fn. 29.
[52] *Cf.* fn. 13: *Vida económica.*
[53] *Cf.* fn. 13: *Veinte himnos.*
[54] *Cf.* fn. 34.
[55] 'En el primer centenario de la publicación del códice dominicano del Ollantay', *Documenta* 3.141-54 (1951-55).
[56] *Cf.* Norman A. McQuown, *AmA* 62.319 (1960).
[57] *Cf.* fn. 35; see J. H. Rowe, *Eleven,* 85.

translation, and the tools for interpreting sixteenth-century Quechua. Aside from the emended text he also gives its transcription in his own phonemicization of Classical Inca[58] and his English translation. But for simplicity's sake he omits giving the critical apparatus necessary for checking on the emendations (there have been several edited versions of the manuscript, not available in facsimile), which are only sparingly explained. A similar attempt by Plinio Ayrosa to reconstruct a text in Old Tupi[59] has been the object of severe criticism by A. Lemos Barbosa:[60] his principal objection, which is undoubtedly right, refers to the fact that Ayrosa has not kept Tupi and Guarani properly differentiated in establishing the text. On the other hand, his opinion that the reconstruction of the text in question is a hopeless task is surely over-pessimistic.

1.2. It is apparent, therefore, that textual criticism has followed very different principles and criteria, and that the results have varied a great deal. The philological problems encountered are possibly never so complex as the ones found in Greek or Latin philology. Most texts are available only in one manuscript or edition, so that problems of collation are few. In spite of this, inaccuracies in, or total disregard for, currently accepted philological procedures and technique are only too common.[61] The standard format of text editions is ignored in most cases; the consequence is that the reader cannot pass judgement on them until he has remade for himself the work the editor was supposed to do. There is a tendency in some editors to obliterate the difference between a paleographic and a critical edition because, so it appears, of the notion that some kinds of mistakes (?) in the manuscript are trivial. But it is at least doubtful whether at this stage of philological work there are in fact any emendations that may be considered obvious. Sometimes this tendency is carried to an extreme, as in the case of J. Hasler's article entitled 'Paleografía',[62] in which two parallel texts — one of them otherwise still in manuscript — are given only in an unexplained modern orthography. The linguistic notes as well often fall short of accuracy but, as we shall see in the next section, this is in part due to the lack of any standard re-elaboration of old grammars, and references to them are sporadic.

The general impression one gets is that the seeming 'triviality', or directly the absence of philological problems is mainly due to cursory research, when not merely to

[58] *Cf.* fn. 4.

[59] P. Ayrosa, 'Colóquio da entrada ou chegada ao Brasil entre a gente do pais chamada Tupinambá e Tupiniquin, em lenguagem Brasílica e Francesa', in Juan de Léry, *Viagem à terra do Brasil*, tradução integral e notas de Sergio Millet (São Paulo, 1941).

[60] Estudos de Tupi. *O 'Diálogo de Léry' na restauração da Plinio Ayrosa* (Rio de Janeiro?, 1944). It is a reprint of three papers that appeared in *Revista Filológica* (Rio de Janeiro) Nos. 16, 19, 25.

[61] We have not been able to see Alfredo Barrera Vázquez and Sylvanus Griswold Morley, *The Maya Chronicles*. Carnegie Inst. of Washington, *Contributions to American Anthropology and History* 10.48-51. Pub. 585 (Washington, D.C., 1949). This seems to be, according to second-hand information, the most serious and accurate study along this line.

[62] Juan Hasler, 'Paleografía', *Archivos Nahuas* 1.303-23 (1958).

the lack of all critical apparatus: in contrast to the frequent absence, in the editions, of all references to difficulties in reading the manuscripts, as soon as philological criticism becomes more detailed in the comparison of different readings, many points of divergence immediately appear, and problems begin to emerge.[63]

As for other aspects of the philological content of these works, such as historical and bio-bibliographical ones, they are usually well covered. Yet we must regret the lack of compact manuals in which all the scattered information contained in the editions could be brought together. Much information on Nahuatl is to be found in Garibay's *Historia de la literatura náhuatl*,[64] but not systematically presented, since the fundamental purpose of the book is literary, not philological.

2.0. *Linguistic studies.* The specifically linguistic contributions have been so few, general, and diverse in their nature or subject, that it seems preferable to discuss them following an order of scope, rather than to classify them according to language or subject matter. Therefore, they will be distributed more or less consistently into full grammars, (structural) outlines, and monographic studies.

2.1. Jakob Schoembs[65] has tried to give 'eine möglichst umfassende Darstellung des Aztekischen' (7), but it is obvious that the book has fallen short of this claim. In the first place, and due to the scarcity of previous studies, a complete grammar would have had to offer detailed philological support, and this is not so in the present case. The phonemics is confusingly handled, with more concern for the orthographic practice than for its interpretation and analysis. The list of sentences (66-9), however useful for analysis it may be, with the corresponding translations, cannot be regarded seriously as a syntax; nor, in a language such as Nahuatl, can the page and a half devoted to stem composition be considered an adequate treatment of the topic. On the other hand, the rest of the morphology is extensively treated; but the description is far from clear, and neither inflection and derivation, nor free and bound forms, are kept properly distinct.[66] Especially useful is the vocabulary to the appended Book XII of Sahagún, with many cross-references to the grammar and including the bound morphemes.

In spite of its title, J. Friedrich's *Kurze Grammatik*,[67] on the contrary, is one of the most complete and detailed grammars of any of the classical languages so far available. Derivation and inflection are thoroughly treated, and in the case of verb inflection exhaustive information is given on the forms actually occurring in the *Popol Vuh* — with regard not only to inflection, but also to the underlying verb stems. The general plan of the book is not entirely satisfactory, in that it reflects a paradigmatic approach

[63] *Cf.* e.g. A. Lemos Barbosa, 'Traduções de poemas tupis', *Revista do Arquivo Municipal de São Paulo* 128.27-44 (1949); A. M. Garibay K., 'Magnum Opus', *Cuadernos Americanos* 17:98.127-38 (1958).

[64] A. M. Garibay K., *Historia de la literatura náhuatl*, 2 vols. (México, 1953-54).

[65] *Aztekische Schriftsprache* (Heidelberg, 1949).

[66] For criticism of special points see the review by Walter Krickeberg, *ZPhon* 5.358-62 (1951).

[67] *Cf.* fn. 7.

somewhat influenced by Indo-European categories. This gives rise to unnecessary complications and repetition and, in the last instance, obscures the general lines of the morphological system. But the discussion of each particular point is, in every case, thorough and clear. In the treatment of inflection and of particles, some syntactic information is implicitly contained, but except for a few sections (such as those on nominal phrases, 28-9; on the copula-like forms, 85-6; on 'absolute' verbs, 93-6; on verb sequences, 112-6), syntax is not independently handled. This omission results in some doubt as to the status of certain forms: it is not clear, for example, whether some forms which the author considers nominal (like the 'participle' in *-m*, 431, or the expression of 'superlative', 127) are in fact so rather than verbal. Phonology is cursorily treated. The section on orthography (12-5) lists with considerable detail the variant spellings, but with no clear distinction between mispellings and morphophonemic or phonological alternations. As it is explicitly admitted in the title, the only source for this grammar was the *Popol Vuh*; this may seem an arbitrary restriction, but due to the scarcity of other edited Quiche sources, it is unlikely that the author could have done otherwise. What seems unjustified is the total neglect of modern Quiche (7), notwithstanding the changes that the language may have undergone. But, on the whole, any shortcomings that this grammar may have are more than enough offset by the copious exemplification, as well as by the systematic cross-references to the text.

The *Curso de Tupi antigo*[68] has been conceived, as the title indicates, as a textbook rather than as a descriptive grammar. That the author has done so is regrettable, for several reasons. In the first place, and apart from the fact that the book is remarkably complete, detailed, and serviceably indexed, those sections in which the discussion is more purely descriptive (392-419) show beyond doubt that the author is much more linguistically sophisticated than one might infer from the rest of the book. In the second place, the introduction makes it clear that he is perfectly aware of the best way in which a grammar of Old Tupi could be philologically grounded, though he undoubtedly felt that the practical character of the book made the task unnecessary: not only does the bibliography attached to each section not conform to the philological requirements he himself set forth, but one even gains the impression (a thorough checking would mean a virtual remaking of the book) that he may have extrapolated a good deal. It is also the pedagogic nature of the book which has led Lemos Barbosa both to dismember the materials in the traditional way — which seems to offer a reasonable graduation of complexities — and to approach the language through its equivalents of Portuguese categories — which is not even justified from the didactic point of view. Finally, we may reasonably ask whether the nature of extant Tupi texts is such as to attract a number of persons so forcibly that they may want to acquire a practical knowledge of the language. Notwithstanding all this, the book is an important contribution to Tupian studies, and it would be unfair, given its acknowledged aim, to insist on defects that the author has purposely incurred. All the

[68] *Cf.* fn. 8.

more because in spite of the fact that the general plan is, as we have said, foreign to the language, the discussion of each particular point is not irreparably distorted. Yet it ought to be mentioned that inefficient treatment does not always derive from the author's pedagogic slant, but from the erroneous underlying analysis: e.g. a somewhat inconsistent orthography; also the treatment of morphophonemics, 34-42, and of the subject of predicative 'verbs', 87-9. Lemos Barbosa rightly stresses the fact that the study of Classical Tupi is fundamentally of a philological type, but, as in the case of Friedrich's Quiche grammar examined above, he is probably mistaken in wholly disregarding modern dialects.[69]

Garibay's *Llave del náhuatl*[70] is neither a full grammar nor a structural sketch, since it has been conceived as a grammatical guide to the accompanying anthology. Nevertheless, even if less complete than Schoembs's grammar, and with a more superficial treatment of orthography and phonetics, it includes a better exposition of morphology: it is concise and clear, and contains a separate section on syntax (80-113). The author outlines a division in periods of the history of the language (313-27) which, though couched in somewhat vague and impressionistic terms, is likely to offer a valuable framework for future research, backed as it is by the author's thorough familiarity with the texts.

2.2. K. Croft, in an unpublished dissertation,[71] has described, for the most part independently, Matlapa and Classical Nahuatl. The section on phonology constitutes a monograph in itself: phonemics is fully discussed in relation to orthography, to the statements by old grammarians, and to the phonology of Spanish and of the modern dialects. The system he establishes is not different from that which can be inferred from other treatments, but it is presented in standard terminology and adequately justified, with precise mention of some allophonic details and clear recognition of the dubious points. Morphology is handled more in outline form. Forms are quoted (with cross-references to the sources) both in the original orthography and in the phonemic transcription proposed by the author. Morphemes are classed by position — this aspect being usually neglected in the description of Classical Nahuatl – and their allomorphs listed. Although the observed morpheme sequences are given in detail, this section is somewhat loosely constructed, and there is no clear reference as to which morphemes are inflectional and which are derivational. The major shortcoming of Croft's analysis is that it is based on a too limited corpus: among the grammars only Olmos and Molina — which are the less specific for certain phonemic points — were taken into consideration, together with the dictionary by the latter.

[69] The reader should be warned, because of the misleading title, that Adaucto Fernandes, *Gramática tupi, histórica, comparada e expositiva*[2] (Rio de Janeiro, 1960) is totally devoid of any merits whatever.
[70] A. M. Garibay K., *Llave del náhuatl*[2]. Colección de trozos clásicos, con gramática y vocabulario, para utilidad de los principiantes (México, 1961). The grammar occupies pp. 19-118.
[71] Kenneth Croft, *Matlapa and Classical Nahuatl: with comparative notes on the two dialects.* Univ. Microfilms Publ. 5858 (Michigan, 1953).

N. McQuown, in his structural sketch of Classical Yucatec,[72] avails himself of the little change undergone by Yucatec, which allows him to deal simultaneously with both the classical and the modern dialect. The language is described under the headings of Phonology and Morphology. Morphophonemic variations are described under the corresponding morphemes. Syntax is not treated independently, but syntactic information is given in the course of the discussion of morphology. (In the particular case of the 'verbal complex', the limit between morphology and syntax is not trenchant, and clitics are classified along with affixes according to their positions around the verbal core.) The phonological system here established is the same for both the classical and the modern stage, and, in the case of the former, is correlated with the orthography of the missionaries (which was under-differentiated). Special sections are devoted to allophones, to phonemic distribution, and to (high and low) tone sequences, the latter mostly intended as a frame of reference for further investigation. Very much detailed is the treatment of phonemic shapes of morphemes. These are classified morphologically into verbs, nouns, and particles, with syntactic subclassification of the latter. Derivation is covered under each morpheme class, and more extensively than is usual in sketches. All mentions of classical forms are referred to the Motul dictionary, and the exemplification is abundant. The wording is terse, with a straightforward presentation that allows for the inclusion of plenty of material notwithstanding the relative brevity of the outline. One only misses some information about sentence types — a fact which gives rise to some doubts as to the use of certain forms.

The outline of Quechua grammar which Galante included in his edition of Jurado Palomino[73] has escaped the risk of forcing the language into foreign molds only at the expense of depriving it almost completely of structure. Fundamentally he presents a list of suffixes, among which only those expressing 'person' offer a glimpse of organization. There is some report on canonical shapes, but they depend on a highly suspicious analysis of roots and stems.

2.3. Dávila Garibi has produced a book on Nahuatl orthography[74] which is informative in many respects, and contains some judicious remarks. But it is more an external account of the changes in graphic representation than of the underlying phonological problems. This approach results in a rather casual interpretation of the statements in old grammars. Besides, the book is not well planned.[75] Elsewhere[76] the

[72] *Cf.* fn. 2.

[73] *Cf.* fn. 29: *op.cit.* 447-73. It is fundamentally the same as that included in his edition of *Ollantay* (Lima, 1938), which has been reissued in Spanish translation: *Gramática quechua (del Ollantay)*, traducida del latín por Fernando Tola y Santiago Erik Antúnez de Mayola; 2ª ed. ampliada y corregida por Teodoro L. Meneses. Publicaciones del Inst. de Filología de la Fac. de Letras de la Univ. Nac. Mayor de San Marcos, *Gramática* No. 1 (Lima, 1959).

[74] J. Ignacio Dávila Garibi, *La escritura del idioma náhuatl a través de los siglos* (México, 1948).

[75] The useful data have been summarized by Croft in his review, *IJAL* 16.103-6 (1950).

[76] J. I. Dávila Garibi, 'Clasificación del verbo náhuatl en grupos afines', *Estudios de Cultura Náhuatl* 4.61-72 (1963).

author has attempted to classify Nahuatl verbs according to the ways in which they form the past tense, but the attempt is not successful because of its exclusive dependence on the orthography. Also several of the subclasses of 'irregular' verbs should be eliminated.

In Classical Nahuatl, stress has been usually assumed to fall on the penultimate syllable of the word, except for certain forms like the vocative. Starting from certain statements in Schoembs's grammar, and with the support of Rincón's grammar and, above all, of a minimal pair found in Molina, W. Barrett[77] has assumed instead a free accent and suggested the possibility of multiple stress in a word. The principal merit of this paper is to have called attention to the problem; its originality lies in the hypothesis of multiple-stressed words. For the rest, and even though his discussion of Nahuatl stress as a whole hardly makes sense,[78] Schoembs had already assembled several minimal pairs differentiated by stress.[79] The problem was re-examined by W. Bright.[80] In his article Rincón's and Carochi's systems of accents are carefully analyzed (with quotation and interpretation of the pertinent passages), and found in agreement with each other. From this the author infers that stresses and pitches were always associated, inside the word, with differences in quantity, whereas the latter seems to be the same as in modern dialects. Bright's conclusion is that only quantity is likely to have been phonemic in Classical Nahuatl, stress and pitch having been subordinated to it. The association of stress with the penultimate syllable would have been a later development. This paper organizes into a coherent system the statements and examples of early grammarians, but at the same time it leaves some questions unanswered: (1) The possibility of dialect differences: in view of the otherwise almost phonemic character of the missionaries' orthography and of the lack of phonemic quantity in some modern dialects, it has been suggested that the absence of phonemic quantity can also be considered possible in Classical Nahuatl;[81] (2) the way in which this analysis affects the picture of Nahuatl metrics, since Garibay has already advanced an interpretation in terms of penultimate stress which would seem to have some consistency;[82] (3) whether there is a relation between the differences in pitch associated with quantity and the contrasts found by Whorf in the dialect of Milpa Alta.[83]

On the basis of statements by early grammarians, of fluctuations in the orthography,

[77] Westbrook Barrett, 'The phonemic interpretation of "Accent" in Father Rincón's "Arte Mexicana"', *GL* 2.22-8 (1956).
[78] *Cf.* fn. 65: *op.cit.* 18.
[79] *Cf.* fn. 65: *op.cit.* 71.
[80] William Bright, '"Accent" in Classical Aztec', *IJAL* 26.66-8 (1960).
[81] Richard S. Pittman, 'The phonemes of Tetelcingo (Morelos) Nahuatl', in *A William Cameron Townsend* 643 fn. 3 (México, 1961). On the other hand, Croft's sources do not indicate quantity, and he knows of the existence of Nahuatl dialects with no phonemic quantity; but he assumes this for Classical Nahuatl on the grounds of its occurring in dialects in and around the Valley of Mexico; *cf.* fn. 71: *op.cit.* 14.
[82] *Cf.* fn. 64: *op.cit.* 1.60-4.
[83] Benjamin L. Whorf, 'The Milpa Alta dialect of Aztec, with notes on the Classical and the Tepoztlan dialects', in Harry Hoijer (ed.), *Linguistic structures of Native America* 369-70 (New York, 1946).

of the testimony of modern dialects, and, recently, of comparative evidence,[84] it has been generally assumed that Classical Nahuatl had a vowel system /i e a o/, with [o], [u] as allophones of /o/. Croft suggested in his sketch[85] the possibility of complementary distribution (though the passages in Olmos and Molina he quotes would rather point to free variation[86]), and Schoembs,[87] even if not within a clearly phonological framework, assumed the existence of a high *o*, represented by either ⟨o⟩ or ⟨u⟩, and a low *o* represented nearly always by ⟨o⟩. This is Seiler and Zimmermann's point of departure in their study of the ⟨o, u⟩ fluctuation.[88] In order to ensure dialectal uniformity they restrict their sources to Molina's dictionary, which is known to have been composed on the basis of only one informant. They assume, in the first place, that Molina heard the Nahuatl sounds consistently in terms of his own Spanish phonemic system, and that the ⟨o, u⟩ fluctuation represents [ʊ], while ⟨o⟩ represents [o]. They then look for the basis of complementation, and find it in the structure of the syllable: the higher allophone would have occurred in checked syllables, and the lower allophone elsewhere. But this interpretation is dependent on the previous acceptance of the authors' characterization of checked syllables in Classical Nahuatl: not only CVC, but also C_1VC_2V where C_2 is a continuant; among the continuants, /č/, /λ/ and, presumably, /c/ are classified. They also consider that the type of consonant C_1 is, is relevant to the definition of the checked syllable. The impression we get from all this is that if some sort of complementation existed, it was more in terms of preceding and following consonants than in terms of a suspicious 'checked syllable'. Quite apart from the main argument of the paper, the authors make some remarks on the correlation they assume between type of morpheme and [o] vs. [u] quality. But these remarks are not always easy to reconcile with the hypothesis of the checked syllable: e.g. the observation that the passive prefix /no/ is [no-], since such a prefix will surely occur attached to stems beginning with /č/. The authors also mention the fact that some other sources present ⟨o⟩ in every case, but this problem is left for further treatment. Finally they call attention to other pending problems of Nahuatl phonology, such as the 'saltillo' and the fluctuation between ⟨i⟩ and ⟨e⟩, ⟨e⟩ and ⟨a⟩. Independently of the degree of conviction the authors' interpretation may carry, this paper, based on a painstaking examination of the sources, is a careful study presenting explicit assumptions and a full discussion of the problems involved.

G. Zimmermann has also contributed to the field with a study on stylistics.[89] It is a

[84] C. F. and F. M. Voegelin, and Kenneth L. Hale, *Typological and Comparative Grammar of Uto-Aztecan: I (Phonology)* 36. Indiana University Publications in Anthropology and Linguistics. Memoir 17 of the *IJAL* (Baltimore, 1962).

[85] *Cf.* fn. 71: *op.cit.* 10.

[86] *Cf.* fn. 71: *op.cit.* 19.

[87] *Cf.* fn. 65: *op.cit.* 14.

[88] Hansjakob Seiler and Günter Zimmermann, 'Studies in the phonology and morphology of Classical Nahuatl: I. Orthographic variation o/u; its phonological and morphological implications', *IJAL* 28.243-50 (1962).

[89] Günter Zimmermann, 'Über einige stereotype Wendungen und Metaphern im Redestil des Aztekischen', *Baessler Archiv* N.F. 3.149-68 (1955).

general setting of the problems of Nahuatl style, focussing on the materials furnished by Sahagún's Book VI. The author states that in speeches we find the intensification of procedures also found in other types of texts — such as metaphors, twin-forms, fixed formulas, as well as some grammatical features: use of the vocative and of special forms of honorifics. He notes the sporadic use of rhetorical 'self-abasement', and suggests that its introduction was due to Spanish influence. Finally he studies the greeting formulas, and for some of them he establishes their precise meaning through observing their uses in the texts. (This paper continues, after a long interval, previous studies by Hölker that fall outside the scope of the present survey.[90])

As for Maya, it is worth mentioning Knorozov's hypothesis[91] that hieroglyphic Maya differs considerably from the classical dialect. Naturally this claim depends on the success of his decipherment, whose evaluation corresponds to a different section of this volume.

So far the only significant study of Classical Quechua has been Rowe's paper on the phonemic system.[92] His sources for the reconstruction are the statements by old grammarians, combined with the internal examination of their orthography, and the phonemic systems of modern Cuzco and Ayacucho Quechua. The system he finally establishes for Classical Quechua agrees in the number and kinds of contrasts with the modern Cuzco dialect, but with the Ayacucho dialect only in certain allophonic details. Two fricatives, represented by ⟨ç, z⟩ and ⟨s,ss⟩ respectively, are assumed, tentatively, on the basis of some consistency in González Holguín's orthography and agreements with the same words in Ecuadorian Quechua. But the author leaves the point as hypothetical, pending further comparative work which may also throw more light on the exact nature of the phonetic content of the fricatives (there is an explicit testimony that Cuzco Quechua had no equivalent for the Spanish ⟨x⟩, i.e. [š]). Rowe purposely dismisses the first Quechua grammar, written by Domingo de Santo Tomás, on the suspicion that it did not reflect Cuzco Quechua. This turns on the problem of dialectal variation, to which only slight consideration has so far been given. In commenting above (§ 1.1) on Galante's edition we mentioned the fact that Ávila's manuscript does not differentiate more than one series among the stops: on the basis of biographical data and of the occurrence in that text of certain nonclassical linguistic forms, Trimborn has suggested[93] that it reflects the dialect referred to by old grammarians as Chinchasuyu. In a later work, on the other hand, Ávila not only used the classical orthography, but also made statements that show he was aware of more than

[90] Georg Hölker, 'Dvandvaähnliche Wortkuppelungen im Aztekischen', *Wiener Beiträge zur Kulturgeschichte und Linguistik* 1.349-58 (1930); 'Einige Metaphern im Aztekischen des P. Sahagúns', *Anthropos* 27.249-59 (1932).

[91] Y. V. Knorozov, 'La lengua de los textos jeroglíficos mayas', *Actas del 33 Congreso Internacional de Americanistas* 2.573-9 (San José, Costa Rica, 1959).

[92] *Cf.* fn. 4.

[93] *Cf.* fn. 3: *op.cit.* 15-6; also 'El manuscrito quichua inédito de Francisco de Ávila', *Actas del* 27 *Congreso Internacional de Americanistas* 1.223-5 (Lima and México, 1939).

one stop series[94] (and Rowe uses this work among his sources for Classical Quechua). Rowe also advances the rather bold hypothesis — given the time elapsed and the differences that the dialects show at present — that modern Quechua dialects do not continue the dialectal differentiation of pre-Inca times, but that they stem from a kind of 'koiné' based on Classical Cuzco Quechua. (On the other hand, there have been no attempts to establish the relation between the divergences called dialectal in the old sources and the modern dialects, nor between these and the old 'nonclassical' features.)

Comparatively, monographic studies in the field of Tupi-Guarani have been quite numerous. Aryón Dall'Igna Rodrigues has devoted separate papers to studying several aspects of Old Tupi morphology: composition, reduplication, voice.[95] He has also studied the phonology, but has so far only published the phonemic chart.[96]

Lemos Barbosa has described the system of demonstratives,[97] which he finds may be classified according to the categories of proximity and visibility. He has concerned himself too with one problem of Tupi-Guarani morphology which has attracted disproportionate attention: the alternation of initial consonants in noun stems, as shown e.g. by ⟨tape⟩ 'road', ⟨xe rape⟩ 'my road', ⟨sape⟩ 'his road'.[98] Some of the entries in the *Vocabulário na língua brasílica* give him cause for the assumption that the initial consonant was a class prefix, dividing nouns into a 'superior' and an 'inferior' class. The original paper has not been available to us, but judging from his discussion of this problem in his *Curso de Tupi antigo*[99] we must conclude that his argument does not carry enough conviction. The same facts have been studied by Ayrosa.[100] Due to his diffuse style, and to the amount of irrelevant digressions, it is difficult to see clearly which points he wants to prove. But it seems that his interpretation is that of ⟨t-⟩ as a determinative, and of ⟨r-, s-⟩ as indicating the noun is possessed. It must be pointed out that it is very questionable whether these alternations can be accurately analyzed other than as morphophonemic variations, and that any reconstruction of a former morphological status should better await the results of comparative work, in view of the parallel complex alternations of other Tupian languages.[101]

In the same paper Ayrosa also touches upon another trite point of Tupian grammar, to which F. Edelweiss has devoted a whole monograph:[102] the fact that the same set of

94 *Cf.* fn. 3: *op.cit.* 16.

95 Aryón Dall'Igna Rodrigues, 'A categoria da voz em Tupi', *Logos* (Curitiba) 2:6.50-3 (1947); 'A composição em Tupi', *ibid.* 6:14.63-70 (1951); 'Analise morfológica de um texto tupi', *ibid.* 7:15.55-7 (1952); 'Morfologia do verbo tupi', *Letras* (Curitiba) 1.121-52 (1953). These papers have not been available to me.

96 Wanda Hanke, Morris Swadesh and Aryón Dal'Igna Rodrigues, 'Notas de fonología mekens', *Miscellanea Paul Rivet Octogenaria Dicata* 2.187-217 (México, 1958).

97 A. Lemos Barbosa, 'Nova categoria gramatical tupi', *Verbum* (Rio de Janeiro) 4:2.67-74 (1947).

98 A. Lemos Barbosa, 'Os índices de classe no tupi', *O Estado de São Paulo* (25-VIII-40).

99 *Cf.* fn. 8: *op.cit.* 105-14, 294-301.

100 *Dos índices de relação determinativa de posse no tupi-guarani. ELTG* No. 1 (1939).

101 *Cf.* Perry N. and Anne M. Priest, and Joseph E. Grimes, 'Simultaneous orderings in Siriono (Guarani)', *IJAL* 27.335-44 (1961).

102 Frederico G. Edelweiss, *O caráter da segunda conjugação tupi* (Bahía, 1958).

prefixes express, according to the class of the following stem, possession, subject, or object. The unawareness of both authors of the widespread character of this phenomenon, added to a total incomprehension of the difference between unstressed prefixes and stressed pronouns, prevent them from making in their respective studies any positive contribution to the description of these facts — and even give to both their papers an amateurish touch. In fact, the real problem here involved — namely, the attributive or predicative function of some nominal (?) stems, sometimes coupled with variations in the stem and, probably, with double stem affiliation — is left not only unsolved but not even well posed. Although the treatment is also unsatisfactory, this problem can be better understood in the exposition made by Lemos Barbosa in his book.[103] The monograph on the particle ⟨haba⟩, by C. Drumond,[104] also exhibits an extremely elementary linguistic technique, but it may be useful as a collection of examples.

In spite of the fact that phonology is the aspect of classical languages of which we at present have a clearer picture, there are still many dubious points of phonemic and phonetic detail. Obviously all the information that may be derived from the study of sixteenth-century Spanish or Portuguese is very helpful for the solution of those points, and many of the papers we have surveyed have profited from that information (usually Canfield and Menéndez Pidal). But for some years past a great many studies have been made, especially on the phonemic system of Spanish, which have modified in several ways the views formerly held on these matters. Yet none of the recent knowledge has so far contributed to the study of classical languages — nor, for that matter, to the study of any other Indian language, since the same problems obviously prevail in the interpretation of all the missionaries' grammars of the sixteenth and seventeenth centuries. Authors have continued to avail themselves of the works of Canfield, Menéndez Pidal, and others which, in this aspect, have become outdated.

2.4. Notwithstanding their reduced number and their various shortcomings, we believe that the works we have just mentioned can, as a whole, be considered signs of a renewal of interest in the linguistic study of classical languages. The majority were published after 1950, and the philological and linguistic technique of some of them is sound enough. The extent of their significance cannot be wholly appreciated unless we bear in mind that we must go as far back as 1921 (Tozzer) for Yucatec, 1884 (Tschudi) for Quechua, or 1876 (Almeida Nogueira) for Tupi-Guarani to find works of real importance for the points covered by them.

3. *Dictionaries.* The most important contribution in this field, which has been scarcely explored, has been the vocabulary inserted by Schultze Jena in his edition of the *Popol Vuh.*[105] In the first place, because the old vocabularies for Quiche are still in manu-

[103] *Cf.* fn. 8: *op.cit.* 144-5.
[104] *Da particula hába do tupi-guarani. ELTG* No. 12 (1946).
[105] *Cf.* fn. 23.

script. But also, what is more important, because the entries include the original spelling with the variants found in the manuscript, the editor's phonetic transcription, cross-references to the text and to some other manuscripts used by the author, and grammatical comments. Schultze Jena has also included glossaries in his other editions.[106]

H. Galante's above mentioned books[107] contain full Quechua glossaries. Their merits are not lexicographic, since only the most general meaning of each entry is given, but lie in the fact that for each root or stem several derived or inflected forms are presented, with cross-references to the text; in this sense they constitute a very useful tool for grammatical and lexical research.

Some other lexicons are also useful, but of reduced scope. E.g. a list of specific domains by Farfán,[108] or the philosophical vocabulary assembled by León-Portilla.[109] The paper by Porras Barrenechea[110] is general, and rather rash in drawing conclusions, but in it the author rightly insists on the necessity of studying more closely the first lexicons for the sake of their cultural content.

L. Cadogan has dealt specifically[111] with the problem of important Guarani words which are buried in the entries of Ruiz de Montoya's *Tesoro*, and has shown the necessity of re-elaborating that dictionary. It is a very apposite paper, as it clearly illustrates the inconveniencies of ancient dictionaries in general (Zimmermann[112] mentions similar difficulties in Molina's dictionary), and its plea could be applied to all the classical languages.

4. *Conclusion.* It may be observed that studies on Tupi-Guarani, as well as all the philological work in this field, are in general more linguistically slanted — whatever their quality — than in the other classical languages. We do not believe this to be casual. Due to the nature and subject-matter characteristics of extant Old Tupi and Guarani texts, it would indeed be difficult to see how they could awake other than a linguistic interest. On the other hand, it is only natural that Nahuatl and Maya texts have attracted attention by their cultural contents, and only in an indirect way by their linguistic aspects. As a result, and in spite of the fact that certainly many more people are able to handle a classical text in Maya or Nahuatl than in Tupi, the total output of linguistic studies is comparatively more reduced in the former than in the latter.

The survey by E. Mengin[113] may be taken to a great extent as illustrative of this

[106] *Cf.* fns. 12 and 20.

[107] *Cf.* fns. 29, 30, and 34.

[108] J. M. B. Farfán, 'Glosario patológico quechua de la "Crónica" de Guaman Poma y un breve vocabulario patológico quechua', *Revista del Museo Nacional* 10.157-64 (Lima, 1941).

[109] Miguel León-Portilla, 'Breve vocabulario filosófico náhuatl', in *La filosofía náhuatl estudiada en sus fuentes*[2] 325-45 (México, 1959).

[110] Raúl Porras Barrenechea, 'El primer vocabulario quechua', *Letras* 49.217-28 (Lima, 1953).

[111] León Cadogan, 'Registro de algunas voces internas del Tesoro de la Lengua Guaraní del P. Antonio Ruiz de Montoya', *BFS* 41:8 (*TILAS* 3) 517-32 (1963).

[112] *Cf.* fn. 89.

[113] *Cf.* fn. 26.

state of affairs: it is manifest that all the emphasis is placed on editions with TRANSLATIONS whereas, although listed in the bibliography, no special mention is made of Friedrich's grammar, which is undoubtedly the most important linguistic contribution to Quiche. Clearly, the best delineated trend so far in the study of classical languages has been translation, and, in keeping with it, there is also the tendency to write grammatical outlines chiefly as a practical guide for reading classical texts. Of course, every translation presupposes a certain linguistic analysis of the original text — and in this respect they are also useful. But the linguistic knowledge they require remains implicit and, to a great extent, noncumulative. Exceptions are Schultze Jena's already mentioned glossary of the *Popol Vuh* and the one appended to his edition of the *Cantares Mexicanos*, where the entries contain all the forms actually occurring in the text, with hyphens marking the boundaries between the component elements.

This situation is not surprising. Linguists working in Indian languages are for the most part chiefly interested in living languages, whereas scholars interested in the classical languages usually have interests other than merely linguistic ones. Nevertheless, the dates of some of the works we have commented on show signs — at least for some of the languages — of an increasing activity of mainly linguistic orientation. Within this activity, research tends — logically, we think — either to descriptive outlines or to the treatment of specific grammatical points (and, surprisingly enough, it is in these papers that the results tend to be better supported philologically than for the rest); an important consequence is that, in some cases, specific problems have begun to take shape. But the points that still need treatment of this sort are so numerous, for each and every language, that it would be useless to attempt their enumeration.

On the whole, we believe the philological aspect is still the weakest: not only because of the shortcomings of most editions, but also because in most works of strictly linguistic nature there is no systematic use of concrete data — from old grammars, texts, or vocabularies — in support of arguments and conclusions. Translations are seldom philologically justified, and the general procedure is to present side by side text and version, with no other comments than those based on the translator's familiarity with the classical language. As for the most advanced and refined stage of philological work, namely the truly critical edition, we believe it would mean, in the present circumstances, a veritable tour de force on the part of some one individual.

If the term 'classical' is taken in its full implication and if, consequently, research in the Old World classical languages is taken as the standard point of reference, it is obvious that what has been done so far in indigenous languages is not much more than preliminaries. There seems to be a long way ahead before we can have standard reference grammars, philological guides, dictionaries with Authorities, and good critical editions.

There are still other aims to pursue. It is obvious that these languages have a privileged position among Indian languages in that they present multiple problems, some of which can at present be but enumerated: the emergence of a written language, its relations with the spoken language and with later dialects, its adaptation to the needs of expressing a different cultural content, the influence of a foreign literary language, the comparison of texts written by native speakers to those written by Europeans, and the control of old descriptions that those texts afford. The solutions to these problems go far beyond the linguistic interest for each particular language, and may represent a significant contribution to general linguistics.

WRITING SYSTEMS

THOMAS S. BARTHEL

None of the native writing systems in the New World has reached the stage of a 'complete writing system' capable of fully mirroring a language. We are dealing with all levels of 'partial writing systems', that is to say, with incomplete systems which attempted in various ways to graphically set down segments of a richer oral transmission. This is the reason for its weakness as compared to the fully developed writing systems of the Old World and the reason for an absolute limitation of knowledge in this field of research, but at the same time it stimulates the task of analytically grasping the early phases and stages in the development of complete writing systems.

This presentation of the current status of research is within the geographic framework of this volume. Thus we are *not* discussing the primitive writing systems of the North American Indians (although they definitely belong to the great process of development of writing systems in the New World), although, on the other hand, we refer to Chile's Easter Island with its inscribed tablets (in spite of the fact that these relics are undoubtedly Polynesian). Our resumé starts with the South American pieces of evidence, moves on to the Mexican material and finally reaches its climax as to extent and intensity of coverage with the Maya hieroglyphs. The deciphering of these hieroglyphs is currently provoking vehement differences of opinion. For all details and further questions please refer to the bibiography. The period covered by this paper is not narrowly restricted in time, but does, however, concentrate mainly on the last 20 years.

I

There is no proof today as to whether or not any partial writing systems existed in the pre-Colombian Andes. The use of knotted strings (Quipus) other than in a mathematical-statistical context has not been attested by concrete pieces of evidence. Nevertheless, a minimum of objective information could be established by the different colors of the strings and special shapes of the knots. The mnemonic principle of such knotted strings is an almost insurmountable barrier for the comprehension of quipus discovered in archeological findings. Only in such cases where astronomical measurements (cycles and calendar units) are to be ascertained can an objective statement be made as to the intended meanings.

Larco Hoyle's suggestion that the Mochicas had an ideographic system has not evoked a positive response. The depictions of beans with extremely varied markings, especially on ceramics but also found on textiles, should be understood rather as gambling counters (analogous to the use by recent Chaco tribes). The interpretation of the rich iconography of ancient Peruvian vessels and textiles or of elaborate stone reliefs can be taken as a legitimate task of Peruvian Studies, but is not within the range of tasks involved in the research on a writing system. The possible hints at older pictographic documents (Cristoval de Molina, Sarmiento de Gamboa) also belong to such studies. The question remains unanswered as to the value of Montesino's report about a pre-Inca writing. Several investigators have postulated possible (genetic?) relationships with the Easter Island writing system, since in both cases it has been reported that banana leaves were used as writing material. Inasmuch as not a single piece of evidence of the 'Montesino writing system' is available, it seems to us that a precept of the most elementary prudence is not to argue *e silento*.

The fact that pictographic representations of Christian-religious texts existed in the southern area of the Andes has been known at least since von Tschudi. But it was not until the modern investigations had been made, especially by Ibarra Grasso, to whom we are indebted for the standard work on such material, that it became evident that this is a problem of interest in the field of writing theory. From a formal point of view, the documents produced by the Aymara and Quechua indians constitute a pictography: the signs are not standardized, they differ per se and from place to place, they resemble certain rock pictures in their realistic configuration, and their inventory can be expanded at any time by random ad-hoc ingenuity. The writing material went through a certain development; for one thing, animal skins painted with the juices of plants or mineral pigments gave way to paper; for another thing, the grouping of clay figurines (human figures or objects) on a stationary disc gave rise, as it were, to a three-dimensional means of communication. Their purpose is a mnemonic device for illiterates and consists of catholic prayers (the Lord's Prayer, catechism, etc.). Now that the proper sounds of the words of the appertaining Indian language have been established, it is possible to determine the precise function of the seemingly equivalent 'pictograms'. Thus it turns out that we are dealing with a 'mixed system': the majority of the pictograms are naturalistic reproductions of persons (also scenes, gestures) and objects, that is to say 'picture-writing' in the literal sense of the word. Elliptical spellings (pars-pro-toto method) are not found. A second group of signs comprises symbols, that is, it makes use of ideographic means of expression. The great surprise, however, is that about 20% of them operate according to a rebus procedure. Homophones are used as well as puns, with the latter allowing quite some latitude in the similarity of the sounds. Not only entire words but also parts of words can be transcribed 'quasi-phonetically' in this manner. In other words: what outwardly appears to be merely a pictography contains the multiple ways of expression used in a partial writing system! There is not always a one-to-one correspondence between a sign and a word and there are even instances in which considerably fewer signs occur than the actual words of the prayer being depicted. This is a case, then, of text condensation with the aid of cues; here the mnemonic goal is especially obvious. Now the question is whether we are dealing with an invention of the colonial period (possibly because of missionaries working with an illiterate people), or whether it is to be accepted that we are dealing with pre-Columbian roots ('Andean Proto-Writing'). The second possibility is not to be ruled out entirely, since the direction in which such texts are read (various types of boustrophedon or in a spiral reading inwards) are suggestive not of European models but rather of Amerindian creations. It is conceivable that a pan-American 'pictographic horizon' extended from Bolivia to North America.

The so-called 'Cuna Writing' could also belong to this category. Its thorough investigation is an accomplishment of the 'Göteborg School' which — following the pioneering analyses of Nordenskjöld — in close cooperation with Cuna informants collected and worked out detailed pictographs with their matching songs. The outward appearance of a picture-writing, which gets additional properties through the use of colors and which obviously follows autochthonous Indian patterns in its utilization of boustrophedon types, leads here also to an underestimation of the basic communication system. As a matter of fact, two principles can be seen at work: the simpler type is strictly pictographic, that is to say, it depicts in imagery the situation which is described in detail in the song. The more developed type (which at present seems to be on the decline) attempts to fix separate words or even parts of words. To do this, the entire range of rebus techniques (homophony, homeophony, a partial sound allusion, especially for the initial syllables) is used. Pictograms can be used ambiguously. Combined forms usually are used to express longer textual statements. There are instances of hybrid systems, when, for example, a pure pictorial element is coupled with a form which is functioning as an indicator of an initial sound. Contrary to the example of the Andean pictographs, the topic matter is autochthonous (songs and prayers of the medicine men in their healing rites and other rituals). Although there is no standardized inventory of obligatory forms, still in all, the differences between the forms used by the various 'schools' is not insurmountable. The function is based upon the mnemonic role of fixing long song texts and narrations by means of 'cues'. But the graphic notation per se seems to enhance the magical appreciation of the oral tradition. The illustrations from the Cuna writings demonstrate the fact that there is a strict barrier to comprehension at the lowest level of partial writing systems: as soon as we know the original text in its complete oral version, we can see right through the multiple expressions of an alleged 'pictography'. As long as we have only the effigy signs before us for consideration, a definitive decipherment is not possible; the rules governing the sound indicators, the condensation of cues, and so on, cannot be understood through the pictograms themselves. Strictly speaking, it's a matter of highly developed mnemonicons for one's personal information, not a matter of objectified information, that is to say, 'messages' which can be reproduced by strangers. The 'Cuna Writing' is the sole existing form of an ancient Indian 'writing' that is still used today in Latin America and is for that reason valuable as a prototype.

Various authors have sought to establish a connection between the Easter Island writing system and the American partial writing systems. These conjectures, however, must be regarded as obsolete, ever since the principal features of the structure, contents, and origin of the Easter Island writing system have been clarified through the work of the present writer. His 'Grundlagen zur Entzifferung' (i.e. Basic Principles for a Decipherment) has been further strengthened and broadened during the course of the last decade. According to those principles the following synthesis of that writing system which was still in use less than a hundred years ago on Easter Island can now be stated:

The classical Easter Island writing, in contradistinction to pictographic systems, comprises a corpus of standardized and conventional signs, which fixed the outlines of the natural or geometric models according to definite rules. Its inventory of about 120 basic graphemes can be combined with each other according to traditional and obligatory rules, resulting in up to 2,000 different composite forms. The texts are normally incised in boustrophedons on both sides of flat wooden tablets; it can be proven, however, that the very 'first writing' was done on fresh banana leaves, that is to say, that the very first writing material was perishable. Thus it is very likely that this writing, which was brought to Easter Island in the fifteenth century A.D. by a wave of Polynesian immigration, has left no evidences of its former existence in the area in which it originated, namely the area of Raiatea-Huahine (the Windward Islands, west of Tahiti). The deciphering of place names and names of deities as well as other bits of graphic evidence prove at any rate that this writing was not invented locally on Easter Island itself. The remote possibility has to be taken into account that the creation of the Central Polynesian protoform of the Easter Island writing is due to a 'stimulus diffusion' from Asia. From a linguistic point of view, the writing on the Easter Island tablets includes various stages of development of the Polynesian language. During the course of 400 years older Central Polynesian words were replaced on Easter Island to some extent by local regionalisms. Therefore, it is necessary in the deciphering work to try to bring in other East Polynesian languages for comparison with the Rapanui vocabulary.

The Easter Island writing merits theoretical interest because of its principles of internal structure. As a rule a grapheme corresponds to the fixed sound value of a radical. Occasionally a polyvalence is noted: in such instances it's a matter of related concepts, which can be concatenated with the pictorial quality of a sign functioning in a like manner. Some associations between the form of the sign and the spoken equivalent are obvious: color values are rendered by objects which are typical of the color in question; at times other properties are expressed pictorially by the shape of the sign itself; supernatural powers can be represented by their prominent characteristics or external features (pars-pro-toto or symbolic signs). Poetic circumlocutions or figurative phraseology are rendered, so to speak, as 'written metaphors'. Since the wealth of homonyms in the Polynesian language is cleverly exploited to its full extent, the nature of the phoneticization is crucial for an understanding of the inscriptions. In the rebus procedure the writers worked not only with homonyms but also with homeophonous elements (within precisely defined rules of sound similarity). Two factors, however, considerably complicate the situation: The first one is the fact that the Easter Island writing system was not able to reproduce a complete spoken sentence but was only able to use its graphic system as cues to the main ideas embodied in the sentences. Thus the profusion of the original oral transmission is reduced to a sort of telegraphic style which naturally causes considerable difficulties for the present day decipherer (with his quite different cultural milieu). Added to this difficulty is the fact that the writer was satisfied more often than not with a 'partial sound indication', that is, for example, with representing in writing only parts of a polysyllabic word. As with all partial writing systems, this then creates an 'information decrease' which is far more serious than, say, the lack of grammatical particles or the intricate variety of the poetic expressions in the Easter Island writing system. As seen from the point of view of the present day decipherer, the cue type inscriptions present a meager 'exteriority'; it is only when we can completely reveal the corresponding 'interiority' through other kinds of ethnographic sources that the original richness of the traditional culture is disclosed. The sequence of signs, through which the songs were transmitted in a fixed structure, had above all a complementary value for the Polynesian writer, the one who was qualified and knowledgeable to read them, whether they were mnemonicons or whether they were a normative means of standardization. Inasmuch as the Easter Island writing system was not constructed, properly speaking, as an autonomous communication system but merely as the auxiliary carrier of the traditions of their culture, it presents a paradox: It is a highly developed stage of mnemonics and a nascent early writing system at one and the same time.

The range of themes dealt with on the inscribed tablets are first and foremost of a ritualistic character revolving about deities, mythical events, and festivals. This results in a considerable yield for a deeper understanding of the Old-Polynesian religion. Sociology and history are harder to understand due to the technique of stereotyped circumlocutions. But even here some light is thrown on the former social functions and especially on the earlier migrations in eastern Polynesia. Even the archeological problems of Easter Island itself, such as the giant stone figures and the cult sites, are at least dealt with indirectly. The task today for research is to interpret and provide commentaries on the structures of the motifs in the long, interrelated texts on the tablets and to specify the linguistic change in the Easter Island writing system. The prospects for doing this may be considered to be favorable.

II

Teotihuacán, the northernmost of the great cult centers during the Meso-American classical period, apparently had a ritual calendar although the majority of the signs for the days have not yet been identified. Hasso von Winning has especially distinguished himself in his attempts to identify the signs. There is a complete lack of longer texts. For this reason an interpretation of the isolated symbols, which occur for the most part on ceramic ware, runs up against considerable difficulties. Regardless of the recalcitrance of the subject matter, individual studies are indispensable for future progress in this field since there are significant cross-connections leading from Teotihuacán to the sign inventories of other classical centers.

Xochicalco can well serve as an example of such cross-connections. Not long ago Sáenz dug up three stelae which, according to the iconography of their deities and their calendar data as well as the concomitant non-calendaric hieroglyphs, can pass as a proto-example of a late classic syncretism. And, last but not least, additional solutions would have a favorable effect on the investigation of the Zapotec hieroglyphs.

We probably reach the greatest time depth in Meso-America with the written monoliths at Monte Alban. The most important name connected with this research is that of Alfonso Caso. Although his first compendium of the Zapotec stone inscriptions (1928) was just restricted to a chronologically non-differentiated presentation which merely discussed the calendaric hieroglyphs, his second synthesis (1947) has brought us, however, quite a distance forward. Monte Alban I presents us with what is to all appearances the oldest Meso-American writing already completely developed without any recognizable preliminary stages. The calendar, starting with a ritual calendar of 260 days, already contains computations as to the year and probably also positions of the months. The signs for the days can be interpreted at least partially from their shapes. Hieroglyphs without concomitant numerals appear singly or in compounds and constitute short inscriptions. An analysis of the shapes of the forms yields three groups: anthropomorphic and zoomorphic heads, hand-forms (apparently for actions), and stylized objects of the material culture. Calendar and non-calendaric statements are already intermingled. The iconography of the figures plays a very important role, i.e. the characteristics of the costume and ornamentation provide essential additional information. Typical structures of the texts can be recognized in Monte Alban II. Such characteristic inscriptions taken from the 'Montículo J' have the following general structure:

1. A reversed human head with death-eyes, individualized especially by the headdress;
2. The hieroglyph 'mountain' with variable additional elements;
3. Dates (year, month, day);
4. Possibly other non-calendaric supplementary signs.

This sequence can be interpreted as 'substantive expression—location information—time information—(further elucidation)', and we can accept Caso's explanation that these are inscriptional proclamations of conquests (defeated opponent—location of the event — date of the triumph), i.e. political history. Hieroglyphic texts of this period occur in double columns, a fact that is familiar in Maya epigraphy. Only attempts at interpretation of the inscriptions of Monte Alban I and II are under consideration. Readings in the literal sense of the word are out of the question since the linguistic connection to Zapotec in the early period is rather problematic. The research suffers especially from a lack of Zapotec codices and of early colonial period commentators (of the level of a Sahagún or a Landa) and is therefore restricted to an inner analysis based on archeology, with at the most an insight — based on shapes — into written elements of other classical cultures. The extremely scanty number of 'Olmec' inscriptions have not yet been subjected to writing system research. Interest is concentrated mainly on questions of a calendar nature, especially the role of the 'Long Count' dating and the order of seniority precedence vis-a-vis the early classical Maya monuments.

The studies concerning the pre-Spanish codices have progressed disproportionately. There are essentially two groups of themes: codices of a religious (ritual and mantic) character and codices with a historical and genealogical content. The first group was the main subject of research at the turn of the century; the art of interpretation reached an apogee that has never been attained since then, especially with the commentary by Edward Seler on the manuscripts of the Codex Borgia-Group. More advanced ideas and methods are found in Novotny and Spranz. Novotny postulates a judicious separation between 'elucidation' and 'interpretation' of this paleographic material. While Novotny accepts Seler's elucidations of the effigies in the codices of the Codex Borgia-Group as appropriate and reliable, many of the earlier 'interpretations' seem to him to be dubious. This is mainly true in regard to the topics concerning astronomy and myths of nature in which there is a reflection of a vogue in the history of science. The re-interpretations which are required today must support the considerations of function, such as the role of the priestly rituals and the techniques of divination. The cataloguing of the manuscripts according to calendaric arrangements and to internal cross-connections creates an objective frame of reference. Another method of analysis is one of a precise and detailed study of the iconographic material. The painted designs on the faces and bodies, hair styles, clothing and ornaments characterize the images (deities or representations of priests as deities) and make it possible to recognize positions which are parallel and substitutable elements. Thus success has been achieved in grouping the deities solely according to their iconographic features, not biased by premature interpretations or conclusions drawn from analogies to sources of the Spanish colonial period. In this manner it is possible to reconstruct in a novel way the arrangement of the pantheon (of deities) according to the time horizon of the Mixteca-Puebla culture. The analyses which have just been outlined are not, strictly speaking, within the narrow scope of writing systems research, but they do show at the same time how a breadth of methods of investigation is essential when dealing with ancient Mexican picture writings. It is absolutely out of the question to talk of a real 'reading' of the codices mentioned above.

A stroke of luck has resulted in a decisive break-through in the Mixtec codices of the historical type. After a series of Anglo-American researchers had already begun to operate with the historicity of such documents (as opposed to the German scholars who had been advocating the thesis of mythological topics), Caso was successful in getting convincing proof that this material consisted of a record of the genealogies of the rulers. The key to the success, in some respects a Mexican 'Rosetta Stone', was a colonial document, a map of Teozacoalco drawn up in about 1580. It contains, along with other information, particulars of historical and genealogical nature about Mixtec kings who were then able to be identified in a number of preserved pre-Spanish codices by the iconographic and calendaric data. With this as a starting point, it was possible to interrelate and make sense out of the contents of longer passages. The genealogies of the Mixtec rulers can be traced back as far as the end of the seventh century and then followed, with a number of genealogical overlappings, up to the sixteenth and seventeenth centuries. What is interesting about the contents is the knowledge of which facts were considered to be 'worthy of noting down'. Given the present status of research, the main things which can be ascertained are birthdates and various types of cognominations the kings were given, their blood relatives (parents, siblings, and progeny) and marital ties, prominent events (enthronement, meetings of assemblies, trips or migrations, and especially military actions, conquests, and sacrificial acts) and, finally, the dates of their deaths. The codices either deal with genealogies of a single locality (e.g. the Codex Vindobonensis Verso provides the genealogy of Tilantongo) or with histories of a number of Mixtec rulers with information covering many localities (e.g. the Bodley Codex); it is possible to set up a number of concordances. The insight gained into this subject matter proves that a true consciousness of history existed in Meso-America. With the pictographic and calendaric system it was possible to pinpoint events temporally and spatially and thus pass them down to their descendants. At any rate an extract, and outline of cues, which called for the far more comprehensive oral treatment, could thus be written down. The main contribution of Caso's pioneering works, from the point of view of writing as a system, is in his determination of the graphic and typological forms for names. The names of persons (the 'nicknames' that signify rank as contrasted to the plain 'calendaric names' indicating the date of birth) and the names of places and localities are the components of the Mixtec codices which can be interpreted and thus make true readings possible. Hence it follows that the Mixtec language is the basis of the writing system (as contrasted to the Aztec speech medium of other Old-Mexican codices) and that, secondly, it involves a phoneticization by means of a rebus procedure. Pictorial elements are sometimes utilized for their phonetic value when it is necessary to differentiate homophonous words. Future research, especially toponymy, will be able to provide further insights into the construction principles of the Mixtec partial writing system; there is no significant difference between this writing and the possibilities of expression of the Aztec era. This also holds true for the usages of ideograms or symbolic graphemes scattered throughout the texts. Neither one of them have hieroglyphic texts which render complete sentences of a spoken language.

Of basic importance for a theoretical understanding of the Meso-American partial writing systems are Novotny's new analyses (1959, 1963) of the hieroglyphs in the Mendoza Codex. As is well known, this is a document from the early period of Spanish colonization in which the pictorial symbolizations (based on Aztec models) were explained by modern commentaries in order to make the document comprehensible. Thus, although no literal decipherment is given, still, thanks to the commentary, it is possible to take exact stock of structural symbolic characters, especially the locality hieroglyphs. It is evident that two-thirds of the hieroglyphs in the Mendoza Codex are clearly 'word pictures', i.e. that the name of the represented object provides the sound value. Further distinctions are introduced with the aid of 'inherent elements', that is to say through the addition of colors, ornaments, or changes in position. Hieroglyphic elements can be polymorphic (several signs can represent the same Aztec base word) or polyphonic (a sign can have several phonetic values). Hieroglyphic elements can be repeated several times for esthetic considerations without causing a corresponding repetition of the sounds. There is a relatively low proportion of 'elliptical writings' based on the pars-pro-toto principle and a relatively restricted inventory of true 'phonetic writings' based on rebus principles. Certain reading aids are used to make up for the ambiguity of the Aztec partial writing system. Hieroglyphs which are similar to each other or polyphonic are made precise by the use of 'double writings', and these double writings are repetitions of the first syllable or of the entire word. Pleonastic writings place the emphasis mainly on the beginning of the word. One can agree with Novotny that the Old-Mexican picture writings are not 'written texts but rather pictograms with interspersed pictures of words'. The heuristic value of such studies, let us say for the deciphering of the Maya hieroglyphs, is based on the fact that Meso-America is invested with a knowledge of hieroglyphic and calendaric means of expression which are structurally related and historically connected.

We will disregard the numerous detailed works covering questions about the Ancient Mexican calendar system since these are relevant only for writing system research proper where the beginnings of both of the two traditions are involved. At any rate the writing system and the calendar system have been closely united with each other in Meso-America since the pre-classical periods; in fact, this connection can be regarded as nothing less than the defining criterion of Ancient Mexico.

III

The endeavors to decipher the Maya writing system are being directed at the present time by a small number of scholars who are unfortunately very widely scattered. If we disregard the founding of the Seminario de Cultura Maya at the National University of Mexico, there has been no institutional center for such research on an international basis since the dissolution of the Department of Archeology of the Carnegie Institution. Those concerned are either former colleagues of the Carnegie Institution or are members of universities and academies. Occasional cooperation usually doesn't involve anything more than two partners in research or casual correspondence; instead of cooperation there have arisen controversies that have, now and then, reached deplorable heights of animosity. Unfortunately this latter situation, just like the lack of cooperation on Maya linguistic research, slows down and impedes progress in this field.

The key figure in efforts at deciphering the Maya heiroglyphs is indubitably Eric

Thompson. Not enough time has elapsed yet for an objective historical and scientific evaluation to be made of his accomplishments and shortcomings. It is incontrovertible that Thompson opened up a way (recognized since 1944) out of the blind alley of mere calendar and astronomical studies during the period between the two World Wars, and once again made the 'texts' themselves, consisting of non-calendaric hieroglyphs, the goal of the main research offensive. To work without his *opus magnum* (1950), a landmark of this new development, is inconceivable, although it is not free of errors, contradictions and illogical reasonings. A broad knowledge of the sources, placed against the broader Meso-American perspective, serves as a background for tracking down the entangled religious and ritual traces of the written elements. The deciphering work itself is occasionally in danger of being overshadowed by an emotional feeling for the intellectual history of the Maya culture. Kelley accepts approximately half of the new interpretations and new readings of the hieroglyphic elements; but even when more rigorous objections are made — we estimate that some 30 to 40% of Thompson's suggestions will be solidly substantiated — his 'quota of successes' is, still in all, considerably higher than all of the other works on the Maya writing system that are known to us. Thompson's articles on his deciphering ideas which have appeared in the last few years are somewhat less convincing than his major work; but we concur in the broad insights as to the character of the Maya hieroglyphs, especially as regards the role of the rebus readings and his observation about the 'pictorial synonyms and homonyms'. Thompson might make a further decisive breakthrough if the way were not blocked, in our opinion, by an over-interpretation of the Yucatec material that is based on Roy's work.

Tatiana Proskouriakoff and Heinrich Berlin succeeded in discovering political and dynastic events in the classical inscriptions and were thus able to bring real history into the discussion once again. This 'breakthrough to historicity' deals with the recognition of two things: 'emblem' hieroglyphs pertaining to specific localities and texts containing the biographies of rulers. The emblem hieroglyphs are for very definite cult centers and consist of individual main signs which occur, as a rule, only in that locality or in neighboring dependencies; they are coupled with ordinary affixes which, as a rule, can be identified throughout the entire area of the classical southern region. These affixes apparently indicate the lineage and rank of individuals while the main signs are surrogates for the various city-states. The biographies of the rulers contain hieroglyphic statements about births, enthronements or changes of official position, successful military actions and so on. The arrangement by dates makes it possible to draw up individual personal histories for particular Maya rulers (e.g. in Yaxchilan). Then too, the not inconsiderable role of female personages in certain inscriptions is starting to become evident. These new realizations have just reached the status of 'interpretations', and there are still considerable advances and refinements to be expected in this field. Nevertheless the basic principles discovered by Proskouriakoff can already be certified as valid today.

The so-called 'Hamburg School' has structural and functionalist methods which are related to those of the researchers named above, but it focuses more on studies of the interpretations and readability of single hieroglyphs. This then is a continuation of the Seler tradition which carefully judges the phenomena of the Maya culture against the larger background of Ancient Mexico and pays stronger attention to the symbolic means of expression and basic ideas they had in common. Only parts of the studies in the paleographic field have been published so far; further results will be forthcoming for the Madrid Codex (Zimmermann) and the Dresden Codex (Barthel). An investigation of worthwhile epigraphic targets (Chichen Itza, Tikal, Palenque) and also an analysis of the hieroglyphic writing present on Maya ceramic artifacts are under way at present in Tübingen.

There is a group of researchers, separated as to location but related in their theoretical position as to the writing system, who could be called, somewhat overstated perhaps, 'the phoneticians'. Knorosov, Kelley and Cordan are following a line of investigation which reflects an old tradition, even if not a too successful one, in the study of Maya hieroglyphs, a tradition that started with the so-called 'Landa alphabet'. The phonetic conception accounts to a considerable degree for the use of syllables or purely alphabetic values, i.e. this principle goes beyond a mere 'word sign writing'. According to this version, hieroglyphic compounds oftentimes consist of sound blends or instances of acrophony. The new readings which have been suggested so far, however, have to be considered as overwhelmingly controversial. The so-called 'Mérida System' approach signifies a step forward, since it deliberately attacks the problem through the philological reconstruction of a Proto-Maya language (that is to say, the spoken form of the language of the period during which the Maya writing system was invented). This approach is, on principle, necessary and most welcome, even if one, like the present writer, views most of the results attained so far with scepticism. The logical incorporation of Maya languages of the non-Yucatec group should undoubtedly open up new perspectives, especially for the epigraphy expert.

The experiment undertaken by the Siberian Academy of Science to decipher the Maya codices with the aid of electronic computers has to be considered as an attempt that failed. The criticism of the specialists is of one voice in the rejection of this attempt. It failed because the original premise was wrong, namely that of equating the lexical material of the Motul dictionary and of the Chilam Balam books *eo ipso* with the graphemes of the Maya paleography and wanting to undertake a schematic transference according to statistical rules. This mechanistic arrangement broke down, moreover, due to an inadequate theoretical grasp of the system of a partial writing mode such as the one represented by the Maya hieroglyphs. The decisive feats of deciphering will still have to be accomplished by researchers using their brains and not by machines in the foreseeable future.

Let us now proceed to a detailed report on the situation: The status of the sources has continued to develop unevenly. A new edition of the Dresden Codex, which is probably on a par with the Förstemann issues, has been published in the field of paleography. The new facsimile editions of the Paris Codex and of the Madrid Codex which have been announced will help facilitate their utilization on a broader basis. Publications on the Maya ceramic artifacts, whose iconography and concomitant hieroglyphic writings are of great heuristic value, are still fragmentary. There is no comprehensive opus of the type done by Gordon and Mason in which the objects scattered out through many private collections are inventoried. The same type of dispersal has to be taken into account when dealing with inscriptions on bones, shells, obsidian and greenstone, although these, as a group, are quite disparate as to subject matter and are less promising of success. The inscriptions of the classical period are still the basic material for epigraphic research, since our future understanding of the history, social structure and religion of the golden age of the Maya theocrats is dependent on their decipherment. Longer inscriptions, especially in the leading cult centers of Tikal and Palenque, have recently been uncovered. The discovery of stele 31 at Tikal has given us an early classical piece of evidence on which are shown influences from Teotihuacán; the iconography and text of this relic both hold out a promise for an approach with a successful solution. New important material is available in Palenque with the discoveries at the palace (Tablero de El Palacio, Tablero de los Esclavos) and in the crypt of the Temple of Inscriptions (sarcophagus texts). The discovery of new sites has provided the epigraphy experts with additional research possibilities of which only a fraction has been exploited so far. These include, among others, Bonampak, Caracol, and the cult centers in the basin of the Río Pasión (Aguateca, Dos Pilas, Machaquilá and Tamarandito). It is discouraging to report that the editing technique used in these and many other classical inscriptions is far inferior to the standard set by Maudslay at the close of the nineteenth century. An urgent list of desiderata for research is headed by a need for publication of larger and clearer photographs of the epigraphic material together with reliable and detailed re-drawing of the hieroglyphic passages. The decipherer lacks a handy working aid at the very beginning of his investigations unless he has adequate volumes of plates, arranged according to site and time depth, in which all of the inadequately covered as well as the unpublished inscriptions are systematically inventoried. Unfortunately even that preparation of series of hieroglyphic texts, for which Beyer established a model with the inscriptions from Chichen Itza, has come to a dead halt. Many of the cult centers have their own typical sequences of hieroglyphs (so-called 'clauses') which deal with expanded versions, abbreviated versions and modified versions of certain topics restricted to a specific locality. By arranging such texts in parallel sets it is possible, at least, to structurally divide an inscription which has not yet been deciphered and determine the possible substitutions in the sets of affixes, main signs, and combinations of signs. H. Berlin has recently begun to reveal such structural arrangements in at least a few of the Palenque texts.

The second step, after an inventory and presentation of the hieroglyphic texts that is justified by the facts, is to catalogue the attested elements of the writing system. The frequencies of occurrence of the individual main signs and affixes, the manner of their association, and the distribution in time and space reveal objective data before the deciphering work proper even begins. Thus a catalogue is not only a proof of the occurrences but as a result of the way in which it is prepared, also contains quantitative indices as to the possible types of writing. Zimmermann's catalogue (1956) is a precise and well thought out working aid that is available when working with the hieroglyphs in the three preserved Mayan manuscripts. Of the original stock of hieroglyphs in the paleographic texts the Madrid Codex has preserved 90%, the Dresden Codex about 85%, but the Paris Codex only about 30%. The main signs and the affixes are in a proportion of about 47 to 53 in the construction of the 5,770 hieroglyphs composed of a total of 14,230 construction elements. But if, from a statistical point of view, the main signs and affixes are almost equally divided, the picture shifts when one looks into the number of basic forms participating in the construction of this writing. There is a maximum of 230 main signs as compared to a stock of some 90 affixes in the paleography. Or in other words: affixes generally occur more frequently in the composition of compound hieroglyphs. Thus a study of the affixation facilitates a deeper penetration into the rules of construction of the Maya writing system, can indirectly connect isolated hieroglyphs, and, finally, can give rise to a sort of 'syntax' of hieroglyphic passages. It is here that one of the main thrusts of future research will be focused. Zimmermann's catalogue uses registration numbers for the indivual hieroglyphic sub-elements which are differentiated and grouped according to affixes or main signs of anthropomorphic, zoomorphic and geometric types. The manner in which the writing elements are combined in the formation of the hieroglyphs is indicated by dots or dashes between the registration numbers.

Unfortunately this catalogue, which is so satisfactory paleographically, has been pushed into the background by a further catalogue by Thompson (1962) which has the advantage of incorporating most of the epigraphic material. This unification was purchased, however, at the price of a completely new system of registration numbers for which a concordance list with the Zimmermann nomenclature gives no comfort, inasmuch as no decipherer can retain two completely different systems of enumeration of hieroglyphic elements in his memory at one and the same time. Furthermore, Thompson's catalogue is incomplete; the evidences for the occurrences of the important group of portraits of the deities is missing and the totality of the affix attestations can be revealed only indirectly. Controversies about the justification of 'splitting and lumping' of hieroglyphic sub-elements should disappear as the epigraphic research is refined further. Catalogue supplements for new inscriptions are indispensable and could be coupled with the elaboration of a real Corpus Inscriptionum Mayarum. Urgently needed, in addition, is access for all researchers to the texts in which the registered hieroglyphs are located. Even if Thompson's catalogue, despite the many years of work expended on it, has not yet achieved the desired completeness and precision, still it has proven to be exceedingly helpful even in the current stage of research for the rapid examination of textual cross-connections, and for a judgement as to the regional (but unfortunately not the temporal) dispersion as well as for a quantitative estimate covering the entire writing system of the Maya culture. Thompson enumerates a total figure of 862 hieroglyphic construction elements, including those types which are dubious. There are said to be 370 affixes with the main signs exceeding this by 30%. The number of main signs will probably exceed 500 when further anthropomorphic and zoomorphic portrait-glyphs, as well as forms which have not yet been inventoried – discovered at the new sites – are taken into consideration. Then, too, there is a part of the signs, notless limited, which occur only a single time. If such 'odd examples' are disregarded (some 80 affixes and 130 main signs), the total number still always works to be at least 650 hieroglyphic elements occurring in various constructions. This limit cannot be lowered any further and thus proves per se that the Maya writing cannot be an alphabet (requiring 20 to 40 signs) nor a syllabary (80 to 160 signs) but has to belong to the category of a 'word sign writing system'.

The constituent elements of the Maya writing system are divided into main signs and affixes. We call the smallest meaningful formal unit a 'grapheme'. A grapheme can have a certain amount of variation in its shape but does exist in a system of relationships to other graphemes. The graphemes follow certain rules of combination and arrangement, a fact that was already obvious from the formal analysis of the Maya hieroglyphs. Any further decomposition of a 'grapheme' into graphic sub-elements of signs generally destroys the semantic content of the grapheme and leads the decipherer away from the integral writing system into a 'world of subhieroglyphic forms'. Hermann Beyer, for example, has been taken in by this temptation for atomism.

The occurrence and distribution of the graphemes yield a statistical picture of the frequencies, favorite positions, and characteristic possibilities of substitution. A comprehensive 'study of the affix' — that is to say, an adequate investigation of the small signs in both the paleographic and the epigraphic material — has not been done, but such a study would afford considerable pre-orientation and clarification for the decipherment proper.

The solving of the Maya writing system is taking place at several levels of understanding. A basic distinction has to be made between 'interpretations' and 'readings'. 'Interpretations' are to a certain degree 'decipherings in the rough' established for a grapheme or compound hieroglyph by the analyst in a certain frame of reference. The degree of interpretation is variable: A good example of this is provided by the so-called 'positional meaning scheme' developed by Zimmermann which has been of value especially in paleography so far but which should be productive even for epigraphy. Sequences of hieroglyphic texts in the codices are often constructed according to a recurring pattern. In the first position in the 'sentence' are the so-called 'thematic hieroglyphs' which often correspond to a predicate. In the second position are the so-called 'nominal hieroglyphs' which designate the subject. The first position is occasionally expanded by the addition of hieroglyphs which give the object of the action or its setting. The second position can be supplemented by hieroglyphic titles or attributives. As for the latter of these, a group of 'attributive hieroglyphs' can be singled out which are often placed systematically at the end of a hieroglyphic sentence, unless this position is filled by a ritualistic expression (sacrifice offering hieroglyphs).

Thus it is often possible for the paleographer to obtain a first interpretation for the category just from the characteristic position in a hieroglyphic sentence. It appears, furthermore, that the graphemes are not distributed according to a choice of thematic, nominal, or attributive hieroglyphs but rather that they often display definite preferences. For example, the hand forms occur predominately as main signs in the first category and head variants in the second category. Also, with the aid of the 'positional meaning scheme', the framework of a rudimentary 'hieroglyphic syntax and grammar' can already be seen at an early stage of investigation. There are certain small signs which are always regulated by either thematic hieroglyphs or by nominal hieroglyphs. In the first instance, there is a limited number of frequently documented affixes (with prefixes occurring more frequently than suffixes) which can be interpreted as verbal formants and which serve to indicate a grammatical connection with the following hieroglyph. In the second instance, we are more likely to come upon affixes with a limited spread of occurrence which are occasionally so closely bound to the main sign of the nominal hieroglyphs that they can be taken as small signs serving as nominal indicators for a person or a deity. And, lastly, the logical exploitation of the positional meaning scheme makes it possible to differentiate the 'primary' and 'secondary' small signs from each other. A 'primary affix' is indispensable in the construction of compound hieroglyphs in which a new idea is thereby created or expressed. In other words: If a primary affix is detached from the other graphemes participating in the construction of a hieroglyph, then the meaning of the whole is lost. A 'secondary affix' on the other hand is not required inasmuch as its absence does not affect the core of the hieroglyphic statement. There are two reasons for this. It may be a matter of reflexes of a linguistic nature which can be interpreted as grammatical elements. Or it may be a matter of additions of artistic writing which function as 'reading aids' but whose use is absolutely facultative.

There is a distinct polarization of meanings in the group of the so-called 'attributive hieroglyphs'. One subgroup of attributive hieroglyphs appears exclusively in textual passages in association with the nominal hieroglyphs of the 'favorable' deities, while a second subgroup is always linked to 'unfavorable' deities. Thus we are able to differentiate the 'positive attributive hieroglyphs' from the 'negative attributive hieroglyphs' in the codices even at the stage of first interpretations before any kind of attempts at a reading are started. In addition, there is another less sharply distinguishable group that belongs here, one which is based not so much on a contrast between qualities as it is on a theme of an agrarian and meteorological nature.

The largest part of the paleographic material can be schematically grouped for the future 'reading' stage by a logical application of the so-called principles of arrangement and of interpretation. Some passages in the codices offer a certain resistance to the process and remain there, like erratic blocks, awaiting a solution. It seems as if it is a matter of expressions of some other topic, as is usually the case in the epigraphic material. A position scheme is applicable to the inscriptions whenever it is a matter of typical sequences of the 'thematic hieroglyph — nominal hieroglyph' type. Further principles of arrangement (clustering of titles, designations of place and kinship relationships, artifact and cult hieroglyphs, etc.) still have to be worked out laboriously in the field of epigraphy. The prospects for this can be said to be favorable.

Most of the specialists in this field probably agree on what has been covered up to this point in the analysis, namely on what we can call the 'structural interpretation process.' The difficulties and controversies start with the diverse suggestions proposed for the 'reading' proper, that is, for the replacement of graphemes by their oral equivalents.

Here we will have to differentiate some of the various complexes of problems and bring out some of the most important questions that are involved in the controversy:

1. Do the hieroglyphic components correspond to whole words, to simple syllables, or do they constitute an alphabet?

2. In compound hieroglyphs which consist of two or more graphemes:

a. Are the oral equivalents strung in a row without any sound loss?

b. At the points of connection is there any sort of fusion or overlapping, that is to say, a partial mutation (alteration or loss) of a final sound or of an initial sound?

c. Is there a system of abbreviation, corresponding to an acrophonic process, whereby only the initial sounds stand for something?

3. For compound hieroglyphs which consist of two or more graphemes, in which order are they read?

a. Does the order of reading correspond to the well known structuring of blocks of hieroglyphic texts from left to right (that is to say, prefix before main sign, or main sign before postfix) and from top to bottom (that is to say, superfix before main sign, or main sign before suffix)?

b. Does the order of reading start off with a main sign with the order based on the sequence of the affixes?

c. Is the order of reading 'arbitrary'; in other words, does the arrangement of the graphemes reflect some traditional, esthetically formal pattern which has nothing whatsoever to do with the order in which the spoken equivalents are uttered?

4. Is an ensemble of graphemes in a compound hieroglyph to be read always as purely 'additive', that is to say, as an accumulation of all the individual oral equivalents, or does one also have to take ideographic processes into account in which the graphemes form a sort of 'Gestalt'? In an 'integrative' reading two or more graphemes are not combined according to their individual sound values but rather express in combination an idea or situation with a new semantic value (example T 561 (544):526, 'sun' interpolated between 'heaven' and 'earth' does not result in an 'addition' of *kin* plus *caan* plus *caban* but rather results in 'integrating' the situation as 'the sun appears between earth and heaven', i.e., 'sunrise' *hatzcab*).

5. With which approach can the system of Maya hieroglyphs in general best reflect the language which forms its basis? The affixes which can be interpreted as grammatical particles are numerically far fewer than the prefixes or suffixes that are

in fact used in the Maya languages. The graphemes also do not occur in those frequencies and permutations which would soon be obvious even on an early analytical level in a syllabic system or an alphabetical system. If one accepts as a general rule that the normal spoken equivalent to a grapheme is a word, and if, furthermore, one brings into account the technique for a rendering of sounds which we call a 'rebus' process, then all of the homophones of the underlying language can be expressed. A strict homophony, by the way, has been authenticated in none of the Old World early writing systems which proceeded from picture to sound with the aid of a rebus process; they always admitted a certain degree of mere 'sound similarity' rather than a rigorous 'identical sound'. The field of possible relationships of meaning is thus broadened to that of 'homeophony'. We do not know a priori what degree of divergence in sound similarities the Maya writer felt was permissible. Puns from Maya texts of the post-Columbus period give a first inkling of the breadth possible in their homeophony. Partial writing systems, which imply a degree of permissible homeophony, are suitable for use as long as they function in passing down and commenting on the cultural pattern to which they owe their creation. For the present-day decipherer, such an obfuscation and paucity of the oral reflex naturally presents a considerable handicap since modern research can be enticed so easily into a morass of possible puns.

6. The question as to which stage of the language the Maya hieroglyphs are to be considered as coordinate is a paleolinguistic problem.

The first problem relates to time depth and the region of origin. Then too a portion or model from non-Maya languages would have to be taken into consideration for the moment of the creation and in the development of the writing system. Furthermore, one has to test the mutation or perseverance of language forms which are portrayed by specific graphemes, as well as the possible reflexes of local designations in the hieroglyphs that are confined to a specific sub area. A fundamental problem to be reckoned with is the growth of contradictions between the graphic forms and the linguistic content over the course of at least 1,200 years of hieroglyphic history. A key to the problem apparently lies in the spatial displacement of the use of hieroglyphs from an older center (Guatemala: Highlands/Pacific Coast) into the region of the classical golden age (the axis Palenque-Copan) and finally to a marginal province (Yucatan) where there was an encounter with Mexican foreign influence and a resultant syncretist decadence. From the point of view of incipient Maya research it was doubtless justified to start at first with the ethnolinguistic findings in Yucatan where a Maya culture using the writing system was still functioning at the time that the Spaniards arrived. But the greatest part of the possibilities contained in such source material have apparently been fully used and exhausted. Today we can state with confidence that Yucatan was NOT the area of origin of the Maya writing system but rather a late and historically accidental repository. Ethnolinguistic data ranging from the Chiapas tribes to the Chorti are coming more and more to the forefront as more worthwhile for new starts. The possibilities of obtaining readings of hieroglyphic components from the Maya languages of the uplands of Guatemala also appear noteworthy.

There still exists, however, at the current stage of investigation the danger of an inadmissible contamination from two different paths of research. It is important now to work hard with the aid of historical and comparative linguistic research to obtain the linguistic base of the Maya languages at a time depth of about 2,000 years in order to use reconstructed forms to tackle a correct time and place reading of the Maya hieroglyphs in the early stage of their invention and development. It is equally important that the epigraphic analysis should remain painstakingly separated from the linguistic analysis. According to our view, one should not start out with hypothetical attempts at reading the graphemes which then lead to the establishment of series of drifts right across the Maya languages, but rather first of all the linguistic reconstruction should be made, based on its own organic autonomies. The decipherer can then test out protoforms in the inscriptions. Of course, such reconstructed material is insufficient to probe the entire breadth of play of possible rebus readings, that is to say, the representation of identical sounding words or similar sounding words by a given grapheme. An etymological, semasiological comparative dictionary of the Maya languages is valuable in itself for its objective and beneficial contents, and its value in the hands of the decipherer working on a solution of the Maya writing system cannot be estimated too highly. Thus while 'interpretations' can be done independently by a researcher on writing systems with a knowledge of the techniques of writing analysis and a knowledge of the historical background of the ethnography and culture, he needs to work in close cooperation on specific systems with linguists in order to attain the goal of proper decipherment, i.e. correct 'readings'.

7. Partial writing systems can only be an extraction from the stream of tradition, and, thus, there is a need for additional sources of information. While the oral teachings in the Maya schools for priests and for scribes are forever lost to us (except for chance bits of isolated information in the ethnological material), we do have available an exceedingly valuable aid in the shape of the pictorial and iconographic representations. A hieroglyphic text never occurs in complete isolation in paleography, and seldom so in epigraphy. As a rule it is coupled with pictorial bits of evidence. The research on the codices, especially, has shown that this is not a simple parallelism between writing and pictures — wherein exactly the same information was merely repeated on two different levels — but rather a display of reciprocal interlocking and supplementation. In other words, the sequences of hieroglyphs are 'backed up' by expressions of imagery and the pictures are 'made clear and decreed' by the accompanying writings. Of course the image is oftentimes more than a mere 'illustration': It is frequently nothing less than a 'painted metaphor'. Figurative locutions from the language medium permeate the representations in the codices to a quite considerable extent. If, however, even the paleographic pictorial material is to be 'read' as pictorial homonyms and synonyms, this shows the compulsion there was to pass down meaningful and additional data that was beyond the capacity of the weaknesses

inherent in the Maya hieroglyphic system and shows furthermore a basic relationship in the techniques of expression. In other words: In the intimate coupling of imagery and writing we see a simple proof of the fact that the Maya hieroglyphs never attained that degree of sophistication required by a syllabic or entirely alphabetic writing system which alone would have allowed for an autonomous and complete representation of the transmission of speech.

8. A complete 'reading' of a hieroglyphic text is the prerequisite for a really profound interpretation. The Maya writing seems to be imbedded in a sort of priest language according to the results which have been achieved so far. There are serious obstacles blocking the real 'understanding' of the system due to the richness of metaphors and the techniques of paraphrasing and cover names. It reminds one of the so-called 'Language of Zuyûa', a knowledge of which was nothing less than a criterion for the right to inherit one of the positions of leadership. Even when we will have succeeded some day in reading the major portion of the Maya hieroglyphs, the investigation of the semantic content, of the ambiguities, and of the esoteric references will still be an especially difficult task.

9. The next task for the current stage of development in deciphering is to clarify whether or not the Maya writing shows evidences of multiple values or redundances, that is to say, pleonasms. Or more precisely:

a. Do we have to take polymorphy into account? That is, can various graphemes be indentified which express the same sound value? In the Landa alphabet we are confronted with an apparent polymorphy (three graphemes for 'a', two graphemes for 'b', etc.), but it appears that the justification for the superficially similar arrangement of sound value and grapheme in this document has not been absolutely proven. Suggestions for decipherment which contain examples of polymorphy (e.g., Thompson's conjectures for affixes 'te 1', 'te 2' and 'te 3') apparently haven't met with much favor. On the other hand, there is one unique instance of polymorphy which can be characterized as the identifying property of the Maya writing system, namely the analogous possibilities of usage of geometrical signs and portraiture hieroglyphs.

b. Do we have to take redundancy into account? That is, is the multiple placement of a grapheme in a hieroglyphic construction to be understood as a repetition of the sound value of the same single grapheme, whether it be 'additive' or 'integrating' at a new level of meaning? Or does it retain the original simple communicative value with the multiple placement merely fulfilling a formal function, that is, some sort of graphic composition technique? Or does the first of the aforementioned apply only to the main signs, and the second only to the small signs? This group would also have to take into account graphemes which are utilized but which are not to be read with the proper sound value. The function of such 'reading aids' would probably consist in helping to make the proper selection when polyphonous main signs were involved. There are even other types of 'pleonastic writings' which cannot be excluded a priori when one thinks about the Aztec examples.

c. Do we have to take polyphony into account? That is, are there graphemes which have various sound values (over and beyond plain homeophony) which are demonstrable in various compositae? Suggestions for polyphonous readings pertain first and foremost to the main signs which function on the one hand especially in the make up of calendaric hieroglyphs and on the other hand in the non-calendaric hieroglyphs. Is such a polyphony historically conditioned (a frozen sound value dating from the beginning stage of development of the Maya hieroglyphs plus another sound value introduced later for other functions within the further developed writing system) or is it an obligatory part of the system itself? It is evident that there is a lack of suggestions concerning the polyphony of affixes. What also has to be tested out is where the boundary of a given postulated polyphony is situated, that is to say, whether clues exist to indicate that there are *more than two* different sound values for the same main sign.

Despite the dangers inherent in making scientific predictions, one dares, even in a most sober assessment of the state of research, to look forward with justified optimism to further advances in the decipherment of the Maya hieroglyphs. The situation has changed greatly since 1945 when Paul Schellhas, after a lifetime devoted to studies of Maya, stated that the Maya hieroglyphs are an insoluble problem. A painstaking re-evaluation of past achievements, a critical separation of the controversial integrations, and improvements in new methods and tools all promise, during the next decade, to bring into sharper focus the way of thinking of the Ancient American world.

BIBLIOGRAPHY

I. *South American Writing Systems*

Barthel, Thomas, 'Bemerkungen zu einem astronomischen Quipu aus Südperu', *Ethnos* 16.153-70 (1951).

——, 'Zwei problematische Schrifttafeln von der Osterinsel', *Z Ethn* 81.287-92 (1956).

——, 'Neues zur Osterinselschrift', *Z Ethn* 84.161-72 (1959).

——, 'Vorläufige Ergebnisse bei der Entzifferung der Kohau-Rongorongo von der Osterinsel', *PICAm* 32. 500-07 (1956). (= 'Resultados preliminares del desciframiento de las Kohau-Rongorongo de la Isla de Pascua', *Runa* 7.233-41 (1956)).

——, *Grundlagen zur Entzifferung der Osterinselschrift* (Hamburg, 1958).

——, 'Diskussionsbemerkungen zu einem Rongorongo-Text', *AEH* 12.65-83 (1963).

——, 'Rongorongo-Studien (Forschungen und Fortschritte bei der weiteren Entzifferung der Osterinselschrift)', *Anthropos* 58.372-436 (1963).

Butinov, N., 'Predvaritel'noe soobščenie ob izučenii pis'mennosti ostrova Pashi', *Sov Ethn* 4.77-91 (1956).

——, 'Ieroglifičeskie teksty ostrova Pashi-Rapanui', *Vestnik istorii* 3.69-80 (1959).

Butinov, N. and Knorozov, Yuri, 'Preliminary report on the study of the written language of Easter Island', *JPS* 66.5-17 (1957).

Heine-Geldern, Robert, 'La escritura de la isla de Pascua y sus relaciones con otras escrituras', *Runa* 8.5-27 (1956-57).
Heyerdahl, Thor, *American Indians in the Pacific* (London, 1952).
Holmer, Nils, Miranda Rivera, Porfirio and Ryden, Stig, 'A modelled picture-writing from the Kechua Indians', *Ethnos* 16.171-84 (1951).
Holmer, Nils and Wassén, Henry, *The complete Mu-igala in picture writing. A native record of a Cuna Indian medicine song* (= *Etnologiska Studier* 21) (Göteborg, 1953).
——, *Dos Cantos Shamanisticos de los Indios Cunas* (= *Etnologiska Studier* 27) (Göteborg, 1963).
Ibarra Grasso, Dick, 'La escritura indigena Andina', *AnnLat* 12.9-124 (1948).
——, 'La escritura jeroglífica de los indios andinos', *CA* 15.157-72 (1956).
Lanyon-Orgill, Peter, 'A catalogue of the inscribed tablets and other artifacts from Easter Island', *JAS* 1.20-39 (1956).
——, 'Addenda to the catalogue of the inscribed tablets and other artifacts from Easter Island', *JAS* 2.15-17 (1958).
Nordenskiöld, Erland, *Picture-writings and other documents by Nele, Paramount Chief of the Cuna Indians, and Ruben Perez Kantule, his Secretary* (= *Comparative Ethnographical Studies* 7:1 (Göteborg, 1928).
——, *Picture-writings and other documents by Nele, Charles Slater, Charlie Nelson, and other Cuna Indians* (= *Comparative Ethnographical Studies* 7:2) (Göteborg, 1930).
Nordenskiöld, Erland and Wassén, Henry, *An historical and ethnological survey of the Cuna Indians* (= *Comparative Ethnographical Studies* 10) (Göteborg, 1938).
Rowe, John, 'Inca culture at the time of the Spanish Conquest'', *HSAI* 2.183-330 (1946).
Wassén, Henry, *Contributions to Cuna ethnography* (= *Etnologiska Studier* 16) (Göteborg, 1949).

II. *Mexican Writing Systems*

Barlow, Robert and MacAfee, Byron, *Diccionario de elementos fonéticos en escritura jeroglífica* (*códice mendocino*) (Mexico, 1949).
Burland, Cottie, 'Einige Bemerkungen über den Codex Vindobonensis Mexic. 1', *Arch V* 2. 101-07 (1948).
——, 'Town foundation dates and historical cross references in Mixtec codices', *AIAK* 34.665-69 (1962).
Burland, Cottie and Kutscher, Gerdt, *The Selden Roll* (= *Monumenta Americana* 2) (Berlin, 1955).
Caso, Alfonso, *Las estelas zapotecas* (Mexico, 1928).
——, 'Calendario y escritura de las antiguas culturas de Monte Albán', *Obras completas de Miguel Othón de Mendizabal* (Mexico, 1947).

——, 'El mapa de Teozacoalco', *CA* 8.145-82 (1949).
——, 'Explicación del Reverso del Codex Vindobonensis', *Memoria de El Colegio Nacional* 5:5.1-46 (1951).
——, 'Base para la sincronología mixteca y cristiana', *Memorias de El Colegio Nacional* 6:6.49-66 (1952).
——, *Interpretacion del Códice Gomez de Orozco* (Mexico, 1954).
——, 'Comentario al Codice Baranda', *Miscellanea Paul Rivet octogenario dedicata* 1.372-93 (Mexico, 1958).
——, 'El calendario mexicano', *Memorias de la Academia Mexicana de la Historia* 17.41-96 (1958).
——, 'Glifos teotihuacanos', *RMEA* 15.51-70 (1959).
——, 'Nuevos datos para la correlación de los años aztecas y christiano', *Estudios de Cultura Nahuatl* 1.9-25 (1959).
——, 'Valor histórico de los códices mixtecos', *CA* 19.139-47 (1960).
——, *Interpretacion del Códice Bodley* 2858 (Mexico, 1960).
——, 'Calendario y escritura en Xochicalco', *RMEA* 18.49-80 (1962).
——, 'Los Señores de Yanhuitlan', *ACIA* 35:1.437-48 (1964).
Dark, Phillip, *Mixtec ethnohistory: A method of analysis of the codical art* (Oxford, 1958).
——, 'Evidence for the date of painting and provenience of Codex Selden and Codex Bodley', *ACIA* 33:2.523-29 (1959).
——, 'El antiguo sistema de escritura en México', *RMEA* 4.105-28 (1940).
——, *Códice Xolotl* (= *Publicaciones del Instituto de Historia* 22) (Mexico, 1951).
——, 'Spanish influence of the Aztec writing system', *Homenaje a R. Garcia Granados* 171-77 (Mexico, 1960).
——, 'Glifos fonéticos del Códice Florentino', *Estudios de Cultura Nahuatl* 4.55-60 (1963).
Franco, José Luis, 'La escritura y los códices', *Esplendor del México Antiguo* 1.361-78 (Mexico, 1959).
Kirchhoff, Paul, 'Calendarios tenochca, tlatelolca y otros', *RMEA* 15.257-67 (1954-55).
Kubler, George and Gibson, Charles, *The Tovar Calendar* (= *Memoirs of the Connecticut Academy of Arts and Sciences* 11) (New Haven, 1951).
Mengin, Ernst, 'Commentaire du Codex Mexicanus nos. 23-4', *JSAm* 41.387-498 (1952).
Miles, Suzanne, 'Sculpture of the Guatemala-Chiapas Highlands and Pacific slopes, and associated hieroglyphs', manuscript prepared for *Handbook of Middle American Indians*.
Nicholson, H. B., 'The Mesoamerican pictorial manuscripts: Research, past and present', *AIAK* 34.199-215 (1962).
Nowotny, Karl, 'Erläuterungen zum Codex Vindobonensis (Vorderseite)', *Arch V* 3.125-200 (1948).
——, 'Der Codex Becker II', *Arch V* 12.172-81 (1957).

——, 'Die Bilderfolge des Codex Vindobonensis und verwandter Handschriften', *Arch V* 13.210-21 (1958).

——, 'Die Hieroglyphen des Codex Mendoza. Der Bau einer mittelamerikanischen Wortschrift', *Mitteilungen, Museum für Völkerkunde Hamburg* 25.97-113 (1959).

——, *Tlacuilolli. Die mexikanischen Bilderhandschriften, Stil und Inhalt* (= *Monumenta Americana* 3) (Berlin, 1961).

——, 'Der Bau der mexikanischen Hieroglyphen', *VIe Congrès International des Sciences Anthropologiques et Ethnologiques* 451-55 (Paris, 1963).

Robertson, Donald, *Mexican manuscript painting of the early colonial period: The metropolitan schools* (New Haven, 1959).

——, 'Los manuscritos religiosos Mixtecos', *ACIA* 35:1.425-35 (1964).

Ruz Lhuillier, Alberto, 'La escritura indígena', *México Prehispánico* 685-93 (Mexico, 1946).

Sáenz, César, 'Las estelas de Xochicalco', *ACIA* 35-2.69-84 (1964).

——, 'Tres estelas en Xochicalco', *RMEA* 17.39-66 (1961).

——, *Xochicalco. Temporada 1960* (= *Instituto Nacional de Antropología e Historia, Informes*, No. 11) (Mexico, 1962).

Spinden, Herbert, 'Indian manuscripts of southern Mexico', *Smithsonian Institution Annual Reports* 429-51 (1933).

Spranz, Bodo, *Göttergestalten in den mexikanischen Bilderhandschriften der Codex Borgia-Gruppe* (= *Acta Humboldtiana, Series Geographica et Ethnographica* Nr. 4) (Wiesbaden, 1964).

Sydow, Eckart von, 'Studien zur Form und Form-Geschichte der mexikanischen Bilderhandschriften', *Z Ethn* 72.197-234 (1941).

Thompson, Eric, *Dating of certain inscriptions of non-Maya origin* (= *Theoretical Approaches to Problems* 1) (Carnegie Institution, Washington, 1941).

Winning, Hasso von, 'Teotihuacan symbols: The reptile's eye glyph', *Ethnos* 26.121-66 (1961).

III. *Maya Hieroglyphic Writing*

Andrews, Wyllys, 'The Maya supplementary series', *PICAm* 29:1.123-41 (1949).

Araujo, R., Rodríguez, M. and Solis, H., *I Chol Kin* (Mérida, 1965).

Barrera Vásquez, Alfredo, 'Investigaciones de la escritura de los antiguos mayas con máquinas calculadoras electrónicas: Síntesis y glosa', *Estudios de Cultura Maya* 2.319-42 (1962).

Barthel, Thomas, *Studien zur Entzifferung astronomischer, augurischer und kalendarischer Kapitel in der Dresdener Mayahandschrift* (Dissertation, Philosophische Fakultät, Universität Hamburg, 1952).

——, 'Maya epigraphy: Some remarks on the affix "al"', *PICAm* 30.45-9 (1952).

——, 'Der Morgensternkult in den Darstellungen der Dresdener Mayahandschrift', *Ethnos* 17.73-112 (1952).

——, 'Regionen des Regengottes', *Ethnos* 18.86-105 (1953).

——, 'Versuch über die Inschriften von Chich'en Itzà Viejo', *Baessler-Archiv N.F.* 3.5-33 (1955).

——, 'Die gegenwärtige Situation in der Erforschung der Maya-Schrift', *JSAm* 45.219-27 (1956). (= *PICAm* 32.476-84 (1956)). 'El estado actual en la investigación de la escritura Maya', *Boletín del Centro de Investigaciones Antropológicas de México* 4.19-28 (1957).

——, 'Die Stele 31 von Tikal', *Tribus* 12.159-214 (1963).

——, 'Comentarios a las inscripciones clásicas tardias de Chich'en-Itzá', *Estudios de Cultura Maya* 4.223-44 (1964).

——, 'Gedanken zu einer bemalten Schale aus Uaxactun', *Baessler-Archiv N.F.* 13.131-70 (1965).

Berlin, Heinrich, 'El glifo "emblema" en las inscripciones Mayas', *JSAm*47.111-19 (1958).

——, 'Glifos Nominales en el Sarcófago de Palenque', *Humanidades* 2:10.1-8 (1959).

——, 'Actualidades de la Epigrafía Maya', *Antropologia e Historia de Guatemala* 14.32-7 (1962).

——, 'The Palenque Triad', *JSAm* 52.91-9 (1963).

——, 'The inscription of the Temple of the Cross at Palenque', *AA* 30.330-42 (1965).

Berlin, Heinrich and Kelley, David, 'The 819-day count and color-direction symbolism among the classic Maya', *Middle American Research Institute* 26.9-20 (1961).

Beyer, Hermann, *Studies on the inscriptions of Chichen Itza* (= *Carnegie Institution Washington Publication 483, Contribution 21*) (Washington, 1937).

Coe, Michael, 'Cycle 7 monuments in Middle America: A reconsideration', *AA* 59.597-611 (1957).

Cook de Leonard, Carmen, 'Dos extraordinarias vasijas del Museo de Villa Hermosa (Tabasco)', *Yan* No. 3.83-104 (1954).

Cordan, Wolfgang, *Götter and Göttertiere der Maya* (Bern-München, 1963).

——, *Introduccion a los Glifos Mayas* (*Sistema de Mérida*) (Mérida, 1963).

——, *La Clave de los Glifos Mayas* (Mérida, 1964).

Cordy, Napoleon, 'Examples of phonetic construction in Maya hieroglyphs', *AA* 108-17 (1964).

Evreinov, E.; Kosarev, Y. and Ustinov, V., *Primenenie elektronnyx wytschiliteljnix maschin b issledowanij pijsmennosti drewnyx Maia*, 3 Vols. (Akademija Nauk CCCR-Sibirskoje otedelenie) (Novosibirsk, 1961).

Genet, Jean, 'Les glyphes symboliques dans l'écriture maya-quichée. Le glyph symbolique de la guerre', *REMQ* 1.23-7 (1934).

——, 'L'écriture maya-quichée et les glyphes phonétiques', *REMQ* 1.37-63 (1934).

Graham, John, 'Sobre la escritura maya', *Desarrollo Cultural de los Mayas* 243-54 (Mexico, 1964).

Kelley, David, 'Fonetismo en la escritura Maya', *Estudios de Cultura Maya* 2.277-317 (1962).

——, 'Glyphic evidence for a dynastic sequence at Quirigua, Guatemala', *AA* 27.323-35 (1962).

——, 'A History of the decipherment of Maya script', *AnL* 4. 1-48 (1962).

Knorozov, Yuri, 'Drevnaja pis'mennost' Central'noj Ameriki', *Sov Etn* 3.100-18 (1952). (= 'La antigua escritura de los pueblos de America Central') (Mexico, 1954).

——, 'Pis'mennost' drevnih Maija (opyt rasšifrovki)', (= *Ancient Maya writing; attempt at decipherment*) *Sov Etn* 1.94-125 (1955).

——, *Sistema pis'ma drevnih maija* (= *La escritura de los antiguos Mayas*) (Moskau, 1955).

——, 'New data on the Maya written language', *JSAm* 45.209-16 (1956). (= *PICAm* 32.467-75 (1956)).

——, 'The problem of the study of the Maya hieroglyphic writing', *AA* 23.284-91 (1958).

——, 'La lengua de los textos jeroglíficos mayas', *ACIA* 33:2.571-79 (1959).

——, *Pis'mennost' indeizev Maija* (Moscow, 1963).

——, 'Aplicación de las matematicas al estudio lingüistico', *Estudios de Cultura Maya* 3.169-85 (1963).

Lizardi Ramos, Cesar, 'Los jeroglíficos Mayas y su descifración', *Esplendor del México Antiguo* 1.243-62 (Mexico, 1959).

Long, Richard, 'Maya and Mexican Writing', *Maya Research* 2.24-32 (1935).

——, 'Maya writing and its decipherment', *Maya Research* 3.309-15 (1936).

Makemson, Maud, *The Maya Correlation Problem* (Vassar College Observatory, Publications V.) (Poughkeepsie, 1946).

——, *The miscellaneous dates of the Dresden Codex* (Vassar College Observatory, Publications VI) (New York, 1957).

Maler, Teobert, *Researches in the central portion of the Usumatsintla Valley* (Piedras Negras, Chinikiha, etc.) (= *Memoirs of the Peabody Museum of Harvard University* 2:1) (Cambridge, 1901).

——, *Researches in the central portion of the Usumatsintla Valley* (*Memoirs of the Peabody Museum of Harvard University* 2:2) (Cambridge, 1903).

Maudslay, A. P., *Archaeology. Biologia Centrali-Americana*, 5 Vols. (London, 1889-1902).

Morley, Sylvanus, *The inscriptions at Copán* (= *Carnegie Institution Washington Publication* 219) (Washington, 1920).

——, *The inscriptions of Petén* (= *Carnegie Institution Washington Publication* 437, 5 Vols.) (Washington, 1937-1938).

Proskouriakoff, Tatiana, 'Historical implications of a pattern of dates at Piedras Negras, Guatemala', *AA* 25.454-75 (1960).

——, 'Portraits of women in Maya art', *Essays in pre-Columbian art and archaeology* 81-99 (Cambridge, Mass., 1961).

——, 'The lords of the Maya realm', *Expedition* 4:1.14-21 (1961).

——, 'Historical data in the inscriptions of Yaxchilan. Part I: The reign of Shield-Jaguar', *Estudios de Cultura Maya* 3.149-67 (1963).

——, 'Historical data in the inscriptions of Yaxchilan. Part II: The reigns of Bird-Jaguar and his successors', *Estudios de Cultura Maya* 4.177-201 (1964).

Sächsische Landesbilbiothek Dresden, Ed., *Maya-Handschrift der Sächsischen Landesbibliothek, Dresden* (Berlin, 1962).

Sáenz, César, *Exploraciones en la pirámide de la Cruz Foliada* (= *Instituto Nacional de Antropologia e Historia Informes*, No. 5) (Mexico, 1956).

Satterthwaite, Linton, *Concepts and structures of Maya calendrical arithmetics* (Philadelphia, 1947).

——, 'The dark phase of the moon and ancient Maya methods of solar eclipse prediction', *AA* 14.230-34 (1949).

——, 'Moon ages of the Maya inscriptions; The problem of their seven-day range of deviation from calculated mean ages', *PICAm* 29:1.142-54 (1949).

——, 'Radiocarbon dates and the Maya correlation problem', *AA* 21.416-19 (1956).

——, 'Five newly discovered carved nomuments at Tikal and new data on four others', *Museum Monographs, Tikal Reports*, No. 4 (Philadelphia, 1958).

——, 'Early "uniformity" Maya moon numbers at Tikal and elsewhere', *ACIA* 33:2.200-10 (1959).

——, 'An appraisal of a new Maya-Christian calendar correlation', *Estudios de Cultura Maya* 2.251-75 (1962).

——, 'Note on hieroglyphs on bone from the tomb below Temple I, Tikal', *Expedition* 6.18-19 (1963).

——, 'Calendrics of the Lowland Maya', Manuscript prepared for *Handbook of Middle American Indians*.

Satterthwaite, Linton and Ralph, E. K., 'New radiocarbon dates and the Maya correlation problem', *AA* 26.165-84 (1960).

Schellhas, Paul, 'Die Entzifferung der Mayahieroglyphen ein unlösbares Problem?' *Ethnos* 10.44-53 (1945).

Smith, Robert, *Ceramic sequence at Uaxactún, Guatemala* (Middle American Research Institute, Tulane University Publication 20, 2 vols.) (New Orleans, 1955).

Termer, Franz, *Die Mayaforschung* (Nova Acta Leopoldina Board 15, No. 105) (Leipzig, 1952).

Thompson, Eric, *The fish as a maya symbol for counting and further discussion of directional glyphs* (= *Theoretical Approaches to Problems* 2) (Carnegie Institution, Washington, 1944).

——, *Maya hieroglyphic writing: Introduction*, Publication 589 (Carnegie Institution, Washington, 1950).

——, 'Aquatic symbols common to various centers of the classic period in Meso-America', *PICAm* 29:1.31-6 (1951).

——, 'La inscripción jeroglífica del Tablero de El Palacio, Palenque', *AnINA* 4.61-8 (1952).

——, Review of Knorozov's 'La Antigua Escritura de los pueblos de America Central', *Yan* 2.174-78 (1953).
——, 'Research in Maya hieroglyphic writing', in Willey, Gordon, *Middle American anthropology* 43-52 (Washington, 1958).
——, 'Symbols, glyphs, and divinatory almanacs for diseases in the Maya Dresden and Madrid codices', *AA* 23.297-308 (1958).
——, 'Systems of hieroglyphic writing in Middle America and methods of deciphering them', *AA* 24.349-64 (1959).
——, 'A blood-drawing ceremony painted on a Maya vase', *Estudios de Cultura Maya* 1.13-20 (1961).
——, *A Catalog of Maya Hieroglyphs* (University of Oklahoma Press, Norman, 1962).
——, 'Pictorial synonyms and homonyms in the Maya Dresden Codex', *Tl* 4.148-56 (1963).
——, 'Algunas consideraciones respecto al desciframiento de los jeroglificos Mayas', *Estudios de Cultura Maya* 3.119-48 (1963).
Ulving, T. 'A new decipherment of the Maya glyphs', *Ethnos* 20.152-58 (1954).
Voegelin, C. F., and F. M., 'Typological classification of systems with included, excluded, and self-sufficient alphabets", *AnL* 3.55-96 (1961).
Whorf, Benjamin Lee, *The Phonetic value of certain characters in Maya writing* (= *Papers of the Peabody Museum of American Archaeology and Ethnology* 13:2 (1933).
——, 'Maya writing and its decipherment', *Maya Research* 2.367-82 (1935).
——, 'Decipherment of the linguistic portion of the Maya hieroglyphs', *Annual Report* 479-502 (Smithsonian Institution, Washington, 1942).
Zimmermann, Günter, *Kurze Formen- und Begriffssystematik der Hieroglyphen der Mayahandschriften* (= *Beiträge zur mittelamerikanischen Völkerkunde I*) (Hamburg, 1953).
——, 'Notas para la historia de los manuscritos Mayas', *Yan* 3.62-4 (1954).
——, *Die Hieroglyphen der Maya-Handschriften* (Hamburg, 1956).
——, 'La escritura jeroglífica y el calendario como indicadores de tendencias de la historia cultural de los Mayas', *Desarrollo cultural de los Mayas* 229-42 (Mexico, 1964).

DESCRIPTIVE LINGUISTICS

JOSEPH E. GRIMES

When Franz Boas introduced the first volume of the *International Journal of American Linguistics* he had to write: '... it is not saying too much if we claim that for most of the native languages of Central and South America the field is practically *terra incognita*. We have vocabularies; but, excepting the old missionary grammars, there is very little systematic work. Even where we have grammars, we have no bodies of aboriginal texts.'[1] The first number of *IJAL* contains a brief but systematic description by Boas himself,[2] and the first two volumes contain four more contributions of the kind Boas asked for.

Since then descriptive linguistics in Latin America has flourished. Vocabularies continue to be produced; grammars in whole or in part are common; entire text collections have been published for numerous languages. This florescence of descriptive studies can be attributed to the vigorous efforts of national institutions, such as the Instituto Nacional de Antropología e Historia of Mexico, the Comisión Indigenista of Venezuela, the Museu Nacional of Brazil, and similar institutions associated with the ministries of education of other nations. International organizations like the Summer Institute of Linguistics and the Instituto Indigenista Interamericano, which sponsor field work in a number of countries, have been an important factor in this growth in the field. Several North American universities have carried on research programs that touch indigenous languages of the area, notably California, Chicago, Cornell, Indiana, Pennsylvania, and Texas.

Periodicals in which descriptive statements on Latin American languages appear include not only *IJAL*, which specializes in such statements, but also *Acta Linguistica*, *American Anthropologist*, *América Indígena*, *Anales del Instituto Nacional de Antropología e Historia* (Mexico), *Anthropological Linguistics*, *Archivum Linguisticum*, *Boletín Indigenista*, *Boletín Indigenista Venezolano*, *Investigaciones Lingüísticas*, *Journal de la Société des Américanistes*, *Kroeber Anthropological Society Publications*, *Language*, *Lingua*, *Lingua Posnaniensis*, *Linguistics*, *El México Antiguo*, *Miscellanea Phonetica*, *Phonetica*, *Proceedings* of the International Congresses of Phonetic Sciences, of the International Congresses of Linguists, of the International Congresses of Americanists, *Revista Colombiana de Antropología*, *Revista Mexicana de Estudios Antropológicos*,

[1] *IJAL* 1.1-8 (1917).

[2] 'El dialecto mexicano de Pochutla, Oaxaca', *IJAL* 1.9-44 (1917).

Studies in Linguistics, Southwestern Journal of Anthropology, Tlalocan, Word, and *Zeitschrift für Phonetik, Sprachwissenschaft und Kommunikationsforschung.* Many universities, museums, and Indian institutes issue bulletins from time to time that contain descriptive material. The *Summer Institute of Linguistics Publications in Linguistics and Related Fields* is a series of monographs almost exclusively dedicated to descriptions made in Latin America; with it is associated a *Serie de Vocabularios Indígenas 'Mariano Silva y Aceves'.* For bibliographic reference the annual *Bibliographie linguistique publiée par le Comité International Permanent des Linguistes* gives coverage in a section on 'Langues Américaines', and the occasional *Bibliography of the Summer Institute of Linguistics* (latest edition dated February 1964) gives a cumulative list of all publications of the Institute's members. *Dissertation Abstracts* contains abstracts of all doctoral dissertations from a number of North American universities, including some on Latin American languages; *Linguistics* also reports dissertations occasionally.

In discussing the current status of descriptive linguistics and the trends the field is taking, then, there is no longer any need to sound as forlorn about the state of things as Boas did in 1917. On the contrary; the problem now is to maintain reasonably complete coverage of the field. In this chapter there is no attempt to mention every descriptive work published on an indigenous language of Latin America, but only to evaluate trends and emphases, citing works that are representative of schools of thought.

The kind of descriptive work done most recently in Latin America has varied in emphasis, depending partly on the end for which the studies were done and in even greater part on the theoretical interests at the moment of the analyst and his circle of colleagues. Thus, a number of descriptive studies have taken shape during the pursuit of some formulation of linguistic theory, while others during the course of field research have brought to light phenomena that required a revision of existing theory in order to account for them. Even these studies, however, reflect the Boasian bias toward getting on record all the data possible from as many languages as possible. Many other studies are routinely Boasian; they do not purport to form part of the continuing debate on the nature of human language, but only to report what the field worker hears and sees. A few studies have been made as preliminary to other linguistic work: preparation of language teaching materials, for example, or comparative linguistic studies.

I. PHONOLOGICAL THEORY

Theories concerning the nature of phonology and its relationship to the rest of language have been tested extensively on Latin American languages. At the same time, some developments in phonological theory have been required by the nature of some of the language systems observed, so that previously unnoticed phenomena could be described adequately.

The best illustration of this interplay between the growth of a theoretical position and the empirical requirement that all languages studied be adequately described is the work of Pike and his associates. The first attempted description in phonology by this group was McIntosh's 'Huichol phonemes', which appeared in 1945, prepared under Pike's guidance.[3] The approach to phonology used there and in subsequent papers from the same period was substantially the one embodied in Pike's *Phonemics* of 1947, a sequentially oriented approach to phonemicizing on the basis of relationships among neighboring phonetic segments.[4] Many descriptions of phonological systems were made using this approach, not only by members of the Summer Institute of Linguistics but also by linguists such as Hildebrandt in Macoita and Hawkins in Waiwai.[5]

A year after *Phonemics*, Pike set forth in *Tone Languages* a methodology that proved helpful in investigating systems of tonal contrasts in a number of languages.[6] He included in this book not only an exposition of his method but also two monograph-length appendices that describe in detail the phonology and the tonal morphophonemics of two Mexican languages. With Eunice V. Pike he also published 'Immediate constituents of Mazateco syllables',[7] which became the model for the development of a hierarchical view of phonological structure. Hockett, although disagreeing vigorously with Pike concerning what the latter insisted were 'grammatical prerequisites to phonemic analysis',[8] took up the hierarchical model in his *Manual of Phonology*,[9] which itself became the basis for several descriptions of phonological systems of Latin American languages.[10] Pike attempted to integrate a hierarchical view of phonology with a general theory of linguistics in 1954.[11] The first description of a Latin American phonological system produced under the impact of his general theory was the McArthurs' 'Aguacatec (Mayan) phonemes within the stress group', in which stress

[3] John B. McIntosh, 'Huichol phonemes', *IJAL* 11.31-5 (1945).

[4] Kenneth L. Pike, *Phonemics: a technique for reducing languages to writing* (Ann Arbor, 1947).

[5] Martha Hildebrandt, *Sistema fonémico del Macoita* (Caracas, 1958). W. Neill Hawkins, *A fonologia da lingua uáiuái* (São Paulo, 1952).

[6] Kenneth L. Pike, *Tone languages: a technique for determing the number and type of pitch contrasts in a language, with studies in tonemic substitution and fusion* (Ann Arbor, 1948).

[7] 'Immediate constituents of Mazateco syllables', *IJAL* 13.78-91 (1947).

[8] Kenneth L. Pike, 'Grammatical prerequisites to phonemic analysis', *Word* 3.155-72 (1947). Charles F. Hockett, 'Two fundamental problems in phonemics', *SIL* 7.29-51 (1949). Pike, 'More on grammatical prerequisites', *Word* 8.106-21 (1952). In perspective it appears that both Pike and Hockett were reacting to high level phonological phenomena without recognizing them as such at the time. Now that they are explicitly taken into account in phonological analysis, this debate has lost most of its significance.

[9] Charles F. Hockett, *A manual of phonology* (=Memoir 11 of the International Journal of American Linguistics, Part I of *IJAL* 21:4) (Baltimore, 1955).

[10] Frank E. Robbins, 'Quiotepec Chinantec syllable patterning', *IJAL* 27.237-50 (1961). Robbins, 'Palabras nasales sin vocales fonéticas en el chinanteco de Quiotepec', *A William Cameron Townsend en el Vigésimoquinto Aniversario del Instituto Lingüístico de Verano* 653-6 (México, 1961). Joseph E. Grimes, 'Huichol tone and intonation', *IJAL* 25.221-32 (1959).

[11] Kenneth L. Pike, *Language in relation to a unified theory of the structure of human behavior* (Glendale, Part 1, 1954; Part 2, 1955; Part 3, 1960). Part 2 is especially concerned with phonology.

group boundaries, rather than grammatical word boundaries, were recognized as a conditioning environment for allophonic variation.[12]

In the analysis of some Indian languages of Peru, in which teams of field investigators worked intensively for several months under Pike's personal guidance, problems came to be recognized concerning the nature of peak and boundary phenomena at higher phonological levels: the possibility that complex foot nuclei consisting of several syllables might have to be recognized in Campa,[13] problems in locating syllable boundaries in Huitoto,[14] and a previously unreported kind of contrast — ballistic versus controlled feet — in Arabela.[15] Not long after this, Crawford, while studying under Pike, attempted to combine certain refinements in Pike's phonological theory with a descriptive dissertation, *Totontepec Mixe phonotagmemics*.[16]

The approach to phonology pioneered by J. R. Firth in Great Britain has been applied in the field of Latin American linguistics in a limited way, notably by Callow in Apinayé and by Bendor-Samuel in Terena.[17] The Terena data have also been discussed from within the Pike-Hockett tradition by Ekdahl and Grimes.[18]

Of other theoretical trends in phonology that are reasonably easy to identify and label, the generative theories of Chomsky are only beginning to be applied to indigenous languages of Latin America. To date nothing has appeared in print.

New linguistic phenomena have turned up in the process of field work in Latin America. They have had a tendency to stretch existing views of language in one direction or another, with the result that any workable linguistic theory must now be able to span a wider typological range than formerly. Among these phenomena can be mentioned the five-way pitch contrasts of Trique and Ticuna,[19] the five-way contrastive system of nasals in Pehuenche,[20] the complex structure of the foot in Shiriana,[21] the influence of syntactic as well as morphological factors in tonal morphophonemics in Huave and Northern Tepehuan,[22] phonetically atypical but distributionally plausi-

[12] Harry and Lucille McArthur, 'Aguacatec (Mayan) phonemes within the stress group', *IJAL* 22.72-6 (1956).

[13] Kenneth L. Pike and Willard Kindberg, 'A problem in multiple stresses', *Word* 12.415-28 (1956).

[14] Eugene Minor, 'Witoto vowel clusters', *IJAL* 22.131-7 (1956).

[15] Kenneth L. Pike, 'Abdominal pulse types in some Peruvian languages', *Lg* 33.30-5 (1957).

[16] John Chapman Crawford, *Pike's tagmemic model applied to Totontepec Mixe phonology* (University of Michigan doctoral dissertation, 1959), reissued as *Totontepec Mixe phonotagmemics* (Norman, Oklahoma, 1963).

[17] John Campbell Callow, *The Apinayé language: phonology and grammar* (University of London, 1962). John T. Bendor-Samuel, 'Some problems of segmentation in the phonological analysis of Terena', *Word* 16.348-55 (1960). Bendor-Samuel, 'Stress in Terena', *Transactions of the Philological Society* (1962), 105-23.

[18] Muriel Ekdahl and Joseph E. Grimes, 'Terena verb inflection', *IJAL* 30.261-8 (1964).

[19] Robert E. Longacre, 'Five phonemic pitch levels in Trique', *Acta Linguistica* 7.62-81 (1952). Lambert Anderson, 'Ticuna vowels with special regard to the system of five tonemes', 76-119 *Publicagoes do Museu Nacional* (Rio de Janeiro, 1959).

[20] Jorge A. Suárez, 'The phonemes of an Araucanian dialect', *IJAL* 25.177-81 (1959).

[21] Ernest Migliazza and Joseph E. Grimes, 'Shiriana phonology', *AnL* 3:6.31-41 (1961).

[22] Kenneth L. Pike and Milton Warkentin, 'Huave, a study in syntactic tone with low lexical functional load', *A William Cameron Townsend en el Vigésimoquinto Aniversario del Instituto Lingüístico de Verano* 627-42 (México, 1961). Burton Bascom, 'Tonomechanics of Northern Tepehuan', *Phonetica* 4.71-88 (1959).

ble variants of phonemes in Amuesha and Maxakalí,[23] three contrastive vowel lengths in Coatlán Mixe,[24] and simple patterns underlying complex consonant sequences in Chatino.[25] As spadework of this kind continues, it is probable that the yield of novel phenomena that have to be fitted into phonological theory by one means or another will increase before it levels off.

II. GRAMMATICAL THEORY

As in phonology, the clearest illustration of the interplay between problems encountered in the description of Latin American indigenous languages and the development of linguistics as a discipline is Pike's development of the so-called tagmemic theory of grammar. Just as his hierarchical view of phonology grew from an attempt to handle data in Mazateco and Mixteco, so his view of grammar was in part molded by the way in which Mixteco refused to fit neatly into a model that assumed a priori a distinction between morphology and syntax, or that required agreement between phonological and grammatical boundaries.[26] The theoretical framework he has developed over the last decade or so leaves open the possibility, therefore, that a language may be treated without reference to a clearcut distinction between levels, or rather (as explicated by Longacre[27]) may be treated with reference to a number of different levels of grammatical configuration. The extreme instance of the kind of phenomena that operate across levels in Mixteco is probably Rosbottom's analysis of Bolivian Guaraní, in which functional elements that form a small closed class, tense markers, are shown to fit into the grammatical system at widely different levels.[28]

Soon after Pike published his general statement of tagmemic theory he had opportunity in Peru to work with a team of field investigators to apply it in a variety of systems; it has since been put to use in many workshop situations. The third number of Volume 23 of *IJAL* (July, 1957), for example, is devoted exclusively to studies made as a test of Pike's theory as applied to five different American Indian languages.[29] Although the entire collection suffers from the ponderous style of Pike's *Language*, and the reader often bogs down in terminological and formulaic apparatus, the papers in it are remarkably thorough demonstrations that Pike's theory is applicable to natural language. More recent papers in the same tradition (for example, Lind's on

[23] Mary Ruth Wise, 'Diverse points of articulation of allophones in Amuesha (Arawak)', *Miscellanea Phonetica* 3.15-21 (1958). Sarah Gudschinsky, paper on Maxakalí presented to the summer meeting of the Linguistic Society of America (Bloomington, 1964).

[24] Searle Hoogshagen, 'Three contrastive vowel lengths in Mixe', *ZPhon* 12.111-5 (1959).

[25] Howard P. McKaughan, 'Chatino formulas and phonemes', *IJAL* 20.23-7 (1954).

[26] Kenneth L. Pike, 'Analysis of a Mixteco text', *IJAL* 10.113-382 (1944). Pike, *Language* 3.28,70.

[27] Robert E. Longacre, *Grammar discovery procedures: a field manual* (The Hague, 1964). This book contains a number of examples of linguistic structures in languages of Latin America viewed tagmemically.

[28] Harry Rosbottom, 'Different-level tense markers in Guaraní', *IJAL* 27.345-52 (1961).

[29] Doris Cox, 'Candoshi verb inflection', *IJAL* 23.129-40 (1957). Helen Long Hart, 'Hierarchical

Sierra Popoluca[30]) have become much more transparent, largely through the introduction of paradigm and matrix presentation of related phenomena and the simplification of formulas. Monograph-length examples of tagmemic analysis by Pike's students are Pickett on Isthmus Zapotec and Waterhouse on Oaxaca Chontal.[31]

The British structure-function approach to grammar, like Firthian phonology, is represented in the work of Callow on Apinayé and Bendor-Samuel on Jebero and Terena.[32] Bendor-Samuel's dissertation on Jebero was the first on an American Indian language to be presented at the University of London.

Pittman introduced a Hjelmslevian note into Latin American linguistics with his grammar of Tetelcingo Náhuatl,[33] but his example was not followed further. Studies made from the point of view of generative or transformational grammar have not been published on languages of Latin America.[33a] The transformation has, however, been used as a descriptive device within a different framework by Gudschinsky and Grimes.[34]

The notion of a morphology-syntax division is still under discussion by linguists who work in Latin America. Hoff deals with it in Carib and Clark finds it not completely relevant in Sayula Popoluca.[35]

Types of grammatical phenomena recently brought to light in languages of the hemisphere include the complex grammar and morphophonemics associated with stem initial position in Otomí reported by Wallis,[36] the discrepancies between morphophonemic domains and grammatical constructions reported by Priest, Priest, and Grimes in Siriono,[37] the compound affixes found by Pike in Ocaina.[38]

---

structuring of Amuzgo grammar', 141-64. Marvin Mayers, 'Pocomchi verb structure', 165-70. Martha Duff, 'A syntactical analysis of an Amuesha (Arawak) text', 171-8. Olive A. Shell, 'Cashibo II: grammemic analysis of transitive and intransitive verb patterns', 179-218.

[30] John O. Lind, 'Clause and sentence level syntagmemes in Sierra Popoluca', *IJAL* 30.341-54 (1964).

[31] Velma Bernice Pickett, *The grammatical hierarchy of Isthmus Zapotec* (Baltimore, 1960). Viola Waterhouse, *The grammatical structure of Oaxaca Chontal* (Bloomington, Indiana, 1962).

[32] See also Footnote 17. John T. Bendor-Samuel, *The structure and function of the verbal piece in the Jebero language* (University of London doctoral dissertation, 1958), reissued as *The verbal piece in Jebero* (Monograph 4, Supplement to *Word* 17), 1961.

[33] Richard S. Pittman, *A grammar of Tetelcingo (Morelos) Nahuatl* (Language Dissertation No. 50, Supplement to *Lg* 30), Baltimore, Linguistic Society of America (1954).

[33a] Since this chapter went to press, John Paul Daly's *Generative Syntax of Mixteco* (Indiana University doctoral dissertation, 1966) has appeared.

[34] Sarah C. Gudschinsky, 'Mazatec kernel constructions and transformations', *IJAL* 25.81-9 (1959). Joseph E. Grimes, *Huichol syntax* (Cornell University doctoral dissertation, 1960), reissued as *Huichol syntax* (The Hague, 1964).

[35] B. J. Hoff, 'The nominal word-group in Carib: a problem of delimitation of syntax and morphology', *Lingua* 11.157-64 (1962). Lawrence E. Clark, 'Sayula Popoluca morpho-syntax', *IJAL* 28.183-98 (1962).

[36] Ethel E. Wallis, 'Simulfixation in aspect markers of Mezquital Otomi', *Lg* 32.453-9 (1956).

[37] Perry N. Priest, Anne M. Priest, and Joseph E. Grimes, 'Simultaneous orderings in Siriono (Guarani)', *IJAL* 27.335-44 (1961).

[38] Kenneth L. Pike, 'Compound affixes in Ocaina', *Lg* 37.570-81 (1961).

III. SEMANTICS

Mathiot's work on the form of a dictionary for Papago and Cowan's notes on a Mazateco text[39] are the most extensive attempts at a theoretically oriented description of semantics yet undertaken in languages of Latin America. Landar made a semantic componential analysis of Tequistlatec kinship terminology; Grimes and Grimes did the same for Huichol.[40] More restricted studies in the field of semantics include those by Pottier, Ramírez, Aschmann, and Wiesemann.[41]

IV. BASES FOR COMPARATIVE STUDIES

A number of linguistic descriptions seem to be made with the primary motivation of providing data for comparative linguistic studies to be made later. This seems to be a focus (though by no means the limit) of interest for a number of Mexican linguists, particularly those who worked with Swadesh.[42] Others such as Fernández de Miranda and Weitlaner, who were not directly associated with Swadesh, agree with his group in this orientation toward descriptive work for comparison's sake.[43] Rodrigues in Brazil has similar interests.[44]

V. DIALECTOLOGY

While no extensive work in the dialectology of Indian languages has been carried out, small projects are reported from several places, and there appears to be continuing interest.[45] John Crawford is directing an extensive set of field surveys in Mexico but has not yet prepared materials for publication.

[39] (Mathiot, reference unavailable.) George M. Cowan, *Some aspects of the lexical structure of a Mazatec historical text* (Norman, Oklahoma, 1965).
[40] Landar, Herbert J., 'Semantic components of Tequistlatec kinship', *IJAL* 26.72-5 (1960). Joseph E. Grimes and Barbara F. Grimes, 'Semantic distinctions in Huichol (Uto-Aztecan) kinship', *AmA* 64.104-14 (1962).
[41] Bernard Pottier, 'Catégories linguistiques et expérience en guarani', *BFS* 39.329-32 (1962), Félix C. Ramírez, *Semántica y mecanismo de construcción de la lengua Phurhembe (Tarasca o Michoacana)* (México, 1955). Herman P. Aschmann, 'Totonac categories of smell', *Tl* 2.187-9 (1946). Ursula Wiesemann, 'Semantic categories of good and bad in relation to Kaingang personal names', *RMPaul*, n.s. 12.177-84 (1960).
[42] For example, Roberto Escalante H., 'El Pima Bajo', *AnINA* 14.349-52 (1962), and similar studies by Manrique and Arana.
[43] María Teresa Fernández de Miranda, *Diccionario Ixcateco* (Instituto Nacional de Antropología e Historia, Dirección de investigaciones antropológicas, Publicación 7, México, 1961). Roberto J. Weitlaner, 'El Otomí de Ixtenco, Tlaxcala', in *Estudios antropológicos publicados en homenaje al doctor Manuel Gamio*, 693-6 (México, Universidad Nacional Autónoma, 1956).
[44] Arion Dall'Igna Rodrigues, 'Morphologische Erscheinungen einer Indianersprache', *MSS* 7.79-88 (1955).
[45] Jacob A. Loewen, 'Dialectología de la familia lingüística Choco', *RCA* 9.9-22 (1960). Marvin K. Mayers, 'The linguistic unity of Pocomam-Pocomchí', *IJAL* 26.290-300 (1960). Bernard Pottier,

VI. PRESERVATION OF DISAPPEARING LANGUAGES

In some areas, notably the southern part of the Amazon basin and the Chaco, a number of languages have but recently gone out of existence, and others seem to be headed for extinction. Rather than allow these languages to be lost, linguists have made a special effort to record them. Much of the work of Nimuendajú had this effect.[46] Sargent and Peeke made a special project of recording Záparo and Shimigae.[47] Fernández de Miranda's Ixcateco field work was done under similar circumstances.[48]

VII. SUMMARY

In the field of descriptive linguistics in Latin America there has been interaction between theoretical development and on-the-spot analysis, particularly in the case of Pike's linguistic theories, and to a lesser extent in the case of the British structure-function school. New types of linguistic phenomena continue to come to light even in the case of routine investigations made without reference to refining any particular theory of language. While little was known about any of the indigenous languages of Latin America thirty to fifty years ago, enough work is now completed, in progress, or planned to insure eventual thorough coverage of the area from a descriptive point of view.

'Problèmes de dialectologie dans le domaine du tupi-guaranai', *Orbis* 10.31-34 (1961). Sarah C. Gudschinsky, 'Mazatec dialect history: A study in miniature', *Lg* 34.469-81 (1958). Juan A. Hasler, 'La posición dialectológica del Pipil como parte del Nahua del Este', *América Indígena* 18.333-9 (1958).

[46] Curt Nimuendajú, 'Reconhecimento dos Rios Içána, Ayarí, e Uaupés, março a julho de 1927. Apontamentos linguísticos', first part in *Revista del Instituto de Etnología de Tucumán* 2.590-618 (1932), second part in *JSAm* 44.149-78 (1955).

[47] Mary Sargent, 'Vocabulario Záparo', in *Estudios acerca de las lenguas Huarani (Auca), Shimigae y Zápara*, 43-8 (Publicaciones científicas del Ministerio de Educación del Ecuador, 1949). Catherine Peeke, 'Structural summary of Záparo', *Studies in Ecuadorian Indian languages I*, 125-216 (Publication 7 of the Linguistic Series of the Summer Institute of Linguistics of the University of Oklahoma, 1962). Catherine Peeke, 'Shimigae, idioma que se extingue', *Perú Indígena* 5.170-8 (1954), reprinted in *Estudios acerca de las lenguas Huarani (Auca), Shimigae y Zápara* 18-28 (1959). Catherine Peeke and Mary Sargent, 'Pronombres personales en Andoa', *Perú Indígena* 5.103-12 (1953), reprinted as 'Pronombres personales en Shimigae', *Estudios acerca de las lenguas Huarani (Auca), Shimigae y Zápara* 29-42 (1959).

[48] María Teresa Fernández de Miranda, *Fonémica del Ixcateco* (Instituto Nacional de Antropología e Historia, Publicación 3), México, 1959). See also Footnote 43, *Diccionario.*

INDIGENOUS DIALECTOLOGY

MARVIN K. MAYERS

Dialect studies in broad perspective have to do with any linguistic study that involves structural or comparative consideration of dialect. Dialectology, or dialect studies more narrowly conceived, involves those linguistic studies that indicate dialect distinction or definition. The goal of such research is to establish a sound base from which to project further structural and historical linguistic studies. Effective dialectology is dependent on two main factors: the provision of extensive diagnostic linguistic materials,[1] and the confirmation of results from various related and supporting disciplines such as geography, anthropology, psychology and sociology.[2] Linguistics has an adequate technique for providing the materials for such study in the dialect survey.[3] Since, however, dialect surveys can be carried out ineffectively as well as effectively, the following paper will attempt to present an ideal approach to dialect survey, and with this as background, discuss a number of attempts to do dialect studies in Ibero-America in light of their successes and shortcomings. It is quite obvious, from a study of the literature, that very little dialectology has been done in this area of the world. That which has been done is of a preliminary nature and itself needs amplification and extension before its validity can be fully established and evaluated.

An ideal approach to dialect studies would involve a careful geographical consideration of the area of interest, with mapping undertaken following the general knowledge of a given language area as provided by government personnel, business interests, missionaries, nationals, etc. Political boundaries need to be kept in mind as well,

[1] There is no intention here of becoming involved in the argument of whether a mass of material is needed to prove genetic relationship, i.e. by eliminating the chance factor, or whether in fact, a single innovation may constitute the entire phonological evidence for proving the unique common history of a given subgroup. The information called for here is all the defining and supporting evidence necessary to convincingly establish dialect boundary.

[2] Linguistics has long recognized the need for adequate geographical orientation to dialect research. Uriel Weinreich in *Languages in contact* (The Hague, 1963) indicates the need for psychological and sociocultural stimuli to structural (or linguistic) stimuli which help to determine linguistic interference, and he also warns that 'the linguist who makes theories about language influence but neglects to account for the sociocultural setting of the language contact leaves his study suspended, as it were, in mid-air'. Further, quoting Haugen, he suggests that 'talk of substrata and superstrata must remain stratospheric unless we can found it solidly on the behavior of living observable speakers'.

[3] Hans Kurath, *Handbook of the linguistic geography of New England*, 48-50, (Providence, R.I., 1939) gives some excellent instruction for field work. New techniques are being developed with the wider usage of the tape recorder, but little is in print describing these techniques.

so that both urban and rural areas might be included in the study. Lines of communication and transportation throughout the area would be plotted since migration is generally effected along lines of easy access.

The survey itself is best carried out in multiple stages, where possible. The initial stage would be a sociolinguistic shallow survey involving sociocultural[4] data; a linguistic word list such as the Swadesh 100 diagnostic word list;[5] a supplementary word list prepared for the local area in mind, to be appended to the basic word list and used as a control for evaluating the results of the 100 list; and a questionnaire involving details of the community involvement for every political unit, i.e. every town, city, etc. in the language area to provide broad background knowledge.[6] Observations made by the field investigators of a sociocultural nature not specified on the various questionnaires would also be noted. The linguistic and sociocultural questionnaires would ideally be elicited from at least two individuals from every distinct geographical or political division within the potential language community. Where the population is larger, or the geographical or political entity more extensive or diversified, more questionnaires[7] would be completed as a safeguard.

During the carrying out of the shallow survey or following its completion, all materials would be processed in a consistent way prior to instituting the second stage. Processing would involve first of all a lexicostatistical analysis of the diagnostic word lists.[8] The purpose of the lexicostatistical study would be primarily synchronic rather than diachronic, in that all the linguistic features would be submerged within the whole, and specific details of the languages would only be projected onto the gross lexicostatistical results.[9] This would be effected by the preparation of a linguistic-geographical map,[10] which would be used as a base map for dialect geography map-

4 The term 'sociocultural' will be used to include details of social organization, cultural information, and physiological information of both individual and society.

5 Any word list could serve so long as it represented 'cultural' items and 'noncultural' items and was recorded systematically and consistently throughout the area of the survey. The Swadesh 100 diagnostic list is satisfactory for this purpose and in fact to be desired as a base list, since it has been used in a wide variety of situations and thus can serve as a 'standard' word list, eliminating the proliferation of word lists with only local impact.

6 As a check on the coverage of the survey, a question such as: 'Are there any towns or villages in this area where the people do not speak exactly as you do?' should be asked of each informant in the survey.

7 Because of the factors of time and finances, it is seldom possible to effect a 'statistically' valid selection of participants in the survey. A survey, however, executed according to the above plan will turn up enough diagnostic details for the preliminary determination of dialect boundary and will be far superior to the 'hit and miss' method employed in dialect survey at the present time.

8 See Sarah C. Gudschinsky, 'The ABC's of lexicostatistics (glottochronology)', *Word* 12.175-210 (1956), and David Henne, 'Quiche dialect survey', ms. Summer Institute of Linguistics (Guatemala, 1965), for two ways of processing the lexical material of the survey.

9 This particular aspect of lexicostatistical method, which is a shortcoming in diachronic studies, becomes a distinct asset in synchronic studies.

10 By permuting columns and rows on a traditional lexicostatistical chart until there was an overall gradation of percentage of shared retention from high to low on the rows and columns, there would result clusterings of similar numbers at the point of intersection of rows and columns. Such clusterings of similar numbers are interpreted as dialect cores. These dialect cores would then be spread on a

ping as well as for other sociolinguistic plotting. Such a map is the base map used in Norman A. McQuown, *Measures of dialect-distance in Tzeltal-Tzotzil*,[11] and Marvin K. Mayers, 'The linguistic unity of Pocomam-Pocomchi'.[12] Isoglosses drawn on a linguistic geographical base map have been found to produce a clearer profile of dialect unity or separation than those drawn on a strictly geographical map. A preliminary attempt should be made at this time also, to correlate sociocultural information with linguistic usage.

Once the shallow survey had been completed, and the results known, a second survey would be planned making maximal usage of the processed data of the first. This would be a depth survey and would be carried out ideally with representatives of the resultant dialect areas selected on the basis of the shallow survey. Approximately one-tenth[13] of the initial participants in the original survey would thus be revisited and restudied. A new word list would be compiled, based on the first and including as many new items as would appear to be fruitful for a comparative study of the dialects. A more extensive sociocultural questionnaire would be prepared involving daily schedules, year cycles, diets, as complete kinship data as possible, etc. A tape recording would be made for each informant and each recording played to the other for mutual intelligibility check, and all played for specialists in the language where these are available. The speech of each individual in the survey would be structurally analyzed as fully as possible in the time available. This would involve not only phonological analysis of the traditional segmental type but also of phonological units more complex than those of the segment, such as the syllable, word, and others. Grammatical structures would also be analyzed for all levels of grammatical analysis.[14] Lexical-semantic analysis should be undertaken as well to the limits of theory, though at present, technique of such analysis follows far behind that of the phonological or grammatical techniques. If possible, psychological tests could also be applied.[15]

A third stage of ongoing linguistic and cultural studies would follow the processing of the material of stage two. Two or more representative speakers of the language whole would be selected to enter into full scale language and cultural analyses in preparation for multi-language diachronic studies in the language family involved, and from this into a multi-family comparison.

---

geographical map and the two be made to coincide with the least amount of distortion of either the linguistic data or of the geographical information.

11 University of Chicago (1958).

12 *IJAL* 26.290-300 (1960a).

13 This percentage would be adjusted in keeping with the extensiveness of the survey.

14 Once analysis is in hand for this aspect of the linguistic whole, any one of the descriptive techniques of the stratificational, tagmemic, or transformational approaches can be applied to the analysis for structural presentation and the phonology oriented to the grammar in the final description. The main requisite is that the material be handled consistently and compared consistently.

15 McQuown, in his *Indian and ladino bilingualism: sociocultural contrasts in Chiapas, Mexico*, mimeo (Chicago, 1964), made use of the conventional T.A.T. as well as a photo test for cultural perception devised especially for the Chicago Chiapas project.

No one study, however carefully made, produces the final answer in language classification.[16] Such a careful preparation for further comparative work, however exhausting and time consuming, will insure more effective results than we are now achieving. The program, further, is totally within the realm of possibility for Ibero-America with the extensive research programs of various universities and of the Summer Institute of Linguistics.

In 1958, McQuown[17] presented some of the linguistic results of the ongoing Chicago project among the Tzeltal and Tzotzil Indian peoples of Chiapas, Mexico. The survey team consisted of a geographer, a botanist, an archaeologist, two social anthropologists and a linguist. The initial survey made use of Swadesh's 100- and 200-word 'basic' vocabulary lists coupled with a list of 400 'cultural words'. To these 600 words were added, in a few instances, more specialized vocabularies covering the geography and the flora and fauna. The purpose of this initial survey was 'to work out a minimal questionnaire of maximally contrastive items for a saturation study of the dialect variation in the project transect'. An intensive dialect distributional survey was planned for the summer of 1958 and was expected to include the social differentiation dimension, as well as the geographical dimension; in this survey it was intended that informants would be so chosen as to represent both 'horizontal and vertical dimensions'.

The processed material, as presented, included a geographical map of the transect, the lexicostatistical results ordered first with an arbitrary geographical ordering and then following an ordering based on the permutation of columns and rows of the geographical chart, until clusters of like numbers (of sameness-difference) appeared at the point of intersection of rows and columns; a geographical linguistic map; and four presentations of dialect geographical studies including two of normalized phonemic isoglosses, and one each of phonetic and lexical isoglosses. The isogloss presentations utilized the geographical linguistic map as a base map.

Further materials, reporting on the survey in depth and its significance, are continuing to appear. McQuown[18] reported on the attempt to correlate linguistic materials with the results of cultural projection tests and sociocultural census information. Though the purpose of the paper was to study bilingualism, it gives invaluable background for proper evaluation of the language contact problem in dialect studies.

Nicholas A. Hopkins[19] has submitted a paper to the Boletin of the Instituto Nacional Indigenista in which he reports on sociocultural aspects of linguistic distributions in the Tzeltal Tzotzil area. He attempts to describe briefly the varieties of Tzeltal and

[16] Though we do agree with Gudschinsky, 'Mazatec dialect history', *Lg* 34.474 (1958), that 'for establishing linguistic subgroups, lexical isoglosses are less reliable than phonological isoglosses. ...' and thus would rank aspects of the total study in terms of 'more helpful, less helpful'; 'more reliable, less reliable' etc.

[17] Norman A. McQuown, *op. cit.* (1958).

[18] Norman A. McQuown, *op. cit.* (1964).

[19] Hopkins, 'Sociocultural aspects of linguistic distributions: a preliminary study of Tzeltal and Tzotzil dialects', ms. (1965).

Tzotzil and the geographical distributions of these varieties; to relate these geographical distributions to social factors which underlie them; to place the contemporary linguistic varieties in the perspective of their historical development; and to draw inferences about the historical development of the indigenous communities themselves. Hopkins finds each community relatively homogeneous internally with some phonological, morphological, or lexical features shared by no other community. Likewise, clusters of geographically contiguous communities share features not found outside the cluster. 'It is suggested that this situation results from a series of splits in speech communities, the single, homogeneous, Proto-Tzeltal-Tzotzil speech community having split into two divisions, the ancestors of Tzeltal and of Tzotzil, each of these further split into several speech communities, the progenitors of the modern dialect clusters, which in turn developed into the modern individual dialects.'

The materials by McQuown and Hopkins are the first of a wealth of material coming from the Chiapas area and in effect set the standard for dialect studies in the Americas. There will be no question in the mind of the reader nor of the scholar who makes use of the material for comparative work as to the representativeness of the data, nor are there likely to be significant dialects left out of major language studies, produced in the area.

Gudschinsky has presented a 'precise analysis, in miniature, of successive dialect splits and of the effects on these splits of the disturbing factors of shift in the boundaries of speech communities'.[20] The analysis is further supported by a high correlation with the word geography of the area and with what is known of the political history of the Mazatecs. Being both a careful comparativist and a thorough field worker, the scholar is not too concerned that he must accept Gudschinsky's word that the material she utilizes is complete as far as diagnostic detail is concerned, representative of the language,[21] and true to each dialect in the languge; but her approach in the hands of a lesser scholar could seriously affect the usefulness of the results.

In 1960[22] I undertook a dialect survey of one of the Mayan languages of Guatemala, first to understand the internal dialect picture of the language and second to prepare a base from which the language itself could be effectively compared with other languages, both within and without the Mayan family of languages. The survey was undertaken in two stages: in the first I made use of few materials with a sampling of fifty individuals. In the second stage, I made use of extensive materials with nine individuals. The purpose of the first stage of the research was to select the individuals who would be most representative of their particular cultural and linguistic subgroup so that I

[20] Sarah C. Gudschinsky, *op. cit.* (1958).

[21] We are informed at the end of the article that 'the earlier study was able to draw on data from only six dialects instead of the present ten', which in itself would be no problem except that because of this, 'the unity of the high dialect was not apparent'. The question naturally arises, are there further dialects that could modify the picture presented in this later article or are we to await new information after further dialects are studied?

[22] Marvin K. Mayers, *The Pocomchi: a sociolinguistic study*, University of Chicago (1960b abstract).

could proceed with depth studies. The purpose of the second stage of the research was to prepare a preliminary phonology, grammar, and lexicon that would be as much as possible representative of the language itself, and to attempt to understand a) the way language interacts with culture and b) the way culture confirms dialect groupings or indicates further dialect divisions based on sociolinguistic criteria. It is with this basic linguistic and sociocultural information that the language itself can be compared beyond the borders of the language, i.e. with other Mayan or non-Mayan languages.

The structural studies produced two distinct dialects,[23] i.e. two dialects, with one having two divisions within the Pocomchi language, based on the phonology and grammar. Only one dialect with three subgroups resulted on the basis of the lexicostatistical counting.[24] Geographical and cultural divisions within this ethnic linguistic group bear out the division into three groups. As might be expected, the group dialects are mutually intelligible, and the dialect division is based on the clustering of features, rather than as a result of any neat break in a scale of sameness-difference.

I took with me into the field three basic tools of research: a linguistic word list, a sociocultural census, and a tape recorder. The linguistic word list consisted of the Swadesh diagnostic one-hundred-word list to show minimum difference between informants and to be the basis for lexicostatistical counts. It also included an additional one-hundred-and-fifty-word list that was intended to show maximum difference between informants. Both word lists were designed to provide phonological, lexical, and grammatical information, which, in turn, would contribute toward descriptive analysis of the speech of these informants. It was further planned that specific linguistic features, isolable in the material in the word lists, would form the basis for dialect distributional studies.

The sociocultural census included one hundred and twenty-six questions designed to give information regarding the person of the informant, his family, his social and civic responsibilities, his occupation and wealth, his religion and religious responsibilities, and the degree of his assimilation into the Latin culture. It also attempted to indicate his preference for dress, for his living situation, i.e. house type and location, and in what relationship to his neighbors he considered himself in terms of wealth, social class, and prestige. The census was to provide the basis for a descriptive statement of the sociocultural placement of the informants. Finally, the results of the census were to be placed side by side with those of the word list, in an attempt to observe whatever correspondences[25] there might be between the two, and to determine just how language indexes culture.

[23] The San Cristobal and the Tactic-Tamahu dialects.

[24] In initial interpretations two subdialects resulted, but final interpretations of the results of the counting showed the necessity for having three groupings of speakers with the Tactic-Tamahu core splitting.

[25] 'Correspondences', as used here, simply refers to the observation that the group of informants utilizing a linguistic feature is the same as, or almost the same as, i.e. corresponds to, the group of informants characterized by a specific sociocultural feature. There was no attempt made to do a statistical evaluation of these correspondences.

The word lists were tape recorded to provide a check on the phonetic transcription by hand of the linguistic materials, to provide material for future research in areas of interest involving linguistic and paralinguistic structures, and to enable the investigator to check on variations within the speech patterns of any particular informant. Ethnographic text material was recorded, whenever possible, to provide material for future research in linguistic and paralinguistic structures, for content analysis studies, and to provide sociocultural information needed for a more complete understanding of the sociocultural census.

I was prepared, in a few intensive studies of selected informants,[26] to add to the basic tools of the first stage of survey a second word list, to provide additional material for a preliminary phonemic and grammatical analysis of the informant's speech; a genealogy, a life history, day schedules, and daily diets. These items of information were sought (1) to provide more information on a smaller number selected from among the same informants, (2) to provide for sociolinguistic comparisons in depth, and (3) to provide, in addition to further text material, the needed background for the interpretation of the results of the survey.

The tools of research, mentioned above, were used in three municipalities or townships in Guatemala. These townships were Tamahu, Tactic, and San Cristobal, all in the department of Alta Verapaz. The predominant ethnic group occupying these three townships is named Pocomchi.[27]

Processing the data provided the following:

1. Assurance that all the major dialects and most of the minor dialects were represented in the survey.

2. Assurance that individuals who were chosen for in-depth studies were representative of their dialects, and that those chosen for ongoing comparative work were representative of their language.

3. Lexicostatistical results coincided basically with structural results, the difference being, as Gudschinsky found, one of 'detail and supporting evidence'.[28]

[26] Informants were selected for the depth studies on the basis of the results of the lexicostatistical counts. Once the counts for a town were completed, and the reordering of the informants on the basis of relative distance were complete, one informant was selected from the first of the list, one from the middle of the list, and one from the bottom of the list. It was hoped in this way to be able to work with an informant who diverged only a little from the others, one who diverged a little more from the others, and an informant who diverged a great deal linguistically from all the others. It was not always possible, however, to arrange to work with an informant so chosen, though it was possible to find a cooperative informant from the same relative position in the count results.

[27] Conservative estimates of the Pocomchi population living in Alta Verapaz, as well as in Baja Verapaz and Quiche, would indicate about 37,500 Pocomchi speakers. Of this number, 3,500 live in the township of Tamahu; 7,000 live in the township of Tactic, and 13,000 live in the township of San Cristobal. The township is an area of jurisdiction over a geographically centrally located town, and any number of rural villages. The majority of the population lives in the rural districts. Only about 300 inhabitants occupy the town of Tamahu; about 1,200 occupy the town of Tactic; and about 3,000 occupy the town of San Cristobal. The remainder of the population lives in three other centers in the same geographical area. A preliminary survey carried out in the six townships of the Pocomchi in 1954 set the stage for the survey carried out in the three representative townships.

[28] Gudschinsky, op. cit., p. 481 (1958).

4. The linguistic-geographical map enabled clear presentations of the detail of linguistic divergence and indicated that the phonemic isoglosses produced the clearest picture of language boundaries, followed by lexical isoglosses, then grammatical isoglosses, and finally phonetic isoglosses.

5. Dialect geographical studies, projected on the linguistic-geographical map, revealed dialect boundaries, confirming again both the lexicostatistical and structural studies.

6. Sociocultural results made it possible to sort out inconsistencies in the handling of the linguistic material, to confirm results of the linguistic studies, and to eliminate, up to a point, chance responses and the possibility of accidental influences in language relationships.

7. These latter results again gave clear indication that culture is indexed by language, though such a process is seen to be highly selective in the case of the Pocomchi.

The Pocomchi study complements another one,[29] placing Pocomchi in a larger frame of reference by relating it to Pocomam. The techniques of lexicostatistics, the comparative method, and dialect geography were utilized to gain an understanding of the relationships existing between the dialects of these languages. The results of the various studies reflect the close relationships of the two languages and indicate the possibility that the San Cristobal dialect of the Pocomchi language is in reality as close to, if not closer to the San Luis dialect of Pocomam than it is to other dialects of the Pocomchi. Unfortunately, a completely new synchronic study of the two languages was not undertaken in preparation for the study and though the results are gratifying, a more thoroughgoing research program, undertaken in the same amount of elapsed time, could have provided even more adequate results.

Bridgeman and Gudschinsky[30] have produced a plan for the study of the Tupi languages in Brazil. The suggestion is advanced that classifications have previously been made on the 'basis of geographical or ethnological factors or in the distribution of given morphemes'. These have been criticized correctly as being inadequate indicators of dialect when taken alone.[31] However, the lexicostatistical technique suffers under the same criticisms when taken as the sole basis for language division, as is pointed out by Bridgeman and Gudschinsky when evaluating an article by Aryón D. Rodrigues on the 'Classification of the Tupi-Guarani'. They propose to follow up Rodrigues' study by doing research in the living languages and to 'verify, by the method of comparison, the validity (or lack of validity) of the groupings made by Rodrigues; and 2) to prepare complete descriptive studies, at least of the most representative languages, in the major groups, in accord with what the results of the inspection, i.e.

[29] Marvin K. Mayers, op. cit. (1960a).

[30] Loraine Bridgeman and Sarah Gudschinsky, 'A plan for study of the Tupi languages', ms. (Brazil, 1965).

[31] Psychological, geographical, or sociocultural materials prove nothing of linguistic groupings when taken alone. They provide, rather, clues to follow in the study of language divergence as well as provide supporting evidence for linguistic conclusions and confirm or suggest further study to confirm division.

analysis or study, may indicate, and on the basis of these results proceed with a definitive and complete reconstruction of the Proto-Macro-Tupi and distribute (or classify) the various languages by subgroups'.[32]

The program of research is being carried out to produce more than just a 'series of little lists'. Because of restrictions in time and money, a special 'Standard or pattern for Tupi Research' has been developed as a supplement to the 'Standard Questionnaire for the Study of the Indigenous Brazilian Languages' organized by the National Museum of Brazil. It contains two parts, the first of which has 'as its goal a rapid verification of phonemic contrasts with each series of words illustrating a phonemic contrast, or the occurrence of important allophones in Guarani; and the second part shows lists of categories of affixes which pertain to Kaiowá to give a reasonably complete picture of the grammatical structure of the dialect being examined'. In spite of the obvious advantage in determining linguistic groups on the basis of linguistic information alone, features of control of representation as well as of verification appear to be missing from this otherwise excellent plan for field survey.

A number of studies have been made dealing with mutual intelligibility as one technique for determining dialect boundaries. Bruce Briggs has utilized such a technique among the Yuman speakers of California and has thus set a pattern that could be followed in Spanish America. 'Briefly, the technique involves asking an informant to respond in the investigator's language to a tape recording of a text in a language different from, but related to the informant's own language. The response is scored against a master translation, and the result expressed as an index of the degree of intelligibility. This is checked with lexicostatistical counts. It is evident that the higher the degree of linguistic similarity, the more likely there is to be a one-to-one correlation of cognate percent and intelligibility percent. The lower the degree of linguistic similarity the more likely the intelligibility percent will fall below the cognate percent.'[33]

The Mexican Branch of the Summer Institute of Linguistics is also carrying on mutual intelligibility testing of the Indian languages of Mexico, directed by John Crawford. This is being effected by the use of questionnaires and tape recordings, though at the moment no material has reached the publication stage.

David Henne has utilized tape recordings to determine mutual intelligibility borders in the Quiche area of Guatemala.[34] He recorded the materials in a 'shallow' survey of the Quiche area, and as he moved from town to town, he would play the tapes and take reaction of informants in an informal way. When he had all the tapes recorded, he worked with a companion who had been studying the Quiche language for twelve years and together they grouped recordings into like groups on the basis of impressionistic reactions to phonological and grammatical features. These coincided almost completely with studies made focusing first on similar features in the language and then focusing on variations in the responses of informants. He derived by this means

[32] *IJAL* 24.231-234 (1958).
[33] Bruce Briggs, 'Testing intelligibility among Yuman languages', *IJAL* 23.57-62 (1957).
[34] Henne, op. cit. (1965).

a three-way verification of dialect boundaries and will be adding a fourth, i.e. dialect geography.

Perhaps the greatest threat to dialect studies in the twentieth century is the possibility that efforts will not be coordinated. With the Summer Institute of Linguistics actively engaged in field research in the majority of the countries of Spanish America, and with some of the greatest Universities of the world now engaged in field research in this area, the future for dialect studies has never been so bright. If there could be (1) basic tools utilized in initial survey so that a broad base could be laid for future work, and (2) if the results of this preliminary survey work, as well as further materials as it became available, could be archived in some accessible, interested University or center, dialect studies and further comparative studies based on the dialect studies could produce research sources and research such as has never been achieved in any other area of the world. Such studies are not foreign to the basic goals of the various institutions working in the area, nor for that matter of the governments sponsoring or cooperating in the research. Dialect studies are vital to the researcher interested in the professional field, in order to enable him to place his work in a broad linguistic framework, as well as a broad cultural and geographical framework. They are necessary to the members of the Summer Institute of Linguistics, since a given Scripture translation should be representative of a given dialect to be utilized effectively; and further, since scientific knowledge must be at hand, indicating need for separate translation projects and in decisions regarding assignment of personnel to a given field. Governments should be vitally interested in (1) the spread of dialects; (2) a field worker's careful estimate of the number of speakers; and (3) the mutual intelligibility. of the dialects. Business interests now using the dialects for their public advertisements need to become apprised of their effectiveness in a given dialect area, or the need for restating the 'ad' in the 'idiom' of the area. Cooperation in this area of linguistic activity is therefore valuable and could result in many side benefits.

Besides the need for standardized research materials and for a center for archiving such materials, the materials that are available in various files, both institutional and individual, should be made available to the rest of the scholastic world (perhaps in a mimeographed form as a publication of the archives), as research is accomplished and later in established journals when there has been time for summarization and synthesis. Unfortunately, at the present time, there is little being produced, and this is either not being published or is finding its way into relatively unknown journals.[35]

[35] The lack of theoretical orientation, its physical bulk and the need for phonetic script that is difficult to reproduce in conventional type is likely keeping this type of material out of the more scholastic journals.

COMPARATIVE RECONSTRUCTION OF INDIGENOUS LANGUAGES

ROBERT E. LONGACRE

0. For many years the accomplishment of Indo-European comparative reconstruction has stood in lonely splendor without a serious rival (in depth and scope) in other linguistic stocks. Current work in Latin America and the Caribbean is, however, now going forward at such a pace that in the near future it will no longer be possible to equate comparative linguistics with Indo-European studies. In Mesoamerica comparative reconstruction is reaching a very mature stage — especially in the Otomanguean and Mayan stocks and in the Mixe-Zoque family. Proto-Otomanguean, embracing some thirty languages grouped into seven component families, is currently on the drawing boards. Meanwhile, phonologies of component families have either been worked out as of several years ago or are currently being completed. Etymological dictionaries — sizeable bodies of cognate sets — will soon be available for component families and the stock as a whole. Current work in the Mayan stock is also very promising with a proven link of Mayan to one South American language. Mixe-Zoque is shaping up well. Good work has been done recently in Utoaztecan but we still lack an etymological dictionary of adequate size for that stock. Less advanced are available comparative studies in Totonac-Tepehua (not to mention the vexed question of 'Mexican Penutian': Mayan, Totonac-Tepehua, Mixe-Zoquean) and in Yuman (Hokan).

In South America and in the Caribbean, comparative projects are at early stages. Arawakan, Tupi-Guaraní, Chibchan, and Carib are scarcely begun. Nevertheless, in Quechua-Aymara and in Pano-Tacanan mature projects with sizeable ensembles of reconstructed forms will soon be forthcoming. A significant beginning has been made in Gê.

A sine qua non of careful comparative reconstruction is adequate synchronic data. It is probably no accident that comparative reconstruction is at an advanced stage in Mesoamerica, where investigators of the Summer Institute of Linguistics are currently working in approximately 100 languages and dialects, and where that organization began work in 1935. In as much as the same organization has been at work in Peru since 1946, Ecuador since 1953, Bolivia since 1955, Brazil since 1956, and Colombia since 1962 (with projected expansion into yet other countries), the descriptive data needed for sound comparative work on an extensive scale are either available already or will be available shortly.

This article does not pretend to be either exhaustive or encyclopedic. I have concentrated on reporting comparative projects that seemed to me to be genuinely significant. Articles which are essentially collations of word lists from two or more languages (or dialects) without application of the comparative method have usually not been mentioned. Such articles, if they contain reliable data, are sources for comparative projects but not themselves such projects. By the same token, the rather extensive literature of lexico-statistics (glottochronology) has been bypassed. Many such articles have been written without application of the comparative method or with a minimum use of that method. Such articles deal with resemblant forms rather than with cognates. Nor have I been concerned to report the varying linguistic classifications found in the literature. Greenberg's and McQuown's classifications have proved useful for providing frames of reference (and occasionally a convenient whipping-boy).

In that some of the most significant comparative work is still unpublished — some even in non-final form — this article cites a much higher proportion of unpublished works than is customary. My defense for this unorthodox procedure is that the sketch would have been most impoverished otherwise. Colleagues of the Summer Institute of Linguistics have been cooperative in providing unpublished materials and letting me quote from them — as have also María Teresa Fernández de Miranda, Terrence Kaufman, and José Rona (who lent me the unpublished Ferrario manuscript on Charruan). Naturally, the citation of so many unpublished works is inevitably accompanied by failure to cite other such works unknown to me.

Current progress in comparative reconstruction throughout Latin America and the Caribbean — along with the prospect of increased momentum in such studies during the immediate future — offers promise of payoff in the following domains: (1) Cultural analysis of reconstructed vocabularies and evidence of past cultural contacts; (2) evidence of past migrations and locations of original homelands of some language groups; (3) scope for application of dialect geography (e.g. Mixtec, Mazatec, Zapotec, Chinantec in Mexico); (4) fresh examination of substratum theory (e.g. Aymara substratum in Quechua); (5) study of late spread of certain languages as linguae francae (Quechua, Tupi-Guarani) vis-a-vis tribal languages on the one hand and Spanish or Portuguese on the other hand; (6) classification of languages and dialects.

The last point needs to be underscored. Consider, e.g. 'Macro-Otomanguean' as set up by Greenberg and predecessors. In this classification, the whole phylum has been divided into the following stocks: Otomanguean, Mixtecan, Chinantecan, Zapotecan. Within Otomanguean stock the following families have been posited: Otomian, Popolocan, Mazatecan, Trique, Chorotegan (Chiapanec-Manguean). The Mixtecan stock is said to contain the Mixteco family: Mixtec, Cuicatec, Amuzgo. Such a classification reflects intuitive groupings, guesses made before adequate descriptive data were available, and before serious comparative work was undertaken in various branches of the phylum. However, it is now evident (see section 6 below) that Popolocan contains Mazatecan (as its most divergent member), that Trique belongs within Mixtecan, and that Amuzgo is not Mixtecan but a separate family in the stock or phylum. Furthermore, the very grouping 'Otomanguean' within 'Macro-Otomanguean' can no longer be justified. Popolocan within 'Otomanguean' shared important developments with Mixtecan which is not in this grouping. Although it is probable that Chorotegan shares developments with Mixtecan-Popolocan, there is no evidence as yet that Otomian is any nearer to these two families than, say, to Zapotecan or Chinantecan. The old Mixtecan-Zapotecan grouping may not be entirely irrelevant. In brief, it is best at present to posit an Otomanguean phylum or stock (discarding the term 'Macro-Otomanguean') with seven component families: Otomian (or better, 'Otopamean'), Popolocan, Mixtecan, Amuzgoan, Chorotegan (or better, 'Chiapanec-Manguean'), Zapotecan, Chinantecan. These are the main pieces. How they mutually relate will be decided when Proto-Otomanguean is published. It will then be possible to trace not only isoglosses as such but shared innovations versus shared retentions. In that shared innovations are crucial to genetic grouping (cf. 4.2 below) it should be possible to make some mature judgments regarding groupings within Otomanguean.

Special mention should be given to those obliged to work with often poorly recorded data of extinct languages in an effort to use such data for comparative reconstruction and language classification. María Teresa Fernández de Miranda and Roberto Weitlaner's comparative reconstruction of Proto-Chiapanec-Manguean (6.3) and Benigno Ferrario's treatment of the scanty data for Charruan (9) are exemplary in this regard.

1. Wonderly's reconstruction of Proto-Zoquean[1] was based on the comparison of Zoque (4 dialects), Tapachulteco, Sierra Popoluca, and Mixe. The Tapachulteco data, characterized by Wonderly as 'scanty and not too reliable', are all we can expect to have in that the language is either already extinct or very close to extinction. In an important little note Nordell[2] presented evidence to show that the Zoquean family does not consist of three branches, Zoque, Popoluca, and Mixe, but basically of two: Zoquean and Mixean. The 'Popolucan' dialects may be parcelled out on one side or the other. In this judgment Kaufman has now concurred and has placed Tapachulteco on the Mixean side as 'Chiapas Mixe'. Kaufman's unpublished study, *Mixe-Zoque diachronic studies*[3] replaces all former work in its detail and scope.

Wonderly set up the phonemic system for Proto-Zoquean (Table 1):

[1] William L. Wonderly, 'Some Zoquean phonemic and morphophonemic correspondences', *IJAL* 15.1-11 (1949).
[2] Norman Nordell, 'On the status of Popoluca in Zoque-Mixe', *IJAL* 28.146-9 (1962).
[3] Terrence Kaufman, unpublished manuscript.

*p	*t	*c	*k	$*k^w$	*ʔ
	*s				*h
*m	*n			*ŋ	
*w	*y				
		*i	*ʌ	*u	
		*e		*o	
		*ä		*a	

Table 1

Of the phonemes in Table 1 (a) $*k^w$ is set up on the basis of the correspondence Zoque and Popoluca k^w ~ Tapachulteco and Mixe p in but one set; (b) *ŋ is set up only in word final; (c) *ä is set up to account for Mixe-Zoque-Popoluca a ~ Tapachulteco e.

Kaufman does not reconstruct these three phonemes. In common with Wonderly, he finds the correspondence Zoque and Popoluca k^w ~ Mixe p in but one set where he posits a Proto-Mixe-Zoque cluster *kw which went to common Mixe p. An allophone *[ŋ] of Proto-Mixe-Zoque *w is considered to have become phonemic in common Zoquean. Concerning Wonderly's posited *ä Kaufman suggests: 'more data on Tapachulteco would probably show the correspondence Tap./e/: other MZ /a/ to be the result of a secondary development in Tap. For instance, if we assume this correspondence to go with MZ *a, we can account for the Tap. forms by the following rules ...' (42).

One of the most marked features of Mixe-Zoque is its complicated morphophonemics: palatalization, metathesis, assimilation, loss or gain of laryngeal (ʔ or h); lengthening or shortening of vowel. One can proceed neither synchronically nor diachronically in this family without attending to such processes. Wonderly's article was significantly entitled 'Some Zoquean phonemic and morphophonemic correspondences'. Kaufman's careful consideration of the morphophonemics is matched by his care in reconstructing affixes both derivational and inflectional; and patterns of word, phrase, and clause structure. In one respect Kaufman was handicapped, however: no published modern description of Oaxaca Mixe was extant when he wrote. A major breakthrough has now been scored in understanding the grammar of Oaxaca Mixe. The clause system described for Tlahuiltoltepec Mixe[4] is in some ways strikingly different from that found in any previously described Mixe-Zoquean dialect. Thus, while Kaufman describes two sets of person markers for verbs, Tlahuiltoltepec Mixe has eight partially similar but functionally distinct sets of such markers.

2.1. The comparative reconstruction of Proto-Mayan has been under way by McQuown for many years. His sketch of 1955[5] (revised somewhat in 1956)[6] outlines a phonemic

[4] Shirley Lyon, 'Tlahuiltoltepec Mixe clause structure' *IJAL* 33.25-33 (1967). A similar analysis is followed in unpublished materials of Searle Hoogshagen and John Crawford for two other Oaxaca Mixe dialects.

[5] Norman McQuown, 'The indigenous languages of Latin America', *AmA* 57.501-70 (1955).

[6] Norman A. McQuown, 'The classification of the Mayan languages', *IJAL* 22.191-5 (1956).

system for Proto-Mayan but cites data only from Mam and Huastec. Kaufman, with access to McQuown's data, has published recently[7] an ensemble of 532 reconstructed forms classified according to semantic domains and accompanied by a chart of the phonemic system. Olson's article on the genetic relation of the Chipaya of Bolivia to Mayan contains a sketch of Proto-Mayan.[8] None of these materials are adequate at present. Kaufman's sketch, the best of the three, needs to be amplified into an etymological dictionary; it cites no actual language forms but gives only reconstructions. Olson's sketch (to which I contributed) is based on a more meager file of reconstructions than is Kaufman's — although some sets have fuller representation and spread. Furthermore, in Olson's article, only those Proto-Mayan sets are given for which Chipaya cognates exist. Olson is able, however, to state in some detail reflexes of Proto-Mayan phonemes in the various Mayan languages. His description of Proto-Mayan reflexes is based on the total corpus of sets, published and unpublished, which Olson and I assembled.

McQuown's inventory of Proto-Mayan phonemes (1955 modified by 1956) follows in Table 2:

*p	*t	*c	*č	*č̣	*k	*ḳ	
*p'	*t'	*c'	*č'	*č̣	*k'	*ḳ'	*ʔ
		*s	*š		*x		*h
*m	*n				*ŋ		
*w			*y				
	*l						
	*r						
*i	*ï	*u					
*e	*a	*o					

Two tones ´and`; Clusters $C_1 C_2$ in which C_1 = any except bilabials, liquids and semivowels; and C_2 = semivowels *y and *w.

Table 2

Kaufman's inventory of phonemes is much the same as McQuown's except (1) that he does not reconstruct retroflexed *č̣ and *č̣'; (2) he does not reconstruct *r; and (3) he posits a threefold contrast among the bilabials: *p, *p', and *b.

Olson's inventory of phonemes includes *ṭ and *ṭ' as well as *ḳ and *ḳ' — all of which McQuown handles as clusters of *t, *t', *k, and *k' with *y. Likewise, Olson reconstructs *h^w and *x^w which McQuown handles as clusters of *h and *x plus *w. Olson also includes a full series of retroflexed affricates and sibilants (č̣, č̣', and ṣ̌). Olson, like McQuown, posits a simple two-way contrast of bilabials (*p versus *b)

[7] Terrence S. Kaufman, 'Materiales lingüísticos para el estudio de las relaciones internas y externas de la familia de idiomas mayanos', Evon Z. Vogt and Alberto Ruz L., eds. *Desarrollo cultural de los Mayas* 31-136 (Mexico City, 1964).

[8] Ronald D. Olson, 'Mayan affinities with Chipaya of Bolivia I: correspondences', *IJAL* 30.313-24 (1964) and 'Mayan affinities with Chipaya of Bolivia II: cognates', *IJAL* 31.29-38 (1965).

and of liquids (*l and *r). As in McQuown's 1955 sketch, he posits five vowels rather than six.

Olson summarizes as follows the sound correspondences on which the threefold distinction among the Proto-Mayan affricates (*c, *č, *ç̌) is based: '*c regularly has reflex c in most languages. ... In M this reflex occurs only root finally. Root initially the M reflexes are č in the environment of high vowels ... and t in the environment of low vowels ... Under obscure conditions, reflex s occurs in P and K ... as well as in C and Tz. Similarly obscure is t ... versus Ø in H.

*č has reflex c in A, Q, C, P, Pm, K, Ch, Chr, Chl, and Tz ... Root initially it has č before front vowels and ç̌ elsewhere in I, Ag, Mm, and J ... Root finally, č occurs in Ag, Mm, and J, but c in I and M.

*ç̌ has reflex č in A, Q, C, Pm, K, Ch, Chr, Chl, Tz, M, and H ... ; it has reflex č in I, Ag, Mm, and J before front vowels ... it has reflex ç̌ in I, Ag, M, and J in other environments' (318).

In brief, *c is based on correspondence of c ~ c throughout the languages with occasional reflex s under conditions as yet not understood; while *ç̌ has reflex č in languages which have no retroflexed affricate but is ç̌ in languages having this phoneme (aside from fronting to č before front vowel). A further affricate *č is reconstructed on the basis of the correspondence c ~ ç̌ (~ č), i.e. the phoneme *č merged with reflexes of *c in some languages and with those of *ç̌ in others.

Olson's reconstruction of *r is based on the correspondence r(A, Q, C, P, Pm, K) ~ y (J, Ch, Chr, Chl, Tz, Mop, H), ~ (with weaker witness) č (I,M) ~ ç̌ (Ag). In words where Olson and I reconstructed *r, Kaufman reconstructed *y — for which Olson posits uniform reflex y in all languages. However, Olson's reconstructions of *y are all contiguous to vowel *a. In that *r — which has wider distribution — also occurs contiguous to *a there is apparent contrast. Here, however, Kaufman reconstructs vowel *ë. Thus, where Olson posits **par* or **pahar* 'skunk' Kaufman posits **pahëy*; and where Olson posits **raṣ* 'green' Kaufman posits **yëš*. A phonemic contrast must be posited here somewhere in the Proto-Mayan forms. Olson accounts for the contrast by positing *r (versus *y); Kaufman, by positing *ë (versus *a).

It is impossible at present to evaluate Kaufman's three-way contrast among bilabials. McQuown and Olson reconstruct only *p versus *b. The phoneme b, which is a reflex of the latter in contemporary Mayan languages, is usually accompanied by glottal friction or closure. In some languages it has a variety of allophones. Thus, in Tzotzil[9] the phoneme varies from [b], to [ʔb], to [ʔm] to [ʔM]. In that Kaufman reconstructs *p' presumably he has found sets of correspondences which justify his assuming that b in contemporary Mayan has two different sources. The slender file of comparative Mayan sets which Olson and I assembled is not sufficient to check this out. All etymons in our present data are forms where Kaufman reconstructs either

[9] Nadine Weathers, 'Tsotsil phonemes with special reference to allophones of B', *IJAL* 13.108-11 (1947).

*p or *b; we do not have sets containing the (relatively few) etymons for which Kaufman reconstructs *p'.

One of the most commendable features of Kaufman's work is his careful attention to the geographical distribution of cognates which do not occur in the entire family. He sets up the following subgroupings in Mayan: (1) Huastecan; (2) Yucatecan; (3) Cholan; (4) Tzeltalan; (5) Tojolabal; (6) Chuj; (7) Kanjobalan (includes Jacaltec); (8) Motocintleco (extinct); (9) Mamean (includes Aguacatec and Ixil); (10) Quichean (includes Kakchiquel, Tzutujil, and Achi); (11) Kekchian (includes Pocoman-Pocomchi).

Excluding Huastecan (which is geographically noncontiguous) Kaufman sets up (2)-(11) as a dialect chain along which certain cognates, not found in the whole family, occur in continuous areas. In this way he is able to group (2)-(5) as a lexical area distinguishable from (6)-(7); and from (8)-(11). Other cognates, which have less than family-wide distribution may reflect sporadic survival of competing Proto-Mayan forms. In the above dialect chain, (2), (4), and (7) are especially singled out as centers of lexical innovation.

Kaufman closes his article with a consideration of extra-Mayan contacts as reflected by the presence of 11 loans from Mixe-Zoque; one from Zapotec; and three from Utoaztecan.

2.2. By far the most interesting feature of Olson's paper is the evidence that it presents that the Uru-Chipaya of the Bolivian altiplano is related to Mayan.[9a] One hundred twenty-one cognate sets are presented in which reconstructed Proto-Mayan forms are given along with Chipaya forms and reconstructed Proto-Mayan-Chipaya forms. Both the present day phonemic system of Chipaya and the reconstructed Mayan-Chipaya system are quite similar to that posited for Proto-Mayan.

The phonemic system of Proto-Mayan-Chipaya follows (Table 3):

*p	*t̯	*t	*c	*č	*č̣	*k̯	*k		*ḳ	*ʔ
*p'	*t̯'	*t'	*c'	*č'	*č̣'	*k̯'	*k'		*ḳ'	
*v			*s	*š	*ṣ̌		*h^w	*h	*x	*x^w
*m		*n					*ŋ			
		*l								
		*r								
*w		*y								
*i	*ʌ									
*e	*a	*o								

Table 3

It is interesting to note in Table 3 that three bilabials are reconstructed (cf. Kaufman's reconstruction of three bilabials in Proto-Mayan); a full set of retroflexed alveopalatals

[9a] Cf. Eric Hamp, 'On Maya-Chipayan', *IJAL* 33-74-76 (1967).

(cf. Olson's Proto-Mayan); *r versus *y (cf. Olson's Proto-Mayan); and six vowels (cf. Mc Quown 1956 and Kaufman). In the above *v deserves special comment. The reflexes in Chipaya are: zero in root-initial; w in root-final in certain special phonemic environments; elsewhere: l after high vowels and r after low vowels. The Proto-Mayan reflex is, according to Olson, *b. It would be interesting to see if Kaufman's reconstruction of *p versus *b corresponds in any sets with Olson's Proto-Mayan-Chipaya *p' versus *v.

The Mayan-Chipaya link undoubtedly will not stand as an isolated example of demonstrated linguistic relationship between Mesoamerica and South America. Indeed, the Mayan-Chipaya tie cannot in itself be evaluated without broader context. It has been assumed that Mayan, Mixe-Zoquean, and Totonacan are related.[10] The day when Mayan and Mixe-Zoquean can be seriously compared should be near, in that both language families are subjects of serious comparative study. When etymological dictionaries of the two families are available, serious comparison of the two will be greatly facilitated.

Olson summarizes the problem of the relation of Uru-Chipaya to these three families as follows: 'At least four solutions are possible. These solutions imply varying estimates of the relative recency of migration to South America. In order of relative recency of migration these four possibilities are:

(1) Is Uru-Chipaya the farthest extension of the Mayan stock, the Tocharian of Mayan?

(2) Does Uru-Chipaya form a sub-grouping with either Mayan, Zoquean, or Totonacan as against the other two, or does Uru-Chipaya form a subgrouping with any two of the three as against the third?

(3) Are Uru-Chipaya, Mayan, Zoquean, and Totonacan all coordinate on the same horizon?

(4) Does Mayan-Zoquean-Totonacan form a grouping against Uru-Chipaya?' (29).

3. Evangelina Arana has reconstructed Proto-Totonacan-Tepehuan on the basis of three Totonac dialects and one Tepehua dialect.[11] She reconstructs the following phonemes (Table 4):

[10] After this article went to the editor I received from Terrence Kaufman some mimeographed sheets which present the first solid evidence yet assembled to demonstrate the affinities of these three linguistic families. He has 131 cognate sets plus sixteen further sets that he regards as possible diffusions. Of the 131 sets, 51 are Mayan and Mixe-Zoquean; 31 are Mayan and Totonacan; 28 are Mayan, Mixe-Zoquean, and Totonacan; and 21 are Mixe-Zoquean and Totonacan. Cognates and reconstructed forms are not given. The catalogue consists rather of a set of English glosses with indications of presence of cognates in the two or three families involved in each set. In that Kaufmann is conservative in what he terms 'cognate' we may feel assured that published evidence regarding 'Macro-Mayan' is forthcoming.

[11] Evangelina Arana O., 'Reconstrucción del Protototonaco', Ignacio y Eusebio Davalos Hurtado Bernal, eds. *Huastecos, Totonacos y sus vecinos*, 123-30 (Mexico City, 1953).

*p	*t	*c	*č	*tl	*k	*ḳ	*ʔ
		*s	*š	*ł	*x		
*m	*n						
*w		*y					
	*l						
*i	*i·	*u	*u·				
	*a	*a·					

Table 4

Initially, certain clusters of spirant plus stop occurred: *sk, *šk, *st, *sḳ, *łk, *łt. Medially, syllable final consonants (*t, *k, *s, *n, *y) followed by the syllable initial consonants and consonant clusters constituted clusters of two or three members.

Proto-Totonacan-Tepehua was characterized by regular morphophonemic alternation among the members of the following sets of consonants: *k/*ḳ; *c/*č/*tl; *s/*š/*ł. Notice that these morphophonemic alternations involve contiguous pairs or triplets of consonants within the stop or spirant series.

While *ʔ is included in the stop series, Arana actually reconstructs glottalized vowels in preference to either a glottal stop or a series of glottalized consonants. The role of the Proto-Totonac-Tepehua laryngeal thus forms an interesting comparison and contrast with laryngeals in other reconstructed languages (cf. Proto-Mayan, Proto-Chipaya-Mayan, and Proto-Mixe-Zoque).

Phonological developments from Proto-Totonacan-Tepehua to the various daughter languages show a minimum of split and merger. Presumably the dialects involved have not diverged far from each other. The Totonac dialect of San Pedro Octlacotla seems to display evidence of borrowing from the adjacent Tepehua.

4.1. For Proto-Utoaztecan we have an early sketch of Whorf's (1935)[12] and the recent work of the Voegelins and Hale (1962).[13] These may be supplemented by an unpublished study of Burton Bascom on the Piman group.[14]

Whorf reconstructed the following phonological entities for Proto-Utoaztecan (Table 5):

*p	*t	*c	*ḳ	*k	*kʷ	*ʔ
*m	*n	*ⁿs	[ñ]	*ŋ	*ŋʷ	
*v	*r	*s				
*w	*l	*y				
	*i			*u		
	*e	*a	*a·	*o		

Table 5

[12] Benjamin L. Whorf, 'The comparative linguistics of Uto-Aztecan', *AmA* 37.600-8 (1935).

[13] C. F. and F. M. Voeglin, and Kenneth L. Hale, 'Typological and comparative grammar of Uto-Aztecan: I (phonology)', Indiana University publications in anthropology and linguistics memoir 17 of *IJAL* 28 (Jan., 1962).

[14] Burton William Bascom Jr., 'Proto-Tepiman', unpublished manuscript, (University of Washington, 1965). I have had access only to an abstract prepared by Bascom.

The Proto-Utoaztecan phonemic inventory of the Voegelins and Hale is somewhat simpler (Table 6):

*p	*t	*c	*k	*kʷ	*ʔ
*m	*n		*ŋ		
		*s			*h
*w	*r	*y			
	*l				
*i	*ï	*u			
	*a	*o			

Table 6

Whorf's reconstruction of k̯ was based on the contrast of k̯ and k in Hopi. The Voegelins and Hale trace this development in Hopi to preceding high vowel versus preceding low vowel: 'Accordingly, we argue that UA *k descends as [Hopi] /k/ when preceded by a high vowel and followed by *a, but as /q/ when preceded by a low vowel and followed by *a. This argument can be extended — if restricted to examples descended from reconstructable forms — to account for the Hopi reflection of *k in all environments: UA *k>/k/ when contiguous to a high vowel; *k>/q/ when initial before a low vowel and when medial and flanked by low vowels, i.e. when not contiguous to a high vowel' (51).

Certain other features of Whorf's reconstruction possibly reflect Hopi bias: (1) *ñ (a reconstruction of which Whorf himself is doubtful) is probably based on Proto-Utoaztecan *ŋ >Hopi /ŋʸ/ after a high vowel. (2) *ŋʷ is based on Hopi reflex of *w in a special morphophonemic environment discussed below. Whorf's *ⁿs and his *p versus *v also involve us in Hopi and Utoaztecan morphophonemics.

Whorf's six vowel system is awkward and off balance with respect to the occurrence of only one long vowel. The Proto-Utoaztecan vowel system of the Voegelins and Hale is more plausible.

Whorf, impressed by the p/v and w/ŋʷ alternations in Hopi, tried to outline a theory to account for these and other alternations: (1) The stop-spirant alternation p/v reflects a stage in which spirant allophones occurred intervocalic and stop allophones elsewhere; (2) Some Utoaztecan stems which contain stops resistant to spirantization probably witness to a lost consonant which occurred in cluster before the nonspirantizing stop; (3) Other Utoaztecan stems, which contain non-spirantizing stops associated with a nasalizing influence, witness to medial clusters of nasal plus stop. Thus *w alternating with *ŋʷ really was originally *w versus nw (or *mw?). For the lost consonants of (2), Whorf suggested '*l, *r, possibly no more' (606).

Whorf seemed to believe that the canonical pattern *CVCVC occurred as well as *CVCV and that final consonants were nasals, *l, and *r. Occurrence of one of these syllable finals accounted for a further *CVCCV pattern. While Whorf's choice of *r and *l as syllable finals is probably a poor choice, his theory of a syllable final consonant (or consonants) is worth serious consideration.

The most regrettable feature of Whorf's study is its brevity. The article is especially deficient in having no catalogue of cognate sets appended to it. However, as an example of careful logic and good writing, the article is still quite relevant.

4.2. The study of the Voegelins and Hale takes account of the following languages in the U.S. and Mexico: Papago, Hopi, Huichol, Cora, Tarahumara, Zacapoaxtla Nahuat, Pochutla Nahuat, Nahuatl, Tübatulabal, Southern Paiute, Comanche, Mono, Bannock, Luiseño, Cahuilla, and Yaqui-Mayo. The varying quality of their sources causes them to treat some languages more fully than others. In their own words 'In our procedure, we have reconstructed where we had evidence to reconstruct, typologized whether or not reconstruction was possible, and quantified rather casually wherever quantification promised to be interpretable' (7). Phonemic systems are typologized, given numerical ratings, and compared with each other. Glottochronology — with a disavowal of interest in dates — is applied along with Grimes-Agard quantifying.[15] Nevertheless, proto forms are reconstructed, phonological developments traced in various Utoaztecan languages, and various horizons carefully distinguished.

Besides Proto-Utoaztecan, the authors also reconstruct Proto-Aztec, Proto-Shoshonean, Proto-Sonoran. The evidence for Proto-Aztec is clear: loss of initial *p and of the laryngeals *h and *ʔ; *s and *c splitting to s, š and c, č; and *l remaining l (instead of at least some allophones becoming n or r). While the split of *s to s, š is shared by a secondary development in Luiseño and that of *c to c, č is shared by Southern Paiute, this does not greatly weaken the argument. Aztec stands out, at all events, as a well-defined group within Utoaztecan — as indeed no one is inclined to doubt.

Proto-Shoshonean (really beyond the scope of this paper) is not so well attested; it is united by shared phonological retentions rather than by shared innovations, while the morphophonemic innovations are not universally shared. The one exclusive universally shared phonological innovation in Shoshonean is medial *l>n.

Although the Voegelins and Hale reconstruct 'Proto-Sonoran', they are unable to cite one exclusive, universally shared innovation in support of the grouping. Thus, while *n and *ŋ merge into /n/ in all Sonoran, they also so merge in Aztec, and in the following Shoshonean languages: Shoshone, Comanche, Mono, and pre-Bannock; in brief this development is found in all branches of Utoaztecan. The merger of morphophonemic $*V^n$ and $*V^u$ is found in all Sonoran and in Aztec. Complete merger of the morphophonemes $*V^s$, $*V^n$, and $*V^u$ is found in Taracahitan (Tarahumara, Yaqui-Mayo, and possibly a number of extinct languages). Other developments are given; none seem to point conclusively to the reality of the Sonoran

[15] Joseph E. Grimes and Frederick B. Agard, 'Linguistic divergence in Romance', *Lg* 35.598-604 (1959).

grouping. On the other hand, merger of *V^{n} and *V^{u} in Sonoran and Aztec cannot be cited in favor of the 'Aztecoidan' (Aztec, Cora-Huichol, and extinct languages) in that this development is found in Taracahitan and in Piman as well.

All in all the evidence suggests that the surviving 'Sonoran' languages might better be considered to constitute three branches of Utoaztecan: Taracahitan; Cora-Huichol; and Piman.[16] The first has at least one solid, exclusive, and universally shared innovation to support it. It is no final objection that 'shared cognates are no more numerous between Tarahumara and Yaqui-Mayo than those between Papago and Yaqui-Mayo, for example' (130).[17] It would be interesting to see whether Varohio (or Guarajio), still spoken by a few bilinguals, is also 'Taracahitan'. Regarding the closeness of Cora-Huichol no one is prepared to object but they scarcely share enough of the characteristic Aztec developments to be called 'Aztecoidan'. Finally, regarding the unity of Piman (Upper Piman, Lower Piman, Northern Tepehuan, Southern Tepehuan) there can be no doubt — as will be presented below.

The Voegelins and Hale treat Utoaztecan morphophonemics very thoroughly. They set up *V^{s} on a broader basis than did Whorf (and Sapir): '*V^{s} is written when a vowel preceding a stop may suspend the stopness of the stop, and when preceding a nasal may suspend the nasal articulation. ... In Sapir's terminology, V^{s} 'spirantizes'; but we use a more general term, since 'suspending' extends all the way from a replacement within the stop series (plosive stop by affricate stop) to a replacement of a consonant by zero. ...' (82). They set up *V^{n} 'when a vowel precedes a consonant which is reflected either by a change of the consonant, or by addition of a nasal in consonant cluster with the unchanged consonant' (82). They wisely choose to write *V^{u} when there is enough data to show that neither of the above takes place.

One who has carefully read Whorf's sketch of Utoaztecan immediately begins to thumb through the Voegelins-Hale monograph to see if their sketch can be shown either to support or to disprove Whorf's theory that Utoaztecan stems, whose medial consonant neither spirantizes nor nasalizes, really contained medial consonant clusters. Does anything in the Voegelins-Hale description bear out this theory of 'lost' or 'ghost' consonants which occurred as first members of medial *CC clusters? Whorf speculated that the ghost consonants may have been *l and *r. Of this there is no hint in the data more recently presented. There is, however, some slight support that other consonants, possibly laryngeals, did occur as first members of medial clusters. The evidence must be sought in stems where the Voegelins and Hale mark the first vowel as *V^{u} — since here was where a 'lost' consonant would have prevented both spirantization and nasalization. It is intriguing to note that in Southern Paiute, -xC- clusters (C=stop) occur after *V^{u}, while in Comanche -hk- clusters also occur

[16] Swadesh has analyzed the available scanty material on the extinct Tamaulipeco language in the south of the state of Tamaulipas. He concludes that Tamaulipeco was an independent division within Utoaztecan. 'El Tamaulipeco', *RMEA* 19.93-104 (1963).

[17] Comparative linguistics, as developed on the terrain of Indo-European studies, has not considered percentages of shared cognates to be decisive of genetic grouping. On the contrary, the principle of shared innovations has been held to be the criterion. See Eric Hamp as quoted in 4.3.

after *V^{u} (85-6). Yaqui-Mayo have a gemination of medial consonants: 'Under certain morphophonemic conditions involving stress and length alternation, medial consonants are doubled (geminated)' (75). It is interesting to note that this gemination occurs only twice after *V^{s}, while after eleven examples of *V^{s} no gemination occurs. After *V^{u} the data are evenly divided: 5 examples of gemination versus 5 examples of single consonant. In brief, Yaqui-Mayo gemination is rare after *V^{s} but not uncommon after *V^{u}. It is possible, therefore, that this gemination has its origin in old laryngeal plus consonant clusters which are reflected as Yaqui-Mayo geminates. The Southern Paiute -xC- clusters and the Comanche -hk- cluster may be direct witness to the existence of such Proto-Utoaztecan clusters. That Proto-Utoaztecan syllables were closed with a laryngeal is not improbable in view of the occurrence of such syllables in some of the language: 'Some of these, as Comanche and Cora, permit a laryngeal consonant final, /h/ or /ʔ/ or both, but no other final consonant' (96). If Proto-Utoaztecan *cvʔ and/or *cvh syllables occurred, then canonical patterns *CVLCV and *CVLCVL (ʔ or h = L) also occurred. The *V^{u} posited by the Voegelins and Hale would be a first syllable vowel which occurred in either of these canonical patterns, while *V^{s} would be a vowel that occurred in the first syllable of *CVCV and *CVCVL. Possibly, *V^{n} was a first syllable vowel which occurred in *CVnCV and *CVnCVL — to reinstate bodily this part of Whorf's 1935 reconstruction. Further work on Utoaztecan morphophonemics is needed to test these hypotheses.[18] The Voegelins and Hale assumed no consonant clusters and no final consonants in Utoaztecan. It may be somewhat whimsically asserted, however, that no reconstruction project of any scope and depth can be engaged in without encountering a laryngeal problem. Perhaps Utoaztecan is no exception?

The Voegelins and Hale give 171 cognate sets. This needs to be expanded with addition of further data. Ultimately we need an etymological dictionary of Uto-aztecan, both for further work within the stock and comparison with other stocks.

4.3. Burton Bascom's recent study *Proto-Tepiman* reconstructs Piman or Piman-Tepehuan on the basis of Upper Piman, Lower Piman, Northern Tepehuan, and Southern Tepehuan. The terminology is misleading in that there apparently is no Piman versus Tepehuan division. Rather, according to Bascom 'There seems to be no clearcut grouping among the Tepiman languages'. Four unique universally shared innovations define 'Tepiman'; **k^{w}>*b; **y>*d; **w>*g; and **c>*s (double asterisk for Proto-Utoaztecan; single asterisk for Proto-Tepiman). The first three innovations yield a new series of consonants in Proto-Tepiman. In no other sub-grouping in Utoaztecan is Hamp's dictum regarding the crucial relevance of exclusive shared innovations so well exemplified: 'The only criterion for genetic proximity consists in the recognition of a decisive set, whether in number or in structural place-

[18] Cf. e.g. Hansjakob Seiler, 'Accent and morphophonemics in Cahuilla and in Uto-Aztecan', *IJAL* 31.50-9 (1965).

ment, of shared structural innovations; and these must be innovations by addition or replacement, rather than by loss.'[19]

A further interesting detail of Bascom's reconstruction is best stated in his own words: 'Probably the most satisfying result of our research was the ability to demonstrate the derivation of Northern Tepehuan tone from Proto-Tepiman stress. This development has resulted, at least in part, from the loss of laryngeals and the resultant vowel clusters with contrastive pitch patterns. In certain environments a Proto-TP contrast in syllable types, *'CVV versus *'CVʔV, has merged into a single syllable in NT. The contrast between proto-syllables, however, has been maintained in NT by the contrasting tone patterns which they manifest, NT CVV́-versus CV́V respectively.'

Bascom's array of 473 Proto-Tepiman cognates might well form the nucleus for a Proto-Utoaztecan etymological dictionary.

5. Recently Alan Wares has made a good beginning towards the systemic comparison of the Yuman languages.[20] Wares characterizes his study as follows: 'The Yuman languages, with which this study deals, are spoken by some four to five thousand Indians living in the southwest United States and the northwest of Mexico ... The corpus of language data that forms the basis for this study covers material in Havasupai, Walapai, Yavapai, Mohave, Maricopa, Yuma, Cocopa, Diegueño, Tipai, Paipai, and Kiliwa ... On phonological and lexical grounds, four groups of languages are posited: (1) Northern Yuman (Havasupai, Walapai, Yuvapai, and also Paipai which, although spoken in Lower California near the southern limit of Yuman speech, exhibits features in common with the other languages in this group); (2) Central Yuman (Mohave, Maricopa, Yuma); (3) Delta-California (Cocopa, Diegueño, Tipai); and (4) Kiliwa ... Chapter XIII deals with a reconstruction of Proto-Yuman phonemes — chiefly consonant phonemes — on the basis of sets of correspondences found in this comparative vocabulary. No attempt has been made here to reconstruct entire forms. ... A comparative vocabulary of 501 cognate sets (some 3000 individual items) concludes the paper.'

While it is evident that the study here summarized is only a beginning, it appears nevertheless to be a good beginning. The size of the comparative vocabulary is gratifyingly large.

6. In published or unpublished form extensive, detailed reconstructions are now completed for all language families considered to belong to the Otomanguean stock of Mesoamerica. Furthermore, Calvin Rensch has now completed the reconstruction of Proto-Otomanguean itself. The publication of this study will give us one language stock of the western hemisphere in which systemic reconstruction has been carried out on a scale somewhat comparable to the scope and depth of Indo-

[19] Eric P. Hamp, 'Protopopoloca internal relationships', *IJAL* 24.151 (1958).

[20] Alan Campbell Wares, 'A comparative study of Yuman consonantism', unpublished manuscript (University of Texas, 1965). I have had access to an abstract prepared by Wares. cf. also Mary R. Haas, 'Shasta and Proto-Hokan', *Lg* 39.40-59 (1963).

European studies — although with a fraction of the manpower involved in the latter.

Some thirty native languages of Middle America are probably included in Otomanguean. The central mass of Otomanguean languages is found in the Mexican state of Oaxaca, and in surrounding areas of Puebla, Veracruz and Guerrero. To the west within this general area are found the Mixtecan (Mixtec, Cuicatec, and Trique), Popolocan (Popoloc, Ixcatec, Choco, and Mazatec), and Amuzgoan (one language) branches. To the east within the central mass lie Chinantecan and Zapotec- Chatino. While Chinantecan and Zapotecan have been spoken of as each consisting of but one language they are in reality complexes of at least six or seven languages each.

The northern outliers of Otomanguean constitute the Otopamean branch (Otomí, Mazahua, Pame, Chichimeco-Jonaz, Matlatzinca, and Ocuilteco); these languages are found in the Mexican states of Hidalgo, México, Queretaro, Guanajato, and San Luis Potosí. Pame lies north of the cultural boundary of Mesoamerica as defined by Kirchhoff in 1943.[21] Two extinct languages, Chiapanec and Manguean, which are southern outliers, constitute the Chiapanec-Manguean branch of Otomanguean. Chiapanec was spoken until fairly recently in and around the town of Chiapa de Corzo in Chiapas, Mexico. Mangue, which became extinct in the late nineteenth century was spoken along the Pacific coast of Central America in Honduras, Nicaragua, Costa Rica, and El Salvador with some extensions into the interior. Chiapanec and Mangue appear to have been very similar. Evidently they comprised a group which emigrated southward from the central mass of Otomanguean. The Chiapanecs stopped off in Chiapas while the Mangue continued to disperse further southward where they formed the southermost continuous extension of Mesoamerica as a cultural area.

Swadesh wrote a brief but suggestive sketch of Proto-Zapotecan in 1947.[22] In 1950, Stanley Newman and Robert Weitlaner published two articles which pioneered in the reconstruction of Proto-Otomi and Proto-Otomi-Mazahua.[23] The first detailed full scale reconstruction of a branch of Otomanguean was my 1957 Proto-Mixtecan.[24] This was followed in 1959 by Sarah Gudschinsky's triple piece of reconstruction (Proto-Mazatec, Proto-Popolocan, and Proto-Popolocan-Mixtecan).[25] In 1961 María Teresa Fernández de Miranda and Robert Weitlaner published a monograph which reconstructed Proto-Chiapanec-Mangue on the basis of extant data from those two

[21] Paul Kirchhoff, 'Mesoamerica', *Acta Americana* 1.92-107 (1943).

[22] Morris Swadesh, 'The phonemic structure of Proto-Zapotec', *IJAL* 13.220-30 (1947).

[23] Stanley Newman and Robert Weitlaner, 'Central Otomian I: Proto-Otomí reconstructions' and 'Central Otomian II: primitive central Otomian reconstructions', *IJAL* 16.1-19 and 73-81 (1950).

[24] Robert E. Longacre, 'Proto-Mixtecan', *IJAL* part III (1957). For an alternative reconstruction of Proto-Mixtecan (based on a narrower empirical base) see Evangelina A. Osnaya, 'Relaciones internas del Mixteco-Trique', *AnINA* 12.219-73 (1960).

[25] Sarah C. Gudschinsky, 'Proto-Popotecan' Indiana University publications in anthropology and linguistics memoir 15 of *IJAL* 25 (April, 1959). Paul Kirk, with access to an enlarged corpus of Mazatec dialect material, has recently completed a more definitive and detailed reconstruction of Proto-Mazatec (Proto-Mazatec Phonology, unpublished dissertation, University of Washington, 1966).

extinct languages, and tied them in convincingly to Proto-Mixtecan, Proto-Popolocan, and Proto-Popolocan-Mixtecan.[26] Rensch's as yet unpublished *Proto-Chinantec phonology* was completed in 1963.[27] Doris Bartholomew published a revision of the Newman-Weitlaner line-up of Proto-Otomian consonants (1960);[28] she has now completed *The reconstruction of Otopamean.*[29] Fernández de Miranda's reconstruction of Proto-Zapotecan is all but complete.[29a] I have argued in several articles that Amuzgo, traditionally considered to Mixtecan, is in reality a separate branch of Otomanguean.[30]

On the basis of Proto-Mixtecan, Proto-Popolocan, and Amuzgo (with a side-glance at Proto-Chiapanec-Mangue), I hazarded a preview of Otomanguean in 1964.[31] The following consonants seemed indicated (Table 7):

*t	*tʸ	*k	*kʷ	*ʔ
*θ	*θʸ	*x	*xʷ	
*n			*[m]	
	*y		*w	

Table 7

In that Proto-Chiapanec-Mangue, Proto-Zapotecan, and Proto-Otopamean all contain *p, the absence of this phoneme in the above scheme, shows an evident bias towards Mixtecan-Popolocan-Amuzgoan. *[m] was an allophone of *n in that *m occurred preposed and postposed while *n occurred in roots.

For a vowel system I guessed six vowels, perhaps *i, *e, *ï, *a, *o, *u.

Taking a clue from Gudschinsky it seemed to me very certain that Proto-Otomanguean had a system of postposed elements that reconstructed as follows (Table 8):

*-m	
*-xm	-*xV
-*xmʔ	-*xVʔ
-*ʔm	-*ʔ/ʔV

Table 8

I considered that postposed elements contained either a syllabic *m or a repeat of the

[26] María Teresa Fernández de Miranda and Roberto J. Weitlaner, 'Sobre algunas relaciones de la familia Mangue', *AnL* 3:7.1-99.

[27] Calvin Ross Rensch, 'Proto-Chinantec phonology', unpublished thesis, (University of Pennsylvania, 1963).

[28] Doris Bartholomew, 'Some revisions of Proto-Otomi consonants', *IJAL* 26.317-29 (1960).

[29] Doris Bartholomew, 'The reconstruction of Otopamean (Mexico)', unpublished dissertation, (University of Chicago, 1965). I have had access only to an abstract prepared by Bartholomew.

[29a] This is fortunate in view of the untimely death of our colleague. Plans have been initiated for posthumous publication of her work.

[30] 'On Linguistic Affinities of Amuzgo', *IJAL* 32.46-49 (1966); 'The Linguistic Affinities of Amuzgo', *Homonaje a Roberto Weitlaner* (Mexico City, 1967); 'Progress in Otomanguean reconstruction', *Proceedings of the Ninth International Congress of Linguists, Cambridge, Mass.*, 1962, 1017-19 (The Hague, 1964).

[31] Longacre, 'Progress in Otomanguean reconstruction', 1016-25.

stem vowel, and that the only other elements involved were laryngeals. I could not, however, fully account for the distribution and development of laryngeals even in Mixtecan.

Calvin Rensch's work in Otomanguean reconstruction indicates rather clearly that several cherished assumptions stated above are either doubtful or wrong. Rensch is challenging the palatal series of consonants, reducing the vowels to four, and reducing to a minimum the posited system of postposed elements. It is possible, however, that the four-level tone system which I reconstructed for Proto-Mixtecan, and Gudschinsky for Proto-Popolocan-Mixtecan, may be a rather primitive feature.

At all events, this is the worst of all times to speculate as to the details of Proto-Otomanguean. When Rensch's study appears — itself based on the work of many predecessors — it will merit careful scrutiny from all those familiar with given branches of Otomanguean. Out of the foment that is certain to ensue, an even better picture of Proto-Otomanguean will be obtained than can be hoped for from Rensch's initial treatment — as brilliant an accomplishment as that is.

Brief reports on the reconstruction of various branches of Otomanguean follow:

6.1. My Proto-Mixtecan reconstructions demonstrated that Trique belongs to Mixtecan properly conceived.[32] Subsequent study has shown that Amuzgo does not belong to the Mixtecan family. There are 279 cognate sets with reconstructions of consonants, vowels, glottal stop, initial consonantal alternations, tone patterns, and postposed elements. Proto-Mixtecan consonants were (Table 9):

*t	*k	*kʷ	*ʔ
*θ	*x	*xʷ	
*ⁿd	*ⁿg	*ⁿgʷ	
*n	*ñ	*m	
*l(?)	*y	*w	

Table 9

Of the above (Table 9) *ñ was eliminated in a joint paper with Mak.[33] While seven vowels were reconstructed, *ɔ was eliminated in a subsequent article of mine.[34] Four tones were reconstructed in fourteen tone couplets, eight of which occurred in basic forms and six only in tone sandhi variants. The highest tone level was apparently restricted to sandhi variants. Especially characteristic of Proto-Mixtecan is its prenasalized series.

The joint paper with Mak was a brief sketch of Proto-Mixtec based on a scattering of data collected from 28 points in the Mixtec-speaking regions of Oaxaca, Puebla,

[32] Cf. the isoglosses considered in my article, 'Swadesh's Macro-Mixtecan hypothesis', *IJAL* 27.9-29 (1961).

[33] Cornelia Mak and Robert Longacre, 'Proto-Mixtec phonology', *IJAL* 26.23-40 (1960).

[34] Robert E. Longacre, 'Amplification of Gudschinsky's Proto-Popolocan-Mixtecan', *IJAL* 28.227-42, especially 231-4 (1962).

and Guerrero. Besides establishing that *ñ and the anomalous *tn cluster were both unnecessary in Proto-Mixtecan and Proto-Mixtec, this brief study (some 100 cognate sets) also revealed that Proto-Mixtecan *i and *e probably never completely merged in Proto-Mixtec *i but remained separate in a few environments. In brief, it showed the relevance of a mass of dialect material in one language to the reconstruction of a language family. The paper also revealed that Mixtec dialect geography will be an engrossing and rewarding study when it can be undertaken.

6.2. Gudschinsky's Proto-Popolocan followed an earlier sketch of Fernández de Miranda which brought together Popoloc, Chocho, and Ixcatec.[35] Gudschinsky first reconstructed Proto-Mazatec on the basis of four dialects and then went directly to the reconstruction of Proto-Popolocan (356 sets). In her own words, 'I have bypassed the fuller reconstruction of PP (Proto-Popoloc), however, and proceeded directly to PPn (Proto-Popolocan). It remains for others to fill in the detail of development in PP and its exact position within the family'[36](2).

Proto-Popolocan consonants are (Table 10):

*t	*t^y	*k	*k^w	*ʔ
*c	*č			
*s	*š	*h	*h^w	
*n	*ñ		*m	
*l(?)	*y		*w	

Table 10

Especially characteristic of Popolocan is its alveopalatal order, and the proliferation of sibilants and affricates. Five oral vowels are reconstructed, *i, *e, *a, *o, *u, as are their nasalized counterparts. While Proto-Mazatec tone is reconstructed in detail with four tones, Proto-Popolocan tone could not be reconstructed in detail because adequate synchronic sketches of present day tone systems were not available. Certain preposed and postposed elements were posited.

For 113 of Gudschinsky's Proto-Popolocan sets she was able to suggest etymologies with Proto-Mixtecan. I subsequently added some seventy further etymologies (1962).[37] Thus, we now can give Proto-Popolocan-Mixtecan etymologies for approximately half of the Proto-Popolocan reconstructions. In the same article in which I proposed these etymologies I suggested a few refinements in the comparative phonology of the two language families.

6.3. The Fernández-Weitlaner reconstruction of Chiapanec-Mangue was based on poorly phonemicized materials recorded by various people before these two languages

[35] María Teresa Fernández de Miranda, 'Reconstrucción del Protopopoloca', *RMEA* 12.61-93 (1951).
[36] Cf. fn. 25.
[37] 'Amplification of Gudschinsky's Proto-Popolocan-Mixtecan', 237-42.

became extinct.[38] They were able to compile some 286 Chiapanec-Mangue sets. For 64 of these sets they suggest etymologies with Proto-Mixtecan, for 75 sets, etymologies with Proto-Popolocan. My inspection of their materials convinces me that more such etymologies could be posited.

The consonants of Proto-Chiapanec-Mangue are (Table 11):

*p	*t	*k	
	*s	*h	*hʷ
*ᵐb	*ⁿd	*ⁿg	
*m	*n(ñ?)		*M[hm]
*w	*y		
	*l/r		

Table 11

Chiapanec-Mangue, unlike Proto-Mixtecan and Proto-Popolocan, had a labial order. The absence of a labiovelar may, however, indicate some relation of Proto-Popolocan-Mixtecan *kʷ to Proto-Chiapanec-Mangue *p and *ᵐb. Like Proto-Mixtecan, Proto-Chiapanec-Manguean has a prenasalized series. Reflexes of *n and *ñ overlap as do those of *l and *r. Five vowels are reconstructed: *i, *e, *ɨ, *a, *u. Three further vowels are reconstructed in the comparison of Proto-Chiapanec-Mangue with Proto-Mixtecan and Proto-Popolocan. Possibly at least two of these vowels can be eliminated in similar fashion to my elimination of *ɔ from Proto-Mixtecan and both *ë and *ɔ from Proto-Popolocan-Mixtecan.[39] Postposed elements containing nasals and the laryngeal h (ʔ was not recorded) are clearly witnessed to.

6.4. Fernández de Miranda's as yet unpublished reconstruction of Proto-Zapotecan (some 300 sets) gives the following system of consonants; all consonants not in italics have a fortis (or according to Swadesh, a geminated[40]) counterpart (Table 12):

*p	*t	**tʸ*	*k	**kʷ*	*ʔ
*c					
	*s	*š			
**m*	*n				
	*l				
	*r				**R*
**w*	**y*				

Table 12

[38] Cf. fn. 26.

[39] 'Amplification of Gudschinsky's Proto-Popolocan-Mixtecan', 231-2.

[40] 'The phonemic structure of Proto-Zapotec', 221.

Swadesh[41] did not reconstruct *m for Proto-Zapotec. While Fernández de Miranda reconstructs *m it is a very rare phoneme and does not have a fortis (or geminated) counterpart. According to my tentative sketch of Proto-Otomanguean (based on Mixtecan, Popolocan, and Amuzgo), *[m] was an allophone of *n and was restricted to preposed and postposed elements. Possibly the scarcity of *m in Proto-Zapotec and the origin of the geminates are related. As I have already suggested: 'Preposed *m, however, could conceivably have coalesced with a following consonant to form a geminate which in time came to pattern as a fortis consonant. I suggest, therefore, that PZ fortis consonants hark back to Proto-Otomanguean *mC clusters while PZ lenis consonants hark back to consonants without the preposed *m.'[42]

Proto-Zapotecan *R was apparently restricted to postposed elements. It is attested somewhat obliquely by divergent developments in a few Zapotecan languages. Apparently it had an uvular or velar quality. In other branches of Otomanguean a velar spirant is found in certain postposed elements.

The contrast of *p and *k^{w} is noteworthy (only *k^{w} in Proto-Mixtecan and Proto-Popolocan; only *p in Proto-Chiapanec-Mangue).

Of some relevance here is Chatino and the extinct Papabuco. Upson and I reconstruct the following consonants for Proto-Chatino[43] (Table 13):

	*t	*t^{y}	*k	*k^{y}	*k^{w}	*ʔ
	*c	*č				
	*s	*š				
	*n	*n^{y}				
	*l	*l^{y}				
*w		*y	*h	*h^{y}	*h^{w}	

Table 13

The extinct Papabuco is considered to be simply a further Chatino dialect. The Papabuco does display, however, rather divergent reflexes from those found in the other Chatino dialects. Fernández de Miranda has pointed out that some of the Papabuco reflexes agree with those posited for Proto-Zapotec. Thus, the commonest Papabuco reflex of Proto-Chatino *k is b which corresponds to *b (lenis p, or ungeminated p) in reconstructed Zapotec forms. Likewise, the commonest Papabuco reflex of Proto-Chatino *t is s — which often corresponds to Proto-Zapotec s. Fernández would, therefore, place Papabuco on the Zapotec, rather than the Chatino side of Zapotec-Chatino.

Two hundred fifty-one sets have been assembled for Proto-Chatino. Papabuco forms, painfully culled from Belmar (1901)[44] are found in only 84 of the sets.

[41] 'The phonemic structure of Proto-Zapotec', 223.

[42] Longacre, 'Progress in Otomanguean reconstruction', 1023.

[43] Bill Upson and Robert Longacre, 'Proto-Chatino phonology', *IJAL* 31.312-22 (1965).

[44] Francisco Belmar, *Breve reseña histórica y geográfica del estado de Oaxaca* (Oaxaca City, 1901).

6.5. Bartholomew's recently completed reconstruction of Proto-Otopamean was preceded by the Newman-Weitlaner Otomi-Mazahua reconstruction (1950)[45] and by Bartholomew's own revision of their consonantal reconstructions for Proto-Otomi-Mazahua.[46] She is able to reduce the consonant inventory from 20 to 16 by eliminating *č, *s, *ñ, *r. Her present reconstruction of Proto-Otopamean consonants is starkly simple [47](Table 14)

*p	*t	*c	*k	*ʔ
	*s			*h
*m	*n			

Table 14

Fortis and lenis forms of the above were environmentally conditioned: Lenis forms occurred intervocalic; fortis forms elsewhere. Nasal influence as well as weakening resulted from addition of an *m/nV- prefix. Clusters of laryngeals (*ʔ or *h) with the above occurred as well.

The vowel system is also the simplest reconstructed for any Otomanguean language yet: *i, *e, *a, *o, and their nasalized counterparts. Vowel clusters *ao, *oa, *ai, *ia, *io, *oi, *eo, and *oe occurred. Reconstruction of these clusters involving *i and *o presumably obviated the need for reconstructing *w, *y, *kʷ, and *hʷ.[48]

Six tones are reconstructed: high, low, falling, and rising, plus two further contours falling plus low, and high plus falling.

Characteristic of Otopamean is the structure: prefix plus root syllable plus stem formative. The latter two are reconstructed in detail; the first only sketchily.

There are 700 cognate sets of which about half contain cognates from the two largest subgroups, Otomian and Pamean. Other languages cited are: Mazahua, Matlatzinca, Ocuilteco, and Chichimeco. A good amount of paradigmatic material is included in the sets. The tone correspondences are based on 147 sets.

Bartholomew's work is of special interest in that she follows the model of generative phonology.

6.6. Rensch's reconstruction of Proto-Chinantec is at once sufficiently important — and unavailable — to require fuller treatment than we have given any of the reconstructed languages above.[49] The reconstructions (773 sets) are based on material from 23 points in the Chinantec language complex. Synchronic descriptions of the present day Chinantec languages (Rensch nowhere attempts to distinguish language from dialect and would probably not be prepared to sustain the thesis that all 23 points on

45 Cf. fn. 23.
46 Cf. fn. 28.
47 Cf. fn. 29.
48 Cf. Longacre, 'Progress in Otomanguean reconstruction', 1023.
49 Rensch's work was preceeded by Roberto Weitlaner and Paul Smith, 'Detalles de la fonología del idioma Proto-Chinanteco', unpublished manuscript (Mexico City, 1957).

his map represent separate languages) is followed by a presentation of the phonemic system of Proto-Chinantec.

The consonants of Proto-Chinantec are (Table 15):

*p	*t	*k	*kʷ	*ʔ
*b	*z	*g	*gʷ	
	*s			
	*l			
*w	*r	*y		

Table 15

Clusters of consonants included *ʔ or *h plus *b, *z, *g, or *l.

Somewhat startling in Table 15 is the absence of nasals. Rensch explains this: 'The sets of correspondences that witness to *[b] reconstruct only with oral vowels. In all Chinantec languages nasals appear only before nasalized vowels and, therefore, sets of correspondences that witness to nasal proto-segments reconstruct only with nasalized vowels. It follows, then, that the sets of correspondences that witness to *[b] and *[m] are in complementary distribution and may be grouped together under the same symbol, say *b. The same may readily be done for sets witnessing *[g] and *[ŋ] in the same way. However, no *[d] and thus, no oral counterpart to *[n] is available. There are, however, three other correspondence sets which are reconstructed only before oral vowels, *gʷ, *z, and *l. Because of the supposed labiovelar articulation of *gʷ it would seem a poor choice, but either *[z] or *[l] could well be matched with *[n] as the oral allophone of the voiced stop in the dental-alveolar area. *[z] has been selected for reasons of clustering with *h and *ʔ which will be discussed in a subsequent section, but the choice is somewhat arbitrary. In summary, then, apart from *gʷ, three voiced stops are postulated for Proto-Chinantec *b, *z, and *g with allophones *[b], *[z], and *[g] respectively before oral vowels and allophones *[m], *[n], and *[ŋ] respectively before nasalized vowels. Phonetically, the oral allophones may have been prenasalized as they are to varying degrees in a number of the modern Chinantec languages' (32-3).

The Proto-Chinantec vowels are (Table 16):

*(i)	*ɨ	*u
*(e)	*ʌ	*a

Table 16

Rensch comments: 'Clusters of vowels include *i plus each of the vowels shown outside the parentheses. The vowels *i and *e correspond to the clusters **iɨ and *iʌ respectively. ... However, since the evidence indicates that they were probably articulated as phonetic units and since the distribution of these correspondence sets is broader than that of the other *iV clusters, these are treated as special members of the inventory of single vocalic elements' (24). In brief, the evidence points to a period (perhaps pre-Proto-Chinantec?) when a four vowel system was extant: (cf. Otopamean above, and Rensch's hypothesis of four vowels for Otomanguean and his desire to reduce Proto-Mixtecan vowels to four).

A consonant, a vowel, and a tone pattern were essential to a Proto-Chinantec syllable. In addition, the syllable could: (a) have ballistic articulation; (b) be lengthened; (c) be checked with *ʔ; (d) have a prepeak vowel *i; (e) be nasalized; and (f) be closed with *z. I have arranged these schematically as follows (Table 17):

(/)
T
C (i) V (·) (ʔ) (z)
(N)

Table 17

The diagram — in which optional elements are in parenthesis — implies that all possible combinations of optional elements with obligatory elements occur. More will be said about this later.

The ballistic articulation is described by Rensch as 'sharp, ballistic, fortisly articulated'; syllables without this feature are 'smooth, controlled, lenisly articulated'. The phonetic description is based, of course, on the phenomenon as observed in several Chinantec languages.

In that ballistic versus controlled articulation, length, and glottal closure are all independent variables, this yields eight syllable patterns: *CV, *CV́, *CV·, *CV́·, *CVʔ, *CV́ʔ, *CV·ʔ, *CV́·ʔ (103).

Apparently, prepeak *i may occur with any of the above also; although it is for example, very rare with *CV́ʔ and *CV·ʔ.

It is of special interest that nasalization and postposed *z appear to be independent variables — since postposed *z is also a source of nasalized vowels in some Chinantec languages. The phoneme *z, as was stated above, belongs to a series of three phonemes (*b, *z, *g) which have nasal allophones (*m, *n, *ŋ) before the phonemically nasalized Proto-Chinantec vowels. Furthermore *z had an allophone *y in cluster with *h or *ʔ before oral vowels. In the various languages the reflexes of postposed *z range from postposed i or y to n, to ŋ, to nasalization, to affecting of vowel quality in various ways.

Rensch reconstructs a system of three level tones (*1, *2, *3 from high to low) and four sequences: *32, *23, *21, and *131.[50] Tone reflexes are radically affected by occurrence of Proto-Chinantec ballistic versus controlled syllables. Further sets of correspondences not fitting in the above scheme are conscientiously listed.

[50] As this goes to press Rensch informs me that he now posits a Proto-Chinantec tone system with two register tones and the following tone sequences: high-low, low-high, and high-low-high.

Although the study is called *Proto-Chinantec phonology*, Rensch gives summary information regarding the Proto-Chinantec verb — even to the point of giving a Proto-Chinantec verb paradigm. Only those who have tried to rationalize the structural vagaries of the verb in any Chinantec language can appreciate Rensch's accomplishment.

Rensch's work is a model in respect to good craftsmanship, carefully reasoned logic, and scope of detail. We can only hope that it will be published soon.

6.7. Swadesh has repeatedly urged that Huave (an unclassified language of Mexico) be considered to be related to Otomanguean.[51] Notwithstanding my initial skepticism, I now am inclined to believe that Swadesh may be correct. Swadesh's flat horizon approach to reconstruction — without taking account of particular developments in the several language families composing Otomanguean — vitiates many of his reconstructions. He sets up, among other features, more alveolar and alveopalatal sibilants and fricatives than the data warrant, and imposes his theory of geminates versus singles (Zapotec bias) on Otomanguean. I have taken his Huave-Otomanguean sets, restated some of them along the lines of the phonology more congenial to me, and added a few sets of my own. The results are not implausible. Possibly, as Swadesh suggests, Huave witnesses to original *p versus *k^w which have been merged into one phoneme or the other in some traditional Otomanguean languages (e.g. in Mixtecan, Popolocan, Amuzgoan, and Zapotecan).

6.8. Reconstructed vocabularies may be subjected to cultural analysis in an effort to reconstruct past cultural horizons. Some of the obvious dangers of this approach can be obviated by reconstructing cultural complexes rather than isolated items. Millon and I examined[52] the vocabulary of reconstructed Proto-Mixtecan and noted six cultural complexes witnessed to by various reconstructed vocabulary items: (1) agricultural; (2) maize; (3) masa preparation; (4) palm; (5) maguey; (6) weaving. Comparing Amuzgo with the above, all complexes except (4) reconstructed. Recent archeological investigations square well with the linguistic reconstruction.[53]

McQuown in three and a half pages[54] succinctly summarizes probable features of Proto-Mayan culture as reflected in reconstructable forms. The resulting picture is typically Mesoamerican. Noteworthy is the variety of cultivated plants: maize (with

[51] 'The Oto-Manguean hypothesis and Macro-Mixtecan', *IJAL* 27.9-29 (January, 1961). 'Interim Notes on Oaxacan phonology', *SJA* 20.168-89 (Summer, 1964). 'Algunos problemas de la lingüística Otomangue', *Anales de antropología* 1.91-123 (1964).

[52] René Millon and Robert E. Longacre, 'Proto-Mixtecan and Proto-Amuzgo-Mixtecan vocabularies: a preliminary cultural analysis', *AnL* 3:2.1-44 (1961).

[53] Richard Stockton MacNeish, 'First' and 'Second annual reports of the Tehuacan archeological-botanical project' (Andover, 1961) cf. MacNeish and Antoninette Nelken, 'Le Mexique et les débuts de l'agriculture au Nouveau Monde', *L'Anthropologie* 65:349-53 (1961).

[54] Norman McQuown, 'Los orígenes y la diferenciación de los Mayas segun se infiere del estudio comparativo de las lenguas Mayanas', *Desarrollo cultural de los Mayas* 49-80, especially 77-80 (Mexico City, 1964).

terms for green ear, dry ear, and cob), squash, sweet potatoes, chile, avocado, maguey, cotton, and cacao. Other terms are suggestive of cooking, weaving, housmaking, and other techniques. Still others suggest nature deities (water, sun, wind), and religious ceremonies (incense, mask).

Without attempting reconstructions of linguistic forms as such, Howard Law had some success in obtaining a sketch of Proto-Yuman culture.[55] In that the Yuman languages have not diverged too radically from each other and most sound correspondences are quite regular, Law was able to proceed somewhat surely in identifying cognates. His attention to culture complexes (in which various items mutually reinforce each other as witnesses) helped him scale his results in terms of probability. The reconstructed horizon is more shallow than for Proto-Mixtecan or Proto-Mayan. Nevertheless, the cultural sketch reveals a culture still largely dependent on hunting but with developing agriculture. Again, the picture is a plausible one.

The reconstruction of Proto-Maya has advanced far enough to invite inquiry as to the homeland of the Mayas. A. R. Diebold, Jr. in an article concerned with the application of migration theory,[56] makes out a plausible argument that the homeland of the Mayas was the Central Guatemalan highlands. Migration theory, as thus exemplified, is based on comparative reconstruction. The latter gives a measure of the closeness of the linguistic relationships. This consideration, taken together with that of the distribution of present day languages, makes possible probability judgments as to original homeland of a language family and migrations from that homeland.

Comparative reconstruction within a family or stock may also yield evidence of past cultural contacts between population groups speaking diverse languages. This is possible in that careful application of the comparative method facilitates recognition of loanwords as opposed to inherited items. Kaufman's summary and analysis of Mixe-Zoque loans in Mayan (cf. 2.1) is suggestive of what can be done. The fact, moreover, that Mixe-Zoque seems to have had more cultural influence on early Mayan than either Zapotecan or Utoaztecan is in itself significant. On a lesser scale my tracing of a few Mixtec loans in Trique is of some interest.[57] In that the Mixtec loans are words referring to pathological states it is possible that the presence of these loans is another evidence of Mixtec cultural domination over the Triques. In this case we infer a situation involving Mixtec shamans and Trique clients.

Isoglosses within Mixtecan are traced in my 1961 article.[58] Shared innovations between Mixtec and Trique are relatively weak while those between Mixtec and Cuicatec, and between Cuicatec and Trique are relatively strong. There is some relevance to culture history and even migration theory here: ... 'Mixtec and Cuicatec

[55] Howard W. Law, 'A reconstructed proto-culture derived from some Yuman vocabularies', *AnL* 3:4.45-57 (1961).

[56] A. Richard Diebold, Jr., 'Determining the centers of disposal of language groups', *IJAL* 26.1-10 (1960).

[57] Longacre, 'Systemic comparison and reconstruction of Middle American Indian languages', to appear in McQuown, ed. *Handbook of Middle American Indians* 5.

[58] 'Swadesh's Macro-Mixtecan Hypothesis', 12-19.

have apparently been in unbroken contact since the common Proto-Mixtecan period. By contrast, Cuicatec-Trique have not been in contact in historical times, while an argument can well be made in favor of the thesis that Mixtec-Trique (now found in contact) were out of contact for a significant period of time. The paucity and weakness of shared Mixtec-Trique innovations versus the comparative wealth and strength of Cuicatec-Trique shared innovations seem to indicate that Cuicatec-Trique, although now not in contact, were actually in longer early contact than were Mixtec-Trique. Apparently Trique moved off from Mixtec during the period of early dialect differentiation (but retained contact for some time with Cuicatec) only to be engulfed on all sides by Mixtec during the later period of Mixtec expansion' (12).

It is apparent that serious linguistic reconstruction has much to offer to the student of culture history. This is evident, e.g. in the recent symposium volume: *Desarrollo cultural de los Mayas*[59] — where articles of linguists McQuown and Kaufman make a crucial contribution.

In a classic article dealing with Mazatec dialect history,[60] Gudschinsky brings together insights of dialect geography with those of comparative reconstruction. Basing her arguments on exclusively shared phonological innovations she traces successive dialect splits and constructs a genealogical tree of the Mazatec dialects. She then considered 'word geography', i.e. lexical innovation versus retention. She then compares her results with what is known or conjectured regarding Mazatec history (480-1). Two periods of dialect development are distinguished before 'the period in which a lowland nation first flourished'. A third period is posited 'in which Low Mazatec developed its characteristic phonological and lexical features'; this period is probably that of the 'Lowland Mazatec Nation'. The fourth period — possibly a period of domination by some non-Mazatec people — saw the development of a 'Valley dialect', and subsequent split into 'Northern Valley' and 'Southern Valley' dialects. The fifth period (possibly 1300-1456) saw the development of a High Mazatec dialect in that both highland and lowland Mazatec kingdoms flourished at this time. One village, which had belonged to the Lowland kingdom and dialect in period three, now was absorbed into the highland kingdom with consequent dialect adjustments. The sixth and seventh periods (Aztec and Spanish domination) have seen further dialect developments.

7. The possible genetic affinity of the highland Andes languages, Quechua and Aymara, has been debated since 1888 when Steinthal affirmed that the two languages 'were genetically related and mutual exchange of loans was secondary'.[61] This has been controverted by others, such as Mason, who, while admitting phonological and morphological parallelism of the two languages, denied genetic affinity. Mason held

[59] cf. fns. 7 and 54.
[60] Sarah C. Gudschinsky, 'Mazatec dialect history, a study in miniature', *Lg* 34.469-81 (1958).
[61] Heymann Steinthal, 'Das verhältniss, das zwischen dem Keschua und Aymara besteht', 7 *Congreso Internacional de Americanistas,* 462-4 (Berlin, 1888).

that 'the lexical roots seem to have little in common, except a large number, perhaps as much as $^1/_4$ of the whole, obviously related and probably borrowed by one or the other language'.[62] Both these contrary evaluations find present day adherents. What is needed is a careful assessment of the dialect situation in Quechua itself (with careful attention to the history of Quechua-Aymara contacts and present dialect geography) plus the culling out and evaluation of resemblant forms between the two languages.[63]

7.1. Benigno Ferrario published a very important article concerning Quechua dialectology.[64] He argued that a basic division must be made between Quechua dialects that are in direct descent from Proto-Quechua and dialects that represent a late spread of Quechua, first as the language of the Inca empire, and secondly as a lingua franca for Spanish administrators and the missionary friars. Thus, he considers Ecuadorian, Colombian, and Argentine Quechua to be largely irrelevant to the reconstruction of Proto-Quechua. To distinguish the lingua franca of these areas from the most relevant dialects he terms the former 'Neo-Quechua' and the latter 'Runa-simi' (i.e. 'the people's language' in Quechua).

Within the dialects of 'Runa-simi' Ferrario recognized a further dichotomy: '... dialetti derivati dalla Proto Runa-simi, ossia: a) le parlate delle popolazioni che circondavano il luogo dove sorse, di poi, il Cuzco; b) quelle dei Chinchas (che già erano una nazione potente, a base federale, quando gli Inca ancora erano occupati a consolidare il loro piccolo Stato locale, nucleo del futuro impero) cioè le varietâ di Ancash, di Huánuco, di Cajamarca ed altri luoghi' (136).

The dialect division posited by Ferrario within 'Runa-simi' was considered to be more relevant to phonology than to morphology. The salient phonological difference is that Cuzco type dialects (including those of Bolivia) have aspirated and glottalized series of stops as well as a simple series, while other dialects have only the latter.

Ferrario argued cogently that the aspirated and glottalized stops of Cuzco Quechua were due to Aymara substratum. He presented two maps. In the first, which represents the linguistic situation in the sixteenth century, the Aymara speaking region of Peru is shown to extend up to the 11° parallel south and to include a fingershaped strip of territory running up to the north of Lima; this region also includes most of Huancavelica, parts of Ayacucho, and Arequipa and extends about half way from Lake Titicaca to Cuzco. On the second map, reflecting the present linguistic situation, the former Aymara region of Peru is shown to be largely Quechua speaking, with Aymara

[62] J. Alden Mason, 'The languages of South American Indians', ed. Julian H. Steward, *Handbook of South American Indians*, 6.157-317 (Washington, 1950).

[63] The Haquearu language of west central Peru (which Ferrario considered to be simply an Aymara dialect) should also be included in the sphere of investigation: cf. José M. Farfán, 'Diccionario conciso Castellano-Haquearu-Quechua', *Revista de Museo Nacional* 30.19-40 (1961).

[64] Benigno Ferrario, 'La dialettologia della Runa-Simi', *Orbis* 5.131-40 (1956). I am indebted to Miss Yolanda Lastra and Mr. Alfred Pietrzyk of the Center for Applied Linguistics (Washington, D.C.) for securing for me copies of this and other articles which were hard for me to obtain under field conditions.

confined to a narrow region north and west of Lake Titicaca (plus of course the Altiplano of Bolivia). Ferrario further argued that many of the placenames of Peru can be shown to be Aymara, while the Haquearu enclave in central Peru can be shown to be a remnant of the original Aymara-speaking population. Ferrario concludes: 'Il gruppo dei dialetti di tipo 'Cuzqueño' rappresenta, invece, una Runa-simi aymarizzata, e non solo foneticamente, ma altresì nel lessico, dovuto alla convivenza, sopra un medesimo territorio, di gente parlante Aymara e Runa-simi, già in epoca pre-incaica' (139-40).

It is probably somewhat inconsistent of Ferrario to draw such a sharp line between his Quechua or 'Neo-Quechua' (as a lingua franca) and dialects of 'Runa-simi' properly constituted. The data that he presents regarding displacement of Aymara by Quechua would indicate that many Quechua-speaking areas of southern Peru represent a recent spread of that language — even as the Quechua dialects of Ecuador, Colombia, and the Argentine. At any rate, Ferrario concludes that the dialects of greatest relevance to Proto-Quechua are the dialects now spoken in Ancash, Húanuco, and Junin.

The current studies of Gary Parker[65] seem to substantiate Ferrario's conclusion. Parker distinguishes Quechua A (including Cuzco, Ayacucho, Bolivia, and Ecuador-Ucayali) from Quechua B (Ancash, Húanuco, and Junin). While Ferrario had argued that all dialects of Quechua were quite similar morphologically, Parker contrasts the two major groups of Quechua dialects in respect to postpositions on nouns, person markers, and verb inflection. He also delineates certain isoglosses that separate the various dialects in each of the two large divisions. Phonologically, Ayacucho in Quechua A is more similar to Quechua B. While the Cuzco and Bolivian dialects have both aspirated and glottalized stops, and central Ecuador-Ucayali dialects have aspirated stops (and one phoneme which is a reflex of a former glottalized stop), Ayacucho has no trace of either aspirated or glottalized stop.

Parker, like Ferrario, considers the aspirated and glottalized stops of Quechua A to be by way of influence from Aymara: 'Aunque se ha presumido que éstas son originales del Quechua, el autor prefiere considerarlas como que fueron prestadas del Aymara, tanto sobre la base de la distribución geográfica como del relativamente bajo rendimiento funcional de estos componentes en el Quechua' (248). He points out the interesting fact that in Quechua no more than one laryngealized (aspirated or glottalized) consonant may occur per word. Possibly of greater relevance is the fact that the laryngealized stops are limited to roots in Quechua while they are also found in affixes in Aymara.

Parker reconstructs Proto-Quechua A, Proto-Quechua B, and Proto-Quechua. Since he groups Ayacucho in 'Quechua A' and does not reconstruct glottalized and aspirated stops in that dialect, the phoneme inventories of the three do not markedly differ.

65 Gary Parker, 'La classificación genética de los dialectos Quechuas', *Revista del Museo Nacional* 32.241-52 (1963).

The phonemes of PQA are as follows (Table 18):

*p	*t	*č	*k	*ḳ
	*s	*š	*x	
*m	*n	*ñ		
	*l	*l^y		
*w	*r	*y		
		*i	*u	
		*a		

Table 18

PQB differs only by virtue of the presence of a further affricate: c. Proto-Quechua is considered to have the phoneme inventory of PQB, plus the phoneme š based on the correspondence: PQA s ~ PQB x in some sets.

Parker considers that the 1560 lexicon of Domingo de Santo Tomás (the first printed work in Quechua) is an early dialect witness to Quechua A. He believes that this was a coastal dialect. Ferrario's description of the linguistic situation in the sixteenth century leaves no room for a 'coastal' dialect of Quechua; in southern Peru the Aymara-speaking strip separated the Quechua region from further languages spoken on the coast. The orthography of Santo Tomás gives no hint of aspirated or glottalized stops, nor of the contrast k:ḳ. While Parker concludes that the dialect in question is obviously QA, (on the basis of morphology?) he admits that the accentual system is that of Quechua B. Presumably, this is a link in his argument for eliminating aspirated and glottalized stops from PQA. Ferrario and Rowe seem to locate Santo Tomás' Quechua dialect in Apurimac — where it would have been contiguous to Ayacucho. Presumably, both the dialect of Santo Tomás and Ayacucho — granting that both can be classified morphologically as Quechua A — are phonologically like Quechua B.

By contrast, the classic 'Inca' dialect ('court dialect' of Cuzco) which Rowe posits on basis of early 17th century documents[66] clearly had aspirated and glottalized stops. Ecuador-Ucayali dialects, some of which preserve aspirated stops and partial witness to existence of a glottalized series, presumably are developments from such Cuzco dialects on spread of the latter northwards.

7.2. The question of Quechua-Aymara genetic affinity is complicated by the undoubted prolonged historical contact of the two peoples and the presence of Aymara substratum in a large area of southern Peru.

In an unpublished study Carolyn Orr has assembled some 300 Proto-Quechua sets of which a bit under 50% can be shown to have resemblant forms in Aymara of Bolivia.[67] These tentative Quechua-Aymara cognate sets include some body parts

[66] John Rowe, 'Sound patterns in three Inca dialects', *IJAL* 16.137-48 (1950).

[67] Since submitting this article, Orr and I have further studied the Quechua-Aymara problem. Our joint paper, 'Proto-Quechumaran', is committed to the thesis that the two languages are genetically related. We now reconstruct glottalization and aspiration as Proto-Quechua features.

(*fist/joint, knee, finger/toenail, skin/hide/back, goiter/mumps/Adam's apple*), kinship terms (*father, man's brother, woman/wife, child/baby, sister/daughter-in-law, relative, brother/son-in-law*, and other items (*carry, put/give, be, want, cut, ripen, gather, walk*) that are usually less suspect of being loans from one language to the other. On the other hand, other items (*money, gold, write, two, three*, and *ten*) might well be loan-words from one of the languages into the other. Furthermore, Orr's sets do not include on the Quechua side, dialect witness from Ancash, Húanuco, and Junin — which according to Ferrario are less 'Aymarized' dialects of Quechua. If, on addition of material from these dialects, it is found that most of the presumed Proto-Quechua forms can be witnessed to in these cruical dialects, then a case can be made for the genetic affinity of Quechua-Aymara.[68] The case will rest heavily on the argument that a form disseminated homogeneously throughout Quechua dialects is not likely to be a loan from Aymara. Loans of this sort should tend to be statistically most frequent in dialects contiguous to Aymara (including Ucayali-Ecuador, if these are derived from Cuzco Quechua) and less frequent in other dialects (Ancash, Húanuco, Junin).

In brief, if — as generally admitted — the two languages are quite similar morphologically, and not so dissimilar phonologically (aside from extra series of aspirates and glottalized consonants in Aymara), and if cognate sets with plausible geographical spread can be assembled from vocabulary domains not highly suspect of containing loans, and if a viable phonology can be reconstructed based on systemic sound correspondences, then there would seem to be little point in continuing to doubt the genetic affinity of the two languages.

8. Olive Shell has made a good beginning at the reconstruction of Proto-Panoan,[69] while Mary Key has completed a sketch of Proto-Tacanan.[70] The two stocks have been assumed to be related (e.g. in Greenberg's Macro-Panoan).[71] This relationship is confirmed by the present studies.

8.1. Olive Shell's unpublished study is based primarily on seven Pano languages for which extensive lexical materials as well as phonological and grammatical analyses exist: Cashinahua, Shipibo, Capanahua, Amahuaca, Marinahua, Cashibo, and Chacobo. The first six are spoken in Peru, the last in Bolivia. Shell describes her procedure as follows: '... the comparative method was applied to data from seven Pano languages in current investigations to obtain a tentative reconstructed primitive Pano. Reversing the process of reconstruction, rules of historical change were noted

68 Since writing this, I have received from Helen Larsen (Summer Institute of Linguistics) a word list in the Quechua dialect of Ancash. Larsen has only recently begun her studies of Ancash Quechua and has incomplete lexical materials. Nevertheless, for almost one half of the Quechua-Aymara sets she readily found cognates in Ancash Quechua.

69 Olive A. Shell, 'Pano reconstruction', unpublished monograph.

70 Mary Ritchie Key, 'Comparative phonology of the Tacanan languages', unpublished dissertation (University of Texas, 1963).

71 Sol Tax, 'Aboriginal languages of Latin America', *CAnthr* 1.430-8 (1960) (reproduces Greenberg's classification of 1956).

which enabled the investigator to predict forms in the daughter languages. By applying these rules and making comparisons with further word lists found in the literature, the latter were evaluated, their symbolization interpreted, and the findings utilized in modifying the first construction' (1). Besides the seven control languages, Shell also had word lists from current investigations in the following Pano languages (all but the first are spoken in Brazil): Isconahua, Marobo, Yaminahua, Chaninahua, Mastanahua. Published word lists of varying quality (many nineteenth century) were available for: Atsahuaca, Yamiaka, Cakobo, Pakaguara, Karipuna, Culino, Mayoruna, Arazaire, Canawary, Poyanawa, Tutxiunaua, Pano, Wariapano, and Nokaman.

Although the published word lists of earlier investigators enter only indirectly into Shell's studies, they enable her to make a careful evaluation (6-39) of previous classifications. This admirably demonstrates the relevance of careful, detailed comparative reconstruction for the classification of languages. It is not necessary that the careful, detailed work embrace the entire family or stock but enough must be done — and done well — to provide a solid core around which other material can nucleate.

Even the mutual classification of the seven Panoan languages entering directly into Shell's study is of considerable interest. The grouping is done on the basis of shared phonological innovations with some attention to shared lexical innovations as well (131-6). On this basis (1) Shipibo-Conibo is first grouped with Capanahua, then (2) these, with (3) Chacobo. (4) This grouping is more or less coordinate with Amahuaca and Cashinahua-Marinahua. Finally, (5) Cashibo ties in on a still earlier horizon. By contrast McQuown[72] groups as follows: (1) Shipibo and Conibo. (2) These, in turn, group with Cashibo (all sub-divisions of his QIA) (3) The preceding comprise a branch roughly coordinate with those branches represented by Capanahua (his Capanahuan is QIC) by Amahuaca (his Amahuacan is QID), and by Marinahua (in his Panoan QIF). Most distantly related of all is Chacobo (QIIIAa of Southwest Panoan QIII). Greenberg's classification — here, as in other places — is geographic rather than linguistic. Chacobo as 'South east Panoan' is separated from the other six languages which are classified as 'Central Panoan'. A glance at the striking difference in the classifications (e.g. Cashibo ties in on the earliest horizon in Shell's classification; Chacobo, in McQuown's) suffices to emphasize the difference between tentative classifications and those coming about as a by-product of the comparative method. Shell modestly entitles her reconstructions 'Reconstructed Panoan' instead of 'Proto-Panoan': 'The reconstruction is not claimed to be final. Further research in Bolivia and Brazil may provide data for a more primitive Pano than can be reconstructed from present data' (2). Needless to say, 'proto-languages' have been posited by other comparativists on a much more slender basis. Granting the inevitable subsequent revision of any pioneer piece of linguistic reconstruction, there is no reason why Shell's reconstructions should not be considered to be for all practical purposes 'Proto-Panoan'.

[72] Norman McQuown, 'The indigenous languages of Latin America', *AmA* 57.501-70 (1955).

After a careful presentation of current phonemic systems in the seven languages, Shell presents the phonemes of 'Reconstructed Panoan' (Table 19):

*p	*t			*k	*k^{w}	*ʔ	
	*c	*č					
*ƀ	*s	*š	*ṣ̌				
*m	*n						
	*r			*i	*ï	*į	*į̈
*w	*y			*a	*o	*ą	*ǫ

Table 19

In a series of charts Shell presents the developments from Reconstructed Pano to each daughter language. There is a minimum of split and merger among the consonantal reflexes in the various languages. The nasals, however, condition nasalized reflexes of vowels in certain environments. The patterns of split and merger involving *b, *w, and *y vary in interesting fashion among the seven languages. Vowel reflexes are fairly consistent from language to language except for (1) loss of final vowels under certain conditions varying in degree and kind from language to language; (2) merging of oral and nasalized vowels in varying degree and under varying conditions; and (3) other miscellaneous developments too detailed to mention here. Development (2) is of special interest in that while it reflects a tendency to lose nasalized vowels, such vowels are developed in all the languages except Chacobo on loss of nasal consonants in third syllable (with nasalization of all second syllable vowels — although vowel nasalization is considered to be an allophone of nasal consonant in Capanahua).

Of the seven Pano languages under consideration, in two a two-way stress contrast is posited; in four a two-way tone contrast; and in one a complex stress-tone contrast. A two-way tone contrast is reconstructed. Shell comments: 'The RP high toneme was probably accompanied by strong stress, except when affected by over-all rhythm patterns' (116).

The Pano languages are very complex morphologically. Shell is able to reconstruct certain morphological features of RP. In current Pano languages there is a difference in the form of the noun when subject of a transitive verb and when either subject of an intransitive verb or object of a transitive — although this is expressed in different ways in the various languages. Shell reconstructs three-syllable forms for the nouns as subjects of transitive verbs versus two syllable forms either as subjects of intransitives or objects of transitives. In two-syllable Reconstructed Pano nouns, she posits a morpheme of high tone and nasalization on the last syllable of forms that were subjects of transitive verbs.

Shell lists 512 cognate sets. Forms from the seven languages on which the study is based are given when extant and available. At the bottom of each page additional cognates are given for languages other than the seven on which the reconstruction is primarily based. We thus have for Proto-Panoan an etymological dictionary of no mean proportions. This should greatly facilitate further comparison of Panoan with Tacanan (see below) and with Macro-Guaycuruan — if Greenberg's Macro-Panoan grouping (Panoan-Tacanan with Macro-Guaycuruan) can be verified.

8.2. Mary Key's *Comparative phonology of the Tacanan languages* is based on three languages of Bolivia: Tacana, Cavineña, and Chama. For these three languages phonological, lexical, and (to some degree) grammatical materials are available, whether published or unpublished. Mary Key herself did some field work in the first two. These data are supplemented by Reyesano and Huarayo word lists recorded phonetically on short field trips. Reyesano may be the same language as that referred to as 'Maropa' by earlier investigators and still occurring as such in McQuown's and Greenberg's classifications: 'Both Armentia (1905) and Cardus (1886) identify the Maropa as the tribe which formed the mission of Reyes. If this is true, Maropa would be the dialect which is known today as Reyesano' (6). On the basis of phonological isoglosses Key feels that Reyesano is closer to Tacana, and Huarayo to Chama. She then posits that Chama-Huarayo, Cavineña, and Tacana-Reyesano, are more or less coordinate on the same horizon of reconstruction.

Current phonemic systems are duly presented, followed by the phonemic system of Proto-Tacanan (I have rearranged Key's chart and changed a few symbols in the interest of consistency with the format followed for the phonemes of Proto-Pano) (Table 20):

*p	*t			*k	*ʔ(?)
*b	*d				
	*c	*č	*ç̌		
	*s	*š	*ş̌	*x	
*m	*n				
	*r	*ř			
*w	*y				
		*i	*o		
		*e	*a		

Table 20

Aside from the inevitable 'obscure reflexes' and 'unexplained residues' which to varying degrees plague all comparativists, the reflexes of Proto-Tacanan phonemes are straightforward with a minimum of split and merger. One outstanding problem is Chama t: 'The status of Chama t is not satisfactorily explained. While it is a fairly common phoneme in the language it is found in only a few cognates. The limited material shows reflex t only occurring after the morpheme e — (which indicates an unidentified possessed form) in stem initial position. ... The conditioning factor cannot be e alone since s also occurs in that circumstance' (54). A further problem is posed by the systemic interchange of certain phonemes in Chama. The problem affects not only Chama but the reconstruction of Proto-Tacanan: 'In almost all of the instances of specific fluctuations listed, corresponding problems are found in the comparative data. Either the sounds involved are proved reflexes of a sister language or remain as unexplained residues in one of the sister languages' (58). Key suggests dialect borrowing as at least a partial explanation of these 'fluctuations'. She adds a rather puzzling comment: 'Often the Panoan languages clarify the Chama problems better than do the Tacanan languages' (58).

Key's cognate sets, for which she gives Proto-Tacanan reconstructions, number about 200. Along with sets of this nature she presents many further sets with obviously resemblant forms among two or three of the languages, but for which she does not attempt specific reconstructions. The entire ensemble of sets are not numbered, but are arranged alphabetically according to English glosses. Forms answering to the glosses are added from various Panoan languages — whether or not the forms are cognate or even resemblant. No reconstructed Proto-Tacanan-Pano forms are given. On casual glance I would say that some 70 of the sets contain Pano forms that would seem to be very plausible cognates with the Tacanan languages.

8.3. Prospects seem bright for reconstruction of Proto-Tacanan-Pano in the near future. The extensive array of materials presented by both Shell and Key will greatly facilitate the task of bringing the two language groups together.

The reconstructed phonemic systems of the two language families are gratifyingly similar. Both have: four stops (*p, *t, *k, *ʔ), a voiced bilabial (Panoan *ƀ; Tacanan *b), five affricates and sibilants (*c, *č, *s, *š, *ʂ), two nasals (*m, *n), one vibrant (*r), two semivowels (*w, *y) and four vowels (*i, *ï, *a, *o in Panoan; *i, *o, *e, *a in Tacanan). In addition, Proto-Pano has the further stop *k^w and four nasalized vowels. Proto-Tacanan has a further voiced stop (*d), a further affricate (*ç), a further vibrant (*ř), and a velar spirant (*x). This resemblance is all the more remarkable in that neither Shell nor Key had access to the materials or conclusions of the other while carrying out her reconstructions. In brief, the converging of the two reconstructions is dictated by the data. The phonemic systems of the two language families are similar, and this similarity is undoubtedly based on linguistic kinship.

9. Benigno Ferrario, in an as yet unpublished manuscript,[73] treated exhaustively the question of the genetic affinity of three extinct languages of Uruguay: Chana, Güenoa, and Charrúa. He believed these languages to have been related to the Matacan

[73] Benigno Ferrario, 'Las lenguas indígenas del Uruguay', unpublished manuscript, 160 handwritten pages.

Antonio Tovar has written two articles on Matacan, but I was not able to obtain access to them in the limited time available before submitting this paper: 'El grupo mataco y su relación con otras lenguas de America del Sur', Congreso Internacional de Americanistas *Actas y memorias* 2.439-52 (1964); 'Relación entre las lenguas del grupo mataco', *Homenaje a Fernando Márquez-Miranda*, 370-7 (Madrid-Sevilla, 1964).

languages of Paraguay and the Argentine (cf. Greenberg's Macro-Guaycuruan, which in turn belongs along with Panoan and Tacanan in his Macro-Panoan).[74]

The extant data are pitifully restricted: 90 words and 26 expressions in Chana; 19 expressions in Güenoa; and 50 words in Charrua. For a fourth language Minuana (presumed to have been related) but one word (a place name) has survived. This small corpus Ferrario analyzed morpheme by morpheme in masterful fashion.

Ferrario had first to dispose of other suggestions regarding the affinities of the 'Charruan' family (listed as 'unclassified' under Macro-Guaycuruan by Greenberg). He does this incisively with cutting criticism of those who confuse social entities and linguistic families, of those who 'leaf through vocabularies' and latch on to superficial resemblances — comparing parts of words willy-nilly and discarding the rest without regard to the morphological structures involved; and of the cavalier handling of data and the semantic confusions found in some so-called 'comparative work'. Specifically he examines and rejects claims of affinity with Tupi-Guarani, Guaycuru, Kaingang (Gê), and Arawakan. These claims are not superficially dismissed; on the contrary, available evidence is painstakingly examined. The Tupi-Guarani claim is seen to be based on place names resultant on spread of Tupi-Guaraní as a lingua franca. Assumed Charruan cognates with Guaycuru and Kaingang are laid in the balances and found wanting. Especially sharp is his criticism of Sixto Perea y Alonso's suggestion that Charruan is Arawakan.[75]

Ferrario's positive argument for Matacan affinities cannot be based on systematic sound correspondences supported by an imposing array of cognate sets — the data are too fragmentary to permit this. He showed, however, that certain basic morphological features of Charruan — and certain specific morphemes — are very similar to those of such Matacan languages as Nocten, Vejoz, Choroti and Mataco. The resemblances are not superficial. Ferrario was especially interested in archaic and nonproductive features rather than in features which may reflect recent analogical spread. Affixes such as first person singular, first person plural, second person common, and pluralizer are examined with care in Charruan and Matacan. Ferrario had the material well in hand. His methodology was sound and his arguments convincing.

10. Comparative Arawakan is scarcely begun as yet.[76] In the words of Douglas

[74] José Pedro Rona, *Nuevos Elementos acerca de la Lengua Charrúa*, (Montevideo, 1964). In this 28-page work, Rona first analyzes some proper names (found in the Jesuit mission records of the town of São Borja, Rio Grande de Sul, Brazil) for names of possible Charruan origin. The restricted nature of extant data on the Charruan languages necessitates efforts of this sort. The second section of the article presents comparative evidence that Charruan pertains to the Lule-Vilelan subdivision of Macro-Guaycuruan rather than to the Matacan sub-division.

[75] Sixto Perea y Alonso, *Filología comparada de las lenguas y dialectos Arawak* 1 (Montevideo, 1942). Reproduces his earlier work 'Apuntes para la prehistoria indígena del Rio de la Plata y especialmente de la banda Oriental del Uruguay, como introducción a la filología comparada de la lengua y dialectos Arawak', *BFM* 1.217-45 (1937) cf. Olaf Blixen, *Acerca de la supuesta filiación Arawak de las lenguas indigenas del Uruguay* (Montevideo, 1958).

[76] After this article went to the editor the following monograph appeared: G. Kingsley Noble,

Taylor: 'No serious work on comparative Arawakan can be undertaken until we have adequate descriptions of some of the more typical Arawakan languages. Recent work on such languages as Amuesha, Campa, Tereno, etc. are little help, as these languages are very far indeed from the type represented by Arawak, Achagua, Goajiro, or the Rio Negro group. It seems to me that in order to make a beginning in any comparative work, one must have reasonably reliable descriptions of at least several languages showing a moderate amount of likely cognates. Outliers can be dealt with only at a later stage' (private correspondence).

Robert Shafer has assembled some 125 sets from some sixty Arawakan languages.[77] Certain languages enter, however, into only a few sets (e.g. Amuesha, which Greenberg considers to be 'unclassified' Arawakan, occurs in only two sets). The data are assembled from published sources which required some interpretation of the phonetically recorded data. Thus, Shafer felt it safe to consider that any given Arawakan language has but one set of stops whether voiced or voiceless. At any rate his sources did not record consistently any such differences if they were contrastive in the data. It now turns out that in at least one of the languages of his sources — Arawak proper — there is an opposition of aspirated and unaspirated consonants.[78] This opposition includes two of the stops (t versus t^h; k versus k^h;) and the lateral (l versus l^h). Thus, in the Arawak word for 'moon' where Shafer's source recorded katti, the tt was not an inconsistency of recording but a way of indicating the aspirated stop (kat^hi). Difficulties of this sort in his sources naturally limit the scope of Shafer's work.

Shafer reconstructed the following consonants (he does not reconstruct vowels): *h, *k, *t, *p, *n, *m, *t', *ś, *ts (doubtful), *d, *y, *w, *r. It is difficult to arrange these in any sort of orderly array. The phoneme *h is a major problem since Shafer's sources indicate a variety of reflexes: h, ø, k, s, z, and t. Maybe it was a fronted k which palatalized to č/c and thereby gave the latter three reflexes. By contrast, *k and *t have fairly consistent reflexes. Aspirated p occurs as a reflex of *p in some sets, while plain p occurs in others. Shafer believed these sets to be in complementary distribution, but the data are fragmentary. For phoneme *n, a puzzling reflex n^h occurs in several languages of one set. The occurrence of *d — one lone voiced stop

'Proto-Arawakan and its Descendants', *IJAL* (July, 1965) (Part II). As the author admits 'The sources of data have often been rather inexact transcriptions. Sometimes, they have represented compilations of several, often unobtainable primary sources' (113). In addition, the book tries to cover an immense area linguistically. Not only is Arawakan proper included, but Uru-Chipayan is assumed to be Arawakan (on the basis of some twenty sets) and included in the line-up along with Tupian and Chapacuran, for which data are given on the assumption that they are related to the Arawakan stock. A brief sketch of Goajiro is included as a control. Nevertheless, the overall result is almost as diffuse as Shafer's brief sketch described in this section. Noble, however, pays some attention to morphological features and to shared innovations — whether phonological, grammatical, or lexical. In this way he obtains a family tree for Arawakan and related languages. It needs to be emphasized, however, that without a detailed reconstruction of a proto-language shared innovations are not surely distinguished from shared retentions. Some use is made of glottochronology.

77 Robert Shafer, 'Algumas equações fonéticas em Arawakan', *Anthropos* 54.542-62 (1959).

78 H. C. van Renselaar and J. Voorhoeve, 'Rapport over een ethnologische studiereis door Mata', *BijdrTLV* 3.328-61 — probably 1959).

— is difficult to systematize. In two-thirds of the languages cited initial *d gives zero; in others, d or t (h in Yukuna). While Shafer labeled *ts as doubtful, the data for the reconstruction of *t' are even scantier. The doubtful status of *ts is due, however, to the fact that in all but two of the thirteen sets where it is posited it occurred before vowel i (probably Proto-Arawakan *i). While Shafer reconstructs only *r, his sets may possibly indicate three phonemes, say, two varieties of r, and an l.

Douglas Taylor has compared (Surinam) Arawak with Island Carib (the language is Arawakan in spite of the name) as culled from historical sources and as now spoken by the 'Black Caribs' of Central America.[79] Taylor is encouraged by the comparative Arawak data to interpret his historical sources as indicating a contrast of aspirated and unaspirated consonants in the stops, nasals, and liquids. He symbolized the consonant systems of Dominican Island Carib (17th century) and Vincentian Island Carib (spoken until 1920) as follows (Table 21):

	DIC:			VIC:	
m	n		m	n	
	n^h			-(?)	
b			b	d	g
	t	k		c	
p^h	t^h	k^h		t^h	k^h
	s	h	f	s	h
	r,l				r,l
	l^h				

Table 21

In VIC, as in Arawak, the f phoneme is probably a development from earlier p^h. DIC, which has no f, has a p^h.

Although Taylor's study is on a narrow front, it may have significance for Arawakan in general. Shafer's n^h residue and apparent contrasts among reflexes of his r might be explained by some such scheme as the above. In current Arawak and in the 17th century DIC, there were three contrasting phonemes: r, l, l^h. Notice also Shafer's sets which witness to *[p^h] in possible contrast with *[p]. Furthermore, in that the contrast — if it existed — could have been fortis-lenis in Proto-Arawakan, Shafer's *h versus *k could be lenis versus fortis velar, while his *d may also have been a lenis alveolar. It is futile to speculate further. As reliable synchronic data become available, the serious reconstruction of Proto-Arawakan will become possible.

11. Irvine Davis' unpublished sketch of Proto-Gê[80] is brief but fulfills many of the

[79] Douglas Taylor, 'Surinam Arawak as compared with different dialects of Island Carib', *BijdrTLV* 3.362-73 (1959?) cf. earlier article 'Some problems of sound correspondence in Arawak', *IJAL* 24. 234-9 (1958).

[80] Irvine Davis, 'Comparative Jê phonology', unpublished manuscript, Brazilian branch of the Summer Institute of Linguistics (1964).

requisites of a good comparative study: (1) presentation of current phonological systems; (2) reconstruction of an earlier phonological system; (3) careful tracing out of reflexes in daughter languages; (4) attention to apparent irregularities of a quasi-systemic sort; (5) presentation of a significant number (112) of cognate sets, and English indexing of cognates.

Davis' Proto-Gê is based on: Apinaye, Canela, Suyá, Xavante, and Kaingang. While the choice of languages was partially dictated by availability of data, the languages chosen are nevertheless well representative of Gê. Thus: 'Apinaye in its relationship to Proto-Jê, is in most respects representative of the Northern Kayapó dialects. ... Most of the facts concerning Canela outlined in the paper are apparently also true of the other members of the Eastern Timbira subgroup. ... So far as it is known, Suyá constitutes in itself a subdivision of Jê lacking other members, while Xavante with its several dialects plus Xerente forms another distinct subgroup' (3).

Regarding Kaingang, Davis says 'For the purposes of phonological reconstruction Kaingang belongs more logically within the Jê family than as a separate family within the Macro-Jê stock. It is obviously more closely related to the traditional Jê languages than are other Macro-Jê languages such as Maxakalí, and in many respects it shows closer conformity to Proto-Jê phonology than does Xavante, an undisputed member of the Jê family' (2). With Kaingang Davis groups Xokleng as 'either a somewhat divergent Kaingang dialect or a separate but closely related language' (2). Ursula Weisemann unhesitatingly places Xokleng (which she spells Xokreng) as a fourth Kaingang dialect (along with Paraná, South Kaingang, and Saõ Paulo).[81]

Davis reconstructs Proto-Gê phonemes as follows (Table 22):

Consonants				*Oral Vowels*			*Nasal Vowels*		
*p	*t	*c	*k	*i	*ɨ	*u	*į	*ɨ̨	*ų
*m	*n	*ñ	*ŋ	*e	*ə	*o	*ę	*ą	*ǫ
*w	*r	*z		*ɛ	*a	*ɔ			

Table 22

The phonetics of the Gê languages is anything but straightforward. In current languages the phonemes symbolized as nasals 'vary from voiced stops or affricates to prenasalized or postnasalized stops, to nasal continuants depending on the environment and on the language' (4). Phonemes transcribed as w/v and y/z vary from non-syllabic vocoids to fricatives. In some languages vowel length, possibly even consonant length, are phonemic. Current phonemic systems are variations on Proto-Gê. Thus, Apinaye adds glottal stop to the consonants and a tenth oral vowel (and seventh nasal vowel). Canela (tentative phonemicization) adds two laryngeals, ʔ and h, and an aspirated velar k^h. The vowel system is identical with that of Proto-Gê. Suya (even more tentatively phonemicized) adds one laryngeal h, a spirant s, two

[81] Ursula Weisemann, 'Notes on Proto-Kaingang: a study of four dialects', unpublished manuscript, Brazilian branch of the Summer Institute of Linguistics.

aspirants, t^h and k^h, and a further vowel (as in Apinayé). Xavante eliminates phonemes corresponding to *n and *z, but adds one laryngeal, h. The glottal stop ʔ occurs instead of the velar k. The system of oral vowels is identical to Proto-Gê, but one nasal vowel is eliminated.

Kaingang raises a few problems due to the uncertainty of phonemic analysis in present-day Kaingang dialects. Weisemann (in what appears to be an early paper) states that possibly some Kaingang dialects and Proto-Kaingang had a voiced obstruent series b, d, g. Since, however, Weisemann collaborated somewhat with Davis in his recent reconstruction, it appears that her more recent thinking would not lead to positing such a series. Davis indicates that, as in the traditional Gê languages, voiced obstruents are allophones of the nasals.[82] Even if the obstruents are phonemic in one or more current Kaingang dialects their sub-phonemic status seems probable in Proto-Kaingang. We may assume, then, that relative to Proto-Gê, Kaingang eliminates one stop *c, adds two laryngeals ʔ and h, and two spirants f and š. The system of oral vowels corresponds to that of Proto-Gê, while one nasal vowel has been eliminated.

Phonological developments — granting the above range of allophonic variation in certain phonemes — are, as a whole, consistent and straightforward. Conditioned sound changes and unexplained residues often involve vertical shunting within an order of consonants. Thus *p is, on occasion, reflected as m or w in certain languages; *m, on occasion as p. Similarly *t is, on occasion, reflected as n or r; *n, on occasion, as t. By conditioned sound change *c splits to c/y in Canela, and ñ/y in Kaingang. Less parallel is the velar order, but even here Kaingang has a few unexplained reflexes ŋ of *k. While these are by no means the only conditioned sound changes and unexplained residues in the reflexes in current Gê languages, nevertheless the parallelism of the above is scarcely fortuitous. It is puzzling that the vertical shunting is neither wholly conditioned by sound change nor wholly irregular and sporadic. If the latter were the case, we could posit Proto-Gê consonantal alternation — possibly marking one or more grammatical categories. Some sort of morphophonemic alternation — partly phonologically conditioned — is nevertheless indicated.

12. Proto-Tupi-Guarani is, like Proto-Arawakan, more of a promise than a reality at present. We have, nevertheless, a phonological sketch by Hanke, Swadesh, and Rodrigues of the Mekens language along with (1) a sketch of the phonology of Tupinambá and Cocama; (2) a page of Proto-Tupi phonemes along with reflexes in thirteen languages; and (3) a Mekens word-list with a scattering of cognates from various other languages.[83]

[82] Cf. Weisemann, Notes on Proto-Kaingang (2,3): 'According to the phonemic analysis now established for Paraná dialects as spoken at Rio dos Cobras however, [b], [d], and [g] do not have phonemic status. They occur only contiguous to homorganic nasals. ...' It is possible that this analysis could also be established for some of the other dialects if sufficient data were available.

[83] Wanda Hanke, Morris Swadesh, and Aryón D. Rodrigues, 'Notas de fonología Mekens', *Miscellanea Paul Rivet octogenario dicata* (Mexico City, 1958).

Although they divided the Tupi stock into seven component families as did Rodrigues, 1958[84] (except that the Tupari family is rechristened Mekens), no attempt is made to distinguish Proto-Tupi as such from Proto-Mekens, nor to proceed step-wise by reconstruction of the phonologies of component families, then of the stock as a whole. The table of reflexes in thirteen languages tabulates reflexes of eight languages of Tupi-Guaraní proper, one of the Yuruna family, one of the Ariken family, two of the Mekens family, and one of the Monde family. Typologically Mekens is compared directly with Tupinamba and Cocama (both of Tupi-Guarani proper) with the comment 'Podemos, pois, ter uma idéia geral de qualquier idioma tupí, examinando o Tupinamba é o Kokama. ...' (192).

The reconstructed consonants are plausibly similar to those found in Tupinambá, Cocama, or Mekens — except for two oddities *t^y and *g (the latter is the only voiced obstruent posited and is very poorly attested). Six oral vowels are reconstructed as against four in Tupinamba and five in Mekens.

In a student paper at Indiana University[85] Loraine Bridgeman lines up comparative data in the following Tupí languages: Urubu, Kamayura, Assurini, Guajajara, and Satare (all Tupi-Guaraní proper). She suggests a few sound correspondences (each one attested in at least five sets involving four or five languages), but does not reconstruct forms. Some 75 sets are given with forms in five languages, some 48 sets with forms in four languages; and some 65 sets with forms in two or three languages.

In a four-page article Bernard Pottier[86] suggests a few sound correspondences in the following Tupi languages: Xeta, Chiriguano, Izozo, Guarayo, Siriono, Guayaki, Cocama, Emerillon, Oyampi, and Tembe (all Tupi-Guarani proper). He proposes a division within Tupi-Guarani (corresponding to the first of Rodrigues' seven main divisions of the Tupi stock) in which the 'South-West' group (Xeta, Guayaki, Chiriguano, Izozo, Guarayo, Siriono) is distinguished from the 'North and East' group (Tupi, Tembé, Oyampi, Emerillon, Cocama) on the basis of certain phonological isoglosses. In that Rodrigues' slightly different grouping within Tupi-Guarani is based on lexical-statistics, while Pottier's is based on phonological isoglosses, the two articles form an interesting comparison.

13. Bruce Moore has compared two Chibchan languages, Colorado and Cayapa, spoken in the Ecuadorian coastal jungle.[87] Sound correspondences are carefully sorted out and classified according to Moore's stated purpose: 'The present study attempts to explain all the differences between 207 cognate pairs' (273). Although Moore never gives the phonemic system which he reconstructs for 'South Barbacoan Chibchan' —

[84] Aryón D. Rodrigues, 'Classification of Tupi-Guaraní', *IJAL* 24.231-4 (1958).

[85] Loraine I. Bridgeman, 'Preliminary notes on a comparative study of five Tupi-Guaraní languages' (1965).

[86] Bernard Pottier, 'Problemes de dialectologie dans le domaine du Tupi-Guaraní', *Orbis* 10:1.31-4 (1961).

[87] Bruce R. Moore, 'Correspondences in South Barbacoan Chibcha', Benjamin Elson, ed., *Studies in Ecuadorian Indian Languages I:* 270-89, (Norman, 1962).

nor a reconstructed form for each of his sets — the following phonemes occur in reconstructed forms scattered through the article (Table 23):

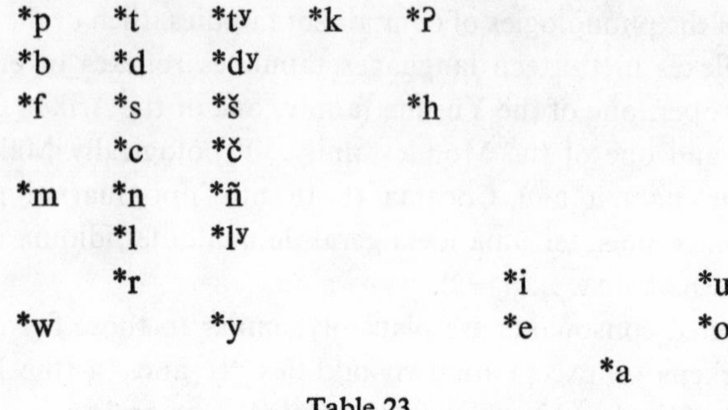

*p	*t	*t^y	*k	*ʔ			
*b	*d	*d^y					
*f	*s	*š		*h			
	*c	*č					
*m	*n	*ñ					
	*l	*l^y					
	*r				*i		*u
*w		*y			*e		*o
						*a	

Table 23

In addition, there occurs an *N which was a syllable final nasal element whose reflexes are vowel nasalization and nasal consonants. An *S is reconstructed to account for two irregular cognate pairs.

The only syllable final elements were *N and *h.

14. Comparative Carib is yet to be initiated. Desmond Derbyshire, however, has written briefly concerning three mutually intelligible dialects of Brazilian Carib: Hiskaryana, Katxhuyana, and Waiwai.[88] Internal reconstruction is employed within each dialect with attention to differences in phoneme inventories, restrictions in distribution of certain phonemes, and the distribution of allophones. On this basis the three dialects are reduced to the same inventory of phonemes. This yields a system considered to be that of the common stage lying back of the three dialects. The comparative method is not employed. Some lexical and grammatical comparisons are given — especially in respect to the structure of verbs.

Without engaging in comparative reconstructions, Jacob Loewen presents several isoglosses dividing the Choco languages of Panama and Colombia (in Greenberg's 'Northwestern Cariban').[89] It is, however, impossible to distinguish shared innovations from shared retentions without prior application of the comparative method. And, to refer again to Hamp's dictum (4.3), shared innovations are the sine qua non of genetic groupings.

[88] Desmond Derbyshire, 'Comparative notes on three Carib dialects', *Boletim do Museu Paraense Emílio Goeldi, nova série, Anthropologia* 14 (1961).

[89] Jacob A. Loewen, 'Chocó I: introduction and bibliography', *IJAL* 29.239-63 (1963).

CREOLE LINGUISTICS

ROBERT A. HALL JR.

I. GENERAL TREATMENTS

Scholarly interest in pidgin and creole languages dates back to the mid-nineteenth century; see extensive bibliography in Reinecke (1937). However, work which would be considered scientific by present-day standards did not begin until the 1930's; even such relatively advanced and extensive treatments as Schuchardt (1914) on Saramaccan or Lenz (1928) on Papiamentu[1] were based largely on traditional categories and analysis. Our discussion will, therefore, treat of developments since the middle 1930's.

Book-length discussions of the nature and function of pidgin and creole languages (for which Reinecke proposed the linguistically and sociologically justified term *marginal languages*) have been furnished by Reinecke (1937) and Hall (1965b). The former treats the subject primarily from a sociologist's stand-point, as was inevitable in view of the type of material available before the middle 1930's. The latter attempts to combine linguistic and anthropological criteria in an over-all presentation. Not all general treatments have shown even an elementary command of the essentials of linguistic analysis (e.g. Faine [1939]). Surveys of the creole languages of the Caribbean have been made by Loftman (1953) and Stewart (1962a). Of specifically bibliographical studies, the only extensive one, covering the entire description and history of a single creole, is Voorhoeve and Donicie (1963) for Sranan (reviewed by Taylor [1965]).

II. DESCRIPTIVE STUDIES

Strictly descriptive analyses have been made of a number of Caribbean creoles since the 1930's. Göbl-Gáldi (1934) attempted an over-all sketch of the grammar of French-based creoles, but with an unsatisfactory analytical approach. Of the French-based creoles, that of Haiti has received the most attention, perhaps because of the independent status of the nation and its literacy-problem. The UNESCO Fundamental Education project at Marbial in 1947-50 included a study of the language-question, out of which came an over-all structural description of Haitian Creole in Hall (1953; reviewed by Taylor [1953] and Zumthor [1957]), which included a large amount of

[1] I use this form, representing the local pronunciation of the name of the language, in preference to the Hispanized *Papiamento*.

descriptive material from earlier studies, especially Sylvain (1936) and McConnell and Swan (1945). Individual aspects of Haitian Creole structure have received occasional treatment: phonetics, by Evans (1938) and Hall (1950c); form-classes, by Hall (1962a);[2] aspect and tense in verbs, by Hall (1952). The dialectal divisions of Haitian Creole received a somewhat sketchy treatment in Hyppolite (1950; reviewed by Hall [1951]); despite the historical implications of its title ('Origines'), it is primarily descriptive.

Of the other French-based creoles, that of Louisiana has been the object of considerable amateurish discussion, but the only sound linguistic treatments have been those of Lane (1935) and Morgan (1959, 1960). Dominican Creole has been studied extensively by Taylor (1947, 1951, 1952, 1955a). Martiniquais Creole has been investigated by two authors, but with only moderate success: Funk (1950) and Jourdain, whose Paris doctoral thesis dated from 1946 but appeared only much later (1954, 1956a, 1956b; reviewed by Taylor [1957a] and Hall [1957b]). For Trinidad Creole, only Goodman (1958) has analyzed its phonetics.

Papiamentu structure has been analyzed in three dissertations: Silva-Fuenzalida (1952), Harris (1953), and Wattman (1953). The only other study of an Ibero-Romance-based marginal language is contained in the brief notes of Riley (1952) on a variety of Venezuelan trade Spanish.

Of the English-based creoles of the region, Jamaican Creole and Sranan (or 'Taki-Taki', the speech of Paramaribo, Suriname) have been the most extensively studied. The former was the object of intensive work in the late 1950's, partly under Fulbright auspices, at the then U.C.W.I., directed by R. B. Le Page and F. G. Cassidy, with the assistance of D. De Camp. Out-growths of these and other studies include a discussion of work done on Caribbean off-shoots of English (Cassidy [1959]), a general discussion of English creoles (Le Page [1957-58]), and book-length presentations of Jamaican Creole in Le Page and De Camp (1960; reviewed by Taylor [1963b]) and Bailey (1965). The *Dictionary of Jamaican English* (Cassidy and Le Page [1967]) affords extensive descriptive and historical documentation. An observation repeatedly made concerning Jamaican Creole in the above discussions, and emphasized by De Camp (1961, 1962), is the absence of a sharp dividing line between Creole and English, and hence the existence of a broad spectrum ranging from 'Bongo talk' to the nearly standard usage of Kingston.[3]

The Krio language of Sierra Leone, an off-shoot of Jamaican Creole taken to Freetown in the 19th century by resettlement of ex-slaves from Jamaica, has also been studied. Its general status was discussed by Jones (1957) and Berry (1959b), and an anthology of texts in phonemic transcription was published by Turner (1964).

Extensive Sranan texts, in phonetic transcription, were published by Herskovits and

[2] Essentially a reply, concerning questions of method and analytical procedure, to Zumthor (1957).

[3] This situation is, however, not peculiar to Jamaica or to creoles, but is found in virtually every area where non-standard and standard varieties of speech have been in contact over long periods of time.

Herskovits (1936); these texts, together with data from Simons (1941), were utilized for the preliminary sketch presented in Hall (1948). Later treatments by Donicie (1954) and Voorhoeve (1953a — reviewed by Taylor [1956b] — 1953b, 1962) have been much more complete and thorough. Specific aspects of Sranan structure have also received separate treatment: phonetics in Pée (1951) and Donicie (1953); the verbal system in Voorhoeve (1957b); the verbal prefixes *sa-* and *de-* in Simons (1954/55) and Donicie (1956); and problems of syntactic analysis in Voorhoeve (1958 and 1961b).

Saramaccan, the speech of the up-country Bush-Negroes in Suriname, has also been studied, though less extensively than Sranan; Voorhoeve (1951d) discusses the presence of phonemically significant syllabic tone in relation to grammatical structure.

III. APPLIED LINGUISTICS

The glottopolitical aspect of creole languages in the Caribbean has not been neglected, since (as elsewhere) it has frequently occasioned the attention paid to them in the first place. The social position and function of creoles, and their relation to the standard language, has been discussed for the English-based creoles by Vérin (1958), and for Haitian Creole by Efron (1954) and Stewart (1962). Pompilus (1961) has analyzed the influence of the Creole substratum on the standard French of Haiti. The potentialities of creoles for literary use, often a topic of debate, have been examined for Krio by Jones (1957) and for Haitian Creole by Pressoir (1947). These and other Caribbean creoles have been the media for a certain amount of literary creation in recent years (cf. Taylor [1957b]).

One of the major problems involved in the official recognition of creoles has been the provision of orthographies which would be both phonologically adequate and inoffensive to users of the most closely related European standard language. The general problems of orthographies for pidgins and creoles was discussed in Hall(1959). For Haitian Creole, the orthography developed by McConnell and adapted to French spelling by Laubach was embodied in McConnell and Swan (1945) and adopted in the late 1940's and early 1950's in sporadic government-backed literacy campaigns. It was later replaced by the further adaptation made by Pressoir (1947) which was recognized in the government decree of 1962 legalizing the use of Creole and is currently used in writing the language throughout the country. For Sranan, a unified missionary orthography has been adopted and is in general use; cf. Pée, Hellinga and Donicie (1953a, 1953b), and Voorhoeve (1957a, 1957c, 1961a). Similar problems connected with the spelling of Saramaccan have been treated by Voorhoeve (1959).

IV. HISTORICAL STUDIES

The French-based creoles as a whole have been studied from a historical-comparative point of view by Goodman (1964; reviewed by Hall [1965a]), in relation to French and

West African languages. Goodman traces them to a pidginized variety of French spoken in West Africa during the early years of the slave-trade. Sylvain (1936) undertook a similar study for Haitian Creole alone, emphasizing the African element, but without much reference to other French-based creoles. In a later study, she and her husband (Comhaire and Sylvain-Comhaire [1955]) demonstrated the survival of numerous African lexical items in Haitian Creole religious terminology, whereas it had been thought that the vocabulary of this language was derived almost wholly from French. Schwartz (1949) and Hall (1950b) treated American lexical influence in Haiti. The value of another early philological study of Haitian Creole (Faine [1937]) was greatly diminished by its author's ignorance of historical method in linguistics. Funk (1953) treated the historical back-ground of Martiniquais Creole. For Dominican Creole, the influence of Carib on its morphology was discussed by Taylor (1945), and the structural status of certain survivals of the French definite article by Taylor (1961a).

In discussions of the history of Papiamentu, the main question has been whether to assign it to Spanish or to Portuguese. Against the earlier assumption (e.g. in Lenz [1928] that Papiamentu developed out of Spanish, several scholars have more recently assigned it to Portuguese, with a heavy later over-lay from Spanish: e.g. Navarro Tomás (1953), van Wijk (1958). It has been suggested by others (Ribeiro [1939], Silva Neto [1949]) that the dialects of northern Brazil were an out-growth of an earlier creole which had resulted from a mixture of Portuguese with West African languages; but this view has been opposed by Révah (1964).

The English-based creoles were rightly included among the 'neue germanische Kultursprachen' whose rise was treated by Kloss (1952). Their origin in West African Pidgin English has been discussed by Cassidy (1962), and a sample reconstruction of some items in Proto-Pidgin-English (based in part on Sranan and Gullah) was made by Hall (1964, ch. 65). The clearly African origin of many personal names and various structural features of Gullah was shown by Turner (1949); reviewed by Hall [1950a]). The history of Jamaican Creole over three centuries and its changing relation to standard English was treated in a semi-popularizing book by Cassidy (1961). The origin of various aspects of Krio vocabulary was discussed by Jones (1959) and Berry (1959a, 1960).

The history of Sranan and Saramaccan has been a particular concern of the Dutch team working in Suriname, as set forth programmatically by Voorhoeve (1961c). An eighteenth-century dictionary of Saramaccan, together with comparisons from modern Saramaccan and town Sranan, forms the basis of Donicie and Voorhoeve (1962; reviewed by Taylor [1964]). The influence of Dutch on Sranan in word-composition was analyzed by Simons and Voorhoeve (1955/56), and that of English in vocabulary by Echteld (1961). Silva-Neto (1938) set forth a theory of Portuguese and African origins for Sranan, analogous to that mentioned above for North Brazilian Portuguese dialects.

The major theoretical problem in the history of the Caribbean creoles has been their relation to European language-structure on the one hand, and that of West African tongues on the other. The common opinion among nonspecialists, that the creoles are 'corruptions' of French, Spanish, or English (as the case may be), with virtually no African influence, is by now prima facie evidence of an amateurish approach (as in the works of, say, Faine or Jourdain). At present, the existence of a considerable African element in the various Caribbean creoles, on all levels of linguistic structure, is recognized by all scholars, e.g. Göbl-Gáldi (1933), Lichtveld (1954), Hall (1955), Sommerfelt (1958), Valkhoff (1960). Where the extent of European elements is studied (e.g. forms from Romance *sapēre* 'to know > to be in the habit of ...', Hall [1957a]), it is or should be with full awareness of the often complicated relationships between European and non-European features.

The point of disagreement among present-day scholars is, rather, the possibility of applying to pidgins and creoles the comparative method, as developed in the field of Indo-European and other 'normal' language-families. Beginning with Sylvain (1936), it has been widely held that (to paraphrase her words slightly) a Caribbean creole is 'une langue éwé à vocabulaire européen', whose structure is essentially African and hence cannot be traced to a European source. Against this point of view, Hall (1950d, 1958, 1965b) has argued for the applicability of the comparative method and the derivation of the creoles from European languages, based on the establishment of regular phonetic correspondences between the morphemes (especially the functors) of the grammatical core of the Creole in question and those of the presumed European source. On the other hand, Taylor (1956, 1959, 1960, 1961b, 1963a) has maintained that the structural relationships of the Caribbean creoles are due to their all having come from a single source in West Africa, and that the creoles have become differentiated through a process of 'relexification', in which elements (including functors) have spread from different European languages to take the place of the original morphemes. Thompson (1961) suggests that the similarities between creoles in many parts of the world are due to their having been out-growths of a single West African Pidgin Portuguese. Weinreich (1958) has seen that there is no fundamental opposition between the two points of view.

V. FUTURE DIRECTIONS OF RESEARCH

The greatest need at present is simply for more investigation, data-gathering, and analysis, and for publication of scholarly descriptions of as many pidgins and creoles as possible. Work of the type already begun for Haitian Creole and Sranan is needed for all the other creoles mentioned in this article, and for some which have been badly neglected in modern times: e.g. the English-based creoles of the Bahamas, the Virgin Islands, and the Lesser Antilles; the French-based creoles of various smaller islands such as Trinidad, and that of French Guiana; and the trade Spanish of countries around the Caribbean, from Mexico to Venezuela. To accompany such studies, bibliographies (based largely on materials accessible only locally) similar to the model work of Voorhoeve and Donicie (1963) are needed for virtually all creoles. Detailed studies of the social function of creoles, in their stratification and use in different environments, are also needed, as are more traditional geographical investigations, with a linguistic atlas of one or more areas.

In historical work, a promising beginning has been made by Goodman (1964), but really extensive work must await thorough investigation of as much earlier documentation as is available,[4] and the availabiliy of more descriptive material. The position of creoles with respect to the general process of 'nativization' (whereby a language becomes native to a group which formerly spoke one or more other tongues) awaits further clarification (what is a 'true creole' as referred to by Taylor [1963b]?). The disagreement over the origins of creoles cannot be resolved until the disputants reach a clearer understanding of the nature of linguistic relationships and the relative weight to be assigned to regular phonetic correspondences in morphemes and regular morphemic correspondences in syntagmata, as opposed to similarities in phrasal and semantic patterns.

BIBLIOGRAPHY

Bailey, Beryl Loftman, 1966. *Jamaican Creole Syntax. A transformational approach* (Cambridge, England).

Berry, Jack, 1959a. 'The origins of Krio vocabulary', *Sierra Leone Studies* NS.3:12 (Dec., 1959).

——, 1959b. 'Creole as a language', *West Africa* Sept. 1959. 745.

——, 1960. 'English loanwords and adaptations in Sierra Leone Krio', *Creole Language Studies* 2.1-16.

Cassidy, Frederic G., 1959. 'English language studies in the Caribbean', *AS* 34.163-171.

——, 1961. *Jamaica talk: three hundred years of the English language in Jamaica* (London and New York).

——, 1962. 'Towards the recovery of early English-African Pidgin', *Symposium on Multilingualism* 267-277.

Cassidy, Frederic G., and R. B. Le Page, 1967. *Dictionary of Jamaica English* (Cambridge [England] and New York).

Comhaire, Jean, and Suzanne Comhaire-Sylvain, 1955. 'Survivances africaines dans le vocabulaire religieux d'Haïti', *ED* 14.3-20.

Creole Language Studies 2. (1961) *Proceedings of the Conference on Creole Language Studies* (London).

De Camp, David, 1961. 'Social and geographical factors in Jamaican dialects', *Creole Language Studies* 2.61-84.

[4] A dictionary of Haitian Creole on a historico-philological basis, utilizing all available earlier documentation, was announced in the late 1940's as being under way, but to the best of my knowledge the project never came to fruition.

De Camp, David, 1962. 'Creole language areas considered as multilingual communities', *Symposium on Multilingualism* 227-231.

Donicie, Antoon, 1953. 'Kanttekeningen bij "De klanken van het Neger-Engels"', *TT* 5.4-7.

——, 1954. *De Creolentaal van Suriname. Spraakkunst*, 2nd ed., *ibid.*, 1959 (Paramaribo).

——, 1956. 'De partikels *sa* en *(de) go* in de Creolentaal van Suriname', *NWIG* 26.183-191.

Donicie, Antoon, and Jan Voorhoeve, 1962. *De saramakaanse Woordenschat.* (Amsterdam) [mimeographed].

Echteld, Johannes Julius Marius, 1961. *The English words in Sranan* (*Negro-English of Surinam*) (Amsterdam and Groningen).

Efron, Edith, 1954. 'French and Creole patois in Haiti', *Caribbean Quarterly* 3.199-214.

Evans, Eileen M., 1938. 'Notes on the phonetics of the Creole language of Haiti', *AvPh* 2.195-210.

Faine, Jules, 1937. *Philologie créole. Etudes historiques et étymologiques sur la langue créole d'Haïti.* Deuxième édition (Port-au-Prince).

——, 1939. *Le créole dans l'univers. Etudes comparatives des parlers français-créoles* (Port-au-Prince).

Funk, Henry, 1950. *The French creole dialect of Martinique. Phonology and morphology* (M. A. thesis, University of Virginia).

——, 1953. *The French Creole dialect of Martinique: its historical background* (Ph. D. dissertation, University of Virginia).

Göbl-Gáldi László, 1933. 'Problemi di sostrato nel creolo francese', *RLR* 9.336-345.

——, 1934. 'Esquisse de la structure grammaticale des patois français-créoles', *ZFSL* 58.257-295.

Goodman, Morris F., 1958. 'On the phonetics of the French Creole of Trinidad', *Word* 14.208-212.

——, 1964. *A comparative study of French creole dialects* (The Hague) (= Janua Linguarum, Series Practica, no. 4.)

Hall, Robert A., Jr., 1948. 'The linguistic structure of Taki-Taki', *Lg* 24.92-116.

——, 1950a. 'African substratum in Negro English', *AS* 25.51-54.

——, 1950b. 'Further English borrowings in Haitian Creole', *AS* 25.150-151.

——, 1950c. 'Nasalization in Haitian Creole', *MLN* 65.474-478.

——, 1950d. 'The genetic relationships of Haitian Creole', *RL* 1.194-203.

——, 1951. Review of Hyppolite (1950), in *RomPh* 4.326-328.

——, 1952. 'Aspect and tense in Haitian Creole', *RomPh* 5.312-316.

——, 1953. *Haitian Creole: Grammar, texts, vocabulary* (= *American Anthropological Association Memoir* no. 74; also issued as *American Folklore Society Memoir* no. 43).

——, 1955. 'Sostrato e lingue créole', *AGI* 40.1-9.

Hall, Robert A., Jr., 1957a. 'Romance *sapēre* in pidgins and creoles', *RomPh* 10.156-157.

——, 1957b. Review of Jourdain (1956a, 1956b). *Lg*.33.226-231.

——, 1958. 'Creole languages and genetic relationships', *Word* 14.367-373.

——, 1959. 'L'ortografia delle lingue pidgin e créole', *Ioanni Dominico Serra ex munere laeto inferiae* 205-214.

——, 1962a. 'The life-cycle of pidgin languages', *Lingua* 11. 151-156 (= Festschrift De Groot).

——, 1962b. 'The determination of form-classes in Haitian Creole', *ZRPh* 78.172-177.

——, 1964. *Introductory linguistics* (Philadelphia).

——, 1965a. Review of Goodman (1964) in *Word* 21.117-123.

——, 1965b. *Pidgin and creole languages* (Ithaca, N.Y.).

Harris, Charles Cleland, 1953. *Papiamentu phonology* (Ph. D. dissertation, Cornell University).

Herskovits, Melville J., and Frances S. Herskovits, 1936. *Surinam Folklore* (=*Columbia University Contributions to Anthropology*, vol. 27) (New York).

Hyppolite, Michelson, 1950. *Les origines des variations du créole haïtien* (Port-au-Prince).

Jones, E. D., 1957. 'The potentialities of Krio as a literary language', *Sierra Leone Studies* 3:9.40-48.

——, 1959. 'Some English fossils in Krio', *Sierra Leone Studies* NS 3.295-297.

Jourdain, Elodie, 1954. 'Le verbe en Créole martiniquais', *NWIG* 35.39-70.

——, 1956a. *Du français aux parlers créoles* (Paris).

——, 1956b. *Le vocabulaire du parler créole de la Martinique* (Paris).

Kloss, Heinz, 1952. *Die Entwicklung neuer germanischer Kultursprachen von 1800 bis 1950* (München).

Lane, George S., 1935. 'Notes on Louisiana French, II. Negro-French dialect', *Lg* 11.5-16.

Le Page, Robert B., 1957-58. 'General outlines of English Creole dialects', *Orbis* 6.373-391; 7.54-64.

Le Page, Robert B., and David De Camp, 1960. *Jamaican Creole* (London and New York). (= *Creole Language Studies* 1.)

Lenz, Rodolfo, 1928. *El papiamento, la lengua criolla de Curazao, la gramática más sencilla* (Santiago de Chile). (Reprinted from *Anales de la Universidad del Chile* II.4.695-768, 1021-1090 [1926] and II.5.287-327, 365-412 ([1927]).

Lichtveld, Lou, 1954. 'Enerlei Creools?', *NWIG* 35.59-71.

Loftman, Beryl I., 1953. *Creole languages of the Caribbean area* (M. A. thesis, Columbia University).

McConnell, H. Ormonde, and E. Swan, 1945. *You can learn Creole* (Port-au-Prince).

Morgan, Raleigh, Jr., 1959. 'Structural sketch of Saint Martin Creole', *AnL* 1:8.20-24.

——, 1960. 'The lexicon of Saint Martin Creole', *AnL* 2:1.7-29.

Navarro Tomás, Tomás, 1953. 'Observaciones sobre el papiamento', *NRFH* 7.183-189.

Pée, Willem, 1951, 'De klanken van het Neger-Engels', *TT* 3.130-192.

Pée, W., W. Gs. Hellinga, and A. Donicie, 1953a. 'Voorstellen tot een nieuwe systematische spelling van het Suriname (Neger-Engels) op linguistische grondslag', *TT* 5.8-18.

——, 1953b. *Het Neger-Engels van Suriname: Bijdragen en Beschouwingen* (Amsterdam). (Reprinted from Pée [1951]; Donicie [1953]; and Pée, Hellinga and Donicie [1953a]).

Pompilus, Pradel, 1961. 'De quelques influences du Créole sur le français officiel d'Haïti', *Creole Language Studies* 2.91-98.

Pressoir, Charles-Fernand, 1947. *Débats sur le créole et folklore* (Port-au-Prince).

Reinecke, John E., 1937. *Marginal languages: a sociological study of creole languages and trade jargons* (Ph. D. dissertation, Yale University).

Révah, I. S., 1964. 'La question des substrats et des superstrats dans le domaine linguistique brésilien: les parlers populaires brésiliens doivent-ils être considérés comme des parlers 'créoles' ou 'semi-créoles'?', *Romania* 84.433-450.

Ribeiro, Joaquim, 1939. *Histôria da romanização da América* (Rio de Janeiro).

Rice, Frank (ed.), 1962. *Study of the rôle of second languages in Asia, Africa, and Latin America* (Washington, D.C.).

Riley, Carroll L., 1952. 'Trade Spanish of the Piñaguero Panare', *SIL* 10.6-11.

Schuchardt, Hugo Ernst Maria, 1914. *Die Sprache der Saramakkaneger in Surinam* (Amsterdam) (*VKNA* 16:4).

Schwartz, William Leonard, 1949. 'American speech and Haitian French', *AS* 24.282-285.

Silva-Fuenzalida, Ismael, 1952. *Papiamentu morphology* (Ph. D. dissertation, Northwestern University).

Silva Neto, Serafim de, 1938. 'O crioulo de Surinam', in *Miscelânea de estudos em honra de Saïd Ali* (Rio de Janeiro). Reprinted in *Cultura* (Rio de Janeiro) 2.57-70 (1949) and in Silva Neto, *Lingua, Cultura e Civilização* 127-153 (1960).

——, 1949. 'Falares crioulos', *Brasilia* 5.

Simons, R. D., 1941. *Het Neger-Engelsch: Spraakkunst en Taaleigen* (Paramaribo).

——, 1954/55. 'Het partikel *sa* in het Surinams', *NWIG* 35.166-170.

Simons, R. D., and J. Voorhoeve, 1955/56. 'Ontlening van Nederlandse samenstellingen in het Surinams', *NWIG* 36.61-64.

Sommerfelt, Alf, 1958. 'Sur le rôle du substrat dans l'évolution d'une langue créole', *Omagiu lui Iorgu Iordan* 815-817 (București).

Stewart, William A., 1962a. 'Creole languages in the Caribbean', in Rice (ed.), 34-53 (1962).

——, 1962b. 'The functional distribution of French and Creole in Haiti', *MSLL* 15.149-159.

Sylvain, Suzanne, 1936. *Le créole haïtien: morphologie et syntaxe* (Port-au-Prince and Wetteren).

Symposium on Multilingualism (Brazzaville, 1962).

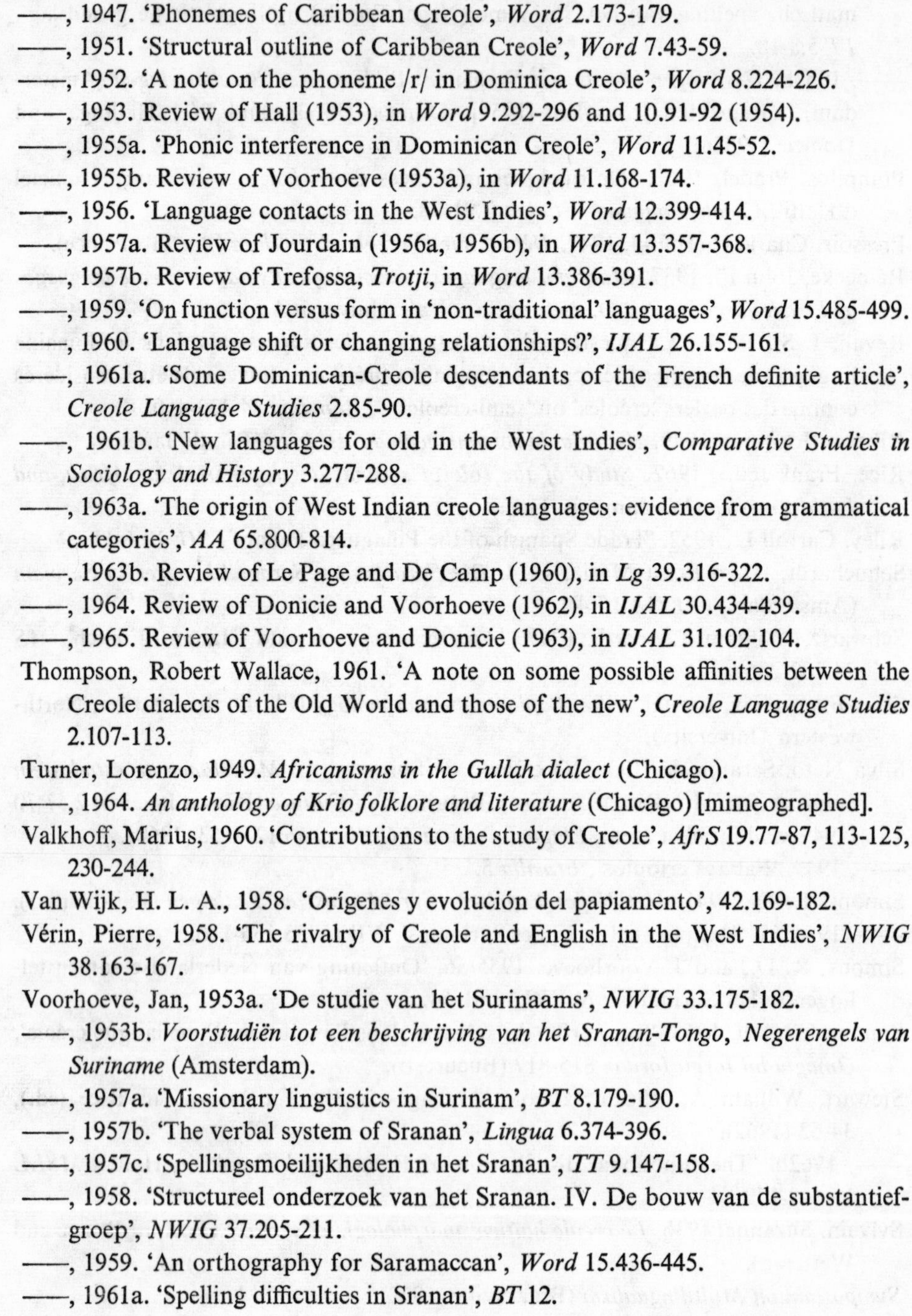

Taylor, Douglas McR., 1945. 'Certain Carib morphological influences on Creole', *IJAL* 11.140-155.

——, 1947. 'Phonemes of Caribbean Creole', *Word* 2.173-179.

——, 1951. 'Structural outline of Caribbean Creole', *Word* 7.43-59.

——, 1952. 'A note on the phoneme /r/ in Dominica Creole', *Word* 8.224-226.

——, 1953. Review of Hall (1953), in *Word* 9.292-296 and 10.91-92 (1954).

——, 1955a. 'Phonic interference in Dominican Creole', *Word* 11.45-52.

——, 1955b. Review of Voorhoeve (1953a), in *Word* 11.168-174.

——, 1956. 'Language contacts in the West Indies', *Word* 12.399-414.

——, 1957a. Review of Jourdain (1956a, 1956b), in *Word* 13.357-368.

——, 1957b. Review of Trefossa, *Trotji*, in *Word* 13.386-391.

——, 1959. 'On function versus form in 'non-traditional' languages', *Word* 15.485-499.

——, 1960. 'Language shift or changing relationships?', *IJAL* 26.155-161.

——, 1961a. 'Some Dominican-Creole descendants of the French definite article', *Creole Language Studies* 2.85-90.

——, 1961b. 'New languages for old in the West Indies', *Comparative Studies in Sociology and History* 3.277-288.

——, 1963a. 'The origin of West Indian creole languages: evidence from grammatical categories', *AA* 65.800-814.

——, 1963b. Review of Le Page and De Camp (1960), in *Lg* 39.316-322.

——, 1964. Review of Donicie and Voorhoeve (1962), in *IJAL* 30.434-439.

——, 1965. Review of Voorhoeve and Donicie (1963), in *IJAL* 31.102-104.

Thompson, Robert Wallace, 1961. 'A note on some possible affinities between the Creole dialects of the Old World and those of the new', *Creole Language Studies* 2.107-113.

Turner, Lorenzo, 1949. *Africanisms in the Gullah dialect* (Chicago).

——, 1964. *An anthology of Krio folklore and literature* (Chicago) [mimeographed].

Valkhoff, Marius, 1960. 'Contributions to the study of Creole', *AfrS* 19.77-87, 113-125, 230-244.

Van Wijk, H. L. A., 1958. 'Orígenes y evolución del papiamento', 42.169-182.

Vérin, Pierre, 1958. 'The rivalry of Creole and English in the West Indies', *NWIG* 38.163-167.

Voorhoeve, Jan, 1953a. 'De studie van het Surinaams', *NWIG* 33.175-182.

——, 1953b. *Voorstudiën tot een beschrijving van het Sranan-Tongo, Negerengels van Suriname* (Amsterdam).

——, 1957a. 'Missionary linguistics in Surinam', *BT* 8.179-190.

——, 1957b. 'The verbal system of Sranan', *Lingua* 6.374-396.

——, 1957c. 'Spellingsmoeilijkheden in het Sranan', *TT* 9.147-158.

——, 1958. 'Structureel onderzoek van het Sranan. IV. De bouw van de substantiefgroep', *NWIG* 37.205-211.

——, 1959. 'An orthography for Saramaccan', *Word* 15.436-445.

——, 1961a. 'Spelling difficulties in Sranan', *BT* 12.

Voorhoeve, Jan, 1961b. 'Linguistic experiments in syntactic analysis', *Creole Language Studies* 2.37-60.

——, 1961c. 'A project for the study of Creole language history in Surinam', *Creole Language Studies* 2.99-106.

——, 1961d. 'Le ton et la grammaire dans le Saramaccan', *Word* 17.146-163.

——, 1962. *Sranan syntax* (Amsterdam).

Voorhoeve, Jan, and Antoon Donicie, 1963. *Bibliographie du négro-anglais du Surinam (avec un appendice sur les langues créoles parlées à l'intérieur du pays)* (Amsterdam).

Wattman, Francine Harriet, 1953. *Papiamentu morphology and syntax*. (M. A. thesis, Cornell University).

Weinreich, Uriel, 1958. 'On the compatibility of genetic relationship and convergent development', *Word* 14.374-379.

Zumthor, Paul, 1957. Review of Hall (1953), in *ZRPh*. 73.515-517.

PART III

APPLIED LINGUISTICS

INTRODUCTION

ROBERT LADO

Applied linguistics is often mentioned in the context of language teaching, and indeed language teaching is a major concern of applied linguistics. But the two are not synonymous and should not be confused. Applied linguistics has an important role in teaching foreign languages, and in teaching the native language, and more recently it is seen to have an equally important place in teaching a standard language to those who, lacking cultural opportunities, have not acquired it, or who speak some Indian or foreign language at home. The field of applied linguistics is a vigorous and expanding one involving computational linguistics, machine translation, literacy and bilingualism, language learning, etc.

Applied linguistics can be defined as the application of the insights, methods and findings of linguistic science to practical language problems. This definition emphasizes the application of the insights and methods of linguistics as well as the findings, and it clearly focuses on practical problems. A paternalistic or nominalistic restriction of applied linguistics to the findings of linguistics would be neither true, nor practical, nor desirable.

As in applied physics, applied mathematics, and other applied sciences the focus is on the problems rather than on the construction of theories, theorems, concepts, and other components of scientific endeavor, and as in the other applied sciences, findings may run ahead of theory, and theory then has to be revised and restated to account for the new evidence. The distinction between pure and applied linguistics is further seen in that the goal of pure linguistics is to arrive at the most powerful theories, theorems, and concepts that are internally and externally consistent, i.e. not in conflict with each other or with experimental evidence; whereas in applied linguistics the goal is the solution of practical problems by means of linguistics. Actually, there can be little pure linguistics without intimate contact with applied problems, and there can be little applied linguistics without pure linguistics. And there are good and bad pure linguists, as there are good and bad applied linguists. Merely addressing oneself to pure linguistic speculation or research does not make a linguist better, nor is applied linguistics easier linguistics.

In fact, the moment one addresses himself to practical problems, other sciences and technology come into play, and experiments become more complex and difficult. The only compensatory fact is that only limited parts of the theory may be involved in any particular problem. In language teaching and learning, psychology must be taken into account. Mathematics, statistics, and the technology of computers are involved in computational linguistics. Sociology and sociological techniques will be needed in problems of national languages. In fact, in these contacts with other sciences and their experimental techniques, linguistic techniques may be thought to be too subjective, almost too anecdotal, and may have to yield to research designs of these other sciences, or combinations of them with those of linguistics.

The question then arises as to whether a problem that requires research designs of psychology or sociology is not applied psychology or applied sociology instead of applied linguistics. The answer lies in how the problem is viewed rather than how it is researched or what other sciences are brought to bear upon it for solution. In applied linguistics the problem is viewed as one of language, with primary classifications based on language units and elements and their use in communication. Paired associate learning is a problem in psychology which happens to use words or nonsense syllables for the learning tasks. The learning of mass versus count nouns by preschool children, on the other hand, is a problem in applied linguistics.

With this focus in mind we include in Part III papers on the chief national languages of the Americas — Spanish and Portuguese, the influence of the language academies, research specifically labelled as applied linguistics in the Spanish-speaking areas of the continent, on computational linguistics, and then specifically on literacy, bilingualism, and on the teaching of foreign languages.

The paper on Spanish as a national language is by Jaime Cisneros of the University of San Marcos of Lima, Peru; that on research on applied linguistics is by Heles Contreras of the University of Concepción, Chile; the one on the role of the academies is by Guillermo L. Guitarte of Argentina, now at Boston College, in collaboration with Rafael Torres Quintero of the Instituto Caro y Cuervo of Bogotá, Colombia.

Leonardo Manrique of the Escuela Nacional de Antropologia e Historia of Mexico wrote the article on Computational Linguistics; Yolanda Lastra of Mexico, at the University of California at Los Angeles, is author of the paper on literacy; and Robert J. Di Pietro of Georgetown University wrote the one on bilingualism. The paper on the teaching of foreign languages is by Leopoldo Wigdorsky of Catholic University of Santiago, Chile, and Francisco Gomes de Matos of the Centro de Linguística Aplicada in São Paulo. The subject required longer and more detailed treatment because there is more activity in this area, and differences among the nations could not always be telescoped and neatly summarized.

From these papers, from the papers of the First Inter-American Symposium on Linguistics and Language Teaching held at Cartagena, Colombia, in 1963, and from subsequent meetings and personal observation, it is not difficult to conclude that the linguistic problems which come under the heading of applied linguistics have economic, social, and educational consequences of great magnitude, and that the work being done is largely preparatory, and is unequal to the tasks at hand. It is also evident that even though there is some increase in interest and activity, neither the amount of increase nor its nature can be expected to cope with the great needs.

The number one linguistic problem according to the conclusions of the Cartagena Symposiun is the teaching of national languages to both those who speak them at home and the large Indian populations who do not. Methods admittedly are casual and ancient, and provisions for applied linguistic research are minimal and haphazard.

Bilingualism is largely at the stage of natural drift with associations of cultural deprivation, and no serious efforts or prospects of development into a cultural asset. Literacy, a major problem in which larger scale efforts have been made and are continuing to be made, depends too much on gimmicks and amateurish cure-alls such as the 'each-one-teach-one' campaigns, radio campaigns, and TV programs, without the necessary integration of literacy into research, materials, and teaching through some system of schooling and vocational training. Where it is integrated, it is under the aegis of some U.S. university which considers it interesting research, but is not likely to have a national or even lasting commitment to it, or those whose work, though carefully structured and well executed, is directed primarily at translating the Bible.

If the language problems are as serious as they seem, there is need to attack them head-on with their solution as the direct goal, and through their national institutions in order to give them permanence. Nothing less than national language and linguistic centers with adequate financial support and personnel and in cooperation with the school systems can be expected to cope with the task.

The Instituto Caro y Cuervo in Bogotá is such an institution. It has carried on research, training, and publication in Spanish. It could plan a research and action program of real consequence. In collaboration with specialists of their own and from abroad, they could prepare up-to-date literacy materials adapted to the needs of Colombia and neighboring countries. The armed forces could become the instrument to teach literacy to new recruits. This approach was highly successful in Turkey where Georgetown University did the research and prepared the basic literacy materials, then trained cadres of recruits who were already teachers, who in turn taught large numbers of illiterate recruits in two-month intensive courses. The number reached in the first two years was 5,000, and until the present some 24,000 have been affected.

It is cause for pause and even alarm that Castro and his communist regime should have immediately instituted a vigorous campaign of literacy with regular classes and some organized approach to the teaching.

Teaching the national language constitutes a different problem when it is directed to those who speak some form of it at home and those who speak an American Indian language in some remote rural area. For the former, research on dialects should gradually permit more realistic and valid standards. The chief remaining problem is to find and disseminate the most effective ways to teach the material and to provide sufficient numbers of qualified teachers and schools to teach all the children.

For the latter — those who must learn it as a second language because they do not speak it at home — again some action research connected with a university or research center and programmed for implementation through public and private schools, the armed forces, and some form of national peace corps would be needed to reach all the native population and give them the opportunity to participate in their national life and economic development.

SPANISH

LUIS JAIME CISNEROS

The preoccupation of scholars with the scientific analysis of the teaching and learning of Spanish is not new in Spanish America. It can be said that the prospects for the development of applied linguistics in Spanish America begun at the time when Bello, in 1847, suggested that attention be given to the 'oficios' and 'funciones' of linguistic elements. However, in spite of the valuable progress which followed the teachings of Rodolfo Lenz in Chile, the application of linguistic criteria to language teaching has only been organized in the last few years.

The results of modern linguistic investigation are only slowly gaining ground, and they are not yet firmly established. Two rather important reasons can explain this situation: (a) the introduction of applied linguistics methodology to the field of Spanish in general, even in Europe, is relatively recent; (b) this is a problem which is connected in America with the training of teachers at the different levels of primary and secondary education. To this, another fact should be added: it cannot be honestly said that in the Spanish-American countries an educational policy exists in language matters (exceptions confirm the rule). In some countries, the problem is further complicated because they are bilingual (Spanish and indigenous language), a reality which may affect the willingness to expand the application of scientific methods.

In order to consider the problem of applied linguistics with regard to Spanish it is necessary to survey, even though briefly, these factors: teachers, programs, methods, and texts.

1. TEACHERS

A typical anecdote in different Spanish American countries goes as follows: A minister of Education offers an old friend a position as a chemistry teacher. 'But I know nothing about science!' says the friend. A conversation follows in which the prospective teacher is invited to teach courses in mathematics, botany, anatomy. The answer is always the same, irrefutable: he doesn't know a word about it. Finally, the minister offers his friend some hours of language teaching. 'That's it, that I can do with pleasure. Who doesn't know grammar?' Leave or take a detail, the anecdote is repeated all over our countries. It helps to illustrate one of the most frequent and visible difficulties encountered by the most serious attempts to apply to the teaching of Spanish the results of modern linguistics.

The importance of this problem does not seem to be clearly understood. The preparation of primary and secondary teachers has different levels in the different countries of America and is related to the state of underdevelopment in many of them. That is why a meaningful comparison is not possible between the methods and programs in the preparation of teachers in Argentina or Chile and those in countries like Bolivia or Peru. Apart from polite declarations and expressions of agreement in the desire for advancement implied in every program, it can hardly be said that the desiderata of a system can be equated with those of another system. A careful analysis of this reality — something not yet seriously undertaken — would reveal the core of early disenchantments experienced by prospective candidates for language teaching. In many countries there is no real system of selection of candidates. Thus, students who originally intended to be in geography, or mathematics, and who did not reach the required minimum grade in these disciplines, end up by joining the courses for language teachers; they take the advantage offered by laws whose spirit is not what the letter says. Beside a situation of this sort, which in fact exists in many South American countries, not to speak of the disastrous interference of national politics in the matter of appointments, it should be considered that not all the countries have a uniform policy for the training of teachers. Thus, while in some countries only the university has that formative mission through the faculty of philosophy and letters, in others this mission is carried out by the faculty of education or pedagogy. There is another system, that of the *Escuelas Normales de Profesores* or the *Institutos Nacionales del Profesorado* working simultaneously with the universities.

On the other hand, the regulations governing the teaching profession, from an official point of view, create some problems which have an impact on education. While in some countries the certificates issued by any of the above mentioned institutions have a standard validity, in some others a preference is given to teachers from the faculties of education or the Escuelas Normales.

This problem is particularly important because many of these institutions are not officially considered institution of higher learning. This means that both their students and professors do not deepen their studies, and this sometimes provides an adequate excuse to avoid expanding ideas and methods which are considered proper to the higher sphere of the university.

This is why until approximately ten years ago, the need had not been felt to approach the language problem scientifically. The need has been felt sporadically, and in each of our countries a bibliographical survey would remind us of the names of some pioneers who in their times called attention to the problem. But it is only now that some clear indications can be observed that the silent labours of certain formative institutions have yielded some fruits. In America, that labour is linked to the teachings of Amado Alonso who, from the Instituto de Filología de Buenos Aires, spread the necessary light and infused in his disciples and followers the responsibility to expose existing deficiencies. This preoccupation counted in the Antilles with the support and tenacity of Rubén del Rosario, and in Chile with the understanding and fertile cooperation of Rodolfo Oroz.

If the new generations of the last decades have gradually understood the advantages of studying the language scientifically in order to be able to teach it efficiently, the reason is that in the higher education programs designed to train future teachers (at universities, Institutos de Profesorado or Escuelas Normales) a special importance was attached to basic disciplines, and also because tape-recorders were introduced as a frequent instrument of every day work — thus facilitating field work and focussing attention on the living language, away from the puristic ideals of the old school; a language that was the best document to show how man was linked to his tradition and culture. It is only fair to say that these new generations initiated their work under difficult circumstances, but, in the end, have found understanding among the teachers of previous generations who were opposed, in general, to any radical reform of methods and principles.

Nonetheless, today, in 1965, victory cannot yet be claimed from the point of view of the teaching profession. The reports read at the Cartagena Symposium (1963) showed the dissimilarities in the training programs of the majority of the Spanish American countries. ('Programa Interamericano de Lingüística y Enseñanza de Idiomas', *El Simposio de Cartagena*, Bogotá, 1965).

2. PROGRAMS

In most Latin American countries, language programs are coordinated, since they are determined by their respective Ministries of Education (or of Public Instruction). Some of these programs are the results of special commissions, whose members are almost always teachers and seldom linguists. In very few occasions are these programs well founded, as is usually the case in France; and although it is true that many of them include directives for the teachers, in most cases these do not refer to methodology but to the general development of education.

Since programs are made for the entire teaching body, no coherent doctrine has yet been found which can guide them. This is the reason why all of them keep adopting an unfortunate perspective: traditional grammar inspired in normative ideals and based on the reality of words as sources of meaning. Language teachers must fight against these programs, while being part of them and while they meet their institutional obligation of satisfying the directives coming from the 'competent' authority.

The disadvantages of those programs which do not adjust to coordinating principles were analized by Amado Alonso in his celebrated article, 'Los nuevos programas de lengua y literatura', *RFH* 2 (1940). In that article, A. Alonso emphasized an idea which, although meant for Argentina, could be applied to the rest of Spanish America: 'Teaching has the double task of informing and forming the student.' In order to achieve that double task, it is necessary that the object of programs 'the language which is both studied and learned', be that they direct the teaching of grammar towards the same practical goal, so that 'that which is learned by the student would in fact serve as an advantage that for the greater and lesser dominance of their mother tongue'. Because it is true language programs, at all levels of education, state that their subject matter should be studied in order to provide the speakers with the best use and knowledge of their language.

But we will see that although the last linguistic advances, with regard to methodology, are gradually gaining ground, they are not fully operative in the making of programs, since these are not usually the result of technical discussions. In this regard, the most advanced steps have been taken by Argentina, where linguistic teaching on structural bases is widespread.

It is clear, on the other hand, that the programs now in force in Latin America, without exceptions, maintain a grammatical teaching which does not clearly define its levels according to primary or secondary students. This linguistic preoccupation has touched those who work mainly in the field of secondary education. The conviction becomes deeper that the ideal grammars for secondary education should be those that describe what Noam Chomsky would call the *competence* (*competencia*) of their users. Only this type of grammar would be the grammar of L described by Chomsky: 'The grammar of L will thus be a device that generates all of the grammatical sequences of L and none of the ungrammatical ones' (*Syntactic Structures*, p. 12, The Hague, 1957). When language programs reflect the perspective of modern linguistics, they emphasize that this perspective is fourfold: hearing, speaking, reading, and writing. But they do not always seem to accept that each of these aspects offers its own peculiarities, its particular atmosphere, and the fact that each requires its own methods. When they do perceive these differences, the teacher does not usually understand that the independence of each of these four aspects is only apparent, since the four are intimately related to one another. Ismael Rodriguez Bou has well realized this interrelationship when he explains the significance of this fourfold linguistic perspective: Listening requires understanding of the spoken word. The oral aspect of language, a most important one because of its social value in communication, demands not only approprieteness and correction, but enough flexibility to adjust itself to different situations. Reading requires learning of the phonetic mechanism as a means to arrive at the interpretation of content. The writer also goes beyond mere correction in order to provide a vehicle for thought'. (*Apuntaciones gramaticales*, p. 2 (Puerto Rico, 1958).

The main problem faced by programs of education, precisely because they are not based on solid scientific postulates, usually is that of the gradual progression of the curricula. A general disarray presides over every program and every one of the reforms that have been attempted. Those responsible for these programs do not consider what it is the student should receive according to his abilities and linguistic needs; rather they devote themselves to the solution of a different problem, i.e. what should be taught by the teacher according to his teaching needs. These needs depend on the set of topics to be developed in an academic year. It is true, though, that there is already a tacit agreement for these programs in most Spanish American countries to begin their language presentation with a study of the sentence, thus abandoning the old custom of beginning with the parts of speech. But in spite of this welcome approach, textbooks — as we will see later — avoid this type of presentation.

Perhaps Puerto Rico is the most progressive country, at least in what concerns the levels of elementary education. Having adopted the teaching of language as something functional, it seeks to present the child with the different aspects of language 'so that the child can use them at any moment as an effective instrument of communication', in the words of Ismael Rodriguez Bou, *Apuntaciones sobre la enseñanza hablada y escrita en la escuela elemental*, p. 27 (Rio Piedras, Puerto Rico, 1954). That is, language is taught functionally, according to its use, which the child should develop; thus, this study means discovering the secrets of the use of language, and not the accumulation of unpalatable information. A type of teaching that would encourage the abilities of the speaker was requested in Peru by José Jiménez Borja, when he stated that the goal of language teaching should not be teaching language quantitatively, but instilling in the soul of the student the capacity to continue to broaden and strengthen his relative command of the language', *Fines de la enseñanza del Castellano y la Literatura en el Perú*, p. 5 (Lima, 1955). Further on, he specifies what the social goal of linguistic teaching should be. It is related to the field of objective language and presupposes a command of my own speech as well as that of others, i.e. of a common instrument, the nexus of social cohesion, which is indispensable for communication and comprehension (*ibid.*, 9).

The specialists, then, have always seen clearly that any program of language courses (an official syllabus seeking to accomplish the objectives of education) should have in mind the needs of those for whom it is intended. They have also seen that it is upon this discipline that the 'necessary [foundation] for communication and comprehension' rest. These foundations are essential in a democracy. But although these specialists are almost always unofficially consulted by administrative authorities, they have very seldom, or ever, been in charge of preparing the programs. This has been for a long time the basic flaw of the system. However, the reforms that are now being implemented in Argentina and Uruguay allow us to think that a new era is in prospect. I do not mean that the preparation of official programs should be left entirely to universities, or that the administrative authorities should relinquish their right and duty to establish such programs. It is simply that those programs should be based on reality, the truth of which can be established by linguists, since it is our duty 'to search for the permanent features of language, those which form its structure and must be kept in mind in the study of language evolution', Pottier, 'La lingüística moderna y los problemas hispánicos', *RFE* 40.224 (1956).

Which could be the natural progression of these studies? In a paper read at the University of San Marcos in 1959, Alberto Escobar proposed the establishment of three cycles in linguistic training through the three levels of primary, secondary, and higher education. The first cycle would deal with linguistic levelling; the second with the equation *language-life*; and the third one would develop around the topic *Language and Culture*, *El lenguaje y la función social de la Universidad* p. 23 (Lima, 1959). The principle that unifies Escobar's conception is the old one which understands language as an activity of the spirit, as *energeia*, as a reelaboration of common traditions, a dynamics between the individual and society. Language is thus understood as the means to realize the goals of culture and man, which are the goals of the university.

In an official report presented by the author of the present paper to the Ministry of Education eight years ago, the following principles were emphasized: 'It is essential that the teaching of language be done simultaneously with that of literature, in one organic course, throughout the period of primary education'; 'The *desideratum* of a language course in primary education should be that the student be able *to read* and *express himself*, where the term 'reading' means 'understanding'. 'The explanation for this only goal lies in the fact that the student should firmly establish his linguistic feeling, which is not only a general problem of good taste, but also of feeling secure in his pronunciation, and expressions, and of being linguistically secure within his environment.' 'To teach how to read is to prepare the student to realize the value of intonation, the significance of melodic units, and of punctuation marks. It is to get him accustomed to articulate properly to make him extricate the meaning of a text, and to reveal this by his oral rendering. With regard to the teachers at that level, the report demanded: 'Technical information: the teacher should be trained in phonetics, and should be familiar with the general principles of linguistics.'

In a study devoted to transformational grammar, Gerardo Alvarez thinks that the acquisition by the child of the use of language at the primary level helps to develop 'a series of organizing principles (grammatical rules) which will enable him to understand and speak the language of the community where he was born. It is not yet well established exactly how the child proceeds, which are the steps he takes in this process of creating a grammar for his native language'. On the basis that even at his most tender age 'any normal child has developped the capacity of a native speaker', and by the fact that, in his own way, the child has organized a grammar of the language, Alvarez thinks that the teaching of transformational grammar at this stage should not at all be discarded (*RLA* 2.21). Needless to say, this notion coincides with that of Chomsky, according to whom the child only needs to be exposed to language for a notably brief period in order to consolidate his capacity as a native speaker. At any rate, and without entering here into a discussion of methods, the important thing is to make this principle clear: that the teaching at primary levels should seek to prepare the child 'to understand and speak the language of the community'. This is not frequently achieved by the official programs for this level in Spanish America.

Language specialists seem to agree that grammatical theory should be taught in secondary school. Discrepancies among them are confined to the priority of some principles over others, but there is a clear notion that the term *grammatical theory* is on the rise. By way of illustration I will only mention the testimony of two authors a few years apart: Mabel Manacorda de Rosetti (1961) and Sergio Echeverría Weasson (1964). Mabel Manacorda states with clarity that the exclusive interest of grammatical theory centers around 'the synchronic study of the functioning of language'; but she admits that since 'the systematic organization of linguistic phenomena requires a very especial mental attitude, a clear and coherent way of organizing knowledge, ... grammatical theory could have an influence in discursive language, which is the language of the community', *La gramática estructural en la escuela secundaria* pp. 71-72 (Buenos Aires, 1961). Grammatical theory should be taught side by side with normative grammar and textual commentaries, as a first aspect of the language program. The basis of this theory is the fact that language is a system in constant reconstruction, hence the immobility to which our analysis subjects it is the result of the linguist's approach rather than a reality of language. That is to say, the language system betrays constantly a creative instability. This allows the student to discover that language has a structure and permits him to appreciate the advantages of a syntactic criterion to analyze the functioning of such system. Basically, language teaching would have here a descriptive character.

In his study 'La Gramática española en la asignatura de Castellano en la educación media' (*RLA* 1. 32-44, 1964) Sergio Echeverría thinks that scientific grammar 'can have a formally descriptive character in secondary education'. According to this approach consideration should be given to the distribution of grammatical elements, 'i.e., where they occur, their possibilities of combination, the substitutions within the same contexts' (p. 41). The linguistic study recommended by this author should have the following characteristics with regard to secondary education: it should be formally descriptive, comparative, and work through the gradual presentation of problems, which would develop a capacity for reflection in the students. Such problems and comparisons could be worked out through a confrontation with unfamiliar languages, such as African languages. This would contribute to the development of the student's reflective power and at the same time awaken his curiosity due to the novelty of the subject (p. 39). Because of the bilingual status of many Spanish American countries, and also because normative ideas prevail over linguistic ones, the problems we have to face are complex and of different nature. Talking about programs, an important observation should therefore be made: Which is the *norm* that educational programs should follow from one level to the next, when such programs stipulate their ideals of correction? Under what category or classification should the indigenous language be placed in those countries where the immense majority does not use the official language, that is, Spanish? This, of course, is not a problem in Argentina or Uruguay, but it is a problem for the Andean countries and for Paraguay. Not all the programs address themselves to this problem, nor are scientific solutions usually proposed, subject as these problems are to other problems of a social nature. In this regard, Sergio Echeverría proposes 'the detailed description of socio-linguistic levels in the Spanish spoken in Chile', as a starting point to establish his teaching program (*op.cit.* 94). Addressing herself to this reality, Berta Vidal de Battini published a crucial study intended for primary school teachers in Argentina, *El español de la Argentina* (Buenos Aires, 1954). A teaching grounded in an accurate knowledge of the language and in an honest and scientific appreciation of it, would yield extraordinary results, such as those which have allowed Argentina to venture into structural methods.

This problem is contemplated in the thoughtful report presented by José Pedro Rona in Cartagena in 1963, during the First Inter-American Symposium in Linguistics and Language Teaching, José Pedro Rona, 'Relación entre la investigacion dialectológica y la enseñanza de la lengua materna', Programa Interamericano de Lingüística y Enseñanza de Lenguas, *El Simposio de Cartagena* 333-343 later published also in Chile (*RLA*, 2.1-12 1965). Rona establishes the connection between language teaching at the elementary level with the results of dialectological investigation: 'dialectology is an aid in determining the characteristics of the language the child possesses before he is taught the literary, academic, or simply learned form of his mother tongue'. Elementary teaching offers him the desired contrast. Applying the ideas of Weinrich and Flydall, the goal of this education consists in offering the child 'another system of the same language, so that he can *also* use it intuitively' (italics are mine). Elementary education would be confined to instructing the child in the learned forms of his own region, that is, the system accepted in that region as a learned one. Here the guiding principle is, of course, the possibility to actually use the language taught. For secondary school the teaching should be 'the scientific teaching of language and above all the forms of literary or academic language'. At this level, reflective knowledge must be imparted (ibid, 4). We are here within the scope of a statement which presides over the Introduction to the *Gramática Castellana* (Buenos Aires, 1942) by Amado Alonso and Pedro Henríquez Ureña, when they make a distinction between 'lengua general' and 'lengua regional'. Regional uses said Alonso 'are not taken as incorrect by those who use them but they are geographically limited and do not belong to the standard language ... When we say *regional language* we mean those particular language peculiarities used by educated people', (*op. cit.* 1.15 1947).

Official programs, on the other hand, make mistakes by not considering the foreseeable relationship between theory and practice. At times, even when the program plans its teaching according to scientific theory, based on a realistic presentation of language as it is observable to the students, the teachers, when preparing their exercises for the students, require them to do such tasks as imitating an artificial literary language far removed from reality. This is perhaps the most deficient part of all the programs, even of those that take into account linguistic teachings. This is a deficiency related to lack of technical preparation in the teachers of a large part of the Spanish American countries. Only a sound linguistic training would enable the teacher to prepare valuable exercises, and to stimulate the students to prepare them on their own.

On the other hand, if it is true that there is a great deal of confusion in elementary and secondary school programs, in spite of some advances through the warnings of specialists, there exists a healthy renovation concerning university programs. What has been done at the University of Puerto Rico by the group headed by Rubén del Rosario, the influence of Angel Rosenblat's teachings in Venezuelan universities, that exercised by Eugenio Coseriu in Uruguay, and the labors in Peru by José Jiménez Borja, Luis Jaime Cisneros, and Alberto Escobar, together with the reputation already achieved by Chilean institutions, and the works of Ana María Barrenechea and Luis J. Prieto in Argentina, can be offered as a testimony that language teaching in higher education certainly travels along the paths opened by scientific investigation. In this regard, and by way of illustration, we can mention the programs published by Luis Jaime Cisneros, *Cátedra de Lengua Española: guía de temas* (Lima, Universidad Católica, 1959), and *Primera Cátedra de Lengua Española; syllabus* (Lima, 1963), and by Ana María Barrenechea, *Guía del curso de Gramática* (Buenos Aires, Facultad de Filosofía y Letras, 1960).

METHODS

Obviously, the need for a new methodology was imposed by the existence of a type of teaching which emphasized memorization and grammatical rules, a fact preventing the realization of the basic objectives of language teaching in all its levels. A situation existed, and still exists in many countries, or in cities far away from the main cultural centers, which repeated what Américo Castro found in Spain many years ago in his book *La enseñanza del español en España* (Madrid, 1922). Castro saw a connection between the backward state of language teaching and the 'the general backwardness that vitiates the very soul of the pedagogical life of the nation'. But we cannot be taken blindly by the sweep of general statements losing sight of another, more specific reality; the problems of language teaching are linked to a conservative routine rooted in a lack of investigation. The importance that Andrés Bello's *Gramática* had in the teaching of Spanish lay precisely in the fact that, for the first time, somebody saw that language is susceptible to description, and that in order to understand it one had to subject it to observation and study, rather than to analogies and parallelisms with Latin.

Methodological preoccupation is an old affair in Spanish America. We can find testimonies both among the adepts to a particular linguistic theory as well as among those whose only serious preparation derives from their teaching experience. I will only offer two illustrations, coming one from a European and the other from a South American professor, neither one a linguist by profession, and both far away from what we understand today as structuralism. Both opinions are only a few years apart, and belong to two different levels, the university and the secondary school. In 1924, Manuel de Montolíu, appointed by the Centro de Estudios Históricos of Madrid to direct the Instituto de Filología of Buenos Aires, said: 'I will not try to discuss or determine the rules of the correct language, I am not going to teach good Castillian dogmatically'; 'Language teaching must be essentially an intense and organized exercise of the natural talent to speak. ... On the other hand, the teaching of grammar consists essentially in abstracting the laws that govern our oral expression and formulating them in a theoretical manner. It is a scientific discipline'; 'By clearly separating language teaching from the teaching of grammar it will be possible to do away with the false orientations that have so far disturbed the latter', *Boletín del Instituto de Filología* 1.90,96,100 (Buenos Aires, 1926). Six years later, Juan B. Selva, publishing his bases for the reform of official plans of education and drawing from his many years of teaching experience, proposed that in secondary education 'language be studied by arriving inductively at the precepts and rules really useful to know the *structure* of language and to speak and write it better', *La enseñanza gramatical* p. 4 (Buenos Aires, 1930). (italics mine). He echoes the ideas presented by Lenz in his famous lecture, *¿Para qué estudiamos gramática?*, delivered at the University of Chile in 1912, insisting in its central thesis: in reality grammar does not accomplish the goals attributed to it by official programs (that is, to think, speak, and write correctly in a given language) because that is assured by the use of the speakers.

I have included these opinions, gathered at random among others of the same time, in order to prove that this methodological preoccupation is an old one in Spanish America. It really is an echo of a similar attitude in Spain (Cf. A. Castro, *Lengua, enseñanza y literatura*, Madrid, 1924). The discussion continues, creating divisions not only among the defenders of official programs, but also among pedagogues and linguists. A clear picture of what the situation is in Venezuela can be found in Angel Rosenblat's *La educación en Venezuela* (Caracas, 1964). What creates that perplexity to which Spanish American students are so used, is, to generalize about this question of language study, the confusion about methodology. It is a question caught in a crossfire between old ideas whose impact still persists. Should grammar be taught in schools, and, on the other hand, the impetus of those who, although granting that something different should be studied, are not in agreement as to whether language education should be conducted with no grammar, i.e. left to pure intuition, or whether a scientific grammar should be taught, in which case they propose to teach it with the methods developed by modern linguistics.

Should grammar be taught? — The controversies in this regard have finally shown that the position of those who favored a reform in methods did not imply a complete termination of all grammatical information. It was only a question of determining the precise scope of the term 'grammar', taking into account the fact that twentieth century education could not use concepts already obsolete. *Grammar* could not mean today what it did among the Greeks or among the preceptists of the sixteenth century. Luis Juan Piccardo has dealt with this problem in a thoughtful study, *Gramática y enseñanza* (Montevideo, 1956); the question is that all acceptable definitions of grammar can be reduced to these two essential types: (a) 'the art of speaking and writing correctly' and (b) 'the science that studies the system of a language'. Piccardo's study greatly clarifies the situation: between the expression, ventured by Lenz, 'to speak well is an art', and that which explains grammar as 'the art of speaking and writing', repeated by all of our official plans, programs, and textbooks, there is an essential difference. Language courses should aim at these goals: 'practical training in the language; discursive knowledge of the language as an integral element of the general culture'. (*op. cit.* 9). The purpose is to develop in the students the command of a certain technique, something which implies a 'saber hacer', and to give them a firm understanding of its procedures, 'un saber cómo hacer'.

What grammar should be taught? — Since Saussure pointed out the scientific shortcomings of normative grammar, the latter has been under continuous attack in the pedagogical field, due to the fact that primary and secondary education has not benefited from scientific advances. It is clear that the reaction to this situation in every country proceeds very slowly because it almost always comes from the university, that is, it is not always associated with the ranks of primary and secondary teachers and thus suffers from lack of experience with that type of students.

It should be said, however, that the reaction against normative grammar, being the result of a reflective attitude critical of established routines, leads to different conclusions in different fields of education. Witness the methods used by teachers graduated from normal schools, whose main preoccupation is with a literary language and who therefore aim their teaching towards the creation of a cultivated style. Graduates from universities, on the other hand, because of their technical preparation, aim at a study of the system of the language. Not to teach normative grammar is by now almost a motto for every progressive teacher all over the Spanish American continent. But the result of this attitude is not uniform with regard to its methodology. Some books on methodology, and certain scattered articles in reviews devoted to education propose pointed reflexions about compositions made upon literary models, and this is an attempt towards the consolidation of grammatical theory, a theory which ends up by being, after all, the same grammar they wanted to avoid.

Furthermore, we should realize what it means to fight against normative grammar in these countries where academic authority is so deeply rooted; where the teachers themselves erroneously believe in the authority and dogmatic principles of an academic Grammar. It is a struggle that reaches beyond education and administrative circles into different social strata, all of them touched by problems of *pundonor gramaticista*—social circles where everybody considers himself to be an authority on this kind of problems. These are the same people that would, of course, hesitate to venture an opinion on modern physics, for example, a science which also carries for them a new social message.

Descriptive grammar. — Undoubtedly, the method which is being proposed by responsible circles of opinion is that of descriptive grammar. Official programs are hesitant about it in most countries, and indeed a great step forward is that which has been done in Argentina, where it has been authorized at two levels of education on an experimental basis. But acceptance is not without discussion. It is easy to convince the teachers that language, while fulfilling 'its main function — that of communication — fulfills also social and cultural purposes. Therefore, it is necessary to have general guidelines understandable to the entire population of one language, without neglecting to emphasize regional manifestations or vacillations determined by the changes of life habits', Ismael Rodríguez Bou, *Apuntaciones gramaticales* p. 10. (Puerto Rico, 1958). The teachers' quick understanding of the problem derives, rather than from the successes of the new method, from the perspectives, incomprehensible to many of them, presented by a kind of methodology which had aimed at a literary language almost never accessible to them in time or space. It is also easy for the students to accept the new method without taking sides with one or another linguistic school, because it is a general fact in any of our countries that the students are confused when they are confronted with a language instruction full of academic norms, far away and different from the 'frequent uses that their communities make of that language', uses through which the student discovers that language 'becomes a means of communication'. This general agreement rests on this truth: only a scientific language teaching offers the possibility to achieve an understanding of the expressive functions of language; an understanding much more valuable than the memorization of general theoretical principles. A dynamic teaching also helps to show the role played by language in the development of democratic principles.

Normative grammar is an obstacle to the understanding of the linguistic phenomenon. To replace it with descriptive grammar does not mean, then, a mere change of terminology, but a radical change of attitude with regard to language. The following observation is important: traditional grammar did not permit taking into consideration the relationship *language-speakers.* The student faced the teacher, and vice-versa; language was between them like an embarrassing wall. Now, descriptive grammar offers a different image: communication among speakers, that is, language and those who use it. Teachers and students as observers and creators of communication, that is, of language. The wall has been destroyed. Grammatical theory becomes now justified because it exercises, at last, a formative influence, since it is concerned with discursive and expressive uses.

What is the scope of the adjective *descriptive* in these new principles adopted by the scientific teaching of language? As we will gradually see, since there is no agreement with regard to the different directions that language study can take, it would seem appropriate to admit that the scope of such an adjective would be that contemplated in the following statement by José Roca Pons: 'the terms descriptive, functional, or structural appropriately refer to true grammar, if we understand these terms correctly, as the description of significant linguistic forms, determined, to a large extent, by their functions — that is, their relations with one another—, so that the whole appears as a structure in which the different elements show their solidarity in relation to the goal pursued by language', *Introducción a la Gramática* 1.69. (Barcelona, 1960). It was to the same thing that Pagliaro was referring when, studying the essentially formative value of grammar, he stated that through it one could know 'the structure and functioning of the sign system' used by men to objectify their own consciousness, *Destino della grammatica* p. 276. (Napoli, 1952). The term *normative*, then, did not cover such a scope, now implied, in general, by the new qualification; the term *descriptive* refers to 'structure' and 'function'. To make these structural and functional goals clear has been the best and most difficult triumph for those who favored the new approach. It carried with it a change of attitude in the teachers and started also a healthy change of attitude in the students, since, by stimulating reflection it placed them in a position to inquire and examine the problems. This spiritual renewal, on the other hand, showed the weak technical information of the teacher, usually not trained to understand a new doctrine, no matter how truthful it could be. More easily did the new ideas triumph in university circles, although this has not been completely easy, nor is it fully established all over Spanish America. However, the nature and ways of university education (seminars, debates) favors anything that means discussion and reflection. In primary and secondary education other questions arise: Teaching function, is it not, perhaps, ignoring vocabulary? Or the usual task of revising dictionaries, by being abandoned, does it not distort the reality of meanings? Where do we include composition and the rigour of orthographic rules? If these are questions and discussions frequently aired in lower levels of education, other questions and problems exist among those with a scientific background. Here the controversy centers on which of the different schools should have a priority (Copenhague, Prague, Bloomfield, Guillaume, with all their variations), and at what level in the life of a student true grammatical training should begin. It is most instructive to see how detailed some of these questions can be.

A clearly Saussurian affirmation presides over all this scientific attitude: language is form rather than substance. Form flows from the relations established among the words of a given context. Meaning has no influence on that form. Grammatical analysis 'is going to center its investigation on the variations of formal moulds, on structure', Mabel Manacorda de Rosetti, *La gramática estructural en la escuela primaria* p. 7. (Buenos Aires, 1965). The equivalence of the terms 'form', 'function', and 'relation' is central in this doctrine. Nothing forbids qualifying this teaching as structural, and to postulate that a grammar of this kind will be a 'systematic and synchronic study of the facts of language' (*ibid.* 8).

The problems posed by modern linguistics in the teaching of Spanish are related to such an approach, to the value that a synchronic approach can have, to the priority of form over meaning. The discussion of these questions, debated only by linguists, has consequences for the methods, and also as we will see later, for the texts used in higher and lower education. The overall heading, structural, under which the new doctrines are grouped, seems to have, in the opinion of Mabel Manacorda, a provisional character, since in fact it indicates mainly an opposition to the old methods. This term will eventually disappear once the term 'grammar' acquires its true meaning: analysis of structures. Grammatical theory strives toward the accurate 'synchronic study of the functioning of language', and in order to analyze such a functioning 'we rely on a syntactic criterion', even though we recognize the existence of other criteria, the morphological and the semantic, to study the linguistic phenomenon, Mabel Manacorda de Rosetti, *La gramática estructural en la escuela secundaria* p. 71, 73 (Buenos Aires, 1961). This explanation alone of the methodological starting point confirms the fact that, in this matter, in Spanish America we still move about in a gulf of visible obscurities.

One of the aspects of modern doctrine open to more objections seems to be its separation from semantics. In his study *La lingüística moderna y los problemas hispánicos* (*RFE* 40.209-229, 1956), Bernard Pottier finds it appropriate to include form (the material aspect of expression), function (the syntax of form), and meaning in the study of language, accepting a strictly morphological theory separated from function and meaning, only for pedagogical reasons — that is, as a methodological abstraction. Besides, he understands this as a grammatical exigency, since after all 'grammar has to consider, in the first place, the functions of the elements of language, without letting itself be carried away by pseudo-semantic impressions' (*ibid.* 217). In other words, description should be made on the basis of the function of linguistic elements, apart from any psychological association (cf. 'impresiones seudosemánticas'), observing these elements in their functional behavior, where they fulfil their syntactic and syntagmatic associations, through which they define their own value. Pottier's observation does not carry with it a complete divorce from semantics, because in his own grammatical theories the ideas of value and function imply a semantic compromise (Cf. *Introduction à l'étude des structures grammaticales fondamentales*, Nancy, 1962; *Systématique des éléments de relation*, Paris, 1963). Some years before, in his study 'Directions in Modern Linguistics', E. Haugen had criticized this tendency to minimize meaning as a factor in the description of language (*Lg* 27,211-22, 1951). The fact is that, even though they may not admit it openly, it is difficult for many professors in Spanish America, having been educated under the influence of the German or French schools, to do away with meaning. It is generally admitted, thinking like Antoine Meillet in his *Linguistique historique et linguistique générale* (Paris, 1948) that, in the end, the grammar of a language is but the body of procedures by which words are grouped; something which can easily suggest the idea of a syntactic structure. However, nobody doubts, when introducing the criteria of formal moulds, that the ways in which words are arranged tend to offer a meaning through this arrangement. In this category are those who address themselves to the problem of the 'boundless nature of thought and the limitations of expressive means'; surely it is this that Amelia Sánchez Garrido is thinking about when, confronting 'the necessity that man has to *articulate his thought*' (italics mine), admits of 'the necessity to study the norms that govern the system, in order to better translate the infinite world of thought', deciding at once that 'to study that system of articulations is to study grammar', *La enseñanza de la gramática* p. 14 (Buenos Aires, 1962).

These criticisms to the abstraction of meanings made by the descriptive method are certainly based on the fact that these meanings are related to the function of communication, essential to language — a function which is indeed very close to the possibilities of a native speaker. Undoubtedly, when transformational grammar proposes to reduce grammar to a description of such competences and the capacity of the speaker to actualize linguistic facts, its positive contribution lies in the fact that it faces the problem of communication in itself, even though Chomsky places the whole problem in the field of syntactic structures. But, what does a well informed professor in Spanish America understand by the function of communication? I want to illustrate it by just quoting one document, from the above mentioned *Apuntaciones* of Ismael Rodriguez Bou: 'In its main function — that of communication — language fulfills social and cultural purposes. Therefore, it is necessary to have general guidelines understandable to the entire population of one language'. The fact is that when we enter the field of communication, by which the word acts upon an interlocutor, Karl Vossler's observations (*Límites de la sociología lingüística*) are still considered in force; thus his name and that of Bally, together with the sequel of philosophers such as Bergson or Croce, appear as prestigeous authorities among those who still consider themselves the promoters of linguistic teaching by descriptive methods.

The second observation formulated concerns synchronic description held by Mabel Manacorda de Rosetti as another one of the great achievements of modern pedagogy. It is no longer a question of teaching the literary language, and especially the literary language of a period of literary excellence, but the living language in actual use. But this is not very easy. It is also true that from the moment grammatical theory disregards artistic and expressive creation, be it oral or written, one cannot say that it is concerned with the synchronic study of the functioning of language, since this functioning, although synchronic, implies a concrete realization (i.e. an expression, oral or written, of a discursive or expressive nature) not an abstraction. There does not exist a synchronic structure since every synchronic state exists within a diachronic frame of reference. This is why Pottier observes that 'it is Utopian to believe that a purely synchronic structure can be established'. He also says that 'the synchronic merely exists with the diachronic' (*op.cit.* 212). To ignore this truth would be to limit a priori the aspects offered by language to our consideration. One can make, and this is of extraordinary pedagogical value, synchronic cuts, but giving this perspective its exact value within a general frame.

This is perhaps the most difficult path yet to be traveled by descriptive teaching, especially among those who are accustomed to think about language using as the only material for observation the literary language (and particularly of by-gone periods: Golden Age and romanticism). If the descriptive method is used to introduce the students to an attitude of reflection, serious risks are taken about the interpretation of the scope and validity of saying that grammar is a systematic and synchronic description.

A clear advantage of the new methods, which base their analysis on the actual language, with attention to spontaneous oral expression rather than the thought-out written expression, consists in the new perspectives offered by regional speeches. The most important work published in this respect is the already mentioned 'Relación entre la investigación dialectológica y la enseñanza de la lengua materna', by José Pedro Rona, inspired in North American pedagogy. The author feels that the child 'should speak the system of the learned language level of the region where he lives', in order for him to be considered by society as a cultivated speaker. This is the scientific thing. But in our countries of Spanish America this worthwhile attempt brings about problems, which Rona analyzes in his work. It happens that in Spanish American countries no studies have yet been made to establish the linguistic features of a learned and a vulgar level in a given place. As Rona clearly sees, it is from these studies 'that a useful didactic material could be obtained by determining descriptively the learned norms of a region'. (*Op.cit.* 6). In Chile, for instance, it would be easy to do it; that is why Sergio Echeverría demands 'the detailed description of each of the cultural levels of Spanish in Chile'. (*Op.cit.* 44), as a starting point for an ordered plan for the scientific teaching of grammar. It would be relatively easy in Argentina, and Amelia Sánchez Garrido understands how in our America the structuralist orientation about colloquial forms leads to the 'comparative presentation of the relationship between structure and expression in the mother tongue and its regional variants' (op.cit. 19), something which would produce those hoped for benefits when the time comes for literary appreciation. And it would not be difficult to carry it through in Colombia, where the advance made in linguistic geography has placed regional speeches at an enviable scientific level. But the problem persists and it is up to the dialectologist to solve it so that the language teacher can work profitably.

Dialectological studies will be most profitable to the teacher with regard to orthography, particularly in those countries with a substantial Indian population. In these countries it is possible to find not only orthographic errors due to the lack of correspondence between the phonemic system and the graphemic systems of the language, but also other errors due to the fact that 'the system of graphemes corresponds to a phonemic system different from that of the local dialect'. (Rona, *op. cit.*, p 11). This type of investigation, already successfully initiated by Mattoso Câmara in Brasil, would open a new horizon for linguistics in education.

The subject of orthography leads to that of correctness. The absence of this topic as a visible preoccupation in descriptive grammar creates strong suspicions among the teachers who favor normative grammar. If correctness is not mentioned (and orthography provides a battleground for this discussion), it is not clearly seen how this new grammar can fulfil the ideals of thinking, speaking, and writing correctly. Contributing to this perplexity is the obvious chaos in the orthography of students at all levels of education, and even some occasional errors in newspapers, even in the most serious ones. It is needless to say that for most teachers, the term 'correctness' is synonymous with 'precept', 'law', 'rule'; it has little to do with the concept of social prestige of culture of which Amado Alonso speaks. When structural methodology is criticized in this respect, the correctness that is mentioned is that which underlies normative grammar, the grammar that is supposed to be avoided. Correctness, however, is not ignored by scientific teaching, since only a scientific knowledge of the language enables the speaker to command his capacity for expression, something more worthy than memorization of general theories. Correctness is indeed a phenomenon which linguistic teaching takes into consideration, but without contemplating errors in themselves; it studies communication and deals with errors with a functional criterion, i.e. insofar as they are an obstacle to effective communication. In doing this, linguistics only concurs with Pooley's old opinion, who in a lively commentary, *These Things shall not pass*, explained that creative teaching with emphasis on communication should replace the obsession with studying errors separately, as if they had any meaning in themselves, apart from their medium. He categorically condemned 'the practice of correcting those errors separated from the real use of the language'. (*The English Journal* 35, 1946). The fact is that correctness was — and is — associated for most teachers and authors of grammar texts, with the idealized image of a literary language. Mabel Manacorda de Rosetti sees the problem clearly when she insists in spreading the idea that correctness is also something synchronic, and that 'in order to determine whether a form is correct or not, we would rely on present actual usage'. She offers a sensible scientific reason: 'without knowing the system there will be no possibility of perceiving expressive deviations or of justifying the norms' (*Op.cit.* 69). Naturally though, this notion that correctness is something synchronic, when applied to orthography, can only be pedagogically valid by keeping in mind that anything synchronic is part of a general diachronic picture. In this respect, I should perhaps mention my work, to come out shortly, *Descripción del sistema de la lengua escrita* (Lima, 1966), which is an explanation of the different combinations of graphemes in modern Spanish, compared with the phonological phenomena of sounds on which they rest.

Since Hjelmslev announced (*Acta Lingüística* 1, 10-22) that the name structural linguistics was 'a program rather than an actual reality', there has been progress in the methods, in the investigation, and in the pedagogical application of these principles. In Spanish America, accustomed through centuries to a teaching based on memorization and subject to vacillating and encyclopedic plans of education, language study has not achieved at the primary and secondary levels the results that could be expected. But this situation is not so deeply related to the validity of the methods sponsored by modern linguistics, as it is with the social and political reality of these countries, and with the situation of their professorial bodies. Nonetheless, a beneficial influence slowly flows from the university, and there are already several countries awakening from past errors to the new ways. Not only is there the contribution of new generations of scholars educated abroad, or by intensive and modern studies at home, but also the brilliant linguistic tradition which claims in America the names of Andrés Bello and Rufino Cuervo, Rodolfo Lenz and Amado Alonso, as models of fruitful work and scientific preoccupation.

THE TEXTS

A general phenomenon about education is repeated in Spanish America: language teaching at the primary and secondary levels is not in general in the hands of linguists. Linguists, on the other hand, with esceptions, do not usually show an interest in providing materials to guide language teaching at those levels. We can repeat here Robert P. Stockwell's observation: 'the job of the linguist is to provide the basis both theoretical and in many instances, directly practical, on which the language teacher should build up his materials and his pedagogy' (*MSLL* 8. 34 (1955). It is also true that the books written by specialists in the hope of providing such guidance have not attained — on the whole — the success that could be expected, among other reasons because they were assimilated as 'linguistic dogmas' in an atmosphere still accustomed to the sad and monstrous pedagogy of irrational memorization.

A quick inventory of the textbooks used in Spanish America for language teaching would produce more than one hundred texts in primary and secondary education. Very few of them can withstand a severe analysis. Just a few follow a sound linguistic line. Perhaps it is in Argentina that these attempts are being more decisive. Teachers there receive an adequate training in specialized institutes; also in Chile, with a serious pedagogical tradition. We are not, however, ignoring the advances made in Puerto Rico, Uruguay, Venezuela, Colombia, and Peru, where there are already textbooks written by university people, linguists by profession. But it will be yet some time before the results of this not yet uniform preparation leave a clear imprint upon the generations of young students.

Something different is happening in the sphere of the university, which has contributed valuable works to higher language teaching, including even texts of descriptive linguistics. Angel Rosenblat in Venezuela, Ruben del Rosario in Puerto Rico, Juan L. Piccardo in Uruguay, Ana María Barrenechea in Buenos Aires, Luis Jaime Cisneros in Peru, Rodolfo Oroz, Félix Morales Pettorino, Félix Martínez Bonatti, and Ambrosio Rabanales in Chile (and it is not my purpose to make a list) are the testimonies of a modelling labor which transcends the limits of language education at the university following the methods of modern investigation, and whose echoes are now reaching the level of secondary teaching.

Rather than denouncing deficient methods and programs, and exposing the meagre preparation of teachers, these complaints about the bad linguistic teaching now offered in Spanish America should serve, in an account as short as this one, to state a general affirmation: it is not easy to teach language in Spanish-speaking America. It is a task bristling with difficulties. It is so, above all, because teachers at all levels are ideologically committed in this regard. It is, nonetheless, a task that linguists must undertake.

5. BIBLIOGRAPHY

Alonso, Amado, 'Los nuevos programas de literatura', *RFH* 2 (1940).

Alonso, Amado and Pedro Henríquez Ureña, *Gramática castellana*, 2 vols. (Buenos Aires, 1942).

Bally, Charles, *La enseñanza de la lengua materna en el lenguaje y la vida*, varias ediciones. (Buenos Aires).
Barrenechea, Ana Maria, *Guía del curso de gramática* (Buenos Aires, 1960).
Castro, Americo, *La enseñanza del español en España* (Madrid, 1922).
——, *Lengua, enseñanza, literatura* (Madrid, 1924).
Chomsky, Noam, *Syntactic Structures* (The Hague, 1962).
Cisneros, Luis Jaime, *Cátedra de Lengua española: guía de temas* (Lima, 1959).
——, *Descripción del sistema de la lengua escrita* (en prensa).
——, *Lengua española*, 3 vols. (Lima, 1962).
——, *Lenguaje* (Lima, 1953).
——, *Lengua y estilo* (Lima, 1959).
——, *Primera Cátedra de Lengua española: syllabus* (Lima, 1964).
Echeverría, Sergio, 'La gramática española en la asignatura de Castellano en la educación media', *RLA* 1 (1964).
Flórez, Luis, *Concepto y enseñanza del castellano* (Bogotá, 1960).
——, *Lecciones de pronunciación* (Bogotá, 1963).
Fradejas Sanchez, Luis, *Gramática española* (Cuenca, 1959).
Gutierrez Eskildsen, Rosario, *Primer curso de Lengua y Literatura española* (México, 1958).
Haugen, Einar, 'Directions in Modern Linguistics', *Lg* 27 (1951).
Jimenez Borja, Jose, *Fines de la enseñanza del castellano y la literatura en el Perú* (Lima, 1955).
Lenz, Rodolfo, *Para qué estudiamos gramática* (Stgo, de Chile, 1912).
Manacorda de Rosetti, Mabel, *La gramática estructural en la escuela primaria* (Buenos Aires, 1965).
——, *La gramática estructural en la escuela secundaria* (Buenos Aires, 1961).
Montoliu, Manuel de, 'Discurso de inauguración', *Boletín Instituto Filología* (Buenos Aires, 1926).
Pagliaro, Antonio, *Destino della grammatica* (Napoli, 1952).
Piccardo, Luis Juan, *Gramática y enseñanza* (Montevideo, 1956).
Pooley, Robert C., 'These Things Shall Not Pass', *The English Journal* 35.76-82 (1946).
Pottier, Bernard, *Introduction à l'étude des structures grammaticales fondamentales* (Nancy, 1962).
——, 'La lingüística moderna y los problemas hispánicos', *RFE* (1956).
——, *Systématique des éléments de relation* (Paris, 1963).
——, Programa Interamericano de Linguistica y Enseñanza de Idiomas, El Simposio de Cartagena (Bogotá, 1965).
Roca Pons, José, *Introducción a la gramática*, 2 vols. (Barcelona, 1960).
Rodríguez Bou, Ismael, *Apuntaciones gramaticales* (Puerto Rico, 1958).
——, *Apuntaciones sobre la enseñanza de la lengua hablada y escrita en la escuela elemental* (Río Piedras, 1954).

Rona, José Pedro, 'Relación entre la investigación dialectológica y la enseñanza de la lengua materna', *RLA* 2 (1965).
Rosenblat, Angel, *La educación en Venezuela* (Caracas, 1964).
Sanchez Garrido, Amelia, *La enseñanza de la gramática* (Buenos Aires, 1962).
Saussure, Ferdinand de, *Curso de Lingüística general* (Buenos Aires, 1944).
Selva, Juan B., *La enseñanza gramatical* (Buenos Aires, 1930).
Toscano, Humberto, *Gramática castellana* (Quito, 1961).
Vidal de Battini, Berta, *El español de la Argentina* (Buenos Aires, 1954).
Vossler, Karl, *Límites de la sociología lingüística* Several edition, Buenos Aires).

BILINGUALISM

ROBERT J. DI PIETRO

1. GENERAL REMARKS

Any treatment of what is termed 'bilingualism' carries with it several rather serious problems of definition. If bilingualism involves the alternate use by an individual of two languages (Weinreich, 1953), it is not always easy to draw a line of demarcation between languages. Hockett (1958) discusses the problem of separating the romance languages, and DeCamp (1961, 1962) and Stewart (1962a) reiterate it when they discuss the various levels lying between standard English and French and their related creoles.

Although Weinreich's reliance on alternate use of two languages by one individual (1953) accurately rules out of any discussion on bilingualism those cases of isolated monolingual communities, such as the German-speaking Mennonites in Paraguay (Krause, 1962) or the Javanese in Surinam, he leaves untreated the degree of language control that is necessary to qualify one as a bilingual. Haugen (1953) suggests that bilingualism begins at the point where the speaker can produce complete meaningful utterances in the 'other' language. Diebold (1961b), developing further the theoretical start of bilingualism and its relationships to cultural change, describes a case of 'incipient' bilingualism in Mexico. McQuown's investigations in Mexico (1962) concern primarily the adjustment of American Indians to a general cultural Mexican norm through the acquisition of Spanish. Haas (1955, as cited in Haugen, 1956) adds some important dimensions in her classification of bilinguals into 'receiving and sending', 'oral and visual', and 'close and distant' types. The concept of receptive bilingualism (where one understands a second language without being able to speak it) is especially useful for describing the situation in which many second generation immigrant children find themselves in both North and South America.

Peal and Lambert (1962) define 'pseudo-bilingualism' as being that condition where the speaker never really learns the second language fully and, in the process, forgets the first one. The present writer has often encountered pseudo-bilinguals in his investigations among aged, semiliterate immigrants. The extent of pseudo-bilingualism, however, has not yet been fully determined.

The term 'bilingualism' is theoretically inappropriate in its implied restriction to a dual language competence. There are many cases in the Americas where more than two recognizably different languages are used by the same individual. In the Caribbean, and specifically in Netherlands America, as many as three or four languages are used daily by many people: a standard language (Dutch), an immigrant language (Hindi-Urdu), a language of wider communication (English or Spanish) and, possibly, a creole language (Papiamentu or Sranan or Saramakkan) (Stewart, 1966). The term 'multilingualism' is coming more into vogue, e.g. in the title of the Brazzaville Conference of 1962 (Symposium on Multilingualism) and Vildomec's book (1963), and is, of course, more appropriate in describing both plurilingual and bilingual situations.

Stewart (1962 and revised 1966) develops a typology for describing the use of each language in multilingual communities. Ferguson (1959) introduces the term 'diglossia' to handle cases involving problems of language status and separation, in which he includes Haitian Creole. Stewart (1962b) differentiates between diglossic and bilingual communities. He reserves bilingualism to describe those situations where the co-occurrent languages are sufficiently unlike to be readily distinguished from each other and possibly function in competitive cultures. Diglossic situations are more stable in comparison with bilingual situations, since each diglossic language is associated with a different cultural situation, e.g. creole used with women and children and French used in business affairs in Haiti.

We briefly define a bilingual (or a multilingual) as an individual who has two (or more) idiolects. We leave open for further study the procedures for testing and evaluating our definition. Bi-dialectalism (control of two or more dialects) might also be considered a type of bilingualism, and we do not wish to exclude this possibility from our definition.

It has not yet been proven that there are psychological aspects separating bilingualism from plurilingualism in regard to either language or dialect control. Involved is the nature of the systems underlying the two idiolects. Daniel Jones (1950) speaks of 'diaphones' as units identifying phonic correspondences between different varieties of the same language. It has been pointed out (by Haugen, 1958 and Stewart, 1962b) that bilingual situations often involve the use of a single 'common core' inventory of phonemes for otherwise diverse linguistic systems. Fries and Pike (1949) use the term 'coexistent phonemic systems'. In some bilingual situations, the evaluation of the speaker can be carried out by comparing his language performance with the performances of monolingual speakers of each language involved. In diglossic situations, however, a bilingual's competence in one language may be justifiably compared only with one style level of a monolingual's command of that language. Lambert's projection (1963) of Weinreich's concept of 'coordinate bilingualism', focusing on equal fluency in all sociocultural areas, is not likely to be equally appropriate in most cases of bilingualism in Latin America, where language use is closely connected with many problems of cultural stratification.

Gumperz (1962) treats the general problem of identifying language with community. He points out that there are no a priori grounds requiring that speech communities be restricted to those having only one language. Gumperz's point is well taken, since bilingualism and multilingualism are typical of many communities in Latin America.

Janet Roberts (1962), in her survey of sociocultural change and problems of communication, points out that communication in Latin America is not as serious a problem as that of Asia and Africa because Spanish and Portuguese extend over almost the entire area as official and widely learned languages. Communication on a larger-than-local scale is acute primarily for Indians who are monolingual in a native language. There remain, nevertheless, places in Latin America where bilingualism and multilingualism are very much in evidence. Paraguay, with its large number of Guaraní speakers, Argentina, with its immigrant groups, and Surinam, with its complex multilingualism, come to the fore as illustrative of three distinct types of language contact. Most of Latin America continues to attract immigrants from both Europe and Asia, although in diminishing numbers. Argentina, Chile, Uruguay and Brazil have long been centers of attraction for Europeans. Japanese have migrated to Brazil in such large numbers that the Centro de Estadística of the Pan American Union rates it as having the largest colony of Japanese outside of the homeland. The sixth census of Brazil (1950) gives the number of Japanese and naturalized Japanese-Brazilians as 129,192 persons. Buenos Aires, São Paulo and Santiago (just to mention a few) are all centers of newspapers and radio broadcasts in languages other than Spanish or Portuguese.

Tempesta (1965) estimates that Italians who emigrated to Argentina between 1861 and 1960 numbered as high as 3,000,000 persons. The high number is especially meaningful when it is compared with the present population of Argentina: 22,045,000. Sadly, data on the actual extent of Spanish/Italian bilingualism are not available. Some work has been published concerning Italian influence on Argentine Spanish (Grossmann, 1926, Wagner, 1949, Castro, 1961), but, generally speaking, there is little on Italian/Spanish language contact. Cocoliche, an Italian/Spanish blend, has been reported for the La Boca section of Buenos Aires. Little more than its existence has been noted, however (Grossmann, 1926, for example). In many cases, the assimilation of Spanish has been evidently rapid for Italian immigrants — in a way analogous to Dutch and German immigrants to North America. The presence of pockets of Germans and Serbo-Croatians in Latin America, especially in Argentina and Chile, reflect a much slower assimilation to a national norm. The Brazilian census of 1950, to cite another example, listed 197,658 Italian nationals living in Brazil, of which only 27,474 indicated that they habitually spoke Italian in the home. There were fewer German nationals (58,399), but the figures for speakers of German in the home in Brazil was proportionately much higher: 45,419 (see also Moraes, 1957, for further discussion).

A survey of the figures available in various national censuses indicates that the majority of bilingual cases involve speakers of native Indian languages who are acquiring control of Spanish. According to the Mexican census of 1960, there are 3,030,254 persons speaking a native Indian language of which 1,925,299 also speak Spanish. The largest number of Indians in Mexico speak Nahuatl (297,285) and the second largest number speak Mixteco (106,545). There are even some cases remaining of bilingualism in two Indian languages, e.g. Nahuatl and Otomí (Diebold 1962a).

Roberts (1962) lists the three most important native Indian languages on the South American continent as being Quechua, Aymará, and Guaraní. Of the three, Quechua is possibly the one spoken over the widest area. It was the official language of the Inca Empire and was taught to conquered peoples. When the Spanish arrived, they used it extensively in their own conquests and in the spreading of Christianity. It is presently spoken throughout the highlands of Ecuador, Peru, and Bolivia and as far south as Santiago del Estero in Argentina (Tovar, 1961). Similarly, Guaraní has had a long history as a language of trade (the term is *língua geral* in Portuguese) throughout Paraguay and Brazil (Rodrigues, 1958).

In some Latin American countries, multilingualism has had an effect on the school curriculum. In Paraguay, Guaraní is used in instruction (Rubin, 1961). English is taught in Puerto Rico. William A. Stewart reports in private conversation that Japanese is being taught in Peru. Both English and Spanish are so widely used in Curaçao and Aruba that instruction in both languages is generally begun as early as the fifth grade (Hauch, 1960).

2. APPROACHES TO THE STUDY OF LANGUAGE CONTACT

Language contact can be discussed from several points of view. The functional distribution of each language in the multilingual community (e.g. in the public media and in education) and the attitudes of the speakers toward the languages they speak constitute what could be called the sociocultural aspect.

Discussions can also focus on measuring the degree of control of each language by the speaker. Testing and evaluating fluency has been carried out chiefly for Canadian French by Lambert (1962). The evaluation of fluency in Spanish of McQuown (1962) and Diebold (1961a, 1962) incorporates fluency within a sociocultural context in a way that the Canadian study does not.

Of great interest to investigators has been the matter of interference of one language on the other(s) in multilingual communities. Taylor (1956) and Weinreich (1953) concentrate on measuring the range of interference.

Haugen (1956) classifies the languages of the Americas as follows: (1) native (exclusively the various Amerindian languages), (2) colonial (e.g. Spanish and Portuguese), (3) immigrant (e.g. German and Italian), and (4) creole (e.g. Papiamentu and French Creole). Although Haugen's classification is based chiefly on the provenance of each language and pertinent historical factors, it can be adapted to serve in describing the major types of multilingual situations if we make a few adjustments: 'colonial' is changed to 'standard' and a class, 'languages of wider communication', is added to describe the special role of both Spanish and English in Latin America.

(1) *Native Languages*. — The total count of Amerindian languages has not been completed yet. There are several useful sources presenting the recent results of field

investigations, notably, Cohen (1952), Carl Voegelin's survey of the languages of the world at Indiana University, the language files of the Center for Applied Linguistics of Washington, D.C. presently being compiled by W. W. Gage, McQuown (1955, Spanish ed. 1961), Tovar (1961), and the work sponsored by the Summer Institute of Linguistics of Harold and Mary Key (1961) on Bolivia and Mary Key (1964) on Chile, Argentina, Paraguay, and Uruguay.

(2) *Standard Languages.* — There are five standard languages in Latin America: Spanish, Portuguese, English, French, and Dutch. Each standard language was also a colonial language. Another colonial language, Danish, spoken in the Virgin Islands, (a Danish possession until 1917, when the Islands were sold to the United States) is no longer functional and is most likely extinct in the area.

It should be pointed out that of all the native languages of Latin America, only the Guaraní of Paraguay is approaching the status of a standard language (Rubin, 1961, Garvin and Mathiot, 1960): Although Spanish is still the only official language of Paraguay, Guaraní is used extensively in everyday communication and is literally the mother tongue of a majority of Paraguayan children. According to the latest figures available, 40.1 percent of the population speak only Guaraní, another 53.8 percent are bilingual in Guaraní and Spanish, and only 4.7 percent are monolingual in Spanish (the small residue consists of speakers of other languages).

Surveying Mexico, Central and South America, and the Caribbean, we observe that the vast majority of the population speak either Spanish or Portuguese. Quechua and French Creole speakers rank third and fourth in number. English is well represented with over 1,000,000 speakers located primarily in the British sphere of control. Standard French is spoken by less people (mostly in the creole areas) but continues to enjoy prestige in many parts of the Caribbean. Dutch, despite its official status as a standard language, has the weakest representation. According to Hauch (1960), Dutch in the Windward Islands of the Netherlands Antilles must be taught as a foreign language. In Surinam, the government has established separate schools for children from non-Dutch speaking homes, and on Aruba, Papiamentu is offered in evening courses for teachers who do not know the language (Hauch, 1960). In all Netherlands America, the use of English seems to be increasing.

(3) *Immigrant Languages.* — According to the tabulations of the Centro de Estadística of the Unión Panamericana, the overwhelming majority of immigrants to Latin America are from Europe (including Russia). Asiatics are second in number. Argentina and Brazil have attracted the greatest number of immigrants. There are, at present, 2,440,000 immigrants in Argentina (accounting for 15 percent of the population) and 1,210,000 in Brazil (2 percent). The latest Brazilian census lists six immigrant languages having more than 1500 speakers: Arabic, German, Italian, Japanese, Polish, and Spanish. Speakers of languages other than Portuguese in Brazil total 1,305,720.

Among the Asiatic languages, Javanese and Hindi-Urdu are spoken in Surinam, and the latter is also found in some British areas (e.g. British Guiana and Trinidad).

Most of the Asiatic languages were first introduced into the Caribbean when numbers of indentured servants were brought in from India and Indonesia by the Dutch and British after the abolition of the slave trade with Africa.

A type of Sephardic Portuguese was once spoken in Surinam by the descendants of Jewish refugees from Portugal and Brazil. In Panama there are numbers of Chinese who have descended from the laborers imported to build railroads and to work on the various canal projects of that country (Doubleday, 1961).

(4) *Creole Languages.* — All of the colonial languages, except Danish, have played a role in the formation of creolized languages: French in the creoles of Haiti, Martinique, Guadeloupe, and Louisiana; Spanish and Portuguese in Papiamentu, English in Sranan, and Portuguese and English in Saramakkan. A Dutch-based creole called Negerhollands is reported for the Virgin Islands but is now presumably extinct (Stewart, 1962a).

(5) *Languages of Wider Communication* (hereafter abbreviated LWC). — Charles Ferguson (1962) suggests the title in offering a taxonomy for language use. Spanish and English are classified here in addition to being called standard languages because of their special role in Latin America as languages of commercial and cultural access among countries. For example, in Cuba and Santo Domingo which are technically monolingual, English is widely known. Perhaps the classic example of bilingualism involving a LWC would be Puerto Rico. In the British and Dutch affiliated areas of the Caribbean, Spanish has been added to the curriculum in many of the secondary schools. In Jamaica, for example, Spanish is presently replacing French as the most popular foreign language taught (Hauch, 1960).

3. THE FATE OF THE AFRICAN LANGUAGES IN LATIN AMERICA

Because of the great numbers of Negro slaves that were transported from Africa to the New World throughout the period of colonization, one would expect to find certain numbers of African languages, especially those of the Niger Congo family, still spoken. Owing, however, to the slavers' technique of separating ethnic communities and even families in order to insure against rebellion, the slaves were forced to rely on their masters' languages and, eventually, on pidginized languages for communication among themselves. Except for Lucumí, a language supposedly related to Yoruba and spoken in the interior of Cuba (Olmsted, 1953) and Nagô, its possible counterpart in Brazil, no native African language has survived. The African languages have, however, made a contribution to the formation of the various creoles. The extent of this contribution is not yet well understood and is presently being discussed by scholars interested in the origins of creole languages, e.g. Taylor (1956), Hall (1958), and Goodman (1965).

4. GEOGRAPHICAL DISTRIBUTION

Surveying the types of language contact situations in Latin America reveals five areas which are more or less distinct geographically:

(1) The non-urban areas of Mexico, Central America, Colombia, Ecuador, Peru, and Bolivia all share a type of bilingualism which centers on problems of acculturation to a western Spanish-speaking society and away from the native Indian culture (cf. the works of Diebold, McQuown and Rubin). Ability to speak Spanish is correlated to a large extent with economic and social advancement. Despite a history of wide use, Quechua in Peru and Bolivia is presently associated with a rural, non-literate, non-western peasant society (Rubin, 1962). Spanish is the standard language in both countries, and all positive values of social and economic advancement accompany the ability to speak it. In many cases of contact between native and standard languages, men tend to be bilingual more often than women — primarily because the men have more opportunities to converse with Spanish-speaking employers and businessmen than do the women. As Rubin puts it (1952), native Indian monolingualism is the 'last rung on the social ladder'.

It is clear that Indians and Mestizos make up the largest body of bilinguals in Latin America. Individuals classified as Indians account for 63 percent of the population of Bolivia, 39 percent of Ecuador, 45.9 percent of Peru and 53 percent of Guatemala. Diebold (1962) reports that communities with bilinguals in two native languages still exist in areas remote from Spanish-speaking centers, such as Southern Mexico.

(2) Paraguay deserves to be put in a special class because it is the only country in Latin America where a native language (Guaraní) is so wide-spread that it competes with Spanish in several socially important ways (Rubin 1961). Although Spanish remains the only official standard language of Paraguay and exerts great influence on Guaraní (Cadogan 1958), all indications are that Guaraní is firmly established and that Guaraní-Spanish bilingualism is relatively stable. Bilingual speakers account for 53.8 percent of the population, while speakers who are monolingual in Spanish make up only 4.7 percent (see Table I).

(3) The Caribbean. Most of the islands of the Caribbean and part of the surrounding land mass display a type of multilingualism characterized chiefly by the presence of creolized languages. We include in the general area of the Caribbean those parts of Louisiana and Southern Alabama where Creole and French are spoken (Morgan 1959, 1960, 1964), British Honduras in Central America, and Surinam and British and French Guiana in South America. We exclude Cuba, Puerto Rico, the Dominican Republic, and most of Central America, where either Spanish or Spanish and Indian languages predominate (see discussion below under Puerto Rico). Four fifths of the world's speakers of creole languages live in the area (Loftman 1953 aptly calls the Caribbean the 'cradle of the creoles'). The Caribbean language situation has been recently investigated by Taylor (1956, et al.), Le Page (1958, 1961), Stewart (1962a),

Voorhoeve (1962), Hall (1965), Lichtveld (1965) and Goodman (1965). Ferguson (1959) cited the case of Haitian Creole in defining diglossia.

Although creolized languages share in part the same social status as native Indian languages in that they are never accepted as official languages, there seems to be much less repression of the creoles, especially in the British and Netherlands Antilles. References are made to the creoles as expressing the 'soul of the people', and a literature in many creoles does exist (Jourdain, 1956). Dillard (1962) observes that some creole speakers have even developed attitudes of prescriptivism and purism toward their language. Some would like to see it made less like any other language and more distinctly creole while others would prefer to make it more like the co-occurrent prestige language. As a result, it is difficult in many places (in Haiti, for example) to separate features of the local creole from those of the local standard.

In addition to creole languages, the general area of the Caribbean contains speakers of immigrant languages from both Europe and Asia and many speakers of LWCs. It is not unlikely to encounter, as in Trinidad, persons who have varying degrees of fluency in a standard (English), an immigrant language (Hindi), an LWC (Spanish), and a creole language (French Creole).

Native Indian languages are practically extinct in the Caribbean. Caribs are found on the island of Dominica, but they are speakers of French Creole. A Carib-speaking Negro population exists in Honduras. They are called 'Black Caribs' and were transported there in the eighteenth century from the island of Saint Vincent (Taylor, 1951). Taylor (1958) cites several instances of Carib verses in ancestral religious rites and in the recounting of dreams by Black Caribs.

(4) Urban Centers in South America. There is a marked tendency in Latin America toward urbanization, with the flow of population toward one or two cities in each country. The United Nations Report on the World Social Situation (1957) indicates that 29.4 percent of Argentina's population lives in Buenos Aires and as much as 44 percent of the population of Uruguay lives in Montevideo. Buenos Aires, for example, has a population of 3,799,200 while the second largest city in Argentina is Rosario with only 761,300. Rio de Janeiro and São Paulo account for the greatest number of urban Brazilians by a wide margin over the other cities of Brazil. Following the population trend, numbers of recent immigrants from Europe and Asia are to be found in or around all Latin American cities.

The two leaders in attracting immigrants have been Argentina and Brazil. Chile has perhaps the most heterogenous population of Europeans in Latin America, having attracted Italians, Germans, Serbo-Croatians, French, Irish, and English in significant numbers. The type of immigrant-standard bilingualism encountered in the urban centers is markedly different from other types of bilingualism discussed above. The immigrants' languages as well as the standard language are literate and have what Stewart (1962a) has termed 'historicity', enabling the speakers to maintain certain cultural values of the home country through private schools, radio broadcasts, newspapers, and commercial enterprises. Tempesta (1965) announces the formation of a university in Argentina where all instruction is given in Italian. It is presumably the first of its kind in existence. Since immigrants (especially European immigrants) generally enjoy economic success in the urban centers, they are also in a position to maintain their national language. Their children are often bilingual from childhood.

The largest group of non-Spanish and non-Portuguese speaking immigrants to Latin America is Italian. The combined migration of Italians to Brazil and Argentina during the last 100 years is estimated at more than 4,600,000 (Tempesta, 1965). The Centro de Estadística of the Pan American Union lists 786,000 Italian nationals living at present in Argentina and 242,000 living in Brazil. The numbers of native Argentines and Brazilians of Italian extraction are not available, but would, of course, be much larger.

(5) Puerto Rico, Cuba, and Santo Domingo. Both Spanish and English are in daily use in Puerto Rico as standard languages. Although Spanish is the only official language and is by far the predominant one (a 1959 estimate lists 83 percent of the population speaking only Spanish — Epstein, 1961), English is constantly reinforced

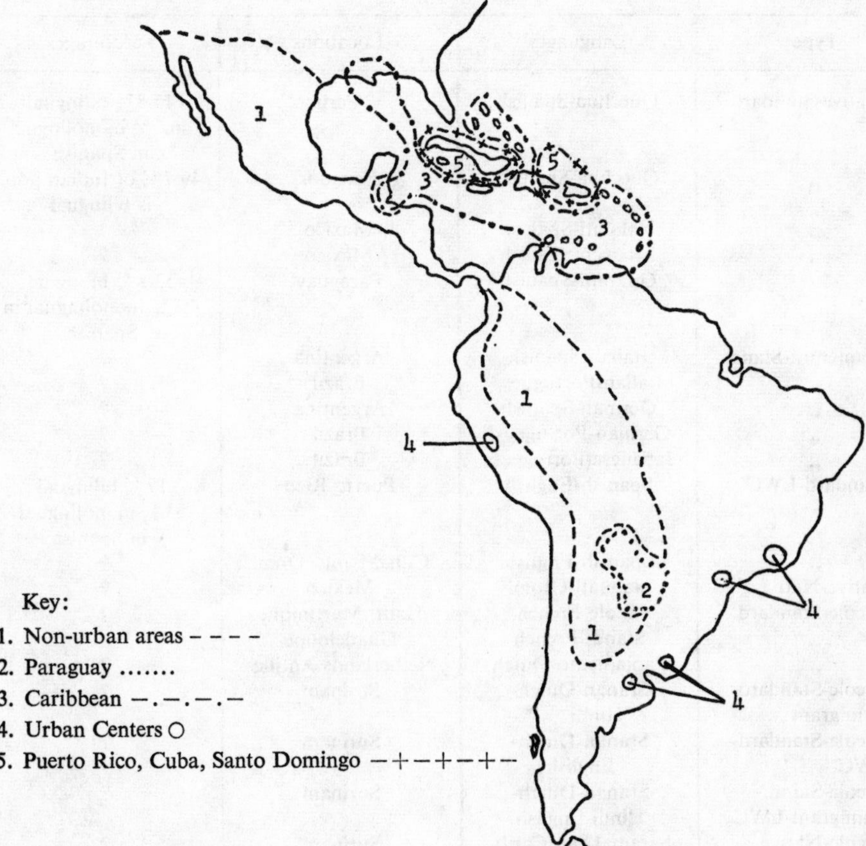

A Sampling of the Geographical Distribution of Language Contact Areas

by close economic ties with the United States. We consider the bilingualism in Puerto Rico to be of the Standard-LWC type, with Spanish the standard and English the LWC. Other instances of Standard-LWC bilingualism are found in Cuba and Santo Domingo where English plays a reduced yet comparable role as a LWC.

5. A SUGGESTED TYPOLOGY FOR BILINGUALISM AND MULTILINGUALISM.

As a result of surveying the instances of language contact in Latin America, ten major types of bilingualism and multilingualism are suggested. In Table I each type is identified and one or more example is given for each. In some cases it was possible to determine actual percentages of speakers.

TABLE I

Type	Languages	Locations	Percentages
1. Native-Standard	Quechua-Spanish	Peru	15.8% bilingual 46.7% monolingual in Spanish
"	Quechua-Spanish	Ecuador	49.7% of Indian pop. is bilingual
"	Nahuatl-Spanish	Mexico	?
"	Mixteco-Spanish	Mexico	?
"	Guaraní-Spanish	Paraguay	53.8% bilingual 4.7% monolingual in Spanish
2. Immigrant-Stand.	Italian-Spanish	Argentina	?
"	Italian-Portuguese	Brazil	?
"	German-Spanish	Argentina	?
"	German-Portuguese	Brazil	?
"	Japanese-Portuguese	Brazil	?
3. Standard-LWC	Spanish-English	Puerto Rico	17% bilingual 83% monolingual in Spanish
"	Spanish-English	Cuba, Santo Dom.	?
4. Native-Native	Nahuatl-Otomí	Mexico	?
5. Creole-Standard	Creole French-Stand. French	Haiti, Martinique Guadeloupe	?
"	Papiamentu-Dutch	Netherlands Antilles	?
6. Creole-Standard-Immigrant	Sranan-Dutch-Hindi	Surinam	?
7. Creole-Standard-LWC	Sranan-Dutch-English	Surinam	?
8. Creole-Stand.-Immigrant-LWC	Sranan-Dutch-Hindi-English	Surinam	?
9. Creole-Native	Saramakkan-Carib.	Surinam	?
10. Immigrant-Creole	Hindi-Sranan	Surinam	?

6. DESIDERATA

Investigations of the range and types of language contact in Latin America have barely begun. There is no work dealing with a bilingual situation in Latin America that approaches the comprehensiveness of Haugen's two volumes on the Norwegian language in America (1953).

As much of the published work shows, bilingual situations reflect important changes in social and cultural structure. Latin America has been one of the world's prime targets for recent immigration. The wide-spread process of urbanization has been throwing together not only the many disparate groups of Asiatic and European immigrants but also native Indians. According to Davies (1965), three quarters of the total population of Latin America lives in only one quarter of the land area. Consequently, there is a need for more study of urban language contact.

The study of native Indian languages has been carried on, but primarily by outside groups. The work of Hildebrandt (1958) is hopeful evidence of increasing interest on a local scale in native languages. Following the suggestion of Diebold (1962), there should be more rigorous testing of acculturation and changes in all multilingual areas. Investigations of diglossia outside of the Caribbean should be conducted on the model of Rona (1965). Detailed contrastive analyses should be undertaken of all the languages involved in multilingual situations in order to understand better the nature and degree of interference of each language on the other. There are many areas in Latin America where investigations of the influence of bilingualism on learning could be conducted on the model of Lambert, Havelka and Crosby (1958), and Fishman (1965). The four volumes of Werner Leopold's study of the language development of a bilingual child (1939-49) have no Latin American counterpart.

A systematic classification is needed of the information which has already been gathered. At present, it is scattered about in places that are often inaccessible.

To conclude, we would like to extend Diebold's suggestion for Mexico (1962) and make all of Latin America a laboratory for language contact.

7. BIBLIOGRAPHY

Haugen (1956) and the 600 items in Weinreich (1953) stand as the bibliographical monuments of bilingual studies including Latin America. Listed below are the sources to which we have referred in this paper and others that have come to our attention and are not included in Haugen. The listing includes several bibliographies that have appeared since Haugen such as Rubin (1963) and Pietryzk (1964).

Alleynde, Mervin C., 1961. 'Language and society in St. Lucia', *Carribbean Studies* 1.1-10.

Allsopp, Richard, 1958. 'The English language in British Guiana', *ELT* 12.59-66.

Argentina, 1947. *IV Censo General de la Nación, Tomo* 1 (Buenos Aires).

Bailey, Beryl, 1964. 'Some problems in the language teaching situation in Jamaica', in Roger W. Shuy (ed.) *Social dialects and language learning* 105-11 (Champaign. Ill.) See also Loffman, Beryl.

Bates, Margeret (ed.), 1957. *The migration of peoples to Latin America* (Washington, D.C.)

'Bilingualism and the bilingual child — A symposium', *MLJ* 49, Nos. 3 and 4 (March, April 1965).

Bouscaren, Anthony T., 1963. *International migrations since* 1945 (New York).

Brazil, 1956. *VI Recenseamento Geral do Brasil*, 1950 (Rio de Janeiro).

Bright, William, 1961. Abstracts from Latin American publications, *IJAL* 27.156-60, 251-4.

Caplow, Theodore, 1952. 'The modern Latin American city', in Sol Tax (ed.), *Acculturation in the Americas, Proceedings of the 29th International Congress of Americanists* 2.255-66.

Cadogan, Leon, 1948. 'En torno al bilingüísmo en el Paraguay', *Revista de Antropología* 6.23-30.

Carter, Marion Elizabeth, 1960. *Segmental Phonemes of Martinique Creole* (Georgetown Univ. M.S. thesis).

Castro, Américo, 1961. *La peculiaridad lingüística rioplatense y su sentido histórico* (Madrid).

Center of Latin American Studies, 1961. *Statistical Abstract of Latin America* (Los Angeles).

Churchill, Margaret Anne, *Haitian Creole: Linguistic analysis and proposed orthography* (Georgetown Univ. M.S. thesis).

Cohen, Marcel, 1952. *Les langues du monde* (Paris).

Davies, Howard (ed.), 1965. *South American Handbook* (London).

DeCamp, David, 1961. 'Social and geographical factors in Jamaican dialects', *Creole Language Studies* 2.61-84.

——, 1962. 'Creole language areas considered as multilingual communities', *Symposium on Multilingualism* 227-31.

Diebold, A. Richard, 1961a. *Bilingualism and biculturalism in a Huave community* (Yale Univ. Ph.D. thesis).

——, 1961b. 'Incipient bilingualism', *Lg* 37.97-112.

——, 1962a. 'Mexican and Guatemalan bilingualism', in Rice (ed.) 26-33.

——, 1962b. 'A laboratory for Language contact', *Anthropological Linguistics* 4.41-51.

Dillard, J. L., 1962. 'Purism and prescriptivism as applied to the Caribbean Creoles: a tentative classification', *Caribbean Studies* 4.3-10.

——, 1963. 'Toward a bibliography of works dealing with the creole languages of the Caribbean area, Louisiana, and the Guianas', *Caribbean Studies* 3:84-95.

——, 1964. 'English in the West Indies, or the West Indies in English?', *Harvard Educational Review* 34.312-15.

Epstein, M. (ed.), 1961. *The Statesman's Yearbook* (London).

Ferguson, Charles A., 1959. 'Diglossia', *Word* 15.325-40.

——, 1962. 'The language factor in national development', *Anthropological Linguistics* 4.23-7.

Fishman, Joshua A., 1965. 'Bilingualism, intelligence and language learning', *MLJ* 49.227-37.

Fries, Charles C. and Kenneth L. Pike, 1949. 'Coexistent Phonemic Systems', *Lg* 25.29-50; (reprinted in Bobbs-Merrill *Reprint Series in Languages and Linguistics*, L-26).

Garvin, Paul L. and Madelaine Mathiot, 1960. 'The urbanization of the Guaraní language: a problem in language and culture', in *Proceedings of the Fifth International Congress of Anthropological Sciences* (Philadelphia).

Goodman, Morris F., 1958. 'On the phonemics of the French creole of Trinidad', *Word* 14.208-12.

——, 1965. *A Comparative Study of Creole French Dialects* (The Hague).

Grossmann, Rudolf, 1926. *Das ausländische Sprachgut im Spanischen des Rio de la Plata* (Hamburg).

Gumperz, John F., 1962. 'Types of Linguistic Communities', *Anthropological Linguistics* 4.28-40.

Hall, Robert A., Jr., 1958. 'Creolized languages and genetic relationships', *Word* 14.367-73.

——, 1959. 'Pidgin Languages', *Scientific American* 200.124-34.

——, 1960. 'Nasalization in Haitian creole', *MLN* 65.474-78.

——, 1962. 'The life cycle of pidgin languages', *Lingua* 11.151-6.

——, 1965. *Pidgin and creole languages* (Ithaca, New York).

Hauch, Charles C., 1960. *Educational trends in the Caribbean: European affiliated areas* (U.S. Office of Education Bulletin No. 26) (Washington, D.C.).

Hellinga, W. G., 1955. *Language Problems in Surinam* (Amsterdam).

Haugen, Einar, 1953. *The Norwegian language in America* (Philadelphia).

——, 1956. *Bilingualism in the Americas* (American Dialect Society, Univ. of Alabama Press).

——, 1958. 'The phoneme in bilingual description', *LL* 7.17-24.

——, 1965. 'Linguistics and language planning', (mimeographed).

Hildebrandt, Martha, 'La lingüística descriptiva aplicada a las lenguas indígenas de Venezuela', *Boletín Indigenista Venezolano* 1-4.109-12.

Hockett, Charles F., 1958. *A course in modern linguistics* (New York).

Horth, Auguste, 1949. *Le patois guyanais* (Cayenne).

Jones, Daniel, 1950. *The phoneme: its nature and use* (Cambridge).

Jourdain, Elodie, 1956. *Du français aux parlers créoles* (Paris).

Key, Harold and Mary Key, 1961. *Bolivian Indian Tribes: Bibliography and Map of Present Language Distribution* (Summer Institute of Linguistics).

Key, Mary, 1964. *Bibliography IV: Indian Tribes of Chile, Argentina, Paraguay, and Uruguay* (Summer Institute of Linguistics).

Krause, Annemarie, 1962. 'Mennonites in the Paraguayan Chaco', *Geographical Review* 599-600.

Lambert, Wallace E., J. Havelka and C. Crosby, 1958. 'The influence of language — acquisition contexts on bilingualism', *Journal of Abnormal Psychology* 56.239-44.

Lambert, Wallace E., 1955. 'Measurement of the linguistic dominance of bilinguals', *Journal of Abnormal and Social Psychology* 50.197-200.

——, 1963. 'Psychological approaches to the study of language, Part II', *MLJ* 47.114-21.

León-Portilla, Miguel, 1959. 'Panorama de la población indígena de México', *América Indígena* 19.1-61.

Leopold, Werner, 1939-49. *Speech Development of a bilingual child*, 4 vols. (Evanston-Chicago).

Le Page, Robert B., 1958. 'General outlines of creole English dialects in the British Caribbean', *Orbis* 6.373-91 and 7.54-64.

——, (ed.), 1960. *Creole language studies I* (London).

——, 1961. *Creole language studies II* (London).

Lichtveld, Lou, 1965. 'National language planning', (mimeographed).

Loftman, Beryl I., 1953. *Creole languages of the Caribbean area* (Columbia Univ. M.A. thesis). See also Bailey, Beryl.

Loriot, James, 1964. *A selected bibliography of comparative American Indian Linguistics* (reprinted from *IJAL* 30:1).

Mackey, William F., 1962. 'The description of bilingualism', *Canadian Journal of Linguistics* 7.51-85.

McQuown, Norman A., 1955. 'The indigenous languages of Latin America', *American Anthropologist* 57.501-70.

——, 1961. 'Los lenguajes indígenas de América Latina', *Revista inter-americana de ciencias sociales* 1.37-207 (transl. of McQuown, 1955).

——, 1962. 'Indian and Ladino bilingualism: sociocultural contrasts in Chiapas, Mexico', *MSLL* 15.85-106.

Mexico, 1962. *VIII Censo general de población*, 1960. *Resumen general* (Mexico City).

Moraes, Octavio Alexander de, 1957. 'Immigration into Brazil: a statistical statement and related aspects', in Margaret Bates (ed.) 49-78.

Morgan, Raleigh, 1959. 'Structural sketch of Saint Martin creole', *Anthropological Linguistics* 1.20-4f (issue No. 8).

——, 1960. 'The Lexicon of Saint Martin creole', *Anthropological Linguistics* 2.7-29 (issue No. 1).

——, 1964. 'Saint Martin creole and genetic relationships', in Albert H. Marckwardt (ed.), *Studies in languages and linguistics* (Ann Arbor, Mich.).

Olmsted, David, 1953. 'Comparative Notes on Yoruba and Lucumí,' *Lg* 29.157-64.

Peal, Elizabeth and Wallace E. Lambert, 1962. *The relation of bilingualism to intelligence* (American Psychological Association 16-27).

Pietrzyk, Alfred (ed.), 1964. *Selected Titles in Sociolinguistics* (mimeographed) (Washington, D.C.).

Pike, Kenneth L., 1960. 'Toward a theory of change and bilingualism', *SIL* 25.1-7.

Pompilus, Pradel, 1961. *La langue française en Haïti* (Paris).

Racine, Daniel, 1965. 'Le créole dans les mers Caraïbes', to appear in D. G. Stuart (ed.), *Preliminary Reconnaissance of the Languages of the World* (*Encyclopédie de la Pléiade*).

Racine, Marie Marcelle Buteau, 1965. *A linguistic study of southern Haitian Creole: phonology* (Howard Univ. M.A. thesis, Washington, D.C.).

Ribeiro, Darcy, 1957. 'The tasks of the ethnologist and the linguist in Brazil', *International Social Science Bulletin* 9.298-312.

Rice, Frank (ed.), 1962. *Study of the role of second languages in Asia, Africa, and Latin America* (Washington, D.C.).

Rodrigues, Aryón D., 1958. 'Classification of Tupi-Guaraní', *IJAL* 24.231-4.

Rona, José Pedro, 1965. *El dialecto 'fronterizo' del Norte del Uruguay* (Montevideo).

Rosales, Juan de Diós, 1959. 'Indígenas de Guatemala', *América Indígena* 19.115-124.

Rosenblat, Angel, 1954. *La población indígena y el mestizaje en América* (Buenos Aires).

Rubin, Joan, 1961. 'Bilingualism in Paraguay', *Anthropological Linguistics* 4.52-58.

——, 1962. 'Bilingualism in Peru', (mimeographed).

——, 1963a. *National Bilingualism in Paraguay* (Yale Univ. Ph.D. thesis, to be published in revised form by Mouton).

——, 1963b. 'A bilbiography of Caribbean creole languages', *Caribbean Studies* 2.51-61.

Rycroft, W. Stanley and Myrtle M. Clemmer, 1962. *A study of urbanization in Latin America* (Commission on Ecumenical Mission and Relations, United Presbyterian Church in the U.S.A., New York).

Sawyer, Janet B., 'Aloofness from Spanish influence in Texas English', *Word* 15.270-81.

Stewart, William A., 1962a. 'Creole Languages in the Caribbean', in Rice (ed.), 34-53.

——, 1962b. 'The functional distribution of creole and French in Haiti', *MSLL* 15.149-59.

——, 1966. 'A sociolinguistic typology for describing national multilingualism' (mimeographed) to appear in Joshua A. Fishman (ed.), *A Reader in Sociolinguistics*.

Stokes, William S., 1959. *Latin American Politics* (New York).

Suárez, Jorge Alberto and Emma G. de, 1961. *A Description of Colloquial Guaraní* (Cornell Univ. Ph.D. thesis).

Symposium on multilingualism (Brazzaville, 1962).

Taylor, Douglas, 1951. *The Black Caribs of British Honduras* (New York).

——, 1956. 'Language contact in the West Indies', *Word* 12.399-414.

——, 1958a. 'More on the consonantal system of Island Carib', *Word* 14.71-83.

——, 1958b. 'Lines by a Black Carib', *IJAL* 24.324-5.

——, 1965. review of Goodman (1964) in *IJAL* 31.363-70.

Tempesta, Luciano, 1965. 'Italiani nel Sud America', *Idea* 10.617-8.

Tovar, Antonio, 1961. *Catálogo de las lenguas de América del Sur* (Buenos Aires).

Unión Panamericana, 1964a. *Estudio Social de América Latina:* 1962. (Washington, D.C.).

——, 1964b. *Caracteristicas de la estructura demográfica de los paises americanos* (Washington, D.C.).

United Nations, 1957. *Report on the world social situation.* E/CN 5:324 (New York).

Valdman, Albert, 1965. review of Pompilus, 1961 in *IJAL* 31.374-8.

Vildomec, Veroboj, 1963. *Multilingualism.*

Voorhoeve, Jan, 1962. *Sranan Syntax* (Amsterdam).

Wagner, M. L., 1949. *Lingua e dialetti dell'America spagnola* (Florence).

Weinreich, Uriel, 1953. *Languages in contact* (New York, third printing, 1964, The Hague).

——, 1958. 'Research frontiers in bilingualism studies', *Proceedings of the Eighth International Congress of Linguists* (Oslo).

Zephir, Jacques-J., 1965. 'La situation de la langue française en Haïti', *Revue de L'université Laval* 19.

LITERACY

YOLANDA LASTRA

0. Universal primary education is the law in most countries in the Americas, yet only about half of the population is literate. Illiteracy is the concern of many people: politicians, economists, educators, missionaries. Linguists have played a relatively minor role, but their contribution has, nevertheless, been important. It is the aim of this paper to point out this contribution while describing the literacy situation in Ibero-America and the Caribbean.[1]

The word 'literacy' means different things to different people. A person who knows how to read and write his own name may be considered literate, but to literacy experts a literate person is one who is 'functionally' literate. In other words, an individual who has mastered the writing system of his language to the extent that he can handle it efficiently in his daily life. Literacy is thus a relative matter, because a peasant who can slowly make out the directions on a fertilizer bag, can sign his name, and write an occasional letter is functionally literate in his community, whereas if he moved to a large urban center he might be considered illiterate.

In what follows, it is important to bear this relativity in mind, even though for practical purposes it is becoming customary to consider a person literate when he has finished four years of primary school or its equivalent. Another factor to bear in mind is that a person who attended school and who never applied what he learned may easily relapse into illiteracy. The statistics below, thus, are related to reality, but may not in fact describe it.

The primary school systems which should ideally be in charge of making every citizen literate are discussed first. Since in practically every country it is necessary to supplement primary education with adult literacy programs or with national literacy campaigns, these are discussed next. It is comparatively easy to educate people in the official language when they are native speakers, but in most countries there are minorities that speak a language other than the official one. Governments approach this problem in different ways: by ignoring it, by trying to teach the minorities the national language and then literacy, or by trying to make them bilingual and biliterate. Private institutions and international organizations have in many instances made it their responsibility to educate minorities. Their activities as well as those of national govern-

[1] A survey such as the present one would have been impossible without the cooperation of many persons and organizations that supplied information and materials. Their help is gratefully acknowledged. Thanks are also due Miss Joy Varley who read the manuscript.

ments are described in turn. The application of linguistics has largely been confined to the problem of making minorities biliterate. The contribution of linguistics is pointed out when appropriate, and the relatively scant literature of a technical sort which has any bearing on the relationship between language and writing, and linguistics and literacy, is reviewed. Finally, some further applications of our discipline to literacy in Latin America and the Caribbean are pointed out.

The countries in the area are discussed from north to south from Mexico through Central America and South America, then north again to the Hispanic and non-Hispanic Caribbean.

1. PRIMARY EDUCATION

1.1. *Ibero-America*

1.11. The legal basis for compulsory education in Latin America was laid down in the nineteenth century, but this principle has only recently begun to become a reality. In 1948 there was a conference of Latin American educators held in Caracas under the sponsorship of UNESCO and OAS at which it was decided that illiteracy should be dealt with at the primary school level and that the schooling of children should take priority over literacy campaigns. At succeeding seminars in Rio de Janeiro and Montevideo in subsequent years, the primary school problem was carefully studied. At the Second Conference of Ministers of Education (Lima, 1956) it was decided to generalize primary schooling. A Third Conference of Ministers of Education was held in Bogotá in 1963. All these meetings have contributed towards the awakening of public interest in primary education and as a result there has been substantial improvement.

The description which follows is drawn primarily from *La educación primaria en América Latina* (1963), prepared by UNESCO and distributed by OAS in mimeographed form, and on the reports of the ministers presented at the Bogotá Conference.

Elementary education is free and compulsory in every Latin American country, but the regulations are not enforced where there are not enough facilities. Almost every country provides for 6 years of schooling, but some provide shorter courses in rural areas. The ages for compulsory attendance vary from country to country. (See Table 1). Rural education is usually inferior; enrollment is lower, and desertion, absenteeism, and irregular attendance are higher in rural than in urban areas. There is a direct correlation between the adult illiteracy rate and the percentage of rural population in a given country. (See Table 2). The percentage of children enrolled in school in Latin America is shown on Table 1.

Enrollments have risen 31% from 1956 to 1961, but this increase reflects a larger enrollment in the lower grades; the percentage of those who finish primary school is about 20%. (See Table 3)

TABLE 1

*Primary School in Ibero-America and the Caribbean**

	Year	Compul-sory	Percent enrol-led**	Ages	Rural diff. from urban	Number of grades***
MEXICO AND CENTRAL AMERICA						
Mexico	1961	Yes	93	6-15		6
Guatemala	1961	Yes	58	7-14		6
El Salvador	1961	Yes	122	7-14		6
Honduras	1961	Yes	76	7-15	Yes	6,3
Nicaragua	1961	Yes	66	7-14		6
Costa Rica	1961	Yes	112	7-14		6
Panama	1961	Yes	104	7-15		6
SOUTH AMERICA						
Colombia	1961	Yes	73	7-14	Yes	5, 2-4
Venezuela	1961	Yes	114	7-14		6
Ecuador	1961	Yes	92	6-14		6
Peru	1961	Yes	85	6-16		6
Bolivia	1961	Yes	93	7-14	Yes	6,4
Chile	1961	Yes	101	7-15	Yes	6,4
Argentina	1961	Yes	119	6-14		7
Paraguay	1961	Yes	105	7-14		6
Uruguay	1961	Yes	184	6-14	Yes	6
Brazil	1961	Yes	80	7-12		5,4
HISPANIC CARIBBEAN						
Cuba	1961	Yes	101	6-12	Yes	6
Dominican Republic	1961	Yes	100	7-14		6
Puerto Rico	1961	Yes		8-14		6
NON-HISPANIC CARIBBEAN						
Haiti	1961	Yes	44	7-14		
British Affiliated areas						
Jamaica		No	80-85	7-15		
Trinidad and Tobago		No	88	5-15		
Bahamas		Yes		14		
Bermuda		Yes		7-12		
British Guiana		Yes	90	6-14		
British Honduras	1964	Yes	95	5-14		
British Virgin Islands		No		5-15		
Barbados		No	98			
Turks and Caicos		Yes				
Leeward Islands		Yes	98	5-14		
Windward Islands		No	70			

TABLE 1 *(continued)*

	Year	Compul-sory	Percent enrol-led**	Ages	Rural diff. from urban	Number of grades***
French Areas						
Guadeloupe	1950	Yes	80	6-14		
Martinique	1950	Yes	99	6-14		
French Guiana	1950	Yes	98	6-14		
Dutch Areas						
Surinam	1955	Yes	80	7-14		
Netherlands Antilles	1962	No	95			

* Sources: OAS, *América en Cifras*; UNESCO, *International Guide*; Hauch (1960); Netherlands Antilles Inspector of Education; Jolly, 'Education'.

** Figures above 100 mean people above the normal age limits attend primary school.

*** The second figure refers to rural schools.

TABLE 2

*Latin America: Income per capita, percentage of rural population, and illiteracy (1950)**

		Percentage of adult illiterates	Income per capita (U.S.cy)
Illiteracy Rate Less than 25% Average Percentage of Rural Population: 40%	Argentina	13	300-449
	Uruguay	15	300-449
	Chile	19	150-299
	Costa Rica	20	100-149
	Cuba	20	300-449
Illiteracy Rate 25-50% Average Percentage of Rural Population: 62%	Panama	30	150-299
	Paraguay	34	-100
	Colombia	37	100-149
	Mexico	38	100-149
	Ecuador	44	-100
	Venezuela	47	300-449
	Brazil	50	100-149
Illiteracy Rate Above 50% Average Percentage of Rural Population: 74%	Peru	53	100-149
	Dominican Republic	57	-100
	El Salvador	60	100-149
	Nicaragua	61	100-149
	Honduras	64	-100
	Bolivia	67	-100
	Guatemala	70	-100
	Haiti	89	-100

* UNESCO (1963), *La educación primaria en América Latina.*

TABLE 3

*Percentage of Children who Finish Primary Schools in Some Latin American Countries**

Panama	1961	31.2%
Chile	1956	24.8%
Venezuela	1959	22.7%
Costa Rica	1955	22.2%
Brazil	1959	18.7%
Peru	1955	18.4%
Colombia	1958	14.2%
Ecuador	1958	14.0%
El Salvador	1957	10.5%
Honduras	1961	6.5%
Nicaragua	1959	5.0%
Haiti	1960	3.2%

* UNESCO (1963), *La educación primaria en América Latina.*

Table 4, which includes the countries of the non-Hispanic Caribbean, summarizes the enrollment situation and classifies countries in three groups: (A) those with total enrollment; (B) those with enrollment of 75% or above; (C) those with enrollment below 75%.

TABLE 4

*Enrollment in Primary School**

Group A	Group B	Group C
100% enrollment of children; minimum absenteeism	Enrollment above 75%; minimum urban absenteeism; considerable rural absenteeism	Enrollment below 75%
El Salvador	Mexico	Guatemala
Costa Rica	Honduras	Nicaragua
Panama	Ecuador	Colombia
Venezuela	Peru	Haiti
Chile	Bolivia	Windward Islands
Argentina	Brazil	
Paraguay	Jamaica	
Uruguay	Trinidad and Tobago	
Cuba	British Guiana	
Dominican Republic	British Honduras	
	Barbados	
	Leeward Islands	
	Guadeloupe	
	Martinique	
	French Guiana	
	Surinam	
	Netherlands Antilles	

* Source for Latin America: UNESCO (1963), *La educación primaria en América Latina.*

With the increase in the number of children attending school, there has been an accompanying decrease of the quality of teaching reflected in the high number of non-certified teachers, which averages 44% (0% in Argentina, 7% in Panama, to 70% in Bolivia and Colombia). The teacher-to-student ratio is generally low (the average is thirty-six students per teacher for Latin America, twenty-three for Argentina, fifty-six for the Dominican Republic), but teachers are not evenly distributed throughout urban and rural areas, and neither are schools, which through poor planning are often built where there is no urgent need for them.

Policy and administration are under Ministries of Education, which are very similar in structure throughout the area. Political upheavals often disturb the education process, especially in those countries where the teaching personnel is not protected by law against becoming unemployed as a result of changes in administration.

The role of private education is very important. About 8% of primary school children are enrolled in private institutions. The proportion varies greatly from country to country. These schools, usually sponsored by religious bodies, follow official programs and are visited by ministry inspectors. Their role is very valuable in remote areas where mission schools are often the only ones available.

Population growth in Latin America (2.5% per year) is higher than in any other area in the world, and the school age population represents 20% of the total, while in Europe it varies between 12 and 15%. The increase in population makes it difficult for Latin American countries with their existing economic resources to supply the necessary schools. Adult illiteracy is the result of lack of schooling or of insufficient or inadequate schooling. There is a correlation between the per capita income of a country on the one hand, and the percentage of its adult illiterates on the other. The correlation is not by any means a cause and effect one, however, as can be seen on Table 2 by taking Paraguay and Venezuela as examples. The former, in the group of countries with low per capita income (less than $ 100) has a comparatively low illiteracy rate (34%) while the latter, in the group of countries with high per capita income ($ 300-449) has an illiteracy rate of 47.8%.[2]

1.12. After the adoption of the Constitution of 1917 by *Mexico*, the Department of Education (Secretaría de Educación Pública, SEP) was organized along its present lines and a series of reforms designed to make education available to all social classes was instituted. The number of schools and the percentage of children of school age enrolled has been steadily increasing since the Revolution (1910) and efforts continue to be made to improve both the quantity and quality of education. Schools are municipal, state, or federal, but matters of policy are all centralized, and the government supervises and inspects all private schools that wish to be officially recognized.

The main problem in education faced by *Honduras* is that among the rural population, which constitutes about 69% of the total, schooling is not considered very im-

[2] For a discussion of the relationship between literacy and economic development see: Adam Curle (1964) and Alfred S. Hayes (1965).

portant. Lack of school attendance is a grave problem and only about 16% of the children finish primary school. There is also a great need for certified teachers since only about 44% have normal school diplomas. Similar problems exist in *Nicaragua*, where 70% of the teachers are uncertified and there are only enough schools for 50% of the children of school age because of lack of funds, and in *Panama*, where there are not enough elementary schools and many do not offer all the primary grades.

In *Colombia* illiteracy is caused by insuffient number of schools and lack of attendance. Out of 100 children only about 19 go through fourth grade and only 14 through fifth grade. These problems are specially true of rural areas.

In *Peru* there is a great need for primary schools. Accordingly many small rural one-grade schools are being built and associated to schools in the same area which offer all primary grades.

Two authorities are responsible for elementary education in *Bolivia:* The Ministry of Education, in charge of urban schools, and the Ministerio de Asuntos Campesinos (Ministry of Peasant Affairs). The percentage of children attending schools is 81% in the urban areas and 43% in the rural ones, primarily because of lack of schools. In the decade between 1951 and 1961 some 3,000 schools were built in rural areas, usually on the peasants' own initiative, but many more are still to be built. The difference between urban and rural schools is that in the rural areas many schools offer only four grades, and only the 'nucleos escolares', to which the smaller schools are associated, offer the complete six grade cycle. Education for the large number of Quechua and Aymara speaking children continues to be in the official language in spite of the fact that the 1956 Bolivian code of education states that literacy must be initiated in the mother tongue.

There are 2,589 schools in *Paraguay* when there should be more than twice as many according to the report of the Ministerio de Educación y de Culto (Ministry of Education and Religion) to the UNESCO-IBE Commission in 1964.[3]

In *Uruguay*, according to a very detailed statistical report prepared by the Comisión de Desarrollo e Inversiones Económicas, *Informe preliminar sobre la situación de la educación en el Uruguay* (Montevideo, 1960) the problem of absenteeism in primary schools is declining, but that of desertion is still a major one. 59.1% of the pupils attending primary school leave without finishing the 6 grades. About one third of these have finished fourth grade. Many children repeat one, two, or three grades; the repeaters usually come from the lower classes and the number is larger in rural areas. Deserters and repeaters who don't reach sixth grade by the time they can legally leave school become potential functional illiterates. Thus we see that even in a country like Uruguay with a high primary school enrollment and a low official illiteracy rate (9.5%) there is still a large number of functional illiterates in rural areas.

A national three-year plan for economic and social development (1963-65) is now in effect in *Brazil*. The following figures are available: 100,000 new school rooms are

[3] UNESCO and International Bureau of Education (1964).

necessary by 1970 for 6,000,000 pupils; 600,000 children finish four grades every year; it would be necessary to have 2,000,000 children have that much schooling.

During Trujillo's rule in the *Dominican Republic* there was a program to create two-year rural schools for both children and adults, called emergency schools, to combat the illiteracy problem. In 1945, 500 such schools were in operation; and in 1954 there were 1,271 with 66,811 pupils.

Elementary education in *Cuba* is free and compulsory for children from the ages of 6 to 12. There are six grades in primary schools. The system of education has undergone considerable reform since 1959, The Ministry of Education is responsible for general policy, but the system has been decentralized. Enrollment has risen considerably in recent years. In 1958 about 737,000 were attending primary school. This number represented about half of the children between the ages of 7 and 14. By 1962 about four fifths of the children of the same age group were enrolled.

1.2. *Non-Hispanic Caribbean*

1.21. The non-Hispanic Caribbean includes Haiti, an independent republic, Trinidad-and-Tobago, and Jamaica, two independent countries which are members of the Commonwealth, and the islands and mainland territories which have close political ties or are political dependencies of the United Kingdom, France, or the Netherlands.

The British affiliated areas, aside from Jamaica and Trinidad and Tobago, are British Honduras and British Guiana on the mainland in Central and South America respectively, the Bahamas and Bermuda which do not consider themselves Caribbean territories, the British Virgin Islands, and the island countries of the Federation of the West Indies, namely Barbados, Turks and Caicos, the Leeward Islands (Antigua, Montserrat, St. Kitts-Nevis-Anguilla), and the Windward Islands (Dominica, Grenada, St. Lucia, St. Vincent, St. Helena).

The French affiliated areas are three overseas departments of France: French Guiana, on the South American mainland, Guadeloupe (two main islands and smaller dependencies), and the island of Martinique.

The Netherlands affiliated areas constitute two political units co-equal with the Netherlands proper since 1954. These are Surinam, on the South American mainland and the Netherlands Antilles which includes the Netherlands Leeward Islands (Curaçao, Aruba, and Bonaire) and the Netherlands Windward Islands (Saba, St. Eustatius, and part of St. Maarten).

Awareness of the basic similarities and needs of the whole area and a desire for economic and cultural cooperation led to the organization of the Caribbean Commission in 1946 by the Netherlands, the United Kingdom, France, and the United States. The Commission established a Secretariat in Trinidad to serve as a center of information in matters such as education. The Fifth Session of the West Indian Conference (1952) recommended that UNESCO be asked to assist the Commission in the field of adult education including literacy training. As a result a UNESCO consultant, H. W. Howes, prepared a *Study of Fundamental, Adult, Literacy, and Community Education in the West Indies* (1955) for the Sixth Session held at Puerto Rico in 1955. A Conference on Education and Small Scale Farming, jointly sponsored by the Commission and UNESCO, recommended that the Sixth Session consider the establishment of a Clearing House for information regarding materials on primary and adult education. Part of its report, dealing with common problems in education and community development, is contained in *Education in the Caribbean* (1956). The Clearing House was set up at the Commission's Secretariat, and it prepared a *Bibliography of Education in the Caribbean* (1959). Unfortunately, the Caribbean Commission has now been dissolved, apparently for political reasons, and the Clearing House was closed down in 1956. UNESCO's *International Guide to Educational Documentation* 1955-60 (1963) provides essential information on the systems of education in this region and Hauch's *Educational Trends in the Caribbean* (1960) includes an excellent summary of the cultural background.

The territories of the non-Hispanic Caribbean share certain political and economic patterns which co-occur with socio-linguistic patterns typical of the area, which give rise to peculiar education problems which have not been adequately met. Generally speaking, the territories have strong cultural, political, and economic ties with Europe, under-developed rural economies coupled with rapid demographic growth, mixed ethnic composition with a large negro element, and official languages (English, French, or Dutch) which are seldom the languages used by the people in their every-day activites (a creole, a non-European imported language, or, less often, an Amerindian language) The problem of teaching people an official language which is not their mother tongue has not been met squarely in any of these areas, although the linguistic naiveté of the authorities varies from country to country: In the French areas the use of the vernacular is forbidden in the classroom whereas in Surinam provision is made for bilingual schools, and the government sponsors a language research institute. In countries with such cultural and linguistic heterogeneity, a low standard of living, and comparatively small budgets devoted to education, one can hardly be surprised to find inadequacies in the education systems and a high percentage of illiteracy.

1.22. The Constitution of 1957, promulgated in *Haiti* shortly after Duvalier took office as president, declares education to be free and compulsory. The period of obligation is declared by law to be between the ages of seven and fourteen, but this provision is not enforced. Education is under the authority of the Minister of Education who is an appointed official. Local communities have no responsibility for the administration of schools. There are a number of church schools which receive small government subsidies.

In 1961 about 33% of the 736,000 children of school age were enrolled in primary school. This is the lowest percentage in the hemisphere. The number of children who finish primary school is much smaller than the number of children who begin. This is particularly true of rural areas where, for instance, in 1962, 60,000 children were enrolled in first grade (about 60% of the total enrollment) and only 700 in sixth grade.[4]

There are not enough schools and not enough teachers; about 15% of the instructors have normal-school diplomas. The teacher — pupil ratio reaches extremely high proportions in rural areas where there are groups of 200-250 children. Those who attend school do not necessarily learn to read. Instruction is given in French, the official language, even though the majority of the population speaks only Creole. No attempt is made to teach children reading in the vernacular or to teach them French before attempting to teach them to read it. Some educators in Haiti are aware of the necessity of changing the system, but they have been faced with the political power of an elite who profit from the ignorance of the masses and prefer to insist on the prestige of French. Due to the lack of schools, the poor quality of the instruction, as well as the growth of the population, the number of adult illiterates increases every year.

Education is free in *Jamaica*, but compulsory (for children between 7 and 15) only in certain areas. In *Trinidad and Tobago* education for children between 5 and 15 is free. At the time of the 1960 census about 75% of the population between 5 and 19 where attending school. The language of instruction of children is English, even though a large part of the population speaks a French-based creole.

In *British Honduras* education is free and compulsory for children 5-14, and this is enforced wherever schools are available. The medium of instruction is English even though a large number of people speak Spanish, Maya, or Chekchí. The population is estimated to be 103,000 and, according to the data furnished by the Ministry of Education, school enrollment represents 95% of the children of school age. This figure seems an extremely high one when one considers that, according to the estimated figure of the American Indianist Institute, when the total population was 64,300 the Indian population numbered 14,500 and there seems to be no adequate provision for the education of the Indians.

In *British Guiana* the Ministry of Community Development and Education is responsible for education policy. Primary education is free and compulsory for children between six and fourteen years of age. The language of about 90% of the population is English. There are Amerindian tribes who speak several languages and who have not been in any way assimilated to the culture of the rest of the population.

The British Caribbean in general has the problem of an increasing population which has to be met by building schools and training teachers. The low enrollment ratios are due to lack of schools in some areas and in others to the fact that education is not compulsory (See Table 1). There are also low attendance records specially in the rural areas. Church schools play a very important role throughout the area. They are usually inspected and subsidized by the government in question.

Martinique and *Guadeloupe* are heavily populated islands with an agricultural economy. The majority of the people are of African descent and speak a French-based creole. In *French Guiana* 90% of the population estimated at 31,000 in 1960, lives on

[4] Edouard C. Paul (1965) 113.

the coast and also speaks a French-based creole. In the interior there are Amerindians (Carib, Arawak, and Tupi-Guarani) and Bush negroes.

Education is free and compulsory between the ages of 6 and 14 in all three departments, but not enforceable in areas where there are no facilities. The cost of education is largely paid by the French national budget, and most of the schools are government-run and not denominational as in the British and Dutch areas. Martinique is the most advanced of the three departments. There has been a tremendous increase in school enrollment, but not in school attendance. At the 1957 West Indian Conference it was remarked that the curriculum was not suited to the Caribbean environment and, according to Hauch, the situation has not changed since: The programs are exactly the same as in France. French is the only medium of instruction and a large number of children spend several years in the first grade and about one fourth of the total never go beyond fourth grade. This means that, official statistics notwithstanding, the number of functional illiterates is extremely high.

Education, compulsory for children aged 7-12, is a responsibility shared by the government and private organizations in *Surinam*. In 1955 enrollment was satisfactory in the urban areas, but not in the rural ones where children worked in the farms and schools were overcrowded.

The complex linguistic situation and its relation to educational policies was described by Hellinga in *Language Problems in Surinam* (1951). More recently, Lichtveld's 'National Language Planning' (1964) is an excellent socio-linguistic description of Surinam. Dutch is the official language and the language of education, but it is spoken natively by about 1.5% of the population. There are about 38% Creoles, native speakers of Sranantongo, an English-based creole; 35% Hindustani, speakers of Hindi-Urdu; 13% Javanese; 1.5% Chinese. These groups live in the costal belt. The interior is populated by Bush negroes (about 9% of the population), descendants of run-away slaves who speak Aukan and Saramakan and by small Carib tribes.

Hellinga found that the denominational schools of the interior left much to be desired because the subjects taught were not adequate for the environment. He also found that the results of entrance examinations to schools of higher education showed insufficient command of Dutch on the part of all non-native speakers, and he advocated bilingual schools. According to Howes, however, the situation in the interior was improving in 1955 and, according to Lichtveld, the matter of deficient knowledge of Dutch is being solved by trying to make the population bilingual at the pre-primary school level. A Linguistic Bureau has been created with partial support from the government. It advises the education authorities on linguistic matters and carries on important research.

Primary education is not compulsory in the *Netherlands Antilles*, but about 95% of the children of school age are enrolled in schools. Dutch is the medium of instruction and the programs are practically the same as those in Holland. Children are taught English and Spanish in the last two grades in elementary school. The vernacular, however, is Papiamento.

2. LITERACY CAMPAIGNS AND ADULT[5] EDUCATION PROGRAMS

2.1. *Latin America*

2.11. *Mexico and Central America*

Besides combating illiteracy at the primary school level there have been a number of adult literacy programs and campaigns. For a summary of illiteracy rates, see Table 5, following.

TABLE 5

*Adult Illiteracy in Ibero-America and the Caribbean**

	Year	Total Population (thousands)	Adult Population (thousands)	Adult Illiterates (thousands)	Percentage of adult illiterates
MEXICO AND CENTRAL AMERICA					
Mexico	1960	34,923	19,471	6,742	34.6
Guatemala	1950	2,805	1,611	1,138	70.6
El Salvador	1961	2,511	1,694	879	52
Honduras	1961	1,866	969	537	55.4
Nicaragua	1950	1,060	599	369	61.6
Costa Rica	1963	1,333	868	126	14.6
Panama	1960	1,075	607	162	26.7
SOUTH AMERICA					
Colombia	1951	11,334	6,450	2,429	37.6
Venezuela	1961	7,523	4,153	1,309	34.2
Ecuador	1950	3,197	1,843	815	43.3
Peru	1961	9,747	5,109	2,014	39.4
Bolivia	1950	3,019	1,633	1,109	67.9
Chile	1960	7,375	4,440	717	16.2
Argentina	1960	21,247	14,199	1,221	8.6
Paraguay	1950	1,397	747	255	34.2
Uruguay	1950	2,407	1,650	250	15
Brazil	1950	51,976	30,249	15,272	50.6
HISPANIC CARIBBEAN					
Cuba	1962	6,933			3.9
Dominican Republic	1950	2,131	1,185	677	57.1
Puerto Rico	1960	2,349	1,345	261	19.4

* Sources: *UN Demographic Yearbook* 1963; Jolly, 'Education'; UNESCO, *World Illiteracy at Mid-century*; OEA, *América en Cifras*; Paul, *L'Alphabétisation*; communications from the Ministries of Education of British Honduras and the Netherlands Antilles.

[5] *Adult* usually means 15 years and over.

TABLE 5 *(continued)*

	Year	Total population (thousands)	Adult population (thousands)	Adult illiterates (thousands)	Percentage of adult illiterates
NON-HISPANIC CARIBBEAN					
Haiti	1965	4,738	2,808		80
British Affiliated Areas					
Jamaica	1960	1,609	947	171	18
Trinidad and Tobago	1950	632	380	76-95	20-25
Bahamas	1950	79	49	10-12	20-25
Bermuda	1960	42	28	.5	2
British Guiana	1950	420	260	52-65	20-25
British Honduras	1965	103			6.5
British Virgin Islands	1960	7	4	.2	7.1
Barbados	1950	209	140	7-14	5-10
Turks and Caicos	1960	5	3	.2	6.9
Leeward Islands					
Antigua	1960	54	30	3	11.3
Montserrat	1960	12	6	1	19.5
St. Kitts	1960	56	30	3	11.8
Windward Islands	1950	276	160	48-56	30-35
French Areas					
Guadeloupe	1950	289	180	54-63	30-35
Martinique	1950	273	170	43-51	25-30
French Guiana	1950	26	16	5-6	30-35
Dutch Areas					
Surinam	1950	219	140	35-42	25-30
Netherlands Antilles					
Curaçao	1960	125			10.7
Aruba	1960	57			15
Bonaire	1960	5.8			23
St Maarten	1960	2.7			25
St Eustatius	1965	1			23
Saba	1965	1			31

In *Mexico* the percentage of illiteracy was 58% in 1940; it was 36% in 1963. A national literacy campaign of the 'each one teach one' (see 4.23) type was begun in 1944. In a few months it became clear that the results were very poor. Fortunately, many literacy centers were established. There were 11,889 in 1962 as well as 100 reading rooms furnished with appropriate materials for new literates. It is claimed that 6,000,000 adults became literate between 1944 and 1963, but the author of a report on Mexico in CREFAL,[6] *Cursillo sobre alfabetización funcional: Informes sobre nueve países* (1964) doubts that these new literates are functional literates.

[6] CREFAL: Centro Regional de Educación Fundamental para el Desarrollo de la Comunidad en América Latina. See 4.13.

On February 24, 1965, a new National Literacy Campaign was begun. It is directed by the Literacy Department of the SEP which requests and receives help from private enterprise, including the press, radio, and television, the army, normal schools, and school children. Its aim is to eradicate illiteracy by 1970. For purposes of the campaign, the nation has been divided in regions and intensive work has begun in four of these. The first phase of the campaign consisted in locating illiterates (there are nine million throughout the country) with the help of fifth and sixth grade school children whose role it was to persuade them to register at the literacy centers. Regular teachers are employed at these centers which offer a ten-month course. The primer uses the syllable approach, but it could conceivably be used with the word approach. Simple directions were given in *Excelsior*, a Mexico City newspaper, which printed a lesson a day, to use the primer with either approach.

Action to promote literacy among adults in *Guatemala* became regular and official in 1948 when the National Literacy Department was created. It set up evening schools which made about 3,000 adults literate in each ten-month course. Due to administrative instability, however, the illiteracy rate which was 65% in 1940 increased to 71% in 1950. Efforts are being made to cope with the problem, but funds from the national budget are not assigned to adult literacy work. Many private institutions set up literacy centers and the army also carries on some work. USIS produces a television literacy program in which the official eclectic primer *Juan* is used.

In *El Salvador* the illiteracy rate decreased by about 8% from 1950 to 1960. The Ministry of Education operated 400 literacy centers from 1961 to 1962 where some 14,000 people were made literate. In 1962 a National Campaign was launched with national budget funds by the Department of Fundamental Education. It was to last five years. Private institutions take part in the campaign and the Catholic Church operates radio schools. In 1962 there were 1,042 such schools which made 1,821 persons literate. These represent 85% of those enrolled. Literacy teachers receive short training courses. The primer, *Vamos a leer*, uses the word approach.

Campaigns against illiteracy began early in the twentieth century in *Honduras*. An intensive one was initiated in 1942 and technical assistance of foreign experts was sought. In 1944 Laubach gave a series of lectures and as a result, a primer *Aprendo a leer*, based on his method, was prepared with the assistance of Honduran teachers. In the same year another group under the direction of the Puerto Rican scholar Ismael Rodriguez Bou brought the technique of teaching fundamental education by means of motion pictures. Literacy work continued through the years. In 1950 the illiteracy rate was 64%; in 1960 it had gone down to 58%. In 1958 4,000 adults registered at literacy centers; 2,500 completed the course successfully. In 1963 not only had the numbers increased, but the percentage of students who dropped out or failed had lowered considerably: 10,200 registered and 9,790 completed the course successfully.

In 1959 a separate Basic Education Section was created within the Ministry of Education. Its professional staff has largely been trained at the CREFAL center in Pátzcuaro, Mexico. These professionals are responsible for the training of teachers who specialize in adult education. These are usually primary school teachers. In 1964 there were 132 assisted by normal-school students in forty-one adult schools in about half of the departments of the country. Recently a Venezuelan mission gave directions concerning literacy education and offered copies of its primer *Abajo cadenas*. Other primers employed are the above mentioned *Aprendo a leer* and *Mi mejor amigo*, published in 1962, which uses the sentence method.

In addition to the literacy work sponsored by the government, private agencies play an important role. The most important group is Popular Cultural Action, formed by priests, representatives from private enterprise and other individuals dedicated to fundamental education in the rural areas. A radio station, La Voz de Suyapa, is operated by this group. It started in 1961 with 17 schools and 306 students. By 1964 there were 500 schools with 8,000 students.

No government funds are assigned to adult education in *Nicaragua*. On the Atlantic there is a region which is sparsely populated, where communications are poor and several languages are spoken (Misquito, Zumo, and English). The Rio Coco Pilot Project for basic education was carried out by UNESCO in collaboration with a national commission of representatives from various ministries of the Nicaraguan government. It included teacher training, literacy work, and the teaching of Spanish. In 1959 it had 90 teachers, had established 90 schools, 45 literacy centers and 12 libraries.

In *Costa Rica*, adult literacy work had been in progress on a small scale for a number of years. In 1963 a ten-year campaign was organized by the Community Education and Development Division of the Ministry of Education. Permission was obtained from the University of Puerto Rico to adapt and print its literacy manual and set of five primers and readers for use in Costa Rica. The cost of the campaign is to be borne by the Ministry of Education (50%), CARE (30%), and the local communities (20%).

In *Panama* there are minorities who speak Amerindian languages and English. The illiteracy rate is 26%. In 1959 a campaign in adult literacy was begun. Evening schools were set up with primary school teachers in charge. From 1959 to 1963 about 21,000 adults had become literate as a result of the campaign.

2.12. *South America*

There had been no organized government effort to combat illiteracy in *Colombia* until 1960 when a CREFAL technician visited the country. As a result new scientific materials designed for adults were prepared. Sometime later, a National Service to Promote Literacy was established and short courses to train teachers were given to 13,000 persons. In 1963, 1,300 adult literacy centers were operating in Colombia.

The most important non-government literacy effort in Colombia is that of Acción Cultural Popular, ACP, organized by Monsignor José Joaquín Salcedo in 1947. This represents an effort of the Catholic Church to raise the standard of living of the Colombian peasant by means of radio-schools. Monitors are trained to supervise the instruction; battery radios, blackboards, primers, notebooks, pencils, etc. are distributed free to each community. The teacher broadcasts a lesson at the appointed hour and the peasants, children and adults, assemble with the monitor at the radio school which is usually outdoors. Between 1954 and 1961 184,206 people were made literate this way. A very impressive film of the ACP program has been made by AID. The primer used by ACP, called *Cartilla de lectura*, uses the synthetic approach. It consists of forty-two lessons and seven supplementary reading lessons.

In *Venezuela* a campaign against adult illiteracy took place in 1946-48, but for the next ten years very little was done. In 1958 the Adult Education Division of the Ministry of Education initiated a new plan: People in the most densely populated areas were to be made literate first. These are also regions which offer best prospects of economic development. The people in sparsely populated regions are not likely to be made literate rapidly.

Non-professional teachers of the following types are engaged in the program: (1) 'literacy legions' consisting of students of fifth and sixth grades, secondary schools, normal schools, and universities; (2) 'civil legions', private individuals. Professional teachers act as advisors. Evening classes are offered at literacy centers. The eclectic primer *Abajo cadenas* (1948) and the reader *Leamos compañeros* are used.

Since 1942 there was a movement for adult literacy in *Ecuador* sponsored by two private organizations encouraged by Laubach: The Unión Nacional de Periodistas, UNP, a group of journalists in Quito; and a group which called itself Liga Ecuatoriana de Alfabetización, LAE (Ecuadorian Literacy League). The first group worked in the Andean and Eastern regions while the latter worked on the Coast. The UNP reduced illiteracy 9% in its area and LAE made about 67,000 people literate in ten years. In addition the army has carried on important literacy work within its ranks.

In 1962 the Ministry of Education created the Department of Adult Education and Literacy and thus assumed responsibility for adult education throughout the country. A plan was drawn up to undertake a campaign by stages as follows: (1) literacy, one year; (2) accelerated primary course, duration not yet established; (3) vocational training. While the first group is in Stage Two a new group will start with Stage One and the process is to be repeated as long as necessary. The plan was put in operation in April 1963 and there are as yet no available reports on the results.

Classes of some thirty students are held in the evening; the teachers are paid in-service teachers; the primer was specially prepared for the campaign. It is an eclectic primer, called *Ecuador* (1964), well suited for adult illiterates. In addition at least the following materials have been prepared:

GENERAL: *Plan nacional de alfabetización y educación de adultos* (1964), a description of the project.
Seis artículos sobre analfabetismo (1963)
Excellent newspaper articles by Fernando Valderrama Martinez designed to awaken the interest of the educated classes.

FIRST STAGE: *Guía didáctica de la cartilla Ecuador* (1964)

A teacher's manual to go along with the primer.

Guía para la enseñanza de cálculo (1964)

A manual to teach arithmetic.

Agenda del alfabetizador (1964)

A manual which includes background material, programs of study, directions to use the primer (same as the *Guía* above), guidelines in teaching geography, history, morals, civics, and hygiene.

SECOND STAGE: *Libro de historia* (1964)

Libro de geografía (1964)

In the *Guía didáctica* the author makes a reference to phonemes on page two, but he fails to point out the relationship between phonemes and graphemes. This author along with many other literacy experts is preoccupied with meaning and interprets reading as the acquisition of meaning from the written symbols without the intermediary step, language, which seems all important to the linguist.

1963 was declared 'literacy year' in *Peru* and the campaign which had started in 1958 was intensified. Its main characteristic seems to have been that employers with twenty employees or more were required by law to set up literacy courses. Teachers were primary school teachers, normal school students, and volunteers. The figures on Table 6, taken from the CREFAL report on Peru, reflect the size and aims of the campaign. No figures on actual results are available yet:

TABLE 6

Kinds of Centers	Number of Centers	Number of Literacy Workers	Number of Students Enrolled
Rented	4,000	4,000	120,000
Voluntary (ie. homes)	1,500	1,500	45,000
Civic service	Industry	70,000	140,000
TOTAL	5,500	75,000	305,000

It was expected that 300,000 adults would be made literate (Report to UNESCO-IBE Commission sent by the Ministry of Education) but from the above figures of enrolled students, this seems hardly probable.

The illiteracy rate has been lowered only slightly in rural areas in *Bolivia* while the absolute number of adult illiterates has actually increased (Table 7). The National Literacy Division of the Ministry of Education, in charge of adult literacy in urban areas, has no funds with which to operate. There is an almost complete lack of trained personnel in adult education and literacy.

TABLE 7

Rural Population 15 *Years and Over*[7]

	Total	Literate	%	Illiterate	%
1951	1,202,139	135,010	11	1,067,129	89
1961	1,359,181	198,149	15	1,160,539	85

Since 1952 the illiteracy rate in *Chile* has been 19.8%. It is caused by absenteeism and desertion at the primary school level. For this reason, the Ministry of Education maintains a permanent adult literacy service with 345 schools, a volunteer corps and four centers of fundamental education and community development. The schools make some 20,000 adults literate every year.

The illiteracy rate is 8.6% in *Argentina.* Illiterates are adult immigrants and people who have not finished primary school and have relapsed into illiteracy or who live in very remote and sparsely populated areas where primary schools are not provided. By Argentinian law, it is the duty of the State to establish schools for adults at factories, barracks, prisons, etc., wherever there are more than forty illiterate persons over fourteen of years age. It has not been necessary to organize literacy campaigns.

The report of the Ministry of Education and Religion of *Paraguay* to the UNESCO-IBE commission in 1964 states that the Ministry does not undertake any adult education projects. There are certain government-sponsored programs within the armed forces and in the prisons, and missionaries carry out some adult education work among some Indian groups. This report does not mention that in spite of the fact that 40.1% of the population is monolingual in Guaraní and 53.8% is bilingual in Guaraní and Spanish, Spanish is the only medium of instruction.

In 1951 the Department of Literacy and Adult Education was created in *Uruguay.* In 1962 it had sixty centers with 4,845 students.

Under the 1963-65 plan now current in *Brazil* it is hoped that persons between fourteen and eighteen years of age will be made literate at the rate of 1,150,000 per year. Volunteer teachers are to be used in this effort.

2.13. *Hispanic Caribbean*

Cuba is the country with the smallest percentage of illiterates in this hemisphere. In 1962 the population of Cuba was approaching seven million, the percentage of people ten years and older who were illiterate was 3.9. The number of illiterates has been drastically and dramatically reduced from 979,207 to 271,788 by means of an intensive country-wide campaign undertaken by the revolutionary government in 1961. The goals of the campaign were to teach the mechanics of reading and writing to every person older than fourteen and anyone under fourteen not attending school.

[7] Burns (1963).

These goals were very nearly met. According to official reports 979,000 illiterates were located in 1961, 894,000 enrolled, 707,212 were made literate and 186,000 were unsuccessfully taught. It must be understood that in the context of this campaign literacy does not mean functional literacy, but only the equivalent of one year of primary school.

The Cuban literacy campaign is described in detail by Richard Jolly, a British economist, trained at Cambridge and Yale, who did research on the island in 1962. The campaign was organized by the National Literacy Commission formed with representatives from the Ministry of Education and the revolutionary organizations. A preparatory census started in November 1960 which attempted to locate and register all illiterates. Four kinds of literacy workers, making a total of 271,000, were involved in the campaign: (1) 'Brigadistas Conrado Benítez', about 100,000 young students given a short training course and sent out to rural areas in groups to work under the supervision of a teacher. (2) 'Alfabetizadores populares', 121,000 volunteers in the towns who taught people in their own neighbourhoods. (3) 'Brigadistas obreros Patria o Muerte', 15,000 workers who served as teachers with the understanding that their fellow workers would make up for their work in the factories. (4) School teachers, 35,000 professionals who served mostly as supervisors and administrators.

The approach which was followed was one of individual instruction, the ratio of students to teacher being about three to one. After a short training period the volunteers were transported all over the island equiped with their teacher's manual, *Alfabeticemos* and a primer, ¡*Venceremos*! Even peasants in the remotest corners of the island were approached. Great enthusiasm was displayed by all concerned. The number of people involved, close to a million, between instructors and pupils, is in itself remarkable. Two million copies of *Venceremos* and one million copies of *Alfabeticemos* were printed. In addition each *brigadista* was supplied with clothing and lamps and many illiterates given eye glasses. The organization required to mobilize so many people and so much equipment and to keep up the morale of the students and volunteers for the eight months which the campaign lasted is also remarkable. As for the quality of the results, those who were declared literate in December 1961 when the campaign came officially to an end, had no doubt mastered the mechanics of reading and writing. They passed a test which consisted of reading a short paragraph and writing a letter. The government realized that much more had to be done to bring the new literates to the level of functional literacy. Accordingly, *Seguimiento* (follow-up) courses were organized. The attendance in these courses in 1962 represents about one third of the new literates. This means that aside from the political gains made by teaching such large numbers of peasants and workers, about two thirds of them were in danger of relapsing into illiteracy unless the enrollment in the *Seguimiento* classes was increased.

¡*Venceremos*![8] is a 111-page primer prepared by the National Literacy Commission

[8] Special thanks are due Professor Richard R. Fagen, of Stanford University, for allowing me to use photographic reproductions of the Cuban primer and manual.

for the 1961 literacy campaign. Its format and presentation are excellent. The material is interesting and varied and suitable for adults. The method is eclectic. The primer consists of 15 units. A typical unit contains a photograph with an appropriate comment of two or three model sentences and a set of three lessons of 6 to 9 parts. The first part analyzes a word of one of the model sentences into syllables and presents other syllables that complete a pattern; the second and third present new words built out of known syllables and new sentences built out of known words; 4 is a fill-in exercise, 5 a dictation, 6 a writing exercise, while 7, 8, and 9 constitute a review. The grading of the material could have perhaps been improved if the relationship between phonemes and graphemes had been more clearly understood.

Alfabeticemos is a teachers' manual prepared by the same commission. It consists of five parts: a preface to the instructor, a list which relates the units of the primer to the topics of the manual, an orientation section which explains clearly and briefly how the primer is used; a series of topics for discussion and a vocabulary list. The topics section is the longest one. The vocabulary section explains terms used in the topics section and is not directly related to the words taught in the primer.

In 1952 a nation-wide literacy campaign was begun in the *Dominican Republic.* It aimed to eradicate illiteracy by 1958. Illiteracy was declared a crime and provisions were made to fine illiterates who did not attend the literacy centers. A word-approach primer called *Cartilla Trujillo de alfabetización de adultos* was prepared. According to Pacheco (1955), *La obra educativa de Trujillo*, there were 7,434 centers with 200,000 students registered in 1955, but he does not say how many people actually learned to read and write. On the other hand, a booklet put out by the campaign directors claimed that the illiteracy rate was 33.9 in 1957. The percentage given in Table 5 refers to census figures.

According to the report sent to the joint UNESCO-IBE Commission in 1964 by the Ministry after the end of the 'Trujillo Era', the task of making people literate had not been entrusted to very competent people. New plans were drawn up in 1962. At the time the report was written, promotion of literacy and adult education, under a program of unlimited duration, was entrusted to the Ministry, 70% of the certified teachers were engaged in adult literacy work and the Puerto Rican primers were being used.

An Adult Literacy Program was created in 1953 in *Puerto Rico.* It functioned under that name until 1960-61 when new regulations created a Program in Elementary Education for Adults. This program under the Ministry of Education is equivalent to primary school education. It aims to reduce the number of illiterates, including functional illiterates over ten years of age.

Classes are held in the afternoon and evening; the first three grades last five months and offer 130 hours of instruction and the last three grades last ten months and offer 260 hours. It was found that with a primary school teacher who has been trained in adult education methodology, an adult has to take sixty two-hour classes to learn the mechanics of reading and writing and that to achieve this end seventy-five to eighty classes have to be planned for. An adult should become an independent reader after 180 two-hour classes.

From 1953 to 1963 almost 300,000 people were enrolled, over 80,000 successfully completed the first grade, and over 13,000 finished the equivalent of primary school. In 1950 there were 526,154 adults ten years or older in Puerto Rico; 24.7% of these were illiterate and 23.8% functionally illiterate. In 1960 the percentages had dropped to 12% and 20% respectively.

The present program is described by Rafael Marcano Blanco (1963) and by Ismael Rodriguez Bou (1960) and in the Annual Report for the Fiscal Year 1963-64. Rodriguez Bou points out some of the false assumptions in the original proposal to the Puerto Rican Legislature in 1960, but considers that the Program has been a very successful one. His report is very detailed and he makes valuable suggestions for the improvement of the program.

The materials that have been prepared in Puerto Rico for the government-sponsored adult education programs include *Manual para la enseñanza de lectura y escritura a adultos analfabetos* (1956), a teacher's manual to be used with the primer *¡A la escuela!* which uses the sentence approach; a series of four readers; teacher manuals for each grade including such subjects as social sciences, arithmetic, Spanish grammar and English; booklets on geography, hygiene, civics, elementary science, etc. The primers and readers deal with subjects which seem appropriate for adults; the manuals are very thorough and should adequately guide teachers.

2.2. *Non-Hispanic Caribbean*

The first attempt to teach literacy in Creole in *Haiti* was made by Christian Beaulieu in 1939. In 1943 McConnell, a Protestant missionary, invited Laubach to visit Haiti and succeeded in interesting the Ministry of Education in his literacy work. For a number of years the writing system proposed by McConnell with minor revisions by Laubach was the only one used. In 1948 the Haitian government asked UNESCO to set up a pilot project in adult education at Marbial. Literacy was one of the components of the project and it was decided that a linguist should be consulted as to the appropriateness of the existing orthography. Robert A. Hall, Jr. endorsed the McConnell-Laubach orthography in a series of articles in the *Nouveliste* and used it in his study of French Creole. This orthography was used in the short-lived UNESCO project and in some Protestant publications. In 1947 Charles Ferdinand Pressoir proposed some changes in the orthography. Faublas adopted them for an adult education program, and the revised orthography came to be called the Faublas orthography. In 1961 adult education became the responsibility of the Office Nationale d'Education Communautaire, ONEC. It uses this revised orthography in all its Creole publications, and it may thus be considered official.

ONEC, a dependency of the Ministry of Education, started its work in 1962 with extremely limited financial resources. Its goal is to eradicate illiteracy by concentrating on separate areas of the country in eleven annual stages. Adults are taught to read and write in Creole for eight months as a first step in their acquisition of French, which is then taught for two years. Thus far, ONEC claims to have reduced illiteracy by 8% in the regions where it has worked.

For a review of the literature on the language situation and the orthography questions in Haiti, see Hall in this volume. The orthography question is further discussed by Paul C. Berry in a mimeographed memorandum to AID in which he maintains that since French will no doubt continue to be the prestige language and the language that people want to learn because it is a language of wider communication, Creole should be used as a tool for the eventual acquisition of French. He argues that the social question is more important than phonemics, and that French spelling conventions are capable of unambiguous representation; he proposes a new orthography which represents the phonemes of Creole in a consistent way such that there would be some problems for the writer but none for the reader and which would facilitate the passage from Creole to French.

In *L'Alphabetisation en Haïti* (1965), E. C. Paul describes the work of ONEC, of which he is the technical director, and the attempts which had previously been made in order to cope with the illiteracy problem. The book, which seems to be addressed to the Haitian elite who have thus far succeeded in maintaining the status quo, proposes to attack the illiteracy problem at the primary school level as well as at the adult level and to use Creole as a means of achieving literacy in French at all levels.

Among the publications of ONEC the following are important: *Guide National d'Alphabétisation des Adultes*, a booklet explaining how every Haitian can cooperate in the fight against illiteracy; *Liv pa nou*, a thirty-lesson primer employing the synthetic method; *Nap li*, a twelve-lesson reader; *Pri liv-la gnou Goud*, an elementary book in history, geography, civics, hygiene, and arithmetic; *Parlons français*, a short beginners' book for speakers of Creole. Charles Ferdnand Pressoir has prepared a French textbook for speakers of Creole: *Méthode de Français Oral.*

Around 1950 it was estimated that *Jamaica* and its dependencies had from 220 to 270 thousand adult illiterates, fifteen years or over, constituting from 25 to 30% of the adult population (900,000) out of an estimated total of 1,417,000. The report made by the Caribbean Commission to the 1955 West Indian Conference stated that about 40% of the population was probably illiterate at the time.

In 1950 the Social Welfare Commission started its work on literacy. The Commission, which began as a private organization, is today financially supported by the government, but it is largely autonomous. It works on community development chiefly in rural areas. Efforts are made to obtain the collaboration of churches and various organizations in the action against illiteracy. Teachers are voluntary workers given some training by the Commission. No statistics on the results thus far obtained seem to be available.

In 1950 it was estimated that between 20-25% of the adult population of *Trinidad and Tobago* was illiterate. At the time of the 1960 census 11.4% of the population had no formal education and 12.9% had roughly five years or less. There has never been a literacy campaign, but there have been five-year development plans which include the provision of adequate facilities for the basic education of children and adults.

The estimated percentage of adult illiterates in *British Honduras* in 1950 was 20-25%. According to recent official estimates this figure has been lowered to 6.5%. An adult literacy program using the Laubach method is operating.

Illiteracy in the British Caribbean is not only the result of insufficient number of schools and poor attendance records, but of the lack of reading materials; people who have attended school very often forget what they have learned. There are very few organized efforts to combat illiteracy and very little information is available. Statistics are untrustworthy, population figures often being estimates rather than actual census figures. Language data is very rarely included. The available information is summarized in Tables 1 and 3.

No adult literacy programs have been reported for the French Areas.

A new Department of Adult Education was set up in *Surinam* in 1958. In the *Netherlands Antilles* illiteracy is rapidly decreasing. In 1960, the percentage of illiterates, defined, in this case, as those who have completed less than three grades of elementary school, was 10.7% in Curaçao. This is the largest and most important island. As may be seen in the following Table 8, the illiteracy rate is much lower among the younger section of the population than among the older people. This means that there should soon be no illiteracy problems in the Netherlands Antilles.

TABLE 8

Percentage of Illiterates Divided in Age-Groups (1960)[9]

	15-19	20-24	25-29	30-39	40-49	50 and older
Curaçao	2.6	3	3.5	4.5	10	29.3
Aruba	4,5	8	8.5	9	21	42.5
Bonaire	3			6	15	48
		15-29		30-49		50 and older
St. Maarten		10		21		45
St. Eustatius		7		18		44
Saba		7		24		62

3. LITERACY IN INDIGENOUS GROUPS

3.1. Every country strives to educate its people and considers literacy a means to this end. In most countries the official language is the only medium of instruction, but in some, literacy in minority languages is considered a bridge for the acquisition of the

[9] Data furnished by the Inspector of Education, Netherlands Antilles.

official language. It is clearly easier to have universal primary education in a monolingual country than in a bilingual one. In America the official languages, all European, are Spanish, Portuguese, French, Dutch, and English. There are three other types of languages: immigrant, creole and indigenous. Immigrant languages are spoken by significant minorities in some countries of the non-Hispanic Caribbean and, to a certain extent, in Central America, Argentina, and Brazil. Argentina, as we have seen, tries to cope with the problem, and immigrants are considered to contribute to a large degree to the increase of the illiteracy rate. In the Creole-speaking areas illiteracy is directly related to the linguistic situation. The indigenous languages constitute the most important group of non-official languages in the area under study. Table 9 lists the languages spoken and the literacy programs and campaigns carried on in each language group.

TABLE 9*

Languages and Adult Literacy Programs and Campaigns

	LANGUAGES			PROGRAMS AND CAMPAIGNS		
	Off. lg.	Major lgs. (10% of pop. or over a million)	Other significant lgs.	Official	Major	Other
MEXICO AND CENTRAL AMERICA						
Mexico	Sp.	—	20 Amerindian	National campaign 1965-	—	Govt., SIL
Guatemala	Sp.	Quiché	16 Amerindian	Private efforts	Govt., SIL	Govt., SIL
El Salvador	Sp.	—	4 Amerindian	National campaign 1962- Catholic Church	—	
Honduras	Sp.	—	11 Amerindian	Govt. program 1959- ACP	—	
Nicaragua	Sp.	—	3 Amerindian English	Rio Coco Pilot Project	—	
Costa Rica	Sp.	—	English	National campaign 1963-	—	
Panama	Sp.	—	English 3 Amerindian	Govt. program 1959-	—	
SOUTH AMERICA						
Colombia	Sp.	—	9 Amerindian	ACP 1947- Govt. prog. 1960-	—	Govt.
Venezuela	Sp.	—	8 Amerindian	Govt. program 1958-	—	Govt.
Ecuador	Sp.	Quechua	6 Amerindian	Govt. campaign 1963-	1956 Andino prog.	SIL
Peru	Sp.	Quechua	Aymara 30 Amerindian	1963 'literacy year'	SIL Govt.	SIL, Govt.

TABLE 9 *(continued)*

	LANGUAGES			PROGRAMS AND CAMPAIGNS		
	Off. lg.	Major lgs. (10% of pop. or over a million)	Other significant lgs.	Official	Major	Other
Bolivia	Sp.	Quechua Aymara	60 Amerindian		1963 Acción Andina	SIL
Chile	Sp.	—	5 Amerindian	Govt. prog.	—	
Argentina	Sp.	—	12 Amerindian Italian and other immigrant languages	Compulsory programs	—	
Paraguay	Sp.	Guaraní	Several Amerindian			
Uruguay	Sp.	—	Portuguese	Govt. prog. 1951-	—	
Brazil	Port.	—	Many Amerindian German	Govt. campaign 1963-1965	—	SIL
HISPANIC CARIBBEAN						
Cuba	Sp.	—	—	1961 National Campaign	—	—
Dominican Rep.	Sp.	—	—	Govt. campaign 1952-1957 Govt. Prog. 1962-	—	—
Puerto Rico	Sp. Eng.	English	—	Govt. Prog. 1953-		—
NON-HISPANIC CARIBBEAN						
Haiti	Fr.	French Creole	—	Govt. and others	Govt. and others	—
BRITISH AFFILIATED						
Jamaica	Eng.	Jamaican English	Immigrant languages	Jamaica Welfare Commission 1950-		
Trinidad and Tobago	Eng.	French Creole	Immigrant languages			
Bahamas	Eng.				—	—
Bermuda	Eng.					
British Guiana	Eng.	—	Several Amerindian Immigrant languages		—	
British Honduras	Eng.	Spanish, Maya	Carib	Laubach		
British Virgin Is.	Eng.	—	—		—	—
Barbados	Eng.					

TABLE 9 *(continued)*

	LANGUAGES			PROGRAMS AND CAMPAIGNS		
	Off. lg.	Major lgs. (10% of pop. or over a million)	Other significant lgs.	Official	Major	Other
Turks and Caicos	Eng.	—	—		—	—
Leeward Islands	Eng.	—	—		—	—
Windward Islands	Eng.	French Creole	—			—
FRENCH AREAS						
Guadeloupe	Fr.	French Creole	—			—
Martinique	Fr.	French Creole	—	Few govt. programs in 1945		—
French Guiana	Fr.	French Creole	Several Amerindian			—
DUTCH AREAS						
Surinam	D	Sranantongo Hindi-Urdu Javanese	English, Carib, Aucan, Saramakan	Govt. programs		Govt. programs
NETHERLANDS ANTILLES						
Curaçao Aruba Bonaire	D	Papiamento	—			—
Saba St. Eustatius St. Maarten	D	English	—			—

* A line means that there are no languages of that type and therefore no campaign or program in the country. A blank space means we have no report on a program or campaign.

There are no reliable statistics on the number of speakers of Indian languages. We do not know how many languages there are. Most countries do not include language data in their censuses. Some countries have statistics on the number of Indians, but 'Indian' is defined in different ways so that the figures are not comparable even where they exist and are seldom an accurate reflection of the language situation. Where 'Indian' is defined culturally, we may have speakers of Spanish who are called Indians; where ethnically, monolingual speakers of an indigenous language may be counted as mestizos as in Paraguay. Since Indians are associated with low prestige their numbers are, consciously or unconsciously, minimized by census respondents and government officials alike.

The figures in Table 10 are taken from the best available sources, *La población indígena y el mestizaje en América* (1954), by Angel Rosenblat, and *Guía de la Población Indígena de América* (1964), a publication of the Inter-American Indianist Institute. They are included here in order to give a vague approximation of the number of speakers of Indian languages and an idea of the number of Indian groups large enough to merit literacy programs geared to their needs.

The sixteen Latin American countries which have an Indian population (Uruguay, Cuba, the Dominican Republic, and Haiti have none) have ratified the creation of the Inter-American Indianist Institute (3.2). This means that every government has shown some concern with Indian well-being and a desire to protect him and incorporate him into the mainstream of national life.

3.2. In *Mexico* cultural missions were first established among Indian groups in 1921. Their aim is to educate people in community development, and literacy was one of the components of the programs they set up. A history of these missions and of other institutions which have been created with the welfare of the Indian in mind, is found in Gonzalo Aguirre Beltrán (1953), *Teoría y práctica de la educación indígena.*

Everyone who has been concerned with education in Mexico has, in one way or another, been concerned with Indian education. There has been much experimenting, and policy has changed from time to time, fluctuating between the extreme Hispanicist view — that all Mexicans are equal, that everyone, both in urban and rural areas, should be entitled to the same opportunities and taught the same subjects in the national language, that Indians should be encouraged to forget their languages as quickly as possible, and that literacy means *castellanización,* — to that of the cultural relativist who is concerned with the poverty and exploitation of the Indian and wants him at the same time to preserve his language and values and to live within Western culture. Bureaucratization was seen by President Cárdenas as a danger that lurked behind every effort to improve the lot of the Indian, and this remains a major problem.

In 1940 the first Interamerican Indianist Congress took place in Pátzcuaro and as a result the Interamerican Indianist Institute was created with participation of all the American republics which have an Indian population. Mexico had taken the lead in Indian affairs in the international field. But in 1946 with a change of administration, the Departamento de Asuntos Indígenas, which had been founded by Cárdenas and which had been active at the time of the Pátzcuaro Congress, disappeared and its domestic functions were taken over by the División General de Asuntos Indígenas of the SEP. On the occasion of the Second Interamerican Congress, the National Indianist Institute (Instituto Nacional Indigenista, INI) was created. Since then there have been two government agencies in charge of Indian education, the SEP, which until recently maintained regular primary schools and used Spanish as medium of instruction everywhere in the country, and the INI, which at present has centers of fundamental education in the following areas:

Tzeltal-Tzotzil, Chiapas, with sub-center at Huáutla de Jiménez
Tarahumara, Chihuaha
Mixteca de la Costa, Oaxaca

TABLE

Amérindian

	Percentage of Indian population 1950	Total estimate 1960	One million or over	500-1000	250-500
Guatemala	55%	1,497,261			Quiché 339
Bolivia	55%	2,450,000	Quechua 1,500,000	Aymara 850	
Peru	40%	3,121,071 excludes jungle, 1954 est: 453,000	Quechua 3,200,000	Aymara 300	
Ecuador	40%	Over one million non-acculturated	Quechua		
British Honduras	23%	5,000			
Mexico	20%	2,447,609			Nahuatl
El Salvador	20%	100,000			
Honduras	6%	107,800			
Panama	6%	60,000			
French Guiana	6%	2,500			
British Guiana	4%	9,292			

10

Population

Thousands			
100-250	50-100	10-50	Less than 10
Mam 178 Cakchiquel 167 Kekchí 153	Pocomam	12 groups	
About 60 groups belonging to 15 linguistic families			
About 30 groups			
		Jivaro Yumbo	
			Yucatec Kekchí Carib Chol
Mixteco Zapoteco Otomí Totonaco Maya	Tzeltal-Tzotzil Mazateco	Mixe Chol Huasteca Mazahua Chinanteca Tlapaneca Tarasco	Chatino Tarahumara Amuzgo Zoque
	Pipil	Nahua Quiché Cakchiquel	
	Misquito		About 10 groups
		Guaymí Cuna	Chocó
			Carib Arawak others
			Carib Arawak others

TABLE 10

Amerindian

	Percentage of Indian population 1950	Total estimate 1960	One million or over	500-1000	250-500
Nicaragua	4%	43,000			
Paraguay	3%	40,000	This percentage does not reflect the linguistic situation. According to 1950 census figures 40.1% of the population is monolingual in Guaraní, 53.8% bilingual in Guaraní and Spanish, and 4.7% monolingual in Spanish.		
Venezuela	2%	98,682 (1950)			
Chile	2%	240,000 (including mestizos)			
Surinam	2%	4,500			
Colombia	1%	200,000			
Argentina	Less than 1%	130,000			
Costa Rica	Less than 1%	7,200			
Brazil	Less than 1%	1,200,000	Some 100 tribes in the Amazon area and some 100 tribes in other areas; census takers do not reach remote areas where the Indians live.		

(continued)

Population

Thousands 100-250	50-100	10-50	Less than 10
		Misquito	Sumo Rama
			Groups belonging to 7 linguistic families
		Guajiro	About 35 groups
			Quechua Aymara Uru
			Carib Arawak others
		Guajiro Chibcha groups	Carib Quechuan others
			Mataco Chorotí Chiriguano Quechua Colla Araucano Tehuelche Macobí Toba
			Bribrí Boruca Guatuso

Mixteca Alta, Oaxaca
Cora-Huichol, Jalisco
Tlapaneca, Guerrero

Native languages are employed as a medium of instruction at all centers, and literacy primers in the indigenous tongues, prepared by Mexican linguists and by Summer Institute of Linguistics personnel, are used in all the centers except the one in the Cora-Huichol area.

The SEP decided in 1963 to adopt as national policy that literacy in the native language be the first step toward literacy in Spanish and planned to publish a series of national primers in Mixteca de la Costa, Otomí, Maya, and Tarasco. In 1964 it initiated a National Literacy Program in Indigenous Languages under the direction of the noted Mexican ethnologist Angélica Castro de la Fuente with the collaboration of linguists of the Summer Institute of Linguistics.

Among the earliest and most significant projects in modern Indian education is the Tarasco Project, which was an experiment in applied linguistics under the direction of Morris Swadesh. The project had these characteristics: Literacy in the vernacular preceded literacy in Spanish; the vernacular was used to teach arithmetic and other subjects; young native bilinguals were trained as teachers. Instead of taking a year to learn to read a language which they did not understand, children would learn to read Tarasco in three or four months and then proceed to learn to read Spanish easily. The first phase of the project was successful, but lasted only a year (1939-40) because of a change in administration; it was continued later and again terminated after a few years. It is described in UNESCO, *The Use of Vernacular Languages in Education* (1953), 77-86.

Julio de la Fuente describes other projects and discusses the work of the INI and the role of anthropology in Indian education in *Educación, antropología y desarrollo de la comunidad* (1964). In 'La alfabetización en idiomas indígenas y los promotores culturales' *A William Cameron Townsend* (1961) 231-49, Angélica Castro de la Fuente describes the work of the Instituto de Alfabetización para Indígenas Monolingües. Her detailed description of the Otomí project is of particular interest.

In connection with literacy work among indigenous groups in Mexico it should be pointed out that linguists and ethnologists have been involved in many ways. The role of the Summer Institute of Linguistics has been significant. The role of the Instituto Nacional de Antropología e Historia and of its School of Anthropology has also been significant. These Mexican institutions carry on research and train ethnologists and linguists who are capable of contributing to the literacy effort when called upon by the government.

Literacy among the large Indian population of *Guatemala* is the concern of the Instituto Indigenista Nacional, a research center, which studies and tries to solve the problems of rural areas, particularly those with numerous indigenous groups, either directly or in collaboration with other institutions such as the Summer Institute of

Linguistics. It publishes a periodical called *Guatemala Indígena* which often features articles on literacy. A statistical study of illiteracy in Guatemala, 'El analfabetismo en Guatemala' was prepared by Jorge Arias B. in *Guatemala Indígena* (1962). A very detailed survey of the problem of illiteracy and of the attempts that have been made to solve it is made by Victor Manuel Valverde, 'El analfabetismo en Guatemala' in *Guatemala Indígena* (1962).

The Summer Institute of Linguistics has also cooperated in the preparation of official alphabets for thirteen important indigenous languages. These are found in an off-print of the *Diccionario Geográfico de Guatemala* as *Alfabetos oficializados de trece principales idiomas indígenas de Guatemala* (1962).

The indigenous population in *Colombia* is very small. The Division of Indian Affairs of the Ministry of the Interior has run eight programs among eight different groups.

In *Venezuela* a campaign has recently been carried on among the Guararunos with the collaboration of a group of Catholic missionaries. The Comisión Indigenista of the Ministry of Justice also concerns itself with Indian literacy: In 1958 and 1959, for instance, it published excellent Guajiro primers prepared by the Peruvian linguist Martha Hildebrandt.

Indians constitute at least one third of the population in *Ecuador*. The largest group is the Quechua group. Even though not all Indians are monolingual, the language problem is an important one which has not yet been faced by the government in any systematic way, although there have been pilot projects in basic education, notably the Andino Program (1956) where several international organizations participated.

The large number of speakers of Indian languages is one of the of the greatest problems in education in *Peru*, although it had been the practice, until very recently, to minimize its importance. An experiment to teach monolingual Quechua children to learn Spanish by audio-lingual methods during the pre-primary year is being carried on jointly by the Ministry of Education and Cornell University at the Quinua school in the Department of Ayacucho. The project director is Donald F. Solá and the director of the experiment is Florián Luque, a Bolivian linguist trained at Cornell. Quechua is used as a medium of instruction, and special dialogue materials have been prepared. The control group is taught in Spanish in the traditional way. The experimental group was progressing more rapidly than the control group in the learning of Spanish, reading, writing, and arithmetic according to the progress reports of the experiment.

The Ministry of Education has been carrying on literacy programs in the jungle area with the cooperation of the Summer Institute of Linguistics for twelve consecutive years. One hundred sixty schools have been established among twenty-one different tribal groups. A training center for native bilingual teachers has been operating since 1953 at Yarinacocha. The center, its history, and its role are briefly described in *El XII curso de capacitación para maestros bilingües de la selva y el fenómeno de cambio*, a speech made by Darío Gutierrez in 1964. A technical description of the program was presented by Gamaniel Arroyo Ponce and Donald Burns at the Fifth Interamerican Indianist Congress (1964).

Recently the bilingual program has been extended to the Highlands where a series of Quechua primers is being used experimentally. Audio-lingual Spanish materials are also being tried. It is hoped that the large number of Quechua speaking children in Peru will soon benefit from the same type of bilingual education which has been proved successful in the experimental areas and which has only been available to very small groups up to now.

The Bolivian education code states that the peasantry and the working class must be incorporated into the stream of national life by means of large-scale projects in literacy and fundamental education, but none have been initiated up to now. In 1963, a National Plan for Rural Development was operating under the administration of a joint committee with the participation of several ministries and UNESCO through Acción Andina. This project insists upon the use of the vernacular as medium of instruction and as a bridge for eventual learning of reading and writing in Spanish. But it affects a very small sector of the rural population.

4. THE LITERACY WORK OF INTERNATIONAL AND PRIVATE ORGANIZATIONS

4.1. *International organizations*

Among the international organizations working for the spread of education in the Americas UNESCO and OAS are the most important. It might also be appropriate to mention here the work of the United States Agency for International Development, AID. It sponsors civic action and teacher education projects in Latin America which may at times be related to literacy. Directly related projects are carried on in Guatemala where there is a literacy adviser and AID has paid for the production of materials, and in Colombia where it has helped purchase TV equipment.

OAS sponsors relevant conferences, research, and publications and sometimes is one of the joint sponsors of particular programs such as Andino, mentioned above.

But UNESCO is the most influential as well as the most active of the international organizations engaged in literacy work. It has been concerned with the problem of illiteracy since its first session in 1946. Its activities include pilot projects in literacy and adult education, research projects, evaluations of national literacy projects, technical advice, and training of experts. UNESCO sponsors an important training center in fundamental education at Pátzcuaro, Mexico: Centro Regional de Educación Fundamental para el Desarrollo de la Comunidad en América Latina, CREFAL. Some of the UNESCO publications which have bearing on our subject have already been mentioned. Others are listed in the bibliography. They do not, by any means, reflect all of UNESCO's activities. Very often it is only one of the sponsors in joint development programs which have literacy as a component and which are described in reports which are not easily available.

In December 1961 the General Assembly of the United Nations adopted a resolution on literacy and asked UNESCO to make a survey of the situation with the object of eradication of illiteracy throughout the world. UNESCO studied the planning, organization, and execution of programs for the eradication of illiteracy. A questionnaire was sent out to member states and its results, 'A Survey of Illiteracy' in the mimeographed document *World Campaign for Universal Literacy* (1963), reveal that there are no adequate data on the extent of illiteracy and that for the time being the 1957 estimates in the UNESCO publication *World Illiteracy at Mid-Century* (1957) are still the only available figures in many cases. In 1962 UNESCO experts met in Paris and prepared 'Recommendations for National Literacy Programmes', published in the same mimeographed document. These recommendations deal with adult literacy (although it is, of course, recognized that universal primary schooling is basic to the eradication of illiteracy) and with the economic aspects of a world campaign.

In December 1962, as a reply to the General Assembly, UNESCO declared its readiness to promote a world campaign for universal literacy during the Development Decade. It seemed as though a massive world wide campaign was about to start, but recently UNESCO'S position has become cautious and realistic. A selective, rather than a massive approach, has been decided upon. UNESCO research teams are visiting prospective pilot areas, among them Ecuador.

4.2. *Private organizations*

4.21. There are many private organizations which are involved in literacy work. Some of these operate in wide areas and are supported, or at least encouraged, by the national governments. Their work has already been mentioned. Many others are local and limit their action to smaller areas. Many of them are inspired by religious motives and sometimes they carry on work in more than one country. Among these the most important is the Summer Institute of Linguistics whose work is described below. There are Catholic missionaries among indigenous groups in every Latin American country, and Protestant missionaries, many Evangelical, and often with United States connections, in several countries. The Evangelical Conference of Churches, for instance, prepared a primer which the Brazilian government adopted and of which four million copies have been printed.

4.22. The Committee for Aymara Literacy and Literature in Bolivia is an interdenominational committee of Protestant missions. It runs a program in literacy education for adults using its own bilingual Aymara-Spanish primer. Recently it has begun to work with Aymara children as well.

4.23. The Laubach Literacy Fund, founded by Frank Laubach, originator of the 'each one teach one' concept,[10] at present has programs in Mexico, Guatemala, Colombia, Ecuador, and Brazil. It has prepared charts, primers, readers, teachers' guides, etc. Laubach methods are often used by other organizations. For instance, the Peace Corps sponsors a literacy program in a prison in Bogotá which is part of a prison reform project, and Laubach literacy methods are used.

4.24. Since 1942 the Committee on World Literacy and Christian Literature of the National Council of Churches has been sponsoring adult literacy programs in connection with the Evengelical churches in Latin America. The organization called ALFALIT came into being in 1962. Its headquarters are in Alajuela, Costa Rica. It prepares literacy materials, distributes a newsletter and holds workshops for the training of literacy workers. Workshops have now been held in Honduras, Nicaragua, Costa Rica, Panama, Bolivia, Chile, and the Dominican Republic.

4.25. The Summer Institute of Linguistics, SIL, is a non-denominational organization which is primarily concerned with translating the Bible into many languages. Besides their well known contributions in descriptive and theoretical linguistics and their work in the training of linguists in the United States and abroad, SIL members prepare primers, readers, and other materials related to literacy and fundamental education. SIL has programs involving literacy in Mexico, Guatemala, Honduras, Colombia, Ecuador, Peru, Bolivia, and Brazil under the auspices of the government agencies which are in charge of Indian education. It is engaged in government sponsored experiments in bilingual education in several countries. The most important of these is the Peru program which has already been mentioned (See 3.2). The Ecuador program, which is similar, started in July 1963 with ten bilingual Indians from four tribal groups attending a teacher training course which is planned for five or six years. The prospective teachers are trained for three months; then they go back to their community to teach under technical supervision for eight months. Their training includes administration of the school, use of teaching materials, and courses in Spanish, history, geography, public health, agriculture, civics, etc. There are now seventeen schools with twenty bilingual teachers and a total attendance of 363 students. The children are taught in their native language until they are ready for the transition from their mother tongue into Spanish.

In Mexico, the members of SIL have been active in the preparation of materials for many government-run literacy programs. The materials may be published by the SEP or the INI and the authors are not involved in the actual teaching once the programs get under way. Max Lathrop has worked in the official Tarasco project, but has also been active among the Tarascos on his own. Ethel Wallis and Nancy Lanier developed the primer for the Otomí which at times has been officially used. It was

[10] Frank Laubach and Robert S. Laubach (1960).

later revised (1963) by Iris Wares who also wrote a workbook. These were published by the SEP. Ethel Wallis and Ellen Carlson collaborated in the preparation of the Tarahumara primer used by the INI. Iris Wares wrote the SEP Maya primer with the help of Moisés Romero, a Mexican linguist. Dow F. Robinson, Iris Wares, and Lois Robinson wrote materials for the Nahuat of Puebla and the Nahuatl of Northern Veracruz (1962-64).

In Guatemala SIL has literacy programs in eleven Indian groups and it is expected that a program of bilingual schools will soon be started in cooperation with the Ministry of Education.

The following list from the 1964 Peru SIL *Bibliography* is indicative of the amount of literacy materials which have recently been produced in Peru in Spanish and thirty indigenous languages:

Basic primers	214
Advanced primers	49
Readers	6
Texts in religion and morals	13
Texts in nature studies and civics	33
Texts in arithmetic	64
Orthography manuals	56
Hygiene manuals	13
Oral Spanish textbooks	3
Teachers guides	4
Materials for training program in bilingual schools	5
TOTAL	460

Table 11 provides a summary of literacy materials in indigenous languages prepared by SIL up to the time of the publication of its 1964 *Bibliography*. Authors' names are omitted in the table. In it we can see that SIL linguists had prepared literacy materials in thirty-two languages (some of them requiring different treatment because of dialect differences) in forty-nine communities in Mexico; ten in Guatemala; one in Ecuador; twenty-three in Peru; six in Bolivia; five in Brazil. The methods for preparing the primers are described in Sarah C. Gudschinsky (1962) *Handbook of Literacy* (Rev. ed.). The primers follow the approach best suited to the language. For instance, the word approach is used in the Mazatec primer, the sentence approach in the Zapotec, the syllable approach in the Mixtec, but the psychophonemic method, developed by Townsend (See section 5 below) is the most commonly used in the SIL primers.

TABLE 11

Literacy Materials in American Languages Prepared by the Summer Institute of Linguistics

Language	Family	Pre-primer	Basic primers 1	2	3	4	5	6	7	Readers	Number book	Other
MEXICO												
Amuzgo	Mixtecan	×										
Chinanteco	Chinantecan											
Lalana			×									
Ojitlán			×	×								
Palantla			×									
Yolox			×									
Chol	Mayan		×	×	×	×						
Chontal de Oaxaca	Hokan		×									
Chontal de Tabasco	Mayan											2
Cora	Utoaztecan		×									
Cuicateco	Mixtecan		×	×	×	×						
Huasteco	Mayan		×									
Huave	Huave											×
Huichol	Utoaztecan	×	×	×	×					×		
Ixcateco	Popolocan		×									
Lacandón	Mayan		×	×	×						×	×
Mazahua	Otomí	×	×	×	×	×						
Mazateco	Popolocan											
Highland			×	×	×	×	×	×	×			5
Jalapa de Diaz			×									
Soyoltepec			×	×	×	×	×	×	×			3
Mixe	Zoque											
Coatlán			×	×							×	×
Totontepec			×									
Mixteco	Mixtecan											
Lowland		×	×	×	×	×	×	×				
S. Esteban			×	×	×	×						
S. Miguel		×	×							2		
S. Tomás												×
Nahuat	Utoaztecan		×	×								
Otomí	Otomí											
Eastern			×	×	×							
Mezquital		×	×									×
State of Mex.			×	×								
Tenango			×	×	×						×	
Pame	Otomí		×	×								
Popoloca	Popolocan	×	×	×	×	×	×	×	×			×
Seri	Hokan		×	×	×	×					×	×
Tarahumara	Utoastecan		×	×	×							×
Tarasco	Tarascan									4		
Tepehua	Totonacan		×	×	×							
Tojolabal	Mayan		×	×	×	×	×	×	×			2

TABLE 11 *(continued)*

Language	Family	Preprimer	Basic primers 1	2	3	4	5	6	7	Readers	Number book	Other
Totonaco	Totonacan											
Northern			×	×								
Sierra			×									
Trique	Mixtecan		×	×	×							
Tzeltal	Mayan		×	×	×	×						
Tzotzil	Mayan											
SanAndrés			×	×								
Zinacantan			×	×								
Yaqui	Utoaztecan		×									
Zapotec	Zapotecan											
Isthmus			×	×	×	×						22
Sierra Juarez			×	×	×	×	×	×	×			2
Villa Alta												×
Zoque	Zoquean		×									
GUATEMALA												
Achí	Mayan		×									
Aguacateco	Mayan		×	×								×
Cakchiquel	Mayan		×									
Chuj	Mayan		×	×								
Ixil	Mayan		×									
Kekchí	Mayan		×	×								
Mopán	Mayan											×
Pocomchí	Mayan		×	×	×	×	×			2		
Quiché	Mayan		×									
ECUADOR												
Quichua	Quechua-Aymaran		×									
PERU												
Aguaruna	Jivaroan		×	×	×	×						
Amahuaca	Central Panoan		×	×								
Amarakaerí	Uncl.		×	×								
Amuesha	Uncl.		×	×	×	×	×	×				×
Arabela	Zaparean		×									
Bora	Huitotoan		×									
Campa	Arawakan		×	×	×	×	×	×				
Candoshi	Zaparoan		×	×	×							
Capanahua	Central Panoan		×	×	×	×						
Cashibo	Central Panoan		×	×	×	×	×	×				×
Chayahuita	Capanahuan		×	×	×							
Cocama	Tupian		×	×	×	×	×					4
Culina	Arawakan		×	×	×							
Huambisa	Jivaroan		×									
Muinane	Huitotoan		×	×	×	×	×	×				
Machiguenga	Arawakan		×	×	×	×	×	×				3
Ocaina	Huitotoan		×	×	×	×	×					
Orejón	Western Tucanoan		×	×	×							
Piro	Arawakan		×	×	×	×	×	×	×		×	73

TABLE 11 *(continued)*

Language	Family	Pre-primer	Basic primers 1 2 3 4 5 6 7	Read-ers	Num-ber book	Other
Quechua	Quechua-Aymaran		× ×			
Shipibo	Panoan		× × × × ×			
Ticuna	Uncl.		× × ×			
Yagua	Peba-Yaguan		× × × × × ×			
BOLIVIA						
Aymara	Quechua-Aymara		× × ×			
Baure	Arawakan		×	×		
Chacobo	Panoan		× × ×			
Chipaya	Macro-Mayan		×			
Guaraní	Guaranian		×			
Sirionó	Guaranian			4		
BRAZIL						
Apinaye	Ge		×			
Hishkaryana	Carib		×			
Kaingang	Ge		× ×			
Kaiwa	Tupí-Guaraní		× × × ×			
Satare	Tupí-Guaraní		× ×			

5. TECHNICAL LITERATURE

Literature on linguistics applied to literacy in Latin America and the Caribbean is rather scanty. Besides the works which have already been mentioned, we note the following dealing with the applications of linguistics to literacy or describing certain literacy projects in which linguists have had a major role in analyzing the socio-linguistic situation, the languages and writing systems, in preparing materials, training teachers, or supervising the actual teaching process: Gudschinsky (1964), 'Techniques for Functional Literacy in Indigenous Languages and National Languages', discusses the contributions of linguistics to the teaching of oral and written control of the national language to speakers of indigenous languages or substandard varieties of the national language. Swadesh (1964), 'El impacto sociológico de la enseñanza en lengua vernácula', deals with recent projects sponsored by the Mexican government to teach literacy in the vernacular as a bridge to literacy in Spanish. Ethel Wallis (1956), 'Sociolinguistics in Relation to Mezquital Otomí Transition Education', describes several socio-linguistic problems which had to be coped with in order to prepare an adequate alphabet which would look like that of the prestige language and at the same time handle all the phonemic contrasts of the language. Margaret Wendel (1962), 'En torno a un programa de alfabetización bilingüe', describes the preparation and use of the Pocomchí eclectic primers and readers in Guatemala.

The book *Recuento de Vocabulario Español I* (1962) by Ismael Rodriguez Bou is a publication of the University of Puerto Rico to which UNESCO and OAS contributed. It is a frequency list which gives the results of a seven million word count which included literary material, but also a large sample of vocabulary from oral and written expression by children and adults, radio programs, newspaper articles, religious literature, and school texts. It is the most comprehensive work of its kind with many practical applications and a valuable source for writers of primers and readers.

The following papers deal with technical problems in devising orthographies: J. Voorhoeve (1959), 'An Orthography for Saramaccan'. Saramaccan is the language of a people descended from escaped slaves, 'bush negroes', now living along the upper reaches of the Surinam river. A phonemic orthography which takes into account tone, nasalization, and length is proposed. In Gudschinsky (1959), 'Toneme representation in Mazatec Orthography', alternative ways of representing Mazatec tones are described. Numbers were found to be the most practical representations. In David G. Fox (1961), 'Some Psycholinguistic Considerations in Quiché Literacy', the relationship between certain morphemes that occur at terminal contours and intonation, and of word order in relation to punctuation in Quiché is studied.

The psychophonemic method devised by William C. Townsend is described in the following articles: W. C. Townsend (1956), 'El método psicofonémico de alfabetización'; Elaine Townsend (1952 and 1948), 'Construction and Use of Readers for Aymara Indians'; 'Accelerating Literacy by Piecemeal Digestion of the Alphabet'. The idea behind this method is to develop the association between sound and symbol and, so to speak, make the student psychologically literate at the initial stages by very carefully grading the material and presenting some of the most frequent graphemes in commonly used words.

The following articles deal with the preparation of literacy materials: William L. Wonderly 1961), 'Some Factors of Meaningfulness in Reading Matter for Inexperienced Readers'. The experienced reader retains parts of a sentence in mind until the whole can be decoded. The inexperienced reader tends to decode in sequential order and while he puzzles over one word he may forget what came before. Materials for beginning readers have to be designed bearing in mind the memory span of the decoder. This is achieved by using short sentences, no improbable collocations and a style that will be meaningful when the sentence is decoded in sequential order. Ethel Wallis (1952), 'Using Linguistic Analysis in Literacy Methods in Mexico', describes several primers which use different approaches because the languages, Tarasco, Tzeltal, Mazateco, and Zapoteco, are all different in their phonological structure. Raymond Eliott (1962) writes of 'Breves observaciones acerca de la relación entre la lingüística y el proceso de alfabetización'. There is no ideal method; each primer has to be designed to suit the language; in areas where an Indian language is spoken and there are no bilingual teachers, materials to acquaint the teacher with the language of the students have proved to be useful. In Catherine Church (1962) 'Algunas observaciones acerca de la elaboración de cartillas de alfabetización en lengua jacalteca', the complications which arose when trying to introduce the CVC pattern early in a Jacalteca primer are discussed. In Gudschinsky (1951-52) 'Solving the Mazateco Reading Problem', the procedures used to make reading easier for Mazatecos are described.

Pedagogical techniques are discussed in Gudschinsky (1958) 'Native Reactions to Tone in Mazatec' and John Beekman (1950) 'The use of Pre-primer Syllable Charts in Chol Literacy Work'. The emphasis in Beekman's article is on the pre-primer stage at which the learner becomes familiar with the graphemes.

6. As we have seen, linguists have not in any way been involved in literacy work for monolinguals in the national languages either within the framework of the primary school systems or of official programs and campaigns. Linguists could play a role by describing the different standard varieties of the official languages. Children could then be taught to write the standard of their community rather than that prescribed by the Academy as is sometimes the case. Research of the type undertaken in Puerto Rico would benefit primer writers in every country. The substandard dialects should also be described and contrastive studies could then be made from which the primary school teachers would benefit. Work of this kind is being undertaken in the United States.[11] The only Latin American linguist to have done any work along these lines is Berta Vidal de Battini in her book *El español de la Argentina* (1954). Methods of teaching literacy to children and adults could be improved by better knowledge of the relationship between speech and writing.

The linguistic situation has been mapped in very few countries in the area. Further research should be done in the non-Hispanic Caribbean where bilingualism is the rule rather than the exception. The linguistic situation in Haiti is well known. Some educators are aware of the linguistic problems and know how they could be solved, but for reasons beyond their control very little has been accomplished. In the European affiliated areas linguists have had very little influence except in Surinam. If the number of monolingual and bilingual speakers of each language were known and if there were adequate descriptions of the languages and contrastive analyses of every vernacular and the appropriate official standard, perhaps governments could be persuaded to undertake programs where literacy in the vernacular would be at least a stepping stone to literacy in the official language or where people would be taught to speak the official language before they were expected to learn to read and write in it.

Of the linguists who have been active in the literacy field in Indian languages, by far the largest number are members of the Summer Institute of Linguistics. Others are Mexican linguists. A handful have been active elsewhere. Besides the efforts of SIL members on their own, and as technical advisers to governments, very few official programs of any linguistic sophistication can be mentioned, although there have been some in Mexico, Guatemala, Venezuela, and Peru. The activities of SIL had been

[11] William A. Stewart (1964).

largely limited to languages with a relatively small number of speakers until recently when work in Quechua was included both in Ecuador and Peru. We can now hope that their work will have wider impact and that governments of countries where Indian languages are spoken will adopt the policy of making minorities bilingual and biliterate. If this ever becomes a reality, more citizens of these countries will need to be trained in linguistics and its applications.

Linguists have shown that their discipline can be valuable in the field of literacy, but remaining tasks of research, training, and application are still to come.

BIBLIOGRAPHY

Aguilera Dorantes, Mario, 'Guacochi: un centro para muchachas tarahumaras,' *A William Cameron Townsend* 209-26 (México, 1961).

Aguirre Beltrán, Gonzalo, *Teoría y Práctica de la Educación Indígena* (México, 1953).

Argentina, Ministerio de Educación y Justicia. *Informe a la Tercera Reunión de Ministros de Educación* (Bogotá, 4-10 de agosto de 1963). (Buenos Aires, 1963).

Arias, Jorge, 'El Analfabetismo en Guatemala', *Guatemala Indígena* 7.7-20 (1962).

Arroyo Ponce, Gamaniel and Donald H. Burns, 'El papel de las lenguas aborígenes en el proceso de incorporación del indígena a la vida nacional'. Paper read at the Fifth Interamerican Indianist Congress. Mimeographed. (Quito, 1964).

Beekman, John, 'The Use of Pre-primer Syllable Charts in Chol Literacy Work', *LL* 3.41-50 (Jan.-June, 1950).

Berry, Paul C., *Writing Haitian Creole: Issues and Proposals for Orthography*. Mimeographed. (Hudson Institute, New York, Dec. 1964).

Bolivia. Ministerio de Asuntos Campesinos. *SCIDE. Compa Conejo* by Toribio Claure. (La Paz, 1954).

Bolivia. Ministerio de Educación y Cultura. *Informe a la Tercera Reunión de Ministros de Educación*, (Bogotá, 4-19 de agosto de 1963). (La Paz, 1963).

Bolivian Indian Mission. *Quechua Silabario* (Adelaide, 1952).

Burns, Donald, 'El Instituto Lingüístico de Verano en la América Latina', Paper read at the First Inter-American Symposium in Linguistics and Language Teaching, Mimeographed (Cartagena, Colombia, Aug., 1963).

Caribbean Commission. *Education in the Caribbean* (Kent House, Trinidad, 1956).

——, *A Bibliography of Education in the Caribbean* (Kent House, Trinidad, 1959).

Castro de la Fuente, Angélica, 'La alfabetización en idiomas indígenas y los promotores culturales', *A William Cameron Townsend* 231-48 (México, 1961).

Chile. Ministerio de Educación Pública. *Informe a la Tercera Reunión de Ministros de Educación* (Bogotá, 4-10 de agosto de 1963). (Santiago, 1963).

Church, Catarina Maas de, 'Algunas observaciones acerca de la elaboración de cartillas de alfabetización en lengua jacalteca', *Guatemala Indígena* 5.29-34 (1962).

Colombia. Ministerio de Educación. *Informe a la Tercera Reunión de Ministros de Educación* (Bogotá, 4-10 de agosto de 1963). (Bogotá, 1963).

Costa Rica. Ministerio de Educación Pública. *Informe a la Tercera Reunión de Ministros de Educación* (Bogatá 4-10 de agosto de 1963). (San José, 1963).

CREFAL (Centro Regional de Educación Fundamental para el Desarrollo de la Comunidad en América Latina). *Cursillo sobre alfabetización funcional. Informes sobre nueve países* (Pátzcuaro, México, 1964).

Cuba. Comisión Nacional de Alfabetización. Ministerio de Educación. *Alfabeticemos. Manual para el alfabetizador* (1961).

——, ¡*Venceremos*! (1961).

Curle, Adam, *World Campaign for Universal Literacy: Comment and Proposal.* Harvard University Occasional Papers in Education and Development, No. 1 (1964).

De la Fuente, Julio, *Educación, antropología y desarrollo de la comunidad* (México, 1964).

Ecuador. Casa de la Cultura Ecuatoriana. *Plan nacional de alfabetización y educación de adultos* (Quito, 1964).

Ecuador. Ministerio de Educación Pública. *Informe a la Tercera Reunión de Ministros de Educación* (Bogotá, 4-10 de agosto de 1963). (Quito, 1963).

——, *Agenda del alfabetizador* (Quito, 1964). *Cartilla Ecuador* by Alberto Jácome in collaboration with Anibal Buitrón (Quito, 1964).

——, *Guía didáctica de la Cartilla Ecuador* (Quito, 1964).

——, *Guía para la enseñanza de cálculo* (Quito, 1964).

——, *Libro de Geografía. Segundo ciclo* (Quito, 1964).

——, *Libro de Historia. Segundo ciclo* (Quito, 1964).

Elliott, Raymond L., 'Breves observaciones acerca de la relación entre la lingüística y el proceso de alfabetización', *Guatemala Indígena* 5.35-44 (1962).

El Salvador. Ministerio de Cultura. *Informe a la Tercera Reunión de Ministros de Educación* (Bogotá, 4-10 de agosto de 1963). (San Salvador, 1963).

——, *Vamos a leer* (San Salvador).

Fagen, Richard R., *The Political Content of Adult Education* (Hoover Institution Studies, Stanford University, Stanford, 1964).

Fox, David G., 'Some Psycholinguistic Considerations in Quiché Literacy', *A William Cameron Townsend*, 256-72.(Mexico, 1961).

Guatemala. Dirección General de Cartografía. *Alfabetos Oficializados de Trece Principales Idiomas Indígenas de Guatemala.* Off-print of the *Diccionario Geográfico de Guatemala* (Guatemala, 1962).

Guatemala. Ministerio de Educación Pública. *Juan* (Guatemala).

Gudschinsky, Sarah C., 'Solving the Mazateco Reading Problem', *LL* 4.61-5 (1951-52).

——, 'Native Reactions to Tones and Words in Mazatec', *Word* 14.338-45 (1958).

——, 'Toneme Representation in Mazateco Orthography', *Word* 15.446-52 (1959).

——, *Handbook of Literacy*. Rev. ed. (Norman, Okla., 1962).

——, 'Techniques for Functional Literacy in Indigenous Languages and the National Languages'. Paper read at the Second Inter-American Symposium in Linguistics and Language Teaching, Mimeographed (Bloomington, Indiana, August, 1964).

Gutierrez, Darío, *El XII curso de capacitación para maestros bilingües de la selva y el fenómeno de cambio* (Yarinacocha, Perú, 1964).

Haiti. Ministère d'Education Nationale. *Rapport à la Troisième Reunion de Ministres d'Education* (Bogotá, août, 1963). (Port-au-Prince, 1963).

Hall, Robert A., *Haitian Creole: Grammar, Texts, Vocabulary. AAA* Memoir No. 74 (1953).

Hauch, Charles C., *Educational Trends in the Caribbean: European Affilitated Areas* (U.S. Department of Health, Education, and Welfare. Office of Education, Washington, 1960).

——, *The Current Situation in Latin American Education* (U.S. Department of Health, Education, and Welfare. Office of Education, Washington, 1963).

Hayes, Alfred S., *Recommendations of the Work Conference on Literacy* (Washington, 1965).

Hellinga, W. G., *Language Problems in Surinam* (Amsterdam, 1955).

Honduras. Ministerio de Educación Pública. *Mi mejor amigo* (Tegucigalpa, 1962).

——, *Informe a la Tercera Reunión de Ministros de Educación* (Bogotá, 4-10 de agosto de 1963). (Tegucigalpa, 1963).

Howes, H. W., *A Study of Fundamental, Adult, Literacy, and Community Education in the West Indies* (Caribbean Commission, Kent House, Trinidad, 1955).

Instituto Indigenista Interamericano. *Boletín Indigenista. Guía de la Población Indígena de América* (México, 1961).

——, 'El Programa Indigenista Andino' *Anuario Indigenista* 23.44-68 (1963).

Instituto Lingüístico de Verano. *A William Cameron Townsend* (México, 1961).

Instituto Lingüístico de Verano and Ministerio de Asuntos Campesinos, Bolivia. *Leesunchej. Cartilla quichua* by Snider Ada (La Paz, 1961).

Instituto Lingüístico de Verano in cooperation with El Instituto Indigenista Nacional, Guatemala, and the Ministerio de Educación Pública. *Guía para maestros. Cartillas de San Sebastián Coatán* (Guatemala, 1962).

Instituto Lingüístico de Verano en el Perú. *Bibliografía.* In collaboration with the Ministerio de Educación Pública del Perú and the University of Oklahoma (Yarinacocha, Peru, 1964).

Jean François, Gabriel, *Historique de la langue créole en Haïti et sa place dans l'enseignement.* Lelio Faublas, ed. (Port-au-Prince, No date).

Johnston, Marjorie, *Education in Mexico.* (U.S. Department of Health, Education, and Welfare, Office of Education, Washington, 1956).

Jolly, Richard, 'Education', *Cuba: The Economic and Social Revolution,* 161-280 Dudley Seers, ed. (Chapel Hill, N.C., 1964).

Jorge, Luis O., 'La escuela rural', *Enciclopedia de la Educación* II. 15. Nos. 1 and 2, 5-106 (Jan.-Dec., 1955).

Laubach Frank C. and Robert S. Laubach, *Toward World Literacy: The Each One Teach One Way* (Syracuse, 1960).

Lichtveld, Lou, 'National Language Planning'. Paper read at the Second Inter-American Symposium in Linguistics and Language Teaching. Mimeographed (Bloomington, Indiana, August, 1964).

Lopez Galarreta, Alberto, 'El plan de trabajo en la selva peruana', *A William Cameron Townsend* 281-92 (Mexico, 1961).

Marcano Blanco, Rafael, *La alfabetización y enseñanza elemental de adultos en Puerto Rico*. Departamento de Instrucción Pública, Mimeographed (Hato Rey, Puerto Rico, 1963).

Marino Flores, Anselmo, 'El monolingüismo indígena según los censos de población de 1930 y 1950', *A William Cameron Townsend*, 293-99 (Mexico, 1961).

Martins, Octavio A. L., 'Analfabetismo y nivel educativo en América Latina', *La Educación* 29 and 30, 60-91 (Jan.-June, 1963).

México. Instituto Nacional Indigenista. *Nueva cartilla mixteca* by Evangelina Arana (Mexico, 1960).

México. Patrimonio Indígena del Valle del Mezquital. *Aprendo a leer* by Emilia Wallis and Angélica Castro (México, 1957).

México. Secretaría de Educación Pública. Campaña Nacional contra el Analfabetismo. *Cartilla* (Mexico, 1965).

——, *Informe a la Tercera Reunión de Ministros de Educación* (Bogotá, 4-10 de agosto de 1963). (México, 1963).

Miñano García, Max H., 'The Rio Coco Pilot Project in Fundamental Education', *Fundamental and Adult Education* 9. 78-84 (April, 1957).

Morote Best, Efraín, 'Trabajo y escuela en la selva peruana', *A William Cameron Townsend* 301-12 (Mexico, 1961).

Navas Matute, Gonzalo, *Guía para la enseñanza del cálculo a los adultos en el primer ciclo de alfabetización* (Quito, 1964).

Nicaragua. Ministerio de Educación Pública. *Informe a la Tercera Reunión de Ministros de Educación* (Bogotá, 4-10 de agosto de 1963). (Managua, 1963).

OEA (Organización de los Estados Americanos). *La educación primaria en América Latina* by UNESCO. Mimeographed (Washington, January, 1963).

OEA. Instituto Interamericano de Estadística. *La estructura demográfica de las naciones americanas, 3: País de nacimiento, nacionalidad y lengua*; *4: Analfabetismo y nivel de educación* (Washington, 1960).

OEA. Unión Panamericana. *América en cifras 1961*. 8. *Estadísticas culturales* (Washington).

ONEC (Office National d'Education Communautaire). *Bulletin d'Information* No. 1 (Nov., 1962).

——, *Guide national d'alphabétization des adultes* (Port-au-Prince, 1962).

——, *Liv pa nou* (Port-au-Prince, 1962).

——, *Parlons français* (Port-au-Prince, 1963).

——, *Nap Li* (Port-au-Prince, 1964).

——, *Pri liv-la gnou Goud* (Port-au-Prince, 1964).

Pacheco, Armando Oscar, *La obra educativa de Trujillo* 1.163-214 (Ciudad Trujillo, 1955).

Panamá. Ministerio de Educación Pública. *Informe a la Tercera Reunión de Ministros de Educación* (Bogotá, 4-10 de agosto de 1963). (Panamá, 1963).

Paraguay. Ministerio de Educación y Culto. *Informe a la Tercera Reunión de Ministros de Educación* (Bogotá, 4-10 de agosto de 1963). (Asunción, 1963).

Paul, Edouard C. *L'alphabetisation en Haiti* (Port-au-Prince, 1965).

Perú. Ministerio de Educación Pública. *Informe a la Tercera Reunión de Ministros de Educación* (Bogotá, 4-10 de agosto de 1963). (Lima, 1963).

——, *Planes y Programas. Curso de capacitación para nativos alfabetizados de la selva peruana* (ILV, Yarinacocha, 1964).

Perú. Ministerio de Educación Pública. Dirección de Educación Primaria y del Adulto. *Planes y Programas para el curso de capacitación ocupacional para indígenas de la selva* (Yarinacocha, 1964).

Posada, Jaime. *La guerra contra la pobreza en América Latina.* Speech delivered in Jan. 1965. Mimeographed (PanAmerican Union, Washington).

Pressoir, Charles F., *Débats sur le Créole et le Folklore* (Port-au-Prince, 1947).

——, *Méthode de français oral à l'usage de l'haitien débutant* (Port-au-Prince, 1954).

Puerto Rico. Consejo Superior de Enseñanza. Unviersidad de Puerto Rico. *A divertirnos sanamente* (Rio Piedras, 1953).

——, *A cuidar la salud* (Rio Piedras, 1953).

——, *Nuestra isla* (Rio Piedras, 1953).

——, *A la escuela!* (Rio Piedras, 1953).

——, *Los trabajadores* (Rio Piedras, 1953).

——, *El ciudadano en una democracia* (Rio Piedras, 1953).

——, *El valor nutritivo de las frutas del país* (S. Juan, Puerto Rico, 1959).

Puerto Rico Departamento de Instrucción Pública. *Manual para la enseñanza de lectura y escritura a adultos analfabetos* (Río Piedras, 1956).

——, *Prontuario para los maestros. Primer nivel Programa de Alfabetización* (1959).

——, *Prontuario para los maestros. Segundo nivel. Programa de Alfabetización.* (1959).

——, *Prontuario para los maestros. Tercer nivel. Programa de Alfabetización.* (1959).

——, *Unidades de ciencia elemental y estudios sociales. Segundo nivel* (1958).

——, *Unidades de ciencia elemental y estudios sociales. Tercer Nivel* (1958).

——, *Catálogo de materiales del Programa de Enseñanza Elemental de Adultos* (Hato Rey, 1964).

——, *Ejemplos de planes para los grados primero, segundo y tercero del programa de enseñanza elemental de adultos* Mimeographed (Hato Rey, 1964).

——, *Informe anual: Programa de Enseñanza Elemental de Adultos, Año Fiscal 1963-1964*. Mimeographed (Hato Rey, 1964).

República Dominicana. Secretaría de Estado de Educación y Bellas Artes. *Campaña Trujillo de Alfabetización Total* (Ciudad Trujillo, 1957).

Rodriguez Bou, Ismael, *Recuento de vocabulario español I* (Rio Piedras, 1952).

——, *El programa de alfabetización y las cooperativas*, Mimeographed (Rio Piedras, 1953).

——, 'Pointers on Literacy'. Paper presented at the Seminar on the Role of Adult Education in the Caribbean Area. Mimeographed (Jamaica, Sept., 1952).

——, *Apuntes sobre el programa de alfabetización*. Speech delivered in 1954. Mimeographed.

——, *El programa de alfabetización. Consideraciones sobre sus metas y logros.* Speech delivered in 1955. Mimeographed.

——, *Illiteracy Freedom and Justice*. Speech delivered in 1959. Mimeographed.

——, *Educación de Adultos*. Mimeographed (Río Piedras, 1960).

Rosenblat, Angel, *La población indígena y el mestizaje en América*. (Buenos Aires, 1954).

Rubio Orbe, Gonzalo, 'Algo sobre la población del Ecuador', *A William Cameron Townsend* 355-86 (Mexico, 1961).

Rycroft, Stanley W. and Myrtle M. Clemmer, 'Literacy and Adult Education', *A Factual Study of Latin America*, 151-55 (United Presbyterian Church, New York).

Seers, Dudley, ed., *Cuba: The Economic and Social Revolution* (Chapel Hill, N.C., 1964).

Les Sociétés Bibliques. *Quatre Lettres de l'apôtre Paul, Kat lèt lapòt pòl té écri* (Paris, 1961).

Solnit, Albert J., 'Educación bilingüe y desarrollo comunal en la Amazonia', *Desarrollo y Democracia* 3.1-7 (1964).

Stewart, William A., ed., *Non-Standard Speech and the Teaching of English* (Washington, 1964).

Summer Institute of Linguistics. *Bibliography* (Santa Ana, Cal., 1964).

Swadesh, Mauricio. 'El impacto sociológico de la enseñanza en lengua vernácula'. Paper read at the Second Inter-American Symposium in Linguistics and Language Teaching. Mimeographed (Bloomington, Indiana, August, 1964).

Townsend, Elaine, 'Accelerating Literacy by Piecemeal Digestion of the Alphabet', *LL* 1.9-19 (July, 1948).

——, 'Construction and Use of Readers for Aymara Indians', *Fundamental and Adult Education* 4.21-6 (Oct., 1952).

Townsend, William C., 'El método psicofonémico de alfabetización', *Homenaje al Dr. Manuel Gamio*, 685-92 (México, 1956).

UN *Demographic Yearbook* 1963 (New York, 1964).

UNESCO. *The Mexican Cultural Mission Programme* by Lloyd Hughes (Paris, 1950).

——, *L'Expérience Témoin d'Haïti* (Paris, 1951).

——, *Social Welfare Work in Jamaica: A Study of the Jamaica Social Welfare Commission* by Roger Marier (Paris, 1953).

——, *The Use of Vernacular Languages in Education* (Paris, 1953).

——, *Literacy Teaching: A Selected Bibliography* (Paris, 1956).

——, *World Illiteracy at Mid-Century* (Paris, 1957).

——, *The Provision of Popular Reading Materials* (Paris, 1959).

——, *Literacy Primers, Construction, Evaluation, and Use,* by Karel Neijs (Paris, 1961).

——, *World Campaign for Universal Literacy: Request Addressed to UNESCO by the General Assembly of the UN at its 16th Session* (Paris, 1962).

——, *World Campaign for Universal Literacy* (Paris, 1963).

——, *International Guide to Educational Documentation* 1955-60 (Paris, 1963).

UNESCO and Bureau of Education. *Literacy and Education for Adults* (Geneva, 1964).

UNESCO and Pan American Union. *La tuberculosis.* Biblioteca Popular Latinoamericana (Washington, 1952).

Uruguay. *Censo general de población y vivienda, 1963* (Montevideo).

Uruguay. Comisión de Desarrollo e Inversiones Económicas. *Informe preliminar sobre la situación en el Uruguay* 1930-60. Mimeographed.

Uruguay. Ministerio de Instrucción Pública. *Informe a la Tercera Reunión de Ministros de Educación* (Bogotá, 4-10 de agosto de 1963). (Montevideo, 1963).

FOREIGN LANGUAGE TEACHING IN LATIN AMERICA

FRANCISCO GOMES DE MATOS and LEOPOLDO WIGDORSKY

I. INTRODUCTION

The difficult task entrusted to us by the editor of this volume has proven to be challenging in far more ways than these reviewers had ever thought of anticipating. Upon being offered the assignment of surveying — in less than eleven months' time, and amidst all sorts of professional commitments in their respective countries — the status and trends of foreign language teaching in the highly diversified complex which is Latin America, the writers began corresponding and exchanging views on how best to divide the assignment and proceed with the data-gathering process; an originally agreed upon outline was thus eventually changed so as to accommodate minor changes.

It was soon discovered how hard it would be to collect statistical data in order to present as objective a report as possible of many countries. Another discovery was that the questionnaire method, ideal in many circumstances, did not — in this case — seem to bring forth the kinds of prompt responses needed. The writers do not wish to sound apologetic at this point but only to make it clear that whatever they have achieved in this article is a result of the contributions of individuals who were asked to interpret the situation in their respective countries rather than of the present writers' original interpretations and analyses, as would have been the case if it had been possible for them to travel to at least some of the leading nations in the field intended to be covered. The shortcomings in the ensuing reports are, obviously, the responsibility of the writers alone but, in all fairness, it should be pointed out that the difficulties encountered in the process of gathering the data forced the writers to focus rather extensively on some countries and make but passing mention of others.

The task of surveying the field of foreign language teaching in Latin America should optimally be carried out in terms of representative regions and then gradually in terms of individual countries. It is the writers' hope that their efforts at compiling the body of fragmentary information presented here will point to the need of a series of detailed surveys. In 1964 the Center for Applied Linguistics of the Modern Language Association of America issued a questionnaire to be sent to representative teachers in Latin America and to all individuals directly involved in the teaching of English as a foreign language in that part of the world; the purpose of that initiative was to obtain information that might enrich the Center's files on the teaching of English as a foreign language. Praiseworthy initiatives such as the one just mentioned are bound to be launched in the near future; only when this has been accomplished shall we truly be able to assess in depth some of the crucial problems affecting the status of foreign language teaching in Latin America.

The difficulty in obtaining information from individuals and from institutions is aggravated by the fact that the published literature on our theme is meager and, at times, virtually inaccessible. Specialized library resources concerning the field of foreign language teaching proved relatively scant in both writers' home countries and, needless to say, information on the status of foreign languages in the Latin American schools proved even harder to obtain. In spite of all these obstacles and shortcomings the writers believe to have succeeded in — at least — doing their assignments on a closer rapport than had been planned. Except for the treatment of four countries (Argentina, Brazil, Chile and Uruguay), where the responsibility of a single writer was possible, this survey was — in general — done on a bilateral basis.

We take this opportunity to express our deepest appreciation to all those who were most cooperative and kind in supplying us with the data requested and, in some cases, in suggesting means of obtaining further information. This should, in fact, be the place for a list of individuals and institutions deserving meritorious credit for their indispensable assistance. The reports received ranged from six-page essays to one-page letters. People representing the fields of English, French, German and Italian as foreign languages, administrators of foreign language schools, heads of teacher training centers, textbook authors, directors of scholarship granting institutions, editors of journals, linguists, educators, these are just some of those who made the present survey possible.

In addition to their disappointment at not being able to obtain as much information as they had planned, the writers can not help feeling frustrated in their intentions to offer a comprehensive view of all of the foreign languages taught in Latin America. The fact that the present work leans so heavily on the status of English as a foreign language is, perhaps, an indicator of the very importance given to that language in the area under consideration. Our efforts to secure data on French as well as on other languages may not have been strong enough, but the fact remains that the generalizations made on the status of foreign languages other than English are based on a geographically broad coverage — which, after all, is a consolation in the long run.

The writers feel deeply grateful to the Editors for having permitted them to share the burden of a challenging — at times, frustrating — but above all gratifying assignment. Needless to say, the present report is to be considered as a mere stimulus for deeper and wider analyses. On the other hand, we are conscious of the fact that considerably improved results might have been obtained from more capable members of the teaching profession: we consequently submit this work to the kind reader in the same spirit of humility which prevailed throughout its preparation.

II. FOREIGN LANGUAGE TEACHING IN BRAZIL

1. *Brief Historical Background: Evolution of FL teaching*

In a survey intended to be informative rather than comprehensively critical it would be impossible to provide the reader with an adequate historical background to the field of FL teaching in Brazil; what can be done instead is to offer an outline presentation of historically significant events which shaped and/or have been shaping the development of the field in Brazil. At the end of this section the reader may find a few bibliographical sources which will help him pursue the desired topic in somewhat greater detail.

It has been stated by an eminent Brazilian educator that the 'evolution of FL teaching in Brazil is closely linked to the history of the Brazilian Secondary School itself'.[1] According to his analysis of the evolution of FL teaching in Brazil two historical stages can be distinguished: one from 1855 to 1931 and another after 1931. Eight years have elapsed since the publication of Professor Valnir Chagas' valuable work, and an event of great importance to Brazilian educational history took place in 1961: the passing and subsequent enforcement of the Law of Foundations and Norms of National Education (Lei de Diretrizes e Bases da Educação Nacional) which has been giving the secondary and university curricula a more flexible and realistic organization than ever before.

It can easily be seen that historically, at least, changes in FL teaching have always gone hand in hand with major educational reforms in Brazil. The first stage described by Professor Chagas was characterized by a complete lack of official concern over the methodology of FL teaching and a greater importance attached to Latin or to a Latin-based teaching of languages, in other words, both classical and modern languages were taught according to the same overall scheme of Grammar-Reading Translation. In 1931 a reform of secondary school teaching was launched which affected somewhat strongly (and for the first time) the teaching of foreign languages. This second stage was characterized by the official recognition of the so-called Direct Method and its derivatives through well thought out teaching-programs "which, notable exceptions notwithstanding, have not ... been put into practice up to now'. The present writer would add a third stage to the two periods proposed by the Brazilian educator referred to above. The third stage can be said to have started in 1961 with the enactment of the law already alluded to and, which is more significant from the point of view of FL teaching, because of the slow but gradual awakening, especially on the part of some institutions, to truly linguistically oriented approaches and resulting improvement in language teaching standards. The predominance of Latin in the curriculum, the teaching of the grammar rather than of the language, the teaching of the written language, translation activities, a growing concern over the

[1] R. Valnir, Chagas, *Didática especial de línguas modernas* (São Paulo, 1957), 504; See esp. Chap. Three: 'Evolução do Ensino das Línguas no Brasil', 84-101.

teaching of spoken skills, initial attempts at systematized FL teaching — all such descriptive phrases could be attributed to the successive steps in the evolution of FL teaching in Brazil. Let's, however, leave history and go into the other topics outlined at the beginning of this section.

2. *The Contemporary Scene: FL Teaching in Secondary Schools, Universities and in Private Institutions*

Practically the only modern or living foreign languages which are taught in the secondary schools in Brazil are English and French in that order of importance. French had reigned supreme throughout the first stage of Brazilian secondary school education and had kept its leadership (although a slight one) up till the outbreak of World War II when the rise of English as a FL in Brazil can be said to start. An example of a humble but pioneering text for the teaching of English was *Inglês para as Américas*[2] (which had been pretested in mimeographed form in the Rio de Janeiro American-Brazilian Cultural Institute and published under its auspices in 1947). Since high school students are now given the option of only one foreign language, English gets to be favored in a ratio of eighty percent or more as against French. It might be interesting to illustrate the present trend with a typical instance: in São Paulo State official secondary schools the educational authorities favored both English and French: the former being taught in the first and second years of "Ginásio" and the latter being offered in the third and fourth grades.

In most private secondary schools in Brazil it may be a safe generalization to state that English is by far predominant and French is often not available at all. Latin and Greek have been eliminated almost entirely from the secondary schools curriculum because of their optional status. Spanish had a short-lived existence in the secondary schools — it was made into a required foreign language upon a Ministry of Education decision in 1943, but did not continue partly because of the overloaded curriculum (as many as eleven subjects) and also because it was offered as a one-year subject, two classes a week. German and Italian, which were featured in the First Stage (1855-1931), the former as a required subject and the latter as an elective, were destined to gradually disappear; so much so that only German is offered under very special circumstances in a few private schools located in Southern Brazilian states where the density of German population is relatively high. Unless another educational policy comes into effect it seems plausible to foresee the evergrowing supremacy of English language teaching in Brazilian secondary schools with most unfortunate consequences for the status of French not only on the secondary but also on the university level. Symptomatic of this trend is the scarcity of textbooks for the teaching of French, especially the locally produced ones, not to mention the almost total absence of recently

[2] Ned Carey Fahs, and S. Raymond Sayers, *Inglês para as américas, A new textbook for Brazilian students* (Rio de Janeiro, 1947), 113.

published ones. The major publishing firms dealing with FL teaching materials in Brazil have already started refraining from the publication of new textbooks for the teaching of French, re-issuing, instead, the same outdated texts already available or catering to the popular taste and predilection for grammars, dictionaries, and teach-yourself type manuals. In spite of its highly privileged position in the high school curriculum, English as it is offered now (two, three, or four years in a seven-year program of studies) leaves much to be desired both quantitatively and qualitatively, turning out to be a victim of the greater educational flexibility now prevailing.

A student who takes English in the lower grades of high school only, will have to face the problem of taking an entrance examination to college some years later, and the time elapsed between his initial acquaintance with the language and the taking of such exam will act as a negative factor in his preparation. What is he to do to prepare for an exam which unrealistically tests reading, comprehension, spoken skills, along with control of grammatical terminology, thus placing heavier demands on the students' incipient knowledge of the language, than he could have possibly acquired after a short - term exposure in high school?

It would be extremely hard for a foreign reader to understand the predicament of Brazilian students as regards taking examinations without a simple explanation of the prevailing cultural attitudes toward examinations and tests in Brazil. Both because of a teaching tradition whereby students are prepared for final exams and in view of the fact that exams are interpreted by students as highly competitive events, a connotation of fearful enterprise becomes invariably attached to the very word "prova" in Brazilian Portuguese. It is not surprising to hear even very bright students state that they are afraid of examinations and, which is more revealing culturally, that they sometimes take tranquilizers the day before the examination is to take place. The knowledge of the above situation is indispensable to an understanding of the causes that hamper teaching in general and especially so foreign language teaching in Brazil. The fact that most teachers adhere or stick slavishly to the contents of a textbook throughout the year leads some students to become indifferent to the language learning process and instead prepare the key parts of the lessons which are to be "officially" included in the exams (instructors often tell students what will be covered) thus reinforcing the age old habit of memorization of conjugations, paradigms, and passages translated into Portuguese. This sad state of affairs is symptomatic of the whole country and points to the absence of psychological orientation on the part of teachers, educators, and parents, concerning attitudes toward learning and testing. The latter figures prominently among the wholly neglected topics (to say "disciplines" would be far too ambitious) in the teacher-training programs given in the Faculdades de Filosofia of Brazilian Universities.

The highly significant trend, to be seen in Brazil to a larger extent than in any other country in South America — for laymen, students, and professional workers, even unskilled laborers to resort to books written in English (even without any previous knowledge of the language) and to try to absorb a little of the valuable information contained in such publications (almost all published in the U.S.) is thus being damagingly offset or counterbalanced by the unsound attitudes developed by students in high schools. The successful taking of exams often means getting oneself rid of something undesirable or frightening. How much motivation for foreign language learning has died prematurely in Brazilian classrooms because of the mixed feelings of indifference and aversion built up in the students' minds through an alleged failure either in language performance or in taking exams?

The students whose parents can afford it turn to private schools of languages where actual language learning takes place or hire a private teacher on an hourly basis. The negative tone expressed in the preceding statements reflects the bitter truth regarding the role of English (and other foreign languages) in Brazilian secondary schools: they are taught more in the fashion of ordinary disciplines than as languages worthy of study in themselves. The secondary school students are mostly prepared to take the exams rather than to develop any kind of skills in the foreign language. Attempts at an improvement of the situation can be seen even on a state-wide basis — the state of São Paulo (Brasil's largest) has commissioned a group of specialists and teachers of English to prepare a syllabus and to work out provisions for the production of adequate materials and modernization of teaching techniques. The little improvement which is to be witnessed in the next few years will certainly be the result of initiatives undertaken at the local or state levels, rather than regional or national ones.

Let's turn now to FL teaching in universities and comment briefly on the status of the more commonly taught languages, that is, English, French, Italian, German, and Spanish.

On the college level English also leads the way and here the qualitative gap between it and its closest competitor (French) is a great deal wider than in the case of secondary school teaching. Students who take English in Brazilian universities are offered more opportunities for efficient learning than do those who take French — this is partly due to teacher training standards being improved by greater specialization and preparation both abroad and at home but it also reflects a number of other complex cultural factors which cannot be dealt with here.

In universities English can be taken as a subject of professional specialization, that is, which leads to a teaching certificate or a licentiate degree or in some cases as a required language for instrumental use in scientific disciplines. The latter case is typical, for example, of the University of Brasília (Brazil's best planned institution of higher learning) where science students take English compulsorily. Ever since the enforcement of the Law of Foundations and Norms there have been some radical changes in the organization of the so-called 'curricula of letters' in most Brazilian universities and although there are differences as to detail, the general plan is pretty much the same: to prepare a student, upon completion of a four-year program of courses, to teach Portuguese and only one foreign language.

In many universities another foreign language is offered along with the one chosen by the student, so as to give him a chance to learn about it (one or two-year offerings only); this is surprisingly done under the guise of 'experimentation', but it actually boils down to a perpetualized remnant of former systems where the teacher-to-be was forced to be exposed to French, Italian, and Spanish in addition to Latin and Portuguese in order to be granted the degree of Licentiate in Neo-Latin Letters. The heavily overloaded curriculum of letters which prevailed until 1961 produced generations of teachers poorly prepared to teach even one language, if any at all. Granted that the present system is far from perfect it has, nevertheless, gone a long way toward a long-dreamed of goal of prospective FL teachers: the possibility of pursuing a less diversified but more concentrated program of studies leading to a reasonable degree of professional competency in the teaching of one foreign language. More changes are bound to be made within the decade under way which may affect not only the organization of the curriculum of letters but, more importantly, the role of the FL teacher and which may perhaps bring about a badly needed revival of interest in other foreign languages, such as German and Spanish, so underservedly neglected, particularly so the latter.

In some Brazilian universities Spanish is not being offered this year or it has a minimum enrollment enough to barely justify one course.

The gradual decline of interest toward Spanish in Brazil can perhaps be explained in terms of a high degree of cultural indifference to a language supposed, by the average Brazilian, to be so similar to Portuguese as not to be worth devoting oneself to and in terms of the relative cultural and linguistic isolation of Brazil in the Southern Hemisphere which favors closer rapport with the United States and (increasingly less now) with Europe.

The ever stronger cultural bonds between Brazil and the United States only adds to the interest in English language learning — English is the window to a world of success in business, industry, science, the arts, international relations. The learning of English, to the average educated Brazilian, represents a chance to make up for the still relatively little international prestige of the mother tongue. It is too soon to make predictions, but with the slow but steadily rising wave of interest for Brazilian Portuguese studies in the United States (witness, for example, the launching in the near future of the first textbook of Modern Portuguese produced by a team of American and Brazilian specialists) more and more Brazilians will reciprocate the attention being given to Portuguese by turning to English. That something needs to be done about this sort of cultural aversion toward Spanish in Brazil is dramatically true, and the opposite holds true about the teaching of Portuguese in Spanish-speaking countries.

Enrollments of German in Faculdades de Filosofia, as the eighty-eight teacher training colleges are still known in Brazil, have been dropping at a frightening rate. Enrollment figures involving foreign languages offered at Faculdade de Filosofia of the University of Brasil (Rio de Janeiro) 1965 were as follows (figures refer to first year courses only):

Portuguese and English (136)
Portuguese and French (99)
Portuguese and Spanish (28)
Portuguese and Italian (13)
Portuguese and German (7)

Needless to say, the above figures can not be taken as universally representative of the Brazilian situation, especially as regards Spanish. Another example is that of one of Brazil's leading Catholic Universities, The Pontifical Catholic University of São Paulo, where in its Faculty of Philosophy the 1965 enrollments for FL's were as follows:

English - 28
French - 18
German - 1
Spanish - No students enrolled
Optional Courses
Italian - 15
German - 14
Spanish - 14

For fear that the above figures may be misleading to the reader it would be well to explain that in Rio de Janeiro alone there are four "Faculdades de Filosofia", three of which are private. The relatively low number of students enrolled in the first year results from the existing conditions: fewer youngsters are attracted into the teaching profession and women students outnumber men in education courses and in foreign languages: in 1957 72% of the total enrollment for the so called "Cursos de Letras Anglo-Germânicas" (Anglo German Letters: English, German, Portuguese, Latin, Literatures and Methodology) in Brazilian Universities was made up of women, and again the female sex constituted 75% of the total enrollment in the "Cursos de Letras Neolatinas" (Neo-Latin letters: Latin, French, Spanish, Italian, Portuguese, Literatures, Methodology). The Faculdades de Filosofia in addition to having a student shortage, have to compete with private institutions where teacher-training standards are high. The Rio de Janeiro American-Brazilian Cultural Institute offers a two-year training program for prospective teachers of English which is considerably more productive than its counterparts in most if not all Faculdades in Brazil. The vocational problem as regards foreign language teaching looms large: perhaps one third or even less of a graduating class in foreign languages will become teachers. The writer recalls that only a male classmate and himself took up teaching as a profession out of a group of nine students who obtained a Licentiate in Anglo-German Letters in 1956 at the Faculdade de Filosofia de Pernambuco of the University of Recife. The overwhelmingly larger proportion of women students to men students in the foreign languages courses at the Brazilian Universities is still characteristic at present even with the more flexible course offerings and the possibility of majoring in only one foreign language. The number of diploma-seeking students in such Faculdades would be surprisingly high to a foreign observer — many of the students would not conceal their proposed objectives, whether the one alluded to, which is culturally disastrous, or just killing time or looking for a husband in the case of women.

The changes being introduced in the university curriculum of letters place heavier demands on teacher-trainers since more time has to be devoted to just one foreign language and the trainees can improve their command of spoken skills — a language laboratory is an asset in such cases but unfortunately only two Brazilian universities could boast of such a resource up till 1964 — and at the same time study the descriptive aspects of the language preceding a concentrated training in methodology of that particular language as well as practice teaching. A cogent discussion of the problems affecting the curriculum of letters in Brazil at present is given in an article written by an eminent Brazilian professor.[3]

In response to a questionnaire sent him, a professor of Italian at a small Brazilian university stated that 'on account of the recent changes made Italian was taught only in the second year (3 hours a week), therefore, it is impossible for students to study literature and everything boils down to grammar, reading, conversation and nomenclature'. Such a quotation is very revealing of the situation in many universities. Whether the position of Italian, German, and Spanish will weaken more and more in terms of students' preference, it is too soon to know — it seems, however, at the present moment that although statistically underprivileged, such languages may have a chance, their first golden chance, to survive on their own in and of themselves, freed from the shackles of a heterogeneous and unrealistic system which put as many as three FL's together in an incipient 3-year Baccalaureate Program. The writer can envisage, consequently, a strengthening and more careful planning of FL courses in universities geared to the needs and free inclinations of young students who no longer feel that they have to adjust to the impositions of the system but instead can pursue a career in the one FL they actually choose.

Other foreign languages taught in (very few) universities, especially in the South where immigration was most channeled to, are Japanese, Arabic, and Hebrew. Except for the five modern languages commonly taught, other FL offerings in the Brazilian university curriculum are exceptional and somewhat conditioned to particular local situations. This panoramic description of FL teaching in secondary schools and universities is obviously incomplete but an attempt to do otherwise would be beyond the goals of a section in a chapter.

Let us proceed, then, to FL teaching in private institutions — a topic deserving of a chapter-length treatment to say the least. 'Private institutions' means 'schools other than those on a secondary or university level whether privately or officially supported and maintained'. Included in the category of private institutions are such FLT centers as the Brazilian-American Cultural Institutes (technically known as Binational

[3] Ataliba de Castilho, 'A reforma dos cursos de letras', *ALFA* (São Paulo, March 1963).

Centers), Brazilian Societies of English Culture, French-Brazilian Cultural Associations, German-Brazilian Cultural Institutes, Hispanic Culture Centers, Brazilian-Italian Institutes, the Yázigi Institute of Languages, to mention only the best known specialized centers of FL teaching in the country. In a report on the first Inter-American Symposium in Linguistics and Language Teaching published in IRAL[4] the present writer mentioned the Binational Center Language Teaching Activities (American English) as one of the typical examples of wholly or partly successful teaching programs in Latin America. It may be appropriate to add now, that this is most vehemently so in the case of Brazil. Some of the outstanding contributions made by Binational Center Language Teaching in Brazil can be summarized as follows:

Over twenty five years' experience in the sponsoring and planning of two-week summer seminars for teachers of English, often with State of Federal government recognition (17 Seminars were held in Brazil in 1963 attended by nearly a thousand teachers) have turned such Centers in the most influential sources of methodological and linguistic inspiration in the country. It is primarily due to the influence of such seminars and other longer teacher-training programs (in Rio de Janeiro, São Paulo, Belo Horizone, Recife among other cities) that secondary teachers of English have become acquainted with newer methodological approaches and teaching techniques and that they are being given the opportunity to take the Michigan Proficiency Examination or to apply for a scholarship to study in the United States, thus helping to disseminate important ideas and concepts to others in the profession. It can be said that the efforts of the Binational Centers scattered all over Brazil have done more to the cause of better English language teaching than any other institution or group of institutions of a similar kind. The production of pioneering textbooks for the learning of spoken English and the preparation of manuals designed to orient the teacher according to present day trends[5] and the almost universal emphasis on the teaching of Spoken English in private institutions is a consequence of the role played by the Brazilian-American Cultural Centers. One of the pioneering sensibly produced high school series for the learning of English in Brazil, *Learning by Doing* (by Heini Wenzel — Rio de Janeiro, 1957) was prefaced by the then English Language Consultant for Binational Centers in Brazil, Mr. John J. Ewing, who actually helped that author by writing a Manual of Pronunciation to be used in conjunction with the four-volume series. In his introduction Mr. Ewing points out that 'the series meets all the requirements considered essential for a good beginning text for secondary school', and he adds that the Rio de Janeiro Binational Center had begun to use such books in demonstration classes in their annual seminars for English teachers. Binational Center officials have been contributing very vigorously to the

[4] Francisco Gomes de Matos, 'Interamerican symposium brings linguists and teachers together', *IRAL* Vol. 1/3 u.4, (Heidelberg, 1964). Reprinted in *English teaching forum*, *USIA* No. 1, (1964).

[5] A. J. Hald Madsen, *Teaching English in Brazil*. Practical Linguistics and Methodology for English teachers. (Rio de Janeiro, Ao Livro Técnico S.A., 1964), 163.

incorporation of the latest scientific techniques in Brazilian classrooms and textbooks. The so-called oral approach has in Brazil been almost overwhelmingly associated with the materials produced by the staff of the English Language Institute of the University of Michigan; no wonder, therefore, that some Brazilian-textbook writers give credit to that center for inspiration. The influence of American methodological approaches has been felt in Brazil especially in the Binational Centers, in the Yázigi Institute of Languages, and in a few universities where one or two faculty members happened to have pursued graduate-level programs of study in the United States through teacher-development grants sponsored by the State Department. In the English departments of some of Brazil's largest universities the visitor from abroad is likely to meet a teacher who has studied in the Universities of Michigan, Texas, Georgetown, and San Francisco State College among others. Names like Fries, Lado, and Prator are relatively well known to Brazilian teachers of English who have studied under specialists trained in the United States. An interesting fact about the influence of the oral approach is that along with it there has arisen an interest in applied linguistics. The only book published in Portuguese dealing with linguistics for language teachers is still the translation of Edwin Cornelius' *Language Teaching* — the Brazilian edition came out four years after the publication of the English original (1957) and it is now out of print. There certainly seems to be a market for books of this sort, whether locally produced or translations of significant American and European works. Eight years have gone by since the appearance of Cornelius' *O Ensino de Idiomas* (São Paulo, Editôra Nacional) but not a single new title in Portuguese has been made available commercially since then. Would this be an indication of publishers' general reluctance to invest in the field of FL teaching manuals or of the lack of competent individuals who could write such books? The first alternative seems to be the plausible answer — the very initial transition of the field as regards privileged private institutions, where some departures are being made from the traditionally used approaches to FL teaching, does not serve as a strong justification for publishers to acknowledge this commercially — witness the general poor quality of textbooks produced for secondary schools — let alone to publish guides to FL teaching which may incorporate some of the principles and findings of the still relatively new field of Applied Linguistics. Those who state that the discipline of Linguistics was prematurely included in the Brazilian University curriculum (the author is bound to sympathize with such view now) without a carefully thought out blueprint for its implantation in the nation's oversurplus of Faculdades de Filosofia, are not surprised to find that publishers reject suggestions for translations of important introductory texts in linguistics because of the low potential market for such works.

Long before the official recognition and introduction of Linguistics in the Brazilian University curriculum (see the Linguistic Reporter article, Oct. 1962) Binational Centers had already stimulated the minds of hundreds of teachers with some of the basic principles of the science of languages, especially as applied to English language teaching. To give credit to all the American and Brazilian teachers who have contributed to the successful evolution of BN centers would call for too lengthy a description, better fitted to a still-to-be written history of Binational Center English Teaching Programs in Latin America, where Brazil would figure prominently.

Although far from being characterized by uniformity of methodological approaches, Binational Centers in Brazil, especially the ones located in the country's largest cities have achieved an enviable degree of efficiency in their English teaching programs. A Teachers' Association has been developed in one of them (see the March 1963 issue of the English Teaching Form) so as to evidence the seriousness of purpose binding teachers together.

The introduction of electronic language laboratories in such centers (7 were in operation in 1964) — added greatly to the already existing assets, although it has brought about a need for the construction of and experimentation with material adequate for use in the laboratory, whether as supplementary to the textbooks used or as fully integrated courses. To say that such labs were operationally ready for use would be more descriptive of the present situation — the Agency for International Development upon donating most of the electronic laboratories now installed in Brazil was certainly well intentioned, but how well prepared were the teachers to use such labs to be able to make their students profit from such resources? The word laboratory, such as the expression audio-visual, has become fashionable, as can be seen in ads publicizing the 'electronic teaching of foreign languages' in some of Brazil's bigger cities such as Rio de Janeiro, São Paulo, Recife, and Porto Alegre. Are language laboratories used as true reinforcers of the teacher's work or is modern technological gadgetry being used for the sake of novelty; thus defeating its very purposes? That laboratories are being misused should not come as a shock to impartial observers — they were as prematurely introduced on the scene in Brazil as was linguistics in the college curriculum. In the case of linguistics, emergency attempts were and are being made to remedy the situation, but in the case of laboratories each institution has the final say, and professional pride often hampers enlightenment if it is offered. A great deal of assistance is needed to see that such costly equipment and installations do not go to waste — the institutions which were generous enough to donate such aids could either provide such training for the proper utilization of laboratories or then try to persuade the Brazilian institutions to finance such badly needed orientation.

In 1963, according to statistics supplied by the United States Information Agency, there were thirty-eight large Binational Centers in Brazil (a third of the total number of such institutions in Latin America) with an estimated total enrollment of 39,957 students. In that year Argentina ranked second with thirteen centers. The number of Anglophil Societies (called Brazilian Societies of English Culture) operating in Brazil totaled ten in 1964 as against thirty-five in Argentina and fifteen in Uruguay. A basic difference between the American and British Centers is that the former are usually given a more substantial material assistance, but it is interesting to note that FL teaching with British attempts to keep up with modern developments are gaining momentum — six language labs had been installed at the time of writing, and plans to equip all the 'Culturas' were well under way. The fact that they are independent organizations (not under the control of the British Council although to some institutes a British Council officer is seconded as Director and a small subsidy is made available) accounts for the difficulty in obtaining statistics for them. The Alliances Françaises, like other institutions maintained by the strong spirit of cultural cooperation and friendship between Brazil and a foreign country, are autonomous entities pursuing a variety of goals, among which is the teaching of French language and civilization.

Generalizations on the quality of instruction prevailing in either British or French institutes are dangerous to make because of the lack of published literature and the difficulty in obtaining reliable, objective reports — personal and, therefore, hasty observations made by the writer resulting from visits paid to centers in the largest Brazilian cities (including interviews with key personnel) can give but a fragmented glimpse of the total picture, which is sufficiently complex and multifaceted, to call for a rather patient and detailed analysis. Instead of risking any critical statements, devoid of objectivity, the writer would rather focus on two facts which have impressed him regarding the operation of the above mentioned centers: attention to the teaching of the spoken language (with utilization of audiovisual materials) and concern over the refining of methodological procedures through specialized seminars and the production of supplementary materials to make up for deficiencies in textbooks used.[6]

Except for the American, British, and French Brazilian Institutes, where FL teaching seems to range qualitatively from fair to excellent, no other Binational Institutes have earned as much prestige with the public and educational authorities at large as those, although some German-Brazilian centers have given evidence that they, too, can offer good quality instruction and want to compete as vigorously as their human and material resources will allow them. Unfortunately the teaching of Italian and Spanish still suffers from all the capital sins of traditional language teaching and the relatively little being done even in their most congenial habitats, such as their respective Cultural Centers or Institutes, leaves too much to be desired from the methodological standpoint. Greater emphasis on cultural and literary activities has characterized such institutions, rendering fruitless any attempts toward better language teaching. In a few instances where such Institutes are affiliated or happen to operate in close relationship with a University (this is, for example, true of the University of Bahia) the teaching of the language (Spanish in this case) can live up to the basic requirements of contemporary methodology. A proliferation of small private 'courses' devoted to the teaching of foreign languages especially English has in the past five years taken place in Brazil's largest cities — FL teaching is becoming more prevalent on the private initiative level, but then, the quality of instruction may range from poor to very good.

The only typically Brazilian institution (with a nation-wide network of schools

[6] *Supplementary lessons to Candlin's English for foreign students, teacher's notes* (mimeographed) (Produced by the staff of the British-Brazilian Center, Rio de Janeiro, 1964).

(branches) which ranks high on the FL teaching field is the Yázigi Institute of Languages (see the article in The Linguistic Reporter, June, 1965), the first organization to have a Department of Studies and Research, and to publish a journal devoted to FLT.

3. *Methods and Materials: Methodological Approaches and the Influence of Textbooks*

The development of FL teaching in Brazil has paralleled to some extent major reforms in both secondary and university education. If we were to trace the adoption of methodological approaches from the earliest days of the secondary school we would have two alternatives: either make an analysis of the most widely sold textbooks from the middle of the nineteenth century up to the time of this writing or then examine the official teaching programs established for FL's by Ministry of Education decrees in 1911, 1915, 1945, and 1951. The second alternative, being the easier one to take advantage of, would reveal that many have been the detours to reach a not entirely inaccessible destination: realistic language teaching. Pedagogical terminology was publicized and expressions like 'Direct Method' and even 'Scientific Method' were applied. There remains no doubt that unknowingly and inaccurately to do so did more harm than good to the well intentioned proponents of such reactions against grammar-translation methods. Complaints against the enforcement of the principles of the Direct Method, explicitly (and later implicitly) embodied in the 'official programs' were sometimes voiced by the textbook writers themselves.

In the preface of one of the textbooks published for secondary students of English in 1954[7] the authors voice their disillusionment over the Direct Method by stating 'we have been most unwilling to prepare this textbook for beginners, according to the Direct Method. We have striven to cut down on the improprieties of an already obsolescent method in the United States.' In spite of their feeling somewhat rebellious against the official programs or their heritage, the authors did not, as is still typical of 90% of textbook writers in Brazil, depart from traditional practices. It is no wonder, then, that the most widely sold series for learning English in Brazilian secondary schools happens to be a product of Direct-Method dominance in Brazil: no less than 800,000 copies of Book I have been sold since its appearance in the market in the 1930's. High school textbooks (only a couple have outlived the school reforms) cling tenaciously to old-fashioned contents because of the almost perennially unchanging pattern of teaching prevalent in schools.

It would not be fair to state that all secondary school textbooks available in Brazil

[7] Brito, Jurandir de and Von Sohsten, Elijah, *The Brazilian teacher of English* (São Paulo, Editôra do Brasil, 1954), 78.

for the learning of FL's lack at least a sprinkling of what Robert Lado wisely labels a scientific approach to language teaching, but even in such cases the book's contents and general organization belie the 'linguistic' tone professed in the Foreword or in the Instructions to the Teacher. Statements such as 'the linguistic aspects of the English language were taken into consideration, 'the classification and grading of this material were based on the sentence patterns of structural linguistics', 'this book is mostly based on the most direct and active method, the Scientific-Linguistic Method (Oral Approach) adapted to the needs of our secondary schools' are all taken from very recent textbooks — this pseudosophistication on the part of the authors is less to be blamed than the introduction of labels such as 'linguistic', and 'oral approach', as counter words in teacher training institutions responsible for the professional preparation of future language teachers, a topic which merits discussion in the next subsection. If the question were put to a well trained FL teacher in Brazil (they are still quite scarce these days) of how best to classify high school textbooks he would probably say that there are those adaptable to oral work and those that aren't. The latter category would, in turn, include those which are word-learning oriented and those which focus on unsystematic completion drills. An examination made by the writer of a dozen recent secondary textbooks of English shows that except for the insistence on the teaching of spoken English such books suffer from the same basic ailments afflicting similar tools produced in other Latin American countries, that is, they are culturally poor, linguistically artificial (witness a sentence in a pattern drill like: the picture of the elephant in the book of this girl is red), entirely unsystematized, ungraded, heavy on grammatical theory, and not amenable to objective testing.

What solutions can be proposed to such problems? Why do secondary school teachers of English and French decide to adopt books produced in the United States, England, or France instead of locally constructed materials? Why are some American books being printed by Brazilian publishing houses in order to supply the market? The answer to these questions lies in the fact that once government decrees ceased to exercise too rigid a control on teaching (through the official programs) with an increasing greater autonomy given to schools and teachers themselves in the organization of curricula, it was only natural that Brazilian FL teachers looked for texts which, already being used in institutions such as the Binational Institutes, helped them teach less and less about the language as the previous generations in the profession had been indulging in.

Such apparently sad state of affairs may turn out to be one of a number of decisive factors which will challenge the educational authorities and all those responsible in the field of FLT to do something about the problem of textbook construction. We can conclude then that in a sense the adoption of foreign produced textbooks will serve a twofold purpose: that of giving FLT a corrective touch, a polishing up, and of awakening the profession's interest in the crucial problems. How influential can one or two sound Brazilian produced textbooks be, now that more foreign books are being made available and plans have been announced for the adaptation of an

American Series to Brazilian needs?[8] The future of FL textbook construction is not to be interpreted as optimistic.

4. *The Status of the FL Teacher: Socio-Economic Standing and Professional Preparation*

The dichotomy between private and official or public school teachers in Brazil needs to be further subdivided in order for one to have an idea of the socioeconomic standing of FL teachers: the majority of FL teachers are employed in private high schools (which made up 72% of the total system of secondary education in Brazil in 1960) according to the Report of the Brazilian Director of Secondary School Teaching.[9]

Only a little more than a fourth of the secondary school teachers work in official or state supervised schools. The official teachers holding permanent jobs (through competitions) are usually underpaid and have to work, just like their colleagues in private schools, in one or two other schools in order to make a decent living. Most teachers put in eight to twelve hours' work a day, five days a week is a normal pattern. How this reflects on professional performance, especially in a dynamic field as FL teaching, can be easily deduced — tired, overburdened instructors produce dull, tiring, reading-and-translation practice. To quote the educator and member of the Brazilian Federal Council of Education, Valnir Chagas: 'What is actually done in our secondary schools about FL teaching, besides the unproductive grammar teaching and the indestructible read-and-translate technique?' In addition to the socioeconomic problems afflicting the secondary school teacher (he works mostly on an hourly basis with a meager paid vacation to compensate for his heroic efforts throughout the school year) a share of the blame goes to the inadequate professional preparation of most teachers hastily absorbed in intensive type courses held every year (especially in small towns in the country) to cope with the evergrowing problem of shortage of officially licensed teachers. By taking such orientation courses and upon successfully passing the final exam the prospective teacher (who usually has only a high school certificate) is qualified to teach in secondary schools. A more privileged position is that of bearers of Proficiency Certificates issued by the Universities of Michigan, Cambridge (England), Nancy and Sorbonne through American, British, and French Cultural Centers where such examinations attract hundreds of candidates every year. The Brazilian legislation is perhaps unique in this respect in all of Latin America: it grants the bearers of such certificates the right not only of teaching the foreign language in secondary schools but also of obtaining credit for the language in the university if the candidate wants to start college in order to become

[8] *English for today* (Books, I, II, III, IV) Produced by the National Council of Teachers of English. (New York, Mc Graw-Hill, Inc. 1963-4-5).

[9] *Relatório da diretoria do ensino secundário* (Rio de Janeiro: Ministério da Educação e Cultura, 1952-1961).

a teacher. The high caliber quality of some of the teacher-training programs administered in American, British, and French Institutes has enabled advanced students registered in those schools to turn to teaching as a career, and the granting of some well deserved privileges to the bearers of the above mentioned certificates resulted, in the long run, from the wise analysis made by the Brazilian Federal Council of Education of the problems of FL teacher shortage.[10]

The demand for FL teachers being great as it is, has brought about praiseworthy initiatives on the part of the Ministry of Education aimed at improving the contents of the existing emergency teacher training courses which lead to the 'Exames de suficiência' (candidates are to pass an exam testing minimal desirable professional competency). The production of updated teachers' manuals for use with the trainees in such intensive programs is an instance of governmental interest in such matters. In two of such methodological manuals for prospective teachers of English[11] the trainees are instructed very sensibly concerning the aims of the teaching of English in secondary schools and are given basic orientation on the teaching of the four skills of listening, speaking, reading, and writing and are supplied with fairly good bibliographies. The title of 'private teacher' in Brazil is usually attached to a person who runs his own private school or language course (considered by the unworthy members of the profession as *good business*). In the case of FL's, and especially so of English, the private teacher has his own share of a booming, thriving market. It is mostly Brazilians who make up the strong contingents of private FL teachers, but natives (Americans, Englishmen, Frenchmen) are sometimes attracted to a professionally and economically rewarding activity. The more successful (and sometimes elaborately equipped) FL courses are usually listed in telephone books of bigger cities. Although such private language teachers have no such advantages as social security, a permanent job, or the academic prestige of a university position or degree they manage to become financially stable and can often plan on either expanding their courses through the opening of branches or merging with another competitor. Aside from the class of economically privileged teachers of foreign languages (English, for that matter) there is the class of part time teachers who teach in one of the American-Brazilian Centers, in a Yázigi School, or in other similar institutions. Up till the end of 1964 the bearers of the Proficiency Certificates issued by the Universities of Michigan, Cambridge, Nancy, and Sorbonne (through American, British, and French Cultural Institutes in Brazil), who had also completed an officially recognized teacher-training program, would be entitled by the decisions of the Brazilian Federal Council on Education to enter a Faculdade de Filosofia's Course of Letters and register in the last year (called 'Didática') so as to take the methodological disciplines which would turn the candidates into teachers of the foreign language which they had had previous

[10] *DOCUMENTA*, journal of the Brazilian Federal Council on Education. See esp. No. 9 (1961), No. 10 (1962) and the 1964 issues for text of decisions.

[11] Lima, Enny and Aragão, Vera de Beaurepaire, *Roteiro de inglês* (Rio de Janeiro, Cades, 1963), 113. Filho, Miguel Azevedo, *Técnicas do ensino de inglês* (Rio de Janeiro, Cades, 1962). 210.

training in. Such privilege granted to an evergrowing number of individuals was destined to help the cause of realistic foreign language teaching in the country and to cope with the problem of teacher shortage for secondary schools (upon completion of the last year in the Faculdade de Filosofia the candidate would be entitled to teach in high schools only). It is a well known fact in Brazilian circles devoted to foreign language teaching that sometimes the professional competence of teachers from private institutions such as the Binational Centers is far superior to that of university teachers themselves. No wonder then that private institutions supply the country's best qualified teachers and that we find the same teacher holding a job in college and teaching part time in such bicultural centers as was mentioned above. The granting of such a privilege has now been revoked, much to the disappointment and disillusionment of hundreds of young people who were hoping to gain access to college through their already proven achievements in a teacher-training course and the successful passing of a universally recognized proficiency exam. The reforms brought about by the Law of Foundations and Norms have made it impossible for the above mentioned privilege to continue being granted. What had been a significant initiative, unprecedented in Latin America, now belongs to history, but only time will tell us whether the revoking of a hitherto healthy trend will become a liability in the country's meager baggage of educational initiatives in the field of foreign language teaching. Hasn't a deadly blow been given to a number of potential vocations for FL teaching by revoking such decisions? This question is often asked now, and so is the following: Is the training of FL teachers to be confined exclusively to Faculdades de Filosofia? How well prepared are such teachers' colleges to perform what is expected of them? Too much remains to be done before even a mildly optimistic answer can be given in the future. The greater flexibility and authenticity expected to characterize the curriculum of letters through a wider choice of offerings in foreign languages than had ever been possible before and the student's majoring in only one foreign language have to go hand in hand with a sincere awareness on the part of university language departments that the invaluable aid of private institutions cannot be dispensed with — it is actually indispensable that colleges and private institutions pool their efforts together for the pursual of a national reform in the field — anything other than this will only lead to continual frustration and pseudoacademic achievements.

The eventual passing by Congress and the President of the Statutes of Higher Education Teaching will surely make it possible for university teachers to work on a fulltime basis, either devoted to teaching or to research, and earn a salary worthy both of their professional responsibilities and achievements. A new era will undoubtedly be started, which is bound to affect education on lower levels in a very positive way.

With the advent of the Statutes of the University Teacher we can, perhaps, envisage similar projects which may benefit the secondary school teacher. It is the latter who are, after all, responsible for most of the teaching in the country — it is they who help shape the minds of youngsters for adjustment in society. As long as secondary school teachers are denied better salaries, and until their training gets strengthened on a nation-wide basis, one can not hope for substantial gains both quantitatively and qualitatively. There have been school reforms which theoretically have tried to alter the course of events, and as regards FL teaching they have attempted to enforce a modern methodological orientation, but in practice, with a few notable exceptions such as the orientation courses already referred to and seminars held under the auspices of Binational Institutions, very little has been achieved. The cry for better preparation, for better materials is very vigorous now and may even be beginning to be heard: in the Sixth Brazilian Congress of Technical and Commercial Teaching (English and French are featured in those curricula, too) held last year, recommendations made by the participants in round table discussions on FL teaching emphasized the need for the holding of specialized seminars on FL's to best orient teachers, in addition to suggesting that the old-fashioned teaching programs be replaced by more linguistically oriented plans.[12]

Opportunities for professional improvement and even specialization in the teaching of FL's do exist, although on a small scale, through scholarships and grants offered by the Brazilian Ministry of Education itself and by the Fulbright Commission, the British Council, other foreign government agencies and/or foundations represented in Brazil through diplomatic missions. The Fulbright Commission, for example, has sent an average of twelve Brazilian teachers of English for study in American universities every year, and the number of applicants awarded grants is increasing. Granted that FL teacher training is a major problem in Brazil, what about the training of teacher trainers? This is an even more painfully acute problem — foreign countries such as the United States, Great Britain, France, Italy, and Spain in that order of importance sometimes make it possible for trainers of FL teachers to specialize abroad or they have specialists brought to Brazil in the capacity of visiting professors to participate in seminars, give semester-length courses, and to contact leading members in the profession in several Brazilian academic centers. The contributions stemming from foreign sources are more significant, in that respect, than those made by the Brazilian government itself. A Brazilian Congress of Foreign Language Teachers has never been held and the only National Convention of Teachers of English was held in Rio de Janeiro in January of 1950. It can be claimed that in a country so big as Brazil things are best accomplished on a regional basis — there was, for instance, a Regional Congress of Teachers of English, held in Recife in 1954 under the auspices of Pernambuco State Association of Teachers of English — but the Ministry of Education can offer more substantial assistance on a nationwide basis to initiatives taken by private institutions such as happened when the Yázigi Institute of Languages sponsored the First Brazilian Seminar in Linguistic Orientation for Secondary and College Teachers of Foreign Languages in Rio de Janeiro in July 1965.

[12] Boletim No. 5, VI Congresso Brasileiro de Ensino Técnico Comercial (Caxambú, Minas Gerais, July 1965).

In a British Council publication[13] we are told that 'It is with teacher training that Britain and other English-speaking countries can help most overseas'. That report points out that 'There is as yet no established method of training teacher-trainers... and in theory the trainers of trainers should be generated by the local and national systems which they serve, in fact they cannot be for many years to come because expansion is too rapid and teachers too few.'

To close our comments on the topic of teacher preparation we can state that during the third stage of FL teaching history in Brazil changes are bound to take place on the regional level which may eventually lead the wave of reform to spread over the whole country. Between now and the time when this materializes a tremendous amount of effort, courage, persuasion, understanding, money, and patience will have to be expended so as to neutralize the influence of bookish traditional approaches in schools and to encourage the government to sponsor the production of texts through the 'team-approach', and to create an atmosphere which will be favorable to the study of a language on an intensive basis for a six-year sequence. For Brazilian students to graduate from high school with a basic speaking and reading knowledge of a major world language such as English, French, or Spanish, what is required is the planning of courses and the greater availability of materials which are conducive to twentieth century language teaching.

The study of Latin should definitely be revived in secondary schools or it will become more and more neglected in college. Prior to the learning of a foreign language in high school, students should be oriented as to the learning process involved and to the reasons for the increase in their exposure to the language, especially in the spoken form. Such an orientation could be made a required high school subject (preferably in the first year) just as linguistics is required of all university students taking languages.

It could be called Introduction to Language Learning and it could feature a series of tests to evaluate the potential learning abilities and inclinations of students so as to help them choose the right foreign language. It might dispel some of the linguistic prejudices inherited by the students from their own parents or from other members of the community where they live.

The effort to revitalize language teaching in Brazil calls for a greater concern on the part of educational authorities toward re-training programs for teachers, for the establishment of re-training centers which will enable language teachers, say five or ten years from now, to meet the minimum requirements demanded of modern language teachers. In short, it is high time that the current of reform begin to be felt through actions and not only through words. Brazilian universities lack competent manpower to help stimulate or step up the effectiveness of language instruction and without financial help they are unable to do their share. The rapprochement — between universities and private language institutions is a notable trend these days; last year the Department of Letters of the University of Minas Gerais signed an agreement with

[13] *The English language abroad* (extracted from the British Council's Annual Report) London 1960-1), 24.

the local branch of the Yázigi Institute of Languages whereby this school would contribute to the English teaching efforts of that university. Similar instances of such inter-institutional understanding and cooperation could be given but the one above will suffice to show that the movement to introduce more realistic language teaching should be blind to hierarchical conditions or to privileges.

5. *Significant Pioneering Attempts to Develop the Field of FL Teaching: Main Present Trends and Future Outlook*

In the preceding subsections we have already touched on some pioneering attempts to foster the development of realistic language teaching in Brazil and have even hinted at some future perspectives. In listing other such attempts we will, due to space limitations, obviously omit some events which would perhaps be worthy of inclusion here; in a future book, intended to cover the field as comprehensively as possible such gaps and omissions will be duly taken care of.

Significant pioneering attempts:

(1) The launching by the Rio de Janeiro Binational Center in the 1960's of the American English Series: six textbooks, a student's workbook, a teacher's manual, and accompanying tapes. The manual was the first of its kind published in Brazil to include an elementary treatment of English linguistics.[14] Such series is being used in some of the American-Brazilian Cultural Centers, high schools, and in some teacher training programs. Although less ambitious than the American-English Course (Mexican Binational Center Series), the Brazilian series has been helping to restore the value of sound pedagogical approaches among many Brazilian teachers. The series' author, A. J. Hald Madsen, English Teaching Consultant for USIS in Brazil, had the valuable cooperation of John Ewing and of Sidney Burks (among others) in the production of that series. Professor Madsen is undoubtedly one of the teachers who have done their very best to promote the oral approach in Brazil.

(2) The holding of a Seminar on Modern Foreign Languages in Maceió, Alagoas State in September 1964, an example of stimulating and inspiring cooperation among foreign cultural missions (U.S., British, French, German, Italian, Spanish), universities, and state authorities. Methodology and linguistics had a chance to be offered to hundreds of secondary school teachers from Alagoas and other neighboring states.

(3) The introduction of linguistics in the Brazilian University Curriculum thanks to a decision of the Federal Council of Education in 1961. A healthy trend in FL teaching in Brazilian universities is the interest in the possible applications of linguistics to that field and, as a result, a larger number of teachers applying for scholarships to study

[14] (See item five above). A. J. Hald, Madsen, *Learn American English* — The American Language Series. (Rio de Janeiro, Ao Livro Técnico S.A., 1962-5).

linguistics in American universities (Michigan, Indiana, Texas, Georgetown are often the favorites), in Great Britain, and in France.

(4) The publication in 1964 of the first methodologically sound English course for children by two British Council officers who work in the Anglo-Brazilian Institute in Rio de Janeiro[15] a fact which may boost somewhat the enrollment in courses for children in English language teaching institutions throughout the country.

(5) The launching in 1961 of the journal ESTUDOS by the Department of Studies and Research of the Yázigi Institute of Languages — the first Brazilian publication to deal specifically with FLT in the light of modern principles of applied linguistics. After December 1965 this publication will take on a broader scope and be changed into Brazil's first journal of theoretical and applied linguistics under the editorial responsibility of three active Brazilian linguists.

(6) The holding of the First Brazilian Seminar in Linguistics for Secondary and University Teachers (Rio de Janeiro, July 1965) under the auspices of Yázigi, The Ministry of Education and Guanabara State Department of Education.

(7) The efforts of a fourteen-year-old Association of Teachers of English (Pernambuco State) toward a reformulation of its goals and greater activity in the field through the establishment of a university-level English Language Institute.

(8) The setting up of a Department of Studies and Research in Yázigi Institute and now in the British Center in São Paulo.

(9) The introduction of language laboratories at the University of Ceará, São José dos Campos Aeronautical Technological Institute, in most American Cultural Institutes, in some British, French, and German Centers.

(10) The pioneering utilization of an experimental language laboratory in a high school (Julio de Castilho) in Porto Alegre, Rio Grande do Sul State, financed partly by USAID and by the school itself. It emphasizes audio-visual learning of English and the materials are produced locally.

(11) The printing in Brazil of widely used American textbooks for the learning of English, among which are *Let's Learn English*, *English This Way*.

(12) The participation of three Brazilian specialists in the InterAmerican Program in Linguistics and Language Teaching as delegates.[16]

(13) The introduction of audiovisual courses (Voix et Images de France) in the French-Brazilian Institutions and the offering of French phonetics in such centers — such efforts will do much to encourage the actual production of visual aids by Brazilian teachers of French themselves and to arouse their enthusiasm toward the valuable contributions of French methodology and applied linguistics.

(14) The establishment of Intensive Language Programs in some universities,

[15] R. D. Fairfax, *Tom and Jane* (Books I, II and Teacher's Text) (Rio de Janeiro, Ao Livro Técnico S.A., 1964-5).

[16] Francisco Gomes de Matos, *Indiana University hosts interamerican symposium in linguistics and language teaching*. Report in *Linguistics*, 13 (The Hague, Mouton & Co., 1965). Reprinted in *Hispania* (Sept. 1965).

catering to students from a variety of schools, such as the courses given in the University of Paraiba.

(15) A truly noteworthy initiative, entirely unprecedented in other Latin American countries, was the establishment in March, 1965 of a Federation of Binational Centers in Brazil. At a meeting of the Presidents of all such institutions in Rio de Janeiro, statutes were drafted so as to give the American-Brazilian Cultural Institutes (hitherto nominally united) a chance for stronger unification and sharing of common goals than had ever been possible before. The implications of this action for English language teaching programs are obvious: we can envisage the holding, in the near future, of regular regional seminars for teachers who have never had access to specialized training or to the literature in the field. The prestigious English Proficiency Examinations (University of Michigan), which are given every year to thousands of people representing the whole range of professions and occupations in Brazil, could for the first time be administered in those small centers as soon as the Federation starts its nationwide activities. The outcome of such enterprise will certainly bring fruitful results to the field of foreign language teaching.

What are, in conclusion, the present trends in FL teaching in Brazil?

With the relative freedom of initiative given to teachers, both on the secondary and university level, to plan their courses, a heterogeneous pattern of approaches is bound to be followed, thus perpetuating some of the outdated methods and techniques still widely prevalent in most schools in the country. On the other hand, such flexibility will afford teachers who have had some pedagogical orientation a change to introduce a few influential practices based on modern scientific approaches to language teaching. The curiosity aroused by the so-called oral approaches has already been reflected in some recently published textbooks for secondary schools and in some materials prepared by the Binational Centers and the Yázigi Language Institute.

The teaching of Portuguese as a FL in Brazil, although limited to American diplomatic and consular posts, to the Catholic University in Rio Grande do Sul, to the Center for Intercultural Formation and a few private institutions like Yázigi is also being influenced by the advent of audio-lingual techniques and materials. The still-to-be established Departments of Foreign Languages in Brazilian universities will enhance the possibilities of curriculum enrichment such as the offering of Master's and Doctoral Programs in Languages, a hitherto utopian goal as far as the majority of universities are concerned. Once such departments are equiped (no matter how modestly) with the appropriate aids and competent personnel to use them, real language learning will take place whether for professional, instrumental, cultural or other purposes. Until the Brazilian universities are prepared to offer foreign language instruction meeting a variety of needs, college students will go on being severely handicapped as regards their ability to read and understand so badly needed technical, scientific, and literary works in English, French, German, Italian, and other languages if necessary.

The linguistic and pedagogical preparation of foreign language teachers poses some difficult challenges because of the very flexibility in the educational system and the strong pressure exerted by traditional practices.

The cry for reform has been voiced and will continue to echo vehemently wherever there are earnest, dedicated language teachers in Brazil. A great deal of ink has been used up in pages of two bulletins published by book companies[17] on the critical problems afflicting the teaching of foreign languages in Brazil. The trend toward narrow specialization or concentration on a single foreign language in the university may turn out to be a blessing from the pedagogical point of view but such practice on the secondary level may be a deadly blow to the cultural preparation of young students who are to contribute to the development of their country according to today's needs and aspirations.

We should not close without a warning that although the field is bustling with enthusiasm, there is too much to be done before a transitional stage can really characterize the scene. It is up to the responsible foreign language teachers to make Brazil embark on such a revolution and a universally significant task.

6. *Bibliographical Suggestions*

Teaching English in secondary schools (São Paulo, União Cultural Brasil-Estados Unidos, 1961), 62. *O Instituto Brasil-Estados Unidos* (The Brazil-United States Institute- History and organization) (Rio de Janeiro, 1961), 72. Gomes de Matos, Francisco, *Reflexões sobre problemas atuais do ensino de línguas no Brasil.* In *Proceedings of the First National Convention of the Yázigi Institute of Languages* (São Paulo, 1964), 36. Lisboa, J. Carlos, *O estudo de letras neolatinas no Brasil.* (Rio de Janeiro, Ministério da Educação e Saúde, 1960), 18.

Rodrigues, Aryón D'Alligna, *Relatório sôbre a linguística e o ensino de línguas no Brasil* Report presented in the 1st Inter-American Symposium in Linguistics and Language Teaching (Cartagena, Colombia). See Annals of such meeting in special edition published by the Instituto Caro y Cuervo (Bogotá, Colombia, 1965).

Werebe, Maria José, *Grandezas e misérias do ensino brasileiro* (São Paulo, Difusão Européia do Livro, 1963), 247.

Melo, J. F., *Look and speak English* (Books I, II and two workbooks). (São Paulo, 1965). See esp. Preface and Instructions to teacher.

Melo, J. F., *English for Brazilians* Segunda série. pp. 176 (São Paulo, Editôra do Brasil, S.A., 1955). See preface and contents for influence of the so-called Michigan School.

Kelly, Celso, 'O ensino das Línguas nas escolas de curso médio', *Mec* (Jan. 1964).

[17] *Atualidades pedagógicas* journal of the Companhia Editôra Nacional (São Paulo) — On the teaching of French see esp. the Sept.-Oct., Nov.-Dec. issues (1950). On Spanish language teaching see the above and the Nov.-Dec. issue (1951). On the teaching of English see the March-April issue (1951) *EBSA*, journal of the Editôra do Brasil (São Paulo). See esp. the following issues: Oct. 1949, Oct. 1950, Nov. 1952.

Simpósio sôbre problemática universitária (University of Recife Press, 1965), 231. See esp. 'A Universidade brasileira: sua idéia e sua realização', by Professor Newton Sucupira.

Escola Secundária, quarterly journal of the Diretoria de Ensino Secundário (Cades). See section devoted to FL teaching, esp. issues No. 6, 7, 8, 12, 13, 15 (Sept. '58-Dec. '60).

III. FOREIGN LANGUAGE TEACHING IN SPANISH-SPEAKING AMERICA AND HAITI

1. *General Considerations*

A few cultural considerations of a general kind are, we believe, necessary before dealing specifically with the teaching of foreign languages in Spanish-speaking America and Haiti.

At the risk of appearing tautological and paradoxical at the same time, it is necessary to point to the fact that all twenty nations are simultaneously similar and contrasting with one another. Thus, for example, with the exception of Haiti they share Spanish as their native language and exhibit, to a large extent, Iberian traditions. All twenty nations have, on the whole, similar problems and cultural targets; relative spacial neighborhood is also relevant to our topic. Brazil, which has been the subject of the first part of this article, shares some of the characteristics described above.

A noteworthy similarity is the desire for independence prevailing in these nations; during the nineteenth century this ideal led to revolt from the colonizing nation and then on to war and political independence. In the twentieth century this desire has led, in different degrees, to the ideals of democracy and, consequently, to relative universal education. The latter is far from being achieved, however, a fact which helps to account for the striking growth of primary and secondary education in most of Latin America. A remarkable rate of increase of population (one of the highest in the world) is also to be considered in this context.

It is a well known fact that none of the Latin American nations has yet achieved an economic development acceptable for European or North American standards. As an indirect result of this, the benefits of elementary education (let alone of secondary education) have not yet reached great portions of the population, this fact having a direct effect upon the status of foreign language teaching in Latin America. We wish to emphasize, however, that we should be particularly cautious of generalizations concerning the Latin American republics, as striking differences are to be found amongst them. It becomes evident, after considering the information provided in Chart I, that foreign language teaching can not but rank far down in the list of problems to be solved by several of these nations.

As it has already been pointed out, Latin America inherited European culture, although the native cultural contribution is important in many of these nations.

European contribution has come not only from Spain and Portugal — the conquering and first-colonizing nations — but also from Italy, Germany, France, Britain and other nations, through important waves of immigration, especially during the nineteenth century. It is also to be observed that the above mentioned nations, particularly Britain, France and Germany, had great influence in Latin America, especially in the fields of politics, education, industry, trade, and the organization of the armed forces. This accounts, in part, for the fact that at least one foreign language is taught at the secondary school level for a minimum of three years virtually everywhere in Latin America.

2. *The social impact of foreign languages*

As elsewhere in the occidental world during the eighteenth century, the knowledge of Latin (and, to a minor extent, Greek) was a sign of social prestige in Spanish-speaking America. The opening years of the nineteenth century, however, witnessed the rather rapid replacement of the 'Classical' languages by French, first, and by English shortly afterwards; the period happened to coincide with the beginnings of economic and political revolt against Spain, and it is a significant fact that the most prominent leaders of the Latin American Revolution mastered either one or both of the above mentioned modern languages. The consolidation of independence (after 1830, for several Latin American nations) actually strengthened the definitive social impact of French and English.

Assessing the influence of these languages today is, unfortunately, a rather subjective task; we tried to be as objective as possible by conducting a quick survey on the actual requirements of the different abilities (i.e. recognizing the spoken language, recognizing the written language, productive ability in the spoken language and productive ability in the written language) on three levels of achievement (poor, fair, good) of just one foreign language — English — on diverse socio-laboral groups.

The above survey, weak as it is, nevertheless provides some information in the nature of a tendency for Haiti and Spanish-speaking America 'as a whole', misleading as this may be. Thus, for example, all four abilities, at a rather high level of achievement, are usually expected from persons belonging in the socio-economic 'élites', particularly in the countries with reduced population. Armed forces officers are expected to have at least a fair command of English in several Latin American nations.[18] University graduates, business executives, and university students are supposed to be able to understand both spoken and written English and, to a minor extent, to be able to speak it. Executive government officials are not, on the whole, expected to master the foreign language concerned, with the possible exception of Puerto Rico, which has direct political ties with the United States of America. English is required in the exercise of the mid-level technical trades in only a few Latin American countries, with the emphasis on the receptive skills; it is not at all required in ordinary

[18] Institutions for the training of military personnel usually possess language laboratories for the teaching of English (e.g. Argentina, Bolivia, Brazil, Chile, Colombia, Ecuador, El Salvador, Guatemala, Honduras, Mexico, Nicaragua, Panama, Paraguay, Peru, Venezuela).

CI

Comparative Socio-Economic Status o

	Total Population 1960	Total Population 1970[a] (thousands)	% Urban Population 1960	% Urban Population 1970[a]	Rate of Increase of Total Population 1960 = 100	% Active Population in middle & higher positions	% Active Population in industry (5 or more workers)	Gross Pro per capi (1950 US
Argentina	21000	24990	64	68	119	36,0	13,5	560
Bolivia	3600	4540	34	37	126	8,0	2,8	78
Brasil	65860	84440	31	37	128	15,0	6,2	270
Colombia	14770	19590	38	48	133	22,0	4,3	306
Costa Rica	1145	1560	29	36	136	22,0	4,8	249
Cuba	6820	8340	49	55	122	22,0	8,0	386
Chile	7635	9660	59	66	127	22,0	8,1	317
Ecuador	4285	5630	28	34	131	10,0	3,5	142
El Salvador	2395	3115	28	35	130	10,0	4,7	169
Guatemala	3980	5325	24	30	134	8,0	3,2	170
Haiti	3725	4620	10	17	124	3,0	1,4	87
Honduras	1755	2305	17	25	131	4,0	1,6	160
Mexico	35115	47330	43	50	135	17,0[d]	6,7	264
Nicaragua	1465	1955	28	37	133	—	2,0	187
Panama	1010	1370	42	47	134	15,0	3,0	280
Paraguay	1625	1975	28	35	122	14,0	3,3	113
Perú	10510	14030	35	41	133	—	4,7	174
Rep. Dominicana	2845	3895	21	28	137	—	3,0	216
Uruguay	2760	3020	79	81	109	33,0[d]	13,0	380
Venezuela	6935	9350	49	61	135	18,0	6,5	1037

* After the proceedings of the Conference on Education and Economic and Social Development in Latin America, CEPAL/UNESCO. Santiago de Chile, 1962. (Unless otherwise indicated).

** *Perspectivas de desarrollo de la educación en 19 países latinoamericanos*, IEDES, Univ. of Paris, 1960; OEA (Pan Am. Union), 1963. (First approximation to a proportional mean combining eight socio-economic indexes: gross national product per inhabitant, 1961; percentage of active population working in industry, 1950; percentage of total population living in rural areas, 1960; percentage of literates in the age group 15 plus, 1947-1952; percentage of individuals registered in primary schools in the age group 5-14, 1957-1960; consumption of energy (electric) per inhabitant; number of daily newspapers per 100 inhabitants; and number of wireless receivers per 100 inhabitants).

[a] Projections on the 1960 or previous census.

[b] Primary school courses administered by institutions other than the State Office of Primary Education have not been considered.

[c] Subsidized or non-subsidized private schools have not been considered.

[d] *Tipología de los países latinoamericanos*, by Roger Vekemans.

[e] 1952.

*American Republics**

ulative te of . cap. -1958	Annual Mortality (Gross & effective). 1950-1955	% Literacy, 15 and above c. 1950	% Population 5-14 registered in Prim. Schools 1956	Scholarity Average in Years c. 1950	No. of Primary school teachers p. 100 inhabitants school age, c. 1960	Socio-economic Ranking** Index, 100
-0,4	10	86	69	3,9	4,0	100,0
-0,7	20	32	40	1,2	1,0	28,1
,7	20	49	40	1,7	1,5	48,9
,5	20	62	39	2,4	1,2	58,0
,3	15	79	60	3,2	3,0	43,9
,3	15	78	53	3,3	1,7	—
,6	15	80	62	4,2	2,0[b]	76,6
,5	20	56	50	2,3	1,5	34,7
,5	25	39	41	1,3	2,0	38,3
,0	25	29	27	1,1	—	27,4
,8	25	11	25	0,5	0,5[c]	14,8
,1	20	35	32	—	1,2	27,5
,1	15	57	51	2,3	1,4	60,9
,4	20	38	36	1,4	—	37,2
,2	20	70	59	3,5	2,2	61,6
,3	15	66	63	2,4	3,1	48,1
,6	20	47	45	—	1,8	47,9
—	20	43	60	1,0	1,0	42,5
,2	—	85[e]	59	—	—	98,7
,0	20	52	43	—	1,5	83,9

office work but, as it is to be expected, it is indispensable in office work in connection with foreign trade. On the whole, emphasis tends to lie on the passive skills, particularly on the comprehension of written English. English is not at all INDISPENSABLE in Latin American social and university life, but it is DESIRABLE. Textbooks for virtually all of the university disciplines come in Spanish or Portuguese; nevertheless, professional journals in the English language (and, to a minor extent in German and French) have a wide circulation.

3. *Foreign language teaching at the elementary school level*

By 'elementary school' we here mean grades first through sixth, covering an age span which varies sharply from nation to nation and, furthermore, from one socio-economic group to another within a country. In Chile, for example, school entering age fluctuates between five (urban areas, higher socio-economic strata) and sixteen (rural); the situation is very much the same in the rest of Latin America.

Only Haiti, Panama and Puerto Rico have a foreign language requirement at the primary school level. English is taught in almost every school in Puerto Rico from grades first through sixth, and in the Republic of Panama, in grades fifth and sixth. In Haiti it is an elective, alongside with Spanish, towards the end of the primary school cycle.[19]

Foreign languages are taught to a much wider extent in the private elementary schools — English, French, German and Italian (in that order of preference) being the most favored ones. It is hard to assess the seriousness and efficiency of foreign language instruction at the elementary school level. Chile illustrates, up to a point, the situation for the rest of Latin America; alongside several highly efficient schools, where the children use a foreign language (i.e. English, French or German) most of the time from the very beginning, there are some schools advertised as especially 'English' schools, where the foreign language is little better than a mere label. Other languages reported as being taught in private elementary schools are Hebrew (e.g. Chile), and Japanese (e.g. Paraguay).

There is, at present, a current of opinion which fosters foreign language teaching at the elementary school level on a compulsory or semi-compulsory basis. It is our opinion that this project is likely to be only partly successful (that is, in some large urban primary schools in the bigger cities of some nations) if we consider that Latin American elementary education really has more vital problems to solve.

4. *Foreign language teaching at the secondary school level*

One foreign language, at least, is required in the great majority of the Latin American secondary schools[20] (grades seventh through eleventh or twelfth, approximately). When only one foreign language is required, the choice is virtually always English. Two foreign languages are demanded in several national systems (e.g. Argentina, Bolivia, Chile, Colombia, Dominican Republic, El Salvador, Venezuela); French almost invariably seconds English, though in many school systems (e.g. Argentinean, Chilean) it becomes an optative with German, Italian or Latin, in that order of preference (exceptionally other languages, such as Portuguese, Hebrew, Japanese or Chinese, are also offered). Three foreign languages are required in Uruguay (English, French and Italian) and, within a limited context, in Panama and Paraguay.

Where one foreign language is required (e.g. Cuba, Ecuador, Guatemala, Haiti, Peru) the course usually lasts five or six years. Where two foreign languages are demanded the general pattern is a five- or six-year course for the first (major) foreign language and a two-year course for the second foreign language (e.g. Argentina, Colombia, Dominican Republic), although the three-year course and two-year course scheme is also common (e.g. El Salvador, Nicaragua, Venezuela). Chile offers a

[19] UNESCO, *La situación educativa en América Latina*: *La enseñanza primaria*: *estado, problemas, perspectivas* (Paris, 1960).

[20] Specialized secondary schools, such as business schools, industrial schools, technical schools, normal (i.e. teacher-training) schools and others have not been taken into consideration.

six-year course for the first foreign language (almost invariably English) plus a five-year course for the second foreign language (French or, less frequently, other languages). In Uruguay the English course and the French course last four years each, while the Italian course lasts two years.

Chart II attempts to show the situation of foreign language teaching, at the secondary school level, in seventeen nations. Although there has been a considerable amount of leveling up and approximation of figures, and in spite of the fact that at least part of the basic information may not be quite up to date, yet this chart gives us some very general tendencies and positions. The average individual foreign language course, extending over the whole secondary school period (five or six years), consists of 358.3 class meetings of an average duration of forty-five minutes; Panama offers the largest individual foreign language course — English — with 810 class periods, while Mexico offers the smallest course, with 90 class periods; Colombia, the Dominican Republic and Ecuador offer the next smallest course, lasting 180 periods. Panama, again, devotes the largest amount of time, over the whole secondary school cycle, to foreign languages, with 1124 class periods, closely followed by Chile, with 1110 periods (17.5% of the whole plan of studies);[21] Ecuador devotes the smallest amount of time — 386 class periods, an 8.5⁰/₀ of the whole plan of studies — to foreign languages; the average amount of time devoted to foreign languages in the countries we have here considered is 611.3 class periods.[22]

Uruguay, where three foreign languages are required, exhibits the highest proportion[23] of the total plan of studies for foreign language instruction, namely 17.7 per cent; the lowest proportion corresponds to Peru and Guatemala, with an 8.3 per cent, the average proportion for the countries here considered being 12.4 per cent.

The above figures and rankings should be considered with reserve on account of the following facts: (a) the whole of Latin America, rather than a simple aleatory sample, should have been taken into consideration; (b) only a section of secondary school education (i.e. the 'humanities', or general schools) were here contemplated, with the exclusion of the special secondary schools;[24] (c) secondary school was indiscriminately estimated in five or six academic years; (d) foreign language requirements in pre- or post-secondary school institutions were not taken into account in the estimate of course lengths; (e) the school year was arbitrarily estimated as consisting of thirty weeks.

The foreign language requirement is partially made extensive to colleges, affecting only some faculties or professional schools, usually for no longer than two years (e.g.

[21] The situation has changed slightly since March, 1967, with less importance given to foreign languages.

[22] Our averages are simple arithmetic means.

[23] Complementary information on the plans of secondary school studies in Panama was unavailable.

[24] English alone is, almost invariably, taught at these schools; the schedule for foreign languages is usually more restricted than its counterpart in the general secondary schools. (See, for example, *Planes y Programas de las Escuelas Normales Latinoamericanas*, published by the Departamento de Asuntos Educativos, Unión Panamericana; Washington, D. C., 1963).

The Situation of Foreign Language Teaching in the Non-Specialized Sec

	Total periods in secondary schoolcourse****	Percentage of total periods devoted to FLL	FIRST FOREIGN LANGUAGE* Average No. of weekly periods****	Duration of course (Years)	Total l of co in peri
Argentina	4660	10.8	3.0	3	27
Bolivia	6120	11.3	2.3	5	34
Colombia	5400	10.5	2.7	6	38
Cuba	—	—	3.4	5	51
Chile[j]	6318	17.5	3.5	6	63
Ecuador	4500	8.5	2.7	6	38
El Salvador			3.0	3	27
Guatemala	6840	8.3	3.8	5	57
Haiti	4860	11.1	3.0[b]	6	54
Mexico[c]	—	—	3.0	3	27
Nicaragua	4350	15.1	4.0	3	36
Panama[e]	—	—	4.5	6	81
Paraguay[c]	—	—	3.0	3[g]	27
Peru	5400	8.3	3.0	5	45
Dominican Republic	4500	14.7	3.2	5	48
Uruguay	5400	17.7	3.0	4	36
Venezuela	4740	15.1	3.3	3	29

* Basic data from the official plans of studies and from *Les langues vivantes dans les écoles secondaires d'enseignement général*, UNESCO, 1964, unless otherwise indicated.
** Usually English ***Usually French **** Usually 45 minutes each period.
[a] On an estimate of 30 weeks per year.
[b] Two foreign languages compulsory in some sections only; details not considered here.
[c] Information privately obtained; there is considerable regional variation; variations in private schools.
[d] Alternatively, this course may be an extension of the first foreign language.

English, at the School of Economics, Universidad de Chile and Universidad Católica de Chile; English, at the Schools of Journalism and Sciences of Education, Universidad Nacional de Nicaragua; Greek and Latin, at the Faculty of the Humanities, Universidad Nacional de Nicaragua; German, in several schools of the same institution).

5. *Contents, methods, procedures and materials*

a. *Programs.* — The great majority of the Latin American nations possess official programs for the foreign languages included in the school plans. As in other aspects of foreign language teaching, however, these programs vary considerably in extension and content. On the one hand, we have rather detailed programs, virtually covering

*ols (Grades 7 through 11-12) of Seventeen Latin-American Nations**

COND FOREIGN LANGUAGE***			THIRD FOREIGN LANGUAGE			Total Number of periods devoted to foreign languages in Sec. School plans
rage No. weekly iods****	Duration of course (Years)	Total length of course, in periods	Average No. of weekly periods****	Duration of course (Years)	Total length of course, in periods	
4.0	2	240				510
2.3	5	345				690
3.0	2	180				566
						510
3.2	5	480				1110
						386
3.0	2	180				450
						570
3.0[b]						540
3.0	1	90[d]				360
5.0	2	300				660
2.6	3	234	3.0	2	180[f]	1124
2.0[h]	3	180	3.0	4[i]	360	810
						450
3.0	2	180				660
3.0	4	360	4.0	2	240[g]	960
3.5	4	420				717

[e] Course of Letters only; information privately obtained.
[f] Latin.
[g] Italian.
[h] Portuguese.
[i] Choice of English, French, (German).
[j] All the figures for Chile will vary considerably as a result of primary school reform (1966) and middle school reform (1968).

all the stages of the method, including directions or suggestions for the teacher, thus approaching the concept of 'curriculum' (e.g. Cuba,[25] Puerto Rico[26]); the opposite tendency is represented by the one-page program, merely listing fairly generalized headings to be approached in class (e.g. Argentina,[27] Nicaragua). A few countries (e.g. Ecuador[28]) do not have an actual program, where the topics or activities are

[25] Ministerio de Educación, Dirección de Enseñanza Secundaria, *Programas de inglés*: *enseñanza preuniversitaria* (La Habana, 1964).
[26] As shown indirectly in *Fries American English Series*, *Teacher's Guide*, prepared by the English Section of the Department of Education of Puerto Rico (Boston, 1957).
[27] República Argentina, Ministerio de Educación y Justicia, *Planes y programas de estudio* (Buenos Aires, 1956). Bureau International d'Éducation and UNESCO, *Les langues vivantes dans les écoles secondaires d'enseignement général* (Paris and Geneva, 1964).
[28] República del Ecuador, Ministerio de Educación Pública, Sección Secundaria y Superior, *Planes*

listed, but merely present a document stating the general methodological tendencies which are considered desirable, but not compulsory.

Chile[29] presents what we might term the 'standard' foreign language program for Latin America: the language is divided into areas or levels (e.g. vocabulary, pronunciation, grammar, contextual orientation), a list of items to be covered being placed under each heading; these items are broken up to some extent (though not sufficiently to prevent different interpretations) and, in several cases, they are further divided into items to be learned for production and recognition, or for recognition only. There is partial correlation of levels, particularly between lexis, grammar, and contextual orientation. These programs do not normally prescribe any particular grading to be followed during the school year, nor do they include any detailed teachers' guide. In the case of Chile, however, there is an optative teachers' guide whose main purpose is to illustrate the program itself and suggest a grading;[30] two of the textbooks in use[31] also contain teachers' guides with similar characteristics, plus suggestions for procedures and techniques; we must remark, however, that these guides are strictly in line with the official programs and with the official aims of foreign language teaching.

The remark is often made that, in the long run, aims, programs, and methods actually depend on the particular textbook, or textbooks, being used. That is the case with Cuba (amongst other nations), where the official program makes constant and regular reference to five textbooks.[32]

b. *Aims of foreign language teaching*. — Where stated, the foreign language programs of practically all the Latin American nations share the general aims of development of personality and furthering of international understanding. As to specific aims (again, where stated), all share comprehension of the written language; in a few cases (e.g. Paraguay[33]) this is the sole aim; in the majority of cases, recognition and production of the oral language are the principal aims during the first years of instruction, recognition of the written language being the principal aim in subsequent years (e.g. Bolivia,[34] Chile, Dominican Republic[35]). Production of the written language is

de estudios para los colegios de bachillerato (Quito, 1955). Bureau International d'Éducation and UNESCO, *Les langues vivantes ... op. cit.*

[29] *Diario Oficial de la República de Chile*, No. 25847 (Santiago, 23rd May 1964). New programs will appear in 1967 and 1968.

[30] Superintendencia de Educación Pública, *Manual para el profesor, anexo al programa de inglés de educación secundaria* (Santiago de Chile, 1963). A new teacher's guide, covering the program of English for the eighth is grade, is scheduled for 1967. Similar material has been planned for French.

[31] Lydia Miquel and Augusto Manríquez, *English through Practice*[4] (Santiago de Chile, 1964).
Elia Díaz and Leopoldo Wigdorsky, *I Speak English*[5] (Santiago de Chile, 1965).

[32] Ministerio de Educación, Dirección de Enseñanza Secundaria, *Inglés* 3 (La Habana, 1964).
Robert Lado, Charles Fries and English Language Institute Staff, *English Sentence Patterns*[3].
Ministerio de Educatión, *English Reading Selections* 3 *and* 4 (La Habana, 1963).
I. A. Richards and C. M. Gibson, *English through Pictures, Book* 2 (La Habana, 1962?).
C. K. Ogden, *The General Basic English Dictionary* (La Habana, 1961).

[33] Privately reported.

[34] *Ibid.*

[35] *Ibid.*

recognized as an aim in a few countries only (e.g. Colombia, Puerto Rico).[36] The above aims are not always overt but usually implied through the teaching methods recommended and the materials used.

c. *Methods.* — The grammar-translation method, the 'direct method', and the 'oral approach' have subsequently predominated in foreign language teaching in Spanish-speaking America and Haiti. At present the situation is a mixture of all three methods, the more active methods prevailing in the earlier stages of foreign language instruction, later to be replaced, almost invariably, by the grammar-translation method. Puerto Rico and Cuba are, perhaps, the only countries where the 'oral approach' is used permanently throughout the foreign language course. Grammar-translation techniques and procedures predominate in the teaching of French, particularly at the secondary school level.

The 'oral approach', as applied by Charles C. Fries and Robert Lado, has certainly outranked the remaining methods in the teaching of English in several countries during the last ten years (e.g. Chile, Cuba, Haiti,[37] Mexico[38]). The methods developed at St. Cloud, for French, and at the Goethe Institut, for German, which may be said to correspond to the 'oral approach', are increasingly being used, particularly at the binational centers.

At this stage, perhaps it is convenient to summarize the characteristics of the 'oral approach', as commonly understood in Latin America: selection of teaching items primarily based on bilingual comparison; the sentence as the unit of instruction; careful grading of teaching items; main stress on grammatical structure, which is functionally approached; concern for the teaching of pronunciation; vocabulary limited to what is strictly necessary to operate the patterns being taught; active presentation techniques, though translation is occasionally permitted exclusively at this stage; constant and active drilling of items, especially through transformation exercises and 'pattern practice'; the oral drilling of items precedes reading and writing; grammatical structures individually presented and drilled; the students — not the teacher — take most of the talking time; the teacher controls the grammatical structures and the vocabulary he uses in class; moderate concern for aspects bearing on situational contexts; and moderate emphasis on choral work. The above characteristics are to be interpreted as general tendencies in the teaching of English as a foreign language rather than as actual achievements.

Most foreign language programs, however, recommend the 'direct method', as traditionally understood, though modified (in the case of the English language) by the structuralist tendencies of Harold Palmer, A. H. Hornby, and other British authors.

[36] *Ibid.*

[37] Bureau International d'Éducation and UNESCO, *Les langues vivantes...*, *op. cit.*

[38] Universidad Nacional Autónoma de México, Escuela Nacional Preparatoria, *Programa de Inglés* (México, D.F., 1965).
Secretaría de Educación Pública, *Plan de estudios y programas de educación normal urbana aprobados por el Consejo Nacional Técnico de Educación* (México, D.F., 1964).

The British approach to the teaching of English as a foreign language has been particularly popular in Argentina, Chile, and Uruguay.

In a very general way, the 'direct method', as commonly understood in Latin America, exhibits the following characteristics: avoidance of the student's native language at *all* stages; rather strict control of vocabulary on a frequency basis;[39] some concern for pronunciation (usually the variety of English known as 'Received Pronunciation', though this is seldom made explicit in the programs); some concern for the structural approach to grammar, especially during the last fifteen years; 'substitution' and, to some extent, 'transformation', as the preferred drilling techniques in the teaching of grammar; the oral aspects of language given theoretical predominance; considerable interest in matters concerning the context of situations. Many of the textbooks produced locally have been, in fact, inspired by the 'direct method' as outlined above.

It is to be understood, however, that virtually nowhere in Latin American public education are either of these methods fully or exclusively used. The 'oral approach' or the 'direct method' (or a combination of both) is usually employed during the first two years of instruction, gradually to be replaced by grammar-translation procedures in the higher forms. The reason for this is primarily to be seen, we believe, in the fact that practically all the Latin American secondary school plans (usually from thirty to thirty-six hours a week) and programs for English are extraordinarily overloaded,[40] this fact possibly accounting for impatience both on the part of the teacher and on the part of the student.

Perhaps it is useful to confront the English program of one Latin American secondary school system against the usual pattern of the stages of foreign language teaching in all four major linguistic levels (Pronunciation, Vocabulary, Grammatical Structure, and Contextual Orientation). We have here chosen the Chilean program as an example, although we wish to reiterate that we should be careful of generalizations to all of Spanish-speaking America.

(1) *Limitation.* — There is no restriction, implicit or explicit, to any one variety of the English language; in actual practice, however, there is a slight tendency in favor of 'Received Pronunciation', this being the variety of English prospective teachers are usually trained in. Selection operates chiefly on the lexical and grammatical levels, the former on frequency-usefulness bases (Thorndike's list[41] and Michael West's list[42] were partially considered in the drafting of the present program, in 1963), grammatical selection being based on teaching experience and partial bilingual analyses. Contextual orientation is handled through general topics (e.g. sports, public holidays, the arts, chief historical events).

(2) *Arrangement.* — Six yearly stages are clearly marked off, covering all four linguistic levels. Only grammar and, to some extent, vocabulary, are graded within

[39] Many Latin American programs for English set quantitative targets for vocabulary; in Chile, for example, students were expected to learn actively approximately four hundred 'words' per year.

[40] See Chart I.

[41] Thorndike and Lorge, *The Teacher's Word Book of 30,000 Words* (New York, 1944).

[42] Michael West, *A General Service List of English Words* (London, 1955).

each stage in a very general way. Two of the most commonly used textbooks,[43] both locally made, complement the official program by presenting all linguistic and colinguistic items in a strictly graded sequence.

(3) *Application.* — Direct association techniques are recommended both for presentation and drilling; teachers are requested to avoid translation, particularly from Spanish into English, but no specific techniques are enforced. The textbooks referred to above complement the official program through 'teacher's guides'.

(4) *Testing.* — Official regulations impose several controls, both written and oral, throughout the school year; with the exception of testing and promotion practices in seven experimental secondary schools, however, there are no standard examinations, although there is a comprehension test of written English, along traditional lines, as a university entrance examination.[44] The program recommends the use of objective tests, responsibility for the building of such tests resting with the English department of each school. In actual practice, however, students are generally asked to answer questions (either in oral or written form) on a given text and to perform several monolingual transformations. Foreign language aptitude tests are not employed.

(5) *General remarks.* — There is an explicit statement of aims, both general and specific (i.e. the use of oral English during the first three years, attention drifting to reading and cultural contents in the three remaining years); there is no systematic attempt at a correlation of levels, but points of contact with other school subjects are apparent, especially with the social sciences. No allowance is made for individual differences nor are specific coprogrammatic activities contemplated. Radio and television do not collaborate directly with English teaching in schools (nor with any other subject),[45] but usually independent programs with either British or United States material are to be found. Experimental secondary schools, business schools, industrial schools, technical schools and normal schools (e.g. institutions for the training of primary school teachers) have English programs of their own, usually differing considerably from the program just outlined. Special programs are also used by the 'foreign' schools,[46] where most of the activities are carried on in the foreign language concerned since kindergarten; most pupils of these schools become virtual ambilinguals by the time they graduate.

Other Latin American nations differ in various degrees from the pattern described above. In Argentina, though the program is not quite specific as to aims and procedures, yet more concern for pronunciation teaching is inferred from existing textbooks

[43] Lydia Miquel and August Manríquez, *English through Practice*, *op. cit.*; Elia Díaz and Leopoldo Wigdorsky, *I Speak English*, *op. cit.*

[44] Until March, 1966, the foreign language examination was a part of a set of examinations conditioning the entrance of candidates to the University of Chile and other universities; since January 1967 the entrance examination system has been entirely modified and a foreign language is no longer required.

[45] The recent arrival of two UNESCO experts on educational television will certainly change this situation.

[46] e.g. The Grange School, St. George's School, Santiago College, Dunalastair School, Deutsche Schule, Lycée de l'Alliance Française, Scuola Italiana.

(Argentina possesses the only Latin American textbook for English printed in phonetic type only for the first five lessons[47]). Colombia tends to favor American English, while vocabulary is rather neglected throughout the stages of the method.[48] In Costa Rica grading is rather neglected but the program is more specific as to both presentation and drilling.[49] Both the Cuban and the Puertorican programs, based directly on Fries's and Lado's work, are much more articulate and specific as to the stages of the method than the Chilean program is; this is particularly so of the grading of lexical and grammatical items in the case of the Cuban program, and of both arrangement (staging and grading) and application (presentation and drilling) in the case of the Puertorican program. Both Ecuador and Nicaragua[50] are explicitly liberal as to the kind of method to be used and as to the aims to be set up, but stress the fact that they should be in consonance with each other; as in other places, here the method is determined by the textbook chosen. Mexico offers a variety of methodological approaches, the tendency being towards the 'oral approach', with some trials being done with the 'situational approach'.[51] Paraguay reports no particular method or approach.[52] In Perú, while selection relatively operates in the fields of pronunciation, vocabulary, and grammatical structure, it is only the latter which — rather freely — passes through the remaining methodological stages.[53] The Venezuelan program is almost exclusively concerned with grammatical structure through the selection, grading, presentation, and drilling stages.[54] The English program of Guatemala[55] resembles its Peruvian counterpart.

Apparently English ranks higher in the use of modern teaching methods and techniques than the remaining foreign languages being offered in the Latin American school systems. Both French and German, however, are making considerable advance in the field and in Chile, at least, active and direct techniques for the teaching of these languages are now unanimously accepted and introduced at an ever increasing speed.

The existence of many variables make it exceedingly difficult to pass judgement as to the efficiency — let alone as to the quality — of foreign language instruction at the secondary school level. Amongst these variables the following may be mentioned:

[47] Josefina Molinelli, *My English Book, Part I* (Buenos Aires, 1950).

[48] Privately reported.

[49] República de Costa Rica, Ministerio de Educación Pública, Inspección General de Enseñanza Media, *Programa de Enseñanza de Inglés* (San José, 1963).

[50] From the official program.

[51] We presume the Mexican small-scale experiment to be based on *English for Newcomers to Australia, Teacher's Book* (Canberra, 1956), and accompanying publications, prepared by The Commonwealth Office of Education for the (Australian) Department of Immigration.

[52] Privately reported.

[53] República del Perú, Ministerio de Educación Pública, *Programas para la Educación Secundaria* (Lima, 1960).

[54] República de Venezuela, Ministerio de Educación, *Programa de Educación Secundaria: Primer Ciclo* (Caracas,).
ibid., *Programas Provisionales de Educación Industrial* (*Ciclo Básico*) (Caracas, 1955).

[55] República de Guatemala, Ministerio de Educación Pública, *Programas de estudio para la educación secundaria: ciclo prevocacional* (Guatemala, 1960).

lack of standardized proficiency tests; frequent absence of clearly defined goals; wide range of actual foreign language requirements in the different Latin American nations; different degrees of exposure to the foreign language outside the classroom; wide range of academic standards within each Latin American nation and among the different Latin American nations; and, finally, individual differences.

Perhaps we may tangentially approach the topic of foreign language teaching efficiency by stating—rather subjectively, of course—what an abstract concept, 'the average Chilean secondary school graduate', is actually capable of comprehending in the English language, on the assumption that it is not too long since he left school. Normally, he should be able to (a) read straight nonidiomatic prose, with frequent recurrence to a dictionary; (b) understand from thirty to fifty per cent of standard, carefully spoken English, such as the special radio programs of the British Broadcasting Corporation or of The Voice of America; context makes a dictionary less necessary here than in the case of written English; (c) understand rather efficiently when he is being addressed to by an English speaker, provided that the latter makes slow and clear use of the language, chooses his vocabulary and grammatical structures carefully, and makes abundant use of colinguistic manifestations (gestures, head shaking, etc.); (d) respond in very, very broken English, but sufficient enough for what he wants to convey, provided that the message is simple and rather concrete. Our abstract being is *not* able to attend, with learning profit, a regular lecture at an English speaking university (but about sixty periods of complementary or remedial English should capacitate him to do so) nor to dissert in easily intelligible English before an audience.

Needless to say, there are many graduates from public secondary schools who rank well above the described 'type' and who are perfectly able to communicate with ease in the English language, with just a few mistakes (particularly in pronunciation), in practically all possible situations. That is the case, for example, with most boys and girls (usually about seventeen or eighteen years old) who are selected to travel to the United States of America on the 'Experiment in International Living' program (although the number of students traveling each year on such program is no larger than twenty).

It is interesting to speculate on how 'the average Chilean secondary school graduate' ranks with his counterparts in the rest of Latin America and in other nations. As shown in Chart II, Chile offered until recently the second largest[56] English course in Spanish speaking America and Haiti; but, on the other hand, outside classroom exposure to English comes to a virtual minimum in Chile, chiefly because of geographical reasons (compare Chile with, say, Mexico, Cuba, Central America, and Panama; or even with Venezuela, Argentina, and Uruguay); because of this, we venture to suggest that the Chilean graduate stands as a Latin American average, if there is such a thing. The average Chilean secondary school graduate ranks certainly higher than his counterpart in the United States of America, as to proficiency in foreign languages, and perhaps lower than his counterparts in Britain, Germany and France. All of

[56] It was actually the third largest course if Puerto Rico is taken into consideration.

this is extremely 'on the average' and on the subjective side, but at least it should give us some information as to what a Chilean teacher of English, with experience outside as well as inside his nation, *feels* about the subject of proficiency.

d. *Teaching materials.* — Our survey of the teaching materials used in Latin American foreign language instruction will concentrate on the educational level where foreign languages are generally taught in Latin America, that is, on the secondary school. Moreover, we have reduced our exposition to the public secondary schools, as the private schools, apart from constituting a relative minority, usually dispose of a larger budget, this fact permitting the acquisition of material which is beyond the reach of the majority of the schools.

Only the blackboard, white chalk, and the textbook are used both extensively and intensively. Color chalk, wall pictures, flashcards, flannel boards, and duplicating machines are found and used occasionally; records, tape recorders, and projection slides are even less frequent. Sound or silent films, language laboratories, close circuit television, and machines for programmed instruction are rare in public secondary school education, with the possible exception of Mexico City. Marionettes are used in several schools.

Although not at all common in secondary schools, language laboratories are to be found in virutally every Latin American country, particularly at the binational centers or institutes (e.g. British Institutes, American Institutes, Alliance Française, German Institutes) offering foreign language courses, at other teaching institutions (e.g. universities, normal schools), and at the institutions training military personnel. A private survey indicates that Colombia and Brazil rank first in the number of language laboratories now in operation (between twenty and thirty, the more sophisticated types of laboratories included); Chile ranks second, with some fifteen laboratories, followed closely by Argentina and Venezuela. It is the authors' impression that, where they exist, language laboratories are not being used to the full extent of their possibilities; apparently the reason for this is to be found in the small amount of taped material now at their disposal. Films, either sound or silent, are very seldom used, at all levels of instruction.

It is to be remarked that, practically everywhere in Latin America, public schools operate below the minimum acceptable costs, the result being that no funds or surprisingly few funds are spent on 'nonessential' items, audiovisual aids amongst them; it is the classroom teacher who frequently buys this material out of his own, usually meager, salary. Furthermore this equipment is extremely expensive in Latin America, as it is almost invariably imported, and severe import restrictions are to be found in virtually every Latin American nation. Thus, for example, an average quality tape recorder costs no less than US. $ 150.00 in Chile, that is, just about a teacher's salary for approximately seven weeks. Yet tape recorders, particularly, are becoming almost popular with language teachers in Chile and in other Latin American nations. Incidentally, only Argentina, Brazil, and Mexico manufacture plastic and optical teaching material (e.g. charts, slides, slide projectors) in any significant output; language records are manufactured in Chile and in other nations as well.

VI. TEXTBOOKS

In order for the reader of this survey volume to have a comprehensive view of the problems concerning both the production and the adoption of FL textbooks in Latin American countries, the present writer would have to have conducted a careful examination of teaching materials in at least two thirds of the Spanish-speaking countries and in Brazil. Although no such comprehensive coverage was made possible, for several reasons already alluded to in the introductory section and elsewhere, an attempt was made, for the views set forth here, to be reasonably broad from the geographical point of view. References made to locally produced textbooks are based on an examination of the format and contents of a dozen FL courses having the following features in common: they are all widely used in the secondary school curricula of the respective countries, were produced by local, that is, native authors, follow officially sanctioned teaching programs and have enjoyed more than three editions since their publication (1955 was taken as the starting point for our purposes). Another feature shared by such sample textbooks was their alleged intention to follow what some authors would label an 'oral approach' whereas others would prefer to call it 'audiovisual'.

The truth of the matter is that a thorough, careful, and detailed analysis of present-day textbooks produced in Latin America (by local teachers and specialists) is a still-to-be-undertaken task, ideally by a team of competent investigators such as one might find on the roster of the Inter-American Program in Linguistics and Language Teaching. Here is a profitable and fruitful area of research which is worthy of immediate attention on the part of that Program's delegates. The carrying out of such an analysis should prove to be very revealing of the weaknesses, the vulnerable aspects of FL textbook making in Latin America, and perhaps more importantly, of the significant breakthroughs already made and perhaps more importantly, in the field by pioneering individuals.

Limitations of space have necessarily forced this writer to curtail his handling of textbooks and to focus rather on two subtopics: first, the description not of all twelve representative textbooks but of four samples supposedly representing Latin American developments; secondly, a brief summary will be given of the main trends in FL textbooks produced locally as well as some comments which will be made on the impact of foreign materials on the Latin American scene. By providing the reader with a summary outline of four books or four language courses from Mexico, Chile, Uruguay, and Brazil it is hoped that he can have at least a glimpse of the organizational features as well as some insight into the philosophies of approach underlying the materials incorporated in each book.

The four courses selected for our purposes are: *Inglés objetivo*. By Maria Luisa Garduño and Carmen Ochoa. A three-book course with accompanying workbooks and records. Primer curso: 1959; segundo curso: 1959; tercer curso: 1960. Mexico: Editorial Victoria, S.A.

I speak English. By Leopoldo Wigdorsky and Elia Díaz. A three-book course. Primer año: 1959; segundo año 1960; tercer año: 1961. Chile: Fondo Editorial Educacion Moderna.

Le Français au lycée. By Maria del Carmen Fontana and María del Carmen Garicoïts de Sayagués Laso. Par la méthode directe. N.d. Approved by the Council on Secondary and Preparatory Education, Sept. 1958. Premier volume.
Montevideo: A. Monteverde y Cia. S.A.

My English book. By Olga Creidy. A two-book course. São Paulo: Editôra do Brasil, S.A. 1964. 3rd edition.

Except for the Chilean textbooks the other three were written by secondary school teachers. *I speak English* was produced by university teachers who have had training both in the United States and in Scotland (Edinburgh). Let's turn, then, to a description of the contents of each course:

Garduño and Ochoa's *Inglés objetivo* has the following (typical) lesson outline:

Oral Practice and/or Reading Passage.
Listing of New Words (English-Spanish equivalents).
Variety of drills emphasizing reading, writing, translation.
Grammatical presentation.
Conversation (questions to be answered by the students).

The Mexican textbooks feature an English-Spanish vocabulary for each book; the drill instructions for the student are translated into Spanish in an appendix at the end of each book.
The accompanying workbooks for *Ingles objetivo* have instructions in Spanish. Drills emphasize writing, conjugation, translation, copying, dictation, etc.
Diaz and Wigdorsky's *I speak English* has the following typical lesson outline:

Short narrative or set of basic sentences and/or dialogues. Grammatical presentation and drills (active structure and passive structure).
Vocabulary (active and passive).
Pronunciation (sound contrasts, stress drills).

Except for assignment instructions given in Spanish through lesson seven (Book 1), this course is all English. The authors state that their work is based upon the linguistic research of Fries, Lado, and on the teaching approach of the *American English Series* (Fries, Rojas). *I speak English* features a Picture Series in Book III, intended for the drilling of tenses. In the Foreword to the Teacher we are told that 'each lesson centers on one grammatical problem and one pronunciation problem at a time'... 'vocabulary was strictly controlled and selected on the basis of usefulness to operate the grammatical patterns in each lesson'. The parts of a typical lesson in *Le Français au lycée* are as follows:

Reading or set of basic sentences.
Pronunciation (explanation of supposedly difficult sounds for the Spanish speaker).
Grammar (explanation, examples, emphasis on terminology).
Exercises.
Vocabulary (glossing of supposedly difficult French words and expressions).

The grammatical exercises are of the fill-in-blanks, conjugate, and simple-structural-change type. There is an index of French words with corresponding Spanish equivalents at the end of the book. Interspersed in the book are a few poems.

The fourth item on our list is Olga Creidy's *My English book*. The typical lesson outline in Volume 2 is as follows:

Reading (about a supposedly cultural topic referring to an English-speaking country).
Exercises (completion, simple transformation or change, questions to be answered).
Notes on Grammar (a listing of grammatical terms and word classes with corresponding examples).

At the end of the book there is a 50-page section called Grammar (the book has 279 pages!).

The above materials are all English. In the Foreword we are told that the 'classification and grading of this material were based on the sentence patterns of structural linguistics'... 'the linguistic aspects of the English language as well as the psychological implications in the mechanism of teaching a foreign language were taken into consideration'. Obviously the description of the four sample textbooks should not imply any comparative value judgments since each course is desgined to meet the needs of different educational systems. A critical analysis or interpretation of such texts could only be made in the light of the whole socio-educational complex in each country.

Turning to the second proposed subtopic: trends in FL textbooks and the impact of foreign materials on the Latin American scene it might be advantageous to speak first of the negative aspects and then of the positive trends. The generalizations are the sole responsibility of the Brazilian writer and reflect his own incomplete and fragmentary study of the problems involved.

Negative aspects characterizing FL textbooks in Latin America: High on the list would come a tendency for local textbook authors to imitate and follow foreign textbooks, especially as to the mechanical aspects of drill procedure. The reasoning that 'if it is foreign it must be good' proves to be more harmful than it should be. The result is that some of the newer textbooks are built on false pretenses, tending to be pseudopatterned after the more sophisticated products of American textbook making. Grammatical drills ignore important contrastive differences between the learner's language and the FL with too much redundant or superfluous material creeping in. Testing is neglected and not integrated with the teaching materials — the absence of review lessons in textbooks often acts as a negative factor against the preparation of tests. Teachers are thus tempted to use the very 'learning exercises' as devices for testing with most unfortunate consequences at times.

The cultural content is uneven and of generally poor quality, ranging from too learned and literary to a rather facetious, ridiculous tone. Bicultural comparisons are often misleading and misstated. There is a general lack of unity in the books as to a central theme (of a cultural nature), and there is also lack of consistency in treatment of linguistic variety (British and American English, for example). There is not a smooth transition from the learning and practicing of spoken skills to written skills.

The generally lengthy lessons lead to overteaching, teaching about the language (grammatical information is passed on, usually of a precarious, useless nature), and to no teaching at all. The authenticity of the foreign language in textbooks often leaves much to be desired — the authors have not taken the trouble to have competent native speakers check the linguistic accuracy or authenticity of the language presented in the books, thus allowing artificial, unnatural patterns to be included and alas to be acquired by the learner. The excessive concentration of grammatical and semantic material throughout the book reinforces the belief held by many students that the textbook is good only as an aid for passing the examinations.

Many more statements having a negative tone could be added to those made above; let us, however, proceed and take a look at the slightly brighter, more promising, more optimistic side.

Positive trends (slowly emerging) in the fields: Responsible textbook authors are beginning to give some attention (and more importantly, some 'space') to the development of spoken skills, by including dialogues and several types of systematized oral drills in their books. Alongside with this initial emphasis on the learning of spoken or conversational language there is a concern over the teaching of pronunciation through fairly simple drills involving common contrast between segmental phonemes. There is an awakening to the realization of the importance of grading of structural patterns and vocabulary control, although attempts to comply with such pedagogical requirements have so far reflected the keenly intuitive practice and experience of language teachers. The inclusion of pattern practice drills (substitution, primarily) and the simplification of grammatical presentation through tables, charts, etc. can be described as a healthy trend.

The avoidance of translation in the more realistic textbooks and the strict separation between the acquisition of active and passive skills as reflected in grammatical and semantic drills may well be a major breakthrough in the field. The addition of workbooks intended to provide the students with more oral practice and the availability of recorded material (records; tapes are prohibitive and unrealistic as yet) may act as powerful stimulus and incentive, thus counter-balancing the strong tradition of teaching of the written language in Latin America. The appearance of teamsponsored textbook projects, whereby local talent may work side by side with competent foreign specialists is bound to be a blessing and to do much to offset the at times harmful influence of commercially powerful imported textbooks. The awakening to the necessity of the establishment of national committees competently prepared to set up policies on FLT textbook construction is another outstanding trend.

V. STATUS AND TRAINING OF THE FOREIGN LANGUAGE TEACHER

Fulltime teaching at the secondary school level is a typical middle class profession, or occupation, in most of Latin America, certainly ranking below, in prestige, the traditional liberal professions, such as medicine, civil engineering, economics, the law; this is so even in countries where secondary school teaching is an established profession (e.g. Chile). Secondary school teachers are reported as occupying a somewhat higher socioeconomic status in Brazil and in Costa Rica. Nevertheless, they are normally trusted — particularly by commerce — above the level of other 'white collar' workers, and this we believe to be an index (if certainly imperfect) of the status of our profession. This should also explain why keeping up to date in the profession, through the attendance of seminars and the purchase of foreign books, usually constitutes a major problem for those in our profession.

The training of foreign language teachers varies considerably from one Latin American nation to another, although there is a general tendency to train them at a special department of languages and education at the local universities. In some nations (e.g. Chile, Costa Rica, Panama) teachers are trained at the universities exclusively;[57] in other nations (e.g. Argentina, Mexico) they are trained either at a university or at a higher section of an 'escuela normal'; still in other nations (e.g. Perú, Dominican Republic) training may take place either at a university or at a binational cultural center (e.g. Instituto Mexicano-Peruano). In Nicaragua the training of teachers of English is not yet clearly established, but teachers of French are trained at the Universidad Nacional de Nicaragua by special arrangement with L'Alliance Française (prospective students spend six semesters at the local university and, subsequently, eight semesters in France).

Chart III shows the plan leading to the professional title of 'Profesor de Inglés'

[57] In Chile, an emergency program to enable primary schoolmasters to teach English was started in March, 1967. This program (which does not grant a degree) aims at making the teaching of English possible, in the seventh and eighth grades, in the rural areas, where professional teachers of English are not usually available.

(Teacher of English), at the Universidad Católica de Chile (Facultad de Filosofía y Ciencias de la Educación, Escuela de Pedagogía, Departamento de Inglés). 'English Language' covers several activities in connection with the *use* of the language—listening comprehension, oral expression, pattern practice, pronunciation and oral drilling, vocabulary and diction, written exercises, conversation and dialogue memorization, theatre or speech, combined activities, extensive (silent) reading, intensive (silent) reading, written composition and laboratory work. The 'literature' course consists of several minor courses: a survey course on British literature, a survey course on United States literature, two elective courses (in 1965 courses on Lyrical Poetry, the Drama in the United States of America, the Short Story in the United States, and the English Novel were offered) and a course on Shakespeare. In 1966 research 'Seminars' on Literature, Grammar and Phonetics were offered on an elective basis. The above plan is complemented with a supervised teaching practice lasting approximately two

CHART III

Plan of Studies at the Department of English, Universidad Católica de Chile

Class periods per week.*

Subject \ Year	First	Second	Third	Fourth	Fifth
English Language	15	12	10	6	6
Phonetic Theory		2	(2)		
Grammatical Theory			2	2	
Applied Linguistics	2				
Literature		4	2	4	5
Lit. Background	2	2			
Preseminar			1		
Seminar				2	
Teaching methods				3	
Pedagogy	4				
General Psychology	2				
Religious Culture	2				
Latin	2	2	2	2	
Psychopedagogy		4			
Sociology		2			
Technique of Teaching			4		
Introduction to Philosophy			2		
Aesthetics			2		
Educational Philosophy				3	
Philosophy of Art				2	
Guidance					2
Seminar on Education					2
Professional Ethics					1
Aesthetic Axiology					1
TOTALS	29	26	27	24	17

* The 'credit' system is not currently used in Chile, nor in the majority of the Spanish speaking nations in Latin America. The information of this chart has been provided in a provisional character by the University authorities.

months (emphasis is on the completion of specific teaching units rather than on actual teaching time), a research thesis and a final degree examination. This curriculum is in a process of change in the direction of working on the basis of levels of proficiency rather than on overall annual promotion.

There are five other universities in Chile offering programs for prospective teachers of English as a foreign language (Universidad de Chile, Universidad del Norte, Universidad Técnica del Estado, Universidad Católica de Valparaíso, Universidad de Concepción);[58] these programs are comparable to the curriculum just outlined, although the Universidad Católica de Chile has succeeded in keeping under control the increase of the so-called 'general' subjects, the extension of which is a regular cause for complaint in most of the foreign language departments in Latin America. Programs for French and German, along similar lines, are also offered at several of the Chilean universities (The Universidad de Chile also offers programs for Italian and Classical Philology).

University courses offered in other Latin American nations resemble the Chilean course just outlined. In the countries where responsibility for the training of foreign language teachers rests with binational institutions, admission to such courses is usually restricted to applicants with training in education (e.g. normal school graduates).

Teaching staffs vary considerably from country to country, and from university to university within a country; yet, along general lines, they consist of an equal proportion of native speakers of English (both British and North American) and local teachers frequently with some kind of postgraduate work either in Britain or in the United States of America. 'Ph. D.' holders, or equivalent, are rare, both amongst the native speakers of English and the local teachers; 'M. A.' holders are scarce.

Most lecturers in the Latin American foreign language teacher training programs work on a parttime, or even on an hourly basis; this negative characteristic accounts, in part, for the fluctuating standards of foreign language teacher training and professional competence. Limited budgets and lack of material facilities cut down on the possibilities for even the larger universities to have a significant number of fulltime faculty members. That both secondary school teachers and university lecturers frequently hold two, and even three positions simultaneously is symptomatic of the general status of foreign language teaching in Latin America.

Amongst the Latin American universities offering courses for the professional training of foreign language teachers the following may be mentioned:

Universidad de Costa Rica
Universidad Autónoma de Santo Domingo
Universidad Autónoma Nacional de México
Universidad Nacional de Panamá
Universidad Nacional de Trujillo (Perú).

[58] Students total approximately nine hundred.

Universidad Nacional de Nicaragua
Universidad de Puerto Rico
Universidad de La Habana
Universidad Central (Caracas, Venezuela)
Universidad de Córdoba (Argentina)
Universidad de Chile
Universidad Católica de Chile (Santiago)
Universidad Católica de Valparaíso (Chile)
Universidad del Norte (Chile)
Universidad de Concepción (Chile)
Universidad Nacional (Bogotá, Colombia)
Universidad Pedagógica Nacional Femenina (Bogotà, Colombia)
Universidad Pedagógica y Tecnológica de Tunja (Colombia)
Universidad del Valle (Cali, Colombia)
Universidad Central del Ecuador
Universidad Nacional (Asunción, Paraguay)
Universidad de Oriente (Cuba)
Universidad Católica Andrés Bello (Caracas, Venezuela).

English is offered in all of the above universities, while French and Latin are offered in only part of them; German and Greek are exceptional; other languages are rare. Some universities in Perú and México offer courses of varying levels on the structure of some American Indian languages. The École Normale Superieur, at Port-au-Prince, Haiti, has programs for teachers of English and for teachers of Spanish; special courses for teachers of English are offered at the Escuela Normal Superior, Mexico City, and at the Instituto Normal Superior, La Paz, Bolivia.

Mixed programs, involving a university and usually a binational institution, are found in some places. Apart from the French program at the Universidad Nacional de Nicaragua, the Universidad Católica Andrés Bello (Caracas, Venezuela) offers a licentiate program in Letters, with a major in English, in collaboration with the Venezuelan-North American Center (four years, using the material of the English Language Institute of the University of Michigan); the Department of Modern Languages at the Universidad del Valle (Cali, Colombia) operates on a binational agreement with the University of Texas.

A brief survey of the textbooks and reference books used at these teacher training programs indicated, amongst others, the following titles for English: *Living English Structure* and *Living English Speech*, by W. Stannard Allen; *English Sentence Patterns*, *English Pattern Practices*, *English Pronunciation*, and *Lessons in Vocabulary*, by Charles C. Fries, Robert Lado, and English Language Institute staff; *Teaching and Learning English as a Foreign Language* and *The Structure of English*, by Charles Fries; *Linguistics across Cultures*, *Language Testing*, and *Language Teaching: A Scientific Approach*, by Robert Lado; *A Guide to Patterns and Usage in English*, *The*

Advanced Learner's Dictionary of Current English and *The Teaching of Structural Words and Sentence Patterns*, by A. S. Hornby; *An English Pronouncing Dictionary*, by Daniel Jones; *The Phonetics of English*, by Ida Ward; *A Pronouncing Dictionary of American English*, by Kenyon and Knott; *Language*, by Edward Sapir; *Language*, by Leonard Bloomfield; *An Introduction to Descriptive Linguistics*, by H. A. Gleason, Jr.; *Roget's Pocket Thesaurus*; *A Grammar of English Words*, by Harold Palmer; *A Handbook of English Grammar*, by R. W. Zandwoort; *English Grammar, Past and Present*, by J. C. Nesfield; *The Use of Tenses in English*, by J. Millington-Ward; *Growth and Structure of the English Language*, by Otto Jespersen; *Exercises in English Patterns and Usage*, by Ronald Mackin; and several literary histories and anthologies.

Textbooks by Mauger, Galichet, Lagarde and Michard, and Castex and Surer have been reported as being used in the beginning stages of the training programs for teachers of French. De Saussure is a standard textbook in virtually all foreign language programs.

Several specialized periodicals reach Latin America, amongst them *English Language Teaching*, *Language Learning*, *IRAL*, Australia's *English, a New Language*, *Le français dans le monde*, *The Linguistic Reporter*, and *The Modern Language Journal*. *Language Learning* reports 173 individual subscribers in Latin America, besides the copies regularly sent to the binational centers and other institutions; *English Language Teaching* possibly doubles that figure. Only a few specialized journals are locally produced; lack of time allowed us to gather information only about two of them, *Lenguaje y Ciencias*, published quarterly by the Universidad Nacional de Trujillo, Perú, and *Revista de Lingüística Aplicada*, published occasionally by the Linguistic Circle of the Universidad de Concepción, Chile. Occasional relevant leaflets are published in almost every Latin American nation.

A modest amount of research, in connection with seminars and theses, takes place at several universities training foreign language teachers.[59]

Tenure of foreign language teaching positions in secondary schools is consonant with the amount and quality of professional instruction offered by each Latin American nation. Thus in Chile, for example, the possession of the professional degree is a requisite for permanent appointment in the public secondary schools. We must remark, however, that Latin America is no exception to the poor economic condition of teachers,[60] this fact making appointment requirements rather illusory. There are approximately three thousand foreign language teachers in Chile, but no more than fifty per cent of them hold a professional title, though approximately fifty per

[59] A brief bookshelf research at the Universidad Católica de Chile revealed, amongst others, the following theses (1961-65): *Prepositions after Nouns, Adjectives and Particles* (pp. 335); *Spanish Translation Equivalents of English Tenses* (pp. 128); *A Comparative Study of Coordinate and Subordinate Clauses in English and Spanish* (pp. 210); *The Importance of Visual Aids in Teaching English, particularly in Chilean Education* (pp. 141).

[60] In Chile, where the per capita income is approximately US $ 317.00 (as estimated from the Gross National Product), fulltime secondary school teachers, lecturing thirty-six hours a week, average a yearly salary of US. $ 920.00.

cent of the remaining half have nearly finished the program leading to the title. Foreign language teachers, however, do have more opportunities outside the teaching profession (e.g. interpreters, translators, specialized clerical work) than their colleagues in the other school subjects, this fact actually working against the status of foreign language teaching as much effort, both human and financial, is spent in the training of specialized teachers.

Shortage of specialized foreign language teachers is reported from Argentina, Bolivia, Cuba, Colombia, Dominican Republic, El Salvador, Guatemala, Venezuela and Nicaragua.[61]

1. *International Cooperation to Foreign Language Teaching*

The United States of America, the United Kingdom, France and, to a minor extent, Germany and Canada render assistance to Latin America in the field of foreign language teaching. Indirectly the Soviet Union, Czechoslovakia, Italy, the United Arabic Republic, Japan, and the People's Republic of China contribute to the diffusion of their respective languages. Inter-Latinamerican assistance comes from Brazil and from some Spanish speaking nations, especially Argentina, Mexico, and Chile. The Organization of American States and the United Nations are increasing considerably their assistance to foreign language projects.

Assistance is provided in four different ways, namely through exchange or study grants abroad, through the binational centers, through the contribution of experts and through grants in didactic material.

The United States of America outranks the other assisting nations as to the number of scholarships granted for foreign language teachers, either through official (e.g. United States State Department, Fulbright Commission)[62] or private (e.g. Ford Foundation, Rotary Club) agencies. Most of these scholarships, ranging in duration from four to eighteen months, cover travel and all other expenses; a significant number of Latin American teachers of English holding twelve or eighteen month scholarships succeed in obtaining a Master's degree. The number of scholarships granted by the United States of America, large as it is, yet appears discouragingly low in relation to the number of teachers of English in Latin America, grossly estimated at seventeen thousand, with the exclusion of Brazil (by far the largest Latin American nation).

These last three or four years the 'Peace Corps', created by President John Kennedy,

[61] *Les langues vivantes dans les écoles secondaires d'enseignement général, op. cit.*

[62] The Fulbright Commission granted sixty-five scholarships (or exchange fellowships) to Chilean teachers of English, from 1957 to 1964. Several of these grantees, however, did not register for programs for teachers of English as a foreign language but for general education courses. The total number of scholarships granted by other United States institutions, both official and private, was approximately ten, during the same period. The number of United States scholarships bestowed on other Spanish speaking American nations is proportionate, roughly, to their population.

has proved a valuable help to English teaching in some Latin American countries.

The United Kingdom grants, through the British Council, approximately eight scholarships every year to teachers of English from Spanish speaking America. These scholarships include voyage expenses and normally last an academic year. The Universities of London, Edinburgh and Bangor, and the Cardiff College of Advanced Technology, seem to receive the highest proportion of Latin American teachers of English.

The Cultural Service of the French Republic granted Chilean teachers of French fifty-seven scholarships from 1959 to 1965, plus one or two positions of 'assistant d'espagnol' every year.[63]

The Soviet Union, Czechoslovakia, and Italy do not grant scholarships to teachers of those languages (teachers of the first two languages are virtually unknown in the public school systems of Spanish speaking America) but to teachers of other subjects, for different fields of specialization (e.g. educational planning), thus indirectly contributing to spread their respective languages. The People's Republic of China has recently entered the scene in a similar way.

Binational centers or institutes — particularly those connected with Great Britain, the United States of America, and France — have played an important role in the Latin American foreign language teaching scene these twenty-five or thirty years. 'American' (that is, connected with the United States of North America) centers function all over Latin America, with the exception of Cuba, while British, French and — less frequently — German institutes (or centers) exist in many Latin American nations. These centers, partly financed by the foreign nation concerned, are structured and function in a fairly similary way, with cultural activities such as art exhibitions, lectures, library services and so on; foreign language teaching is a major activity in virtually all of these centers.

There are seven 'American'-Mexican binational centers, the largest being the one in Mexico City with an approximate enrollment of twelve thousand students. Courses on English at different levels are offered, either intensively or at a regular pace; they have produced the *American English Course* (chiefly based on the material of the University of Michigan English Language Institute), which is used in many Mexican secondary schools and in the 'American Institutes' of other Latin American nations. One of the most positive constributions of the 'American'-Mexican center is the regular meeting of two-week seminars for teachers of English every year, attendance varying between two hundred and fifty and three hundred teachers.

The Haitian-'American' Institute, at Port-au-Prince, is reported as one of the leading foreign language teaching institutions in that country, with an approximate enrollment of eight hundred students in the courses on English language and United States literature. As in virtually all of the 'American Institutes' in Latin America, the oral-aural approach is regularly used, with the aid of a language laboratory. The

[63] There are approximately five additional scholarships per year for teachers of French belonging in the religious orders of French origin.

Institute sponsored television programs on the *Let's Learn English* and *Let's Speak English* series, with great success. The Instituto Chileno-Norteamericano de Cultura, at Santiago de Chile, enrolls approximately four thousand five hundred students (both adults and children) in fifteen different courses, amongst them a course on Spanish for speakers of English.

In Colombia, apart from the regular activities of the Centro Colombo-Americano, there is an Instituto Lingüístico Colombo-Americano operating under the joint auspices of the National Ministry of Education and the University of California at Los Angeles. In 1962 the Instituto was officially requested to prepare a series of six *Teacher's Guides* for the teaching of English in the Colombian secondary schools. We read in the preface to the first Guide that the objective of the enterprise was 'to introduce in the secondary schools of the nation an entire complex of those new methods in language teaching which have proven most effective in promoting rapid learning'. We are also told that the materials were tested throughout their production in experimental and demonstration classes at the Instituto Pedagógico of the Universidad Pedagógica Nacional, at Bogotá. The Guides were given official approval by the Ministry of Education for wider application in the public and private schools of Colombia. In the Introduction to the Guides Dr. John Martin, Director of the Instituto Lingüístico Colombo-Americano and member of the Inter-American Program in Linguistics and Language Teaching, sets out the qualifications required of the teacher who is to use the First Year Guide, namely, that he should have a satisfactory command of English pronunciation, that he should possess a knowledge of the interference created by native language habits, and that he should master the special techniques required for conducting effective oral practice.[64] The Brazilian co-author of this survey has had the fortune to examine a copy of the *Guía para la enseñanza del inglés en las escuelas de nivel medio, primer año* (Guide to the Teaching of English in Secondary Schools, First Year) and has been favorably impressed by the thorough and systematic treatment of pedagogical procedures; the wealth of suggestions and sound advice on grammatical, phonological, orthographic and semantic points leads the impartial observer to lay great faith and confidence in such an ambitious — and, apparently, successful — enterprise. ILCA also offers a one-year course on Applied Linguistics for teachers already in the possession of an official degree.

'British Institutes' function in many Latin American republics, with a major emphasis on the teaching of English. These Institutes are subsidized by the British Council in different degrees, usually covering salaries and rather expensive equipment, such as language laboratories. Our report from Mexico City indicates the existence of the Instituto Anglo-Mexicano de Cultura, founded in 1944, with an approximate enrollment of three thousand students in the English courses; above seven hundred of the above figure are children between ten and fifteen.[65] The interesting remark is made

[64] Compare with the Qualifications for Secondary School Teachers of Modern Languages stated by the Modern Language Association in PMLA, vol. 70, No. 4, part 2, September 1955.

[65] Figures for the First Term of 1965.

that enrollment has been increasing steadily slightly above the rate of ten per cent for the last six years. There are three kinds of English language courses: a regular course with two and a half hours a week, lasting thirty-six weeks; an intensive course which meets five hours a week; and a still more intensive course, meeting daily for ninety minutes, from December through January. There are special courses also, such as history and translation. The 'oral-direct' method is used in the language courses, although an experiment is being done with the 'situational approach'. English language students are prepared for the 'Lower Certificate', the 'Certificate of Proficiency in English', and the 'Diploma of English Studies'; in 1964 fifty-nine out of eighty-seven candidates passed the Lower Certificate examination, and eight out of ten candidates passed the Proficiency Examination. Our informant reports that negotiations are being made with the Ministry of Education and the National University of Mexico to have these certificates officially recognised, a situation which exists in a few Latin American nations.

The Instituto Chileno-Británico, at Santiago, founded in 1938, has an approximate enrollment of 2700 students (September 1965), about 700 of them being children between ten and sixteen. The Institute offers three kinds of English language courses, viz. the regular eight-semester course, meeting three hours a week, and two intensive courses, one of them meeting five hours a week during four semesters, and the remaining course meeting ten hours a week for a year. Apart from the English language courses there are Spanish courses for speakers of English, business courses, literature courses, and a course on Scientific English.

The Instituto Chileno-Británico, together with its counterparts in Argentina and Uruguay, has recently started the A.C.U. (Argentina-Chile-Uruguay) project, consisting of an 'experimental approach' to English language teaching based on the principles of bilingual analysis, emphasis on the oral-aural aspects of language, and direct techniques of presentation and drilling. The Basic ACU course meets three times a week for three (possibly four) years. A provisional textbook has been prepared in mimeographed form, with its corresponding teacher's guide. It is worth mentioning that the ACU course is being tried in some classes of the experimental secondary school run by the Universidad de Chile.

Apart from the British Institutes in Chile (three main branches), Argentina (three main branches), Uruguay and Mexico, there are similar Institutes in Brasil (three main branches), Colombia, Perú, and Venezuela. British Institutes indirectly connected with the British Council exist in other places as well.

French cultural institutes are in operation in Argentina, Chile, Colombia, Cuba, Costa Rica, Ecuador, Haiti, Mexico, Nicaragua, Uruguay and other Latin American nations. The Instituto Chileno-Francés de Cultura, at Santiago, has an approximate enrollment of 1300 students (September 1965) in the four main kinds of courses offered, namely the regular seven-semester course, the audiovisual course (based on the material prepared at St. Cloud), the 'conversation' course, and the higher course leading to the 'Certificat Practique de Langue Française' and the 'Diplome d'Études

Françaises'; on the other hand, valuable assistance is given to the local secondary school teachers of French through the loan of books, slides, records and, less frequently, films.

The remaining part of our survey of the binational institutes will concentrate on the situation in Santiago de Chile which, because of its population (at present estimated at two and a half million), is fairly representative of a large Latin American city. The Chilean-Italian Institute offers a course lasting approximately five semesters; the Chilean-Soviet Institute offers a two-year Russian language course meeting three hours a week, and a three-year course meeting two hours a week. The Chilean-Brazilian Institute offers a four-month language course, meeting two hours a week, and additional courses in conversation and literature. The Chilean-Chinese Institute and the Chilean-Japanese Institute offer shorter elementary courses, usually lasting no longer than six months. The German Cultural Institute enrolls approximately 1000 students in the regular eight-semester course, meeting three hours a week, and in the four semester course, meeting six hours a week; modern teaching techniques and a language laboratory are used.

We wish to finish this section with a few words on the situation in Cuba. A recent report indicates the existence of the state operated Abraham Lincoln Institute and John Reed Institute, where instruction on several languages (English and Russian included) is offered, particularly to adult students.

2. *Foreign language teacher organizations*

Associations of teachers of individual foreign languages exist in the majority of the Latin American nations, though their degree of operativeness varies considerably. The Association of Teachers of English of Uruguay is reported as one of the most active, holding regular meetings and constantly striving for professional improvement.

The situation in most of the Latin American nations is not too satisfactory, however: on the one hand, the excess of class periods actually prevents teachers from devoting any significant portion of their time to meeting and, on the other hand, practically no financial assistance has ever been given to these associations. Such is the situation in Chile, where the National Association of Teachers of English and the National Association of Teachers of French function irregularly and survive under precarious conditions; an Association of Teachers and Research Workers in Language, Linguistics and Literature (APIL, 'Asociación de Profesores e Investigadores de Lenguas, Lingüística y Literatura') has just been formed under the auspices of the Chilean Ministry of Education, the Chilean universities, the organizations of teachers of individual languages (Spanish included), and a private international Foundation; APIL's plans are ambitious (long scale reserch projects are contemplated) but the survival of the association rests with the materialization of promised financial assistance.

VI. FOREIGN LANGUAGE TEACHING IN ARGENTINA

1. *The General Situation*

At the outset it should be pointed out that this brief survey is basically a summary of reports sent to the writer by responsible individuals holding key positions in the field of FL teaching in Argentina. The difficulties met with in the process of data-gathering through private correspondence or through published literature are perhaps characteristic of the Latin American situation. There is a great deal of interest and curiosity regarding the field but very little has actually been done to describe it. The writer hopes that, by summarizing what is actually a more complex situation than he presents here, others may pursue the task in as great detail, degree of accuracy, and realism as is called for. Limitations of space are also partly responsible for the sketchy treatment of topics, and the focus on a particular institution rather than on another only reflects the availability of data. Omissions and gaps are bound to be noticeable but it is to be hoped that the general aims here as in other sections of the chapter are at least satisfactorily achieved. The most commonly taught foreign languages in Argentina are English, French, Italian and German in that order of importance. Reports indicate that in the last decades English has aroused an enormous interest in all circles and fields of activity and that it is by far the most popular choice among students for both economic and intellectual reasons. It has been suggested that English be taught in elementary schools, but state-controlled primary schools do not as a rule include the teaching of foreign languages in their curriculum. According to T. B. Gregori 'In Argentina, foreign language study has not as yet been integrated in the primary school curriculum'. She adds that there are some private institutions, however, that offer a foreign language course outside school hours, and she explains that the reasons for the growing interest in teaching English to children may be found in the zeal of parents to equip their children better for today's world. Another pertinent comment of hers is that 'the fact that English is the most widely used language, which has gained such importance lately in conducting world affairs, leads parents to prefer it to other foreign languages'.

Some institutions where children can take foreign languages are the Escuela Normal de Maestras John F. Kennedy, Escuela Normal de Professores Mariano Acosta, and the Instituto de Lenguas Vivas, all three in Buenos Aires, the Escuela Graduada Joaquín V. González attached to the Facultad de Humanidades at La Plata, and the Escuela Normal de Professores in Rosario. In such pilot-schools children begin studying the foreign tongue in Upper First Grade, i.e., their second year in school, when the majority are seven years old. A report states that several attempts have been made at adding a foreign tongue to the curriculum of primary schools in other parts of the country and drafts for bills to make this practice compulsory are known to have been lying unheeded for years at various provincial legislatures.

As regards the situation in secondary schools, they all include English as a subject in their curriculum. In some schools the students are given a choice between English and French, of even Italian, but the general tendency is for students to take English. In secondary schools students usually take 3-4 years of English with an average of 3-4 teaching periods a week. Depending on the type of secondary school, however, the foreign language, may sometimes be studied for five or even six years totaling an average of one hundred classes a year.

At the end of the secondary school FL course a student should have acquired the basic structures of the language together with an adequate vocabulary that will allow him to pursue his studies at a higher level. By and large the results achieved by the type of instruction given in Argentinian secondary schools do not differ significantly from those of other similar Latin American institutions that is, the incipient development of reading and translation skills rather than some control of the spoken language. As Gregori says 'pupils often meet with disappointment at their failure to understand and to speak the second language, and parents are often confronted with the problem of having them coached by private teachers'. Regulations require the use of Argentine textbooks but foreign textbooks, such as those by Hornby, Gatenby, and Hicks, in the case of English, are sometimes allowed at the request of the corresponding language departments.

2. *Some Typical Instances*

The Ministry of Education, in its great concern over the status and quality of FL instruction, has always given a great deal of responsibility to the Inspector General de Idiomas Extranjeros, a top ranking official who inspects, supervises the teaching of FL's in government-run schools, and who is in a position to contribute toward realistic changes in methodology by supporting or by launching himself pioneering initiatives which turn out to be beneficial to the status of FL teaching in Argentinian schools.

An example of the training of secondary school teachers of English is that provided by the University of Cuyo in the city of Mendoza. According to a report prepared by Mrs. T. B. Gregori, Lecturer in Methodology and Practice in the above mentioned institution, the training of foreign language teachers extends over a period of five years of which the last two make up the professional training proper. In the case of the training of reachers of English care is taken that by the fourth year the trainees have already become fairly fluent in the language so that they can be exposed to a theoretical study of the problems involved in teaching English as a foreign language and that they have teaching practice for at least three semesters.

The course outline given for Teaching English as a FL lists as major topics the following items: Introduction to the teaching of FL's. The Psychology of FLL, Specific Problems in the Teaching and Learning of English as a FL, the teaching of Grammar, the teaching of Vocabulary, Technological Aids, Reading, the Teaching of Composition, The teaching of Literature, and The Training of Modern Language Teachers.

In addition to attending lectures and doing research assignments the trainees are required to attend classes in secondary schools under the supervision of an instructor. A great deal of actual teaching practice and lesson planning is emphasized and only upon successful completion of both theoretical and practical classroom work can the trainee be permitted to sit for his examination which consists of a class in the presence of three professors.

Except for the Teacher-Training institutions, devoted to the preparation of FL teachers, at most Argentine universities foreign languages are now taught to enable students to read the vast foreign bibliography and to eventually facilitate travel and study abroad. In the Escuela Superior de Lenguas y Literaturas Extranjeras of the Universidad Nacional de Cuyo, prospective FL teachers take an average of five subjects a year in a five-year program leading to a degree of 'Professor' in the language and literature of his or her choice. English, French and Italian are the most commonly taught languages in that model institution.

The Departamento of Aplicación is a section of the Escuela Superior de Lenguas Extranjeras where a practical knowledge of English, French, German, and Italian is imparted to over 1500 students distributed into courses for adults and children. The teaching staff is made up entirely of University teachers carefully selected through a rigorous competitive examination. According to a report by the Head of that Department 'the method employed for the teaching of English is the pattern practice approach'. She adds that teachers of English in her Department availed themselves of the linguistic principles underlying that new approach, and experiments are continually being carried out on the bases supplied by the modern linguistic sciences. it is interesting to note that in such scheme an emphasis has also been placed on the teaching of culture on anthropological principles.

As for the situation involving German, Italian and French we are told that such languages are taught 'according to the direct method' because of the difficulty in obtaining materials based on the findings of linguists, which can be successfully applied to that school.

The task of supplying schools all over Argentina with well trained FL teachers has been making greater demands on teacher-training institutions than ever before, in spite of the natural shortage of material (and sometimes human) resources which afflict such centers. Only one of such teacher-training-centers, for example, was equipped with an electronic language laboratory until the time of this writing: the outstanding and well known Instituto de Lenguas Vivas in Buenos Aires.

On the subject of language laboratories it is well to add that only ten such elaborate installations existed in the country in 1964 distributed as follows: four laboratories in military training institutions, two labs in the Universities of Buenos Aires and of Cuyo, one lab in the Instituto Nacional de Tecnologia Agropecuaria (Buenos Aires), one lab in the Argentinian American Cultural Institute, one in USAID and one in the

U.S. Federal Aviation Agency. A plea for the establishment of language laboratories is made by heads of important teacher-training centers; Professor Lidia Tubino de Toso, Director of the Escuela Superior de Lenguas y Literaturas Extranjeras (Universidad de Cuyo), in an unpublished report read to the participants of the Regional Summer School sponsored by the British Council in Montevideo (January 1964), states that 'it is high time all the teacher-training centers were fitted with technological aids, but costs and bureaucracy are heavy odds and success seems to be still a long way off'.

Teacher-training colleges in Argentina are interested in offering courses in linguistics for teachers, and some pioneering attempts have already been made. In 1964 a semester course in linguistics was given to graduate-level teachers of the Escuela Superior de Lenguas (Universidad de Cuyo) by a local Faculty member who holds an M. A. degree from an American University. It was aimed, according to a communication from the instructor, at introducing teachers of English to the principles of synchronic linguistics underlying the new approach for the teaching of English as a foreign language.

Argentina's evergrowing core of competent teacher-trainers is very fortunate in having had a well balanced background of both European and American methodological traditions. It is said that British English has traditionally been the variety of English taught in Argentina's fine training colleges, but the impact of American applied linguistics and the dissemination of teaching materials produced in the United States is beginning to be felt. There were thirty-six British Institutes in Argentina as against fifteen American Centers in 1965.

By and large the teaching of foreign languages is successfuly carried out at the various British, American, French, German and Italian Cultural Institutes with varying degrees of emphasis on the so-called audio-lingual approach. Such centers have branches in most major towns in Argentina and generally work hand in hand with state-run educational centers for the purposes of strengthening the cultural bonds between the respective countries. With the evergrowing interest in the learning of English more of such American and British Institutes are bound to open in the near future.

The thirty-six '*Culturas* Inglesas' throughout the country are attended by some 30,000 students and the American-Argentinian centers by some 22,000 students, mainly young adults and children of school-leaving age. At the time of this writing considerable progress was being made on the preparation of a common basic English language teaching syllabus for the British Cultural Institutes located not only in Argentina but also in Chile and Uruguay. The draft text of this ACU scheme, as it is called, was prepared by a team of experts from the three countries and tested in pilot groups at the 'Culturas'.

A short seminar was held in July 1965 for fifty teachers from provinces who would be teaching from ACU material next year. The unprecedented initiative of preparing an English textbook series to serve three Spanish-speaking countries (and others possibly) is a fine example of professional cooperation and solidarity on a hemispheric basis. The British Council arranged for the Argentinian, Chilean and Uruguayan experts to be oriented in the constrative analysis of River Plate Spanish and British English, by British linguists from the University College, Bangor, Wales.

The study of linguistics, structural grammar, and the audio-lingual approach have all been given impetus by the seminars held especially by the American- Argentinian Centers and by the active Culturas Inglesas. It is primarily through scholarships given by binational institutions that high-caliber Argentinian teachers pursue graduate and postgraduate courses in American and European universities. It is mainly to private institutions that foreign language teachers are indebted for enlightenment and for improvement of their professional qualifications. The writer could observe for himself the great concern of Argentine teachers of English over developments in their field: he was very impressed by the sincere eagerness and anxiety of a highly select group who attended the British Summer School held in Montevideo, January of 1965.

Their almost unquenchable professional thirst to learn more about more scientifically oriented approaches to language teaching and to be better informed as to bibliographical sources is but one of the optimistic symptoms now pervading the small but steadily growing body of leaders in the profession. An example of sincere willingness to experiment with more linguistically sophisticated textbooks for the learning of English can be seen in the adoption by all Argentine-American Cultural Institutes last year (1965) of the NCTE sponsored series English for Today. In that respect the Binational Centers in Argentina have gone a step farther than its counterparts in most Latin American countries, including Brazil where the heterogeneity of textbooks used, even in such centers, accounts for the multiplicity of sometimes conflicting approaches with resulting inherent obstacles to a fruitful assessment of textbook efficacy. It may be argued that in a Continentsized country like Brazil it is almost impossible to take steps of a similar nature but something on a regional basis at least could be striven for.

Some progress has been made in Teacher-Training Programs at institutions of higher learning but the quality of instruction in secondary schools has not been improved upon significantly: locally produced textbooks still capitalize on the direct method approach and give much importance to learning about the language. A sequel to Robert Lado's Annotated Bibliography for Teachers of English as a Foreign Language (Department of Health, Education and Welfare—Washington: 1955, pp. 224), especially as regards his description of textbooks produced for Spanish and Brazilian Portuguese-speaking students (he covers a period from 1946 to the end of 1963) would be quite revealing of the minor but realistic changes which have been taking place in textbooks — particularly so the transition from a heavily British-orientated textbook to a more balanced tool. Teacher's Manuals accompanying textbooks are beginning to come into fashion — surely an indication of the atmosphere of unrest and ferment where FL teachers work and live.

Both because of high standards of its teacher-training institutions and on account of the active participation and sharing on the part of a few outstanding Argentinian teachers and linguists in Interamerican activities leading to an eventual improvement of FLT conditions in Central and South America, Argentina is destined to rank among the leading nations in the field of FL Teaching in the Americas. As is true of its sister country Brazil, the road ahead is filled with detours — much assistance will be needed both from Argentine educational authorities and from foreign entities to boost FLT, to remedy, and to correct its present ailments, but above all it is on the teachers' shoulders that there lies the hardest task of all.

Two significant facts evidencing the great interest displayed by Argentine university authorites, linguists, and FL teacher trainers, in the development of programs of linguistic training and research in that country are given herein: First, the letter by the Rector of the University of Buenos Aires addressed to the Executive Committee of the Interamerican Program in Linguistics and Language Teaching (Minutes of Executive Committee Meeting, October 25-27, 1964), stating that his institution 'assigns the highest value' to the goals of the Program and recommends the establishment of a regional center for linguistic research and training in Buenos Aires; secondly, the offers to support the Program's goals from The University's Centers of La Plata, Córdoba, Rosario, and Cuyo and from the Instituto Nacional de Lenguas Vivas (Buenos Aires). The latter Institution has published its own journal (Lenguas Vivas) since 1957, devoted to the dissemination of present day FLT methodology and applied linguistics. The 61-year old teacher-training Center has been a veritable pioneer in the field of FLT in the Southern Hemisphere — particularly so in the utilization of the language laboratory for phonetic training and FL drill.

The former Technical Advisor to the Instituto de Lenguas Vivas, Professor Adriana Gandolfo, has been a delegate to the Interamerican Program in Linguistics and LT since its official launching in 1963. She is now a member of the Foreign Languages Committee. FLT in Argentina owes a great deal to her painstaking efforts of an entire professional life dedicated to FLT and teacher-training: she both planned and helped found the model language laboratory in the above mentioned Institute of Modern Languages. She has set an example to a generation of fellow Argentinians, who, upon returning from specialization courses in The United States, England, France, Italy, Germany, and other countries, contribute to the strengthening of the already existing top quality programs in FL teaching and linguistics.

The summary statement about the Latin American situation in second language learning (Washington, 1961, Language Information Series I, Pp. 18) to the effect that 'up to this time local linguists have shown little active interest in the application of linguistics to the methodology of language teaching' (p. 9) would have to be slightly changed and given an optimistic tone if only four years later: local linguists and FL teachers, especially in universities, teacher-training centers, and Binational institutions are beginning to show an active interest in what the above mentioned report describes.

In this too short section we might mention some more higher level institutions where such active interest is gaining momentum in Argentina: Universidad Nacional del

Sur, Universidad Nacional de Tucumán, Universidad Nacional del Litoral, Universidad Nacional del Nordeste. In the Second Inter-american Symposium in Linguistics and Language Teaching, held in Bloomington, (Aug. 2-8, 1964) Argentina was represented by six delegates. In the Third Symposium (to be held in Montevideo January 1965) the delegation from the third-largest Spanish country in the world will be almost twice as large, thus attesting to the recognition by the Program of the great potential human resources to be found in Argentina.

The evergrowing rapprochment between Argentine and Brazilian specialists in FL teaching and linguistics, made possible by joint Interamerican efforts, will pave the way for the performance of tasks of the utmost relevance biculturally, such as, for example, the implementation of the teaching of Portuguese in Argentina's universities and of Spanish of the River Plate variety in Brazilian institutions of higher learning.

Continental solidarity, based on the pursual of common objectives and aspirations must stimulate the introduction (no matter how slow and gradual) of Spanish and Brazilian Portuguese as tools of intercultural understanding. Portuguese in its Brazilian variety is as deserving of a stable place in the Argentine (or in other Spanish-speaking countries) university curriculum as other languages and the same is true of Spanish in Brazil. It is high time that the educational authorities of the respective countries awaken to the potentialities of the two languages as foreign languages instead of sitting back and letting them follow their course of languages usually taught in private institutions under government auspices.

The craving on the part of Argentine teachers for possibilities of further training and specialization in their own country is greater than ever before. It is not uncommon nowadays to hear of roundtable discussions in leading university Departments of languages focused on the planning of 'cursos de perfeccionamiento para graduados' and even of courses leading to a doctorate. University statutes and bylaws sometimes present themselves as obstacles to such visionary movements but, strong as the teachers' urge is, such legislation is bound to be revitalized.

It might be too premature to think that Argentine teachers are ready to pursue postgraduate level courses in their own country — in terms of financial expenditure the enterprise would now prove to be prohibitive, but as regards the human potential to carry out such task, there should be no question about it. The very existence and successful operation of some higher learning institutions devoted exclusively to FL teaching in Argentina leads us to predict that within the next five years or so a small center for Applied Linguistics will be set up to best coordinate individual and institutional efforts on both regional and national bases. The 1970's may well bear witness to the emergence in Argentina, as well as in Brazil of students whose interest in foreign languages will be focused on research, thus opening up a new era for the field in South America.

It is high time that Argentine universities pool their efforts together and aim at mutually rewarding goals in the field of FL teaching: the creation of a Center for Applied Linguistics is not a new ideal but from thought to reality there is a long way to go. The research potential of Argentine FL teachers lies mostly dormant awaiting for forces which may bring them out — the stimulation of the publishing of specialized journals and the contributions by Argentine teachers to foreign journals may do much to arouse the admiration (already expressed) of specialists and institutions abroad.

An Association of Latin American teachers of foreign languages might be a useful means to draw continental efforts together and strengthen existing programs on how best to disseminate information and share valuable undertakings by getting to know one another better. Argentina can assume a position of leadership in some areas of the field just as Brazil, Uruguay, and other countries. The challenge is here and now but it is here to stay, unless adequate steps are taken to meet and fight such challenge.

VII. FL TEACHING IN URUGUAY

In Uruguay as in most Latin American countries, 'teaching programs' for the secondary school subjects are organized under government auspices or at least have to bear some kind of official sanction. In the case of Uruguay it is the Consejo de Enseñanza Secundaria (Council of Secondary School Teaching) which grants permission for textbooks to be published. Government supervision of secondary school teaching is carried out through the Inspección de Enseñanza Secundária and there is accordingly an inspector in charge of FL teaching just as there is in Argentina. In some respects the FLT situation in Uruguay is quite unique and some of the generalizations made about other Latin American countries hold good only to a very small extent, if at all. Our report here, which in turn is based on impressions and some data gathered mostly from Uruguayan teachers of English, is focused on the status of English as a FL.

At the British Council Summer School Held in Las Toscas, Uruguay, (January 1965) the writer heard a report given by the Inspector of FL Teaching, Dr. Aquiles Guerra, on the situation of the teaching of English in Uruguay and what is being done by the Council of Secondary School Teaching to improve the quality of instruction. The tradition of the Direct Method (an often loosely employed term) can still be seen as a textbook 'qualifier' or descriptive phrase. Some textbook authors do not hesitate to claim 'that the merits of such method, its fruits, are unquestionable and the authors' own experiences can but testify such efficiency' (Preface of Le Français au Lycée — By Maria del Carmen Neiro Fontana and Maria del Carmen Garicoits de Sayagués Laso. Montevideo: 1958. Premier Volume — p. 111).

As was pointed out above, the Uruguayan FLT situation differs from that of other Latin American countries: French is taught for three years, but there are only two years of English in the secondary schools, and this is the only language teaching provided by the State, with the exception of the English and French courses at the teacher training college. There is practically no university-level teaching of English, although there is an English literature course at the Facultad de Humanidades y Ciencias, which has a Department of Linguistics under the competent direction of

Dr. Jose Pedro Rona, delegate to the Inter-American Program in Linguistics and Language Teaching.

Before summarizing Dr. Guerra's Plans (to be submitted to the Uruguayan Council of Secondary School Teaching) of a New Methodology for teaching of English to be followed in pilot-liceos (government schools), it may be appropritate to describe the situation as regards the teaching of FL's in private institutions.

Although there is no complete list of FLT institutions in Uruguay it is commonly known that English, French, German, Italian, and Russian are taught in binational schools, especially in Montevideo. Thus The Alliançe Française, the Italian-Uruguayan Institute, etc., are engaged in teaching language and civilization courses. The French Institute is also active through teacher-training programs. The teaching of Portuguese is conducted mainly at the Brazilian-Uruguayan Cultural Center, maintained by the Brazilian Embassy but there's some teaching of Portuguese in the Facultad de Humanidades y Ciencias, too.

There are eleven British-Uruguayan Institutes in Uruguay as against one U.S. Binational Centre (Alianza Cultural Uruguay-Estados Unidos). As concerns methods used: the American-Uruguayan Centre uses the oral-aural approach to language teaching. The Anglo-Uruguayan Institute in Montevideo is in transition; it uses a grammar-translation method in the upper grades, and an audio-lingual method based on contrastive analysis (River-Plate Spanish-RP English) in the lower grades. Other FLT institutes use a melange of approaches, combining direct method, audiolingual, and grammar translation.

In 1965 the textbooks used in the U.S. Binational Centre were as follows: Children-American English Course (Mexico BNC)

Adults — Fries American English Series (Fries, Rojas-Puerto Rico).

The Instituto Cultural Anglo-Uruguayo used: Learning English (Miller) for children and Oxford Progressive English (Hornby) for adults. The Erwy School and the Crandon Institute teach English to children. Both the American and the British Centre in Montevideo had a language laboratory; the only other institution which could boast of such an aid was the Ministry of Defense.

Uruguayan teachers of English have their own professional Association which promotes seminars, round table discussions, publishes important papers and conducts longer teacher-training programs. The Summer School for Teachers of English has been held every year since 1945. It is an edifying example of international cooperation in the field of English language teaching: the courses are sponsored by the Consejo Nacional de Enseñanza Secundaria, the British Council, the United States Information Service, and the general organization is in charge of the Uruguayan Association of Teachers of English. The emphasis in such summer schools (2 week-long) is on the modern approaches to the teaching of English. There are several lectures dealing with English and literature, English linguistics for teachers and some round table discussions.

At the time of this writing the very active Association referred to above was sponsoring a course in Introductory Linguistics so as to best prepare Montevideo teachers of English to take advantage of the First Latin American Institute of Linguistics to be held there from December 27, 1965, to February 28, 1966, under the auspices of the Latin American Association of Philology and Linguistics, the Inter-American Program in Linguistics and Language Teaching and the Facultad de Humanidades y Ciencias of the Universidad de la Republica. Uruguay will have an important role to play in the development of modern methods of textbook construction in the field of English as a foreign language. The participation of highly competent Uruguayan teachers in the A.C.U. scheme (the joint production by Argentina, Chile, and Uruguay's British Institutes of a series for the teaching of English under modern linguistic principles) is strong evidence of the high caliber professional status achieved by some of its leading teachers. There is a need for professional associations of teachers of foreign languages (there are only a half dozen truly active ones in Latin America) to make one another's goals and achievements better known. The Association of Teachers of English can set an example, through its well organized teacher-training program, to be followed in other countries. There can be no doubt that Latin American Teachers of FL's have a great potential both methodologically and linguistically but such potential is largely unexplored. It is through undertakings such as professional associations that great initiatives bear fruit.

Before closing this brief series of statements on Uruguay it is well to name an institution that has been active in French language teaching for forty years and has achieved reasonably good results — The Lycée Français of Montevideo. A full description of its goals, organization of courses, results obtained, etc, appeared in the June issue (1965) of *Le Français dans le Monde*.

Reports on institutions where teaching based on bilingualism is carried out are scant. Although the organization of such institutions differs from that of exclusively monolingual foreign language centers, they can not be ignored in a survey such as this — it is in institutions of such a type that Latin American children can be exposed to a foreign language, whether it be French or English or even German, from kindergarten age. If foreign language teaching on an elementary level is to have any chances of a gradual realistic introduction throughout Latin-American countries the experience of schools such as the Lycée Français of Montevideo will prove to be valuable for the planning and development of courses.

Seriously handicapped by the evergrowing prestige of English all over the world and particularly so in Latin America, French as a foreign language cannot compete quantitatively, no one can deny, but it can be placed on a methodologically sound basis of equality with English. In countries where the Alliance Française is becoming more and more active there may be a revival of interest in the language, especially at the university level.

The longer-span recommended for the learning of foreign languages is to be seen in private institutions such as the Lycée and in experimental schools — FLES is still too far off for most if not all Latin American countries but the experience of the few active centers in such a field deserve closer attention and imitation. Foreign governments and local Latin American governments could well stimulate the opening of more bilingual schools to promote not only the learning of languages but the acquisition of so badly needed crosscultural insights. To conclude this section on Uruguay the writer would like to stress the need for the introduction and upkeeping of programs of foreign language teaching at the university level.

The manpower reservoir of Uruguay in the field of FL teaching is of as good quality as that in other Latin American countries. There is a lack of opportunities for graduate and postgraduate work in foreign languages, especially English. Governmental assistance on the university level could be as significant as on the secondary school level. The installation of electronic laboratories in institutions of higher learning and in pilot secondary schools would facilitate the training and re-training of teachers in the spoken skills, thus paving the way for the gradual utilization and production of audiovisual resources in the schools throughout the country.

Badly needed in Uruguay as well as in other Latin American and Caribbean countries is the planning of follow up or advanced courses in the civilization and literature for students of foreign languages. Professor R. A. Cowling, former professor of English Literature at the University of Montevideo, in an article for *English Language Teaching* (Oct. 1962) 'Observations on the Teaching of English Literature to Foreigners with special reference to South American', states that 'the time has come to pay serious attention to the next stage in English teaching: to offer literature courses, talks about books in the library, classes in which the students themselves can take part, so as to keep their English alive and make them feel that their long years of study have not been wasted.' (p. 27). The problem of letting a foreign language rust away through disuse, as Prof. Cowling puts it, can not be neglected. Some language institutes favor social contacts between teachers and students outside classroom hours so as to enable the latter to use the foreign language in more realistic and more pleasant situations. Modern advertising made by foreign language institutions, particularly that of the British Cultural Institutes, draws the learners' attention to Conversation Tea where they can practice their English in a leisurely, informal fashion. The emphasis on cultural values closely linked to the learning of a foreign language needs a more rigorous structuring in the training of teachers in Latin America.

In short, the situation in Uruguay, although being in some respects similar to that of other Latin American countries, has, on the other hand, major gaps to fill, thus calling for the concerted efforts of educational authorities, teachers, and institutions devoted to the field of foreign language teaching. The establishment of a small center of applied linguistics in Montevideo, under official and private auspices or even on a binational basis, would be a decisive factor to correct the existing mistakes and to improve and expand, perhaps on a short term basis, the prevailing conditions. The functioning of such centers in key cities in the Americas may be veritable springboards for the launching of a continental revolution in language teaching.

VIII. CONCLUDING REMARKS

Upon completion of a necessarily fragmentary and incomplete survey of a too comprehensive field in a highly complex situation, the writers feel rather reluctant to come up with a set of concluding remarks which, whether or not intended to have the flavor of generalizations, will inevitably thus be considered by the readers who were curious and patient enough to take this journey across the still partially explored lands of foreign language teaching in Latin America.

A cursory glance at some of the shortcomings of foreign language teaching is needed, we believe, at this point.

Promising as the situation may appear in the Latin American universities, binational institutes, and larger secondary schools, there is an acute shortage of duly qualified foreign language teachers. The absence of rewards, both material and in the nature of the recognition of an appropriate social status, drives away from the profession many meritorious young persons. The same reason accounts, at least in part, for the difficulty graduate teachers have in keeping abreast of new developments; 'follow-up' and 'refresher' courses do exist, but they are not usually paralleled by the administrative and pecuniary measures which should secure the participation of a significant number of teachers, particularly of those who live and labor in the smaller cities. This situation has deleterious consequences in the Latin American nations, usually with large sparsely-populated areas, as teachers tend to resist appointments in the provinces. And in this way is another typically Latin American circle closed.

Undeservedly low socioeconomic status still has another negative consequence. It is not unusual for foreign language teachers, particularly of those working in secondary schools, to add some ten to twenty (sometimes even more) hours of private tutoring to their 'regular' thirty or thirty-six weekly hours at school. We hardly need go into the eventual loss of human capital this unnatural amount of work means to the Latin American communities; let us solely consider the evil consequences which lack of time has on any person who has been entrusted with a profession. The average Latin American foreign language teacher has no time to read journals, to visit classes by his colleagues, to write about his own experiences — let alone to attend professional meetings with any regularity; he is usually faced with — to the European or North-American reader — unbelievable alternatives: dinner or the meeting of the foreign language association; the daily newspaper or the professional journal; talking to the children before they go to sleep or preparing classes for tomorrow. Homely as all this may sound, it reflects a very serious situation whose remedy should be considered with absolute priority if anything is to be done concerning the improvement of foreign language instruction in these parts of the New World.

Books constitute another problem. Money and time are not the only barriers between Latin American foreign language teachers and books printed in Europe or in the United States of America; import restrictions arising from unfavorable 'terms of exchange' make foreign books ever more scarce. There is little that the Latin

American governments can do in this case, but the financially more powerful nations could do much in, for example, the form of currency exchange facilities for foreign language teachers who wish to buy specialized books (or subscribe to specialized magazines). On the pessimistic assumption that rationing of time is bound to continue for some time, we all know that browsing a book is better than not having it at all. Or why not jointly assist in the publication of a 'foreign language digest' for all of Latin America?

This brings us to the vital issue of communications between groups of foreign language teachers in the different Latin American countries. Communications do exist within the reduced group of lecturers and experts, and even there usually at the cost of great personal economic sacrifice — for distances are very, very long in America.

In some Latin American areas more coordination, based on mutual respect and understanding, is needed between the binational centers and the local teachers in the public schools. Frictions have not uncommonly arisen when the binational center authorities have failed to realize that each Latin American republic presents peculiarities, or when such authorities have tried to center, monitor, or patronize foreign language teaching in the absence of the consent of the local teachers, or in the absence of an open dialogue. The practice, existing in some places, of having the local teachers working in the binational centers examine their colleagues in the local schools who apply for scholarships is particularly deleterious for good relations, especially if the personnel at the binational institution happen to be nongraduate or newly graduated.

The number of foreign language teaching grants for study or stay abroad is surprisingly low, especially in relation to the scholarships or fellowships granted in the technical and scientific areas. We certainly need not enlarge upon this point. To the largest possible extent the policies governing the granting of scholarships should correlate with the hierarchical expectations of teachers; selecting bodies do not necessarily become objective when local personalities are asked to integrate them.

Not infrequently have absolute statements about new foreign language teaching principles bewildered the Latin American teacher. Perhaps we should try and restore his confidence by stating clearly what we all know, namely, that there is no substitute for the hard-working and enthusiastic teacher. An open-minded attitude is indeed required from professors and supervisors.

It has become commonplace to speak of 'revolutions' in Latin America from a political point of view and to describe major attempts at changes in the socioeconomic systems in terms of the aspirations of the lower and middle classes, such as the eradication of illiteracy and more educational opportunities. Although educational reforms have often characterized both the secondary school and the university curricula of many if not most countries in these regions, the impact that such reforms have had on the role of foreign languages has been slight. Reform in the field of foreign language teaching and in the attitude of the authorities towards foreign languages is urgently needed, no matter how advanced a few institutions may be and regardless of the outstanding initiatives stemming either from individuals or from official sources.

Above all, and in consideration of the gap between needs and resources in all of Latin America, this reform movement should be carefully planned.

The preceding survey should have proven sufficiently revealing of the acute problems afflicting the overall position of foreign language instruction in the Latin American secondary schools; it must have also indicated that there is a growing concern both on the part of private and official institutions over the gradual elimination of difficulties to be found within the profession itself — the too short foreign language programs, the frequent lack of adequate teacher training, and the emphasis on the reading-translation aim, to name just a few.

Global solutions which could bring about a drastic reorganization of foreign language instruction in the Latin American countries can not be possibly contemplated, even on a long term basis, on account of the striking diversity of educational systems and of the complexity of cultural patterns characterizing Haiti, the Spanish-speaking countries and large, Portuguese-speaking Brazil.

Diversity, however, should be no obstacle to planned reform, which should start in the countries where the prevailing educational practices leave ample room for greater flexibility in the secondary and university curricula, where, in other words, the educational atmosphere is more congenial and conductive to not only generating interest in foreign language learning but especially to sustaining, expanding, strengthening, and orienting such interest on a nation-wide basis. What the writers are proposing here is the inception of a generative reform movement involving realistic attitudes towards foreign language learning and teaching. Every country in Latin America is in a position to contribute to the preparatory stages of such an enterprise, (witness, for instance, the great cooperative efforts of individuals connected with the Inter-American Program in Linguistics and Language Teaching) but some countries are in a more privileged position than others to launch reforms in foreign language teaching in the near future; these reform movements are bound to be fruitfully contagious to other Latin American nations.

The establishment of carefully planned national policies regulating foreign language instruction in the official or government schools would be a major step toward the eradication of a multiplicity of pseudo approaches to language teaching. Attempts on the part of individual Ministries of Education to improve both linguistically and pedagogically the official programs for the teaching of foreign languages should be made known to other Latin American nations, as part of the reform movement here proposed.

The production of methodological manuals, or teacher's guides, could also be turned into a powerful tool for the fulfillment of the aims we suggest. The ever growing importance and hemispheric recognition of the goals of the Inter-American Program in Linguistics and Language Teaching might eventually persuade the educational authorities in a number of countries to devote more time and to spend more funds on projects carried out on a teamwork basis rather than resulting from individual contributions.

A listing of key figures, outstanding institutions, and main trends characterizing foreign language teaching in Latin America would fail for its many omissions and noticeable gaps, but it would not sin as regards the seriousness of purpose which has led the writers to pursue this challenging task to an end.

Foremost on our list come those scholars who, directly or indirectly, have been in charge of specialized training programs in the United States or in Europe. The names of distinguished personalities such as Charles Fries, Robert Lado, Albert Marckwardt, Bruce Pattison, J. C. Catford, Randolph Quirk, A. H. King, and André Martinet deserve special mention amongst many linguists of renown. Amongst the authors of published materials which have been of paramount importance to foreign language teaching in Latin America we may now mention, besides the personalities referred to above, I. A. Richards, Christine Gibson, Ralph Robinett, Betty Wallace Robinett, William Slager, Pauline Rojas, Edward Cornelius, Clifford H. Prator Jr., Frederick B. Agard, Kenneth Croft, Audrey Wright, James McGillivray, Michael West, Harold Palmer, A. S. Hornby, F. G. French, W. S. Allen, E. V. Gatenby, E. E. Eckersley, Roger Kingdon, Ronald Mackin, David Abercrombie, Peter Strevens, M. A. K. Halliday, Angus McIntosh, S. Pit Corder, R. W. Zandvoort, Fr. Closset, A. Mauger and, most particularly, the editors of and contributors to *English Language Teaching* and *Language Learning*. We also remain in deep gratitude to the course directors and supervisors who, appointed by their respective governments, have labored enthusiastically and fruitfully in the binational institutes all the way from Mexico to Argentina.

Initiatives such as the 1964 seminar offered jointly by the Université de Besançon and the Universidad de Concepción, Chile, are worthy of imitation. Latin American teachers of foreign languages have been and will always be most responsive to the linguistic and pedagogical achievements of those countries where great academic importance is attached to modern language teaching and research. The United States of America, Great Britain, France, and other nations can do much to enrich the programs of the teacher training centers in Latin America; they are already doing a great deal in the promotion of higher professional standards through the granting of specialized scholarships. Conferences, meetings, congresses, round tables, and symposia on the role of foreign language teaching will be more numerous and more badly needed in Latin America.

Although some local enterprises might be considerably improved as regards their immediate outcomes, stimulating and contagious ideas usually arise from them; these ideas, once elaborated, may turn out to become effective weapons against official indifference and the unwholesome perpetuation of outdated methods of instruction. Ferment is evident in several Latin American centers for the teaching of foreign languages, amongst them the Instituto Lingüístico Colombo-Americano, in Bogotá; co-sponsorship of the Colombian Ministry of Education in the Institute's project is an outstanding example of the confidence with which the local authorities may welcome the collaboration of a foreign institution of higher studies in the development of programs attuned to modern trends of foreign language teaching and to the realities of the classroom.

The appearance of teachers' guides such as the ones produced by the Instituto Lingüístico Colombo-Americano attest to the productivity in the field of foreign language teaching in Latin America. Foreign language teachers are beginning to demand that their voices be heard, that their ideas be incorporated in textbooks which promote efficient and rapid learning.

Team-sponsored textbooks produced locally are still gargantuan tasks for many Latin American countries and, until the much expected advent of more favorable conditions, the art of foreign language textbook-making will continue to be the easy profit of many and the pioneering idealism of a neglected few. A Brazilian author of an English textbook for secondary schools complained to one of the present writers that the pressure of conservative standards of textbook construction and the business mindedness of some publishing firms make it difficult for an author to innovate or even to minimize the poor contents of traditional materials.

In 1961 the Chilean Ministry of Education appointed a committee of foreign language teachers to take charge of the planning of the official programs for foreign language courses in the secondary school (different teachers constituted the committee in subsequent years); as a result of this decision a major emphasis was given to the acquisition of the audio-oral skills for the first three years of instruction. The production of more adequate locally produced textbooks was the immediate outcome of the shift of emphasis in the foreign language programs. The A.C.U. (Argentina-Chile-Uruguay) course, soon to be published, will mark a memorable date in the history of international cooperation for the production of foreign language teaching material. Some binational centers sponsored by the United States of America (e.g. Mexico, Brazil) have already produced materials of wide appeal.

The Yázigi Institute of Languages, in Brazil, has been winning national recognition, and it may well have an influential role to play in the badly needed reform of foreign language teaching in Latin America's largest nation, especially because of the Institute's pioneering attempts to promote greater dissemination of the findings of applied linguistics.

To close this listing of some representative institutions it is edifying to point out that the Uruguayan Association of Teachers of English was, by the time of the elaboration of the present review, preparing its members to be able to participate in the Instituto Lingüístico Latino-Americano, to be held in Montevideo from the 27th of December of 1965 to the 28th of February of 1966, and in the Third Inter-American Symposium in Linguistics and Language Teaching. The latter program, established in Cartagena, Colombia, in 1963, has been bringing together key figures in the field of foreign language teaching in the Americas, so that when the phase of productivity is launched, the long-cherished dream of radical reform in foreign language teaching may not seem an unattainable goal for Latin Americans.

What remains to be said about present trends in foreign language teaching in these parts of the world can be summarized as follows:

The introduction of the audio-lingual approach or of linguistically sound techniques alone will not solve the problems afflicting the profession. High and above such meritorious goals (to be pursued on a long-range basis) is a sincere examination of conscience on the part of the educational authorities regarding the status of foreign language teaching in their respective countries.

As it was stressed before, the heaviest burden of responsibility for the reform movement here preconized lies on the shoulders of the privileged language teachers who have had good training in their countries or abroad; theirs is the revolution and theirs is the destiny of foreign language teaching in Latin America. It is up to those revolutionists to win both the popular and the official recognition for their objectives. Linguistics can aid in such a campaign by orienting and enlightening the minds of teachers, but the heterogeneity of teaching procedures will not be neutralized without much cooperative effort and dedication.[66]

[66] At the time the proofs for this section were being corrected the authors received a copy of a rather detailed and carefully prepared report on Foreign Language Teaching in Peru, written by Ernesto Zierer, Head of the Department of Foreign Languages and Linguistics in the National University of Trujillo. This excellent survey, published in Spanish by that institution, should prove an extremely useful guide to the preparation of similar national surveys on FL Teaching in Latin America and the Caribbean in the near future. A summarized version of such report has appeared recently in the October issue of *The Linguistic Reporter*, Newsletter of the Center for Applied Linguistics, 1717 Massachusetts Avenue, N.W. Washington, D.C.

Readers interested in FL Teaching in Argentina should also read an article on the Lenguas Vivas Institute by Prof. Adriana Gandolfo (*Linguistic Reporter*, Aug., 1966) and should look forward to the appearance of other brief but highly informative articles on FL teaching in other Latin American countries to appear in the above mentioned newsletter.

APPLIED LINGUISTIC RESEARCH

HELES CONTRERAS

0. INTRODUCTION

Very little has been done in the area of applied linguistics research in Ibero-America, as will become apparent from this chapter.[1] On writing this report, our purpose is not only to record the little work that HAS been done, but also to call the attention of our colleagues to the vast area of research that lies before us in this field.

Two criteria seem to underlie the distinction between applied linguistics and theoretical linguistics: a) the criterion suggested by the names themselves, i.e. the opposition between theory and application; b) the distinction between what Trager (1949)[2] has termed microlinguistics and metalinguistics,[3] i.e. between studies concerned exclusively with language, and studies which view language in relation to something else.

If we take the first criterion alone, a difference is established between, say, works on theoretical linguistics and grammatical descriptions of specific languages, which are normally not considered applied linguistics, in spite of their nontheoretical[4] nature, presumably because they are not at the same time exolinguistic.

Taking the second criterion by itself, we would consider as applied linguistics such interdisciplinary studies as psycholinguistics, mathematical linguistics, sociolinguistics, etc. Although occasionally these areas are in fact so classified,[5] the most general tendency is to distinguish between exolinguistic studies and applied linguistics.

It is only by using both criteria that we define an area corresponding to what most people do in fact call applied linguistics. Our definition of applied linguistics (non-theoretical and exolinguistic) will thus cover the linguistic aspects involved in techniques such as language teaching, automatic translation, psychiatric diagnosis, etc., but

[1] I express my gratitude to the following colleagues for very valuable information: Adriana Gandolfo, F. Gomes de Matos, Joseph Grimes, Yolanda Lastra, John W. Martin, Jorge Luis Porras Cruz, Rafael Posada, and Inés Pozzi-Escot de John.

[2] See the bibliography for full references.

[3] We prefer the term *exolinguistics* suggested by J. B. Carroll in *The Study of Language*, Cambridge: Harvard University Press (1953), because of Trager's strange use of the prefix *meta-*, which deviates from the more usual meaning in such words as *metalanguage*, *metatheory*, etc.

[4] We should say *non-metatheoretical*, since a grammar is a theory of a language based on a particular linguistic metatheory.

[5] See, for instance, the first volume of *Current Trends in Linguistics*, where, under the heading *Applied Linguistics*, in addition to 'Machine Translation' and 'Foreign Language Teaching', we find chapters on 'Mathematical Linguistics' and 'Metrics'. (*Soviet and East European Linguistics*, Thomas A. Sebeok, Editor, The Hague, Mouton, 1963).

it will exclude areas such as psycholinguistics and sociolinguistics as well as straight grammatical descriptions.

The scope of this particular chapter is further limited by the fact that it deals with *research* as opposed to more practical matters such as the problem of literacy or the teaching of foreign languages, which are discussed in other chapters of this volume.

We do not have to go too far back in time to trace the development of applied linguistics research in Ibero-America. The reasons are obvious: on the one hand, applied linguistics is a new discipline even in the United States; on the other, modern structural linguistics is a recent import (both from Europe and the United States) and, clearly, there cannot be much application where the theoretical foundation is not very firmly established. Although the names of Andrés Bello, Rodolfo Lenz, Federico Hanssen and Rufino José Cuervo suggest a respectable philological and grammatical tradition in Ibero-America, the fact is that the linguistic theories associated with them are not a good foundation for an applied linguistics. It is only with the very recent introduction of various brands of structuralism and functionalism that the way has been opened for research in the field of applied linguistics. The strongest stimuli in this kind of endeavor have come, no doubt, from the so-called American structuralism. More recent trends, such as transformationalism, which has already made its way into some applied linguistics publications in the United States,[6] are just being introduced to Ibero-America, and some time will have to elapse before they can really become part of the active knowledge of applied linguistics researchers.[7]

1. PUBLISHED RESEARCH

Our report will cover books and articles published by Ibero-American authors regardless of the place of publication, and by foreigners if published in Ibero-America.

1.1 *Second-Language learning*

The impact of American structuralism, represented mainly by Fries and Lado, is apparent in several articles of this section. This is true of Skoberg (1962), which discusses second-language learning as the acquisition of new speech habits on the basis of quotations from Lado, Fries and Sapir; of Garon (1962a) and Garon (1962b), the first being a description of the method employed at the Yázigi Institute of Languages in São Paulo, preceded by some theoretical discussion, and the second being a comment on Fries' definition of grammar as '... the devices that signal structural meaning'.

Of a more general nature is Cintra (1963), a discussion of the noncongruent struc-

[6] See, for instance, Stockwell, Bowen, and Martin (1965), Roberts (1964), and various articles in the latest issues of *Language Learning*.

[7] In the bibliography discussed below, only one item, Alvarez (1964), refers to transformationalism.

ture of different languages, supported by many examples both phonological and grammatical.

A classification of types of interference, based partly on Weinreich (1953) is found in Contreras (1963).

A recent contribution to the theoretical foundation of second-language teaching is Alvarez (1964), which discusses modern transformational theory from the point of view of its usefulness for the language teacher.

1.2. *Contrastive analysis*

Although mostly descriptive, we will mention here Cintra (1962) and Alvarez (1963), because of their relevance for contrastive analysis. The former deals with the phonology of Brazilian Portuguese, and the latter with the suffixes *-al* and *-el* in French.

The most common second language is English. The following are Portuguese-English studies: Cintra (1964), dealing with segmental phonemes; Gomes de Matos (1964), dealing with syntax; and Bichels (1962) and Candido and Neto (1962), dealing with deceptive cognates. Spanish-English studies are Rodríguez (1950), dealing with vocabulary, and Wolff (1950), dealing with phonology.

French as a second language is represented by the already cited Alvarez (1963) and by Bianchi and Bordagorry (1963).

Finally, Balan (1962-63) is a comparison of English and Japanese consonants, and Larson (1963), a grammar of Spanish for Aguaruna[8] speakers.

1.3 *The standard language*

A few works have appeared dealing with the problem of teaching the standard language, both in its oral and written form, to speakers of substandard varieties. Of a general nature are Rona (1964), Echeverría (1963) and Porras (1962), dealing respectively with the relationship between dialectological research and the teaching of the standard language, the teaching of the standard language in the secondary school, and the teaching of the standard language in general.

Rodríguez (1949) is a study of themes written by elementary school children in Puerto Rico and a discussion of the most frequent errors.

Rodríguez (1952) and Santos (1959) are descriptions of the language spoken by elementary school children in Puerto Rico. The same study for Puerto Rican secondary school students has been done by Mauleón (1948).

1.4 *Literacy*

Although the work done in this area especially by members of the Summer Institute

[8] A Peruvian Indian tribe.

of Linguistics has been impressive, we have found only two references which will fit the framework of this report: Gudschinsky (1951-52) and Townsend (1952), dealing with the reading problems of the Mazateco and Aymara Indians respectively. The rest of the work mentioned, for instance, in the Bibliography of the Summer Institute of Linguistics is either straight description or pedagogical.

1.5 *Pedagogical*

In this section, we include materials dealing directly with teaching problem both of native and foreign languages.

On foreign language teaching, we will mention the Portuguese translation of Cornelius' *Language Teaching* (Cornelius, 1957) and Chagas (1957), both of which are primarily methodological. Here again, like in the section on contrastive analysis, English is the most common foreign language. This is the case with Garon (1963), Garon (1964), Machuca (1953-54), Madsen (1964), Rojas (1954), and Skoberg (1963). The subject matter is apparent from the titles, so no comment is needed.

Pesaresi (1962) deals with the problem of selecting a standard for the teaching of Italian.

Rodríguez (1954) deals with the teaching of Spanish in Puerto Rican elementary schools.

1.6. *Information*

There are a few articles containing information on the development and present status of theoretical and applied linguistics in Ibero-America.

The main source for this is the Proceedings of the First Symposium of the Inter-American Program in Linguistics and Language Teaching, to be published by the Instituto Caro y Cuervo in Bogotá, Colombia.

Church (1960) and Loos (1963) report on the activities of the Summer Institute of Linguistics in Guatemala and Perú, respectively. More information on this can be obtained from the Bibliography of the Summer Institute of Linguistics.

Gomes de Matos (1963) and (1965) deal, respectively, with the place of linguistics in the Brazilian University curricula and with the activities of the Yázigi Institute of Languages in São Paulo.

Rodríguez (1962) reports on the research carried out by the Consejo Superior de Enseñanza of the University of Puerto Rico on the teaching of Spanish.

Finally, Rabanales (1964) is an exhaustive report on the status of linguistics in Chile.

1.7 *Journals*

There are two journals devoted to the application of linguistics to the teaching of languages. One, *Estudos* (subtitled *Revista de lingüística e metodologia do ensino de línguas*), is published by the Departamento de Estudos e Pesquisas of the Yázigi Institute of Languages in Sãa Paulo.[9] It is a quarterly publication initiated in 1962. Its editorship has been recently taken over by three of the top Brazilian linguists, Joaquim Mattoso Câmara Jr., Aryon Rodrigues, and F. Gomes de Matos, and they intend to change it into a journal of theoretical and applied linguistics aimed at a much wider public than it has reached so far.[10] Articles are published mostly in English and Portuguese. The other journal, *Revista de Lingüística Aplicada* (*RLA*), is published annually by the Círculo Lingüístico at the Universidad de Concepción, Chile.[11] Two issues have appeared so far, and as the number of contributions increases, it is hoped that more than one annual issue will be published. Articles are mainly in Spanish. The editorship is in charge of Gerardo H. Alvarez and Heles Contreras.

Another journal, *Lenguas Vivas*, published by the Instituto Nacional del Profesorado en Lenguas Vivas 'Juan R. Fernández' in Buenos Aires,[12] also contains some articles of interest for our purpose, together with materials of a more pedagogical and practical nature.

2. RESEARCH IN PROGRESS

The following projects have come to our attention:

a) F. Gomes de Matos is working on an Introduction to Applied Linguistics, in Portuguese, for the use of Brazilian teachers of English and French mainly. The tentative completion date is the spring of 1966.

b) John W. Martin, Director of the Instituto Lingüístico Colombo-Americano, in Bogotá, is working on an English-Spanish contrastive study based on the descriptive studies of English which he has carried out as a basis for syllabi intended for the use of English teachers throughout Colombia.

c) The Quechua program, carried out by the University of Cornell and the Universidad de San Marcos, in Quinua, Perú, is experimenting with new methods in the teaching of Spanish to speakers of Quechua. The traditional method has been teaching the oral language, reading, and writing simultaneously. Under the new approach, the native language is used at the beginning while the students receive some oral instruction in Spanish. Exercises in reading and writing do not begin until the fifth month. The results so far have been highly satisfactory. The experiment will continue until December 1966.

d) The Cuzco program, in Kuyo Chico, Perú, is being carried out by the Peruvian Ministerio de Trabajo y Asuntos Indígenas. It is a literacy program which, like the

[9] The address is Rua Aurora, 713, 80. andar, São Paulo, Brazil.
[10] Information provided by F. Gomes de Matos.
[11] The address is Instituto Central de Lenguas, Universidad de Concepción, Concepción, Chile.
[12] Address: Carlos Pellegrini 1455, Buenos Aires, Argentina.

Quechua program, gives importance to the native language, and introduces Spanish gradually.

e) The Summer Institute of Linguistics is constantly engaged in research in applied linguistics through the efforts of many field workers in several Ibero-American countries. The tangible results are numerous descriptive studies and subsequent didactic materials for the teaching of reading through the native language.

3. INSTITUTIONS

We have already referred in passing to some institutions connected with applied linguistics research. Certainly one of the most important ones is the Summer Institute of Linguistics, both for the quality and the bulk of the work being done. We should mention also, without identifying them, various government agencies, which, either by themselves or through other institutions, play an important role in the encouragement of applied linguistics research. A good example of fruitful cooperation between the local government and an outside institution is the already mentioned Instituto Lingüístico Colombo-Americano, jointly sponsored by the Colombian Ministerio de Educación Nacional and the University of California in Los Angeles.

The natural sources of stimulation for research in our area of interest, namely, the local universities, are really quite inactive in this respect, due to a long tradition where linguistics has had nothing to do with the business of teaching languages.

4. PROBLEMS AND PROSPECTS

Our problems may be summarized in a simple sentence: There is a lot of work to be done and not enough people to do it. An intensification of training in linguistics is, therefore, urgently needed. So is more communication between linguists and teachers.

Another aspect has to do with the linguist's 'image'. Both government and university officials have to become aware of the potential contribution of linguists to the solution of practical problems. This is up to us linguists, of course. If we keep hiding in our ivory towers there is not much chance of a change of image.

The advent of the Inter-American Program in Linguistics and Language Teaching, which is about to celebrate its third Symposium and its first Linguistic Institute, has really made an impact in the development of linguistics in Latin America. From isolationism we have moved to fruitful exchange. We will have a true measure of the importance of this movement if, ten years from now, a report like this is a truly an optimistic one.

5. BIBLIOGRAPHY

Alvarez, Gerardo H., 'Los sufijos *-al* y *-el* en francés actual', *Revista de Lingüística Aplicada* 1:1.24-32 (1963).

——, 'La gramática transformacional y la enseñanza de idiomas extranjeros', *Revista de Lingüística Aplicada* 2:1.13-25 (1964).

Balan Scemes, Diana, 'A Comparison of English and Japanese Consonant Phonemes', *Estudos* 1:2.7-17 (1962), 2:1.19-26 (1963).

Bianchi, Marta, and Claudette Bordagorry, 'Interferencias en la pronunciación del francés', *Revista de Lingüística Aplicada* 1:1.14-24 (1963).

Bichels, Hélio O., 'Trouble Spots in Vocabulary', *Estudos* 1:2.27-30, 1:3.33-4 (1962).

Cândido, Luiz A., and Michel H. Neto, 'Trouble Spots in Vocabulary', *Estudos* 1:4.13-4 (1962).

Chagas, R. Valnir C., *Didática especial de línguas modernas* (São Paulo, Companhia Editôra Nacional, (1957).

Church, Clarence, 'El Instituto Lingüístico de Verano en Guatemala', *Boletín Indigenista* 20.133-5 (1960).

Cintra, Geraldo, 'Ensaios sôbre a estrutura do português do Brasil (1)', *Estudos* 1:1.17-31, 1:3.19-31, 1:4.15-25 (1962).

——, 'Why Contrastive Analysis?', *Estudos* 2:1.8-14 (1963).

——, 'Consonantes e vogais do português e do inglês: estudo comparativo', *Estudos* 3:1.5-16 (1964).

Contreras, Heles, 'La lingüística aplicada a la enseñanza de idiomas', *Revista de Lingüística Aplicada* 1:1.1-14 (1963).

Cornelius, Edwin T., Jr., *O Ensino do Idioma* (São Paulo, Companhia Editôra Nacional, 1957).

Echeverría, Sergio, 'La gramática española en la asignatura de castellano de la educación media', *Revista de Lingüística Aplicada* 1:1.32-44 (1963).

Garon, Ernest, 'The Yázigi Method', *Estudos* 1:1.7-16, 1:3.5-18 (1962a).

——, 'Grammar and Modern Language Teaching', *Estudos* 1:4.7-12 (1962b).

——, 'A Program for the Preparation of Language Teachers', *Estudos* 2:1.5-7 (1963).

——, 'Types of Pattern Practices', *Estudos* 3:1.25-9 (1964).

Gomes de Matos, F., 'Linguistics in Brazilian University Curriculum', *The Linguistic Reporter* 5:5 (1963).

——, 'Some Cases of Structural Interference: A Clash of Portuguese and English Syntactical Patterns', *Estudos* 3:1.17-23. (1964)

——, 'Yázigi: Brazil's Leading Institute of Languages', *The Linguistic Reporter* 7:3 (1965).

Gudschinsky, Sarah C., 'Solving the Mazateco reading problem', *Language Learning* 4.61-5 (1951-2).

Larson, Mildred, *Pedagogical Grammar of Spanish for Aguaruna Speakers*, (multilithed) (Serie Lingüística Peruana I, 1963).

Loos, Eugenio E., 'Actividades del Instituto Lingüístico de Verano en el Perú', *Perú Indígena*, 126-36 (1963).

Machuca, Belén, 'Teaching English Reading in Puerto Rico', *Language Learning* 5.22-8 (1953-54).

Madsen, A. J. Hald, *Teaching English in Brazil* (Rio de Janeiro, Ao Livro Técnico S. A., 1964).

Mauleón Benítez, Carmen Cecilia, *La lengua oral en la escuela intermedia*, M.A. thesis, (University of Puerto Rico, 1948).

Pesaresi, Marisa, 'Problemi dell'insegnamento della lingua italiana', *Estudos* 1:2.39-40 (1962).

Porras Cruz, Jorge Luis, 'Algunos presupuestos teóricos en la enseñanza de la lengua', *Extramuros* 1:1.7-11 (1962).

Rabanales, Ambrosio, 'Pasado y presente de la investigación lingüística y filológica en Chile', *Boletín de Filología*, Universidad de Chile 16.121-43 (1964).

Roberts, Paul, *English Syntax* (New York, 1964).

Rodríguez Bou, Ismael, *La composición escrita en la escuela elemental. Estudio de los temas y errores más frecuentes* (Río Piedras, P.R., Consejo Superior de Enseñanza de la Universidad de Puerto Rico, 1949).

——, *A Study of the Parallelism of English and Spanish Vocabularies* (Río Piedras, P.R., Consejo Superior de Enseñanza de la Universidad de Puerto Rico, 1950).

——, *La lengua hablada en la escuela elemental* (Río Piedras, P.R., Universidad de Puerto Rico, 1952).

——, *Apuntes sobre la enseñanza de la lengua hablada y escrita en la escuela elemental* (Río Piedras, P.R., Consejo Superior de Enseñanza de la Universidad de Puerto Rico, 1954).

——, *La labor de investigación que sobre la enseñanza del español ha hecho el Consejo Superior de Enseñanza* (Río Piedras, P.R., Universidad de Puerto Rico, 1962).

Rona, José Pedro, 'Relación entre la investigación dialectológica y la enseñanza de la lengua materna", *Revista de Lingüística Aplicada* 2:1.1-12 (1964).

Rojas, Pauline, *Sobre la enseñanza del inglés en Puerto Rico* (San Juan, P.R., Editorial del Departamento de Instrucción Pública, 1954).

Santos de Robert, Carmen L., *La lengua hablada en la escuela elemental*, M.A. thesis (University of Puerto Rico, 1959).

Skoberg, Norman E. P., 'Language Learning as the Acquisition of New Speech Habits', *Estudos* 1:1.33-5 (1962).

——, 'Some Fine Points in Correcting Mistakes', *Estudos* 2:1.15-8 (1963).

Stockwell, Robert P., J. Donald Bowen, and John W. Martin, *The Grammatical Structures of English and Spanish* (Chicago, 1965).

Townsend, Elaine M., 'The construction and use of readers for the Aymara Indians', *Fundamental and Adult Education* 4:4.21-5 (1952).

Trager, George L., *The Field of Linguistics* (Norman, Oklahoma, 1949).

Weinreich, Uriel, *Languages in Contact* (New York, Linguistic Circle of New York, 1953).

Wolff, Hans, 'Partial Comparison of the Sound Systems of English and Puerto-Rican Spanish', *Language Learning* 3:1.38-40 (1950).

COMPUTATIONAL LINGUISTICS

LEONARDO MANRIQUE CASTAÑEDA

A more accurate, if more cumbersome, expression for 'computational linguistics' would be: 'the handling of linguistic material with the aid of electronic computers'.

In reference to both pure and applied linguistcs, electronic computers have been used all over the world. Since it is necessary to formulate the programs with great attention to detail, work with computers has led to the formalization of many of the assumptions underlying linguistic research. Sometimes problems were clarified through new formulations of linguistic theories (e.g. the transformational theory), in other instances totally new theories and formulations had to be devised in order to adjust the data to the requirements of the input, processing, and output of computers. By way of illustration, we will mention a few of the applications of computers in linguistic research.

First of all, we must discuss the attempts made in the field of machine translation. So far, the proposed end has not been attained, but the project has stimulated a great deal of research. There are now many descriptive studies available, in which the analysis of a language (the source) is made in accordance with a supposed algorithm of translation into another language (the target); or, when it is assumed that an intermediate stage will save time and effort, the analysis is made with this intermediate target in mind. The analysis of languages for machine translation has imposed new criteria for the recognition of roots, stems, and affixes, since a traditional definition has proved, in most instances, not suitable for computer processing. Computers have led to the formulation of new kinds of dictionaries, formulas of syntactic constructions, and the like, but we cannot examine all of them here.

If machine translations are not yet possible, research has led, in several instances, and with varying degrees of success, to 'machine aided translations'. In many instances, the correction of the machine 'translation draft' by a human translator is more expensive, instead of saving time and effort. In a few cases the machine has translated the greater part of the text and has given two or three (rarely more) alternate translations to ambiguous expressions, so that the human corrector only has to choose that expression which fits the context as a whole. This is possible, in many cases, without referring to the source.

The attempts to obtain machine translations involve many fields or aspects of linguistics. The use of computers in linguistic research is, however, more varied. One of these uses is the description of languages.

Usually, descriptions begin with the phonemics of a language. At first, computers were not employed for this kind of work, but now attempts are made to give the machine all the phonetic information gathered in the field, so that it may identify phones that are in complementary distribution or that are not in contrast, and reduce them to phonemes. As far as I know, phonemization with computers is more expensive in terms of time and effort than phonemization without computers. Nevertheless, it demonstrates the variety of possible applications of computers.

Another application of computers for research in descriptive linguistics is the analysis of grammatical structures. One way of doing such an analysis is to depend on a previous analysis that lists the classes of elements of that language (which has, in all probability, a provisional analysis of the grammatical structure underlying it). If each class of elements has an identification key, then the processing of a text gives us a series of all the possible locations of the elements of the classes in constructions; with a good classification of elements and with some criteria for distinguishing cases of homophony, the computer is able to render an analysis not only of stems, but of affixes. Attempts have been made to do the analysis on the basis of a phonemic (or graphemic) transcription of the language only, and with more elaborate machine programs, but we cannot go into the details of the process, nor into the results obtained.

Grammatical description also has improved with machine-made concordances. A concordance is an index of all the occurrences of the units (usually words, but also morphemes, phonemes, phrases, or other purposely defined units) of a text. The traditional concordances of the Bible used to cite only the places where a word was to be found; the concordances made for modern linguistic research usually cite the whole element and more or less long parts of the text preceding and following it. A concordance of this type implicitly gives the total number of occurrences of a given unit, but there are concordance programs that explicitly count the number of occurences of the item and print it immediately preceding or following the list.

In examining a concordance, the linguist can easily see which other elements do, or do not, appear with the unit under consideration and from this he can gather some interesting facts as to the description of a language, e.g. the mutual dependence of units or their exclusiveness, the frequent association of certain units versus others, the relative order of the elements in these units, and the like. With a tentative analysis of the grammatical structure of the language under study, programs developed to bring two lines into concordance (one containing the text and the other some appropriate identification marks) to permit the easy checking of the previous analysis and a reinterpretation of those parts that do not fit.

Concordances have also been used in attempts to decipher ancient scripts. By codifying each one of the graphemes and, in case of non-linear arrangement, their relative positions, scholars have developed a kind of file in which each grapheme, or series of graphemes, appears grouped in a block and included in a segment of the text.

It is not possible to mention the numerous applications of the statistical studies of a language, both in linguistics and literary research. Let us only remember that the computer can do the counting and mathematical operations involved with more accuracy and in much less time than human beings.

Computers have aided in historical linguistics also. Provided with rules for counting correspondent determinate phonemes of two languages, the machine can go through a whole dictionary and search for cognates and print them. The linguist can then use them for reconstructing ancient meanings and continue the customary work. Phonemic reconstruction is also feasible with a method developed by Swadesh, giving a key to types of phonemes; the machine groups together all words with the same combination of keys and prints them; then the linguist looks at the printed list and proposes protoforms. Although, as far as I know, the computer has not yet been used to check the resultant hypothesis, it should be easy to do so.

The examples given, though very sketchy, are sufficient to show that today computers are a most valuable instrument in linguistic research, and that there is no field in linguistics which has no room for them. Let us now look at a few of the difficulties encountered in their use and at a few of the future possibilities.

The greatest obstacle faced by linguists who want to process their materials with an electronic computer is the fact that not many computers are available. All important universities in the United States, the European countries, and the Soviet Union have at least one computer, but usually it is devoted only a small part of the time to linguistic research. Many research institutions in the above mentioned countries and in most Asian, African, and Ibero-American countries cannot afford the great cost implied in the use of computers.

Another great problem is, that computers are not designed for use by linguists. Without entering into details on computer parts, annexes, and operations, we can say that not one of the computers now in use has a 'fast reaching memory', capable of containing the bulky information required for most linguistic problems; this means that one must very frequently revert to the 'slow reaching memory', extending the operating time and increasing the expenses. The designers have constantly been increasing the capacity of the 'fast reaching memory', so that we may hope that machines, suitable for the majority of linguistic problems, will soon be available; nevertheless, computational linguistics will continue to dream of a computer expressly designed to fit its needs.

A computer of this kind would be capable of 'recognizing' and operating with more signs. The machines manipulate now about forty signs. In many instances the linguist may use numbers and mathematical symbols instead of the linguistic symbols. It is not very difficult, if one is adjusted to symbols, to read the sequence *te 6abi o2mal u tunile7* as the Maya sentence /te č'abi oc'mal u tunileʔ/, but it is not so easy for other linguists; this makes it necessary for computational linguists to convert their material to the limited set of signs available and then to convert the material back to the usual form when he wants to publish the results. It is possible to make some adaptations to existing computers so that they may work with the phonetic or phonemic symbols, but, as most computers are not devoted to linguistic work alone, one can imagine the problems this would create. The best solution would be to have specially designed computers (and designed at low cost, of course).

The present computers use as input punched cards or tape, and also magnetic tape (which commonly records information first punched on cards or paper tape). This causes much trouble in processing linguistic material, because it takes a long time to transcribe material, written in the traditional scripts (phonetic, Roman with inconsistent orthography, or symbols not commonly handled by the staff used to the Roman alphabet, e.g. cyrillic) into suitable symbols. After the transcription it takes again a long time to do the punching (which frequently is made with many mistakes that require several revisions). To overcome these difficulties, at least in part, it is conceivable to construct input units capable of 'reading' printed or typed material, i.e. to identify the symbols and to convert them into combinations of holes on a card or tape, or to the appropriate magnetic impulses; some of these 'reading' devices have been used experimentally, but they are not yet available for normal work.

As far as I know, computers are not used in geographical linguistics. Nevertheless, analogical computers (probably better than digital computers) may trace maps of the distribution of linguistic traits, and the corresponding isoglosses, saving much time if the material is copious.

In sum, computational linguistics is now a reality. However, the processing of linguistic material with electronic computers is more expensive in terms of human work, time, and money, than the traditional manual handling of the same material, provided the material is not bulky enough. There are no computers yet specifically designed for linguistics; machines of this kind would save human work and time more than the computers now in use, but they would probably be more expensive. The hope of computational linguist is to have computers designed for their work and that they will be cheap enough to be within the reach of all departments of linguistics in the world.

A. CURRENT COMPUTATIONAL LINGUISTICS IN IBERO-AMERICA

As pointed out above, there are few universities in Ibero-America and the Caribbean Area which are in a position to make use of digital computers (the type of computer most commonly known and the only one which, as far as I know, has been employed in linguistic work). However, access to these machines is vital to the existence of computational linguistics.

To this we must add that only about half of the countries in this area have well organized institutions devoted to modern linguistic research. There are, it must be pointed out, many groups with philologically oriented interests, and a few groups or individuals interested in modern linguistics, but although some of them are remarkable for the quality of their studies, their interests and/or their usually limited funds exclude work in computational linguistics.

This makes the handling of linguistic materials with the aid of computers very rare in the area which concerns us. It must be noted that of the approximately one dozen modern linguistic research centers in Ibero-America and the Caribbean only five seem to be interested in computational linguistics, and only two of them are actually engaged in research in this field.

In the following part a brief description (sometimes extremely short, because of lack of information) is presented of the few projects of computational linguistics in Ibero-America. The Caribbean, to my knowledge, is not at all engaged in this kind of research. The data are presented under the headings of the countries, which appear in alphabetical order; ALILEME appears after the countries, on the basis of its international character.

1. *Argentina*

a. *Instituto de Cálculo, Universidad de Buenos Aires*

The Instituto de Cálculo de la Universidad de Buenos Aires has done work in computational linguistics, centering on a project of automatic translation from Russian to Spanish. The project is directed by an engineer, Eugenia Fisher, and work is executed with a Mercury computer; this computer has a 'fast reaching memory' of medium capacity, which limits its possibilities for linguistic work.

This project works with a body of mathematical texts of 40 000 words, punched on tape. The words are in Russian and comprehend texts taken from books and titles of diverse publications.

There are four machine programs used for the linguistic analysis of texts. The first program calculates the frequency of a predetermined number of words of a given vocabulary, but I am not sure if it gives only a counting of the words, if it calculates its percentage, or if it does other kinds of calculation (such as the rank order, the ratio of each word to the total body, etc.). This first program has been applied to the calculation of the frequency of Russian prepositions; it is designed to operate with any volume of data.

The second machine program selects contexts under certain preestablished conditions, i.e. it is a kind of concordance which does not cite the location of the selected lines. The preestablished conditions may consist of a previously selected vocabulary or of previously analyzed suffixes. It is easy to see that this selection of contexts allows the linguist to extract the word or suffixes he wants to study, along with their environment. Since this program also works with any volume of data, the analyst may count on a considerable amount of material, selected within a very short time and without the mistakes human beings usually make. The results are not given in alphabetical order, but in the order of first occurrence of the words or suffixes selected.

The third program is a concordance program. It works by following a preestablished vocabulary, as the program just mentioned, but it also gives the name of the book, and the page and line numbers, from which the word and its context are taken. Owing to the limited capacity of the 'fast reaching memory' (this computer does not yet have a 'slow reaching memory'), the program can store a total of 800 contexts of 60 signs each. When the 'memory' is full, it stops. It is being improved, however, to output partial results and to continue work with larger amounts of data.

A further program looks for predetermined suffixes in a text and counts the stems that occur with them, or it does the inverse operation, i.e. it looks for the stems and counts the associated suffixes.

Besides these programs already in use, the Instituto de Cálculo de la Universidad de Buenos Aires runs experimental programs. The first program orders alphabetically as many as 2 000 words; its usefulness as a complement to the second of the programs mentioned above is obvious.

The second of the experimental programs (its complexity makes me assume that, in fact, it consists of several different programs) has two aspects: a) the construction of a vocabulary with all pertinent information for translation; the information relative to the words will be in another block than the vocabulary proper, probably for higher speed in the second aspect of this program; b) search of words in the vocabulary: as just pointed out, the search is faster if the information relative to each word is recorded separately, so that the machine goes to the information only when it has found the desired word; the cases of internal homonymy will be solved by deciding whether the elements (stem and affixes) of the complex are compatible or not.

It is clear that a program such as the one just described represents a great step in the direction of automatic translation. The information I have pertains only to the resolution of cases of internal homonymy, but the same principle may be applied to cases in which the resolution of the homonymy depends on an external context.

Finally, we must mention several machine programs for statistical manipulation of data, but I have no information on their number or the operations they perform.

b. *Instituto de Filología, Universidad de la Plata*

A member of this institution, Nejama L. de Sager, is working on an analysis of gender and number in Spanish, specifically designed to be used in machine translation. The Universidad de La Plata does not have a computer, so that the results of this investigation cannot be applied there. Nevertheless, this project shows the interest linguists now have in computational linguistics, and undoubtedly, the results that cannot be used in the places where they were obtained will be useful to other scholars.

It should be noted that these two Argentinian Universities (Buenos Aires and La Plata) are oriented towards the methods used by the CETA of Grenoble, whose director, Bernard Vauquois, has taught in Buenos Aires.

2. *Brazil*

The last news I had on this subject was that Aryón D. Rodrigues, of the University of Brasilia, together with the cooperation of some members of the Summer Institute of Linguistics, had definite plans for working on computational linguistics there. People who have observed the installation and working of a computer know the multiple problems implied. For this reason, I suppose, work has not yet actually begun.

3. *Mexico*

a. *Centro de Cálculo Electrónico*

The Centro de Cálculo Electrónico (CCE) de la Universidad Nacional Autónoma de México, directed by an engineer, Sergio Beltrán, is an institution devoted to computer research and to its application in all fields. In 1958, soon after its creation, the CCE processed the first linguistic materials at the request of Morris Swadesh, using mainly the equipment peripheral to the computer. This experiment and the interest of linguists and students of linguistics led, in 1960, to the creation of a 'Sección de Investigaciones Lingüísticas' (Linguistic Research Section) of the CCE, directed by Swadesh.

The CCE has given lectures and short courses to linguists and students of linguistics. The courses dealt with the general characteristics of computers and their functioning, the limitations of input and output, and remarks on programming. They were not intended to transform linguists into computation engineers, but to give them the necessary information to get a fruitful cooperation from people specializing in computer research and in linguistics.

In May, 1963, the CCE organized under the auspices of UNESCO a 'Simposio Latinoamericano sobre la Utilización de las Calculadoras Electrónicas en la Investigación Lingüística' (Latin-American Symposium on the Use of Electronic Computers in Linguistic Research) attended by linguists from several South American countries and from Mexico; the Symposium had some of the best known European and American specialists in this field as teachers. The Symposium directly led to the formation of ALILEME (see under this heading below) and the 'Comisión para el estudio de la escritura Maya' (see under this subhead below). It also promoted the programs in computational linguistics in Montevideo (Uruguay) and La Plata (Argentina).

Today the 'Sección de Investigaciones Lingüísticas' of the CCE (hereafter referred to as CCE), devoted to linguistic research, is engaged in several projects on computational linguistics: 1) machine translation, 2) general linguistics. It works closely with the 'Comisión para el estudio de la escritura Maya' and is of help to other institutions.

(1) *Machine Translation*

The CCE has been working on a dictionary to translate Russian into Spanish. The basis for this dictionary is similar to the one prepared for translating Russian into English, developed at Berkeley. Up to the present, the dictionary gathered by the staff of the CCE has not been used in Mexico but in Berkeley, as a cooperative enterprise of the two institutions in the field of machine translation. At the same time, Berkeley offered the CCE all its dictionaries and machine programs, so that the CCE will be able to use them when necessary.

The CCE has its own project of automatic translation in which it is advised by and basically follows the procedures of the Centre d'Etudes pour la Traduction Automatique du Centre National de la Recherche Scientifique (CETA). For the planning of this program the CCE sent two members of its staff to the CETA in Grenoble, France and after their return two members of the CETA went to Mexico to help set up the project.

The CCE has received from the CETA a Russian dictionary which contains in two separate blocks the bases and their morphological keys. As the CDC-G-20 Magnetic Tape System computer of the CCE which will be used in these projects has characteristics which differ from the computers of the CETA, the staff of the CCE has reduced the form of the morphological keys. They have also translated the Russian bases into the corresponding 'canonical' forms of Spanish (a 'canonical' form is a complete form, not a base or stem, arbitrarily chosen to represent a whole series of derived or inflected forms of a base). It has also been necessary to reduce the derivational system, excluding many of the derivative affixes and creating, in their stead, new and longer bases. These projects are near completion and it is hoped they will soon be applied.

Other investigations related to machine translation have only begun. One of them is an analysis of Spanish, following the same principles applied by the CETA to other languages, and specifically designed to serve in automatic translations. So far, only the analysis of substantives, adjectives, and verbs in a base and of flective elements is in progress.

Although the cooperation of the CETA and the University of California (Berkeley) with the CCE is quite close, the CCE also interchanges information with many other institutions which are working on automatic translation.

(2) *General Linguistics*

The CCE began by developing for grammatical analysis a very rudimentary way of handling linguistic material with the electromechanic IBM classifier of cards. It was a tentative analysis of the words of a language for which cards were punched in three different fields. The first contained a coded identification of the language, the second had the lexeme as it occurred in the vocabulary or dictionary from which it was taken, and the third had the supposed root or affix. A card was punched for each constituent. By classifying the cards according to the third field, the linguist had a file in which all cards containing the tentatively defined element were put together, permitting him to check the hypothesis. For easy handling of the materials the information on the cards could be printed automatically.

After this first attempt, Swadesh programmed a concordance able to handle as context only a sentence. As it was designed for the study of the ancient Maya script, this was not really a handicap. Today the CCE has several concordance programs which can be used for many purposes. The best of these programs, developed by Joseph Grimes, of the Summer Institute of Linguistics, admits tentatively analyzed materials in which different levels of analysis are marked with different signs, so that the same punched material may be used for concordance at the 'fossilized' morpheme- (i.e. ancient morphemes not active now), morpheme-, word-, phrase-, and sentence-levels. Each element appears printed with a codified key, indicating the source from which it is taken. The program developed by Grimes is to be used in the CDC-G-20 computer; another concordance program was prepared for the Bull-Gamma-30-C computer by María Eugenia Reyes.

With the systems mentioned (from the rudimentary use of peripheral equipment to the sophisticated concordance programs) several grammars have been worked out: Cuitlateco, by Roberto Escalante; Tzeltal from Bachajón, by Carlos Robles; Matlatzinca, by Daniel Cazes. Another grammar, that of Tarahumara, is in process, with a body of 15 000 sentences supplied by David Brambila, who will also do the final analysis. The concordance programs are also applied to the study of Spanish written in Mexico during the first years after the Conquest, and they will produce an index of names very useful to those who work with the sources of the Ancient History of Mexico. This last project is also done by Daniel Cazes.

The CCE has been compiling 'traditional' dictionaries, i.e. it has punched on cards the entries of common dictionaries, largely of Mexican Indian languages. The cards are divided into four fields: the first field contains an identification key of the language (sometimes it specifies also the dialect), in the second field is punched a 'phonetic key', used for comparative linguistics, in the third field is punched the lexeme (which not unfrequently consists of more than a morpheme), and in the fourth field is found the translation of the lexeme into Spanish. Usually each entry needs no more than one card, but when necessary, two or more cards are used.

Of course, the compiling of these dictionaries does not simply consists of punching existing printed dictionaries or vocabularies. Experience has shown that bilingual dictionaries (especially those of the 16th, 17th, and 18th centuries, e.g. the well-known *Vocabulario en lengua mexicana y castellana*, written by Alonso de Molina) have frequently under entries in the Indian language meanings that do not appear under the entries in Spanish, and vice versa. So, although the nucleus of each entry is an aboriginal lexeme, the card contains not only the translation as it appears in the Indian-Spanish section of the original dictionary, but also the meanings that appear exclusively in the Spanish-Indian section. At the same time, as a superficial analysis shows that the 'words' in the original vocabularies are frequently not lexemes but phrases, the punched entries are correspondingly reduced. We must add that, when there are several sources, the dictionaries give all the information provided by each source. The process of checking each new entry against all other entries of the original dictionary and of looking for a meaning not mentioned in that entry is long and tedious, and new meanings are easily overlooked. Thus, the human compiler makes many entries, without paying much attention if he includes information previously recorded, but he is careful not to omit new information. The cards are ordered alphabetically by the machine, after which the human compiler looks at them and eliminates redundant information.

These 'traditional' punched dictionaries have been printed with the printing machine which is part of the output equipment of all computers and linguists have used them in their work. They have not gone to press because they would be very bulky (although less so than the original ones) and would not add much new information. Instead of it, the CCE has made 'compact' dictionaries.

It has always been desirable, for easy handling and low cost, to have complete but not too large dictionaries. Common dictionaries usually have an entry for each uninflected word of a language. New dictionaries have reduced their bulk by making no entries for a number of derivatives, providing at the same time indications on how to build derivatives on the basis of the entries in the dictionary. Considerations of the difficulties and the reduction of the bulk usually determine the number of derivatives not included. Another way of reducing a dictionary (used along with the method just mentioned) consists in making entries for the bases (commonly roots and stems, compound of roots plus prefixes) and citing only those derivational suffixes along with the resultant meanings that greatly change the meaning of the base.

M. Swadesh has constructed the smallest dictionaries possible: the 'compact' dictionaries. Under his direction, the CCE (with the aid of outside staff) has reduced the size of 'traditional' dictionaries. One way of doing so is to apply the principle of listing only the stems of roots, without affixes (the affixes are, of course, listed too, but separately). The reduction has gone so far as to analyze what seemed at first glance unitary roots, dividing them into what I have here called 'fossilized' morphemes. The resulting dictionary is called a 'dictionary of elements', whose pros and cons we cannot discuss here. The computer has been used in this process of reduction in several recurrent steps. In the first step a series of affixes or elements which obviously entered in compounds were determined; then the machine detected them in the lexemes of the 'traditional' dictionary and 'erased' them, leaving a base which the same computer entered in an alphabetically ordered list. A revision of this list showed other possible elements which were then used as the affixes or elements used in the first step, and so on. It is clear that the linguist had to check after each step, whether an element had been indicated as the homophonous part of a root when it should not, and he had to correct the mistake if it had occurred. Up to now, the CCE has compiled the compact dictionaries of classical Nahuatl, Mixtec, and Tzeltal (which have been printed by the Instituto de Historia, the Instituto Nacional Indigenista, and the

Instituto Nacional de Antropología e Historia respectively) and one of classical Tarascan. The dictionaries of Spanish and classical Zapotec are in the initial stages, and there are plans for dictionaries of the classical form of Matlatzinca and of some Mayan and Semitic languages. The printed dictionaries are complemented by a grammar of the language and an index of the Spanish meanings of the elements.

Also under the direction of Swadesh, the CCE has been forming the 'Archivo Mexicano de Lingüística Mundial' (Mexican Files of the Languages of the World), largely based on material by Swadesh, collected in the field, from printed sources, or from colleagues all over the world. The majority of the languages on these files is represented by 100-item or 200-item diagnostic lists, employed in lexicostatistic calculations, but there are also languages with much more material. Plans are to enlarge the files by including new languages or dialectal variants and new material of languages already filed. The files are up to now punched on cards, but when they get bulkier, they will be put on magnetic tape. The cards for these archives have five fields: a) an identification key of the language; b) a phonetic key of the form(s) entered; c) the head word or form; d) a semantic key; e) a field in which is punched first the translation into Spanish of the head word, and then all additional information pertinent to the case, such as related meanings, variant forms of the head word, references to the source, reconstructed protoforms of the head word, etc.

These files are a general source of information for all linguistic purposes, but their actual form makes them specially suitable for comparative linguistics, especially for comparative phonology, lexicography, and structure of the word, but less so for comparative 'syntax' (meaning by 'syntax' the arrangement of words in constructions).

Using the materials of the just mentioned archives, Swadesh has looked for cognate words in dictionaries of many languages. The phonetic key punched on the second field of each card is the most valuable aid in this task; this key uses ten letters, corresponding to ten broad classes of consonantal phonemes. Not more than three phonemes of the head word are indicated. Some of the features of those phonemes which are usually marked in linguistic notation with diacritics are here recorded with the use of digits. Vowels are not codified because of their frequent change of quality through time, unless they are supposed reflexes of ancient consonants. The computer groups together and prints all words in two or more languages which have the same phonetic key, i.e. which have phonemes of the same broad classes. The linguist then examines the printed lists and is able to set up the correspondences, eliminating the cases that do not fit the established pattern and changing the phonetic keys that prove wrong.

The first allotting of phonetic keys may be wrong in some cases, when, for example, the same keys were assigned to words that must have different keys, and vice versa. The semantic key proves useful to bring these together. Swadesh has developed fifteen fields of meaning which are codified with two letters; further subdivisions are marked with an additional letter and number 67. The semantic key of a word does not codify the meaning it has now, but its most archaic meaning. Swadesh says, for example, that the English word *thumb*, instead of being codified as PND (=PN, the broad semantic field of 'punctus', plus D which specifies the field as 'digit, finger, nail, hand, foot') should have the key PNB (=PN, plus B 'ball, bumb, stone'), because it is related to Lat. *tumor* and to the Indo-European root which means 'bulbous, swollen'.[1]

It is possible, of course, that, after groupings according to the phonetic and the semantic keys, two related words may be left apart. Translation may help in those cases. If the translations were punched in the same form as they appear in the source, as, for example, 'a kind of tree', 'pine tree', etc. the sorting and alphabetical ordering would not bring them together; for this reason the translations are rearranged as 'tree sp.' and 'tree pine'. With a third examination of the materials, now grouped according to their translation, it is very difficult for two cognates to be overlooked, especially if the linguist knows that he must look for them in semantic areas which commonly have some cognate elements, such as 'water', 'rain', 'river', 'sea', 'tear'; and 'stone', 'egg', 'bone', etc.

Following the procedure I just described, Swadesh has investigated a large amount of material from several linguistic groups and he has carefully established sets of correspondences, reconstructed protophonemes, and with all these preliminary results has constructed the respective linguistic fields. The groups so investigated are: Indo-European, Coahuiltecan, Savizaa (which comprises Mixtecan, Zapotecan, and Popolocan-Mazatecan).

Less thorough comparisons have been done through the CCE, also by Swadesh, of all linguistic groups of America. They resulted in six broad linguistic fields, five of which belong to this continent, and another one which comprises languages of the Old and the New Worlds, with, however, more representatives in the former (the proposed Vasco-Dené). More superficial comparisons have led to the establishment of six other fields of the same rank of complexity which, with the six fields proposed for America, comprise all the existing languages of the world.

b. *Comisión para el Estudio de la Escritura Maya*

The meeting of linguists and computer engineers in the 'Primer Simposio Latinoamericano sobre la Aplicación de Computadoras a la Investigación Lingüística' raised the question of applying computers in the study of the ancient Maya writings. The work done in Novosibirsk was known to some of the participants of the Symposium, as well as the failure to decipher the Maya hieroglyphs. It is assumed that Mexican scholars (linguists, archeologists, computation engineers), working in their own country, where many elements for their research are at hand (native speakers of Mayan languages, Maya monuments, etc.), would be in a better position than their European colleagues to solve the problem. Therefore, the 'Comisión para el Estudio de la Escritura Maya' (Commission for the Study of Maya Writing) was created.

[1] M. Swadesh, 'Algunos sistemas para la comparación lingüística', *CINCO* 1.1 (1956). (Apr.-June, 1966).

The 'Comisión para el Estudio de la Escritura Maya' (CEEM) has gathered, since its creation, scholars of several institutions, such as the Instituto Nacional de Antropología, Centro de Cálculo Electrónico, Instituto de Historia de la UNAM, Seminario de Cultura Maya, Instituto Yucateco de Antropología e Historia, and Universidad de Yucatán. All these institutions have participated in the research by providing staff, funds, or instruments. The CEEM has approached the problem in three ways simultaneously which will later have to be correlated: a) internal analysis of the Maya system of writing to define its meaningful units and 'syntax'; b) study of the evolution of the Maya script and its relation to other Mexican scripts, to other elements of Maya, and other Mesoamerican cultures; c) thorough analysis of Yucatec Maya, Lacandon, Itza, Mopan, and other Mayan languages, and reconstruction of proto-languages at several appropriate stages.

It is outside the scope of this report to discuss all the work done by the CEEM, although a great portion of it has been executed with the help of computers. A short review of the use of computers in the linguistic research done by the CEEM may suffice. The staff of the CEEM consists of Leonardo Manrique, Alberto Ruz, Daniel Cazes, Marta Frías, Juan José Rendón, María Cristina Alvarez, Juan Ramón Bastarrachea, and Marisela Ayala; the first three persons named constitute a directing board with Manrique as coordinator. The planning and assessment on computer processing is the work of Manrique, Cazes, and Rendón. The machine programs are made by the staff of the Centro de Cálculo Electrónico.

All written material, whether in the Roman alphabet (which was already modified in the sixteenth century because of the need of representing Mayan phonemes), painted in the known codices, in ceramics, and on buildings, or sculpted, has a long coded identification which indicates the kind of object or building bearing the inscription, the location of the writing on the object or building, the site where it is or was found, and its age.

Since the CEEM wants to analyze the structure of the glyphic writings without any bias, it has begun its work by classifying and giving a code to each grapheme (minimal significant graphic unit), voluntarily ignoring the work of other scholars. The preliminary work was done without the aid of computers, but as soon as 14 pages of the Dresden Codex were transcribed (giving for each provisionally identified grapheme its code number and an indication of its position on a block or 'cartouche'), the graphemes were arranged in concordance with an experimental concordance machine program, made by Swadesh. The results permitted better classification of graphemes and the development of a transcription system which fits the research needs more adequately. The catalog of graphemes with their code number, equivalences with other catalogs, and introductory remarks is now published in the *Estudios de Cultura Maya V* (Mexico, 1965). By now, the CEEM has transcribed the Dresden and Madrid Codices (the Paris Codex requires the results of the two others to define boundaries in constructions) which will soon be set up in a concordance by a program kindly made for the CEEM by Joseph Grimes, of the Summer Institute of Linguistics. As explained above, this concordance will permit us to write a 'grammar' of the glyphic expressions, defining the various possible constructions, the classes of elements (whether simple graphemes or fixed combinations), the permitted sequences, etc. A first attempt to do this with the scarce experimental material of 14 pages has been published by Rendón and Manrique in *Anales de Antropología III* (Mexico, 1965).

The same kind of analysis will be applied to the Colonial Maya documents. Up to the present, the CEEM has transcribed the Books of Chilam Balam from Chumayel, Tizimín, and Ixil, using instead of the traditional modified symbols of the Roman alphabet some letters and numbers. Besides the phonemic transcription, morpheme boundaries, both living and 'fossilized', have been marked with distinct signs for each one, since the same punched materials will be used for different tasks. A concordance of words (as traditionally defined in Maya) and another one of morphemes will be the foundations of a grammar of Colonial Yucatec Maya. Here again, the previously existing works will be purposely ignored in order to avoid any bias.

The CEEM has machine programs to count the frequency of occurrence of elements and of sequences of elements. Up to now, the program has been applied to calculate the frequencies of occurrence of the phonemes of the Book of Chilam Balam of Chumayel. The results are given not only in absolute numbers, but also in percentages, not only considering the total number of occurrences, but also, whether they appear as initial, medial, or final in words and in morphemes within words. Very soon a similar experiment to calculate frequencies of occurrence of sequences of two, three, four, and five phonemes will be set up. It is easy to see that these calculations done with phonemes are the basis for constructing Markov Chains which will correct or redefine the value(s) of the graphemes of the Maya script when the research is in a more advanced stage. But at this stage, these calculations will prove useful for attributing tentative values to some of the graphemes according to their number and distribution.

The mechanical calculations of frequencies of other elements (morphemes, words) and their sequences, along with the concordances, will help in writing the grammar of Colonial Maya. The same kind of calculations, made with the coded graphemes, will similarly help in the analysis of glyphic writing. The programmers of the CCE are writing for the CEEM a program which will correlate each of the frequency of occurrence calculations of Colonial Maya with each of the frequency of occurrence calculations of glyphic Maya. It is known that the relatively scarce glyphic material of the codices will produce many spurious correlations due to chance alone, but others will undoubtedly be right; the spurious correlations must be checked against the established 'glyphic grammar', the names of personages (gods, animals, etc.), and other results.

The method developed by Swadesh for the search of cognates as well as new programs will be used for the mentioned reconstructions of Mayan at different levels. It is worth noting that although several machine programs have been and will be planned expressly for the needs of the CEEM, they will be available for processing other linguistic material, just as the CEEM may use other existing programs.

Although not exclusively related to computational linguistics, the 'Primer Seminario Internacional para el Estudio de la Escritura Maya', which included several sessions on the use of computers in decipherment, must be mentioned. This 'Seminario' was held in December, 1966, in Mexico City, and is organized by the directing board of the CEEM jointly with Alfredo Barrera-Vázquez and Ramón Arzápalo, both members of the CEEM. During this 'Seminario' about thirty specialists in the decipherment of Maya writing from several countries met.

c. *Other institutions*

(1) *Centro Nacional de Cáculo*

The Centro Nacional de Cáculo del Instituto Politécnico Nacional was, during 1963 and 1964, interested in the possibilities of processing nonnumerical data with electronic computers, in a study of the 'grammaticality' of the so-called machine languages and formal langues, in the possibilities of applying the methods of descriptive linguistics to their analysis, and in the feasibility of using the results of the analysis in the development of new formal languages, designed for processing several specific kinds of data Most interested in these problems was David Alfaro, who aroused the enthusiasm of two young members of the staff of the Centro Nacional de Cálculo and had a mild response of other people. The writer of these lines was called by Alfaro to collaborate with him and his two close followers, he gave them some information on linguistics and discussed with them the problems just pointed out in weekly sessions held during 1963 and 1964. Unfortunately, the group disintegrated when Alfaro was assigned new tasks in other sections of the Instituto Politécnico Nacional. The Centro Nacional de Cálculo set up an experimental program for the counting of phonemes at the request of the CEEM and applied it to a short sample of about 1600 characters (a character is either a sign or a blank) of the Chilam Balam of Chumayel. The disintegration of the small team interested in nonnumerical computation did not permit the continued cooperation between the Centro Nacional de Cálculo and the CEEM.

(2) *Escuela Nacional de Antropología e Historia*

The Escuela Nacional de Antropología e Historia recognized, since 1958, the possibilities opened for linguistic research by the use of computers. Not being able to change its curricula, it has encouraged the students of linguistics to follow the courses on this subject given jointly at the CCE by members of its staff and teachers of the above mentioned school, where the activities of the CCE are well known. The curricula are now being revised, and a course on computational linguistics is probably going to be included.

Although the following remark does not relate to computational linguistics proper, it must be mentioned that the computer work of teachers and students of linguistics has aroused the interest of other scholars in this research tool of our era. The new curricula have four academic semesters in which students of all four branches of anthropology participate, and one of the first courses taught is on the systematization of research and the aids now available, including electronic computers. It is possible that other branches will include special courses on computer processing of their data, just as linguists have a course in computational linguistics.

(3) *Instituo Lingüistico de Verano (Summer Institute of Linguistics)*

It is not easy to decide whether the Mexican branch of the Summer Institute of Linguistics (ILV) should be included, in a discussion of computational linguistics in Ibero-America. As is known, the ILV was created by Americans in Mexico, its staff consists of Americans who have done and are doing valuable work in Mexican aboriginal languages, have taught reading, writing, and Spanish to many monolinguals, but now they have their headquarters in Oklahoma, where much of their work in computational linguistics is done.

Faced with this difficulty, I have decided to mention that Grimes, of the ILV, has, many times, used the machines of the CCE for processing his own material on Huichol and, as I recall, material of some of his colleagues. He has established a true cooperation by discussing some problems with the staff of the CCE and by directly helping toward a solution. He has also offered some machine programs and, as already mentioned, elaborated a concordance program at the request of the CEEM and the CCE.

(4) *Colegio de México*

Although the Colegio de México has many times been invited to have its linguistic materials processed by the staff working in computational linguistics at the CCE and the Escuela Nacional de Antropología e Historia, it has accepted only recently. In 1954, José Pedro Rona taught a course on Ibero-American dialectology at the Colegio de México. The complementary fieldwork consisted of a study of the dialectal variant of Spanish in Chiapas, in which more than 50 hours of texts were recorded on tape. The students made the transcription of the texts and began their analysis under the direction of Rona; when he had to go back to Montevideo, his place was filled, as planned, by Margit F. de Alatorre. Now Daniel Cazes and Leonardo Manrique are advising Alatorre and her students in the preparation of the materials to obtain better results in the concordances. The concordance will be done in the Bull Gamma-30-C computer of the CCE, with the program Grimes made for the CEEM. Before January 1966, the concordance will serve for analyzing and writing a report on the use of the Spanish pronoun *mi* in the Chiapas dialect; later it will be used for a complete structural study of that dialect.

4. *Peru*

Ernesto Zierer, Director of the Instituto de Idiomas y Linguística de la Universidad Nacional de Trujillo (Institute of Languages and Linguistics, National University of

Trujillo), has planned to do work on mathematical linguistics — which in certain areas is a synonym for computational linguistics. He has not yet begun work in this field, but it is hoped that we will soon become acquainted with his first achievements. As the University of Trujillo does not have a computer, his materials will be processed in other places.

5. *Uruguay*

The Director of the Departamento de Lingüística de la Facultad de Humanidades y Ciencias de la Universidad de la República (Department of Linguistics, Humanities and Sciences Faculty, University of the Republic) in Montevideo, José Pedro Rona, has promoted computational linguistics in Uruguay, and is himself participating in several related activities.

Rona has arranged three courses on machine programming, in which the University and the IBM branch in Montevideo have had a part — presumably IBM has provided instructors in programming and the University has provided the majority of participants. As a result, several participants are now interested in nonnumerical computation. Afterwards Rona himself taught in his department a course in computational linguistics.

Rona is doing research on the syntax of the preposition *a* in the dialect of the Northern border of Uruguay with Brazil, as compared with the use of the same preposition in the Spanish spoken in the Rio de la Plata region and in the Portuguese spoken in the Brazilian State of Rio Grande do Sul. This research will be based on concordances. The transcription and other preliminary work with the materials is now completed. They will be processed in the comupter of the Instituto de Cálculo de la Universidad de Buenos Aires.

Another project is planned by Rona and a student of his, Celia Carmen García. It will be a concordance of the 'poetas gauchescos primitivos' (that is, the first poets who wrote about the *gauchos*, employing many of the speech forms peculiar to them).

The Centro Lingüístico de Montevideo has a section devoted to computational linguistics, which is directed by Mario H. Otero. I am not familiar with any of the work done there.

In October 1966, there was, in Montevideo, a Round Table meeting, with the attendance of scholars from Argentina, Brazil, and Uruguay, who work in linguistics and other sciences. The topic of the meeting was: 'Percepción e identificación en el lenguaje' ('Perception and identification in language'). A general conclusion reached was that the human brain identifies linguistic messages basically in the same manner as an electronic computer. This is not the place to discuss such a conclusion, but we may note the bearing it has on the design of computers for linguistic purposes, on programming, and on many other subjects which need not concern us here. It should be pointed out that four of the six scholars who met attended the 'Primer Simposio Latinoamericano sobre la Aplicación de Computadoras a la Investigación

Lingüística' in Mexico, 1963 (see under the heading: Mexico, Centro de Cálculo Electronico).

B. ALILEME

In a way a byproduct of the 'Primer Simposio Latinoamericano sobre la Aplicación de Computadoras a la Investigación Linguística', the 'Asociación Latinoamericana para la Investigación Lingüística con Equipo Mecánico y Electrónico' (ALILEME, 'Latin-American Association for Linguistic Research with Mechanic and Electronic Equipment') deserves to be mentioned in its own right. As mentioned before, in the 'Primer Simposio...', held in Mexico in 1963, under the auspices of the CCE and UNESCO, scholars of Argentina, Brazil, Colombia, Guatemala, Mexico, and Uruguay met. These scholars, interested in the perspectives opening in linguistic research through the use of computers and peripheral equipment, decided to constitute an organism to promote computer-aided research in the countries which were not represented at the Symposium, and to mutually exchange general information, programs, etc. Rona was appointed President of the newly created ALILEME, with Swadesh, Fisher, and Luis J. Prieto (from the Universidad de Córdoba, Argentina) in other directing functions.

ALILEME has not had the expected success. Communication between people interested in computational linguistics in Ibero-America has not increased much above the level existing before the creation of ALILEME. Few institutions, if any, have joined the first ones. Nevertheless, it seems to me that nobody on the directing board is responsible for this fact. It seems rather that there are relatively few people now working in computational linguistics and the difficulties all of them have to face make new gains, worthy of communication, slow to come. So far, personal contacts have made the use of the chanels ALILEME should provide, unnecessary, but it is very probable that with more people from more countries working on computational linguistics, ALILEME will prove to be the useful information pool and promoting agency it is intended to be.

C. PERSPECTIVES

Computational linguistics is just beginning to be a reality in Ibero-America and the interest in it is spreading at an increasing rate. Every day more research centers plan the use of computers to make linguistic work easier and faster.

The high cost of processing linguistic data with the aid of computers will always hamper their broad utilization in the geographic area which concerns us, but this problem will hopefully be solved, at least in part, when the research institutions which cannot afford computers will send their material to those centers where these machines do, or will in the future, exist.

It seems probable that cooperation will be established between those institutions which do have a computer and those which do not. This kind of cooperation is even now established, but on a small scale, as for example, between the Centro de Cálculo

Electrónico (Mexico City) and the Escuela Nacional de Antropología e Historia (Mexico City), or between the Centro de Cálculo de la Universidad de Buenos Aires and the Departamento de Lingüística de la Universidad de la República (Montevideo). Up to now, the cooperation has been limited to the aid given by institutions with computers to those without, but some true cooperative work is already taking place, as, for example, when research done by the 'Comisión para el Estudio de la Escritura Maya' has led to improved machine programs of the Centro de Cálculo Electrónico. Other cooperative work is in sight in the grammatical analysis of gender and number in Spanish, realized at the La Plata University, which will be very useful for the work on automatic translation that the Centro de Cálculo de la Universidad de Buenos Aires is doing.

The interchange of information between the few computational linguistic centers or institutions interested in computational linguistics in different countries has been scarce, because the progress of each of these institutions is relatively slow. When the amount of information increases, the interchange will be much greater and will, probably, involve ALILEME, which will then grow and carry out all the functions it is supposed to serve.

Up to the present, the Centro de Cálculo Electrónico (Mexico) and the Centro de Cálculo de la Universidad de Buenos Aires (Argentina), have received aid in information, direct assessment on concrete problems, and visiting staff, from similar centers in Europe and the United States; also, the CCE has collaborated with the University of California at Berkeley. In the future, with the expansion of computational linguistics, the aid from countries outside of Ibero-America will undoubtedly increase, but the institutions within this area will also be more on a par with those from the United States and Europe and may be able to give information and suggestions on certain problems.

Finally, it should be stressed that all future developments of computational linguistics in Ibero-America (and possibly also in the Caribbean) will be based on two pioneering institutions of which so much has been written here: the Centro de Cálculo Electrónico of the University of Mexico, and the Centro de Cálculo de la Universidad de Buenos Aires. I feel not quite at ease in making this remark, being a close collaborator of Swadesh and of the CCE, but when everything is considered, the aid given to other institutions, the organization of the 'Primer Simposio Latinoamericano sobre la Aplicación de Computadoras a la Investigación Lingüística', and the part it had in the consitution of ALILEME, the CCE is the more advanced of the two pioneering institutions and the more active in promoting computational linguistics.

A final remark must be made: this paper was written in November, 1965, but will be edited after the third volume of *Current Trends in Linguistics*, where, probably, a paper discussing computational linguistics will appear. This will make the introductory part of the present paper unnecessary, poor, and redundant. Nevertheless, it may always prove useful to have a short and general view of the status of computational linguistics up to the present.

LINGUISTIC CORRECTNESS AND THE ROLE OF THE ACADEMIES

GUILLERMO L. GUITARTE and RAFAEL TORRES QUINTERO*

1. HISTORY OF THE LATIN AMERICAN ACADEMIES

1.1. *Antecedents*

The work of the Latin American academies should be considered in relation to that of the Royal Spanish Academy, since these academies share the latter's aims, employ its means of action, and are statutorily linked with it. On one hand the Royal Spanish Academy,[1] founded in 1713, continues the literary life which developed in academies or literary groups during the sixteenth and seventeenth centuries.[2] On the other hand

* Thanks are due to Hernán Lozano Hormaza for his help to Rafael Torres Quintero in the preparation of this paper.

[1] For the history of the Royal Spanish Academy, see: [José Casani], 'Historia de la Real Academia Española', *Diccionario de autoridades* 1.IX-XLI (1726) and 6.I-XXIV (1739); [Mariano Roca de Togores,] Marqués de Molins, 'Reseña histórica de la Academia Española', *Memorias de la Academia Española* 1.1-128 (1870); Emilio Cotarelo y Mori, 'La fundación de la Academia Española y su primer director D. Juan Manuel F. Pacheco, Marqués de Villena', *BAE* 1.4-38 and 89-127 (1914); F. Gil Ayuso, 'Nuevos documentos sobre la fundación de la Real Academia Española', *BAE* 14.593-9 (1927); Armando Cotarelo Valledor, 'Bosquejo histórico de la Real Academia Española', *Sesión conmemorativa del rey don Felipe V celebrada por el Instituto de España en los salones de la Real Academia de la Historia el dia 26 de octubre de 1946* 9-50 (Madrid, 1947); Didier Ozanam, 'L'idéal académique d'un poète éclairé: Luzán et son projet d'Académie Royale des Sciences, Arts et Belles Lettres', *BHi* 64 bis. 188-208 (1962); Gerardo Diego, 'Un cuarto de milenio en la Academia Española', *BAE* 43.413-29 (1963).

[2] On the literary associations of the Golden Age, the two most recent general descriptions are: José Sánchez, *Academias literarias del Siglo de Oro español* (Madrid, 1961) and Willard F. King, *Prosa novelistica y academias literarias en el siglo XVII* (Madrid, 1963). Given the early establishment of literature in the Spanish settlements of Latin America and the fidelity with which, generally speaking, the literary activity of the peninsula was reproduced in them during those centuries, it is not surprising that academies have also arisen in the New World. The first academy of the Spanish Renaissance for which there exists a record, and which may have functioned in Madrid and Seville between 1544 and 1547, is a curious case, for it owes its existence to an *indiano* [a person back from the New World with great wealth], none other than the great conqueror of Mexico, Hernán Cortés (cf. Sánchez, ibid. 196-9 and King, *ibid.* 22-4). Unfortunately, the Latin American literary academies of the sixteenth and seventeenth centuries have not been studied extensively. Although it does not seem possible to us that many others have not existed in the old Viceroyship of New Spain, we know only of the 'royal and flourishing Mexican Academy' of Mexico City mentioned by Francisco Bramón in *Los sirgueros de la Virgen* 27 (Mexico, 1620; we quote the 1944 edition), and the 'Inner Academy of Good Taste and Fine Arts', formed at the Conciliar Pontifical Seminary of Puebla, which existed and was famous around the year 1650 (cf. José Sánchez, *Academias y sociedades literarias de México* 19-20 [Chapel Hill, 1951]) The 'Antarctic Academy of the City of Lima, Peru', which brought together people of out-

it is now, after the model of the French Academy, an organization representative of the most outstanding part of the country's literary life and is protected by the state so that it can guide the linguistic activity of the country after the manner of a supreme tribunal. Finally, it represents the new sense of the individual's responsibility, born in the era of national states, to collaborate collectively and institutionally in the development and glory of his nation.[3] The motto of the Spanish Academy: 'Purifies, stabilizes and gives splendor', sums up these aspirations of establishing and giving dignity to a national medium of expression and communication. The instruments which the Academy utilized to achieve these ends were its *Diccionario*,[4] its *Ortografía*[5] and its *Gramática*,[6] and, in addition, its editions of classics and its literary competitions.[7]

---

standing talent and flourished between 1590 and 1610, stands out in South America. The academy that met during 1709 and 1710 in the Lima palace of the viceroy of Peru, the Marqués de Castell-dos-Rius, can be considered a continuation of the literary academies of that time. Concerning the Antarctic Academy one can consult: M. Menéndez Pelayo, *Antología de poetas hispano-americanos* 3.CLXXIX-CXCV (Madrid, 1894), José de la Riva-Agüero, 'Diego Mexía de Fernangil y la segunda parte de su *Parnaso Antártico*', *Obras completas* 2.107-63 (Lima, 1962) and Alberto Tauro, *Esquividad y gloria de la Academia Antártica* (Lima, 1948). Leopoldo A. de Cueto, *Historia crítica de la poesía castellana en el siglo XVIII*[3] 1.83-91 (Madrid, 1893) and M. Menéndez Pelayo, ibid. 3.CCXIII-CCXX, give information about the academy of the Marqués de Castell-dos-Rius. Ricardo Palma, *Flor de Academias y Diente del Parnaso* 1-332 (Lima, 1899), published its complete transactions. The existence of literary groups during this period in various other South American cities, such as the gathering that Juan de Castellanos brought together in Tunja and the nuclei of literary people that existed in Santo Domingo, Arequipa, La Paz, Potosí, and Santiago, Chile, is known, but information is lacking to decide if they constituted true academies.

[3] Karl Vossler, *Frankreichs Kultur und Sprache*[2] 328-9 (Heidelberg, 1929).

[4] *Diccionario de la Lengua Castellana*, en que se explica el verdadero sentido de las voces, su naturaleza y calidad, con las phrases o modos de hablar, los proverbios o refranes, y otras cosas convenientes al uso de la lengua. Dedicado al Rey Nuestro Señor Don Phelipe V (que Dios guarde) a cuyas reales expensas se hace esta obra. 6 volumes (Madrid, 1726-39). This work, more simply known by the name *Diccionario de Autoridades* because the definitions of each word were followed by quotations of passages by the writers who used them, was published in a single volume in 1780 without these quotations. In this reduced form, and with fitting additions and deletions to reflect the linguistic usage of the moment, it was later republished, reaching its eighteenth edition in 1956.

It was intended that the *Diccionario de Autoridades* be republished and the first volume was issued in 1770, but this plan was abandoned. To replace it, at the beginning of the twentieth century the Spanish Academy began to prepare a *Diccionario histórico de la lengua castellana*, of which volumes I (letter *A*, 1933) and II (letters *B-Cev*, 1936) were published. The work was not felt to be satisfactory and was interrupted in order to start a new *Diccionario histórico* following a different plan. This undertaking has been successful and beginning with 1960 the first fascicles of this work have begun to be published (cf. 2.2.3.1).

[5] *Ortographía española.* Compuesta y ordenada por la Real Academia Española (Madrid, 1741). This work is an amplification of the *Discurso proemial de la Ortographía de la Lengua Castellana* by Adrián Connink, which appeared in the *Diccionario de Autoridades* 1.LXI-LXXXIV (Madrid, 1726). The orthographic rules of the Spanish Academy, modified various times of course with the passing of time, are today printed as a chapter of its *Gramática.*

[6] *Gramática de la Lengua Castellana*, compuesta por la Real Academia Española (Madrid, 1771). Its authors were Juan de Iriarte and Ignacio de Luzán. The *Gramática* underwent various other revisions in the course of time; the last is that represented by the 1920 edition, which is still reprinted today.

[7] The complete list of works published by the Spanish Academy can be found in Emilio Cotarelo y Mori, *Discurso acerca de las obras publicadas por la Real Academia Española*, leído en la junta pública

With these works the Spanish Academy achieved full success in its task of regulating the language after the spontaneity of the Golden Age, doctrinairely fixing an orthographic, grammatical and lexical point of reference for linguistic usage, and succeeded in banishing bad taste by eliminating the excesses of the *culteranismo* and *conceptismo* of the baroque era. At the end of the eighteenth century and beginning of the nineteenth, the prose of Jovellanos and the poetry of Cienfuegos and Quintana, which represent the first examples of modern style in Spanish, were now triumphant.

The work of the Spanish Academy in its first century of life affected the entire Hispanic world, both Spain and Latin America.[8] This is evident just in reviewing the writings that appeared in Spanish America around 1810 when the wars of independence begin. When independence was won in 1824, the state of the language in the former colonies was similar to that found in the mother country. However, political separation turned the Royal Spanish Academy into a foreign institution, a situation which made it especially distasteful to admit its authority in countries that had just fought a long and bloody war against Spain. Nevertheless, the academic spirit, which Mathew Arnold defined as 'that effort to set up a recognized authority, imposing on us a high standard in matters of intellect and taste',[9] had taken deep roots in the Latin America nations. The fact that Latin Americans would be unable to count on the Spanish Academy in the future to direct their aspirations for a dignified language was immediately felt to be a problem which required an

---

de 7 de octubre de 1928 (Madrid, 1928), in its *Anuario* for the years 1953, 1956, 1958, 1961, or in the more recent editions of its *Gramática*.

[8] It should be remembered that during the period prior to independence there were academy members from Latin America. Miguel Reina Ceballos (Mexico, 1739) and Mariano Carvajal, Conde del Puerto (Peru, 1773) were honorary academy members. The Mexican Manuel de Lardizábal (1775), who was the sixth secretary of the association, and the Peruvian Diego de Villegas y Saavedra (1733), Joaquín de Lamo y Castañeda, Conde de Castañeda de los Llanos (1787), and José de Carvajal, Duque de San Carlos (1814), who was its tenth president, belonged to the Spanish Academy as regular members. Even after independence, various Latin Americans who had taken up residence in Madrid also joined the Academy as regular members: the Argentine Ventura de la Vega (1845), the Peruvian Juan de la Pezuela, Conde de Cheste (1847), the Mexican Fermín de la Puente y Apezechea (1850) and the Venezuelan Rafael María Baralt (1853).

Shortly after the political separation between Spain and her former overseas possessions, the Spanish Academy resumed its relations with the literary men of Latin America, beginning the movement that at the end of the century would result in the creation of the associate academies. In 1840 José Gómez de la Cortina, Conde de la Cortina was named an honorary academy member in Mexico. In 1851 Andrés Bello received this title in Chile. The category of associate member, to which Bello was admitted in 1861, was created shortly after. Prior to the regulation that on November 24, 1870 established associate academies in Latin America, the Peruvian Felipe Pardo y Aliaga (1860), the Mexicans Bernardo Couto (1860) and Joaquín Pesado (1860), the Venezuelan Cecilio Acosta (1869) and the Chilean José Victorino Lastarria (1870) had also received appointments as associate academy members. (The majority of these facts were compiled by Miguel Antonio Caro, 'Fundación de la Academia Colombiana', *Obras completas* 2.137-8 [Bogotá, 1920], based on the lists of academy members published in *Memorias de la Academia Española* 1.36-55 [1870]. We also use this source, except for the date of Bello's appointment as an honorary academy member, for which we utilize Miguel Luis Amunátegui, *Vida de don Andrés Bello* 543 [Santiago de Chile, 1882]).

[9] 'The literary influence of Academies', *Essays in Criticism*, First Series 50 (London, 1903).

urgent solution. In 1823 it had already been proposed in Buenos Aires that decisions about matters of language should be made by the literary Society of this city.[10] In 1825, in Bogotá, a much more ambitious project, the creation of an Academy of the Latin American Language, was called for. It would be formed by the most distinguished literary men of the new republics and have as its object the preservation and perfection of Spanish (that language 'full of nobility, expression and majesty') in the New World.[11] A similar proposal was advanced in Mexico during the same period.[12]

But proposals such as those mentioned above did not manage to be more than a *pium desiderium*. Immediately after emancipation all the energies of the Spanish American nations were absorbed by the urgent tasks of institutionally organizing the new countries, and the projects for independent academy activity to guide the development of the Spanish language in Latin America vanished in the political turmoil.[13] When a few decades had elapsed, a weakening of the Spanish linguistic tradition took place, which could be observed in the neglect of traditional vocabulary, the development of neologisms and solecisms and an inundation of Gallicisms which managed to emerge in the literary language. Several factors contributed to the creation of this situation. First there was contempt for Spanish language and literature, which were considered a manifestation of a culture which was opposed to the progress of civilization, and, therefore, not appropriate to express the needs of the Latin American people. To this can be added the penetration in Latin America of the currents of thought, skills and customs of various European countries, principally France and England, and, finally, an incipient adherence to local peculiarities of language, now considered dignified since they had become converted into characteristics of a nations' speech. It remained for a figure from the era of independence, a moment in which the problem posed for the preservation and dignity of the language by Spain's political separation has been discerned, to confront these centrifugal tendencies and attain a memorable success in support of the traditional system and usages of the Spanish language. This victorious defender of the Spanish language in Latin America was Andrés Bello, a Venezuelan residing in Chile. His principal work in this vein is the *Gramática de la lengua castellana, destinada al uso de los americanos* (Santiago de Chile, 1847), which is

[10] *El Argos de Buenos Aires* 2:15.4 (February 19, 1823).

[11] *La Miscelánea*, núm. 13 (December 11, 1825); cited by Fernando A. Martínez in 'Estudio preliminar' to R. J. Cuervo, *Obras* 1.XXXVIII-XL, notes 50 and 51 (Bogotá, 1954).

[12] Fernando A. Martínez, ibid. XL, note 52. It is an interesting fact that during this period a Spaniard also proposed the establishment of a Latin American Academy of Language, as a means of avoiding the fragmentation of the language that might occur when the bonds that united Spain with her Latin American offspring were broken; cf. Mariano José Sicilia, *Lecciones elementales de Ortologia y Prosodia* 1.18 and 2.26, note a (Paris, 1827-28).

[13] Thus, the Literary Society of Buenos Aires, which was founded in January, 1822, began to decline in 1823 due to political dissent and finally died out about the middle of the following year (cf. Carlos Ibarguren, *Las sociedades literarias y la revolución argentina (1800-25)* 108-19 [Buenos Aires, 1938]). Marco Fidel Suárez, 'Cómo se fundó la Academia Colombiana', *Obras* 1.715 (Bogotá, 1958), mentions two attempts which were unsuccessful, to found a Colombian Academy of Language in 1860 and 1865, respectively.

the most perfect exposition of the Spanish system and is still of great value today. It is based on classical Spanish usage such as the Spanish Academy, whose authority Bello acknowledged as best, followed.

With Bello's *Gramática de la lengua castellana*, an attitude of moderate respect toward the Spanish Academy and the model of speech proposed by it is deliberately restored by the scholars of the language in Latin America. The unequalled success of this work, a bedside book for all those Latin Americans who were concerned with questions of language, gave prestige to the criteria it defended and spread them throughout Latin America. In this sense, Bello's *Gramática* announces the end of a stage of trial and error or of confusion which, in the field of language, followed Spanish American emancipation, and prepares the way for the following period.

1.2. *Founding and development of the academies*

The strength of the ideals defended by the Spanish Academy, which independence could weaken but not destroy, was supported by the success with which Bello's work upheld correct usage of the language. However, Bello's influence, and that of those who shared his attitude, remained restricted to the orbit of what could be attained through purely personal action. That is, many Latin Americans accepted the efforts to unify and purify the language as urged by the Spanish Academy and freely adopted the linguistic usage it proposed. However, the fundamental basis for its regulatory activities was lacking. This should have been the recognition of the peninsular association as the sole authority, not by various individuals who in turn could only take action personally, but rather as an institution which supersedes individual wills and encompasses, *de jure*, an entire national domain. Given this state of affairs, a break in the unity of the Spanish language or territorial losses in the areas it occupied in Latin America were still dangers. An attempt was made to remedy this situation through the creation of Latin American academies as associates of the Spanish Academy. The initial idea seems to have originated with the Colombian writer José María Vergara y Vergara and the Spanish Academy member Juan Eugenio Hartzenbusch.[14] In the 1860's the Spanish Academy had created the category of associate member for Spaniards and foreigners who had distinguished themselves either by their excellence in the study of the language or by their brilliance as writers. In a session on November 24, 1870, the Spanish Academy resolved that the associate academy members — three at the least — of each of the Latin American countries could establish an academy which at its own request would be recognized by the Madrid association as an associate institute in that particular Latin American republic. These Latin American academies would be organized and governed wholly by their members. Their operation would be analogous to that of the peninsular organization, they would have the same goals and

[14] Cf. Guillermo L. Guitarte, 'Cartas desconocidas de M. A. Caro, J. M. Gutiérrez y E. Uricoechea', *Thesaurus* 17.300-1 (1962).

would collaborate on a national scale in the fulfillment of these goals.[15] In this way the gap that independence had created in the influence of the Spanish Academy in Latin America is closed: its doctrines and linguistic ideals are in the future represented and defended by the Latin Americans themselves, through their own institutions that multiply the image of the original academy throughout Latin America.

The thoughts of the founders of the Latin American associate academies were essentially patriotic. 'Language is the mother country!' exclaimed Miguel Antonio Caro, explaining the reasons that had prompted the creation of the Colombian Academy.[16] On stating the object of his *Apuntaciones críticas sobre el lenguaje bogotano*,[17] a work which with Bello's *Gramática* has had the greatest influence in the task of bringing the language of Latin America closer to that of Spain, Rufino José Cuervo for his part said: 'Nothing, in our opinion, so fully symbolizes the mother country as does its language'. Those who founded the academies in Latin America saw with surprise that the accelerated process of modernization through contact with Western Europe and the disappearance, after political independence, of a unanimously recognized center for the Hispanic world, unleashed a great many centrifugal tendencies with respect to language. Moreover, this situation favored all kinds of innovations and borrowings, which were checked only with difficulty by the tradition of literary language that was maintained in Latin America. Deliberate separation from the Spanish language was even suggested, which would have provided a clear path for the centrifugal linguistic forces so that 'national' languages could have succeeded in establishing themselves in the various Latin American republics.[18] For the supporters of

[15] Fermín de la Puente y Apezechea, 'Academias Americanas correspondientes de la Española', *Memorias de la Academia Española* 4.274-89 (1873); here one will find the Spanish Academy's resolution and the 'spirit that presided at its adoption'.

[16] 'Fundación de la Academia Colombiana', *Anuario de la Academia Colombiana* 1 (1874) and in *Obras completas* 2.131 (Bogotá, 1920).

[17] 'Prólogo', *Obras* 1.6 (Bogotá, 1954).

[18] This 'linguistic nationalism' is usually considered to be a phenomenon which occurs only in Argentina. Arturo Costa Alvarez has written the best history of this subject: *Nuestra lengua* 20-154 (Buenos Aires, 1922). But this desire for 'one's own language' is not an Argentine peculiarity. There is no lack of evidence for Chile: Julio Saavedra, *Nuestro idioma patrio* (Santiago de Chile, 1907), defends the idea. Miguel de Unamuno, 'El idioma nacional', *Obras completas* 6.180 (Madrid, 1958), copies a passage by a Chilean author from an article published in *La Nación* of Buenos Aires on December 23, 1907, in which 'This very pronounced inclination we have always had in Chile to create our own language' is spoken of. We believe this observation to be accurate since J. V. Lastarria in his inaugural address to the Literary Society of Santiago, delivered in 1842, censures those who 'have believed that our emancipation from the mother country should lead us even to scorn her language and to form upon its ruins another language which will be more fitting for us, which will represent our needs, our feelings'. (*Recuerdos literarios*[2] 107 [Santiago de Chile, 1885]). In Peru, the position of Manuel González Prada with respect to matters of language is very similar to that of Sarmiento, Alberdi and Gutiérrez in Argentina. He resembles the latter even in having refused the opportunity to become an associate member of the Spanish Academy. See, by Prada: 'Conferencia en el Ateneo de Lima' (1886) and 'Notas acerca del idioma' (1889), *Páginas libres* 3-32 and 256-72 (Lima, 1946). It seems likely to us that a search through other Latin American writings would uncover similar evidence. In any case, with what has been said above, we believe this to be sufficient reason to consider the reference to 'linguistic nationalism' as an Argentine phenomenon to be inaccurate: Argentina was only the country in which an attitude shared also by other republics reached its greatest intensity.

the academies, language was the expression of the cultural personality of the Latin American countries. To accept its decadence and resign oneself to its probable fragmentation was to abandon their own historic substance, and to renounce participation in the highest forms of civilization by declaring themselves powerless to keep alive a language of culture. Finally, it meant breaking the ties that united the Latin American republics among themselves and with Spain and showing themselves to be incapable of sustaining one of the great creations of history.

Other Latin Americans interpreted the situation in a different way. Their patriotism made them reject an alliance of language academies which would strive to generalize in the New World the doctrines of an institution they considered characteristic of Spain. It was felt that this would constitute meddling by the former mother country in the affairs of the new nations. Other motives, moreover, were involved in this opposition to the associate academies. The old rivalry between Spaniards and Latin Americans was augmented at times by a political dimension: the liberalism dominant in many Latin American republics gave rise to a disdainful attitude toward the Spanish cultural tradition. There were struggles to eliminate this tradition in many areas of life; with respect to language, attitudes varied. Above it was seen how, after the war of independence, some people wanted to guard the language from anti-Spanish feeling by putting it under the protection of a Latin American Academy of Language, which would have been independent of the association in Madrid. This idea and other similar ones were not carried out. Later, around the 1840's, the invasion by romanticism added a new aspect to the dispute. The doctrine of romanticism, with its exaltation of artistic liberty, was essentially anti-academy. Its rejection of the models of speech proposed by the Spanish Academy, its scorn for rules and its war on purism coincided with Latin-American feelings of opposition to the actions of the Spanish Academy. The 'emancipation' of the Spanish language in Latin America, which was spoken of then at times, and which should have been a consequence of political emancipation, in good part represents the same struggle that was carried out contemporaneously in Spain to create styles different from those cultivated in the literature of Spain's Golden Age which the Academy offered as models. To consider Spanish literature as a reflection of a world of ideas unconnected with the modern age in which one desired to live and to try to 'emancipate' the Spanish language from the burden of this tradition is what, for example, Larra preached and practiced in Spain. The Latin American authors[19] who opposed Spanish literature and considered its language incapable of

Bear in mind, moreover, that the expression 'linguistic nationalism' is not a felicitous one, because it does not capture the full meaning of this attitude. In it were included, in addition to patriotism (which is not exactly 'nationalism'), various other motives, some of which we schematically outline in the text. Linguistic ideas in Latin America still await a serious and systematic treatment.

[19] For example, the Argentines Juan Bautista Alberdi and Domingo F. Sarmiento; cf. Arturo Costa Alvarez, *Nuestra lengua* 34 and 47 (Buenos Aires, 1922). The literary influence of Larra on Alberdi has been thoroughly studied by José A. Oría, 'Alberdi *Figarillo*: Contribución al estudio de la influencia de Larra en el Río de la Plata', *Humanidades* (La Plata) 25:2.223-83 (1936). Also J. V. Lastarria, *Recuerdos literarios*[2] 106-7 (Santiago de Chile, 1885), in his address delivered in 1842 at the

being the medium of expression for the new ideas of science and democracy, chose *Fígaro* as their standard-bearer in the campaign against the language of the academy. Finally, for a whole variety of reasons, the continuing ties with Spain through the associate academies seemed to many Latin Americans to be a return to dependence on the former mother country and an obstacle to the advance of the Latin American nations on the path of progress. Voices of protest were heard in Latin America against the associate academies, that reached their highest pitch in 1875 when the Argentine Juan María Gutiérrez turned down the diploma of associate member in the Spanish Academy because he did not agree with the aims of this institution and because it did not seem proper to him for Latin American writers to be associated with it.[20]

In spite of this opposition, those in favor of the associate academies in Latin America carried forward their plans. After the regulation of November 24, 1870, these institutes began to appear in Latin American countries, if not in all of them during the nineteenth century, in a good number of them. The Colombian Academy, first of the Latin American associate academies, was founded in 1871; those of Mexico (1875), Ecuador (1875), El Salvador (c. 1880), Venezuela (1881), Chile (1886), Peru (1887) and Guatemala (1888) followed it. In general, these academies brought together the most select of the men of letters and those who concerned themselves with matters of language who lived in the capital of each republic. Membership in them, of course, was based only on literary merit, as in the Spanish Academy. The frequent participation in the academies of members of the liberal party not only provided the academies with a complete representation with regard to national letters, but also quieted the distrust that writers of this political orientation felt at the beginning for these institutes, and helped them understand the genuine sense of high culture that animated the academies.

The academies of that period were formed around a nucleus of a dozen individuals, who received no money for their work; generally they held their meetings in the president's house. Sometimes the national government or one of the academy members defrayed the cost of its publications; on other occasions the works of the members appeared at private cost, or a literary magazine allowed them to announce their activities and welcomed their work: thus, for example, in Colombia *El Repertorio Colombiano* (1878-99) during its years of publication was the organ of the Colombian

---

inauguration of the Literary Society of Santiago, borrows a phrase from Larra to establish that Latin Americans should reject Spanish literature as not being 'useful and progressive' and should rely only on a small number of 'reasoned writers'. Lastarria, however, advises studying the former because it presents models that should be imitated to prevent the language from declining to a barbaric state.

[20] On the refusal by Juan María Gutiérrez to join the academy and his opposition to the formation in Río de la Plata of an associate academy, an episode which is very illustrative of the position of many Latin Americans with regard to the matter, see Arturo Costa Alvarez, *Nuestra lengua* 57-70 (Buenos Aires, 1922) and Guillermo L. Guitarte, 'Cartas desconocidas de M. A. Caro, J. M. Gutiérrez y E. Uricoechea', *Thesaurus* 17.237-312 (1962). The opposite position, that taken by the defenders of the Latin American associate academies, found its best expression in Miguel Antonio Caro's polemic article: 'Americanismo en el lenguaje', *El Repertorio Colombiano* 1.3-21 (1878), and in his *Obras completas* 5.120-37 (Bogotá, 1928).

Academy. In spite of so many difficulties, the work of the Latin American academies in the final decades of the nineteenth century was valuable and firmly established these institutions in Latin American life. Many great Latin Americans devoted their talents and energy to encouraging the academies in this stage of their creation and development: Joaquín García Icazbalceta and Rafael Angel de la Peña in Mexico, Julio Calcaño in Venezuela, Miguel Antonio Caro, Rufino José Cuervo and Marco Fidel Suárez in Colombia, Pedro Fermín Cevallos in Ecuador, Ricardo Palma in Peru, Miguel Luis Amunátegui in Chile. In the face of indifference, contempt, and even at times opposition to the Spanish language, the movement initiated by the Latin American academies performed the task of consolidating the intractable Latin American linguistic tradition of the nineteenth century. It would be unfair to overlook the academies' service to Latin American culture, and their historical significance as a counterbalance to what has rather vaguely been labelled 'nationalist' tendencies in matters of language.

The disappearance of the academies' founding generation at the beginning of the twentieth century resulted in the *de facto* disintegration of many of them. Both the Royal Spanish Academy and local Latin American circles provided the initiative to reorganize the academies that had ceased to exist and to found them in the countries that still lacked these organizations. Thus, those of Chile (1914), Peru (1918), Ecuador (c. 1923), El Salvador (c. 1923), Guatemala (c. 1930) and Venezuela (c. 1930) were reactivated. Associate academies were founded in Bolivia (1920), Costa Rica (1923), Cuba (1926), Panama (1926), the Dominican Republic (1927), Paraguay (1927), Honduras (1948) and Puerto Rico (1952).[21] In 1931, by a decree of the national government, and as one of the country's organs of high culture, the Argentine Academy of Letters was founded in Buenos Aires. It succeeded an associate Argentine academy that was founded in 1910 and disappeared soon after without leaving a trace. The present Argentine Academy of Letters, therefore, has no institutional ties with the Spanish Academy; it is not an 'associate' academy but works in harmony with it and with the other Latin American associate academies and is officially certified as a 'collaborator' of the peninsular institution. The National Academy of Letters of Uruguay, founded by a decree of the government of this country in 1943, has the same status. An associate academy has also existed in the Philippines since 1925, and the possibility of founding institutions of this kind in Tel Aviv for the Sephardic Jews, and in the cities of the United States that have large Spanish-speaking communities is being considered,[22] so that there will remain no sizable group with a Spanish-speaking population that doesn't have its own organ for the control and defense of the language.

[21] The dates we give in the text for the founding of the associate academies for the most part come from the pamphlet *Asociación de Academias de la Lengua española. Comisión Permanente (1953-56)* 36-62 (Mexico, 1956).

[22] The plans developed by the Permanent Comission of the Association of Academies to organize Leagues for the defense of the language in the cities of the United States that have large Hispanic nuclei, such as Los Angeles, San Antonio, Texas, Chicago and New York, are related on page 17 of the pamphlet cited in the previous note.

1.3. *The Association of Academies of the Spanish Language*

A new trend in the activity of the academies has been embarked on starting with the congresses of academies which were held from 1951 on. During this year the then president of Mexico, Miguel Alemán, called a meeting of all the academies of the Spanish language, under the auspices and at the expense of the Mexican government. He was guided by advanced and enlightened aims. In a modern world dominated by great political blocs, he felt the best way of serving the aspirations and interests of the Hispanic countries was to unite them all in one group, so that their voice would attain sufficient volume to be heard in the world. Given that the community of language is the basis for unity between Spain and the nations she founded, the Mexican president's idea took the form of a meeting of the representatives of the institutions entrusted with the elucidation and defense of the Spanish language, thus officially assigning an important role to the academies in the life of the Spanish-speaking nations. The plan to hold congresses of academies was completely successful; up to the present there have been meetings, with almost total regularity, every four years: in Mexico (1951), in Madrid (1956), in Bogotá (1960) and in Buenos Aires (1964), and the next meeting is planned for Quito (1968). The aim of the academy members is to keep themselves well-informed about the state of the Spanish language through these periodic contacts and to elaborate joint plans to guide its development. There is no doubt that these congresses have stimulated the life of the academies and have accorded a greater influence to their work. In the congresses opportunities were found to discuss language problems and to adopt measures in defense of the unity of Spanish that would have a systematic nature, with the assurance that they were shared by the representatives of all the academies.

The most important achievements of the congresses to date have been the establishment of the Association of Academies of the Spanish Language and the creation of the Permanent Commission of this Association. In the congress held in Mexico, it was decided to revise the bases that governed the relations between the Royal Spanish Academy and its associate academies.[23] In this manner the old regulation of November 24, 1870 that had created the associate academies and guided their work up to that moment was set aside, and a new stage in the life of the Latin American academies began. The Spanish Academy and its associate academies were organized as an Association of Academies of the Spanish Language, 'whose purpose is to work assiduously for the defense, unity and integrity of our common language, and to see that its natural growth follows the traditional paths of the Spanish language'.[24] In the Madrid con-

[23] Resolución XLII, *Memoria del Primer Congreso de Academias de la Lengua Española* 368 (Mexico, 1952).

[24] Estatutos de las academias correspondientes de la Real Academia Española, art. 1, *Memorias del Primer Congreso de Academias de la Lengua Española* 495 (Mexico, 1952). The complete statutes can be found on pages 495-7 of that volume.

gress it was decided to request[25] that this Association and its Permanent Commission be recognized, by a multilateral agreement between the countries to which the various academies belonged, as organizations of an international nature. To date this agreement has been signed by Honduras, Costa Rica, Paraguay, Panama, Spain, Colombia, Guatemala, Argentina and Nicaragua.[26]

In this new organization the Latin American associate academies acknowledge that the Spanish Academy 'is the one naturally designated to direct the collective work of defending and promoting the Spanish language',[27] and that their task consists in 'collaborating with the Spanish Academy, according to its instructions, in the writing of the *Gramática* and *Diccionario*.'[28] It is certain that the creation of the Association allows one to detect a tendency to diminish the distance between the Spanish Academy and its Latin American associates. In this spirit it has been agreed that each time the Royal Spanish Academy considers a serious resolution in grammatical matters or in any other linguistic area, it will submit the resolution to the associate academies so that they may express their opinion about the proposed change.[29] But it is equally certain that relations between the associate and Spanish academies, in spite of courtesies such as that mentioned above, are still fundamentally on the same level as they were when the regulation of 1870 established them. Rather, the Association of Academies implies a change in the procedures designed to accomplish the goals that were adopted in the creation of the Latin American associate academies. It is hoped that this change will better adapt the organization to a situation which is now different from and perhaps of greater danger than that of the preceding century. The Association, of course, promotes academy action since it unites the Spanish and associate academies in one whole to which all belong, instead of maintaining bilateral relations between the peninsular institution and each one of the Latin American academies. This encourages an increase in responsibility in the face of work which is now collectively discussed and approved every four years by all the academies, and has the great advantage that the recommendations arrived at are simultaneously put into effect (or are supposed to be) throughout the domain of the Spanish language. Similarly, an organization in the form of an association has a legal character which gives more authority to the academies' decisions and favors any measure of support for its projects from the respective national governments. In short, the Association has injected new life into the academies and has supplied them with better means of action.

The Permanent Commission is the organ entrusted with implementing the decisions

[25] Resolución XXVII, *Memoria del Segundo Congreso de Academias de la Lengua Española* 426 (Madrid, 1956).

[26] Oscar Echeverri Mejía, *Nuestro idioma al dia*[2] 19 (Cali, 1965).

[27] Estatutos de las academias correspondientes de la Real Academia Española, art. 2, *Memoria del Primer Congreso de Academias de la Lengua Española* 495 (Mexico, 1952).

[28] Estatutos de las academias correspondientes de la Real Academia Española, art. 3, c, *Memoria del Primer Congreso de Academias de la Lengua Española* 495 (Mexico, 1952).

[29] Resolución XIX, *Memoria del Segundo Congreso de Academias de la Lengua Española* 419 (Madrid, 1956).

of the Association of Academies. It was created in Mexico in 1951, following the first congress of academies, when the new organization of academies was established as an Association. It met in Mexico City from 1951 to 1956 through the generosity of the Mexican government, which had committed itself to being responsible for its maintenance expenses until the next congress of academies. The Commission was then composed of eight Latin American academy members and one Spaniard who presided over it, and its work consisted principally in organizing the new life of the academies and dictating its own statutes and standards for action. This Permanent Commission ceased to meet after 1956, possibly due to difficulties in obtaining the funds to support it in the future. In 1964, during the Fourth Congress in Buenos Aires, a satisfactory formula was devised for its reconstitution and operation. Now the Permanent Commission will have fixed headquarters, in order to facilitate its regular operation, and it will be located in Madrid, although it may meet elsewhere in the Hispanic world. It will be composed of a minimum of five members, of which two will be from the Royal Spanish Academy and three from the remaining academies. Of the non-Spanish delegates, one will be permanent and will hold office until the meeting of the next congress of academies; the two remaining delegates will be elected by their academies for annual terms, in accord with a rotating order among the academies, which will be established by casting lots. The Royal Spanish Academy will defray the travel and maintenance expenses of the non-Spanish delegates.[30]

Beginning in April, 1965 this new Permanent Commission has started to work again in Madrid, with the following membership: President, Dámaso Alonso (Spain); Secretary, Luis Alfonso (Argentina); Treasurer, Rafael Lapesa (Spain); voting members, Baltasar Isaza Calderón (Panama) and Luis Flórez (Colombia). The Commission coordinates and channels the activities of the academies, takes charge of seeing that the agreements arrived at by the academies in their congresses are carried out, serves as a consultative body to the Spanish Academy and keeps watch over the development of the life of the language. Without a doubt the stable organization of the Permanent Commission offers an opportunity for the recently established Association of Academies of the Spanish Language to unfold all the capacity for action that it can develop.

2. THE WORK OF THE LATIN AMERICAN ACADEMIES

2.1. *Theoretical work*

The work of the associate academies is carried out in accord with the aims that direct the action of the Royal Spanish Academy, although these aims are in general adapted to conditions of Latin American life. Their purpose lies in fulfilling the program of the

[30] See the agreement by which the Permanent Commission was reorganized in 'IV Congreso de Academias de la Lengua', *BAE* 44.560-3 (1964).

parent institute within the limits of their own national territories. Due to the appearance of the academies, centers for the cultivation and elucidation of Hispanic language and literature arose in various parts of Latin America. Perhaps a few existed before the academies and others probably would have been formed without their establishment having coincided with that of the academies, but with regard to this point, each case would have to be individually investigated. It seems likely to think, however, that the idea of creating associate academies in many cases provided the stimulus that led a group of writers, who without this stimulus perhaps might not have found the opportunity, to establish these literary centers, and that gave them the support and prestige they might only with difficulty have attained by themselves.

Before reviewing the work of the academies, it must be pointed out that, possibly due to the economic poverty in which the academies have existed and continue to exist, a large part of the members' works have appeared in publications that are not connected with the academies or have been isued by private publishing houses. On occasion they have even been paid for by the authors themselves: Cuervo paid for the printing of the two volumes of his *Diccionario de construcción y régimen* out of his own pocket. In these circumstances it is difficult to decide to what extent these works are directly inspired by the academies, or to what degree the ideas expressed in them represent the criterion of the academies and not simply the author's personal point of view. For the moment it is not possible to give a satisfactory answer to this question, since a full knowledge of the history of each academy, which we do not currently have available, would be necessary.[31] Therefore, the description below of the academies' work could perhaps be called 'work of the academy members' rather than 'work of the academies'. We do not feel this would be an incorrect presentation, however, because in reality, it shows very clearly how the work of the academies frequently developed: often it was due to the efforts of isolated individuals and it is important to interpret

[31] In reality, the only Latin American academies whose histories have been written are the Mexican Academy: Alberto María Carreño, *La Academia Mexicana, correspondiente de la Española (1875-1945)* (Mexico, 1945), and the Chilean Academy: Miguel Luis Amunátegui Reyes, *La Academia Chilena en el cincuentenario de su fundación* (Santiago de Chile, 1937), a work which should be supplemented by the next work, written by the same author, *La Real Academia Española y sus relaciones con sus hijas de América* (Santiago de Chile, 1943). For the Bolivian Academy we rely on some notes by Porfirio Díaz Machicao, 'Breve historia de la Academia Boliviana correspondiente de la Real Española', *BAC* 9.287-92 (1959). Luis Alfonso gives a historical synopsis of the life of the academies in Argentina, *Presente y futuro de la lengua española* 1.161-5 (Madrid, 1964). The study by Marco Fidel Suárez, 'Cómo se fundó la Academia Colombiana', *Obras* 1.747-54 (Bogotá, 1958), although a summary, offers an excellent picture — the only one that exists — of the historical-linguistic situation which led to the creation of the associate academies in Latin America, giving a detailed account of the successive events in this process; however, it can hardly be considered a history of the Colombian Academy, which on the other hand was not the author's objective. Some brief works give information about the life of this association; see, for example, Oscar Echeverri Mejía, 'La Academia Colombiana de la Lengua, baluarte del idioma español', *Presente y futuro de la lengua española* 2.103-8 (Madrid, 1964). Fernando Galvis Salazar, an associate member of the Colombian Academy, has a completed but unpublished *Historia de la Academia Colombiana* (1871-1966), written to carry out a resolution of the Bogotá Congress of Academies (1960), which urges those institutions that have not yet traced their own histories to do so.

this work, *lato sensu*, as analogous to the deeds of the knights-errant: that is, as different undertakings, separately carried out by men who, nevertheless, belonged to the same order.

2.1.1. *Literary studies*

The decisive role that literature fills in the formation of a national language and in the establishment of its literary norm is well-known. Hence the preservation and elucidation of the general linguistic norm, as expressed in the literary language, is one of the fundamental tasks of the academies. This work is carried out in the first place by the academy members themselves by participating in their country's life, practicing that general linguistic norm in their writings and lending it the prestige of their names. The group of academy members that aspires to represent that which is most select in each nation with regard to letters should constitute a center of influence for the literary language. This effect, which is difficult to gauge, but whose existence it would be false to deny, is of unfailing importance insofar as it grants value and prestige to the general linguistic norm, in all of a country's cultural activities.

The efforts to elucidate this tradition in each of the respective Latin American republics, that is, to trace the literary history of each country and study the authors who have cultivated the language with the greatest brilliance, constitute a special area within the academies' work on behalf of the literary language. Their studies of literature have been one of the most fruitful activities of the academies, and these organizations are credited with a substantial contribution to the knowledge of Latin American letters. A classic representative of this type of literary criticism is the Colombian Miguel Antonio Caro.[32] Also the name of the Argentine Calixto Oyuela is worth mentioning.[33] It should not be forgotten that in several countries the history of the national literature was begun by academy members[34] and that members of the associate academies are responsible for what are still the best histories of literature of several republics.[35]

[32] See his *Estudios literarios*, volumes 2 and 3 of his *Obras completas* (Bogotá, 1920 and 1921). His study of Bello is famous and was originally published as an introduction to Bello's *Poesías* (Madrid, 1881). This work and the equally notable biography by Miguel Luis Amunátegui, *Vida de don Andrés Bello* (Santiago de Chile, 1882), have been the fundamental works for an understanding of the life and work of the Venezuelan teacher.

[33] Recall, for example, his great work on Latin American poetry: *Antología poética hispano-americana*, 3 volumes (Buenos Aires, 1919).

[34] The works of José María Vergara y Vergara, *Historia de la literatura en la Nueva Granada* (Bogotá, 1867), José Toribio Medina, *Historia de la literatura colonial de Chile* (Santiago de Chile, 1878) and Francisco Pimentel, *Historia crítica de la literatura y de las ciencias en México. Poetas* (Mexico, 1883), have this initiating character.

[35] To this category belong: Julio Jiménez Rueda, *Historia de la literatura mexicana*[4] (Mexico, 1945); Antonio Gómez Restrepo, *Historia de la literatura colombiana*, 4 volumes (Bogotá, 1938-43); Isaac Barrera, *La literatura ecuatoriana* (Quito, 1960); Enrique Finot, *Historia de la literatura boliviana* (Mexico, 1943). Another part of the academies' work in the field of literature has been the publication of texts; along this line we recall the *Antología ecuatoriana. Poetas* (Quito, 1892) and *Cantares del pueblo ecuatoriano*, compiled by Juan León Mera (Quito, 1892), both publications of the Ecuadorian

Possibly the most mature product of the academy efforts in literary history was the *Antología de poetas hispano-americanos*, 4 volumes (Madrid, 1893-95), by the extraordinary Spanish scholar Marcelino Menéndez Pelayo. This work, conceived as a gift from the Spanish Academy to Latin America on the occasion of the fourth centennial of the discovery of the New World, presents a view of Latin American letters in which poetry is emphasized. Menéndez Pelayo's capacity for order and comprehension caused this book to become the basis for a new view of Latin American literary development, offering future scholars a clear path for criticism of an imposing breadth and plentiful culture. Menéndez Pelayo composed this *Antología* as a result of the idea, which was an old one with him, of not conceiving of Spanish literature as being limited solely to the Iberian peninsula, but as including the literary production of all Spanish-speaking peoples. In order to carry out the Latin American part of his project, Menéndez Pelayo relied on his friends who were academy members in Latin America to send him information and books.[36] It can be said then without much danger of exaggerating that the *Antología de poetas hispano-americanos* represents on the literary plane an achievement similar to that which began to be reached with the academy's *Diccionario* after the founding of the associate academies. At that time the *Diccionario* began to make room for the Latin-Americanisms that were forwarded by its Latin American correspondents, so that the work would include the entire domain of the Spanish language and not just Spain. Menéndez Pelayo, with similar collaboration by Latin American academy members, extended the academy work in the field of literary history to include all of the poetry in the Spanish language. The only difference lies in the fact that Menéndez Pelayo worked alone in the sphere of literature, on behalf of the entire institute.[37]

Academy; Pedro de Oña, *Arauco domado*, a critical edition published by the Chilean Academy, annotated by José Toribio Medina (Santiago de Chile, 1917); *Poemas de Colombia*, an anthology published by the Colombian Academy (Medellín, 1959); finally, the Argentine Academy of Letters published a *Biblioteca* in whose series 'Clásicos argentinos' six volumes have now appeared.

[36] Above all he counted on his close Latin American friend, the Colombian academy member Miguel Antonio Caro. See the correspondence between them in *Epistolario de Miguel Antonio Caro* 179-283 (Bogotá, 1941), studied by Ciriaco Pérez Bustamente, 'Sobre la génesis de la *Antología de poetas hispano-americanos*', *Finisterre* (2ª época) 3.22-37 (1948). See also the article by Emilio Carilla cited in the next note, pp. 279-90.

[37] The errors in detail and in point of view, which are due to the period and the author's on occasion excessively Spanish criterion, in no way diminish the merit and importance of this notable work. Its influence, which seems unquestionable to anyone who is familiar with works of Latin American literary history, remains to be thoroughly studied. Contributions in this vein can be found in Emilio Carilla, 'Menéndez Pelayo y la cultura argentina', *BAAL* 21.271-314 (1956), John E. Englekirk, 'La *Antología de poetas hispano-americanos* y el hispanismo norteamericano', *Arbor* 34.456-82 (1956), and Manuel Olguín, 'Menéndez Pelayo y la literatura hispanoamericana', *Révista Iberoamericana* 22.27-39 (1957). It will not be superfluous to recall that the Dominican Pedro Henríquez Ureña, the last great historian of Latin American literature, in 1909 wrote to Menéndez Pelayo: 'Personally, I consider it my duty to make known to you the admiration I have always had for you. More than admiration, I would say devotion ... I have not read the works of any critic, in our language or in any other, as much as I have yours' (*Menéndez Pelayo y la hispanidad*[2] 154 [Santander, 1955]). In 1911, on sending him the *Antología del Centenario* which he had compiled in collaboration with Luis G.

2.1.2. *Theoretical study of the language*

To establish and maintain a national linguistic norm, which is specifically an academy task, a theoretical understanding of the usage proposed is of fundamental importance. Some of the greatest contributions made by the associate academy members to an understanding of the Spanish language belong to this area of grammatical studies. Outstanding in this respect is the work of two extraordinary individuals, Andrés Bello and Rufino José Cuervo, as well as that of a group of lesser figures who are still of the first magnitude. The *Gramática de la lengua castellana, destinada al uso de los americanos* (Santiago de Chile, 1847) by Andrés Bello is still today the best grammar of Spanish; it surpassed both the Spanish Academy's volume of the same period, which was still too attached to the Latin model, and Vicente Salvá's fine *Gramática de la lengua castellana según ahora se habla* (Paris, 1830), due to the profundity of its conception. This work of Bello's is the classic exposition of the system of the Spanish language. With it, its author, very much against his intention, created a point of friction between Spain and Latin America, since there were many cases in which, because of Latin American patriotism, people preferred to follow Bello's *Gramática* rather than that of the Academy.

It has been said of Bello that he was born in Venezuela, taught in Chile and had his disciples in Colombia. And, in effect, the movement of linguistic studies and of concern for correct usage of the language initiated by him found its most talented followers in the group formed in Bogotá during the last decades of the nineteenth century. Rufino José Cuervo, Miguel Antonio Caro and Marco Fidel Suárez found in Bello's works, which they revered and kept by their bedsides,[38] the stimulus that inspired their

---

Urbina and Nicolás Rangel, he says: 'It will not escape your notice that your own studies on Latin America and, in general, on Spanish letters, have been our best models' (*ibid.* 157). Henríquez Ureña remained devoted to Menéndez Pelayo all his life. In the years when opinion was against the latter, the Dominican had the intellectual integrity, which ennobles his name, to defend the value of Menéndez Pelayo's work (cf. *En la orilla. Mi España* [Mexico, 1922], reproduced in *Obra crítica* 226-9 [Mexico, 1960]). The influence of the Spanish critic is evident through Henríquez Ureña's last books, such as his great study *Las corrientes literarias en la América hispánica* (Mexico, 1949), where Menéndez Pelayo is the author most quoted and forthrightly used to characterize personalities and events.

[38] Marco Fidel Suárez, *Obras* 1.814 (Bogotá, 1958), recounts that 'one can characterize as personal affection that which our great compatriot professed for the famous teacher of Bolívar and of the Chilean nation'; with a felicitous expression he calls the deep veneration that Caro felt for Bello 'intellectual fondness'. Cuervo's words in the 'Introducción' to the *Notas* he wrote for Bello's *Gramática* are well-known: 'Having studied this grammar in school and having kept it always at hand, when I have found something significant in my reading, I have noted it in the margin ... I wish it might be brought about that Bello's name would always be the symbol of the scientific teaching of Spanish, as it has been up to today, and that his work might be preserved in the hands of the young as an expression of the teachings most verified and accepted by philologists!' (*Obras* 1.913 [Bogotá, 1954]). Almost until his death, which occurred in 1911, Cuervo had Bello's *Gramática* constantly at hand, as is evidenced by the fact that in the copy from his library, hand-written annotations appear added to the last edition of the *Notas*, that of 1907. As for Suárez, who developed along with Caro and Cuervo, it is not surprising that he has considered Bello as an 'honored teacher, a kind of oracle and somewhat of a deity and a person with remarkable insight' (*Obras* 1.726 [Bogotá, 1958]).

great linguistic works. This 'triumvirate of Colombian culture' — according to Menéndez Pidal's expression[39] — at the height of their investigations kept Bello's work alive and transmitted it to new generations. Cuervo did so in his classic *Notas*[40] to the *Gramática*, which has constituted, ever since its appearance, an inseparable whole with the work of the Venezuelan; Caro, a poet as well as a scholar, enriched Bello's *Principios de la Ortología y métrica de la Lengua Castellana* (Santiago de Chile, 1835) with his *Notas*,[41] which like Cuervo's *Notas* on the *Gramática*, later on formed a whole with the work on which it is based. The *Estudios gramaticales*, Introducción a las obras filológicas de don Andrés Bello (Madrid, 1885) by M. F. Suárez is an extremely clear exposition of Bello's doctrine, carried out by a scholar of sound cultural formation and notable insight, which still maintains a pre-eminent place for the understanding of the *Gramática*.[42]

In the field of language studies, the most outstanding figure without doubt was Cuervo. His first work, *Apuntaciones críticas sobre el lenguaje bogotano* (Bogotá, 1867-72), has a normative aim, but goes beyond that, especially in later republications of the work.[43] In effect, the *Apuntaciones* not only elucidates the usage of Bogotá which Cuervo describes but also the classic usage with which the learned Colombian contrasts it. Moreover, by constantly comparing the speech of the city of his birth with that of other places in Latin America and with the information provided by the colonial chroniclers, Cuervo traced the first lines of the dialect studies and linguistic history of the Spanish of Latin America. Various monographs which were classics on the subjects they treated, and his *opus magnum*, the *Diccionario de construcción y*

[39] 'En memoria de Don Marco Fidel Suárez, con ocasión del primer centenario de su nacimiento', *BAE* 35.164 (1956).

[40] The *Notas* appeared for the first time in the Bogotá reprinting of Bello's *Gramática* in 1874. In successive editions, Cuervo made numerous additions to and revisions of the *Notas*. The complete bibliographical history can be found in Rafael Torres Quintero, 'Bibliografía de R. J. Cuervo', in R. J. Cuervo, *Obras* 2.1764-67 (Bogotá, 1954).

[41] Published for the first time in the 1882 edition of Bello's *Principios* which was printed in Bogotá.

[42] The *Estudios gramaticales* is an amplification of the work with which Suárez won the competition sponsored by the Colombian Academy in 1881 to celebrate the centennial of Bello's birth. It can also be found in his *Obras* 1.117-409 (Bogotá, 1958). Bello's *Gramática* has constantly received attention from Latin American grammarians. Among the works that have been dedicated to him we will mention: Manuel A. Bonilla (member of the Colombian Academy), 'Ensayo sobre la *Gramática de la lengua castellana* de D. Andrés Bello', *Boletín de la Academia Venezolana* 15.3-60 (1948); José Ramón Ayala (member of the Venezuelan Academy), 'Obra gramatical de D. Andrés Bello', *Boletín de la Academia Venezolana* 15.251-352 (1948); Juan B. Selva (associate member of the Argentine Academy of Letters), *Trascendencia de la* Gramática *de Bello y estado actual de los estudios gramaticales* (Buenos Aires, 1950); Amado Alonso (associate member of the Argentine Academy of Letters), 'Introducción a los estudios gramaticales de Andrés Bello', in Bello's *Obras completas* 4.IX-LXXXVI (Caracas, 1951); Baltasar Isaza Calderón (member of the Panamanian Academy), *La doctrina gramatical de Bello* (Panama, 1960). Although the author is not a member of an academy, the work of Angel Rosenblat, *El pensamiento gramatical de Bello* (Caracas, 1961), cannot be omitted from a list of studies dedicated to Bello.

[43] Cuervo managed to prepare six editions of the *Apuntaciones*; the sixth appeared in 1914 after the death of its author. See the bibliographic history of the book in Rafael Torres Quintero, 'Bibliografía de R. J. Cuervo', in R. J. Cuervo, *Obras* 2.1749-50 (Bogotá, 1954).

régimen de la lengua castellana (Paris, Vol. I, 1886, *A-B*; Vol. II, 1893, *C-D*), along with the *Apuntaciones*, later brought Cuervo his deserved fame as the first Spanish-speaking philologist of the nineteenth century.[44]

On a level with Cuervo's works are the studies by his contemporary, Miguel Antonio Caro, 'Tratado del participio',[45] by Marco Fidel Suárez, 'El pronombre posesivo',[46] and by the Mexican Rafael Angel de la Peña, 'Tratado del gerundio'.[47] As the twentieth century advances, the number of academy grammarians decreases and the academy philologists begin to appear. This fact is undoubtedly related to the transatlantic influence of the school of philology created in Spain by Menéndez Pidal, which was spread and established in Latin America by such notable scholars as his disciple Amado Alonso. The latter, who directed the Institute of Philology of Buenos Aires from 1927 to 1946, continued the teachings of the learned Spanish master and in turn formed a brilliant school of Latin American philologists. The incorporation of philologists in the academies, on the other hand, reflects a process similar to that which has occurred in the Spanish Academy. The latter, under the influence of Menéndez Pelayo,[48] began to be more a center for scholars of Spanish language and literature than a gathering of the most outstanding representatives of proper usage.

The work of the great Latin American grammarians has been kept in mind by the Spanish Academy in writing its *Gramática*,[49] which is the work that officially gives the grammatical norm for Spanish. The writing of the *Gramática* has been traditionally in the hands of the Spanish Academy, and this situation has not changed with the creation of the associate academies, nor with the subsequent reorganization of the latter and the parent academy into one Association.[50] The Spanish Academy, in line with the climate of activity and renewal which has characterized the life of the academies for the last few decades, is working on a revision of its present edition of the *Gramática*. This revision will include both recommended usage and grammatical principles. With regard to the latter the aim is to present an interpretation of the

[44] The Caro and Cuervo Institute in Bogotá, using materials in part already assembled by Cuervo, has undertaken the continuation of the *Diccionario*. Fernando A. Martínez is in charge of the work and up to now two fascicles have appeared, corresponding to the letter *E- ea-empeorar* (1959) and *emperezar-émulo* (1961).

[45] *Anales de la Universidad Nacional de los Estados Unidos de Colombia* 3.419-99 (1870) and in *Obras completas* 5.23-100 (Bogotá, 1928).

[46] *El Repertorio Colombiano* 10.123-50 (1883) and in *Obras* 1.89-116 (Bogotá, 1958).

[47] *Memorias de la Academia Mexicana* 3.201-47 (1886). It was republished as a book (Mexico, 1889), reprinted by the Permanent Commission of the Association of Academies of the Spanish Language in 1955 when it met in Mexico.

[48] Ramón Menéndez Pidal, 'Don Emilio Cotarelo', *BAE* 23.6-7 (1936).

[49] The Spanish Academy has recognized its debt to Bello beginning with the 1854 edition of its *Gramática*. On the gradual appearance of Bello's teachings in successive versions of the *Gramática* of the Royal Spanish Academy, see Juan B. Selva, *Trascendencia de la* Gramática *de Bello y estado actual de los estudios gramaticales*, passim (Buenos Aires, 1950).

[50] In the second congress of academies a resolution was adopted by which associate academy members, appointed for the purpose by their respective academies, can participate in the writing of the *Gramática*; cf. *Memoria del Segundo Congreso de Academias de la Lengua Española* 410 (Madrid, 1956).

grammatical facts that takes into account recent developments in linguistics, in particular those subsumed under the label of 'structuralism', without embracing any one trend. All studies of Spanish grammar which have been done up to the present time will be systematically taken into account, with care being taken that the ideas of Latin American writers are incorporated, so that Latin American speakers of Spanish can see their point of view represented in the *Gramática*, will not feel they have been ignored, and will consider the work as their own. In this respect, for example, the nomenclature of verb tenses, regarding which Bello's *Gramática* and that of the Academy differ, has always constituted a source of controversy which has deprived the Spanish Academy's work of some of its authority. The Spanish Academy also proposes to broaden and bring up to date the usage that will be reflected in its future *Gramática*. The most recent authority cited in the present version is Juan Valera († 1905). This means that although the Spanish language was greatly altered beginning with the period of literary modernism at the end of the past century, recent usages are not found in the current version of this grammar. This absence of twentieth century usage in the Academy's *Gramática* is a serious defect, which fortunately this institution now proposes to remedy. Moreover, in this new version of the *Gramática* not only Spanish writers but also Latin Americans and Filipinos will be utilized as authorities, so that the language common to Spain, Latin America and the Philippines can present its varied usages through the representatives of all of these countries. The collaboration of the Latin American and Philippine academies is solicited just as much to provide examples of contemporary authors now considered classics, as to provid information about the range and social value of usages concurrent in each country.[51]

2.1.3. *Study of the Latin American lexicon*

Together with their literary studies, the most fruitful activity of the associate academies has been their contribution to a knowledge of the regional lexicon of Latin America. This work entails their direct collaboration in the editing of the *Diccionario*, one of the language's regulatory instruments, and figures as one of their obligations according to the regulation by which the associate academies of Latin America were created.[52] Thus the abundance of the lexicographic work done by the academies, which was

[51] On this reform of the *Gramática*, see Rafael Lapesa, 'Sugestiones relacionadas con la futura edición de la *Gramática* de la Academia. Conveniencia de tener en cuenta otras gramáticas de mérito notable', *Memoria del Segundo Congreso de Academias de la Lengua Española* 83-8 (Madrid, 1956). Provisional samples of this new edition of the *Gramática* have been published by Salvador Fernández Ramírez; see by this Spanish academy member, 'La revisión de la *Gramática* de la Real Academia Española' [chapter on the pronoun], *Tercer Congreso de Academias de la Lengua Española. Actas y labores* 399-420 (Bogotá, 1960), and 'Para la futura *Gramática*' [I. El acento ortográfico. II. Morfología. Generalidades], *BAE* 44.431-48 (1964). The work of the Colombian academy member Rafael Torres Quintero, 'Unificación de la terminología gramatical', *Tercer Congreso de Academias de la Lengua Española. Actas y labores* 378-98 (Bogotá, 1960), represents a Latin American contribution to the academy project of revising the *Gramática*.

[52] Fermín de la Puente y Apezechea, 'Academias americanas correspondientes de la Española', *Memorias de la Academia Española* 288-9 (1873).

already in evidence in the first edition of the Academy's *Diccionario* published after the foundation of the associate academies, is explained. This twelfth edition, of 1884, was enriched by provincialisms from Mexico, Colombia and Venezuela, sent by the academy members of those countries. In the prologue to the work, Manuel Tamayo y Baus, secretary of the Spanish Academy at that time, could say with satisfaction that 'now for the first time Spain and Spanish America have joined hands to work together on behalf of the language which is the common property of both. This is an event which fills both with indescribable happiness and which deserves eternal commemoration'.[53]

With regard to this work, as for other activities of the academies, it is difficult to say to what extent it was stimulated by the creation of the associate academies, since the work of gathering regionalisms was begun before these academies were founded, and on the other hand, has been abundant in the southern republics of Spanish America, where either there was no associate academy for many years (as in Argentina) or where after a short time the institute which has been founded in the country disappeared (such was the case for the Chilean Academy). Without disregarding the different situation of each Latin American republic, it seems certain that the creation of the associate academies and the Spanish Academy's summons to enrich the *Diccionario* with Latin American provincialisms encouraged the collection of local words. Furthermore we know, for example, that Joaquín García Icazbalceta might not have written his *Provincialismos mexicanos*, the first collection of regionalisms from Mexico, if the obligation for the associate academies to collaborate in the compilation of the Spanish Academy's *Diccionario* had not existed.[54]

In many cases, this lexicographic work was carried out by people who had no professional training as linguists. This cannot be said, of course, about the lexicon in Cuervo's *Apuntaciones*, nor of the works of the philologists who have joined the academies in recent decades. In order to give some idea of what the work in this field has been, we list below, without presuming to be exhaustive, various lexicographic works by academy members from the Latin American republics. Many have been the classic works on the regional vocabulary of their countries for a long time, and in some cases continue to be even up to today. A critical bibliography of dictionaries of Latin American regionalisms can be found in Rodolfo Lenz, *Diccionario etimológico de las voces chilenas derivadas de lenguas indígenas americanas* 58-89 (Santiago de Chile, 1904-10), and Miguel de Toro y Gisbert, *Americanismos* 169-219 (Paris, 1912). These works should be supplemented by bibliographies that are not exclusively lexical as are the preceding ones, such as those by Charles Carroll Marden, 'Notes for a bibliography of American Spanish', *Studies in honor of A. Marshall Elliott* 2.267-92

[53] Quoted by Ramón Menéndez Pidal, 'Acta de la solemne sesión de apertura del segundo Congreso de Academias de la Lengua', *Memoria del Segundo Congreso de Academias de la Lengua Española* 467 (Madrid, 1956).

[54] Alberto María Carreño, *La Academia Mexicana, correspondiente de la Española (1875-1945)* 26 (Mexico, 1945).

(Baltimore, [1911]), Id., 'A bibliography of American Spanish (1911-21)', *Homenaje a Menéndez Pidal* 1.589-665 (Madrid, 1925), Madaline W. Nichols, *A bibliographical guide to materials on American Spanish* (Cambridge, Massachusetts, 1941), Lawrence B. Kiddle, 'Bibliografía adicional para la obra de la Srta. Nichols', *Revista Iberoamericana* 7.213-40 (1943), and Max Leopold Wagner, 'Crónica bibliográfica hispanoamericana', in M. de Paiva Boléo (ed.), *Os estudos de lingüística românica na Europa e na América desde 1939 a 1948* 369-98 (Coimbra, 1951). The section on Latin American Spanish in Homero Serís, *Bibliografía de la lingüística española* (Bogotá, 1964), is worth consulting.

WEST INDIES

CUBA. — Esteban Pichardo, *Diccionario provincial, casi razonado, de voces y frases cubanas* (Matanzas, 1836), the first collection of provincialisms from a Latin American country, which was republished by the Cuban Academy in 1953, with corrections and ample annotations by the academy member Esteban Rodríguez Herrera; Juan Manuel Dihigo, *Léxico cubano* (Habana, Vol. I [letter *A*], 1928; Vol. II [letter *B*], 1946).

DOMINICAN REPUBLIC. — Manuel A. Patín Maceo, *Dominicanismos* (Santo Domingo, 1940).

PUERTO RICO. —Augusto Malaret, *Vocabulario de Puerto Rico* (San Juan, 1937). Malaret is the author of a *Diccionario de americanismos*[3] (Buenos Aires, 1946) which is the best general work on the subject.

MEXICO AND CENTRAL AMERICA

MEXICO. — Joaquín García Icazbalceta, 'Provincialismos mexicanos', *Memorias de la Academia Mexicana* 3.170-90, 296-301 and 436-32 (1886); Id., *Vocabulario de mexicanismos* (Mexico, 1899-1905). This work, which Icazbalceta managed to carry out through the letter *G*, was continued by Francisco J. Santamaría, *Diccionario de mejicanismos* (Mexico, 1959); Manuel G. Revilla, 'Provincialismos de expresión en México', *Memorias de la Academia Mexicana* 6.352-67 (1910); Cecilio Robelo, *Diccionario de aztequismos*[3] (Mexico, 1912); Darío Rubio [Ricardo del Castillo], *Los llamados mexicanismos de la Academia Española* (Mexico, 1917).

GUATEMALA. — Antonio Batres Jáuregui, *Vicios del lenguaje. Provincialismos de de Guatemala* (Guatemala, 1892); Lisandro Sandoval, *Semántica guatemalense o diccionario de guatemaltequismos*, 2 volumes (Guatemala, 1941-42).

HONDURAS. — Alberto Membreño, *Hondureñismos* (Tegucigalpa, 1895; 2nd ed., 1897; 3rd ed., Mexico, 1912).

COSTA RICA. — Carlos Gagini, *Diccionario de barbarismos y provincialismos de Costa Rica* (San José, 1982-93; 2nd ed., with the title *Diccionario de costarriqueñismos*, 1919).

SOUTH AMERICA

VENEZUELA. — Julio Calcaño, *El castellano en Venezuela* (Caracas, 1897); Baldomero Rivodó, *Voces nuevas en la lengua castellana* (Paris, 1889); Gonzalo Picón-Febres, *Libro raro: Voces, locuciones y otras cosas de uso frecuente en Venezuela*[2] (Curazao, 1912); Lisandro Alvarado, *Glosario de voces indígenas de Venezuela* (Caracas, 1921); Id., *Glosario del bajo español en Venezuela* (Caracas, 1929).

COLOMBIA. — Rufino José Cuervo, *Apuntaciones críticas sobre el lenguaje bogotano* (Bogotá, 1867-72; there is a ninth edition, 1955); Rafael Uribe Uribe, *Diccionario abreviado de galicismos, provincialismos y correcciones de lenguaje* (Medellín, 1887); Emilio Robledo, 'Un millar de papeletas lexicográficas relativas a los departamentos de Antioquia y Caldas', *Repertorio Histórico* (Medellín) 13.1-165 (1934); Leonardo Tascón, *Diccionario de provincialismos del Valle del Cauca* (Bogotá, 1935; 2nd ed., Cali, 1961); Julio Tobón Betancourt, *Colombianismos y otras voces de uso general* (Medellín, 1947; 2nd ed., Bogotá, 1953); Luis Flórez, *Habla y cultura popular en Antioquia* [Cosas y palabras: 115-363] (Bogotá, 1957); Abilio Lozano Caballero, 'Vocabulario de lenguaje popular colombiano', *BAC* 9.367-94 (1959); Luis Flórez, *Léxico de la casa popular urbana en Bolívar, Colombia* (Bogotá, 1962); Mario Alario di Filippo, *Lexicón de colombianismos* (Cartagena, 1964).

ECUADOR. — Pedro Fermín Cevallos, *Breve catálogo de errores en orden a la lengua y al lenguaje castellanos* (one of the oldest records of Latin-Americanisms, progressively enriched since its original publication in 1861 up to its fifth edition which was published in Ambato in 1880); Pablo Herrera, 'Voces provinciales del Ecuador', *Memorias de la Academia Ecuatoriana* 1.51-69, 33-45, 159-64, 221-6 (1884) [probably continued in vol. 2, which we could not check]; Carlos R. Tobar, *Consultas al Diccionario de la lengua* (Quito, 1900; 2nd ed., Barcelona, 1907-8; 3rd ed., 1911); Gustavo Lemos Ramírez, *Semántica o ensayo de lexicografía ecuatoriana* (Guayaquil, 1920).

PERU. — Juan de Arona [Pedro Paz-Soldán y Unanue], *Diccionario de peruanismos* (Lima, 1871; 2nd ed., 1883; 3rd ed., Paris, 1938); Id., *Suplemento al* Diccionario de peruanismos (Lima, 1957); Ricardo Palma, *Neologismos y americanismos* (Lima, 1896; reprinted in *Recuerdos de España* 223-309 [Lima, 1899]); Id., *2.700 voces que hacen falta en el Diccionario; papeletas lexicográficas* (Lima, 1903); Rubén Vargas Ugarte, *Glosario de peruanismos* (Lima, 1953).

CHILE. — Zorobabel Rodríguez, *Diccionario de chilenismos* (Santiago de Chile, 1875); Aníbal Echeverría y Reyes, *Voces usadas en Chile* (Santiago de Chile, 1900); Manuel A. Román, *Diccionario de chilenismos y de otras voces y locuciones curiosas*, 5 volumes (Santiago de Chile, 1901-18); Miguel Luis Amunátegui, *Apuntaciones lexicográficas*, 3 volumes (Santiago de Chile, 1907-08); José Toribio Medina, *Chilenismos, apuntes lexicográficos* (Santiago de Chile, 1928); José Miguel Irarrázaval Larraín, *Chilenismos* (Santiago de Chile, 1945).

ARGENTINA. — Although this country has one of the richest bibliographies of regional lexicons in Latin America, the majority of these dictionaries was written before, or on the periphery of, the Argentine associate academy which was founded in 1910. It had an ineffectual life and soon vanished without a trace. The Argentine Academy of Letters, founded in 1931, a collaborator though not an associate of the Spanish Academy, has been, on the other hand, extremely active. Its *Boletín,* of all the journals of the Latin American academies, is the one that has had the longest life. It has been published regularly since 1933, except for a four-year interruption beginning with 1952, due to political conditions. The *BAAL,* which could often be classified as a philological journal, frequently publishes studies of Argentine lexicography and, also, works on the lexicon of other Latin American countries. Today the *BAAL* is an indispensable source to consult on this subject.

URUGUAY. — Daniel Granada, *Vocabulario rioplatense razonado* (Montevideo, 1889; 2nd ed., 1890; 3rd ed., 1957); Id., *Apuntamientos sobre lexicografía americana y otros estudios filológicos* (Buenos Aires, 1948); Adolfo Berro García, 'Prontuario de voces del lenguaje campesino uruguayo', *BFM* 1.23-46, 163-97, 395-416 (1936-37), 2.27-38(1938), and 3.389-412 (1939); Id., 'Lexicografía rochense', *BAAL* 5.43-70 (1937).

2.2. *Normative and prescriptive work*

The Spanish Academy was founded to establish and generalize one model of speech in the entire domain of the Spanish language, a model that would represent the most refined, most 'correct' form of elevated literary and conversational language and to preserve it, brought up-to-date, through time. Such has continued to be its task up to the present in Spain itself. The creation of the Latin American associate academies beginning in 1870 in response to the new situation that arose with the independence of Spain's former Latin American colonies, added a new dimension to the tasks of the Spanish Academy: that of defending the unity of the language, that is, to preserve the tradition of the Spanish language in Latin America, defending it against the dangers that threatened its survival. In this effort of maintaining fidelity to the Spanish language in Latin America, the academies took the speech of Castile as its model in the nineteenth century. In a now independent Latin America, which had very few contacts with Spain, this in fact amounted to no more than the literature (above all of the Golden Age), and the Academy's *Gramática* and *Diccionario.* There is no doubt that this situation at times gave rise to what Bello called 'superstitious purism'. But it would be wrong to consider this attitude to be a general one. Above all it was not the position of the leading figures such as Bello[55] and Cuervo,[56] who seem to have pre-

[55] 'I feel it is important to preserve the language of our fathers in as pure a condition as possible, as a providential means of communication and a fraternal bond between the various nations of Spanish origin distributed over two continents. But what I venture to recommend to you is not a superstitious purism' ('Prólogo' to the *Gramática,* in *Obras completas* 4.11 [Caracas, 1951]).

[56] 'We are as far then from thinking that one should today write the same as in the time of the Philips, as from the opposite extreme of accepting the ill-advised innovations of those writers who, not being able to attract the attention of the public with new ideas, disfigure and variously color the language with exotic or outlandish words and phrases' ('Prólogo' to *Apuntaciones críticas,* in *Obras*

ferred a compromise of approximating rather than identifying with the Spanish model. Today the educated usage of each republic is accepted as correct Spanish.

Only Miguel Antonio Caro and Cuervo devoted careful thought to deliberate intervention in usage. The former develops the subject in his magnificent essay 'Del uso en sus relaciones con el lenguaje',[57] and the latter does so in the prologue to the *Apuntaciones críticas sobre el lenguaje bogotano*.[58] Caro shows, with abundant erudition, that Horace's well-known opinion on respect for usage as the 'arbiter, judge and standard of the language', must not be taken to mean the capricious usage of the common people or of the ignorant masses, but rather the creative usage (*genitor usus*) of those who know the language and are qualified to direct it and lay out guidelines for it, as are skilled writers and people who are experts in matters of language. In this usage there is — he says — a factor of 'greater value than instinctive spontaneity, namely the rational freedom of those people of superior talent who with generous efforts clarify and broaden the limits of their native language'.[59] For his part, Cuervo maintains that 'it is necessary to distinguish between usage, which creates a rule, and abuse, which should be eradicated. Being respectable, general and up-to-date are characteristics of the former. No one doubts that in matters of language the common people can never challenge the pre-eminence of cultured persons; but it is also certain that something from the sphere of the former can spread to that of the latter in special circumstances and places.'[60]

Such notable agreement and assurance in the opinions of these two leaders who are counted among the first members of the Colombian Academy, which is the dean of the Latin American associate academies, without doubt must have decisively influenced the criterion utilized by these associations in directing linguistic usage. This criterion did not differ in general outline from that which guided the Spanish Academy's normative work since its founding.

The theoretical position of the current presidents of the academies has continued to be the same as that of the founders, perhaps with a greater breadth of criteria, owing to an increase in linguistic studies and the access the specialists in this discipline

---

1.13 [Bogotá, 1954]). The same idea is advanced, with further elaborations, in the 'Prólogo' to *Apuntaciones*[7] [ibid. 1.32-3]. The evolution of Cuervo's thoughts on utilizing Castilian Spanish as the model of speech is well-known. Adopting as his motto at the beginning of his work a phrase by Puigblanch which summed up this thought, the linguist from Bogotá reached this conclusion at the end of his life: 'When the Spaniards faithfully maintain the official model, their authority is reason itself; when we Latin Americans maintain it and the Spaniards depart from it, we can properly call them to order and not change our own usages' ('Prólogo' to *Apuntaciones*[7] [ibid. 1.44]).

[57] An address read before the Colombian Academy in the inaugural session of August 6, 1881, and published in *El Repertorio Colombiano* 7.89-136 (1881); also in his *Obras completas* 5.234-75 (Bogotá, 1928).

[58] *Obras* 1.19-101 (Bogotá, 1954). This prologue reproduces the manuscript that Cuervo had left prepared for the sixth edition, but which the publishers did not include in it.

[59] *Obras completas* 5.257 (Bogotá, 1928).

[60] *Obras* 1.11 (Bogotá, 1954). It is to be noted that Cuervo preserved these sentences in his text from the first edition (1867-72) to the last edition prepared by him before his death in 1911, which proves the continuity of his thought in a matter of such importance.

have had to the traditional associations. With the linguists' counseling or direct intervention, all aspects of the language have been the object of study and have been subjected to the normative efforts of the academies. The latter have employed other means to disseminate their ideas to a wider public which is not composed of professional men of letters. In their watchfulness over the purity and correctness of the language they have attempted to influence (of course not always with success) the modern means of communication such as radio broadcasts, motion pictures, television, the press, public posters and announcements and the signs on businesses and stores. The Colombian Academy succeeded in getting the National Congress to pass Law 002 of August 6, 1960, called *Ley de defensa del idioma,* and a subsequent statutory decree in 1964. The use of foreign languages in documents of official business and in the names of educational establishments, cultural, social or sports centers, hotels, restaurants and, in general, in concerns or services open to the public is prohibited.[61] In the Fourth Congress of Academies held in Buenos Aires, on the iniciative of Nicaragua and Costa Rica, a recommendation to the academies of countries where legislation to uphold the Spanish language does not exist was approved, so that these academies might take steps to bring about the adoption of laws relating to this matter.[62] And Adolfo Berro García affirms: 'In the Municipality of Montevideo, the advertisements and signs to be exhibited by merchants in front of their businesses are subjected to a prior examination'.[63]

In the newspapers of some Latin American capitals articles on correct usage, written by academy members, frequently appear. Arturo Capdevila maintains a permanent column in *La Prensa* of Buenos Aires on this subject and so does Luis Flórez in the Bogotá *El Tiempo.* Also the Venezuelan Academy publishes a periodical leaflet, *La limpieza de la lengua,* to correct expressions common in that country.

A very generalized form of spreading linguistic norms is employed by the more active academies, especially the Argentine Academy and the Colombian Academy, which are consistent in considering the public's opinion. The Argentine Academy has now been able to prepare two volumes of its *Acuerdos acerca del idioma*[64] and the Colombian Academy publishes in its bimonthly *Boletín* the solutions to major written questions, and takes care of many others verbally. By a legal arrangement, the Colombian Academy is a consultative body to the government in matters of language and is entrusted with 'the work of continuing, extending and intensifying the campaign for the defense and purity of the Spanish language'. The matters discussed ordinarily involve the lexicon, neologisms, technical terms, trade-marks and patents, but also

[61] The texts of the law and of the decree can be found in Oscar Echeverri Mejía, *Nuestro idioma al día*[2] 20-5 (Cali, 1965).

[62] Informe de la Comisión de enseñanza y moralidad del idioma del Ministerio de Justicia e Instrucción Pública, *Conclusiones del Cuarto Congreso de Academias de la Lengua* 23 (Buenos Aires, 1965).

[63] 'Vigilancia para la conservación de la pureza del idioma castellano', *Memoria del Primer Congreso de Academias de la Lengua Española* 131 (Mexico, 1952).

[64] The first volume (Buenos Aires, 1947) brings together the agreements reached from 1931 to 1943 and the second (Buenos Aires, 1954) assembles those from 1944 to 1951. These agreements also appear conveniently in *BAAL.*

frequently relate to problems of grammatical theory and to doubts about the legitimacy of certain constructions or the interpretation of legal texts.

The Hispanic people, in general, have a deep-rooted feeling of affection for their language, in spite of the feelings of indifference or snobbishness that penetrate deeply in certain environments. Responsible people in government and in institutions try to stimulate and educate this kind of protective instinct, above all among those in the schools, but also among the public in large cities. To this end frequent literary and philological contests are held which are reported by the press or broadcast over the radio. In some countries a 'Language Day' is celebrated (on April 23rd, the anniversary of Cervantes' death, in Argentina, Colombia, Cuba, and perhaps in other countries as well) and public events such as lectures, radio broadcasts, cultural weeks, provincial conventions and literary contests in which academy members often participate are frequent. At any rate the role the academy associations play in this work as guides and educators of society in matters of language is evident. This role correctly belongs to them on account of their historical background, the ends to which they are dedicated and the tradition they defend on the basis of worthy spiritual values.[65]

We will present below a panorama of what this work has concretely been in the areas of orthography, pronunciation, lexicon and grammar. We hope this presentation will bring to light the community's determined will with regard to the protection of its own language system.

2.2.1. *Orthography*

Angel Rosenblat has aptly said that Spanish orthography 'is a historical product that undergoes continual change'.[66] Its agitated history, before and after the Academy, indicates that this has been a sore point which has always disturbed the theoreticians of the language and points out the difficulties inherent in trying to establish a practical norm that will be respected by everyone. Certainly the Royal Spanish Academy has had the greatest influence, for obvious historical reasons, and it can even be said that we live with the system it imposed and disseminated. But to achieve this many difficulties had to be overcome.

The dispute over orthographic questions between the partisans of etymology and

[65] The distinction between the linguistic fact and the fact that concerned the academy was expounded in its true dimension by Ramón Menéndez Pidal in his address before the Chilean Academy on November 8, 1914: 'Everything that is said is a *linguistic fact* that is acceptable for a historical grammar, but not everything that is said is *good linguistic usage*, acceptable for a prescriptive grammar. The latter is the grammar entrusted with educating and instructing new generations, and with seeing that the language, as a basic function of the human spirit, has the greatest possible worth, effectiveness and significance' (see *Boletín de la Academia Chilena* 1:1.1-7 [1915]). Amado Alonso develops the point in his article 'Intereses filológicos e intereses académicos en el estudio de la lengua', *BAAL* 1.7-14 (1933), reprinted in *Universidad de Antioquia* (Medellín) 4.95-100 (1937) and in his book *La Argentina y la nivelación del idioma* 73-83 (Buenos Aires, 1943).

[66] 'Las ideas ortográficas de Bello', in Andrés Bello, *Obras completas* 5.IX-CXXXVIII (Caracas, 1951). This work is an excellent historico-critical outline of Castilian orthography.

those of pronunciation found support for both points of view among the writings of sixteenth and seventeenth century Spanish grammarians. At the beginning, the Madrid association decided in favor of etymology; but it then amended its theories until it arrived, little by little, through various editions of its *Ortografía*, at an intermediate solution which, though giving primary emphasis to pronunciation and usage, does not wholly reject etymology.

In 1823 Juan García del Río and Andrés Bello's important paper, 'Indicaciones sobre la conveniencia de simplificar y uniformar la ortografía en América', was published.[67] The two illustrious Latin Americans firmly defend the criterion of pronunciation and oppose the criteria of etymology and usage. Their aim is simplification, which implies both simplicity and uniformity, conditions which they esteem as the most effective means to improve the educational level of the Latin American people. They go even further than the Academy in the direction of reform because they are concerned with the specific problems of Latin America and with harmonizing the political liberty of the new states with submission to the basic norms of the literary language of Spain.

In 1842 the militant figure of the Argentine Domingo Faustino Sarmiento appears in Santiago, Chile. He resolutely demands a *Latin American reform* of the orthography, that is, a total accommodation to the pronunciation of the New World users of the language, who 'with regard to letters will have nothing to do with the Language Academy or with the Spanish nation, either now or in the future'.[68] After bitter polemics in which Bello has to adopt the position of arbiter in the face of Sarmiento's extremism, the School of Philosophy and Humanities of the University of Chile decided on a reform which, while audacious, does not go as far as that defended by Sarmiento. Rather, it coincides with that of Bello and García. But the outcries of rebellion against the Academy do not persist long and the Venezuelan leader himself begins to yield until, in his capacity as President of the University of Chile, he ends by asking the Minister of Public Instruction to abandon the revised orthography 'in order to obviate the difficulties of a useless teaching and of a lack of uniformity'.[69] The academy orthography is not fully generalized until near the end of the century. In Chile, which was the last holdout of the Latin American reform, the norm of the academy is adopted in public documents by an official decree in 1927.

The creation of associate academies contributes to the stabilization of usage in the sense that these organizations promote uniformity by encouraging the sacrifice of deep-rooted political and national prejudices. However, there were occasional attacks against the academy's usage, even after the founding of the first associations, since an eagerness for new spellings has always persisted. In his time, this tendency was fought against by such polemic pens as that of Miguel Antonio Caro, the defender of the

[67] Published for the first time in *La Biblioteca Americana* (London) 1.50-62 (1823), and soon reprinted with some additions in *El Repertorio Americano* (London), 1.27-41 (1826). See Bello's *Obras completas* 5.71-87 (Caracas, 1951).

[68] Quoted by Rosenblat from Bello's *Obras completas* 5.CVII (Caracas, 1951).

[69] Rosenblat, *ibid.*, 5.XXI.

academies, who in 1867 expressed the opinion that 'to surrender the scepter of orthography exclusively to pronunciation amounts to delivering it to a monster with a hundred heads'.[70] The reformist urge as well as the tenacious defense of any system whatsoever, no matter how arbitrary it might be, were at all times motivated by the good intention of putting an end to *orthographic anarchy*, which was considered to be one of the greatest calamities for the dissemination of culture and an open door to incomprehensibility and isolation.[71]

The most important event in the present century is the publication by the Royal Spanish Academy of the *Nuevas normas de prosodia y ortografía* (Madrid, 1952). This work constitutes an effort to further the academy's aim of making the Spanish orthographic system ever more coherent and of avoiding differences between what is practiced by the *Gramática* and by the *Diccionario*. It sanctions, moreover, many of the innovations defended by the Latin American philologists since Bello's time. This publication produced a generally favorable reaction in Latin America, although there were observations and criticisms, some of which were quite reasonable, such as those related to the freedom in which the Academy left stress, prosody and orthography in certain cases of vowel clusters.[72]

The *Nuevas normas* achieved wide acceptance at the time of the eighteenth edition of the *Diccionario* (1956). The latter was already in print when the Association of Academies resolved, in the Congress of Madrid, that the *Nuevas normas* were of a provisional nature until they were coordinated and incorporated in the next edition of the *Gramática* and until the observations of scholars and the practice of writers made

[70] 'Reacción ortográfica', *La República* (Bogotá), núm. 24 (diciembre de 1867) and in *Obras completas* 5.9 (Bogotá, 1928). 'In Spain and Latin America the *v* will be eliminated because it is a dead letter so far as pronunciation is concerned. In part of Spain and in all of Latin America the *z* will disappear. In some places the *x* will disappear, in others, the *ll*, or the *s* (*hablamo* is said for *hablamos* ['we speak'] on the coasts), or the *d* in certain words (*ciudá* [instead of *ciudad* 'city'], *soldao* [instead of *soldado* 'soldier'])'.

[71] Complaints about the anarchy prevailing in matters of orthography, especially due to the reformist efforts, are constant among academy writers of the past century. The Colombian José María Samper, on inviting eminent Chileans in 1885 to found an academy of the language, cites this fact as one of the most convincing reasons that academies are needed (See Miguel Luis Amunátegui Reyes, *La Real Academia Española y sus relaciones con sus hijas de América* 15-6 [Santiago de Chile, 1943]). On the same subject, in 1884, José María Izaguirre in behalf of the Ministry of Education of Guatemala and José Manuel Marroquín, president of the Colombian Academy, had exchanged interesting letters (see *Anuario de la Academia Colombiana* 1:2.50-3 [1874-1910]).

[72] For example, *período* or *periodo* ['period'], *alvéolo* or *alveolo* ['alveolus], *gladíolo* or *gladiolo* ['gladiolus']. This work also allowed either penultimate or antepenultimate stress for words such as *omoplato* and *omóplato* ['shoulder blade'], *pentagrama* and *pentágrama* ['musical staff'], etc. See Julio Casares, 'Las *Nuevas Normas de Prosodia y Ortografía* y su repercusión en América', *BAE* 35.321-46 (1955). In the Second Congress of Academies in Madrid (1956), the *Nuevas Normas* were extensively discussed. In the *Memoria* of this meeting, see the papers by the Colombian Academy (pp. 139-44), by the Mexican Alfonso Junco (pp. 150-60), by the Argentine Rodolfo M. Ragucci S. D. B. (pp. 160-88), by the Colombian Roberto Restrepo (pp. 188-96), by the Uruguayan Adolfo Berro García (pp. 197-204) and by the Spaniard Julio Casares (pp. 204-10). The Colombian Academy approved its own norms for the disputed points 'until the Association of Academies of the Spanish Language arrives at a definitive solution'; see the pamphlet: Academia Colombiana, *Nuevas normas de ortografía* (Bogotá, 1956).

them uniform. They have no obligatory effect on disputed areas in which individuals and the academies maintain their freedom of decision, as long as unanimous and definitive agreement has not been reached.

Those who favor total agreement in matters of pronunciation make use of various arguments in their attempts to win acceptance for their point of view. The Cuban Academy presented a new 'orthography reform project'[73] to the Third Congress of Academies in Bogotá (1960), designed to obtain a maximal simplification of the orthography that would facilitate the teaching of writing to the common people. The assembly, after careful study, decided that this project could only be considered as a document the Spanish Academy should have in mind when it takes a new step 'in the process of simplifying the orthography in a prudent and gradual manner, as it has been doing since the middle of the eighteenth century'. In the Congress of Buenos Aires (1964) the Philippine Academy proposed a radical simplification of the orthography to facilitate the learning of Spanish by non-Spanish speakers. This proposal was rejected but due to the Philippine delegate's insistence, the use of phonetic symbols as a temporary step preliminary to the acquisition of a knowledge of the general orthography was authorized for the teaching of Spanish in his country. It was even admitted that this orthographic simplification might be extended to other uses if it contributed to the survival of Spanish in the Philippines. However, the Philippine Academy was warned that the adoption of a different orthographic system could presuppose a cultural isolation which would be more serious than the damage it tried to avoid.[74]

Spanish orthography nowadays is acceptably uniform and can pride itself on being one of the orthographies that has best succeeded in reconciling the written and verbal signs. Vacillations continue to exist, above all in the marking of orthographic accents or tildes. There is no dispute, in spite of the *seseo* [the pronunciation of Spanish *c* and *z* like *s*] and *yeísmo* [the pronunciation of Spanish *ll* like *y*], with regard to the writing of *s*, *c*, *z*, and *x*, or of *ll* as opposed to *y*; nor with regard to the use of *b* and *v* even though there is no difference in how they are pronounced, or of *j* and *g*, in spite of their phonetic identity in a large number of cases. The silent *h* in initial or medial position, although much opposed, continues to maintain itself with notable firmness. The use of capital letters and other symbols, as well as punctuation, undergo the

[73] See *Tercer Congreso de Academias de la Lengua Española. Actas y labores* 265-75 (Bogotá, 1961). The resolution of the Congress with regard to this project is found on p. 174.

[74] See 'IV Congreso de Academias de la Lengua', *BAE* 44.558-9 (1964). In all the congresses of academies, ample and well-reasoned studies have been presented to defend the motto: 'for each phoneme one symbol and for each symbol one phoneme'. See in the *Memoria del Primer Congreso* (Mexico, 1952) the following: Adolfo Berro García (Uruguay), 'Reforma ortográfica de la lengua española' (pp. 138-47), Gustavo Adolfo Mejía Ricart (Mexico), 'Simplificación ortográfica' (pp. 172-4), Roberto Restrepo (Colombia), 'Modificaciones en ortografía castellana' (pp. 185-6). In the *Memoria del Segundo Congreso* 130-5 (Madrid, 1956) another report by Adolfo Berro García on the same subject appears. Since the *Memoria del Cuarto Congreso* of Buenos Aires (1964) has not yet been published, we are only acquainted with the reform project presented by the Philippine delegate José Lauchengco to which we refer in the text.

natural alternations that result from writer's expressive aims or, at times, from the whims of typesetters and publishers. But even in these details a unifying tendency prevails.

This result, subject of course to further improvement, is due principally to the work of the academies of language, both Spanish and Latin American, along with the contribution of eminent philologists from both sides of the Atlantic. The latter, with their arguments and criticisms, have succeeded in showing the convenience of adopting this or that symbol. What is certain is that on this point more than any other, the authority of the academy is respected by governments, institutions, teachers, publishers and individual writers, who are all agreed upon seeking the greatest simplicity and uniformity of the system until it is obtained.

2.2.2. *Pronunciation*

Although some aspects of Spanish pronunciation, such as that of stress, are intimately and necessarily connected with questions of orthography, it is preferable to study the problem of pronunciation separately. In general, this is a much more complex and difficult problem than that of the physical writing of the words, since it involves an aspect of language in which, more than in any other, the perennial changeability of the language is evident. The work of the academies in this area is limited by natural dialectal barriers and is much more conditioned by social and geographical variations than are matters of orthography or grammar. Modes of pronunciation exist, such as the Latin American *seseo* and *yeísmo*, which is a city phenomenon found both in Spain and Latin America. Both *seseo* and *yeísmo* are so deeply rooted that the academies have given up their determination to correct them and have chosen to legitimize them, by assigning them full value as cultured variants of the same pronunciation.[75]

Still, it seems that two fairly well-defined periods can be distinguished in normative work with regard to matters of pronunciation: the first corresponds to the period of the academies' prosody and orthoëpy and the second to that of the modern studies of phonetics and phonology. In 1852, when Andrés Bello had already circulated two editions (1835 and 1850) of his famous *Principios de la Ortología y Métrica de la Lengua Castellana*, in Santiago, Chile, the Spanish Academy a little tardily became concerned with the problem of pronunciation. Another edition of this work had also been circulated in Caracas in 1844. Bello's doctrines were already so highly regarded by the Madrid association that the latter found no better course than to ask the Latin American for authorization to adopt his treatise as the official text on the subject. Even though this project did not turn out well in its entirety, the foundation for the academy's teachings, as set forth for the first time in the *Gramática* of 1870, is basically

[75] For *seseo*, see Resolución IX, *Memoria del Segundo Congreso de Academias de la Lengua Española* 412 (Madrid, 1956); for *yeísmo*, 'IV Congreso de Academias de la Lengua', *BAE* 44.558 (1964).

Bello's.[76] The latter, naturally, had channeled the tradition that originated during the Spanish Renaissance, without deviating from the scientific principle that guided him in all his works on language, that of describing language as an autonomous system without relying on the Latin model. On that and on his carefully considered pedagogical and Latin-Americanist aims rests much of his originality. We have already seen in 2.1.2. how Bello's book had its fitting complement in M. A. Caro's *Notas*, published in Bogotá in 1882. Together with the *Notas*, Bello's work continued to be a point of reference for everything concerning prosody and orthoëpy, at least until the development of experimental phonetics, which removed orthoëpic studies from their routine and provided them with new scientific bases.[77]

During the period of orthoëpic studies there were determined efforts to correct certain pronunciations, such as displacements of stress, that invaded Castilian Spanish during the eighteenth century and were also common in Spanish America. The mania for stressing the antepenultimate syllable (*méndigo* [for *mendigo* 'beggar'], *périto* [for *perito* 'expert'], *médula* [for *medula* 'marrow']), for example, was stubbornly opposed by prescriptivists everywhere and censured as a pedantic or barbarous innovation. The establishment of penultimate stress in a great many words that at the end of the century showed a strong tendency to change their stress is a good indication of how much the academies accomplished. These organizations were supported with regard to this matter by the schools and by the best writers and poets. Due to this energetic repression, the acoustic physiognomy of a good part of the Spanish lexicon was successfully preserved, at least among educated speakers and reading aloud, in recitations, and in the theater.

The scientific trend which was initiated with the works of Wulff, Lenz, Araujo and other philologists of the past century,[78] has culminated in the studies by Tomás

[76] One can read the letters exchanged by the Spanish Academy and Bello in Samuel Gili Gaya, 'Introducción a los estudios ortológicos y métricos de Bello', of Bello's *Obras completas* 6.XXI-XXV (Caracas, 1954). It is only proper to mention Mariano José Sicilia, *Lecciones elementales de Ortologia y Prosodia*, 2 volumes (Paris, 1827-28), among the principal predecessors of Bello in the matter of orthoëpy.

[77] Felipe Robles Dégano's *Ortología clásica de la lengua castellana* (Madrid, 1905) should also be mentioned as one of the most important works on this subject.

[78] The first phonetic descriptions of Spanish appeared at the end of the nineteenth century, in works by foreign philologists, and were basically dialectal studies. For example, those of the Swede Fredrik Wulff, 'Un Chapitre de phonétique andalouse', *Recueil de mémoires philologiques présenté à Monsieur Gaston Paris par ses élèves suédois* 211-60 (Stockholm, 1889) and of the German Rudolf Lenz, 'Chilenische Studien', *Phonetische Studien* 5.272-92 (1891-92), 6.18-34, 151-66, and 274-301 (1892-93), to which can be added the valuable observations contained in Hugo Schuchardt, 'Die Cantes Flamencos', *ZRPh* 5.249-322 (1881). The first Spanish phonetician was Fernando Araujo, but neither his *Estudios de fonética castellana* (Toledo, 1894) nor the later books by F. M. Josselyn, *Etudes de phonétique espagnole* (Paris, 1907), and M. A. Colton, *La phonétique castillane* (Paris, 1909), can be considered satisfactory. The true study of Spanish phonetics begins with the work of Tomás Navarro Tomás and his disciples, carried out within the framework of the philological school of Menéndez Pidal in Madrid.

Under the simple title of antecedents we will mention the work of two Latin Americans in the field of phonetics during this period. The Colombian Academy associate member Ezequiel Uricoechea wrote *El alfabeto fonético de la lengua castellana* (Madrid, 1872), in which there are skillful observations

Navarro and other experts on phonetics. These studies mark a different phase in the search for a type of correct pronunciation that will be respected as a model and will be as remote from affectation as from provincial vulgarisms.[79] The Latin American academies are familiar with the movement to renovate pronunciation and have tried to accommodate their purifying work to modern trends. In 1952 the Permanent Commission of the Association of Academies which met in Mexico appealed to Tomás Navarro to prepare a practical guide which would contain the principal rules needed to obtain the most respectable and uniform phonetic usage possible. The illustrious philologist acceded to the academy's petition and wrote his *Guía de la pronunciación española* (Mexico, 1956), although he accepted the fact that 'it would be an illusory ambition to hope to subject the pronunciation of all Spanish-speakers to a uniform discipline'. He affirmed, however, that one could speak of an attainable phonetic correctness, although not by reason 'of the place in which a person is born, but by reason of the education he receives'.[80]

The report that Rafael Lapesa presented to the Congress in Bogotá on behalf of the Spanish Academy, 'Medios para poner en ejecución el acuerdo No. XX del Congreso de México sobre la enseñanza y práctica en escuelas y colegios de la fonética normal del castellano literario',[81] provided a fully conscious examination of the problem. In this report it is recommended that the speech used in radio broadcasts should conform to some sort of cultivated diction; that records with the correct pronunciation for each country, 'minus its most notable peculiarities', be used to aid the teaching of this diction; and that recordings by literary men who represent the best diction in their respective regions also be utilized, so that by exchanging these recordings among the Hispanic countries, 'linguistic uniformity rather than diversity will be encouraged'. The group of measures that would need to be adopted was assigned in a

that show the acuteness of his singular talent. Cuervo, who in the first semester of 1894 had taken a phonetics course in Paris with Paul Passy, between 1892 and 1895 and in 1898 and 1899 worked on a vast dialectology of the Spanish of Europe and Latin America, part of which was published posthumously under the title of *Castellano popular y castellano literario* (see *Obras* 1.1321-660 [Bogotá, 1954]). Material from this work has been incorporated in the *Apuntaciones* beginning with the fifth edition of 1907. In this work, of which only the part on phonetics has been preserved, following an extensive and excellent chapter on general phonetics, based on Sweet, Sievers and Passy, Cuervo examines all the phenomena of the popular speech of the peninsula and of Latin America, demonstrating a complete command of this discipline. Naturally, the work is not based on direct observation but rather on dialectal forms gleaned from printed works.

[79] The classic work in this respect is the book by the patriarch of Spanish phonetics, Tomás Navarro Tomás, *Manual de pronunciación*[4] (Madrid, 1932). The various subsequent reprintings of this work in Madrid and New York follow this edition. The author has added to the New York edition, beginning with 1957, an appendix to bring the observations in the text up to date. In the *Manual* the correct pronunciation of the Spanish of Madrid during the first quarter of the twentieth century, as recommended by educated people, is described with a didactic aim (cf. Diego Catalán, *RomPh* 18.186, note 36 [1964-65]). The pamphlet by the same Navarro Tomás, *Compendio de ortología española* para la enseñanza de la pronunciación normal en relación con las diferencias dialectales[2] (Madrid, 1928), is a summary of this work, written for a lay audience.

[80] *Tercer Congreso de Academias de la Lengua Española. Actas y labores* 429 (Bogotá, 1961).

[81] *Tercer Congreso de Academias de la Lengua Española. Actas y labores* 428-32 (Bogotá, 1961).

recommendation to the Spanish Academy so that in the next edition of its *Gramática* it could specify 'vulgarisms that should be avoided and idiosyncratic expressions that need to be discouraged'. Meanwhile, in this respect, recourse should be had to the guidelines given by the previously mentioned *Guía* of Tomás Navarro and the *Lecciones de pronunciación española* (Bogotá, 1960; 2nd ed., 1963) by the Colombian academy member Luis Flórez.

Latin Americans and Spaniards are urged to make a maximum effort to moderate idiosyncratic features of pronunciation and intonation as a necessary sacrifice in the struggle against dissociative tendencies. But the total exclusion of the popular and local variations that give the language life and expressive charm is not considered. Study and moderation are needed. Let both Spaniards and Latin Americans observe, compare, analyze and strive to unite in a dialogue that will be both cultivated and normalizing.

Lexicon.

2.2.3.1. *Provincialisms.* — The copious provincial and regional vocabulary of Latin America has been the object of countless studies and has offered abundant material for the formation of collections in which the most varied criteria prevail. Some attempt only to note words that the authors judge to be native to their own soil and consider descriptive of its nature and customs; others try to get these words admitted to the Royal Academy's *Diccionario*; and finally, some try to contrast the words, as belonging either to vulgar speech or to a language of inferior lineage, with the purest and most proper words that are found in literature, serious discourse or the conversation of people in high positions. In any case, this effort by lexicographers as well as amateurs to emphasize the Latin American contribution to Spanish vocabulary has great utility as an attempt to classify and explain the facts, as a contribution of material for the compilation of an ideal dictionary of Latin-Americanisms, and, above all, as a means to dispel the danger of the fragmentation of the language prophesied by Cuervo and the other philologists of the past century. Evidently all those explanations of provincialisms, localisms, ruralisms and all sorts of popular words, upon multiplying and spreading, have succeeded in showing how the 'barbaric' element can be incorporated in the Hispanic cultural heritage.

In effect, the substrata of indigenous Latin American languages, Latin-Americanisms in the strict sense or native words (*canoa* ['canoe'], *cacique* ['chief'], *bohío* ['hut'], *yuca* ['yucca'], etc.), entered the Spanish lexicon as easily as those words that added prefixes and suffixes of Latin origin to their indigenous roots (*saban-ero* ['savanna dweller'], *cot-udo* ['goitrous'], *macan-ear* ['to exaggerate, boast, joke'], *enchich-ado* ['drunk with *chicha*' (drink made from fermented corn)], etc.) or those that were traditionally used names in Spain and were now applied to kinds of animals or vegetables in Latin America (*gallinazo* ['turkey buzzard'], *armadillo* ['armadillo'], *piña* ['pineapple'], *higuera* ['fig tree'], etc.).[82] The Spanish Academy has been incorporating a growing number of these words in the general dictionary and continues to do so in each edition of its work as soon as the stability, spread, geographical area and social level of these items are verified. If the labels 'Latin-Americanism' or 'Mexicanism', 'Colombianism', etc. (indicating their origin in a specific country) by which those words are designated are not always exact and are even at times incorrect, it is due to the lack of information from which the editors of the *Diccionario* suffer. As Rafael Lapesa lamented in the report he presented to the Third Congress of Academies on the *Diccionario histórico*:[83] 'Those complaints with fear of disregard and unjust disdain! Those pamphlets with four hundred or six hundred errors from the "Madrid Dictionary", most of which are true, but many of which are unjustly heralded'.

The problem of Latin-Americanisms and their incorporation in the general dictionary must be related to the present huge undertaking of the Royal Spanish Academy: the *Diccionario Histórico de la Lengua Española*, 'the most complete inventory possible of the lexicon coined by the Spanish-speaking people in eleven centuries of history and over an area of two continents'.[84] In this work the Latin-Americanisms with literary endorsement that the Madrid lexicographers succeed in documenting should have their own place. In the first fascicle alone of those published, 220 Latin American writers are cited and seven hundred titles of works by Latin Americans are utilized. The academies, especially those of Argentina, Colombia, Chile and Bolivia, have aided in the task of compiling this dictionary by providing regular contributions and continue to be concerned that the lexicons of their respective countries are included in this important lexicographic treasure. But 'we would like to have' — says Lapesa — 'more evidence on Latin American lexical usage, whether it be identical to or different from peninsular usage'.[85]

The complete and documented recording of the common vocabulary, and even of that which is limited to certain regions, is considered a necessity by the Spanish-speaking people. And this is a task that is considered well-suited to the academies, which it is acknowledged have sufficient authority to carry it out. The lack of a work of this nature (the Spanish *Webster*, as has often been said) causes some people to suppose that Spanish is a language of less richness than English or French, without having taken into account the normative character that our dictionary has today. That selection of words, legitimate and illegitimate, as well as the distinction between good and bad usage, constitutes the principal weapon in the defense of linguistic integrity.

[82] The bibliography on this subject is very extensive and exceeds the limits of this work. For academy work in this field, see 2.2.3.1.

[83] 'Informe relativo al Diccionario Histórico de la Lengua Española', *Tercer Congreso de Academias de la Lengua Española. Actas y labores* 103-7 (Bogotá, 1961).

[84] Ibid. 103. A detailed exposition of the aims, plan and method of this work can be seen in Julio Casares, *Introducción a la lexicografía moderna* 245-310 (Madrid, 1950).

[85] Ibid. 107. On the present state of the writing of the *Diccionario Histórico* and of the rest of the lexicographic works of the Spanish Academy, see the paper presented by Rafael Lapesa at the Fourth Congress of Academies in Buenos Aires (1964), 'Los diccionarios de la Academia', *BAE* 44.425-30 (1964).

The academies cannot leave it in the hands of just anyone, allowing the proliferation of dictionaries with the goal of commercial distribution on a large scale and doubtful scientific backing, since these dictionaries spread anarchism and confusion in the criterion of the public, on the pretext of filling the needs of contemporary life.[86]

This normative policy concerning the lexicon is not opposed to an exhaustive compilation such as that of the *Diccionario histórico*, a modern version of the *Diccionario de Autoridades* with which the Spanish Academy began its lexicographic work. The six fascicles that have appeared up to now (eight hundred pages, from *a* to *aducción* [Madrid, 1960-65]; beginning with 1965, the Academy hopes to be able to publish three fascicles per year) are a magnificent example of what this ambitious work, conceived as a gigantic monument to Hispanic unity, will become, without affecting the continuation of the parallel enrichment of the common *Diccionario* that represents the spirit and the governing intention of the academies.

2.2.3.2. *Neologisms.* — If the concepts of *casticismo* and 'purism' are closely linked to the image that the great majority of people have of the language academies, it is due above all to the academies' determination to purify the lexicon. Nevertheless those concepts are sufficiently blurred and confused even in the Spanish Academy's own dictionary (*casticista* is there defined as: 'a purist in the way the language is used'). And it is certain that each concept has sufficiently clear and distinguishing connotative nuances. *Casticismo* is related to what is traditional and of high breeding, to what is historical and national; 'purism', in general, is the negative position of he who rejects a neologism only because of the fact that it is strange. *Casticismo* is opposed to 'barbarism', but also to *culteranismo*, 'regionalism', and to everything which does not have roots in classical literary usage; it excludes any baroque or excessively modernizing efforts. 'Purism' especially confined itself to rejecting the admission of linguistic borrowings at the time of the Gallic invasion of the eighteenth century and today limits itself to the repudiation of Anglicisms. Both are a foundation for the 'purity of the language', whose exaggerations irritated Padre Feijoo: 'Purity! It should sooner be called *poverty*, nakedness, misery and dullness'.[87]

In the beginning the Spanish Academy was decidedly purist for reasons of national defense and because of the conviction that the Spanish language was sufficient to express all that one might want to say. The Latin American academies supported these ideas, although national honor caused them to compromise with regard to the native vocabulary, which was tolerated much more than similar phenomena pertinent to morphology and syntax. The well-known change of criterion that has taken place

[86] Consult R. Menéndez Pidal, 'El diccionario que deseamos', prologue to *Vox. Diccionario general ilustrado de la lengua española* (Barcelona, 1945) by Samuel Gili Gaya, which is an outstanding synthesis and masterly exposition of Spanish lexicographic theory. In it are established legitimate criteria for neologisms and archaisms, technical terms, barbarisms, localisms, etymology and chronology, synonymy and the emotional and social values of words.

[87] Quoted by Fernando Lázaro Carreter, *Las ideas lingüísticas en España durante el siglo XVIII* 263 (Madrid, 1949), a work in which is found the same differentiation of concepts we have expounded.

during this century in the organizations that govern the language perhaps has not spread enough for the public to be aware of it. The academies continue to be considered by many as organizations that constrain speech and restrict freedom of expression. They are 'Cerberuses of the language', someone sarcastically remarked. This opinion is supported by exaggerations that persist as the remains of the former impoverishing attitude and by the formalism the academies still maintain in their official procedures. But frequently the narrowness of criteria originates instead with certain authors of scholastic manuals, reporters or professors of Spanish who, with excessive zeal, take upon themselves the prescriptive mission. And it is very likely that a good part of the blame usually assigned to the work of the academy for encouraging archaisms, and for being formalistic or reactionarily conservative, actually lies with overzealous academy members, partisans of purity at any cost, rather than with the directors and leaders of the real governing action of usage. What is certain is that the academy associations today show a great permeability to new linguistic ideas, which produces a scandal among those spirits who insist on dogmatic censure, which is always an easier and more expeditious way to resolve problems of correctness or incorrectness.

The traditional aim of 'purity of language' which reached its apogee in the fight against Gallicisms is continued today in the aim of 'defense of the language'. And this defense, first of all, is against Anglicisms, considered to be one of the greatest threats to the denaturalization and fragmentation of the Spanish language. This is the case above all in Spanish America, where in many places the influence of English is felt, for obvious reasons, with an enslaving force. The Spanish American academies have intensified their efforts in this difficult struggle against Anglicisms because they consider them to be dangerous for the fundamental unity of the language.[88] The three volumes of the *Memorias* in which the resolutions and reports of the congresses of academies are compiled, abound with works on the correction of Anglicisms and the same thing is true of the *Anuarios* and *Boletines* that are published as the official organs of these organizations. Of all of them, it is worth mentioning the *Diccionario de anglicismos* (Panama, 1950; 2nd ed., Madrid, 1964) by the Panamanian academy member Ricardo J. Alfaro, as the most successful work because it is both complete and systematic. Some thirteen hundred items are included and condemned usages are classified into eleven categories such as unnecessary borrowings or Spanish words whose phonetics or meaning have been altered by the influence of English. The problem of Anglicisms, like that of the Gallicisms of long ago, is the subject of long controversies in Spanish-speaking nations and constitutes the specific object of one of the principal missions of the academies: that of *cleansing* the language of impurities. However,

[88] In countries distant from the United States which have had a high rate of non-Spanish speaking European immigration, principally Italian, the battle against foreign words has been above all a struggle against Italianisms, which generally exist as vulgarisms. Such is the case in Argentina and Uruguay. Giovanni Meo Zilio has been studying these Italianisms in the Spanish of Latin America for several years; see his overall description: 'Italianismos generales en el español rioplatense', *Thesaurus* 20.68-119 (1965).

this intent is no longer being fulfilled, as Dámaso Alonso, thinking of the improvement and upkeep of a house, graphically expressed it: 'The problem is quite different: that the house does not collapse upon us'.[89]

To prevent 'the house from collapsing', or the disintegration of Spanish from taking place, Dámaso Alonso proposes an academy program based on two points: 1) *the preservation of all that is common to the language of educated Latin Americans*, that is, to not fight against the dissimilarities that already exist in their speech, which for the moment do not endanger the linguistic community; 2) *any new element accepted should be held in common.* One of the most active factors in the lexical differentiation of the Hispanic world has been the avalanche of words that designate objects of modern technical civilization. In this respect Alonso sees a marked division in the Spanish of Latin America: the upper half of Spanish America has terms relating to modern civilization that come from English, while those of the lower half come from French (Spain generally falls into this category). But even within these categories there exist differences from country to country, because in some countries the English or French word has been adapted and in others it has been translated, so that at times if two different manufacturers introduce a new product in two different nations, the product will be given a different name in each country. Alonso proposes a coordinated emergency service among all the academies of the Hispanic world to uniformly baptize the equipment that modern technology develops at such a rapid pace, before terms limited to one national practice are generalized. The task that Dámaso Alonso proposes for an interacademy organization such as the Association of Academies of the Spanish Language is to preserve the unity of the language. In his opinion, this should be the principal concern of the academies today, and in the presence of this task, any other type of linguistic interest must occupy a secondary position: 'The struggle for the purity of the language could be the password and sign of the nineteenth century but cannot be our principal objective today: our struggle must be to prevent the disintegration of our common language. We welcome impurities or foreign words if they adapt well to our phonetic pattern and if all Spanish-speakers adopt them of one accord! "Linguistic unity"; that should be our principal concern.'[90]

As for Anglicisms, the criterion for dealing with them is widely variable, since this matter involves speakers from such different geographical areas, of such varied interests and widely different educational and cultural levels. This is the case because Anglicisms constitute a common matter, about which everyone feels he is qualified to pass judgment. While many English words have gained total acceptance in Latin America and in one way or another have been adapted to Spanish phonetics and spelling: (*fútbol* ['football'], *béisbol* ['baseball'], *suéter* ['sweater'], *overol* ['overall(s)']),

[89] 'Unidad y defensa del idioma', *Memoria del Segundo Congreso de Academias de la Lengua Española* 36 (Madrid, 1956). One should read this fundamental work by Dámaso Alonso which includes pages 33-48 of the previously cited *Memoria*, in order to understand the linguistic policy of the academies in recent years.

[90] Ibid. 39-46 and the paper presented to the Fourth Congress of Academies in Buenos Aires (1964) with the same title, 'Unidad y defensa del idioma', *BAE* 44.392 (1964).

others are accepted in one place and rejected in another: (*record* ['(sport) record'], *chance* ['chance'], *score* ['score'], *parquear* ['to park']), or are the object of polemics with regard to their translation, substitution or accommodation (hall = *vestíbulo*, *recibidor*, etc.; closet = *alacena*, *ropero*, etc.; hobby = *pasatiempo*, *afición*, etc.). The academies, following the example of the Spanish Academy, have adopted a tolerant policy and have accepted a large amount of this Anglicized vocabulary which becomes official with its admission to the dictionary, as willful usage or necessity sanction it.[91] An attempt is made to avoid falling into one of the two untenable extremes of recalcitrant purism or excessive liberty. And although this attempt frequently results in the nonconformity of both extremes, the academies strive to maintain this difficult equilibrium and trust that the vitality of the language will little by little aid in the assimilation of the great mass of foreign words, as has happened in other periods with similar characteristics.

2.2.3.3. *Technical terms.* — A specific problem of present-day Spanish has been that of absorbing the abundant vocabulary arising from the developments of modern science and technology, almost all of which is of foreign origin. In the eighteenth century Feijoo recognized that while the language had been sufficient unto itself 'without the aid of another language', it was necessary to exempt 'some special words whose loan from one nation to another is indispensable'.[92] Padre Feijoo's *special words* had ample space in the later works of Terreros[93] and Capmany.[94] But the preoccupation with the subject of scientific and technical vocabulary died in the nineteenth century and has been resurrected only in our time. Spanish and Latin American academy members have sounded a new warning and have promoted the study of a problem which, if annoying fifty years ago, is today grievous and almost maddening, due to the unexpected increase of theoretical knowledge and its practical application in all areas.[95]

A new formulation was adopted in the Second Congress of Academies in Madrid, in 1956, when Dr. Gregorio Marañón delivered his paper, 'Utilidad de aumentar en el diccionario los vocablos técnicos y científicos de uso corriente'.[96] Four years later, at the Congress in Bogotá (1960), a decisive step was taken upon approving Resolution XX in which is recommended the creation within each academy of a Commission on

[91] See Julio Casares, *Nuevas voces en el Diccionario Académico* 24-7 (Madrid, 1963). The present secretary of the Spanish Academy, Rafael Lapesa, has written an interesting article on foreign words in modern Spanish, which classifies their types and postulates the criteria that should be adopted in order to assimilate them, to the extent that this is possible; see his '*Kahlahtahyood.* Madariaga ha puesto el dedo en la llaga', *Revista de Occidente* (2ª época) 4.373-80 (1966).

[92] Quoted by Fernando Lázaro Carreter, *Las ideas lingüísticas en España durante el siglo XVIII* 251 (Madrid, 1949).

[93] Esteban de Terreros y Pando, *Diccionario castellano con las voces de ciencias y artes y sus correspondientes en las tres lenguas francesa, latina e italiana*, 4 volumes (Madrid, 1786-93).

[94] Antonio de Capmany, *Nuevo diccionario francés-español* (Madrid, 1805). It adapts words from French technical terminology.

[95] See Blas Cabrera, *Evolución de los conceptos físicos y lenguaje* (Madrid, 1936) and Esteban Terradas, *Neologismos, arcaísmos y sinónimos en plática de ingenieros* (Madrid, 1946).

[96] *Memoria del Segundo Congreso de Academias de la Lengua Española* 234-9 (Madrid, 1956).

Technical Vocabulary, composed of academy members and representatives of the technical and scientific associations that exist in each country. The purpose of these comissions is to engage in the study of scientific terminology and to propose admission to the dictionary for new technical terms, together with the revision of those terms already in the dictionary and their definitions.[97] In the Congress of Buenos Aires (1964), a report by the Argentine Academy of Letters on 'the study of technical and scientific expressions'[98] was approved and the Spanish academy member Julio Palacios again emphasized the danger of allowing unrestrained technical neologisms, the need for the academies to seek advice in this area from technical people and the urgency for interacademy collaboration in this field.[99]

The Colombian Academy, responding to this need, in November, 1961 created its Commission on Technical Vocabulary, composed of four academy members and four scientists from various organizations.[100] They have worked actively in biweekly conferences and have presented to the Colombian Academy a series of terms, which, when approved there, are then sent on to be studied by the Spanish Academy. The latter up to now has given its approval to about two hundred terms and many of them will be included in the next edition of the general dictionary.[101] Since the Permanent Commission of the Association of Academies resumed its activities in Madrid in 1965, it has been, with regard to matters of technical vocabulary, the liason between the academies and has begun a series of consultations on the use of certain technical terms, since its mission is to give information about the preferences of each nation or professional group in order to then produce the widest agreement.

In this area the Royal Academy of Exact, Physical and Natural Sciences of Madrid contributes in an effective manner to the work of the Spanish Academy. The former has been publishing in its *Revista*, since 1959, a special chapter on 'Terminología científica'. The express desire of this organization is for all those who want to collaborate in this undertaking of general interest, to offer without delay their knowledge and experience.

There are two very clear goals that are pursued above all else in this campaign: 1) to see that present-day Spanish does not remain on the edge of the scientific and tech-

[97] *Tercer Congreso de Academias de la Lengua Española. Actas y labores* 182-3 (Bogotá, 1961). This recommendation is based on the report presented by the Colombian academy member Alfredo Bateman, 'Vigilancia de las academias sobre el crecimiento del lenguaje, especialmente sobre el vocabulario técnico' (*ibid.* 374-8).

[98] 'IV Congreso de Academias de la Lengua', *BAE* 44.559 (1964).

[99] 'Los neologismos en la ciencia y en la técnica', *BAE* 44.421-4 (1964).

[100] The original members were: Father Félix Restrepo, S. J., as Director of the Academy and later Eduardo Guzmán Esponda, as Director in Charge of the Academy; Alfredo Bateman (who is also a civil engineer); Oscar Echeverri Mejía and Rafael Torres Quintero. Also Leopoldo Guerra Portocarrero, replaced at his death by Gustavo Perry Zubieta, for the Colombian Society of Engineers; Luis Patiño Camargo, for the National Academy of Medicine; Daniel Mesa Bernal, for the Colombian Academy of Exact, Physical and Natural Sciences, and Alvaro Daza, since 1966, for the Colombian Society of Economists.

[101] See Oscar Echeverri Mejía, *Nuestro idioma al día*[2] 62-99 (Cali, 1965).

nical developments of the contemporary world; 2) to see that this incorporation of technical terms is accomplished by following the natural channels and character of the language. This process must take place so that the language does not suffer a violent period of growth and so that the multiplicity of new concepts and objects, as utilized by such a heterogeneous multitude of people, will not result in losses in the necessary unity of understanding, which is a key point in the campaigns in defense of the language. What has been accomplished up to now, while proportionally very little, is a good beginning and is largely owed to the watchfulness of the academy associations. Only the active participation of the Spanish-speaking nations in the creation and development of modern technology could provide a thoroughgoing solution, as those who have treated the problem in depth have accurately observed.[102]

2.2.4. *Grammar*

For centuries grammar has been conceived of as an essentially normative discipline: 'the art of speaking and writing correctly'. Only the revolution brought about in linguistic studies in the last fifty years has caused the revision of a concept that seemed definitely established. Today grammar is considered to consist of the objective study of the functioning of a given linguistic system, within certain limits of space and time. (We do not here take a stand with regard to generative grammar, with all that it signifies of a return, in large part, to traditional grammar.) This conception has favored the acquisition of a scientific knowledge of one of the fundamental aspects of language. But we do not believe that this new conception should be cause for casting aside correction, which traditional experience has demonstrated to be an effective principle of behavior with regard to language usage. Awareness of speaking well or speaking badly has such a deep significance for the regular users of a language of culture such as Spanish, that it would be an error to ignore it. One can look for very deep roots for this fact, or attribute it to social, geographic or esthetic prejudices, or to the spontaneous gregarious tendency of the masses.[103] In any case, it is evident that the language academies continue to have in grammar, conceived of as an art, a powerful instrument of action to plan the course to be followed by those who, from generation to generation, receive the inheritance of language.

In Latin America this prerogative has been disputed by the texts of the Spanish Academy and of Andrés Bello. Many other texts have followed that repeat, summarize or revise one or the other of these two works, without adding any new content in their exposition of these two doctrines. At most, they raise simple questions of detail or of

[102] See Samuel Gili Gaya, 'El lenguaje de la ciencia y de la técnica', *Presente y futuro de la lengua española* 2.269-76 (Madrid, 1964).

[103] See chapters V and VI, 'Criterios de corrección' and 'Buen lenguaje y lenguaje correcto', in Otto Jespersen, *Humanidad, nación e individuo desde el punto de vista lingüístico* 109-88 (Buenos Aires, 1947). The excellent paper that Angel Rosenblat presented on the same subject at the Second Inter-American Symposium on Linguistics and Language Teaching, held in Bloomington, Indiana in August of 1964, will soon be published by the Caro and Cuervo Institute of Bogotá, together with the other papers read at that meeting.

pedagogical method.[104] It can be said that the academies have made those two manuals official, often complementing them with the teachings of other philologists, but always in line with the corrective criterion of repudiating that which is felt to be an error. The description of the grammatical system, usually divided into *analogy* (today called morphology) and *syntax*, basically has as its object the comparison of 'legitimate' forms of speech with those that are rejected as corruptions introduced by uneducated persons. It is inculcated in the student at every level, in the journalist, in the speaker in general of every class, that grammar is a kind of code in which certain forms are prescribed, while others are condemned.

The discussion of this criterion, which many scorn as typical of the academies but to which most programs and texts conform, even those prepared by people outside of the academies, has no place here. It is certain that its results relate to that kind of social criticism that is directed toward those who use, for example, abnormal numerical formations such as *el víver* or *los pieses* for *los víveres* ['the food, provisions'] or *los pies* ['the feet']; analogies in gender such as *la testiga* or *la clienta* for *la testigo* ['the (female) witness'] or *la cliente* ['the (female) client']; constructions such as *más mejor* ['*more better'] or *más peor* ['*more worse'] for *mejor* ['better, best'] and *peor* ['worse, worst'], or *hubieron fiestas* for *hubo fiestas* ['there were celebrations']; inflections of verbs that don't correspond to literary usage such as *forza* for *fuerza* ['he forces'], *suerbe* for *sorbe* ['he sips'], *apreta* for *aprieta* ['he squeezes'] and the many variations that afflict conjugation, government or concord. There are cases in which the complexity of the rules, which are not at all easy to keep in mind, causes speakers or writers who are fearful of committing some error, to prefer to avoid the difficulty by having recourse to some other construction. Such a situation occurs, for example, with the so-called 'Gallic *que*' or with the 'incorrect gerunds'[105] or with the 'use of the preposition *a* in the accusative'. Some special problems that present themselves because of divergent usages in Spain and Spanish America, such as that of certain forms of address (*vosotros* ['you', familiar plural] vs. *ustedes* ['you', polite plural]) or that of the so-called *leísmo* [the use of *le* instead of *lo* as the masculine third person singular object pronoun], *loísmo* [the use of *lo* as the masculine third person singular object pronoun], and *laísmo* [the use of *la* and *las* instead of *le* and *les* as the feminine third person indirect object pronouns], do not generally enter into consideration in normative grammars or are explained as linguistic habits which are prevalent in one or another region. On the other hand, the changes in conjugation and in the pronoun system occasioned by the *voseo* [the use of *vos* instead of *tú* as the second person sin-

[104] Perhaps the only exception in all that time would be the *Gramática castellana*, 2 volumes (Buenos Aires, 1938; which has had numerous subsequent reprintings) by Amado Alonso and Pedro Henríquez Ureña, in which the solid linguistic background of its authors is transferred to the field of education. But even in this work Alonso and Ureña affirm that they want to conform principally to Bello, 'who is closest to the modern criterion', and maintain that normative grammar 'is what is most important in the elementary and secondary schools' (*Gramática castellana* 1.10).

[105] See Raúl Quintana, 'El miedo al gerundio en los escritores argentinos', *BAAL* 4.405-17 (1936), reprinted in *Universidad de Antioquia* (Medellín) 4.176-85 (1937).

gular pronoun], which is used so widely in the familiar speech of Latin America, especially in Río de la Plata and in Central America, have not become reconciled with the patterns required by precepts of the academy which have prevailed since the time of Bello.[106]

It has still not been possible to extend the notion of grammar considered as a special branch of linguistics, deliberately separated from any normative aim, beyond the circle of specialists in this field. Moreover, it has been questioned whether this is a desirable goal, or if, on the contrary, it is preferable that grammatical instruction, at least on the lower levels, retain its normative character.[107] Perhaps it will be necessary to search for a reasonable compromise in which different kinds of truths are placed in a hierarchy, since the need to know a language in its most intimate structure is just as scientifically valid as, in the sphere of practical life, to give that language, by means of suitable institutions, the direction that the speakers outline, so that it is not left without guidance or authority, at the mercy of all the forces of change, both positive and negative.[108]

At the present time, there is no doubt that for the majority of Spanish-speakers the normative will prevails. Accordingly, the orthographic representation of words has acquired a notable stability which it lacked in the so-called golden ages. Syntax, as the basic mechanism and control for linguistic functioning, does not in general cause insurmountable difficulties in comprehension. Vocabulary, in its double aspects of morphology and semantics, despite enormous geographic distribution and confrontations with new ways of life, is gradually enriched without monstrous deformations, due to the growing economic and cultural interrelations of the Spanish American countries. Even pronunciation and intonation, which are much more difficult to control since they transmit emotion and thus are strongly embedded in the regional and individualistic spirit, have found an intermediate area of open agreement. The reasons, then, for restrained optimism about the future of the language appear to be stronger than those that would lead one to predict the catastrophe of linguistic confusion.[109]

[106] In this respect Dámaso Alonso, 'Unidad y defensa del idioma', *Memoria del Segundo Congreso de Academias de la Lengua Española* 46 (Madrid, 1956), arrives at this conclusion: 'Personally, I do not believe (although I could be mistaken) that the attempts to restore the *tuteo* [addressing people with the second person singular pronoun *tú*] in Argentina have the slightest advantage; I feel that the *voseo* should be maintained there (and in the other areas where it exists), as it is practiced in educated circles'.

[107] In the Fourth Congress of Academies in Buenos Aires, the Spanish academy member Samuel Gili Gaya proposed that the new grammatical theories be considered as a fitting subject for higher education. 'Structural grammar' — he said — 'is not sufficiently stabilized, and therefore, it is not advisable to teach it at the primary and secondary levels'; see his paper 'Sobre nomenclatura y enseñanza de la Grámatica', *BAE* 44.449-53 (1964).

[108] Very illustrative in this respect is the address presented before the Colombian Academy in 1961 by its Perpetual Secretary, José Manuel Rivas Sacconi, with the title 'Academia, lengua, cultura, nación', *BAC* 12.5-25 (1962).

[109] A record of the opinions expressed in the Philological Assembly of the First Congress of Hispanic Institutions, which met in Madrid in June, 1962, gives a quite favorable balance to the prognoses

This preoccupation with the linguistic unity of the nations of Spanish origin has in large part been, and continues to be, the concern of the Language Academies of Spain, Spanish America and the Philippines, jointly involved as never before in linguistic instruction, methods and programs. The academies, supported by institutions and individuals who are prominent in society, valiantly carry out their work of protection and unification and feel that their language engenders an active and dynamic cohesive force, constitutes their richest heritage and is the bond that joins the Hispanic people with universal culture.

---

concerning the unitary preservation of Spanish, with a tendency to feel that unity of language parallels the preservation of the traditional forms of our culture. See the proceedings of this Assembly, published under the title *Presente y futuro de la lengua española*, 2 volumes (Madrid, 1964), and the review by José Joaquín Montes, *Thesaurus* 19.333-42 (1964).

Dámaso Alonso, 'Unidad y defensa del idioma', *Memoria del Segundo Congreso de Academias de la Lengua Española* 43 (Madrid, 1956), is concerned about the destiny of Spanish: 'Divisions are occurring everywhere within the organism of the Spanish language ... The edifice of our linguistic community is cracked'. Nevertheless, he believes that 'much can be done ... The final breach in the Spanish linguistic community can be postponed several centuries if we take action with decision and with sensible energy'. He has reaffirmed his position before those who brand him as pessimistic in 'Unidad y defensa del idioma', *BAE* 44.395 (1964). Angel Rosenblat, on the other hand, is optimistic: he believes there is no danger of 'linguistic disintegration' because the language deviations in Latin America occur only in popular and familiar speech, while educated speech is dominated by a general ideal of 'Hispanic universality'; certainly he later sees a 'real danger' of 'the rupture of our old norms, and of the relaxation of the expressive ideal' in 'the dizzy ascent of people from the lower levels, who burst in, legitimately motivated by new appetites' (*El castellano de España y el castellano de América. Unidad y diferenciación* 52-3 and 57 [Caracas, 1962]). Rafael Lapesa reveals himself to be cautiously optimistic. He believes that the linguistic background common to Spanish Americans is much more powerful than their individual characteristics, and thinks that with good will, mutual influences can be promoted that will lead to the formation of a *koiné* throughout the domain of the Spanish language. 'That *koiné* would guarantee for some centuries more — perhaps not many — the survival of Spanish as a unified language' ('América y la unidad de la lengua española', *Revista de Occidente* (2ª época) 4.300-10 [1966]).

PART IV

SOURCES AND RESOURCES

THE ORGANIZATION OF LINGUISTIC ACTIVITIES

YOLANDA LASTRA

0. There are several aspects of linguistic activities which may be considered from the point of view of organization: research, the teaching of linguistics, the various applied fields, notably language teaching, and, finally, the reporting of all these activities in writing (journals) or verbally at congresses and meetings of various kinds. In addition, linguists and language teachers have recently begun organizing in order to cooperate with each other and to learn about each other's activities.

In this volume, Coseriu reviews the organization of research; Contreras reviews recent or current research in applied linguistics; Wigdorsky and Gomes discuss language teaching; Manrique describes the activities in the field of computational linguistics; and journals are described in detail in Coseriu's chapter.

In order to present a more complete picture of the organization of linguistic activities there only remains to list some of the most important institutions where linguistics is taught; to mention some of the most important programs in language teaching or teacher training programs with a linguistic approach or with emphasis on oral competence, and finally to give a brief description of the professional organizations which have recently been established. In addition, a list of journals and bulletins which are currently being published is supplied.

1. *The teaching of linguistics.*[1] – Table 1 lists the most important institutions where linguistics is taught. There are only three countries where it is possible to pursue graduate studies in linguistics leading to a degree or certificate: Mexico, Peru, and Colombia. Linguistics is taught as a subject in many of the Faculties of Letters, normal schools, and the like, and there is also the possibility of specializing in philology in many of the Latin American universities. In Bolivia, linguistics was offered for the first time in 1965 by Martha Hardman-de-Bautista, Fulbright lecturer; in Paraguay at the University of Asunción there are no courses in linguistics, the subject being treated only by the anthropologist Branca Sušnik as a part of a more general anthropological course.

[1] The information given here is largely taken from Programa Interamericano de Lingüística y Enseñanza de Idiomas. *El Simposio de Cartagena* (Bogotá, 1965). This book should be consulted for more detail on institutions where languages and linguistics are taught. Some countries are treated in more detail than others, but, as a whole, the information given is complete and reflects the situation up to 1963.

2. *Language teaching.* – English, French, Italian, and German are offered in most university programs in Latin America. A few other institutions offer other languages. Table 2 lists training institutions for language teachers and institutions where languages are taught with a linguistic approach or at least with emphasis on oral competence. Bi-national centers are not included. The United States Information Agency partly sponsors bi-national centers in practically every important Latin American city. English is taught at these centers and many of them hold short seminars for English teachers which often provide their only opportunity for contact with recent scientific methodology the teachers ever have. Other countries sponsor similar centers or institutes. For instance, French is taught in most cities at the Alliance Française where oral competence is usually emphazised.

3. *Professional organizations.* – On the occasion of the Ninth International Congress of Linguists, fifteen linguists unanimously called for the establishment of the Asociación de Lingüística y Filología de América Latina, ALFAL. Its first secretary general was Gastón Carrillo Herrera of Chile and its first treasurer Luis J. Prieto of Argentina. Since then practically every philologist and linguist in Latin America and many Americans and Europeans interested in the language field in Latin America have joined this membership organization.

ALFAL's first meeting was held at Viña del Mar, Chile (January, 1964) and its second meeting in Montevideo (January, 1966). Its present Executive Committee has the following members:

Joaquim Mattoso Câmara, Universidade do Brasil, Chairman
Ambrosio Rabanales, Universidad de Chile, Secretary
Luis Flórez, Instituto Caro y Cuervo, Bogotá
Robert Lado, Georgetown University
Juan M. Lope Blanch, Universidad Nacional Autónoma de México and El Colegio de México
Luis J. Prieto, Universidad de Córdoba, Córdoba, Argentina
José Pedro Rona, Universidad de la República, Montevideo.

ALFAL plans to publish a bulletin and to continue to hold professional meetings and to sponsor linguistic institutes and other activities which will foster the development of linguistics in Latin America.

In May, 1963 the Asociación Latinoamericana para la Investigación Lingüística mediante Equipos Mecanico-Electrónicos, ALILEME was first organized in Mexico City. ALILEME held its first meeting in Montevideo (January, 1966) during which José Pedro Rona of the Universidad de la República, Uruguay, was elected president and Daniel Cazés of the Centro de Cálculo Electrónico, Universidad Nacional Autónoma de México, secretary. ALILEME has published its first mimeographed bulletin and has as one of its aims the diffusion of the technique of using computers as an aid in linguistic analysis.

The Inter-American Program in Linguistics and Language Teaching was established in Cartagena, Colombia, in August, 1963 at the First Inter-American Symposium in Linguistics and Language Teaching. The Symposium was sponsored by the U.S. Department of State, the Ford Foundation, and the Colombian Ministry of Education through the Instituto Lingüístico Colombo-Americano, ILCA. Its local host was the Instituto Caro y Cuervo. The idea of an international organization which would gather information about the human and institutional resources in the language sciences in Latin America and the Caribbean, which would encourage the cooperation among specialists, and which would provide a mechanism for those interested to be able to cooperate in furthering language studies, had been latent for many years. But it was not until November, 1962 at a meeting of a small number of scholars at the Center for Applied Linguistics, Washington, D.C. that the plans for organizing what was to become the Inter-American Program began to take shape. Donald F. Solá, of Cornell University accepted the task of being Coordinator and began planning the First Inter-American Symposium with the cooperation of key institutions and individuals in Latin America, the Caribbean, and the United States.

At the general assembly of the Cartagena Symposium the Inter-American Program was established, an Executive Committee elected, scholarly papers read, and the Cartagena Reports presented. These had been prepared by the Regional Coordinators, a group of linguists acquainted with the area they reported on, who visited institutions and interviewed scholars and administrators in order to gather information on the human and institutional resources in their area. A set of recommendations leading to the improvement of the channels of communication among language specialists and to the fostering of linguistics and its applications was made by the assembled delegates on the basis of the regional reports.

The Second Inter-American Symposium was held in Bloomington, Indiana (August, 1964) and the Third Symposium took place in Montevideo (January, 1966). Recommendations were made including plans for a Fourth Symposium and the Second Inter-American Linguistic Institute to be held in Mexico City and the Fifth Symposium and Third Institute to be held at São Paulo.

The present (1966) Executive Committee of the Inter-American Program has the following members:

Norman A. McQuown, University of Chicago, Chairman
Aryón Dall'Igna Rodrigues, Museu Nacional, Rio de Janeiro, Secretary
Robert Lado, Georgetown University
Juan M. Lope Blanch, Universidad Nacional Autónoma de México and El Colegio de México
Angel Rosenblat, Universidad Central, Caracas
Donald F. Solá, Cornell University
Rafael Torres Quintero, Instituto Caro y Cuervo, Bogotá.

The most notable achievement of the Inter-American Program has been the sponsorship of the First Inter-American Linguistic Institute held in Montevideo, January-February, 1966. The Institute was also sponsored by ALFAL. The host institution was the Universidad de la República and the director of the Institute was J. P. Rona. Twenty eight courses were taught by well known specialists. Over 300 students attended the Institute. These included many auditors who were established scholars and nearly 200 younger scholars who took the courses for credit.

The Program's symposia have provided a means for the majority of the linguists of Latin America and the Caribbean and many of their North American counterparts to meet together to discuss common interests. The symposia have, in many cases, been the first opportunity for scholars who have long known about one another to meet, or for linguists who were interested in the same types of problems to discuss them face to face with their colleagues from other countries. The Program has set up a number of committees of specialists in fields such as theoretical linguistics, national languages, computational linguistics, foreign languages, literacy, socio-linguistics, etc. which constitute a mechanism where particular research or experimental projects can be discussed and then presented to the whole assembly of delegates for endorsement. This is a means of achieving professional excellence, avoiding duplication of efforts, and providing for genuine inter-American cooperation.

In addition to the three international organizations just described, there is the Summer Institute of Linguistics, SIL, a non-denominational religious organization which is primarily interested in translating the Bible into many languages. It operates in eight Latin American countries under the auspices of government agencies which are in charge of Indian education. The work of SIL members is important not only in the field of bilingual education, but also in those of research and of training. SIL frequently encourages its members to teach linguistics in the local institutions when the institutions request it.

Chile is the only Latin American country which has a professional organization of language specialists, the Asociación Chilena de Profesores e Investigadores de Lengua y Literatura which was founded in 1965.

USIS encourages associations of English teachers, and there are, no doubt, other local professional organizations, but there is, nevertheless, a lack of communication among language specialists.

Scholars in different countries who are interested in the same fields have few opportunities to communicate with one another and within a given country, language teachers of different special ties seldom meet to discuss common interests.

The only country in the area which has an organization similar to the Center for Applied Linguistics in the United States is Brazil. The Centro de Lingüística Aplicada was inaugurated at the Instituto Yazigi of São Paulo in March, 1966. Francisco Gomes de Matos is the Director of the Centro which will carry on research, prepare teaching materials, train language teachers, and publish a journal.

The Linguistic Bureau of Surinam directed by Christian H. Eersel is a government sponsored institution which carries on research and which often plays a role similar to that of a Center for Applied Linguistics by organizing conferences and advising the government on linguistic matters.

4. *Journals.*[2] – Journals which are currently being published are listed below. The abbreviations given are those used in the *Linguistic Bibliography*.

Alfa, *Alfa*. Marília, Brasil.
América Indígena. México.
Anales de Filología Clásica. Buenos Aires.
Anales del Instituto de Lingüística de la Universidad Nacional de Cuyo, *AIL*. Mendoza, Argentina.
Anales del Instituto Nacional de Antropología e Historia, *AnINA*. México.
Anuario. Universidad Central de Venezuela. Facultad de Humanidades y Educación. Instituto de Antropología e Historia. Caracas, Venezuela.
Antropológica, *Antropológica*. Caracas.
Anuario de Letras, *AdL*. México.
Anuario Indigenista. Instituto Indigenista Interamericano. México.
Anuario de Filología. Universidad del Zulia. Facultad de Humanidades y Educación. Maracaibo, Venezuela.
Archivos Venezolanos de Folklore. Caracas, Venezuela.
Boletín del Instituto Riva-Agüero. Lima.
Boletín de Filología. Instituto de Filología de la Universidad de Chile, *BFUCh*. Santiago de Chile.
Boletín de Filología, *BFM*. Montevideo.
Boletín de la Academia Argentina de Letras, *BAAL*. Buenos Aires.
Boletín de la Academia Colombiana, *BAC*. Bogotá.
Boletín de la Academia Costarricense de la Lengua. San José.
Boletín de la Academia Cubana de la Lengua. La Habana.
Boletín de la Academia Salvadoreña de la Lengua. San Salvador.
Boletín de la Academia Venezolana de la Lengua. Caracas.
Boletín del Instituto de Antropología. Medellín, Colombia.
Boletín Indigenista. Instituto Indigenista Interamericano. México.
Boletín Indigenista Venezolano, *BIV*. Caracas.
Cuadernos del Instituto Nacional de Investigaciones Folklóricas. Instituto Nacional de Antropología. Buenos Aires.
Diógenes, *Diogenes*. Buenos Aires.
Filología, *FF*. Buenos Aires.
Guatemala Indígena. Guatemala.

[2] This list was compiled at the library of the Instituto Caro y Cuervo. The journals mentioned are those listed in the *Linguistic Bibliography* and those currently (1966) being received by the Instituto. Literary journals which publish articles on language or linguistics only occasionally are not included. Thanks are due Hernan Lozano for his help.

Humanidades. Universidad Nacional de la Plata. Facultad de Humanidades y Ciencias de la Educación. La Plata, Argentina.
Humanidades. Montevideo.
Humanitas. Universidad Nacional de Tucumán. Tucumán, Argentina.
Humanitas. Curitaba, Brasil.
Iberída. Río de Janeiro.
Indianoromania. Lima.
Inter-Pret. Universidad de Puerto Rico. Río Piedras, Puerto Rico.
Jornal de Filología. São Paulo.
Lenguage y Ciencia. Trujillo, Perú.
Noticias Culturales. Instituto Caro y Cuervo. Bogotá.
Nueva Revista de Filología Hispánica, NRFH. México.
Revista Brasileira de Filología, RBF. Río de Janeiro.
Revista Colombiana de Antropología, RCA. Bogotá.
Revista Colombiana de Folklore. Instituto Colombiano de Antropología. Bogotá.
Revista de Estudios Clásicos. Instituto de Lenguas y Literaturas Clásicas. Facultad de Filosofía y Letras. Universidad Nacional de Cuyo. Mendoza, Argentina.
Revista de Humanidades. Universidad Nacional de Córdoba. Facultad de Filosofía y Letras. Córdoba, Argentina.
Revista de Letras, RdL. Assis, São Paulo, Brasil.
Revista de Lingüística Aplicada. Concepción, Chile.
Revista del Museo Nacional, RMNac. Lima.
Revista de Museu Paulista, RMPaul. São Paulo.
Revista Mexicana de Estudios Antropológicos, RMEA. México.
Romanitas, Revista de cultura romana, *Romanitas*. Río de Janeiro.
Sphinx, Anuario del Departamento de Filología de la Universidad de San Marcos. Lima.
Thesaurus, Boletín del Instituto Caro y Cuervo, *Thesaurus*. Bogotá..

TABLE 1

Institutions where Linguistics is Taught

Programs leading to a degree or certificate	*Courses offered in facultades de filosofía, facultades de educación, normal schools, etc.*
Puerto Rico	
	Universidad de Puerto Rico, Río Piedras.
Mexico	
Escuela Nacional de Antropología e Historia, Mexico City (*maestría*, 4 years); Instituto de Historia, Universidad Nacional Autónoma de México, Mexico City (doctorate in Anthropology with major in linguistics); Centro de Estudios Lingüísticos y Literarios, El Colegio de México, Mexico City (doctorate); Univerversidad de Veracruz, Jalapa (*maestría*)	Facultad de Filosofía, Universidad Nacional Autónoma de México, Mexico City; Universidad Iberoamericana, Mexico City; Universidad de Yucatán, Mérida
Colombia	
Instituto Caro y Cuervo, Bogotá	Instituto de Antropología, Bogotá; Universidad de los Andes, Bogotá; Universidad Nacional, Bogotá; Universidad Pedagógica, Tunja; Universidad de Antioquia, Medellín; Universidad Pedagógica del Caribe, Barranquilla; Universidad Pedagógica Nacional Femenina, Bogotá.
Venezuela	
	Universidad Central, Caracas.
Peru	
Universidad de San Marcos, Lima	Universidad de Huamanga, Ayacucho.
Ecuador	
	Universidad de Cuenca.

TABLE 1 (*continued*)

Programs leading to a degree or certificate	*Courses offered in facultades de filosofía, facultades de educación, normal schools, etc.*
Bolivia	
	Instituto Nacional de Estudios Lingüísticos, La Paz.
Brazil	
	Universidade do Brasil, Rio de Janeiro; Universidade do Brasilia; about 81 other universities.
Argentina	
	Universidad de Buenos Aires; Universidad de la Plata; Universidad de Córdoba; Universidad de Tucumán; Universidad de Cuyo; Universidad del Litoral, Rosario; Universidad del Sur, Bahía Blanca; Instituto Superior del Profesorado en Lenguas Vivas, Buenos Aires.
Uraguay	
	Universidad de la República, Montevideo; Instituto de Estudios Superiores, Montevideo. Instituto de Profesores 'Artigas', Montevideo.
Chile	
	Universidad de Chile, Santiago and Valparaíso; Universidad Católica de Valparaíso; Universidad de Concepción; Universidad Austral de Valdivia.

TABLE 2

Institutions with language teaching programs or teacher training programs with a linguistic approach, or with emphasis on oral competence

Puerto Rico

Universidad de Puerto Rico, Río Piedras;
Universidad Católica de Santa María, Ponce;
Universidad Interamericana, San Germán.

México

Escuela Normal Superior, Mexico City;
El Colegio de México, Mexico City;
Universidad Iberoamericana, Mexico City;
Universidad de las Américas, Estado de México.

Nicaragua

Universidad Central Americana, Managua.

Colombia

Instiuto Lingüístico Colombo-Americano, Bogotá;
Centro de Estudios Universitarios Colombo-Americano, Bogotá;
Universidad del Valle, Cali;
Universidad de los Andes, Bogotá;
Universidad Javeriana; Bogotá;
Universidad de Antioquia, Medellín.

Venezuela

Universidad Católica Andrés Bello, Caracas.

Peru

Facultad de Educación, Universidad de San Marcos, Lima;
Universidad Agraria, La Molina;
Universidad de Trujillo.

Ecuador

Universidad Central, Quito.

Brazil

Instituto de Idiomas Yazigi, São Paulo.

Argentina

Instituto Superior del Profesorado en Lenguas Vivas, Buenos Aires.

PRESENT STATE OF LINGUISTICS

ALBERTO ESCOBAR

0. A work such as has been done in this volume by its scholarly contributors, an ambitious undertaking indeed by its scope and the interest it will raise, necessarily exposes the reader to certain risks of interpretation which I would like to discuss here.

1.0.0. The partial conclusions sketched by the authors of the different chapters, even though they deal with different aspects of language, offer, nonetheless, certain common features, that can be viewed as *constants*, as typically revealing of the general state of linguistics in Latin America. By way of illustration, I could mention, for instance, the references to the shortage of technically qualified personnel; the scarcity of books and inefficient planning of our libraries; the disproportionate amount of foreign collaborations in our periodicals; the lack of familiarity with untranslated bibliography; the almost inexistent contacts between Brazilian and Spanish American scholars; the difficulties in achieving a certain professional status with sufficient economic guaranties for the teacher and the scholar; an attitude of insecurity with regard to our own work and a blind acceptance of foreign works. Let all this suffice for the moment to evoke an image that keeps reappearing in almost every chapter. It would be easy, and also wrong, to conclude from all this that the present state of affairs or its immediate future, is such that it would allow us to discard without remorse the linguistic work already accomplished, or in progress, in Latin America. My approach will be different: when we discuss the tasks, the institutions, and the men that in this part of the continent have dedicated or are dedicating themselves to the study of language, it becomes imperative, lest we distort the meaning of facts, to view such linguistic endeavors within the wider frame of the entire cultural and scientific activity of a social panorama characterized, with differences of degree only, by the phenomenon known as *underdevelopment*.[1]

1.0.1. On the other hand, our acceptance of this generic characteristic could unwittingly reinforce an erroneous practice in the way in which foreigners view the totality of what we call Latin America. Thus, I should immediately warn that nothing of what I have said has anything to do with the cliché of Latin American 'unity' or 'uni-

[1] We will understand the term *underdevelopment* as the inability to reach a state of *socio-economic* development, distinguishing between 'development' and simple 'growth'. *Development* will be 'growth' + 'change'. Among the typical characteristics of *underdevelopment* we recognize social disintegration, economic and political subordination, and a situation of human injustice.

formity'. On the contrary, it questions that assumption, since the phenomenon of underdevelopment does not presuppose either uniformity or unity. In fact, we have to deal with a plural panorama differentiated within itself by degrees and shades which reveal, not only the stronger or lesser contact with Europe and North America, but also the different socio-cultural composition of our nations: a fact that draws to the foreground the questions of society versus culture.

1.0.2. It is then necessary to discard any simplistic idea about a homogeneous whole of which the peculiarities or antecedents of any of its parts could be equally predicated. Otherwise, we could end up with a series of superficial, excessively generic traits, the product of inveterate stereotypes.

Therefore, we should put aside the external and deceiving series of negative coincidences, which strike so bluntly the unprepared spectator, and decide in favor of a less simple, more instructive critical approach. That is, we should turn to a historic perspective that would show, however partially, what distant discrepancies are at the basis of a panorama so varied and little integrated, in spite of its apparent crust of epidermic coincidences. That is, let us keep this in mind, we are not only facing a panorama of diversified variants and regional styles — such as happens in Europe —, even less a variety of schools or theoretical premises, but also are we faced with the complex panorama that Latin America is, physically, culturally, and socially, as a remote and operative background, both at its origins and at present.

1.0.2.1. Today, when a Mexican, an Argentinian, and a Puertorican linguist converse, usually the same factors operate on them that distort the proper communication among the educated citizens of these countries. In my opinion, this means that there exists an implicit cultural experience, in which certain cultural patterns and prejudices are grounded; a cultural experience that erases individual antecedents and predetermines the attitude of these men to a large extent.

1.0.3. This is not the place, nor am I the proper authority, to trace the boundaries that delineate the socio-cultural substratum of the different areas; a most significant, and frequently disregarded substratum. But very roughly speaking, it seems obvious that at least Central America and the Andean regions have organized themselves socially along an axis of 'long duration', preceding by 10,000 or 15,000 years the establishment of those high culture empires which European man found there, and which were at that point the end of a long period of 4 or 5 thousand years. Empires, furthermore, in which a series of cultures participated which are very little known today to non-specialists. Thus, this feature that assimilates these regions among themselves, visibly differentiates them from those other countries which, as those in the southern triangle, base their historic development upon the Spanish discovery, and the formation of the Spanish city, in which the waves of European migration would arrive later. It is likewise clear that Paraguay is a singular phenomenon in Spanish America, and also that the Caribbean area typifies another historic development, one of traditionally outlying territory and maritime transit. A historically a midway region, exposed to the migration and influences from other areas. And, finally, nobody would doubt how deeply isolated Brazil is from the rest of Latin America, because of its vinculation to Portugal, which does not fit with that of Spanish America to Spain, and because of its connections with Africa, which are different from those of the Caribbean.

If we accept this fragmentation of Latin America in principle, although it could be discussed and perfected, we would be in a better position to understand to what extent the historic make up of our societies has consistently influenced, as it still does, our cultural development and the state of linguistics in our countries.

1.1.0. From all this, it can be inferred that a mere comparison of institutions, fields of activity, quantity, and level of publications, between, on the one hand, Latin American centers and, on the other, European, North-American, or Soviet centers would not be very productive, since it would explain little and distort much. The reason lies in the fact that our societies have not reached a degree of integration that would create in them a cultural superstructure conducive to a rich, independent, continuous, and creative dedication to science and, within it, to philology and linguistics. This means that our societies do not recognize clearly the importance of language studies, and that linguists, where they exist, do not quite understand their place in the social context in which they live. Consequently, the role attached to the study of language and the function assumed by the specialists remain undefined, incidental, euphemistically labeled as activities of 'high cultural level', 'very disinterested', of 'refined technical knowledge', or of 'plausible erudition'; something which, in my opinion, does nothing but covertly show mutual disinterest, the lack of coincidence between the objectives of linguistic disciplines and their exponents on the one hand, and the values and ideals of the different Latin American societies on the other.

1.1.1. If my second premise is correct, and, though unfortunate, valid for us, we can see how out of place a comparison would be between the state of linguistics and philology in Latin America and what has flourished in Europe, the United States, and the Soviet Union. We can say however that it would be possible to mention the names of scholars who were born in Latin America, or came to it from abroad, and resided and worked among us, and whose individual work deserves great respect and satisfies the technical exigencies of the moment. But this does not affect the state of our disciplines, the role of the professionals, or the activity of our institutions, taken as a whole and seen in their continuity. One might also add that, if we disregard the preceding considerations, the comparison with foreign centers would only produce the finding of muffled echoes, of incidental and late resonances.

1.2.0. There is another aspect worthy of consideration when, as is the case now, we ask ourselves about the state of linguistic disciplines in Latin America. An image such as we are looking for presupposes a cut, an inventory, an interpretation and accounting of certain points which serve as a limit, and in the selection of which, somehow, our contemporary judgement, our way of perceiving their temporal frequency has an influence. The authors of the different essays collected in this volume have all faced the same question. The answers point to the particular reasons linked to the nature of each topic, or to individual preferences to consider a date or a phenomenon the starting point of their respective expositions. Or also, in order to alleviate the effort of the reader by proposing a certain parallelism with developments which occurred especially in the Iberian Peninsula or in Europe. In each case, the authors have had to decide on an initial point from which their exposition proceeds.

It is not my intention to propose the year X as an exact boundary, while the years Y or Z would be false. I do not pretend either to say that from a certain period the work done is 'scientific' and that the rest is not. Unfortunately, the framework that occurs to me is more complex, but, at the same time, more natural and in consonance with the premises I have stated.

1.2.1. It is my impression that wherever the authors of this volume may have effected the cut that introduces a particular period, such operation will acquire its full meaning if we remember that what we call the *tradition* of Latin American linguistics, although weak and occasionally broken, is wider and goes back, at least, to the XIXth century, to Bello, Cuervo, Lenz, Hanssen: isolated names rather than the supporters of schools or movements, but who nonetheless placed the study of language among us at a level equal to that of the most highly developed centers of their time. It could also be said, perhaps with some audacity, that the sizable and little known endeavors of the authors of the first grammars and vocabularies of pre-Hispanic languages, throughout the XVIth, XVIIth and a good part of the XVIIIth centuries, truly represent in their own times an augural effort in our continent. And this in spite of the fact that they forced the nature of the languages studied into the Latin frame; even if today they are called pre-scientific.

1.2.2. Today it would be fruitful to turn our attention to that first stage, and to integrate it into what in some form we admit as our *tradition.* Not because those books would necessarily be acceptable today, but because we could perhaps recognize that their value exceeds that of their immediacy to the oral sources that nourished them. They offer us a fundamental lesson because of their attitude and inspiration. A reencounter with those works, with all the pertinent adjustments, would still be healthy for the future of linguistics in Latin America.

If the reader can conceive and retain in his mind a process as long and discontinuous as the one suggested here, each of the chapters of this book will afford a better view of the present state of that linguistic aspect with which each one deals, and will also help him to fit such a state in the trajectory we have traveled to arrive at our present moment.

2.0.0. Our XIXth century and the great many adventures undergone by the different urban centers founded during the European rule give our political history a synchronism which is more apparent than real. Thus, the weakening of Peninsular groups matches the self-defining movement of 'criollo' circles. These circles, stimulated by the crisis in the Peninsula, become progressively aware of their own identity, their interests, and their virtual power. The political and administrative system resulted in the hegemony of those capitals over a particular network of dependencies. A fact which sanctions the disarticulation of vast territories, and makes such capitals centers of direct contact with the metropolis. Printing, the universities, the academic societies, European travelers with a scientific mission, strengthened those circles which cultivated classical erudition, and inspired a local awareness reluctant to accept colonial rigidity. It is then that the metropolitan pattern is fragmented, and an educated 'criollo' class proclaims the ideals of the emancipation and breaks the politico-administrative apparatus of European domination. But what really happens in this process, though covertly, is only the consolidation of the traditional power structure, resulting only in the substitution of a 'criollo' group for that of the Peninsula, without altering the social structure, and without advancing the integration of those sectors that made up colonial society.

In Central America and the Andean region, those human sectors had been hierarchically structured in a system similar to that of castes. This fact, which seems in itself so distant from our linguistic problem, has a very close connection with it, since this is also an ethnic fact carrying with it a cultural differentiation of languages relative to Spanish. In other Latin American areas the slight importance of an aboriginal language and culture determines that the effect of the distribution of powers would not have the same depth or cultural repercussions. In still other areas, a Negro population determines the existence of a different set of circumstances whose main characteristic would be the lack of a native tongue associated with the preservation of a traditional culture. Finally, in countries like those in the Southern Triangle, one would have to add a strong European immigration, which certainly creates a problem of linguistic stabilization, but which is both linguistically and socially, different from that of the confrontation of an aboriginal language with Spanish.

2.1.0. Against the background afforded by all these historical circumstances, a process can be outlined that explains, although not in the manner of a historical survey of linguistics and philology in Latin America, the *attitudes* and *value-judgements* that Latin Americans have assumed with regard to the problem of language and linguistic disciplines.

This process can best be observed with regard to certain preoccupations about the future of the language in this part of the continent. For example, the possible fragmentation of Castilian in America, or the Brazilian preoccupation to maintain a philological continuity along Portuguese lines. Attitudes, on the other hand, that occasionally produce works which either reflect or improve those done in Spain and Portugal. It is a general attitude towards language and its study based on certain premises: a) the consideration of Spanish and Portuguese as the general languages of their respective territories, an idea inherited from the last colonial period. And this happened before the social integration of the different linguistic groups had been achieved, and without the existence of an effective linguistic stabilization. b) the fear in some groups that such overall unity, the privilege of the urban and educated class, would be lost in a process of linguistic *decomposition*; as well as the belief in other groups that the new independent political status had to be perfected also through linguistic independence leading to the creation of new national languages.

2.1.1. This *fear* and this *illusion* only distorted reality and motivated such partial outlooks as purism, anti-purism, and regionalism. They fomented such efforts as the insistent search for provincial linguistic traits as differentiated from the Peninsular model; they instigated the attempt to govern the contemporary use of the language through historical interpretations; they created the tendency towards *prescriptivism* and atomized compilations in the Romance languages spoken in Latin America, rather than the formation of global inventories; they made scholarly work to concentrate on the lexical level quite commonly using written sources, to the prejudice of the rich testimoney of the spoken language. Finally, they determined that in the scale of values of our linguists the highest rank was given to exemplary Castilian, something indicative of the fact that our societies were following a process of *transculturation* instead of the desirable *aculturación*. Something that can also explain the reason why the method used, with more or less technical virtuosity (both in the expert and the dilettante), was primarily philological.

2.2.0. A similar attitude is also found at the origin of the slight importance that Latin Americans attached, particularly after the independence, to the study of the non-European languages spoken in the continent. One would have to say that not only were a great many misconceptions and puerile rivalries widespread, but also that the fabulous laboratory that those other languages could have provided was abandoned to the almost exclusive interest of foreign scholars, especially German at the beginning, and North American later.

2.2.1. It is only after the second decade of the XXth century that the situation I have outlined begins to change. Latin American scholars and institutions begin to operate over a less exclusive and circumscribed panorama. A new preoccupation sets in in some circles, such as the Institute of Philology of Buenos Aires, about a systematic formation of scholars, a work methodically planned, translation series, and a well-reasoned orientation towards linguistic currents not strictly Hispanic or extending from the Peninsula. About the same time, though in an isolated way and with a limited influence, a few North American linguists begin to take an interest in the aboriginal languages of Mexico, and some links are established with scholars from the social sciences, thus attracting towards language study a scholarly sector that had not previously participated in these tasks. Finally, the Summer Institute of Linguistics undertakes a work initially observed with indifference, that would eventually attract the curiosity, emulation, and respect of those who, until that time, thought of European languages as the only material worthy of serious study and the almost exclusive field of linguistic interest to Latin Americans.

3.0.0. It is as a consequence of the upheaval which took place after the second world war, that we begin to detect some signs insinuating tendencies towards a change in society and in culture: a) in the social structure, b) in attitudes and values, c) in motivations, methods, and technical objectives.

3.1.0. a) With regard to social change, sociological factors linked to the rapid growth of urban centers, the migration of rural masses to the big cities, as well as an incipient industrialization requiring specially qualified personnel, gave birth to a social dynamics inconceivable in the XIXth century. Parallel to these developments, a series of others forewarns of an approaching crisis that will question, for the first time, the entire socio-economic structure of our countries. These are, among others the migration of workers from the countryside with its subsequent reduction in agricultural activity, the spreading hunger, the demographic explosion, the unemployment and frustration of peasants in the cities, the sharpening of social tensions and political instability, the outgrowth of a civic awareness in the masses and the awakening of further expectations, the inefficiency of the reform movements together with the obstinacy of the privileged groups and the obstructions suffered by the Alliance for Progress. All these factors operate each with different intensity, according to specific circumstances, but all have, in any case, created an atmosphere of anxiety and uncertainty which, in its turn, motivates a reexamination and reinterpretation of our social reality, not only in terms of an immediate or remote past but of the future towards which we travel at the accelerated and complex rythm imposed on us anew each day.

3.1.1. While this brief account has referred to national, internal situations, it would not be honest to ignore the situation at an international level without which we could not have the total panorama.

The events occurring in the hemisphere as well as outside, have made evident the state of dependency in which Latin American nations find themselves in the face of pressures playing a role in the cold (or hot) war between capitalist countries (especially the U.S.) and communist countries (especially Russia and China). The dramatic fate of Cuba and Santo Domingo; the situation in Venezuela, Colombia, and Peru; the Argentinian, Brazilian or Ecuadorian crises; political developments in Europe and the development of the new nations in Africa and Asia, as a whole, are all factors in a tight network in the face of which it is impossible not to admit that the position of each country is determined by the general outlook of the distribution of forces at a world level. However, this discovery of being a part of a universal destiny has aroused, paradoxically, the outgrowth of a nationalist tendency which is the counterpart and complement of our universal awareness.

3.2.0. b) With regard to the *attitudes* and *values* of those devoted to language studies, step by step a more exact understanding of our linguistic reality is gaining ground; that is, an understanding of the proper functions of Spanish and Portuguese, which will have to continue as the general means of language communication in our countries; and at the same time, a better understanding of the obvious plurilingualism that defines our continent. This change of outlook has led to a rearrangement of our linguistic concerns, not now in philological terms (without affecting the *raison d'être* and validity of Philology) but rather within a larger and more complex anthropological framework, such as that implied in the terms 'communication' and 'linguistic barriers'.

Through different channels, in the field of education, of research, or both, professionals are becoming progressively convinced that the *lack of communication* created by the *linguistic barrier* reflects, at the level of language, a cultural and social disintegration and disarticulation. Thus, the *fear* and *illusion* of the XIXth century are becoming now a *conviction*: that the propagation and expansion of Castilian and Portuguese, as means of general communication, has not been achieved; that, therefore, it has to be undertaken, and that insofar as this is possible and we can contribute to it, we are by the same token defining a very important part of the role of the linguist within the socio-cultural context of our countries. That is to say, it is now more clearly understood that if, on the one hand, the lack of communication and the linguistic barriers, as something feeding social discrimination, are not enough to determine a state of underdevelopment (the case of Belgium, for instance), on the other hand, there is no doubt that underdevelopment carries with it the absence or insufficiency of a general language (the case of India, for example) and the lack of social integration and identity.

3.2.1. We may add that for the reasons mentioned with regard to the international panorama, the desire becomes stronger every day to redirect the interest of students and that of educational policies in the sense of fomenting massive training in foreign languages, first of all in English, French, and German, for their extreme usefulness in taking advantage of technological, scientific, commercial, and touristic advances. With regard to English, while the number of people interested in learning the language grows constantly, there are still understandable reasons of political and cultural preferences which create a certain distrust, or resistance, among professionals, towards what has been wrongly called 'North American Linguistics'.

3.3.0. c) With regard to institutional incentives, one has to mention first of all the activity of those centers which in an almost heroic effort, although distant from one another and poorly communicated, have established the validity of linguistic work. That their respective orientations are divergent, and that the intensity and scope of their work have not been continuous or similar, are facts that cannot be denied. But the impact that centers such as the Caro y Cuervo Institute and the Andres Bello Seminar have had cannot be measured exclusively in terms of quantity, the degree of perfection, and the scholarly rank of their publications, although this also already reveals a level superior to that of many other countries, but it is an impact to be also understood in what such activity has meant as an institutionalization of research and teaching; as a strengthening of team work and the awareness of a supra-national dimension; as an opening — so difficult among us — towards the coexistence of the new directions of descriptive linguistics side by side with the older philological line. A similar statement could be made with regard to the work accomplished in Montevideo, which is undoubtedly connected with the pioneering work of Coseriu, of enormous theoretical influence, whether accepted or disputed, that is at present as powerful or even more as that exercised by Amado Alonso from the Buenos Aires Institute in the decades from the 30s to the 50s.

Glancing at the Spanish American horizon, the institutions I have mentioned, plus the Colegio de México and the NRFH, without minimizing the local importance of other institutions, are responsible today for the adoption of certain irreversible standards in linguistic works, the direct beneficiaries of which (members, students, scholarship holders), or those who receive their influence in an indirect way, are beginning to approach their work with a professional attitude. Besides, such institutions have attracted the visits of foreign specialists, mainly European, that, although not as frequent as would be desired, have had a testing role while, at the same time, have renovated the links with institutions in the continent.

3.3.0.1. Together with this internal source of incitements and stimuli, we could add the effect of a sizable increment in scholarships and cultural exchange trips. Something which has notably fostered, since the end of the second world war, the discovery of the international scientific panorama; a discovery accompanied sometimes by painful frustrations, and some other times by an obvious improvement. In brief, we believe that the essential and specific characteristic of this new period is without a doubt the greater contact and exchange of persons and institutions within the continent and outside. In this sense, although *Alfal* may not have satisfied the expectations of its founders, we cannot deny that it has been a valuable symptom, perhaps premature, but revealing of a determined attitude that could lead, if its goals are redefined, to the outgrowth of an effective and dynamic professional association.

3.3.1. Talking about 'methods' and 'objectives' I will not dare survey, even briefly, the diversified picture offered by all the groups, institutes, universities, and individual people that are now working in Latin America. But I do want to underline certain tendencies, certain currents, especially worthy of mention for their vigor or their novelty. From this standpoint we can see: a) that together with the traditional work in Spanish and Portuguese, an already appreciable advance has been made in the analysis of indigenous languages;[2] b) that it has been in this field where structural linguistics has operated, of a post-Bloomfieldian inspiration, as well as tagmemics, spread by Pike's followers and the members of the Summer Institute of Linguistics; c) that structural linguistics of European or North American inspiration, in the few analyses devoted to Spanish or Portuguese, has not achieved any higher results than those obtained in a more traditional way. This situation has become more palpable since, until recently, those analyses had been confined to phonological presentation, or to limited contrastive studies serving the pedagogical needs of the teaching of English.[3]

[2] "Descriptive Linguistics" by Joseph E. Grimes; "Indigenous Dialectology: 1955-1965" by Marvin K. Mayers; and, "Comparative reconstruction of indigenous languages" by Robert E. Longacre. chapters and collaborators of this volume, they offer an eloquent synopsis of the research done and the theoretical consequences which have resulted in some cases.

[3] Erica García comments in this volume on the studies devoted to phonology. Among the works done with pedagogical purposes, I will mention: *Introducción a una comparación fonológica del español y del inglés* by Daniel Cárdenas. (Washington, 1960); *Patterns of Spanish Pronounciation* by J. D. Bowen and R. Stockwell (Chicago, 1963). More comprehensive works are: *Modern Spanish* by Bolinger et al. (New York, 1960): *Modern Approach to Spanish* by F. B. Agard (New York, 1964). *The Grammatical Structure of English and Spanish* by R. Stockwell, D. Bowen, and J. Martin (Chicago, 1965) offers the novelty of applying in part the transformational method; but, like the other books mentioned, finds itself limited by its specific purpose. Therefore, it will not be able to influence effectively the grammatical tradition of Spanish America, in spite of its valuable analyses.

d) It should also be noted that there begins to be propagated in Latin America André Martinet's version of the structuralism of Prague, through translations of this author's work and the activity of scholars who studied under his direction in Paris. e) With regard to linguistics applied to education, what exists still leaves much to be desired, be it with regard to the teaching of the native language or of second languages. However, we cannot ignore the technical progress implied in the existence of institutions such as Buenos Aires department of Living Languages, the Yazigi Institute in São Paulo, and the recent Center for Applied Linguistics in that city. It may be said, then, that, although slowly, an essential change is taking place, whose main objective consists in the founding of language teaching on an adequate combination of linguistics and pedagogy. In order to do this, apart from the necessary basic investigation, the training system of language teachers has to be modified, *curricula* have to be modernized, and the appropriate teaching materials will have to be written on similar premises.[4] These considerations apply to the teaching of foreign languages, but also to the teaching of national languages, especially, for example, in order to Castilianize and make literate the indigenous populations.

3.3.2. Looking at this global picture, it is astonishing that the studies about Spanish and Portuguese are not at a level of development on a par with that of the indigenous languages.[5] It would seem that, beside those socio-cultural factors already mentioned, a combination of circumstances has impeded this desirable and to be expected advance; two of these possible circumstances may be: 1) the weak state of structural linguistics and the inability of its followers to show new ways and new goals in the investigation of the Spanish and Portuguese spoken in America; and 2) the pertinacity with which scholars in these fields have clung to certain 'problems' of language in America; an attitude which has led time and again to the consideration of such questions as the origin of American Spanish, or the historical analysis of isolated words, or to the compilation and semantic commentary of lexicon. No impartial observer could say that the study of American Spanish and Portuguese has truly reached a higher level and a new perspective beyond those already achieved by Cuervo, the Colombian master. It is most unfortunate, but both languages continue to be, using and expanding the meaning of a reflection by Lope Blach, 'great strangers', in spite of the efforts

[4] Concerning the teaching of foreign languages, Fracisco Gómez de Matos and Leopoldo Wigdorsky show with recent data the obstacles facing the modernization of this activity, as well as the advantages obtained specially in Brasil, Chile, Colombia, and Argentina, by the use of applied linguistics criteria. Complementing this is Yolanda Lastra's report on 'Literacy', insofar as the author reviews the situation of illiteracy and the steps taken to eliminate it, as well as the serious problem of non-standard language speakers. These authors emphasize the existence not only of adverse technical factors, but also the sociological premises affecting the status of language teachers. This observation should not be confined to the teacher of foreign languages since it also applies to those of the official language, particularly in the elementary grades.

[5] It seems to me a significant fact that the classic accounts of A. Rosenblat, M. L. Wagner, and B. Malmberg (see Malkiel's essay) continue to be the indispensable source for any global outlook. Another similar argument would be the still unquestioned validity of A. Alonso and P. Henríquez Ureña's *Gramática Castellana*, the use of which is still imperative for lack of better works, in spite of its obvious debt to the logic of Pfänder.

of many scholars who are reluctant to work with the living oral language, and countless studies which, unfortunately, are uneven and atomistic.

4.0.0. The years of 1965 and 1966 will be remembered as a defining milestone in the progress of Latin American Linguistics. We may very well use these dates to effect a diagnosis of the state of our discipline, and to establish which are its real prospects.

The commemoration of Andrés Bello's centenary reactualized in the continent the work and stature of the Caracas master. Many brilliant or modest pages were written or read in his honor, and, finally, his spirit presided over the Congress of *Alfal*, the session of the Third Symposium of the Interamerican Program of Linguistics and Language Teaching, as well as the labors of the First Institute of Interamerican Linguistics, events all of them which took place in Montevideo.

This collective reflection on the works of the Venezuelan linguist, as well as the analysis of his thought, particularly that of his famous *Grammar*, are of capital importance. This happens at a moment when the exchange promoted by the *I.P.*, and the meeting of and discussion among men of Latin America, the United States, and Europe, reactivates the interest in the destiny and task that await Linguistics in our countries. It stimulates the desire to examine the progress made to the present and, in the light of all this, it invites us to a thoughtful awareness about the different theoretical options that exist and so many concrete tasks, within an atmosphere of cooperation, mutual information, and a work well planned.[6]

Such a coincidence of possibilities never occurred in Latin America. What will come of this will depend greatly on those of us who believe that it is urgent to consolidate this propitious outlook at the level of specific exchanges, and concrete work, without sectarianism, emotional positions or rivalries of school or nationality. At this moment, Bello's lesson becomes exemplary: a) because nobody doubts that his work is a most essential part of our tradition; and b) because, this being so, Bello affords us from inside such tradition the possibility for a synchronic, descriptive, and formal study to compensate and diversify the influence of our historical and semantic tendency.[7] In other words, this means that our approach to any tendency of modern linguistics can find its roots in Bello as a legitimate starting point; the man who in his successes and failures offers us the brilliant lesson of his scientific determination and the acceptance of change as an inherent factor in the progress of science. Andrés Bello's prologue to his *Grammar* is a sort of declaration of principles that hundreds of

[6] Such is the purpose animating the Inter-American Program of Linguistics and Language Teaching, And also in that spirit has the study of the Spanish of large Spanish American capitals been conceived, upon the suggestion of Juan Lope Blanch. With similar attitude, the Plan de Fomento Lingüístico of the University of San Marcos is committed to the systematic description of Quechua and Castilian dialects in the Peruvian Andes. Likewise, to the already old translation of Sapir's *Language* (Mexico, 1954), we must add the recent translation of Bloomfield's *Language* (Lima, 1964), *Phonetics* by Malmberg (Buenos Aires, 1964), and the now imminent *A Course in Modern Linguistics* by Hockett (Buenos Aires) and *Principios de Fonología* by Trubetzkoy (Buenos Aires).

[7] Cf. Guillermo L. Guitarte, "Bosquejo histórico de la filología hispanoamericana", in *El Simposio de Cartagena* (1963) (Instituto Caro y Cuervo, 1965), pp. 230-44.

scholars and students have begun to reexamine only recently. It is our proper accreditation as heirs, in our own right, not only to the tradition of philology, but also to the attempts to formalize the structure of language at a level of independent abstraction.

If Latin American linguists follow the line of Bello, the future of our discipline will be cast in the mold of a constant reexamination and reevaluation of the different linguistic currents prevalent today in linguistic theory, fostering our critical ability, strong in the face of prejudices and irrational antagonisms. It is quite true that to this date we are consumers of linguistic theory, from Europe or the United States, and it is quite possible that this situation will not change in the immediate future. But if we adopt a conscious attitude before this fact; if we accept the plurilingualism of Latin America; if we proceed to an organic analysis of national tongues as they are spoken; if we recognize our interdisciplinary situation and our serious commitment to pedagogy, in an atmosphere of ideological freedom and critical respect for the old and the new, we will be in a privileged position with regard to Europe and the United States. From our concrete work with the problems of today and the history of our languages a new era could be born that would harmonize our work of linguistic description with, perhaps, the elaboration of original and creative thought. Then, together with our countries and their cultures, we will have become actors in the great history of science, we will accede to the level of universality through the recognition of our own individuality.

San Marcos University, Lima

BIOGRAPHICAL NOTES

THOMAS S. BARTHEL (1923-), a native of Berlin, studied social anthropology under Thurnwald and American archaeology under Termer, and received his doctorate at the University of Hamburg. His main fields of interest are primitive writing systems, especially the "Talking Boards" of Easter Island (where he did fieldwork in 1957-58) and Maya hieroglyphic writing, dealt with in a monograph and many articles. Since 1959, he is Professor of Ethnology at the University of Tübingen and Director of the newly founded Ethnological Institute. He has recently started a research project on trans-Pacific contacts.

LUIS JAIME CISNEROS (1921-) was born in Lima, he studied in Buenos Aires under Amado Alonso, Raimundo Lida, and Pedro Henriquez Ureña. He is head of the Department of Linguistics and Philology at the Universidad de San Marcos, where he is also Professor of Linguistics and Romance Philology. He has taught and lectured in Germany, The Netherlands, France, Romania, Belgium, and in several countries of Latin America. He is the author of eight books and more than two hundred articles which have appeared in European and Latin American journals. He is the editor of the journal *Indianoromania* of the Seminario de Filologia of the Instituto Riva Agüero in Lima.

HELES CONTRERAS (1933-), a native of Chile, completed his doctoral studies at Indiana University, and is currently Associate Professor of Linguistics and Romance Languages at the University of Washington. He has also taught at the Universidad de Concepción, Chile. His main interests are linguistic theory and the structure of Spanish. He is co-editor of the *Revista de Lingüística Aplicada*, a publication of the Círculo Lingüístico de Concepción.

EUGENIO COSERIU (1921-) was born in Romania and first studied at the University of Iași. In 1940, he moved to Italy, where he studied Romance and Slavic Philology at the University of Rome, and Philosophy at the Universities of Rome, Padua, and Milan. From 1951 to 1963, he was Director of the Department of Linguistics and Professor of General and Indoeuropean Linguistics at the University of Montevideo, Uruguay. Since 1963, he has been Professor of Romance Linguistics at the University of Tübingen, Germany. His publications deal mainly with linguistic theory and

Romance linguistics. In recent years he has been concerned above all with linguistic typology, structural grammar (syntax) and structural semantics.

ROBERT JOSEPH DI PIETRO (1932-) was born in Endicott, New York, holds the B.A. from the State University of New York (Harpur College, 1954), the M.A. from Harvard (1955), and the Ph. D. from Cornell (1960). From 1960 to 1961, he was project linguist with the Center for Applied Linguistics and concurrently held a Fulbright Lectureship at the University of Rome. Since September 1961, he has been at Georgetown University's Institute of Language and Linguistics. From 1963 to 1964, he served as Senior Fulbright Lecturer in linguistics at the University of Madrid, and as the first Coordinator of the English Language Program sponsored jointly by Georgetown University and the American Commission. In 1965, he conducted Spanish proficiency tests of Peace Corps workers and other personnel in Caracas, Venezuela. He is the editor of Monograph 16 in the *Georgetown Series on Languages and Linguistics* and co-author of two volumes, *The Sounds of English and Italian* and *The Grammatical Structures of English and Italian* (1965). He has also written several articles on contrastive analysis, language contact, and the analysis of Italian, Spanish, and Catalan. In 1965, he was elected to appear in the biography, *Outstanding Young Men of America.*

ALBERTO ESCOBAR (1929-) born in Lima, did graduate work at the University of San Marcos, and at the Universities of Florence, Madrid, and Munich. He has specialized in Hispanic philology, stylistics, and, subsequently, descriptive linguistics. He is particularly interested in problems of bilingualism. At the invitation of the Quechua Language Program, he was a Visiting Fellow in the Division of Modern Languages at Cornell University for two years. He has been Visiting Professor at the University of Puerto Rico and is now Director of the Plan de Fomento Lingüístico (sponsored by The Ford Foundation) and Professor of Descriptive Linguistics at the Universidad de San Marcos. He is a member of the Executive Committee of the Inter-American Program.

ERICA GARCÍA (1934-) a native of Argentina, came to the United States in 1958. She studied in the Universidad Nacional de La Plata and at Columbia University, where she took her doctorate and now teaches linguistics.

FRANCISCO GOMES DE MATOS (1933-) is Director of the "Centro de Lingüística Aplicada" of the Yázigi Institute of Languages in the city of São Paulo, Brazil. He also teaches Linguistics in São Paulo's Catholic University. He is Chairman of the Foreign Languages Committee of the Inter-American Program in Linguistics and Language Teaching. His present activities include his participation in MLA's supported Modern Portuguese textbook project and the publication of English textbooks for Yázigi schools in Brazil.

JOSEPH E. GRIMES (1928-) received degrees from Wheaton College (Illinois) and Cornell University. Since 1950, he has been actively engaged in field work in Mexico as a member of the Summer Institute of Linguistics, with primary concentration on Huichol. He teaches regularly in the Summer Institute of Linguistics at the University of Oklahoma, and, in addition, conducts periodic seminars at the Universidad Nacional Autónoma de México. His publications include descriptive linguistic studies and investigations of the process of language change.

GUILLERMO L. GUITARTE (1923-) was born in Buenos Aires and received his degree at the University of his native city. He spent two years in Spain improving his training. He has been secretary of the Institute of History of Spain and of the Institute of Hispanic Philology of the University of Buenos Aires, and has taught Hispanic Philology at this University, at the National University of the South (Bahía Blanca), at the Andrés Bello Seminar of the Instituto Caro y Cuervo (Bogotá), and at Harvard University. His publications include works on Spanish-American phonetics and phonemics, dialectology, and the history of linguistics.

ROBERT A. HALL JR. (1911-) is Professor of Linguistics at Cornell University. He holds degrees from Princeton University, the University of Chicago, and the University of Rome. His training was in German, French, and later Italian literature and linguistics. The first work he did on pidgin and creole languages dates from 1942, beginning with Melanesian Pidgin English and extending later to other varieties of English- and French-based pidgins and creoles, and consideration of the problems of pidginization, creolization, and nativization in general.

ROBERT LADO (1915-), born in Tampa, Florida, of Spanish parents, received his M.A. degree at the University of Texas and his Ph. D. at the University of Michigan, in 1950. He was Professor of English and Director of the English Language Institute, University of Michigan, and is now Professor of Linguistics and Dean of the Institute of Languages and Linguistics at Georgetown University. He has published books on applied linguistics, language teaching, and language testing, and more than fifty articles and tests in linguistics applied to language teaching. He was co-founder of the journal *Language Learning*. He lectured in six Latin American countries as well as in Japan, Thailand, Spain, Germany, England, and Scotland. He is an elected member of the Executive Committees of the Inter-American Program in Linguistics and Language Teaching and of the Asociación de Filología y Lingüística de América Latina (ALFAL).

YOLANDA LASTRA (1932-) was born in Mexico City, obtained an M.S. degree at Georgetown University and her Ph. D. at Cornell University. She has been active in the organization of the Inter-American Program in Linguistics and Language Teaching. She has taught at Georgetown University and is now Assistant Professor of Linguistics at the University of California at Los Angeles. She is interested in the applications of linguistics to the problems resulting from the contact of Spanish and the indigenous languages of Spanish America.

ROBERT E. LONGACRE (1922-) took undergraduate degrees in liberal arts and theology before going to Mexico in 1946 under the auspices of the Summer Institute of Linguistics. His immediate field of research has been Trique, into which he has now completed the translation of the New Testament. In 1955, he received his doctorate from the University of Pennsylvania. Since the publication of his dissertation on Proto-Mixtecan (1957) he has written numerous articles on Mesoamerican comparative linguistics. Besides teaching at the University of Michigan (1960-61) and at the University of Buffalo (1966-67), he has taught descriptive grammar at sessions of the Summer Institute of Linguistics at the Universities of Oklahoma and North Dakota. He is chief linguistic consultant for the Mexican branch of the same Institute. Recent publications (including a manual of field procedures) reflect interest in further development of Pike's tagmemics by incorporating insights from transformational grammar.

JUAN M. LOPE BLANCH (1927-) was born in Madrid, where he studied at the Universidad Central. In 1951, he went to the University of Mexico with a fellowship from Spain's Consejo Superior de Investigaciones Científicas. He has since held the chairs of Spanish Grammar and Romance Philology at the University of Mexico. He has published several studies on topics in Spanish Philology and Mexican Spanish Dialectology. He is a researcher at the Colegio de México, secretary of the *Nueva Revista de Filología Hispánica* and editor of the *Anuario de Letras* of the National University of Mexico.

YAKOV MALKIEL (1914-), a native of Kiev, received his secondary education in Berlin (1924-1933), majoring in Latin and French, and studied at the Friedrich-Wilhelm Universität Romance, Slavic, and Semitic philology, earning his Ph. D. in 1938. Early in 1940, he moved to the United States where, after a brief period of employment by the University of Wyoming (1942) as a teacher of six languages, he has been consistently associated with the University of California at Berkeley (Dept. of Spanish and Portuguese, of Italian, of Slavic; Romance Philology Group), receiving an appointment as Professor of Romance Philology in 1952 and a concurrent three-year appointment as Associate Dean of the Graduate Division. In 1966 he joined Berkeley's Department of Linguistics while retaining full membership in the Romance Philology Group. Since 1947 he has been founding Editor-in-Chief of the *Romance Philology* Quarterly, the first, and to this day, only journal of its kind in the English-speaking world. He has been Vice-President (1955) and President (1965) of the Linguistic Society of America, First Vice-President (1964) and President (1965) of the Philological Association of the Pacific Coast, co-founder of the 'Comparative

Romance Linguistics' Group within the Modern Language Association (1946), senior post-doctoral fellow of the National Science Foundation (1966), and recipient on three occasions (1948-49, 1959, 1967), of either a travelling or a resident fellowship from the John Simon Guggenheim Memorial Foundation. He has taught for shorter periods of time at the Universities of Southern California, Texas, and Colorado, and at Mills College; has been associated, over the years, with five Linguistic Institutes; has lectured extensively in Europe (esp. in 1959 and 1966); was one of the key speakers at the First International Congress of Hispanists (Oxford, 1962); and acted as a co-initiator and co-organizer of the University of Texas' 'Symposium on Historical Linguistics' (1966).

LEONARDO MANRIQUE (1934-) was born in Mexico City. He received his M.A. from the Escuela Nacional de Anthropología e Historia and has finished his Ph. D. course work at the Universidad Nacional Autónoma de México. He has taught General Anthropology and Linguistics as Visiting Professor at the Universidad Nacional de Asunción, Paraguay, and is currently Associate Director and Professor of Linguistics at the Escuela Nacional de Antropología. He has done fieldwork on ethnology and linguistics in Oaxaca and the Otomian area, and his papers reflect his interests. Currently coordinator of the Comisión para el Estudio de la Escritura Maya, he is himself doing research on the statistical properties of Mayan languages with the aid of computers.

FERNANDO ANTONIO MARTINEZ (1917-), has his Ph. D. from the Pontificia Universidad Católica Javeriana (Bogotá). Since 1945, he has worked with the Instituto Caro y Cuervo and contributed to its journal, *Thesaurus*. At present, he serves as Head of the Lexicography Department at this Institute and is in charge of the continuation of the Rufino José Cuervo's *Diccionario de construcción y régimen de la lengua castellana*. He is interested in the Spanish literary language, particularly certain aspects of vocabulary and syntax.

JOAQUIM MATTOSO CÂMARA JR. (1904-) received his doctorate at the Universidade de Brasil, in Rio de Janeiro. Since 1950, he has taught linguistics at the Faculdade de Filosofia of that University. In 1943, he came from Brazil to the United States as a graduate student where he worked at Columbia University. He has been a Visiting Professor at the Universidade de Lisboa, in Portugal, at the University of Washington, and at Georgetown University. He has published several papers and books on general linguistics and Portuguese linguistics, among them *Principios de Linguistica Geral*, now in its 4th edition.

MARVIN K. MAYERS (1927-) completed his graduate studies in Linguistics and Anthropology at the University of Chicago. These studies interrupted a twelve year program of field research in Guatemala, Central America, under the auspices of the Summer Institute of Linguistics, during which period he studied Pocomchí, the subject of a number of his publications in general linguistics and folklore. His responsibilities as Chairman of the Technical Studies Program of this Institute made him acquainted with the language problem in Guatemala and as a result he has edited a book entitled *Languages of Guatemala*. He has received Fellowships from the Organization of American States and the National Science Foundation. He has taught at the University of Washington and is at present Associate Professor of Sociology and Anthropology at Wheaton College.

NORMAN A. MCQUOWN (1914-) is a native of Illinois, studied linguistics at Yale University, where he received his doctorate in 1940. His main field of interest is the indigenous linguistics of Middle America (chiefly Nahuatl and Maya), and he has carried on field work in Mexico and in Guatemala since 1938. Since 1946, he has been Director of the Mayan Studies Program at the University of Chicago where he is also Professor of Anthropology and of Linguistics.

SOL SAPORTA (1925-) received his undergraduate degree from Brooklyn College, and his graduate degrees from the University of Illinois. He taught at Indiana University, and is currently Professor of Linguistics and Romance Languages at the University of Washington. He was a Fellow at the Center for Advanced Study in the Behavioral Sciences, and in 1965, delivered the State of Oregon Condon Lectures. His publications reflect his interest in Spanish linguistics, linguistic theory, and psycholinguistics.

SEBEOK, THOMAS A. (1920-) is a native of Budapest who has lived in the United States since 1937. After studying literary criticism, anthropology, and linguistics at the University of Chicago, he earned his doctorate at Princeton University in Oriental languages and civilizations. He has been a member of the Indiana University faculty in Linguistics since 1943, since 1967 with the rank of Distinguished Professor. He also serves as Chairman of the University's Research Center for the Language Sciences. During its formative years, he was also Chairman of Uralic and Altaic Studies, served as the first Director of the Uralic and Altaic Language and Area Center, and has continued, since 1960, as Editor of the Uralic and Altaic Series. He has held fellowships from the John Simon Guggenheim Memorial Foundation (1958-59), the Center for Advanced Study in the Behavioral Sciences, (1960-61), and was a Senior Postdoctoral Fellow of the National Science Foundation (1966-67). In 1964, he was Director of the Linguistic Institute of the Linguistic Society of America. He organized and, until 1963, was Chairman of the Committee on Linguistic Information. Beginning 1968, he became Editor-in-Chief of *Studies in Semiotics*. His major research interest has centered on the Uralic languages and peoples; his contributions also include works on the history of linguistics, psycholinguistics, and semiotics, especially the study of animal communication; in addition, he has worked with Aymara, and published, in 1957, a dictionary of this language.

JORGE A. SUÁREZ (1927-) received his academic training at the University of Buenos Aires, and completed graduate studies in linguistics and anthropology at Cornell University. He has taught at the Universities of Buenos Aires and Tucumán, and is currently Professor of Spanish Philology and Linguistics at the Universidad Nacional del Sur (Argentina). In 1963, he was elected Fellow of the Editorial Board of *Romance Philology*. He has been invited to preside over the Permanent Committee on American Indian Languages of the Inter-American Program in Linguistics and Language Teaching. His major research interest centers on the indigenous languages of South America. He has published articles and reviews on Araucanian, and written (in collaboration) a description of Paraguayan Guaraní, now in press.

RAFAEL TORRES QUINTERO (1909-), Ph. D. from the Pontificia Universidad Católica Javeriana (Bogotá), has been Professor of Spanish Language and Literature in several schools and universities in Bogotá. He joined the Instituto Caro y Cuervo in 1942, when it was founded. He is presently its Associate Director and also Dean of the Centro Andrés Bello, its teaching section. He is also Associate Director of the Academia Colombiana de la Lengua, to which he has belonged since 1951. He attended the first three Symposia of the Inter-American Program in Linguistics and Language Teaching, in Cartagena (Colombia), Bloomington (U.S.A.), and Montevideo (Uruguay). He directed the edition of *El Antijovio* by G. Jiménez de Quesade and of the *Obras* de Rufino J. Cuervo and of Hernando Domínguez Camargo. He has published several works on Spanish and Spanish American philology in *Thesaurus*, the journal of the Instituto Caro y Cuervo.

LEOPOLDO WIGDORSKY (1929-) was born in Santiago, Chile. With wide and intensive experience as a teacher of English as a foreign language, he lectures at present on applied linguistics and on English grammar at Teachers College, Universidad Católica de Chile, as well as the Universidad Técnica del Estado, Santiago. He received his undergraduate and graduate training at the Universities of Chile, Michigan, and Edinburgh.

INDEX OF LANGUAGES

INDEX OF NAMES